PROPERTY
CONCISE EDITION

ASPEN CASEBOOK SERIES

PROPERTY
CONCISE EDITION

Third Edition

JESSE DUKEMINIER
Late Maxwell Professor of Law
University of California
Los Angeles

JAMES E. KRIER
Earl Warren DeLano Professor of Law Emeritus
University of Michigan

GREGORY S. ALEXANDER
A. Robert Noll Professor of Law Emeritus
Cornell University

MICHAEL H. SCHILL
President and Professor of Law
University of Oregon

LIOR JACOB STRAHILEVITZ
Sidley Austin Professor of Law
University of Chicago

 Wolters Kluwer

Published by Wolters Kluwer in New York.

Wolters Kluwer Legal & Regulatory U.S. serves customers worldwide with CCH, Aspen Publishers, and Kluwer Law International products. (www.WKLegaledu.com)

To contact Customer Service, e-mail customer.service@wolterskluwer.com, call 1-800-234-1660, fax 1-800-901-9075, or mail correspondence to:

Wolters Kluwer
Attn: Order Department
PO Box 990
Frederick, MD 21705

Printed in the United States of America.

1 2 3 4 5 6 7 8 9 0

ISBN 978-1-5438-2631-9

Library of Congress Cataloging-in-Publication Data

Library of Congress Cataloging-in-Publication Data application is in process.

Certified Chain of Custody
Promoting Sustainable Forestry
www.sfiprogram.org
SFI-01681

SFI label applies to the text stock

About Wolters Kluwer Legal & Regulatory U.S.

Wolters Kluwer Legal & Regulatory U.S. delivers expert content and solutions in the areas of law, corporate compliance, health compliance, reimbursement, and legal education. Its practical solutions help customers successfully navigate the demands of a changing environment to drive their daily activities, enhance decision quality and inspire confident outcomes.

Serving customers worldwide, its legal and regulatory portfolio includes products under the Aspen Publishers, CCH Incorporated, Kluwer Law International, ftwilliam.com and MediRegs names. They are regarded as exceptional and trusted resources for general legal and practice-specific knowledge, compliance and risk management, dynamic workflow solutions, and expert commentary.

To my grandson, Zane

—G.S.A.

Summary of Contents

Contents

List of Illustrations

Chapter 8

Chapter 10

Chapter 11

Chapter 12

Preface to the Concise Third Edition

From the time of its first edition in 1981, *Property* was warmly embraced by law professors and students around the country. Compared with casebooks that had preceded it, Jesse Dukeminier and Jim Krier served up to casebook users a refreshing combination of intellectual rigor, wit, humor, history, and an interest in human behavior. Over 30 years later, the latest edition to this legendary casebook remains a favorite of professors across the country.

This Concise Version of *Property* strives to retain all of the same characteristics of its parent volume while responding to changed needs of both instructors of the Property course and their students. Beginning with its first edition, *Property* has been noted for its eclectic combination of economic analysis, history, and philosophy, as well as rigorous doctrinal analysis. The Concise Version retains that eclecticism even while reducing the length of the book. The reduced amount of space devoted to some of the interdisciplinary material has not sacrificed coverage of the core insights of the theories studied. Throughout, the aim is to retain the main book's intellectual integrity while making the material more accessible to students.

Why a Concise Version?

The Property course has changed greatly over the years. In many, probably most, law schools it now carries only four or even three credits. With this contraction many teachers have come to realize that a concise teaching tool is not a mere luxury but a necessity. This Concise Version is aimed at meeting the need for such a compact course.

Not only has the Property course changed, but law students have changed as well since the book's first appearance. Today's law students have needs that differ from their counterparts of three decades ago. They are accustomed to a wide variety of visual cues and have been exposed to diversified textual formats rather than a single undifferentiated presentation of pedagogical material. I have shaped the Concise Version with this background in mind.

Features of the Concise Version

Longtime users of the casebook will note that the Concise Version is substantially shorter than its parent. I have achieved this by editing down topical coverage consistently throughout the book. The doctrinal coverage remains basically the same as in the parent book, but I have significantly reduced the number of pages devoted to some topics.

Keeping in mind the needs of contemporary law students, I have also done some significant editing in the casebook's Notes. My goal has been to make the Notes in the Concise Version as brief as possible without sacrificing coverage of core topics. I have deleted all string case citations and omitted many references to law review articles and other legal literature. The citations that remain were selected for specific pedagogic reasons. The overall result is Notes that are quite concise. Many of the cases included in this Concise Version will be familiar to users of past editions of the main book. I have striven for as much continuity as possible. To add freshness to the book, however, I have replaced several cases that have reappeared in multiple past editions of *Property* with new, more recent cases. The reason for these substitutions is not solely to introduce cases of more recent vintage (although that is part of it) but also because the new cases are, in my view, better vehicles for discussion of the doctrinal points covered in those cases. Users of past editions of the main book may disagree with me, of course, and choose to revert to some of the old cases in past editions of the main book.

As for excerpted material, many of the lengthy excerpts from law review articles and other literature that the parent book includes have been omitted in the Concise Version. This material is unquestionably valuable, but, taking into account the goals of the Concise Version, I decided to conserve time and space by summarizing for students the basic points that this material makes. In some instances students more easily grasp the points by reading such summaries rather than reading lengthy excerpts.

In response to changes in student pedagogical needs, I have introduced several new features in this Concise Version. The book has a look and feel that distinguishes it not only from the parent book but from most casebooks as well. Its new layout includes several design features, which include:

- *two-color interior design*
- *boxed side material*, which enriches student understanding without interrupting the flow of the main text
- *graphic designs*, which clarify complex doctrinal topics
- *bulleted items*, to emphasize especially important points
- *highlighted introductory* and *follow-up material*, which lay doctrinal groundwork or follow to completion the human stories involved in cases.

In addition to these design innovations, the book includes many new maps, drawings, and photos to enhance student understanding of and interest in cases.

Changes in the Third Concise Edition

Users of previous editions of the Concise Version will notice a number of changes throughout the book. There are several recent cases, including U.S. Supreme Court cases on copyright and takings. Where I have substituted cases, I have done so in the interest of providing better teaching vehicles. This new edition also adds some new topics, including the implications of Covid-19 for various aspects of Property, Airbnbs, and the problem of homelessness. My aim is to keep the book as current and relevant as possible. I have rewritten textual material at various points, hoping to add greater clarity. Many of these changes are the result of very helpful comments and suggestions that users of previous editions of the Concise Version were kind enough to offer me. I hope that I have adequately responded to these suggestions. Doubtless there remains plenty of room for further improvement, so I encourage users to send me their thoughts regarding future changes.

Throughout, I have been mindful of the great tradition of the parent book. My hope is that the Concise Version will continue that tradition, extending it for a new generation of teachers and students. I invite your comments and suggestions. Many users of past editions of the parent book have been kind enough to offer suggestions, and these comments have greatly improved that book. I invite all users to share with me your thoughts about ways to make this a better book.

Gregory S. Alexander

Healdsburg, CA
July 2020

Author's Note: The Pandemic

As we go to press, the global Covid-19 pandemic continues. This catastrophic event, unprecedented in modern times, has affected every aspect of society, the law included. Regarding property law in particular, areas especially affected thus far are landlord and tenant, mortgages, and governmental takings. We will discuss these developments in the relevant chapters, but we emphasize that the pandemic's implications for property law are at this point very much uncertain. Consequently, much of what we have to say is tentative and subject to change.

Acknowledgments

This Third Concise Edition, like all books, is the result of a collaborative effort. In the case of this edition, the most obvious collaboration is that among my co-authors, including the late Jesse Dukeminier, and me. Although I have done the majority of the revisions necessary to prepare this edition alone, I literally co-wrote the Third Concise Edition. Not only was the parent edition the indispensable foundation for the Concise Edition, but my current co-authors, Jim Krier and particularly Lior Strahilevitz, were invaluable and gracious contributors to my efforts. Quite literally, I could not have prepared this book without them.

The team at Wolters Kluwer has been truly indispensable. I am also deeply grateful to them all for their indefatigable efforts and patience during the production of this book.

I am also grateful to the many users, past and present, who very kindly provided enormously helpful feedback regarding the book's strengths and weaknesses. In particular, I wish to thank Mary Sarah Bilder, David Favre, and Jeffrey Gaba. In developing this Concise Edition, I have tried to respond directly to their and other comments. Whatever merits the book has, it is a far stronger product because of their feedback.

Gregory S. Alexander
September 2020

The authors acknowledge the permissions kindly granted to reproduce excerpts from, or illustrations of, the materials indicated below.

Books and Articles

American Law Institute, Restatement (Third) of Property, Servitudes (2000). Copyright © 2000 by the American Law Institute.

Baird, Douglas G., *Common Law Intellectual Property and the Legacy of International News Service v. Associated Press*, 40 U. Chi. L. Rev. 411 (1983). Copyright © 1983 by University of Chicago Law Review. Reproduced with permission of the University of Chicago Law School via Copyright Clearance Center.

Multi-Board Residential Real Estate Contract, REALTOR Association of the Western Suburbs. Used with permission.

Perry, Sandra White, Letter to editors regarding Jessie Lide's house (1988).
Posner, Richard A., *Economic Analysis of Law* (9th ed. 2014). Copyright © 2014 CCH
Incorporated. Reprinted with permission of Wolters Kluwer Law & Business.

Illustrations

Aerial View of Ft. Trumbull, photograph. Courtesy Andrew Kull, of the University
of Texas at Austin.
AP Newsroom, circa 1920, photograph. Reproduced with permission of AP/Wide
World Photos.
Apartment building in Greenwich Village, Manhattan, New York City, photograph
courtesy of iStock Photo/Robert Crum.
Blackstone, Sir William, portrait by Sir Joshua Reynolds. Copyright © National
Portrait Gallery, London. Reproduced with permission.
Brandeis, Louis Dembitz, photograph, collection of the Supreme Court of the
United States.
Collapsed House photograph, courtesy of Andrew Kull, of the University of Texas
at Austin Law School. http://kullproperty.weebly.com/pennsylvania-coal-co-
v-mahon.html.
Decoyman driving wild duck up the pipe, Vincent Brooks Day & Son, Lith., drawn
by Sir Ralph Payne-Gallwey. Used with permission of Providence Press.
de Lamerie, Paul, Tureen and Cover (1736-37), photograph courtesy of Virginia
Museum of Fine Arts, Richmond. Gift of Rita R. Gans. Photograph by
Katherine Wetzel. Copyright © Virginia Museum of Fine Arts. Reproduced
with permission.
Delfino v. Vealencis, Bristol, Connecticut, map of land, from Manuel Baucells
& Steven A. Lippman, *Justice Delayed is Justice Denied: A Co-operative Game
Theoretic Analysis of Hold Up in Co-Ownership*, 22 Cardozo L. Rev. 1191, 1222
(2001).
Doonesbury © 2001 G. B. Trudeau. Reprinted with permission of Andrews McMeel
Universal. All rights reserved.
Emporia, Kansas, Berkley Hills Addition, house, 1991, photograph by Chad
Johnson.
Euclid zoning map, photograph. Courtesy Andrew Kull, of the University of Texas
at Austin.
For sale by owner, photograph courtesy of iStock Photo/CHRISsadowski.
Grand Central Station, statue of Mercury (Hermes) with clock, photograph
courtesy of iStock Photo/mdwarren.
Grand Central Terminal, circa 1930, photograph courtesy of the Library of
Congress.
Grand Central Terminal construction, 1906, photograph courtesy of the Library
of Congress.
Gravesite of Noah Phelps in Revolutionary War cemetery in Austerlitz, New York,
photograph courtesy of Getty Images/Fotosearch.
Gray's Mansion, Chanute, Kansas, photograph by Vernon R. Parham, M.D.
Gulf Terrace Condominium, Destin, Florida, photograph by Lucy Howell.

Gwernhaylod House, Overton-on-Dee, Wales, photograph, 1956. © Crown Copyright: Royal Commission of the Ancient and Historical Monuments of Wales, reproduced with permission of the National Monuments Record of Wales.

Haunted House, Nyack, New York, photograph. AP/Wide World Photos.

Hickeringill, Edmund, possibly by R.C. Roffe, after J. Jull, from the National Portrait Gallery, London. Copyright © National Portrait Gallery, London. Reproduced with permission.

Holmes, Oliver Wendell, photograph, collection of the Supreme Court of the United States.

Home Owner's Loan Corp., map. Mapping Inequality Project, University of Richmond.

Howard v. Kunto, Washington, map © 1995 by Barry C. Nelson.

Kelo house, New London, Connecticut, photograph. Used with permission of the Institute for Justice (www.ij.org).

Klimt, Gustav, painting entitled "Schloss Kammer am Attersee II." Private collection. Reproduced with permission of Galerie St. Etienne, New York.

Ladue, Missouri, residences, 1999, photographs by Stuart Banner.

Lakeside Village Condominiums, Culver City, California, photograph by Jesse Dukeminier.

Leicester Square, London, etching, from the British Museum, London.

Leicester Square, London, 2012, photograph by Kim K. Alexander.

Lide, Jessie, Knoxville, Tennessee, house, 1956 photograph, courtesy of Sandra White Perry.

Loretto's Apartment House, New York City, photograph by Michael S. Gruen.

Lucas v. South Carolina Coastal Council, lots, 2000, photograph by David S. Sanders.

Map of land claims in Johnson v. M'Intosh. Reproduced with permission of Eric Kades.

Map of North America, circa 1784, attributed to William Faden. Courtesy of the Library of Congress.

Map of the disputed land in Fulkerson v. Van Buren. Reproduced with permission of John G. Sprankling.

Maslin, Michael, cartoon. Michael Maslin/The New Yorker Collection/The Cartoon Bank. Reproduced by permission of Condé Nast.

Marshall, John, portrait by Chester Harding. Reproduced with permission of the Boston Athenæum.

Messersmith, Caroline, Dickinson, North Dakota, house, 1999 photograph by Richard Volesky.

Mortgage records in canvas binders from a government records center, photograph courtesy of iStock Photo/wsmahar.

Nahrstedt, Natore, photograph by Alan J. Duignan from Los Angeles Times, Dec. 24, 1992. Reproduced with permission.

O'Brien, John, cartoon. John O' Brien/The New Yorker Collection/The Cartoon Bank. Reproduced by permission of Condé Nast.

O'Keeffe, Georgia, painting entitled "Seaweed," 1926. Copyright © 2020 Georgia O'Keeffe Museum / Artists Rights Society (ARS), New York. Reprinted by permission.

O'Keeffe, Georgia, photograph. Science History Images / Alamy Stock Photo.

Oxford House, Edmonds, Washington, photograph, courtesy of Oxford House.

Pierre Apartments, Hackensack, New Jersey, photograph by David S. Sanders.

Pepys, Charles, First Earl of Cottenham, by Charles Robert Leslie. Copyright © National Portrait Gallery, London. Reproduced with permission.

The Progressive Church, photograph. Reproduced with permission of John G. Sprankling.

Railroad tracks, photograph courtesy of iStock Photo/mbbirdy.

Real estate agent giving keys to new property owners, photograph courtesy of iStock Photo/LDProd.

Residences on lots 19, 20, and 4, Chanute, Kansas, photograph by Vernon R. Parham, M.D.

River View Towers, Fort Lee, New Jersey, photograph by David S. Sanders.

Seawall in Bay Head, N.J., photograph by David Gard, from The Star-Ledger, Jul. 18, 2013. Copyright © 2013 NJ Advance Media. All rights reserved. Used under license.

Shelley House in St. Louis, Missouri, street level view, photograph by FrancisNancy. Reproduced via Creative Commons.

Steiner, Peter, cartoon. Peter Steiner/CartoonCollections//https://www.cartooncollections.com. Reproduced with permission.

Stoyanoff house, Ladue, Missouri, 2001 drawing by Stephen Harby.

Van Pelt, J. F., photograph, from The Steve Hill Collection, Mitchell Community College, North Carolina. Reproduced with permission of Bill Moose.

Van Pelt Residence, Statesville, North Carolina, etching, courtesy of Bill Moose.

Van Sandt v. Royster, Lots 19, 20, and 4, map by Greg R. Vetter and Marcilynn A. Burke.

Vealencis, Helen, photograph from Manel Baucells & Steven A. Lippman, *Justice Delayed is Justice Denied: A Cooperative Game Theoretic Analysis of Hold-Up in Co-Ownership*, 22 Cardozo L. Rev. 1191, 1249 (2001).

Weber, Robert, cartoon. Robert Weber/The New Yorker Collection/The Cartoon Bank. Reproduced by permission of Condé Nast.

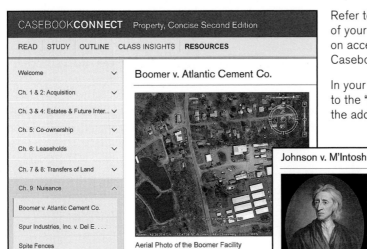

▲ Navigation

Refer to the sticker in the front of your book for instructions on accessing the resources at CasebookConnect.com.

In your Connected Casebook, go to the "Resources" tab to explore the additional materials.

The website is geared to the book chapter by chapter, and within each chapter by topic.

Photo of the parcel in the Delfino v. Vealencis case

▲ Co-ownership, Chapter 5

Acquisition, Chapters 1 & 2 ▲

We welcome any comments or suggestions you might have about improving the site and making it more useful and interesting to you.

Please email your feedback to Lior@Chicago.edu

PROPERTY
CONCISE EDITION

PART I

AN INTRODUCTION TO SOME FUNDAMENTALS

The first two chapters of this book pursue a common theme—how someone might acquire property other than by purchase—across a wide range of legal terrain. One purpose of the exercise is to lay down the chief doctrinal foundations of property law. Another is to introduce some basic concepts, issues, and analytic methods of ongoing importance.

First Possession: Acquisition of Property by Discovery (or Conquest), Capture, and Creation

Qui prior est tempore potior est jure.
(The one who is prior in time is stronger in right.)—

> *Maxim of Roman Law*

First come, first served.—

> *Henry Brinklow,*
> Complaynt of Roderick Mors,
> Ch. 17 (c. 1545)

How does property come to be, and why, and so what? Most of us most of the time take these questions for granted, which is to say that we take property for granted. But taking something for granted is not exactly the best path to understanding it. So we begin with the origins of property.

A. ACQUISITION BY DISCOVERY/CONQUEST

Thus in the beginning all the world was *America*—

> *John Locke*
> Two Treatises of Government,
> Book II, Ch. V ("Of Property") (c. 1690)

JOHNSON v. M'INTOSH

Supreme Court of the United States, 1823
21 U.S. (8 Wheat.) 543

Error to the District Court of Illinois. This was an action of ejectment for lands in the State and District of Illinois, claimed by the plaintiffs under a purchase and conveyance from the Piankeshaw Indians, and by the defendant, under a [later] grant from the United States. It came up on a case stated, upon which there was a judgment below for the defendant. . . .

3

MARSHALL, C.J. The plaintiffs in this cause claim the land, in their declaration mentioned, under two grants, purporting to be made, the first in 1773, and the last in 1775, by the chiefs of certain Indian tribes, constituting the Illinois and the Piankeshaw nations; and the question is, whether this title can be recognised in the Courts of the United States?

> ## Sidebar
>
> The lawsuit in Johnson v. M'Intosh, one of the most famous (infamous?) cases in all of American property law, was actually collusive. The plaintiffs were a consortium of land speculators (land speculation in the Old Northwest was common in the years just prior to the Revolution), and their nominal opponent was an Illinois resident who allegedly owned a parcel of land within one of the huge tracts that the consortium had purchased. M'Intosh had several motives for colluding with the consortium, including their agreement to give him a share of the companies. The consortium's motive? To test the validity of their title, which was considered insecure. For more background on *Johnson*, see Stuart Banner, How the Indians Lost Their Land: Law and Power on the Frontier (2005); Lindsay G. Robertson, Conquest by Law: How the Discovery of America Dispossessed Indigenous Peoples of Their Lands (2005); Eric Kades, History and Interpretation of the Great Case of *Johnson v. M'Intosh*, 19 Law & Hist. Rev. 67 (2001).

The facts, as stated in the case agreed, show the authority of the chiefs who executed this conveyance, so far as it could be given by their own people; and likewise show, that the particular tribes for whom these chiefs acted were in rightful possession of the land they sold. The inquiry, therefore, is, in a great measure, confined to the power of Indians to give, and of private individuals to receive, a title which can be sustained in the Courts of this country.

As the right of society, to prescribe those rules by which property may be acquired and preserved is not, and cannot be drawn into question; as the title to lands, especially, is and must be admitted to depend entirely on the law of the nation in which they lie; it will be necessary, in pursuing this inquiry, to examine, not singly those principles of abstract justice, which the Creator of all things has impressed on the mind of his creature man, and which are admitted to regulate, in a great degree, the rights of civilized nations, whose perfect independence is acknowledged; but those principles also which our own government has adopted in the particular case, and given us as the rule for our decision.

On the discovery of this immense continent, the great nations of Europe were eager to appropriate to themselves so much of it as they could respectively acquire. Its vast extent offered an ample field to the ambition and enterprise of all; and the character and religion of its inhabitants afforded an apology for considering them as a people over whom the superior genius of Europe might claim an ascendency. The potentates of the old world found no difficulty in convincing themselves that they made ample compensation to the inhabitants of the new, by bestowing on them civilization and Christianity, in exchange for unlimited independence. But, as they were all in pursuit of nearly the same object, it was necessary, in order to avoid conflicting settlements, and consequent war with each other, to establish a principle, which all should acknowledge as the law by which the right of acquisition, which they all asserted, should be regulated as between themselves. This principle was, that discovery gave title to the government by whose subjects, or by whose authority, it was made, against all other European governments, which title might be consummated by possession.

The exclusion of all other Europeans, necessarily gave to the nation making the discovery the sole right of acquiring the soil from the natives, and establishing settlements upon it. It was a right with which no Europeans could interfere. It was a

William McIntosh (1775-April 30, 1825) was a prominent chief of the Creek Nation
between the turn of the nineteenth century and his execution in 1825. He was
sentenced to execution by the Creek National Council for violating Creek law when
he negotiated to cede remaining Creek land to the United States.

right which all asserted for themselves, and to the assertion of which, by others, all
assented.

Those relations which were to exist between the discoverer and the natives, were
to be regulated by themselves. The rights thus acquired being exclusive, no other
power could interpose between them.

In the establishment of these relations, the rights of the original inhabitants were,
in no instance, entirely disregarded; but were necessarily, to a considerable extent,
impaired. They were admitted to be the rightful occupants of the soil, with a legal
as well as just claim to retain possession of it, and to use it according to their own

Map of North America (c. 1784), attributed to William Faden, London 1793
Source: Library of Congress

discretion, but their rights to complete sovereignty, as independent nations, were necessarily diminished, and their power to dispose of the soil at their own will, to whomsoever they pleased, was denied by the original fundamental principle, that discovery gave exclusive title to those who made it.

While the different nations of Europe respected the right of the natives, as occupants, they asserted the ultimate dominion to be in themselves; and claimed and exercised, as a consequence of this ultimate dominion, a power to grant the soil, while yet in possession of the natives. These grants have been understood by all, to convey a title to the *grantees*, subject only to the Indian right of occupancy.

. . .

[O]ur whole country been granted by the [British] crown while in the occupation of the Indians. These grants purport to convey the soil as well as the right of dominion to the grantees. In those governments which were denominated royal, where the right to the soil was not vested in individuals, but remained in the crown, or was vested in the colonial government, the king claimed and exercised the right of granting lands, and of dismembering the government at his will. . . . It has never been objected to this, or to any other similar grant, that the title as well as possession was in the Indians when it was made, and that it passed nothing on that account.

. . .

Thus, all the nations of Europe, who have acquired territory on this continent, have asserted in themselves, and have recognised in others, the exclusive right of the discoverer to appropriate the lands occupied by the Indians. Have the American States rejected or adopted this principle?

By the treaty which concluded the war of our revolution, Great Britain relinquished all claim, not only to the government, but to the "propriety and territorial rights of the United States," whose boundaries were fixed in the second article. By this treaty, the powers of government, and the right to soil, which had previously been in Great Britain, passed definitively to these States. We had before taken possession of them, by declaring independence; but neither the declaration of independence, nor the treaty confirming it, could give us more than that which we before possessed, or to which Great Britain was before entitled. It has never been doubted, that either the United States, or the several States, had a clear title to all the lands within the boundary lines described in the treaty, subject only to the Indian right of occupancy, and that the exclusive power to extinguish that right, was vested in that government which might constitutionally exercise it.

Virginia, particularly, within whose chartered limits the land in controversy lay, passed an act, in the year 1779, declaring her

> exclusive right of pre-emption from the Indians, of all the lands within the limits of her own chartered territory, and that no person or persons whatsoever, have, or ever had, a right to purchase any lands within the same, from any Indian nation, except only persons duly authorized to make such purchase; formerly for the use and benefit of the colony, and lately for the Commonwealth.

The act then proceeds to annul all deeds made by Indians to individuals, for the private use of the purchasers.

. . .

The States, having within their chartered limits different portions of territory covered by Indians, ceded that territory, generally, to the United States, on conditions expressed in their deeds of cession, which demonstrate the opinion, that they ceded the soil as well as jurisdiction, and that in doing so, they granted a productive fund to the government of the Union. The lands in controversy lay within the chartered limits of Virginia, and were ceded with the whole country northwest of the river Ohio. This grant contained reservations and stipulations, which could only be made by the owners of the soil; and concluded with a stipulation, that "all the lands in the ceded territory, not reserved, should be considered as a common fund, for the use and benefit of such of the United States as have become, or shall become, members of the confederation," &c. "according to their usual respective proportions in the general charge and expenditure, and shall be faithfully and *bona fide* disposed of for that purpose, and for no other use or purpose whatsoever."

The ceded territory was occupied by numerous and warlike tribes of Indians; but the exclusive right of the United States to extinguish their title, and to grant the soil, has never, we believe, been doubted. . . .

The United States, then, have unequivocally acceded to that great and broad rule by which its civilized inhabitants now hold this country. They hold, and assert in themselves, the title by which it was acquired. They maintain, as all others have maintained, that discovery gave an exclusive right to extinguish the Indian title of occupancy, either by purchase or by conquest; and gave also a right to such a degree of sovereignty, as the circumstances of the people would allow them to exercise.

The power now possessed by the government of the United States to grant lands, resided, while we were colonies, in the crown, or its grantees. The validity of the titles given by either has never been questioned in our Courts. It has been exercised uniformly over territory in possession of the Indians. The existence of this power must negative the existence of any right which may conflict with, and control it. An absolute title to lands cannot exist, at the same time, in different persons, or in different governments. An absolute must be an exclusive title, or at least a title which excludes all others not compatible with it. All our institutions recognise the absolute title of the crown, subject only to the Indian right of occupancy, and recognise the absolute title of the crown to extinguish that right. This is incompatible with an absolute and complete title in the Indians.

We will not enter into the controversy, whether agriculturists, merchants, and manufacturers, have a right, on abstract principles, to expel hunters from the territory they possess, or to contract their limits. Conquest gives a title which the Courts of the conqueror cannot deny, whatever the private and speculative opinions of individuals may be, respecting the original justice of the claim which has been successfully asserted. The British government, which was then our government, and whose rights have passed to the United States, asserted a title to all the lands occupied by Indians, within the chartered limits of the British colonies. It asserted also a limited sovereignty over them, and the exclusive right of extinguishing the title which occupancy gave to them. These claims have been maintained and established as far west as the river Mississippi, by the sword. The title to a vast portion of the lands we now hold, originates in them. It is not for the Courts of this country to question the validity of this title, or to sustain one which is incompatible with it.

Although we do not mean to engage in the defence of those principles which Europeans have applied to Indian title, they may, we think, find some excuse, if not justification, in the character and habits of the people whose rights have been wrested from them.

The title by conquest is acquired and maintained by force. The conqueror prescribes its limits. Humanity, however, acting on public opinion, has established, as a general rule, that the conquered shall not be wantonly oppressed, and that their condition shall remain as eligible as is compatible with the objects of the conquest. Most usually, they are incorporated with the victorious nation, and become subjects or citizens of the government with which they are connected. The new and old members of the society mingle with each other; the distinction between them is gradually lost, and they make one people. Where this incorporation is practicable, humanity demands, and a wise policy requires, that the rights of the conquered to property should remain unimpaired; that the new subjects should be governed as equitably as the old, and that confidence in their security should gradually banish the painful sense of being separated from their ancient connexions, and united by force to strangers.

. . .

But the tribes of Indians inhabiting this country were fierce savages, whose occupation was war, and whose subsistence was drawn chiefly from the forest. To leave them in possession of their country, was to leave the country a wilderness; to govern them as a distinct people, was impossible, because they were as brave and as high spirited as they were fierce, and were ready to repel by arms every attempt on their independence.

What was the inevitable consequence of this state of things? The Europeans were under the necessity either of abandoning the country, and relinquishing their pompous claims to it, or of enforcing those claims by the sword, and by the adoption of principles adapted to the condition of a people with whom it was impossible to mix, and who could not be governed as a distinct society, or of remaining in their neighbourhood, and exposing themselves and their families to the perpetual hazard of being massacred.

Frequent and bloody wars, in which the whites were not always the aggressors, unavoidably ensued. European policy, numbers, and skill prevailed. As the white population advanced, that of the Indians necessarily receded. The country in the immediate neighbourhood of agriculturists became unfit for them. The game fled into thicker and more unbroken forests, and the Indians followed. The soil, to which the crown originally claimed title, being no longer occupied by its ancient inhabitants, was parcelled out according to the will of the sovereign power, and taken possession of by persons who claimed immediately from the crown, or mediately, through its grantees or deputies.

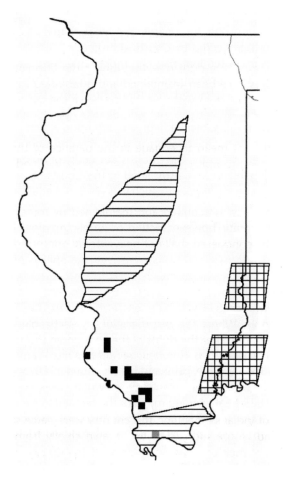

Map of land claims in Johnson v. M'Intosh. The areas in horizontal lines are the tracts purchased by the Illinois Company (1773). The areas in the hashed lines are the tracts purchased by the Wabash Company (1775). The areas in black are the townships containing McIntosh purchases of 1815, at issue in the case.

(Courtesy of Professor Eric Kades.)

That law which regulates, and ought to regulate in general, the relations between the conqueror and conquered, was incapable of application to a people under such circumstances. The resort to some new and different rule, better adapted to the actual state of things, was unavoidable. Every rule which can be suggested will be found to be attended with great difficulty.

However extravagant the pretension of converting the discovery of an inhabited country into conquest may appear; if the principle has been asserted in the first instance, and afterwards sustained; if a country has been acquired and held under it; if the property of the great mass of the community originates in it, it becomes the law of the land, and cannot be questioned. So, too, with respect to the concomitant principle, that the Indian inhabitants are to be considered merely as occupants, to be protected, indeed, while in peace, in the possession of their lands, but to be deemed incapable of transferring the absolute title to others. However this restriction may be opposed to natural right, and to the usages of civilized nations, yet, if it be indispensable to that system under which the country has been settled, and be adapted to the actual condition of the two people, it may, perhaps, be supported by reason, and certainly cannot be rejected by Courts of justice. . . .

It has never been contended, that the Indian title amounted to nothing. Their right of possession has never been questioned. The claim of government extends to the complete ultimate title, charged with this right of possession, and to the exclusive power of acquiring that right. . . .

After bestowing on this subject a degree of attention which was more required by the magnitude of the interest in litigation, and the able and elaborate arguments of the bar, than by its intrinsic difficulty, the Court is decidedly of opinion, that the plaintiffs do not exhibit a title which can be sustained in the Courts of the United States; and that there is no error in the judgment which was rendered against them in the District Court of Illinois.

Judgment affirmed, with costs.

THE REST OF THE STORY . . .

William McIntosh (1775-1825), also known as *Tustunnugge Hutke* (White Warrior), was a highly prominent chief of the Creek Nation between 1800 and his execution in 1825. He was a commander of a police force and also became a planter who owned slaves. He led the group that negotiated and signed the 1825 treaty ceding much of the remaining Creek lands to the United States in violation of Creek law, and for that, the Creek National Council ordered that he be executed. See William McIntosh, https://en.wikipedia.org/wiki/William_McIntosh (last visited May 6, 2020).

There is some evidence that Chief Justice John Marshall was sympathetic to the plight of Native Americans. In an 1828 letter to Justice Joseph Story, for example, Marshall mentioned some reasons to be forgiving of the "conduct of our forefathers in expelling the original occupants of the soil," but went on to state his view that "every oppression now exercised on a helpless people depending on our magnanimity and justice for the preservation of their existence impresses a deep stain on the American character." Quoted in The Political and Economic Doctrines of John Marshall 124-125 (John E. Oster ed. 1914).

Notes and Questions

1. *Discovery or conquest?* Chief Justice Marshall's opinion in the *Johnson* case mentions both discovery and conquest. These are terms of art referring to methods of acquiring territory in international law. Acquisition by discovery entails "the sighting or 'finding' of hitherto unknown or uncharted territory; it is frequently accompanied by a landing and the symbolic taking of possession," acts that give rise to an inchoate title that must (on one view) subsequently be perfected, within a reasonable time, by settling in and making an effective occupation. (new) Note 14 Encyclopedia of Public International Law 839-840 (1992). The discovery doctrine is highly controversial these days, although several countries continue to adhere to it. See Robert J. Miller, Lisa LeSage & Sebastián López Escarcena, The International Law of Discovery, Indigenous Peoples, and Chile, 80 Neb. L. Rev. 819 (2011). Conquest is the taking of possession of enemy territory through force, followed by formal annexation of the defeated territory by the conqueror. See Parry & Grant, Encyclopaedic Dictionary of International Law 96 (2000). The doctrine of conquest has long been abandoned by international law. See Oona A. Hathaway & Scott I. Shapiro, The Internationalists: How a Radical Plan to Outlaw War Remade the World 312-315 (2017).

With respect to the "discoverer" and the status of the Native Americans' land title, what work does the doctrine of discovery do? That is, what is its effect—does it trump the Native Americans' title? If not, how does it work together with conquest?

2. *The discovery doctrine and the principle of first possession.* Marshall's application of the discovery doctrine was based on a Eurocentric assumption—that Europeans were the first finders of an undiscovered land. In this respect, the discovery doctrine is an application of the broader legal principle of first possession. As we shall see, that principle continues to have a great deal of practical importance. As one theorist puts it, "The notion that being there first somehow justifies ownership rights is a venerable and persistent one." Lawrence C. Becker, Property Rights: Philosophical Foundations 24 (1977). You will see it running throughout the materials in this book, particularly in the next section, "Acquisition by Capture (and the Right to Exclude)." (For an overview of its active role in contemporary property law, see Lawrence Berger, An Analysis of the Doctrine That "First in Time Is First in Right," 64 Neb. L. Rev. 349 (1985).)

3. *Chain of title.* To resolve conflicting claims to title to the same parcel of land, courts sometimes construct a chain of title for each claimant to determine which one has the stronger claim. Each link in the chain represents a different owner of the land in question. Each chain is traced back, link by link, until we reach the "root of title." The traditional rule is that if both claims trace back to the same root of title, i.e., a common grantor (such as the United States government), the party whose predecessor was the prior grantee from the common grantor prevails. The later grantee takes nothing because a grantor cannot convey title that he has already transferred to another. This principle is sometimes called the *nemo dat* principle, short for *nemo dat quod non habet* ("you cannot give that which you do not have").

In Johnson v. M'Intosh, the plaintiff, Johnson, traced his title back to the Piankeshaw and Illinois Tribes, while the defendant, McIntosh, traced his to the United States government. The government in turn acquired its rights from the Piankeshaw and Illinois Tribes by treaty in 1795, so there is a common grantor—the Tribes. Under the traditional *nemo dat* principle, Johnson, whose predecessor was the prior grantee from a common grantor, should prevail. Why, then, did he lose to McIntosh?

John Marshall
Chief Justice of the United States, 1801-1835
by Chester Harding (1828)
Collection of the Boston Athenaeum

4. *Dominion and occupancy.* Marshall's opinion in *Johnson* frequently mentions the discoverer's right of dominion, which seems to imply sovereign title to the land. The opinion also mentions, more than once, the Indians' right of occupancy. What is the relationship between dominion and occupancy? Is Marshall saying that the Indians have the right of possession but that the United States has title? If so, how can this be? See Oneida Indian Nation of New York v. State of New York, 691 F.2d 1070, 1075 (2d Cir. 1982) ("Thus the concept of fee title in the context of Indian lands does not amount to absolute ownership, but rather is used interchangeably with 'right of preemption' or the preemptive right over all others to purchase the Indian title or right of occupancy from the inhabitants.") See also Michael C. Blumm, Why Aboriginal Title Is a Fee Simple Absolute, 15 Lewis & Clark L. Rev. 975 (2011).

5. *Back to conquest.* Chief Justice Marshall's opinion states that one of the ways in which the Indians' right to occupancy may be extinguished is by *conquest.* Is this basically a statement that might makes right? What do you think Marshall means in his curious statement, "Conquest gives a title which the Courts of the conqueror cannot deny"?

Given that the European settlers had superior might, why did they not instead simply conquer the Indians altogether, and grant them nothing? In his article, The Dark Side of Efficiency: *Johnson v. M'Intosh* and the Expropriation of American Indian Lands, 148 U. Pa. L. Rev. 1065 (2000), Professor Eric Kades argues that the settlers' objective was efficient expropriation; they wanted to get land at the least cost to themselves, with "cost" defined broadly to include lives lost in battle, diversion of capital to military production, and so on. In this light, purchase was often the cheapest course. To see why, consider that the decision in *Johnson*, echoing a long line of colonial statutes, royal proclamations, and administrative rulings, decreed that the sovereign (first Britain, then the United States) was the only buyer empowered to purchase Indian lands. The government was a so-called monopsonist—a sole buyer—and this fact helped reduce the price paid for the Indian title of occupancy. Moreover, major portions of early American land law (favorable financing, squatters' rights, and Homestead Acts) had the purpose and effect of weakening Indian resistance by luring settlers to the frontier. They brought with them European diseases against which tribes had no immunity; they cleared land and hunted prodigiously to get hides and fur. A native population decimated by sickness and deprived of sources of food and other necessities had little bargaining power. The title of occupancy went for a pittance. See also Eric Kades, History and Interpretation of the Great Case of *Johnson v. M'Intosh*, 19 Law & Hist. Rev. 67 (2001). For in-depth examinations of *Johnson* and the doctrines of discovery and conquest, see Lindsay G. Robertson, Conquest by Law: How the Discovery of America Dispossessed Indigenous Peoples of Their Lands (2005); Stuart Banner, How the Indians Lost Their Land: Law and Power on the Frontier (2005); Jedediah Purdy, Property and Empire: The Law of Imperialism in *Johnson v. M'Intosh*, 75 Geo. Wash. L. Rev. 329 (2007).

6. *"Fierce savages" or "agriculturists"?* One justification that Marshall gives for the decision is the character of Native Americans and their use of land. Toward the end of his opinion, he describes Native Americans as "fierce savages," "whose subsistence was drawn chiefly from the forest." Marshall contrasted this use of the land with that of the European settlers, whom he described as "agriculturists" who parceled out the land in private plots. The Indians' use of land (or what Marshall thought was the Indians' use of land) was not considered to constitute ownership.

Marshall's view was widely shared by his contemporaries, but that view has now been discredited. William Cronon, for example, has shown that New England Indians did recognize boundaries, at least between village territories, and in southern New England, they did engage in extensive farming, recognizing something like exclusive control rights for families over fields. See William Cronon, Changes in the Land: Indians, Colonists and the Ecology of New England 58-63 (1983).

7. *Possession as a "text."* As Johnson v. M'Intosh illustrates, the practical effect of the first possession principle often depends on just what we mean by *possession*. In one sense of the term (probably the obvious sense), the Indians were in possession of the land first, but as Marshall's opinion indicates, the Indians' use of land (according to Marshall) did not count as possession from the point of view of common law. Carol Rose suggests that *Johnson* illustrates that acts of possession are a kind of "text" that have to be interpreted. "It is not enough," Rose writes, "for the property claimant to say simply, 'It's mine' through some act or gesture; in order for the 'statement' to have any force, some relevant world must understand the claim it makes and take that claim seriously." Carol M. Rose, Possession as the Origin of Property, 52 U. Chi. L. Rev. 73, 84-85 (1985). In *Johnson*, the "relevant world" was the U.S. Supreme Court, and that world did not understand the Native Americans' uses of land as fitting the meaning of property that British and American lawyers had given to the "text" of possession. This is an important point that we will encounter again.

8. *Johnson v. M'Intosh in retrospect.* Commentators today generally take a dim view of *Johnson*. For example, Eric Kades argues that Marshall's decision to allow Indians to sell their land to non-Indians only with the permission of the United States government was "one element of a calculated, rational, unemotional effort to obtain Indian lands at the least costs," to the detriment of the Indians. Eric Kades, The Dark Side of Efficiency: *Johnson v. M'Intosh* and the Expropriation of American Indian Lands, 148 U. Pa. L. Rev. 1065, 1109 (2000).

B. ACQUISITION BY CAPTURE

Most things in the world are already owned by someone. But not always. Fish in navigable waters, for example, are considered unowned. How do people come to acquire property rights in fish and other unowned resources? And what property rights do people acquire in such resources? This part explores these foundational questions.

1. The Rule of Capture

[handwritten annotation: → Original plaintiff]

[handwritten annotation: Original defendant ←]

PIERSON v. POST

Supreme Court of New York, 1805
3 Cai. R. 175, 2 Am. Dec. 264

This was an action of trespass on the case commenced in a justice's court, by the present defendant against the now plaintiff.

The declaration stated that Post, being in possession of certain dogs and hounds under his command, did, "upon a certain wild and uninhabited, unpossessed and

Fact:

waste land, called the beach, find and start one of those noxious beasts called a fox," and whilst there hunting, chasing and pursuing the same with his dogs and hounds, and when in view thereof, Pierson, well knowing the fox was so hunted and pursued, did, in the sight of Post, to prevent his catching the same, kill and carry it off. A verdict having been rendered for the plaintiff below, the defendant there sued out a *certiorari*, and now assigned for error, that the declaration and the matters therein contained were not sufficient in law to maintain an action. . . .

Case history
↳ Post won and now Pierson appeals

TOMPKINS, J. This cause comes before us on a return to a *certiorari* directed to one of the justices of Queens county.

ISSUE

The question submitted by the counsel in this cause for our determination is, whether Lodowick Post, by the pursuit with his hounds in the manner alleged in his declaration, acquired such a right to, or property in, the fox, as will sustain an action against Pierson for killing and taking him away?

The cause was argued with much ability by the counsel on both sides, and presents for our decision a novel and nice question. It is admitted that a fox is an animal *ferae naturae*, and that property in such animals is acquired by occupancy only. These admissions narrow the discussion to the simple question of what acts amount to occupancy, applied to acquiring right to wild animals? If we have recourse to the ancient writers upon general principles of law, the judgment below is obviously erroneous. Justinian's Institutes, lib. 2, tit. 1, s.13, and Fleta, lib. 3, c.2, p. 175, adopt the principle, that pursuit alone vests no property or right in the huntsman; and that even pursuit, accompanied with wounding, is equally ineffectual for that purpose, unless the animal be actually taken. The same principle is recognised by Bracton, lib. 2, c.1, p. 8.

Novel question

Ancient legal position

Sidebar

Daniel Tompkins (1774-1825) was an important figure in the early Republic, especially in New York politics. A self-made man of humble origins, he graduated first in his class from Columbia College. He was an enormously popular figure with the electorate, served twice as Governor of New York State (1807-1817), and was the sixth Vice President of the United States (1817-1825) during James Monroe's administration. Throughout his public service, Tompkins had serious financial problems and was a heavy drinker. During his tenure as Vice President, he occasionally presided over the Senate while inebriated. He died in 1825, disgraced, deeply in debt, and probably alcoholic. See Ray W. Irwin, Daniel D. Tompkins: Governor of New York and Vice President of the United States (1968).

Puffendorf, lib. 4, c.6, s.2, and 10, defines occupancy of beasts *ferae naturae*, to be the actual corporal possession of them, and Bynkershoek is cited as coinciding in this definition. It is indeed with hesitation that Puffendorf affirms that a wild beast mortally wounded, or greatly maimed, cannot be fairly intercepted by another, whilst the pursuit of the person inflicting the wound continues. The foregoing authorities are decisive to show that mere pursuit gave Post no legal right to the fox, but that he became the property of Pierson, who intercepted and killed him.

It therefore only remains to inquire whether there are any contrary principles, or authorities, to be found in other books, which ought to induce a different decision. Most of the cases which have occurred in England, relating to property in wild animals, have either been discussed and decided upon the principles of their positive statute regulations, or have arisen between the huntsman and the owner of the land upon which beasts *ferae naturae* have been apprehended; the former claiming them by title of occupancy, and the latter *ratione soli*. Little satisfactory aid can, therefore, be derived

no direct applicable English authority

by reason of the land/soil

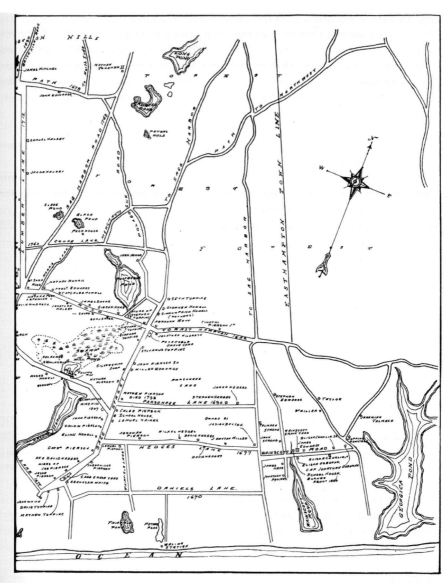

1800 map of a portion of Southampton, Long Island. The home of Jesse Pierson, the defendant, is shown on the extreme lower part of Sagg Street (left side of the map). Lodowick Post's home is on the Main Road (middle of the page, far left side). Pierson killed the fox as it hid in an old well near Peter's Pond, near the ocean shore.
Source: William D. Halsey, Sketches from Local History ("Map Extending from Water Mill to Wainscott") (Southampton, NY, 1966).

from the English reporters. Barbeyrac, in his notes on Puffendorf, does not accede to the definition of occupancy by the latter, but, on the contrary, affirms, that actual bodily seizure is not, in all cases, necessary to constitute possession of wild animals. He does not, however, *describe* the acts which, according to his ideas, will amount to an appropriation of such animals to private use, so as to exclude the claims of all other persons, by title of occupancy, to the same animals; and he is far from averring that pursuit alone is sufficient for that purpose. To a certain extent, and as far as Barbeyrac appears to me to go, his objections to Puffendorf's definition of occupancy are reasonable and correct. That is to say, that actual bodily seizure is not indispensable to acquire right to, or possession of, wild beasts; but that, on the contrary, the mortal wounding of such beasts, by one not abandoning his pursuit, may, with the utmost propriety, be deemed possession of him; since, thereby, the pursuer manifests an unequivocal intention of appropriating the animal to his individual use, has deprived him of his natural liberty, and brought him within his certain control. So also, encompassing and securing such animals with nets and toils, or otherwise intercepting them in such a manner as to deprive them of their natural liberty, and render escape impossible, may justly be deemed to give possession of them to those persons who, by their industry and labour, have used such means of apprehending them. Barbeyrac seems to have adopted, and had in view of his notes, the more accurate opinion of Grotius, with respect to occupancy. . . . The case now under consideration is one of mere pursuit, and presents no circumstances or acts which can bring it within the definition of occupancy by Puffendorf, or Grotius, or the ideas of Barbeyrac upon that subject.

The case cited from 11 Mod. 74-130, I think clearly distinguishable from the present; inasmuch as there the action was for maliciously hindering and disturbing the plaintiff in the exercise and enjoyment of a private franchise; and in the report of the same case, (3 Salk. 9) Holt, Ch. J., states, that the ducks were in the plaintiff's decoy pond, and so in his possession, from which it is obvious the court laid much stress in their opinion upon the plaintiff's possession of the ducks, *ratione soli.*

We are the more readily inclined to confine possession or occupancy of beasts *ferae naturae*, within the limits prescribed by the learned authors above cited, for the sake of certainty, and preserving peace and order in society. If the first seeing, starting, or pursuing such animals, without having so wounded, circumvented or ensnared them, so as to deprive them of their natural liberty, and subject them to the control of their pursuer, should afford the basis of actions against others for intercepting and killing them, it would prove a fertile source of quarrels and litigation.

However uncourteous or unkind the conduct of Pierson towards Post, in this instance, may have been, yet his act was productive of no injury or damage for which a legal remedy can be applied. We are of opinion the judgment below was erroneous, and ought to be reversed.

LIVINGSTON, J. My opinion differs from that of the court. Of six exceptions, taken to the proceedings below, all are abandoned except the third, which reduces the controversy to a single question. Whether a person who, with his own hounds, starts and hunts a fox on waste and uninhabited ground, and is on the point of seizing his prey, acquires such an interest in the animal, as to have a right of action against another, who in view of the huntsman and his dogs in full pursuit, and with knowledge of the chase, shall kill and carry him away?

This is a knotty point, and should have been submitted to the arbitration of sportsmen, without poring over Justinian, Fleta, Bracton, Puffendorf, Locke, Barbeyrac, or Blackstone, all of whom have been cited; they would have had no difficulty in coming to a prompt and correct conclusion. In a court thus constituted, the skin and carcass of poor *reynard* would have been properly disposed of, and a precedent set, interfering with no usage or custom which the experience of ages has sanctioned,

Of the good
say nothing unless
it is good

and which must be so well known to every votary of Diana. But the parties have referred the question to our judgment, and we must dispose of it as well as we can, from the partial lights we possess, leaving to a higher tribunal, the correction of any mistake which we may be so unfortunate as to make. By the pleadings it is admitted that a fox is a "wild and noxious beast." Both parties have regarded him, as the law of nations does a pirate, "*hostem humani generis,*" and although "*de mortuis nil nisi bonum,*" be a maxim of our profession, the memory of the deceased has not been spared. His depredations on farmers and on barn yards have not been forgotten; and to put him to death wherever found, is allowed to be meritorious, and of public benefit. Hence it follows, that our decision should have in view the greatest possible encouragement to the destruction of an animal, so cunning and ruthless in his career. But who would keep a pack of hounds; or what gentleman, at the sound of the horn, and at peep of day, would mount his steed, and for hours together, "*sub jove frigido,*"

under the
cold sky

or a vertical sun, pursue the windings of this wily quadruped, if, just as night came on, and his stratagems and strength were nearly exhausted, a saucy intruder, who had not shared in the honours or labours of the chase, were permitted to come in at the death, and bear away in triumph the object of pursuit? Whatever Justinian may have thought of the matter, it must be recollected that his code was compiled many hundred years ago, and it would be very hard indeed, at the distance of so many centuries, not to have a right to establish a rule for ourselves. In his day, we read of no order of men who made it a business, in the language of the declaration in this cause, "with hounds and dogs to find, start, pursue, hunt, and chase," these

Laws of
Rome too
old -
times have
changed

animals, and that, too, without any other motive than the preservation of Roman poultry; if this diversion had been then in fashion, the lawyers who composed his institutes would have taken care not to pass it by, without suitable encouragement. If any thing, therefore, in the digests or pandects shall appear to militate against the defendant in error, who, on this occasion, was the foxhunter, we have only to say *tempora mutantur;* and if men themselves change with the times, why should not laws also undergo an alteration?

It may be expected, however, by the learned counsel, that more particular notice be taken of their authorities. I have examined them all, and feel great difficulty in determining, whether to acquire dominion over a thing, before in common, it be sufficient that we barely see it, or know where it is, or wish for it, or make a declaration of our will respecting it; or whether, in the case of wild beasts, setting a trap, or lying in wait, or starting, or pursuing, be enough; or if an actual wounding, or killing, or bodily tact and occupation be necessary. Writers on general law, who have favoured us with their speculations on these points, differ on them all; but, great as is the diversity of sentiment among them, some conclusion must be adopted on the question immediately before us. After mature deliberation, I embrace that of Barbeyrac, as the most rational, and least liable to objection. If at liberty, we might imitate the courtesy of a certain emperor, who, to avoid giving offence to the advocates of any of these different doctrines, adopted a middle course, and by ingenious distinctions, rendered it difficult to say (as often happens after a fierce and angry contest) to whom the palm of victory belonged. He ordained, that if a beast be followed with *large dogs and hounds,* he shall belong to the hunter, not to the chance occupant; and in like manner, if he be killed or wounded with a lance or sword; but if chased with *beagles only,* then he passed to the captor, not to the first pursuer. If slain with a dart, a sling, or a bow, he fell to the hunter, if still in chase, and not to him who might afterwards find and seize him.

Now, as we are without any municipal regulations of our own, and the pursuit here, for aught that appears on the case, being with dogs and hounds of *imperial stature,* we are at liberty to adopt one of the provisions just cited, which comports also with the learned conclusion of Barbeyrac, that property in animals *ferae naturae* may be acquired without bodily touch or manucaption, provided the pursuer be within reach, or have a *reasonable* prospect (which certainly existed here) of taking, what he has *thus* discovered with an intention of converting to his own use.

[handwritten margin note: should be reasonable prospect of taking what he has discovered with intention of converting it]

When we reflect also that the interest of our husbandmen, the most useful of men in any community, will be advanced by the destruction of a beast so pernicious and incorrigible, we cannot greatly err, in saying, that a pursuit like the present, through waste and unoccupied lands, and which must inevitably and speedily have terminated in corporal possession, or bodily *seisin,* confers such a right to the object of it, as to make any one a wrongdoer, who shall interfere and shoulder the spoil. The justice's judgment ought, therefore, in my opinion, to be affirmed.

Judgment of reversal.

THE REST OF THE STORY . . .

A considerable amount of background on Pierson v. Post, one of the old chestnuts of property law, has emerged from several law review articles. It turns out that the encounter between Pierson and Post occurred on a stretch of public beach on Long Island, near Southampton, today one of the wealthiest resort communities in the country—hardly a "waste land." Neither party actually wanted the fox. Post, whose family was a kind of early version of nouveau riche, simply wanted to run a hunt free of interference from others, whereas Pierson, a farmer, wanted to get rid of these animals, which raided his nearby farm. See Andrea McDowell, Legal Fictions in *Pierson v. Post,* 105 Mich. L. Rev. 735 (2007). Similarly, Professor Bethany R. Berger argues that the real dispute in the case had little to do with rights to a fox; the issue, rather, was whether the use of local common areas should be determined by the tastes of the newly wealthy (Post) or the old agricultural traditionalists (Pierson). See Bethany Berger, It's Not About the Fox: The Untold History of *Pierson v. Post,* 55 Duke L.J. 1089 (2006). Finally, Professor Angela Fernandez argues that the length of time the case took to be heard on appeal, plus the procedural error involved in the original finding for Post, which could easily have led to a quick and simple reversal for Pierson, suggest that something besides just the legal merits was at work in the case; specifically, that the judges and lawyers involved with it at the appellate level saw an opportunity for a learned debate. The chief justice of the court at the time of the appeal, James Kent, demonstrated considerable interest in the case, as evidenced by annotations he made on a later copy of the case and his treatment of it in his famous Commentaries on American Law (four volumes, 1826-1830). Professor Fernandez speculates that Kent was the mastermind behind the case in 1805. See Angela Fernandez, *Pierson v. Post*: A Great Debate, James Kent, and the Project of Building a Learned Law for New York State, 34 Law & Soc. Inquiry 301 (2009).

Notes and Questions

1. *Who are these guys?* The majority and dissenting opinions in Pierson v. Post are peppered with references to a number of obscure legal works and legal scholars. Justinian's Institutes is a Roman law treatise of the sixth century; Bracton was the author of a thirteenth-century tome on English law; Fleta refers to a Latin textbook on English law written in 1290 or thereabouts, supposedly in Fleet prison and possibly by one of the corrupt judges Edward I put there. Barbeyrac, Bynkershoek, Grotius, and Pufendorf (sometimes spelled Puffendorf) were legal scholars who wrote in the seventeenth and eighteenth centuries; the last two of them figured in our discussion of Johnson v. M'Intosh, as did John Locke, the English philosopher (1632-1704), and William Blackstone (1723-1780). Blackstone was the first professor of English law at an English university. His famous and highly influential treatise, Commentaries on the Laws of England (1765-1769), the first accessible general statement of English law, was popular and influential in both England and the United States, despite being scorned by the likes of Jeremy Bentham (about whom see page 242) for uncritical acceptance of previous writers and blind admiration of the past. After resigning a professorship at Oxford, Blackstone was appointed to the bench.

2. *First possession again.* The discussion in Note 2 on page 11 briefly discussed the principle of first possession. As the majority opinion tells us, both sides in Pierson v. Post agreed that property in wild animals is acquired by "occupancy," i.e., first possession. On what issue, then, did the two sides disagree? And what views did the majority and dissenting justices take on that issue?

The majority held as it did "for the sake of certainty, and preserving peace and order in society." See page 17. How did its opinion (that mere chase is insufficient to confer the rights of first possession) advance those goals? Consider the dissenting opinion of Justice Livingston, who wanted to promote the destruction of "pernicious beasts." He believed that his approach would do that more effectively than the rule of the majority opinion. Do you think he was right?

3. *Custom.* Livingston was also of the view that the question in *Pierson* "should have been submitted to the arbitration of sportsmen." See page 17. In that event, Post probably would have won, because "it appeared from the record that all hunters in the region regarded hot pursuit as giving rights to take an unimpeded first possession." Richard A. Epstein, Possession as the Root of Title, 13 Ga. L. Rev. 1221, 1231 (1979). The local custom, in short, was contrary to the rule adopted by the majority. Should the majority have abided by the custom?

4. *John Locke and the labor theory of property.* Why should first possession confer property rights in unowned resources, rights that everyone else has to respect? One historic answer to this old question is the famous *labor theory of property*, commonly attributed to the English philosopher John Locke (1632-1704). In his influential work, Two Treatises of Government (1690), Locke argued that humans have natural rights to their own bodies and, by derivation, their own labor. So, Locke reasoned, when a person appropriates some resource—say, an apple—from the common stock (a common stock because in the beginning, Locke thought, all the earth and its resources existed as a commons), that person acquires a property right in the apple because he has mixed his labor (which he owns) with the previously unowned apple and thereby made the apple his own.

Sir William Blackstone
Attributed to Sir Joshua Reynolds
Source: National Portrait Gallery, London

Locke's labor theory has been subject to many criticisms. For example, just what sort of property rights—how broad or how narrow—does one acquire by mixing one's labor with some unowned resource? Why is mixing what one owns (one's labor) with what one doesn't own a way of gaining what a person doesn't own, rather than losing what a person does own? More fundamentally, why should we assume, as Locke does, that a person owns his or her own "Person" and, by extension, "the Labour of his Body and the Work of his Hands"? See Gregory S. Alexander & Eduardo M. Peñalver, An Introduction to Property Theory 46-51 (2012). Still, though, the labor theory has its appeal, and the law of property continues to feel its influence.

In *Pierson*, both Pierson and Post expended labor trying to capture the "wily quadruped." In whose favor, then, does the labor theory seem to run—Pierson's or Post's? Which opinion, the majority or the dissent, appears to place greater weight on the expenditure of labor?

5. *The labor theory illustrated: the doctrine of accession.* The labor theory is illustrated by the common law doctrine of *accession*. This doctrine comes into play where *A* in good faith applies labor alone or labor plus materials to some object that *B* owns. If *A* adds labor alone, the final product is generally awarded to *B* unless *A*'s labor (1) transforms the original item into a fundamentally different article or (2) greatly increases the value of *B*'s original item. A typical example of accession in which the final product is usually awarded to *A*, the accessioner, is where *A* innocently uses *B*'s grapes to make wine. If *A* is awarded the final product, *B* is entitled to damages equal to the value of the original material before transformation. If *A* adds both labor and other materials to *B*'s object, the final product is awarded to the owner of the "principal" material. Just what the "principal" material is often proves difficult to determine.

6. *The doctrine of increase.* Suppose that a doe belonging to *A* roams onto a neighbor's land, takes up with a buck in the neighbor's herd, is fed by the neighbor, and eventually bears a fawn sired, presumably, by the neighbor's buck. Who owns the fawn, *A* or the neighbor? According to the *doctrine of increase*, *A* does. The doctrine of increase provides that "the offspring or increase of tame or domestic animals belongs to the owner of the dam or mother. . . . Furthermore, the increase of the increase, ad infinitum, of domestic animals comes within the rule and belongs to the owner of the original stock." Carruth v. Easterling, 150 So. 2d 852, 855 (Miss. 1963). The doctrine of increase is one of those rules that is recognized in every legal system in the world that has addressed the issue. See Felix Cohen, Dialogue on Private Property, 9 Rutgers L. Rev. 357, 365-369 (1954). What reasons do you suppose explain the doctrine's universal appeal?

Problems: More on the Rule of Capture of Wild Animals

1. In *Pierson*, we encountered the doctrine of *constructive possession* (or *ratione soli*, as the court called it). This doctrine provides that a landowner is considered as being in possession of a resource that is on or in her land even if she does not have physical possession of it. Under this doctrine, a trespasser who captures a wild animal on the land of another might still have no rights to the animal as against the landowner, even though the landowner never had actual physical possession or control and even though the trespasser does. The court might say that the landowner had constructive possession of the animal. What policy does this obviously fictitious doctrine serve? See Ray A. Brown, The Law of Personal Property 17 (Walter B. Raushenbush ed. 3d ed. 1975).

2. Suppose that *T,* a trespasser, captures a wild animal on the land of *O,* a landowner, and carries it off to her own land where she confines it in a cage. Subsequently, *T1* trespasses on *T*'s land and takes away the animal. In a suit by *T* against *T1* for return of the animal, *T1* defends on the ground that *T* had no rights of ownership in the animal. How would you respond, and why? Would your response be different if *O* had gone onto to the land of *T* and taken the animal back, and *T* is now suing *O* for its return?

3. *F* has established a herd of deer that she keeps for pleasure and an occasional roast of venison. The deer roam about on open government grazing land during the day, but are sufficiently tame and domesticated that they return to a large shelter on *F*'s land in the evening. *H*, a hunter, licensed to hunt deer on the land, shoots one of *F*'s deer one day during the hunting season. *F* sues *H* for return of the carcass. Who prevails? See Brown, supra, at 18. What policies might be served by holding for *F*? For *H*?

4. *P* imports two silver gray foxes, a male and a female, from Canada for breeding purposes on her Mississippi ranch. The natural habitat of the animals is the north central United States and Canada. The foxes are wild and once having escaped any captivity have no inclination to return. For this reason, *P* keeps her pair securely confined in a floored pen with plank walls five feet high. Despite these measures, the male gnaws his way out. *P* sets traps to recapture him, but to no avail. Sometime later *D* kills the fox in a pine thicket 15 miles from *P*'s ranch. *D* skins the fox and preserves the hide. *P*, learning of this, sues for return of the hide. Who should prevail, and why? See Brown, supra, at 18.

KEEBLE v. HICKERINGILL

Queen's Bench, 1707   *Queen Anne*
11 East 574, 103 Eng. Rep. 1127
11 Mod. 74, 130 (as Keble v. Hickringill)
3 Salk. 9 (as Keeble v. Hickeringhall)

Action upon the case. Plaintiff declares that he was, 8th November in the second year of the Queen, lawfully possessed of a close of land called Minott's Meadow, [containing] a decoy pond, to which divers wildfowl used to resort and come: and the plaintiff had at his own costs and charges prepared and procured divers decoy ducks, nets, machines and other engines for the decoying and taking of the wildfowl, and enjoyed the benefit in taking them: the defendant, knowing which, and intending to damnify the plaintiff in his vivary, and to fright and drive away the wildfowl used to resort thither, and deprive him of his profit, did, on the 8th of November, resort to the head of the said pond and vivary, and did discharge six guns laden with gunpowder, and with the noise and stink of the gunpowder did drive away the wildfowl then being in the pond: and on the 11th and 12th days of November the defendant, with design to damnify the plaintiff, and fright away the wildfowl, did place himself with a gun near the vivary, and there did discharge the said gun several times that was then charged with the gunpowder against the said decoy pond, whereby the wildfowl were frighted away, and did forsake the said pond. Upon not guilty pleaded, a verdict was found for the plaintiff and 20*l.* damages.

HOLT, C.J. I am of opinion that this action doth lie. It seems to be new in its instance, but is not new in the reason or principle of it. For, 1st, this using or making a decoy is lawful. 2dly, this employment of his ground to that use is profitable to the plaintiff, as is the skill and management of that employment. As to the first, every man that hath a property may employ it for his pleasure and profit, as for alluring and procuring decoy ducks to come to his pond. To learn the trade of seducing other ducks to come there in order to be taken is not prohibited either by the law of the

To face page 34.

Drawn by Author.   Vincent Brooks Day & Son lith.

DECOYMAN DRIVING WILD DUCK UP THE PIPE.

Source: Sir Ralph Payne-Gallwey, The book of duck decoys, their construction,
management, and history (London, 1886).

Edmund Hickeringill
Possibly by R.C. Roffe; after J. Jull
Source: National Portrait Gallery, London.

land or the moral law; but it is as lawful to use art to seduce them, to catch them, and destroy them for the use of mankind, as to kill and destroy wildfowl or tame cattle. Then when a man useth his art or his skill to take them, to sell and dispose of for his profit; this is his trade; and he that hinders another in his trade or livelihood is liable to an action for so hindering him. . . .

[W]here a violent or malicious act is done to a man's occupation, profession, or way of getting a livelihood, there an action lies in all cases. But if a man doth him damage by using the same employment; as if Mr. Hickeringill had set up another decoy on his own ground near the plaintiff's, and that had spoiled the custom of

Sidebar

Chief Justice John Holt was one of the greatest English judges. After the flight of James II to France, abandoning the throne, Holt, as a member of the House of Commons, played a leading role in establishing a constitutional monarchy under William and Mary, a system that survives today. Subsequently, he was appointed Chief Justice, an office he held from 1689 to 1710. He was noted for his integrity and independence and for his common sense, as well as his deep learning in the law. Holt laid down the rule that the status of slavery could not exist in England; as soon as a slave breathed the air of England, he was free. Smith v. Brown & Cooper, 2 Salk. 666, 90 Eng. Rep. 1172 (1703). Chief Justice Holt was the first of a line of enlightened judges who, in the eighteenth century, shaped English law to accommodate the needs of a mercantile society that would dominate world trading. Lord Mansfield, who served as Chief Justice from 1756 to 1788, was perhaps the most notable of these.

the plaintiff, no action would lie, because he had as much liberty to make and use a decoy as the plaintiff. This is like the case of 11 H. 4, 47.[1] One schoolmaster sets up a new school to the damage of an antient school, and thereby the scholars are allured from the old school to come to his new. (The action was held there not to lie.) But suppose Mr. Hickeringill should lie in the way with his guns, and fright the boys from going to school, and their parents would not let them go thither; sure that schoolmaster might have an action for the loss of his scholars. 29 E. 3, 18. A man hath a market, to which he hath toll for horses sold: a man is bringing his horse to market to sell: a stranger hinders and obstructs him from going thither to the market: an action lies, because it imports damage. . . .

And when we do know that of long time in the kingdom these artificial contrivances of decoy ponds and decoy ducks have been used for enticing into those ponds wildfowl, in order to be taken for the profit of the owner of the pond, who is at the expence of servants, engines, and other management, whereby the markets of the nation may be furnished; there is great reason to give encouragement thereunto; that the people who are so instrumental by their skill and industry so to furnish the markets should reap the benefit and have their action. But, in short, that which is the true reason is that this action is not brought to recover damage for the loss of the fowl, but for the disturbance; as 2 Cro. 604, Dawney v. Dee. So is the usual and common way of declaring.

Notes and Questions

1. *Early English reports.* There were no official reports of judicial decisions in England prior to the nineteenth century; entrepreneurs gathered up information about cases in one way or another and published them on their own. Students of the matter consider some of these unofficial sources to be more reliable than others. We have not indicated all the reports of *Keeble*. That from East (reprinted in Volume 103 of the English Reports), which we have used, is thought to be particularly trustworthy, the reporter claiming that his account came directly from a copy of Chief Justice Holt's manuscript. Modern (Mod.) is not esteemed, nor is the third volume of Salkeld (Salk.). See generally John W. Wallace, The Reporters (4th ed. 1882).

---

1. The citation indicates a case decided in the eleventh year of the reign of Henry IV (1410). A variant is Y.B. 11 H.IV, 47. *Y.B.* refers to one of the Year Books, a collection (running from 1283 to 1535) of anonymous notes reporting cases. — EDS.

2. Keeble *and* Pierson. Go back to page 17, and you will see that the court in Pierson v. Post reckoned with *Keeble*, though it referred to it not by name but only by citation—the "case cited from 11 Mod. 74-130" and "the report of the same case, (3 Salk. 9)." The report in 3 Salk. 9 suggested to the court that the result in *Keeble* was influenced by the fact that the ducks were in the plaintiff's decoy pond, such that the plaintiff had possession of the ducks "*ratione soli.*" *Ratione soli* refers to the conventional view that an owner of land has possession—*constructive* possession, that is—of wild animals on the owner's land; in other words, landowners are regarded as the prior possessors of any animals *ferae naturae* on their land, until the animals take off.

We shall return to property *ratione soli* shortly. The point for now is that it appears to have had little, if any, bearing on the final decision in *Keeble*, the statement of the court in Pierson v. Post to the contrary notwithstanding. The *Keeble* case was argued several times, and there was indeed a stage at which Chief Justice Holt seemed to be of the view that the plaintiff had (constructive) possession of the ducks in question. The arguments of counsel led him to change his mind, however, and to rest the judgment on the theory spelled out in the opinion from East that you have read—the theory of malicious interference with trade.

But the East report was unavailable at the time of Pierson v. Post; it was not published until 1815, a decade after the decision in *Pierson* was handed down. Hence the court had to rely on the accounts in Modern and Salkeld, which, as we saw, are probably untrustworthy.

Suppose East had been available.

Sidebar

The Parties of Keeble v. Hickeringill

The plaintiff, Samuel Keeble, was a yeoman from Bradfield, England, who owned a number of properties. Not much is known about him, outside of his ongoing battles with the defendant over the decoy ponds. Much more is known about Edmund Hickeringill.

Though a minister, it is not surprising that Hickeringill would come into conflict with his neighbor Keeble. He was "not a man of peaceable and quiet temper," and would come into conflict with those around him throughout his life. If, as some have speculated, Keeble moved his decoy pond close to that of Hickeringill, it would not be out of character for Hickeringill to attempt to remove the competition from Keeble's pond.

After college, Hickeringill became a Baptist preacher. His views would soon run into conflict with those of his parish, and he was eventually excommunicated. He would go on to become a Quaker, and then a Deist, at which point he gave up religious service all together.

Hickeringill performed clandestine marriages, poached tithes, and intercepted funeral processions (so as to be able to perform the service himself). He also unleashed a flurry of pamphlets, criticizing the Bishop and the religious courts of England. His extensive use of pamphlets garnered him the title "the great scribbler of the nation."

Along with this title, the pamphlets also brought Hickeringill legal difficulties. Hickeringill's endless legal problems eventually got the better of him when he was convicted of forgery in 1707. He died a year later in 1708. His tombstone read, "Reverndus admodum Dominus," or "a master greatly to be respected." In a final act of retribution, his bishop, who was one of his main rivals, had this inscription removed from the tombstone. Thus Hickeringill, who found himself entrenched in legal and social rivalries his entire life, was the victim of such a rivalry in the end.

Would the outcome of *Pierson* have been different? Should it have been? Was it essential to the outcome in *Keeble* that the plaintiff was engaged in something like a trade, as opposed to mere sport? Suppose *X* is an avid hunter who tracks down a deer on a piece of open hunting land during the hunting season. The deer is at very close range, and just as *X* is about to shoot it, another hunter, *Y*, appears and does so. Who gets the deer? Was it essential to the outcome in *Keeble* that the ducks were frightened off, rather than captured by a competitor of the plaintiff?

POPOV v. HAYASHI

Superior Court of California, County of San Francisco, 2002
2002 WL 31833731

McCarthy, J.

Facts

In 1927, Babe Ruth hit sixty home runs. That record stood for thirty four years until Roger Maris broke it in 1961 with sixty one home runs. Mark McGwire hit seventy in 1998. On October 7, 2001, at PacBell Park in San Francisco, Barry Bonds hit number seventy three. That accomplishment set a record which, in all probability, will remain unbroken for years into the future.

The event was widely anticipated and received a great deal of attention.

The ball that found itself at the receiving end of Mr. Bonds' bat garnered some of that attention. Baseball fans in general, and especially people at the game, understood the importance of the ball. It was worth a great deal of money and whoever caught it would bask, for a brief period of time, in the reflected fame of Mr. Bonds.

With that in mind, many people who attended the game came prepared for the possibility that a record setting ball would be hit in their direction. Among this group were plaintiff Alex Popov and defendant Patrick Hayashi. They were unacquainted at the time. Both men brought baseball gloves, which they anticipated using if the ball came within their reach.

They, along with a number of others, positioned themselves in the arcade section of the ballpark. This is a standing room only area located near right field. It is in this general area that Barry Bonds hits the greatest number of home runs. The area was crowded with people on October 7, 2001 and access was restricted to those who held tickets for that section.

Barry Bonds came to bat in the first inning. With nobody on base and a full count, Bonds swung at a slow knuckleball. He connected. The ball sailed over the right-field fence and into the arcade. . . .

When the seventy-third home run ball went into the arcade, it landed in the upper portion of the webbing of a softball glove worn by Alex Popov. While the glove stopped the trajectory of the ball, it is not at all clear that the ball was secure. Popov had to reach for the ball and in doing so, may have lost his balance.

Even as the ball was going into his glove, a crowd of people began to engulf Mr. Popov. He was tackled and thrown to the ground while still in the process of attempting to complete the catch. Some people intentionally descended on him for the purpose of taking the ball away, while others were involuntarily forced to the ground by the momentum of the crowd. . . .

Mr. Hayashi was standing near Mr. Popov when the ball came into the stands. He, like Mr. Popov, was involuntarily forced to the ground. He committed no wrongful act. While on the ground he saw the loose ball. He picked it up, rose to his feet and put it in his pocket. . . .

It is important to point out what the evidence did not and could not show. Neither the camera nor the percipient witnesses were able to establish whether Mr. Popov retained control of the ball as he descended into the crowd. Mr. Popov's testimony on this question is inconsistent on several important points, ambiguous on others and, on the whole, unconvincing. We do not know when or how Mr. Popov lost the ball.

Perhaps the most critical factual finding of all is one that cannot be made. We will never know if Mr. Popov would have been able to retain control of the ball had the crowd not interfered with his efforts to do so. Resolution of that question is the work of a psychic, not a judge.

Legal Analysis

Plaintiff has pled causes of actions for conversion, trespass to chattel, injunctive relief and constructive trust.

Conversion is the wrongful exercise of dominion over the personal property of another. There must be actual interference with the plaintiff's dominion. Wrongful withholding of property can constitute actual interference even where the defendant lawfully acquired the property. If a person entitled to possession of personal property demands its return, the unjustified refusal to give the property back is conversion.

The act constituting conversion must be intentionally done. There is no requirement, however, that the defendant know that the property belongs to another or that the defendant intends to dispossess the true owner of its use and enjoyment. Wrongful purpose is not a component of conversion. . . .

Trespass to chattel, in contrast, exists where personal property has been damaged or where the defendant has interfered with the plaintiff's use of the property. Actual dispossession is not an element of the tort of trespass to chattel.

In the case at bar, Mr. Popov is not claiming that Mr. Hayashi damaged the ball or that he interfered with Mr. Popov's use and enjoyment of the ball. He claims instead that Mr. Hayashi intentionally took it from him and refused to give it back. There is no trespass to chattel. If there was a wrong at all, it is conversion.

Conversion does not exist, however, unless the baseball rightfully belongs to Mr. Popov. One who has neither title nor possession, nor any right to possession, cannot sue for conversion. The deciding question in this case then, is whether Mr. Popov achieved possession or the right to possession as he attempted to catch and hold on to the ball.

The parties have agreed to a starting point for the legal analysis. Prior to the time the ball was hit, it was possessed and owned by Major League Baseball. At the time it was hit it became intentionally abandoned property. The first person who came in possession of the ball became its new owner.

The parties fundamentally disagree about the definition of possession. In order to assist the court in resolving this disagreement, four distinguished law professors participated in a forum to discuss the legal definition of possession.[2] The professors also disagreed. . . .

---

2. They are Professor Brian E. Gray, University of California, Hastings College of the Law; Professor Roger Bernhardt, Golden Gate University School of Law; Professor Paul Finkelman, The Chapman Distinguished Professor of Law, The University of Tulsa School of Law; and Professor Jan Stiglitz, California Western School of Law. . . .

The focus of the analysis in this case is not on the thoughts or intent of the actor. Mr. Popov has clearly evidenced an intent to possess the baseball and has communicated that intent to the world. The question is whether he did enough to reduce the ball to his exclusive dominion and control. Were his acts sufficient to create a legally cognizable interest in the ball?

Mr. Hayashi argues that possession does not occur until the fan has complete control of the ball. Professor Brian Gray suggests the following definition: "A person who catches a baseball that enters the stands is its owner. A ball is caught if the person has achieved complete control of the ball at the point in time that the momentum of the ball and the momentum of the fan while attempting to catch the ball ceases. A baseball, which is dislodged by incidental contact with an inanimate object or another person, before momentum has ceased, is not possessed. Incidental contact with another person is contact that is not intended by the other person. The first person to pick up a loose ball and secure it becomes its possessor."[3]

Mr. Popov argues that this definition requires that a person seeking to establish possession must show unequivocal dominion and control, a standard rejected by several leading cases.[4] Instead, he offers the perspectives of Professor Bernhardt and Professor Paul Finkelman who suggest that possession occurs when an individual intends to take control of a ball and manifests that intent by stopping the forward momentum of the ball whether or not complete control is achieved.

Professors Finkelman and Bernhardt have correctly pointed out that some cases recognize possession even before absolute dominion and control is achieved. Those cases require the actor to be actively and ably engaged in efforts to establish complete control. Moreover, such efforts must be significant and they must be reasonably calculated to result in unequivocal dominion and control at some point in the near future.

This rule is applied in cases involving the hunting or fishing of wild animals or the salvage of sunken vessels. The hunting and fishing cases recognize that a mortally wounded animal may run for a distance before falling. The hunter acquires possession upon the act of wounding the animal not the eventual capture. Similarly, whalers acquire possession by landing a harpoon, not by subduing the animal.

In the salvage cases, an individual may take possession of a wreck by exerting as much control "as its nature and situation permit." Inadequate efforts, however, will not support a claim of possession. Thus, a "sailor cannot assert a claim merely by boarding a vessel and publishing a notice, unless such acts are coupled with a then present intention of conducting salvage operations, and he immediately thereafter proceeds with activity in the form of constructive steps to aid the distressed party."[5]

These rules are contextual in nature. They are crafted in response to the unique nature of the conduct they seek to regulate. Moreover, they are influenced by the custom and practice of each industry. The reason that absolute dominion and control is not required to establish possession in the cases cited by Mr. Popov is that such a rule would be unworkable and unreasonable. The "nature and situation" of the property at issue does not immediately lend itself to unequivocal dominion and control. It is impossible to wrap one's arms around a whale, a fleeing fox or a sunken ship.

---

3. This definition is hereinafter referred to as Gray's Rule.

4. Pierson v. Post 3 Caines R. (N.Y. 1805); Young v. Hitchens 6 Q.B. 606 (1844); State v. Shaw (1902) 67 Ohio St. 157, 65 N.E. 875.

5. Brady v. S.S. African Queen 179 F. Supp. 321, 324 (E.D. Va. 1960).

The opposite is true of a baseball hit into the stands of a stadium. Not only is it physically possible for a person to acquire unequivocal dominion and control of an abandoned baseball, but fans generally expect a claimant to have accomplished as much. The custom and practice of the stands creates a reasonable expectation that a person will achieve full control of a ball before claiming possession. There is no reason for the legal rule to be inconsistent with that expectation. Therefore Gray's Rule is adopted as the definition of possession in this case.

The central tenant of Gray's Rule is that the actor must retain control of the ball after incidental contact with people and things. Mr. Popov has not established by a preponderance of the evidence that he would have retained control of the ball after all momentum ceased and after any incidental contact with people or objects. Consequently, he did not achieve full possession.

That finding, however, does not resolve the case. The reason we do not know whether Mr. Popov would have retained control of the ball is not because of incidental contact. It is because he was attacked. His efforts to establish possession were interrupted by the collective assault of a band of wrongdoers. . . .

As a matter of fundamental fairness, Mr. Popov should have had the opportunity to try to complete his catch unimpeded by unlawful activity. To hold otherwise would be to allow the result in this case to be dictated by violence. That will not happen. . . .

Here Mr. Popov seeks, in effect, a declaratory judgment that he has either possession or the right to possession. In addition he seeks the remedies of injunctive relief and a constructive trust. These are all actions in equity. A court sitting in equity has the authority to fashion rules and remedies designed to achieve fundamental fairness.

Consistent with this principle, the court adopts the following rule. Where an actor undertakes significant but incomplete steps to achieve possession of a piece of abandoned personal property and the effort is interrupted by the unlawful acts of others, the actor has a legally cognizable pre-possessory interest in the property. That pre-possessory interest constitutes a qualified right to possession which can support a cause of action for conversion. . . .

Mr. Hayashi was not a wrongdoer. He was a victim of the same bandits that attacked Mr. Popov. The difference is that he was able to extract himself from their assault and move to the side of the road. It was there that he discovered the loose ball. When he picked up and put it in his pocket he attained unequivocal dominion and control.

If Mr. Popov had achieved complete possession before Mr. Hayashi got the ball, those actions would not have divested Mr. Popov of any rights, nor would they have created any rights to which Mr. Hayashi could lay claim. Mr. Popov, however, was able to establish only a qualified pre-possessory interest in the ball. That interest does not establish a full right to possession that is protected from a subsequent legitimate claim.

On the other hand, while Mr. Hayashi appears on the surface to have done everything necessary to claim full possession of the ball, the ball itself is encumbered by the qualified pre-possessory interest of Mr. Popov. At the time Mr. Hayashi came into possession of the ball, it had, in effect, a cloud on its title.

An award of the ball to Mr. Popov would be unfair to Mr. Hayashi. It would be premised on the assumption that Mr. Popov would have caught the ball. That assumption is not supported by the facts. An award of the ball to Mr. Hayashi would unfairly penalize Mr. Popov. It would be based on the assumption that Mr. Popov would have dropped the ball. That conclusion is also unsupported by the facts.

Both men have a superior claim to the ball as against all the world. Each man has a claim of equal dignity as to the other. We are, therefore, left with something of a dilemma.

Thankfully, there is a middle ground. . . .

The concept of equitable division has its roots in ancient Roman law. . . . [I]t is useful in that [the concept of equitable ownership] "provides an equitable way to resolve competing claims which are equally strong." Moreover, "[i]t comports with what one instinctively feels to be fair."[6] . . .

Mr. Hayashi's claim is compromised by Mr. Popov's pre-possessory interest. Mr. Popov cannot demonstrate full control. . . . Their legal claims are of equal quality and they are equally entitled to the ball.

The court therefore declares that both plaintiff and defendant have an equal and undivided interest in the ball. Plaintiff's cause of action for conversion is sustained only as to his equal and undivided interest. In order to effectuate this ruling, the ball must be sold and the proceeds divided equally between the parties.

THE REST OF THE STORY . . .

According to a July 19, 2005 report on CourtTV.com, the judge ordered that the ball be sold and the proceeds divided equally between the two men. The ball was estimated to be worth as much as $1.5 million, but ended up selling at auction for $450,000. The shortfall, according to the CourtTV account, gave rise to another legal battle. Popov's attorney obtained a freeze on his client's half of the money to help pay a legal bill of $473,530.32.

Notes and Questions

1. *Reasoning by analogy.* The court in *Popov* analyzed the case in part by analogizing the case to disputes over rights in wild animals. Are cases like Pierson v. Post proper analogies for the dispute between Popov and Hayashi?

2. *Custom again.* Recall that in *Pierson*, the dissent suggested that the dispute between Pierson and Post should have been decided on the basis of the custom of hunters. Was *Popov* an appropriate case for decision on the basis of custom? If custom should be given weight, whose custom should count? For example, the custom among baseball players is that if the ball is hit to the outfield and one outfielder signals his intention to catch the ball, by calling out or waving his teammates away, the other outfielders must defer to him and give him the first chance to catch the ball. Should that custom apply to and bind the fans in the stands as well? Even assuming that one small community's custom is sensible, how are

---

6. [R.H. Helmholz, Equitable Division and the Law of Finders, 52 Fordham L. Rev. 313] at 315 [(1983)].

people outside that community to know what the custom is? See Henry E. Smith, Community and Custom in Property, 10 Theoretical Inq. in L. 5 (2009).

3. *Equitable division—half-measures.* The court in *Popov* reached the Solomonic solution of dividing the proceeds from the sale of the baseball between Messrs. Popov and Hayashi. Although this "equitable division" remedy might seem to be the sensible approach to take in situations like *Popov*, where both parties have made some (more than trivial) movement toward reducing the object to physical custody (is Pierson v. Post such a case?), it is highly unusual. Courts rarely adopt half-measure remedies in these cases. Should they do so more often, or is it just a way of avoiding a difficult decision?

The Rule of Capture Applied to Other "Fugitive" Resources

Courts have extended the analogy to wild animals to various "fugitive" resources, using the rule of capture as the means of acquiring property rights for the first time. Two examples are the common law doctrines governing oil and gas and water in common pools.

Oil and gas. Oil and natural gas commonly collect in reservoirs that underlie many acres of land owned by many different people. The resources have a fugitive character, in that they wander from place to place. Oil or gas once under the land of *A* might migrate to space under the land of *B* as the result of natural circumstances or because *B* drops a well and mines a common pool beneath *A's* and *B's* land. The oil or gas mined by *B* may even have been placed in the pool by *A* (gas and oil extracted elsewhere are often reinjected for storage or secondary recovery).

When these obviously problematic situations first led to litigation—usually (but not always) a suit by someone like *A* to recover the value of gas or oil drawn away by someone like *B*—the fugitive nature of the resources led courts to analogize them to wild animals. And because ownership of wild animals had long been settled in terms of the rule of capture, the courts reasoned that ownership of oil and gas should be determined in the same manner; i.e., under the rule of capture. According to this common law approach, oil and gas in natural underground reservoirs are not considered owned by anyone until reduced to physical possession. Any surface owner whose land lies above the reservoir is free to pump oil or gas so long as the drilling remains within the imaginary column of space projected down from the boundaries of his land. Slant drilling, which is drilling at an angle so that the well bottoms beneath a neighbor's parcel, is considered trespass.

Scholars and policy analysts have criticized this common law rule of capture on the ground that it tends to create a race to pump. If *A*, *B*, and *C* are all surface owners whose parcels lie above a pool of oil, each one has incentives to continue pumping oil as soon as the first begins to do so for fear that otherwise no oil will remain when she needs it. The result will be a "tragedy of the commons," a phenomenon that we discuss shortly. See page 35 infra. Theoretically, *A*, *B*, and *C* could agree among themselves upon a rate of drilling that optimizes the value of the oil over time, but, as we will soon discuss, there are problems reaching such agreements. Even where the parties do reach an agreement, it will be costly to monitor and enforce. As a result of these and other problems, many states have modified the capture rule in various ways.

Water. The rule of capture has played a formative role in the case of another migratory resource—water. Water law distinguishes between two basic different categories of water: surface water and groundwater.

Surface water. There are two different systems governing water in a defined channel (or body): *riparianism* and *prior appropriation.*

- *Riparianism.* This system assigns water rights on the basis of ownership of riparian land; i.e., land that abuts the watercourse. Under this system, water rights are derivative of rights to the land. Each owner of riparian land has a right to use the water, subject to the rights of other riparians. At first glance, riparian rights have no relation to a rule of capture, or first in time, but on a closer look they do—because the claims of riparians rest on their underlying holdings of riparian land, and the land itself was originally acquired by first possession. See Richard A. Epstein, Possession as the Root of Title, 13 Ga. L. Rev. 1221, 1234 (1979).
- *Prior appropriation.* The riparian system has been adopted mainly in the Eastern states, where water is abundant. Many Western states, where water is scarcer, have adopted the prior appropriation method. The basic principle is that the person who first appropriates (captures) water and puts it to reasonable and beneficial use has a right superior to later appropriators. Prior appropriation is a straightforward application of the idea behind the rule of capture. (Obviously, complications can arise. Suppose that *A* begins efforts to appropriate water from a stream—starts building diversion works—before *B*, but that *B* finishes her works and puts the water to beneficial use before *A*. Who is prior to whom? What would Pierson v. Post say?)

Neither system is perfect. Riparian rights, for example, take little or no account of the relative productivity of the land the water services, encourage the development of uneconomical "bowling-alley" parcels of land perpendicular to the banks of a stream, and ration poorly when stream levels are low. Prior appropriation encourages premature development and excessive diversion. It also rations poorly when supplies dwindle periodically.

Groundwater (water found in underground aquifers). Groundwater was governed early on by the English rule of absolute ownership, which allowed each landowner over an aquifer to withdraw freely without regard to effects on neighbors. "[F]ramed in property language, the rule was in reality a rule of capture, for a landowner's pump could induce water under the land of his neighbor to flow to his well—water that was in theory the neighbor's property while it remained in place." Restatement (Second) of Torts ch. 41, commentary at 256 (1977). Whoever first captured the water, then, was really its owner. The so-called *English rule* was adopted by a number of states, but virtually all others followed the American rule of reasonable use, itself a rule of capture, but with the slight addition that wasteful uses of water, if they actually harmed neighbors, were considered unreasonable and hence unlawful. As with the English rule, there was no principle of apportionment among overlying users. Today groundwater extraction is commonly governed by legislative and administrative programs.

What might be the consequences of applying the rule of capture to wild animals—and then to oil, gas, water, and other natural resources? What might those consequences have to do with the concept of "common property"? Consider the following discussion.

The Tragedy of the Commons and the Economic Theory of Property

The rule of capture operates in the context of the relevant resource being unowned, a context frequently termed a "commons." The term "commons" itself is somewhat ambiguous and needs some clarification. An important distinction is between limited-access commons and open-access commons. Limited-access commons limit access to and use of some resource (say, pasture land) to members of a relatively small group, all of whose members have equal privileges to use the pasture land. But the group has the right to exclude outsiders from access to and use of the land. In open-access commons, no single individual and no group has the right to exclude anyone; the land is open for anyone to use.

The open-access commons is thought to create a "tragedy of the commons," a phrase that derives from the eponymous (and influential) article by a biologist, Garrett Hardin, published in 1968. To illustrate his model, he imagines a pasture open to all. Viewing the situation from the perspective of each herder, whom he assumes to be rational (i.e., self-interest maximizing), Hardin observed that each herder benefits directly from his animals and suffers only delayed costs from the deterioration of the commons when his and other herders' cattle overgraze. Hence, Hardin reasoned, each herder, acting rationally, will add more and more animals to the grazing herd because doing so maximizes his own direct gains while bearing only a share of the costs of overgrazing. "Therein is the tragedy," Hardin concluded. "Each man is locked into a system that compels him to increase his herd without limit—in a world that is limited. Ruin is the destination toward which all men rush, each pursuing his own best interest in a society that believes in the freedom of the commons." Garrett Hardin, The Tragedy of the Commons, 162 Science 1243, 1244 (1968). What is the solution for this dilemma? Hardin's solution was coercive intervention by the government, which then institutes either a system of central regulation or private property rights.

Some analysts have argued that the tragic consequences do not always occur in a limited-access commons. These scholars, notably the late Elinor Ostrom, who won the Nobel Prize for Economics in 2009, have found that in a limited-access commons people are often able to cooperate with each other in arrangements that avoid tragic consequences for the group. Limited numbers and shared outlooks tend to reduce strategic behavior among the group members, thus facilitating constructive collective action. See generally Elinor Ostrom, Governing the Commons: The Evolution of Institutions for Collective Action (1990).

The tragedy of the commons illustrates an important concept in the economic analysis of property—*externalities*. Externalities exist whenever some person, say X, makes a decision about how to use resources without taking full account of the effects of the decision. X ignores some of the effects—some of the costs or benefits that would result from a particular activity, for example—because they fall on others. They are "external" to X, hence the label "externalities." As a consequence of externalities, resources tend to be misused or "misallocated," which is to say used in one way when another would make society as a whole better off.

Externalities can be negative or positive. Externalities are commonly thought of in negative terms. Air and water pollution, overharvesting of fish and other resources in common areas, littering, and cutting in line are all examples of negative externalities (also called "social costs"). But externalities can be positive as well. For example, think of street performers who make music in a public space, hoping for tips from those who sit and watch. They provide a positive externality for anyone who enjoys the performance as they walk by on their way somewhere else.

The concept of externalities is at the heart of the economic theory of property rights, which has gained much attention over the past several decades. According to this theory, the purpose of property rights is to enhance social welfare by maximizing the value of scarce resources. Property rights are thought to perform this value-maximizing function by "internalizing externalities," to use the economics jargon—i.e., bringing the costs of the resource's use to bear on the user. See Harold Demsetz, Toward a Theory of Property Rights, 57 Am. Econ. Rev. 347-357 (Pap. & Proc. 1967). They do so in two ways: first, property rights concentrate the costs and benefits of the use on owners, giving them greater incentives to use their own resources more efficiently; second, by reducing the costs of negotiating with others over remaining externalities. In a commons, agreements to reduce external costs require the consent of everyone having a right to use the resource. Such agreements encounter high *transaction costs* by virtue of the sheer number of users involved. Even if the number of users is low, however, there are other types of transaction costs. One is the problem of freeriders, which occurs when efforts are made to extract contributions *from* members of a group in order to carry out transactions that will confer collective or nonexclusive benefits on the group—on contributors and noncontributors alike. Collective or nonexclusive effects are typical of many (but not all) externalities. Another is the problem of holdouts, which arises when payments must be made *to* a group in order to carry out a transaction, and where, unless each member of the group accepts payment, the transaction fails entirely. Suppose X wishes to change to a land use that will increase his profits by $1,000 but impose $50 in costly effects on each of 10 neighbors. Suppose, too, that X is prohibited by law from engaging in the use unless he first obtains the permission of each person affected. X will be inclined to offer payments (between $50 and $100) to each neighbor, but each has an incentive to "hold out" for an exorbitantly higher amount, knowing that without his permission X cannot pursue a venture worth far more to X than $100. Holding out can frustrate transactions, the completion of which would, as in the example posed, be beneficial to all concerned. The general point is this: when transaction costs become sufficiently high, the external effects of using resources are unlikely to be taken into account through any sort of bargaining process, and the resources are likely to be misused.

The economic theory of property derives from the utilitarian account of property, the theoretical foundations of which trace back to the work of Jeremy Bentham and earlier to David Hume in the eighteenth century. Utilitarian theory marked the break of philosophies of property from their earlier natural rights foundations. Unlike natural law theorists, utilitarians regard the concept of property as a mere artifact—a human invention, a social institution. Utilitarian theory is the dominant view of property today, at least among lawyers and legal scholars who believe that a primary function of property rights is to promote the efficient use of resources.

The utilitarian theory of property certainly has its share of critics. One frequent objection to utilitarian theory generally, one that applies with equal force to utilitarian property theory, is that it does not give adequate weight to the interests of individuals. Utilitarianism has long been criticized for a willingness to trade on individual well-being to enhance aggregate utility. Another criticism is that utilitarians treat goods as always substitutable. This is because in order to aggregate individual utility, the theory requires some unitary measure of value. Other theories, however, view human well-being as multivalent, such that multiple goods cannot be measured against each other and, therefore, cannot be easily substituted for each other. See Gregory S. Alexander & Eduardo M. Peñalver, An Introduction to Property Theory 31-33 (2012).

Finally, critics of economic analysis have challenged its behavioral foundation, the rational actor model of individual motivation. According to a common version of this model, individuals base their decisions on a private cost-benefit calculation in which they invariably opt for the course of action that will yield them the greatest individual net wealth. (This is the behavioral assumption that underlies the Tragedy of the Commons thesis, for example.) Social scientists conducting empirical work have found, however, that human behavior doesn't always work this way. People do not always act on the basis of self-interest alone; they care, or act as if they care, about others in some circumstances. Moreover, there are systematic gaps between observed actual judgments and the unbiased judgments that utilitarian theory posits. For example, people commonly rely on rules of thumb and similar shortcuts in making judgments, and although these are often useful, they can lead to incorrect conclusions. For example, using the so-called availability heuristic, people tend to conclude that the probability of an event (e.g., a car accident) is greater if they have recently witnessed an occurrence of that event than if they have not. See Amos Tversky & Daniel Kahneman, Judgment Under Uncertainty: Heuristics and Biases, in Judgment Under Uncertainty (Daniel Kahneman, Paul Slovic & Amos Tversky eds. 1982).

> ### In Brief
>
> #### Externalities
>
> An effect of one person's activity on another person that the first person does not take into account. For example, when someone decides to drive her car to work, she contributes to local traffic congestion, slowing down the commutes of everyone else who uses those same roads at roughly the same time. Externalities are important in the economic analysis of property because they tend to encourage inefficient use of resources.

C. CONSTITUTING OWNERSHIP

If you were to ask an ordinary layperson what property is, perhaps the most common answer you would get is "things." Although there is some element of truth in the ordinary notion that property is about things, from the lawyer's point of view ownership is more complex than that simple equation. In preparing you for the remaining materials in this book, it will help to introduce you to the conventional legal understanding of the concept of ownership. We emphasize, however, that there is no single universally agreed-upon definition or conception of ownership and that legal theorists have struggled, without success, to come up with a definitive model of ownership. What we present here is what we take to be a view of ownership that is most widely accepted among American lawyers today.

1. Ownership as a "Bundle of Rights"

JOSEPH WILLIAM SINGER, PROPERTY AND SOCIAL RELATIONS: FROM TITLE TO ENTITLEMENT
Property and Values: Striking an Equitable Balance of Public and Private Interests 75-76 (Charles Geisler ed. 2000) (footnotes omitted)

According to the legal realists, from [Wesley Newcomb] Hohfeld to (Arthur L.] Corbin to the American Law Institutes' [sic] Restatement of Property to Thomas Grey's famous article on the disintegration of property, property has been exploded as a useful concept. It merely describes a collection of legally protected interests which can be disaggregated into their component parts. Under this conception of legal rights, the crucial steps are: (1) identifying the interests for which individuals seek legal protection and (2) using policy analysis to adjudicate conflicts among those interests and to determine the appropriate extent of legal protection for each interest. Further, it describes legal relations among people with regard to control of valued resources, rather than relations between persons and things. Under this conception, property as a category has no utility except to obfuscate the underlying policy choices which must be done at the level of the detailed individual rules. Specific entitlements and policy concerns should replace the formalist and conceptualist attempt to imbue the concept of "property" with operative force in its own right.

HENRY E. SMITH, PROPERTY AS THE LAW OF THINGS
125 Harv. L. Rev. 1691, 1691-1692, 1694, 1696, 1697 (2012)

According to th[e] conventional wisdom, property is a bundle of rights and other legal relations available between persons. Things form the mere backdrop to these social relations, and a largely dispensable one at that. Particularly with the rise of intangible property, so this story goes, the notions of ownership and property have become so fragmented and untethered to things that property is a mere conclusion, a label that we affix to the cluster of entitlements that result from intelligent policymaking. . . .

[T]he bundle of rights by itself is more a description than a theory[,] and . . . the more extreme versions of the bundle of rights fail to be a theory at all. . . .

As an analytical device the bundle picture can be very useful. It provides a highly accurate description of who can do what to whom in a legal (and perhaps nonlegal) sense. . . .

The problem with the bundle of rights is that it is treated as a theory of how our world works rather than as an analytical device or as a theoretical baseline. . . . [I]n the most tendentious versions of the picture, the traditional baselines of law were mocked, and the idea was to dethrone them in order to remove them as barriers to enlightened social engineering. In this version of the bundle picture, Hohfeldian sticks . . . are posited to describe the relations holding between persons; the fact that the relations hold with respect to a thing is relatively unimportant or, in some versions, of no importance. "Property" is simply a conclusory label we might attach to the collection.

Notes and Questions

1. *Wesley Newcomb Hohfeld and the origins of the "bundle of rights" picture.* Both Professors Singer and Smith refer to Wesley Newcomb Hohfeld and "Hohfeldian" analysis. Hohfeld (1879-1918) was a law professor whose legal writings, though limited in number, were highly influential not only among his peers, but subsequent generations of legal scholars. Hohfeld pointed out that rights such as the right to property are not simple at all but have a complex internal structure. If *A* owns land, then *A* generally has the privilege of entering that land along with a right to prevent *B* from using that land without *A*'s permission. *B*, then, not only has no right to enter the land, but even owes a duty to *A* to stay off the land. Hohfeld noted that one could not logically recognize privileges without imposing duties on others. And in deciding whether particular individual privileges ought to be recognized, lawmakers should consider whether imposing duties on others is justified. Since property rights are usually "in rem" (i.e., good against the entire world), duties associated with others' ownership could be particularly burdensome on society.

Hohfeld's contemporaries at Yale, and later at Columbia and elsewhere, used this approach to critique the then-dominant conception of ownership, which is often loosely called "formalist" or "conceptualist." Hohfeld's followers, the so-called Legal Realists, objected to that conception, among other reasons, because it lumped all of the constituent elements of the right of property into a single unitary interest. The Realists used Hohfeld's approach to break down what it means to own property into a bundle of constituent elements—hence, the "bundle of rights."

> **Sidebar**
>
> Hohfeld was not the first to use the term "bundle of rights." In fact, he never used it at all. Apparently the first legal scholar to use the term was John Lewis, who coined it in his treatise on eminent domain (John Lewis, A Treatise on the Law of Eminent domain in the United States (1888)) several years before Hohfeld published his work on jural opposites and correlatives.

2. *Two views of the bundles picture—Singer and Smith.* The excerpts from Professors Singer and Smith reflect different attitudes toward the bundle of rights conception of property. Is one right and the other wrong, or do both have valuable insights about the bundle conception?

3. *A bundle of rights or things?* Are you convinced that the bundle of rights is the better way to think about owning property, or do you consider ownership a matter of things over which a person has near-absolute control? In thinking about this question, consider the cases and materials that follow in the next subpart.

2. Some Basic Aspects of Ownership

a. The Right to Exclude

It is often said that the right to exclude is one of the most important incidents of ownership. But no property right is absolute, including the right to exclude. The two cases that follow illustrate both the importance of the right to exclude and its limits.

JACQUE v. STEENBERG HOMES, INC.
Supreme Court of Wisconsin, 1997
563 N.W.2d 154

BABLITCH, J. Steenberg Homes had a mobile home to deliver. Unfortunately for Harvey and Lois Jacque (the Jacques), the easiest route of delivery was across their land. Despite adamant protests by the Jacques, Steenberg plowed a path through the Jacques' snow-covered field and via that path, delivered the mobile home. Consequently, the Jacques sued Steenberg Homes for intentional trespass. Although the jury awarded the Jacques $1 in nominal damages and $100,000 in punitive damages, the circuit court set aside the jury's award of $100,000. The court of appeals affirmed, reluctantly concluding that it could not reinstate the punitive damages because . . . an award of nominal damages will not sustain a punitive damage award. We conclude that when nominal damages are awarded for an intentional trespass to land, punitive damages may, in the discretion of the jury, be awarded. . . .

I.

Plaintiffs, Lois and Harvey Jacque, are an elderly couple, now retired from farming, who own roughly 170 acres near Wilke's Lake in the town of Schleswig. The defendant, Steenberg Homes, Inc. (Steenberg), is in the business of selling mobile homes. In the fall of 1993, a neighbor of the Jacques purchased a mobile home from Steenberg. Delivery of the mobile home was included in the sales price.

Steenberg determined that the easiest route to deliver the mobile home was across the Jacques' land. Steenberg preferred transporting the home across the Jacques' land because the only alternative was a private road which was covered in up to seven feet of snow and contained a sharp curve which would require sets of "rollers" to be used when maneuvering the home around the curve. Steenberg asked the Jacques on several separate occasions whether it could move the home across the Jacques' farm field. The Jacques refused. The Jacques were sensitive about allowing others on their land because they had lost property valued at over $10,000 to other neighbors in an adverse possession action in the mid-1980's. Despite repeated refusals from the Jacques, Steenberg decided to sell the mobile home, which was to be used as a summer cottage, and delivered it on February 15, 1994.

On the morning of delivery, Mr. Jacque observed the mobile home parked on the corner of the town road adjacent to his property. He decided to find out where the movers planned to take the home. The movers, who were Steenberg employees, showed Mr. Jacque the path they planned to take with the mobile home to reach the neighbor's lot. The path cut across the Jacques' land. Mr. Jacque informed the movers that it was the Jacques' land they were planning to cross and that Steenberg did not have permission to cross their land. He told them that Steenberg had been refused permission to cross the Jacques' land. . . .

At that point, the assistant manager asked Mr. Jacque how much money it would take to get permission. Mr. Jacque responded that it was not a question of money; the Jacques just did not want Steenberg to cross their land. Mr. Jacque testified that he told Steenberg to "[F]ollow the road, that is what the road is for." Steenberg employees left the meeting without permission to cross the land.

At trial, one of Steenberg's employees testified that, upon coming out of the Jacques' home, the assistant manager stated: "I don't give a _____ what [Mr. Jacque] said, just get the home in there any way you can." The other Steenberg employee confirmed this testimony and further testified that the assistant manager told him to park the company truck in such a way that no one could get down the town road to see the route the employees were taking with the home. The assistant manager denied giving these instructions, and Steenberg argued that the road was blocked for safety reasons.

The employees, after beginning down the private road, ultimately used a "bobcat" to cut a path through the Jacques' snow-covered field and hauled the home across the Jacques' land to the neighbor's lot. One employee testified that upon returning to the office and informing the assistant manager that they had gone across the field, the assistant manager reacted by giggling and laughing. The other employee confirmed this testimony. The assistant manager disputed this testimony.

When a neighbor informed the Jacques that Steenberg had, in fact, moved the mobile home across the Jacques' land, Mr. Jacque called the Manitowoc County Sheriff's Department. After interviewing the parties and observing the scene, an officer from the sheriff's department issued a $30 citation to Steenberg's assistant manager. . . .

This case presents [two] issues: (1) whether an award of nominal damages for intentional trespass to land may support a punitive damage award and, if so; (2) . . . whether the $100,000 in punitive damages awarded by the jury is excessive. . . .

II.

. . . Steenberg argues that, as a matter of law, punitive damages could not be awarded by the jury because punitive damages must be supported by an award of compensatory damages and here the jury awarded only nominal and punitive damages. The Jacques contend that the rationale supporting the compensatory damage award requirement is inapposite when the wrongful act is an intentional trespass to land. We agree with the Jacques.

[After noting that the traditional rule in Wisconsin had been that a plaintiff may not recover punitive damages where only nominal compensatory damages are found, the court continued:]

The Jacques argue that the rationale for not allowing nominal damages to support a punitive damage award is inapposite when the wrongful act involved is an intentional trespass to land. The Jacques argue that both the individual and society have significant interests in deterring intentional trespass to land, regardless of the lack of measurable harm that results. We agree with the Jacques. An examination of the individual interests invaded by an intentional trespass to land, and society's interests in preventing intentional trespass to land, leads us to the conclusion that the Barnard rule should not apply when the tort supporting the award is intentional trespass to land.

We turn first to the individual landowner's interest in protecting his or her land from trespass. The United States Supreme Court has recognized that the private landowner's right to exclude others from his or her land is "one of the most essential sticks in the bundle of rights that are commonly characterized as property." Kaiser Aetna v. United States, 444 U.S. 164, 176 (1979). . . . This court has long recognized "[e]very person['s] right to the exclusive enjoyment of his own property for any purpose which does not invade the rights of another person." Diana Shooting Club v. Lamoreux, 114 Wis. 44, 59 (1902). Thus, both this court and the Supreme Court recognize the individual's legal right to exclude others from private property.

Yet a right is hollow if the legal system provides insufficient means to protect it. . . . Harvey and Lois Jacque have the right to tell Steenberg Homes and any other trespasser, "No, you cannot cross our land." But that right has no practical meaning unless protected by the State, [and a nominal dollar] does not constitute state protection. . . .

In sum, the individual has a strong interest in excluding trespassers from his or her land. Although only nominal damages were awarded to the Jacques, Steenberg's intentional trespass caused actual harm. We turn next to society's interest in protecting private property from the intentional trespasser.

Society has an interest in punishing and deterring intentional trespassers beyond that of protecting the interests of the individual landowner. Society has an interest in preserving the integrity of the legal system. Private landowners should feel confident that wrongdoers who trespass upon their land will be appropriately punished. When landowners have confidence in the legal system, they are less likely to resort to "self-help" remedies. . . .

Moreover, what is to stop Steenberg Homes from concluding, in the future, that delivering its mobile homes via an intentional trespass and paying the resulting Class B forfeiture, is not more profitable than obeying the law? Steenberg Homes plowed a path across the Jacques' land and dragged the mobile home across that path, in the face of the Jacques' adamant refusal. A $30 forfeiture and a $1 nominal damage award are unlikely to restrain Steenberg Homes from similar conduct in the future. An appropriate punitive damage award probably will.

In sum, as the court of appeals noted, the [traditional] rule sends the wrong message to Steenberg Homes and any others who contemplate trespassing on the land of another. It implicitly tells them that they are free to go where they please, regardless of the landowner's wishes. As long as they cause no compensable harm, the only deterrent intentional trespassers face is the nominal damage award of $1 . . . and the possibility of a Class B forfeiture. . . . We conclude that both the private landowner and society have much more than a nominal interest in excluding others from private land. . . .

COMMONWEALTH v. MAGADINI

Supreme Judicial Court of Massachusetts, 2016
52 N.E.3d 1041

HINES, J. We recite the facts the jury could have found, reserving certain details for our discussion of the specific issues raised. In 2014, the defendant was charged with trespassing on three properties in Great Barrington—Barrington House, Castle Street, and SoCo Creamery.[7] Barrington House is a mixed-use building with several different restaurants, an enclosed atrium, and apartments above the businesses. Castle Street is a three-story building with retail establishments, offices, and apartments. SoCo Creamery is an ice cream shop. The defendant was barred from each property by no trespass orders. The owner of the Castle Street building had the defendant served with a no trespass order in July, 2008; the manager of Barrington House had the defendant served in June, 2012; and the owner of SoCo Creamery had the defendant served in January, 2014. All of the no trespass orders were in effect at the time the charges were brought against the defendant.

Four charges related to the defendant's presence at Barrington House. On February 21, March 4, and March 6, police found the defendant lying in a hallway by a heater during the evening, nighttime, or early morning hours of days described as "cold" or "very cold." At approximately noon on April 8, a day described as "cool," police responded to a report and observed the defendant walking through a common area in the Barrington House toward the front door. Two charges stemmed from the defendant's presence at Castle Street, where police had found the defendant lying on the floor in the lobby next to a heater during periods of cold weather. The first incident occurred between 8 A.M. and 10 A.M. on February 20, 2014; the defendant was awake. The second incident occurred at approximately 6:30 A.M. on March 28; the defendant was sleeping. The seventh charge was based on conduct that occurred on June 10, 2014, when the defendant entered SoCo Creamery, ignored requests by the clerk to leave the premises, and used the bathroom for ten to fifteen minutes. The defendant did not dispute that he violated all of the trespass orders, focusing his case instead on the necessity defense in cross-examination and his direct testimony.

The defendant, a lifelong resident of Great Barrington, became homeless after he moved out of his parents' home in 2004. His purpose in moving out was to "reorganize." He planned to return to his parents' home, but he was unable to do so because the "landlord," who "wanted [the defendant] out" refused to allow it. After leaving his parents' home, he generally lived outside year-round, but during the winter months, he tried to "find a more sheltered area" from the "ice and a snow storm." During the cold weather, the defendant used blankets, gloves, and scarves to try to stay warm, but when the weather was "so severe . . . that [it was] not possible," he would seek shelter in private buildings.

For a two- to three-month period in the winter of 2007, the defendant stayed at the local homeless shelter, called the Construct. Three days before he began staying there, he had gone to that shelter at approximately 3 A.M. following a blizzard. He was refused entry, and he stayed on the porch for about an hour before being asked to leave. A few days later, he spoke with someone from the shelter, and he was allowed to stay for a few months before he was told to leave because of "certain issues." Therefore, the defendant had no other place to stay in Great Barrington. For a period of "three to four years," he lived outdoors, first at Stanley Park and later at the outdoor gazebo behind the Great Barrington Town Hall, where he had been living at

---

7. The state criminal trespass statute reads in relevant part: "Whoever, without right enters or remains in or upon the dwelling house [or] buildings . . . of another . . . after having been forbidden so to do by the person who has lawful control of said premises . . . shall be punished." Mass. Gen. L. Ann. c. 266, § 120 (2020).

the time of the trespass incidents. He considered the gazebo his home and registered to vote from that address.

At the time of the trial, the defendant was a sixty-seven year old unemployed college graduate. He had worked in the past, but he was not employed at the time he was charged with the trespassing offenses. The defendant had attempted to obtain an apartment almost "every week for about seven years." Although he had money to pay for an apartment depending on the day, he explained that it was very difficult to find an apartment in Great Barrington because of the upfront fees. Accordingly, he was unable to obtain an apartment. He was aware of a homeless shelter in Pittsfield, but he did not consider renting lodging or staying at a homeless shelter outside of Great Barrington. He testified, "I was born here and I intend to stay here." He does not have a driver's license.

Discussion

1. Necessity Defense

The defendant claims that the judge erroneously denied his request for a jury instruction on the defense of necessity and that he improperly excluded evidence relevant to the defense. The common-law defense of necessity "exonerates one who commits a crime under the 'pressure of circumstances' if the harm that would have resulted from compliance with the law . . . exceeds the harm actually resulting from the defendant's violation of the law." Commonwealth v. Kendall, 883 N.E.2d 269 (Mass. 2008), quoting Commonwealth v. Hood, 452 N.E.2d 188 (Mass. 1983). As such, the necessity defense may excuse unlawful conduct "where the value protected by the law is, as a matter of public policy, eclipsed by a superseding value. . . ." Kendall, supra, quoting Hood, supra.

For a defendant to be entitled to a necessity defense instruction, he or she must present "some evidence on each of the four underlying conditions of the defense," Kendall, 883 N.E.2d 269: "(1) a clear and imminent danger, not one which is debatable or speculative"; (2) [a reasonable expectation that his or her action] will be effective as the direct cause of abating the danger; (3) there is [no] legal alternative which will be effective in abating the danger; and (4) the Legislature has not acted to preclude the defense by a clear and deliberate choice regarding the values at issue." Id. at 13-14, 883 N.E.2d 269, quoting Hood, 452 N.E.2d at 188. If the defendant satisfies these foundational conditions, "the burden is on the Commonwealth to prove beyond a reasonable doubt the absence of necessity." Commonwealth v. Iglesia, 525 N.E.2d 1332 (1988).

The judge focused only on the third element in his denial of the defendant's request for a necessity defense instruction at the close of all the evidence. The judge ruled that the defendant had other available legal alternatives, "motels, and hotels, the police station," and that the evidence was lacking on the defendant's inability to "rent a hotel room on these isolated evenings." We conclude that the judge erred in ruling that the defendant failed to meet his burden to provide some evidence that showed the lack of an available legal alternative to the trespasses.

a. Clear and Imminent Danger

Before we address the third element, we review the first element, "clear and imminent danger," because the Commonwealth contends that the defendant failed to meet the foundational requirement for this element as to the seventh offense, which occurred on June 10, 2014.

There appears to be little question that the weather conditions on the dates of the offenses in February and March presented a "clear and imminent danger" to a homeless person. The temperatures on the dates of the offenses were not admitted at trial, but the weather on the February and March dates was described as "cold," "really cold," and "very cold." Moreover, the timing of each of those incidents, in the early morning or late evening hours when the defendant was either sleeping or lying down, suggests the dangerousness of the circumstances where sleeping may place one in the same position for an extended period and, thus, increases the potential harm from the weather. See Jones v. Los Angeles, 444 F.3d 1118, 1138 (9th Cir. 2006) ("involuntary sitting, lying, or sleeping on public sidewalks . . . is an unavoidable consequence of being human and homeless without shelter"). See also In re Eichorn, 81 Cal. Rptr. 2d 535 (Cal. App. 1998) ("Sleep is a physiological need, not an option for humans"). Moreover, the Commonwealth concedes that the defendant met his burden of demonstrating a "clear and imminent danger" for these six incidents.

We agree with the Commonwealth that the defendant did not meet his burden to show a "clear and imminent danger" for the incident on June 10, where the evidence showed only that he had to use the bathroom. Accordingly, we do not include the incident on June 10 in our analysis requirements of the availability of "legal alternatives" to trespass.

b. Availability of Lawful Alternatives

We have explained previously that satisfaction of the third element requires a defendant to demonstrate that he "ma[d]e himself aware of any available lawful alternatives, 'or show[ed] them to be futile in the circumstances.'" *Kendall*, 883 N.E.2d 269, quoting Commonwealth v. Pike, 701 N.E.2d 951 (Mass. 1998). On that point, the defendant must present "some evidence," enough that "supports at least a reasonable doubt" whether the unlawful conduct was justified by necessity. *Kendall*, 883 N.E.2d 269. In other words, the defendant must present enough evidence to demonstrate at least a reasonable doubt that there were no effective legal alternatives available before being entitled to an instruction on the necessity defense. This does not require a showing that the defendant has exhausted or shown to be futile all conceivable alternatives, only that a jury could reasonably find that no alternatives were available. See *Kendall*, 883 N.E.2d 269 (Cowin, J., dissenting), citing *Iglesia*, 525 N.E.2d 1332.

. . .

[T]he defendant's evidence was sufficient to meet his burden. . . . In determining whether there has been sufficient evidence of the foundational conditions to the necessity defense, "all reasonable inferences should be resolved in favor of the defendant, and, no matter how incredible his testimony, that testimony must be treated as true." *Pike*, 428 Mass. at 395, 701 N.E.2d 951. Taken in this light, there is at least "some evidence" that the defendant lacked effective legal alternatives to trespass during cold days and nights. The defendant testified that he stayed at an outdoor gazebo "[p]retty much" year round, that in 2007 he was told to leave the only local homeless shelter and had previously been denied entry to the shelter in the middle of the night following a blizzard, that no other places "want [him] in . . . their facility," that he was unable to rent an apartment despite repeated attempts, and that there was nowhere besides public parks where he could stay. Additionally, the officer who asked the defendant to leave the Barrington House at approximately 9:30 P.M. on February 21 testified that the defendant had to go back outside, and the judge sustained an objection to defense counsel's question about whether the officer offered to transport him to any other shelter or facility. The manager of Castle Street corroborated the defendant's attempt to rent an apartment by his testimony that he called police to have the defendant removed from the building after the defendant "forced his way onto the third floor of the building, flashing money in hand, demanding I rent him an apartment."

The Commonwealth argues that the defendant failed to meet his burden because he presented no evidence that he was unable to rent an apartment outside of Great Barrington, that he was unable to gain entry to the Pittsfield shelter, and that he would still be excluded from the local homeless shelter in 2014. The Commonwealth's argument is unavailing. We do not require an actor facing a "clear and imminent danger" to conceptualize all possible alternatives. So long as the defendant's evidence, taken as true, creates a reasonable doubt as to the availability of such lawful alternatives, the defendant satisfies the third element. The defendant has done so here.

Additionally, we note that the options proposed by the Commonwealth do not appear to be effective alternatives on the record before us. Where the only local homeless shelter had previously denied the defendant entry at 3 A.M. following a blizzard and had later told him he had to leave, the law does not require the defendant to continue to seek shelter there in order to demonstrate that doing so is futile. Moreover, the defendant's conduct is viewed at the time of the danger, and actions that the defendant could have taken to find shelter before the dangerous condition arose do not negate the conclusion that there were no lawful alternatives available at the time of his unlawful conduct.

We do not view the requirement that a defendant consider lawful alternatives as broadly as suggested by the Commonwealth. Our cases do not require a defendant to rebut every alternative that is conceivable; rather, a defendant is required to rebut alternatives that likely would have been considered by a reasonable person in a similar situation.[8] Moreover, we are not prepared to say as a matter of law that a homeless defendant must seek shelter outside of his or her home town in order to demonstrate a lack of lawful alternatives. Our law does not permit punishment of the homeless simply for being homeless. Once the foundational requirements are met, the necessity defense allows a jury to consider the plight of a homeless person against any harms caused by a trespass before determining criminal responsibility.[9]

---

8. As the level of harm that could arise from the unlawful conduct increases, so does the requirement for considering lawful alternatives. See *Commonwealth v. Hutchins*, 575 N.E.2d 741 (Mass. 1991) (discussing weighing of "competing harms"). We recognize that the defendant's conduct may not have been appreciated by owners, managers, and residents of the private buildings in which the defendant sought cover, but there was no evidence that the defendant's presence did, or had the potential to, cause physical harm to any persons. Accordingly, the requirement to consider alternatives may be viewed more leniently where the potential harm was only property-related than it would be viewed where the unlawful conduct, as in *Kendall*, had the potential to harm both persons and property. The doctrine of necessity has its roots in the notion that "[t]he law deems the lives of all persons far more valuable than any property." *United States v. Ashton*, 24 F. Cas. 873, 874 (C.C.D. Mass. 1834) (No. 14,470).

9. Allowing a defendant to defend his trespassing charges by claiming necessity will not, of course, condone all illegal trespass by homeless persons. It simply allows a jury of peers to weigh the "competing harms" to determine criminal responsibility. See *Hutchins*, 575 N.E.2d 741. In *Hutchins*, this court reviewed different circumstances where the balance of harms was considered. *Id.* at 575 N.E.2d 741, discussing *Commonwealth v. Thurber*, 418 N.E.2d 1253 (1981), and *Commonwealth v. Iglesia*, 525 N.E.2d 1332 (1988). Specifically, the court noted that a prison escape would likely be justified where a prisoner was in imminent danger at the prison and submitted himself directly to authorities after escape or where an individual who was unlawfully carrying a firearm would likely be justified where the carrier "wrested the gun" from an attacker and immediately went to the police station. *Id.* Here, whether a homeless person's trespass in a privately-owned building where he previously had been barred from entry is a greater or lesser harm than the intrusion suffered by the owner and occupiers of the building is a question properly decided by a jury where the defendant met the foundational elements for the necessity defense. *Iglesia*, 525 N.E.2d 1332 (jury instructed on whether defendant made "better choice" by acting illegally).

Accordingly, in the circumstances of this case, we conclude that the judge erred in denying the defendant's request for an instruction on the defense of necessity. As the defendant satisfied the foundational elements entitling him to the defense, the judge's failure to instruct the jury about the defendant's principal defense requires a new trial. We therefore vacate the defendant's convictions of the charges occurring in February, March, and April, 2014.

. . .

Conclusion

Because we conclude that the judge erred in denying the defendant's request for a jury instruction on the defense of necessity for the trespassing charges that occurred in February, March, and April, 2014, we vacate those six convictions and remand for a new trial. We affirm the conviction stemming from conduct that occurred on June 10, 2014.

Notes and Questions

1. *Trespass.* Both *Jacque* and *Magadini* involve trespass, which is the cause of action that most obviously involves the right to exclude. *Jacque* is a case of civil trespass, while *Magadini* involves criminal trespass. Civil trespass consists of an unprivileged intentional encroachment upon property owned by another. "Intentional" simply means that the defendant engaged in a voluntary act, such as walking. It does not require that the defendant specifically intended to commit trespass. Hence, a mistaken entry upon another's land can still be trespass. Trespass is unprivileged when the encroachment is (1) without the owner's consent; (2) lacks necessity as a justification; and (3) is not otherwise justified by public policy. Simple examples of privileged intentional encroachments include firefighters entering a building to stop it from burning and police officers entering a private home to prevent a crime.

Trespass is criminal only when the defendant enters another's land knowing that he lacks a privilege to do so, or if the defendant refuses to leave another's land after being asked to do so.

2. *Despotic owners?* Did Jacque have an objectively good reason for refusing permission to cross his land? Does this matter?

William Blackstone (see pages 20-21) grandly defined the right of property as "that sole and despotic dominion which one man claims and exercises over the external things of the world, in total exclusion of the right of any other individual in the universe." 2 Commentaries *2. Two centuries later, the U.S. Supreme Court, in *Kaiser Aetna*, cited and quoted in *Jacque* (see page 40), described the right to exclude as an essential feature of property. Why could the owners in *Jacque* be despotic, but the owner of Barrington House in *Magadini* could not? What value or values support the idea that the right to exclude is central to ownership? For an argument that the owner in *Jacque* should not have been allowed to be despotic (i.e., to exclude Steenberg), see John Makdisi, Uncaring Justice: Why *Jacque v. Steenberg Homes* Was Wrongly Decided, 51 J. Cath. L. Stud. 111 (2012).

3. *Limits on the right to exclude.* No right is absolute, including the right to exclude. Even in Blackstone's time, there were limitations on the right to exclude.

Today there are many more. *Magadini* illustrates one important defense to criminal trespass, i.e., necessity. In a famous case, State v. Shack, 277 A.2d 369 (N.J. 1971), the New Jersey Supreme Court recognized another limit on trespass. In that case, two employees of government-funded organizations entered upon a private farm for the purpose of providing aid, medical and legal, to migrant farm workers who were living on the farm owner's land. When the owner demanded that they leave, they refused, and he summoned state police to eject them. He initiated criminal prosecution for trespass. The New Jersey Supreme Court overturned their convictions, finding that their entry was privileged under state law. The court stated, "Property rights serve human values. They are recognized to that end, and are limited by it. . . . Here we are concerned with a highly disadvantaged segment of our society. . . . [W]e find it unthinkable that the farmer-employer can assert a right to isolate the migrant worker in any respect significant for the worker's well-being. The farmer, of course, is entitled to pursue his farming activities without interference, and these defendants readily concede. But we see no legitimate need for a right in the farmer to deny the worker the opportunity for aid available from federal, State, or local services, or from recognized charitable groups seeking to assist him." Id. at 372, 374.

You will encounter other examples of limits on the right to exclude as you work your way through this book. Here are a few: civil rights legislation forbidding various forms of discrimination; rent controls and other limitations on a landlord's right to evict tenants; the law of adverse possession; bodies of doctrine granting public rights of access to private beaches (which we will encounter in this chapter); and legislation protecting homeowners who have defaulted on mortgage payments.

Homelessness in America. The plight of David Magadini has become all too familiar in the United States today. The problem of homelessness is visible from coast to coast and everywhere in between. Numbers can hardly tell the entire story, of course, but they tell us something. The most recent Homeless Assessment Report from the U.S. Department of Housing and Urban Development (2019) stated that on a single night in 2019, roughly 568,000 people were experiencing homelessness in the United States. U.S. Department of Housing and Urban Development Office of Community Planning and Development, The 2019 Annual Homeless Assessment Report (AHAR) to Congress 1 (January 2020). Homelessness in most states declined, by varying percentages, between 2018 and 2019, but increased in California by 16 percent, or 21,306 people. African Americans have remained considerably overrepresented among the homeless population compared to the U.S. population, accounting for 40 percent of all people experiencing homelessness in 2019. Id.

The roots of homelessness are complex and varied, including structural problems in the housing market affecting both the supply and the demand side, mental illness and substance abuse problems, and other factors. To the list of factors contributing to homelessness we might now add the Covid-19, which has led to high numbers of unemployed persons, some of whom are no longer able to afford rent or mortgage payments. As we go through the materials in the remaining chapters, we will come back to the homelessness problem as it bears upon particular topics.

b. The Right to Transfer

ANDRUS v. ALLARD

Supreme Court of the United States, 1979
444 U.S. 51

BRENNAN, J. The Eagle Protection Act and the Migratory Bird Treaty Act are conservation statutes designed to prevent the destruction of certain species of birds.[10] Challenged in this case is the validity of regulations promulgated by appellant Secretary of the Interior that prohibit commercial transactions in parts of birds legally killed before the birds came under the protection of the statutes. The regulations provide in pertinent part:

50 CFR § 21.2(a) (1978):

"Migratory birds, their parts, nests, or eggs, lawfully acquired prior to the effective date of Federal protection under the Migratory Bird Treaty Act . . . may be possessed or transported without a Federal permit, but may not be imported, exported, purchased, sold, bartered, or offered for purchase, sale, trade, or barter. . . ."

50 CFR § 22.2(a) (1978):

"Bald eagles, alive or dead, or their parts, nests, or eggs lawfully acquired prior to June 8, 1940, and golden eagles, alive or dead, or their parts, nests, or eggs

---

10. The Eagle Protection Act, § 1, 54 Stat. 250, as amended, as set forth in 16 U.S.C. § 668(a), provides in pertinent part:

"Whoever, within the United States or any place subject to the jurisdiction thereof, without being permitted to do so as provided in this subchapter, shall knowingly, or with wanton disregard for the consequences of his act take, possess, sell, purchase, barter, offer to sell, purchase or barter, transport, export or import, at any time or in any manner any bald eagle commonly known as the American eagle or any golden eagle, alive or dead, or any part, nest, or egg thereof of the foregoing eagles, or whoever violates any permit or regulation issued pursuant to this subchapter, shall be fined not more than $5,000 or imprisoned not more than one year or both: . . . Provided further, That nothing herein shall be construed to prohibit possession or transportation of any bald eagle, alive or dead, or any part, nest, or egg thereof, lawfully taken prior to June 8, 1940, and that nothing herein shall be construed to prohibit possession or transportation of any golden eagle, alive or dead, or any part, nest, or egg thereof, lawfully taken prior to the addition to this subchapter of the provisions relating to preservation of the golden eagle."

The Migratory Bird Treaty Act, § 2, 40 Stat. 755, as amended, as set forth in 16 U.S.C. § 703, similarly provides:

"Unless and except as permitted by regulations made as hereinafter provided in this subchapter, it shall be unlawful at any time, by any means or in any manner, to pursue, hunt, take, capture, kill, attempt to take, capture, or kill, possess, offer for sale, sell, offer to barter, barter, offer to purchase, purchase, deliver for shipment, ship, export, import, cause to be shipped, exported, or imported, deliver for transportation, transport or cause to be transported, carry or cause to be carried, or receive for shipment, transportation, carriage, or export, any migratory bird, any part, nest, or eggs of any such bird, or any product, whether or not manufactured, which consists, or is composed in whole or part, of any such bird or any part, nest, or egg thereof, included in the terms of the conventions between the United States and Great Britain for the protection of migratory birds concluded August 16, 1916 (39 Stat. 1702), the United States and the United Mexican States for the protection of migratory birds and game mammals concluded February 7, 1936, and the United States and the Government of Japan for the protection of migratory birds and birds in danger of extinction, and their environment concluded March 4, 1972."

lawfully acquired prior to October 24, 1962, may be possessed, or transported without a Federal permit, but may not be imported, exported, purchased, sold, traded, bartered, or offered for purchase, sale, trade or barter. . . ."

Appellees are engaged in the trade of Indian artifacts: several own commercial enterprises, one is employed by such an enterprise, and one is a professional appraiser. A number of the artifacts are partly composed of the feathers of currently protected birds, but these artifacts existed before the statutory protections came into force. After two of the appellees who had sold "pre-existing" artifacts were prosecuted for violations of the Eagle Protection Act and the Migratory Bird Treaty Act, appellees brought this suit for declaratory and injunctive relief in the District Court for the District of Colorado. The complaint alleged that the statutes do not forbid the sale of appellees' artifacts insofar as the constituent birds' parts were obtained prior to the effective dates of the statutes. It further alleged that if the statutes and regulations do apply to such property, they violate the Fifth Amendment.

A three-judge court, convened pursuant to 28 U.S.C. § 2282 (1970 ed.), held that because of "grave doubts whether these two acts would be constitutional if they were construed to apply to pre-act bird products," the Acts were to be interpreted as "not applicable to preexisting, legally-obtained bird parts or products therefrom. . . ." Accordingly, the court ruled that "the interpretive regulations, 50 C.F.R. §§ 21.2(a) and 22.2(a) [are] void as unauthorized extensions of the Migratory Bird Treaty Act and the Eagle Protection Act and [are] violative of the [appellees'] Fifth Amendment property rights." Judgment was entered declaring "the subject regulations to be invalid and unenforceable as against the [appellees'] property rights in feathers and artifacts owned before the effective date of the subject statute," and enjoining appellants "from any interference with the exercise of such rights, including the rights of sale, barter or exchange." . . . We reverse.

I

Appellant Secretary of the Interior contends that both the Eagle Protection and Migratory Bird Treaty Acts contemplate regulatory prohibition of commerce in the parts of protected birds, without regard to when those birds were originally taken. Appellees respond that such a prohibition serves no purpose, arguing that statutory protection of wildlife is not furthered by an embargo upon traffic in avian artifacts that existed before the statutory safeguards came into effect.

A

[In this section, the Court interpreted the scope of Eagle Protection Act. It read the statute as providing that "with respect to pre-existing artifacts, Congress specifically declined to except any activities other than possession and transportation from the general statutory ban." It further regarded the prohibition against the sale of bird parts lawfully taken before the effective date of federal protection "[a]s fully consonant with the purposes of the Eagle Protection Act. The Court stated: "[T]he possibility of commercial gain presents a special threat to the preservation of the eagles because that prospect creates a powerful incentive both to evade statutory prohibitions against taking birds and to take a large volume of birds. The legislative draftsmen might well view evasion as a serious danger because there is no sure means by which to determine the age of bird feathers; feathers recently taken can easily be passed off as having been obtained long ago."]

B

[The Court next turned to the Migratory Bird Treaty Act, which it interpreted similarly to the Eagle Protection Act.]

II

We also disagree with the District Court's holding that, as construed to authorize the prohibition of commercial transactions in pre-existing avian artifacts, the Eagle Protection and Migratory Bird Treaty Acts violate appellees' Fifth Amendment property rights because the prohibition wholly deprives them of the opportunity to earn a profit from those relics.

Penn Central Transportation Co. v. New York City, 438 U.S. 104 (1978), is our most recent exposition on the Takings Clause. That exposition need not be repeated at length here. Suffice it to say that government regulation — by definition — involves the adjustment of rights for the public good. Often this adjustment curtails some potential for the use or economic exploitation of private property. To require compensation in all such circumstances would effectively compel the government to regulate by purchase. "Government hardly could go on if to some extent values incident to property could not be diminished without paying for every such change in the general law." Pennsylvania Coal Co. v. Mahon, 260 U.S. 393, 413 (1922).

The Takings Clause, therefore, preserves governmental power to regulate, subject only to the dictates of "'justice and fairness.'" Ibid. There is no abstract or fixed point at which judicial intervention under the Takings Clause becomes appropriate. Formulas and factors have been developed in a variety of settings. Resolution of each case, however, ultimately calls as much for the exercise of judgment as for the application of logic.

The regulations challenged here do not compel the surrender of the artifacts, and there is no physical invasion or restraint upon them. Rather, a significant restriction has been imposed on one means of disposing of the artifacts. But the denial of one traditional property right does not always amount to a taking. At least where an owner possesses a full "bundle" of property rights, the destruction of one "strand" of the bundle is not a taking, because the aggregate must be viewed in its entirety. In this case, it is crucial that appellees retain the rights to possess and transport their property, and to donate or devise the protected birds.

It is, to be sure, undeniable that the regulations here prevent the most profitable use of appellees' property. Again, however, that is not dispositive. When we review regulation, a reduction in the value of property is not necessarily equated with a taking. In the instant case, it is not clear that appellees will be unable to derive economic benefit from the artifacts; for example, they might exhibit the artifacts for an admissions charge. At any rate, loss of future profits — unaccompanied by any physical property restriction — provides a slender reed upon which to rest a takings claim. Prediction of profitability is essentially a matter of reasoned speculation that courts are not especially competent to perform. Further, perhaps because of its very uncertainty, the interest in anticipated gains has traditionally been viewed as less compelling than other property-related interests.

. . .

We hold that the simple prohibition of the sale of lawfully acquired property in this case does not effect a taking in violation of the Fifth Amendment.

Reversed.

Notes and Questions

1. *The "Takings" Clause.* We will study the Just Compensation Clause of the Fifth Amendment to the U.S. Constitution, commonly called the "Takings" Clause, in Chapter 12, but for now, a brief bit of background will help you to understand the issue in Andrus v. Allard. The clause simply provides: "nor shall private property be taken for public use, without just compensation." The implication, of course, is that government may "take" "private property" so long as it does so for "public use" and with payment of "just compensation." In Andrus v. Allard, the owners argued that the federal government had de facto "taken" their property (i.e., their artifacts made with eagle parts) by virtue of prohibiting commercial transactions in those artifacts, thereby substantially diminishing their value to the owners. Hence, the focus of the Court's analysis was on the meaning of "property" under the Takings Clause.

2. *The bundle of rights and Andrus v. Allard.* The Court in Andrus v. Allard relied on the bundle-of-rights conception of ownership in analyzing whether the federal regulations in question had taken the appellees' property. The Court concluded that the regulations had not done so because they had only removed one twig from the bundle: the right to sell. The owners of the artifacts still had many other rights, including possession, use (other than commercially bought or sold), display, give, devise by will, and others.

3. *Ownership and market value.* The Court in Andrus v. Allard conceded that the challenged regulations deprived the owners of the most profitable use of the artifacts. The effect of that deprivation, of course, would have been to decrease the market value of the artifacts, likely quite substantially. We will study the question of the role of reduction in market value on takings analysis in greater detail in Chapter 12. For now, it is enough to note that the Court's response to this question in *Allard*—"a reduction in the value of property is not necessarily equated with a taking"—is the Court's usual response. Should that be the response? Should ownership be equated with market value?

c. The Right to Destroy

How far can property rights go? Is there even a right to destroy what you own? May you, for example, tear down your house if you wish? Suppose instead that you leave instructions in your will that the house be torn down after you die. Should your rights in these instances differ, and, if so, how? Consider the following case.

EYERMAN v. MERCANTILE TRUST CO.
Missouri Court of Appeals, 1975
524 S.W.2d 210

RENDLEN, J. Plaintiffs appeal from denial of their petition seeking injunction to prevent demolition of a house at #4 Kingsbury Place in the City of St. Louis. The action is brought by individual neighboring property owners and certain trustees for the Kingsbury Place Subdivision. We reverse.

Louise Woodruff Johnston, owner of the property in question, died January 14, 1973, and by her will directed the executor "to cause our home at 4 Kingsbury Place . . . to be razed and to sell the land upon which it is located . . . and to transfer the proceeds of the sale . . . to the residue of my estate." Plaintiffs assert that razing the home will adversely affect their property rights, violate the terms of the subdivision trust indenture for Kingsbury Place, produce an actionable private nuisance and is contrary to public policy.

The area involved is a "private place" established in 1902 by trust indenture which provides that Kingsbury Place and Kingsbury Terrace will be so maintained, improved, protected and managed as to be desirable for private residences. The trustees are empowered to protect and preserve "Kingsbury Place" from encroachment, trespass, nuisance or injury, and it is "the intention of these presents, forming a general scheme of improving and maintaining said property as desirable residence property of the highest class." The covenants run with the land and the indenture empowers lot owners or the trustees to bring suit to enforce them.

Except for one vacant lot, the subdivision is occupied by handsome, spacious two and three-story homes, and all must be used exclusively as private residences. The indenture generally regulates location, costs and similar features for any structures in the subdivision, and limits construction of subsidiary structures except those that may beautify the property, for example, private stables, flower houses, conservatories, play houses or buildings of similar character.

4 Kingsbury Place

On trial the temporary restraining order was dissolved and all issues found against the plaintiffs. . . .

Whether #4 Kingsbury Place should be razed is an issue of public policy involving individual property rights and the community at large. The plaintiffs have pleaded and proved facts sufficient to show a personal, legally protectible interest.

Demolition of the dwelling will result in an unwarranted loss to this estate, the plaintiffs and the public. The uncontradicted testimony was that the current value of the house and land is $40,000.00; yet the estate could expect no more than $5,000.00 for the empty lot, less the cost of demolition at $4,350.00, making a grand loss of $39,350.33 if the unexplained and capricious direction to the executor is effected. Only $650.00 of the $40,000.00 asset would remain.

Kingsbury Place is an area of high architectural significance, representing excellence in urban space utilization. Razing the home will depreciate adjoining property values by an estimated $10,000.00 and effect corresponding losses for other neighborhood homes. The cost of constructing a house of comparable size and architectural exquisiteness would approach $200,000.00.

The importance of this house to its neighborhood and the community is reflected in the action of the St. Louis Commission on Landmarks and Urban Design designating Kingsbury Place as a landmark of the City of St. Louis. This designation, under consideration prior to the institution of this suit, points up the aesthetic and historical qualities of the area and assists in stabilizing Central West End St. Louis. It was testified by the Landmarks Commission chairman that the private place concept, once unique to St. Louis, fosters higher home maintenance standards and is among the most effective methods for stabilizing otherwise deteriorating neighborhoods. The executive director of Heritage St. Louis, an organization operating to preserve the architecture of the city, testified to the importance of preserving Kingsbury Place intact:

> The reasons (sic) for making Kingsbury Place a landmark is that it is a definite piece of urban design and architecture. It starts out with monumental gates on Union. There is a long corridor of space, furnished with a parkway in the center, with houses on either side of the street. . . . The existence of this piece of architecture depends on the continuity of the (sic) both sides. Breaks in this continuity would be as holes in this wall, and would detract from the urban design qualities of the streets. . . . Many of these houses are landmarks in themselves, but they add up to much more. . . . I would say Kingsbury Place, as a whole, with its design, with its important houses . . . is a most significant piece of urban design by any standard.
>
> To remove #4 Kingsbury from the street was described as having the effect of a missing front tooth. The space created would permit direct access to Kingsbury Place from the adjacent alley, increasing the likelihood the lot will be subject to uses detrimental to the health, safety and beauty of the neighborhood. The mere possibility that a future owner might build a new home with the inherent architectural significance of the present dwelling offers little support to sustain the condition for destruction.

[N]o individual, group of individuals nor the community generally benefits from the senseless destruction of the house; instead, all are harmed and only the caprice of the dead testatrix is served. Destruction of the house harms the neighbors, detrimentally affects the community, causes monetary loss in excess of $39,000.00 to the estate and is without benefit to the dead woman. No reason, good or bad, is suggested by the will or record for the eccentric condition. This is not a living person who seeks to exercise a right to reshape or dispose of her property; instead, it is an attempt by will to confer the power to destroy upon an executor who is given no other interest in the property. To allow an executor to exercise such power stemming from apparent whim and caprice of the testatrix contravenes public policy.

The Missouri Supreme Court held in State ex rel. McClintock v. Guinotte, 204 S.W. 806, 808 (Mo. en banc 1918), that the taking of property by inheritance or will is not an absolute or natural right but one created by the laws of the sovereign power. The court points out the state "may foreclose the right absolutely, or it may grant the right upon conditions precedent, which conditions, if not otherwise violative of our Constitution, will have to be complied with before the right of descent and distribution (whether under the law or by will) can exist." Further, this power of the state is one of inherent sovereignty which allows the state to "say what becomes of the property of a person, when death forecloses his right to control it." Id. at 808, 809. While living, a person may manage, use or dispose of his money or property with fewer restraints than a decedent by will. One is generally restrained from wasteful expenditure or destructive inclinations by the natural desire to enjoy his property or to accumulate it during his lifetime. Such considerations however have not tempered the extravagance or eccentricity of the testamentary disposition here on which there is no check except the courts.

In the early English case of Egerton v. Brownlow, 10 Eng. Rep. 359, 417 (Queen's Bench 1853), it is stated: "The owner of an estate may himself do many things which he could not (by a condition) compel his successor to do. One example is sufficient. He may leave his land uncultivated, but he cannot by a condition compel his successor to do so. The law does not interfere with the owner and compel him to cultivate his land, (though it may be for the public good that land should be cultivated) so far the law respects ownership; but when, by a condition, he attempts to compel his successor to do what is against the public good, the law steps in and pronounces the condition void and allows the devisee to enjoy the estate free from the condition." . . .

In the case of In re Scott's Will, Board of Commissioners of Rice County v. Scott et al., 93 N.W. 109 (Minn. 1903), the Supreme Court of Minnesota stated, when considering the provision of a will directing the executor to destroy money belonging to the estate: "We assume, for purpose of this decision, that the direction in the codicil to the executor to destroy all of the residue of the money or cash or evidences of credit belonging to the estate was void." Id. at 109. See also Restatement, Second, Trusts § 124, at 267: "Although a person may deal capriciously with his own property, his self interest ordinarily will restrain him from doing so. Where an attempt is made to confer such a power upon a person who is given no other interest in the property, there is no such restraint and it is against public policy to allow him to exercise the power if the purpose is merely capricious." . . .

The term "public policy" cannot be comprehensively defined in specific terms but the phrase "against public policy" has been characterized as that which conflicts with the morals of the time and contravenes any established interest of society. Acts are said to be against public policy "when the law refuses to enforce or recognize them, on the ground that they have a mischievous tendency, so as to be injurious to the interests of the state, apart from illegality or immorality." . . .

Public policy may be found in the Constitution, statutes and judicial decisions of this state or the nation. In re Rahn's Estate, 291 S.W. 120 (Mo. 1927). But in a case of first impression where there are no guiding statutes, judicial decisions or constitutional provisions, "a judicial determination of the question becomes an expression of public policy provided it is so plainly right as to be supported by the general will." In re Mohler's Estate, 22 A.2d 680, 683 (Pa. 1941). In the absence of guidance from authorities in its own jurisdiction, courts may look to the judicial decisions of sister states for assistance in discovering expressions of public policy. . . .

Although public policy may evade precise, objective definition, it is evident from the authorities cited that this senseless destruction serving no apparent good purpose is to be held in disfavor. A well-ordered society cannot tolerate the waste and destruction of resources when such acts directly affect important interests of other members of that society. It is clear that property owners in the neighborhood of #4 Kingsbury, the St. Louis Community as a whole and the beneficiaries of testatrix's estate will be severely injured should the provisions of the will be followed. No benefits are present to balance against this injury and we hold that to allow the condition in the will would be in violation of the public policy of this state.

Having thus decided, we do not reach the plaintiffs' contentions regarding enforcement of the restrictions in the Kingsbury Place trust indenture and actionable private nuisance, though these contentions may have merit.

The judgment is reversed and the cause remanded to the Circuit Court to enter judgment as prayed.

DOWD, P.J., concurs.

CLEMENS, J., dissenting. . . . The simple issue in this case is whether the trial court erred by refusing to enjoin a trustee from carrying out an explicit testamentary directive. In an emotional opinion, the majority assumes a psychic knowledge of the testatrix' reasons for directing her home be razed; her testamentary disposition is characterized as "capricious," "unwarranted," "senseless," and "eccentric." But the record is utterly silent as to her motives.

The majority's reversal of the trial court here spawns bizarre and legally untenable results. By its decision, the court officially confers a "benefit" upon testamentary beneficiaries who have never litigated or protested against the razing. The majority opinion further proclaims that public policy demands we enjoin the razing of this private residence in order to prevent land misuse in the City of St. Louis. But the City, like the beneficiaries, is not a party to this lawsuit. The fact is the majority's holding is based upon wispy, self-proclaimed public policy grounds that were only vaguely pleaded, were not in evidence, and were only sketchily briefed by the plaintiffs.

The only plaintiffs in this case are residents of Kingsbury Place and trustees under its indenture. In seeking to enjoin the removal of testatrix' home at #4 Kingsbury Place, these plaintiffs claim they are entitled to an injunction first, by virtue of language in the trust indenture; secondly, because the razing would constitute a nuisance; and thirdly on the ground of public policy. But plaintiffs have not shown the indenture bars razing testatrix' home or that the razing would create a nuisance. And no grounds exist for ruling that the razing is contrary to public policy.

The Trust Indenture. Kingsbury Place is a "private place" established in 1902 by trust indenture. Except for one well-tended vacant lot (whose existence the majority ignores in saying the street minus #4 Kingsbury Place would be like "a missing front tooth") the trust indenture generally regulates size, constructions and cost of structures to be built on Kingsbury Place. It empowers the trustees to maintain vacant lots and to protect the street from "encroachment, trespass, nuisance and injury." The indenture's acknowledgment that vacant lots did and would exist shows that such lots were not to be considered an "injury." The fact the indenture empowers the trustees to maintain vacant lots is neither an express nor an implied ban against razing residences. The indenture simply recognizes that Kingsbury Place may have vacant lots from time to time—as it now has—and that the trustees may maintain them—as they now do. The indenture itself affords plaintiffs no basis for injunctive relief.

. . . Plaintiffs opined the home's removal would be detrimental to neighbors' health and safety, would lower property values in the area and would be undesirable aesthetically, architecturally, socially and historically. These opinions were based upon conjecture rather than upon a reasonable degree of certainty; hence, they were not binding on the trial court. . . . The record reveals the one existing vacant lot on Kingsbury Place is well-maintained by the trustees. . . . There is no reason to presume a second vacant lot would be left untended or that private police would cease patrolling. The facts do not support an inference that plaintiffs' rights in the use of their own lands would be invaded by removing the Johnston home. They are not entitled to injunctive relief on the basis of imagined possibilities.

Public Policy. The majority opinion bases its reversal on public policy. But plaintiffs themselves did not substantially rely upon this nebulous concept. Plaintiffs' brief contends merely that an "agency of the City of St. Louis has recently (?) designated Kingsbury Place as a landmark," citing § 24.070, Revised Code of the City of St. Louis. Plaintiffs argue removal of the Johnston home would be "intentional . . . destruction of a landmark of historical interest." Neither the ordinance cited in the brief nor any action taken under it were in evidence. Indeed, the Chairman of the Landmarks and Urban Design Commission testified the Commission did not declare the street a landmark until after Mrs. Johnston died. A month after Mrs. Johnston's death, several residents of the street apparently sensed the impending razing of the Johnston home and applied to have the street declared a landmark. The Commissioner testified it was the Commission's "civic duty to help those people."

The majority opinion . . . suggests the court may declare certain land uses, which are not illegal, to be in violation of the City's public policy. And the majority so finds although the City itself is not a litigant claiming injury to its interests. The majority's public-policy conclusions are based not upon evidence in the lower court, but upon incidents which may have happened thereafter.

The court has resorted to public policy in order to vitiate Mrs. Johnston's valid testamentary direction. But this is not a proper case for court-defined public policy. . . .

The leading Missouri case on public policy as that doctrine applies to a testator's right to dispose of property is In re Rahn's Estate. . . . There, an executor refused to pay a bequest on the ground the beneficiary was an enemy alien, and the bequest was therefore against public policy. The court denied that contention: "We may say, at the outset, that the policy of the law favors freedom in the testamentary disposition of property and that it is the duty of the courts to give effect to the intention of the testator, as expressed in his will, provided such intention does not contravene an established rule of law." And the court wisely added, "it is not the function of the judiciary to create or announce a public policy of its own, but solely to determine and declare what is the public policy of the state or nation as such policy is found to be expressed in the Constitution, statutes, and judicial decisions of the state or nation, . . . not by the varying opinions of laymen, lawyers, or judges as to the demands or the interests of the public." And, in cautioning against judges declaring public policy the court stated: "Judicial tribunals hold themselves bound to the observance of rules of extreme caution when invoked to declare a transaction void on grounds of public policy, and prejudice to the public interest must clearly appear before the court would be warranted in pronouncing a transaction void on this account." In resting its decision on public-policy grounds, the majority opinion has transgressed the limitations declared by our Supreme Court in *Rahn's Estate*.

. . . It requires judicial imagination to hold, as the majority does, that the mere presence of a second vacant lot on Kingsbury Place violates public policy.

As much as our aesthetic sympathies might lie with neighbors near a house to be razed, those sympathies should not so interfere with our considered legal judgment as to create a questionable legal precedent. Mrs. Johnston had the right during her lifetime to have her house razed, and I find nothing which precludes her right to order her executor to raze the house upon her death. . . .

Notes and Questions

1. *Aftermath.* The house at #4 Kingsbury Place still stands. As of 2020, it was listed for sale at $939,900. See https://www.stlouisrealty.net/neighborhood/homes-for-sale-in-central-west-end-mo/.

2. *Do justifications matter?* If you were representing a client in Missouri who earnestly wished to live in his home until his death and then to have it destroyed, would there be any way to help him accomplish this goal under *Eyerman*? Would articulating a rationale in the will for the destruction of the house convince the courts to permit enforcement? See National City Bank v. Case Western Reserve University, 369 N.E.2d 814, 818-819 (Ohio Com. Pl. 1976).

3. *What about pro-destruction social norms?* How should the law respond if someone wants to be buried wearing her diamond wedding ring and other jewelry, as is commonly the case? See Meksras Estate, 63 Pa. D. & C. 2d 371 (C.P. Phila. County 1974). For that matter, if someone elects *not* to be an organ donor, should *Eyerman*'s rule apply? These questions and related ones are considered in Lior Jacob Strahilevitz, The Right to Destroy, 114 Yale L.J. 781 (2005). The same source considers the right to destroy artistic works of the owner's creation, as does Joseph L. Sax, Playing Darts with a Rembrandt: Public and Private Rights in Cultural Treasures (1999).

d. The Public Trust and the Public Domain in Land

Cases like *Jacque* indicate that private property rights are very strong, but other cases like *Magadini*, *Andrus*, and *Eyerman* suggest that ownership rights are not absolute when particular uses of property might reduce society's welfare. Some public-spirited limitations on absolute ownership are longstanding, tracing their back to the Roman Empire. One such doctrine is considered in Matthews v. Bay Head Improvement Association. *Matthews* will perform double duty in this chapter by emphasizing ways in which the kinds of limits on absolute ownership that we encountered in cases like State v. Shack (Note 3, page 48) may grant rights to a broader public, and also by serving as a bridge to the ownership of intellectual property and other intangible assets. In those contexts, as on the New Jersey beachfront, the concept of an inalienable public domain looms large. So, as you progress through the chapter, think about the connection between *Matthews* and cases like *I.N.S.*, *White*, *Feist*, *Eldred*, and *Booking.com*.

MATTHEWS v. BAY HEAD IMPROVEMENT ASSOCIATION

Supreme Court of New Jersey, 1984
471 A.2d 355

SCHREIBER, J. The public trust doctrine acknowledges that the ownership, dominion and sovereignty over land flowed by tidal waters, which extend to the mean high water mark, is vested in the State in trust for the people. The public's right to use the tidal lands and water encompasses navigation, fishing and recreational uses, including bathing, swimming and other shore activities. Borough of Neptune City v. Borough of Avon-by-the-Sea, 61 N.J. 296, 309, 294 A.2d 47 (1972). In *Avon* we held that the public trust applied to the municipally-owned dry sand beach immediately landward of the high water mark. The major issue in this case is whether, ancillary to the public's right to enjoy the tidal lands, the public has a right to gain access through and to use the dry sand area not owned by a municipality but by a quasi-public body.

The Borough of Point Pleasant instituted this suit against the Borough of Bay Head and the Bay Head Improvement Association (Association), generally asserting that the defendants prevented Point Pleasant inhabitants from gaining access to the Atlantic Ocean and the beachfront in Bay Head. The proceeding was dismissed as to the Borough of Bay Head because it did not own or control the beach. Subsequently, . . . Stanley Van Ness, as Public Advocate, joined as plaintiff-intervenor. When the Borough of Point Pleasant ceased pursuing the litigation, the Public Advocate became the primary moving party. The Public Advocate asserted that the defendants had denied the general public its right of access during the summer bathing season to public trust lands along the beaches in Bay Head and its right to use private property fronting on the ocean incidental to the public's right under the public trust doctrine. The complaint was amended on several occasions, eliminating the Borough of Point Pleasant as plaintiff and adding more than 100 individuals, who were owners or had interests in properties located on the oceanfront in Bay Head, as defendants. . . .

I. Facts

The Borough of Bay Head (Bay Head) borders the Atlantic Ocean. Adjacent to it on the north is the Borough of Point Pleasant Beach, on the south the Borough of Mantoloking, and on the west Barnegat Bay. Bay Head consists of a fairly narrow strip of land, 6,667 feet long (about 1 1/4 miles). A beach runs along its entire length adjacent to the Atlantic Ocean. There are 76 separate parcels of land that border the beach. All except six are owned by private individuals. Title to those six is vested in the Association.

The Association was founded in 1910 and incorporated as a nonprofit corporation in 1932. . . . Its constitution delineates the Association's object to promote the best interests of the Borough and "in so doing to own property, operate bathing beaches, hire life guards, beach cleaners and policemen. . . ."

Bay Head's sea wall, constructed in 1882
Source: David Gard/Newark Star-Ledger

Nine streets in the Borough, which are perpendicular to the beach, end at the dry sand. The Association owns the land commencing at the end of seven of these streets for the width of each street and extending through the upper dry sand to the mean high water line, the beginning of the wet sand area or foreshore. In addition, the Association owns the fee in six shore front properties, three of which are contiguous and have a frontage aggregating 310 feet. Many owners of beachfront property executed and delivered to the Association leases of the upper dry sand area. These leases are revocable by either party to the lease on thirty days' notice. Some owners have not executed such leases and have not permitted the Association to use their beaches. . . .

The Association controls and supervises its beach property between the third week in June and Labor Day. It engages about 40 employees who serve as lifeguards, beach police and beach cleaners. Lifeguards, stationed at five operating beaches, indicate by use of flags whether the ocean condition is dangerous (red), requires caution (yellow), or is satisfactory (green). In addition to observing and, if need be, assisting those in the water, when called upon lifeguards render first aid. Beach cleaners are engaged to rake and keep the beach clean of debris. Beach police are stationed at the entrances to the beaches where the public streets lead into the beach to ensure that only Association members or their guests enter. Some beach police patrol the beaches to enforce its membership rules.

Membership is generally limited to residents of Bay Head. Class A members are property owners. Class B are non-owners. . . . Upon application residents are routinely accepted. . . .

Except for fishermen, who are permitted to walk through the upper dry sand area to the foreshore, only the membership may use the beach between 10:00 A.M. and 5:30 P.M. during the summer season. The public is permitted to use the Association's beach from 5:30 P.M. to 10:00 A.M. during the summer and, with no hourly restrictions, between Labor Day and mid-June.

No attempt has ever been made to stop anyone from occupying the terrain east of the high water mark. During certain parts of the day, when the tide is low, the foreshore could consist of about 50 feet of sand not being flowed by the water. The public could gain access to the foreshore by coming from the Borough of Point Pleasant Beach on the north or from the Borough of Mantoloking on the south. . . .

II. The Public Trust

In Borough of Neptune City v. Borough of Avon-by-the-Sea, 61 N.J. 296, 303, 294 A.2d 47 (1972), Justice Hall alluded to the ancient principle "that land covered by tidal waters belonged to the sovereign, but for the common use of all the people." The genesis of this principle is found in Roman jurisprudence, which held that "[b]y the law of nature" "the air, running water, the sea, and consequently the shores of the sea," were "common to mankind." Justinian, Institutes 2.1.1 (T. Sandars trans. 1st Am. ed. 1876). No one was forbidden access to the sea, and everyone could use the seashore "to dry his nets there, and haul them from the sea. . . ." Id., 2.1.5. The seashore was not private property, but "subject to the same law as the sea itself, and the sand or ground beneath it." Id. This underlying concept was applied in New Jersey in Arnold v. Mundy, 6 N.J.L. 1 (Sup. Ct. 1821).

[I]n *Arnold* . . . Chief Justice Kirkpatrick, in an extensive opinion, . . . concluded that all navigable rivers in which the tide ebbs and flows and the coasts of the sea, including the water and land under the water, are "common to all the citizens, and that each [citizen] has a right to use them according to his necessities, subject only to the laws which regulate that use. . . ." Id. at 93. Regulation included erecting docks, harbors and wharves, and improving fishery and oyster beds. This common property . . . [belonged] to the Crown of England, and upon the Revolution these royal rights became vested in the people of New Jersey. Later in Illinois Central R.R. v. Illinois, 146 U.S. 387, 453 (1892), the Supreme Court, in referring to the common property, stated that "[t]he State can no more abdicate its trust over property in which the whole people are interested . . . than it can abdicate its police powers. . . ."

In *Avon*, Justice Hall reaffirmed the public's right to use the waterfront as announced in *Arnold v. Mundy*. He observed that the public has a right to use the land below the mean average high water mark where the tide ebbs and flows. These uses have historically included navigation and fishing. In *Avon* the public's rights were extended "to recreational uses, including bathing, swimming and other shore activities." 61 N.J. at 309, 294 A.2d 47. . . . Extension of the public trust doctrine to include bathing, swimming and other shore activities is consonant with and furthers the general welfare. The public's right to enjoy these privileges must be respected.

In order to exercise these rights guaranteed by the public trust doctrine, the public must have access to municipally-owned dry sand areas as well as the foreshore. The extension of the public trust doctrine to include municipally-owned dry sand areas was necessitated by our conclusion that enjoyment of rights in the foreshore is inseparable from use of dry sand beaches. See Lusardi v. Curtis Point Property Owners Ass'n, 86 N.J. 217, 228, 430 A.2d 881 (1981). In *Avon* we struck down a municipal ordinance that required nonresidents to pay a higher fee than residents for the use of the beach. We held that where a municipal beach is dedicated to public use, the public trust doctrine "dictates that the beach and the ocean waters must be open to all on equal terms and without preference and that any contrary state or municipal action is impermissible." 61 N.J. at 309, 294 A.2d 47. The . . . Court depended on the public trust doctrine, impliedly holding that full enjoyment of the foreshore necessitated some use of the upper sand, so that the latter came under the umbrella of the public trust.

In Van Ness v. Borough of Deal, 78 N.J. 174, 393 A.2d 571 (1978), we stated that the public's right to use municipally-owned beaches was not dependent upon the municipality's dedication of its beaches to use by the general public. The Borough of Deal had dedicated a portion of such beach for use by its residents only. We found such limited dedication "immaterial" given the public trust doctrine's requirement that the public be afforded the right to enjoy all dry sand beaches owned by a municipality. 78 N.J. at 179-80, 393 A.2d 571.

Public Rights in Privately-Owned Dry Sand Beaches

In *Avon* and *Deal* our finding of public rights in dry sand areas was specifically and appropriately limited to those beaches owned by a municipality. We now address the extent of the public's interest in privately-owned dry sand beaches. This interest may take one of two forms. First, the public may have a right to cross privately owned dry sand beaches in order to gain access to the foreshore. Second, this interest may be of the sort enjoyed by the public in municipal beaches under *Avon* and *Deal*, namely, the right to sunbathe and generally enjoy recreational activities. . . .

Exercise of the public's right to swim and bathe below the mean high water mark may depend upon a right to pass across the upland beach. Without some means of access the public right to use the foreshore would be meaningless. To say that the public trust doctrine entitles the public to swim in the ocean and to use the foreshore in connection therewith without assuring the public of a feasible access route would seriously impinge on, if not effectively eliminate, the rights of the public trust doctrine. This does not mean the public has an unrestricted right to cross at will over any and all property bordering on the common property. The public interest is satisfied so long as there is reasonable access to the sea. . . .

The bather's right in the upland sands is not limited to passage. Reasonable enjoyment of the foreshore and the sea cannot be realized unless some enjoyment of the dry sand area is also allowed.[11] The complete pleasure of swimming must be accompanied by intermittent periods of rest and relaxation beyond the water's edge. See State ex rel. Thornton v. Hay, 254 Or. 584, 599-602, 462 P.2d 671, 678-79 (1969) (Denecke, J., concurring). The unavailability of the physical situs for such rest and relaxation would seriously curtail and in many situations eliminate the right to the recreational use of the ocean. This was a principal reason why in *Avon* and *Deal* we held that municipally-owned dry sand beaches "must be open to all on equal terms. . . ." *Avon*, 61 N.J. at 308, 294 A.2d 47. We see no reason why rights under the public trust doctrine to use of the upland dry sand area should be limited to municipally-owned property. It is true that the private owner's interest in the upland dry sand area is not identical to that of a municipality. Nonetheless, where use of dry sand is essential or reasonably necessary for enjoyment of the ocean, the doctrine warrants the public's use of the upland dry sand area subject to an accommodation of the interests of the owner.

We . . . perceive the public trust doctrine not to be "fixed or static," but one to "be molded and extended to meet changing conditions and needs of the public it was created to benefit." *Avon*, 61 N.J. at 309, 294 A.2d 47.

Precisely what privately-owned upland sand area will be available and required to satisfy the public's rights under the public trust doctrine will depend on the circumstances. Location of the dry sand area in relation to the foreshore, extent and availability of publicly-owned upland sand area, nature and extent of the public demand,

---

11. Some historical support for this proposition may be found in an analogous situation where fishermen, in exercising the right of public fishery in tidal waters, were permitted to draw nets on the beach above the ordinary high water mark in the act of fishing. S. Moore & H. Moore, The History and Law of Fisheries 96 (1903).

and usage of the upland sand land by the owner are all factors to be weighed and considered in fixing the contours of the usage of the upper sand.

Today, recognizing the increasing demand for our State's beaches and the dynamic nature of the public trust doctrine, we find that the public must be given both access to and use of privately-owned dry sand areas as reasonably necessary. While the public's rights in private beaches are not co-extensive with the rights enjoyed in municipal beaches, private landowners may not in all instances prevent the public from exercising its rights under the public trust doctrine. The public must be afforded reasonable access to the foreshore as well as a suitable area for recreation on the dry sand.

. . .

V. The Beaches of Bay Head

The Bay Head Improvement Association, which services the needs of all residents of the Borough for swimming and bathing in the public trust property, owns the street-wide strip of dry sand area at the foot of seven public streets that extends to the mean high water line. It also owns the fee in six other upland sand properties connected or adjacent to the tracts it owns at the end of two streets. In addition, it holds leases to approximately 42 tracts of upland sand area. The question that we must address is whether the dry sand area that the Association owns or leases should be open to the public to satisfy the public's rights under the public trust doctrine. Our analysis turns upon whether the Association may restrict its membership to Bay Head residents and thereby preclude public use of the dry sand area. . . .

The Association's activities paralleled those of a municipality in its operation of the beachfront. . . . When viewed in its totality—its purposes, relationship with the municipality, communal characteristic, activities, and virtual monopoly over the Bay Head beachfront-the quasi-public nature of the Association is apparent. The Association makes available to the Bay Head public access to the common tidal property for swimming and bathing and to the upland dry sand area for use incidental thereto, preserving the residents' interests in a fashion similar to *Avon*. . . .

Accordingly, membership in the Association must be open to the public at large. In this manner the public will be assured access to the common beach property during the hours of 10:00 A.M. to 5:30 P.M. between mid-June and September, where they may exercise their right to swim and bathe and to use the Association's dry sand area incidental to those activities. . . .

The Public Advocate has urged that all the privately-owned beachfront property likewise must be opened to the public. Nothing has been developed on this record to justify that conclusion. We have decided that the Association's membership and thereby its beach must be open to the public. That area might reasonably satisfy the public need at this time. We are aware that the Association possessed, as of the initiation of this litigation, about 42 upland sand lots under leases revocable on 30 days' notice. If any of these leases have been or are to be terminated, or if the Association were to sell all or part of its property, it may necessitate further adjudication of the public's claims in favor of the public trust on part or all of these or other privately-owned upland dry sand lands depending upon the circumstances. . . .

. . . It is not necessary for us to determine under what circumstances and to what extent there will be a need to use the dry sand of private owners who either now or in the future may have no leases with the Association. Resolution of the competing interests, private ownership and the public trust, may in some cases be simple, but in many it may be most complex. In any event, resolution would depend upon the specific facts in controversy. . . .

The judgment of the Appellate Division is reversed in part and affirmed in part. Judgment is entered for the plaintiff against the Association. Judgment of dismissal against the individual property owners is affirmed without prejudice.

Notes and Questions

1. *Post-*Matthews *developments regarding beach access in New Jersey.* Subsequent to its decision in *Matthews*, the New Jersey Supreme Court expanded the public trust doctrine. In Raleigh Avenue Beach Assn. v. Atlantis Beach Club, 879 A.2d 112 (N.J. 2005), the court held that the public's right to reasonable access to beaches extends to the dry-sand portion of beaches owned by strictly private entities as well as quasi-public entities such as the Bay Head Improvement Association. In *Raleigh Avenue*, the beach owner, Atlantis Beach Club, was strictly private, performing no city-like functions and having no symbiotic relationship with the municipality. The beach on the Atlantis property was the only beach in the township, and it was open to the public free of charge until 1996, when the beach club was established. The court stated that "*Matthews* established the framework for application of the public trust doctrine to private-owned upland sand beaches." Id. at 121. Is this a satisfactory explanation of the extension of *Matthews* to *Raleigh Avenue*? For an argument that such a right is justified on the basis of promoting human flourishing through improved public health and enhanced sociability, see Gregory S. Alexander, The Social-Obligation Norm in American Property Law, 94 Cornell L. Rev. 745, 801-810 (2009).

2. *Origins of the public trust doctrine.* Though its roots lie in Roman law, the modern version of the public trust doctrine is conventionally traced to the 1892 U.S. Supreme Court decision in Illinois Central Railroad Co. v. Illinois, 146 U.S. 387 (1892). In that case the Illinois legislature in 1886 granted to the railroad in fee simple submerged lands comprising virtually the entire Chicago lakefront. Four years later, regretting the grant, the legislature revoked it. The Supreme Court upheld the revocation, explaining that the legislature did not have the power to convey the entire city lakefront free of trust, thus barring all future legislatures from protecting the public interest. For a fuller account of *Illinois Central*, see Joseph D. Kearney & Thomas W. Merrill, The Origins of the Public Trust Doctrine: What Really Happened in *Illinois Central*, 71 U. Chi. L. Rev. 799 (2004). The seminal article that revived interest in the public trust doctrine is Joseph L. Sax, The Public Trust Doctrine in Natural Resource Law: Effective Judicial Intervention, 68 Mich. L. Rev. 471 (1970).

3. *Scope of the public trust.* The public trust doctrine in *Matthews* creates an *easement* that gives rights to the public generally. An easement provides someone other than the owner(s) of land with rights to use the land or an opportunity to prevent land from being used in a particular manner. We will consider easements in more depth in Chapter 10.

The public trust doctrine extends to all land covered by the ebb and flow of the tide and, in addition, all inland lakes and rivers that are navigable. Phillips Petroleum Co. v. Mississippi, 484 U.S. 469 (1988). In Michigan, the public trust doctrine protects the public right of access to privately owned beaches along the Great Lakes. In Glass v. Goeckel, 703 N.W.2d 58 (Mich. 2005), the court held that public access along the shore is permitted between the current edge of the lake and the "ordinary high water mark." Any prior state grants of private property rights inconsistent with this public easement, the court said, are invalid. See Kenneth K. Kilbert, The Public Trust Doctrine and the Great Lakes Shores, 58 Clev. St. L. Rev. 1 (2010).

4. *Homelessness and the right to access public space.* In connection with the public access issues raised in *Matthews*, consider Martin v. City of Boise, 902 F.3d 1031, 1035 (9th Cir. 2018), amended by 920 F.3d 584 (9th Cir. 2019), cert. denied. City of Boise v. Martin, 140 S. Ct. 674 (2019). In that case, the Ninth Circuit held that a city ordinance that allowed for the "imposition of criminal penalties for sitting, sleeping, or lying outside on public property for homeless individuals who cannot obtain shelter" was unconstitutional under the Eighth Amendment's prohibition of cruel and unusual punishment by criminalizing homeless status. The holding was limited to involuntary conduct: the Eighth Amendment bars punishing a person only "for lacking the means to live out the 'universal and unavoidable consequences of being human,'" the court stated. Id. at 1048 n.8 (quoting Jones v. City of Los Angeles, 444 F.3d 1118, 1136 (9th Cir. 2006), vacated, 505 F.3d 1006 (9th Cir. 2007)). The court's decision did not nullify the range of laws that punish homeless people, nor prevent the political process from addressing the problem of homelessness. As Judge Berzon noted, "[O]nly . . . municipal ordinances that criminalize sleeping, sitting, or lying in all public spaces, when no alternative sleeping space is available, violate the Eighth Amendment." *Martin*, 920 F.3d at 589 (Berzon, J., concurring in the denial of rehearing en banc).

Is this decision a hollow victory for homeless people and their advocates, or will it have a practical impact? More broadly, what are its implications for the right of public access to public spaces such as city parks?

D. ACQUISITION BY CREATION: AN INTRODUCTION TO INTELLECTUAL PROPERTY

Another method of acquiring property rights is by creation. The idea is that if you create something—if in that sense you are first in time—then that something is yours to exploit because of your investment of labor and money. This idea is commonly associated with John Locke, who argued that you own the fruits of your labor by virtue of having "a property in your own person." See Note 4 on page 21.

The trouble is that the fruits of your labor are *not* always yours alone to exploit. In fact, you do *not* always have full rights of property in your own person. Why? The materials in this section address that question.

The principle of acquisition of property rights by creation is the domain of intellectual property. In this section, we will briefly survey three types of intellectual property: copyrights, patents, and trademarks. These are all governed by federal statutes, but there are common law copyrights in addition to statutory ones. Moreover, trademarks are regulated through a mixed system of state common law rules and optional federal registration. The Federal Constitution authorizes Congress to "promote the progress of science and useful arts, by securing for limited times to authors and inventors the exclusive right to their respective writings and discoveries." U.S. Const. art. I, § 8, cl. 8. Pursuant to this authorization, Congress has passed legislation for patents and copyrights. *Patent* legislation protects inventions that are novel, useful, and non-obvious. *Copyright* legislation grants exclusive rights in original literary and artistic works, including books, poetry, music, dance, movies, paintings, and computer programs. *Trademark* law protects words or symbols that identify the source of goods or services. Trademark law began as part of state common law (specifically, unfair competition law), and although federal trademark statutory law now exists, generally it supplements rather than replaces the common law. We begin, however, with three interests that were not conventionally recognized as part of intellectual property but that have gained prominence in recent years.

The law of intellectual property grants limited monopolies over protected material. The point of the monopolies is to promote creative activity; the point of the limits is to advance competition (which in turn facilitates consumption by holding prices down). The design of the systems involves difficult trade-offs.

Intellectual property rights are rights in information. Such rights differ from property rights in tangible resources in several ways. Two characteristics in particular distinguish information assets from real and chattel property. Information assets are:

- *non-excludable*—meaning that once a resource has been created, people cannot be prevented from gaining access to it even though they have not paid for it; and
- *non-rivalrous*—meaning that the resource may be used by one person without preventing simultaneous use by others.

In economic terms, goods that are both non-excludable and non-rivalrous are called "public goods" (national defense is a common example—my being protected by the U.S. Armed Forces doesn't diminish your protection). Goods that are rivalrous and excludable are "private goods" (my use of my computer diminishes your ability to use it, and I can exclude you from using my computer by locking it away). Most tangible goods are both excludable and rivalrous, but not so information—the stuff of intellectual property.

The distinction between public and private goods is important because, according to conventional economic theory, the market will produce goods that are excludable and rivalrous but will undersupply those that are non-excludable and non-rivalrous. The reason is that the market creates incentives to produce private goods by allowing producers to capture the excess of what buyers are willing to pay for such goods over the production costs. Not so with respect to public goods. If a good is non-excludable, no one will pay for it, and a rational actor will not produce a good unless he can capture some of the benefits associated with its production.

Intellectual property rights are a potential solution to this problem. Their primary purpose is to create incentives for inventors, writers, and others involved in similarly creative enterprises to produce goods that would, at least in theory, otherwise not be produced. Intellectual property law does this by transforming public goods into goods that are excludable but non-rivalrous.

While intellectual property rights solve one problem, they create another. By giving producers of goods in information monopolies over their products, intellectual property rights stifle competition and thus harm consumers. This tension between competing threats to consumer welfare runs throughout intellectual property law. Concerns about monopolization helps explain why the law sometimes relies on other mechanisms to incentivize the creation of information assets, such as government grants, prizes, first-mover advantages, and social production. Alas, each of these alternatives to intellectual property has drawbacks of its own.

1. Three Non-Traditional Intellectual Property Interests

a. Misappropriation

INTERNATIONAL NEWS SERVICE v. ASSOCIATED PRESS
Supreme Court of the United States, 1918
248 U.S. 215

PITNEY, J. The parties are competitors in the gathering and distribution of news and its publication for profit in newspapers throughout the United States. The Associated Press [or AP, complainant] . . . gathers in all parts of the world, by means of various instrumentalities of its own, by exchange with its members, and by other appropriate means, news and intelligence of current and recent events of interest to newspaper readers and distributes it daily to its members for publication in their newspapers. . . .

Defendant [INS] is a corporation organized under the laws of the State of New Jersey, whose business is the gathering and selling of news to its customers and clients, consisting of newspapers published throughout the United States, under contracts by which they pay certain amounts at stated times for defendant's service. . . .

The parties are in the keenest competition between themselves in the distribution of news throughout the United States; and so, as a rule, are the newspapers that they serve, in their several districts. . . .

The bill was filed to restrain the pirating of complainant's news by defendant in three ways: First, by bribing employees of newspapers published by complainant's members to furnish AP news to INS before publication, for transmission by telegraph and telephone to defendant's clients for publication by them; Second, by inducing AP members to violate its by-laws and permit defendant to obtain news before publication; and Third, by copying news from bulletin boards and from early editions of complainant's newspapers and selling this, either bodily or after rewriting it, to defendant's customers.

The District Court, upon consideration of the bill and answer, with voluminous affidavits on both sides, granted a preliminary injunction under the first and second heads; but refused at that stage to restrain the systematic practice admittedly pursued by INS, of taking news bodily from the bulletin boards and early editions of AP's newspapers and selling it as its own. The court expressed itself as satisfied that this practice amounted to unfair trade, but as the legal question was one of first impression it considered that the allowance of an injunction should await the outcome of an appeal. . . .

[The Court of Appeals modified and sustained the injunction.]

AP newsroom circa 1920
Source: Associated Press

The only matter that has been argued before us is whether INS may lawfully be restrained from appropriating news taken from bulletins issued by AP or any of its members, or from newspapers published by them, for the purpose of selling it to INS clients. AP asserts that INS's admitted course of conduct in this regard both violates AP's property right in the news and constitutes unfair competition in business. And notwithstanding the case has proceeded only to the stage of a preliminary injunction, we have deemed it proper to consider the underlying questions, since they go to the very merits of the action and are presented upon facts that are not in dispute. As presented in argument, these questions are: 1. Whether there is any property in news; 2. Whether, if there be property in news collected for the purpose of being published, it survives the instant of its publication in the first newspaper to which it is communicated by the news-gatherer; and 3. Whether defendant's admitted course of conduct in appropriating for commercial use matter taken from bulletins or early editions of AP publications constituted unfair competition in trade. . . .

AP's news matter is not copyrighted. It is said that it could not, in practice, be copyrighted, because of the large number of dispatches that are sent daily; and . . . news is not within the operation of the copyright act. Defendant, while apparently conceding this, nevertheless invokes the analogies of the law of literary property and copyright, insisting as its principal contention that, assuming AP has a right of property in its news, it can be maintained (unless the copyright act be complied with) only by being kept secret and confidential, and that upon the publication with AP's consent of unco-pyrighted news by any of AP's members in a newspaper or upon a bulletin board, the right of property is lost, and the subsequent use of the news by the public or by INS for any purpose whatever becomes lawful. . . .

In considering the general question of property in news matter, it is necessary to recognize its dual character, distinguishing between the substance of the information and the particular form or collocation of words in which the writer has communicated it.

No doubt news articles often possess a literary quality, and are the subject of literary property at the common law; nor do we question that such an article, as a literary production, is the subject of copyright by the terms of the act as it now stands.

But the news element—the information respecting current events contained in the literary production—is not the creation of the writer, but is a report of matters that ordinarily are *publici juris*; it is the history of the day. It is not to be supposed that the framers of the constitution, when they empowered Congress "to promote the progress of science and useful arts, by securing for limited times to authors and inventors the exclusive right to their respective writings and discoveries" (Const., Art. I, § 8, par. 8), intended to confer upon one who might happen to be the first to report a historic event the exclusive right for any period to spread the knowledge of it.

We need spend no time, however, upon the general question of property in news matter at common law, or the application of the copyright act, since it seems to us the case must turn upon the question of unfair competition in business. . . . The peculiar value of news is in the spreading of it while it is fresh; and it is evident that a valuable property interest in the news, as news, cannot be maintained by keeping it secret. Besides, except for matter improperly disclosed, or published in breach of trust or confidence, or in violation of law, none of which is involved in this branch of the case, the news of current events may be regarded as common property. What we are concerned with is the business of making it known to the world, in which both parties to the present suit are engaged. . . . The parties are competitors in this field; and, on fundamental principles, applicable here as elsewhere, when rights or privileges of the one are liable to conflict with those of the other, each party is under a duty so to conduct its own business as not unnecessarily or unfairly to injure that of the other.

. . . The question here is not so much the rights of either party as against the public but their rights as between themselves. And although we may and do assume that neither party has any remaining property interest as against the public in uncopyrighted news matter after the moment of its first publication, it by no means follows that there is no remaining property interest in it as between themselves. For, to both of them alike, news matter, however little susceptible of ownership or dominion in the absolute sense, is stock in trade, to be gathered at the cost of enterprise, organization, skill, labor, and money, and to be distributed and sold to those who will pay money for it, as for any other merchandise. Regarding the news, therefore, as but the material out of which both parties are seeking to make profits at the same time and in the same field, we hardly can fail to recognize that for this purpose, and as between them, it must be regarded as *quasi* property, irrespective of the rights of either as against the public. . . .

The peculiar features of the case arise from the fact that, while novelty and freshness form so important an element in the success of the business, the very processes of distribution and publication necessarily occupy a good deal of time. AP's service, as well as defendant's, is a daily service to daily newspapers; most of the foreign news reaches this country at the Atlantic seaboard, principally at the city of New York, and because of this, and of time differentials due to the earth's rotation, the distribution of news matter throughout the country is principally from east to west; and, since in speed the telegraph and telephone easily outstrip the rotation of the earth, it is a simple matter for defendant to take complainant's news from bulletins or early editions of complainant's members in the eastern cities and at the mere cost of telegraphic transmission cause it to be published in western papers issued at least as early as those served by complainant. Besides this, and irrespective of time differentials, irregularities in telegraphic transmission on different lines, and the normal consumption of time in printing and distributing the newspaper, result in permitting pirated news to be placed in the hands of defendant's readers sometimes simultaneously with the service of competing AP papers, occasionally even earlier.

A Look Back

Recall Keeble v. Hickeringill, which we saw earlier in this chapter (see page 23). That case involved the principle of unfair competition. Does *INS* represent anything more than a straightforward application of the principle of that case?

INS insists that when, with the sanction and approval of complainant, and as the result of the use of its news for the very purpose for which it is distributed, a portion of AP's members communicate to the general public by posting it upon bulletin boards so that all may read, or by issuing it to newspapers and distributing it indiscriminately, complainant no longer has the right to control the use to be made of it; that when it thus reaches the light of day it becomes the common possession of all to whom it is accessible; and that any purchaser of a newspaper has the right to communicate the intelligence which it contains to anybody and for any purpose, even for the purpose of selling it for profit to newspapers published for profit in competition with complainant's members.

The fault in the reasoning lies in applying as a test the right of the complainant as against the public, instead of considering the rights of complainant and defendant, competitors in business, as between themselves. The right of the purchaser of a single newspaper to spread knowledge of its contents gratuitously, for any legitimate purpose not unreasonably interfering with complainant's right to make merchandise of it, may be admitted; but to transmit that news for commercial use, in competition with complainant—which is what defendant has done and seeks to justify—is a very different matter. In doing this defendant, by its very act, admits that it is taking material that has been acquired by complainant as the result of organization and the expenditure of labor, skill, and money, and which is salable by complainant for money, and that defendant in appropriating it and selling it as its own is endeavoring to reap where it has not sown, and by disposing of it to newspapers that are competitors of complainant's members is appropriating to itself the harvest of those who have sown. Stripped of all disguises, the process amounts to an unauthorized interference with the normal operation of complainant's legitimate business precisely at the point where the profit is to be reaped, in order to divert a material portion of the profit from those who have earned it to those who have not; with special advantage to defendant in the competition because of the fact that it is not burdened with any part of the expense of gathering the news. The transaction speaks for itself, and a court of equity ought not to hesitate long in characterizing it as unfair competition in business. . . .

The contention that the news is abandoned to the public for all purposes when published in the first newspaper is untenable. Abandonment is question of intent, and the entire organization of the AP negatives such a purpose. The cost of the service would be prohibitive if the reward were to be so limited. No single newspaper, no small group of newspapers, could sustain the expenditure. Indeed, it is one of the most obvious results to defendant's theory that, by permitting indiscriminate publication by anybody and everybody for purposes of profit in competition with the news-gatherer, it would render publication profitless, or so little profitable as in effect to cut off the service by rendering the cost prohibitive in comparison with the return. . . .

It is said that the elements of unfair competition are lacking because there is no attempt by defendant to palm off its goods as those of the complainant, characteristic of the most familiar, if not the most typical cases of unfair competition. But we cannot concede that the right to equitable relief is confined to that class of cases. In the present case the fraud upon complainant's rights is more direct and obvious. Regarding news matter as the mere material from which these two competing parties are endeavoring to make money, and treating it, therefore, as *quasi* property for the purposes of their business because they are both selling it as such, defendant's conduct differs from the ordinary case of unfair competition in trade principally in this that, instead of selling its own goods as those of complainant, it substitutes misappropriation in the place of misrepresentation, and sells complainant's goods as its own. . . .

The decree of the Circuit Court of Appeals will be Affirmed.

[The concurring opinion of Justice Holmes, joined by Justice McKenna, and the dissenting opinion of Justice Brandeis are omitted.]

THE REST OF THE STORY . . .

Contrary to conventional accounts, there was no evidence that INS was copying bulletins on the East Coast and transmitting them to newspapers on the West Coast. INS was just a convenient defendant that AP needed to establish a broad legal precedent that would protect its position as a natural monopoly. In the early twentieth century, the wire service was primary a large network of leased telegraph lines. The cost of creating that network of telegraph lines was a large, fixed cost that dwarfed the cost of gathering the news, an activity that AP spent little time or effort actually doing. Enhancing its market power even further, AP was a member of an international cartel that gave it exclusive rights to bulletins of foreign news services and access to foreign government communiqués. Technological and economic changes (e.g., substituting teletype machines for telegraph operators) threatened AP's monopoly position, opening it up to previously unknown competition. To block its potential competitors, AP sought a broad legal principle that recognized a property right in news. What it needed was a ready defendant whom it could charge with copying "its" news. It found one in INS. The chief of INS's bureau in Cleveland had bribed an AP reporter to provide him with the news there. As for copying, INS had copied some of AP's material, but actually very little copying was done. In truth, that was just a convenient excuse for bringing the lawsuit.

After the decision, AP and INS settled. It was in their self-interest to do so because their relationship was mutually advantageous. INS, which was owned by William Randolph Hearst, wanted to continue to obtain the benefits of AP's service. On the other side, the members of AP, which was a cooperative of subscribing members, did not wish to offend the powerful Hearst. At the end of the day, the case had very little effect on the way INS did business. For a full account of the story, see Douglas G. Baird, The Story of *INS v. AP*: Property, Natural Monopoly, and the Uneasy Legacy of a Concocted Controversy, in Intellectual Property Stories 9 (Jane C. Ginsburg & Rochelle Cooper Dreyfuss eds. 2006).

Notes and Questions

1. *Design protection.* In Cheney Brothers v. Doris Silk Corp., 35 F.2d 279 (2d Cir. 1929), the plaintiff sought protection of designs of silks that it manufactured. Some of the silks succeeded commercially and some of them did not, and even commercially successful patterns did not last more than eight or nine months on the market. The defendant, Doris Silk, made copies of Cheney Brothers's successful prints and sold them at a cheaper price. Cheney Brothers asked for an injunction, although only for the duration of one season. Neither patent nor copyright law then provided protection, for practical and legal reasons, so Cheney Brothers relied on *INS.*

The Second Circuit, in an opinion by Learned Hand, denied relief, stating that the basic rule is: "In the absence of some recognized right at common law, or under the statutes . . . a man's property is limited to the chattels which embody his invention. Others may imitate these at their pleasure." The court distinguished *INS* by limiting it to its facts.

Today, in general, fashion designs are not protected under intellectual property law in the United States. However, legislation is pending in both houses of Congress to provide such protection under the federal Copyright Act.

2. *The "hot news" doctrine.* If the general principle today is that of *Cheney Brothers*—in the absence of some recognized right, people are free to imitate or copy the original—then what is the current status of *INS*? The misappropriation doctrine fell into disuse following the decision, but in recent years, it has experienced a revival of sorts. Led by the Second Circuit, a few courts have developed a "hot news" doctrine, largely on the basis of *INS.* Under the Second Circuit's hot news doctrine, a newsgatherer may recover from a defendant when (1) the newsgathering or collection process involves significant expenditures; (2) the collected news or information is time-sensitive; (3) the defendant free rides on the collected material; (4) the freeriding directly competes with the newsgatherer's market; and (5) the freeriding is likely to diminish incentives to collect news/information in a timely fashion. National Basketball Assn. v. Motorola, Inc., 105 F.3d 841, 852-853 (2d Cir. 1997). See also Barclays Capital, Inc. v. Theflyonthewall.com, Inc., 650 F.3d 876 (2d Cir. 2011) (no misappropriation found when tfotw.com leaked stock tips; claim was preempted by the Copyright Act). See generally Shyamkrishna Balganesh, "Hot News": The Enduring Myth of Property in the News, 111 Colum. L. Rev. 419 (2011).

3. *Intellectual property and the labor theory.* Intellectual property is often defended on the basis of John Locke's labor theory of property. Indeed, from one perspective intellectual creation seems more like creation out of nothing than creation of tangible products from resources removed from an original commons. Hence intellectual property does not seem to involve the same complications of trying to separate out the relative contributions of the individual laborer and the materials on which he has labored. See Gregory S. Alexander & Eduardo M. Peñalver, An Introduction to Property Theory 192 (2010).

How strong is this argument? It rests substantially on the assumption that intellectual creations are creations out of nothing. Is that assumption correct? See id. at 193-194. Are there other reasons why a person should not always be able to reap where she has sown? Consider:

> That an individual has the right to reap what he has sown . . . is far from self-evident even as applied to tangible property. . . . We typically can reap only the wheat we sow on our own land, and how land becomes private property in the first place remains a mystery. In any event, wheat and information are fundamentally different from one another. It is the nature of wheat or land or any other tangible property that possession by one person precludes possession by anyone else. . . . Many people, however, can use the same piece of information. . . .
>
> [G]ranting individuals exclusive rights to the information they gather conflicts with other rights in a way that granting exclusive rights to tangible property does not. In a market economy, granting individuals exclusive rights to property is an effective way of allocating scarce resources. Saying that someone should be able to own a particular good or piece of land and should be able to keep others from getting it unless they pay him is unobjectionable once one accepts the desirability of a market economy. Granting exclusive rights to information does not, however, necessarily promote a market economy. Competition depends upon imitation. One person invests labor and money to create a product, such as a food processor, that people will buy. Others may imitate him and take advantage of the new market by selling their own food processors. Their machines may incorporate their own ideas about how such machines should be made. As a result, the quality of the machines may rise and their price may fall. The first person is made worse off than he would be if he had had an exclusive right to his idea, because his competitors are enjoying the fruits of his labor and are not paying for it. Nevertheless, the public as a whole may be better off, as long as this freedom to imitate does not destroy the incentive for people to come up with new devices.

Douglas G. Baird, Common Law Intellectual Property and the Legacy of International News Service v. Associated Press, 50 U. Chi. L. Rev. 411, 413-414 (1983).

b. Property in One's Persona: The Right of Publicity

Most states now recognize the right of publicity as a kind of property interest, assignable during life and descendible at death, either as a matter of common law or statute. The right of publicity prevents the unauthorized commercial use of one's name, likeness, and other aspects of one's "identity" and gives the individual the exclusive right to license the commercial use of these personal features. The right of publicity seems to be rooted in the right of privacy. Judge Richard Posner observes that the courts first recognized an explicit right of privacy in a case where the defendant, without consent, used the plaintiff's name and picture in an advertisement. "Paradoxically, this branch of the right of privacy is most often invoked by celebrities avid for publicity . . .; they just want to make sure they get the highest possible price for the use of their name and picture." Richard A. Posner, Economic Analysis of Law 411 (9th ed. 2014).

WHITE v. SAMSUNG ELECTRONICS AMERICA, INC.
United States Court of Appeals, Ninth Circuit, 1992
971 F.2d 1395

GOODWIN, J. This case involves a promotional "fame and fortune" dispute. . . .

Plaintiff Vanna White is the hostess of "Wheel of Fortune," one of the most popular game shows in television history. An estimated forty million people watch the program daily. Capitalizing on the fame which her participation in the show has bestowed on her, White markets her identity to various advertisers.

The dispute in this case arose out of a series of advertisements prepared for Samsung by Deutsch. The series ran in at least half a dozen publications with widespread, and in some cases national, circulation. Each of the advertisements in the series followed the same theme. Each depicted a current item from popular culture and a Samsung electronic product. Each was set in the twenty-first century and conveyed the message that the Samsung product would still be in use by that time. By hypothesizing outrageous future outcomes for the cultural items, the ads created humorous effects. For example, one lampooned current popular notions of an unhealthy diet by depicting a raw steak with the caption: "Revealed to be health food. 2010 A.D."

The advertisement which prompted the current dispute was for Samsung videocassette recorders (VCRs). The ad depicted a robot, dressed in a wig, gown, and jewelry which Deutsch consciously selected to resemble White's hair and dress. The robot was posed next to a game board which is instantly recognizable as the Wheel of Fortune game show set, in a stance for which White is famous. The caption of the ad read: "Longest-running game show. 2012 A.D." Defendants referred to the ad as the "Vanna White" ad. Unlike the other celebrities used in the campaign, White neither consented to the ads nor was she paid.

Following the circulation of the robot ad, White sued Samsung and Deutsch in federal district court under: (1) California Civil Code § 3344; (2) the California common law right of publicity; and (3) § 43(a) of the Lanham Act, 15 U.S.C. § 1125(a). The district court granted summary judgment against White on each of her claims. White now appeals.

I. Section 3344

White first argues that the district court erred in rejecting her claim under section 3344. Section 3344(a) provides, in pertinent part, that "any person who knowingly uses another's name, voice, signature, photograph, or likeness, in any manner, . . . or purposes of advertising or selling, . . . without such person's prior consent . . . shall be liable for any damages sustained by the person or persons injured as a result thereof."

White argues that the Samsung advertisement used her "likeness" in contravention of section 3344. . . . Samsung and Deutsch used a robot with mechanical features, and not, for example, a manikin molded to White's precise features. Without deciding for all purposes when a caricature or impressionistic resemblance might become a "likeness," we agree with the district court that the robot at issue here was not White's "likeness" within the meaning of section 3344. Accordingly, we affirm the court's dismissal of White's section 3344 claim.

II. Right of Publicity

White next argues that the district court erred in granting summary judgment to defendants on White's common law right of publicity claim. In Eastwood v. Superior

Portion of the 1988 Samsung ad in *Smithsonian* magazine.

Court, 409, 198 Cal. Rptr. 342 (Cal. App. 1983), the California court of appeal stated that the common law right of publicity cause of action "may be pleaded by alleging (1) the defendant's use of the plaintiff's identity; (2) the appropriation of plaintiff's name or likeness to defendant's advantage, commercially or otherwise; (3) lack of consent; and (4) resulting injury." Id. at 417 (citing Prosser, Law of Torts (4th ed. 1971) § 117, pp. 804-807). The district court dismissed White's claim for failure to satisfy Eastwood's second prong, reasoning that defendants had not appropriated White's "name or likeness" with their robot ad. We agree that the robot ad did not make use of White's name or likeness. However, the common law right of publicity is not so confined. . . .

The "name or likeness" formulation referred to in *Eastwood* originated not as an element of the right of publicity cause of action, but as a description of the types of cases in which the cause of action had been recognized. The source of this formulation is Prosser, Privacy, 48 Cal. L. Rev. 383, 401-07 (1960), one of the earliest and most enduring articulations of the common law right of publicity cause of action. In looking at the case law to that point, Prosser recognized that right of publicity cases involved one of two basic factual scenarios: name appropriation, and picture or other likeness appropriation. . . .

Even though Prosser focused on appropriations of name or likeness in discussing the right of publicity, he noted that "it is not impossible that there might be appropriation of the plaintiff's identity, as by impersonation, without the use of either his name or his likeness, and that this would be an invasion of his right of privacy." Id. at 401, n.155. At the time Prosser wrote, he noted however, that "no such case appears to have arisen." Id.

Since Prosser's early formulation, the case law has borne out his insight that the right of publicity is not limited to the appropriation of name or likeness. . . .

In Carson v. Here's Johnny Portable Toilets, Inc., 698 F.2d 831 (6th Cir. 1983), the defendant had marketed portable toilets under the brand name "Here's Johnny"—Johnny Carson's signature "Tonight Show" introduction—without Carson's permission. The district court had dismissed Carson's Michigan common law right of publicity claim because the defendants had not used Carson's "name or likeness." Id. at 835. In reversing the district court, the sixth circuit found "the district court's conception of the right of publicity . . . too narrow" and held that the right was implicated because the defendant had appropriated Carson's identity by using, inter alia, the phrase "Here's Johnny." Id. at 835-37.

The cases teach not only that the common law right of publicity reaches means of appropriation other than name or likeness, but that the specific means of appropriation are relevant only for determining whether the defendant has in fact appropriated the plaintiff's identity. The right of publicity does not require that appropriations of identity be accomplished through particular means to be actionable. . . .

. . . As the *Carson* court explained: "the right of publicity has developed to protect the commercial interest of celebrities in their identities. The theory of the right is that a celebrity's identity can be valuable in the promotion of products, and the celebrity has an interest that may be protected from the unauthorized commercial exploitation of that identity. . . . If the celebrity's identity is commercially exploited, there has been an invasion of his right whether or not his "name or likeness" is used. *Carson*, 698 F.2d at 835.

It is not important how the defendant has appropriated the plaintiff's identity, but whether the defendant has done so. . . . A rule which says that the right of publicity can be infringed only through the use of nine different methods of appropriating identity merely challenges the clever advertising strategist to come up with the tenth.

Indeed, if we treated the means of appropriation as dispositive in our analysis of the right of publicity, we would not only weaken the right but effectively eviscerate it. The right would fail to protect those plaintiffs most in need of its protection. Advertisers use celebrities to promote their products. The more popular the celebrity, the greater the number of people who recognize her, and the greater the visibility for the product. The identities of the most popular celebrities are not only the most attractive for advertisers, but also the easiest to evoke without resorting to obvious means such as name, likeness, or voice. . . .

Viewed separately, the individual aspects of the advertisement in the present case say little. Viewed together, they leave little doubt about the celebrity the ad is meant to depict. The female-shaped robot is wearing a long gown, blond wig, and large jewelry. Vanna White dresses exactly like this at times, but so do many other women. The robot is in the process of turning a block letter on a game-board. Vanna White dresses like this while turning letters on a game-board but perhaps similarly attired Scrabble-playing women do this as well. The robot is standing on what looks to be the Wheel of Fortune game show set. Vanna White dresses like this, turns letters, and does this on the Wheel of Fortune game show. She is the only one. Indeed, defendants themselves referred to their ad as the "Vanna White" ad. We are not surprised.

Television and other media create marketable celebrity identity value. Considerable energy and ingenuity are expended by those who have achieved celebrity value to exploit it for profit. The law protects the celebrity's sole right to exploit this value whether the celebrity has achieved her fame out of rare ability, dumb luck, or a combination thereof. . . . Because White has alleged facts showing that Samsung and

Deutsch had appropriated her identity, the district court erred by rejecting, on summary judgment, White's common law right of publicity claim. . . .

[The court then turned to White's claim under the Lanham Act, under which White had to show that the robot ad created a likelihood of confusion. The court concluded that the trial court erred in rejecting White's claim at the summary judgment stage, because there was a genuine issue of fact regarding a likelihood of confusion as to her endorsement; the question was one for the jury.]

Judge ALARCON concurred in part and dissented in part.

The defendants in the *White* case subsequently petitioned for a rehearing, which was denied. White v. Samsung Electronics America, Inc., 989 F.2d 1512 (9th Cir. 1992), cert. denied, 508 U.S. 951 (1993). The denial of rehearing prompted the following dissent by Judge Kozinski.]

Something very dangerous is going on here. Private property, including intellectual property, is essential to our way of life. It provides an incentive for investment and innovation; it stimulates the flourishing of our culture; it protects the moral entitlements of people to the fruits of their labors. But reducing too much to private property can be bad medicine. Private land, for instance, is far more useful if separated from other private land by public streets, roads and highways. Public parks, utility rights-of-way and sewers reduce the amount of land in private hands, but vastly enhance the value of the property that remains.

So too it is with intellectual property. Overprotecting intellectual property is as harmful as underprotecting it. Creativity is impossible without a rich public domain. Nothing today, likely nothing since we tamed fire, is genuinely new: Culture, like science and technology, grows by accretion, each new creator building on the works of those who came before. Overprotection stifles the very creative forces it's supposed to nurture.

The panel's opinion is a classic case of overprotection. Concerned about what it sees as a wrong done to Vanna White, the panel majority erects a property right of remarkable and dangerous breadth: Under the majority's opinion, it's now a tort for advertisers to remind the public of a celebrity. Not to use a celebrity's name, voice, signature or likeness; not to imply the celebrity endorses a product; but simply to evoke the celebrity's image in the public's mind. This Orwellian notion withdraws far more from the public domain than prudence and common sense allow. It conflicts with the Copyright Act and the Copyright Clause. It raises serious First Amendment problems. It's bad law, and it deserves a long, hard second look. . . .

The ad that spawned this litigation starred a robot dressed in a wig, gown and jewelry reminiscent of Vanna White's hair and dress; the robot was posed next to a Wheel-of-Fortune-like game board. The caption read "Longest-running game show. 2012 A.D." The gag here, I take it, was that Samsung would still be around when White had been replaced by a robot.

Perhaps failing to see the humor, White sued, alleging Samsung infringed her right of publicity by "appropriating" her "identity." Under California law, White has the exclusive right to use her name, likeness, signature and voice for commercial purposes. But Samsung didn't use her name, voice or signature, and it certainly didn't use her likeness. The ad just wouldn't have been funny had it depicted White or someone who resembled her—the whole joke was that the game show host(ess) was a robot, not a real person. No one seeing the ad could have thought this was supposed to be White in 2012.

The district judge quite reasonably held that, because Samsung didn't use White's name, likeness, voice or signature, it didn't violate her right of publicity. Not so, says the panel majority: The California right of publicity can't possibly be limited to name and likeness. If it were, the majority reasons, a "clever advertising strategist" could avoid using White's name or likeness but nevertheless remind people of her with impunity, "effectively eviscerat[ing]" her rights. To prevent this "evisceration," the panel majority holds that the right of publicity must extend beyond name and likeness, to any "appropriation" of White's "identity"—anything that "evoke[s]" her personality.

But what does "evisceration" mean in intellectual property law? Intellectual property rights aren't like some constitutional rights, absolute guarantees protected against all kinds of interference, subtle as well as blatant. They cast no penumbras, emit no emanations: The very point of intellectual property laws is that they protect only against certain specific kinds of appropriation. I can't publish unauthorized copies of, say, Presumed Innocent; I can't make a movie out of it. But I'm perfectly free to write a book about an idealistic young prosecutor on trial for a crime he didn't commit. . . . All creators draw in part on the work of those who came before, referring to it, building on it, poking fun at it; we call this creativity, not piracy.

The majority isn't, in fact, preventing the "evisceration" of Vanna White's existing rights; it's creating a new and much broader property right, a right unknown in California law. It's replacing the existing balance between the interests of the celebrity and those of the public by a different balance, one substantially more favorable to the celebrity. Instead of having an exclusive right in her name, likeness, signature or voice, every famous person now has an exclusive right to anything that reminds the viewer of her. After all, that's all Samsung did: It used an inanimate object to remind people of White, to "evoke" [her identity].

Consider how sweeping this new right is. What is it about the ad that makes people think of White? It's not the robot's wig, clothes or jewelry; there must be ten million blond women (many of them quasi-famous) who wear dresses and jewelry like White's. It's that the robot is posed near the "Wheel of Fortune" game board. Remove the game board from the ad, and no one would think of Vanna White. But once you include the game board, anybody standing beside it—a brunette woman, a man wearing women's clothes, a monkey in a wig and gown—would evoke White's image, precisely the way the robot did. It's the "Wheel of Fortune" set, not the robot's face or dress or jewelry that evokes White's image. The panel is giving White an exclusive right not in what she looks like or who she is, but in what she does for a living.

This is entirely the wrong place to strike the balance. Intellectual property rights aren't free: They're imposed at the expense of future creators and of the public at large. . . . This is why intellectual property law is full of careful balances between what's set aside for the owner and what's left in the public domain for the rest of us: The relatively short life of patents; the longer, but finite, life of copyrights; copyright's idea-expression dichotomy; the fair use doctrine; the prohibition on copyrighting facts; the compulsory license of television broadcasts and musical compositions; federal preemption of overbroad state intellectual property laws; the nominative use doctrine in trademark law; the right to make soundalike recordings. All of these diminish an intellectual property owner's rights. All let the public use something created by someone else. But all are necessary to maintain a free environment in which creative genius can flourish.

The intellectual property right created by the panel here has none of these essential limitations: No fair use exception; no right to parody; no idea-expression dichotomy.

It impoverishes the public domain, to the detriment of future creators and the public at large. Instead of well-defined, limited characteristics such as name, likeness or voice, advertisers will now have to cope with vague claims of "appropriation of identity," claims often made by people with a wholly exaggerated sense of their own fame and significance. Future Vanna Whites might not get the chance to create their personae, because their employers may fear some celebrity will claim the persona is too similar to her own. The public will be robbed of parodies of celebrities, and our culture will be deprived of the valuable safety valve that parody and mockery create.

Moreover, consider the moral dimension, about which the panel majority seems to have gotten so exercised. Saying Samsung "appropriated" something of White's begs the question: Should White have the exclusive right to something as broad and amorphous as her "identity"? Samsung's ad didn't simply copy White's schtick—like all parody, it created something new. True, Samsung did it to make money, but White does whatever she does to make money, too; the majority talks of "the difference between fun and profit," but in the entertainment industry fun is profit. Why is Vanna White's right to exclusive for-profit use of her persona—a persona that might not even be her own creation, but that of a writer, director or producer—superior to Samsung's right to profit by creating its own inventions? Why should she have such absolute rights to control the conduct of others, unlimited by the idea-expression dichotomy or by the fair use doctrine?

Finally, I can't see how giving White the power to keep others from evoking her image in the public's mind can be squared with the First Amendment. Where does White get this right to control our thoughts? The majority's creation goes way beyond the protection given a trademark or a copyrighted work, or a person's name or likeness. All those things control one particular way of expressing an idea, one way of referring to an object or a person. But not allowing any means of reminding people of someone? That's a speech restriction unparalleled in First Amendment law. . . .

For better or worse, we are the Court of Appeals for the Hollywood Circuit. Millions of people toil in the shadow of the law we make, and much of their livelihood is made possible by the existence of intellectual property rights. But much of their livelihood—and much of the vibrancy of our culture—also depends on the existence of other intangible rights: The right to draw ideas from a rich and varied public domain, and the right to mock, for profit as well as fun, the cultural icons of our time.

Notes and Questions

1. *What are the boundaries of publicity rights?* One of Judge Kozinski's concerns in *White* is that Vanna White was seeking an intellectual property right in "what she does for a living" rather than "what she looks like or who she is." One concern here might be that White could sue the creators of another game show who have another person performing the "Vanna White" role in a different format. This would grant her a monopoly in a function—the sort of monopoly that ought to be protected by patent law or trade secret law, not the right of publicity. Another concern of Kozinski's was that White may be monopolizing an identity that was arguably created by Wheel of Fortune's producers, writers, or directors. The argument for someone other than White owning the rights becomes stronger if she is conceptualized as claiming a monopoly over "what she does for a

living" as opposed to what she looks and sounds like when appearing on the show. Similar concerns arose in Wendt v. Host International, 125 F.3d 806 (9th Cir. 1997), where the actors who played Norm and Cliff on the popular 1980s situation comedy "Cheers" sued the proprietors of a chain of Cheers-replica airport bars that had robots resembling Norm and Cliff perched on barstools. The bar owners had licensed the rights to Cheers's set and characters from Paramount, the studio that created the television show. The actors conceded that Paramount had the exclusive rights to their characters, but the actors noted that the robots resembled them as they portrayed the fictitious characters, thereby implicating their publicity rights as well as Paramount's copyrights. The lines, as you can see, get blurry rather quickly. Judge Kozinski dissented again from the Ninth Circuit's opinion allowing the right of publicity suit to proceed, beginning his dissent with a colorful opening sentence: "Robots again." Wendt v. Host International, 197 F.3d 1284, 1285 (9th Cir. 1999) (Kozinski, J., dissenting from denial of rehearing en banc).

2. *The posthumous right of publicity.* In many jurisdictions, the right of publicity persists after death (for 20 to 100 years, depending on the state), and can descend by will or intestacy. Most states extend the right of publicity to everyone, although usually it has substantial value only to celebrities—even (or especially!) dead ones. For some time, *Forbes* has issued annual reports on the top-earning dead celebrities. In 2015, Michael Jackson's copyrights and publicity rights brought in $115 million for his heirs and assignees. Elvis Presley earned $55 million in 2015, good for second place on the list, despite the passage of 38 years since his death.

3. *The right of publicity and the First Amendment.* The First Amendment, including its state counterparts, may limit publicity rights. In 1982, the Georgia Supreme Court had upheld a publicity rights claim brought by the estate of Martin Luther King, allowing the estate to block the sale of plastic busts of Dr. King by a seller whom the estate had not authorized to conduct such sales. Martin Luther King Jr. Center for Social Change v. American Heritage Products, 296 S.E.2d 697 (Ga. 1982). More recently, however, the federal Court of Appeals for the Eleventh Circuit (which includes Georgia) found that the Michigan Constitution's guarantee of free speech rights prevented recognition of publicity rights in the estate of Rosa Parks. In that case, the seller marketed various items showing Rosa Parks's image, including a plaque showing Parks with Dr. Martin Luther King. The court found that Michigan's state constitutional protections for free speech included a "qualified privilege to report on matters in the public interest" and that the items, including the plaque, contained information of a historical nature protected by this constitutional right.

c. Property in One's Person: Body Parts

Remember the foundation of Locke's labor theory of property, stated on page 20: "every man has a property in his own person." Slavery, obviously, was in opposition to that proposition (and so, it appears, were some of Locke's activities), but slavery has been abolished. So, can we now say, without qualification, that you have property in yourself? Consider the following case.

Strictly speaking, the case does not involve intellectual property. We include it because it relates to aspects of traditional intellectual property, such as patents and genes. More fundamentally, subsection C as a whole deals with acquisition of property rights by creation and with Locke's idea of having property rights in one's own body. *Moore* puts that idea front and center.

MOORE v. REGENTS OF THE UNIVERSITY OF CALIFORNIA
Supreme Court of California, 1990
793 P.2d 479

[*Background*: In 1976, John Moore sought treatment for hairy-cell leukemia at the Medical Center of the University of California, Los Angeles. (We shall at times refer to the doctors at the Center and to the Regents of the University who own the Center collectively as "defendants.") The defendants conducted tests, took blood and tissue samples, confirmed the diagnosis, and told Moore that his condition was life-threatening and that his spleen should be removed. What they did not tell Moore was that his cells were unique and that access to them was of great scientific and commercial value.

Moore consented to the splenectomy and to some seven years of follow-up tests and procedures that he was led to believe were important to his treatment. His spleen was retained for research purposes without his knowledge or consent, and during the post-operative period samples of tissue and blood and other fluids were taken on each of Moore's visits. At some point, Moore was informed that his bodily substances were being used for research, but he was never informed of the commercial value of the research or of the defendants' financial interest in it. The defendants subsequently established a cell line from Moore's cells (named the Mo cell line, after Moore), received a patent for it, and entered into various commercial agreements. Hundreds of thousands of dollars had been paid to the defendants under these agreements by the mid-1980s, and the potential market for products from Moore's cell line is estimated to run into the billions of dollars.

Moore sued for damages in 1984, his complaint stating a number of causes of action, including conversion (wrongful exercise of ownership rights over the personal property of another; Moore alleged that his blood and bodily substances, and the cell line derived from them, were "his tangible personal property"), lack of informed consent, breach of fiduciary duty, fraud and deceit, unjust enrichment, intentional infliction of emotional distress, negligent misrepresentation, and others. The trial court sustained the defendants' demurrers to the conversion cause of action and held that because the conversion cause of action was incorporated into all the other causes of action, those too were defective.

The court of appeal reversed, finding that Moore had adequately stated a cause of action for conversion. Moore v. Regents of the University of California, 249 Cal. Rptr. 494 (Cal. App. 1988). The court could find "no legal authority, public policy, nor universally known facts of biological science . . . which compel a conclusion that this plaintiff cannot have a sufficient legal interest in his own bodily tissues amounting to personal property. Absent plaintiff's consent to defendants' disposition of the tissues, or lawful justification, such as abandonment, the complaint adequately pleads all the elements of a cause of action for conversion."

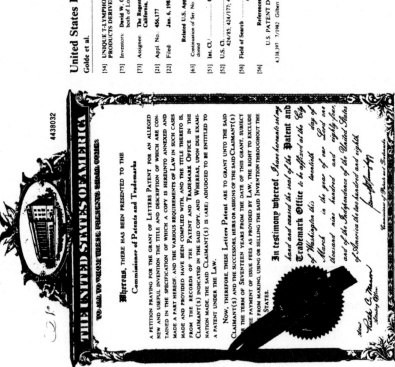

4438032

THE UNITED STATES OF AMERICA

TO ALL TO WHOM THESE PRESENTS SHALL COME:

Whereas, THERE HAS BEEN PRESENTED TO THE

Commissioner of Patents and Trademarks

A PETITION PRAYING FOR THE GRANT OF LETTERS PATENT FOR AN ALLEGED NEW AND USEFUL INVENTION THE TITLE AND DESCRIPTION OF WHICH ARE CONTAINED IN THE SPECIFICATION OF WHICH A COPY IS HEREUNTO ANNEXED AND MADE A PART HEREOF AND THE VARIOUS REQUIREMENTS OF LAW IN SUCH CASES MADE AND PROVIDED HAVE BEEN COMPLIED WITH, AND THE TITLE THERETO IS, FROM THE RECORDS OF THE PATENT AND TRADEMARK OFFICE IN THE CLAIMANT(S) INDICATED IN THE SAID COPY, AND WHEREAS, UPON DUE EXAMINATION MADE, THE SAID CLAIMANT(S) IS (ARE) ADJUDGED TO BE ENTITLED TO A PATENT UNDER THE LAW.

NOW, THEREFORE, THESE **Letters Patent** ARE TO GRANT UNTO THE SAID CLAIMANT(S) AND THE SUCCESSORS, HEIRS OR ASSIGNS OF THE SAID CLAIMANT(S) FOR THE TERM OF SEVENTEEN YEARS FROM THE DATE OF THIS GRANT, SUBJECT TO THE PAYMENT OF ISSUE FEES AS PROVIDED BY LAW, THE RIGHT TO EXCLUDE OTHERS FROM MAKING, USING OR SELLING THE SAID INVENTION THROUGHOUT THE UNITED STATES.

In testimony whereof I have hereunto set my hand and caused the seal of the **Patent and Trademark Office** to be affixed at the City of Washington this twentieth day of March in the year of our Lord one thousand nine hundred and eighty-four, and of the Independence of the United States of America the two hundred and eighth.

United States Patent [19]

Golde et al.

[11] **4,438,032**
[45] **Mar. 20, 1984**

[54] **UNIQUE T-LYMPHOCYTE LINE AND PRODUCTS DERIVED THEREFROM**

[75] Inventors: **David W. Golde; Shirley G. Quan,** both of Los Angeles, Calif.

[73] Assignee: **The Regents of the University of California,** Berkeley, Calif.

[21] Appl. No.: **456,177**

[22] Filed: **Jan. 6, 1983**

Related U.S. Application Data

[63] Continuation of Ser. No. 229,900, Jan. 30, 1981, abandoned.

[51] Int. Cl.³ C12P 21/00; C12N 15/00; C12R 1/91; C07G 7/00

[52] U.S. Cl. .... 260/112 R; 260/112 B; 424/85, 424/177; 435/68, 435/172, 435/240; 435/241, 435/948

[58] Field of Search .... 260/112 R, 112 B, 435/68, 172, 240, 241, 948

[56] **References Cited**

U.S. PATENT DOCUMENTS

4,338,397 7/1982 Gilbert 435/68

OTHER PUBLICATIONS

Saxon et al., Annals of Internal Medicine. (1978), 58:323-326.
Weisbart et al., Clin. Immunology & Immunopathology. (1979), 14:441-448.
Weisbart et al., J. Lab. Clin. Med., (1979), 93:622-626.
Lusis et al., In Viva and In Vitro Erythropoesis, 1980, pp. 97-106.
Golde et al., Blood, (1978), 51:1068-1071.
Golde et al., PNAS, USA, (1980), 77:593-596.
Golde et al., Annals of Internal Medicine, (1980), 92:650-662.

Primary Examiner—Howard E. Schain
Attorney, Agent, or Firm—Bertram I. Rowland

[57] **ABSTRACT**

Human T-lymphoblast cell line. Proteinaceous products produced therefrom. messenger RNA and DNA expressing the proteinaceous products. A human T-lymphoblast cell line (Mo) maintained as a continuous culture constitutively produces proteins, including immune interferon, neutrophal migration inhibition factor, granulocyte-macrophage colony-stimulating activity and erythroid-potentiating activity, as well as other proteins produced by T-cells.

22 Claims, No Drawings

Pages from the Mo Cell Line Patent

Appeal Court

"We have approached this issue with caution," the court said. "The evolution of civilization from slavery to freedom, from regarding people as chattels to recognition of the individual dignity of each person, necessitates prudence in attributing the qualities of property to human tissue. There is, however, a dramatic difference between having property rights in one's own body and being the property of another. . . . We are not called on to determine whether use of human tissue or body parts ought to be 'gift based' or subject to a 'free market.' That question of policy must be determined by the Legislature. In the instant case, the cell line has already been commercialized by defendants. We are presented a *fait accompli,* leaving only the question of who shares in the proceeds. . . ."

The court then considered the meaning of property and concluded that the essential element is dominion, or rights of use, control, and disposition. It went on to discuss the "many cases" (involving search and seizure, consent to medical procedures, rights to dead bodies, and other instances) that recognize "rights of dominion over one's own body, and the interests one has therein. . . . These rights and interests are so akin to property interests that it would be a subterfuge to call them something else."

The court concluded by dealing with a series of contentions by defendants. There were no grounds to infer that Moore had abandoned his tissue or consented to its use in research unrelated to his treatment. And the fact that the defendants' skill and effort had enhanced the value of Moore's tissue went not to the issue of conversion but to the measure of damages for the conversion. "Plaintiff's cells and genes are a part of his person," the court said, citing the right of publicity cases that " 'afford legal protection to an individual's proprietary interest in his own identity.' " To hold that patients do not have the ultimate power to control the destiny of their tissues "would open the door to a massive invasion of human privacy and dignity in the name of medical progress." The court saw no reason to believe that medical research would suffer by requiring the consent of the donor of tissue before it can be appropriated. True, a potential donor, once informed, might refuse consent, but the court "would give the patient that right. As to defendants' concern that a patient might seek the greatest economic gain for his participation, this argument is unpersuasive because it fails to explain why defendants . . . are any more to be trusted with these momentous decisions than the person whose cells are being used." If giving patients a financial interest in their tissues inhibited donations and increased the costs of medical care, that problem could be addressed by the legislature.

Upon petition by the defendants, the court of appeal's judgment was reviewed by the California Supreme Court. Of particular interest here are the views of the various justices regarding the cause of action for conversion.]

PANELLI, J. We granted review in this case to determine whether plaintiff has stated a cause of action against his physician and other defendants for using his cells in potentially lucrative medical research without his permission. . . . We hold that the complaint states a cause of action for breach of the physician's disclosure obligations, but not for conversion. . . .

Holding

A. Breach of Fiduciary Duty and Lack of Informed Consent

Moore repeatedly alleges that Golde [the attending physician] failed to disclose the extent of his research and economic interests in Moore's cells before obtaining consent to the medical procedures by which the cells were extracted. These allegations, in our view, state a cause of action against Golde for invading a legally protected interest of his patient. This cause of action can properly be characterized either as the breach of a fiduciary duty to disclose facts material to the patient's consent or, alternatively, as the performance of medical procedures without first having obtained the patient's informed consent. . . .

B. Conversion

Moore also attempts to characterize the invasion of his rights as a conversion—a tort that protects against interference with possessory and ownership interests in personal property. He theorizes that he continued to own his cells following their removal from his body, at least for the purpose of directing their use, and that he never consented to their use in potentially lucrative medical research. Thus, to complete Moore's argument, defendants' unauthorized use of his cells constitutes a conversion. As a result of the alleged conversion, Moore claims a proprietary interest in each of the products that any of the defendants might ever create from his cells or the patented cell line.

No court, however, has ever in a reported decision imposed conversion liability for the use of human cells in medical research. While that fact does not end our inquiry, it raises a flag of caution. In effect, what Moore is asking us to do is to impose a tort duty on scientists to investigate the consensual pedigree of each human cell sample used in research. To impose such a duty, which would affect medical research of importance to all of society, implicates policy concerns far removed from the traditional, two-party ownership disputes in which the law of conversion arose. Invoking a tort theory originally used to determine whether the loser or the finder of a horse had the better title, Moore claims ownership of the results of socially important medical research, including the genetic code for chemicals that regulate the functions of every human being's immune system.

We have recognized that, when the proposed application of a very general theory of liability in a new context raises important policy concerns, it is especially important to face those concerns and address them openly. . . .

Accordingly, we first consider whether the tort of conversion clearly gives Moore a cause of action under existing law. We do not believe it does. Because of the novelty of Moore's claim to own the biological materials at issue, to apply the theory of conversion in this context would frankly have to be recognized as an extension of the theory. Therefore, we consider next whether it is advisable to extend the tort to this context.

1. Moore's Claim Under Existing Law

"To establish a conversion, plaintiff must establish an actual interference with his *ownership* or *right of possession.* . . . Where plaintiff neither has title to the property alleged to have been converted, nor possession thereof, he cannot maintain an action for conversion." . . .

Since Moore clearly did not expect to retain possession of his cells following their removal, to sue for their conversion he must have retained an ownership interest in them. But there are several reasons to doubt that he did retain any such interest. First, no reported judicial decision supports Moore's claim, either directly or by close analogy. Second, California statutory law drastically limits any continuing interest of a patient in excised cells. Third, the subject matters of the Regents' patent—the patented cell line and the products derived from it—cannot be Moore's property.

Neither the Court of Appeal's opinion, the parties' briefs, nor our research discloses a case holding that a person retains a sufficient interest in excised cells to support a cause of action for conversion. We do not find this surprising, since the laws governing such things as human tissues, transplantable organs,[12] blood, fetuses, pituitary glands, corneal tissue, and dead bodies deal with human biological materials as objects sui generis, regulating their disposition to achieve policy goals rather than abandoning them to the general law of personal property. It is these specialized statutes, not the law of conversion, to which courts ordinarily should and do look for guidance on the disposition of human biological materials.

Lacking direct authority for importing the law of conversion into this context, Moore relies, as did the Court of Appeal, primarily on decisions addressing privacy rights. One line of cases involves unwanted publicity. (Lugosi v. Universal Pictures (1979) 25 Cal. 3d 813, 160 Cal. Rptr. 323, 603 P.2d 425; Motsehenbacher v. R.J. Reynolds Tobacco Company (9th Cir. 1974) 498 F.2d 821.) These opinions hold that every person has a proprietary interest in his own likeness and that unauthorized, business use of a likeness is redressible as a tort. But in neither opinion did the authoring court expressly base its holding on property law. Each court stated, following Prosser, that it was "pointless" to debate the proper characterization of the proprietary interest in a likeness. For purposes of determining whether the tort of conversion lies, however, the characterization of the right in question is far from pointless. Only property can be converted.

Not only are the wrongful-publicity cases irrelevant to the issue of conversion, but the analogy to them seriously misconceives the nature of the genetic materials and research involved in this case. Moore, adopting the analogy originally advanced by the Court of Appeal, argues that "[i]f the courts have found a sufficient proprietary interest in one's persona, how could one not have a right in one's own genetic material, something far more profoundly the essence of one's human uniqueness than a name or a face?" However, as the defendants' patent makes clear—and the complaint, too, if read with an understanding of the scientific terms which it has borrowed from the patent—the goal and result of defendants' efforts has been to manufacture lymphokines. Lymphokines, unlike a name or a face, have the same molecular structure in every human being and the same important functions in every human being's immune system. Moreover, the particular genetic material which is responsible for the natural production of lymphokines, and which defendants use to manufacture lymphokines in the laboratory, is also the same in every person; it is no more unique to Moore than the number of vertebrae in the spine or the chemical formula of hemoglobin.

. . . [T]he Court of Appeal in this case concluded that "[a] patient must have the ultimate power to control what becomes of his or her tissues. To hold otherwise would open the door to a massive invasion of human privacy and dignity in the name of medical progress." Yet one may earnestly wish to protect privacy and dignity without accepting the extremely problematic conclusion that interference with those interests amounts to a conversion of personal property. Nor is it necessary to force the round

---

12. See the Uniform Anatomical Gift Act, Health and Safety Code sections 7150 et seq. The act permits a competent adult to "give all or part of [his] body" for certain designated purposes, including "transplantation, therapy, medical or dental education, research, or advancement of medical or dental science." (Health & Saf. Code, §§ 7151, 7153.) The act does not, however, permit the donor to receive "valuable consideration" for the transfer. (Health & Saf. Code, § 7155.)

pegs of "privacy" and "dignity" into the square hole of "property" in order to protect the patient, since the fiduciary-duty and informed-consent theories protect these interests directly by requiring full disclosure.

The next consideration that makes Moore's claim of ownership problematic is California statutory law, which drastically limits a patient's control over excised cells. Pursuant to Health and Safety Code section 7054.4, "[n]otwithstanding any other provision of law, recognizable anatomical parts, human tissues, anatomical human remains, or infectious waste following conclusion of scientific use shall be disposed of by interment, incineration, or any other method determined by the state department [of health services] to protect the public health and safety." Clearly the Legislature did not specifically intend this statute to resolve the question of whether a patient is entitled to compensation for the nonconsensual use of excised cells. A primary object of the statute is to ensure the safe handling of potentially hazardous biological waste materials. Yet one cannot escape the conclusion that the statute's practical effect is to limit, drastically, a patient's control over excised cells. By restricting how excised cells may be used and requiring their eventual destruction, the statute eliminates so many of the rights ordinarily attached to property that one cannot simply assume that what is left amounts to "property" or "ownership" for purposes of conversion law.

. . . A fully informed patient may always withhold consent to treatment by a physician whose research plans the patient does not approve. That right, however, as already discussed, is protected by the fiduciary-duty and informed-consent theories.

Finally, the subject matter of the Regents' patent—the patented cell line and the products derived from it—cannot be Moore's property. This is because the patented cell line is both factually and legally distinct from the cells taken from Moore's body. Federal law permits the patenting of organisms that represent the product of "human ingenuity," but not naturally occurring organisms. . . . It is this *inventive effort* that patent law rewards, not the discovery of naturally occurring raw materials. Thus, Moore's allegations that he owns the cell line and the products derived from it are inconsistent with the patent, which constitutes an authoritative determination that the cell line is the product of invention. . . .

2. Should Conversion Liability Be Extended?

. . . There are three reasons why it is inappropriate to impose liability for conversion based upon the allegations of Moore's complaint. First, a fair balancing of the relevant policy considerations counsels against extending the tort. Second, problems in this area are better suited to legislative resolution. Third, the tort of conversion is not necessary to protect patients' rights. For these reasons, we conclude that the use of excised human cells in medical research does not amount to a conversion.

Of the relevant policy considerations, two are of overriding importance. The first is protection of a competent patient's right to make autonomous medical decisions. That right, as already discussed, is grounded in well-recognized and long-standing principles of fiduciary duty and informed consent. . . . This policy weighs in favor of providing a remedy to patients when physicians act with undisclosed motives that may affect their professional judgment. The second important policy consideration is that we not threaten with disabling civil liability innocent parties who are engaged in socially useful activities, such as researchers who have no reason to believe that their use of a particular cell sample is, or may be, against a donor's wishes.

To reach an appropriate balance of these policy considerations is extremely important. In its report to Congress the Office of Technology Assessment emphasized that

> [u]ncertainty about how courts will resolve disputes between specimen sources and specimen users could be detrimental to both academic researchers and the infant biotechnology industry, particularly when the rights are asserted long after the specimen was obtained. The assertion of rights by sources would affect not only the researcher who obtained the original specimen, but perhaps other researchers as well.
>
> Biological materials are routinely distributed to other researchers for experimental purposes, and scientists who obtain cell lines or other specimen-derived products, such as gene clones, from the original researcher could also be sued under certain legal theories [such as conversion]. Furthermore, the uncertainty could affect product developments as well as research. Since inventions containing human tissues and cells may be patented and licensed for commercial use, companies are unlikely to invest heavily in developing, manufacturing, or marketing a product when uncertainty about clear title exists. . . .

Indeed, so significant is the potential obstacle to research stemming from uncertainty about legal title to biological materials that the Office of Technology Assessment reached this striking conclusion: "[R]egardless of the merit of claims by the different interested parties, resolving the current uncertainty may be more important to the future of biotechnology than resolving it in any particular way." . . .

We need not, however, make an arbitrary choice between liability and nonliability. Instead, an examination of the relevant policy considerations suggests an appropriate balance: Liability based upon existing disclosure obligations, rather than an unprecedented extension of the conversion theory, protects patients' rights of privacy and autonomy without unnecessarily hindering research.

To be sure, the threat of liability for conversion might help to enforce patients' rights indirectly. This is because physicians might be able to avoid liability by obtaining patients' consent, in the broadest possible terms, to any conceivable subsequent research use of excised cells. Unfortunately, to extend the conversion theory would utterly sacrifice the other goal of protecting innocent parties. Since conversion is a strict liability tort, it would impose liability on all those into whose hands the cells come, whether or not the particular defendant participated in, or knew of, the inadequate disclosures that violated the patient's right to make an informed decision. In contrast to the conversion theory, the fiduciary-duty and informed-consent theories protect the patient directly, without punishing innocent parties or creating disincentives to the conduct of socially beneficial research.

Research on human cells plays a critical role in medical research. This is so because researchers are increasingly able to isolate naturally occurring, medically useful biological substances and to produce useful quantities of such substances through genetic engineering. These efforts are beginning to bear fruit. Products developed through biotechnology that have already been approved for marketing in this country include treatments and tests for leukemia, cancer, diabetes, dwarfism, hepatitis-B, kidney transplant rejection, emphysema, osteoporosis, ulcers, anemia, infertility, and gynecological tumors, to name but a few. . . .

The extension of conversion law into this area will hinder research by restricting access to the necessary raw materials. Thousands of human cell lines already exist in tissue repositories. . . . At present, human cell lines are routinely copied and distributed to other researchers for experimental purposes, usually free of charge. This exchange of scientific materials, which still is relatively free and efficient, will surely be compromised if each cell sample becomes the potential subject matter of a lawsuit.

To expand liability by extending conversion law into this area would have a broad impact. The House Committee on Science and Technology of the United States Congress found that "49 percent of the researchers at medical institutions surveyed used human tissues or cells in their research." . . . In addition, "there are nearly 350 commercial biotechnology firms in the United States actively engaged in biotechnology research and commercial product development and approximately 25 to 30 percent appear to be engaged in research to develop a human therapeutic or diagnostic reagent. . . . Most, but not all, of the human therapeutic products are derived from human tissues and cells, or human cell lines or cloned genes." . . .

In deciding whether to create new tort duties we have in the past considered the impact that expanded liability would have on activities that are important to society, such as research. . . .

[T]he theory of liability that Moore urges us to endorse threatens to destroy the economic incentive to conduct important medical research. If the use of cells in research is a conversion, then with every cell sample a researcher purchases a ticket in a litigation lottery. Because liability for conversion is predicated on a continuing ownership interest, "companies are unlikely to invest heavily in developing, manufacturing, or marketing a product when uncertainty about clear title exists." . . .

If the scientific users of human cells are to be held liable for failing to investigate the consensual pedigree of their raw materials, we believe the Legislature should make that decision. . . .

[T]here is no pressing need to impose a judicially created rule of strict liability, since enforcement of physicians' disclosure obligations will protect patients against the very type of harm with which Moore was threatened. So long as a physician discloses research and economic interests that may affect his judgment, the patient is protected from conflicts of interest. Aware of any conflicts, the patient can make an informed decision to consent to treatment, or to withhold consent and look elsewhere for medical assistance. As already discussed, enforcement of physicians' disclosure obligations protects patients directly, without hindering the socially useful activities of innocent researchers.

For these reasons, we hold that the allegations of Moore's third amended complaint state a cause of action for breach of fiduciary duty or lack of informed consent, but not conversion. . . .

LUCAS, C.J., EAGLESON, J., and KENNARD, J., concurred.

ARABIAN, J., concurring. I join in the views cogently expounded by the majority. I write separately to give voice to a concern that I believe informs much of that opinion but finds little or no expression therein. I speak of the moral issue.

Plaintiff has asked us to recognize and enforce a right to sell one's own body tissue for profit. He entreats us to regard the human vessel—the single most venerated and protected subject in any civilized society—as equal with the basest commercial commodity. He urges us to commingle the sacred with the profane. He asks much. . . .

It is true, that this court has not often been deterred from deciding difficult legal issues simply because they require a choice between competing social or economic policies. . . . The difference here, however, lies in the nature of the conflicting moral, philosophical and even religious values at stake, and in the profound implications of the position urged. The ramifications of recognizing and enforcing a property interest in body tissues are not known, but are greatly feared—the effect on human dignity of a marketplace in human body parts, the impact on research and development of competitive bidding for such materials, and the exposure of researchers to potentially limitless and uncharted tort liability. . . .

Whether, as plaintiff urges, his cells should be treated as property susceptible to conversion is not, in my view, ours to decide. . . .

Where then shall a complete resolution be found? Clearly the Legislature, as the majority opinion suggests, is the proper deliberative forum. Indeed, a legislative response creating a licensing scheme, which establishes a fixed rate of profit sharing between researcher and subject, has already been suggested. Such an arrangement would not only avoid the moral and philosophical objections to a free market operation in body tissue, but would also address stated concerns by eliminating the inherently coercive effect of a waiver system and by compensating donors regardless of temporal circumstances. . . .

[The concurring and dissenting opinion of Justice Broussard is omitted.]

MOSK, J. I dissent. Contrary to the principal holding of the Court of Appeal, the majority conclude that the complaint does not—in fact cannot—state a cause of action for conversion. I disagree with this conclusion for all the reasons stated by the Court of Appeal, and for additional reasons. . . .

The concepts of property and ownership in our law are extremely broad. . . .

Being broad, the concept of property is also abstract: rather than referring directly to a material object such as a parcel of land or the tractor that cultivates it, the concept of property is often said to refer to a "bundle of rights" that may be exercised with respect to that object—principally the rights to possess the property, to use the property, to exclude others from the property, and to dispose of the property by sale or by gift. . . . But the same bundle of rights does not attach to all forms of property. For a variety of policy reasons, the law limits or even forbids the exercise of certain rights over certain forms of property. For example, both law and contract may limit the right of an owner of real property to use his parcel as he sees fit. Owners of various forms of personal property may likewise be subject to restrictions on the time, place, and manner of their use. Limitations on the disposition of real property, while less common, may also be imposed. Finally, some types of personal property may be sold but not given away,[13] while others may be given away but not sold,[14] and still others may neither be given away nor sold.[15]

In each of the foregoing instances, the limitation or prohibition diminishes the bundle of rights that would otherwise attach to the property, yet what remains is

---

13. A person contemplating bankruptcy may sell his property at its "reasonably equivalent value," but he may not make a gift of the same property. (See 11 U.S.C. § 548(a).)

14. A sportsman may give away wild fish or game that he has caught or killed pursuant to his license, but he may not sell it. (Fish & G. Code, §§ 3039, 7121.)
The transfer of human organs and blood is a special case discussed below.

15. E.g., a license to practice a profession, or a prescription drug in the hands of the person for whom it is prescribed.

still deemed in law to be a protectible property interest. . . . The same rule applies to Moore's interest in his own body tissue. . . . Above all, at the time of its excision he at least had *the right to do with his own tissue whatever the defendants did with it*: i.e., he could have contracted with researchers and pharmaceutical companies to develop and exploit the vast commercial potential of his tissue and its products. . . .

Having concluded—mistakenly, in my view—that Moore has no cause of action for conversion under existing law, the majority next consider whether to "extend" the conversion cause of action to this context. Again . . . I respectfully disagree with [their reasoning].

. . . [O]ur society acknowledges a profound ethical imperative to respect the human body as the physical and temporal expression of the unique human persona. One manifestation of that respect is our prohibition against direct abuse of the body by torture or other forms of cruel or unusual punishment. Another is our prohibition against indirect abuse of the body by its economic exploitation for the sole benefit of another person. The most abhorrent form of such exploitation, of course, was the institution of slavery. Lesser forms, such as indentured servitude or even debtor's prison, have also disappeared. Yet their specter haunts the laboratories and boardrooms of today's biotechnological research-industrial complex. It arises wherever scientists or industrialists claim, as defendants claim here, the right to appropriate and exploit a patient's tissue for their sole economic benefit—the right, in other words, to freely mine or harvest valuable physical properties of the patient's body. . . .

A second policy consideration adds notions of equity to those of ethics. Our society values fundamental fairness in dealings between its members, and condemns the unjust enrichment of any member at the expense of another. This is particularly true when, as here, the parties are not in equal bargaining positions. . . . Yet defendants deny that Moore is entitled to any share whatever in the proceeds of this cell line. This is both inequitable and immoral. . . .

There will be . . . equitable sharing if the courts recognize that the patient has a legally protected property interest in his own body and its products: "property rights in one's own tissue would provide a morally acceptable result by giving effect to notions of fairness and preventing unjust enrichment. . . ."

I do not doubt that the Legislature is competent to act on this topic. The fact that the Legislature may intervene if and when it chooses, however, does not in the meanwhile relieve the courts of their duty of enforcing—or if need be, fashioning—an effective judicial remedy for the wrong here alleged. . . .

The inference I draw from the current statutory regulation of human biological materials, moreover, is the opposite of that drawn by the majority. By selective quotation of the statutes the majority seem to suggest that human organs and blood cannot legally be sold on the open market—thereby implying that if the Legislature were to act here it would impose a similar ban on monetary compensation for the use of human tissue in biotechnological research and development. But if that is the argument, the premise is unsound: contrary to popular misconception, it is not true that human organs and blood cannot legally be sold.

As to organs, the majority rely on the Uniform Anatomical Gift Act (Health & Saf. Code, § 7150 et seq., hereafter the UAGA) for the proposition that a competent adult may make a post mortem gift of any part of his body but may not receive "valuable consideration" for the transfer. But the prohibition of the UAGA against the sale of a body part is much more limited than the majority recognize: by its terms (Health &

Saf. Code, § 7155, subd. (a)) the prohibition applies only to sales for "transplantation" or "therapy." Yet a different section of the UAGA authorizes the transfer and receipt of body parts for such additional purposes as "medical or dental education, research, or advancement of medical or dental science." (Health & Saf. Code, § 7153, subd. (a)(1).) No section of the UAGA prohibits anyone from selling body parts for any of those additional purposes; by clear implication, therefore, such sales are legal.[16] Indeed, the fact that the UAGA prohibits *no* sales of organs other than sales for "transplantation" or "therapy" raises a further implication that it is also legal for anyone to sell human tissue to a biotechnology company for research and development purposes. . . .

It follows that the statutes regulating the transfers of human organs and blood do not support the majority's refusal to recognize a conversion cause of action for commercial exploitation of human blood cells without consent. On the contrary, because such statutes treat both organs and blood as property that can legally be sold in a variety of circumstances, they impliedly support Moore's contention that his blood cells are likewise property for which he can and should receive compensation, and hence are protected by the law of conversion.

The majority's final reason for refusing to recognize a conversion cause of action on these facts is that "there is no pressing need" to do so because the complaint also states another cause of action that is assertedly adequate to the task. . . .

I disagree, however, with the majority's further conclusion that in the present context a nondisclosure cause of action is an adequate—in fact, a superior—substitute for a conversion cause of action. . . .

The majority do not spell out how those obligations will be "enforced"; but because they arise from judicial decision (the majority opinion herein) rather than from legislative or administrative enactment, we may infer that the obligations will primarily be enforced by the traditional judicial remedy of an action for damages for their breach. . . .

The remedy is largely illusory. "[A]n action based on the physician's failure to disclose material information sounds in negligence. As a practical matter, however, it may be difficult to recover on this kind of negligence theory because the patient must prove a *causal connection* between his or her injury and the physician's failure to inform." (Martin & Lagod, Biotechnology and the Commercial Use of Human Cells: Toward an Organic View of Life and Technology (1989), 5 Santa Clara Computer & High Tech L.J. 211, 222, fn. omitted, italics added.) There are two barriers to recovery. First, "the patient must show that if he or she had been informed of all pertinent information, he or she would have declined to consent to the procedure in question." (Ibid.) . . .

The second barrier to recovery is still higher, and is erected on the first: it is not even enough for the plaintiff to prove that he personally would have refused consent to the proposed treatment if he had been fully informed; he must also prove that in the same circumstances *no reasonably prudent person* would have given such consent. . . .

The second reason why the nondisclosure cause of action is inadequate for the task that the majority assign to it is that it fails to solve half the problem before us: it

---

16. "By their terms . . . the statutes in question forbid only sales for transplantation and therapy. In light of the rather clear authorization for donation for research and education, one could conclude that sales for these non-therapeutic purposes are permitted. Scientists in practice have been buying and selling human tissues for research apparently without interference from these statutes." (Note, "She's Got Bette Davis['s] Eyes": Assessing the Nonconsensual Removal of Cadaver Organs Under the Takings and Due Process Clauses, 90 Colum. L. Rev. 528, 544, fn.75 (1990).)

gives the patient only the right to *refuse* consent, i.e., the right to prohibit the commercialization of his tissue; it does not give him the right to *grant* consent to that commercialization on the condition that he share in its proceeds. . . .

Reversing the words of the old song, the nondisclosure cause of action thus accentuates the negative and eliminates the positive: the patient can say no, but he cannot say yes and expect to share in the proceeds of his contribution. . . .

Third, the nondisclosure cause of action fails to reach a major class of potential defendants: all those who are outside the strict physician-patient relationship with the plaintiff. Thus the majority concede that here only defendant Golde, the treating physician, can be directly liable to Moore on a nondisclosure cause of action. . . .

In sum, the nondisclosure cause of action (1) is unlikely to be successful in most cases, (2) fails to protect patients' rights to share in the proceeds of the commercial exploitation of their tissue, and (3) may allow the true exploiters to escape liability. It is thus not an adequate substitute, in my view, for the conversion cause of action. . . .

THE REST OF THE STORY . . .

After losing on his conversion claim, Moore eventually resolved his remaining claims in a confidential settlement. There were reports that he received between $20,000 and $600,000, but doubtless much of the amount went to pay attorneys' fees. He later became an advocate for patients' rights. In 2001, his battle with cancer ended when he died at the age of 56.

Notes and Questions

1. *Losing ownership of one's body (and parts).* The majority holds that Moore has no cause of action for conversion because he did not retain an ownership interest in his cells following their removal. Did Moore have an ownership interest in his spleen and cells when they were still in his body? If so, exactly how did he lose that interest? Did he do so because he abandoned his cells? The elements of *abandonment* are intent to permanently relinquish to no one in particular and a voluntary act effectuating that intent. Were both of these elements met here? If not, on what other basis did Moore lose ownership of his cells?

2. *The bundle of rights, again.* In his concurring opinion, Justice Arabian states that recognition of property rights in one's cells would necessarily entail "a right to sell one's own body tissue *for profit*." Is this correct? Consider Justice Mosk's response to this argument in his dissenting opinion (see page 89). Justice Mosk's approach rests on the bundle-of-rights conception of ownership, which we discussed previously (see Note 1 at page 39). Not all of the entitlements that may be included in the bundle are necessary for property. Consider the right to transfer. Although property may usually be transferred by sale or by gift, this is not always the case. As Justice Mosk explained, sometimes gifts alone are permitted, sometimes only sales, and sometimes neither. Notwithstanding, we are still talking about property. When sales are prohibited but gifts allowed, property is sometimes said to be "market-inalienable." What was the effect of the California

statute discussed in both the majority and dissenting opinions on the market-alienability of human body parts?

Could not the majority in *Moore* have used these observations to craft a more satisfactory opinion? If the majority had used Justice Mosk's bundle-of-rights approach, it could first have held the cells still to be Moore's property and then gone on to consider the question of alienability. Framing the matter in this way would readily allow the conclusion that because the cells were Moore's, they were not some doctor's to take, but neither were they Moore's *to sell in a market transaction*. In other words, the majority could have limited Moore's property rights but nevertheless acknowledged and protected them through the cause of action for conversion. Concerns about the impact of conversion liability on medical research and development could in turn have been eased by an appropriately tailored measure of damages. The literature mentions any number of alternatives, such as royalties, a percentage of profits, or a lump sum.

3. *The cell line and the law of accession.* The majority distinguishes between Moore's cells and the cell line, and states that even if Moore owned his cells after removal, he cannot own the cell line, which, the court says, is the product of "inventive effort." This reasoning suggests that the law of accession, which we saw earlier (see page 22), has a role to play here. Recall that under the doctrine of accession, when a person (*A*) in good faith applies labor alone or labor plus materials to some object that another person (*B*) owns to create a fundamentally different product, *A* acquires ownership of the new product. Did the defendants acquire ownership of the cell line on the basis of this doctrine? If so, they would owe Moore the fair market value of his cells. How would one value that asset?

4. *Commodification and the limits of the market.* Justice Arabian's opinion raises an important policy question—should non-replenishable human body parts be subject to market exchange? The question is part of the broader debate regarding the role of markets and commodification. Prohibitions of slavery, child labor, and prostitution are all examples of situations in which resources have been legally removed from the domain of the market, largely for moral reasons, including those to which Justice Arabian alludes. Of course, this issue was mooted by the fact that Moore's cells had already been commodified. But suppose Moore had known that his spleen was worth millions and that its removal was not medically necessary. Should he be allowed to contract with UCLA to sell it and develop research applications, all for a handsome profit? What arguments might be made in favor of allowing him to do so?

5. *Institutional competence.* The policy issue regarding commodification raises a further question. Which institution, courts or the legislature, is more competent to make the decision about this policy issue? Consider what Justice Arabian says about this. Do you agree with him?

6. *Property in fossils.* What is the status of prehistoric fossils, discovered under-ground, as property? As we will see in the next chapter (see page 148), according to the *ad coelum* doctrine, the owner of the surface also owns minerals and other resources below the surface. The surface owner may convey, lease or license the right to extract subsurface minerals lying beneath his land. Do minerals include fossils? In Murray v. BEJ Minerals LLC, 464 P.3d 80 (Mont. 2020), the Montana Supreme Court said no. The Seversons were farmers and ranchers who sold two-thirds of the mineral rights on their land to the Murrays. When the

Murrays discovered rare dinosaur fossils worth millions of dollars on the land, both parties sought declaratory judgment over who owned the fossils. Both parties conceded that they were not contemplating dinosaur fossils when they entered into a transaction over mineral rights. Ultimately, the Montana Supreme Court held that fossils are not considered minerals under the ordinary and natural meaning of the term "mineral." Because the fossil was not included within the surface owner's grant of "mineral" rights, the conveyance did not alter who owned them, leaving the Seversons with complete ownership of the valuable fossils.

The case of Henrietta Lacks. The issue of lack of informed consent in *Moore* was raised in another prominent controversy involving the cells of Ms. Henrietta Lacks (1920-1951), an African American woman who was raised by her grandparents in a log cabin that was a former slave dwelling. In 1951, when Ms. Lacks was stricken with an aggressive form of cervical cancer, doctors from Johns Hopkins University Hospital, where she was being treated, took cells from her tumor without her permission or her knowledge (as was common practice at the time). The physician found that the cells, somewhat similarly to Mr. Moore's, kept replicating at a high rate, making them greatly valuable to researchers. The researcher to whom the cell were given developed a cell line, which he named the "HeLa" line (after the initial letters of Henrietta Lacks's name), The HeLa line proved to be an enormous boon to medical and biological research. On October 4, 1951, Henrietta Lacks died. By 1954, Dr. Jonas Salk had used it to develop a vaccine for polio. Demand for the HeLa cells quickly grew, and soon they were sent to researchers around the world for research on cancer, AIDS, gene mapping, and other scientific endeavors. Almost 11,000 patents involve HeLa cells.

In the early 1970s, Ms. Lacks's family started getting calls from researchers who wanted blood samples from them to learn about the family's genetics. The family soon learned about the removal and use of Ms. Lacks's cells. Despite the fact that medical science had widely used and distributed the cells and that the cells had launched a multibillion-dollar industry, the Lacks family has been completely shut out of the informational loop and the decisional process.

That changed in August 2013, when the family reached an agreement with the National Institutes of Health (NIH) restricting NIH-funded research on the genome of HeLa cells. Two family members were placed on a committee to approve such research. Lacks family members had stated that their greatest concern was protecting their privacy interest in their genetic information. With the agreement in place, researchers will still be able to publish the results of their work. See Carl Zimmer, A Family Consents to a Medical Gift, 62 Years Later, N.Y. Times, Aug. 7, 2013. For a full discussion of the saga of Henrietta Lacks, see Rebecca Skloot, The Immortal Life of Henrietta Lacks (2010).

2. Three Core Intellectual Property Interests

a. Patents

The background and basics of patent law. The patent system is usually thought to be rooted in utilitarian reasons. The U.S. Constitution supports this view: "[t]o promote the Progress of Science and the useful Arts. . . ." U.S. Const. art. I, § 8. As we indicated earlier (see page 67), patent law involves a trade-off: it grants a limited monopoly to the patentee on the assumption that doing so creates an incentive for the patentee to engage in a creative and socially useful enterprise. The specific protection that the federal patent statute grants to the patent holder is the right to prevent others from making, using, selling, etc., the invention during the term of the patent. (Note, however, that the patentee's *use* of the item or product may be regulated or even prohibited by law.) Currently, the term of patents is 20 years from the date the application is filed with the U.S. Patent and Trademark Office (PTO).

Under the federal patent statute, patent applications must meet five requirements in order for the patent to be granted: (1) patentability; (2) novelty; (3) utility; (4) non-obviousness; and (5) enablement.

- ► *Patentability* means that the invention fits in one of the general categories of patentable subject matter. Patentable inventions are limited to these four: "process, machine, manufacture, or any composition of matter." 35 U.S.C. § 101.
- ► *Novelty* means that it has not been preceded in identical form in public prior art.
- ► *Utility* is a minimal requirement that is easily met so long as the invention offers some actual benefit to humans.
- ► *Non-obviousness* is the most important requirement; it asks whether the invention is a sufficiently big technical advance over the prior art.
- ► *Enablement* requires the patent application to describe the invention in sufficient detail so that "one of ordinary skill in the art" would be able to use the invention.

In recent years, one of the major controversies in patent law has concerned the scope of patentable subject matter. Courts have taken an expansive view of the statutory subject matter requirement so that today eligible subject matter includes genetic materials such as DNA sequences, proteins, and business methods. However, the laws of nature and abstract ideas such as $E=mc^2$ are not patentable. Biotechnology-related inventions have been among the most interesting—and controversial—topics in recent decades.

DIAMOND v. CHAKRABARTY

Supreme Court of the United States, 1980
447 U.S. 303

BURGER, C.J. We granted certiorari to determine whether a live, human-made microorganism is patentable subject matter under 35 U.S.C. § 101.

I.

In 1972, respondent Chakrabarty, a microbiologist, filed a patent application, assigned to the General Electric Co. The application asserted 36 claims related to Chakrabarty's invention of "a bacterium from the genus Pseudomonas containing therein at least two stable energy-generating plasmids, each of said plasmids providing a separate hydrocarbon degradative pathway." This human-made, genetically engineered bacterium is capable of breaking down multiple components of crude oil. Because of this property, which is possessed by no naturally occurring bacteria, Chakrabarty's invention is believed to have significant value for the treatment of oil spills.

Chakrabarty's patent claims were of three types: first, process claims for the method of producing the bacteria; second, claims for an inoculum comprised of a carrier material floating on water, such as straw, and the new bacteria; and third, claims to the bacteria themselves. The patent examiner allowed the claims falling into the first two categories, but rejected claims for the bacteria. His decision rested on two grounds: (1) that micro-organisms are "products of nature," and (2) that as living things they are not patentable subject matter under 35 U.S.C. § 101.

Procedural history

Chakrabarty appealed the rejection of these claims to the Patent Office Board of Appeals, and the Board affirmed the examiner on the second ground. . . . [The Court of Customs and Patent Appeals, by a divided vote, reversed this decision, and Diamond, as Commissioner of Patents and Trademarks, petitioned the Supreme Court for certiorari.]

II.

The Constitution grants Congress broad power to legislate to "promote the Progress of Science and useful Arts, by securing for limited Times to Authors and Inventors the exclusive Right to their respective Writings and Discoveries." Art. I, §8, cl. 8. The patent laws promote this progress by offering inventors exclusive rights for a limited period as an incentive for their inventiveness and research efforts. Kewanee Oil Co. v. Bicron Corp., 416 U.S. 470, 480-481 (1974); Universal Oil Co. v. Globe Co., 322 U.S. 471, 484 (1944). The authority of Congress is exercised in the hope that "[the] productive effort thereby fostered will have a positive effect on society through the introduction of new products and processes of manufacture into the economy, and the emanations by way of increased employment and better lives for our citizens." *Kewanee*, supra, at 480.

The question before us in this case is a narrow one of statutory interpretation requiring us to construe 35 U.S.C. § 101, which provides:

> Whoever invents or discovers any new and useful process, machine, manufacture, or composition of matter, or any new and useful improvement thereof, may obtain a patent therefor, subject to the conditions and requirements of this title.

Specifically, we must determine whether respondent's micro-organism constitutes a "manufacture" or "composition of matter" within the meaning of the statute.

III.

[T]his Court has read the term "manufacture" in § 101 in accordance with its dictionary definition to mean "the production of articles for use from raw or prepared materials by giving to these materials new forms, qualities, properties, or combinations, whether by hand-labor or by machinery." American Fruit Growers, Inc. v. Brogdex Co., 283 U.S. 1, 11 (1931). Similarly, "composition of matter" has been construed consistent with its common usage to include "all compositions of two or more substances and . . . all composite articles, whether they be the results of chemical union, or of mechanical mixture, or whether they be gases, fluids, powders or solids." Shell Development Co. v. Watson, 149 F. Supp. 279, 280 (D.C. 1957). . . . In choosing such expansive terms as "manufacture" and "composition of matter," modified by the comprehensive "any," Congress plainly contemplated that the patent laws would be given wide scope.

The relevant legislative history also supports a broad construction. The Patent Act of 1793, authored by Thomas Jefferson, defined statutory subject matter as "any new and useful art, machine, manufacture, or composition of matter, or any new or useful improvement [thereof]." Act of Feb. 21, 1793, § 1, 1 Stat. 319. The Act embodied Jefferson's philosophy that "ingenuity should receive a liberal encouragement." 5 Writings of Thomas Jefferson 75-76 (Washington ed. 1871). See Graham v. John Deere Co., 383 U.S. 1, 7-10 (1966). Subsequent patent statutes in 1836, 1870, and 1874 employed this same broad language. In 1952, when the patent laws were recodified, Congress replaced the word "art" with "process," but otherwise left Jefferson's language intact. The Committee Reports accompanying the 1952 Act inform us that Congress intended statutory subject matter to "include anything under the sun that is made by man." S. Rep. No. 1979, 82d Cong., 2d Sess., 5 (1952); H.R. Rep. No. 1923, 82d Cong., 2d Sess., 6 (1952).

This is not to suggest that §101 has no limits or that it embraces every discovery. The laws of nature, physical phenomena, and abstract ideas have been held not patentable. Thus, a new mineral discovered in the earth or a new plant found in the wild is not patentable subject matter. Likewise, Einstein could not patent his celebrated law that $E = mc^2$; nor could Newton have patented the law of gravity. Such discoveries are "manifestations of . . . nature, free to all men and reserved exclusively to none." Funk [Brothers Seed Co. v. Kalo Inoculant Co., 333 U.S. 127 (1948)], at 130.

Judged in this light, respondent's micro-organism plainly qualifies as patentable subject matter. His claim is not to a hitherto unknown natural phenomenon, but to a nonnaturally occurring manufacture or composition of matter—a product of human ingenuity "having a distinctive name, character [and] use." Hartranft v. Wiemann, 121 U.S. 609, 615 (1887). . . .

Here, by contrast, the patentee has produced a new bacterium with markedly different characteristics from any found in nature and one having the potential for significant utility. His discovery is not nature's handiwork, but his own; accordingly it is patentable subject matter under § 101.

IV.

[Petitioner argues] that micro-organisms cannot qualify as patentable subject matter until Congress expressly authorizes such protection. His position rests on the fact that genetic technology was unforeseen when Congress enacted § 101. From this it is argued that resolution of the patentability of inventions such as respondent's should be left to Congress. The legislative process, the petitioner argues, is best equipped to weigh the competing economic, social, and scientific considerations involved, and to determine whether living organisms produced by genetic engineering should receive patent protection. . . .

It is, of course, correct that Congress, not the courts, must define the limits of patentability; but it is equally true that once Congress has spoken it is "the province and duty of the judicial department to say what the law is." Marbury v. Madison, 1 Cranch 137, 177 (1803). Congress has performed its constitutional role in defining patentable subject matter in § 101; we perform ours in construing the language Congress has employed. In so doing, our obligation is to take statutes as we find them, guided, if ambiguity appears, by the legislative history and statutory purpose. Here, we perceive no ambiguity. The subject-matter provisions of the patent law have been cast in broad terms to fulfill the constitutional and statutory goal of promoting "the Progress of Science and the useful Arts" with all that means for the social and economic benefits envisioned by Jefferson. Broad general language is not necessarily ambiguous when congressional objectives require broad terms. . . .

. . . This Court frequently has observed that a statute is not to be confined to the "particular [applications] . . . contemplated by the legislators." Barr v. United States, 324 U.S. 83, 90 (1945). This is especially true in the field of patent law. A rule that unanticipated inventions are without protection would conflict with the core concept of the patent law that anticipation undermines patentability. Mr. Justice Douglas reminded that the inventions most benefiting mankind are those that "push back the frontiers of chemistry, physics, and the like." Great A. & P. Tea Co. v. Supermarket Corp., 340 U.S. 147, 154 (1950) (concurring opinion). Congress employed broad general language in drafting § 101 precisely because such inventions are often unforeseeable.

To buttress his argument, the petitioner, with the support of amicus, points to grave risks that may be generated by research endeavors such as respondent's. The briefs present a gruesome parade of horribles. Scientists, among them Nobel laureates, are quoted suggesting that genetic research may pose a serious threat to the human race, or, at the very least, that the dangers are far too substantial to permit such research to proceed apace at this time. We are told that genetic research and related technological developments may spread pollution and disease, that it may result in a loss of genetic diversity, and that its practice may tend to depreciate the value of human life. These arguments are forcefully, even passionately, presented; they remind us that, at times, human ingenuity seems unable to control fully the forces it creates—that, with Hamlet, it is sometimes better "to bear those ills we have than fly to others that we know not of."

It is argued that this Court should weigh these potential hazards in considering whether respondent's invention is patentable subject matter under § 101. We disagree. The grant or denial of patents on micro-organisms is not likely to put an end to genetic research or to its attendant risks. The large amount of research that has already occurred when no researcher had sure knowledge that patent protection would be available suggests that legislative or judicial fiat as to patentability will not deter the scientific mind from probing into the unknown any more than Canute could command the tides. Whether respondent's claims are patentable may determine whether research efforts are accelerated by the hope of reward or slowed by want of incentives, but that is all.

What is more important is that we are without competence to entertain these arguments—either to brush them aside as fantasies generated by fear of the unknown, or to act on them. The choice we are urged to make is a matter of high policy for resolution within the legislative process after the kind of investigation, examination, and study that legislative bodies can provide and courts cannot. That process involves the balancing of competing values and interests, which in our democratic system is the business of elected representatives. Whatever their validity, the contentions now pressed on us should be addressed to the political branches of the Government, the Congress and the Executive, and not to the courts.

Accordingly, the judgment of the Court of Customs and Patent Appeals is Affirmed.

BRENNAN, J., dissenting. . . . The only question we need decide is whether Congress, exercising its authority under Art. I, § 8, of the Constitution, intended that he be able to secure a monopoly on the living organism itself, no matter how produced or how used. Because I believe the Court has misread the applicable legislation, I dissent.

The patent laws attempt to reconcile this Nation's deep-seated antipathy to monopolies with the need to encourage progress. Given the complexity and legislative nature of this delicate task, we must be careful to extend patent protection no further than Congress has provided. In particular, were there an absence of legislative direction, the courts should leave to Congress the decisions whether and how far to extend the patent privilege into areas where the common understanding has been that patents are not available. . . .

The Court protests that its holding today is dictated by the broad language of § 101, which cannot "be confined to the 'particular [applications] . . . contemplated by the legislators.'" Ante . . . quoting Barr v. United States, 324 U.S. 83, 90 (1945). But as I have shown, the Court's decision does not follow the unavoidable implications of the statute. Rather, it extends the patent system to cover living material even though Congress plainly has legislated in the belief that § 101 does not encompass living organisms. It is the role of Congress, not this Court, to broaden or narrow the reach of the patent laws. This is especially true where, as here, the composition sought to be patented uniquely implicates matters of public concern.

THE REST OF THE STORY . . .

The patent on Dr. Chakrabarty's invention was finally issued in March 1981. In the meantime, General Electric, which owned the patent, had announced that new techniques had made Chakrabarty's invention obsolete and that the company had no plans to develop his method.

Notes and Questions

1. Chakrabarty *and the then-nascent biotechnology industry.* Chakrabarty is important, among other reasons, because it provided a significant boost to the biotechnology industry, which was then in its nascent stage. In holding that a living, genetically altered microorganism constituted a patentable subject matter, the Supreme Court opened the door to subsequent waves of patent applications involving rapid advances in biotechnology. Prior to Chakrabarty, the patentability of genetically engineered organisms had seemed doubtful because of the long-established exclusion for "products of nature." See Funk Bros. Seed Co. v. Kalo Inoculant Co., 333 U.S. 127 (1948). Chakrabarty put those doubts to rest.

2. *After* Chakrabarty, *what counts as a "product of nature"?* The Supreme Court addressed that issue in Association for Molecular Pathology v. Myriad Genetics, Inc., 569 U.S. 576 (2013). Myriad discovered genetic mutations that were associated with substantially elevated risks of breast and ovarian cancers. Myriad

then obtained patents on the DNA sequences whose presence indicated a heightened cancer risk. The Court held that isolating a sequence that already existed in human DNA did not satisfy *Chakrabarty*'s requirements. "In *Chakrabarty*, scientists added four plasmids to a bacterium, which enabled it to break down various components of crude oil. . . . In this case, by contrast, Myriad did not create anything. To be sure, it found an important and useful gene, but separating that gene from its surrounding genetic material is not an act of invention." *Id.* at 590-591. The case was not a total defeat for Myriad, though. Coding exons and adjacent noncoding introns combine to form human DNA, and Myriad also had removed the introns from naturally occurring DNA sequences, resulting in cDNA sequences that do not appear naturally in the human body. The Court held that such cDNA could be patented: "[T]he lab technician unquestionably creates something new when cDNA is made. cDNA retains the naturally occurring exons of DNA, but it is distinct from the DNA from which it was derived." *Id.* at 595. In a footnote, the Court mentioned that inventors seeking to patent cDNA would still need to establish other elements of patentability such as novelty, non-obviousness, and specification. *Id.* at 595 n.9. Creators of novel cDNA sequences may encounter particular difficulties satisfying patent law's non-obviousness requirement.

3. *Legislative superfluousness?* As the Court states, the 1930 Plant Patent Act extended patent protection to certain asexually reproduced plants, and the 1970 Plant Variety Protection Act authorized protection for certain sexually reproduced plants. The PTO argued that if plants and other living things could already be patented under these acts, then these two pieces of legislation were superfluous. Was the PTO right about this?

4. *Legislature versus courts:* Moore *and* Chakrabarty *compared.* In *Moore*, the court says that "if the scientific users of human cells are to be held liable for failing to investigate the consensual pedigree of their raw materials, we believe the legislature should make that decision." In *Chakrabarty*, on the other hand, the Court in effect says, "The legislature has worded the statute broadly, thereby making the decision for us. Unless genetically engineered bacteria are explicitly excluded from patentable subject matter, they can be patented." Do the two courts share an assumption regarding the proper role of the legislature vis-à-vis courts?

Was there any evidence that Congress ever weighed the patentability of genetically engineered bacteria? If not, which approach, the more cautious approach of the *Moore* court or the bolder approach of the Court in *Chakrabarty*, is likely to lead Congress to investigate the pros and cons of patenting genetically engineered bacteria and other living things? A related but separate question: which step is harder to undo—creating property rights (*Chakrabarty*) or refusing to recognize a property right (*Moore*)?

b. Copyright

The background and basics of copyright law. Copyright law, like patent law, primarily serves utilitarian purposes, although it has also been defended on other grounds, including natural law, as well. The Federal Constitution identifies its utilitarian goal: to "promote the Progress of Science and the Useful Arts. . . ." U.S. Const. art. I, § 8. By and large, copyright law is statutory law, and the federal copyright statute has been amended many times since it was first enacted in 1790. As in patent law, copyright law serves the goal stated in the Constitution by creating incentives for creativity by granting the reward of a limited monopoly.

The copyright holder has the right to prevent others from (1) reproducing the work; (2) creating derivative works; (3) distributing copies of the work to the public; (4) performing the work publicly; (5) displaying the work publicly; and (6) performing the work by digital audio transmission. Of course, copyright holders may and frequently do sell others licenses to use their works in particular ways. A copyright holder may also assign her copyright to another.

Federal law imposes three requirements for copyright protection: (1) originality; (2) work of authorship; and (3) fixation.

- ▶ *Originality* means that (a) the work must be an independent creation of the author and (b) must demonstrate at least some minimal degree of creativity.
- ▶ *Work of authorship* is a fairly broad term. The federal statute identifies eight types of such works: literary works; musical works; dramatic works; pantomimes and choreographic works; pictorial, graphic, and sculptural works; motion pictures and other audio-visual works; sound recordings; and architectural works. The term "literary works" is interpreted to include computer programs. What is not covered is important. First, it includes any "idea, procedure, process, system, method of operation, concept, principle, or discovery." 17 U.S.C. § 102(b). Running throughout copyright law is the idea-expression distinction. Copyright law protects expressions, not ideas. It protects the form or mode by which ideas are expressed rather than the ideas themselves. Second, strictly functional works, such as systems or procedures, are protected by patent law, not copyright.
- ▶ *Fixation* means that the work must be fixed in some kind of tangible medium.

In recent years, the Supreme Court has expressed concerns about the importance of not unduly restricting public access to information. The following case concerns the question of whether copyright protection is available for collections of basic information; in this case, telephone numbers. Consider the implications of the decision for intellectual property protection of other types of databases.

FEIST PUBLICATIONS, INC. v. RURAL TELEPHONE SERVICE CO.

Supreme Court of the United States, 1991
499 U.S. 340

O'CONNOR, J. This case requires us to clarify the extent of copyright protection available to telephone directory white pages.

I

Rural Telephone Service Company is a certified public utility that provides telephone service to several communities in northwest Kansas. It is subject to a state regulation that requires all telephone companies operating in Kansas to issue annually an updated telephone directory. Accordingly, as a condition of its monopoly franchise,

Rural publishes a typical telephone directory, consisting of white pages and yellow pages. The white pages list in alphabetical order the names of Rural's subscribers, together with their towns and telephone numbers. The yellow pages list Rural's business subscribers alphabetically by category and feature classified advertisement of various sizes. Rural distributes its directory free of charge to its subscribers, but earns revenue by selling yellow pages advertisements.

Feist Publications, Inc., is a publishing company that specializes in areawide telephone directories. Unlike a typical directory, which covers only a particular calling area, Feist's areawide directories cover a much larger geographical range, reducing the need to call directory assistance or consult multiple directories. The Feist directory that is the subject of this litigation covers 11 different telephone service areas in 15 counties and contains 46,878 white pages listings—compared to Rural's approximately 7,700 listings. Like Rural's directory, Feist's is distributed free of charge and includes both white pages and yellow pages. Feist and Rural compete vigorously for yellow pages advertising.

As the sole provider of telephone service in its service area, Rural obtains subscriber information quite easily. Persons desiring telephone service must apply to Rural and provide their names and addresses; Rural then assigns them a telephone number. Feist is not a telephone company, let alone one with monopoly status, and therefore lacks independent access to any subscriber information. To obtain white pages listings for its areawide directory, Feist approached each of the 11 telephone companies operating in northwest Kansas and offered to pay for the right to use its white pages listings.

Of the 11 telephone companies, only Rural refused to license its listings to Feist. Rural's refusal created a problem for Feist, as omitting these listings would have left a gaping hole in its areawide directory, rendering it less attractive to potential yellow pages advertisers. In a decision subsequent to that which we review here, the District Court determined that this was precisely the reason Rural refused to license its listings. The refusal was motivated by an unlawful purpose "to extend its monopoly in telephone service to a monopoly in yellow pages advertising." Rural Telephone Service Co. v. Feist Publications, Inc., 737 F. Supp. 610, 622 (Kan. 1990).

Unable to license Rural's white pages listings, Feist used them without Rural's consent. Feist began by removing several thousand listings that fell outside the geographic range of its areawide directory, then hired personnel to investigate the 4,935 that remained. These employees verified the data reported by Rural and sought to obtain additional information. As a result, a typical Feist listing includes the individual's street address; most of Rural's listings do not. Notwithstanding these additions, however, 1,309 of the 46,878 listings in Feist's 1983 directory were identical to listings in Rural's 1982-1983 white pages. Four of these were fictitious listings that Rural had inserted into its directory to detect copying.

Rural sued for copyright infringement in the District Court for the District of Kansas, taking the position that Feist, in compiling its own directory, could not use the information contained in Rural's white pages. . . . The District Court granted summary judgment to Rural. . . . [T]he Court of Appeals for the Tenth Circuit affirmed "for substantially the reasons given by the district court." We granted certiorari, 498 U.S. 808 (1990), to determine whether the copyright in Rural's directory protects the names, towns, and telephone numbers copied by Feist.

II.

A.

This case concerns the interaction of two well-established propositions. The first is that facts are not copyrightable; the other, that compilations of facts generally are. Each of these propositions possesses an impeccable pedigree. That there can be no valid copyright in facts is universally understood. The most fundamental axiom of copyright law is that "[n]o author may copyright his ideas or the facts he narrates." Harper & Row, Publishers, Inc. v. Nation Enterprises, 471 U.S. 539, 556 (1985). Rural wisely concedes this point, noting in its brief that "[f]acts and discoveries, of course, are not themselves subject to copyright protection." Brief for Respondent 24. At the same time, however, it is beyond dispute that compilations of facts are within the subject matter of copyright. Compilations were expressly mentioned in the Copyright Act of 1909, and again in the Copyright Act of 1976.

There is an undeniable tension between these two propositions. Many compilations consist of nothing but raw data—i.e., wholly factual information not accompanied by any original written expression. On what basis may one claim a copyright in such a work? Common sense tells us that 100 uncopyrightable facts do not magically change their status when gathered together in one place. Yet copyright law seems to contemplate that compilations that consist exclusively of facts are potentially within its scope.

The key to resolving the tension lies in understanding why facts are not copyrightable. The *sine qua non* of copyright is originality. To qualify for copyright protection, a work must be original to the author. . . . To be sure, the requisite level of creativity is extremely low; even a slight amount will suffice. The vast majority of works make the grade quite easily, as they possess some creative spark, "no matter how crude, humble or obvious" it might be. Id. § 1.08[C]. . . . Originality does not signify novelty; a work may be original even though it closely resembles other works, so long as the similarity is fortuitous, not the result of copying. To illustrate, assume that two poets, each ignorant of the other, compose identical poems. Neither work is novel, yet both are original and, hence, copyrightable. . . .

It is this bedrock principle of copyright that mandates the law's seemingly disparate treatment of facts and factual compilations. . . . This is because facts do not owe their origin to an act of authorship. The distinction is one between creation and discovery: the first person to find and report a particular fact has not created the fact; he or she has merely discovered its existence. . . . Census-takers, for example, do not "create" the population figures that emerge from their efforts; in a sense, they copy these figures from the world around them. . . . Census data therefore do not trigger copyright, because these data are not "original" in the constitutional sense. . . .

Factual compilations, on the other hand, may possess the requisite originality. The compilation author typically chooses which facts to include, in what order to place them, and how to arrange the collected data so that they may be used effectively by readers. These choices as to selection and arrangement, so long as they are made independently by the compiler and entail a minimal degree of creativity, are sufficiently original that Congress may protect such compilations through the copyright laws. . . . Thus, even a directory that contains absolutely no protectible written expression, only facts, meets the constitutional minimum for copyright protection if it features an original selection or arrangement. . . . This protection is subject to an important limitation. The mere fact that a work is copyrighted does not mean that every element of the work may be protected. Originality remains the *sine qua non* of copyright; accordingly, copyright protection may extend only to those components of a work that are original to the author. . . .

This inevitably means that the copyright in a factual compilation is thin. Notwithstanding a valid copyright, a subsequent compiler remains free to use the facts contained in another's publication to aid in preparing a competing work, so long as the competing work does not feature the same selection and arrangement. . . .

It may seem unfair that much of the fruit of the compiler's labor may be used by others without compensation. . . . The primary objective of copyright is not to reward the labor of authors, but "[t]o promote the Progress of Science and useful Arts." Art. I, § 8, cl. 8. To this end, copyright assures authors the right to their original expression, but encourages others to build freely upon the ideas and information conveyed by a work. This principle, known as the idea/expression or fact/expression dichotomy, applies to all works of authorship. As applied to a factual compilation, assuming the absence of original written expression, only the compiler's selection and arrangement may be protected; the raw facts may be copied at will. This result is neither unfair nor unfortunate. It is the means by which copyright advances the progress of science and art. . . .

Most courts . . . understood from this Court's decisions that there could be no copyright without originality. . . .

But some courts misunderstood the [copyright] statute. . . . [They inferred] erroneously that directories and the like were copyrightable per se, "without any further or precise showing of original-personal-authorship." . . . [They] developed a new theory to justify the protection of factual compilations. Known alternatively as "sweat of the brow" or "industrious collection," the underlying notion was that copyright was a reward for the hard work that went into compiling facts. . . .

B.

[This] "sweat of the brow" doctrine had numerous flaws, the most glaring being that it extended copyright protection in a compilation beyond selection and arrangement—the compiler's original contributions—to the facts themselves. Under the doctrine, the only defense to infringement was independent creation. A subsequent compiler was "not entitled to take one word of information previously published," but rather had to "independently wor[k] out the matter for himself, so as to arrive at the same result from the same common sources of information." [Jeweler's Circular Publishing Co. v. Keystone Publishing Co., 281 F. 83 (2d Cir. 1922)] at 88-89 (internal quotations omitted). "Sweat of the brow" courts thereby eschewed the most fundamental axiom of copyright law—that no one may copyright facts or ideas. . . .

Decisions of this Court applying the 1909 Act make clear that the statute did not permit the "sweat of the brow" approach. The best example is International News Service v. Associated Press, 248 U.S. 215 (1918). In that decision, the Court stated unambiguously that the 1909 Act conferred copyright protection only on those elements of a work that were original to the author. International News Service had conceded taking news reported by Associated Press and publishing it in its own newspapers. Recognizing that § 5 of the Act specifically mentioned "[p]eriodicals, including newspapers," § 5(b), the Court acknowledged that news articles were copyrightable.

Id., at 234. It flatly rejected, however, the notion that the copyright in an article extended to the factual information it contained: "[T]he news element—the information respecting current events contained in the literary production—is not the creation of the writer, but is a report of matters that ordinarily are *publici juris*; it is the history of the day." *Ibid.* . . .

III.

There is no doubt that Feist took from the white pages of Rural's directory a substantial amount of factual information. At a minimum, Feist copied the names, towns, and telephone numbers of 1,309 of Rural's subscribers. Not all copying, however, is copyright infringement. To establish infringement, two elements must be proven: (1) ownership of a valid copyright, and (2) copying of constituent elements of the work that are original. The first element is not at issue here; Feist appears to concede that Rural's directory, considered as a whole, is subject to a valid copyright because it contains some foreword text, as well as original material in its yellow pages advertisements.

The question is whether Rural has proved the second element. In other words, did Feist, by taking 1,309 names, towns, and telephone numbers from Rural's white pages, copy anything that was "original" to Rural? Certainly, the raw data does not satisfy the originality requirement. Rural may have been the first to discover and report the names, towns, and telephone numbers of its subscribers, but this data does not "'ow[e] its origin'" to Rural. . . . Rather, these bits of information are uncopyrightable facts; they existed before Rural reported them, and would have continued to exist if Rural had never published a telephone directory. . . .

The question that remains is whether Rural selected, coordinated, or arranged these uncopyrightable facts in an original way. As mentioned, originality is not a stringent standard; it does not require that facts be presented in an innovative or surprising way. It is equally true, however, that the selection and arrangement of facts cannot be so mechanical or routine as to require no creativity whatsoever. The standard of originality is low, but it does exist. . . .

The selection, coordination, and arrangement of Rural's white pages do not satisfy the minimum constitutional standards for copyright protection. As mentioned at the outset, Rural's white pages are entirely typical. Persons desiring telephone service in Rural's service area fill out an application and Rural issues them a telephone number. In preparing its white pages, Rural simply takes the data provided by its subscribers and lists it alphabetically by surname. The end product is a garden-variety white pages directory, devoid of even the slightest trace of creativity.

Rural's selection of listings could not be more obvious: It publishes the most basic information—name, town, and telephone number—about each person who applies to it for telephone service. This is "selection" of a sort, but it lacks the modicum of creativity necessary to transform mere selection into copyrightable expression. Rural expended sufficient effort to make the white pages directory useful, but insufficient creativity to make it original. . . .

Nor can Rural claim originality in its coordination and arrangement of facts. The white pages do nothing more than list Rural's subscribers in alphabetical order. This arrangement may, technically speaking, owe its origin to Rural; no one disputes that Rural undertook the task of alphabetizing the names itself. But there is nothing remotely creative about arranging names alphabetically in a white pages directory. It is an age-old practice, firmly rooted in tradition and so commonplace that it has come to be expected as a matter of course. It is not only unoriginal, it is practically inevitable. This time-honored tradition does not possess the minimal creative spark required by the Copyright Act and the Constitution.

We conclude that the names, towns, and telephone numbers copied by Feist were not original to Rural and therefore were not protected by the copyright in Rural's combined white and yellow pages directory. As a constitutional matter, copyright protects only those constituent elements of a work that possess more than a *de minimis* quantum of creativity. Rural's white pages, limited to basic subscriber information and arranged alphabetically, fall short of the mark. As a statutory matter, 17 U.S.C. § 101 does not afford protection from copying to a collection of facts that are selected, coordinated, and arranged in a way that utterly lacks originality. Given that some works must fail, we cannot imagine a more likely candidate. Indeed, were we to hold that Rural's white pages pass muster, it is hard to believe that any collection of facts could fail. . . .

The judgment of the Court of Appeals is *Reversed.*

Notes and Questions

1. *The originality requirement, the "sweat-of-the-brow" doctrine, and the labor theory.* Feist is perhaps the most important recent copyright decision dealing with the requirement that the work be original. Until *Feist,* several decisions had applied the "sweat-of-the-brow" doctrine. Under that doctrine, an author gains copyright protection simply on the basis of effort and expense; no originality is required. *Feist* is important, among other reasons, because it rejects that doctrine: "[O]riginality, not 'sweat of the brow,' is the touchstone of copyright protection in directories and other fact-based works. . . ." 449 U.S. at 359-360. *Feist* is also important because of the Court's interpretation of originality. The test for originality, the Court indicates, is creativity. Compilations of preexisting data may be copyrighted if they displayed sufficient creativity.

This is not the first time that we have seen the idea behind the sweat-of-the-brow doctrine. As the Court in *Feist* indicated, it is certainly evident in INS v. AP. But even prior to that, we saw it in Pierson v. Post. Sweat-of-the-brow reasoning is the thrust of Justice Livingston's dissenting opinion in that case. There is some appeal to the idea that a person should be rewarded for her efforts, but recall Douglas Baird's observation, made in connection with INS v. AP (see page 73 supra), that we do not always reap where we sow. Why did the Court in *Feist* reject the sweat-of-the-brow doctrine? And what about creativity—is that a better approach? (If so, better in what respect?)

2. *Databases.* Feist throws into question the status, vis-à-vis copyright protection, of various sorts of factual compilations. For example, what is the status of automated databases after *Feist*? Are they entitled to protection, or do they lack sufficient creativity? The status of such factual compilations is unclear after *Feist*. The lower federal courts have interpreted *Feist* in quite different ways. Compare, e.g., BellSouth Advertising & Publishing Corp. v. Donnelley Information Publishing, 999 F.2d 1436 (11th Cir. 1993) (yellow pages directory unprotectable because act of separating categories of businesses would "merge with the idea of listing such entities as a class of businesses in a business directory"), with Key

Publications, Inc. v. Chinatown Today Publishing Enterprises, 945 F.2d 508 (2d Cir. 1991) (court protected copied directory that differed from BellSouth directory only by solely including businesses thought to be of interest to Chinese Americans).

Owners of databases and other factual compilations sometimes rely on alternative legal means of protecting their "sweat-of-the-brow" investments. Proprietary databases are routinely kept confidential and protected under trade secrets law—another major branch of intellectual property law. Contract law has been especially popular in the wake of *Feist*. See, e.g., ProCD, Inc. v. Zeidenberg, 86 F.3d 1447 (7th Cir. 1996). Some cases hold that a person who copies a database may be liable for breach of contract even though the database is composed entirely of unprotectable facts.

3. *Infringement.* The copyright holder must satisfy three requirements to prevail in an infringement action: (1) he holds a valid copyright in the work; (2) defendant copied the work; and (3) the copying was an "improper appropriation." The final element—"improper appropriation"—requires that the copyright holder show that the defendant copied so much of the original material that the two works are substantially similar.

4. *Fair use.* The most important defense in a copyright infringement action is fair use. As the name implies, fair use authorizes users of copyrighted material to exploit the work for some purposes without needing to obtain the permission of the copyright holder. Classic fair uses include quoting portions of a manuscript in a book review, invoking parts of a well-known song in a musical parody, or creating an abstract painting based on an iconic photograph. When considering a fair use defense, the courts consider (1) the purpose and character of the use; (2) the nature of the copyrighted work; (3) the substantiality of the portion used in relation to the copyrighted work as a whole; and (4) the effect on the potential market for or value of the copyrighted work. See Harper & Row Publishers, Inc. v. Nation Enterprises, 471 U.S. 539 (1985).

5. *Copyright duration.* The patent monopoly generally runs for 20 years from the date on which the patent application is filed. The copyright monopoly is much longer-lived. Works created by living authors are now protected for the author's lifetime and the first 70 years after her death. Is that term too long? Consider the following case.

ELDRED v. ASHCROFT
Supreme Court of the United States, 2003
537 U.S. 186

GINSBURG, J. This case concerns the authority the Constitution assigns to Congress to prescribe the duration of copyrights. The Copyright and Patent Clause of the Constitution, Art. I, § 8, cl. 8, provides as to copyrights: "Congress shall have Power . . . [t]o promote the Progress of Science . . . by securing [to Authors] for limited Times . . . the exclusive Right to their . . . Writings." In 1998, in the measure here under inspection, Congress enlarged the duration of copyrights by 20 years. Copyright Term Extension Act (CTEA), Pub. L. 105298, § 102(b) and (d), 112 Stat. 2827-2828 (amending 17 U.S.C. §§ 302,

304). As in the case of prior extensions, principally in 1831, 1909, and 1976, Congress provided for application of the enlarged terms to existing and future copyrights alike.

Petitioners are individuals and businesses whose products or services build on copyrighted works that have gone into the public domain. They seek a determination that the CTEA fails constitutional review under . . . the Copyright Clause's "limited Times" prescription. . . . Under the 1976 Copyright Act, copyright protection generally lasted from the work's creation until 50 years after the author's death. Pub. L. 94-553, § 302(a), 90 Stat. 2572 (1976 Act). Under the CTEA, most copyrights now run from creation until 70 years after the author's death. 17 U.S.C. § 302(a). Petitioners do not challenge the "life-plus-70-years" time span itself. "Whether 50 years is enough, or 70 years too much," they acknowledge, "is not a judgment meet for this Court." Brief for Petitioners 14. Congress went awry, petitioners maintain, not with respect to newly created works, but in enlarging the term for published works with existing copyrights. The "limited Tim[e]" in effect when a copyright is secured, petitioners urge, becomes the constitutional boundary, a clear line beyond the power of Congress to extend. . . .

In accord with the District Court and the Court of Appeals, we reject petitioners' challenges to the CTEA. In that 1998 legislation, as in all previous copyright term extensions, Congress placed existing and future copyrights in parity. In prescribing that alignment, we hold, Congress acted within its authority and did not transgress constitutional limitations.

I.

A.

We evaluate petitioners' challenge to the constitutionality of the CTEA against the backdrop of Congress' previous exercises of its authority under the Copyright Clause. The Nation's first copyright statute, enacted in 1790, provided a federal copyright term of 14 years from the date of publication, renewable for an additional 14 years if the author survived the first term. Act of May 31, 1790, ch. 15, § 1, 1 Stat. 124 (1790 Act). The 1790 Act's renewable 14-year term applied to existing works (i.e., works already published and works created but not yet published) and future works alike. Congress expanded the federal copyright term to 42 years in 1831 (28 years from publication, renewable for an additional 14 years), and to 56 years in 1909 (28 years from publication, renewable for an additional 28 years). Act of Feb. 3, 1831, ch. 16, §§ 1, 16, 4 Stat. 436, 439 (1831 Act); Act of Mar. 4, 1909, ch. 320, §§ 23-24, 35 Stat. 1080-1081 (1909 Act). Both times, Congress applied the new copyright term to existing and future works, 1831 Act §§ 1, 16; 1909 Act §§ 23-24; to qualify for the 1831 extension, an existing work had to be in its initial copyright term at the time the Act became effective, 1831 Act §§ 1, 16.

In 1976, Congress altered the method for computing federal copyright terms. 1976 Act §§ 302-304. For works created by identified natural persons, the 1976 Act provided that federal copyright protection would run from the work's creation, not—as in the 1790, 1831, and 1909 Acts—its publication; protection would last until 50 years after the author's death. § 302(a). . . . For anonymous works, pseudonymous works, and works made for hire, the 1976 Act provided a term of 75 years from publication or 100 years from creation, whichever expired first. § 302(c).

. . .

The measure at issue here, the CTEA, installed the fourth major duration extension of federal copyrights. Retaining the general structure of the 1976 Act, the CTEA enlarges the terms of all existing and future copyrights by 20 years. For works created by identified natural persons, the term now lasts from creation until 70 years after the author's death. 17 U.S.C. § 302(a). . . . For anonymous works, pseudonymous works, and works made for hire, the term is 95 years from publication or 120 years from creation, whichever expires first. 17 U.S.C. § 302(c).

Paralleling the 1976 Act, the CTEA applies these new terms to all works not published by January 1, 1978. §§ 302(a), 303(a). For works published before 1978 with existing copyrights as of the CTEA's effective date, the CTEA extends the term to 95 years from publication. § 304(a) and (b). Thus, in common with the 1831, 1909, and 1976 Acts, the CTEA's new terms apply to both future and existing copyrights.

B.

Petitioners' suit challenges the CTEA's constitutionality under . . . the Copyright Clause. . . . On cross-motions for judgment on the pleadings, the District Court entered judgment for the Attorney General (respondent here). 74 F. Supp. 2d 1 (D.D.C. 1999). The court held that the CTEA does not violate the "limited Times" restriction of the Copyright Clause because the CTEA's terms, though longer than the 1976 Act's terms, are still limited, not perpetual, and therefore fit within Congress' discretion. . . .

The Court of Appeals for the District of Columbia Circuit affirmed. . . . We granted certiorari to address . . . whether the CTEA's extension of existing copyrights exceeds Congress' power under the Copyright Clause. . . . We now . . . affirm.

II.

A.

We address first the determination of the courts below that Congress has authority under the Copyright Clause to extend the terms of existing copyrights. Text, history, and precedent, we conclude, confirm that the Copyright Clause empowers Congress to prescribe "limited Times" for copyright protection and to secure the same level and duration of protection for all copyright holders, present and future.

The CTEA's baseline term of life plus 70 years, petitioners concede, qualifies as a "limited Tim[e]" as applied to future copyrights. Petitioners contend, however, that existing copyrights extended to endure for that same term are not "limited." Petitioners' argument essentially reads into the text of the Copyright Clause the command that a time prescription, once set, becomes forever "fixed" or "inalterable." The word "limited," however, does not convey a meaning so constricted. At the time of the Framing, that word meant what it means today: "confine[d] within certain bounds," "restrain[ed]," or "circumscribe[d]." S. Johnson, A Dictionary of the English Language (7th ed. 1785); see T. Sheridan, A Complete Dictionary of the English Language (6th ed. 1796) ("confine[d] within certain bounds"); Webster's Third New International Dictionary 1312 (1976) ("confined within limits"; "restricted in extent, number, or duration"). Thus understood, a time span appropriately "limited" as applied to future copyrights does not automatically cease to be "limited" when applied to existing copyrights. . . .

To comprehend the scope of Congress' power under the Copyright Clause, "a page of history is worth a volume of logic." New York Trust Co. v. Eisner, 256 U.S. 345, 349

(1921) (Holmes, J.). History reveals an unbroken congressional practice of granting to authors of works with existing copyrights the benefit of term extensions so that all under copyright protection will be governed evenhandedly under the same regime. As earlier recounted, see supra, at 775, the First Congress accorded the protections of the Nation's first federal copyright statute to existing and future works alike. 1790 Act § 1. Since then, Congress has regularly applied duration extensions to both existing and future copyrights. 1831 Act §§ 1, 16; 1909 Act §§ 23-24; 1976 Act §§ 302-303; 17 U.S.C. §§ 302-304.

. . .

Congress' consistent historical practice of applying newly enacted copyright terms to future and existing copyrights reflects a judgment stated concisely by Representative Huntington at the time of the 1831 Act: "[J]ustice, policy, and equity alike forb[id]" that an "author who had sold his [work] a week ago, be placed in a worse situation than the author who should sell his work the day after the passing of [the] act." 7 Cong. Deb. 424 (1831). . . . The CTEA follows this historical practice by keeping the duration provisions of the 1976 Act largely in place and simply adding 20 years to each of them. Guided by text, history, and precedent, we cannot agree with petitioners' submission that extending the duration of existing copyrights is categorically beyond Congress' authority under the Copyright Clause.

Satisfied that the CTEA complies with the "limited Times" prescription, we turn now to whether it is a rational exercise of the legislative authority conferred by the Copyright Clause. On that point, we defer substantially to Congress. *Sony*, 464 U.S., at 429 ("[I]t is Congress that has been assigned the task of defining the scope of the limited monopoly that should be granted to authors . . . in order to give the public appropriate access to their work product").

The CTEA reflects judgments of a kind Congress typically makes, judgments we cannot dismiss as outside the Legislature's domain. As respondent describes, see Brief for Respondent 37-38, a key factor in the CTEA's passage was a 1993 European Union (EU) directive instructing EU members to establish a copyright term of life plus 70 years. EU Council Directive 93/98, p. 4; see 144 Cong. Rec. S12377-S12378 (daily ed. Oct. 12, 1998) (statement of Sen. Hatch). Consistent with the Berne Convention, the EU directed its members to deny this longer term to the works of any non-EU country whose laws did not secure the same extended term. See Berne Conv. Art. 7(8); P. Goldstein, International Copyright § 5.3, p. 239 (2001). By extending the baseline United States copyright term to life plus 70 years, Congress sought to ensure that American authors would receive the same copyright protection in Europe as their European counterparts. The CTEA may also provide greater incentive for American and other authors to create and disseminate their work in the United States. . . .

In addition to international concerns, Congress passed the CTEA in light of demographic, economic, and technological changes, Brief for Respondent 25-26, 33, and nn. 23 and 24,[17] and rationally credited projections that longer terms would encourage

---

17. Members of Congress expressed the view that, as a result of increases in human longevity and in parents' average age when their children are born, the pre-CTEA term did not adequately secure "the right to profit from licensing one's work during one's lifetime and to take pride and comfort in knowing that one's children—and perhaps their children—might also benefit from one's posthumous popularity." 141 Cong. Rec. 6553 (1995) (statement of Sen. Feinstein); see 144 Cong. Rec. S12377 (daily ed. Oct. 12, 1998) (statement of Sen. Hatch) ("Among the main developments [compelling reconsideration of the 1976 Act's term] is the effect of demographic trends, such as increasing longevity and the trend toward rearing children later in life, on the effectiveness of the life-plus-50 term to provide adequate protection for American creators and their heirs."). . . .

copyright holders to invest in the restoration and public distribution of their works, id., at 34-37; see H.R. Rep. No. 105-452, p. 4 (1998) (term extension "provide[s] copyright owners generally with the incentive to restore older works and further disseminate them to the public").[18]

In sum, we find that the CTEA is a rational enactment; we are not at liberty to second-guess congressional determinations and policy judgments of this order, however debatable or arguably unwise they may be. Accordingly, we cannot conclude that the CTEA—which continues the unbroken congressional practice of treating future and existing copyrights in parity for term extension purposes—is an impermissible exercise of Congress' power under the Copyright Clause.

B.

Petitioners' Copyright Clause arguments rely on several novel readings of the Clause. We next address these arguments and explain why we find them unpersuasive.

1

Petitioners contend that even if the CTEA's 20-year term extension is literally a "limited Tim[e]," permitting Congress to extend existing copyrights allows it to evade the "limited Times" constraint by creating effectively perpetual copyrights through repeated extensions. We disagree.

As the Court of Appeals observed, a regime of perpetual copyrights "clearly is not the situation before us." 239 F.3d, at 379. Nothing before this Court warrants construction of the CTEA's 20-year term extension as a congressional attempt to evade or override the "limited Times" constraint. Critically, we again emphasize, petitioners fail to show how the CTEA crosses a constitutionally significant threshold with respect to "limited Times" that the 1831, 1909, and 1976 Acts did not. . . . Those earlier Acts did not create perpetual copyrights, and neither does the CTEA.

2

Petitioners dominantly advance a series of arguments all premised on the proposition that Congress may not extend an existing copyright absent new consideration from the author. . .

---

18. Justice Breyer urges that the economic incentives accompanying copyright term extension are too insignificant to "mov[e]" any author with a "rational economic perspective." Calibrating rational economic incentives, however, like "fashion[ing] . . . new rules [in light of] new technology," *Sony*, 464 U.S., at 431, is a task primarily for Congress, not the courts. Congress heard testimony from a number of prominent artists; each expressed the belief that the copyright system's assurance of fair compensation for themselves and their heirs was an incentive to create. See, e.g., House Hearings 233-239 (statement of Quincy Jones); Copyright Term Extension Act of 1995: Hearings before the Senate Committee on the Judiciary, 104th Cong., 1st Sess., 55-56 (1995) (statement of Bob Dylan); id., at 56-57 (statement of Don Henley); id., at 57 (statement of Carlos Santana). We would not take Congress to task for crediting this evidence which, as Justice Breyer acknowledges, reflects general "propositions about the value of incentives" that are "undeniably true."

Congress also heard testimony from Register of Copyrights Marybeth Peters and others regarding the economic incentives created by the CTEA. According to the Register, extending the copyright for existing works "could . . . provide additional income that would finance the production and distribution of new works." House Hearings 158. "Authors would not be able to continue to create," the Register explained, "unless they earned income on their finished works. The public benefits not only from an author's original work but also from his or her further creations. Although this truism may be illustrated in many ways, one of the best examples is Noah Webster[,] who supported his entire family from the earnings on his speller and grammar during the twenty years he took to complete his dictionary." Id., at 165.

[P]etitioners contend that the CTEA's extension of existing copyrights does not "promote the Progress of Science" as contemplated by the preambular language of the Copyright Clause. Art. I, § 8, cl. 8. To sustain this objection, petitioners do not argue that the Clause's preamble is an independently enforceable limit on Congress' power. . . . Rather, they maintain that the preambular language identifies the sole end to which Congress may legislate; accordingly, they conclude, the meaning of "limited Times" must be "determined in light of that specified end." Brief for Petitioners 19. The CTEA's extension of existing copyrights categorically fails to "promote the Progress of Science," petitioners argue, because it does not stimulate the creation of new works but merely adds value to works already created.

As petitioners point out, we have described the Copyright Clause as "both a grant of power and a limitation," Graham v. John Deere Co. of Kansas City, 383 U.S. 1, 5 (1966), and have said that "[t]he primary objective of copyright" is "[t]o promote the Progress of Science," Feist, 499 U.S., at 349. The "constitutional command," we have recognized, is that Congress, to the extent it enacts copyright laws at all, create a "system" that "promote[s] the Progress of Science." *Graham*, 383 U.S., at 6.

We have also stressed, however, that it is generally for Congress, not the courts, to decide how best to pursue the Copyright Clause's objectives. . . . The justifications we earlier set out for Congress' enactment of the CTEA, provide a rational basis for the conclusion that the CTEA "promote[s] the Progress of Science."

On the issue of copyright duration, Congress, from the start, has routinely applied new definitions or adjustments of the copyright term to both future works and existing works not yet in the public domain. Such consistent congressional practice is entitled to "very great weight, and when it is remembered that the rights thus established have not been disputed during a period of [over two] centur[ies], it is almost conclusive." Burrow-Giles Lithographic Co. v. Sarony, 111 U.S., at 57. . . . Congress' unbroken practice since the founding generation thus overwhelms petitioners' argument that the CTEA's extension of existing copyrights fails per se to "promote the Progress of Science."

Closely related to petitioners' preambular argument, or a variant of it, is their assertion that the Copyright Clause "imbeds a quid pro quo." Brief for Petitioners 23. They contend, in this regard, that Congress may grant to an "Autho[r]" an "exclusive Right" for a "limited Tim[e]," but only in exchange for a "Writin[g]." Congress' power to confer copyright protection, petitioners argue, is thus contingent upon an exchange: The author of an original work receives an "exclusive Right" for a "limited Tim[e]" in exchange for a dedication to the public thereafter. Extending an existing copyright without demanding additional consideration, petitioners maintain, bestows an unpaid-for benefit on copyright holders and their heirs, in violation of the quid pro quo requirement.

We can demur to petitioners' description of the Copyright Clause as a grant of legislative authority empowering Congress "to secure a bargain—this for that." . . . But the legislative evolution earlier recalled demonstrates what the bargain entails. Given the consistent placement of existing copyright holders in parity with future holders, the author of a work created in the last 170 years would reasonably comprehend, as the "this" offered her, a copyright not only for the time in place when protection is gained, but also for any renewal or extension legislated during that time. Congress could rationally seek to "promote . . . Progress" by including in every copyright statute an express guarantee that authors would receive the benefit of any later legislative extension of the copyright term. Nothing in the Copyright Clause bars Congress from creating the same incentive by adopting the same position as a matter of unbroken practice.

. . .

IV.

If petitioners' vision of the Copyright Clause held sway, it would do more than render the CTEA's duration extensions unconstitutional as to existing works. Indeed, petitioners' assertion that the provisions of the CTEA are not severable would make the CTEA's enlarged terms invalid even as to tomorrow's work. The 1976 Act's time extensions, which set the pattern that the CTEA followed, would be vulnerable as well.

As we read the Framers' instruction, the Copyright Clause empowers Congress to determine the intellectual property regimes that, overall, in that body's judgment, will serve the ends of the Clause. . . . Beneath the facade of their inventive constitutional interpretation, petitioners forcefully urge that Congress pursued very bad policy in prescribing the CTEA's long terms. The wisdom of Congress' action, however, is not within our province to second guess. Satisfied that the legislation before us remains inside the domain the Constitution assigns to the First Branch, we affirm the judgment of the Court of Appeals.

It is so ordered.

BREYER, J., dissenting. The Constitution's Copyright Clause grants Congress the power to "*promote* the *Progress* of Science . . . by securing for *limited* Times to *Authors* . . . the exclusive Right to their respective Writings." Art. I, § 8, cl. 8 (emphasis added). The statute before us, the 1998 Sonny Bono Copyright Term Extension Act, extends the term of most existing copyrights to 95 years and that of many new copyrights to 70 years after the author's death. The economic effect of this 20-year extension—the longest blanket extension since the Nation's founding—is to make the copyright term not limited, but virtually perpetual. Its primary legal effect is to grant the extended term not to authors, but to their heirs, estates, or corporate successors. And most importantly, its practical effect is not to promote, but to inhibit, the progress of "Science"—by which word the Framers meant learning or knowledge,

The majority believes these conclusions rest upon practical judgments that at most suggest the statute is unwise, not that it is unconstitutional. Legal distinctions, however, are often matters of degree. . . . And in this case the failings of degree are so serious that they amount to failings of constitutional kind. Although the Copyright Clause grants broad legislative power to Congress, that grant has limits. And in my view this statute falls outside them.

The "monopoly privileges" that the Copyright Clause confers "are neither unlimited nor primarily designed to provide a special private benefit." Sony Corp. of America v. Universal City Studios, Inc., 464 U.S. 417, 429 (1984). . . . This Court has made clear that the Clause's limitations are judicially enforceable. And, in assessing this statute for that purpose, I would take into account the fact that the Constitution is a single document, that it contains both a Copyright Clause and a First Amendment, and that the two are related.

The Copyright Clause and the First Amendment seek related objectives—the creation and dissemination of information. When working in tandem, these provisions mutually reinforce each other, the first serving as an "engine of free expression,"

Harper & Row, Publishers, Inc. v. Nation Enterprises, 471 U.S. 539, 558 (1985), the second assuring that government throws up no obstacle to its dissemination. At the same time, a particular statute that exceeds proper Copyright Clause bounds may set Clause and Amendment at cross-purposes, thereby depriving the public of the speech-related benefits that the Founders, through both, have promised.

. . . I would find that the statute lacks the constitutionally necessary rational support (1) if the significant benefits that it bestows are private, not public; (2) if it threatens seriously to undermine the expressive values that the Copyright Clause embodies; and (3) if it cannot find justification in any significant Clause-related objective. Where, after examination of the statute, it becomes difficult, if not impossible, even to dispute these characterizations, Congress' "choice is clearly wrong." Helvering v. Davis, 301 U.S. 619, 640 (1937).

Because we must examine the relevant statutory effects in light of the Copyright Clause's own purposes, we should begin by reviewing the basic objectives of that Clause. The Clause authorizes a "tax on readers for the purpose of giving a bounty to writers." 56 Parl. Deb. (3d Ser.) (1841) 341, 350 (Lord Macaulay). Why? What constitutional purposes does the "bounty" serve?

The Constitution itself describes the basic Clause objective as one of "promot[ing] the Progress of Science," i.e., knowledge and learning. The Clause exists not to "provide a special private benefit," *Sony,* supra, at 429, but "to stimulate artistic creativity for the general public good," Twentieth Century Music Corp. v. Aiken, 422 U.S. 151, 156 (1975). It does so by "motivat[ing] the creative activity of authors" through "the provision of a special reward." *Sony,* supra, at 429. The "reward" is a means, not an end. And that is why the copyright term is limited. It is limited so that its beneficiaries—the public—"will not be permanently deprived of the fruits of an artist's labors." Stewart v. Abend, 495 U.S. 207, 228 (1990).

. . .

This statute, like virtually every copyright statute, imposes upon the public certain expression-related costs in the form of (1) royalties that may be higher than necessary to evoke creation of the relevant work, and (2) a requirement that one seeking to reproduce a copyrighted work must obtain the copyright holder's permission. The first of these costs translates into higher prices that will potentially restrict a work's dissemination. The second means search costs that themselves may prevent reproduction even where the author has no objection. Although these costs are, in a sense, inevitable concomitants of copyright protection, there are special reasons for thinking them especially serious here.

First, the present statute primarily benefits the holders of existing copyrights, i.e., copyrights on works already created. And a Congressional Research Service (CRS) study prepared for Congress indicates that the added royalty-related sum that the law will transfer to existing copyright holders is large. E. Rappaport, CRS Report for Congress, Copyright Term Extension: Estimating the Economic Values (1998) (hereinafter CRS Report). In conjunction with official figures on copyright renewals, the CRS Report indicates that only about 2% of copyrights between 55 and 75 years old retain commercial value—i.e., still generate royalties after that time. But books, songs, and movies of that vintage still earn about $400 million per year in royalties. CRS Report 8, 12, 15. Hence, (despite declining consumer interest in any given work over time) one might conservatively estimate that 20 extra years of copyright protection will mean the transfer of several billion extra royalty dollars to holders of existing copyrights—copyrights that, together, already will have earned many billions of dollars in royalty "reward." See id., at 16.

The extra royalty payments will not come from thin air. Rather, they ultimately come from those who wish to read or see or hear those classic books or films or recordings that have survived. Even the $500,000 that United Airlines has had to pay for the right to play George Gershwin's 1924 classic Rhapsody in Blue represents a cost of doing business, potentially reflected in the ticket prices of those who fly. . . .

A second, equally important, cause for concern arises out of the fact that copyright extension imposes a "permissions" requirement—not only upon potential users of "classic" works that still retain commercial value, but also upon potential users of any other work still in copyright. Again using CRS estimates, one can estimate that, by 2018, the number of such works 75 years of age or older will be about 350,000. See Brief for Petitioners 7. Because the Copyright Act of 1976 abolished the requirement that an owner must renew a copyright, such still-in-copyright works (of little or no commercial value) will eventually number in the millions. . . .

The potential users of such works include not only movie buffs and aging jazz fans, but also historians, scholars, teachers, writers, artists, database operators, and researchers of all kinds—those who want to make the past accessible for their own use or for that of others. The permissions requirement can inhibit their ability to accomplish that task. Indeed, in an age where computer-accessible databases promise to facilitate research and learning, the permissions requirement can stand as a significant obstacle to realization of that technological hope.

The reason is that the permissions requirement can inhibit or prevent the use of old works (particularly those without commercial value): (1) because it may prove expensive to track down or to contract with the copyright holder, (2) because the holder may prove impossible to find, or (3) because the holder when found may deny permission either outright or through misinformed efforts to bargain.

. . . The older the work, the less likely it retains commercial value, and the harder it will likely prove to find the current copyright holder. The older the work, the more likely it will prove useful to the historian, artist, or teacher. The older the work, the less likely it is that a sense of authors' rights can justify a copyright holder's decision not to permit reproduction, for the more likely it is that the copyright holder making the decision is not the work's creator, but, say, a corporation or a great-grandchild whom the work's creator never knew. . . . And the qualitative costs to education, learning, and research will multiply as our children become ever more dependent for the content of their knowledge upon computer-accessible databases—thereby condemning that which is not so accessible, say, the cultural content of early 20th-century history, to a kind of intellectual purgatory from which it will not easily emerge.

. . .

What copyright-related benefits might justify the statute's extension of copyright protection? First, no one could reasonably conclude that copyright's traditional economic rationale applies here. The extension will not act as an economic spur encouraging authors to create new works. . . . No potential author can reasonably believe that he has more than a tiny chance of writing a classic that will survive commercially long enough for the copyright extension to matter. After all, if, after 55 to 75 years, only 2% of all copyrights retain commercial value, the percentage surviving after 75 years or more (a typical pre-extension copyright term)—must be far smaller. . . . Using assumptions about the time value of money provided us by a group of economists (including five Nobel prize winners), Brief for George A. Akerlof et al. as Amici Curiae 5-7, it seems fair to say that, for example, a 1% likelihood of earning $100 annually for 20 years, starting 75 years into the future, is worth less than seven cents today.

What potential Shakespeare, Wharton, or Hemingway would be moved by such a sum? What monetarily motivated Melville would not realize that he could do better for his grandchildren by putting a few dollars into an interest-bearing bank account? The Court itself finds no evidence to the contrary. . . .

Regardless, even if . . . somehow, somewhere, some potential author might be moved by the thought of great-grandchildren receiving copyright royalties a century hence, so might some potential author also be moved by the thought of royalties being paid for two centuries, five centuries, 1,000 years, "'til the End of Time." And from a rational economic perspective the time difference among these periods makes no real difference. The present extension will produce a copyright period of protection that, even under conservative assumptions, is worth more than 99.8% of protection in perpetuity (more than 99.99% for a songwriter like Irving Berlin and a song like Alexander's Ragtime Band). . . . The lack of a practically meaningful distinction from an author's ex ante perspective between (a) the statute's extended terms and (b) an infinite term makes this latest extension difficult to square with the Constitution's insistence on "limited Times." . . .

. . .

In any event, the incentive-related numbers are far too small for Congress to have concluded rationally, even with respect to new works, that the extension's economic-incentive effect could justify the serious expression-related harms earlier described. And, of course, in respect to works already created—the source of many of the harms previously described—the statute creates no economic incentive at all.

. . .

Finally, the Court mentions as possible justifications "demographic, economic, and technological changes"—by which the Court apparently means the facts that today people communicate with the help of modern technology, live longer, and have children at a later age. The first fact seems to argue not for, but instead against, extension. The second fact seems already corrected for by the 1976 Act's life-plus-50 term, which automatically grows with lifespans. . . . And the third fact—that adults are having children later in life—is a makeweight at best, providing no explanation of why the 1976 Act's term of 50 years after an author's death—a longer term than was available to authors themselves for most of our Nation's history—is an insufficient potential bequest. The weakness of these final rationales simply underscores the conclusion that emerges from consideration of earlier attempts at justification: There is no legitimate, serious copyright-related justification for this statute.

. . .

This statute will cause serious expression-related harm. It will likely restrict traditional dissemination of copyrighted works. It will likely inhibit new forms of dissemination through the use of new technology. It threatens to interfere with efforts to preserve our Nation's historical and cultural heritage and efforts to use that heritage, say, to educate our Nation's children. It is easy to understand how the statute might benefit the private financial interests of corporations or heirs who own existing copyrights. But I cannot find any constitutionally legitimate, copyright-related way in which the statute will benefit the public. Indeed, in respect to existing works, the serious public harm and the virtually nonexistent public benefit could not be more clear.

I have set forth the analysis upon which I rest these judgments. This analysis leads inexorably to the conclusion that the statute cannot be understood rationally to advance a constitutionally legitimate interest. The statute falls outside the scope of legislative power that the Copyright Clause, read in light of the First Amendment, grants to Congress. I would hold the statute unconstitutional.

I respectfully dissent.

[A separate dissent by Justice Stevens is omitted.]

"I Got You Babe"
Sonny and Cher

THE REST OF THE STORY . . .

The statute that was challenged in the case, the Copyright Term Extension Act, was popularly known as the "Sonny Bono Act." Congressman Bono had been a co-sponsor of the original bill in the House of Representative prior to his untimely death in 1998 by skiing into a tree in Nevada. His widow, Mary Bono, who succeeded him in the House, carried on his support for the bill through its passage. The act was also sometimes derisively called the "Mickey Mouse Act" because the Disney Company was a major force behind its passage.

Notes and Questions

1. *Subsequent legal developments.* In *Golan v. Holder*, 565 U.S. 302 (2012), by a 6-to-2 vote, the Supreme Court extended *Eldred*, holding that the Constitution didn't prevent Congress from permitting foreign works that had fallen into the public domain to become copyrighted once again, in accordance with the Berne Convention for the Protection of Literary and Artistic Works.

2. *Purpose of the CTEA.* Does it matter why Congress enacted the CTEA? Suppose Congress's motivation was to enrich the owners of copyrights of preexisting works about to fall into the public domain. Given the language of Article I, section 8 of the Constitution ("promote the Progress of Science and the Useful Arts . . ."), would this be a legitimate reason? Does that matter?

3. *Outer temporal limits?* After *Eldred*, are there any outer limits to how long Congress may extend the duration of copyrights, short of a literally infinite copyright term? Suppose Congress decided to extend the copyright term to 1,000 years; would that be unconstitutional?

c. Trademarks

The background and basics of trademark law. Volkswagen's VW, MGM's lion, Nike's swoosh, Pepsi-Cola's script-written name—all are examples of trademarks. Trademarks have been around almost as long as trade itself. Marks such as a potter's mark have been found on artifacts from ancient civilizations in China, India, Greece, Egypt, and elsewhere, dating back as far as 4,000 years ago.

Modern trademark law defines a trademark as any "word, name, symbol, or device" used by a person "to identify his or her goods" from those sold by others, and "to identify the source of the goods." 15 U.S.C. § 1127. The reasons for protecting trademarks resemble important rationales for the right of publicity but differ from the policies behind patent and copyright. As we have seen, patents and copyrights are intended to encourage creativity, invention, and expression. Trademark law, by contrast, protects the first to use a distinctive mark in commerce (the first-in-time principle, again). As the Supreme Court has said, trademark protection "does not depend upon . . . invention, discovery, or any work of the brain." *Trade-Mark Cases*, 100 U.S. 82, 94 (1879). Three main policies underlie trademark law. First, exclusive rights to trademarks prevent consumer confusion about the origin of the goods or service. Second, they encourage trademark owners to invest in and maintain a consistent level of quality. Finally, they prevent competitors from freeriding on the trademark owner's goodwill.

Originally, trademark protection was a matter of the state common law of unfair competition. This common law foundation is now supplemented by the federal Lanham Act, which has been amended several times and is based on the Commerce Clause. The Lanham Act allows a trademark owner to register the mark with the Patent and Trademark Office, but registration is not required for the mark's validity.

Generally speaking, words, symbols, jingles, and other sounds can be trademarked. The Supreme Court has even held that colors can be trademarked under specific circumstances. See Qualitex v. Jacobson Products Co., Inc., 514 U.S. 159 (1995). As a rule, three requirements must be met for trademark protection: (1) distinctiveness; (2) non-functionality; and (3) first use in trade.

► *Distinctiveness*—This means that the mark must distinguish the good or service of one person from those of another. The Lanham Act categorizes marks according to varying degrees of distinctiveness. It is easiest to demonstrate distinctiveness fanciful marks that coin a new word for a brand (like Exxon gasoline) or arbitrary marks that use an existing word to describe a product that has nothing to do with the product (like Apple computers). Fanciful and arbitrary marks typically get the strongest protection. Suggestive marks are also considered inherently distinctive. They evoke the nature of the good subtly but still require the consumer to use "imagination and perception" to determine the nature of the product being sold. Examples include Citibank or Tide detergent. Descriptive marks describe a purpose or characteristic of the product. Think of Almond Joy candy bars or Bed Bath & Beyond stores. Descriptive marks can still be protected if the product has acquired "secondary meaning" in the relevant marketplace. For example, Coca-Cola started off as a description of the kind of beverage being sold but has come to be synonymous with a particular drink sold by a particular company. So, too, with Sharp television sets.

► *Non-functionality*—Trademark law does not protect on the basis of functionality. That is what patent law does. Hence, if an aspect of a good is exclusively functional, it cannot be protected by trademark law. A product feature is functional "if it is essential to the use or purpose of the article or if it affects the cost or quality of the article, that is, if exclusive use of the feature would put competitors at a significant non-reputation-related disadvantage." Id. at 165.

► *First use in trade*—An exclusive right to use a mark requires first use, not just first adoption, of the mark in a particular geographic market. Moreover, under the Lanham Act, the use must be in commerce, which has a narrower scope than trade.

Just as the public trust doctrine prevents some types of real property from being privatized (e.g., navigable waterways), patent law prevents patentees from monopolizing some ideas (e.g., laws of nature), and copyright law prohibits people from obtaining a copyright in ideas themselves (as opposed to expressions), there are limits on what words can be trademarked. A generic term is synonymous with a product itself, rather than with a particular maker of that product. In order to promote competition in the marketplace, the Lanham Act treats generic terms as part of the public domain. Policing the boundaries of generic versus non-generic marks is an important task for the Patent and Trademark Office and, ultimately, the courts.

UNITED STATES PATENT AND TRADEMARK OFFICE v. BOOKING.COM B.V.

Supreme Court of the United States, 2020
2020 WL 3518365 (U.S. 6/30/2020)

GINSBURG, J. This case concerns eligibility for federal trademark registration. Respondent Booking.com, an enterprise that maintains a travel-reservation website by the same name, sought to register the mark "Booking.com." Concluding that "Booking.com" is a generic name for online hotel-reservation services, the U.S. Patent and Trademark Office (PTO) refused registration.

A generic name—the name of a class of products or services—is ineligible for federal trademark registration. The word "booking," the parties do not dispute, is generic for hotel-reservation services. "Booking.com" must also be generic, the PTO maintains, under an encompassing rule the PTO currently urges us to adopt: The combination of a generic word and ".com" is generic.

In accord with the first- and second-instance judgments in this case, we reject the PTO's sweeping rule. A term styled "generic.com" is a generic name for a class of goods or services only if the term has that meaning to consumers. Consumers, according to lower court determinations uncontested here by the PTO, do not perceive the term "Booking.com" to signify online hotel-reservation services as a class. In circumstances like those this case presents, a "generic.com" term is not generic and can be eligible for federal trademark registration.

I

A trademark distinguishes one producer's goods or services from another's. Guarding a trademark against use by others, this Court has explained, "secure[s] to the owner of the mark the goodwill" of her business and "protect[s] the ability of consumers to distinguish among competing producers." Trademark protection has roots in common law and equity. Today, the Lanham Act, enacted in 1946, provides federal statutory protection for trademarks. 15 U.S.C. § 1051 et seq. We have recognized that federal trademark protection, supplementing state law, "supports the free flow of commerce" and "foster[s] competition."

The Lanham Act not only arms trademark owners with federal claims for relief; importantly, it establishes a system of federal trademark registration. The owner of a mark on the principal register enjoys "valuable benefits," including a presumption that the mark is valid. The supplemental register contains other product and service designations, some of which could one day gain eligibility for the principal register. The supplemental register accords more modest benefits; notably, a listing on that register announces one's use of the designation to others considering a similar mark.

Prime among the conditions for registration, the mark must be one "by which the goods of the applicant may be distinguished from the goods of others." § 1052; see § 1091(a) (supplemental register contains "marks capable of distinguishing . . . goods or services"). Distinctiveness is often expressed on an increasing scale: Word marks "may be (1) generic; (2) descriptive; (3) suggestive; (4) arbitrary; or (5) fanciful." *Two Pesos, Inc. v. Taco Cabana, Inc.,* 505 U.S. 763, 768 (1992).

The more distinctive the mark, the more readily it qualifies for the principal register. The most distinctive marks—those that are "'arbitrary' ('Camel' cigarettes), 'fanciful' ('Kodak' film), or 'suggestive' ('Tide' laundry detergent)"—may be placed on the principal register because they are "inherently distinctive." "Descriptive" terms, in contrast, are not eligible for the principal register based on their inherent qualities alone. The Lanham Act, "liberaliz[ing] the common law," "extended protection to descriptive marks." But to be placed on the principal register, descriptive terms must achieve significance "in the minds of the public" as identifying the applicant's goods or services—a quality called "acquired distinctiveness" or "secondary meaning." *Wal-Mart Stores,* [*Inc. v. Samara Brothers, Inc.,* 529 U.S. 205, 211 (2000)]; see § 1052(e), (f). Without secondary meaning, descriptive terms may be eligible only for the supplemental register. § 1091(a).

At the lowest end of the distinctiveness scale is "the generic name for the goods or services." §§ 1127, 1064(3), 1065(4). The name of the good itself (e.g., "wine") is incapable of "distinguish[ing] [one producer's goods] from the goods of others" and is therefore ineligible for registration. § 1052; see § 1091(a). Indeed, generic terms are ordinarily ineligible for protection as trademarks at all. See Restatement (Third) of Unfair Competition § 15, p. 142 (1993).

Booking.com is a digital travel company that provides hotel reservations and other services under the brand "Booking.com," which is also the domain name of its website. Booking.com filed applications to register four marks in connection with travel-related services, each with different visual features but all containing the term "Booking.com."

Both a PTO examining attorney and the PTO's Trademark Trial and Appeal Board concluded that the term "Booking.com" is generic for the services at issue and is therefore unregistrable. "Booking," the Board observed, means making travel reservations, and ".com" signifies a commercial website. The Board then ruled that "customers would understand the term BOOKING.COM primarily to refer to an online reservation service for travel, tours, and lodgings." Alternatively, the Board held that even if "Booking.com" is descriptive, not generic, it is unregistrable because it lacks secondary meaning.

Booking.com sought review in the U.S. District Court for the Eastern District of Virginia, invoking a mode of review that allows Booking.com to introduce evidence not presented to the agency. Relying in significant part on Booking.com's new evidence of consumer perception, the District Court concluded that "Booking.com"—unlike "booking"—is not generic. The "consuming public," the court found, "primarily understands that BOOKING.COM does not refer to a genus, rather it is descriptive of services involving 'booking' available at that domain name." *Booking.com B.V. v. Matal,* 278 F. Supp. 3d 891, 918 (2017). Having determined that "Booking.com" is descriptive, the District Court additionally found that the term has acquired secondary meaning as to hotel-reservation services. For those services, the District Court therefore concluded, Booking.com's marks meet the distinctiveness requirement for registration.

The PTO appealed only the District Court's determination that "Booking.com" is not generic. Finding no error in the District Court's assessment of how consumers perceive the term "Booking.com," the Court of Appeals for the Fourth Circuit affirmed the court of first instance's judgment. In so ruling, the appeals court rejected the PTO's contention that the combination of ".com" with a generic term like "booking" "is necessarily generic." 915 F.3d 171, 184 (2019). Dissenting in relevant part, Judge Wynn concluded that the District Court mistakenly presumed that "generic.com" terms are usually descriptive, not generic.

We granted certiorari . . . and now affirm the Fourth Circuit's decision.

II

Although the parties here disagree about the circumstances in which terms like "Booking.com" rank as generic, several guiding principles are common ground. First, a "generic" term names a "class" of goods or services, rather than any particular feature or exemplification of the class. Second, for a compound term, the distinctiveness inquiry trains on the term's meaning as a whole, not its parts in isolation. Third, the relevant meaning of a term is its meaning to consumers. Eligibility for registration, all agree, turns on the mark's capacity to "distinguis[h]" goods "in commerce." § 1052. Evidencing the Lanham Act's focus on consumer perception, the section governing cancellation of registration provides that "[t]he primary significance of the registered mark to the relevant public . . . shall be the test for determining whether the registered mark has become the generic name of goods or services." § 1064(3).

Under these principles, whether "Booking.com" is generic turns on whether that term, taken as a whole, signifies to consumers the class of online hotel-reservation services. Thus, if "Booking.com" were generic, we might expect consumers to understand Travelocity—another such service—to be a "Booking.com." We might similarly expect that a consumer, searching for a trusted source of online hotel-reservation services, could ask a frequent traveler to name her favorite "Booking.com" provider.

Consumers do not in fact perceive the term "Booking.com" that way, the courts be-low determined. The PTO no longer disputes that determination. That should resolve this case: Because "Booking.com" is not a generic name to consumers, it is not generic.

III

Opposing that conclusion, the PTO urges a nearly per se rule that would render "Booking.com" ineligible for registration regardless of specific evidence of consumer perception. In the PTO's view, which the dissent embraces, when a generic term is combined with a generic top-level domain like ".com," the resulting combination is generic. In other words, every "generic.com" term is generic according to the PTO, absent exceptional circumstances.

The PTO's own past practice appears to reflect no such comprehensive rule. Existing registrations inconsistent with the rule the PTO now advances would be at risk of cancellation if the PTO's current view were to prevail. See § 1064(3). We decline to adopt a rule essentially excluding registration of "generic.com" marks. As explained below, we discern no support for the PTO's current view in trademark law or policy.

The PTO urges that the exclusionary rule it advocates follows from a common-law principle, applied in *Goodyear's India Rubber Glove Mfg. Co. v. Goodyear Rubber Co.*, 128 U.S. 598 (1888), that a generic corporate designation added to a generic term does not confer trademark eligibility. In *Goodyear*, a decision predating the Lanham Act, this Court held that "Goodyear Rubber Company" was not "capable of exclusive appropriation." *Id.*, at 602. Standing alone, the term "Goodyear Rubber" could not serve as a trademark because it referred, in those days, to "well-known classes of goods produced by the process known as Goodyear's invention." *Ibid.* "[A]ddition of the word 'Company'" supplied no protectable meaning, the Court concluded, because adding "Company" "only indicates that parties have formed an association or partnership to deal in such goods." Ibid. Permitting exclusive rights in "Goodyear Rubber Company" (or "Wine Company, Cotton Company, or Grain Company"), the Court explained, would tread on the right of all persons "to deal in such articles, and to publish the fact to the world." *Id.*, at 602–603.

"Generic.com," the PTO maintains, is like "Generic Company" and is therefore ineligible for trademark protection, let alone federal registration. According to the PTO, adding ".com" to a generic term—like adding "Company"—"conveys no additional meaning that would distinguish [one provider's] services from those of other providers." The dissent endorses that proposition: "Generic.com" conveys that the generic good or service is offered online "and nothing more."

That premise is faulty. A "generic.com" term might also convey to consumers a source-identifying characteristic: an association with a particular website. As the PTO and the dissent elsewhere acknowledge, only one entity can occupy a particular Internet domain name at a time, so "[a] consumer who is familiar with that aspect of the domain-name system can infer that BOOKING.COM refers to some specific entity." Thus, consumers could understand a given "generic.com" term to describe the corresponding website or to identify the website's proprietor. We therefore resist the PTO's position that "generic.com" terms are capable of signifying only an entire class of online goods or services and, hence, are categorically incapable of identifying a source.

The PTO's reliance on *Goodyear* is flawed in another respect. The PTO understands *Goodyear* to hold that "Generic Company" terms "are ineligible for trademark protection as a matter of law"—regardless of how "consumers would understand" the term. But, . . . whether a term is generic depends on its meaning to consumers. That bedrock principle of the Lanham Act is incompatible with an unyielding legal rule that entirely disregards consumer perception. Instead, *Goodyear* reflects a more modest principle harmonious with Congress' subsequent enactment: A compound of generic elements is generic if the combination yields no additional meaning to consumers capable of distinguishing the goods or services.

The PTO also invokes the oft-repeated principle that "no matter how much money and effort the user of a generic term has poured into promoting the sale of its merchandise . . . , it cannot deprive competing manufacturers of the product of the right to call an article by its name." *Abercrombie & Fitch Co. v. Hunting World, Inc.*, 537 F.2d 4, 9 (CA2 1976). That principle presupposes that a generic term is at issue. But the PTO's only legal basis for deeming "generic.com" terms generic is its mistaken reliance on *Goodyear*.

While we reject the rule proffered by the PTO that "generic.com" terms are generic names, we do not embrace a rule automatically classifying such terms as nongeneric. Whether any given "generic.com" term is generic, we hold, depends on whether consumers in fact perceive that term as the name of a class or, instead, as a term capable of distinguishing among members of the class.

The PTO, echoed by the dissent, objects that protecting "generic.com" terms as trademarks would disserve trademark law's animating policies. We disagree.

The PTO's principal concern is that trademark protection for a term like "Booking.com" would hinder competitors. But the PTO does not assert that others seeking to offer online hotel-reservation services need to call their services "Booking.com." Rather, the PTO fears that trademark protection for "Booking.com" could exclude or inhibit competitors from using the term "booking" or adopting domain names like "ebooking.com" or "hotel-booking.com." The PTO's objection, therefore, is not to exclusive use of "Booking.com" as a mark, but to undue control over similar language, i.e., "booking," that others should remain free to use.

That concern attends any descriptive mark. Responsive to it, trademark law hems in the scope of such marks short of denying trademark protection altogether. Notably, a competitor's use does not infringe a mark unless it is likely to confuse consumers. See §§ 1114(1), 1125(a)(1)(A). In assessing the likelihood of confusion, courts consider the mark's distinctiveness: "The weaker a mark, the fewer are the junior uses that will trigger a likelihood of consumer confusion." [2 J. McCarthy, Trademarks and Unfair Competition § 11.76 (5th ed. 2019)]. When a mark incorporates generic or highly descriptive components, consumers are less likely to think that other uses of the common element emanate from the mark's owner. *Ibid.* Similarly, "[i]n a 'crowded' field of look-alike marks" (e.g., hotel names including the word "grand"), consumers "may have learned to carefully pick out" one mark from another. *Id.*, § 11:85. And even where some consumer confusion exists, the doctrine known as classic fair use, see *id.*, § 11:45, protects from liability anyone who uses a descriptive term, "fairly and in good faith" and "otherwise than as a mark," merely to describe her own goods. 15 U.S.C. § 1115(b)(4).

These doctrines guard against the anticompetitive effects the PTO identifies, ensuring that registration of "Booking.com" would not yield its holder a monopoly on the term "booking." Booking.com concedes that "Booking.com" would be a "weak" mark. The mark is descriptive, Booking.com recognizes, making it "harder . . . to show a likelihood of confusion." Furthermore, because its mark is one of many "similarly worded marks," Booking.com accepts that close variations are unlikely to infringe. And Booking.com acknowledges that federal registration of "Booking.com" would not prevent competitors from using the word "booking" to describe their own services.

The PTO also doubts that owners of "generic.com" brands need trademark protection in addition to existing competitive advantages. Booking.com, the PTO argues, has already seized a domain name that no other website can use and is easy for consumers to find. Consumers might enter "the word 'booking' in a search engine," the PTO observes, or "proceed directly to 'booking.com' in the expectation that [online hotel-booking] services will be offered at that address." Those competitive advantages, however, do not inevitably disqualify a mark from federal registration. All descriptive marks are intuitively linked to the product or service and thus might be easy for consumers to find using a search engine or telephone directory. The Lanham Act permits registration nonetheless. See § 1052(e), (f). And the PTO fails to explain how the exclusive connection between a domain name and its owner makes the domain name a generic term all should be free to use. That connection makes trademark protection more appropriate, not less. . . .

The PTO challenges the judgment below on a sole ground: It urges that, as a rule, combining a generic term with ".com" yields a generic composite. For the above-stated reasons, we decline a rule of that order, one that would largely disallow registration of "generic.com" terms and open the door to cancellation of scores of currently registered marks. Accordingly, the judgment of the Court of Appeals for the Fourth Circuit regarding eligibility for trademark registration is

Affirmed.

[Justice Sotomayor's concurring opinion is omitted.]

Breyer, J., dissenting. What is Booking.com? To answer this question, one need only consult the term itself. Respondent provides an online booking service. The company's name informs the consumer of the basic nature of its business and nothing more. Therein lies the root of my disagreement with the majority.

Trademark law does not protect generic terms, meaning terms that do no more than name the product or service itself. This principle preserves the linguistic commons by preventing one producer from appropriating to its own exclusive use a term needed by others to describe their goods or services. Today, the Court holds that the addition of ".com" to an otherwise generic term, such as "booking," can yield a protectable trademark. Because I believe this result is inconsistent with trademark principles and sound trademark policy, I respectfully dissent.

. . .

In *Goodyear*, 128 U.S. 598, we held that appending the word "'Company'" to the generic name for a class of goods does not yield a protectable compound term. The addition of a corporate designation, we explained, "only indicates that parties have formed an association or partnership to deal in such goods." *Id.*, at 602. . . .

I cannot agree with respondent that the 1946 Lanham Act "repudiate[d] *Goodyear* and its ilk." It is true that the Lanham Act altered the common law in certain important respects. Most significantly, it extended trademark protection to descriptive marks that have acquired secondary meaning. But it did not disturb the basic principle that generic terms are ineligible for trademark protection, and nothing in the Act suggests that Congress intended to overturn *Goodyear*. We normally assume that Congress did not overturn a common-law principle absent some indication to the contrary. I can find no such indication here. . . .

More fundamentally, the *Goodyear* principle is sound as a matter of law and logic. *Goodyear* recognized that designations such as "Company," "Corp.," and "Inc." merely indicate corporate form and therefore do nothing to distinguish one firm's goods or services from all others'. 128 U.S. at 602. It follows that the addition of such a corporate designation does not "magically transform a generic name for a product or service into a trademark, thereby giving a right to exclude others." 2 McCarthy § 12:39. In other words, where a compound term consists simply of a generic term plus a corporate designation, the whole is necessarily no greater than the sum of its parts.

This case requires us to apply these principles in the novel context of internet domain names. . . . The question at issue here is whether a term that takes the form "generic.com" is generic in the ordinary course. In my view, appending ".com" to a generic term ordinarily yields no meaning beyond that of its constituent parts. Because the term "Booking.com" is just such an ordinary "generic.com" term, in my view, it is not eligible for trademark registration. . . .

. . . The majority believes that *Goodyear* is inapposite because of the nature of the domain name system. Because only one entity can hold the contractual rights to a particular domain name at a time, it contends, consumers may infer that a "generic.com" domain name refers to some specific entity.

That fact does not distinguish *Goodyear*. A generic term may suggest that it is associated with a specific entity. That does not render it nongeneric. For example, "Wine, Inc." implies the existence of a specific legal entity incorporated under the laws of some State. Likewise, consumers may perceive "The Wine Company" to refer to some specific company rather than a genus of companies. But the addition of the definite article "the" obviously does not transform the generic nature of that term. True, these terms do not carry the exclusivity of a domain name. But that functional exclusivity does not negate the principle animating *Goodyear*: Terms that merely convey the nature of the producer's business should remain free for all to use.

. . .

In addition to the doctrinal concerns discussed above, granting trademark protection to "generic.com" marks threatens serious anticompetitive consequences in the online marketplace.

The owners of short, generic domain names enjoy all the advantages of doing business under a generic name. These advantages exist irrespective of the trademark laws. Generic names are easy to remember. Because they immediately convey the nature of the business, the owner needs to expend less effort and expense educating consumers. And a generic business name may create the impression that it is the most authoritative and trustworthy source of the particular good or service. These advantages make it harder for distinctively named businesses to compete.

Owners of generic domain names enjoy additional competitive advantages unique to the internet—again, regardless of trademark protection. Most importantly, domain name ownership confers automatic exclusivity. Multiple brick-and-mortar companies could style themselves "The Wine Company," but there can be only one "wine.com." And unlike the trademark system, that exclusivity is worldwide.

Generic domains are also easier for consumers to find. A consumer who wants to buy wine online may perform a keyword search and be directed to "wine.com." Or he may simply type "wine.com" into his browser's address bar, expecting to find a website selling wine. . . .

Granting trademark protection to "generic.com" marks confers additional competitive benefits on their owners by allowing them to exclude others from using similar domain names. Federal registration would allow respondent to threaten trademark lawsuits against competitors using domains such as "Bookings.com," "eBooking.com," "Booker.com," or "Bookit.com." Respondent says that it would not do so. But other firms may prove less restrained.

. . .

Under the majority's reasoning, many businesses could obtain a trademark by adding ".com" to the generic name of their product (e.g., pizza.com, flowers.com, and so forth). As the internet grows larger, as more and more firms use it to sell their products, the risk of anticompetitive consequences grows. Those consequences can nudge the economy in an anticompetitive direction. At the extreme, that direction points towards one firm per product, the opposite of the competitive multifirm marketplace that our basic economic laws seek to achieve.

Not to worry, the Court responds, infringement doctrines such as likelihood of confusion and fair use will restrict the scope of protection afforded to "generic.com" marks. This response will be cold comfort to competitors of "generic.com" brands. Owners of such marks may seek to extend the boundaries of their marks through litigation, and may, at times succeed. Even if ultimately unsuccessful, the threat of costly litigation will no doubt chill others from using variants on the registered mark and privilege established firms over new entrants to the market.

In sum, the term "Booking.com" refers to an internet booking service, which is the generic product that respondent and its competitors sell. No more and no less. The same is true of "generic.com" terms more generally. By making such terms eligible for trademark protection, I fear that today's decision will lead to a proliferation of "generic.com" marks, granting their owners a monopoly over a zone of useful, easy-to-remember domains. This result would tend to inhibit, rather than to promote, free competition in online commerce. I respectfully dissent.

Notes and Questions

1. *"The consumer is king."* As the Court in *Booking.com* explains, trademark law does not extend protection to words or symbols that are the generic names for goods or services. However, although generic terms are not protected, a word or symbol that is "descriptive" may be protected if it has come to acquire a secondary meaning, i.e., consumers have come to identify it with a single producer of that product, rather than merely as a description of its characteristics.

How does one determine whether a word or symbol is generic or descriptive? The trademark statute does not define these terms. The Court in *Booking.com* rejected the PTO's argument that a per se rule should be applied, declaring instead that whether a word or symbol is generic turns on consumer perception: "[W]hether 'Booking.com' is generic turns on whether the term, taken as a whole, signifies to consumers the class of hotel reservations services." Now that consumer perception is decisive, what role(s) will consumer surveys play in trademark litigation and registration?

2. *Generic + generic = non-generic?* In *Goodyear*, the Supreme Court previously had established the principle that "a generic corporate designation added to a generic term does not confer trademark eligibility." Justice Breyer believes that principle controls here. Why does the majority not think so?

3. *Pro- or anti-competitive?* In his dissent, Justice Breyer argues that the Court's holding risks a "proliferation of 'generic.com' marks" that would grant monopolies over easy-to-remember domain names to their owners. "This result," he concluded, "would tend to inhibit, rather than to promote, free competition in online commerce." Is he right about this? Consider the majority's comments regarding the strength of the mark.

4. *Immoral or offensive trademarks?* A provision of the Trademark Act prohibited federal registration of marks that are "immoral or scandalous." In Iancu v. Brunetti, 139 S. Ct. 2294 (2019), the Supreme Court held that the Constitution prohibits statutory distinctions between commercial speech based on its "viewpoint" and therefore that provision of the Trademark Act violates the First Amendment. Brunetti established a clothing line under the label "F-U-C-T," and he sought to register that trademark but was prohibited from doing so under the contested provision of the Trademark Act.

Previously, the Court held as unenforceable under the First Amendment a provision of the federal Lanham Act that denied trademark registration to names or marks that "disparage" a person or "bring [them] into contempt or disrepute." Matal v. Tam, 137 S. Ct. 1744 (2017). An Asian-American rock band named "The Slants" sought trademark protection for its name. As the Court stated, the band believed that "by taking that slur as the name of their group, they will help to 'reclaim' the term and drain its denigrating force." Id. at 1751. The Court held that this provision of the statute violated the Free Speech Clause of the First Amendment.

Subsequent Possession: Acquisition of Property by Find, Adverse Possession, and Gift

Possession, as we saw in the preceding chapter, is a powerful concept in the law of property. By virtue of *first* possession one can make an unowned thing, or a thing before enjoyed only by all in common, one's own. But suppose the principle of first in time, so dominant in Chapter 1, no longer holds. Suppose that something *already* owned by someone else, say *A*, *subsequently* comes into the possession of *B*, and without *A*'s consent. Surprisingly enough, *B* might still become the thing's "owner," as the first two sections of this chapter make clear. Even without being declared the owner, *B* might nevertheless be granted considerable protection by the legal system. But when does *B* have "possession," so as to enjoy this favored position, and why are possessors favored anyway? These important questions figured in the last chapter, and they do so again in this one.

Another common theme persists. Chapter 1 was concerned, among other things, with acquisition of property other than by purchase, and this chapter is as well—right through to its final section, where we examine the law of gifts. Possession plays a role there, too.

A. ACQUISITION BY FIND

Possession is eleven points in the law.—

> *Colley Cibber,*
> Woman's Wit, Act I (1697)

Possession is very strong; rather more than nine points of the law.—

> *Lord Mansfield,*
> Corporation of Kingston-upon-Hull v. Horner,
> 98 Eng. Rep. 807, 815 (1774)

Finders keepers, losers weepers.—

> *Old Scottish proverb*

ARMORY v. DELAMIRIE

King's Bench, 1722
1 Strange 505

The plaintiff being a chimney sweeper's boy found a jewel and carried it to the defendant's shop (who was a goldsmith) to know what it was, and delivered it into the hands of the apprentice, who under pretence of weighing it, took out the stones, and calling to the master to let him know it came to three halfpence, the master offered the boy the money, who refused to take it, and insisted to have the thing again; whereupon the apprentice delivered him back the socket without the stones. And now in trover against the master these points were ruled:

1. That the finder of a jewel, though he does not by such finding acquire an absolute property or ownership, yet he has such a property as will enable him to keep it against all but the rightful owner, and consequently may maintain trover.

2. That the action well lay against the master, who gives a credit to his apprentice, and is answerable for his neglect.

3. As to the value of the jewel several of the trade were examined to prove what a jewel of the finest water that would fit the socket would be worth; and the Chief Justice (Pratt) directed the jury, that unless the defendant did produce the jewel, and shew it not to be of the finest water, they should presume the strongest against him, and make the value of the best jewels the measure of their damages: which they accordingly did.

Notes and Questions

1. *The legal principle of Armory v. Delamirie.* Based on judicial statements like that in the *Armory* case, it is often said "that the title of the finder is good as against the whole world but the true owner. . . ." Ray A. Brown, The Law of Personal Property 26 (Walter B. Raushenbush ed. 3d ed. 1975). Is that an accurate or satisfactory statement of the principle of the case? To test it, suppose that *F1* loses a watch he had earlier found and that it is subsequently found by *F2*. *F1* sues *F2* for return of the watch. Who wins? The answer, as it happens, is that *F1* wins. Knowing this, how would you revise the statement so that it accurately states the law?

In answering this question, it will be helpful to make explicit an important point that is implicit in much of what we saw earlier: property rights are relational. See, e.g., Note 3, page 47. The *F1-F2* problem illustrates a basic principle that builds on that insight: *title, or ownership, is relative.* The meaning of the phrase *true owner* depends upon who the other claimants are: *B* can have title as against *C* but not as against *A*.

2. *The* jus tertii *defense.* The relativity-of-title concept raises another important point involved in the question "Who is the 'true' owner of the jewel?" Although the court doesn't tell us what the goldsmith's defense was, he probably argued that he didn't have to return the jewel to the sweep (the plaintiff) because the sweep could not prove ownership. In other words, the goldsmith asserted the rights of the absent true owner as a defense. This is sometimes known as the *jus tertii* (Latin for "rights of a third party") defense, and, like the court in *Armory*, courts usually reject it. They require that the defendant stand on his own rights rather than those of a third party. Are the reasons for the rejection of the *jus tertii* defense substantive or procedural, or both? Suppose the identity of the true owner is known; should the court then be more willing to accept the *jus tertii* defense?

3. *The cause of action in* Armory—*trover.* In Armory v. Delamirie, the plaintiff sued defendant in trover. *Trover* is the old common law action for money damages resulting from the defendant's conversion to his own use of a chattel owned or possessed by the plaintiff. The plaintiff waives his right to obtain the return of the chattel and insists that the defendant be subjected to a forced purchase of the chattel from him. If the defendant loses, he must pay money damages to the plaintiff. Today trover is basically obsolete. It has largely been replaced by the tort of conversion.

4. *The measure of damages.* The court awarded Armory the value of a "jewel of the finest water." That means a jewel of the highest quality. So, Armory recovered damages equal to the full value of a jewel of the finest quality. Was that equal to the value of his interest in the jewel, or was the value of his interest equal to the value of the jewel discounted by the probability that the true owner will appear and reclaim it? If it was the latter, why did the court award him the full value of the jewel?

5. *Bailment.* When Armory left the jewel with de Lamerie he created a bailment—the rightful possession of goods by a person who is not the owner. The person who delivers the chattel is called the *bailor,* and the person who receives it is called the *bailee.* A bailee has possession but not title to the chattel. The creation of a bailment requires that the bailee both intend to possess and actually possess the chattel.

Bailments are voluntary or involuntary. Voluntary bailments are very common. When you take your clothes to the laundry for cleaning, this creates a voluntary bailment. So, too, when you leave your car keys with a valet parking attendant. Involuntary bailments are less common, but they certainly do occur in ordinary life. A finder of a lost or mislaid chattel, such as Armory, is an involuntary bailee because the bailor has not voluntarily transferred possession to him.

The standard of care that a bailee owes to a bailor depends upon who benefits from the bailment. If the bailor is the sole beneficiary (i.e., the bailee is not

> ### In Brief
>
> A bailment transfers possession but not title to the bailee. The bailee has the duty to take extraordinary care, reasonable care, or to avoid acting in gross negligence or bad faith with respect to the property, depending upon who benefits from the arrangement.

compensated), the bailee is a "gratuitous" bailee, and the bailee is liable only if the property is damaged through his or her gross negligence. If the bailment benefits both parties, as in a car rental arrangement, then the bailee is liable if the property is damaged as a result of his or her ordinary negligence. Finally, if the relationship benefits only the bailee (e.g., the bailee borrows the bailor's property without paying for it), then liability results from damage caused by the bailee's "slight negligence."

Which type of bailment was involved in *Armory*?

6. *Rights of the true owner.* Suppose that in 1723 the true owner of the jewel involved in the *Armory* case appeared at the goldsmith's shop and demanded return of the jewel. What are the rights of the goldsmith and the true owner as against each other and as against the chimney sweeper's boy? Generally, the subsequent possessor's payment to the finder bars any later action by the true owner against the subsequent possessor. The true owner may, however, compel the finder to transfer the payment, which takes the place of the bailed chattel, to the true owner.

7. *Prior possessor as a thief.* Would it have made any difference in *Armory* if the chimney sweeper's boy had taken the jewel off a dressing table in the house where he was cleaning the chimney? Generally, courts say no. In Anderson v. Gouldberg, 53 N.W. 636 (Minn. 1892), the plaintiffs trespassed upon the timberland of a third party, cut logs, and hauled them to a mill, where the defendants took them. Ruling for the trespassing plaintiff, the court said that "bare possession of property, though wrongfully obtained, is sufficient title to enable the party enjoying it to" prevail over the party who takes it from him. "Any other rule would lead to an endless series of unlawful seizures and reprisals in every case where property had once passed out of the possession of the rightful owner," the court reasoned. Id. at 637. See also Payne v. TK Auto Wholesalers, 911 A.2d 747 (Conn. App. 2006) (citing *Anderson* favorably and recognizing the possessory interest of a wrongdoer as against all but the true owner of the property in question).

HANNAH v. PEEL
King's Bench Division, 1945
[1945] K.B. 509

Action tried by Birkett, J. On December 13, 1938, the freehold of Gwernhaylod House, Overton-on-Dee, Shropshire, was conveyed to the defendant, Major Hugh Edward Ethelston Peel, who from that time to the end of 1940 never himself occupied the house and it remained unoccupied until October 5, 1939, when it was requisitioned [for quartering soldiers], but after some months was released from requisition. Thereafter it remained unoccupied until July 18, 1940, when it was again requisitioned, the defendant being compensated by a payment at the rate of 250*l.* a year. In August, 1940, the plaintiff, Duncan Hannah, a lance-corporal, serving in a battery of the Royal Artillery, was stationed at the house and on the 21st of that month, when in a bedroom, used as a sick-bay, he was adjusting the black-out curtains when his hand touched something on the top of a window-frame, loose in a crevice, which he thought was a piece of dirt or plaster. The plaintiff grasped it and dropped it on the outside window ledge. On the following morning he saw that it was a brooch covered with cobwebs and dirt. Later, he took it with him when he went home on leave and his wife having told him it might be of value, at the end of October, 1940, he informed his commanding officer of his find and, on his advice, handed it over to the police, receiving a receipt for it.

In August, 1942, the owner not having been found the police handed the brooch to the defendant, who sold it in October, 1942, for 66*l*., to Messrs. Spink & Son, Ltd., of London, who resold it in the following month for 88*l*. There was no evidence that the defendant had any knowledge of the existence of the brooch before it was found by the plaintiff. The defendant had offered the plaintiff a reward for the brooch, but the plaintiff refused to accept this and maintained throughout his right to the possession of the brooch as against all persons other than the owner, who was unknown. By a letter, dated October 5, 1942, the plaintiff's solicitors demanded the return of the brooch from the defendant, but it was not returned and on October 21, 1943, the plaintiff issued his writ claiming the return of the brooch, or its value, and damages for its detention. By his defence, the defendant claimed the brooch on the ground that he was the owner of Gwernhaylod House and in possession thereof. . . .

BIRKETT, J. There is no issue of fact in this case between the parties. As to the issue in law, the rival claims of the parties can be stated in this way: The plaintiff says: "I claim the brooch as its finder and I have a good title against all the world, save only the true owner." The defendant says: "My claim is superior to yours in as much as I am the freeholder. The brooch was found on my property, although I was never in occupation, and my title, therefore, ousts yours and in the absence of the true owner I am entitled to the brooch or its value." Unhappily the law on this issue is in a very uncertain state and there is need of an authoritative decision of a higher court. Obviously if it could be said with certainty that this is the law, that the finder of a lost article, wherever found, has a good title against all the world save the true owner, then, of course, all my difficulties would be resolved; or again, if it could be said with equal certainty that this is the law, that the possessor of land is entitled as against the finder to all chattels found on the land, again my difficulties would be resolved. But, unfortunately, the authorities give some support to each of these conflicting propositions. . . .

Gwernhaylod House, Overton-on-Dee
"Gwernhaylod," a Welsh word, means "sunny marsh." Gwernhaylod House was
originally built in 1460, rebuilt in 1740, and torn down in 1950.
Source: National Monuments Record of Wales

The case of Bridges v. Hawkesworth, 21 L.J. (Q.B.) 75, 15 Jur. 1079, was . . . an appeal against a decision of the county court judge at Westminster. The facts appear to have been that in the year 1847 the plaintiff, who was a commercial traveller, called on a firm named Byfield & Hawkesworth on business, as he was in the habit of doing, and as he was leaving the shop he picked up a small parcel which was lying on the floor. He immediately showed it to the shopman, and opened it in his presence, when it was found to consist of a quantity of Bank of England notes, to the amount of 65*l.* The defendant, who was a partner in the firm of Byfield & Hawkesworth, was then called, and the plaintiff told him he had found the notes, and asked the defendant to keep them until the owner appeared to claim them. Then various advertisements were put in the papers asking for the owner, but the true owner was never found. No person having appeared to claim them, and three years having elapsed since they were found, the plaintiff applied to the defendant to have the notes returned to him, and offered to pay the expenses of the advertisements, and to give an indemnity. The defendant refused to deliver them up to the plaintiff, and an action was brought in the county court of Westminster in consequence of that refusal. The county court judge decided that the defendant, the shopkeeper, was entitled to the custody of the notes as against the plaintiff, and gave judgment for the defendant. Thereupon the appeal was brought which came before the court composed by Patteson, J., and Wightman, J. Patteson, J., said: "The notes which are the subject of this action were incidentally dropped, by mere accident, in the shop of the defendant, by the owner of them. The facts do not warrant the supposition that they had been deposited there intentionally, nor has the case been put at all upon that ground. The plaintiff found them on the floor, they being manifestly lost by someone. The general right of the finder to any article which has been lost, as against all the world, except the true owner, was established in the case of Armory v. Delamirie, 1 Str. 505, which has never been disputed. This right would clearly have accrued to the plaintiff had the notes been picked up by him outside the shop of the defendant and if he once had the right, the case finds that he did not intend, by delivering the notes to the defendant, to waive the title (if any) which he had to them, but they were handed to the defendant merely for the purpose of delivering them to the owner should he appear." Then a little later: "The case, therefore, resolves itself into the single point on which it appears that the learned judge decided it, namely, whether the circumstance of the notes being found inside the defendant's shop gives him, the defendant, the right to have them as against the plaintiff, who found them." After discussing the cases, and the argument, the learned judge said: "If the discovery had never been communicated to the defendant, could the real owner have had any cause of action against him because they were found in his house? Certainly not. The notes never were in the custody of the defendant, nor within the protection of his house, before they were found, as they would have been had they been intentionally deposited there; and the defendant has come under no responsibility, except from the communication made to him by the plaintiff, the finder, and the steps taken by way of advertisement. . . . We find, therefore, no circumstances in this case to take it out of the general rule of law, that the finder of a lost article is entitled to it as against all persons except the real owner, and we think that that rule must prevail, and that the learned judge was mistaken in holding that the place in which they were found makes any legal difference. Our judgment, therefore, is that the plaintiff is entitled to these notes as against the defendant."

It is to be observed that in Bridges v. Hawkesworth, which has been the subject of immense disputation, neither counsel put forward any argument on the fact that the notes were found in a shop. Counsel for the appellant assumed throughout that the position was the same as if the parcel had been found in a private house, and the learned judge spoke of "the protection of his" (the shopkeeper's) "house." The case for the appellant was that the shopkeeper never knew of the notes. Again, what is curious is that there was no suggestion that the place where the notes were found was in any way material; indeed, the judge in giving the judgment of the court expressly repudiates this and said in terms "The learned judge was mistaken in holding that the place in which they were found makes any legal difference." It is, therefore, a little remarkable that in South Staffordshire Water Co. v. Sharman, [1896] 2 Q.B. 44, Lord Russell of Killowen, C.J., said: "The case of Bridges v. Hawkesworth stands by itself, and on special grounds; and on those grounds it seems to me that the decision in that case was right. Someone had accidentally dropped a bundle of banknotes in a public shop. The shopkeeper did not know they had been dropped, and did not in any sense exercise control over them. The shop was open to the public, and they were invited to come there." That might be a matter of some doubt. Customers were invited there, but whether the public at large was, might be open to some question. Lord Russell continued: "A customer picked up the notes and gave them to the shopkeeper in order that he might advertise them. The owner of the notes was not found, and the finder then sought to recover them from the shopkeeper. It was held that he was entitled to do so, the ground of the decision being, as was pointed out by Patteson, J., that the notes, being dropped in the public part of the shop, were never in the custody of the shopkeeper, or 'within the protection of his house.'" Patteson, J., never made any reference to the public part of the shop and, indeed, went out of his way to say that the learned county court judge was wrong in holding that the place where they were found made any legal difference. . . .

With regard to South Staffordshire Water Co. v. Sharman, [1896] 2 Q.B. 44, the first two lines of the headnote are: "The possessor of land is generally entitled, as against the finder, to chattels found on the land." I am not sure that this is accurate. The facts were that the defendant Sharman, while cleaning out, under the orders of the plaintiffs, the South Staffordshire Water Company, a pool of water on their land, found two rings embedded in the mud at the bottom of the pool. He declined to deliver them to the plaintiffs, but failed to discover the real owner. In an action brought by the company against Sharman in detinue it was held that the company was entitled to the rings. Lord Russell of Killowen, C.J., said: "The plaintiffs are the freeholders of the locus in quo [literally, the place in which], and as such they have the right to forbid anybody coming on their land or in anyway interfering with it. They had the right to say that their pool should be cleaned out in any way that they thought fit, and to direct what should be done with anything found in the pool in the course of such cleaning out. It is no doubt right, as the counsel for the defendant contended, to say that the plaintiffs must show that they had actual control over the locus in quo and the things in it; but under the circumstances, can it be said that the Minster Pool and whatever might be in that pool were not under the control of the plaintiffs? In my opinion they were. . . . The principle on which this case must be decided, and the distinction which must be drawn between this case and that of Bridges v. Hawkesworth, is to be found in a passage in Pollock and Wright's essay on Possession in the Common Law, p. 41: 'The possession of land carries with it in general, by our law, possession of everything which is attached to or under that land, and, in the absence of a better title elsewhere, the right to possess it also. . . .'" And it makes no difference that the possessor is not aware of the thing's existence. . . .

Then Lord Russell cited the passage which I read earlier in this judgment and continued: "It is somewhat strange"—I venture to echo those words—"that there is no more direct authority on the question; but the general principle seems to me to be that where a person has possession of house or land, with a manifest intention to exercise control over it and the things which may be upon or in it, then, if something is found on that land, whether by an employee of the owner or by a stranger, the presumption is that the possession of that thing is in the owner of the locus in quo." It is to be observed that Lord Russell there is extending the meaning of the passage he had cited from Pollock and Wright's essay on Possession in the Common Law, where the learned authors say that the possession of "land carries with it possession of everything which is attached to or under that land." Then Lord Russell adds possession of everything which may be on or in that land. South Staffordshire Water Co. v. Sharman, which was relied on by counsel for the defendant, has also been the subject of some discussion. It has been said that it establishes that if a man finds a thing as the servant or agent of another, he finds it not for himself, but for that other, and indeed that seems to afford a sufficient explanation of the case. The rings found at the bottom of the pool were not in the possession of the company, but it seems that though Sharman was the first to obtain possession of them, he obtained them for his employers and could claim no title for himself.

The only other case to which I need refer is Elwes v. Brigg Gas Co., 33 Ch. D. 562, in which land had been demised to a gas company for ninety-nine years with a reservation to the lessor of all mines and minerals. A pre-historic boat embedded in the soil was discovered by the lessees when they were digging to make a gasholder. It was held that the boat, whether regarded as a mineral or as part of the soil in which it was embedded when discovered, or as a chattel, did not pass to the lessees by the demise, but was the property of the lessor though he was ignorant of its existence at the time of granting the lease. Chitty, J., said: "The first question which does actually arise in this case is whether the boat belonged to the plaintiff at the time of the granting of the lease. I hold that it did, whether it ought to be regarded as a mineral, or as part of the soil within the maxim above cited, or as a chattel. If it was a mineral or part of the soil in the sense above indicated, then it clearly belonged to the owners of the inheritance as part of the inheritance itself. But if it ought to be regarded as a chattel, I hold the property in the chattel was vested in the plaintiff, for the following reasons." Then he gave the reasons, and continued: "The plaintiff then being thus in possession of the chattel, it follows that the property in the chattel was vested in him. Obviously the right of the original owner could not be established; it had for centuries been lost or barred, even supposing that the property had not been abandoned when the boat was first left on the spot where it was found. The plaintiff, then, had a lawful possession, good against all the world, and therefore the property in the boat. In my opinion it makes no difference, in these circumstances, that the plaintiff was not aware of the existence of the boat."[1]

---

1. "Thus the case ended," says a comment on *Elwes* written a century later. "Mr. Elwes, having gained possession of the boat, exhibited it in a specially constructed brick building in the estate yard, near Brigg Station. There for twenty-three years many thousands of visitors paid for admission to see

A review of these judgments shows that the authorities are in an unsatisfactory state. . . .

It is fairly clear from the authorities that a man possesses everything which is attached to or under his land. Secondly, it would appear to be the law from the authorities I have cited, and particularly from Bridges v. Hawkesworth, that a man does not necessarily possess a thing which is lying unattached on the surface of his land even though the thing is not possessed by someone else. A difficulty, however, arises . . . because the rule which governs things an occupier possesses as against those which he does not, has never been very clearly formulated in our law. . . .

There is no doubt that in this case the brooch was lost in the ordinary meaning of that term, and I should imagine it had been lost for a very considerable time. Indeed, from this correspondence it appears that at one time the predecessors in title of the defendant were considering making some claim. But the moment the plaintiff discovered that the brooch might be of some value, he took the advice of his commanding officer and handed it to the police. His conduct was commendable and meritorious. The defendant was never physically in possession of these premises at any time. It is clear that the brooch was never his, in the ordinary acceptation of the term, in that he had the prior possession. He had no knowledge of it, until it was brought to his notice by the finder. A discussion of the merits does not seem to help, but it is clear on the facts that the brooch was "lost" in the ordinary meaning of that word, that it was "found" by the plaintiff in the ordinary meaning of that word, that its true owner has never been found, that the defendant was the owner of the premises and had his notice drawn to this matter by the plaintiff, who found the brooch. In those circumstances I propose to follow the decision in Bridges v. Hawkesworth, and to give judgment in this case for the plaintiff for 66*l.*

Judgment for plaintiff.

Notes and Questions

1. *Back to* Armory. Armory v. Delamarie was a well-known case at the time of the decision in *Hannah*. In fact, the court in Bridges v. Hawkesworth, which the *Hannah* court discusses, cites *Armory*. Yet apparently the court in *Hannah* thought that *Armory* did not decide the issue posed in *Hannah*. Why not?

2. *Ownership versus actual possession.* Major Peel owned Gwernhaylod House, but the court did not give much weight to this factor, apparently because he never occupied it. So, if Major Peel had resided in the house prior to the government requisitioning it, would he have won? See Parker v. British Airways Bd., [1982] 2 W.L.R. 503, 516-517: "I would be inclined to say that the occupier of a house will almost invariably possess any lost article on the premises. He may not have taken any positive steps to demonstrate his *animus possidendi*, but so firm is his control that the *animus* can be seen to attach to it" (per Eveleigh, L.J.). Should the owner's actual possession be necessary? Recall that in Elwes v. Brigg Gas Co.,

---

it." Subsequently, Elwes gave the boat to a public museum at Hull. "[I]t was carefully removed to Hull, via the River Ancholme (appropriately enough), though in a rather different method from the trip it made on the same river some two thousand or more years ago. Would that it had remained in Brigg! In 1943 the boat was destroyed in an air raid on the museum premises. . . ." Michael L. Nash, Are Finders Keepers? One Hundred Years Since *Elwes v. Brigg Gas Co.*, 137 New L.J. 118, 119 (1987).—EDS.

cited in *Hannah*, the court awarded the prehistoric boat to the owner despite the fact that as the landlord of a 99-year lease he was very definitely out of posses-sion. Consider also the fact that Major Peel intended to live in the house, but the military requisitioned it before he had a chance to move in. Should that matter?

3. *Lost versus mislaid property.* American courts sometimes decide between the finder and the owner of the locus in quo on the basis of categorizing the found item as lost or mislaid. (English courts have never adopted this distinction.) See, e.g., McAvoy v. Medina, 93 Mass. (11 Allen) 548 (1866). An item is said to be *mislaid* if the owner intentionally placed it in some location and then forgot to retrieve it. An item is said to be *lost* when the owner inadvertently loses possession of it. If the item is mislaid, the owner of the locus in quo wins. The rationale is that this result aids return of the item to the true owner, who will usually retrace his steps to where he last left the item. Lost property usually goes to the finder because the true owner, who does not know the item's whereabouts, is unlikely to retrace his steps and find it. Moreover, this result rewards the finder's honesty. Was the brooch in *Hannah* lost or mislaid? Can you tell? Should it matter?

Yet another category of found property is *abandoned* property. Property is abandoned when the owner intentionally relinquishes all legal rights to it with no intention to confer rights on any particular person. Abandonment occurs all the time, of course, such as when you toss an item in the trash. According to the blackletter, when a person finds abandoned property, ownership goes to the finder. The policy of facilitating return of the item to the true owner is irrelevant in this context.

4. *Treasure trove.* Suppose you are helping a friend dig a new garden in your friend's yard when you find, buried several inches below the surface, an old tin box containing silver coins. It turns out that the tin box dates to Civil War times and the coins are silver dollars. The total value of all of these items is nearly $25,000. Who is entitled to the box and the coins, you or your friend? The scenario involves yet a fourth category of found property, called *treasure trove.* Treasure trove is gold, silver, bullion, or money that has been concealed in a private place. At English common law, treasure trove (derived from the Old French *tresor trové*, found treasure) belonged to the king. Nowadays, it appears, the practice of the British Crown is to auction treasure trove to British museums and divide the receipts equally between the finder and the owner of the land where the treasure was discovered. Most American jurisdictions reject the treasure trove doctrine and treat it as either lost or mislaid property. In cases where the found item was buried, American courts usually give it to the owner of the land where it was found. See, e.g., Morgan v. Wiser, 711 S.W.2d 220 (Tenn. App. 1985).

5. *Legislation.* Many states have legislation covering lost, mislaid, and aban-doned property—sometimes very lengthy and complicated legislation. A typical statute might require finders to deposit the property at a designated place, pro-vide for notice to possible owners, and provide for an award of title—say to the finder—if the property owner does not appear within a specified period. Some statutes apply only to "lost property." These statutes have often been construed narrowly to apply only to "lost" property as defined by common law and not to abolish the common law distinctions between types of found property.

6. *Shipwrecks.* Sunken treasure from ships sunk at sea is governed either by finders law or maritime law. The law of finders has usually been applied to ships lost in territorial waters, and the finder held entitled to an abandoned shipwreck

unless the wreck was embedded in land owned or possessed by another. Given this, the United States and individual states have successfully asserted claims to shipwrecks embedded in their territorial waters and thus constructively possessed. In the Abandoned Shipwreck Act of 1987, 43 U.S.C.A. §§ 2101-2106, the United States asserts title to any abandoned shipwreck embedded in submerged lands of a state and simultaneously transfers its title to the state in which the wreck is located. The purpose is to turn over management of embedded shipwrecks in state waters to the states and permit them to develop their own rules for salvage or preservation unimpeded by the general law. (The act provides that the law of finds and the law of salvage shall not apply to abandoned shipwrecks covered by its provisions.) For criticism of the act, see Forrest Booth, Who Owns Sunken Treasure? The Supreme Court, the Abandoned Shipwreck Act, and the Brother Jonathan, 11 U.S.F. Mar. L.J. 77 (1998-1999).

The evidentiary standard required for proof of abandonment is high, so in most cases maritime law, with its principle of salvage awards, applies. Under maritime law, a ship lost at sea and settled on the seabed remains the owner's property—unless title to the vessel was abandoned—but anyone subsequently reducing the ship or its cargo to possession is entitled to a salvage award. The law of salvage contrasts sharply with property law, which awards a finder all or nothing, subject to the rights of the true owner. Should the law of finders be changed so that the finder is entitled to an award (a reward) if the property in question is returned to its owner or held to be in possession of the owner of the locus?

"There's my wallet—right where I left it."

Was the wallet lost, or mislaid?

©Michael Maslin/Condé Nast Publications/www.cartoonbank.com

B. ACQUISITION BY ADVERSE POSSESSION

This section continues the inquiry begun in the last, concerning the effect of possession on some asset that another person owns. Suppose, for example, that *B* owns a parcel of land but never visits it. *A* occupies *B*'s land without *B*'s consent for a period of 20 years. Who owns the land at the end of the 20-year period? It is possible that *A* will, under the doctrine of adverse possession.

1. The Theory of Adverse Possession

The idea that a property owner may lose title to another person who possesses the property without the owner's permission is likely to seem strange at first. As one authority observed, "Title by adverse possession sounds, at first blush, like title by theft or robbery, a primitive method of acquiring land without paying for it." Henry W. Ballantine, Title by Adverse Possession, 32 Harv. L. Rev. 135, 135 (1918). Plainly, such a doctrine requires some explanation.

Three policies, or theories, are commonly offered for the doctrine of adverse possession:

- *Avoiding stale claims.* The foundation of adverse possession law is statutory; specifically, the statute of limitations for recovering possession of land in cases of trespass. Like all other statutes of limitations, this statute's purpose is to bar the assertion of claims based on old, unreliable evidence by limiting the time frame within which they may be brought to some reasonable period. If the owner's claim for possession is not filed within this period, the owner loses title, and the adverse possessor gains a new and valid legal title.
- *Quiet titles/correct title errors.* Deeds and other legal instruments of title sometimes contain errors that affect the transferee's title. The deed may be defective because it was improperly executed, or it may contain an error in the description of the property being conveyed. Adverse possession resolves these problems and quiets title after a period of time.
- *Protecting personal attachments.* U.S. Supreme Court Justice Oliver Wendell Holmes once wrote, "A thing which you have enjoyed and used as your own for a long time, whether property or an opinion, takes root in your being and cannot be torn away with your resenting the act and trying to defend yourself, however you came by it." Oliver Wendell Holmes, The Path of the Law, 10 Harv. L. Rev. 457, 477 (1897). Cognitive psychologists now explain Holmes's point in terms of "prospect theory," which holds in part that people regard loss of an asset in hand as more significant than forgoing the opportunity to realize an apparently equivalent gain.

Bear in mind that adverse possession does *not* function as a means of "transferring" ownership, at least not in a straightforward way. The running of the statute of limitations not only bars an action by the erstwhile owner, but also vests a *new* title, created by operation of law, in the adverse possessor. Once acquired, this new title "relates back" to the date of the event that started the statute of limitations running, and the law acts as though the adverse possessor were the owner from that date.

2. Elements of Adverse Possession

Adverse possession law is a synthesis of statutory and judge-made law, with judicial rules supplementing the statutes of limitation that make up the core of adverse possession. These supplemental rules vary somewhat from state to state, but typically they state the following elements, or requirements, of adverse possession:

- *Actual entry.* One obvious reason that an actual entry is required is that adverse possession depends on a statute of limitations running against a cause of action, and the entry (without permission, adverse to the rights of the property owner, but more on this when we get to the fourth item) creates that cause of action—for trespass—and thereby triggers the statute. Entry also helps stake out what it is the adverse possessor might end up claiming. Moreover, some case law and academic commentary seem to suggest the idea that entry manifests an interloper who at least is working the property, making it productive, and by these means *earning* some rights.
- *Exclusive possession.* The exclusivity requirement does *not* mean that only the adverse possessor may use the property for the statutory period. Absolute exclusivity is not required. What exclusivity requires is that the adverse claimant's possession and use cannot be shared with the true owner or with the public in general.
- *Open and notorious.* The meaning and purpose of this requirement is to assure that the adverse possessor's entry and subsequent acts of use are of the sort that would put reasonably attentive property owners on notice that someone is on their property. The notoriety requirement is aimed at constructive, not actual, notice; the test of notoriety is objective. If the adverse possessor's acts would be noticed by an ordinary person, then the owner is regarded as knowing what should have been known. This requirement reflects another rationale sometimes offered for adverse possession—the *sleeping* principle, according to which the purpose of adverse possession is "to penalize the negligent and dormant owner for sleeping upon his rights." Ballantine, Title by Adverse Possession, supra, at 135.
- *"Hostile and adverse" possession.* This does not mean that the adverse possessor must dislike the true owner. The term "hostile and adverse" (the term "claim of right" is also sometimes synonymously used) is a term of art. Its precise meaning is complex, and, as we will discuss below, courts do not agree on what evidence is required to satisfy this requirement. What the courts do agree on is that the claimant's possession cannot be with the true owner's permission. The owner's permission gives a possessor a license, which negates the hostility requirement.
- *Continuous and uninterrupted.* Possession must be continuous for the statutory period, but not literally constant. An adverse possessor is permitted to come and go in the ordinary course, given the nature of the property in question (being on the farm most of the time; using the summer fishing camp

> ### In Brief
>
> Requirements of adverse possession:
>
> 1) Actual
> 2) Exclusive
> 3) Open and notorious
> 4) Hostile and under claim of right (adverse)
> 5) Continuous and uninterrupted

for regular summer fishing trips, etc.). The true owner may interrupt the statute before it has run by bringing a successful ejectment action against the adverse possessor, or by re-entering the property. In the case of a successful ejectment action, the lawsuit interrupts the period of possession even if the owner does not thereafter actually oust the adverse possessor, who must start all over. See, e.g., Irving Pulp & Paper Ltd. v. Kelly, 654 A.2d 416 (Me. 1995). As to re-entry by the true owner, it must be open and hostile and effective. See 3 American Law of Property § 15.9.

———————

The adversity requirement and the adverse possessor's state of mind. By far the most confusing element of adverse possession law is the requirement that possession be "adverse" or "hostile" or "adverse and under claim of right." Just what does this mean? A good way to approach the inquiry is in terms of the state of mind required of the adverse possessor, and in this respect existing doctrine reflects three different views:

1. State of mind is irrelevant. All that matters is the conduct of the adverse possessor. If the adverse possessor occupied and used the land in the way that one would expect of the true owner of land of that character, then that evidence is sufficient to establish adversity. The point behind this view is simple: once there is an entry against the true owner, she has a cause of action. Given that, shouldn't the statute of limitations be running, *whatever* the entrant's state of mind? See 3 American Law of Property § 15.4 (1952), endorsing the view and suggesting it is the majority position in the United States.

2. The required state of mind is, "I thought I owned it." This view requires a good-faith claim. It is voiced from time to time in American decisions. E.g., Halpern v. Lacy Inv. Corp., 379 S.E.2d 519, 521 (Ga. 1989) ("We hold that the correct rule is that one must enter upon the land claiming in good faith the right to do so. To enter upon the land without any honest claim of right to do so is but a trespass and can never ripen into prescriptive title."). It is also codified in a few statutes. E.g., N.Y. Real Prop. Acts. & Proc. § 501(3) (McKinney 2008).

3. The required state of mind is, "I thought I didn't own it, but I intended to make it mine." According to this view, to qualify as adverse possessors, occupants must intend to take the property even if they know it doesn't belong to them.

These different views have been called, respectively, "the *objective standard,* the *good-faith standard,* and the *aggressive trespass standard.*" Margaret Jane Radin, Time, Possession, and Alienation, 64 Wash. U. L.Q. 739, 746-747 (1986) (emphasis added). Think about which view the court in the next case adopts, and whether that view seems appropriate in light of the underlying purposes of adverse possession.

FULKERSON v. VAN BUREN
Court of Appeals of Arkansas, 1998
961 S.W.2d 780

JENNINGS, J. Appellant Floyd H. Fulkerson appeals the Pulaski County Circuit Court's judgment awarding title to a 4.5-acre parcel of real estate to appellee the Progressive Church, Inc. The church claimed title to the land by adverse possession. We reverse and remand.

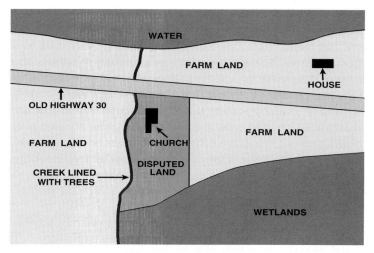

Map of the disputed land
Source: John G. Sprankling

The Progressive Church
Source: John G. Sprankling

The 4.5 acres at issue are situated in Pulaski County, near the town of Scott. The parcel is irregularly configured and has eleven sides. The northernmost part of the parcel abuts Old Highway 30 for approximately 115 feet. A single-story church building is situated near the highway. This building is the meeting place for appellee, the Progressive Church, Inc. When the litigation between the parties began, appellant Fulkerson had held legal title to the parcel since December 1949. Sometime in 1985, the congregation of the Progressive Church, without obtaining permission from Fulkerson, began using the church building on the property as their place of worship. Over the next several years, the congregation greatly improved the church building itself and the surrounding land. . . .

In November 1994, Fulkerson sent to Reverend Van Buren a letter demanding that he and the church congregation immediately vacate the church building located on the parcel. The church did not vacate the premises. In May 1995, Fulkerson filed in Pulaski County Circuit Court a complaint in which he requested that the court eject the congregation from the church building and from the rest of the parcel at issue. . . . [The church filed a response and a counterclaim] assert[ing] that it owned the parcel of land at issue by adverse possession and requested that the matter be transferred to chancery court to quiet title to the land after recognition of its ownership of the parcel. In October 1996, trial was held in Pulaski County Circuit Court in connection with Fulkerson's complaint and the church's counterclaim. After hearing testimony from witnesses presented by both parties, the circuit court subsequently caused to be entered a judgment in which the court determined that . . . the Progressive Church owned the parcel of land by adverse possession.

The legal principles governing establishment of title to land by adverse possession are well established. We recently set forth these principles as follows:

> It is well settled that, in order to establish title by adverse possession, appellee had the burden of proving that she had been in possession of the property continuously for more than seven years and that her possession was visible, notorious, distinct, exclusive, hostile, and with intent to hold against the true owner. The proof required as to the extent of possession and dominion may vary according to the location and character of the land. It is ordinarily sufficient that the acts of ownership are of such a nature as one would exercise over her own property and would not exercise over that of another, and that the acts amount to such dominion over the land as to which it is reasonably adapted. . . .

Moses v. Dautartas, 922 S.W.2d 345 (1996). . . . For possession to be adverse, it is only necessary that it be hostile in the sense that it is under a claim of right, title, or ownership as distinguished from possession in conformity with, recognition of, or subservience to the superior right of the holder of title to the land. *Id.* Possession of land will not ordinarily be presumed to be adverse, but rather subservient to the true owner of the land. *See* Dillaha v. Temple, 590 S.W.2d 331 (1979). Therefore, mere possession of land is not enough to adversely possess the land, and there is every presumption that possession of land is in subordination to the holder of the legal title to the land. *Id.* The intention to hold adversely must be clear, distinct, and unequivocal. *Id.* . . .

The core of the church's proof of adverse possession of the 4.5 acres at issue was provided by appellee, Reverend Sylvester Van Buren. As noted above, the intent required for adverse possession is the intention to claim the land at issue under right, title, or ownership as distinguished from possession in conformity with, recognition of, or subservience to the superior right of the true owner of the land. We conclude that Reverend Van Buren's testimony shows that, from the time the congregation occupied the church building on the parcel until November 1994, the church congregation was unsure of the precise nature of its interest in the land and, moreover, recognized that Fulkerson owned the land.

On cross-examination, Reverend Van Buren testified that in 1990 or 1991 he first realized that the church did not have a deed to the land at issue. He testified further that, prior to this time, he made no assumptions about whether the church was on the land with permission or whether the church had purchased the land. Reverend

Van Buren specifically stated in this regard, "I didn't know how or what kind of possession they had." In order to clarify the matter of the church's right to occupy the land, Reverend Van Buren contacted appellant Fulkerson. He asked Fulkerson to give a quitclaim deed to the church, which Fulkerson refused to do. Reverend Van Buren testified further that, after Fulkerson told him that he (Fulkerson) held legal title to the land, he (Van Buren) "accepted that as a fact." In this regard, Reverend Van Buren testified:

> I had no way of knowing. I did some research on the layout of the land and saw where he had acquired the land from a relative somewhere's . . . between 1940 and '59 or somewhere like that. So I saw he acquired the land. And I saw no other records. During this time the courthouse was taken down and they had moved to another temporary location and everything they had was on microfilm and a lot of things wasn't clear. But as far as I knew he clearly had possession. And this is after we had talked and all. And even some weeks before we went to court. That this took place which is just a couple of years ago. Last year rather.

With regard to the time at which the church congregation decided to claim the land at issue, Reverend Van Buren testified:

> Once the term adverse had been positioned and he [Fulkerson] had caused us to be evicted or had asked us out of the church and we had no other alternatives. I just wondered what we should do. It wasn't a decision that was made impulsively at that time. We made the decision that we wanted the land once we found out it wasn't ours. And as far as adverse, adverse only came into play when no other avenue worked.

When asked whether this decision would have been reached in 1994 to 1995, Reverend Van Buren replied, "If you say so, that's close."

Given this testimony by Reverend Van Buren, given that a possessor of land does not possess adversely if, while in possession, he recognizes the ownership right of the titleholder to the land, and given that proof of the possessor's intention to hold adversely must be clear, distinct, and unequivocal and must have lasted seven years, we conclude that the circuit court's finding of fact that the congregation of the Progressive Church possessed for seven years the requisite intent to possess the land at issue adversely to appellant Fulkerson is clearly against the preponderance of the evidence. Because the church congregation did not possess the land with the requisite intent for seven years, the church congregation did not adversely possess the land.

For the reasons set forth above, we reverse the Pulaski County Circuit Court's judgment in favor of appellee the Progressive Church, Inc., on its counterclaim for adverse possession, and remand to the circuit court for further proceedings not inconsistent with this opinion.

Reversed and remanded.

MEADS, J., dissenting. The trial court determined that appellees established their claim for adverse possession of the tract of land they had occupied since 1985. Because I do not believe the trial court's findings of fact are clearly erroneous or clearly against the preponderance of the evidence, I would affirm.

Reverend Van Buren testified that he became pastor of The Progressive Church in 1985 and that he and other church members immediately began cleaning up the premises, which he described as a "wilderness" and "dumping site." The land was overgrown with vines and littered with storm debris, and the church building was infested with snakes. They cut down trees, cleared out debris, and cleaned up the highway frontage so that the building became visible from the road. They repaired the building by installing central heat and air, and by replacing the roof, siding, windows, and floor. They added a 40-foot building and office. After two years, the property was in "immaculate" condition, and the congregation received compliments for their efforts from the local community. When asked whether he had treated the property as his own, Reverend Van Buren asserted: "There's no way that I would have gone to this property and cleared it by hand . . . if I had assumed we didn't have business being there, the right to be there, or if the church didn't have the needed possession."

Reverend Van Buren further testified that he had no dealings whatsoever with appellant until sometime in the early nineties, when appellant stopped by the church, asked to speak to the preacher, complimented him on the church's efforts to improve the appearance of the church and grounds, but was silent as to his ownership of the site. It was not until 1992 that appellant, through his attorney, notified appellee that he (appellant) owned the land and was willing to negotiate a lease with the church. Subsequently, appellant personally spoke to Reverend Van Buren about a lease. Ultimately, appellant's attorney sent appellees a demand to vacate dated November 4, 1994, and filed the ejectment action in May 1995. All during this time, The Progressive Church steadfastly refused to negotiate with appellant, asserted its intent to remain in possession, and defied eviction efforts. Reverend Van Buren repeatedly asked appellant for a quitclaim deed to the premises. He contended there were never any "negotiations" with appellant for a lease, and "the only reason lease was mentioned is because Mr. Fulkerson dominated the conversation. You only talk about what Mr. Fulkerson wants to talk about. It doesn't matter what you say."

To establish adverse possession which ripens into ownership, the claimant must prove possession for seven years that has been actual, open, notorious, continuous, hostile, and exclusive, accompanied with an intent to hold against the true owner. Utley v. Ruff, 502 S.W.2d 629, 632 (1973). The majority believes appellee failed to establish the requisite intent to hold against the true owner, because once appellant asserted his ownership and the church "recognized" appellant's ownership right, the church's occupancy ceased to be adverse, thus interrupting the seven-year statutory period. I disagree.

First, I do not believe the church recognized appellant's ownership. Church members began to occupy the premises in 1985, using the building regularly, without interruption, and without notice of appellant's ownership until 1992. After being notified of appellant's title and after receiving a demand to vacate and later an eviction notice, they continued to occupy the premises, using the building regularly and without interruption. By their actions, the congregation continued to repudiate appellant's ownership even through the date of trial and beyond. To date, they have been in continuous possession for almost thirteen years.

Second, I believe the church clearly demonstrated a hostile intent within the meaning of the law. As this court stated in Walker v. Hubbard, 787 S.W.2d 251 (1990):

> The word hostile, as used in the law of adverse possession, must not be read too literally. For adverse possession to be hostile, it is not necessary that the

possessor have a conscious feeling of ill will or enmity toward his neighbor. Claim of ownership, even under a mistaken belief, is nevertheless adverse. (Citation omitted.)

Id. [31 Ark. App.] at 46-47. Additionally, for possession to be adverse, it is only necessary that it be hostile in the sense that it is under a claim of right, title, or ownership as distinguished from possession in conformity with, recognition of, or subservience to, the superior right of the owner. Barclay v. Tussey, 532 S.W.2d 193, 195 (1976). For the reasons stated in the previous paragraph, I cannot say that appellee's possession was "in conformity with, recognition of, or subservience to" appellant's rights.

Third, it appears to me that appellee established seven years of possession with all the qualifying factors before appellant ever asserted his ownership.

I would affirm.

THE REST OF THE STORY . . .

Fulkerson had previously allowed another church group, Bailey's Chapel, to use his land. In 1981, that group had signed an agreement with Fulkerson in which the group acknowledged that its use of the land was with Fulkerson's permission. Some time later, at an unknown date in the 1980s, Bailey's Chapel dissolved and discontinued use of Fulkerson's land without informing Fulkerson. The Progressive Church moved its location to the Fulkerson property in 1985, but Fulkerson did not realize that they, not Bailey's Chapel, were in possession until 1990. The Progressive Church eventually moved to a different location a few miles away. Recently, the building on the Fulkerson site remained unoccupied and is in dilapidated condition. The vegetation that the Progressive Church members cleared away is slowly taking over again. See William Hayden Spitler, Note, Over a Century of Doubt and Confusion: Adverse Possession in Arkansas, 53 Ark. L. Rev. 459 (2000).

Notes and Questions

1. *Which view?* Which of the three views described above—the objective standard, the good-faith standard, and the aggressive-trespasser standard—did the court adopt? Did it clearly adopt any one of the three? Does the dissent agree with the majority about which standard applies? As we indicated earlier, the objective standard is, by most authority, the majority approach. Under that approach, how would *Fulkerson* be decided?

2. *Effectuating adverse possession's objectives.* Go back to the various rationales for adverse possession that we described earlier. Does the result in *Fulkerson* effectuate any of them? Does it undermine any of them? If so, which ones?

3. *The bad-faith approach—the better view?* Professor Lee Anne Fennell argues that the aggressive-trespasser standard is the best approach; that is, that bad faith should be required in all adverse possession cases. She reasons that the real goal of adverse possession law is maximizing economic efficiency to giving title to the party who values it more highly. She seeks to eliminate the inefficient trespass; i.e., one that harms the record owner more than it benefits the

trespasser, and to encourage the efficient trespass; i.e., one that benefits the trespasser more than it harms the record owner. To accomplish this goal, she would insert a knowing-trespass requirement, which the trespasser must satisfy through documented evidence, such as a written purchaser offer. See Lee Anne Fennell, Efficient Trespass: The Case for "Bad Faith" Adverse Possession, 100 Nw. U. L. Rev. 1037, 1043 (2006). Is this a good idea?

———————

The open and notorious requirement. Notoriety is usually straightforward, but not always. Consider an instance where adverse possession is underground. Suppose that *A* and *B* are neighbors whose parcels of land lie over a cave, the entrance to which is on *A*'s land. *A* discovers the entrance, explores the full domain of the cave, and then opens it up to the public for a fee. *A*'s business, well known to *B*, runs for many years. After the statute of limitations has expired, *B* learns that part of the cave is under his land and brings suit to quiet his title to that part; *A* in turn claims title to the entire cave by adverse possession. Was *A*'s possession open and notorious? Not according to Marengo Cave Co. v. Ross, 10 N.E.2d 917 (Ind. 1937). The court gave three reasons for this conclusion. First, although *B* long knew of the cave's existence, he did not know whether any portion of the cave lay underneath his land, a fact that would require a survey of the land. But because the entrance to the cave was under *A*'s land, *B* could not obtain a survey without *A*'s permission. So, the cost of obtaining the survey was high relative to the value of the property at stake. The second reason was the discovery rule, according to which the statute of limitations does not start to run until the plaintiff knew or should have known of the defendant's wrong. The implication is that *B* did not know and should not be charged with knowledge that *A* was trespassing under his land until the survey results were revealed. Third, in the court's view, underground trespass is a form of fraud. Are these reasons persuasive? In thinking about this question, bear in mind the following points: (1) In cost-benefit terms in *Marengo*, *B* did eventually get a court order directing *A* to permit a survey. Such an order could have been obtained at any time before the statute ran out. (2) The question of when *B* reasonably could have discovered *A*'s wrongdoing boils down to whether it was reasonable to require *B* to seek a court order authorizing a survey, which we know *B* eventually got. (3) Fraud is an intentional tort that requires a showing that the wrongdoer intentionally or recklessly deceived the victim. Here, we have a finding that *A* did not know that the cave extended under *B*'s land.

Owning below and above the surface: the ad coelum *doctrine.* It is implicit in *Marengo* that the owner of a surface parcel also owns the part of a common cave underlying the parcel. This follows from the so-called *ad coelum* doctrine: *Cujus est solum, ejus est usque ad coelum et ad infernos* ("to whomsoever the soil belongs, he owns also to the sky and to the depths"). Would it make more sense to say that the owner of the land on which sits the entrance to a cave owns the cave? To say that whoever discovers a cave and opens it to access owns the cave? To say that all the overlying landowners own the cave together, in common? Given *ad coelum* and the three alternatives, which is best? For contending views on that question, see the majority, concurring, and dissenting opinions in Edwards v. Sims, 24 S.W.2d 619 (Ky. 1929), and Edwards v. Lee's Admr., 96 S.W.2d 1028 (Ky. 1936).

According to the *ad coelum* doctrine, the surface owner also owns the airspace above his land. Of course, this doctrine is not applied literally today. A landowner certainly owns the airspace immediately above his land, but how much higher? Think of airplanes, for example. In United States v. Causby, 328 U.S. 256 (1946), the Court held that the federal government effectively took part of the landowner's airspace when military airplanes continuously flew over the land at a very low altitude during World War II. The Court said that the landowner "owns at least as much of the space above the ground as he can occupy or use in connection with the land." More recently, the question of ownership of airspace has come up with the growing popularity of small unmanned aircraft known as drones. In June 2016, the Federal Aviation Administration issued a new rule regulating the operation of drones. The rule provides, among other things, that the drone must remain within the operator's visual line of sight, may not operate over persons not involved in its operation, and may not operate higher than 400 feet above ground level. See 14 CFR Parts 21, 43, 61, 91, 101, 107, 119, 133, and 183.

Color of title and constructive adverse possession. All states provide certain advantages to the adverse possessor whose possession is under color of title. *Color of title* refers to a claim founded on a written instrument (a deed, a will) or a judgment or decree that is for some reason defective and invalid (as when the grantor does not own the land conveyed by deed or is incompetent to convey, or the deed is improperly executed). Claim under color of title was not required by English law and is not required in most American jurisdictions. In a few states, color of title is essential to acquiring title by adverse possession.

In some states, a shorter statute of limitations is applicable to adverse possessors with color of title than to those without. In all states, entry with color of title may have an advantage where the adverse possessor enters into possession of only a part of the property. Actual possession under color of title of only a part of the land covered by the defective writing is *constructive* possession of all that the writing describes. The advantage that a person may gain from constructive possession is that the activities relied upon to establish adverse possession reach not only the part of the premises actually occupied, but the entire premises described in a deed to the claimant. This doctrine of constructive adverse possession under color of title, established by judicial rule in some states and by statute in others, is, however, subject to some limitations.

Problems

1. *O* owns all of and has been in possession of a portion of a 100-acre farm since 1975. In 1994, *A* entered the back 40 acres under color of an invalid deed from *Z* (who had no claim to the land) for the entire 100 acres. Since her entry, *A* has occupied and improved the back 40 in the usual manner for the period required by the statute of limitations. *A* brings suit to evict *O* from the farm, claiming title by constructive adverse possession. What result? See Patrick v. Goolsby, 11 S.W.2d 677 (Tenn. 1928). Suppose that in 1975, *O* took title to the farm under an invalid deed and has been in possession for a period sufficient to satisfy the statute of limitations. Would the result in the suit by *A* be different?

2. Two contiguous lots, 1 and 2, are owned by *X* and *Y* respectively. (*X* and *Y* are not in possession.) The lots are conveyed by an invalid deed from *Z* to *A*, who enters lot 1 and occupies it in the usual manner for the period required by the statute of limitations. Subsequently, *A* sues *X* and *Y* to quiet title to lots 1 and 2. What result? Would it matter if *X* had executed the deed? If *X* had executed the deed and *A* had entered lot 2? See Wheatley v. San Pedro, Los Angeles & Salt Lake Railroad, 147 P. 135 (Cal. 1915); Brock v. Howard, 200 S.W.2d 734 (Ky. 1947).

Boundary disputes. The case that follows concerns a *boundary dispute*, now the most frequently litigated of adverse possession claims. You will notice that the question of the claimant's state of mind, a matter we have already considered, comes up once again, in the special context of mistaken boundaries.

HOLLANDER v. WORLD MISSION CHURCH OF WASHINGTON, D.C.
Supreme Court of Virginia, 1998
498 S.E.2d 419

HENRY H. WHITING, S.J. This adverse possession case involves the effect of a mistake as to the location of an actual boundary line upon the intent to hold disputed land adversely.

The World Mission Church of Washington, D.C. (the church), filed a motion for judgment seeking to recover possession of a strip of its land in Fairfax County. The church claimed that Carolyn Hollander, an adjoining property owner, "unlawfully withheld" the land. Hollander responded by claiming title by adverse possession.

At a trial before the court, the evidence indicated that the church had record title to the land in dispute. The dispute arose because Hollander and her predecessors in title (the claimants) had used the disputed land mistakenly believing that their property ran to a line of trees at the edge of woods on the church's property.

After hearing both parties' evidence, the court concluded that all the elements necessary to establish title by adverse possession had been clearly established except for the requirement of an adverse or hostile possession. Because the claimants' possession of the land was based on a mistake as to the ownership of the land, the trial court determined that the possession was not adverse since "there was no intent of the claimant in this case to oust the true owner of the title of the property." Hence, the court entered final judgment for the church. Hollander appeals.

Hollander's evidence disclosed that the claimants had mowed, gardened, and otherwise maintained the strip of land up to the tree line as a part of their residential property for more than 15 years, believing that it was the common boundary between their property and the church's property. The evidence also indicated that the claimants intended to claim title to the land extending to that line as a part of the property they thought was conveyed to them.

Hollander contends that this evidence is sufficient to show that the claimants did not base their claim solely on their deed descriptions; rather, it shows their intention to claim title to a definite line on the ground. Hence, Hollander maintains that this case is controlled by our decision in Christian v. Bulbeck, 90 S.E. 661 (1916). On the other hand, the church, relying primarily on our ruling in Chaney v. Haynes, 458 S.E.2d 451, 453, contends that the claimants' mistake precludes a finding that their possession was with the necessary adverse or hostile intent.

The following principles govern our decision in this case.

"To establish title to real property by adverse possession, a claimant must prove actual, hostile, exclusive, visible, and continuous possession, under a claim of right, for the statutory period of 15 years." Grappo v. Blanks, 400 S.E.2d 168, 170-71 (1991). See Code § 8.01-236. The burden is upon the claimant to prove all of the foregoing elements by clear and convincing evidence.

One who possesses the adjoining land of another under a mistake as to his own boundaries with no intention to claim land that does not belong to him, but only intending to claim to the true line, wherever it may be, does not adversely hold the land in question. Christian, 90 S.E. at 670; Clinchfield Coal Co. v. Viers, 68 S.E. 976, 977 (1910); Schaubuch v. Dillemuth, 60 S.E. 745, 746 (1908).

However, as we held in Christian:

> The rule in Virginia [ ] may be taken to be that, where the proof is that the location of the line in question was caused in the first instance by a mistake as to the true boundary, the other facts and circumstances in the case must negative by a preponderance of evidence the inference which will otherwise arise that there was no definite and fixed intention on the part of the possessor to occupy, use and claim as his own the land up to a particular and definite line on the ground. That is to say, on the whole proof a case must be presented in which the preponderance of evidence as to the character of the possession, how held, how evidenced on the ground, how regarded by the adjoining land owner, etc., etc., supplies the proof that the definite and positive intention on the part of the possessor to occupy, use and claim as his own the land up to a particular and definite line *on the ground* existed, coupled with the requisite possession, for the statutory period, in order to ripen title under the statute. Whether the positive and definite intention to claim *as one's own* the land up to a particular and definite line *on the ground* existed, is the practical test in such cases.

The collateral question whether the possessor would have claimed title, claimed the land as his own, had he believed the land involved did not belong to him, but to another, that is, had he not been mistaken as to the true boundary line called for in his chain of title, is not the proximate but an antecedent question, which is irrelevant and serves only to confuse ideas.

Although in Chaney we said that "use of property, under the mistaken belief of a recorded right, cannot be adverse as long as such mistake continues," we noted that "the present record shows that the [claimants] based their use of Chaney's land *solely* on their mistaken belief that it was the land described in their express easement." 458 S.E.2d at 454 (emphasis added). As we have stated, the claimants in this case based their claim not only on the deed descriptions, but also on their belief that their property line ran to the line of woods. Accordingly, we hold that the claimants' possession was accompanied by the requisite adverse or hostile intent. . . .

Notes and Questions

1. *State of mind, again.* The adversity (or hostility) requirement has proven to be especially problematic in the context of boundary dispute cases. Most jurisdictions follow the objective standard, which, as we saw earlier, provides that the adverse possessor's subjective state of mind is irrelevant. Adversity is judged solely on the basis of the adverse possessor's conduct. A significant minority of jurisdictions follow the "Maine doctrine," however. It is so called because it was first adopted by the courts in Maine, which have since repudiated it in favor of the "Connecticut doctrine," which is the objective approach. Under the Maine doctrine, to prove adversity, the adverse possessor must have "an intention to claim title to all land within a certain boundary on the face of the earth, whether it shall eventually be found to be the correct one or not." Preble v. Maine Cent. R. Co., 27 A. 149, 150 (Me. 1893). Under this approach, an adverse possessor whose possession of part of his neighbor's property was the result of a mistake loses: mistake negates adverse intent.

Did the Virginia court in *Hollander* accept or reject the Maine doctrine? What was its approach to the adversity requirement?

2. *Mistaken improvers.* A problem that can occur in the context of both boundary disputes and adverse possession of larger areas is that of the innocent improver, someone who mistakenly builds on land belonging to another. The early common law on this matter was rather harsh: anything built on the wrong land, whether in good faith or not, became the property of the landowner (subject to the usual exceptions for delay, acquiescence, and estoppel). The modern tendency is to ease the plight of innocent improvers—in that case, by forcing a conveyance (at market value) of land from the owner to the improver. A variation is to give the landowner the option to buy the improvement (again, at market value) instead. Some states have legislation (often called "occupying claimant" or "betterment" acts) that set out these and other remedies.

If the inconvenience caused by an innocent encroachment is so minor as to be trivial, relief might be denied altogether. If, on the other hand, the encroachment takes up a substantial part of the land in question, removal might be ordered notwithstanding the good faith of the encroaching party, depending upon how the court in a particular case strikes a balance between competing considerations. See, e.g., Amkco Ltd., Co. v. Wellborn, 21 P.3d 24 (N.M. 2001), involving an unintentional encroachment that took up almost 10 percent of the plaintiff's land. The court applied a two-part test. First, the plaintiff has to show that it would suffer irreparable harm if removal were denied. But even if irreparable harm is proved, still the relief might be denied under a balancing test that compares the hardship to the plaintiff if removal is denied to the hardship to the defendant if it is granted. If this relative hardship test precludes removal of the encroachment, the encroaching party acquires either title or an easement in the land and pays damages accordingly.

Compare intentional encroachments, as to which most courts require removal of the offending structure, no matter how costly that might be. Why treat intentional encroachers so harshly? See Stewart E. Sterk, Property Rules, Liability Rules, and Uncertainty About Property Rights, 106 Mich. L. Rev. 1285, 1296-1297, 1319-1323 (2008).

Agreed boundaries, acquiescence, and estoppel. Boundary disputes may also be resolved by the doctrines of *agreed boundaries, acquiescence,* and *estoppel.* The doctrine of agreed boundaries provides that if there is uncertainty between neighbors as to the true boundary line, an oral agreement to settle the matter is enforceable if the neighbors subsequently accept the line for a long period of time. The doctrine of acquiescence provides that long acquiescence—though perhaps for a period of time shorter than the statute of limitations—is evidence of an agreement between the parties fixing the boundary line. The doctrine of estoppel comes into play when one neighbor makes representations about (or engages in conduct that tends to indicate) the location of a common boundary, and the other neighbor then changes her position in reliance on the representations or conduct. The first neighbor is then estopped to deny the validity of his statements or acts. Estoppel has also been applied when one neighbor remains silent in the face of expenditures by another that suggest the latter's notion of the boundary's location. The three doctrines are commonly interwoven by the courts, leaving the law vague and tricky to apply.

3. The Mechanics of Adverse Possession

a. Tacking

HOWARD v. KUNTO

Court of Appeals of Washington, 1970
477 P.2d 210

PEARSON, J. Land surveying is an ancient art but not one free of the errors that often creep into the affairs of men. In this case, we are presented with the question of what happens when the descriptions in deeds do not fit the land the deed holders are occupying. Defendants appeal from a decree quieting title in the plaintiffs of a tract of land on the shore of Hood Canal in Mason County.

At least as long ago as 1932 the record tells us that one McCall resided in the house now occupied by the appellant-defendants, Kunto. McCall had a deed that described a 50-foot wide parcel on the shore of Hood Canal. The error that brings this case before us is that the 50 feet described in the deed is not the same 50 feet upon which McCall's house stood. Rather, the described land is an adjacent 50-foot lot directly west of that upon which the house stood. In other words, McCall's house stood on one lot and his deed described the adjacent lot. Several property owners to the west of defendants, not parties to this action, are similarly situated.

Over the years since 1946, several conveyances occurred, using the same legal description and accompanied by a transfer of possession to the succeeding occupants. The Kuntos' immediate predecessors in interest, the Millers, desired to build a dock. To this end, they had a survey performed which indicated that the deed description and the physical occupation were in conformity. Several boundary stakes were placed as a result of this survey and the dock was constructed, as well as other improvements. The house as well as the others in the area continued to be used as summer recreational retreats.

The Kuntos then took possession of the disputed property under a deed from the Millers in 1959. In 1960 the respondent-plaintiffs, Howard, who held land east of that of the Kuntos, determined to convey an undivided one-half interest in their land to the Yearlys. To this end, they undertook to have a survey of the entire area made. After expending considerable effort, the surveyor retained by the Howards discovered that according to the government survey, the deed descriptions and the land occupancy of the parties did not coincide. Between the Howards and the Kuntos lay the Moyers' property. When the Howards' survey was completed, they discovered that they were the record owners of the land occupied by the Moyers and that the Moyers held record title to the land occupied by the Kuntos. Howard approached Moyer and in return for a conveyance of the land upon which the Moyers' house stood, Moyer conveyed to the Howards record title to the land upon which the Kunto house stood. Until plaintiffs Howard obtained the conveyance from Moyer in April, 1960, neither Moyer nor any of his predecessors ever asserted any right to ownership of the property actually being possessed by Kunto and his predecessors. This action was then instituted to quiet title in the Howards and Yearlys. The Kuntos appeal from a trial court decision granting this remedy.

Situation in
Howard v. Kunto:

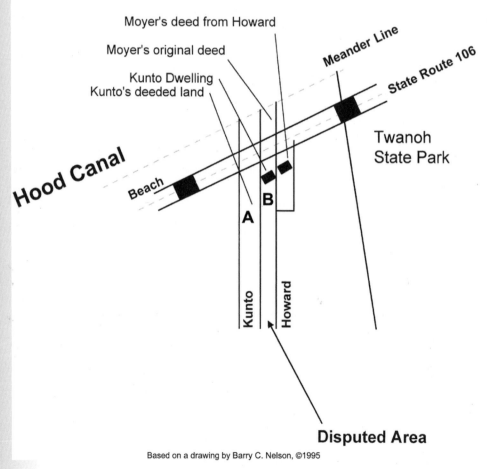

Based on a drawing by Barry C. Nelson, ©1995

Figure 2-1

At the time this action was commenced on August 19, 1960,[2] the defendants had been in occupance of the disputed property less than a year. The trial court's reason for denying their claim of adverse possession is succinctly stated in its memorandum opinion: "In this instance, defendants have failed to prove, by a preponderance of the evidence, a continuity of possession or estate to permit tacking of the adverse possession of defendants to the possession of their predecessors."

Finding of fact 6,[3] which is challenged by defendants, incorporates the above concept and additionally finds defendant's possession not to have been "continuous" because it involved only "summer occupancy."

Two issues are presented by this appeal:

(1) Is a claim of adverse possession defeated because the physical use of the premises is restricted to summer occupancy?

(2) May a person who receives record title to tract A under the mistaken belief that he has title to tract B (immediately contiguous to tract A) and who subsequently occupies tract B, for the purpose of establishing title to tract B by adverse possession, use the periods of possession of tract B by his immediate predecessors who also had record title to tract A?

In approaching both of these questions, we point out that the evidence, largely undisputed in any material sense, established that defendant or his immediate predecessors did occupy the premises, which we have called tract B, as though it was their own for more than the 10 years as prescribed in RCW 4.16.020.[4]

We also point out that finding of fact 6 is not challenged for its factual determinations but for the conclusions contained therein to the effect that the continuity of

---

2. The inordinate delay in bringing this matter to trial appears from the record to be largely inexcusable. However, neither counsel who tried the case was at fault in any way. We have intentionally declined to consider defendant's motion (probably well founded) to dismiss this case for want of prosecution . . . for the reason that a new trial of the same issues would be inevitable and in light of our disposition of the case on the merits, defendants are not prejudiced by disregarding the technical grounds.

3. "In the instant case the defendants' building was not simply over the line, but instead was built wholly upon the wrong piece of property, not the property of defendants, described in Paragraph Four of the complaint herein, but on the property of the plaintiffs, described in Paragraph Three of the complaint and herein. That the last three deeds in the chain of title, covering and embracing defendants' property, including defendants' deed, were executed in other states, specifically, California and Oregon. And there is no evidence of pointing out to the grantees in said three deeds, aforesaid, including defendants' deed, of any specific property, other than the property of defendants, described in their deed, and in Paragraph Four (4) of the complaint, and herein; nor of any immediate act of the grantees, including defendants, in said three (3) deeds, aforesaid, of taking possession of any property, other than described in said three (3) deeds, aforesaid; and the testimony of husband defendant, was unequivocally that he had no intention of possessing or holding anything other than what the deed called for; and, that there is no showing of any continuous possession by defendants or their immediate predecessors in interest, since the evidence indicates the property was in the nature, for use, as a summer occupancy, and such occupancy and use was for rather limited periods of time during comparatively short portions of the year, and was far from continuous."

4. This statute provides:

4.16.020 Actions to be commenced within ten years. The period prescribed in RCW 4.16.010 for the commencement of actions shall be as follows:
Within ten years;
Actions for the recovery of real property, or for the recovery of the possession thereof; and no action shall be maintained for such recovery unless it appears that the plaintiff, his ancestor, predecessor or grantor was seized or possessed of the premises in question within ten years before the commencement of the action.

possession may not be established by summer occupancy, and that a predecessor's possession may not be tacked because a legal "claim of right" did not exist under the circumstances.

We start with the oft-quoted rule that: "[T]o constitute adverse possession, there must be actual possession which is *uninterrupted*, open and notorious, hostile and exclusive, and under a *claim of right* made in good faith for the statutory period." (Italics ours.) Butler v. Anderson, 71 Wash. 2d 60, 64, 426 P.2d 467, 470 (1967).[5]

We reject the conclusion that summer occupancy only of a summer beach home destroys the continuity of possession required by the statute. It has become firmly established that the requisite possession requires such possession and dominion "as ordinarily marks the conduct of owners in general in holding, managing, and caring for property of like nature and condition." Whalen v. Smith, 183 Iowa 949, 953, 167 N.W. 646, 647 (1918). . . .

We hold that occupancy of tract B during the summer months for more than the 10-year period by defendant and his predecessors, together with the continued existence of the improvements on the land and beach area, constituted "uninterrupted" possession within this rule. To hold otherwise is to completely ignore the nature and condition of the property. . . .

We find such rule fully consonant with the legal writers on the subject. In F. Clark, Law of Surveying and Boundaries, § 561 (3d ed. 1959) at 565: "Continuity of possession may be established although the land is used regularly for only a certain period each year." Further, at 566:

> This rule . . . is one of substance and not of absolute mathematical continuity, provided there is no break so as to sever two possessions. It is not necessary that the occupant should be actually upon the premises continually. If the land is occupied during the period of time during the year it is capable of use, there is sufficient continuity.

We now reach the question of tacking. The precise issue before us is novel in that none of the property occupied by defendant or his predecessors coincided with the property described in their deeds, but was contiguous.

In the typical case, which has been subject to much litigation, the party seeking to establish title by adverse possession claims *more* land than that described in the deed. In such cases it is clear that tacking is permitted.

In Buchanan v. Cassell, 53 Wash. 2d 611, 614, 335 P.2d 600, 602 (1959), the Supreme Court stated: "This state follows the rule that a purchaser may tack the adverse use of its predecessor in interest to that of his own where the land was intended to be included in the deed between them, but was mistakenly omitted from the description." El Cerito, Inc. v. Ryndak, 60 Wash. 2d 847, 376 P.2d 528 (1962).

The general statement which appears in many of the cases is that tacking of adverse possession is permitted if the successive occupants are in "privity." See Faubion v. Elder, 49 Wash. 2d 300, 301 P.2d 153 (1956). The deed running between the parties purporting to transfer the land possessed traditionally furnishes the privity of estate

---

5. In 1984, the Washington Supreme Court overruled Howard v. Kunto to the extent that the case suggests a *good-faith* requirement for adverse possession. See Chaplin v. Sanders, 676 P.2d, 431, 436 (Wash. 1984). — EDS.

which connects the possession of the successive occupants. Plaintiff contends, and the trial court ruled, that where the deed does not describe *any* of the land which was occupied, the actual transfer of possession is insufficient to establish privity.

To assess the cogency of this argument and ruling, we must turn to the historical reasons for requiring privity as a necessary prerequisite to tacking the possession of several occupants. Very few, if any, of the reasons appear in the cases, nor do the cases analyze the relationships that must exist between successive possessors for tacking to be allowed. See W. Stoebuck, The Law of Adverse Possession in Washington in 35 Wash. L. Rev. 53 (1960).

The requirement of privity had its roots in the notion that a succession of trespasses, even though there was no appreciable interval between them, should not, in equity, be allowed to defeat the record title. The "claim of right," "color of title" requirement of the statutes and cases was probably derived from the early American belief that the squatter should not be able to profit by his trespass.

However, it appears to this court that there is a substantial difference between the squatter or trespasser and the property purchaser, who along with several of his neighbors, as a result of an inaccurate survey or subdivision, occupies and improves property exactly 50 feet to the east of that which a survey some 30 years later demonstrates that they in fact own. It seems to us that there is also a strong public policy favoring early certainty as to the location of land ownership which enters into a proper interpretation of privity.

On the irregular perimeters of Puget Sound exact determination of land locations and boundaries is difficult and expensive. This difficulty is convincingly demonstrated in this case by the problems plaintiff's engineer encountered in attempting to locate the corners. It cannot be expected that every purchaser will or should engage a surveyor to ascertain that the beach home he is purchasing lies within the boundaries described in his deed. Such a practice is neither reasonable nor customary. Of course, 50-foot errors in descriptions are devastating where a group of adjacent owners each hold 50 feet of waterfront property.

The technical requirement of "privity" should not, we think, be used to upset the long periods of occupancy of those who in good faith received an erroneous deed description. Their "claim of right" is no less persuasive than the purchaser who believes he is purchasing *more* land than his deed described.

In the final analysis, however, we believe the requirement of "privity" is no more than judicial recognition of the need for some reasonable connection between successive occupants of real property so as to raise their claim of right above the status of the wrongdoer or the trespasser. We think such reasonable connection exists in this case.

Where, as here, several successive purchasers received record title to tract A under the mistaken belief that they were acquiring tract B, immediately contiguous thereto, and where possession of tract B is transferred and occupied in a continuous manner for more than 10 years by successive occupants, we hold there is sufficient privity of estate to permit tacking and thus establish adverse possession as a matter of law.

We see no reason in law or in equity for differentiating this case from Faubion v. Elder, 49 Wash. 2d 300, 301 P.2d 153 (1956), where the appellants were claiming *more* land than their deed described and where successive periods of occupation were allowed to be united to each other to make up the time of adverse holding. . . .

This application of the privity requirement should particularly pertain where the holder of record title to tract B acquired the same with knowledge of the discrepancy.

Judgment is reversed with directions to dismiss plaintiffs' action and to enter a decree quieting defendants' title to the disputed tract of land in accordance with the prayer of their cross-complaint.

Notes and Questions

1. *Tacking and privity of estate.* As the court in *Howard* states, under American law, tacking between successive adverse possessors is usually permitted only when they are in *privity of estate* with each other. Privity clearly exists where *A*, who possesses for a period of time less than the statutory period, voluntarily transfers the property to *B*, who then possesses for a period that, together with that of *A*, exceeds the statutory period. On the other hand, privity clearly does not exist if *A* abandons possession after less than the statutory period and *B* takes over possession. Why should these two situations be treated differently? English common law does not require privity for tacking. Is this the better approach?

2. *Privity in Howard v. Kunto.* Howard v. Kunto involves a fact situation somewhere between the two extremes described in Note 1: the Kuntos did take possession after receiving a deed, but the deed described land that was not the same as the land they possessed. In what sense, then, was there privity of estate between the Kuntos and their predecessors? Are there good reasons to allow tacking in this situation?

3. *Continuity.* The requirement of continuity was also at issue in Howard v. Kunto because the Kuntos were in possession only during the summer months. Suppose that instead of building a summer house on "their" lot, the Kuntos and their predecessors had camped every summer on the lot and, being good environmentalists, had left no traces when they removed their camp in the fall. Would this satisfy the requirement of continuity? Compare Ray v. Beacon Hudson Mountain Corp., 666 N.E.2d 532 (N.Y. 1996).

For an argument that adverse possession rules favor economic exploitation of wild lands by permitting successful claims of adverse possession of wild lands to rest on limited, sporadic activities that would not be sufficient for developed lands, see John G. Sprankling, An Environmental Critique of Adverse Possession, 79 Cornell L. Rev. 816 (1994). Inasmuch as strengthening the standard for adverse possession of wild lands might result in claimants inflicting more environmental injury, Professor Sprankling suggests exempting wild lands altogether from adverse possession. See also Alexandra B. Klass, Adverse Possession and Conservation: Expanding Traditional Notions of Use and Possession, 77 U. Colo. L. Rev. 283 (2006).

b. Disabilities

In every state, the statute of limitations is extended if specified disabilities are present. Disability provisions differ, but the following example is typical:

An action to recover the title to or possession of real property shall be brought within twenty-one years after the cause thereof accrued, but if a person entitled to bring such action, at the time the cause thereof accrues, is within the age of minority, of unsound mind, or imprisoned, such person, after the expiration of twenty-one years from the time the cause of action accrues, may bring such action within ten years after such disability is removed.

Particularly note two matters: A disability is immaterial unless it existed at the time when the cause of action accrued. And after the words "such person," you should insert, as a result of judicial construction, the words "or anyone claiming from, by, or under such person." (Do you see why a court would read those words into the statute?)

Problems

When in the following situations would the adverse possessor acquire title under the statute set out above? In each case, *O* is the owner in 1994, and *A* enters adversely on May 1, 1994. The age of majority is 18.
1. *O* is insane in 1994. *O* dies insane and intestate in 2017.
   (a) *O*'s heir, *H,* is under no disability in 2017.
   (b) *O*'s heir, *H,* is six years old in 2017.
2. *O* has no disability in 1994. *O* dies intestate in 2012. *O*'s heir, *H,* is two years old in 2012.

Adverse possession against the government. Under the common law rules, adverse possession does not run against the government—local, state, or federal. In England, the maxim *nullum tempus occurrit regi* (no time runs against the king) barred the running of the statute of limitations against the sovereign. In barring adverse possession against the government, American courts have relied on this rule as well as state constitutional provisions restricting the alienation of state lands. Courts often say, in justification, that the state owns its land in trust for all the people, who should not lose the land because of the negligence of a few state officers or employees.

A number of states, however, have changed the common law rules, whether by legislation or judge-made law. A few permit adverse possession against government land on the same terms as against private land. Others permit it only if possession continues for a period much longer than that applied in the case of private lands. Still others permit it only against government lands held in a proprietary (as opposed to a public or governmental) capacity. See, e.g., American Trading Real Estate Properties, Inc. v. Town of Trumbull, 574 A.2d 796 (Conn. 1990); Devins v. Borough of Bogota, 592 A.2d 199 (N.J. 1991).

Are there good reasons to treat government lands differently from those privately owned? What types of land might justifiably be subjected to adverse possession and what types not?

4. Adverse Possession of Chattels

O'KEEFFE v. SNYDER

Supreme Court of New Jersey, 1980
416 A.2d 862

POLLOCK, J. This is an appeal from an order of the Appellate Division granting summary judgment to plaintiff, Georgia O'Keeffe, against defendant, Barry Snyder, d/b/a Princeton Gallery of Fine Arts, for replevin of three small pictures painted by O'Keeffe. In her complaint, filed in March, 1976, O'Keeffe alleged she was the owner of the paintings and that they were stolen from a New York art gallery in 1946. Snyder asserted he was a purchaser for value of the paintings, he had title by adverse possession, and O'Keeffe's action was barred by the expiration of the six-year period of limitations . . . pertaining to an action in replevin. Snyder impleaded third party defendant, Ulrich A. Frank, from whom Snyder purchased the paintings in 1975 for $35,000.

The trial court granted summary judgment for Snyder on the ground that O'Keeffe's action was barred because it was not commenced within six years of the alleged theft. The Appellate Division reversed and entered judgment for O'Keeffe. A majority of that court concluded that the paintings were stolen, the defenses of expiration of the statute of limitations and title by adverse possession were identical, and Snyder had not proved the elements of adverse possession. Consequently, the majority ruled that O'Keeffe could still enforce her right to possession of the paintings.

. . . We reverse and remand the matter for a plenary hearing in accordance with this opinion.

The record, limited to pleadings, affidavits, answers to interrogatories, and depositions, is fraught with factual conflict. Apart from the creation of the paintings by O'Keeffe and their discovery in Snyder's gallery in 1976, the parties agree on little else.

O'Keeffe contended the paintings were stolen in 1946 from a gallery, An American Place. The gallery was operated by her late husband, the famous photographer Alfred Stieglitz.

An American Place was a cooperative undertaking of O'Keeffe and some other American artists identified by her as Marin, Hardin, Dove, Andema, and Stevens. In 1946, Stieglitz arranged an exhibit which included an O'Keeffe painting, identified as Cliffs. According to O'Keeffe, one day in March, 1946, she and Stieglitz discovered Cliffs was missing from the wall of the exhibit. O'Keeffe estimates the value of the painting at the time of the alleged theft to have been about $150.

About two weeks later, O'Keeffe noticed that two other paintings, Seaweed and Fragments, were missing from a storage room at An American Place. She did not tell anyone, even Stieglitz, about the missing paintings, since she did not want to upset him.

Before the date when O'Keeffe discovered the disappearance of Seaweed, she had already sold it (apparently for a string of amber beads) to a Mrs. Weiner, now deceased. Following the grant of the motion for summary judgment by the trial court in favor of Snyder, O'Keeffe submitted a release from the legatees of Mrs. Weiner purportedly assigning to O'Keeffe their interest in the sale.

O'Keeffe testified on depositions that at about the same time as the disappearance of her paintings, 12 or 13 miniature paintings by Marin also were stolen from An

American Place. According to O'Keeffe, a man named Estrick took the Marin paintings and "maybe a few other things." Estrick distributed the Marin paintings to members of the theater world who, when confronted by Stieglitz, returned them. However, neither Stieglitz nor O'Keeffe confronted Estrick with the loss of any of the O'Keeffe paintings.

There was no evidence of a break and entry at An American Place on the dates when O'Keeffe discovered the disappearance of her paintings. Neither Stieglitz nor O'Keeffe reported them missing to the New York Police Department or any other law enforcement agency. Apparently the paintings were uninsured, and O'Keeffe did not seek reimbursement from an insurance company. Similarly, neither O'Keeffe nor Stieglitz advertised the loss of the paintings in Art News or any other publication. Nonetheless, they discussed it with associates in the art world and later O'Keeffe mentioned the loss to the director of the Art Institute of Chicago, but she did not ask him to do anything because "it wouldn't have been my way." O'Keeffe does not contend that Frank or Snyder had actual knowledge of the alleged theft.

Stieglitz died in the summer of 1946, and O'Keeffe explains she did not pursue her efforts to locate the paintings because she was settling his estate. In 1947, she retained the services of Doris Bry to help settle the estate. Bry urged O'Keeffe to report the loss of the paintings, but O'Keeffe declined because "they never got anything back by reporting it." Finally, in 1972, O'Keeffe authorized Bry to report the theft to the Art Dealers Association of America, Inc., which maintains for its members a registry of stolen paintings. The record does not indicate whether such a registry existed at the time the paintings disappeared.

In September, 1975, O'Keeffe learned that the paintings were in the Andrew Crispo Gallery in New York on consignment from Bernard Danenberg Galleries. On February 11, 1976, O'Keeffe discovered that Ulrich A. Frank had sold the paintings to Barry Snyder, d/b/a Princeton Gallery of Fine Art. She demanded their return and, following Snyder's refusal, instituted this action for replevin.

Frank traces his possession of the paintings to his father, Dr. Frank, who died in 1968. He claims there is a family relationship by marriage between his family and the Stieglitz family, a contention that O'Keeffe disputes. Frank does not know how his father acquired the paintings, but he recalls seeing them in his father's apartment in New Hampshire as early as 1941-1943, a period that precedes the alleged theft. Consequently, Frank's factual contentions are inconsistent with O'Keeffe's allegation of theft. Until 1965, Dr. Frank occasionally lent the paintings to Ulrich Frank. In 1965, Dr. and Mrs. Frank formally gave the paintings to Ulrich Frank, who kept them in his residences in Yardley, Pennsylvania and Princeton, New Jersey. In 1968, he exhibited anonymously Cliffs and Fragments in a one day art show in the Jewish Community Center in Trenton. All of these events precede O'Keeffe's listing of the paintings as stolen with the Art Dealers Association of America, Inc. in 1972.

Frank claims continuous possession of the paintings through his father for over thirty years and admits selling the paintings to Snyder. Snyder and Frank do not trace their provenance, or history of possession of the paintings, back to O'Keeffe.

As indicated, Snyder moved for summary judgment on the theory that O'Keeffe's action was barred by the statute of limitations and title had vested in Frank by adverse possession. For purposes of his motion, Snyder conceded that the paintings had been stolen. On her cross motion, O'Keeffe urged that the paintings were stolen, the statute of limitations had not run, and title to the paintings remained in her. . . .

The Appellate Division accepted O'Keeffe's contention that the paintings had been stolen. However, in his deposition, Ulrich Frank traces possession of the paintings to his father in the early 1940s, a date that precedes the alleged theft by several years. The factual dispute about the loss of the paintings by O'Keeffe and their acquisition by Frank, as well as the other subsequently described factual issues, warrant a remand for a plenary hearing. . . .

Without purporting to limit the scope of the trial, other factual issues include whether . . . the paintings were not stolen but sold, lent, consigned, or given by Stieglitz to Dr. Frank or someone else without O'Keeffe's knowledge before he died; and [whether] there was any business or family relationship between Stieglitz and Dr. Frank so that the original possession of the paintings by the Frank family may have been under claim of right.

On the limited record before us, we cannot determine now who has title to the paintings. The determination will depend on the evidence adduced at trial. Nonetheless, we believe it may aid the trial court and the parties to resolve questions of law that may become relevant at trial.

Seaweed (1926)
Georgia O'Keeffe
Copyright © 2017 Georgia O'Keeffe Museum
Artists Rights Society (ARS), New York

Our discussion begins with the principle that, generally speaking, if the paintings were stolen, the thief acquired no title and could not transfer good title to others regardless of their good faith and ignorance of the theft. Proof of theft would advance O'Keeffe's right to possession of the paintings absent other considerations such as expiration of the statute of limitations.

Another issue that may become relevant at trial is whether Frank or his father acquired a "voidable title" to the paintings under N.J.S.A. 12A:2-403(1). That section, part of the Uniform Commercial Code (U.C.C.),[6] does not change the basic principle that a mere possessor cannot transfer good title. Nonetheless, the U.C.C. permits a person with voidable title to transfer good title to a good faith purchaser for value in certain circumstances. If the facts developed at trial merit application of that section, then Frank may have transferred good title to Snyder, thereby providing a defense to O'Keeffe's action. . . .

On this appeal, the critical legal question is when O'Keeffe's cause of action accrued. The fulcrum on which the outcome turns is the statute of limitations . . . , which provides that an action for replevin of goods or chattels must be commenced within six years after the accrual of the cause of action.

The trial court found that O'Keeffe's cause of action accrued on the date of the alleged theft, March, 1946, and concluded that her action was barred. The Appellate Division found that an action might have accrued more than six years before the date of suit if possession by the defendant or his predecessors satisfied the elements of adverse possession. As indicated, the Appellate Division concluded that Snyder had not established those elements and that the O'Keeffe action was not barred by the statute of limitations. . . .

The purpose of a statute of limitations is to "stimulate to activity and punish negligence" and "promote repose by giving security and stability to human affairs." Wood v. Carpenter, 101 U.S. 135, 139, 25 L. Ed. 807, 808 (1879). A statute of limitations achieves those purposes by barring a cause of action after the statutory period. In certain instances, this Court has ruled that the literal language of a statute of limitations should yield to other considerations.

To avoid harsh results from the mechanical application of the statute, the courts have developed a concept known as the discovery rule. The discovery rule provides that, in an appropriate case, a cause of action will not accrue until the injured party

---

6. Uniform Commercial Code § 2-403 provides:

§ 2-403. *Power to Transfer; Good Faith Purchase of Goods; "Entrusting."*
    (1) A purchaser of goods acquires all title which his transferor had or had power to transfer except that a purchaser of a limited interest acquires rights only to the extent of the interest purchased. A person with voidable title has power to transfer a good title to a good faith purchaser for value. When goods have been delivered under a transaction of purchase the purchaser has such power even though
        (a) the transferor was deceived as to the identity of the purchaser, or
        (b) the delivery was in exchange for a check which was later dishonored, or
        (c) it was agreed that the transaction was to be a "cash sale," or
        (d) the delivery was procured through fraud punishable as larcenous under the criminal law.
    (2) Any entrusting of possession of goods to a merchant who deals in goods of that kind gives him power to transfer all rights of the entruster to a buyer in the ordinary course of business.
    (3) "Entrusting" includes any delivery and any acquiescence in retention of possession regardless of any condition expressed between the parties to the delivery or acquiescence and regardless of whether the procurement of the entrusting or the possessor's disposition of the goods have been such as to be larcenous under the criminal law. — EDS.

discovers, or by exercise of reasonable diligence and intelligence should have discovered, facts which form the basis of a cause of action. The rule is essentially a principle of equity, the purpose of which is to mitigate unjust results that otherwise might flow from strict adherence to a rule of law. . . .

[W]e conclude that the discovery rule applies to an action for replevin of a painting. . . . O'Keeffe's cause of action accrued when she first knew, or reasonably should have known through the exercise of due diligence, of the cause of action, including the identity of the possessor of the paintings. . . .

In determining whether O'Keeffe is entitled to the benefit of the discovery rule, the trial court should consider, among others, the following issues: (1) whether O'Keeffe used due diligence to recover the paintings at the time of the alleged theft and thereafter; (2) whether at the time of the alleged theft there was an effective method, other than talking to her colleagues, for O'Keeffe to alert the art world; and (3) whether registering paintings with the Art Dealers Association of America, Inc. or any other organization would put a reasonably prudent purchaser of art on constructive notice that someone other than the possessor was the true owner.

The acquisition of title to real and personal property by adverse possession is based on the expiration of a statute of limitations. . . .

To establish title by adverse possession to chattels, the rule of law has been that the possession must be hostile, actual, visible, exclusive, and continuous. . . . There is an inherent problem with many kinds of personal property that will raise questions whether their possession has been open, visible, and notorious. . . . For example, if jewelry is stolen from a municipality in one county in New Jersey, it is unlikely that the owner would learn that someone is openly wearing that jewelry in another county or even in the same municipality. Open and visible possession of personal property, such as jewelry, may not be sufficient to put the original owner on actual or constructive notice of the identity of the possessor.

The problem is even more acute with works of art. Like many kinds of personal property, works of art are readily moved and easily concealed. O'Keeffe argues that nothing short of public display should be sufficient to alert the true owner and start the statute running. Although there is merit in that contention from the perspective of the original owner, the effect is to impose a heavy burden on the purchasers of paintings who wish to enjoy the paintings in the privacy of their homes. . . .

The problem is serious. According to an affidavit submitted in this matter by the president of the International Foundation for Art Research, there has been an "explosion in art thefts" and there is a "worldwide phenomenon of art theft which has reached epidemic proportions."

The limited record before us provides a brief glimpse into the arcane world of sales of art, where paintings worth vast sums of money sometimes are bought without inquiry about their provenance. There does not appear to be a reasonably available method for an owner of art to record the ownership or theft of paintings. Similarly, there are no reasonable means readily available to a purchaser to ascertain the provenance of a painting. It may be time for the art world to establish a means by which a good faith purchaser may reasonably obtain the provenance of a painting. An efficient registry of original works of art might better serve the interests of artists, owners of art, and bona fide purchasers than the law of adverse possession with all of its uncertainties. Although we cannot mandate the initiation of a registration system, we can develop a rule for the commencement and running of the statute of limitations that is more responsive to the needs of the art world than the doctrine of adverse possession.

We are persuaded that the introduction of equitable considerations through the discovery rule provides a more satisfactory response than the doctrine of adverse possession. The discovery rule shifts the emphasis from the conduct of the possessor to the conduct of the owner. The focus of the inquiry will no longer be whether the possessor has met the tests of adverse possession, but whether the owner has acted with due diligence in pursuing his or her personal property.

For example, under the discovery rule, if an artist diligently seeks the recovery of a lost or stolen painting, but cannot find it or discover the identity of the possessor, the statute of limitations will not begin to run. The rule permits an artist who uses reasonable efforts to report, investigate, and recover a painting to preserve the rights of title and possession.

Properly interpreted, the discovery rule becomes a vehicle for transporting equitable considerations into the statute of limitations for replevin. . . .

It is consistent also with the law of replevin as it has developed apart from the discovery rule. In an action for replevin, the period of limitations ordinarily will run against the owner of lost or stolen property from the time of the wrongful taking, absent fraud or concealment. Where the chattel is fraudulently concealed, the general rule is that the statute is tolled. . . .

A purchaser from a private party would be well-advised to inquire whether a work of art has been reported as lost or stolen. However, a bona fide purchaser who purchases in the ordinary course of business a painting entrusted to an art dealer should be able to acquire good title against the true owner. Under the U.C.C. entrusting possession of goods to a merchant who deals in that kind of goods gives the merchant the power to transfer all the rights of the entruster to a buyer in the ordinary course of business. In a transaction under that statute, a merchant may vest good title in the buyer as against the original owner. The interplay between the statute of limitations as modified by the discovery rule and the U.C.C. should encourage good faith purchases from legitimate art dealers and discourage trafficking in stolen art without frustrating an artist's ability to recover stolen art works.

The discovery rule will fulfill the purposes of a statute of limitations and accord greater protection to the innocent owner of personal property whose goods are lost or stolen. . . .

By diligently pursuing their goods, owners may prevent the statute of limitations from running. The meaning of due diligence will vary with the facts of each case, including the nature and value of the personal property. For example, with respect to jewelry of moderate value, it may be sufficient if the owner reports the theft to the police. With respect to art work of greater value, it may be reasonable to expect an owner to do more. In practice, our ruling should contribute to more careful practices concerning the purchase of art.

The considerations are different with real estate, and there is no reason to disturb the application of the doctrine of adverse possession to real estate. Real estate is fixed and cannot be moved or concealed. The owner of real property knows or should know where his property is located and reasonably can be expected to be aware of open, notorious, visible, hostile, continuous acts of possession on it.

Our ruling not only changes the requirements for acquiring title to personal property after an alleged unlawful taking, but also shifts the burden of proof at trial.

Georgia O'Keeffe grew up in the rural Midwest. After studying art in Chicago and New York, she decided to paint shapes that, she claimed, were "in [her] head." In 1915, she sent some of her drawings—of budding and organic shapes, reflecting an intense feminine sensibility—to a friend in New York, admonishing her to show them to no one. The friend, disregarding O'Keeffe's wishes, showed them to Alfred Stieglitz, the noted New York photographer and gallery owner. Upon seeing the drawings, Stieglitz remarked, "At last, a woman on paper," and promptly displayed them in his gallery. When, shortly thereafter, O'Keeffe came to New York and learned of this, she was furious. She rushed to the gallery and demanded that her private work be taken down. Stieglitz refused, and the paintings remained. Stieglitz, obsessed with this woman 20 years his junior, soon left his wife and daughter and moved in with her. "He photographed me until I was crazy," O'Keeffe recalled in her nineties. He photographed every square inch of O'Keeffe nude, then exhibited the pictures in a show, creating a scandal and bringing O'Keeffe instant fame.

O'Keeffe and Stieglitz married in 1924. When, a few years later, Stieglitz entered into a liaison with a woman half O'Keeffe's age, and put her in charge of his gallery, O'Keeffe found that New Mexico was where she belonged, but she could not leave Stieglitz. She returned to New York every fall to renew her bond with him. When Stieglitz died in 1946, at age 82, O'Keeffe moved to New Mexico for good. She died in 1986 at age 99.

Under the doctrine of adverse possession, the burden is on the possessor to prove the elements of adverse possession. Under the discovery rule, the burden is on the owner as the one seeking the benefit of the rule to establish facts that would justify deferring the beginning of the period of limitations. . . .

Read literally, the effect of the expiration of the statute of limitations . . . is to bar an action such as replevin. The statute does not speak of divesting the original owner of title. By its terms the statute cuts off the remedy, but not the right of title. Nonetheless, the effect of the expiration of the statute of limitations, albeit on the theory of adverse possession, has been not only to bar an action for possession, but also to vest title in the possessor. There is no reason to change that result although the discovery rule has replaced adverse possession. History, reason, and common sense support the conclusion that the expiration of the statute of limitations bars the remedy to recover possession and also vests title in the possessor. . . . Before the expiration of the statute, the possessor has both the chattel and the right to keep it except as against the true owner. The only imperfection in the possessor's right to retain the chattel is the original owner's right to repossess it. Once that imperfection is removed, the possessor should have good title for all purposes. . . .

We next consider the effect of transfers of a chattel from one possessor to another during the period of limitation under the discovery rule. Under the discovery rule, the statute of limitations on an action for replevin begins to run when the owner knows or reasonably should know of his cause of action and the identity of the possessor of the chattel. Subsequent transfers of the chattel are part of the continuous dispossession of the chattel from the original owner. The important point is not that there has been a substitution of possessors, but that there has been a continuous dispossession of the former owner. . . .

For the purpose of evaluating the due diligence of an owner, the dispossession of his chattel is a continuum not susceptible to separation into distinct acts. Nonetheless, subsequent transfers of the chattel may affect the degree of difficulty encountered by a diligent owner seeking to recover his goods. To that extent, subsequent transfers and their potential for frustrating diligence are relevant in applying

Georgia O'Keeffe, 1968
© Arnold Newman/Getty Images

the discovery rule. An owner who diligently seeks his chattel should be entitled to the benefit of the discovery rule although it may have passed through many hands. Conversely an owner who sleeps on his rights may be denied the benefit of the discovery rule although the chattel may have been possessed by only one person.

We reject the alternative of treating subsequent transfers of a chattel as separate acts of conversion that would start the statute of limitations running anew. At common law, apart from the statute of limitations, a subsequent transfer of a converted chattel was considered to be a separate act of conversion. . . . Adoption of that alternative would tend to undermine the purpose of the statute in quieting titles and protecting against stale claims.

The majority and better view is to permit tacking, the accumulation of consecutive periods of possession by parties in privity with each other. . . .

We reverse the judgment of the Appellate Division in favor of O'Keeffe and remand the matter for trial in accordance with this opinion.

[Dissenting opinions by Justice Sullivan and Justice Handler are omitted.]

THE REST OF THE STORY . . .

The parties subsequently settled before a retrial. The paintings were divided. O'Keeffe took *Seaweed*, Snyder took another painting, and the third was sold at auction at Sotheby's to pay lawyers' bills.

Notes and Questions

1. *Different approaches.* Various courts have developed several different approaches to determining the time when the statute of limitations begins to run for purposes of adverse possession of personal property:

- *The conversion rule.* This is the simplest rule and the one most closely tied to the statute of limitations itself. According to this rule, the statute begins to rule against the true owner as soon as the property is converted. This is the rule that the trial court in *O'Keeffe* applied.
- *The adverse possession approach.* This is the traditional approach. Under it the limitation period begins to run when the adverse possessor takes possession of the chattel, and the usual requirements of adverse possession are applied. This was the approach that the Appellate Division in *O'Keeffe* applied. That court found that defendant Snyder had failed to satisfy the open and notorious requirement.
- *The discovery rule.* According to this rule, the cause of action for conversion does not accrue, triggering the running of the statute of limitations, until the owner "discovers, or by exercise of reasonable diligence and intelligence should have discovered, facts which form the basis of a cause of action." *O'Keeffe*, 416 A.2d at 869. This is the rule that the New Jersey Supreme Court in *O'Keeffe* adopted. As a general matter, it gives the owner a longer interval of time to recover the property than the conversion rule.
- *The demand rule.* Under this rule, the statute of limitations does not begin to run until the true owner makes a demand for the return of the property and the demand is refused. The New York Court of Appeals adopted the demand rule in Solomon R. Guggenheim Found. v. Lubell, 569 N.E.2d 426 (N.Y. 1991).

Which of these three rules is most protective of the true owner? In *Guggenheim*, the court stated that it rejected the discovery rule on the ground that it provides insufficient protection for owners of stolen artwork (New York is probably the site of most purchases of major works of art in the United States). Should protection of good-faith purchasers of stolen goods be the primary objective of this area of adverse possession law?

2. *Applying the discovery rule to* O'Keeffe. According to the court in *O'Keeffe*, under the discovery rule "the focus of the inquiry [is] whether the owner has acted with due diligence in pursuing his or her personal property." Will Georgia O'Keeffe likely be able to satisfy that requirement?

3. *U.C.C. § 2-403.* The court in *O'Keeffe* stated that upon remand, one issue will be whether Frank or his father had *voidable title* to the paintings under U.C.C. § 2-403. It is important to distinguish between *voidable* title and *void* title. The *void title rule* is that if a person acquires possession of a good where the true owner did not intend to transfer title to the good, then the possessor acquires no title to that good and cannot transfer good title to it to anyone else. Title that was void in the transferor's hands is void in the transferee's hands as well. So, a thief, for example, has void title. *Voidable title* is an exception to this rule. Voidable title exists where the true owner intends to transfer the good, even though transfer of possession was procured through fraud or misrepresentation. Unlike void title,

with voidable title delivery is voluntary. Voidable title is a defective title, but it is a title that, although the true owner can rescind, becomes a good title if transferred to a good-faith purchaser for value. The idea is not simply to protect innocent parties, but to protect commercial transactions, which depend upon the ability of innocent purchasers to rely upon the apparently good title of their sellers. U.C.C. § 2-403(1), reprinted in full in footnote 6 on page 163 supra, provides four specific circumstances for the creation of voidable title. For example, suppose that *O* sells a Georgia O'Keeffe painting that *O* owns for $150,000 to *A*. *A* hands *O* a check for that amount, and then sells the painting to *B* for $200,000. However, *A*'s bank account is insufficient to cover the amount of the check, and the check bounces. Under U.C.C. § 2-403(1)(b), *B* owns the painting. *A* had voidable title, giving him the power to transfer good title to *B*, a good-faith purchaser.

Another issue on remand will be whether O'Keeffe "entrusted" the paintings to a "merchant who deals in goods of that kind." U.C.C. § 2-403(2). The UCC defines "entrusting" as any delivery "regardless of any condition expressed between the parties to the delivery" and regardless of the fact that the procurement of the entrusting or the possessor's disposition of the goods may have been larcenous. Suppose that it turns out that O'Keefe gave the paintings to Stieglitz for safekeeping and that Stieglitz sold them to Frank's father without O'Keeffe's consent. Who would prevail under § 2-403?

C. ACQUISITION BY GIFT

To complete our study of possession, we turn to gifts of personal property, where, as we shall see, possession plays a very important role. There are three requirements for a gift:

- *intent*,
- *delivery*, and
- *acceptance*.

Intent—The donor must intend to make a present transfer of an existing interest in the property. That is, the donor must intend to be legally bound now, not in the future. Intent is commonly a problem in litigated gift cases.

Delivery—The law has long required that, to make a gift of personal property, the donor must transfer possession ("hand over the property") to the donee with the manifested intention to make a gift to the donee. Delivery and intent interact and overlap with each other to a considerable degree, but they are discrete requirements nevertheless. Both must be present.

Acceptance—Acceptance by the donee is also required but seldom an issue. Courts presume acceptance upon delivery, unless a donee expressly refuses a gift. Intention to make a gift may be shown by oral evidence; delivery requires objective acts.

More on delivery. The requirement of transfer of possession is feudal in origin. In feudal times, when few could read or write, a symbolic ceremony transferring possession was an important ritual signifying the transfer. Land could be transferred only by delivering a clod of dirt or a branch to the grantee on the land itself. The ceremony was called "livery of seisin" (see page 197); chattels had to be handed over. In 1677, the Statute of Frauds abolished livery of seisin and initiated the requirement of a deed to pass title to land. However, the visual ceremony of transferring possession still survives if the object transferred is on top of the land. In a famous article, Professor Mechem suggested the following reasons for the survival of the delivery requirement in gifts of personal property:

> 1. Handing over the object makes vivid and concrete to the donor the significance of the act performed. By feeling the "wrench of delivery," the donor realizes an irrevocable gift has been made.
>
> 2. The act is unequivocal evidence of a gift to the actual witnesses of the transaction.
>
> 3. Delivery of the object to the donee gives the donee, after the act, prima facie evidence in favor of the alleged gift. [Philip Mechem, Gifts of Chattels and of Choses in Action Evidenced by Commercial Instruments, 21 Ill. L. Rev. 341, 348-349 (1926).]

If manual delivery is not practicable because of the size or weight of the object, or its inaccessibility, constructive or symbolic delivery may be permitted. *Constructive* delivery is handing over a key or some object that will open up access to the subject matter of the gift. *Symbolic* delivery is handing over something symbolic of the property given. The usual case of symbolic delivery involves handing over a written instrument declaring a gift of the subject matter; for example, Joe hands to Marilyn a paper reading, "I give my grand piano to Marilyn. s/ Joe." The traditional rule of gifts is: If an object can be handed over, it must be. But there are indications that the rule is eroding. For example, one court found valid *constructive* delivery where a donor who had received a check from another endorsed the check in blank and put it on a table in her apartment, which she shared with the donee, along with a note giving the check to the donee, and then left with the intention of committing suicide (which she did). Scherer v. Hyland, 380 A.2d 698 (N.J. 1977). Under the traditional rule, constructive delivery would not be recognized here. (Do you see why?) However, the court stated that it would find a constructive delivery adequate "when the evidence of donative intent is concrete and undisputed, when there is every indication that the donor intended to make a present transfer of the subject-matter of the gift, and when the steps taken by the donor to effect such a transfer must have been deemed by the donor as sufficient to pass the donor's interest to the donee."

In Brief

▶ *Manual delivery*. Manual delivery is sometimes called *actual delivery*. It occurs when the donor physically transfers possession of the object to the donee. Manual delivery is the primary method of delivery for most items of tangible personal property.

▶ *Constructive delivery*. Constructive delivery occurs when the donor physically transfers to the donee the means of access to or control of the gifted object, such as when *A* gives *B* the keys to a car that *A* intends to give *B*. Constructive delivery is permitted when manual delivery is impossible or impracticable.

▶ *Symbolic delivery*. Symbolic delivery occurs when the donor physically transfers to the donee an object that represents or symbolizes the subject matter of the gift. This includes a writing. Most jurisdictions recognize symbolic delivery. Traditionally, symbolic delivery is permitted only if manual delivery is not feasible, but the modern trend is to permit it even when manual delivery is possible.

The restriction on *symbolic* delivery has also been relaxed somewhat. Some states have statutes providing that symbolic delivery by a writing is always permitted. E.g., Cal. Civ. Code § 1147 (West 2020).

With only three requirements, gift law is beguilingly simple, and we shall see that the requirements of donative intent and delivery are far more complex than meets the eye. In studying the materials that follow, it will be helpful to keep in mind this observation from one commentator: "[A] close examination of the cases leaves a reader with a sense that ad hoc considerations of fairness and justice or propriety do much of the work in leading judges to decisions." Roy Kreitner, The Gift Beyond the Grave: Revising the Question of Consideration, 101 Colum. L. Rev. 1876, 1906 (2001).

Problems

1. *O* owns a pearl ring. While visiting her daughter *A*, *O* leaves the ring on the bathroom sink. After *O* leaves, *A* discovers the ring. When *A* telephones *O* to tell her of the discovery, *O* tells *A* to keep the ring as a gift. Has *O* made a gift to *A*? If so, can *O* change her mind the next day and require *A* to return the ring?

Suppose that *A* does not telephone *O* to tell her the ring has been found. A week later, at a dinner with friends, *A* surprises *O* by producing the ring. *O* takes the ring, looks at it, then gives it back to *A*, saying, "I want you to have it. It's yours." *A* tries the ring on, but it is too large for *A*'s finger. *O* then says, "Let me wear it until you can get it cut down to fit you." *O* leaves the dinner wearing the ring, is struck by a car, and is killed. *A* sues *O*'s executor for the ring. What result? Garrison v. Union Trust Co., 129 N.W. 691 (Mich. 1910).

Suppose that at the dinner above, *O* had not said the words quoted, but instead had said, "I promise to leave you this ring when I die." What result? For criticism of the distinction between gifts and gift promises, see Jane B. Baron, Gifts, Bargains, and Form, 64 Ind. L.J. 155 (1989). The traditional rule that gift promises are legally unenforceable for lack of consideration is defended in Melvin Eisenberg, The World of Contract and the World of Gift, 85 Cal. L. Rev. 821 (1997).

Suppose *A* gives *B* a $21,000 engagement ring. Later the engagement is broken. Does it matter who broke the engagement in determining who now owns the ring? See Lindh v. Surman, 742 A.2d 643 (Pa. 1999) (4 to 3, adopting a no-fault approach, holding that the ring must be returned to the donor regardless of who broke the engagement, in an opinion by "Madame Justice Newman," dissent by "Mr. Justice Cappy in which Messrs. Justice Castillo and Saylor join" (Law French resurrected?)). The traditional rule is that the donor cannot recover the ring if the donor is at fault. See Annot., 44 A.L.R.5th 1 (1996).

2. *O* writes a check to *B* on her checking account and hands it to *B*. Before *B* can cash the check, *O* dies. What result? See Woo v. Smart, 442 S.E.2d 690 (Va. 1994) (holding no gift until check paid, because donor retains dominion and control of funds; donor could stop payment or die, revoking command to bank to pay the money). But see In re Estate of Smith, 694 A.2d 1099 (Pa. Super. Ct. 1997) (holding valid gifts of checks on facts similar to those in *Woo*).

3. Suppose that *O*, while wearing a wristwatch, hands *A* a signed writing saying: "I hereby give *A* the wristwatch I am wearing." Is this a valid gift?

The traditional rule is that the watch must be handed over, if practicable. Restatement (Third) of Property, Wills and Other Donative Transfers § 6.2 illustration 22 (2003), says that a gift of a watch by a document is valid, even though it would be easy to take it off and hand it over. Although without case support at present, the Restatement rule may be the rule of the future. Which is the better rule? Should the donor be made to feel the "wrench of manual delivery"? Would the average person know the difference between a paper reading, "I give you my watch," which the Restatement says should be a good gift, and a paper reading, "I will give you my watch," which is an unenforceable gratuitous promise?

4. Robert Hocks rented a safe deposit box jointly with his sister Joan. He planned to give her everything he put in the box. At a restaurant, Robert handed Joan four $5,000 bearer bonds, saying, "I want to give these to you." Joan put the bonds in the safe deposit box. Subsequently, Robert clipped the coupons and collected the interest on the bonds.

During the next several years, Robert added 22 more bonds to the box, as well as a diamond ring. Only Robert, not Joan, went into the box, though Joan had a right to do so. To avoid "a lot of hassle" from Robert's wife, Joan suggested to Robert that he should leave a note in the box indicating her interest. Robert placed a handwritten note in the box: "Upon my death, the contents of this safety deposit box #7069 will belong to and are to be removed only by my sister Joan Jeremiah." Upon Robert's death, is Joan entitled to the contents of the box? See Hocks v. Jeremiah, 759 P.2d 312 (Or. App. 1988) (holding Joan entitled only to the first four bonds that were hand delivered to her; the remaining contents were not delivered even though Joan was a joint tenant of the box).

NEWMAN v. BOST

Supreme Court of North Carolina, 1898
29 S.E. 848

Action tried before COBLE, J., and a jury. . . . The plaintiff alleged in her complaint that the intestate of the defendant, while in his last sickness, gave her all the furniture and other property in his dwelling-house as a gift *causa mortis*. Among other things claimed, there was a policy of insurance of $3,000 on the life of intestate and other valuable papers, which she alleged were in a certain bureau drawer in intestate's bedroom. She alleged that defendant administrator has collected the policy of life insurance and sold the household and kitchen furniture, and this suit is against *defendant as administrator* to recover the value of the property alleged to have been converted by him. There are other matters involved, claims for services, claim for fire insurance collected by intestate in his lifetime, etc.

On the trial it appeared that the intestate's wife died about ten years before he died, and without issue; that the intestate lived in his dwelling, after his wife's death, in Statesville until his death, and died without issue; that about the last day of March, 1896, he was stricken with paralysis and was confined to his bed in his house and was never able to be out again till he died on 12 April, 1896; that shortly after he was stricken he sent for Enos Houston to nurse him in his last illness; that while helpless in his bed soon after his confinement and *in extremis* he told Houston he had to go—could not stay here—and asked Houston to call plaintiff into his room; he then asked the plaintiff to hand him his private keys, which plaintiff did, she having gotten them from a place over the mantel in intestate's bedroom in his presence and by his direction; he then handed plaintiff the bunch of keys and told her to take them and keep them, that he desired her to have them and everything in the house; he then pointed out the bureau, the clock and other articles of furniture in the house and asked his chamber door to be opened and pointed in the direction of the hall and other rooms and repeated that everything in the house was hers—he wanted her to have everything in the house; his voice failed him soon after the delivery of the keys and these declarations, so that he could never talk again to be understood, except to indicate yes and no, and this generally by a motion of the head; the bunch of keys delivered to the plaintiff, amongst others, included one which unlocked the bureau pointed out to plaintiff as hers (and other furniture in the room), and the bureau drawer which this key unlocked, contained in it a life insurance policy, payable to intestate's estate, and a few small notes, a large number of papers, receipts, etc., etc., and there was no other key that unlocked this bureau drawer; this bureau drawer was the place where intestate kept all his valuable papers; plaintiff kept the keys as directed from time given her and still has them; at the death of intestate's wife he employed plaintiff, then an orphan about eighteen years old, to become his housekeeper, and she remained in his service for ten years and till his death, and occupied rooms assigned her in intestate's residence; in 1895 the intestate declared his purpose to marry plaintiff within twelve months; nobody resided in the house with them; immediately after the death of intestate, Houston told of the donation to Mr. Burke, and the plaintiff informed her attorney, Mr. Burke, of it, and she made known her claim to the property in the house and kept the keys and forbade the defendant from interfering with it in any way, both before and after he qualified as administrator.

Sidebar

J.F. Van Pelt was a man of some standing in Statesville, North Carolina. He moved there in 1859 and entered the grocery business. When the Civil War broke out, his partner joined the Confederate army, and Van Pelt stayed at home to run their business. He was mayor of the town from 1873 to 1877 and from 1883 to 1885. He was also manager of Statesville's Opera Hall.

Van Pelt was 62 years old when he died in his home on Front Street, having moved there when his Walnut Street residence burned. (In the Walnut Street house was a piano, which the plaintiff, Julia Newman, claimed had been given her and on which Van Pelt had collected the fire insurance proceeds.) Van Pelt died intestate (that is, without a will). His heirs were a sister living in China Grove, North Carolina, and a brother living in Alabama.

The trial in Newman v. Bost occupied four days. The attorneys for the parties took over one day making their closing arguments to the jury. Julia Newman's lawyer, in closing, "spoke for about two and a half hours, finishing at 2 o'clock, when court adjourned for dinner." Id., January 18, 1898. After dinner and lengthy deliberation, the jury unanimously found for Julia.

Sometime after the trial, Julia Newman left Statesville. About a month before Van Pelt's death, Julia had bought 36 acres of land from him. She sold the land in 1907, at a nice profit. The deed listed Julia, still unmarried, as living in Maryland. The information in this footnote was furnished to the editors by Bill Moose of Mitchell Community College, Statesville, N.C. The photograph of Van Pelt is from the collection of Steve Hill in Statesville.

Other facts in relation to the plaintiff's claim appear in the opinion. There was a verdict, followed by judgment for the plaintiff, and defendant appealed.

Furches, J. The plaintiff in her complaint demands $3,000 collected by defendant, as the administrator of J.F. Van Pelt, on a life insurance policy, and now in his hands; $300, the value of a piano upon which said Van Pelt collected that amount of insurance money; $200.94, the value of household property sold by defendant as belonging to the estate of his intestate, and $45, the value of property in the plaintiff's bedroom and sold by the defendant as a part of the property belonging to the intestate's estate.

The $3,000, money collected on the life insurance policy, and the $200.94, the price for which the household property sold, plaintiff claims belonged to her by reason of a donatio causa mortis from said Van Pelt. The $45, the price for which her bedroom property sold, and the $300 insurance money on the piano, belonged to her also by reason of gifts inter vivos.

The rules of law governing all of these claims of the plaintiff are in many respects the same, and the discussion of one will be to a considerable extent a discussion of all.

To constitute a donatio causa mortis, two things are indispensably necessary: an intention to make the gift, and a delivery of the thing given. Without both of these requisites, there can be no gift causa mortis. And both these are matters of fact to be determined by the jury, where there is evidence tending to prove them. The intention to make the gift need not be announced by the donor in express terms, but may be inferred from the facts attending the delivery—that is, what the donor said and did. But it must always clearly appear that he knew *what he was doing*, and that he intended a gift. So far, there was but little diversity of authority, if any.

As to what constitutes or may constitute delivery, has been the subject of discussion and adjudication in most or all the courts of the Union and of England, and they have by no means been uniform—some of them holding that a symbolical delivery—that is, some other article delivered in the name and stead of the thing intended to be given, is sufficient; others holding that a symbolical delivery is not sufficient, but that a constructive delivery, that is, the delivery of a key to a locked house, trunk or other receptacle is sufficient. They distinguish this from a symbolical delivery, and say that this is in *substance* a delivery of the thing, as it is the means of using and enjoying the thing given; while others hold that there must be an actual manual delivery to perfect a gift causa mortis.

This doctrine of donatio causa mortis was borrowed from the Roman Civil Law by our English ancestors. There was much greater need for such a law at the time it was incorporated into the civil law and into the English law than there is now. Learning was not so general, nor the facilities for making wills so great then as now. . . .

It seems to us that, . . . after the statute of fraud and of wills, this doctrine of causa mortis is in direct conflict with the spirit and purpose of those statutes—the prevention of fraud. It is a doctrine, in our opinion, not to be extended but to be strictly construed and confined within the bounds of our adjudged cases. We were at first disposed to confine it to cases of actual *manual* delivery, and are only prevented from doing so by our loyalty to our own adjudications. . . .

Many of the cases cited by the plaintiff are distinguishable from ours, if not all of them. Thomas v. Lewis (a Virginia case), 37 Am. St., 878, was probably more relied on by the plaintiff than any other case cited, and for that reason we mention it by name. This case, in its essential facts, is distinguishable from the case under consideration.

There, the articles present were taken out of the bureau drawer, handed to the donor, and then delivered by him to the donee. According to all the authorities, this was a good gift causa mortis. The box and safe, the key to which the donor delivered to the donee, were not present but were deposited in the vault of the bank; and so far as shown by the case it will be presumed, from the place where they were and the purpose for which things are usually deposited in a bank vault, that they were only valuable as a depository for such purposes, as holding and preserving money and valuable papers, bonds, stocks and the like. This box and safe would have been of little value to the donee for any other purpose. But more than this, the donor expressly stated that all you find *in this box and this safe is yours.* There is no mistake that it was the intention of the donor to give what was contained in the box and in the safe.

As my Lord Coke would say: "Note the diversity" between that case and the case at bar. There, the evidence of debt contained in the bureau, which was present, was taken out, given to the donor, and by him delivered to the donee. This was an actual manual delivery, good under all the authorities. But no such thing was done in this case as to the life insurance policy. It was neither taken out of the drawer nor mentioned by the donor, unless it is included in the testimony of Enos Houston who, at one time, in giving his testimony says that Van Pelt gave her the keys, saying "what is in this house is yours," and at another time on cross-examination, he said to Julia, "I intend to give you this furniture in this house," and at another time, "What property is in this house is yours." The bureau in which was found the life insurance policy, after the death of Van Pelt, was present in the room where the keys were handed to Julia, and the life insurance policy could easily have been taken out and handed to Van Pelt, and by him delivered to Julia, as was done in the case of Thomas v. Lewis, supra. But this was not done. The safe and box, in Thomas v. Lewis, were not present, so that the contents could not have been taken out and delivered to the donee by the donor. The ordinary use of a stand of bureaus is not for the purpose of holding and securing such things as a life insurance policy, though they may be often used for that purpose, while a safe and a box deposited in the vault of a bank are. A bureau is an article of household furniture, used for domestic purposes, and generally belongs to the ladies' department of the household government, while the safe and box, in Thomas v. Lewis, are not. The bureau itself, mentioned in this case, was such property as would be valuable to the plaintiff. . . .

It is held that the law of delivery in this State is the same in gifts inter vivos and causa mortis. Adams v. Hayes, 24 N.C. 361. . . . [T]here can be no gift of either kind without both the intention to give and the delivery. . . .

The leading case in this State is Adams v. Hayes. . . .

Following this case, . . . we feel bound to give effect to *constructive delivery,* where it plainly appears that it was the intention of the donor to make the gift, and where the things intended to be given are *not* present, or, where present, are incapable of *manual* delivery from their size or weight. But where the articles are present and are capable of manual delivery, *this must be had.* This is as far as we can go. It may be thought by some that this is a hard rule—that a dying man cannot dispose of his own. But we are satisfied that when properly considered, it will be found to be a just rule. But it is not a hard rule. The law provides how a man can dispose of all his property, both real and personal. To do this, it is only necessary for him to observe and conform to the requirements of these laws. . . . The law provides that every man may dispose of all of his property by will, when made in writing. And it is most singular how guarded the law is to protect the testator against fraud and impositions by requiring that every word of the will must be written and signed by the testator, or, if written by someone else, it must be attested by at least *two* subscribing witnesses who shall sign the same in his presence and at his request, or the will is void. . . .

In gifts causa mortis it requires but one witness, probably one servant as a witness to a gift of all the estate a man has; no publicity is to be given that the gift has been made, and no probate or registration is required.

The statute of wills is a statute against fraud, considered in England and in this State to be demanded by public policy. And yet, if symbolical deliveries of gifts causa mortis are to be allowed, or if constructive deliveries be allowed to the extent claimed by the plaintiff, the statute of wills may prove to be of little value. For such considerations, we see every reason for restricting and none for extending the rules heretofore established as applicable to gifts causa mortis.

It being claimed and admitted that the life insurance policy was present in the bureau drawer in the room where it is claimed the gift was made, and being capable of actual manual delivery, we are of the opinion that the title of the insurance policy did not pass to the plaintiff, but remained the property of the intestate of the defendant.

But we are of the opinion that the bureau and any other article of furniture, locked and unlocked by any of the keys given to the plaintiff, did pass and she became the owner thereof. This is upon the ground that while these articles were present, from their size and weight they were incapable of actual manual delivery; and that the delivery of the keys was a constructive delivery of these articles, equivalent to an actual delivery if the articles had been capable of manual delivery.

[W]e are of the opinion that the other articles of household furniture (except those in the plaintiff's private bed chamber) did not pass to the plaintiff, but remained the property of the defendant's intestate.

We do not think the articles in the plaintiff's bed chamber passed by the donatio causa mortis for the same reason that the other articles of household furniture did not pass—want of delivery—either constructive or manual. But as to the furniture in the plaintiff's bedroom ($45) it seems to us that there was sufficient evidence of both gift and delivery to support the finding of the jury, as a gift inter vivos. The intention to give this property is shown by a number of witnesses and contradicted by none.

Residence of Mr. F. Van Pelt, Walnut Street
from The (Statesville, N.C.) Landmark Trade Edition, May 22, 1890
This house, and with it "Miss Julia's piano," burned between 1890 and 1896.

The only debatable ground is as to the sufficiency of the delivery. But when we recall the express terms in which he repeatedly declared that it was hers; that he had bought it for her and had given it to her; that it was placed in her private chamber, her bedroom, where we must suppose that she had the entire use and control of the same, it would seem that this was sufficient to constitute a delivery. There was no evidence, that we remember, disputing these facts. But, if there was, the jury have found for the plaintiff, upon sufficient evidence at least to go to the jury, as to this gift and its delivery. As to the piano there was much evidence tending to show the intention of Van Pelt to give it to the plaintiff, and that he had given it to her, and we remember no evidence to the contrary. And as to this, like the bedroom furniture, the debatable ground, if there is any debatable ground, is the question of delivery. It was placed in the intestate's parlor where it remained until it was burned. The intestate insured it as his property, collected and used the insurance money as his own, often saying that he intended to buy the plaintiff another piano, which he never did. It must be presumed that the parlor was under the dominion of the intestate, and not of his cook, housekeeper, and hired servant. And unless there is something more shown than the fact that the piano was bought by the intestate, placed in his parlor, and called by him "Miss Julia's piano," we cannot think this constituted a delivery. But, as the case goes back for a new trial, if the plaintiff thinks she can show a delivery she will have an opportunity of doing so. But she will understand that she must do so according to the rules laid down in this opinion—that she must show actual or constructive delivery equivalent to actual manual delivery. We see no ground upon which the plaintiff can recover the insurance money, if the piano was not hers.

We do not understand that there was any controversy as to the plaintiff's right to recover her services, which the jury have estimated to be $125. The view of the case we have taken has relieved us from a discussion of the exceptions to evidence, and as to the charge of the Court. There is no such thing in this State as *symbolical delivery* in gifts either inter vivos or causa mortis. . . .

New trial.

Note

Gifts causa mortis. In Newman v. Bost, some of the alleged gifts were gifts *causa mortis* (the term the court used, *donatio causa mortis*, is synonymous). A gift *causa mortis* (Latin for "on the occasion of death") is a gift made in contemplation of and in expectation of immediately approaching death. Gifts *causa mortis* are presumed to be revocable. Under the modern view, if the donor survives without revoking the gift within a reasonable time after the donor is no longer in apprehension of imminent death, the power of revocation terminates. See Restatement (Third) of Property, Wills and Other Donative Transfers § 6.2 comment zz. However, older authority has held that the donor's recovery automatically revokes the gift.

According to some modern cases, the "contemplation of death" requirement is met even where the donor intended to commit suicide. E.g., In re Estate of Smith, 694 A.2d 1099 (Pa. Super. Ct. 1997); Scherer v. Hyland, 380 A.2d 698 (N.J. 1977). Older cases widely held otherwise on the ground that suicide was against public policy. The court in Scherer v. Hyland, a leading decision, explains the modern view: "[D]eath is no less impending because of the resolve to commit suicide. Nor does that fixed purpose constitute any lesser or less imminent peril than does a ravaging disease." Id. at 702.

Because the courts see upholding gifts *causa mortis* as undercutting the safe-guards of the Statute of Wills, traditionally they have more strictly applied the requirements for a valid gift *causa mortis* than for a gift inter vivos. They also have placed restrictions on gifts *causa mortis* not applicable to inter vivos gifts. For example, if the donee already is in possession of the property, there must be a redelivery to effect a valid gift *causa mortis,* but not if the gift is inter vivos. If, in *Newman,* Van Pelt had put a small cinnabar box in Julia's bedroom, he could during his lifetime, before death drew near, declare that he was giving the box to Julia. But if he waited until he was on his deathbed, he would have to deliver the box to her again.

Given changes in the law of wills, the strict approach to gifts *causa mortis* may no longer be justified. The modern trend is to enforce the decedent's intent even if there is evidence of some failure to comply with the wills act formalities, so long as there is clear and convincing evidence of donative intent. See, e.g., Uniform Probate Code § 2-503 (2008).

Problems

1. Suppose that Van Pelt had said to Julia, "I want to give you my insurance policy in that bureau over there, so Enos, please get it and give it to her." Enos, however, leaves the policy where it was. Is there a valid gift? See Wilcox v. Matteson, 9 N.W. 814 (Wis. 1881). What if Van Pelt instead had said, "I want to give you my bureau there. Enos, move it into her room." Enos does so. The bureau contains the life insurance policy. On the reasoning of Newman v. Bost, is there a valid gift?

2. Suppose that Van Pelt had called Julia in and said, "I want to give you my bureau and the insurance policy locked in it. Here is the key." Julia takes the key, but the bureau stays where it is. On the reasoning of Newman v. Bost, has a valid gift been made? *No because the policy could have been delivered*

3. Suppose that Van Pelt had called Julia in and said, "I want to give you my little strongbox here and the insurance policy locked in it. Here is the key." Julia takes the key, but the box stays where it is. On the reasoning of Newman v. Bost, has a valid gift been made? See Bynum v. Fidelity Bank of Durham, 19 S.E.2d 121 (N.C. 1942).

4. If Van Pelt had said to his wife before she died, "Dear, I give you the piano," would there be a gift? See Restatement (Third) of Property, Wills and Other Donative Transfers § 6.2 illustration 7 (2003). Would this be sufficient for a gift to Julia? If not, how could Van Pelt give the piano to Julia?

GRUEN v. GRUEN
Court of Appeals of New York, 1986
496 N.E.2d 869

Simons, J. Plaintiff commenced this action seeking a declaration that he is the rightful owner of a painting which he alleges his father, now deceased, gave to him. He concedes that he has never had possession of the painting but asserts that his father made a valid gift of the title in 1963 reserving a life estate for himself. His father retained possession of the painting until he died in 1980. Defendant, plaintiff's stepmother, has the painting now and has refused plaintiff's requests that she turn it over to him. She contends that the purported gift was testamentary in nature and invalid insofar as the formalities of a will were not met or, alternatively, that a donor may not make a valid inter vivos gift of a chattel and retain a life estate with a complete right of possession. Following a seven-day nonjury trial, Special Term found that plaintiff had failed to establish any of the elements of an inter vivos gift and that in any event an attempt by a donor to retain a present possessory life estate in a chattel invalidated a purported gift of it. The Appellate Division held that a valid gift may be made reserving a life estate and, finding the elements of a gift established in this case, it reversed and remitted the matter for a determination of value (104 A.D.2d 171, 488 N.Y.S.2d 401). That determination has now been made and defendant appeals directly to this court, pursuant to CPLR 5601(d), from the subsequent final judgment entered in Supreme Court awarding plaintiff $2,500,000 in damages representing the value of the painting, plus interest. We now affirm.

The subject of the dispute is a work entitled "Schloss Kammer am Attersee II" painted by a noted Austrian modernist, Gustav Klimt. It was purchased by plaintiff's father, Victor Gruen, in 1959 for $8,000. On April 1, 1963 the elder Gruen, a successful architect with offices and residences in both New York City and Los Angeles during most of the time involved in this action, wrote a letter to plaintiff, then an undergraduate student at Harvard, stating that he was giving him the Klimt painting for his birthday but that he wished to retain the possession of it for his lifetime. This letter is not in evidence, apparently because plaintiff destroyed it on instructions from his father. Two other letters were received, however, one dated May 22, 1963 and the other April 1, 1963. Both had been dictated by Victor Gruen and sent together to plaintiff on or about May 22, 1963. The letter dated May 22, 1963 reads as follows:

Dear Michael:

I wrote you at the time of your birthday about the gift of the painting by Klimt. Now my lawyer tells me that because of the existing tax laws, it was wrong to mention in that letter that I want to use the painting as long as I live. Though I still want to use it, this should not appear in the letter. I am enclosing, therefore, a new letter and I ask you to send the old one back to me so that it can be destroyed.

> ## Sidebar
>
> Gustav Klimt (1862-1918) was one of the founders of the Vienna Secession, a group of young fin-de-siècle Viennese artists who sought to liberate Viennese art from the dominance of naturalist style, opening it to such contemporary European influences as *art nouveau*. He created many murals for public buildings, both in Vienna and elsewhere, but perhaps his greatest fame was as a painter of portraits and landscapes that exhibited an exotic and often erotic style. See Gerbert Frodl, Klimt (Alexandra Campbell trans. 1990). In 2006, a Klimt painting, *Adele Block-Bauer I,* was purchased by cosmetics magnate Ronald S. Lauder for $135 million. It was at the time the highest sum ever paid for a painting. The work purchased by Lauder had been the subject of an extensive restitution battle between the Austrian government and a niece of Ms. Block-Bauer, who contended, successfully, that the Nazis had stolen the painting and four other Klimt works during World War II.
>
> Schloss Kammer, the subject of the painting in dispute, was Klimt's favorite vacation spot. It is located in the Salzkammergut, a beautiful lake district outside of Salzburg, Austria. We owe this information to Professor Susan French, who has told the whole (and fascinating) story of the case in her essay, Susan F. French, *Gruen v. Gruen*: A Tale of Two Stories, in Property Stories 75 (Gerald Korngold & Andrew P. Morriss eds. 2d ed. 2009).

I know this is all very silly, but the lawyer and our accountant insist that they must have in their possession copies of a letter which will serve the purpose of making it possible for you, once I die, to get this picture without having to pay inheritance taxes on it.

Love,

s/Victor

Enclosed with this letter was a substitute gift letter, dated April 1, 1963, which stated:

Dear Michael:

The 21st birthday, being an important event in life, should be celebrated accordingly. I therefore wish to give you as a present the oil painting by Gustav Klimt of Schloss Kammer which now hangs in the New York living room. You know that Lazette and I bought it some 5 or 6 years ago, and you always told us how much you liked it.

Happy birthday again.

Love

s/Victor

Plaintiff never took possession of the painting nor did he seek to do so. Except for a brief period between 1964 and 1965 when it was on loan to art exhibits and when restoration work was performed on it, the painting remained in his father's possession, moving with him from New York City to Beverly Hills and finally to Vienna, Austria, where Victor Gruen died on February 14, 1980. Following Victor's death plaintiff requested possession of the Klimt painting and when defendant refused, he commenced this action.

The issues framed for appeal are whether a valid inter vivos gift of a chattel may be made where the donor has reserved a life estate in the chattel and the donee never has had physical possession of it before the donor's death and, if it may, which factual findings on the elements of a valid inter vivos gift more nearly comport with the weight of the evidence in this case, those of Special Term or those of the Appellate Division. The latter issue requires application of two general rules. First, to make a valid inter vivos gift there must exist the intent on the part of the donor to make a present transfer; delivery of the

Sidebar

Victor Gruen, born in Vienna, was an urban designer and architect who came to this country in 1933. His firm, Victor Gruen Associates, has been one of the most influential in shaping the urban environment since World War II. It designed the first regional shopping center, Northland, near Detroit, which inspired similar plans for enormous enclosed shopping malls in other cities. Gruen was the author of several books on urban planning, in which he said his main aim was to design cities that were worthwhile to live in as well as functional. "Some say there is no need for a city, a center," Gruen once said. "They say you can communicate in the future with television phones. You may be able eventually to talk to your girlfriend by television, but you can't kiss her that way." His best book is The Heart of Our Cities (1964).

Gruen viewed Vienna as the most livable of cities, largely because the automobile—which he disliked—had been banned from downtown. In the last years of his life, he returned to live in Vienna, where he died in 1980. See generally M. Jeffrey Hardwick, Mall Maker: Victor Gruen, Architect of an American Dream (2003).

gift, either actual or constructive to the donee; and acceptance by the donee (Matter of Szabo, 10 N.Y.2d 94, 98, 217 N.Y.S.2d 593, 176 N.E.2d 395; Matter of Kelly, 285 N.Y. 139, 150, 33 N.E.2d 62 [dissenting in part opn.]). Second, the proponent of a gift has the burden of proving each of these elements by clear and convincing evidence.

Donative Intent

There is an important distinction between the intent with which an inter vivos gift is made and the intent to make a gift by will. An inter vivos gift requires that the donor intend to make an irrevocable present transfer of ownership; if the intention is to make a testamentary disposition effective only after death, the gift is invalid unless made by will.

Defendant contends that the trial court was correct in finding that Victor did not intend to transfer any present interest in the painting to plaintiff in 1963 but only expressed an intention that plaintiff was to get the painting upon his death. The evidence is all but conclusive, however, that Victor intended to transfer ownership of the

Schloss Kammer am Attersee II
Gustav Klimt
Courtesy of Galerie St. Etienne, New York

painting to plaintiff in 1963 but to retain a life estate in it and that he did, therefore, effectively transfer a remainder interest in the painting to plaintiff at that time. Although the original letter was not in evidence, testimony of its contents was received along with the substitute gift letter and its covering letter dated May 22, 1963. The three letters should be considered together as a single instrument (see Matter of Brandreth, 169 N.Y. 437, 440, 62 N.E. 563) and when they are they unambiguously establish that Victor Gruen intended to make a present gift of title to the painting at that time. But there was other evidence for after 1963 Victor made several statements orally and in writing indicating that he had previously given plaintiff the painting and that plaintiff owned it. Victor Gruen retained possession of the property, insured it, allowed others to exhibit it and made necessary repairs to it but those acts are not inconsistent with his retention of a life estate. . . . Victor's failure to file a gift tax return on the transaction was partially explained by allegedly erroneous legal advice he received, and while that omission sometimes may indicate that the donor had no intention of making a present gift, it does not necessarily do so and it is not dispositive in this case.

Defendant contends that even if a present gift was intended, Victor's reservation of a lifetime interest in the painting defeated it. . . .

Defendant recognizes that a valid inter vivos gift of a remainder interest can be made not only of real property but also of such intangibles as stocks and bonds. Indeed, several of the cases she cites so hold. That being so, it is difficult to perceive any legal basis for the distinction she urges which would permit gifts of remainder interests in those properties but not of remainder interests in chattels such as the Klimt painting here. The only reason suggested is that the gift of a chattel must include a present right to possession. The application of *Brandreth* to permit a gift of the remainder in this case, however, is consistent with the distinction, well recognized in the law of gifts as well as in real property law, between ownership and possession or enjoyment. Insofar as some of our cases purport to require that the donor intend to transfer both title and possession immediately to have a valid inter vivos gift (see Gannon v. McGuire, 160 N.Y. 476, 481, 55 N.E. 7; Young v. Young, 80 N.Y. 422, 430), they state the rule too broadly and confuse the effectiveness of a gift with the transfer of the possession of the subject of that gift. The correct test is " 'whether the maker intended the [gift] to have *no effect* until after the maker's death, or whether he intended it to transfer *some present interest*' " (McCarthy v. Pieret, 281 N.Y. 407, 409, 24 N.E.2d 102 [emphasis added]; see also 25 N.Y. Jur., Gifts, § 14, at 156-157). As long as the evidence establishes an intent to make a present and irrevocable transfer of title or the right of ownership, there is a present transfer of some interest and the gift is effective immediately. Thus, in Speelman v. Pascal, [10 N.Y.2d 313, 222 N.Y.S.2d 324, 178 N.E.2d 723], we held valid a gift of a percentage of the future royalties to the play "My Fair Lady" before the play even existed. There, as in this case, the donee received title or the right of ownership to some property immediately upon the making of the gift but possession or enjoyment of the subject of the gift was postponed to some future time.

Defendant suggests that allowing a donor to make a present gift of a remainder with the reservation of a life estate will lead courts to effectuate otherwise invalid testamentary dispositions of property. The two have entirely different characteristics, however, which make them distinguishable. Once the gift is made it is irrevocable and the donor is limited to the rights of a life tenant not an owner. Moreover, with the gift of a remainder title vests immediately in the donee and any possession is postponed until the donor's death whereas under a will neither title nor possession vests immediately.

Finally, the postponement of enjoyment of the gift is produced by the express terms of the gift not by the nature of the instrument as it is with a will (see Robb v. Washington & Jefferson Coll., 185 N.Y. 485, 493, 78 N.E. 359).

Delivery

In order to have a valid inter vivos gift, there must be a delivery of the gift, either by a physical delivery of the subject of the gift or a constructive or symbolic delivery such as by an instrument of gift, sufficient to divest the donor of dominion and control over the property. As the statement of the rule suggests, the requirement of delivery is not rigid or inflexible, but is to be applied in light of its purpose to avoid mistakes by donors and fraudulent claims by donees. Accordingly, what is sufficient to constitute delivery "must be tailored to suit the circumstances of the case" (Matter of Szabo, supra, 10 N.Y.2d at p.98, 217 N.Y.S.2d 593, 176 N.E.2d 395). The rule requires that "'[t]he delivery necessary to consummate a gift must be as perfect as the nature of the property and the circumstances and surroundings of the parties will reasonably permit'" (id.).

Defendant contends that when a tangible piece of personal property such as a painting is the subject of a gift, physical delivery of the painting itself is the best form of delivery and should be required. Here, of course, we have only delivery of Victor Gruen's letters which serve as instruments of gift. Defendant's statement of the rule as applied may be generally true, but it ignores the fact that what Victor Gruen gave plaintiff was not all rights to the Klimt painting, but only title to it with no right of possession until his death. Under these circumstances, it would be illogical for the law to require the donor to part with possession of the painting when that is exactly what he intends to retain.

Nor is there any reason to require a donor making a gift of a remainder interest in a chattel to physically deliver the chattel into the donee's hands only to have the donee redeliver it to the donor. As the facts of this case demonstrate, such a requirement could impose practical burdens on the parties to the gift while serving the delivery requirement poorly. Thus, in order to accomplish this type of delivery the parties would have been required to travel to New York for the symbolic transfer and redelivery of the Klimt painting which was hanging on the wall of Victor Gruen's Manhattan apartment. Defendant suggests that such a requirement would be stronger evidence of a completed gift, but in the absence of witnesses to the event or any written confirmation of the gift it would provide less protection against fraudulent claims than have the written instruments of gift delivered in this case.

Acceptance

Acceptance by the donee is essential to the validity of an inter vivos gift, but when a gift is of value to the donee, as it is here, the law will presume an acceptance on his part. Plaintiff did not rely on this presumption alone but also presented clear and convincing proof of his acceptance of a remainder interest in the Klimt painting by evidence that he had made several contemporaneous statements acknowledging the gift to his friends and associates, even showing some of them his father's gift letter, and that he had retained both letters for over 17 years to verify the gift after his father died. Defendant relied exclusively on affidavits filed by plaintiff in a matrimonial action with his former wife, in which plaintiff failed to list his interest in the painting as an asset. These affidavits were made over 10 years after acceptance was complete and they do not even approach the evidence in Matter of Kelly (285 N.Y. 139, 148-149, 33 N.E.2d 62 [dissenting in part opn.], supra) where the donee, immediately upon delivery of a diamond ring, rejected it as "too flashy." We agree with the Appellate Division that interpretation of the affidavit was too speculative to support a finding of rejection and overcome the substantial showing of acceptance by plaintiff.

Accordingly, the judgment appealed from and the order of the Appellate Division brought up for review should be affirmed, with costs.

THE REST OF THE STORY . . .

When Michael finally received the painting from his stepmother, Kamija, he immediately arranged for Sotheby's to auction it in London. Sotheby's sold the painting on June 30, 1987, for $5.3 million, then a record price for Klimt's work. Ten years later, the buyer sold the painting at auction for $23.5 million. The painting ended up in Galleria Nazionale d'Arte Moderna, in Rome, Italy. See French, A Tale of Two Stories, supra, at 95.

Source: © The New Yorker Collection, The Cartoon Bank

Notes and Questions

1. *Life estates and remainders.* Gruen v. Gruen introduces you to the concept of a life estate (in Victor) and a remainder (in Michael). Each of these estates is a separate interest in the same property, entitling first the life tenant to possession, and then, after his death, the remainderman. We will closely examine these estates in Chapters 3 and 4.

2. *Gift of complete ownership by letter?* If Victor Gruen had wanted to give Michael the complete ownership of the painting and not reserve a life estate, could he have done so by a letter sent to Michael at Harvard?

3. *Gift of a remainder versus a will.* Suppose that Victor Gruen had typed and signed a letter to Michael: "I give you the Klimt painting when I die." Would this be a valid lifetime gift? It would not. The letter is a will. It shows no intention to give Michael any rights *now*, but only when Victor dies. As a will, the instrument is not valid unless properly executed as a will, with witnesses.

Review Problems

1. On July 9, 1776, a group of patriots, hearing the news of the Declaration of Independence, toppled a large statue of King George III that was located in lower Manhattan, New York City. The group cut the statue, which was made of lead, into pieces and transported it to Connecticut to be melted down and cast into bullets. While the patriots paused to imbibe, some Loyalists managed to steal the pieces of the statue and carry them away. The Loyalists scattered the pieces in the Davis Swamp in Connecticut, and fragments of the statue have turned up from time to time ever since then.

In 1995, James Abel learned that part of the statue might be located on Shondra Brown's property, specifically, the Davis Swamp. Although he knew that the Swamp was private property, he entered the area and, using a metal detector, located a large fragment of the statue, which was embedded nearly a foot below the soil. Abel dug up the fragment and removed it from Brown's property. Brown did not learn about these events until much later when a newspaper article appeared describing what had occurred. In the meantime, Abel sold the piece to the Museum of the City of New York for $10,000. The museum continues to hold the piece pending resolution of the dispute.

Recently, Brown brought an action to have the statue fragment returned to her. Identify the key issue in Brown v. Abel, then analyze that issue using the cases, legal doctrines, and any relevant statutes you have studied so far. Who do you think should prevail?

2. On August 1, 2000, Jorge Arroz purchased, by a legally valid deed, a 200-acre parcel of land that he used for farming. Arroz's deed correctly described the half acre of land now in dispute. On April 1, 2012, Brianna Bourne purchased a 100-acre parcel of land which adjoined and bordered Arroz's land along the entire common boundary. That common boundary was open, with no fence or other structure separating the two parcels. Brianna bought the land from her parents,

the Bournes, who had purchased the land in 2005. Neither the deed to Brianna from the Bournes nor the deed to the Bournes from their predecessors described the half acre of land in dispute.

Soon after the Bournes acquired their land, they began to farm it in the usual way for agricultural land in that area, planting and growing crops and the like. The area that they plowed and planted included a half-acre strip of Arroz's land, right along their common boundary. After the Bournes deeded their land to Brianna, she, like her parents, farmed the half-acre strip in the usual manner. Both Brianna and her parents believed that they owned all of the land that they were farming, including the half-acre strip.

In 2016, Arroz had his land surveyed, and in the course of that survey he discovered that Brianna, and before her, the Bournes, were encroaching upon his land. He brought an action to eject Brianna Bourne from the half-acre strip of land that Arroz claims is his. The period under the local statute of limitations for ejectment actions is 10 years. Identify and analyze the main issue(s), using the legal doctrines and materials you have studied so far. Based on your analysis, who do you think has the stronger legal position?

PART II

THE SYSTEM OF ESTATES (EXCLUDING LEASEHOLDS)

For property law, the system of estates represents the most obvious of many links between past and present. The very word *estate*, drawn from and implying *status*, signifies the feudal origins of the system—origins that we will consider on brief occasions in the following chapters. So does the distinction, still current, between *freehold* and *nonfreehold* estates—the first referring to normal tenures of feudal times, the second to mere leases.

From its feudal origins the system of estates evolved into an elaborate hierarchy of interests in land, accompanied by an equally elaborate taxonomy by which to classify them. Those who held estates in land, free or otherwise, found it to their advantage to create new estates and new interests, or they managed to do as much without knowing they had. It became commonplace for two or more persons to have interests in the same land—for example, one person with a right to possession now (present interest) and another person with a right to possession later (future interest), or two or more persons with rights to concurrent possession, now or in the future (co-ownership or cotenancy). The various estates developed as a consequence of the language or other facts giving rise to their creation, and each estate carried with it characteristics different from the others. The feudal English lawyers apparently thought it was necessary to have some grand scheme to keep everything straight. Hence the taxonomy that you will be studying.

Regarding that taxonomy, we will see that much of it is obsolete today, dealing with distinctions that have, or should have, lost their relevance. Unfortunately, the unduly elaborate classification of the estate system persists. (Why do you suppose that is so?) Justice Holmes once said, "It is revolting to have no better reason for a rule than that it was laid down in the time of Henry IV. It is still more revolting if the grounds upon which it was laid down have vanished long since, and the rule simply persists from imitation of the past." Oliver Wendell Holmes, The Path of the Law, 10 Harv. L. Rev. 457, 469 (1897). Holmes was speaking in another context, but he might as well have been talking about the system of estates. As we shall see, the estates system is riddled with rules that have lost their purpose (though the situation is much better now than it was in Holmes's time and is likely to improve still more). Labels have been even more enduring, a good example of the triumph of form over substance.

Leaseholds—landlord-tenant estates—are an element of the estate system, but the rules governing landlord-tenant relations are sufficiently distinct to merit separate treatment. Accordingly, we save the topic for close study in Part III.

CHAPTER 3

Possessory Estates

Historical origins of the doctrine of estates. The Norman Conquest in 1066 determined to considerable degree the central features of English law, particularly the system of estates. Beginning with William the Conqueror's reign, the English, influenced by Norman, French, and Roman ideas, developed a legal system that spread throughout the English-speaking world, America included.

Immediately following the Conquest, William faced a challenge even greater perhaps than conquering England—securing and consolidating his gains. He quickly began to distribute land among his Norman supporters, but he did so with strings attached. These strings made the barons to whom William distributed land his tenants-in-chief, holding rather than owning land and owing certain duties to their lord, William. These duties took two forms: *services* and *incidents*.

Services. There were three major types of services—military, economic, and religious. The principal military service was *knight service*, which required the tenant to provide a specified number of men to fight for the king. A tenant in chief could provide knights by paying them and keeping them in his household ready to fight, but more commonly he met his quota by *subinfeudation.* This took the form of the tenant in chief granting a parcel of his land to a subtenant in exchange for the service of one or more knights or for some other service necessary to support the land lord. A tenant in chief and a lesser tenant could not shift a service from the land, which was forfeited if the service was not performed, but they could, as between themselves, determine who would perform it. The lesser tenants might also subinfeudate, so that a pyramid was built up, with services flowing to the king at the top and protection extending downward to the actual occupants of the land at the bottom. The title to one tract of land might look like this:

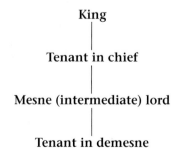

King

|

Tenant in chief

|

Mesne (intermediate) lord

|

Tenant in demesne

The tenant in demesne had possessory use of the land (so-called *seisin*, of which more later); the lords above him had the rights to services.

Another type of service was economic and was intended to provide subsistence and maintenance for overlords. Economic services varied quite widely, ranging from money rent to 10 days of plowing to keeping a bridge in repair to delivering a dish of mushrooms fresh for the king's breakfast in London. The important point was that, upon a grant of land, some service—even if merely symbolic—was thought to be due. A father granting land to a younger son might require annual delivery of an arrow with eagle's feathers, or a rose every midsummer.

Finally, for a society ruled as much by the cross as the sword, it was important to bestow land on the church. Here again, however, the notion that land must be held to enhance the power of a temporal lord required some service from the ecclesiastics, and so there were religious tenures with such services as singing Mass every Friday.

Incidents. The other type of obligation that a tenant owed to his lord was called *incidents*. Feudal services were fixed obligations. In the course of the Middle Ages, the economic importance of services declined because they could not be changed when social conditions or money values made them outmoded. Many of the services were commuted into money rents, which lost value with inflation. On the other hand, feudal incidents, which gave the lord possession of the land or its equivalent, kept pace with inflation and maintained their value. Thus the feudal incidents, jealously guarded by the Crown, lasted long after the feudal services disappeared.

As with the service, there were various forms of incidents. One that is still with us today and so bears mention is *escheat*. If a tenant died without heirs, the land returned to the lord from whom it was held. A modified form of escheat is in force today: when a person dies intestate (that is, without a will) and without heirs, the person's property escheats to the state.

Some things never change, it seems. One is that the rich have always tried to avoid taxes. In medieval times, this meant avoidance of feudal incidents. For example, in the early Middle Ages in England, there were two ways to transfer possession of land. A tenant in demesne could *substitute* for himself some new tenant who would hold the land from his lord. Substitution required the lord's consent and homage to the lord from the new tenant. The second way was for the tenant to subinfeudate, becoming a mesne lord himself and having a tenant who rendered him services. He could do this without the lord's consent. Subinfeudation could not diminish the feudal *services* because a lord could proceed directly against the tenant in possession. But subinfeudation could be used to avoid the feudal *incidents*. The king and the barons, with much to lose by subinfeudation, took steps to curb the practice, finally succeeding with the enactment of the Statute Quia

Emptores in 1290. The statute prohibited subinfeudation altogether, and thus the mischief of devaluing feudal incidents by this route was stopped.

Feudalism and its decline. Both of these basic types of obligations, services and incidents, were characteristic of *feudalism*, the social, economic, military, and legal system that William transplanted to England from Normandy. Feudalism was a strictly organized, hierarchical system in which everyone's place was fixed and, more important for our purposes, was defined in terms of one's relationship to land—a matter of status.

Sidebar

Actually, subinfeudation was not completely abolished. As you may know and as we will see in Chapter 6, pages 298-305, today a tenant can sublease her apartment to a sublessee. This is a modern form of subinfeudation. Quia Emptores abolished subinfeudation only as to the fee simple, which, as we will see, is the largest possible estate, but it allowed subinfeudation as to lesser estates.

The Statute Quia Emptores (which got its name from the first two words of the statute, written in Latin) was intended to shore up the feudal system, but actually it marked the beginning of feudalism's end. It prohibited subinfeudation in fee simple. But as a price for putting an end to subinfeudation, the great lords had to concede to all free tenants the right to substitute a new tenant for all or part of their land without the lord's consent. The new tenant would hold of the lord by the same services as the old, and if only part of the land was conveyed to a new tenant, the feudal services were to be apportioned.

Quia Emptores produced two major historic consequences. First, it established the foundational principle of free alienation of land, which turned out to be a major force in the development of property law. Second, over the course of time, most existing mesne lordships gradually disappeared, and most land came to be held directly from the Crown.

After Quia Emptores permitted free substitution, the forms of landownership that we now refer to as "estates" gradually developed. The tenant was now the "owner"; services and incidents were simply a form of taxes or wages. Yet so important a social system as feudalism, which governed people's lives for several centuries, did not perish outright. Feudalism has its continuations in the law, as we shall see.

The modern relevance of estates. The estate system is central to our laws, both in theory and in practice. It is an essential part of the processes by which property interests are transferred from one party to another during life (inter vivos, as property lawyers say) or at death. Lawyers explicitly refer to the type of estate that is being transferred when they draft deeds, wills, and other legal instruments involved in property transactions. So too for laypeople who undertake a transfer (one hopes correctly) without any legal assistance beyond a form book. The estate system is designed to make clear who is transferring what to whom—not

Sidebar

Occasionally, in this country, one runs across feudal services reserved by a grantor before the American Revolution. Here's one instance: In 1772, Henry William Stiegel and his wife conveyed to their fellow Lutherans in Manheim, Pennsylvania, a plot of ground on which to build a church. The consideration was five shillings and "in the month of June yearly forever hereafter the rent of one red rose if the same shall be lawfully demanded." On the second Sunday in June, each year, the Zion Evangelical Lutheran Church of Manheim would pay the feudal obligation of one red rose to a Stiegel descendant. Professor Craig Oren tells us that this practice still continues.

just what physical parcel of land or item of personal property, but also what sort of ownership, measured in terms of the duration of the transferee's interest.

The estates system developed gradually over the course of several centuries, and the process has rendered it frustratingly complex. Happily, various simplifying measures have been adopted, and still others proposed. Among the latter, perhaps the most significant is the Restatement (Third) of Property, Wills and Other Donative Transfers. We will discuss relevant provisions of the Third Restatement as we go along. (We are advised that the forthcoming Restatement (Fourth) provisions on estates and future interests will continue the substance of the Third Restatement.)

Today an estate represents a means of measuring ownership in terms of time. Each estate is defined by the length of time it may endure. Modern law recognizes only four estates: the *fee simple*, the *fee tail*, the *life estate*, and the *leasehold*. The four estates form a hierarchy in terms of their potential duration, with the fee simple at the top and the leasehold at the bottom. We start with the fee simple absolute, usually just called the "fee simple," the largest estate that the common law recognizes. (As we will see later in this chapter, there are other types of fees simple as well, called "defeasible" fees simple.)

A. THE FEE SIMPLE

The fee simple is by far the most common estate. The vast majority of land in the United States today is held in fee simple. So, just what does it mean to say that you own land "in fee simple"?

To help explain possessory estates (and, in Chapter 4, future interests), we will use graphical depictions. All of the depictions are based on a metaphor sometimes used to explain estates, the "plane of time." In these terms, and taking ∞ to signify infinity, the fee simple absolute looks like this:

Time line 3-1

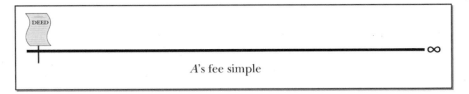

Characteristics of the fee simple. As the above graph suggests, the fee simple is the largest possible estate because its potential duration is infinite. But what does it mean, as a practical matter, to say that an estate may last forever? Won't the fee simple end when its owner dies? The short answer is no, and here is why. The key characteristics of the fee simple are *heritability* and *alienability*, meaning that it is inheritable and alienable. Historically, heritability developed first.

Heritability. Suppose O owns a parcel of land in fee simple. What happens to the fee simple when O dies? As we will see shortly, O might leave a valid will that transfers it to another person(s). But if O does not leave a valid will, the fee simple — the same fee simple that *O* owned rather than a new one — passes to *O*'s legal heirs. This is what it means to say that the fee simple is heritable.

Sidebar

The plane of time metaphor was first developed by two famous nineteenth-century English legal historians, Sir Frederick Pollock and Frederic W. Maitland. Since they first introduced it, students have found it helpful in grasping the complex and abstract concepts of estate. Perhaps you will too.

Heritability developed out of a custom by which a lord would give advance consent to his tenant's heir for the right to succeed to the estate upon the tenant's death. This advance consent, which the lord usually gave for a fee, was denoted by a conveyance from the lord "to *A* and his heirs." During early feudal times, the lord was under no obligation to give this consent because tenants held land only for their lifetime, but gradually this custom ripened into a right so that inheritance of a fee became a matter of right by the beginning of the thirteenth century.

Alienability. In the first 200 years after the Conquest, the fee simple was not freely alienable inter vivos (that is, during life) and was not devisable by will; hence the practical effect of a conveyance (i.e., a lifetime transfer of an interest in land, usually done today by a deed) "to *A* and his heirs" was to give *A* a fee that would pass to *A*'s heir, to the heir's heir, and so on through the centuries. But as the demand for land increased, the idea that a tenant should be able to convey the fee to another during his life openly and without the lord's consent gained favor. By 1290, Quia Emptores settled that the fee was freely alienable.

Once the fee became alienable, the feudal reasons for a conveyance to *A* "and his heirs" disappeared. *A* was now the owner of an estate that was freely transferrable both during *A*'s lifetime and at death to his heirs.

It is important to bear in mind that the estate that *A*'s heirs or *A*'s transferees take is the *same estate* that *A* had. They do not receive a new one. Lawyers think of estates, which, of course, are nothing more than abstract concepts, as "things" that have existence apart from the land itself. It will help you to understand the rest of the material in this chapter and Chapter 4 if you indulge in the same flight of fancy.

Creation of a fee simple. At early common law, a grantor could transfer a fee simple estate only by adding the words "and his heirs" to the words "to *A*." A conveyance "to *A*" transferred a life estate, not a fee estate. A conveyance "to *A* and his heirs" transferred a fee simple to *A*. It transferred no interest of any kind whatsoever to *A*'s heirs. The only reason for adding the words "and his heirs" was to indicate that the grantor's intent was to give *A* a fee simple rather than a life interest. Lawyers express this idea by calling the phrase "and his heirs" *words of limitation.* Words of limitation simply denote what estate the grantor has given *A*. Words of limitation are distinguished from *words of purchase*, "to *A*." Words of purchase denote who is the transferee of the grant. In the grant "to *A* and his heirs," there is one and only one transferee of any property interest — *A*.

Today it is not necessary to put words of inheritance in a deed in any state. A grant by *O* "to *A*," without more, conveys a fee simple to *A*. Still, although the phrase "and his heirs" is no longer required, lawyers, being creatures of habit, continue to insert it.

In Brief

Words of *purchase* = <u>who?</u> ("To A and his heirs")

Words of *limitation* = <u>what?</u> ("To **A and his heirs**")

Interests in personal property. Although the law of estates grew out of dispositions of land, courts permitted the same kinds of interests to be created in personal property. For historical reasons, there is a fee simple only in land, not in personal property. But sometimes people speak of a fee simple in personal property, and no great harm is done.

Problems

(Throughout this chapter, always assume that *O* has a fee simple absolute unless indicated otherwise.)

1. In 1600, *O* conveys Blackacre "to *A* for life, then to *B* forever." What estates do *A* and *B* have? If *A* dies and then *B* dies, who owns Blackacre? Suppose the conveyance takes place in 2002?

2. *O* conveys Greenacre "to *A* and her heirs." *A*'s only child, *B*, is a spendthrift and runs up large, unpaid bills. *B*'s creditors can attach *B*'s property to satisfy their claims. Does *B* have an interest in Greenacre, reachable by *B*'s creditors? Suppose *A* wishes to sell Greenacre and use the proceeds to take a trip around the world. Can *B* prevent *A* from doing this?

Inheritance of a fee simple. Suppose *O* owns land in fee simple and dies without a valid will (i.e., intestate). What happens to the fee simple? The short answer is that it passes to *O*'s *heirs*. (If *O* left a valid will—that is, died *testate*—the fee simple would pass under the will to the beneficiaries designated in that instrument.) Heirs are persons who survive the decedent, and they are designated under the state's statute of intestate succession. No one is an heir of the living; a living person has no heirs (yet!). So, if there is a conveyance "to *A*'s heirs" (*not* "to *A* and his heirs") and *A* is alive at the time of the conveyance, we do not yet know who are the transferees of the conveyance. We will ascertain them only when *A* dies.

Modern intestacy statutes vary in their patterns of who, among a decedent's surviving relatives, are the heirs and what shares of the estate they take, but some generalizations are possible:

▶ *Spouse.* In all states, the surviving spouse is designated as an intestate successor of some share in the decedent's land; the size of the share often depends on who else survives. For example, the surviving spouse might take one-half if the decedent leaves one child, one-third if the decedent leaves two or more children, and all if the decedent leaves no children, no more remote issue, and no parents.

In Brief

Heirs = the persons who are entitled to succeed to a decedent's estate on the basis of the local statute of intestate succession when the decedent has died without a valid will

Intestate succession = succession at death to the estate of a person who dies without a legally valid will

Testate succession = succession at death to the estate of a person who dies with a legally valid will; the beneficiaries under the will are called *devisees*

Issue/descendants = the surviving children, grandchildren, great-grandchildren, and so on, of a decedent

▶ *Issue.* After any surviving spouse takes a share, surviving issue (a synonymous term is "descendants") take the rest of the estate to the exclusion of all other relatives. Issue include not only children but grandchildren, and so on down the line of descent. Issue take by right of representation, meaning that if any child of the decedent dies before the decedent leaves children who survive the decedent, those children (the decedent's grandchildren) take in their parent's place.

▶ *Ancestors.* Parents usually take as heirs if the decedent leaves no issue.

▶ *Collaterals.* All persons related by blood to the decedent who are neither descendants nor ancestors are collateral kin. This includes brothers, sisters, nephews, nieces, uncles, aunts, and cousins. If a decedent leaves no spouse, no issue, and no parents, the decedent's brothers and sisters (and their descendants by representation) take in all jurisdictions. The rules for determining which of the more remote collateral kindred take were rather complicated at common law and remain so today.

▶ *Escheat.* If a person dies intestate without any legal heirs, the person's property escheats to the state where the property is located.

Problems

1. *O*, owner of Blackacre, has two children, *A* and *B*. Subsequently, *B* dies testate, devising all his property to *W*, his wife. *B* is survived by three children, *B1*, *B2*, and *B3*. *A1* is born to *A*. Then *O* dies intestate. Who owns Blackacre under modern American law?

2. *O* conveys Blackacre "to *A* and her heirs." If *A* dies intestate without issue, will Blackacre escheat to the state?

B. THE FEE TAIL

One of the great and continuing conflicts in the development of English property law arose out of the desire of the heads of rich families to keep property within the family—specifically, within the line of lineal descendants. Land was family power, status, and wealth, and those who controlled it wanted to make it impossible—or, if not impossible, at least very difficult—for their descendants to alienate it. The family bond was strong; the family was thought of as a chain of ancestors and descendants extending through time. The best way to keep land from passing outside the family was to make it impossible for descendants to transfer the land. That is what the fee tail estate did. The fee tail prevented the current owner from cutting off the inheritance rights of his issue. If all went well, it assured that the land would pass to the grantee's eldest son, then to his eldest son, generation after generation.

A fee tail is an estate in land created by a conveyance "to *A* and the heirs of his body." It is an estate precisely tailored to the desires of the medieval dynasts. The fee tail descends to *A*'s lineal descendants ("heirs of the body") generation after generation, and it expires when the original tenant in fee tail, *A*, and all of *A*'s lineal descendants are dead. When *A*'s bloodline runs out and the fee tail ends, the land will revert to the grantor or the grantor's heirs by way of reversion or, if specified in the instrument, will go to some other branch of the family. For example, *O* might convey land "to my son *A* and the heirs of his body, and if *A* dies without issue, to my daughter *B* and her heirs." By this conveyance *A* is given a fee tail, and *B* is given a remainder in fee simple to become possessory when and if the fee tail expires. Every fee tail has a reversion or a remainder after it.

Time line 3-2

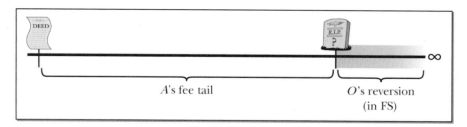

In this country, the fee tail has nearly disappeared. The vast majority of states abolished it beginning in the eighteenth century, both because it clogged the alienability of land and it appeared to be an instrument for perpetuating aristocracy. Today the fee tail can be created only in Delaware, Maine, Massachusetts, and Rhode Island. In these states, a fee tail tenant can convert a fee tail into a fee simple by a deed executed during life, but cannot bar the entail by will. Even in these states, a fee tail is rarely encountered, however.

About the only problem related to the fee tail that arises in modern times is this: when an instrument uses language that would have created a fee tail at common law, what estate is thereby created today? Suppose that *O* conveys "to my son *A* and the heirs of his body, and if *A* dies without issue, to my daughter *B* and her heirs." What interests are created under modern law? In each state in which the fee tail is abolished, a statute specifies what estate is created in *A* by the language of *O*'s conveyance and what interest, if any, is created in *B*. Although a few states provide that *A* takes a life estate, and *A*'s issue take a remainder in fee simple, the large majority of states fall into one of two categories:

(1) In states falling into the first category, statutes provide that a limitation "to *A* and the heirs of his body" creates a fee simple in *A* and that any gift over on *A*'s death without issue is void. Neither *A*'s issue nor *B* takes anything under the above conveyance. The justification for this type of statute is that inasmuch as *A* could disentail and destroy the interests of *A*'s issue and *B*, the statute does it automatically.

(2) In states in the second category, statutes provide that a limitation "to *A* and the heirs of his body" creates a fee simple in *A*, but they further provide that a gift over to *B* if *A* dies without issue will be given effect in one circumstance. *B* will take the fee simple if, and only if, *at A's death*, *A* leaves no surviving issue (and not, as at common law, when *A*'s whole line of issue runs out). *B*'s future interest is known as a divesting executory interest, which will shift the fee simple to *B* if *A* leaves no issue at his death. (Executory interests are explained beginning at page 232.) If *A* leaves surviving issue at his death, *B*'s interest fails, and *A*'s fee simple cannot be divested thereafter. In such case, *A* can devise his fee simple to whomever he chooses.

The Restatement (Third) of Property provides that "[t]he fee tail estate is not recognized in American law." Restatement (Third) of Property, Wills and Other Donative Transfers § 24.4 (2011). It goes on to state that language that would have created a fee tail at common law creates a fee simple absolute. This means that any gift over following what would, at common law, have been a fee tail is void. A comment to the Restatement observes that even under its new rule, it is possible to create a substantially equivalent estate by a disposition such as "to *A* for life, then to *A*'s issue from time to time living forever." Id. § 24.4 comment c. Such a disposition is valid except to the extent restricted by the Rule Against Perpetuities, which we take up in Chapter 4. In recent years, several states have abolished the Rule Against Perpetuities, making it possible in these states to create the substantial equivalent of the old fee tail.

Problems

1. In Massachusetts, *O* conveys Blackacre "to *A* and the children of his body." *A* has three children. What is the state of title in Blackacre?

2. *O* conveys Blackacre "to *A* for life, then to *B* and heirs of his body, but if *B* dies without issue, then to *C* and his heirs." What is the state of title in Blackacre in Delaware? What is the state of title in the first category of those states that have abolished the fee tail? In the second category?

C. THE LIFE ESTATE

The early common law had little difficulty recognizing a *life estate*. Early feudal relations between a lord and his tenant, after all, were only a lifetime matter. Judicial recognition of a life estate had two important consequences. First, it meant that the grantor of a life estate could control who takes the property at the life tenant's death. The life estate ultimately supplanted the fee tail as a device to control inheritance. Second, as land and stocks and bonds came to be viewed as income-producing capital, trust management for the life tenant developed. As we will see in Chapter 4, in the modern

Sidebar

Seisin—The fee simple, the fee tail, and the life estate are *freehold estates*. The chief significance of this, at common law, was that a freeholder had *seisin*. Seisin was possession of a particular kind and with particular consequences. Tenants seised of the land were responsible for feudal services, and feudal land law decreed that someone must always be seised. In early common law, a freehold estate could be created or transferred only by a ceremonial known as "feoffment" with *livery of seisin*. This usually included both the grantor and the grantee going on the land, and the grantor, before witnesses, delivering seisin to the grantee by some symbolic act such as handing over a clod of dirt or some stalks, or putting the grantee's hand on the ring of the door and uttering such words as "Know ye that I have given this land to (the grantee)." Even though livery was often accompanied by a written charter of feoffment, the act of turning over possession before witnesses attested a change of ownership in the clearest possible way. Today, happily, seisin is no longer significant.[1]

---

1. If this ceremony strikes you as quaint, consider that manual delivery may still be required for gifts of tangible personal property. See pages 169-170. And with respect to modern transfers by will, just the right things must be said and done when the will is executed, or the will cannot be probated. See Thomas P. Gallanis, Family Property Law: Wills, Trusts, and Future Interests 110-138 (5th ed. 2011).

trust, one person (often a corporate person such as a bank) manages property for the benefit of the life tenant, paying the life tenant the income therefrom. Today most life estates are created in trust.

A conveyance "to *A* for life" gives *A* a life estate that lasts for the duration of *A*'s life. *A* can transfer his life estate to *B*, in which case *B* has a life estate *pur autre vie*—that is, an estate that is measured by *A*'s life-span, not *B*'s. If *B* dies during *A*'s lifetime, the life estate passes to *B*'s heirs or devisees until *A* dies.

Every life estate is followed by a future interest—either a *reversion* in the transferor or a *remainder* in a transferee, or both. Hence, suppose that *O* conveys Blackacre "to *A* for life." *A* has a life estate, and *O* has a reversion.

Time line 3-3

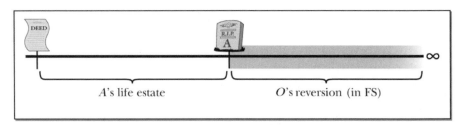

Usually, it is quite clear when an instrument such as a deed or a will creates a life estate rather than some other estate. But sometimes the language used in instruments is less than clear as to what estate the transferor intended to give the transferee. The next case illustrates this problem.

WHITE v. BROWN
Supreme Court of Tennessee, 1977
559 S.W.2d 938

BROCK, J. This is a suit for the construction of a will. The Chancellor held that the will passed a life estate, but not the remainder, in certain realty, leaving the remainder to pass by inheritance to the testatrix's heirs at law. The Court of Appeals affirmed.

Mrs. Jessie Lide died on February 15, 1973, leaving a holographic [handwritten] will which, in its entirety, reads as follows:

April 19, 1972

I, Jessie Lide, being in sound mind declare this to be my last will and testament. I appoint my niece Sandra White Perry to be the executrix of my estate.

I wish Evelyn White to have my home to live in and <u>not</u> to be <u>sold</u>.

I also leave my personal property to Sandra White Perry. My house is not to be sold.

Jessie Lide

(Underscoring by testatrix)

Mrs. Lide was a widow and had no children. Although she had nine brothers and sisters, only two sisters residing in Ohio survived her. These two sisters quitclaimed any interest they might have in the residence to Mrs. White. The [twelve] nieces and nephews of the testatrix, her heirs at law [other than her two sisters and Sandra White Perry], are defendants in this action.

Mrs. White, her husband, who was the testatrix's brother, and her daughter, Sandra White Perry, lived with Mrs. Lide as a family for some twenty-five years. After Sandra married in 1969 and Mrs. White's husband died in 1971, Evelyn White continued to live with Mrs. Lide until Mrs. Lide's death in 1973 at age 88.

> ### Sidebar
>
> The court in White v. Brown apparently misspoke. The interest that is created in the heirs when the owner of the fee simple estate in land devises only a life estate in the land is a *reversion*, not a remainder, as we shall see in Chapter 4. We are grateful to Professor Louise Halper for bringing the court's mistake to our attention.

Mrs. White, joined by her daughter as executrix, filed this action to obtain construction of the will, alleging that she is vested with a fee simple title to the home. The defendants contend that the will conveyed only a life estate to Mrs. White, leaving the remainder to go to them under our laws of intestate succession. The Chancellor held that the will unambiguously conveyed only a life interest in the home to Mrs. White and refused to consider extrinsic evidence concerning Mrs. Lide's relationship with her surviving relatives. Due to the debilitated condition of the property and in accordance with the desire of all parties, the Chancellor ordered the property sold with the proceeds distributed in designated shares among the beneficiaries.[1]

I.

Our cases have repeatedly acknowledged that the intention of the testator is to be ascertained from the language of the entire instrument when read in the light of surrounding circumstances. But, the practical difficulty in this case, as in so many other cases involving wills drafted by lay persons, is that the words chosen by the testatrix are not specific enough to clearly state her intent. Thus, in our opinion, it is not clear whether Mrs. Lide intended to convey a life estate in the home to Mrs. White, leaving the remainder interest to descend by operation of law, or a fee interest with a restraint on alienation. Moreover, the will might even be read as conveying a fee interest subject to a condition subsequent (Mrs. White's failure to live in the home).

In such ambiguous cases it is obvious that rules of construction, always yielding to the cardinal rule of the testator's intent, must be employed as auxiliary aids in the courts' endeavor to ascertain the testator's intent.

In 1851 our General Assembly enacted two such statutes of construction, thereby creating a statutory presumption against partial intestacy.

Chapter 33 of the Public Acts of 1851 (now codified as T.C.A. §§ 64-101 and 64-501) reversed the common law presumption[2] that a life estate was intended unless the

---

1. The brief for the appellee states that the chancellor ordered the proceeds divided between the life tenant, Evelyn White, and the testatrix's heirs, as remaindermen, according to the value of their respective interests ascertained from life expectancy tables. See page 203. — EDS.

2. Because the feudal lord granted land solely as compensation for personal services, the grant was for no longer than the life of the grantee. Later the grant was extended to the sons and other issue of the grantee under the designation of "heirs." Heirs were thus entitled to stand in the place of their

intent to pass a fee simple was clearly expressed in the instrument. T.C.A. § 64-501 provides:

> Every grant or devise of real estate, or any interest therein, shall pass all the estate or interest of the grantor or devisor, unless the intent to pass a less estate or interest shall appear by express terms, or be necessarily implied in the terms of the instrument.

Chapter 180, Section 2 of the Public Acts of 1851 (now codified as T.C.A. § 32-301) was specifically directed to the operation of a devise. In relevant part, T.C.A. § 32-301 provides:

> A will . . . shall convey all the real estate belonging to [the testator] or in which he had any interest at his decease, unless a contrary intention appear by its words and context.

Thus, under our law, unless the "words and context" of Mrs. Lide's will clearly evidence her intention to convey only a life estate to Mrs. White, the will should be construed as passing the home to Mrs. White in fee. " 'If the expression in the will is doubtful, the doubt is resolved against the limitation and in favor of the absolute estate.' " Meacham v. Graham, 98 Tenn. 190, 206, 39 S.W. 12, 15 (1897) (quoting Washbon v. Cope, 144 N.Y. 287, 39 N.E. 388).

Several of our cases demonstrate the effect of these statutory presumptions against intestacy by construing language which might seem to convey an estate for life, without provision for a gift over after the termination of such life estate, as passing a fee simple instead. In Green v. Young, 163 Tenn. 16, 40 S.W.2d 793 (1931), the testatrix's disposition of all of her property to her husband "to be used by him for his support and comfort during his life" was held to pass a fee estate. Similarly, in Williams v. Williams, 167 Tenn. 26, 65 S.W.2d 561 (1933), the testator's devise of real property to his children "for and during their natural lives" without provision for a gift over was held to convey a fee. And, in Webb v. Webb, 53 Tenn. App. 609, 385 S.W.2d 295 (1964), a devise of personal property to the testator's wife "for her maintenance, support and comfort, for the full period of her natural life" with complete powers of alienation but without provision for the remainder passed absolute title to the widow.

II.

Thus, if the sole question for our determination were whether the will's conveyance of the home to Mrs. White "to live in" gave her a life interest or a fee in the home, a conclusion favoring the absolute estate would be clearly required. The question, however, is complicated somewhat by the caveat contained in the will that the home is "not to be sold" — a restriction conflicting with the free alienation of property, one of the most significant incidents of fee ownership. We must determine, therefore, whether Mrs. Lide's will, when taken as a whole, clearly evidences her intent to convey only a life estate in her home to Mrs. White.

---

ancestor after his death if mentioned in the grant—but only if specifically mentioned. Thereafter, the word "heirs," when used in a conveyance to a man "and his heirs," came to include collateral as well as lineal heirs, ultimately indicating that such grantee took an estate which would pass to his heirs or the heirs of anyone to whom he aliened it. That is, "heirs" ceased to be a word of purchase and became a word of limitation. 1 Tiffany, Real Property §28 (3d ed. 1939).

Jessie Lide's House, 1956
Jessie Lide on right, Sandra White in middle

Under ordinary circumstances a person makes a will to dispose of his or her entire estate. If, therefore, a will is susceptible of two constructions, by one of which the testator disposes of the whole of his estate and by the other of which he disposes of only a part of his estate, dying intestate as to the remainder, this Court has always preferred that construction which disposes of the whole of the testator's estate if that construction is reasonable and consistent with the general scope and provisions of the will. A construction which results in partial intestacy will not be adopted unless such intention clearly appears. It has been said that the courts will prefer any reasonable construction or any construction which does not do violence to a testator's language, to a construction which results in partial intestacy.

The intent to create a fee simple or other absolute interest and, at the same time to impose a restraint upon its alienation can be clearly expressed. If the testator specifically declares that he devises land to A "in fee simple" or to A "and his heirs" but that A shall not have the power to alienate the land, there is but one tenable construction, viz., the testator's intent is to impose a restraint upon a fee simple. To construe such language to create a life estate would conflict with the express specification of a fee simple as well as with the presumption of intent to make a complete testamentary disposition of all of a testator's property. By extension, as noted by Professor Casner in his treatise on the law of real property:

> Since it is now generally presumed that a conveyor intends to transfer his whole interest in the property, it may be reasonable to adopt the same construction [conveyance of a fee simple], even in the absence of words of inheritance, if there is no language that can be construed to create a remainder. [6 American Law of Property § 26.58 (A.J. Casner ed. 1952).]

In our opinion, testatrix's apparent testamentary restraint on the alienation of the home devised to Mrs. White does not evidence such a clear intent to pass only a life estate as is sufficient to overcome the law's strong presumption that a fee simple interest was conveyed.

Accordingly, we conclude that Mrs. Lide's will passed a fee simple absolute in the home to Mrs. White. Her attempted restraint on alienation must be declared void as inconsistent with the incidents and nature of the estate devised and contrary to public policy.

The decrees of the Court of Appeals and the trial court are reversed and the cause is remanded to the chancery court for such further proceedings as may be necessary, consistent with this opinion. Costs are taxed against appellees.

Harbison, J., dissenting. With deference to the views of the majority, and recognizing the principles of law contained in the majority opinion, I am unable to agree that the language of the will of Mrs. Lide did or was intended to convey a fee simple interest in her residence to her sister-in-law, Mrs. Evelyn White.

The testatrix expressed the wish that Mrs. White was to have my home to live in and *not* to be *sold.* The emphasis is that of the testatrix, and her desire that Mrs. White was not to have an unlimited estate in the property was reiterated in the last sentence of the will, to wit: "My house is not to be sold."

The testatrix appointed her niece, Mrs. Perry, executrix and made an outright bequest to her of all personal property.

The will does not seem to me to be particularly ambiguous, and like the Chancellor and the Court of Appeals, I am of the opinion that the testatrix gave Mrs. White a life estate only, and that upon the death of Mrs. White the remainder will pass to the heirs at law of the testatrix. . . .

In the present case the testatrix knew how to make an outright gift, if desired. She left all of her personal property to her niece without restraint or limitation. As to her sister-in-law, however, she merely wished the latter have her house "to live in," and expressly withheld from her any power of sale.

The majority opinion holds that the testatrix violated a rule of law by attempting to restrict the power of the donee to dispose of the real estate. Only by thus striking a portion of the will, and holding it inoperative, is the conclusion reached that an unlimited estate resulted.

In my opinion, this interpretation conflicts more greatly with the apparent intention of the testatrix than did the conclusion of the courts below, limiting the gift to Mrs. White to a life estate. I have serious doubt that the testatrix intended to create any illegal restraint on alienation or to violate any other rules of law. It seems to me that she rather emphatically intended to provide that her sister-in-law was not to be able to sell the house during the lifetime of the latter—a result which is both legal and consistent with the creation of a life estate.

In my opinion the judgment of the courts below was correct and I would affirm.

THE REST OF THE STORY . . .

Jessie Lide's niece, Sandra White Perry, has provided us with the following information concerning the fate of her aunt's house: "I moved to that house when I was nine months old along with my parents (my father was Jessie Lide's brother). I lived in that house until I married at age 22. The house originally had four rooms—living room, dining room, kitchen, and one bedroom. Mama, Daddy, and I lived in one room of Jessie's four-room house. She also lived in one room—originally the kitchen. Jessie cleaned the living room every day. We never sat in it. The only time Jessie unlocked it was for a death in the family. In 1957, after renting the house for $3 a week for 38 years, Jessie purchased the house from her landlord for a price of $3,000 cash. At that time, the house had no hot water and no electrical plugs. After she purchased the house, three more rooms were added on—a bedroom for me, a kitchen for my mother, and a room to be used for storing things.

"In 1964 the Chrysler Corporation offered her a price of $35,000 for the property. The company had purchased more than half the block and this house stood in the way. She refused to sell, stating this was her home. [Jessie died in 1973.]

"In 1976 my mother had a serious stroke, therefore making it impossible for her to live alone anymore. I had her move into my home and we rented out the Gratz Street house—after spending $8,000 on improvements.

"In 1981 my mother died. My husband and I were unemployed at the time. We put the house up for sale. Being desperate along with threats from the bank (regarding the home improvement loan on the house), we were forced to sell to anyone that would have it. We sold it to a fellow named Brewster for $10,000. In 1986 he sold the house to the Chrysler Company next door for a price of $40,000. I had contacted the Chrysler Company in 1981, but they were not interested at that time in buying the property." [Letter from Sandra White Perry to the editors, dated Aug. 1, 1988.]

Notes and Questions

1. *The testator's intent.* When construing language in a will, a court's primary objective is supposed to be carrying out the testator's intention. If Jesse Lide were able to express her intent to the court, knowing of all the circumstances present in the case, what do you think she would say? Did the court's decision fulfill her probable intention?

2. *Valuing life estates.* It is possible to calculate the monetary value of a life estate. In *White*, the chancellor ordered the proceeds divided between the life tenant, Evelyn White, and Jesse Lide's heirs, as remainder beneficiaries. What is the value of her life estate? Assume that the house is worth $10,000. Since we do not know how long the life tenant will actually live, to value the life estate we based her life expectancy on mortality tables. We also need an interest rate, so let's assume the market interest rate is 6 percent. Now we can value the life estate. To calculate its value, we need to determine the present value of the right to receive $600 annually (6 percent of $10,000) for the life tenant's life expectancy. We seek a sum that, invested for the life tenant's life expectancy at 6 percent, will pay $600 for the given number of years and exhaust itself on final payment—in short, the price of an annuity. To simplify the problem let us assume that the life tenant has a life expectancy of only three years. The right to $1 one year from now is not worth $1 now, but only the amount that, if increased by the interest it can earn in a year, will equal $1. Assuming a 6 percent rate of interest, 94 cents will grow to $1 a year from today. A dollar due in two years is worth 89 cents today (at 6 percent interest); by reinvesting interest, 89 cents today will grow into 94 cents one year from now, which will grow into $1 two years from now. The present value of the right to receive $1 per year for three years is the sum of 94 cents and 89 cents and

84 cents, or $2.67. Now what is the present value of the right to receive $600 a year for the next three years? $600 × 2.67 = $1,600, which is the present value of the life estate.

Another method, which courts, taxing authorities, and insurance companies use to value life estates, is to rely on life expectancy tables. Under Treasury regulations applicable at the time of Jessie Lide's death, if the life tenant had been 70 years old, the life estate would have been worth 48 percent of the asset value (the remainder would have been worth 52 percent). If Evelyn White had been given a life estate in *White* and were 70 years old, why might she and the remainder beneficiaries not be willing to sell the house voluntarily and divide the proceeds 48 percent to 52 percent?

3. *Restraints on alienation.* The rule prohibiting direct restraints on alienation is an old one and fundamental to American property law. It grows directly out of the foundational policy of promoting free alienability of property. Direct restraints on alienation make property unmarketable, preventing it from moving through market transactions to its highest and best use. There are three types of restraints on alienation: *disabling* restraints, *forfeiture* restraints, and *promissory* restraints. A *disabling restraint* withholds from the grantee the power of transferring his interest (e.g., O conveys Blackacre "to A and his heirs, but any transfer hereafter in any manner of an interest in Blackacre shall be null and void"). A disabling restraint was involved in White v. Brown. A *forfeiture restraint* provides that if the grantee attempts to transfer his interest, it is forfeited to another person (e.g., O conveys Blackacre "to A and his heirs, but if A attempts to transfer the property by any means whatsoever, then to B and her heirs"). A *promissory restraint* provides that the grantee promises not to transfer his interest (e.g., O conveys Blackacre "to A and his heirs, and A promises for himself, his heirs, and successors in interest that Blackacre will not be transferred by any means"). A promissory restraint, if valid, is enforceable by the contract remedies of damages or an injunction. Promissory restraints on alienation of land are rare except in the landlord-tenant context (see pages 305-312).

BAKER v. WEEDON

Supreme Court of Mississippi, 1972
262 So. 2d 641

PATTERSON, J. This is an appeal from a decree of the Chancery Court of Alcorn County. It directs a sale of land affected by a life estate and future interests with provision for the investment of the proceeds. The interest therefrom is to be paid to the life tenant for her maintenance. We reverse and remand.

John Harrison Weedon was born in High Point, North Carolina. He lived throughout the South and was married twice prior to establishing his final residence in Alcorn County. His first marriage to Lula Edwards resulted in two siblings, Mrs. Florence Weedon Baker and Mrs. Delette Weedon Jones. Mrs. Baker was the mother of three children, Henry Baker, Sarah Baker Lyman and Louise Virginia Baker Heck, the appellants herein. Mrs. Delette Weedon Jones adopted a daughter Dorothy Jean Jones, who has not been heard from for a number of years and whose whereabouts are presently unknown.

John Weedon was next married to Ella Howell and to this union there was born one child, Rachel. Both Ella and Rachel are now deceased.

Subsequent to these marriages John Weedon bought Oakland Farm in 1905 and engaged himself in its operation. In 1915 John, who was then 55 years of age, married Anna Plaxico, 17 years of age. This marriage, though resulting in no children, was a compatible relationship. John and Anna worked side by side in farming this 152.95-acre tract of land in Alcorn County. There can be no doubt that Anna's contribution to the development and existence of Oakland Farm was significant. The record discloses that during the monetarily difficult years following World War I she hoed, picked cotton and milked an average of fifteen cows per day to protect the farm from financial ruin.

While the relationship of John and Anna was close and amiable, that between John and his daughters of his first marriage was distant and strained. He had no contact with Florence, who was reared by Mr. Weedon's sister in North Carolina, during the seventeen years preceding his death. An even more unfortunate relationship existed between John and his second daughter, Delette Weedon Jones. She is portrayed by the record as being a nomadic person who only contacted her father for money, threatening on several occasions to bring suit against him.

With an obvious intent to exclude his daughters and provide for his wife Anna, John executed his last will and testament in 1925. It provided in part:

> Second; I give and bequeath to my beloved wife, Anna Plaxico Weedon all of my property both real, personal and mixed during her natural life and upon her death to her children, if she has any, and in the event she dies without issue then at the death of my wife Anna Plaxico Weedon I give, bequeath and devise all of my property to my grandchildren, each grandchild sharing equally with the other.
>
> Third; In this will I have not provided for my daughters, Mrs. Florence Baker and Mrs. Delette Weedon Jones, the reason is, I have given them their share of my property and they have not looked after and cared for me in the latter part of my life.

Subsequent to John Weedon's death in 1932 and the probate of his will, Anna continued to live on Oakland Farm. In 1933 Anna, who had been urged by John to remarry in the event of his death, wed J.E. Myers. This union lasted some twenty years and produced no offspring which might terminate the contingent remainder vested in Weedon's grandchildren by the will.

There was no contact between Anna and John Weedon's children or grandchildren from 1932 until 1964. Anna ceased to operate the farm in 1955 due to her age and it has been rented since that time. Anna's only income is $1000 annually from the farm rental, $300 per year from sign rental and $50 per month by way of social security payments. Without contradiction Anna's income is presently insufficient and places a severe burden upon her ability to live comfortably in view of her age and the infirmities therefrom.

In 1964 the growth of the city of Corinth was approaching Oakland Farm. A right-of-way through the property was sought by the Mississippi State Highway Department for the construction of U.S. Highway 45 bypass. The highway department located Florence Baker's three children, the contingent remaindermen by the will of John Weedon, to negotiate with them for the purchase of the right-of-way. Dorothy Jean Jones, the adopted daughter of Delette Weedon Jones, was not located and due to the long passage of years, is presumably dead. A decree pro confesso was entered against her.

Until the notice afforded by the highway department the grandchildren were unaware of their possible inheritance. Henry Baker, a native of New Jersey, journeyed to Mississippi to supervise their interests. He appears, as was true of the other grandchildren, to have been totally sympathetic to the conditions surrounding Anna's existence as a life tenant. A settlement of $20,000 was completed for the right-of-way bypass of which Anna received $7500 with which to construct a new home. It is significant that all legal and administrative fees were deducted from the shares of the three grandchildren and not taxed to the life tenant. A contract was executed in 1970 for the sale of soil from the property for $2500. Anna received $1000 of this sum which went toward completion of payments for the home.

There was substantial evidence introduced to indicate the value of the property is appreciating significantly with the nearing completion of U.S. Highway 45 bypass plus the growth of the city of Corinth. While the commercial value of the property is appreciating, it is notable that the rental value for agricultural purposes is not. It is apparent that the land can bring no more for agricultural rental purposes than the $1000 per year now received.

The value of the property for commercial purposes at the time of trial was $168,500. Its estimated value within the ensuing four years is placed at $336,000, reflecting the great influence of the interstate construction upon the land. Mr. Baker, for himself and other remaindermen, appears to have made numerous honest and sincere efforts to sell the property at a favorable price. However, his endeavors have been hindered by the slowness of the construction of the bypass.

Anna, the life tenant and appellee here, is 73 years of age and although now living in a new home, has brought this suit due to her economic distress. She prays that the property, less the house site, be sold by a commissioner and that the proceeds be invested to provide her with an adequate income resulting from interest on the trust investment. She prays also that the sale and investment management be under the direction of the chancery court.

The chancellor granted the relief prayed by Anna under the theory of economic waste. His opinion reflects:

> . . . [T]he change of the economy in this area, the change in farming conditions, the equipment required for farming, and the age of this complainant leaves the real estate where it is to all intents and purposes unproductive when viewed in light of its capacity and that a continuing use under the present conditions would result in economic waste.[3]

The contingent remaindermen by the will, appellants here, were granted an interlocutory appeal to settle the issue of the propriety of the chancellor's decree in divesting the contingency title of the remaindermen by ordering a sale of the property.

---

3. What does the chancellor mean by "economic waste"? Is it the same as the legal concept of waste? See Note 3 on pages 209-210. — EDS.

The weight of authority reflects a tendency to afford a court of equity the power to order the sale of land in which there are future interests. Simes, Law of Future Interests, section 53 (2d ed. 1966), states:

> By the weight of authority, it is held that a court of equity has the power to order a judicial sale of land affected with a future interest and an investment of the proceeds, where this is necessary for the preservation of all interests in the land. When the power is exercised, the proceeds of the sale are held in a judicially created trust. The beneficiaries of the trust are the persons who held interests in the land, and the beneficial interests are of the same character as the legal interests which they formally held in the land.

See also Simes and Smith, The Law of Future Interests, § 1941 (2d ed. 1956).

This Court has long recognized that chancery courts do have jurisdiction to order the sale of land for the prevention of waste. Kelly v. Neville, 136 Miss. 429, 101 So. 565 (1924). In Riley v. Norfleet, 167 Miss. 420, 436-437, 148 So. 777, 781 (1933), Justice Cook, speaking for the Court and citing *Kelly*, supra, stated: ". . . The power of a court of equity on a plenary bill, with adversary interest properly represented, to sell contingent remainders in land, under some circumstances, though the contingent remaindermen are not then ascertained or in being, as, for instance, to preserve the estate from complete or partial destruction, is well established."

While Mississippi and most jurisdictions recognize the inherent power of a court of equity to direct a judicial sale of land which is subject to a future interest, nevertheless the scope of this power has not been clearly defined. It is difficult to determine the facts and circumstances which will merit such a sale.

It is apparent that there must be "necessity" before the chancery court can order a judicial sale. It is also beyond cavil that the power should be exercised with caution and only when the need is evident. Lambdin v. Lambdin, 209 Miss. 672, 48 So. 2d 341 (1950). These cases, *Kelly, Riley* and *Lambdin*, supra, are all illustrative of situations where the freehold estate was deteriorating and the income therefrom was insufficient to pay taxes and maintain the property. In each of these this Court approved a judicial sale to preserve and maintain the estate. The appellants argue, therefore, that since Oakland Farm is not deteriorating and since there is sufficient income from rental to pay taxes, a judicial sale by direction of the court was not proper.

The unusual circumstances of this case persuade us to the contrary. We are of the opinion that deterioration and waste of the property is not the exclusive and ultimate test to be used in determining whether a sale of land affected by a future interest is proper, but also that consideration should be given to the question of whether a sale is necessary for the best interest of all the parties, that is, the life tenant and the contingent remaindermen. This "necessary for the best interest of all parties" rule is gleaned from Rogers, Removal of Future Interest Encumbrances — Sale of the Fee Simple Estate, 17 Vanderbilt L. Rev. 1437 (1964); Simes, Law of Future Interests, supra; Simes and Smith, The Law of Future Interests, § 1941 (1956); and appears to have the necessary flexibility to meet the requirements of unusual and unique situations which demand in justice an equitable solution.

Our decision to reverse the chancellor and remand the case for his further consideration is couched in our belief that the best interest of all the parties would not be served by a judicial sale of the entirety of the property at this time. While true that such a sale would provide immediate relief to the life tenant who is worthy of this aid in equity, admitted by the remaindermen, it would nevertheless under the circumstances before us cause great financial loss to the remaindermen.

We therefore reverse and remand this cause to the chancery court, which shall have continuing jurisdiction thereof, for determination upon motion of the life tenant, if she so desires, for relief by way of sale of a part of the burdened land sufficient to provide for her reasonable needs from interest derived from the investment of the proceeds. The sale, however, is to be made only in the event the parties cannot unite to hypothecate the land for sufficient funds for the life tenant's reasonable needs. By affording the options above we do not mean to suggest that other remedies suitable to the parties which will provide economic relief to the aging life tenant are not open to them if approved by the chancellor. It is our opinion, shared by the chancellor and acknowledged by the appellants, that the facts suggest an equitable remedy. However, it is our further opinion that this equity does not warrant the remedy of sale of all of the property since this would unjustly impinge upon the vested rights of the remaindermen.

Reversed and remanded.

THE REST OF THE STORY . . .

After the Mississippi Supreme Court handed down its opinion in Baker v. Weedon, John's grandchildren relented and agreed to sell all of the land except the five acres where Anna lived. Anna and her lawyer were appointed trustees, to invest the proceeds and pay the income to Anna for life. The land became the site of a printing plant printing *National Geographic* magazines. In her nineties, Anna Weedon fell and broke her hip and was confined to a wheelchair, but she managed to live alone in her house until her death in 1996 at age 98. She survived two of her husband's three grandchildren.

Apparently, the case caused quite a stir in Corinth, starting when Weedon's Northern family members came down and began making demands. One of the issues not raised in the case involved Anna's desire to bequeath to her church the new house that she had built. The relatives fought her on that and won. [We owe this information to Professor Donald Campbell, of the Mississippi College School of Law.]

Notes and Questions

1. *Problems with legal life estates.* You will rarely encounter the type of life estate (called a *legal life estate*) that John Weedon created in his will, and for good reason. Such legal life estates create problems that the life tenant cannot adequately solve. Here are some examples of some of these problems:

Sale. Circumstances might change so that a sale of the property is advantageous. The life tenant cannot sell a fee simple unless all other persons having an interest in the property consent, or unless a court of equity orders sale and reinvestment of the proceeds.

Lease. It might be advantageous for the life tenant to lease the property for a period extending beyond the life tenant's death.

Mortgage. If the life tenant has no capital of her own, she may be unable to improve the property without borrowing from a bank and giving the bank a mortgage on the property. A bank ordinarily does not lend money if the security is a life estate rather than a fee simple.

Waste. The life tenant may want to take minerals out of the land, cut timber, or take down a still usable building. The actions may constitute waste, entitling the remainder beneficiaries to an injunction or damages. See Note 3 below.

Insurance. The life tenant is under no duty to insure buildings on the land. If the life tenant does insure buildings and the buildings are destroyed by fire, the life tenant has been held entitled to the whole proceeds and the remainder beneficiaries nothing. Ellersbusch v. Myers, 683 N.E.2d 1352 (Ind. App. 1997).

The person creating a legal life estate can draft the instrument so as to give the life tenant a power to sell or mortgage a fee simple or to lease beyond the duration of the life estate. A life estate can be coupled with any number of powers to do specific acts not otherwise permitted the life tenant. However, if the life tenant is given the power to sell a fee simple, the drafter should consider what is to be done with the proceeds of sale and draft appropriate provisions. Should the proceeds be given outright to the life tenant or held by a trustee in trust for the life tenant's life?

2. *An alternative—the trust.* These problems can all be avoided by creating a trust which confers an equitable life estate upon the first beneficiary, such as Anna Weedon. (The life estate is called "equitable" because courts of equity have jurisdiction over trusts.) A trust is a more flexible and usually more desirable property arrangement than a legal life estate. *A trustee holds the legal fee simple,* and as the "manager" of the property may be directed to pay all the income to the life tenant or to let the life tenant into possession. As manager, the trustee will have powers spelled out in the instrument creating the trust, or supplied by law, to administer the trust for the benefit of the life tenant and remainder beneficiaries. These powers usually give the trustee power to sell, lease, mortgage, remove minerals, or do whatever a prudent person would do with respect to the property. If the trustee sells the property, the trustee invests the proceeds of sale, paying the income therefrom to the life tenant. The great majority of life estates today are equitable life estates.

We will look at the basic structure of the trust in the next chapter, at page 238, but it will help you to be introduced to the trust at this point because cases like Baker v. Weedon illustrate why legal life estates (i.e., life estates created outside of a trust), should almost always be avoided.

3. *The doctrine of waste.* Another problem with legal life estate concerns the doctrine of *waste.* The law of waste can become relevant whenever two or more persons have rights to possess property at the same time. Suppose, for example, *O* conveys land "to *A* for life, then to *B* and his heirs." The central idea of the waste concept is that *A* should not be able to use the property in a manner that *unreasonably* interferes with the expectations of *B.* What if *A* wants to take minerals out of the land, cut timber, or take down a still usable building? The actions may constitute waste, entitling *B* to an injunction or damages.

The law of waste is aptly named, because it is designed to avoid just that—uses of property that fail to maximize the property's value. See Richard A. Posner, Economic Analysis of Law 74-75 (9th ed. 2014):

> [T]he common law doctrine of waste . . . mediates between the competing interests of life tenants and remaindermen. A life tenant will have an incentive

to maximize not the value of the property—that is, the present value of the entire stream of future earnings obtainable from it—but only the present value of the earnings stream obtainable during his expected lifetime. So [h]e'll want to cut timber before it has attained its mature growth even though the present value of the timber would be greater if the cutting of some or all of it were postponed. The law of waste forbids the life tenant to alter the property in a way that reduces the value of the property as a whole.

. . .

There might seem no need for such a law because the life tenant and the remainderman could negotiate an optimal plan for exploiting the property. But since the tenant and remainderman . . . [are locked into dealing with each other—a so-called bilateral monopoly], transaction costs may be high. And the remaindermen may be children, who do not have the legal capacity to make binding contracts; they may even be unborn children.

The precise application of the waste doctrine turns on a number of variables, including the nature of the property interests of the competing parties, the conduct in question, and the remedy sought. In general, the common law has recognized three categories of waste:

- *Affirmative waste*—arises from voluntary acts liability results from injurious acts that have more than trivial effects. Generally, "injurious" has meant acts that substantially reduce the value of the property in question.
- *Permissive waste*—arises from a failure to act. It is essentially a question of negligence—failure to take reasonable care of the property (e.g., failure to make minor repairs).
- *Ameliorative waste*—arises from substantial changes to the property by a tenant that increase rather than decrease the market value of the land. The traditional view was that such actions by the tenant gave rise to liability on the theory that the fee holder was entitled to take possession of the land in substantially the same condition as it was when first transferred to the tenant. Today a significant number of courts reject this view.

D. LEASEHOLD ESTATES

Historically, leases were regarded as personal contracts between lessor and lessee. They were classified as personal property ("chattels real"), and leasehold tenants did not have seisin. Fortunately, none of this has practical importance today.

Today leases are considered to be conveyances of estates, although, as we will see in Chapter 6, they are contracts as well. We defer our study of study of leasehold estates—the foundation of landlord-tenant relations—until Chapter 6.

E. DEFEASIBLE ESTATES

A fee simple may be *absolute*, meaning that it cannot be divested nor will it end upon the occurrence of any future event. Or a fee simple may be *defeasible*. Any estate may be made to be *defeasible*, meaning it will terminate, prior to its natural end point, upon the occurrence of some specified future event. For example, a life estate ends naturally at the death of the life tenant, whereas a defeasible life estate might end earlier than that (as in a conveyance that states, "*O* to *A* for life so long as the property is used only for residential purposes"). The most common defeasible freehold estates are the fees simple defeasible ("defeasible fees," as we will sometimes call them).

The modern relevance of defeasible fees. Although, like estates generally, the origins of defeasible fees are ancient, their functions remain relevant today. The primary reason why landowners create defeasible fees these days is to control the use of the land after it has been transferred. To a lesser extent, defeasible fees are used to control behavior not related to any particular use of land (for example, "to *A* and his heirs so long as *A* never drinks alcoholic beverages"). As instruments of land use control, defeasible fees are rather blunt instruments, because their violation may result in forfeiture of ownership. To a substantial extent, the land use function of defeasible fees has been overtaken by restrictive covenants, which we will study in Chapter 10. But landowners still use them often enough to justify studying them.

Types of defeasible fees. There are three types of defeasible fees simple: the *fee simple determinable*, the *fee simple subject to condition subsequent*, and the *fee simple subject to executory limitation* (or, as some say it, *subject to executory interest*).

- A *fee simple determinable* is a fee simple so limited that it will end *automatically* when a stated event happens. Example: *O* conveys Blackacre "to the Hartford School Board, its successors and assigns, so long as the premises are used for school purposes." The fee simple may continue forever, but if the land ceases to be used for school purposes, the fee simple will come to an end or, using the old word, determine, and the fee simple will revert back to *O*, the grantor. A fee simple determinable is sometimes called a fee simple "on a special limitation," indicating that the fee simple will expire by this limitation if it occurs.

  The key to a fee simple determinable is that it is created by durational language, such as "so long as," "during," or "while." Such words connote that the transferor is conveying a fee simple only until an event happens. These are *words of limitation* that cause the fee simple to terminate automatically upon the occurrence of the stated event. Words that merely state the motive of the transferor in making a gift do not create a determinable fee; for example, a conveyance "to the Hartford School Board for school purposes" gives the Board a fee simple absolute and not a fee simple determinable. Every fee simple determinable is accompanied by a future interest. In the ordinary case, the future interest is retained by the transferor (*O* in the above example) or his heirs, and called a *possibility of reverter*. The possibility of reverter may be expressly retained or, as in the above example, arise by operation of law. It arises by operation of law because *O* has transferred less than his entire interest in Blackacre when he creates a determinable fee in the School Board. (In the next two time lines and in several of the time lines both in this chapter and the next, represents the possessory estate's termination by operation of a limitation; and represents the possessory estate's termination by operation of a condition.)

Time line 3-4

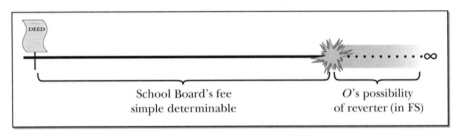

 School Board's fee
 simple determinable

 O's possibility
 of reverter (in FS)

- A *fee simple subject to condition subsequent* is a fee simple that does not automatically terminate but *may be cut short* or "divested," as lawyers say, at the transferor's election when a stated condition happens. Example: O conveys Whiteacre "to the Hartford School Board, its successors and assigns, but if the premises are not used for school purposes, the grantor has a right to re-enter and retake the premises." Notice that we have used a different verbal formula than that creating a determinable fee. The Board's fee simple may be cut short if O elects to exercise the right of entry, but it is not automatically terminated when the stated event happens. Unless and until entry is made, the fee simple continues. That is the essential difference between these two defeasible fees.

Time line 3-5

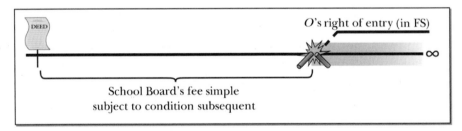

 O's right of entry (in FS)

 School Board's fee simple
 subject to condition subsequent

A *fee simple subject to condition subsequent* is created by a conveyance of a fee simple, followed by language providing that the fee simple may be divested by the transferor if a specified event happens. In the above example, the clause beginning with "but if . . ." states a condition subsequent. Other language creating a condition subsequent, after conveying a fee simple, includes "provided, however, that when the premises . . .," "on condition that if the premises . . .," or other words indicating that the estate may be cut short at the transferor's election. The difference between language creating a determinable fee and language creating a fee simple subject to condition subsequent is extremely subtle, but millions of dollars have turned on this difference in language.

The future interest retained by the transferor to divest a fee simple subject to condition subsequent is called a *right of entry* (also known as a *power of termination*). A right of entry, like a possibility of reverter, may be retained initially only by the transferor or his heirs. It may not be created in a transferee. The right of entry may be expressly retained or it may be implied if the words of the instrument are reasonably susceptible to the interpretation that this type of forfeiture estate was contemplated by the parties. It is always wise, of course, to avoid litigation by expressly including a right of entry, if that is intended.

- A *fee simple subject to executory limitation* is created when a grantor transfers what appears to be a fee simple subject to condition subsequent and in the same instrument creates a future interest in a third party rather than in himself. The future interest in the third party is called an *executory interest*. (We will study executory interests in Chapter 4.) Thus, if O conveys land "to the Hartford School Board, but if it ceases to use the land as a school, to the City Library," the School Board has a fee simple subject to executory limitation, and the City Library has an executory interest. A fee simple subject to condition subsequent and a fee simple subject to executory limitation are created by the same language. The distinction between the two is based on the type of future interest following it. A fee simple subject to condition subsequent is followed by a right of entry, whereas a fee simple subject to executory limitation is followed by an executory interest.

  Confusingly, however, if an executory interest follows a fee simple determinable, we call the fee simple a fee simple determinable, *not* a fee simple subject to executory limitation (or interest). Example: O conveys Whiteacre "to the Hartford School Board, its successors and assigns, so long as the premises are used for teaching purposes; otherwise, to the City Library."

Note well an important practical difference between the fee simple subject to condition subsequent and the fee simple subject to executory limitation: if the condition is breached the former is forfeited only if the right of entry is exercised, but the latter is forfeited immediately, regardless of any action on the part of the holder of the executory interest to take possession. The reason for this difference grows out of the English Statute of Uses (1536), which we will discuss in Chapter 4.

Time line 3-6

Lawyers, when using the term "fee simple," ordinarily have in mind a fee simple absolute. We follow that practice. When we have a fee simple defeasible in mind, we say so.

MAHRENHOLZ v. COUNTY BOARD OF SCHOOL TRUSTEES
Appellate Court of Illinois, 1981
417 N.E.2d 138

JONES, J. This case involves an action to quiet title to real property located in Lawrence County, Illinois. Its resolution depends on the judicial construction of language in a conveyance of that property. The case is before us on the pleadings, plaintiffs' third amended complaint having been dismissed by a final order. The pertinent facts are taken from the pleadings.

On March 18, 1941, W.E. and Jennie Hutton executed a warranty deed in which they conveyed [1½ acres out of 40 acres they owned], to be known here as the Hutton School grounds, to the Trustees of School District No. 1, the predecessors of the defendants in this action. The deed provided that "this land to be used for school purpose only; otherwise to revert to Grantors herein." W.E. Hutton died intestate on July 18, 1951, and Jennie Hutton died intestate on February 18, 1969. The Huttons left as their only legal heir their son Harry E. Hutton.

The property conveyed by the Huttons became the site of the Hutton School. Community Unit School District No. 20 succeeded to the grantee of the deed and held classes in the building constructed upon the land until May 30, 1973. After that date, children were transported to classes held at other facilities operated by the District. The District has used the property since then for storage purposes only. . . .

[In July 1941, W.E. and Jennie Hutton conveyed to Earl and Madeline Jacqmain the remaining 38½ acres of the 40-acre tract from which the 1½ acres conveyed to the school board were taken. In addition to the land surrounding the school, this deed purported to convey to the Jacqmains the reversionary interest the Huttons held in the school land. On October 9, 1959, the Jacqmains executed a warranty deed conveying the 38½ acres adjacent to the school grounds to the plaintiffs, Herbert and Betty Mahrenholz. This deed also purported to convey to the plaintiffs the reversionary interest in the school land.]

On May 7, 1977, Harry E. Hutton, son and sole heir of W.E. and Jennie Hutton, conveyed to the plaintiffs all of his interest in the Hutton School land. This document was filed in the recorder's office of Lawrence County on September 7, 1977. On September 6, 1977, Harry Hutton disclaimed his interest in the property in favor of the defendants. The disclaimer was in the form of a written document entitled "Disclaimer and Release." It contained the legal description of the Hutton School grounds and recited that Harry E. Hutton disclaimed and released any possibility of reverter or right of entry for condition broken, or other similar interest, in favor of the County Board of School Trustees for Lawrence County, Illinois, successor to the Trustees of School District No. 1 of Lawrence County, Illinois. The document further recited that it was made for the purpose of releasing and extinguishing any right Harry E. Hutton may have had in the "interest retained by W.E. Hutton and Jennie Hutton . . . in that deed to the Trustees of School District No. 1, Lawrence County, Illinois dated March 18,

1941, and filed on the same date. . . ." The disclaimer was filed in the recorder's office of Lawrence County on October 4, 1977.

The plaintiffs filed a complaint in the circuit court of Lawrence County . . . in which they sought to quiet title to the school property in themselves. . . . On March 21, 1979, the trial court entered an order dismissing this complaint. In the order the court found that the

> [W]arranty deed dated March 18, 1941, from W.E. Hutton and Jennie Hutton to the Trustees of School District No. 1, conveying land here concerned, created a fee simple subject to a condition subsequent followed by the right of entry for condition broken, rather than a determinable fee followed by a possibility of reverter.

Plaintiffs have perfected an appeal to this court.

The basic issue presented by this appeal is whether the trial court correctly concluded that the plaintiffs could not have acquired any interest in the school property from the Jacqmains and Harry Hutton. Resolution of this issue must turn upon the legal interpretation of the language contained in the March 18, 1941, deed from W.E. and Jennie Hutton to the Trustees of School District No. 1: "this land to be used for school purpose only; otherwise to revert to Grantors herein." In addition to the legal effect of this language we must consider the alienability of the interest created and the effect of subsequent deeds.

The parties appear to be in agreement that the 1941 deed from the Huttons conveyed a defeasible fee simple estate to the grantee, and gave rise to a future interest in the grantors (see Restatement of the Law, Property, sec. 153), and that it did not convey a fee simple absolute, subject to a covenant. The fact that provision was made for forfeiture of the estate conveyed should the land cease to be used for school purposes suggests that this view is correct. Dunne v. Minsor (1924), 312 Ill. 333, 143 N.E. 842; Newton v. Village of Glen Ellyn (1940), 374 Ill. 50, 27 N.E.2d 821. Restatement of the Law, Property, secs. 44, 45.

The future interest remaining in this grantor or his estate can only be a possibility of reverter or a right of re-entry for condition broken. As neither interest may be transferred by will or by inter vivos conveyance (Ill. Rev. Stat., ch. 30, par. 37b), and as the land was being used for school purposes in 1959 when the Jacqmains transferred their interest in the school property to the plaintiffs, the trial court correctly ruled that the plaintiffs could not have acquired any interest in that property from the Jacqmains by the deed of October 9, 1959.

Consequently this court must determine whether the plaintiffs could have acquired an interest in the Hutton School grounds from Harry Hutton. The resolution of this issue depends on the construction of the language of the 1941 deed of the Huttons to the school district. As urged by the defendants and as the trial court found, the deed conveyed a fee simple subject to a condition subsequent followed by a right of reentry for condition broken. As argued by the plaintiffs, on the other hand, the deed conveyed a fee simple determinable followed by a possibility of reverter. In either case, the grantor and his heirs retain an interest in the property which may become possessory if the condition is broken. We emphasize here that although sec. 1 of An Act relating to Rights of Entry or Reentry for breach of condition subsequent and possibilities of reverter effective July 21, 1947 (Ill. Rev. Stat., ch. 30, par. 37b) provides that rights of re-entry for condition broken and possibilities of reverter are neither alienable or devisable, they are inheritable. (Deverick v. Bline (1950), 404 Ill. 302, 89 N.E.2d 43.) The type of interest held governs the mode of reinvestment with title if reinvestment is to occur. If the grantor had a possibility of reverter, he or his heirs become the owner of the property by operation of law as soon as the condition is broken. If he has a right of re-entry for condition broken, he or his heirs become the owner of the property only after they act to retake the property.

It is alleged, and we must accept, that classes were last held in the Hutton School in 1973. Harry Hutton, sole heir of the grantors, did not act to legally retake the premises but instead conveyed his interest in that land to the plaintiffs in 1977. If Harry Hutton had only a naked right of re-entry for condition broken, then he could not be the owner of that property until he had legally re-entered the land. Since he took no steps for a legal re-entry, he had only a right of re-entry in 1977, and that right cannot be conveyed inter vivos. On the other hand, if Harry Hutton had a possibility of reverter in the property, then he owned the school property as soon as it ceased to be used for school purposes. Therefore, assuming (1) that cessation of classes constitutes "abandonment of school purposes" on the land, (2) that the conveyance from Harry Hutton to the plaintiffs was legally correct, and (3) that the conveyance was not pre-empted by Hutton's disclaimer in favor of the school district, the plaintiffs could have acquired an interest in the Hutton School grounds if Harry Hutton had inherited a possibility of reverter from his parents.

The difference between a fee simple determinable (or, determinable fee) and a fee simple subject to a condition subsequent, is solely a matter of judicial interpretation of the words of a grant. . . . [T]he Huttons would have created a fee simple determinable if they had allowed the school district to retain the property *so long as* or *while* it was used for school purposes, or *until* it ceased to be so used. Similarly, a fee simple subject to a condition subsequent would have arisen had the Huttons given the land *upon condition that* or *provided that* it be used for school purposes. In the 1941 deed, though the Huttons gave the land "to be used for school purpose only, otherwise to revert to Grantors herein," no words of temporal limitation, or terms of express condition, were used in the grant.

The plaintiffs argue that the word "only" should be construed as a limitation rather than a condition. The defendants respond that where ambiguous language is used in a deed, the courts of Illinois have expressed a constructional preference for a fee simple subject to a condition subsequent. (Storke v. Penn Mutual Life Ins. Co. (1945), 390 Ill. 619, 61 N.E.2d 552.) Both sides refer us to cases involving deeds which contain language analogous to the 1941 grant in this case.

We believe that a close analysis of the wording of the original grant shows that the grantors intended to create a fee simple determinable followed by a possibility of reverter. Here, the use of the word "only" immediately following the grant "for school purpose" demonstrates that the Huttons wanted to give the land to the school district only as long as it was needed and no longer. The language "this land to be used for school purpose only" is an example of a grant which contains a limitation within the granting clause. It suggests a limited grant, rather than a full grant subject to a condition, and thus, both theoretically and linguistically, gives rise to a fee simple determinable.

The second relevant clause furnishes plaintiff's position with additional support. It cannot be argued that the phrase "otherwise to revert to grantors herein" is inconsistent with a fee simple subject to a condition subsequent. Nor does the word "revert" automatically create a possibility of reverter. But, in combination with the preceding phrase, the provisions by which possession is returned to the grantors seem to trigger a mandatory return rather than a permissive return because it is not stated that the grantor "may" re-enter the land. See City of Urbana v. Solo Cup Co. (4th Dist. 1979), 66 Ill. App. 3d 45, 22 Ill. Dec. 786, 383 N.E.2d 262.

The terms used in the 1941 deed, although imprecise, were designed to allow the property to be used for a single purpose, namely, for "school purpose." The Huttons intended to have the land back if it were ever used otherwise. Upon a grant of exclusive use followed by an express provision for reverter when that use ceases, courts and commentators have agreed that a fee simple determinable, rather than a fee simple subject to a condition subsequent, is created. (1 Simes and Smith, The Law of Future Interests (2nd ed. 1956) sec. 286 n.58.) Our own research has uncovered cases from other jurisdictions and sources in which language very similar to that in the Hutton deed has been held to create a fee simple determinable:

> A conveyance "for the use, intent and purpose of a site for a School House [and] whenever the said School District removes the School House from said tract of land or whenever said School House ceases to be used as the Public School House . . . then the said Trust shall cease and determine and the said land shall revert to the grantor and his heirs." [Consolidated School District v. Walter (1954), 243 Minn. 159, 66 N.W.2d 881, 882.]
>
> [I]t being absolutely understood that when said land ceases to be used for school purposes it is to revert to the above grantor, his heirs. [U.S. v. 1119.15 Acres of Land (E.D. Ill. 1942), 44 F. Supp. 449.]
>
> That I, S.S. Gray (Widower), for and in consideration of the sum of Donation to Wheeler School District to be used by said Wheeler Special School District for school and church purposes and to revert to me should school and church be discontinued or moved. [Williams v. Kirby School District (Ark. 1944), 181 S.W.2d 488, 490.]
>
> It is understood and agreed that if the above described land is abandoned by the said second parties and not used for school purposes then the above described land reverts to the party of the first part. [School District No. 6 v. Russell (1964), 156 Colo. 75, 396 P.2d 929, 930.]
>
> [T]o B and C [trustees of a school district] and their heirs and successors for school purposes and to revert to the grantor when it ceases to be so used. [Restatement of Property, sec. 44, comment 1, illustration V (1936).]

Thus, authority from this state and others indicates that the grant in the Hutton deed did in fact create a fee simple determinable. We are not persuaded by the cases cited by the defendants for the terms of conveyance in those cases distinguish them from the facts presented here. . . .

The estate created in Latham v. Illinois Central Railroad Co. (1912), 253 Ill. 93, 97 N.E. 254, was held to be a fee simple subject to a condition subsequent. Land was conveyed to a railroad in return for the railroad's agreement to erect and maintain a passenger depot and a freight depot on the premises. The deed was made to the grantee, "their successors and assigns forever, for the uses and purposes hereinafter mentioned and for NONE other." Those purposes were limited to "railroad purposes only." The deed provided "that in case of non-user of said premises so conveyed for the uses and purposes aforesaid, that then and in that case the title to said premises shall revert back to [the grantors], their heirs, executors, administrators and assigns." The property was granted to the railroad to have and hold forever, "subject, nevertheless, to all the conditions, covenants, agreements and limitations in this deed expressed." The estate in *Latham* may be distinguished from that created here in that the former was a grant "forever" which was subjected to certain use restrictions while the Hutton deed gave the property to the school district only as long as it could use it. . . .

The defendants also direct our attention to the case of McElvain v. Dorris (1921), 298 Ill. 377, 131 N.E. 608. There, land was sold subject to the following condition: "This tract of land is to be used for mill purposes, and if not used for mill purposes the title reverts back to the former owner." When the mill was abandoned, the heirs of the grantor brought suit in ejectment and were successful. The Supreme Court of Illinois did not mention the possibility that the quoted words could have created a fee simple determinable but instead stated,

> Annexed to the grant there was a condition subsequent, by a breach of which there would be a right of re-entry by the grantor or her heirs at law. [Citations.] A breach of the condition in such a case does not, of itself, determine the estate, but an entry, or some act equivalent thereto, is necessary to revest the estate, and bringing a suit in ejectment is equivalent to such reentry. [298 Ill. at 379, 131 N.E. 608.]

It is urged by the defendants that McElvain v. Dorris stands for the proposition that the quoted language in the deed creates a fee simple subject to a condition subsequent. We must agree with the defendants that the grant in *McElvain* is strikingly similar to that in this case. However, the opinion in *McElvain* is ambiguous in several respects. First, that portion of the opinion which states that "Annexed to the grant there was a condition subsequent . . ." may refer to the provision quoted above, or it may refer to another provision not reproduced in the opinion. Second, even if the court's reference is to the quoted language, the holding may reflect only the court's acceptance of the parties' construction of the grant. (A similar procedure was followed in Trustees of Schools v. Batdorf (1955), 6 Ill. 2d 486, 130 N.E.2d Ill., as noted by defendants.) After all, as an action in ejectment was brought in *McElvain*, the difference between a fee simple determinable and a fee simple subject to a condition subsequent would have no practical effect and the court did not discuss it.

To the extent that *McElvain* holds that the quoted language establishes a fee simple subject to a condition subsequent, it is contrary to the weight of Illinois and American authority. A more appropriate case with which to resolve the problem presented here is North v. Graham (1908), 235 Ill. 178, 85 N.E. 267. Land was conveyed to trustees of a church under a deed which stated that "said tract of land above described to revert to the party of the first part whenever it ceases to be used or occupied for a meeting house or church." Following an extended discussion of determinable fees, the court concluded that such an estate is legal in Illinois and that the language of the deed did in fact create that estate.

North v. Graham, like this case, falls somewhere between those cases in which appears the classic language used to create a fee simple determinable and that used to create a fee simple subject to a condition subsequent. . . .

Although the word "whenever" is used in the North v. Graham deed, it is not found in a granting clause, but in a reverter clause. The court found this slightly unorthodox construction sufficient to create a fee simple determinable, and we believe that the word "only" placed in the granting clause of the Hutton deed brings this case under the rule of North v. Graham.

We hold, therefore, that the 1941 deed from W.E. and Jennie Hutton to the Trustees of School District No. 1 created a fee simple determinable in the Trustees followed by a possibility of reverter in the Huttons and their heirs. Accordingly, the trial court erred in dismissing plaintiffs' . . . complaint which followed its holding that the plaintiffs could not have acquired any interest in the Hutton School property from Harry Hutton. We must therefore reverse and remand this cause to the trial court for further proceedings.

We refrain from deciding the following issues: (1) whether the 1977 conveyance from Harry Hutton was legally sufficient to pass his interest in the school property to the plaintiffs, (2) whether Harry Hutton effectively disclaimed his interest in the property in favor of the defendants by virtue of his 1977 disclaimer, and (3) whether the defendants have ceased to use the Hutton School grounds for "school purposes." . . .

Reversed and remanded.

THE REST OF THE STORY . . .

In the sequel case to *Mahrenholz*, the court held that use of the Hutton School property to store school equipment and supplies, primarily used desks, was for a school purpose, and therefore the Mahrenholzes were not entitled to the property. Mahrenholz v. County Bd. of School Trustees, 544 N.E.2d 128 (Ill. App. 1989).

Notes, Questions, and Problem

1. *FSD or FSCS—why did it matter?* Why did it matter in *Mahrenholz* whether the Huttons had originally conveyed a fee simple determinable (FSD) or a fee simple subject to condition subsequent (FSCS)? To see this, trace the path of the fee simple as it passed through the various owners and see what different legal consequence follows from calling it one type of defeasible fee or the other.

2. *The grantor's intent.* In cases of ambiguous language in a deed, the court is supposed to look for evidence of the grantor's intent. But intent as to what—whether the grantor intended to convey a FSD or a FSCS, or intent as to the practical consequence of the stated event occurring? Do you think the Huttons specifically intended to convey one type of defeasible fee rather than the other (do you think they knew or understood the difference)?

3. *Transferability of possibilities of reverter and rights of entry.* The most important reason why different legal consequences might result from classifying an estate as a fee simple determinable with a possibility of reverter concerns the transferability of the future interest—the problem in *Mahrenholz*. At common law, a possibility of reverter and a right of entry descended to heirs upon the death of the owner of such interests. But, curiously enough, neither interest was transferable during life. In most American states, the possibility of reverter and the

right of entry, like other property interests, are transferable inter vivos, but, as *Mahrenholz* illustrates, a few states adhere to the old common law rule.

Suppose that in *Mahrenholz,* Illinois followed the modern majority rule, which allows both possibilities of reverter and rights of entry to be freely transferred during lifetime. Would it have mattered then whether the fee simple was an FSD or an FSCS?

4. *Should the distinction matter?* As *Mahrenholz* vividly illustrates, disputes and litigation can easily arise when lawyers are less careful than they should be in selecting precisely correct legal terminology as they draft deeds and other legal instruments used to transfer estates. Language matters—but perhaps sometimes too much. Given the trouble it invites, is it sensible to continue the distinction between the fee simple determinable and the fee simple subject to condition subsequent? Should dramatically different consequences turn on fine distinctions unwittingly overlooked? California and Kentucky have abolished the fee simple determinable with statutes providing that language creating a fee simple determinable at common law creates a fee simple subject to condition subsequent. Cal. Civ. Code § 885.020 (West 2020); Ky. Rev. Stat. Ann. § 381.218 (2020). The Restatement (Third) of Property abolishes the distinctions among the three types of defeasible fees (the fee simple determinable, fee simple subject to a condition subsequent, and fee simple subject to an executory limitation). It replaces them with a single estate, the *fee simple defeasible,* defined as "a present interest that terminates upon the happening of a stated event that might or might not occur." Restatement (Third) of Property, Wills and Other Donative Transfers § 24.3 (2011). Hence, if *O* conveys land "to Grantee School District so long as the land is used for school purposes; upon the land being used for non-school purposes, the land is to revert to the Grantor," under the Restatement this would create a fee simple defeasible, rather than a fee simple determinable; the School District's interest would terminate upon the occurrence of an event that might or might not occur (the District using the land for non-school purposes). Id. comment g.

5. *Duration of possibilities of reverter and rights of entry in Illinois.* At the time of the decision in *Mahrenholz,* Illinois had a statute that placed a 40-year limit on the duration of possibilities of reverter and rights of entry. The time limit applied to reverters and rights of entry existing at the time of enactment. The current version of the statute is Ill. Comp. Stat. Ann. c. 765, 330/4 (2020). We discuss this type of statute in Chapter 4. See page 250.

Review Problems

(The answers to these Problems appear in Appendix A, beginning at page 683.)

1. *O* conveys Blackacre "to *A* and her heirs, but if Blackacre is used for any purpose other than agricultural purposes, then *O* has the right to re-enter and take possession of the land." What is the state of title in Blackacre at common law?

2. Taking the facts of Problem 1, suppose that some years after the conveyance, *A* begins construction of several residences on Blackacre. *O* has died and devised her entire estate to *B*. What is the state of title in Blackacre at common law?

3. *O* conveys Blackacre "to *A* and her heirs so long as Blackacre is used for residential purposes only." What is the state of title in Blackacre at common law?

4. Taking the facts of Problem 3, suppose that some years after the conveyance, A begins construction of a factory on Blackacre. O has died and devised her entire estate to B. What is the state of title in Blackacre at common law?

5. O conveys Greenacre "to the Finger Lakes Land Trust [a charitable organization] on condition that Greenacre remains forever undeveloped and in its natural condition; in the event Greenacre is ever developed, residentially, commercially, or otherwise, then to the Land Conservancy [also a charitable organization] in fee simple absolute." What is the state of title in Greenacre at common law?

6. O conveys Wiseacre "to A and her heirs, and A promises, on behalf of her heirs and assigns forever, that Wiseacre shall be used solely for agricultural purposes." What is the state of title in Wiseacre at common law?

7. Taking the facts of Problem 6, suppose that some years after the conveyance, A begins construction of a factory on Wiseacre. What is the state of title in Wiseacre at common law when A begins construction? What remedies does O have against A?

8. O conveyed Whiteacre "to A and his heirs; but if A ever drinks alcohol or alcoholic beverages, then to B and her heirs." Later, B executes and delivers a deed purporting to convey her interest in Whiteacre to C. Later still, A drinks whiskey and gets drunk. What is the state of title in Whiteacre at common law?

9. O devises Whiteacre "to A on condition that A lives; in the event that A dies, then to B and his heirs." What is the state of title in Whiteacre at common law?

10. O devises Blackacre "to A for life, upon A's death to B and her heirs so long as B does not drink any alcoholic beverage." What is the state of title in Blackacre at common law?

11. O conveys Greenacre "to A and the heirs of his body." What is the state of title today in Delaware? What is the state of title in California?

12. O conveys Greenacre "to A and the heirs of his body, but if A should die without issue, then to B and her heirs." Assume that the conveyance occurs today in Massachusetts. Following the conveyance, A died leaving two surviving children, B and C. Fifty years after A's death, both B and C died, and neither left any surviving issue. Both of them devised their entire estates to their respective spouses. Assuming that none of the relevant parties made any conveyance of Greenacre following the conveyance from O, what is the state of title today?

13. O conveyed Greenacre "to A and her heirs so long as Greenacre is used for residential purposes only." A thereafter constructed a single-family house on Greenacre in which she and her family lived for some years. Later, A decided to move to another state and sold Greenacre to X, who took the property by a deed with exactly the same terms as in O's original deed. X tore down the house and constructed an office building on Greenacre. Which of the following statements is most completely correct?

(a) X acquired a fee simple absolute from A.

(b) X acquired the same type of estate as A had, and it remained legally valid following X's construction of the office building until and unless O took action to recover possession from X.

(c) X acquired the same type of estate as A had, but the estate was automatically terminated, without any action on O's part, as a result of X's construction of the office building. The title reverted to O.

(d) None of the above.

14. In 2000, O devised Blackacre "to A and his heirs." In 2015, A died with a legally valid will that left his entire estate to his wife, W. A was also survived by his three children, X, Y, and Z, and by O. Who is entitled to Blackacre following A's death? Choose the answer that is most completely correct:

(a) W, because A had a fee simple absolute, which A was free to devise by his will.

(b) O, because upon A's death, title in Blackacre reverts to the grantor.

(c) W, X, Y, and Z, assuming that under local statutory law they are A's legal heirs. They take by purchase, under the words "and his heirs," rather than under the intestacy statute.

(d) None of the above.

CHAPTER 4

Future Interests

A. THE MODERN RELEVANCE OF FUTURE INTERESTS

We turn now to future interests, which confer rights to the enjoyment of property at a future time. Although future interests have ancient origins, they are very relevant to modern law practice. Most future interests are created in the context of family wealth transfer transactions, particularly those implemented through a trust (to which you were briefly introduced in the last chapter, in Note 2 at page 209). Virtually every family property trust today involves one or more future interests. Such interests usually follow a life estate given to a designated beneficiary, commonly the grantor's spouse, or a class of beneficiaries such as the grantor's children.

We will study the trust in more detail later (see page 238), but to illustrate the relationship between a trust and future interests, consider this simple example. Suppose that W, a woman married to H, has two adult children and no grandchildren (yet). She wishes to plan her estate so that upon her death all of the income from her assets, currently valued at approximately $750,000, and so much of her assets as H needs for his support, health, and maintenance will be paid to H for his lifetime. Upon H's death, all of W's remaining assets are to go to her children.

The best way to implement W's plan is through a trust, which we briefly encountered in Chapter 3. Using the trust form, W can give the trustee, a person or institution in whom she has confidence, the power to invest the trust principal and the discretion to pay the appropriate amount of principal to H. W's will might provide that she devises her estate to a named trustee, in trust, with directions to pay all income and so much of the trust principal as H needs for his support, health, and maintenance to H for his lifetime, providing further that upon H's death the trust shall terminate and the trustee shall distribute all of the trust assets outright to W's children. During the term of the trust the trustee holds the legal title to the trust assets in fee simple, subject to the beneficial interests of H and W's children. H has a life estate, and W's children have a remainder (more precisely, a vested remainder). Future interests in trusts are sometimes referred to as "equitable" because, as we will discuss later (see page 238), trusts and trust interests are enforced by courts of equity. Today life estates followed by future interests are the foundation blocks of wills and estate planning.

Modern future interests are divided into two basic groups, according to the identity of the person who was the first holder of the interest:

(1) Interests initially retained by the transferor
   (a) Reversion
   (b) Possibility of reverter
   (c) Right of entry (also known as "power of termination")
(2) Interests created in a transferee
   (a) Vested remainder
   (b) Contingent remainder
   (c) Executory interest

As you study the materials in this chapter, bear in mind that a future interest is always attached to some estate of the types considered in Chapter 3 (fee simple, life estate, etc.). For example, a person might have a remainder (the future interest) for life (the future interest is attached to, or is "in," a life estate) or in fee simple absolute or in some other estate. And this is true of all the future interests listed above, so be careful to label any future interest fully, identifying not just the interest but also the estate.

It is very important to understand that a future interest is a presently existing property interest. It is a future interest in the sense that the right of possession is delayed to some future time. A future interest gives legal rights to its owner, and it is protectable by courts as such. Take this case: *O* conveys Blackacre to *A* for life, then to *B* and her heirs. *B* has present legal rights and liabilities. *B* can sell or give away her remainder. She can enjoin *A* from committing waste. She can sue third parties who are injuring the land. If *B* dies during the life of *A*, *B*'s remainder will be transmitted to *B*'s heirs or devisees, and a federal estate tax or state inheritance tax may be levied upon its value.

B. FUTURE INTERESTS RETAINED BY TRANSFEROR

1. Reversion

Historically, the earliest future interest to develop was a reversion. If *O*, a fee simple owner, granted the land "to *A* for life," the land would revert ("come back") to *O* at *A*'s death. *O*'s right to future possession is called a reversion. If *O* dies during *A*'s life, *O*'s reversion passes under his will or to his heirs, and at *A*'s death whoever owns the reversion is entitled to possession of the land.

In a general sense, then, a reversion is the interest left in an owner when he carves out of his estate a lesser estate and does not provide who is to take the property when the lesser estate expires. But a more precise definition is necessary. "A reversion is," in the words of Professor Lewis Simes, "the interest remaining in the grantor, or in the successor in interest of a testator, who transfers a *vested estate of a lesser quantum* than that of the vested estate which he has." 1 American Law of Property § 4.16 (1952) (emphasis added). The hierarchy of estates determines what is a lesser estate. The fee simple is a greater estate than a fee tail, which is a greater estate than a life estate, which is a greater estate than the leasehold estates. Hence if *O*, owning a fee simple, creates a fee tail, a life estate, or a term of years, and does not at the same time convey away a vested remainder in fee simple, O has a reversion. If A, owning only a life estate, creates a term of years, A has a reversion.

Because reversions result from the hierarchy of estates, they are thought of as the remnant of an estate that has not entirely passed away from the transferor. Hence all reversions are retained interests, which remain vested in the transferor.

When a reversion is retained, it may or may not be certain to become possessory in the future. Thus:

> *Example 1.* O conveys Blackacre "to A for life." O has a reversion in fee simple that is certain to become possessory. At A's death, either O or O's successors in interest will be entitled to possession.

Time line 4-1

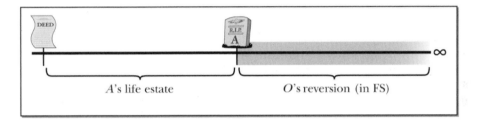

> *Example 2.* O conveys Whiteacre "to A for life, then to B and her heirs if B survives A." O has a reversion in fee simple that is not certain to become possessory. If B dies before A, O will be entitled to possession at A's death. On the other hand, if A dies before B, O's reversion is divested on A's death and will never become possessory.

Time line 4-2

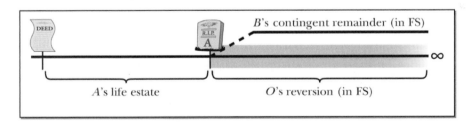

In the above examples, the *value* of the reversions may differ, because one is certain to become possessory and the other is not, but the *name* of O's interest in both examples—a reversion—is the same.

Note well: There is no such interest as a "possibility of *reversion*," and you should never use that phrase. Such talk is likely to produce confusion of a reversion with an entirely different interest, the possibility of reverter, which follows a determinable fee. Remember that the names of future interests are names arbitrarily given, like first names to children. Call the future interest by its correct name. At common law, a reversion was transferable during life and descendible and devisable at death. It remains so today.

Problems

(Throughout this chapter, always assume that O has a fee simple absolute unless indicated otherwise.)

1. O owns a fee simple and makes the following transfers. In which cases is there a reversion?

   (a) O conveys "to A for life, then to B and her heirs."

   (b) O conveys "to A for life, then to B and the heirs of her body."

   (c) O conveys "to A for life, then to B and her heirs if B attains the age of 21 before A dies." At the time of the conveyance B is 15 years old. (If there is a reversion, what happens to it if B reaches 21 during A's life?)

   (d) O conveys "to A for 20 years."

2. O conveys Blackacre "to A for life, then to B for life." O subsequently dies with a will devising all of O's property to C. Then A dies and B dies. Who owns Blackacre?

2. Possibility of Reverter

A possibility of reverter arises when an owner carves out of his estate a *determinable* estate of the same quantum. Theoretically, a possibility of reverter can be retained when a life tenant conveys his life estate to another, determinable on the happening of an event, but the cases, almost without exception, deal with carving a fee simple determinable out of a fee simple absolute. Thus, for all practical purposes, a possibility of reverter is a future interest remaining in the transferor or his heirs when a fee simple determinable is created. Example: O conveys Blackacre "to Hartford School Board so long as used for school purposes." O has a possibility of reverter.

Time line 4-3

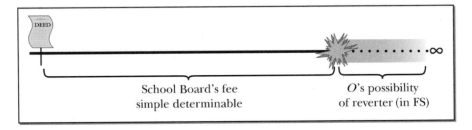

School Board's fee simple determinable

O's possibility of reverter (in FS)

The possibility of reverter has been previously discussed in connection with its correlative possessory estate, the fee simple determinable. See pages 211, 214-219.

3. Right of Entry

When an owner transfers an estate subject to condition subsequent and retains the power to cut short or terminate the estate, the transferor has a right of entry. Example: *O* conveys Whiteacre "to Hartford School Board, but if it ceases to use the land for school purposes, *O* has the right to re-enter and retake the premises."

Time line 4-4

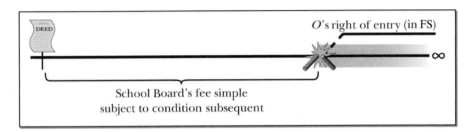

The right of entry has been previously discussed in connection with the fee simple subject to condition subsequent. See pages 213, 214-219.

C. FUTURE INTERESTS IN TRANSFEREES

There are three types of future interests in transferees: *vested remainders, contingent remainders,* and *executory interests.* A remainder or executory interest cannot be retained by the transferor; these interests are created only in transferees. Once created, a remainder or executory interest can be transferred back to the grantor, but the name originally given the interest does not change.

To help you understand the differences among the various future interests that we will examine in the materials that follow in this section, it may help to use a device sometimes called a "decision tree." In classifying a future interest initially created in a transferee, follow the steps in order, making your decision about the correct choice. As you will see, depending on the type of future interest involved, it may not be necessary to go through all of the steps.

A Decision Tree for Classifying Future Interests

Step 1:

Remainder (REM) _____ or _____ executory interest (EI)?

Step 2:

If REM, vested remainder (VR) or contingent remainder (CR)?

Step 3:

If VR, vested how?

Indefeasibly or subject to open or subject to complete divestment or more than one?

In Brief

▶ *Remainders* are *capable of* (i.e., do not do so necessarily) taking effect in possession upon the natural expiration of the possessory estate immediately before them,
  versus
▶ *Executory interests*, which take effect in possession only by *divesting* (i.e., cutting short) the interest before them.

1. Introduction

A remainder is a future interest that waits politely until the termination of the preceding possessory estate, at which time the remainder moves into possession if it is then vested. A remainder is a future interest that is capable of becoming possessory at the termination of the prior estate. It is not required that the future interest be certain of future possession, only that it be possible for the interest to become possessory when the prior estate ends. If, at the time the future interest is created, it is not possible for it to become possessory upon the termination of the prior estate, the future interest is not a remainder.

Not long after the contingent remainder was recognized by the courts, the executory interest arose to complicate matters further. The executory interest developed to do what a remainder cannot do: divest or cut short the preceding interest. An executory interest is a future interest in a transferee that can take effect only by divesting another interest. The difference between taking possession as soon as the prior estate ends and divesting the prior estate is the essential difference between a remainder and an executory interest. More on executory interests shortly.

Problem

In Brief

Vested remainders:

▶ Given to an ascertained person,
  and
▶ not subject to a condition *precedent* (although may be subject to a condition subsequent)

Contingent remainders:

▶ Given to an unascertained (or unborn) person
  or
▶ subsequent to a condition *precedent*

O conveys Blackacre "to *A* for life, then to *B* if *B* gives *A* a proper funeral."[1] Does *B* have a remainder or an executory interest? If it is an executory interest, whose interest will be divested if *B* gives *A* a proper funeral?

2. Remainders

Now that you have a general idea of what a remainder is, the next step to explore the technical aspects of remainders further. With respect to the decision tree on page 227, we are at Steps 2 and 3.

Remainders are classified into two general types: *vested* and *contingent*. A remainder is *vested*

---

1. What is a "proper funeral"? We don't know, but in Seaton v. Commonwealth, 149 S.W. 871 (Ky. 1912), the court reversed a criminal misdemeanor conviction for failing to provide the defendant's infant child with a "decent," "proper," and "Christian" burial. The child was born two weeks premature and lived only two weeks. The defendant, evidently a poor man but able nevertheless to afford a coffin, constructed a crude box out of scrap wood, and buried the box with the baby's body in it in a hole that he dug in some woods on his farm. There was no ceremony, and no family, including the child's mother, or friends, were present for the burial. The defendant, whom the court described as "miserly," was trying to save money. The court held that however offensive to the community's sense of propriety the defendant's conduct might be, it violated no law.

if (1) it is given to an ascertained person and (2) it is not subject to a condition precedent (other than the natural termination of the preceding estates). Or, to put it another way, a remainder is vested if it is created in an ascertained person and is ready to become possessory whenever and however all preceding estates expire. A remainder is *contingent* if (1) it is given to an unascertained person or (2) it is made contingent upon some event occurring other than the natural termination of the preceding estates. In the latter situation the remainder is said to be subject to a condition precedent. In either situation (owner unascertained or subject to condition precedent), the remainder is not now ready to become possessory upon the expiration of the preceding estate.

In terms of our decision tree, we have now completed Step 2. Let's assume that you have correctly classified the future interest as a vested remainder (VR). This decision takes us to Step 3.

About vested remainders. A remainder may be *indefeasibly vested*, meaning that the remainder is certain of becoming possessory in the future and cannot be divested. Thus:

> *Example 3.* O conveys "to A for life, then to B and her heirs." B has an indefeasibly vested remainder certain to become possessory upon termination of the life estate. If B dies during A's life, on B's death B's remainder passes to B's devisees, or, if B dies without a will, passes to B's heirs, or, if B dies without a will and without heirs, escheats to the state. B or B's successor in interest is certain to take possession upon A's death.

Time line 4-5

A's life estate   B's remainder (in FS)

Observe that the full state of B's title in *Example 3* is "B has a vested remainder in fee simple absolute." "Remainder" tells us the kind of future interest; "in fee simple absolute" tells us the kind of estate held as a remainder (and what kind of possessory estate the remainder will become when it becomes possessory).

A remainder may be vested but not certain of becoming possessory. It can be vested subject to being divested if an event happens. *Example 8*, on page 231, is an illustration.

A remainder created in a class of persons (such as in A's children) is vested if one member of the class is ascertained, and there is no condition precedent. The remainder is *vested subject to open* or *vested subject to partial divestment* if later-born children are entitled to share in the gift. Thus:

> *Example 4.* O conveys "to A for life, then to A's children and their heirs." A

Sidebar

Who owns this remainder? Can unborn persons own property? Restatement of Property § 153 comment a (1936) says we cannot accurately say that an unborn person has a future interest. Yet it is quite clear that the law treats the limitation as if a future interest has been created.

has one child, *B*. The remainder is vested in *B* subject to open to let in later-born children. *B*'s exact share cannot be known until *A* dies. If *A* has no child at the time of the conveyance, the remainder is contingent because no taker is ascertained.

About contingent remainders. A remainder that is contingent because its takers are unascertained is illustrated by the following example:

> *Example 5.* *O* conveys "to *A* for life, then to the heirs of *B*." *B* is alive. The remainder is contingent because the heirs of *B* cannot be ascertained until *B* dies.

Time line 4-6

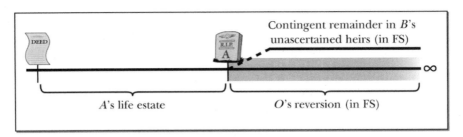

A remainder that is contingent because it is subject to a condition precedent is illustrated in *Examples 6* and *7* below:

> *Example 6.* *O* conveys "to *A* for life, then to *B* and her heirs if *B* survives *A*." The language "if *B* survives *A*" subjects *B*'s remainder to a condition precedent. *B* can take possession only if *B* survives *A*.
>
> *Example 7.* *O* conveys "to *A* for life, then to *B* and her heirs if *B* survives *A*, and if *B* does not survive *A* to *C* and his heirs." The language "if *B* survives *A*" subjects *B*'s remainder to the condition precedent of *B* surviving *A*, and the language "and if *B* does not survive *A*" subjects *C*'s remainder to the opposite condition precedent. Here we have *alternative contingent remainders* in *B* and *C*. If the remainder in *B* vests, the remainder in *C* cannot, and vice versa.

Problems

1. *O* conveys "to *A* for life, and in the event of *A*'s death to *B* and her heirs." Is *B*'s remainder vested or contingent? If *B* subsequently conveys her interest back to *O*, what does *O* have?

2. *O* conveys "to *A* for life, then to *B* for life, then to *C* and her heirs." What interests are created? Suppose the remainder to *C* had been "then to *C* and her heirs if *C* survives *A* and *B*." What interests are created?

3. *O* conveys "to *A* and *B* for their joint lives, then to the survivor in fee simple." Is the remainder vested or contingent?

4. *O* conveys "to *A* for life, then to *A*'s children who shall reach 21." *A*'s oldest child, *B*, is 17. Is the remainder vested or contingent? *B* subsequently reaches 21. Is

the remainder vested or contingent? (For what happens if *A* dies before *B* reaches 21, see pages 239-240.)

About vesting subject to divestment. Example 8 illustrates the fine distinction in modern law between a contingent remainder and a vested remainder subject to divestment:

> *Example 8. O* conveys "to *A* for life, then to *B* and her heirs, but if *B* does not survive *A* to *C* and his heirs." Note carefully: *B* does *not* have a contingent remainder. *B* has a *vested remainder* in fee simple subject to divestment; *C* has a shifting executory interest which can become possessory only by divesting *B*'s remainder.

The different classification of *B*'s remainder in *Example 7* and in *Example 8* results *solely* from the way the conveyance is phrased. *O*'s intent is exactly the same in both cases, but it is expressed differently. *Examples 7* and *8* illustrate the very important point: in classifying a future interest *the form of the language will often (but not always) dictate what type of interest it is.*

The key to understanding why *B*'s interest is contingent in *Example 7* and vested in *Example 8* is this: You must classify interests in sequence as they are written. You start reading to the right, classify the first interest, move on to the second interest and classify it, and then move to the next interest. Gray put it this way: "Whether a remainder is vested or contingent depends upon the language employed. If the conditional element is incorporated into the description of, or into the gift to, the remainderman, then the remainder is contingent; but if, after words giving a vested interest, a clause is added divesting it, the remainder is vested." John C. Gray, The Rule Against Perpetuities § 108 (4th ed. 1942). We have made it easy for you to see what language is "incorporated" into the gift by inserting commas in the conveyance indicating where you should stop and classify, before moving on to the next interest. In *Example 8*, stopping at the comma after the phrase "then to *B* and her heirs," you find that *B* has a vested remainder because there is no condition precedent within the commas setting off *B*'s gift. The phrase "but if *B* does not survive *A*," coming after the comma marking the end of *B*'s gift, is language incorporated into *C*'s gift, not *B*'s. The phrase thus states a condition subsequent (or divesting condition) with respect to *B*'s interest; it states a condition precedent with respect to *C*'s interest.

In classifying future interests after a life estate, you can bet on this rule: If the first future interest created is a contingent remainder in fee simple (as in *Example 7* above), the second future interest in a transferee will also be a contingent remainder. If the first future interest created is a vested remainder in fee simple (as in *Example 8* above), the second future interest in a transferee will be a divesting executory interest.

Here are two shortcut rules to help you when classifying a series of future interests:

→ *Shortcut rule 1*: If LE + FI_1 + FI_2, and FI_1 = CR (in a FS), then FI_2 = CR.

→ *Shortcut rule 2*: If LE + FI_1 + FI_2, and FI_1 = VR (in a FS), then FI_2 = EI.

Question

In *Example 7* above, there is a reversion in *O*; in *Example 8* there is no reversion. In *Example 7*, under what circumstances will the property revert to *O*? Realistically, none. So, the type of reversion that follows alternative contingent remainders is sometimes called a *technical reversion*; "technical" in the sense that it has no practical significance. Why do we even recognize it, then? It is a vestige of a feudal rule that no longer exists. At early common law, a life estate can terminate prior to the death of the life tenant if the life tenant tried to convey a greater estate than he had. Such an attempted conveyance was a tort that triggered forfeiture of his life estate. Even though this rule no longer applies, for purposes of classifying remainders, modern law continues to assume that a life estate can end prior to the death of the life tenant. So, we can use a third shortcut rule of classification:

→ *Shortcut rule 3*: If LE + CR (FS) + CR (in FS), then REV (in FS).

Why does the distinction matter? There are four reasons why at common law the distinction between contingent remainders and vested remainders subject to divestment was important. First, a vested remainder *accelerates* into possession whenever and however the preceding estate ends—either at the life tenant's death or earlier if the life estate ends before the life tenant's death. A contingent remainder cannot become possessory *so long as it remains contingent*. For example, where there is a conveyance "to *A* for life, then to *B*, but if *B* dies under 21 to *C*," *B*, holding a vested remainder, is entitled to possession at *A*'s death, even though *B* is under 21. If *B* is under 21, *B*'s possessory estate remains subject to divestment until *B* reaches 21. If, on the other hand, the conveyance had read "to *A* for life, then to *B* if *B* reaches 21," *B* would not be entitled to possession at *A*'s death prior to *B*'s reaching 21.

Second, at early common law, a contingent remainder, with a few exceptions, was *not assignable* during the remainderman's life and hence was unreachable by creditors. A contingent remainder was thought of as a mere possibility of becoming an interest and not as an interest that could be transferred. Today, however, contingent remainders are alienable, devisable, and descendible.

The third difference between vested and contingent remainders is that at common law, contingent remainders were *destroyed* if they did not vest upon termination of the preceding life estate, whereas vested remainders were not destructible in this manner. But, as we shall see later in this chapter, this old rule has been abolished in nearly all jurisdictions.

The fourth difference is that contingent remainders are subject to the *Rule Against Perpetuities*, whereas vested remainders are not. In applying this rule, the distinction between vested and contingent remainders remains very important in many jurisdictions today. We consider the Rule Against Perpetuities at the end of this chapter.

3. Executory Interests

An executory interest is a future interest in a transferee that must, in order to become possessory,

(1) divest or cut short some interest in another *transferee* (this is known as a "shifting" executory interest), or

(2) divest the *transferor* in the future (this is known as a "springing" executory interest).

The distinction between a shifting and a springing executory interest has no legal consequence. Still, it's useful in identifying exactly what interest the executory interest will divest if it takes effect, an interest originally created in a transferor.

BACKGROUND, BRIEFLY

Executory interests could not be created at early common law. The common law courts had developed two rules based on their ideas about estates: (1) no future interest could be created in favor of a transferee if that interest could take effect by way of divesting a preceding estate in another transferee (e.g., *O* conveys Whiteacre, a small tract of land, "to my eldest son *A* and his heirs, but if *A* inherits Blackacre (the family manor), then Whiteacre is to go to my second son *B* and his heirs"); (2) no future interest could be created in favor of a transferee if that interest could take effect by way of divesting an estate in the transferor (e.g., *O* conveys "to *A* and her heirs when *A* marries *B*"). To get around these rules, landowners relied on the *use*, a device that had developed centuries earlier to evade other legal rules. Courts of law did not enforce uses; courts of equity did. Equitable judges were not concerned with the original reasons behind the two rules above. When a court of equity thought persons should be required to perform their moral duties, it would step in and protect a transferee, regardless of what his legal rights might be. So, the following method for creating shifting uses developed:

> *Example 9.* Before the Statute of Uses, *O* goes on the land and enfeoffs (conveys) "*X* and his heirs to hold to the use of *A* and his heirs, but if *A* inherits the family manor, then to the use of *O*'s second son *B* and his heirs."

Springing uses (divesting the transferor) were also enforceable in equity. Hence there developed in equity a protected interest known as a "use" (meaning benefit).

Although uses were a convenient device for landowners, they created problems for the king. Most important, they were a means of evading feudal taxes and so depleted badly needed revenues. When Henry VIII ran short of money, he prevailed on Parliament to enact the Statute of Uses (effective in 1536), which effectively abolished uses, converting them into legal interests. One important effect of the statute was to expand legal future interests by converting what were "shifting uses" and "springing uses" in equity before 1536 into legal "shifting executory interests" and "springing executory interests."

One effect of the Statute of Uses was to permit the creation of a new estate: *a fee simple subject to an executory limitation*. This is a fee simple that, upon the happening of a stated event, is automatically divested by an executory interest in a *transferee*. Such a fee simple can be created either in possession or in remainder. Thus:

> *Example 10.* *O* conveys "to *A* and his heirs, but if *A* dies without issue surviving him, to *B* and her heirs." *A* has a possessory fee simple subject to an executory limitation (or subject to divestment by *B*'s executory interest). *B*'s future interest can become possessory only by divesting *A*.

Time line 4-7

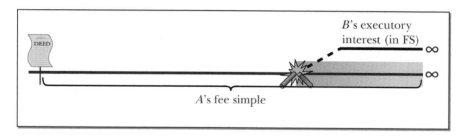

Example 11. O conveys "to A for life, then to B and her heirs, but if B dies under the age of 21, to C and her heirs." B is age 15. B has a vested remainder in fee simple subject to an executory limitation (or subject to divestment by C's executory interest if B dies under age 21). Also see *Example 8* above.

Time line 4-8

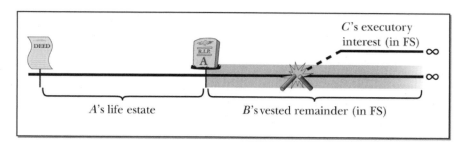

Executory interests are ordinarily treated as contingent interests, because they are subject to a condition precedent and do not vest until they become possessory.

Problems

1. O, owner of Wiseacre, comes to you to draft an instrument of gift. O tells you he wants to convey Wiseacre to his son A for life, and upon A's death, O wants Wiseacre to go to A's children if any are alive or, if none are then alive, to O's daughter B. Consider the following conveyances, all carrying out O's intent, but each creating different future interests. Identify the future interests.

(a) O conveys "to A for life, then to A's children and their heirs, but if at A's death he is not survived by any children, then to B and her heirs." At the time of the conveyance, A is alive and has no children. What is the state of the title?

Two years after the conveyance, twins, C and D, are born to A. What is the state of the title?

Suppose that C dies during A's lifetime, and that A is survived by B and D. What is the state of the title?

(b) O conveys "to A for life, then to such of A's children as survive him, but if none of A's children survives him, to B and her heirs." At the time of the conveyance, A is alive and has two children, C and D. What is the state of the title?

(c) O conveys "to A for life, then to B and her heirs, but if A is survived at his death by any children, then to such surviving children and their heirs." At the time of the conveyance, *A* is alive and has two children, *C* and *D*. What is the state of the title?

2. *T* devises $10,000 "to my cousin, Don Little, if and when he survives his wife." What does Don Little have? In re Little's Estate, 170 A.2d 106 (Pa. 1961). Why do you suppose that the testator would make such a devise?

Review Problems

(The answers to these Problems appear in the Appendix, beginning on page 683.)

Applying the traditional system of estates and future interests, for each problem below, identify all present estates and future interests in existence at the times indicated and on the basis of the facts stated.

1. *O* conveys "to *A* for life, then to *B* for life, then to *C*'s heirs." *A*, *B*, *C*, and *O* are all alive at the time of the conveyance. *C* is unmarried and has two living children, *X* and *Y*.

2. *O* conveys "to *A* upon her first wedding anniversary." *A* is alive and unmarried at the time of the conveyance. *O* is also then alive.

3. *O* conveys "to *A* for 10 years, then to such of *A*'s children as attain age 21." At the time of the conveyance, *A* and *O* were alive. *A* had two children, *X* and *Y*, ages 20 and 17, respectively.

4. Applying the same facts as in Problem 3, assume that *X* later attains age 21 and *Y* is still under age 21. *A* and *O* are both still alive.

5. Applying the same facts as in Problem 3, assume that *X* dies when *X* is age 22 and *Y* is age 19. *O* is still alive.

6. *O* conveys "to *A* for life, then to *A*'s children." *A* and *O* are alive at the time of the conveyance. *A* has one child, *X*.

7. Applying the same facts as in Problem 6, assume that *A* has another

A Look Back

In our discussion of defeasible fees at page 213, we noted that executory interests might be created to follow those interests, rather than a possibility of reverter or a right of entry. A possibility of reverter or a right of entry can be created only in the transferor; an executory interest can be created only in a transferee. Thus, if the transferor wants to create a future interest in a transferee after a defeasible fee, it will necessarily be an executory interest.

Example 12. O conveys "to Hartford School Board, but if the premises are not used for school purposes during the next 20 years, to Town Library." The School Board has a fee simple subject to an executory interest that will automatically divest the Board's fee simple if the condition happens. (In this respect, the executory interest differs from a right of entry in *O*, which is optional, not automatic in divesting.)

Example 13. O conveys "to Hartford School Board so long as the premises are used for school purposes, then to Town Library." The School Board has a determinable fee. Town Library has an executory interest. (For an explanation of why the School Board has a determinable fee in *Example 13* but a fee simple subject to executory limitation in *Example 12*, see page 213, in Chapter 3.)

The interest given to Town Library in *Example 13* is not a divesting interest and should logically be classified as a remainder. It stands ready to *succeed* on the natural expiration of the preceding estate; it does *not divest* the determinable fee, which expires automatically. But the future interest cannot be a remainder because of the rule, laid down before the Statute of Uses, that a remainder cannot follow a vested fee simple. On the other hand, the future interest does not fit into our definition of an executory interest as a divesting interest. Forced to violate one rule or the other, courts chose to give the future interest the label of "executory interest."

child, *Y*, and then *A* dies survived by *X*, *Y*, and *O*. Identify all of the estates and future interests existing as of *A*'s death.

8. *O* conveys "to *A* for life, then to *B* and her heirs; but if *B* marries *Z*, then to *C* and his heirs."

9. *O* conveys Blackacre "to *A* for life, then to *B* and her heirs so long as Blackacre is organically farmed."

10. *O* conveys a sum of money "to *A* if she graduates from college." *A* is not yet enrolled in college.

11. *T* devises "to *S* for life, then to my children for their lives, then to my then-surviving grandchildren. At the time of *T*'s death, *T* had two children, *B* and *C*, and three grandchildren, *X*, *Y*, and *Z*, who survived *T*. Identify all of the estates and future interests existing as of *T*'s death.

12. *T* devises "to *S* for life; then to *B* if *B* marries *Z* by *B*'s 30th birthday; otherwise, to *C* and her heirs." At the time of *T*'s death, *B* is 25 years old and is unmarried. *C* is alive (as are *S* and *Z*). Identify all of the estates and future interests existing as of *T*'s death.

13. *O* conveys Blackacre "to *S* for life, then to *S*'s children and their heirs, but if any of *S*'s children fails to survive *S*, then his/her share to his/her legal heirs." At the time of the conveyance, *S* was alive and had three children, *A*, *B*, and *C*. Identify all of the estates and future interests existing as of the time of the conveyance. Choose the option below that is most completely correct.

(a) Life estate in *S*; vested remainder (in fee simple) in *A*, *B*, and *C* subject to open and subject to divestment by the executory interest in the heirs of any child of *S* who did not survive *S*.

(b) Life estate in *S*; vested remainder in *A*, *B*, and *C* subject to open and subject to divestment by the executory interest in the heirs of any child of *S* who did not survive *S*; reversion (in fee simple) in *O*.

(c) Life estate in *S*; contingent remainder (in fee simple) in *S*'s children; alternative contingent remainder (in fee simple) in the heirs of each of those of *S*'s children who do not survive *S*.

(d) Life estate in *S*; contingent remainder (in fee simple) in *S*'s children; executory interest (in fee simple) in the heirs of each of those of *S*'s children who do not survive *S*.

(e) None of the above.

14. *O* conveys Blackacre "to *S* for life, then to *S*'s children, but if none of them survive *S*, then to *X* and his heirs." At the time of the conveyance, *S* was alive and had two children, *A* and *B*. *X* was also alive. Identify all of the estates and future interests existing as of the time of the conveyance. Choose the option below that is most completely correct.

(a) Life estate in *S*; vested remainder (in fee simple) in *A* and *B* subject to open and subject to complete divestment; executory interest (in fee simple) in *X*.

(b) Life estate in *S*; vested remainder (in fee simple) in *A* and *B* subject to open and subject to complete divestment; executory interest (in fee simple) in *X*; reversion (in fee simple) in *O*.

(c) Life estate in *S*; contingent remainder (in fee simple) in which *A* and *B* have an interest; contingent remainder (in fee simple) in *X*; reversion (in fee simple) in *O*.

(d) Life estate in *S*; contingent remainder (in fee simple) in which *A* and *B* have an interest; alternative contingent remainder (in fee simple) in *X*; reversion (in fee simple) in *O*.

(e) None of the above.

THE SYSTEM OF ESTATES AND FUTURE INTERESTS

Suppose that a transferor who owns land in fee simple absolute conveys one of the possessory estates listed in the left column below. What future interests, if any, might then arise? The middle column shows the possible future interests in the transferor, and the right column shows the possible future interests in transferees.

| POSSESSORY ESTATES | POSSIBLE COMBINATIONS OF FUTURE INTERESTS | |
	In Transferor	In Transferee
Fee simple absolute	None	None
Defeasible fee simple:		
• Fee simple determinable	Possibility of reverter	None
• Fee simple subject to a condition subsequent	Right of entry (power of termination)	None
• Fee simple subject to an executory limitation	None	Executory interest
Fee tail	Same as with life estate	Same as with life estate
Life estate	Reversion [indefeasibly vested] (when no remainder created)	
	Reversion [vested subject to defeasance] (when contingent remainder(s) created)	Contingent remainder(s)
	Reversion [vested subject to defeasance or indefeasibly vested]	Remainder vested subject to open
		Remainder vested subject to divestment
	None	Executory interest (if any)
		Remainder vested subject to limitational defeasance
	None	Executory interests in unborn class members
		Indefeasibly vested remainder
Leasehold	Same as with life estate	Same as with life estate

The trust. The use, which the Statute of Uses never did completely abolish, is the basis for the modern trust, a fundamental device in estate planning today. Trusts allow settlors to arrange their assets in ways that maximize flexibility in property management as well as transfer wealth to future generations.

The core of the trust is separation of "legal" and "equitable" title. The trustee holds legal title to the trust property and manages that property for the benefit of the beneficiaries, who have the right of beneficial enjoyment of the property. In the usual trust, the trustee has the power to sell trust assets and reinvest the proceeds in other assets. The net income of the trust is paid to the beneficiaries, and upon termination of the trust the trust assets as they then exist are handed over to the designated beneficiaries, free of the trust.

The dual ownership of the trust property was possible because of the existence of separate courts of law and equity. Although the trustee is the legal owner, it is subject to orders of an equity court, which enforces the trustee's duties to the beneficiaries, who are said to hold equitable interests; that is, interests enforceable by courts of equity.

In the typical trust, the beneficiaries hold equitable interests that correspond to the legal possessory estates and future interests you have studied. Thus:

> *Example 14.* O conveys Blackacre "to X in trust to pay the income to A for life, and then to pay the principal to A's children who survive A." X is given the express power to sell Blackacre. X has the legal fee simple in Blackacre; A has an equitable life estate and is entitled to all the income generated by the property. A's children have an equitable contingent remainder, and O has an equitable reversion. If X sells Blackacre for $200,000 and reinvests the $200,000 in Whiteacre and General Motors stock, the trust property then consists of these latter items. Upon A's death X conveys the trust property to the persons entitled thereto, A's children if any are alive or O if A has no surviving children.

We can depict this arrangement graphically in the following way:

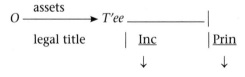

The trustee is a fiduciary and thus subject to stringent duties in managing trust property. Most important is the duty of loyalty. The trustee must act for the exclusive benefit of the beneficiaries and is not permitted to benefit personally. For breach of this or any other fiduciary duty the trustee is subject to personal liability to the beneficiaries and may be removed by a court.

D. RULES FURTHERING MARKETABILITY BY DESTROYING CONTINGENT FUTURE INTERESTS

One of the constant themes of Anglo-American property law for centuries has been the effort of courts to curb excessive "dead hand" control of property by the wealthy. As we have already seen, free alienability of property is a bedrock policy of a market economy, and the common law has long sought to promote that policy. During the late sixteenth and early seventeenth centuries, contingent remainders and executory interests posed a threat to that policy.

The problem is easy enough to see. When *O* conveyed Blackacre "to *A* for life, remainder to *B* and his heirs," a fee simple could be conveyed to a purchaser *A*, the life tenant, and *B*, with the vested remainder, simply by having *A* and *B* join in the deed. But with respect to contingent interests, obstacles to sale were much greater. If *O* conveyed land "to *A* for life, then to *A*'s heirs," the land could not be sold during *A*'s life because the heirs could not be ascertained until *A*'s death. If *T* devised land "to *A* for life, then to *B* if *B* survives *A*," *A* and *B* and *T*'s heir (who had a reversion) would have to agree to sell the land and how to divide the proceeds. Agreement was not likely, thanks mostly to high transaction costs (to use the parlance developed in Chapter 1). On top of these practical difficulties, the legal alienability of contingent interests was uncertain.

To destroy contingent interests and make land more marketable, judges developed four rules. We will quickly summarize the first three because they have been abolished, either by statute or judicial decision, in most states. The fourth rule, the Rule Against Perpetuities, is another matter.

1. Destructibility of Contingent Remainders

Here is a simple statement of the rule of destructibility of contingent remainders: *A legal remainder in land is destroyed if it does not vest at or before the termination of the preceding freehold estate.* If the remainder is still subject to a condition precedent when the preceding estate terminates, the remainder is wiped out, and the right of possession moves on to the next vested interest.

The destructibility doctrine is illustrated in the following example:

> *Example 15.* *O* conveys Blackacre "to *A* for life, then to *B* and her heirs if *B* reaches 21." If at *A*'s death *B* is under the age of 21, *B*'s remainder is destroyed. *O* now has the right of possession.

Contingent remainders could also be destroyed another way. English courts held that the life estate could be terminated before the life tenant's death by forfeiture or merger. The life tenant therefore had the power to destroy contingent remainders whenever he wished. Thus:

> *Example 16.* *O* conveys Whiteacre "to *A* for life, then to *B* and her heirs if *B* survives *A*." *A* conveys his life estate to *O*, the life estate merges into the reversion, destroying *B*'s contingent remainder.

The doctrine of *merger* (which is still in effect) requires a little explanation. It provides that if the life estate and the next vested estate in fee simple come into the hands of one person, the lesser estate is merged into the larger. Suppose there is a conveyance "to *A* for life, remainder to *B* and her heirs." If *A* conveys her life estate to *B*, the life estate and remainder merge, giving *B* a fee simple. This makes good sense, as there is no reason for keeping the estates separate. The courts extended the doctrine from situations like this to the very different situation where the life estate was followed by a contingent remainder and a reversion. Applying the destructibility doctrine in *Example 16* makes land alienable now rather than at *A*'s death.

Because of the mysteries of the concept of seisin (see page 197), the destructibility doctrine did not apply to executory interests. However, to give the destructibility doctrine as extensive a reach as possible, the courts held that *you must construe a limitation as creating a contingent remainder rather than an executory interest if that construction is possible.*

After the Rule Against Perpetuities was fully developed in the nineteenth century, it appeared to be a good idea to subject all contingent future interests in transferees to one rule, the Rule Against Perpetuities, and abolish the destructibility doctrine. The new Restatement does not recognize the destructibility rule and states that it has been abolished by statute or case law in nearly all states. Restatement (Third) of Property, Wills and Other Donative Transfers § 25.5 Reporter's Notes (2011).

To see the effect of abolition of the destructibility doctrine, suppose that *O* conveys Blackacre "to *A* for life, then to such of *A*'s children as attain the age of 21." Two years later *A* dies leaving two children: *C*, age 8, and *D*, age 4. Under the destructibility doctrine, the contingent remainders would be destroyed because they had not vested by the time of *A*'s death. If the doctrine has been abolished, however, the result is different. Upon *A*'s death, *C* and *D* have executory interests that will divest *O*'s possessory fee simple if either or both *C* and *D* reach age 21. (*Question*: If *C* reaches 21 and *D* is still alive, what interest in Blackacre does *C* have?)

2. The Rule in Shelley's Case

The Rule in Shelley's Case can be simply stated. It provides that if

(1) one instrument
(2) creates a life estate in land in *A*, and
(3) purports to create a remainder in persons described as *A*'s heirs (or the heirs of *A*'s body), and
(4) the life estate and remainder are both legal or both equitable,

the remainder becomes a remainder in fee simple (or fee tail) in *A*. (*Note well*: This is all that the Rule in Shelley's Case does.) The doctrine of merger may then come into play. According to this doctrine, a life estate in *A* merges into a vested remainder in fee (a larger estate) held by *A*. Thus:

> *Example 17. O* conveys Blackacre "to *A* for life, then to *A*'s heirs." The Rule in Shelley's Case gives *A* a vested remainder in fee simple. *A*'s life estate then merges into the remainder, leaving *A* with a fee simple in possession. The land is immediately alienable by *A* and not tied up for *A*'s lifetime.

The life estate cannot merge into a vested remainder in fee simple if there is an intervening vested life estate, blocking merger. The Rule in Shelley's Case is a rule of property, not a rule of construction; that is, it is intent-overriding.

The Rule in Shelley's Case has been abolished in an overwhelming majority of states. See Restatement (Third) of Property, Wills and Other Donative Transfers § 16.2 Reporter's Note (2004).

3. The Doctrine of Worthier Title

The Doctrine of Worthier Title provides that where there is an inter vivos conveyance of land by a grantor to a person, with a limitation over to the *grantor's own heirs* either by way of remainder or executory interest, no future interest in the heirs is created; rather, a reversion is retained by the grantor. Thus:

> *Example 18. O* conveys Blackacre "to *A* for life, then to *O*'s heirs." In the absence of the Worthier Title Doctrine, there is a contingent remainder in favor of *O*'s unascertained heirs. Under the Worthier Title Doctrine, however, no such remainder exists. Rather, *O* has a reversion.

The doctrine furthers alienability; *O* could convey a reversion, whereas *O*'s heirs, not being ascertained, could not convey the future interest. The doctrine also prevented feudal tax evasion; the feudal incidents were due only if *O*'s heir acquired his interest by descent from *O* and not by purchase. Because these reasons were inapplicable to personal property, the doctrine was a rule of law that applied only to land. It has been abolished in many states and survives only as a rule of construction in other states. See Restatement (Third) of Property, Wills and Other Donative Transfers § 16.3 Reporter's Note (2011).

4. The Rule Against Perpetuities

a. The Common Law Rule

The culmination of the long struggle between landowners who wanted to keep land within the family and the judges who for centuries had tried to stand firm against these efforts is the Rule Against Perpetuities. The Rule originated in the Duke of Norfolk's Case, 22 Eng. Rep. 931 (Ch. 1681), and as fleshed out in the next 200 years, it took the form of a compromise between the landed class and the judges. At the time of the formulation of the Rule Against Perpetuities, heads of families were much concerned about securing family land from incompetent children. The judges accepted this and over time developed a period during which the father's wishes would prevail. He could realistically and perhaps wisely assess the capabilities of *living* members of his family. So, with respect to them, the father's informed judgment was given effect. But the head of family could know nothing of unborn persons. Hence the father was permitted to control only so long as his judgment was informed with an understanding of the capabilities and needs of persons alive when the judgment was made. Later, judges permitted testators to extend their control beyond lives in being if any of the persons in the next generation was actually a minor. Finally, after about 150 years, the judges fixed the period as lives in being plus 21 years thereafter.

LEWIS SIMES, PUBLIC POLICY AND THE DEAD HAND
32-36 (1955)

In the halls of University College, University of London, prominently displayed within a glass case, are the bones of the great legal philosopher, Jeremy Bentham. The skeleton is clad in the garments which the great man wore in life. A wax replica of his head is substituted for his skull. His bony fingers grasp the walking stick, which he called "Dapple." On the glass case is a typewritten extract from his will, stating that the testator desired to have his preserved figure, on certain occasions, placed in a chair at gatherings of his friends and disciplines, for the purpose of commemorating his philosophy. It is said that this direction is still observed at banquets in his honor. I know of no more vivid illustration of the influence of the dead hand. One can picture that extraordinary scene in which the skeleton of a man, dead for over a century, sits at the head of the board. Literally the hand of the dead presides.

> **Sidebar**
>
> Jeremy Bentham (1748-1832) was a highly influential British philosopher, jurist, and social reformer. Best known for the doctrine of utilitarianism, Bentham was a social critic as well as a philosopher. He was an outspoken advocate of both legal and political reform, attacking ideas such as natural law and promoting universal suffrage and decriminalization of homosexuality.

When the subject of dead hand control is not philosophical ideas, but property, much less bizarre devices than Bentham's corpse are employed. The testator, by terms of his will, uses the trust, the condition, the special limitation, and the future interest. By these means, he seeks to impose his wishes upon the property of future generations.

But our legal system, having recognized all these devices of remote control, also provides a whole arsenal of rules, designed to strike down unwanted creations of the dead hand. There are rules against direct restraints on alienation, against conditions in restraint of marriage, against conditions and limitations generally contrary to public policy. . . .

By far, the most important of these rules, however, is that which restricts the creation of contingent future interests. It is the Rule against Perpetuities. . . .

In the concise formulation made famous by John Chipman Gray, the Rule Against Perpetuities is: "*No interest is good unless it must vest, if at all, not later than twenty-one years after some life in being at the creation of the interest.*" John C. Gray, The Rule Against Perpetuities § 201 (4th ed. 1942). The compromise it strikes is that property may be tied up with contingent interests for lives in being plus 21 years thereafter, but no longer. The

> **Sidebar**
>
> John Chipman Gray was not only an influential scholar of property law and Professor of Law at Harvard Law School, but also a leading practitioner. He was co-founder of Ropes & Gray, one of the leading law firms in Boston.

Jeremy Bentham's "auto-icon" in University College London. The auto-icon was made using Bentham's skeleton, padded with hay, and a wax head fitted with some of Bentham's own hair.
Source: en-wikipedia

effect was to permit a donor "[to] provide for all of those in his family whom he personally knew and the first generation after them upon attaining majority." 6 American Law of Property § 24.16 (1952). When you think about it, permitting this extensive period of dead hand control represents a considerable victory for the rich desirous of controlling their fortunes after death.

(1) Mechanics of the Rule

In applying the common law version of the Rule Against Perpetuities to a given future interest, it may prove helpful to proceed through the following steps, sequentially:

▶ **Step 1:** *Which interests?*

The first step is to determine whether the future interest in question is even subject to the Rule. The Rule applies only to interests that are not vested at the time of the conveyance that creates them. This boils down to saying that only three interests are subject to the Rule:

→ contingent remainders

→ executory interests

→ class gifts

Contingent remainders and executory interests are subject to the Rule because they are not vested interests. Class gifts are a special case that we will consider later (see page 247).

▶ **Step 2:** *What is the "perpetuity period"? (When does the perpetuity clock begin to run?)*

The next step is to determine the perpetuity period of "lives in being plus 21 years." The phrase "perpetuity period" is a bit misleading because there is no actual fixed or finite period of time allotted for the vesting or termination of the interest. Validity of an interest under the common law version of the Rule does not depend on what point in the future the interest does in fact vest or terminate, but rather on whether it *might* do so too remotely. The essential thing to grasp about the Rule is that *it is a rule of logical proof.* You must prove that a contingent interest is certain to *vest or terminate* no later than 21 years after the death of some person alive at the creation of the interest. If you cannot prove that, then the contingent interest is void from the outset.

Regarding the phrase "some person alive at the creation of the interest," which we just used, to what time does "the creation of the interest" refer? In other words, when must the "life in being" be alive? It depends. If the contingent interest is created by will, the life in being must be a person alive at the testator's death. If the contingent interest is created by an irrevocable inter vivos transfer, the life in being must be a person alive at the time of the transfer. In case of a revocable transfer, the Rule Against Perpetuities does not apply until the transfer becomes irrevocable (e.g., the death of the person who has the power to revoke), and hence the life in being must be a person alive when the power of revocation ceases.

▶ **Step 3:** *What is/are the relevant future event(s)?*

Make sure that you clearly understand what future event(s) (there may be more than one such event) must occur in order to resolve the contingency of the interest. Sometimes the event will be obvious from the language of the transfer itself. E.g., *O* conveys Blackacre "to *A* for life, then to *B* if *B* is then alive." There is only one event here that is made a condition precedent to the vesting of *B*'s remainder—*B* surviving *A*. We need not look very closely to see that. But suppose instead *O* conveys Blackacre "to *A* for life, then to such of *A*'s children as survive *A*," and at the time of the conveyance *A* has no children. Here it is not quite as apparent as to what are the event(s) that are relevant to resolve the uncertainty of vesting. Actually, there are two: (1) all of *A*'s unborn children must either be born or remain unborn (i.e., *A* must die either with or without children); and (2) any children born to *A* must survive *A* or predecease him (terminating the child's interest).

▶ **Step 4:** *The search for a validating life*

What you are looking for is a person (it only takes one) who will enable you to prove that the contingent interest will vest or fail within the life, or at the death, of that person, or within 21 years after that person's death. This person, if found, is called the *validating* life. The validating life is sometimes referred to as the "measuring life," but this term is misleading because it may be read to imply that the law "measures" a "perpetuity period" for each case, which isn't so. A life is a "measuring life" only if it *validates* the interest. Hence, only valid interests have "measuring lives." Invalid interests are invalid because there exists no measuring life that makes them valid. Hence the search is for a *validating* life.

→ *Look only at causally connected lives*

Anyone in the world can be a validating life, so long as that anyone was in being (which includes in gestation) at or before the time at which the interest in question was created. But inasmuch as a validating life will be found, if found at all, among persons whose lives are somehow *causally connected* with the vesting or termination of the interest, you look only at them in searching for a validating life. These include the preceding life tenant, the taker or takers of the contingent interest, anyone who can affect the identity of the takers (such as *A* in a gift to *A*'s children), and anyone else who can affect events relevant to the condition precedent.

→ *Test each such life with the "what-might-happen" question*

Now test each candidate for a validating life among this group by asking the "what-might-happen" question: for that person, *is there some possible (not necessarily probable) chain of post-creation events such that the contingency might still remain unresolved, one way or the other, after that person's death plus 21 years have passed?* If you find that there is one person in this group (it only takes one) as to whose life you can answer no to this question, then you have found a validating life. If there is no person among this group of relevant lives by whom the requisite proof can be made, the interest is void.

Anyone who has read the foregoing will no doubt agree that the Rule Against Perpetuities really cannot be understood merely by parsing, however diligently, an explanatory text. Examples are crucial, so begin by considering the two that follow:

> *Example 19. O* transfers a sum "in trust for *A* for life, then to *A*'s first child to reach 21." *A* is the validating life. You can prove that any child of *A* who reaches 21 will necessarily reach 21 within 21 years of *A*'s death. The remainder must vest or fail within this period; it cannot possibly vest more than 21 years after *A* dies. The remainder is valid.

> *Example 20. O* transfers a sum "in trust for *A* for life, then to *A*'s first child to reach 25." *A* has no child age 25 or older. There is no validating life; the contingent remainder is void. You cannot prove that *A*'s first child to reach 25 will do so within 21 years after *A*'s death.

In thinking about the invalidating chain of events involved in *Example 20*, it many help to visualize the possible scenario through the following graphic which depicts a timeline of possible post-creation events:

Time line 4-9

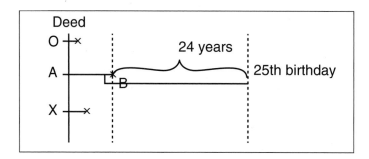

Example 20 illustrates a very important point about the search for a validating life. In looking at persons whose lives are in some way causally connected with the vesting or termination of the interest, we ask whether there is with respect to a given person an invalidating chain of possible events after the interest's creation. We ask what *might* happen, without regard to what, in the end, actually did happen. If what might happen is that the interest remains unvested following that person's life plus 21 years, then that person cannot be the validating life. All possible post-creation events, no matter how unlikely, must be taken into account. In *Example 20*, there is an invalidating chain of possible events. Here is what might happen: *A*'s presently living children (all under 25) die; *A* has another child, *B*, a year later; *A* dies, leaving *B*, age 3, alive. *B* will not reach 25 within 21 years after *A*'s death. If the gift vests in *B*, it will vest 22 years after *A*'s death, and this is too remote. No other life enables you to make the proof required. Since the contingent remainder is void, it is struck from the instrument, leaving a life estate in *A*, with a reversion in *O*.

Sometimes a validating life will be a person who is not mentioned in the instrument. The key is that to be a validating life, a person must be someone who can affect vesting or termination of the interest. Thus:

In Brief

One famous scholar of the Rule Against Perpetuities dubbed this type of Perpetuity violation "the case of the precocious toddler." See W. Barton Leach, Perpetuities in a Nutshell, 51 Harv. L. Rev. 638, 643-644 (1938).

Another variation on the presumption of lifetime fertility is the possibility that a person may conceive a child after her or his death through artificial insemination. Whether a person who deposits an egg or sperm in an artificial insemination bank is a parent of any child conceived after the depositor's death has not been decided. In perpetuities cases to date, courts have ignored the possibility of posthumous parentage of a child *en ventre sa frigidaire.* (Leach's term again! See W. Barton Leach, Perpetuities in the Atomic Age: The Sperm Bank and the Fertile Decedent, 48 ABA J. 942 (1962).) In many states, statutes handle the problem by simply stating that the possibility of a child being born to a dead person is ignored. See Uniform Statutory Rule Against Perpetuities § 1(d).

Example 21. *T* devises property "to my grandchildren who reach 21." *T* leaves two children and three grandchildren under 21. The validating life is the survivor of *T*'s two children. All of *T*'s grandchildren must reach 21, if at all, within 21 years after the death of the survivor of *T*'s two children. Therefore, the gift is valid. (*Question:* Would it make any difference if the transfer had been by deed rather than by will?)

Under the what-might-happen test, an interest may be invalid on the basis of a seemingly absurd invalidating chain of events. Consider this example:

Example 22. *T* devises a sum "in trust for *A* for life, then to *A*'s children for the life of the survivor of them, then upon the death of the last surviving child of *A*, to *A*'s grandchildren." At the time of *T*'s death, *A* is an 80-year-old woman with two living children, *B* and *C*. The remainder to *A*'s grandchildren is void. The invalidating chain of possible events is the following: After *T*'s death, *A* might have a child, *X*, who in turn has a child, *Y*, conceived and born more than 21 years after the death of the survivor of *A*, *B*, and *C*. It matters not how unlikely it is that an 80-year-old woman would conceive a child. Under the common law Rule Against Perpetuities, it must be assumed that a person of any age can have a child, no matter what the person's physical condition. The presumption of lifetime fertility is conclusive, notwithstanding contrary evidence. A variation on this consequence of the lifetime fertility presumption is the possibility that a child, even an infant, might conceive a child.

If a transfer creates more than one interest subject to the Rule Against Perpetuities, you must test the validity of each interest separately. One interest may be valid and another one not. Moreover, the same person may or may not be the validating life for all interests. Different lives may validate different interests.

Time line 4-10

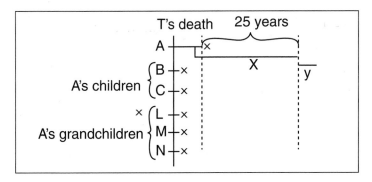

(2) Class Gifts

Gifts to classes present a special case under the Rule Against Perpetuities. A corollary rule known as the "all-or-nothing rule" holds that if a gift to one member of the class might vest too remotely, the whole class gift is void. Or, to put it another way, under the Rule Against Perpetuities, a class gift is not vested in *any member* of the class until the interests of *all members* have vested. A gift that is vested subject to open is *not* vested under the Rule Against Perpetuities. For a class gift to be vested under the Rule, the class must be closed (that is, each and every member of the class must be in existence and identified), and all conditions precedent for each and every member of the class must be satisfied, within the perpetuities period. Thus suppose a gift "to A for life, then to A's children," and A has one living child, B. B's remainder is vested subject to open, but it is not vested under the Rule Against Perpetuities until A dies and all of A's children are then in existence and identified. But because the remainder beneficiaries will all be ascertained at A's death, the remainder is valid.

Problems and Notes

We said earlier that examples help when one is trying to understand the Rule Against Perpetuities. So do problems. Apply the Rule to determine the validity of each interest in the following dispositions. (Assume that all parties designated by a capital letter (e.g., "A") have been born by the time of the transfer.)

1. O conveys "to A for life, then to B if B attains the age of 30." B is now 2 years old.

2. O conveys "to A for life, then to A's children for their lives, then to B if B is then alive, and if B is not then alive, to B's heirs." Assume that A has no children at the time of conveyance.

3. O, a teacher of property law, declares that she holds in trust $1,000 "for all members of my present property class who are admitted to the bar." Is the gift good? Suppose that O had said "for the first child of A who is admitted to the bar."

4. O conveys "to A for life, then to A's children who reach 25." A has a child, B, age 23, living at the time of the conveyance. Is the remainder valid?

5. O conveys "to A for life, then to A's widow, if any, for life, then to A's issue then living." Is the gift to A's issue valid? See Dickerson v. Union Natl. Bank of Little Rock, 595 S.W.2d 677 (Ark. 1980).

6. T devises property "to A for life, and on A's death to A's children for their lives, and upon the death of A and A's children, to [the person or persons indicated in the bracketed examples below]."

A and B survive T. A has one child, X, who also survives T. Is the devise of the remainder in fee simple valid or void under the Rule Against Perpetuities if the following words are inserted in the brackets?

(a) ["*B* if *A* dies childless"]
(b) ["*B* if *A* has no grandchildren then living"]
(c) ["*B*'s children"]
(d) ["*B*'s children then living"]
(e) ["*A*'s grandchildren"]
(f) ["*T*'s grandchildren"]

In solving the class gift problems above, focus first on when all the class members will be ascertained (within lives in being plus 21 years?) and second on when all conditions precedent, if any, will be met for all members of the class (within lives in being plus 21 years?).

Saving clause in a trust. In drafting a trust creating future interests, experienced lawyers almost always include a perpetuities saving clause. A saving clause is designed to terminate the trust, and distribute the assets, at the expiration of specified measuring lives plus 21 years, if the trust has not earlier terminated. Suppose that the testator wants to create a trust paying income to her only child *A* for life, then income to *A*'s children for their lives, then distributing the principal to *A*'s grandchildren. Here is a saving clause that might be inserted in the trust:

> Notwithstanding any other provision in this instrument, this trust shall terminate, if it has not previously terminated, 21 years after the death of the survivor of *A* and *A*'s issue living at my death. In case of such termination, the then remaining principal and undistributed income of the trust shall be distributed to *A*'s issue then living per stirpes, or, if no issue of *A* is then living, to the American Red Cross.

If *A* actually has an afterborn child who lives more than 21 years after the death of *A* and all *A*'s issue living at the testator's death (the possibility that causes the gift of trust principal to violate the Rule), the trust will terminate under the saving clause and the principal will then be distributed.

You can use extraneous lives in a saving clause if you want to. If you want a trust to continue for a very long period of time, you might end the trust 21 years after the death of the survivor of the descendants of John D. Rockefeller living at the creation of the trust. In either case, all interests in the trust will necessarily vest, if at all, within the perpetuities period.

(3) Reversionary Future Interests; Executory Interests Following Defeasible Fees

Future interests retained by the *transferor*—reversions, possibilities of reverter, and rights of entry—are not subject to the Rule Against Perpetuities. They are treated as vested as soon as they arise. This exemption leads to some startling differences in result when the transferor attempts to create an equivalent executory interest in a transferee. Compare these two cases involving future interests in the grantor:

> *Example 23.* O conveys Blackacre "to the School Board so long as it is used for a school." The School Board has a fee simple determinable; O has a possibility of reverter exempt from the Rule Against Perpetuities.

> *Example 24.* O conveys Blackacre "to the School Board, but if it ceases to use Blackacre for school purposes, O has a right to re-enter." The School Board has a fee simple subject to condition subsequent; O has a right of entry exempt from the Rule Against Perpetuities.

Now compare these two cases involving future interests in *transferees:*

> *Example 25.* O conveys Blackacre "to the School Board so long as it is used for a school, then to A and her heirs." A's executory interest violates the Rule Against Perpetuities. It will not necessarily vest within A's lifetime or within 21 years after A's death. It may vest and become possessory centuries from now. When an interest violates the Rule Against Perpetuities, it is struck out and the remaining valid interests stand. Take a pencil and line out the void gift, "then to A and her heirs." This leaves a fee simple determinable in the School Board. Since O has not given away O's entire interest, O has a possibility of reverter.
>
> *Example 26.* O conveys Blackacre "to the School Board, but if it ceases to use Blackacre for school purposes to A and her heirs." The School Board has a fee simple subject to (an apparent) executory interest. A's executory interest violates the Rule Against Perpetuities for the reason given in *Example 25.* Strike it out, beginning with "but if it ceases. . . ." This leaves standing a conveyance "to the School Board." The School Board has a fee simple absolute!

If you were counsel for O in *Examples 25* and *26,* how would you carry out O's desires exactly, using two pieces of paper rather than one?

Should the Rule Against Perpetuities apply to possibilities of reverter and rights of entry? A number of states have limited these interests to a specified number of years, usually 30, after which the possessory fee becomes absolute. See, e.g., Cal. Civ. Code § 885.030 (West 2020); Mass. Ann. Laws ch. 184A, § 7 (2020); N.C. Gen. Stat. § 41-32 (2020) (60 years). Some of these statutes permit a possibility of reverter or right of entry to be preserved for additional periods by recording in the courthouse, before the end of the allowable period, a notice of intent to preserve the future interest. See N.Y. Real Prop. Law § 345 (McKinney 2020). The Uniform Statutory Rule Against Perpetuities, enacted in 30 states and the District of Columbia (see page 252), validates executory interests in *Examples 25* and *26* for 90 years, but it does not change the common law exemption granted to interests in the transferor.

(4) Commercial Transactions

Most of the commercial cases finding violations of the Rule involve options to purchase and rights of first refusal (preemptive options). An *option to purchase*, which is specifically enforceable in equity, creates an interest in the property involved. A purchase option is treated like a future interest, contingent upon exercise of the option. The general view is that purchase options are subject to the Rule Against Perpetuities and are void if exercisable beyond lives in being plus 21 years.

Unlike an option to purchase, a *right of first refusal* (sometimes called a *preemptive right*) does not give the holder the power to compel the owner to sell. It only requires the owner, if and when she decides to sell, to offer the property first to the holder of the right. Courts have generally held that rights of first refusal are not subject to the Rule Against Perpetuities. The reason commonly given is that because the holder of the right may choose to purchase the property on the same terms as a bona fide offer, if and when the owner decides to sell, the holder of the right has no power to encumber an owner's ability to sell the property for an undue length of time. The right casts no uncertainty on the title, nor does it inhibit a sale of the property. See Bortolotti v. Hayden, 866 N.E.2d 882 (Mass. 2007). Some courts, though, hold that rights of first refusal are subject to the Rule and invalidate them if they are exercisable beyond the perpetuities period. See, e.g., Low v. Spellman, 629 A.2d 57 (Me. 1998); Arundel Corp. v. Marie, 860 A.2d 886 (Md. App. 2004). In New York, market-price rights of first refusal created in commercial or government transactions are not subject to the Rule, but are subject to the common law rule against unreasonable restraints on alienation (on which recall the discussion on page 204). See Metropolitan Transp. Co. v. Bruken Realty Corp., 492 N.E.2d 379 (N.Y. 1986).

Does it make sense to subject commercial transactions to the Rule Against Perpetuities? Professor Stake argues that it does not. In his insightful account of *Symphony Space*, he states:

> [T]here is little reason to apply the Rule to commercial options. There is also a reason that the Rule should *not* apply, as opposed to just an absence of reasons for applying it. The Rule invalidates some divisions of rights, divisions that are probably inefficient in the sense that the sum of the parts is less than the whole. The parts are very likely worth less than the whole because those kinds of divisions are rarely created by the market. With commercial options, however, it is less likely that the transfer has been designed to consume some of the value of the land by dividing it. Commercial actors usually want to increase the value of the land. [Jeffrey Evans Stake, Upper West Side Story: The Symphony Space, Inc. v. Pergola Properties, Inc., 669 N.E.2d 799 (1996), in Property Stories 265, 295 (Gerald Korngold & Andrew P. Morriss eds. 2d ed. 2009).]

b. Perpetuities Reforms

Most jurisdictions today have reformed the common law version of the Rule Against Perpetuities in one way or another. Some others have outright abolished it. These reforms can be somewhat complex, and we can only sketch them here.

(1) Specific Statutory Reforms

A few states have enacted statutes that correct technical Perpetuity violations. These technical violations usually result from highly unrealistic assumptions that the common law Rule made, such as the presumption of lifetime fertility. So, for example, a New York statute establishes a presumption that a woman cannot have a child over the age of 55 or under age 12 and that a man cannot produce a child under the age of 14. N.Y. Est. Powers & Trusts Law § 9-1.3(e)(1) (McKinney 2020).

(2) Wait-and-See

Recall that the common law version of the Rule requires absolute certainty that the contingency will be resolved no later than lives in being plus 21 years, and that in applying the "what-might-happen" test, all possible future events are taken into account. There is no second chance for an interest that fails the "what-might-happen" test. But that is precisely the insight of the first type of Perpetuity reform: we wait and see whether the interest does in fact remain contingent too long. Under this approach, if an interest is void under the common law Rule, it is invalid only if the contingency has not been resolved by the end of "lives in being plus 21 years." The key insight is that we look at what *actually* happens rather than what *might* happen.

The main problem with wait-and-see has been the wait-and-see period—how long to wait for the interest to vest or not. Recall that there is no limitation on who can be a life in being, and there is no built-in perpetuity period under the common law Rule (see pages 245-246). So, there is no waiting period that is inherent in the Rule itself.

(3) The Uniform Statutory Rule Against Perpetuities

The waiting-period problem led to another reform: the Uniform Statutory Rule Against Perpetuities (USRAP), first promulgated in 1986. USRAP adopts a fixed waiting period. This approach also avoids the need to trace any designated group of actual lives and to determine which of them is in fact the longest survivor and when she died. USRAP's permissible vesting period is 90 years. Why 90 years? The basic reason is that it approximates the period of time that would result under a well-drafted perpetuity savings clause. Under USRAP, if at the end of the 90-year period (in the unlikely event that it is necessary to wait that long) the interest has still not vested, the court is authorized to reform the offending language of the instrument to allow the interest to vest by that time.

USRAP has been enacted in over 30 jurisdictions. However, a number of enacting states have modified USRAP in various ways.

(4) The Restatement (Third)'s Two-Generations Approach

The Restatement (Third) breaks new ground by adopting a different approach to implement the policy against excessive dead hand control. Although continuing the basic wait-and-see reform, it rejects both a lives-in-being and USRAP's period-in-gross measures. Instead, it adopts a two-generations approach. It provides: "A trust or other donative disposition of property is subject to judicial modification . . . to the extent that [it] does not terminate on or before the expiration of the perpetuity period. . . ." Restatement (Third) of Property, Wills and Other Donative Transfers § 27.1(a) (2011). It goes on to define "perpetuity period" as "expir[ing] at the death of the last living measuring life." The "measuring lives" are comprised of a group consisting of the transferor, the beneficiaries who are related to the transferor and no more than two generations younger than the transferor, and the beneficiaries who are unrelated to the transferor and no more than the equivalent of two generations younger than the transferor. Id. § 27.1(b).

Unlike the common law Rule, the two-generations approach focuses on the *time of termination* rather than the time of vesting. The rationale given for this shift is that the time of termination "coordinates more purposely with the Rule's objective of limiting dead-hand control, because the time of termination is when the property comes under the control of the ultimate beneficiaries." Id. An incidental benefit of the shift is that it makes the distinction between contingent and vested future interests irrelevant.

(5) Qualified Abolition of the Rule, and the Rise of the Perpetual Trust
Nearly one-quarter of the states have now enacted statutes either abolishing (actually or virtually) the Rule Against Perpetuities in the case of trusts containing a power of sale in the trustee, this at least being the characteristic pattern. (The Rule remains in force for legal interests—that is, other than the equitable interests created in a trust—but legal future interests are almost never found in practice today.) Where such statutes exist, perpetual (or virtually perpetual) trusts are now permitted. The primary force behind the movement to abolish the Rule is a generous exemption from the federal generation-skipping tax, which we will leave for you to study in a course on Trusts and Estates or Estate and Gift Taxation.

CHAPTER 5

Co-ownership and Marital Interests

As we have seen, ownership may be divided among two or more persons in the sense that they have *consecutive* rights of possession. The division results in possessory and future interests, not co-ownership. The latter term refers to situations when two or more persons have *concurrent* rights of present or future possession, and those situations are the central subject of this chapter.

A. COMMON LAW CONCURRENT INTERESTS

1. Types, Characteristics, Creation

There are three modern concurrent estates: the tenancy in common, the joint tenancy, and the tenancy by the entirety. Let's consider each in turn.

Tenancy in common. Tenants in common have separate but undivided interests in the property; the interest of each is descendible and may be conveyed by deed or will. There are no survivorship rights between tenants in common. Example: *T* devises Blackacre "to *A* and *B*." *A* and *B* are tenants in common. If *A* conveys his interest to *C*, *B* and *C* are tenants in common. If *B* then dies intestate, *B*'s heir is a tenant in common with *C*. Each tenant in common owns an undivided share of the whole (a situation that, whatever its conceptual difficulties, gives rise to a host of practical ones).

Joint tenancy. Unlike tenants in common, joint tenants have the right of survivorship, the outstanding characteristic of a joint tenancy. The theory underlying this right is rather peculiar, but still important in several instances. By a common law fiction, joint tenants together are regarded as a single owner; each tenant is seised *per my et per tout* (by the share or moiety and by the whole). In theory, then, each owns the undivided whole of the property; this being so, when one joint tenant dies *nothing passes* to the surviving joint tenant or tenants. Rather, the estate simply continues in survivors freed from the participation of the decedent, whose interest is extinguished.

Since the original notion was that all joint tenants were seised together as one owner, the common law insisted that their interests be equal in all respects. In particular, four "unities" were essential to a joint tenancy—time, title, interest, and possession. The meaning of each unity is as follows:

Time	The interest of each joint tenant must be acquired or vest at the same time.
Title	All joint tenants must acquire title by the same instrument or by a joint adverse possession. A joint tenancy can never arise by intestate succession or other act of law.
Interest	All must have equal undivided shares and identical interests measured by duration.
Possession	Each must have a right to possession of the whole. After a joint tenancy is created, however, one joint tenant can voluntarily give exclusive possession to the other joint tenant. (The unity of possession is essential to a tenancy in common as well; none of the other three unities is.)

At common law, and in many states today, if these four unities do not exist, a joint tenancy is not created; instead, a tenancy in common is created. Statutes in some jurisdictions abolish the requirement of the four unities and provide that a joint tenancy may be created simply by stating explicitly the intent to do so.

If the four unities exist at the time the joint tenancy is created but are later severed, the joint tenancy turns into a tenancy in common when the unities cease to exist. Hence joint tenants can change their interests into a tenancy in common by a mutual agreement destroying one of the four unities. Indeed, any one joint tenant can convert a joint tenancy into a tenancy in common unilaterally by conveying his interest to a third party; this *severs* the joint tenancy as between the third party and his cotenants because it destroys one or more of the unities. (Which one or ones?)

If tenants in common or joint tenants cannot solve their problems by mutual agreement, any one of them can bring an action for judicial partition. In a partition action, a court will either physically partition the tract of land into separately owned parts or order the land sold and divide the proceeds among the tenants.

Tenancy by the entirety. A tenancy by the entirety can be created only in husband and wife, although several states have legislation permitting a tenancy by the entirety between unmarried persons prohibited from marrying each other. The tenancy by the entirety is like the joint tenancy in that the four unities (plus a fifth—the unity of marriage) are required, and the surviving tenant has the right of survivorship. However, husband and wife are considered to hold as one person at common law. Because husbands and wives were considered to be of "one flesh," they held by the entirety; there were no individual interests. As a result, neither husband nor wife can defeat the right of survivorship of the other by a conveyance of a moiety to a third party. Only a conveyance by husband and wife together can do so. Neither husband nor wife, acting alone, has the right to judicial partition of property held as tenants by the entirety. Divorce terminates the tenancy by the entirety because it terminates the marriage, which is a requisite for a tenancy by the entirety; absent some agreement to the contrary, the parties usually become tenants in common.

Tenancy by the entirety exists today in fewer than half the states. Because tenancy by the entirety gives rise to marital interests of importance in many states, we will be investigating it further in section B of this chapter, where we discuss marital property.

Presumptions. At common law, a transfer to two or more persons was presumed to create a joint tenancy. Today the situation is reversed, with the presumption in cases of unmarried persons favoring tenancies in common. The presumption can be rebutted, but this requires clear and unambiguous language. Between married persons, the common law presumed an intention to create a tenancy by the entirety, absent some clear indication to the contrary. The presumption still applies in most, but not all, states that retain the tenancy.

Problems

1. *O* conveys Blackacre "to *A*, *B*, and *C* as joint tenants." Subsequently, *A* conveys his interest to *D*. Then *B* dies intestate, leaving *H* as his heir. What is the state of the title? See Cortelyou v. Dinger, 310 N.Y.S.2d 764 (Sup. Ct. 1970). What if *B* had died leaving a will devising his interest to *H*?

2. *T* devises Blackacre "to *A* and *B* as joint tenants for their joint lives, remainder to the survivor." What interests are created by the devise? See Problem 3, page 230. How does a joint tenancy in fee simple differ?

Avoidance of probate. Joint tenancies are popular, particularly between married couples, because a joint tenancy is the practical equivalent of a will, but at the joint tenant's death, probate of the property is avoided. Probate is the judicial supervision of the administration of the decedent's property that passes to others at the decedent's death, and it can be costly and time-consuming. A joint tenancy avoids probate because *no interest passes* on the joint tenant's death. Under the theory of joint tenancy, the decedent's interest ends at death, and the survivor's ownership of the whole continues without the decedent's participation.

A joint tenant cannot pass her interest in a joint tenancy by will. Inasmuch as the joint tenant's interest ceases at death, a joint tenant has no interest that can pass by will. The idea that a joint tenant's interest ceases at death also has important consequences for creditors. If a creditor acts during a joint tenant's life, the creditor can seize and sell the joint tenant's interest in property, severing the joint tenancy. If the creditor waits until after the joint tenant's death, the decedent joint tenant's interest has disappeared, and there is nothing the creditor can seize.

Unequal shares. One of the four unities of a joint tenancy is equal shares. At common law if *A* owned a one-third share and *B* a two-thirds share, *A* and *B* could not hold as joint tenants. They would hold as tenants in common. This result is justifiable solely on historical grounds and makes no sense today. It is increasingly ignored by courts in situations where it counts. If *A* and *B* take title as joint tenants and *A* furnishes one-third of the purchase price and *B* two-thirds, and the parties intend the proceeds from sale of the joint tenancy property to be divided one-third and two-thirds if sold during their joint lives, a joint tenancy is created, and, if the property is sold, the court will divide the proceeds according to their intent.

Severance of joint tenancies. Clearly, a conveyance of a joint tenant's entire interest severs the joint tenancy as to that joint tenant, but what about transfers of less than the joint tenant's entire interest? The question usually comes up in two contexts, leases and mortgages.

Suppose *A* and *B* own a building and lot as joint tenants and *A* leases to *Z* for five years without obtaining *B*'s consent. Is the lease valid, and, if so, does it sever the joint tenancy? The answer to the first question is a clear yes (do you see why?), but the law on the second question is less clear. Tenhet v. Boswell, 554 P.2d 330 (Cal. 1976), is a leading decision for one response. The court held that although the lease was valid, it did not effect a severance. The lease was subject to the cotenant's right of survivorship, and when the lessor cotenant died the lease was terminated. Other cases hold that the lease effects a severance because the unity of interest is lost. See Alexander v. Boyer, 253 A.2d 359 (Md. App. 1969).

Now suppose that *A*, a joint tenant with *B*, unilaterally grants a mortgage on the property to *Z*. Does the mortgage sever the joint tenancy? The answer depends on which theory of mortgages the jurisdiction follows, the title theory or the lien theory of mortgages (more on this at page 393). Under the traditional title theory, a mortgage effects a severance because it transfers title, thereby terminating the unities of time and title. Under the theory that the mortgage creates only a lien, no severance results. Notice how formalistic this approach is. A more functional approach considers the likely intent of the party giving the mortgage. Since a mortgage, as opposed to a conveyance, is an ambiguous sort of conveyance in this respect, it would seem to follow that a mortgage, absent any other evidence of intent, should not work a severance.

Secret severance. Not only may one joint tenant unilaterally sever a joint tenancy, but she may do so without giving notice to the other tenant(s). In Riddle v. Harmon, 162 Cal. Rptr. 530 (Cal. App. 1980), a husband and wife owned real estate as joint tenants. The wife wished to dispose of her interest by will. Rather than using a straw to effect a severance, she secretly deeded her interest to herself and then executed a will in which she devised her interest to her daughter. A few weeks later she died. The court held that a straw is not required to sever a joint tenancy.

Suppose that the wife writes out the deed in her own handwriting: "I convey my interest in [Blackacre] to myself, to terminate the joint tenancy with my husband." Telling only her daughter of it, the wife puts the deed under some papers in her desk drawer. Subsequently, the husband dies, and the wife destroys the deed. What result? Some states (now including California) require recordation to sever a joint tenancy under some circumstances. See Cal. Civ. Code § 683.2 (2020); N.Y. Real Prop. Law § 240-c (2016) (McKinney 2020). Would these statutes avoid the problem posed by the hypothetical?

2. Multiple-Party Bank Accounts

Multiple-party accounts with financial institutions, including banks, generally take one of three forms—*joint* accounts ("*A* and *B*," or "*A* or *B*"), *savings account trusts*, called "Totten trusts" in some states ("*A*, in trust for *B*"), or *payable-on-death* (P.O.D.) accounts ("*A*, payable on death to *B*"). Of the three, joint accounts are the most common. Joint bank accounts have been the subject of much litigation. The primary reason is that the joint bank account is used by depositors with different intentions and for a variety of purposes. Suppose that O deposits $5,000 in a joint bank account, with O and A as joint tenants. O may intend to make a present gift to A of one-half the sum deposited in addition to survivorship rights to the whole sum on deposit. Courts sometimes refer to this as a "true joint tenancy" bank account. Or O may intend to make a gift to A only of survivorship rights. This may be called a P.O.D. account and will likely be invalid unless there is a state statute expressly authorizing P.O.D. accounts (many states have such statutes). Or O may intend that A only have power to draw on the account to pay O's bills and not have survivorship rights. This is often called a "convenience" account. The bank card signed by O and A usually says either O or A has the right to withdraw all money on deposit during their joint lives, and the balance goes to the survivor.

Why do you suppose banks usually do not offer depositors an account tailored to specific desires, but instead suggest the all-purpose joint bank account? An account expressly giving A survivorship rights only is in reality a will; A's name is put on the account solely for the purpose of passing the property at death. In some jurisdictions, a P.O.D. account is not permitted because it is viewed as a testamentary instrument that is not signed and witnessed in accordance with the requirements of the Statute of Wills. Only in recent years have P.O.D. accounts become legally acceptable, largely because of the influence of the Uniform Probate Code, which first authorized them in 1969 in its original version. In jurisdictions that do not permit P.O.D. accounts, depositors sometimes create a joint bank account with the intention that it be a P.O.D. account in disguise.

If O wants a convenience account, what O really intends is an account owned by O with a power in A to draw on the account during O's life. Because a power of attorney expires at the death of the principal, many banks are wary of power-of-attorney accounts and prefer joint accounts. With a joint account, the bank is safe in paying all the money on deposit to any joint tenant or to the survivor. For the bank, a joint account has little risk.

Because the joint account is an all-purpose account, it invites litigation to establish the true intention of the depositor. The agreement signed with the bank, providing that the account belongs to the survivor, is, in most states, not controlling. It is viewed as intended merely to protect the bank if it makes payment to the survivor. It does not determine the realities of ownership between the joint tenants. After the death of the depositor, disappointed heirs may claim that the joint tenant's name was put on the account merely for the purpose of paying the decedent's bills; if they can establish this, the money in the account belongs to the decedent's estate and not to the surviving joint tenant. For an illustrative case, see Estate of Shea, 848 N.E.2d 185 (Ill. App. 2006).

A majority of jurisdictions holds that the surviving joint tenant takes the sum remaining on deposit in a joint account unless there is clear and convincing evidence that a convenience account was intended. The burden of proof is placed upon persons challenging the surviving joint tenant. In some jurisdictions, to prevent litigation, the presumption that survivorship rights were intended in a joint bank account is conclusive. See Wright v. Bloom, 635 N.E.2d 31 (Ohio 1994).

During the lifetime of the parties, litigation may arise over what present rights the parties to a joint account have in the sum on deposit. In most jurisdictions, during the lifetime of the parties the presumption is that the joint account belongs to the parties in proportion to the net contribution of each party. See Uniform Probate Code § 6-211 (2015). Hence if O deposits $5,000 in a joint bank account with A, it is presumed that O does not intend a gift to A of $2,500 but intends A to have survivorship rights only. If A withdraws from this account without O's permission or later ratification, O can force A to return the amount withdrawn. The presumption that O did not intend a gift to A can be overcome by clear and convincing evidence of a different intent. In a few jurisdictions, the parties to a joint account own, during the lifetime of the parties, equal fractional shares in the account (as in a joint tenancy in real property).

Problems

1. O, a widower, opens a joint bank account with his niece, A. O tells A, "I'll want your name on this account so that in case I am sick you can go and get the money for me." O dies. Is A entitled to the money in the bank account? See Franklin v. Anna Natl. Bank of Anna, 488 N.E.2d 1117 (Ill. App. 1986). Suppose that O also gives A a right of access to O's safe deposit box by adding A's name to the signature card giving access; the lease agreement signed with the bank provides that the contents of the box are owned in joint tenancy with right of survivorship. The box contains $324,000 in U.S. savings bonds and $4,000 in cash. Is A entitled to the bonds and cash? See Newton County v. Davison, 709 S.W.2d 810 (Ark. 1986).

2. H and W and their son, S, open a joint savings account. H and W are in their sixties. The money deposited in the savings account comes from savings from H's salary that H formerly had in a separate savings account. H dies. W, claiming that the entire amount in the savings account is hers, withdraws the balance. Does S have any rights to the money? See Allen v. Gordon, 429 So. 2d 369 (Fla. App. 1983).

3. A and B have a joint savings account of $40,000. How much of the account can A's creditor reach? See Maloy v. Stuttgart Memorial Hosp., 872 S.W.2d 401 (Ark. 1994).

3. Relations Among Concurrent Owners

Suppose that A and B are the concurrent owners of a piece of property. What are their rights and liabilities as to the property and as to each other? Courts commonly make such statements as: "Each tenant owns an equal interest in all of the fee and each has an equal right to possession of the whole. . . . 'Neither a joint tenant nor a tenant in common can do any act to the prejudice of his cotenants in their estate.'" Swartzbaugh v. Sampson, 54 P.2d 73, 75, 76 (Cal. App. 1936). Even if these statements were not misleading, they would not be very helpful. If A cannot do as he wishes because it would prejudice B, then B, in having her way, harms A. How should the inherent conflict of reciprocal rights be resolved?

a. Partition

Concurrent owners might decide for any number of reasons to terminate a cotenancy. If they can agree on a division of the property or the proceeds from its sale, no problem arises; the termination can be accomplished through a voluntary agreement. But in the not unlikely event that such an arrangement is impossible, recourse to the equitable action of partition is necessary. The action is available to any joint tenant or tenant in common; it is unavailable to tenants by the entirety. The following materials explore some of the dimensions of partition.

DELFINO v. VEALENCIS

Supreme Court of Connecticut, 1980
436 A.2d 27

HEALEY, J. The central issue in this appeal is whether the Superior Court properly ordered the sale, pursuant to General Statutes § 52-500,[1] of property owned by the plaintiffs and the defendant as tenants in common.

The plaintiffs, Angelo and William Delfino, and the defendant, Helen C. Vealencis, own, as tenants in common, real property located in Bristol, Connecticut. The property consists of an approximately 20.5 acre parcel of land and the dwelling of the defendant thereon. The plaintiffs own an undivided 99/144 interest in the property, and the defendant owns a 45/144 interest. The defendant occupies the dwelling and a portion of the land, from which she operates a rubbish and garbage removal business.[2] Apparently, none of the parties is in actual possession of the remainder of the property. The plaintiffs, one of whom is a residential developer, propose to develop the property, upon partition, into forty-five residential building lots.

In 1978, the plaintiffs brought an action in the trial court seeking a partition of the property by sale with a division of the proceeds according to the parties' respective interests. The defendant moved for a judgment of in-kind partition[3] and the

---

1. General Statutes § 52-500 states: "Sale of Real or Personal Property Owned by Two or More. Any court of equitable jurisdiction may, upon the complaint of any person interested, order the sale of any estate, real or personal, owned by two or more persons, when, in the opinion of the court, a sale will better promote the interests of the owners. The provisions of this section shall extend to and include land owned by two or more persons, when the whole or a part of such land is vested in any person for life with remainder to his heirs, general or special, or, on failure of such heirs, to any other person, whether the same, or any part thereof, is held in trust or otherwise. A conveyance made in pursuance of a decree ordering a sale of such land shall vest the title in the purchaser thereof, and shall bind the person entitled to the life estate and his legal heirs and any other person having a remainder interest in the lands; but the court passing such decree shall make such order in relation to the investment of the avails of such sale as it deems necessary for the security of all persons having any interest in such land."

2. The defendant's business functions on the property consist of the overnight parking, repair and storage of trucks, including refuse trucks, the repair, storage and cleaning of dumpsters, the storage of tools, and general office work. No refuse is actually deposited on the property.

3. Such a partition is authorized by General Statutes § 52-495 which states: "Partition of Joint and Common Estates. Courts having jurisdiction of actions for equitable relief may, upon the complaint of any person interested, order partition of any real estate held in joint tenancy, tenancy in common or coparcenary, and may appoint a committee for that purpose, and may in like manner make partition of any real estate held by tenants in tail; and decrees aparting entailed estates shall bind the parties and all persons who thereafter claim title to such estate as heirs of their bodies."

appointment of a committee to conduct said partition. The trial court, after a hearing, concluded that a partition in kind could not be had without "material injury" to the respective rights of the parties, and therefore ordered that the property be sold at auction by a committee and that the proceeds be paid into the court for distribution to the parties.

On appeal, the defendant claims essentially that the trial court's conclusion that the parties' interests would best be served by a partition by sale is not supported by the findings of subordinate facts, and that the court improperly considered certain factors in arriving at that conclusion. In addition, the defendant directs a claim of error to the court's failure to include in its findings of fact a paragraph of her draft findings.

General Statutes § 52-495 authorizes courts of equitable jurisdiction to order, upon the complaint of any interested person, the physical partition of any real estate held by tenants in common, and to appoint a committee for that purpose.[4] When, however, in the opinion of the court a sale of the jointly owned property "will better promote the interests of the owners," the court may order such a sale under § 52-500. See Kaiser v. Second National Bank, 123 Conn. 248, 256, 193 A. 761 (1937); Johnson v. Olmsted, 49 Conn. 509, 517 (1882).

Helen Vealencis (right), her mother, and her brother, John

---

4. If the physical partition results in unequal shares, a money award can be made from one tenant to another to equalize the shares. 4A Powell, Real Property ¶ 612, pp.653-54; 2 American Law of Property, Partition § 6.26, p.113.

It has long been the policy of this court, as well as other courts, to favor a partition in kind over a partition by sale. See Harrison v. International Silver Co., 78 Conn. 417, 420, 62 A. 342 (1905); Johnson v. Olmsted, supra; 2 American Law of Property, Partition § 6.26, pp.112-14; 4A Powell, Real Property ¶ 612, p.650; 59 Am. Jur. 2d, Partition § 118, pp.864-65; 68 C.J.S., Partition §125. The first Connecticut statute that provided for an absolute right to partition by physical division was enacted in 1720; Statutes, 1796, p.258; the substance of which remains virtually unchanged today. Due to the possible impracticality of actual division, this state, like others, expanded the right to partition to allow a partition by sale under certain circumstances. See Penfield v. Jarvis, 175 Conn. 463, 470-71, 399 A.2d 1280 (1978); see also Restatement, 2 Property c. 11, pp.658-61. The early decisions of this court that considered the partition-by-sale statute emphasized that "[t]he statute giving the power of sale introduces . . . no new principles; it provides only for an emergency, when a division cannot be well made, in any other way. The Earl of Clarendon v. Hornby, 1 P. Wms., 446.4 Kent's Com., 365." Richardson v. Monson, 23 Conn. 94, 97 (1854); see Penfield v. Jarvis, supra, 471, 399 A.2d 1280; Harrison v. International Silver Co., 78 Conn. 417, 420, 62 A. 342 (1905); Vail v. Hammond, 60 Conn. 374, 379, 22 A. 954 (1891). The court later expressed its reason for preferring partition in kind when it stated: "[A] sale of one's property without his consent is an extreme exercise of power warranted only in clear cases." Ford v. Kirk, 41 Conn. 9, 12 (1874). See also 59 Am. Jur. 2d, Partition § 118, p.865. Although under General Statutes § 52-500 a court is no longer required to order a partition in kind even in cases of extreme difficulty or hardship; see Scovil v. Kennedy, 14 Conn. 349, 360-61 (1841); it is clear that a partition by sale should be ordered only when two conditions are satisfied: (1) the physical attributes of the land are such that a partition in kind is impracticable or inequitable; Johnson v. Olmsted, supra; and (2) the interests of the owners would better be promoted by a partition by sale. Kaiser v. Second National Bank, supra; see Gold v. Rosenfeld, Conn. (41 Conn. L.J., No. 4, p.18) (1979). Since our law has for many years presumed that a partition in kind would be in the best interests of the owners, the burden is on the party requesting a partition by sale to demonstrate that such a sale would better promote the owners' interests. Accord, 4A Powell, Real Property ¶ 612, p.651; 59 Am. Jur. 2d, Partition § 118, p.865.

The defendant claims in effect that the trial court's conclusion that the rights of the parties would best be promoted by a judicial sale is not supported by the findings of subordinate facts. We agree.

Under the test set out above, the court must first consider the practicability of physically partitioning the property in question. The trial court concluded that due to the situation and location of the parcel of land, the size and area of the property, the physical structure and appurtenances on the property, and other factors,[5] a physical partition of the property would not be feasible. An examination of the subordinate findings of facts and the exhibits, however, demonstrates that the court erred in this respect.

It is undisputed that the property in question consists of one 20.5 acre parcel, basically rectangular in shape, and one dwelling, located at the extreme western

---

5. These other factors included the present use and the expected continued use by the defendant of the property, the property's zoning classification, and the plaintiffs' proposed subdivision plans. We consider these factors later in the opinion.

end of the property. Two roads, Dino Road and Lucien Court, abut the property and another, Birch Street, provides access through use of a right-of-way. Unlike cases where there are numerous fractional owners of the property to be partitioned, and the practicability of a physical division is therefore drastically reduced; see, e.g., Penfield v. Jarvis, 175 Conn. 463, 464-65, 399 A.2d 1280 (1978); Lyon v. Wilcox, 98 Conn. 393, 394-95, 119 A. 361 (1923); Candee v. Candee, 87 Conn. 85, 89-90, 86 A. 758 (1913); in this case there are only two competing ownership interests: the plaintiffs' undivided 99/144 interest and the defendant's 45/144 interest. These facts, taken together, do not support the trial court's conclusion that a physical partition of the property would not be "feasible" in this case. Instead, the above facts demonstrate that the opposite is true: a partition in kind clearly would be practicable under the circumstances of this case.

Although a partition in kind is physically practicable, it remains to be considered whether a partition in kind would also promote the best interests of the parties. In order to resolve this issue, the consequences of a partition in kind must be compared with those of a partition by sale.

The trial court concluded that a partition in kind could not be had without great prejudice to the parties since the continuation of the defendant's business would hinder

Figure 5-1
Subdivision plot plan for the 20.5-acre parcel

or preclude the development of the plaintiffs' parcel for residential purposes, which the trial court concluded was the highest and best use of the property. The court's concern over the possible adverse economic effect upon the plaintiffs' interest in the event of a partition in kind was based essentially on four findings: (1) approval by the city planning commission for subdivision of the parcel would be difficult to obtain if the defendant continued her garbage hauling business; (2) lots in a residential subdivision might not sell, or might sell at a lower price, if the defendant's business continued; (3) if the defendant were granted the one-acre parcel, on which her residence is situated and on which her business now operates, three of the lots proposed in the plaintiffs' plan to subdivide the property would have to be consolidated and would be lost; and (4) the proposed extension of one of the neighboring roads would have to be rerouted through one of the proposed building lots if a partition in kind were ordered. The trial court also found that the defendant's use of the portion of the property that she occupies is in violation of existing zoning regulations. The court presumably inferred from this finding that it is not likely that the defendant will be able to continue her rubbish hauling operations from this property in the future. The court also premised its forecast that the planning commission would reject the plaintiffs' subdivision plan for the remainder of the property on the finding that the defendant's use was invalid. These factors basically led the trial court to conclude that the interests of the parties would best be protected if the land were sold as a unified unit for residential subdivision development and the proceeds of such a sale were distributed to the parties.

Before we consider whether these reasons are sufficient as a matter of law to overcome the preference for partition in kind that has been expressed in the applicable statutes and our opinions, we address first the defendant's assignment of error directed to the finding of subordinate facts relating to one of these reasons. The defendant claims that the trial court erred in finding that the defendant's use of a portion of the property is in violation of the existing zoning regulations, and in refusing to find that such use is a valid nonconforming use. . . . [The court concluded that there was insufficient evidence to support the trial court's finding that the defendant would be unable lawfully to continue her garbage hauling operation as a nonconforming use begun before the zoning ordinance was enacted.] We are left, then, with an unassailed finding that the defendant's family has operated a "garbage business" on the premises since the 1920s and that the city of Bristol has granted the defendant the appropriate permits and licenses each year to operate her business. There is no indication that this practice will not continue in the future.

Our resolution of this issue makes it clear that any inference that the defendant would probably be unable to continue her rubbish hauling activity on the property in the future is unfounded. We also conclude that the court erred in concluding that the city's planning commission would probably not approve a subdivision plan relating to the remainder of the property. Any such forecast must be carefully scrutinized as it is difficult to project what a public body will decide in any given matter. See Rushchak v. West Haven, 167 Conn. 564, 569, 356 A.2d 104 (1975). In this case, there was no substantial evidence to support a conclusion that it was reasonably probable that the planning commission would not approve a subdivision plan for the remainder of the property. Cf. Budney v. Ives, 156 Conn. 83, 90, 239 A.2d 482 (1968). Moreover, there is no suggestion in the statute relating to subdivision approval; see General Statutes § 8-25; that the undeveloped portion of the parcel in issue, which is located in a residential neighborhood, could not be the subject of an approved subdivision plan notwithstanding the nearby operation of the defendant's business. The court's finding indicates that only garbage trucks and dumpsters are stored on the property; that no garbage is brought there; and that the defendant's business operations involve "mostly containerized . . . dumpsters, a contemporary development in technology which has substantially reduced the odors previously associated with the rubbish and garbage hauling industry." These facts do not support the court's speculation that the city's planning commission would not approve a subdivision permit for the undeveloped portion of the parties' property. See Rogers Co. v. F.W. Woolworth, 161 Conn. 6, 12, 282 A.2d 882 (1971); White v. Herbst, 128 Conn. 659, 661, 25 A.2d 68 (1942).

The court's remaining observations relating to the effect of the defendant's business on the probable fair market value of the proposed residential lots, the possible loss of building lots to accommodate the defendant's business and the rerouting of a proposed subdivision road, which may have some validity, are not dispositive of the issue. It is the interests of all of the tenants in common that the court must consider; see Lyon v. Wilcox, 98 Conn. 393, 395-96, 119 A. 361 (1923); 59 Am. Jur. 2d, Partition § 118, p. 865; and not merely the economic gain of one tenant, or a group of tenants. The trial court failed to give due consideration to the fact that one of the tenants in common has been in actual and exclusive possession of a portion of the property for a substantial period of time; that the tenant has made her home on the property; and that she derives her livelihood from the operation of a business on this portion of the property, as her family before her has for many years. A partition by sale would force the defendant to surrender her home and, perhaps, would jeopardize her livelihood. It is under just such circumstances, which include the demonstrated practicability of a physical division of the property, that the wisdom of the law's preference for partition in kind is evident.

As this court has many times stated, conclusions that violate "law, logic, or reason or are inconsistent with the subordinate facts" cannot stand. Russo v. East Hartford, 179 Conn. 250, 255, 425 A.2d 1282 (1979); Connecticut Coke Co. v. New Haven, 169 Conn. 663, 675, 364 A.2d 178, 185 (1975). Since the property in this case may practicably be physically divided, and since the interests of all owners will better be promoted if a partition in kind is ordered, we conclude that the trial court erred in ordering a partition by sale, and that, under the facts as found, the defendant is entitled to a partition of the property in kind.

There is error, the judgment is set aside and the case is remanded for further proceedings not inconsistent with this opinion.

THE REST OF THE STORY . . .

Apparently, the physical partition resulting from the litigation left Helen Vealencis with the short end of the stick. She was awarded three lots, including the homestead at 311 Birch Street, for a total of approximately one acre, worth $72,000 altogether. This land appears as lot 135-1, located at the far left-hand side of the 20.5-acre parcel inside the bold lines on Figure 5-1. Helen's award was further reduced by a requirement that she pay $26,000 in owelty to the Delfinos to compensate them for the adverse impact of her garbage operation on their proposed subdivision. (Is this fair? Should Helen receive her fractional share of the total acreage as valued with the garbage hauling business on it?) Thus Helen's net benefit was $46,000, less than one-fourth of what was due her for her 5/16 interest in the total value of the land.

The Delfinos received approximately 19 acres, which they sold some three years later for $725,000 to a developer who laid out a subdivision of 42 lots. Helen's lot was separated from the rest of the subdivision by a two-foot-wide strip of land made part of lots 39 and 40, depriving her land of access to Dino Road, with its water and sewage connections (see Figure 5-1). This strip also prevented Helen's garbage trucks from entering the subdivision, thus avoiding a loss in market value of the homes, but this was damage she had already paid for in the settlement! Helen's only access to her land was a one-rod (16.5-foot) easement over lot 9C on the figure. The Vealencis house today uses an artesian well and a septic tank.

Helen Vealencis died of a heart attack at age 55 in 1990, still running the garbage disposal business. This information, as well as other insights, is provided in the valuable article, Manel Baucells & Steven A. Lippman, Justice Delayed Is Justice Denied: A Cooperative Game-Theoretic Analysis of Hold-up in Co-Ownership, 22 Cardozo L. Rev. 1191, 1220-1243 (2001).

Notes and Questions

1. *Modern partition practice.* Although it is usually said, as in Delfino v. Vealencis, that partition in kind is preferred, the modern practice is to decree sales in partition actions in a great majority of cases, either because the parties all wish it or because courts are convinced that sale is the fairest method of resolving the conflict. In this connection, see Manel Baucells & Steven A. Lippman, Justice Delayed Is Justice Denied: A Cooperative Game-Theoretic Analysis of Hold-up in Co-Ownership, 22 Cardozo L. Rev. 1191, 1120-1243 (2001).

2. *Weighting emotional attachments.* In *Delfino,* the court protected Helen Vealencis's subjective attachment to her land. Not all courts do this, however, even when a family homestead is involved. Consider Johnson v. Hendrickson, 24 N.W.2d 914 (S.D. 1946). In 1904, Henry Bauman died intestate. His 160-acre farm passed one-third to his widow, Katie, and two-ninths to each of his three children. In 1908, Katie married Karl Hendrickson and had twin sons by him. The whole family lived in the homestead on a corner of the farm. The Bauman children grew up and left home. Karl and his sons bought an adjacent farm across the road from the family homestead. In 1944, Katie died, devising her one-third interest in the Bauman farm to Karl and his two sons.

The Bauman children brought an action for partition, requesting sale of the whole farm. Karl and his two sons asked for partition in kind, and particularly for allocation to them of the homestead where they lived, which was across the road from their adjacent farm. The court ordered a partition sale under a statute authorizing sale if physical partition "cannot be made without great prejudice to the owners."

> The language of this statute means that a sale may be ordered if it appears to the satisfaction of the court that the value of the share of each cotenant, in case of partition, would be materially less than his share of the money equivalent that could probably be obtained for the whole. . . . Under the terms of the statute quoted above a sale is justified if it appears to the satisfaction

of the court that the value of the land when divided into parcels is substantially less than its value when owned by one person. This land is now owned by six persons. The largest individual interest is two-ninths and the smallest is one-twelfth. Partition in kind would require the division of the land into not less than four parcels: Two-ninths to each of the three respondents, and one-third to appellants, collectively. It is a matter of common knowledge in this state that the division of this quarter section of land, located as it is, into four or more separate tracts would materially depreciate its value, both as to its salability and as to its use for agricultural purposes. The fact that it would be an advantage to appellants to have the farm partitioned according to their demands because of their ownership of adjoining land is immaterial. [24 N.W.2d at 916.]

The court gave no weight to the interest of Karl and his sons in remaining in the family homestead. See also Wizner v. Pavlin, 719 N.W.2d 770 (S.D. 2006).

3. *An alternative approach.* If a court orders partition, whether by sale or in kind, it might also order compensation (called "owelty") in order to make appropriate adjustments—say, to compensate for the fact that partition in kind results in one cotenant getting a more valuable part than other cotenants, or that partition by sale yields a higher price than it otherwise would because one of the cotenants made certain valuable improvements. In some jurisdictions, the principle behind this approach yields an alternative to standard partition in kind or by sale. If a court finds (1) that partition in kind is impractical or wasteful, and (2) that sale would not protect the interests of all parties, then the court may assign all of the property to one or more of the cotenants, provided they pay the other cotenant(s) compensation in an amount set by the court (and presumably equal to fair market value). See, e.g., Zimmerman v. Marsh, 618 S.E.2d 898 (S.C. 2005); Wilk v. Wilk, 795 A.2d 1191 (Vt. 2002).

4. *Agreements not to partition.* A and B own Blackacre as tenants in common. Each agrees in writing with the other never to bring an action to partition the land. A subsequently brings a partition action. What result? Suppose instead that the agreement provides for no partition until certain clouds on the title to the land are resolved in a pending lawsuit. Same result? Traditionally, courts viewed agreements not to partition as invalid restraints on alienation. Today most courts enforce them if they are reasonable in purpose and duration. See Restatement (Second) of Property, Donative Transfers § 4.5 (1983).

African American "heirs' property" and partition. There is considerable evidence that partition sales have worked to the disadvantage of poor African American farmers who own "heirs' property," so called because black farmers, perhaps distrustful of the legal system, commonly die intestate. Their heirs take the family farm as tenants in common, and after several generations the number of cotenants owning any particular farm can become unmanageably large. Currently, 76 percent of all African Americans do not have a will, more than twice the percentage of white Americans. See Lizzie Presser, Their Family Bought Land One Generation After Slavery, ProPublica, available at https://features.propublica.org/black-land-loss/heirs-property-rights-why-black-families-lose-land-south/. By one estimate, heirs' property makes up more than a third of all Southern black-owned land, worth more than $28 billion. Id. The problem is that after several generations ownership of the land has become fragmented into many small shares of undivided interest. A buyer, not uncommonly a white developer or speculator, purchases one share and then sues for partition. The property is sold (the fractionated pattern of ownership makes division in kind impracticable), and the black families seldom have the resources to compete with white buyers at auction. Between 1910 and 1997, African Americans lost about 90 percent of their farmland. Id.

To address this problem, the Uniform Law Commission has promulgated the Uniform Partition of Heirs Property Act (UPHPA). The Act, which has been adopted in over 20 jurisdictions, makes major changes to partition laws that provide heirs' property owners with significantly enhanced property rights. See Thomas W. Mitchell, Restoring Hope for Heirs Property Owners: The Uniform Partition of Heirs Property Act, State & Local Law News (Fall 2016), at 6; Faith Rivers, Inequity in Equity: The Tragedy of Tenancy in Common for Heirs' Property Owners Facing Partition in Equity, 17 Temp. Pol. & Civ. Rts. L. Rev. 1 (2007); John G. Casagrande, Jr., Acquiring Property Through Forced Partitioning Sales: Abuses and Remedies, 27 B.C. L. Rev. 755 (1986).

b. Sharing the Benefits and Burdens of Co-ownership

Concurrent owners might enter into an agreement concerning their rights and duties with respect to use, maintenance, and improvement of the property. These matters would then be governed by the law of contracts. Suppose, however, that there arises some problem not touched upon by the agreement, or that the rights of third parties are in question, or that there was never any agreement in the first place. Then there is a need for independent (property) rules to determine how the benefits and burdens of ownership are to be shared by the co-owners. The following materials explore some of these rules.

SPILLER v. MACKERETH
Supreme Court of Alabama, 1976
334 So. 2d 859

[John Spiller and Hettie Mackereth owned a building in downtown Tuscaloosa as tenants in common. When a lessee, Auto-Rite, which had been renting the building, vacated, Spiller entered and began using the structure as a warehouse. Mackereth then wrote a letter demanding that Spiller either vacate half of the building or pay half of the rental value, and, when Spiller did neither, she brought suit. The trial court awarded Mackereth $2,100 in rent. Spiller appealed.][6]

JONES, J. . . . On the question of Spiller's liability for rent, we start with the general rule that in absence of an agreement to pay rent or an ouster of a cotenant, a cotenant in possession is not liable to his cotenants for the value of his use and occupation of the property. Fundaburk v. Cody, 261 Ala. 25, 72 So. 2d 710, 48 A.L.R.2d 1295 (1954); Turner v. Johnson, 246 Ala. 114, 19 So. 2d 397 (1944). Since there was no

---

6. The facts have been slightly altered to eliminate extraneous issues. —EDS.

agreement to pay rent, there must be evidence which establishes an ouster before Spiller is required to pay rent to Mackereth. The difficulty in this determination lies in the definition of the word "ouster." Ouster is a conclusory word which is used loosely in cotenancy cases to describe two distinct fact situations. The two fact situations are (1) the beginning of the running of the statute of limitations for adverse possession and (2) the liability of an occupying cotenant for rent to other cotenants. Although the cases do not acknowledge a distinction between the two uses of "ouster," it is clear that the two fact situations require different elements of proof to support a conclusion of ouster.

The Alabama cases involving adverse possession require a finding that the possessing cotenant asserted complete ownership of the land to support a conclusion of ouster. The finding of assertion of ownership may be established in several ways. Some cases find an assertion of complete ownership from a composite of activities such as renting part of the land without accounting, hunting the land, cutting timber, assessing and paying taxes and generally treating the land as if it were owned in fee for the statutory period. See Howard v. Harrell, 275 Ala. 454, 156 So. 2d 140 (1963). Other cases find the assertion of complete ownership from more overt activities such as a sale of the property under a deed purporting to convey the entire fee. Elsheimer v. Parker Bank & Trust Co., 237 Ala. 24, 185 So. 385 (1938). But whatever factual elements are present, the essence of the finding of an ouster in the adverse possession cases is a claim of absolute ownership and a denial of the cotenancy relationship by the occupying cotenant.

In the Alabama cases which adjudicate the occupying cotenant's liability for rent, a claim of absolute ownership has not been an essential element. The normal fact situation which will render an occupying cotenant liable to out of possession cotenants is one in which the occupying cotenant refuses a demand of the other cotenants to be allowed into use and enjoyment of the land, regardless of a claim of absolute ownership. Judd v. Dowdell, 244 Ala. 230, 12 So. 2d 858 (1943); Newbold v. Smart, 67 Ala. 326 (1880).

The instant case involves a cotenant's liability for rent. Indeed, the adverse possession rule is precluded in this case by Spiller's acknowledgment of the cotenancy relationship as evidenced by filing the bill for partition. We can affirm the trial Court if the record reveals some evidence that Mackereth actually sought to occupy the building but was prevented from moving in by Spiller. To prove ouster, Mackereth's attorney relies upon the letter of November 15, 1973, as a sufficient demand and refusal to establish Spiller's liability for rent. This letter, however, did not demand equal use and enjoyment of the premises; rather, it demanded only that Spiller either vacate half of the building or pay rent. The question of whether a demand to vacate or pay rent is sufficient to establish an occupying cotenant's liability for rent has not been addressed in Alabama; however, it has been addressed by courts in other jurisdictions. In jurisdictions which adhere to the majority and Alabama rule of non-liability for mere occupancy, several cases have held that the occupying cotenant is not liable for rent notwithstanding a demand to vacate or pay rent. Grieder v. Marsh, 247 S.W.2d 590 (Tex. Civ. App. 1952); Brown v. Havens, 17 N.J. Super. 235, 85 A.2d 812 (1952).

There is a minority view which establishes liability for rents on a continued occupancy after a demand to vacate or pay rent. Re Holt's Estate, 14 Misc. 2d 971, 177 N.Y.S.2d 192 (1958). We believe that the majority view on this question is consistent with Alabama's approach to the law of occupancy by cotenants. As one of the early Alabama cases on the subject explains:

> Tenants in common are seized *per my et per tout.* Each has an equal right to occupy; and unless the one in actual possession denies to the other the right to enter, or agrees to pay rent, nothing can be claimed for such occupation. [Newbold v. Smart, supra.]

Thus, before an occupying cotenant can be liable for rent in Alabama, he must have denied his cotenants the right to enter. It is axiomatic that there can be no denial of the right to enter unless there is a demand or an attempt to enter. Simply requesting the occupying cotenant to vacate is not sufficient because the occupying cotenant holds title to the whole and may rightfully occupy the whole unless the other cotenants assert their possessory rights.

Besides the November 15 letter, Mackereth's only attempt to prove ouster is a showing that Spiller put locks on the building. However, there is no evidence that Spiller was attempting to do anything other than protect the merchandise he had stored in the building. Spiller testified that when Auto-Rite moved out they removed the locks from the building. Since Spiller began to store his merchandise in the building thereafter, he had to acquire new locks to secure it. There is no evidence that either Mackereth or any of the other cotenants ever requested keys to the locks or were ever prevented from entering the building because of the locks. There is no evidence that Spiller intended to exclude his cotenants by use of the locks. Again, we emphasize that as long as Spiller did not deny access to his cotenants, any activity of possession and occupancy of the building was consistent with his rights of ownership. Thus, the fact that Spiller placed locks on the building, without evidence that he intended to exclude the other cotenants, is insufficient to establish his liability to pay rent.

After reviewing all of the testimony and evidence presented at trial, we are unable to find any evidence which supports a legal conclusion of ouster. We are, therefore, compelled to reverse the trial Court's judgment awarding Mackereth $2,100 rental.

Notes and Questions

1. *The ouster requirement—competing views.* When a cotenant is in sole possession of concurrently owned property, the majority holds that unless there has been an ouster, the cotenant in possession does not have to pay a proportionate share of the rental value to the cotenants out of possession. A few jurisdictions take the view that a cotenant in exclusive possession must pay rent to cotenants out of possession even in the absence of ouster. See Cohen v. Cohen, 106 N.E.2d 77 (Ohio 1952). Which view makes better sense?

For an illuminating and searching analysis of whether the cotenant in sole possession should pay rent to the other cotenants, which shows, among other things, that the majority rule is not nearly so clear in operation as it is in the stating, see Evelyn A. Lewis, Struggling with Quicksand: The Ins and Outs of Cotenant Possession Value Liability and a Call for Default Rule Reform, 1994 Wis. L. Rev. 331.

2. *The ouster requirement—what standard?* What constitutes an ouster? Does *Spiller* set too high a threshold? Would it be better to trigger liability for

rental value rather quickly and easily, on grounds of fairness? Efficiency? Suppose a brother and sister inherit a house from their mother, and the sister moves in. The brother writes, as in *Spiller*, asking for rent. Should a refusal to pay, or even a failure to respond, amount to ouster? What if the sister's occupation makes occupation by the brother infeasible? Suppose a husband and wife own a home as joint tenants. The wife moves out because of abusive treatment by the husband. Ouster?

3. *Sharing rents, profits, and costs.* One cotenant may seek to recover from another cotenant rents realized from leases to third parties, profits realized from using the property for business purposes, and value realized by one or more of the cotenants in occupying the property as a residence. A cotenant making various expenditures, such as taxes and mortgage payments, repairs, and improvements, might also seek to recoup some or all of them through a partition action or an action for an accounting (brought independently or incident to a partition action) or an action for contribution from the other cotenants.

> ▶ *Rents and profits.* In all states, a cotenant who collects from third parties rents and other payments arising from the co-owned land must account to cotenants for the amounts received, net of expenses. Thus, if one cotenant leases a farm to a third party, executes a mineral lease, or cuts and sells timber, he must account for net rents, royalties, and other proceeds in excess of his share. See 2 American Law of Property § 6.14 (1952). Absent ouster, however, the accounting is usually based only on actual receipts, not fair market value.
>
> ▶ *Taxes, mortgage payments, and other costs.* A cotenant paying more than his share of expenses such as taxes and mortgage costs is entitled to recover to contributions from other cotenants, at least up to the amount of the value of their share in the property. Also, such a cotenant receives a credit for the excess payments in an accounting or partition action.
>
> ▶ *Repairs and improvements.* As to *necessary repairs*, some jurisdictions provide for contribution if the repairing cotenant gives notice to the other cotenants; most, however, recognize no affirmative right to contribution from the other cotenants in the absence of an agreement. As to *improvements*, a cotenant has no right to contribution from other cotenants for expenditures for improvements; beyond this (and unlike the case of repairs), no credit for the cost of the improvements is given as such in an accounting or partition action. This does not mean, however, that an improving cotenant is always without means to recapture the costs or realize the value of

improvements. The general rule is that the interests of the improver are to be protected if this can be accomplished without detriment to the interests of the other cotenants. Thus, if property is physically divided pursuant to a partition action, the improved portion is awarded to the improving cotenant if such a distribution would not diminish the interests of the other cotenants as they stood prior to the making of the improvements. If physical partition is impossible or would result in injustice to one of the cotenants, the property is sold and the proceeds distributed in such a way as to award to the improver the added value (if any) resulting from his improvements.

B. MARITAL INTERESTS

The common law separate property system was accepted in the large majority of American states. In eight states influenced by French or Spanish law (Arizona, California, Idaho, Louisiana, Nevada, New Mexico, Texas, and Washington) and in two johnnies-come-lately (Wisconsin and Alaska), a community property system exists. In the late twentieth century, the common law marital property system came under pressure to reform itself so that the results resemble those reached under a community property system. The community property idea of treating husband and wife as an economic unit has more or less triumphed when spousal property is divided upon divorce, but it has less effect on division of property at the death of a spouse. Moreover, great differences between these marital property systems remain and cause complications when a couple moves from a common law property state to a community property state, or vice versa.

BACKGROUND, BRIEFLY

Two different systems of marital property emerged out of the medieval period in Europe. One was the *separate property* system, developed in England. Under this system, the husband and wife own property separately; ownership is given to the spouse who acquires the property. The other was the Continental system of *community property*. Community property rests on the notion that husband and wife are a marital partnership (a "community") and should share their acquisitions equally. In Europe, community property originated among the Germanic tribes and was carried by the Visigoths into Spain in the fifth century. Gradually, over hundreds of years, community property customs grew and spread throughout the continent of Europe but never took root in England. Under the pressure of a militaristic feudalism with a powerful king on top, the English royal judges suppressed any tendencies toward community property. The presumed necessities of the great lords dictated the subordination of the wife, and this became the common law for all. See Charles Donahue, Jr., What Causes Fundamental Legal Ideas? Marital Property in England and France in the Thirteenth Century, 78 Mich. L. Rev. 59 (1979).

"They have this arrangement. He earns the money and she takes care of the house."
© *The New Yorker Collection 1977 Robert Weber from cartoonbank.com.*

1. The Common Law System

Under the common law system of separate property, the property rights of each spouse are classified according to three categories: (1) rights during the marriage; (2) rights upon divorce; and (3) rights at death.

a. During Marriage

The historical common law reflected a patriarchal society. A married woman was generally not entitled to exercise powers of ownership. Her property relationship to her husband was one of dependency.

At the instant of marriage, a woman moved under her husband's protection. She ceased to be a legal person for the duration of the marriage. Husband and wife were regarded as one, and that one was the husband. Except for clothes and ornaments, all personal property owned by the wife at the time of the marriage or acquired thereafter, including her earnings, became the property of the husband. The husband had the right of possession to all the wife's lands during marriage, including land acquired after marriage. That right, known as *jure uxoris*, was alienable by the husband and reachable by his creditors. In the 1800s, most common law property states enacted Married Women's Property Acts. These statutes gave a married woman, like a single woman, control over all her property. Such property was her separate property, immune from her husband's debts. The wife also gained control of all her earnings outside the home.

The Married Women's Property Acts did not give the wife full equality. The husband remained head of the family; the wife, although given control over her property, was unlikely, as an unpaid homemaker, to have much property.

SAWADA v. ENDO
Supreme Court of Hawaii, 1977
561 P.2d 1291

MENOR, J. This is a civil action brought by the plaintiffs-appellants, Masako Sawada and Helen Sawada, in aid of execution of money judgments in their favor, seeking to set aside a conveyance of real property from judgment debtor Kokichi Endo to Samuel H. Endo and Toru Endo, defendants-appellees herein, on the ground that the conveyance as to the Sawadas was fraudulent.

On November 30, 1968, the Sawadas were injured when struck by a motor vehicle operated by Kokichi Endo. On June 17, 1969, Helen Sawada filed her complaint for damages against Kokichi Endo. Masako Sawada filed her suit against him on August 13, 1969. The complaint and summons in each case was served on Kokichi Endo on October 29, 1969.

On the date of the accident, Kokichi Endo was the owner, as a tenant by the entirety with his wife, Ume Endo, of a parcel of real property situate at Wahiawa, Oahu, Hawaii. By deed, dated July 26, 1969, Kokichi Endo and his wife conveyed the property to their sons, Samuel H. Endo and Toru Endo. This document was recorded in the Bureau of Conveyances on December 17, 1969. No consideration was paid by the grantees for the conveyance. Both were aware at the time of the conveyance that their father had been involved in an accident, and that he carried no liability insurance. Kokichi Endo and Ume Endo, while reserving no life interests therein, continued to reside on the premises.

On January 19, 1971, after a consolidated trial on the merits, judgment was entered in favor of Helen Sawada and against Kokichi Endo in the sum of $8,846.46. At the same time, Masako Sawada was awarded judgment on her complaint in the amount of $16,199.28. Ume Endo, wife of Kokichi Endo, died on January 29, 1971. She was survived by her husband, Kokichi. Subsequently, after being frustrated in their attempts to obtain satisfaction of judgment from the personal property of Kokichi Endo, the Sawadas brought suit to set aside the conveyance which is the subject matter of this controversy. The trial court refused to set aside the conveyance, and the Sawadas appeal.

The determinative question in this case is, whether the interest of one spouse in real property, held in tenancy by the entireties, is subject to levy and execution by his or her individual creditors. This issue is one of first impression in this jurisdiction.

A brief review of the present state of the tenancy by the entirety might be helpful. Dean Phipps, writing in 1951, pointed out that only nineteen states and the District of Columbia continued to recognize it as a valid and subsisting institution in the field of property law. Phipps, Tenancy by Entireties, 25 Temple L.Q. 24 (1951). Phipps divided these jurisdictions into four groups. He made no mention of Alaska and Hawaii, both of which were then territories of the United States.

In the Group I states (Massachusetts, Michigan, and North Carolina) the estate is essentially the common law tenancy by the entireties, unaffected by the Married

Women's Property Acts. As at common law, the possession and profits of the estate are subject to the husband's exclusive dominion and control. . . . In all three states, as at common law, the *husband* may convey the entire estate subject only to the possibility that the wife may become entitled to the whole estate upon surviving him. . . . As at common law, the obverse as to the wife does not hold true. Only in Massachusetts, however, is the estate in its entirety subject to levy by the husband's creditors. . . . In both Michigan and North Carolina, the use and income from the estate is not subject to levy during the marriage for the separate debts of either spouse. . . .

In the Group II states (Alaska, Arkansas, New Jersey, New York, and Oregon) the interest of the debtor spouse in the estate may be sold or levied upon for his or her separate debts, subject to the other spouse's contingent right of survivorship. . . . Alaska, which has been added to this group, has provided by statute that the interest of a debtor spouse in any type of estate, except a homestead as defined and held in tenancy by the entirety, shall be subject to his or her separate debts. . . .

In the Group III jurisdictions (Delaware, District of Columbia, Florida, Indiana, Maryland, Missouri, Pennsylvania, Rhode Island, Vermont, Virginia, and Wyoming) an attempted conveyance by either spouse is wholly void, and the estate may not be subjected to the separate debts of one spouse only. . . .

In Group IV, the two states of Kentucky and Tennessee hold that the contingent right of survivorship appertaining to either spouse is separately alienable by him and attachable by his creditors during the marriage. . . . The use and profits, however, may neither be alienated nor attached during coverture.

It appears, therefore, that Hawaii is the only jurisdiction still to be heard from on the question. Today we join that group of states and the District of Columbia which hold that under the Married Women's Property Acts the interest of a husband or a wife in an estate by the entireties is not subject to the claims of his or her individual creditors during the joint lives of the spouses. In so doing, we are placing our stamp of approval upon what is apparently the prevailing view of the lower courts of this jurisdiction.

Hawaii has long recognized and continues to recognize the tenancy in common, the joint tenancy, and the tenancy by the entirety, as separate and distinct estates. See Paahana v. Bila, 3 Haw. 725 (1876). That the Married Women's Property Act of 1888 was not intended to abolish the tenancy by the entirety was made clear by the language of Act 19 of the Session Laws of Hawaii, 1903 (now HRS § 509-1). See also HRS § 509-2. The tenancy by the entirety is predicated upon the legal unity of husband and wife, and the estate is held by them in single ownership. They do not take by moieties, but both and each are seized of the whole estate. Lang v. Commissioner of Internal Revenue, 289 U.S. 109, 53 S. Ct. 534, 77 L. Ed. 1066 (1933).

A joint tenant has a specific, albeit undivided, interest in the property, and if he survives his cotenant he becomes the owner of a larger interest than he had prior to the death of the other joint tenant. But tenants by the entirety are each deemed to be seized of the entirety from the time of the creation of the estate. At common law, this taking of the "whole estate" did not have the real significance that it does today, insofar as the rights of the wife in the property were concerned. For all practical purposes, the wife had no right during coverture to the use and enjoyment and exercise of ownership in the marital estate. All she possessed was her contingent right of survivorship.

The effect of the Married Women's Property Acts was to abrogate the husband's common law dominance over the marital estate and to place the wife on a level of equality with him as regards the exercise of ownership over the whole estate. The tenancy was and still is predicated upon the legal unity of husband and wife, but the Acts converted it into a unity of equals and not of unequals as at common law. . . . No longer could the husband convey, lease, mortgage or otherwise encumber the property without her consent. The Acts confirmed her right to the use and enjoyment of the whole estate, and all the privileges that ownership of property confers, including the right to convey the property in its entirety, jointly with her husband, during the marriage relation. They also had the effect of insulating the wife's interest in the estate from the separate debts of her husband.

Neither husband nor wife has a separate divisible interest in the property held by the entirety that can be conveyed or reached by execution. Fairclaw v. Forrest, 76 U.S. App. D.C. 197, 130 F.2d 829 (1942). A joint tenancy may be destroyed by voluntary alienation, or by levy and execution, or by compulsory partition, but a tenancy by the entirety may not. The indivisibility of the estate, except by joint action of the spouses, is an indispensable feature of the tenancy by the entirety. . . .

We are not persuaded by the argument that it would be unfair to the creditors of either spouse to hold that the estate by the entirety may not, without the consent of both spouses, be levied upon for the separate debts of either spouse. No unfairness to the creditor is involved here. We agree with the court in Hurd v. Hughes, 109 A. 418 (Del. Ch. 1920): "But creditors are not entitled to special consideration. If the debt arose prior to the creation of the estate, the property was not a basis of credit, and if the debt arose subsequently the creditor presumably had notice of the characteristics of the estate which limited his right to reach the property." 109 A. at 420.

We might also add that there is obviously nothing to prevent the creditor from insisting upon the subjection of property held in tenancy by the entirety as a condition precedent to the extension of credit. Further, the creation of a tenancy by the entirety may not be used as a device to defraud existing creditors. In re Estate of Wall, 440 F.2d 215 (D.C. Cir. 1971).

Were we to view the matter strictly from the standpoint of public policy, we would still be constrained to hold as we have done here today. In Fairclaw v. Forrest, supra, the court makes this observation: "The interest in family solidarity retains some influence upon the institution [of tenancy by the entirety]. It is available only to husband and wife. It is a convenient mode of protecting a surviving spouse from inconvenient administration of the decedent's estate and from the other's improvident debts. It is in that protection the estate finds its peculiar and justifiable function." 130 F.2d at 833.

It is a matter of common knowledge that the demand for single-family residential lots has increased rapidly in recent years, and the magnitude of the problem is emphasized by the concentration of the bulk of fee simple land in the hands of a few. The shortage of single-family residential fee simple property is critical and government has seen fit to attempt to alleviate the problem through legislation. When a family can afford to own real property, it becomes their single most important asset. Encumbered as it usually is by a first mortgage, the fact remains that so long as it remains whole during the joint lives of the spouses, it is always available in its entirety for the benefit and use of the entire family. Loans for education and other emergency expenses, for example, may be obtained on the security of the marital estate. This would not be possible where a third party has become a tenant in common or a joint tenant with one of the spouses, or where the ownership of the contingent right of survivorship of one of the spouses in a third party has cast a cloud upon the title of the marital estate, making it virtually impossible to utilize the estate for these purposes.

If we were to select between a public policy favoring the creditors of one of the spouses and one favoring the interests of the family unit, we would not hesitate to choose the latter. But we need not make this choice for, as we pointed out earlier, by the very nature of the estate by the entirety as we view it, and as other courts of our sister jurisdictions have viewed it, "[a] unilaterally indestructible right of survivorship, an inability of one spouse to alienate his interest, and, importantly for this case, a broad immunity from claims of separate creditors remain among its vital incidents." In re Estate of Wall, supra, 440 F.2d at 218.

Having determined that an estate by the entirety is not subject to the claims of the creditors of one of the spouses during their joint lives, we now hold that the conveyance of the marital property by Kokichi Endo and Ume Endo, husband and wife, to their sons, Samuel H. Endo and Toru Endo, was not in fraud of Kokichi Endo's judgment creditors. Cf. Jordan v. Reynolds, supra.

Affirmed.

KIDWELL, J., dissenting. . . . The majority reaches its conclusion by holding that the effect of the Married Women's Act was to equalize the positions of the spouses by taking from the husband his common law right to transfer his interest, rather than by elevating the wife's right of alienation of her interest to place it on a position of equality with the husband's. I disagree. I believe that a better interpretation of the Married Women's Acts is that offered by the Supreme Court of New Jersey in King v. Greene, 30 N.J. 395, 412, 153 A.2d 49, 60 (1959):

> It is clear that the Married Women's Act created an equality between the spouses in New Jersey, insofar as tenancies by the entirety are concerned. If, as we have previously concluded, the husband could alienate his right of survivorship at common law, the wife, by virtue of the act, can alienate her right of survivorship. And it follows, that if the wife takes equal rights with the husband in the estate, she must take equal disabilities. Such are the dictates of common equality. Thus, the judgment creditors of either spouse may levy and execute upon their separate rights of survivorship.

One may speculate whether the courts which first chose the path to equality now followed by the majority might have felt an unexpressed aversion to entrusting a wife with as much control over her interest as had previously been granted to the husband with respect to his interest. Whatever may be the historical explanation for these decisions, I feel that the resultant restriction upon the freedom of the spouses to deal independently with their respective interests is both illogical and unnecessarily at odds with present policy trends. Accordingly, I would hold that the separate interest of the husband in entireties property, at least to the extent of his right of survivorship, is alienable by him and subject to attachment by his separate creditors, so that a voluntary conveyance of the husband's interest should be set aside where it is fraudulent as to such creditors, under applicable principles of the law of fraudulent conveyances.

Notes

1. *Four different approaches.* As the court in Sawada v. Endo points out, various jurisdictions have taken four different approaches regarding the effect of the Married Women's Property Acts on the tenancy by the entirety. These different approaches have important consequences for general creditors because a creditor can reach only such property as the debtor can voluntarily assign. In a majority of states, a creditor of one spouse cannot reach a tenancy by the entirety because one spouse cannot assign his or her interest. Doubtless this exemption from creditors is one of the main reasons for the survival of the tenancy by the entirety. The tenancy serves to protect the family home as well as other property from transfer by one spouse and from creditors of one spouse. The tenancy by the entirety, where recognized, can be created in any amount of real property and, in many states, in any amount of personal property.

2. *Taxes, taxes, taxes.* There is one creditor who can reach the interest of a debtor spouse in tenancy-by-the-entirety property: the IRS. In United States v. Craft, 535 U.S. 274 (2002), the United States Supreme Court held that a husband's interest in Michigan land that he and his wife owned as tenants by the entirety was "property" to which a federal tax lien could attach.

b. Termination of Marriage by Divorce

At common law, upon divorce property of the spouses remained the property of the spouse holding title. Property held by the spouses as tenants in common or as joint tenants remained in such co-ownership. Because the unity of marriage was severed by divorce, property held in tenancy by the entirety was converted into a tenancy in common. Inasmuch as the husband owed the wife a duty of support, a duty undertaken upon marriage, the wife was usually entitled to a continuation of support (called "alimony"), though it might be denied her if she were at fault.

In the last 40 years, dramatic changes have taken place in divorce law. Legislatures in every state have replaced the common law division of property with "equitable distribution." Under equitable distribution, property is divided by the court, in its discretion, on equitable principles. Many equitable division statutes authorize a court to divide *all* property owned by the spouses, regardless of the time and manner of acquisition. Other statutes authorize a court to divide only "marital property." Marital property is defined in some states to include all property acquired during marriage by whatever means (earnings, gifts, or inheritances); in others it includes only property acquired from the earnings of either spouse during marriage.

In equitably dividing property, there is a movement toward equal distribution of marital property upon divorce. In some states, equal division is required; in others, it is only a presumptive rule.

c. Termination of Marriage by Death

Historically, with respect to personal property, the common law gave a surviving widow one-third if there were surviving issue and one-half otherwise. A surviving widower took all his wife's personal property absolutely. As to land, the common law gave the widow the right of *dower*. This was a limited right: only a life estate in one-third of each parcel of land of which the husband was seised during marriage and that was inheritable by the issue of husband and wife.

Dower attaches to land at the moment of marriage, if the land is then owned, or thereafter when the land is acquired. It is "inchoate" until the husband dies. If the wife predeceases the husband, or they are divorced, her inchoate dower is extinguished. If she survives the husband, the wife becomes entitled to her dower in possession. After inchoate dower has attached, the husband is powerless to defeat it. Any purchaser from, or creditor of, the husband takes subject to it unless the wife releases her dower.

The widower's analogous common law interest is *curtesy*. This is a right to a life estate in each piece of the wife's real property if certain conditions were fulfilled. Curtesy, like dower, attached to all freehold land of which the wife was seised during marriage and that was inheritable by the issue of husband and wife. Unlike dower, however, curtesy did not attach to land unless issue of the marriage capable of inheriting the estate were born alive.

Dower and curtesy have been abolished in all but a small number of American jurisdictions. Nearly all jurisdictions have replaced these interests with the statutory elective share. Under the conventional type of elective-share statute, the surviving spouse can renounce the will, if any, and elect to take a statutory share, which is usually one-half or one-third or some other fractional share. By contrast, under the Uniform Probate Code the surviving spouse is entitled to keep any property that the will devised to him or her. The value of such property is credited against the elective-share amount. See Uniform Probate Code §§ 2-204, 2-209 (2012). States retaining dower give the surviving spouse the right to elect dower or a statutory forced share; the statutory share is usually larger.

2. The Community Property System

Nine states—Arizona, California, Idaho, Louisiana, Nevada, New Mexico, Texas, Washington, and Wisconsin—use a system of community property. Although there are substantial differences in details among the community property states, the fundamental idea of community property is that the *earnings* of each spouse during marriage should be owned equally, in undivided shares, by both spouses. For example, if the husband earns $1,000, one-half belongs to the wife. If the husband subsequently buys 10 shares of stock with the money, taking title in his name alone, the stock is marital property, and the wife owns one-half of it. The basic assumption is that both husband and wife contribute equally to the material success of the marriage, and thus each should own an equal share of property acquired during the marriage by their joint efforts. Community property includes earnings during marriage and the rents, profits, and fruits of earnings. Whatever is bought with earnings is community property. All property that is not community is separate. Separate property is property acquired before marriage and property acquired during marriage by gift, devise, or descent. Property acquired or possessed during marriage by either husband or wife is presumed to be community property. This is a strong presumption and can be overcome only by a preponderance of the evidence. Where there has been a commingling of separate and community property, the party contending for separate property may have a very difficult tracing burden. Recitals in a deed prepared by one spouse that property is separate property are not controlling; otherwise a self-serving spouse could take his or her earnings and unilaterally convert them into separate property.

In most states, the husband and wife can freely change ("transmute") the character of their property by written agreement and, in some states, by oral agreement. They can convert community property into separate property, or vice versa.

If marriage is terminated by divorce, some states require an equal division of community property. Other community property states authorize a divorce court to make equitable division of community property.

3. Same-Sex Marriage

Until recently, marriage of same-sex couples was everywhere illegal, and intimate relations between persons of the same sex was even a crime in some states. All that has changed. In Obergefell v. Hodges, 576 U.S. 644 (2015), the United States Supreme Court struck down as unconstitutional an Ohio law banning same-sex marriage. The Court emphasized both the symbolic and practical consequences of marriage, and pointed out that many material benefits are attached to the institution of civil marriage. Marriage also confers certain obligations on legally married parties. These property rights and duties exist under both state and federal law.

In Goodridge v. Department of Public Health, 798 N.E.2d 941 (Mass. 2003), the Massachusetts Supreme Judicial Court struck down, under the equality, liberty, and due process provisions of its state constitution, a Massachusetts marriage licensing statute that prohibited granting marriage licenses to same-sex couples. In *Goodridge*, the court emphasized the property dimension of civil marriage, stating:

> The benefits accessible only by way of a marriage license are enormous, touching nearly every aspect of life and death. The department [of public health] states that "hundreds of statutes" are related to marriage and to marital benefits. With no attempt to be comprehensive, we note that some of the statutory benefits conferred by the Legislature on those who enter into civil marriage include, as to property: joint Massachusetts income tax filing; tenancy by the entirety (a form of ownership that provides certain protections against creditors and allows for the automatic descent of property to the surviving spouse without probate); extension of the benefit of the homestead protection (securing up to $300,000 in equity from creditors) to one's spouse and children; automatic rights to inherit the property of a deceased spouse who does not leave a will; the rights of elective share and of dower (which allow surviving spouses certain property rights where the decedent spouse has not made adequate provision for the survivor in a will); entitlement to wages owed to a deceased employee; eligibility to continue certain businesses of a deceased spouse; the right to share the medical policy of one's spouse; thirty-nine week continuation of health coverage for the spouse of a person who is laid off or dies; preferential options under the Commonwealth's pension system; preferential benefits in the Commonwealth's medical program; access to veterans' spousal benefits and preferences; financial protections for spouses of certain Commonwealth employees; the equitable division of marital property on

> divorce; temporary and permanent alimony rights; the right to separate support on separation of the parties that does not result in divorce; and the right to bring claims for wrongful death and loss of consortium, and for funeral and burial expenses and punitive damages resulting from tort actions.

Id. at 955-956. The court noted other benefits related to property that are directly tied to marital status, including the presumptions of legitimacy and parentage of children born to a married couple.

Federal law also provides certain benefits to parties who are legally married. Among these are the right to file a joint tax return, the unlimited marital deduction under the federal gift and estate tax, and the right to create a "family partnership" (which allows married taxpayers the right to divide business income among family members) under federal tax law, to name just a few.

4. Rights of Domestic Partners

The marital property regimes we have just discussed traditionally have applied only to persons who are legally married to each other. Unmarried cohabitants do not acquire any rights in each other's property on the basis of their status alone, although their cohabitation may allow them to become legally married under the doctrine of common law marriage.

Common law marriage is now recognized in only 10 jurisdictions. To have a common law marriage, the cohabiting parties must manifest their intent to be husband and wife and hold themselves out to the public as husband and wife. If the jurisdiction recognizes common law marriage, the couple married by common law has the same rights as a couple married with license and ceremony. Common law marriage was abolished in most states because it was thought to encourage perjured testimony about an alleged agreement to marry.

But status isn't the only basis for acquiring rights in a partner's property. In recent years, courts in many jurisdictions have adopted the view that unmarried partners may acquire certain property rights on the basis of contract. The leading case beginning this trend was the California Supreme Court's well-known "palimony" decision in *Marvin v. Marvin*, 557 P.2d 106 (Cal. 1976). In that case, the court held that an enforceable contract for property division or support can be implied from the conduct of the parties. An express contract is not necessary. "[T]he better approach is to presume . . . that the parties intended to deal fairly with each other." *Id.* at 121. "[T]he parties' intention can only be ascertained by a . . . searching inquiry into the nature of the relationship." *Id.* at 117 n.11. Some courts have limited the contract theory to situations in which a written or express oral agreement exists, rejecting *Marvin*'s implied contract theory. See, e.g., *Morone v. Morone*, 413 N.E.2d 1154 (N.Y. 1980). Other courts have relied on different theories, such as constructive trust, to prevent unjust enrichment. See, e.g., *Watts v. Watts*, 405 N.W.2d 303 (Wis. 1987).

As an alternative to marriage, some jurisdictions recognize domestic partnerships (sometimes called civil unions). Although the details of domestic partnership statutes vary, they confer many of the practical benefits of marriage under state law, including property rights such as the right of survivorship. They are not recognized by federal law, however, so federal benefits such as Social Security survivor benefits are not available.

PART III

LEASEHOLDS: THE LAW OF LANDLORD AND TENANT

Leaseholds—or nonfreeholds, or tenancies—are a part of the larger estates system considered in Part II. Like the freehold estates, leaseholds have roots that run deep into feudal times (hence the notion of a *tenant* who holds under a *landlord*). And again like freeholds, leaseholds have been fairly static over the years in terms of their formal characteristics. In terms of relations between landlord and tenant, however, there have been regular and significant developments. The most important of these, together with the body of conventional law in the background, make up the bulk of the next chapter. The chapter considers, step by step, the nature and incidents of leaseholds, and then concludes with a selective look at the persistent problem of affordable rental housing.

CHAPTER 6

Tradition, Tension, and Change in Landlord-Tenant Law

A. THE LEASEHOLD ESTATES

Leaseholds, or tenancies, are the so-called nonfreehold estates briefly introduced in Chapter 3 (at page 210). The principal leaseholds are the term of years, the periodic tenancy, the tenancy at will, and the tenancy at sufferance. We consider them in turn.

1. The Term of Years

A *term of years* is an estate that lasts for some fixed period of time or for a period computable by a formula that results in fixing calendar dates for beginning and ending, once the term is created or becomes possessory. The period can be one day, two months, five years, or 3,000 years. These are all terms of years. At common law, there was no limit on the number of years permitted, but in some American states, statutes limit the duration of terms of years. A term must be for a fixed period, but it can be terminable earlier upon the happening of some event or condition. Because a term of years states from the outset when it will terminate, no notice of termination is necessary to bring the estate to an end. Ordinarily, the death of either party does not terminate the lease, but statutes may provide otherwise. See Tex. Prop. Code § 92.0162 (eff. Jan. 1, 2020) (tenant's death termi-nates the lease if the tenant's estate gives notice to the landlord of the death and removes the deceased tenant's belong-ings within 30 days).

2. The Periodic Tenancy

A *periodic tenancy* is a lease for a period of some fixed duration that continues for succeeding periods until either the landlord or tenant gives notice of termi-nation. Examples: "to *A* from month to

> **A Look Back**
>
> Bear in mind that when any of the leasehold estates is created, a future interest—in the landlord or in a third party—necessarily arises. Ordinarily, the landlord has retained the right to possession at the end of the leasehold, and the landlord's future interest is a reversion. But it is possible for a third party to take possession immediately upon termination of the leasehold. In that case, the future interest will be a remainder.

month." The period is automatically extended for another period unless either the landlord or the tenant gives proper notice. Usually, the required notice for termination is the length of one period, but many states impose a limit such as one month. Some tenants have no written leases or have no specified end to their tenancy but pay rent monthly. These arrangements create month-to-month tenancies and terminate only upon proper notice by either party. The death of the landlord or tenant has no effect on the duration of a term of years or periodic tenancy, but it does on the tenancy at will.

3. The Tenancy at Will

A *tenancy at will* is a tenancy of no fixed period that endures so long as both landlord and tenant desire. If the lease provides that it can be terminated by one party, it is necessarily at the will of the other as well *if* a tenancy at will has been created. Note, however, that a unilateral power to terminate a lease can be engrafted on a term of years or a periodic tenancy; for example, a lease by L to T for 10 years or until L sooner terminates creates a term of years determinable.

The tenancy at will ends, among other ways, when one of the parties terminates it. (It also ends, as suggested above, at the death of one of the parties.) Modern statutes ordinarily require a period of notice—say 30 days or a time equal to the interval between rent payments—in order for one party or the other to terminate a tenancy at will. If under a tenancy for no fixed period rent is reserved or paid periodically, a periodic tenancy, rather than a tenancy at will, arises in most jurisdictions by implication.

4. The Tenancy at Sufferance: Holdovers

A tenant who is rightfully in possession but wrongfully remains after termination is called a *tenant at sufferance*, or more simply, a *holdover tenant*. Common law rules give the landlord confronted with a holdover essentially two options—eviction (plus damages) or consent (express or implied) to the creation of a new tenancy. Today many jurisdictions have changed these rules and replaced them with statutory rules the details of which vary. Some statutes specify the length of the holdover tenancy. See, e.g., Cal. Civ. Code § 1945 (West 2020) ("not exceeding one month when the rent is payable monthly, nor in any case one year").

5. A Fifth Leasehold Estate?

KAJO CHURCH SQUARE, INC. v. WALKER
Court of Appeals of Texas, 2003
2003 WL 1848555

GRIFFITH, J. Don and Patsy Walker and Joe and Meriam Eakin (hereinafter collectively referred to as "Appellees") filed a declaratory judgment action in which they pleaded that they had a life estate or a leasehold for life in certain property owned by Kajo Church Square, Inc. and the Kajo Trust (hereinafter collectively referred to as "Kajo"). . . .

Appellees transferred ownership of two parcels of land in Whitehouse, Texas to Grace Covenant Fellowship Church ("Grace" or "church"). Part of the transfer was a gift, and part was a sale. The deed does not include any language which would indicate that the couples had reserved a life estate for themselves. Contemporaneously, the church leased one of the parcels of land back to Appellees. The document stated that the lease would continue in effect until "the date of death of the last of the Lessees to die."

Four years later, the church sold the acreage to Kajo Church Square, Inc. and the church building to Kajo Trust. One week after purchasing the property, Kajo notified Appellees that it was terminating the lease. The two couples filed a declaratory judgment action against Kajo, asking the court to declare the rights and responsibilities of all parties as to the property. They sought a declaratory judgment that they had retained a life estate interest in the property or, in the alternative, that their lease of the property was a lease for life, terminable only upon the death of all four Appellees. They also pleaded that if, in fact, the property interest was a lease, Kajo breached that contract when it gave Appellees notice of termination of that lease. . . .

Appellees filed a motion for summary judgment, as did Kajo. Both motions averred that there were no disputed issues of material fact, and that each of the parties was entitled to judgment as a matter of law. The trial court granted Appellees' motion and denied Kajo's, which decisions Kajo now appeals. . . .

Life Estate, Leasehold for Life, or Tenancy at Will

In its first two issues, Kajo argues that the trial court erred when it construed the nature of Appellees' interest in the property. The cardinal rule applied in construing written instruments, including deeds, is to give effect to the intention of the parties as expressed by the language used by them in the instrument. When the terms of a deed plainly and clearly disclose the intention of the parties, or the language used is not fairly susceptible to more than one interpretation, the intention of the parties must be ascertained by the court as a matter of law from the language used in the writing. . . .

In its [sic] motion for summary judgment Appellees attached the deed transferring ownership of the property from Appellees to Grace. The deed states the following:

> Grantors, for the consideration and subject to the reservations from and exceptions to conveyance and warranty, grant, sell, and convey to Grantees the property, together with all and singular the rights and appurtenances thereto in any wise belonging, to have and hold it to Grantees, Grantees' heirs, executor, administrators, successors, or assigns forever.

Appellees also attached the condition statement signed by Kajo when it purchased the property from Grace. It gives notice to Kajo that the "[s]mall out-building on west side of premises and parking lot between said building and E. Main Street are subject to a life estate use agreement between The Church and previous owners."

As illustrated above, there is no language in the deed of record evidencing Appellees' alleged life estate interest in the property. Further, the deed is not ambiguous; consequently, extrinsic evidence such as the condition statement may not be used to determine the intent of the parties. We hold, therefore, that Appellees failed to conclusively establish that it was entitled to judgment as a matter of law. Because Appellees failed in their burden, it was not necessary for Kajo to show that there was a disputed material fact issue precluding summary judgment. We hold, therefore, that the trial court erred when it granted Appellees' motion on this issue. . . .

Also in its [sic] summary judgment motion, and in the alternative, Appellees maintained that the lease creates a leasehold for life. They attached the lease which they signed concurrently with the transfer of the property to Grace, which states that:

> the said Lessor does by these presents Lease and Devise unto the said Lessee the following described property . . . for the term of January 1, 1996 and ending at the date of death of the last of the Lessees to die. . . .

They also attached the lease assignment between Grace and Kajo, which states:

> Assignee agrees to assume Assignor's obligations under the Lease and to accept the premises in their present "AS IS" condition.

. . . Additionally, Appellees offered the warranty deed from Grace to Kajo as evidence that Kajo accepted the transfer of the property from Appellees to Grace with all encumbrances, including the lease for life. With the above-described evidence, Appellees showed that there was no disputed fact issue as to a lease for life, and that they were entitled to judgment as a matter of law.

However, in its response, Kajo argued that the lease creates no more than a tenancy at will. It cited Nitschke v. Doggett, 489 S.W.2d 335 (Tex. Civ. App.-Austin 1972), vacated on other grounds, 498 S.W.2d 339 (Tex. 1973), for the proposition that the lease document does not, in fact, create a lease or tenancy for life. In *Nitschke*, the court stated the following:

> That we shall die, we know; only the hour of death's arrival is unknown. But, an event certain to occur, but uncertain as to the time of its occurrence, as the death of appellee, may not be used to mark the termination of a lease.

Id. at 337. Consequently, a lease which terminates upon the death of a lessee is a tenancy at will rather than a tenancy for life. . . .

Although there is a dearth of authority to support Kajo's position, it is bolstered by landlord-tenant law, which recognizes only four types of leases: the term of years, the periodic tenancy, the tenancy at will, and the tenancy at sufferance. Thomas W. Merrill and Henry E. Smith, Optimal Standardization in the Law of Property: The Numerus Clausus Principle, 110 Yale L.J. 1, 11 (2000). . . . Thus, a leasehold for life is not a recognized property right. Therefore, as a matter of law, the lease constitutes a tenancy at will. Consequently, the trial court erred when it granted Appellees' motion and denied Kajo's motion on this issue. Accordingly, we hold that Kajo owns the property in fee simple, encumbered only by a tenancy at will. . . .

Breach of Lease

Kajo asserts that its termination of the lease was not a breach of contract. In Kajo's motion in which it sought judgment that it had not breached the lease, Kajo attached a letter to Appellees which provided them notice that it was terminating the lease, and gave Appellees a month in which to vacate the premises. . . .

A tenancy at will is terminable by either party. Therefore, Kajo conclusively established the absence of any genuine question of material fact and that it was entitled to judgment as a matter of law that it was not liable for breach of contract. In response, Appellees asserted that they held a lease for life and that, consequently, Kajo could not lawfully terminate the lease. They attached the lease as evidence that Kajo had breached their contract when it terminated their lease. However, since we hold that the lease is, in fact, a tenancy at will, and because Kajo has the right to terminate the lease and it gave Appellees the requisite notice to do so, Appellees failed in its burden to show that there was a disputed material fact issue precluding summary judgment. Consequently, the trial court erred when it denied Kajo's motion on Appellees' breach of contract claim. . . .

Notes and Questions

1. *The parties' intentions.* When interpreting ambiguous or otherwise unclear language in instruments of voluntary transfers, courts normally try to carry out the intentions of the parties. Did the court do so in *Kajo Church Square*? If not, why not?

2. *A leasehold for life?* When faced with language like that *Kajo Church Square*, most courts react as the Texas court did, by trying to construe the interest as fitting one of the established estate forms (and perhaps in the process doing violence to the parties' intentions). But there have been exceptions. For example, in Garner v. Gerrish, 473 N.E.2d 223 (N.Y. 1984), a lease described its duration this way: "for

> ### A Look Back
>
> Recall the *numerus clausus* principle, which we briefly saw on page 210. This is the principle of standardization—the number of property interests that the law recognized is fixed and closed. No novel property interests will be recognized. Consider how the court's decision in *Kajo Church Square* reflects the *numerus clausus* principle. There is no leasehold for life estate at common law.

A Lease, a License, or What?

The legal nature of some arrangements is often unclear. Consider billboards, for example. Suppose, for example, that A "rents" from B the right to erect a billboard on land owned by B. Is the arrangement a lease, or is it something else, such as a license or still some other legal category? Or what about a cosmetics concession in a department store? In answering such questions, courts look at a number of different variables, including the intention of the parties, the number of restrictions on use, the exclusivity of possession, the degree of control retained by the granting party, the presence or absence of incidental services, and so on. The typical billboard situation creates an easement or a license, not lease, for example, because although there is exclusive possession it doesn't really interfere with the grantor's right of possession in any substantial way. See 1 American Law of Property §§ 3.3-3.8 (1952 & Supp. 1977). Or consider short-term rental platforms such as Airbnb or Vrbo. Are guests who rent through these platforms tenants or licensees or guests? The answer depends on local laws, but generally guests who stay in a home or apartment for more than 30 days may establish rights as a tenant. Why might it matter whether any given arrangement amounts to a lease, as opposed to something else? The answer, for now, has to be limited to a pretty empty generalization: it matters primarily because leases give rise to the landlord-tenant relationship, which carries with it certain incidents—certain rights and duties and liabilities and remedies—that do not attach to other relationships. Those incidents are the chief concern of the balance of this chapter.

and during the term of *quiet enjoyment* from the *first* day of *May*, 1977 which term will end—*Lou Gerrish has the privilege of termination* [sic] *this agreement at a date of his own choice.*" The court held that the language created a unilateral tenancy at will for the life of the tenant (Gerrish). Does that interpretation fit any of the recognized common law estates? The interest could also be called a "determinable life estate," determinable by the tenant. Does that interpretation conform to the parties' intent? In the end, does it matter which interpretation, a tenancy at will or a life estate, the court adopts, so long as it gets closest to what the parties wanted? It may. As we will see later in this chapter, certain rules that protect landlords or tenants do not apply to life estates, which, recall, are freehold estates, unlike leaseholds.

The Lease—Contract or Conveyance?

Here is another question you will see playing a part in much of the material that follows: Is a lease a *conveyance* or a *contract*? Actually, of course, it is both. A lease transfers a possessory interest in land, so it is a conveyance that creates property rights. But it is also the case that leases usually contain a number of promises (or covenants, which originally referred to promises under seal)—such as a promise by the tenant to pay rent or a promise by the landlord to provide utilities—so the lease is a contract, too, thus creating contract rights. Historically, it was lease-as-conveyance that the courts tended to stress, but over the last several decades this has changed, to some degree, in favor of a view emphasizing the contractual nature of leases. The objective of the new orientation has been to reform the "property law" of landlord and tenant by importing into it much of the modern law of contracts. Courts today commonly rely, explicitly, on contract principles to reshape the law of leases with respect to such questions as the following: (1) Are the covenants in leases "mutually dependent," such that (as in contract doctrine) a material breach by one party excuses further performance by the other party, even if the lease does not so provide? (2) If the tenant wrongfully abandons the leased premises, must the landlord take steps to mitigate (reduce) the damages, say by searching for a suitable new tenant? (3) Is a warranty of quality—that the leased premises are habitable or fit for their purpose—to be implied in leases? We shall be addressing questions like these in subsequent sections of this chapter.

The Statute of Frauds. Every state has a Statute of Frauds patterned in one way or another after the English Statute of Frauds enacted in the seventeenth century. Commonly, the American statutes provide that leases for more than one year must be in writing. All but a few jurisdictions permit oral leases for a term less than a year; those that do not usually hold that entry under an oral lease plus payment of rent creates a periodic tenancy that is not subject to the statute.

Form leases and the question of "bargaining power." The written lease can be a long document. Unlike a deed, by which (in the usual case) all of the seller's interest is conveyed to the buyer forever, a lease contemplates a continuing relationship between landlord and tenant. Thus deeds are commonly brief, whereas leases can be wordy, full of clauses to handle various contingencies. Quite typically, landlords use form leases—standardized documents offered to all tenants on a take-it-or-leave-it basis, with no negotiation over terms. Does this indicate that tenants lack bargaining power, such that harsh terms can be forced upon them by landlords? Some commentators argue that the motives behind adhesion contracts are not necessarily sinister. The reason may simply be that the seller is trying to avoid the costs of negotiating and drafting a separate agreement with each purchaser. "[W]hat is important is not whether there is haggling in every transaction but whether competition forces sellers to incorporate in their standard contracts terms that protect the purchasers." Richard A. Posner, Economic Analysis of Law 125 (9th ed. 2014). On this view, the underlying problem is not form leases but monopoly power—created, say, by a shortage of rental housing.

The sharing economy and rental housing. One of the striking developments in the American economy in recent years has been the rise of the so-called sharing economy, defined as short-term peer-to-peer transactions to share use of idle assets and services or to facilitate collaboration. The basic model involves an on-line platform that pairs people with some asset to be shared, such as space in a car (e.g., Lyft or Uber) or, in the housing sector (e.g., Airbnb, Vrbo), a room or an apartment to occupy for short stays. The costs and benefits of the sharing economy have been widely debated, with advocates arguing that it works to reduce the carbon footprint of consumption while critics point to the ways in which it undermines consumer welfare protection as well as labor and employment rights.

In the housing sector, the sharing model has been criticized for potentially reducing the supply of available housing, especially in tight markets. Critics have also pointed to safety concerns. Some local governments have taken steps to limit the amount of shared housing. See, e.g., N.Y. Dwelling Law § 4(8)(a) (making it illegal in certain types of buildings for residents to have paying guests for fewer than 30 consecutive days). Shared housing arrangements such as Airbnb have raised several legal issues. For example, do they violate lease covenants? The courts are divided on the question. Some courts find short-term rentals to be compatible with "residential use" and not a violation of such restrictive covenants. See Wilkinson v. Chiwawa Communities Assn., 327 P.3d 614 (Wash. 2014); Santa Monica Beach Property Owners Assn. v. Acord, 219 So. 3d 111 (Fla. Dist. Ct. App. 2017). Other courts have held that short-term rentals violate covenants that restrict the property to "residential use," finding them to be closer to hotel use and thus commercial in nature. See Vonderhaar v. Lakeside Place Homeowners Assn., 2014 WL 3887913 (Ky. App. 2014).

B. SELECTION OF TENANTS AND FAIR HOUSING LAW

Landlords, once free to discriminate as they wished in selecting tenants—whether on grounds of race, gender, national origin, or whatever—are today constrained in a number of respects. Perhaps the most significant constraints (but not, as we shall see, the only ones) are imposed by the federal Fair Housing Act, 42 U.S.C.A. §§ 3601-3619, 3631, originally enacted in 1968 and amended several times since. Portions of the legislation provide as follows:

§ 3603. [Exemptions]

(a) Application to certain described dwellings
Subject to the provisions of subsection (b) of this section and section 3607 of this title [section 3607 exempts religious organizations and private clubs under certain circumstances, and also states that provisions regarding familial status do not apply to housing for older persons], the prohibitions against discrimination in the sale or rental of housing set forth in section 3604 of this title shall apply. . . .

(b) Exemptions
Nothing in section 3604 of this title (other than subsection (c)) shall apply to—

(1) any single-family house sold or rented by an owner: *Provided*, That such private individual owner does not own more than three such single-family houses at any one time. . . . *Provided further*, That after December 31, 1969, the sale or rental of any such single-family house shall be excepted from the application of this subchapter only if such house is sold or rented (A) without the use in any manner of the sales or rental facilities or the sales or rental services of any real estate broker, agent, or salesman, or of such facilities or services of any person in the business of selling or renting dwellings, or of any employee or agent of any such broker, agent, salesman, or person and (B) without the publication, posting or mailing, after notice, of any advertisement or written notice in violation of section 3604(c) of this title; but nothing in this proviso shall prohibit the use of attorneys, escrow agents, abstractors, title companies, and other such professional assistance as necessary to perfect or transfer the title, or

(2) rooms or units in dwellings containing living quarters occupied or intended to be occupied by no more than four families living independently of each other, if the owner actually maintains and occupies one of such living quarters as his residence. . . .

§ 3604. Discrimination in the Sale or Rental of Housing and Other Prohibited Practices

As made applicable by section 3603 of this title and except as exempted by sections 3603(b) and 3607 of this title, it shall be unlawful—

(a) To refuse to sell or rent after the making of a bona fide offer, or to refuse to negotiate for the sale or rental of, or otherwise make unavailable or deny, a dwelling to any person because of race, color, religion, sex, familial status, or national origin.

(b) To discriminate against any person in the terms, conditions, or privileges of sale or rental of a dwelling, or in the provision of services or facilities in connection therewith, because of race, color, religion, sex, familial status, or national origin.

(c) To make, print, or publish, or cause to be made, printed, or published any notice, statement, or advertisement, with respect to the sale or rental of a dwelling that indicates any preference, limitation, or discrimination based on race, color, religion, sex, handicap, familial status, or national origin, or an intention to make any such preference, limitation, or discrimination. . . .

(f)(1) To discriminate in the sale or rental, or to otherwise make unavailable or deny, a dwelling to any buyer or renter because of a handicap . . .

(2) To discriminate against any person in the terms, conditions, or privileges of sale or rental of a dwelling, or in the provision of services or facilities in connection with such dwelling, because of a handicap . . .

(3) For purposes of this subsection, discrimination includes—

(A) a refusal to permit, at the expense of the handicapped person, reasonable modifications of existing premises occupied or to be occupied by such person if such modifications may be necessary to afford such person full enjoyment of the premises except that, in the case of a rental, the landlord may where it is reasonable to do so condition permission for a modification on the renter agreeing to restore the interior of the premises to the condition that existed before the modification, reasonable wear and tear excepted;

(B) a refusal to make reasonable accommodations in rules, policies, practices, or services, when such accommodations may be necessary to afford such person equal opportunity to use and enjoy a dwelling; or

(C) in connection with the design and construction of covered multifamily dwellings for first occupancy after the date that is 30 months after September 13, 1988, a failure to design and construct those dwellings in such a manner that [common and public areas of the dwellings are readily accessible to handicapped persons, doors within the dwellings are wide enough for wheelchairs, and other features of "adaptive design," such as easily reached light switches, are provided].

Notes and Questions

1. *Other aspects of the Fair Housing Act.* Portions of the Fair Housing Act not set out above prohibit discrimination in the financing of housing and in the provision of brokerage services. Anyone injured by a discriminatory practice may commence a civil suit for injunctive relief and damages (including punitive damages). Other enforcement measures include conference and conciliation proceedings, suits by the U.S. Attorney General, and criminal penalties.

2. *Civil Rights Act of 1866.* Attempts by the federal government to combat discrimination, *racial* discrimination in particular, date back to adoption of the Fourteenth Amendment and its guarantee of equal protection. The Fourteenth Amendment prohibits only state (not private) action, but the Supreme Court's decision in Shelley v. Kraemer, 334 U.S. 1 (1948), effectively eliminated at least some private discrimination as well. (In *Shelley*, which we will study in Chapter 10, at page 540, the Court held that state courts could not enforce racially restrictive land use agreements entered into by neighbors.) Much earlier, a section of the Civil Rights Act of 1866, 42 U.S.C.A. § 1982, had promised to do more, at least with respect to property transactions. It provided:

> All citizens of the United States shall have the same right, in every State and Territory, as is enjoyed by white citizens thereof to inherit, purchase, lease, sell, hold, and convey real and personal property.

This measure had essentially no impact on private housing discrimination during the first century of its life, but the situation changed with Jones v. Alfred H. Mayer Co., 392 U.S. 409 (1968), decided the same year the original Fair Housing Act became law. In *Jones*, the Court held that the 1866 provision bars *all* racial discrimination, private and public, in the sale or rental of property. The 1866 law is narrower than the Fair Housing Act in that it reaches only racial discrimination, does not deal with discrimination in the provision of services and facilities, and does not prohibit discriminatory advertising; it is broader, however, in that it is not limited to dwellings and contains none of the exemptions found in the Fair Housing Act.

3. *Is proof of discriminatory intent required?* A discriminatory motive need not be proved in order to make out a prima facie case under the Fair Housing Act; proof of *disparate impact* or *disparate treatment* is sufficient. The Supreme Court

Sidebar

During congressional deliberations on the Fair Housing Act, the exemptions were discussed in terms of "an imagined 'Mrs. Murphy's boardinghouse,' run by a Mrs. Murphy who did not wish to rent to Blacks." Diane J. Klein & Charles Doskow, Housingdiscrimination.Com?: The Ninth Circuit (Mostly) Puts Out the Welcome Mat for Fair Housing Suits Against Roommate-Matching Websites, 38 Golden Gate U. L. Rev. 329, 334 n.17 (2008).

confirmed the availability of disparate impact proof in Texas Department of Housing and Community Affairs v. The Inclusive Communities Project, 135 S. Ct. 2507 (2015). *Disparate impact* claims allege that the defendant's actions have a disproportionate, exclusionary impact on members of a protected group and that such impact is not justified by a legitimate business or governmental purpose. *Disparate treatment* cases assert that the defendant has intentionally treated members of a protected class differently from others with the effect of denying particular persons housing opportunities. In disparate treatment cases, courts often use a three-part approach: (1) the plaintiff establishes a prima facie case of discrimination; (2) the burden then shifts to the defendant to prove a legitimate, non-discriminatory reason for the conduct; and (3) if the defendant satisfies the burden under step 2, then the plaintiff must show that the defendant's reason is merely pretextual. Claims under the Civil Rights Act of 1866 probably do require proof of intentional or purposeful discrimination. On the use of testers to show discrimination, see Teresa Coleman Hunter & Gary L. Fischer, Fair Housing Testing—Uncovering Discriminatory Practices, 28 Creighton L. Rev. 1127 (1995).

4. *Problems on the Fair Housing Act and the Civil Rights Act of 1866.* In the wake of the 1968 Fair Housing Act and Jones v. Alfred H. Mayer Co. (see Note 2), courts considered a variety of cases involving facts that tested the limits of 1968 and 1866 Acts. The following problems illustrate some of those factual circumstances.

(a) Ms. Smith has an apartment to rent in her home. She puts the following advertisement in a local newspaper:

> *For rent:* Furnished basement apartment in private White home. Call 376-7410.

An African American couple applies and is rejected by Ms. Smith because of race. Are there any violations of 42 U.S.C.A § 1982 or § 3604? See United States v. Hunter, 459 F.2d 205 (4th Cir.), cert. denied, 409 U.S. 934 (1972) (discriminatory advertisement). Suppose the advertisement had not contained the word "white." What result? See Bush v. Kaim, 297 F. Supp. 151 (N.D. Ohio 1969) (discussing discriminatory actions). Suppose the advertisement had not said "in private White home," but had said "rented only to persons speaking Polish, German, or Swedish." What result? See Holmgren v. Little Village Community Reporter, 342 F. Supp. 512 (N.D. Ill. 1971) (discrimination based on national origin).

(b) Suppose Ms. Smith discriminates *against*, say, German people in renting the apartment in her home. This would not violate the Fair Housing Act. Do you see why? Would it violate the Civil Rights Act of 1866, 42 U.S.C.A § 1982? See Shaare Tefila Congregation v. Cobb, 481 U.S. 615 (1987) (taking "race" to mean what it meant in 1866).

(c) Suppose that *L* places the following advertisement in a campus newspaper: "Wanted: Female to share 2-bdrm. 2-bath apt. near campus. $500/mo. plus half utilities. Call Pat at 917-4513." Does this language violate the federal Fair Housing Act (should it matter whether Pat is a single woman looking for a roommate)? The advertisement aside, may Pat discriminate in selecting someone with whom to share the apartment and the rent? Does the answer turn on whether the "2-bdrm. 2-bath apt." is in a large multi-unit complex or, instead, is one of two apartments in an owner-occupied duplex? See Fair Housing Council of San Fernando Valley v. Roommate.com, LLC., 666 F.3d 1216 (9th Cir. 2012). In *Roommate.com*, the court held that the Fair Housing Act does not regulate roommate choices or advertisements expressing preferences with respect to roommates. The court interpreted "dwelling" as not including shared living spaces. The court stated, "[I]t's not unlawful to discriminate in selecting a roommate." Does this mean that it's okay to reject a potential roommate on the basis of race?

(d) Housing advertising is increasingly handled on-line. Advertisements posted on-line generally are covered by § 3604(c), even if the underlying transaction falls within the § 3603(b) exemption. A 2010 study of about 10,000 Craigslist ads in 10 cities found that "a significant number of on-line housing ads — roughly several hundred on any given day — violate [§ 3604(c)]." Rigel C. Oliveri, Discriminatory Housing Advertisements On-Line: Lessons from Craigslist, 43 Ind. L. Rev. 1125, 1127-1128 (2010).

For an insightful and sensitive discussion of how on-line rental advertising can lead to subsequent problems of communication between landlords and African Americans looking for housing, see the blog post by Professor Lolita Buckner Inniss, Ain't I a Feminist Legal Scholar Too? Dialing Mrs. Murphy (Or, Me Talk Pretty One Day), Nov. 20, 2008, available at http://innissfls.blogspot.com/2008/11/dialing-mrs-murphy-or-me-talk-pretty-one-day/ (discussing the experience of "phone passing").

(e) Suppose the owner of a large apartment complex reserves a certain number of units exclusively for white applicants, the objective being to guard against "white flight" and thus maintain integrated housing conditions. Does the practice violate the Fair Housing Act? See United States v. Starrett City Associates, 840 F.2d 1096 (2d Cir.), cert. denied, 488 U.S. 946 (1988).

5. *Discrimination on grounds other than race, religion, or national origin.* As originally enacted in 1968, the Fair Housing Act did not prohibit discrimination on the grounds of sex, handicap, or familial status. Sex discrimination was added to the act in 1974; amendments in 1988 added the prohibitions regarding familial status and handicapped persons. The discussion below suggests how the courts have resolved common allegations involving these sorts of discrimination.

▶ *Discrimination based on family status and on sex*

(a) Landlords, a retired couple, have eight single family houses for rent. They limit the number of occupants in each house depending upon its size, number of bedrooms, layout, and yard size. Their business strategy is to maintain their houses well and to rent them for slightly below market in order to give tenants an incentive to stay, thereby avoiding turnover. One of their houses is a 1,200-square-foot house, consisting of a living room, master bedroom, another 10 × 10 bedroom, two baths, a den opening directly into the living room (which could be used as a bedroom), and very little yard. The landlords limit occupancy of this house to four persons and refuse to rent to a couple with three children. See Pfaff v. H.U.D., 88 F.3d 739 (9th Cir. 1996) (even if the numerical occupancy limitations have a disparate impact on families with children, they could be justified on the ground of maintaining the economic value of the property).

(b) *L* regularly rents one-bedroom apartments to households consisting of two adults, and two-bedroom apartments to households of two adults and two children, but will not rent one-bedroom units to one adult and one child, nor two-bedroom units to one adult and three children. See Glover v. Crestwood Lake Section 1 Holding Corps., 746 F. Supp. 301 (S.D.N.Y. 1990) (practice described violates prohibition against discrimination based on familial status).

(c) *L* refuses to rent to a heterosexual couple because they are unmarried. See James A. Kushner, The Fair Housing Amendments Act of 1988: The Second Generation of Fair Housing, 42 Vand. L. Rev. 1049, 1106-1107 (1989) (refusal to rent to unmarried couples is clearly not covered by the FHA unless it can be demonstrated to have a disproportionate racial, ethnic, religious, or gender-based impact; the act does not cover discrimination on the basis of marital status).

(d) *L* refuses to rent to a gay couple because he objects to the partners' sexual orientation. See Kushner, supra, at 1108 (the FHA does not prohibit sexual-orientation discrimination).

(e) *L* rents to a woman who lived with her husband and four children in low income housing. *L* subjects her to what the court described as "unwelcome sexual harassment," including unwanted sexual touching, making sexually suggestive comments, rubbing his genitals in front of her, and calling her repeatedly in the middle of the night. When she asks to be released from the lease and for her deposit to be returned, *L* "flutter[s] his hand against [*T*'s] stomach" and says, "My eagle eyes have not seen everything yet." In Quigley v. Winter, 598 F.3d 938 (8th Cir. 2010), the court concluded that hostile housing environments are actionable under the FHA and there was sufficient evidence to support the jury's verdict that such a hostile environment existed here.

(f) Many homeless shelters and battered women's shelters operate on a single-sex basis, and some place restrictions on familial status. Do these restrictions violate the Fair Housing Act? Notice that the language of the statute speaks of "dwellings." That term, in turn, is defined in terms of a "residence." 42 U.S.C.A. § 3602. Are homeless shelters and battered women's shelters "dwellings" or "residences" within the meaning of the FHA? See Turning Point, Inc. v. City of Caldwell, 74 F.3d 941, 942 (9th Cir. 1996) (applying the FHA to a shelter); but see Community House, Inc. v. City of Boise, 490 F.3d 1041, 1044 n.2 (9th Cir. 2007) ("We have never squarely addressed the issue of whether all temporary shelters fit within the Act's definition of 'dwelling,' see 42 U.S.C. § 3602(b); nevertheless, we decline to do so here.").

▶ *Discrimination based on "handicap"*

"Handicap" is defined by § 3602(h) of the Fair Housing Act, which states that the term means "a physical or mental impairment which substantially limits one or more of [the handicapped person's] major life activities, a record of having such an impairment, or being regarded as having such an impairment, but such term does not include current, illegal use of or addiction to a controlled substance." Proposed amendments that would have excluded alcoholism and infectious, contagious, and communicable diseases from the definition failed to pass.

(g) *L* wants to evict *T* because *T* has a mental disability that results in seemingly threatening behavior. See Roe v. Housing Authority of the City of Boulder, 909 F. Supp. 814 (D. Colo. 1995) (dwellings need not be made available to people whose condition would create a direct threat to the health and safety of others or result in substantial damage to property, but landlords must try to make reasonable accommodations).

(h) *L*, owner of an apartment building with a no-pets policy, refuses to allow *T* to have a dog in his apartment. *T*, who has HIV/AIDS, suffers from resulting depression, anxiety, and isolation and depends on his dog as a companion. See Massachusetts Commission Against Discrimination v. Brighton Gardens Apartments, LP, Massachusetts Commission Against Discrimination, Mass. Lawyers Weekly, Apr. 1, 2011, available at https://masslawyersweekly.com/2011/04/01/landlord-and-tenant-reasonable-accommodation-emotional-support-dog/ (HIV/AIDS is a "handicap" for Fair Housing Act purposes and landlord must make reasonable accommodation, meaning here keeping his emotional support dog).

(i) *T*'s emotional support dog, trained as a guard dog, displayed aggressive behavior toward other dogs and other tenants, lunging forward, flaring up, and baring teeth. Other tenants in the apartment complex were afraid of the dog, staying inside when the dog was outside. *L* sought to terminate the lease for violation of a no-pets policy. See Gill Terrace Retirement Apts., Inc. v. Johnson, 177 A.3d 1087 (Vt. 2017) (reasonable accommodation did not require permitting the dog where the animal posed a direct threat to the safety or health of others or would cause substantial physical damage to the property of others).

6. *State and local legislation.* Many states and localities prohibit discrimination in the sale or leasing of housing. State and local measures may not, of course, operate to narrow the rights and remedies available under federal law, but they may and sometimes do have a broader reach, covering, for example, discrimination based on age, sexual orientation, marital status—and, at least in Austin, Texas, status as a student! Once again, the discussion below suggests the range of problems and judicial responses.

(a) *L* owns an apartment building in an area where state and local law forbid discrimination on the basis of marital status. *L* refuses because of religious convictions to rent a unit to an unmarried couple and argues that to enforce the state and local measures would constitute an unconstitutional interference with his right to free exercise of religion. What result? See Smith v. Fair Employment & Housing Commission, 913 P.2d 909 (Cal. 1996); Swanner v. Anchorage Equal Rights Commission, 874 P.2d 274 (Alaska 1994) (*Smith* and *Swanner* both held that the freedom of religion clause of the Constitution does not exempt landlords from complying with a neutral law of general applicability); Note, The Religious Landlord and the Conflict Between Free Exercise Rights and Housing Discrimination Laws—Which Interest Prevails? 47 Hastings L.J. 1669 (1996).

(b) *T* leases a house from *L* and under the lease is authorized to sublease to others as housemates. *S* applies to *T* as housemate, but *L* refuses when she learns that *S* is a lesbian. *S* files a complaint with the local Equal Opportunity Commission alleging discrimination on the basis of sexual orientation. See State ex rel. Sprague v. City of Madison, 555 N.W.2d 409 (Wis. App. 1996) (holding that the local city ordinance unambiguously prohibits refusal to rent to any person because of that person's sexual orientation and that the ordinance applied here).

C. SUBLEASES AND ASSIGNMENTS

The tenant's interest is, as we have seen, an estate, and as such, it is generally transferable to third parties. This is in keeping with the common law's basic policy favoring alienability of property interests. There are two types of tenant transfers to third parties: *subleases* and *assignments*. The distinction between the two can have important legal consequences, as the next case illustrates.

ERNST v. CONDITT

Court of Appeals of Tennessee, 1964
390 S.W.2d 703

CHATTIN, J. Complainants, B. Walter Ernst and wife, Emily Ernst, leased a certain tract of land in Davidson County, Tennessee, to Frank D. Rogers on June 18, 1960, for a term of one year and seven days, commencing on June 23, 1960.

Rogers went into possession of the property and constructed an asphalt race track and enclosed the premises with a fence. He also constructed other improvements thereon such as floodlights for use in the operation of a Go-Cart track.

We quote these paragraphs of the lease pertinent to the question for consideration in this controversy:

3. Lessee covenants to pay as rent for said leased premises the sum of $4,200 per annum, payable at the rate of $350 per month or 15% of all gross receipts, whether from sales or services occurring on the leased premises, whichever is the larger amount. The gross receipts shall be computed on a quarterly basis and if any amount in addition to the $350 per month is due, such payment shall be made immediately after the quarterly computation. All payments shall be payable to the office of Lessors' agent, Guaranty Mortgage Company, at 316 Union Street, Nashville, Tennessee, on the first day of each month in advance. Lessee shall have the first right to refusal in the event Lessors desire to lease said premises for a period of time commencing immediately after the termination date hereof. . . .

5. Lessee shall have no right to assign or sublet the leased premises without prior written approval of Lessors. In the event of any assignment or sublease, Lessee is still liable to perform the covenants of this lease, including the covenant to pay rent, and nothing herein shall be construed as releasing Lessee from his liabilities and obligations hereunder. . . .

9. Lessee agrees that upon termination of this contract, or any extensions or renewals thereof, that all improvements above the ground will be moved at Lessee's expense and the property cleared. This shall not be construed as removing or digging up any surface paving; but if any pits or holes are dug, they shall be leveled at Lessors' request.

Rogers operated the business for a short time. In July, 1960, he entered into negotiations with the defendant, A.K. Conditt, for the sale of the business to him. During these negotiations, the question of the term of the lease arose. Defendant desired a two-year lease of the property. He and Rogers went to the home of complainants and negotiated an extension of the term of the lease which resulted in the following amendment to the lease, and the sublease or assignment of the lease as amended to Conditt by Rogers:

> By mutual consent of the parties, the lease executed the 18th day of June 1960, between B. Walter Ernst and wife, Emily H. Ernst, as Lessors, and Frank D. Rogers as Lessee, is amended as follows:
>
> 1. Paragraph 2 of said lease is amended so as to provide that the term will end July 31, 1962 and not June 30, 1961.
>
> 2. The minimum rent of $350 per month called for in paragraph 3 of said lease shall be payable by the month and the percentage rental called for by said lease shall be payable on the first day of the month following the month for which the percentage is computed. In computing gross receipts, no deduction or credit shall be given the Lessee for the payment of sales taxes or any other assessments by governmental agencies.
>
> 3. Lessee agrees that on or prior to April 1, 1961, the portion of the property covered by this lease, consisting of about one acre, which is not presently devoted to business purposes will be used for business purposes and the percentage rent called for by paragraph 3 of the original lease will be paid on the gross receipts derived therefrom. In the event of the failure of the Lessee to devote the balance of said property to a business purpose on or before April 1, 1961, then this lease shall terminate as to such portion of the property.
>
> 4. Lessee agrees to save the Lessor harmless for any damage to the property of the lessor, whether included in this lease or not, which results from the use of the leased property by the Lessee or its customers or invitees. Lessee will erect or cause to be erected four (4) "No Parking" signs on the adjoining property of the Lessor not leased by it.
>
> 5. Lessor hereby consents to the subletting of the premises to A.K. Conditt, but upon the express condition and understanding that the original Lessee, Frank D. Rogers, will remain personally liable for the faithful performance of all the terms and conditions of the original lease and of this amendment to the original lease.
>
> Except as modified by this amendment, all terms and conditions of the original lease dated the 18th day of June, 1960, by and between the parties shall remain in full force and effect.
>
> In witness whereof the parties have executed this amendment to lease on this the 4th day of August, 1960.
>
> > *B. Walter Ernst*
> > *Emily H. Ernst*
> > Lessors
> > *Frank D. Rogers*
> > Lessee

For value received and in consideration of the promise to faithfully perform all conditions of the within lease as amended, I hereby sublet the premises to A.K. Conditt upon the understanding that I will individually remain liable for the performance of the lease.

This 4th day of Aug, 1960.

Frank D. Rogers
Frank D. Rogers

The foregoing subletting of the premises is accepted, this the 4th day of Aug, 1960.

A.K. Conditt
A.K. Conditt

Conditt operated the Go-Cart track from August until November, 1960. He paid the rent for the months of August, September and October, 1960, directly to complainants. In December, 1960, complainants contacted defendant with reference to the November rent and at that time defendant stated he had been advised he was not liable to them for rent. However, defendant paid the basic monthly rental of $350.00 to complainants in June, 1961. This was the final payment received by complainants during the term of the lease as amended. The record is not clear whether defendant continued to operate the business after the last payment of rent or abandoned it. Defendant, however, remained in possession of the property until the expiration of the leasehold.

On July 10, 1962, complainants, through their Attorneys, notified Conditt by letter the lease would expire as of midnight July 31, 1962, and they were demanding a settlement of the past due rent and unless the improvements on the property were removed by him as provided in paragraph 9 of the original lease, then, in that event, they would have same removed at his expense. Defendant did not reply to this demand.

On August 1, 1962, complainants filed their bill in this cause seeking a recovery of $2,404.58 which they alleged was the balance due on the basic rent of $350.00 per month for the first year of the lease and the sum of $4,200.00, the basic rent for the second year, and the further sum necessary for the removal of the improvements constructed on the property.

The theory of the bill is that the agreement between Rogers, the original lessee, and the defendant, Conditt, is an assignment of the lease; and, therefore, defendant is directly and primarily liable to complainants.

The defendant by his answer insists the agreement between Rogers and himself is a sublease and therefore Rogers is directly and primarily liable to complainants.

The Chancellor heard the matter on the depositions of both complainants and three other witnesses offered in behalf of complainants and documentary evidence filed in the record. The defendant did not testify nor did he offer any evidence in his behalf.

The Chancellor found the instrument to be an assignment. A decree was entered sustaining the bill and entering judgment for complainants in the sum of $6,904.58 against defendant.

Defendant has appealed to this Court and has assigned errors insisting the Chancellor erred in failing to hold the instrument to be a sublease rather than an assignment.

To support his theory the instrument is a sublease, the defendant insists the amendment to the lease entered into between Rogers and complainants was for the express purpose of extending the term of the lease and obtaining the consent of the lessors to a "subletting" of the premises to defendant. That by the use of the words "sublet" and "subletting" no other construction can be placed on the amendment and the agreement of Rogers and the acceptance of defendant attached thereto.

Further, since complainants agreed to the subletting of the premises to defendant "upon the express condition and understanding that the original lessee, Frank D. Rogers, will remain personally liable for the faithful performance of all the terms and conditions of the original lease and this amendment to the original lease," no construction can be placed upon this language other than it was the intention of complainants to hold Rogers primarily liable for the performance of the original lease and the amendment thereto. And, therefore, Rogers, for his own protection, would have the implied right to re-enter and perform the lease in the event of a default on the part of the defendant. This being true, Rogers retained a reversionary interest in the property sufficient to satisfy the legal distinction between a sublease and an assignment of a lease.

It is then urged the following rules of construction of written instruments support the above argument:

> Where words or terms having a definite legal meaning and effect are knowingly used in a written instrument the parties thereto will be presumed to have intended such words or terms to have their proper legal meaning and effect, in the absence of any contrary intention appearing in the instrument. [12 Am. Jur., Contracts, Section 238.]
>
> Technical terms or words of art will be given their technical meaning unless the context, or local usage shows a contrary intention. [3 Williston on Contracts, Section 68, Sub S. 2.]

As stated in complainants' brief, the liability of defendant to complainants depends upon whether the transfer of the leasehold interest in the premises from Rogers is an assignment of the lease or a sublease. If the transfer is a sublease, no privity of contract exists between complainants and defendant; and, therefore, defendant could not be liable to complainants on the covenant to pay rent and the expense of the removal of the improvements. But, if the transfer is an assignment of the lease, privity of contract does exist between complainants and defendant; and defendant would be liable directly and primarily for the amount of the judgment. . . .

The general rule as to the distinction between an assignment of a lease and a sublease is an assignment conveys the whole term, leaving no interest nor reversionary interest in the grantor or assignor. Whereas, a sublease may be generally defined as a transaction whereby a tenant grants an interest in the leased premises less than his own, or reserves to himself a reversionary interest in the term.

The common law distinction between an assignment of a lease and a sublease is succinctly stated in the case of Jaber v. Miller, 219 Ark. 59, 239 S.W.2d 760: "If the instrument purports to transfer the lessee's estate for the entire remainder of his term it is an assignment, regardless of its form or the parties' intention. Conversely, if the

Sidebar

Whoops! Where the opinion reads "privity of *contract*," substitute the words "privity of *estate*." Privity of estate is what the court means to say; the problems on page 305 explore the distinction between the two concepts.

instrument purports to transfer the lessee's estate for less than the entire term — even for a day less — it is a sublease, regardless of its form or of the parties' intention."

The modern rule which has been adopted in this State for construing written instruments is stated in the case of City of Nashville v. Lawrence, 153 Tenn. 606, 284 S.W. 882: "The cardinal rule to be followed in this state, in construing deeds and other written instruments, is to ascertain the intention of the parties."

In Williams v. Williams, 84 Tenn. 164, 171, it was said: "We have most wisely abandoned technical rules in the construction of conveyances in this State, and look to the intention of the instrument alone for our guide, that intention to be arrived at from the language of the instrument read in the light of the surrounding circumstances." . . .

It is our opinion under either the common law or modern rule of construction the agreement between Rogers and defendant is an assignment of the lease.

The fact that Rogers expressly agreed to remain liable to complainants for the performance of the lease did not create a reversion nor a right to re-enter in Rogers either express or implied. The obligations and liabilities of a lessee to a lessor, under the express covenants of a lease, are not in anywise affected by an assignment or a subletting to a third party, in the absence of an express or implied agreement or some action on his part which amounts to a waiver or estops him from insisting upon compliance with the covenants. This is true even though the assignment or sublease is made with the consent of the lessor. By an assignment of a lease the privity of estate between the lessor and lessee is terminated, but the privity of contract between them still remains and is unaffected. Neither the privity of estate or contract between the lessor and lessee are affected by a sublease. 32 Am. Jur., Landlord and Tenant, Sections 356, 413, pages 310, 339.

Thus the express agreement of Rogers to remain personally liable for the performance of the covenants of the lease created no greater obligation on his part or interest in the leasehold, other than as set forth in the original lease.

The argument that since the agreement between Rogers and defendant contains the words, "sublet" and "subletting" is conclusive the instrument is to be construed as a sublease is, we think, unsound.

> A consent to sublet has been held to include the consent to assign or mortgage the lease; and a consent to assign has been held to authorize a subletting. [51 C.J.S. Landlord and Tenant §36, page 552.]

Prior to the consummation of the sale of the Go-Cart business to defendant, he insisted upon the execution of the amendment to the lease extending the term of the original lease. For value received and on the promise of the defendant to perform all of the conditions of the lease as amended, Rogers parted with his entire interest in the property. Defendant went into possession of the property and paid the rent to complainants. He remained in possession of the property for the entire term. By virtue of the sale of the business, defendant became the owner of the improvements with the right to their removal at the expiration of the lease.

Rogers reserved no part or interest in the lease; nor did he reserve a right of re-entry in event of a breach of any of the conditions or covenants of the lease on the part of defendant.

It is our opinion the defendant, under the terms of the agreement with Rogers, had a right to the possession of the property for the entire term of the lease as amended, including the right to remove the improvements after the expiration of the lease. Rogers merely agreed to become personally liable for the rent and the expense of the removal of the improvements upon the default of defendant. He neither expressly, nor by implication, reserved the right to re-enter for a condition broken by defendant.

Thus, we are of the opinion the use of the words, "sublet" and "subletting" is not conclusive of the construction to be placed on the instrument in the case; it plainly appearing from the context of the instrument and the facts and circumstances surrounding the execution of it the parties thereto intended an assignment rather than a sublease.

It results that the assignments are overruled and the decree of the Chancellor is affirmed with costs.

Notes and Problems

1. *The sublease/assignment distinction—why did it matter?* Both the parties and the court agreed that the result of the case turned on whether the transfer from Rogers to Conditt was a sublease or an assignment. Do you see why it mattered whether the transfer was one or the other? Let's trace the legal relations among all three parties, Ernst, Rogers, and Conditt, in terms of privity of contract and privity of estate first if the transfer was a sublease, then an assignment:

2. *Sublease or assignment: two tests.* The *Ernst* case indicates the two tests courts have used to determine whether a transfer from a lessee to a third party is a sublease or an assignment. The first (and most commonly used) test is formalistic: an *assignment* arises when the lessee transfers his entire interest under the lease—when, that is, he transfers the right to possession for the duration of the term. If the lessee transfers anything less than his entire interest (if two years remain on the lease and the lessee transfers for a term of one year), a *sublease* results. In the latter case, the lessee is said to have retained a reversion; the right to possession goes back (reverts) to him at the end of the period designated in the transfer. Suppose the lessee transfers all of his interest in some physical part of the premises; is this a sublease or a partial assignment? Most courts, quite correctly, say the latter. Suppose the lessee transfers his entire interest, but the instrument of transfer provides that if the transferee breaches any obligation of the lease, the original lessee may terminate the arrangement and retake possession (such a provision is called a power of termination or right of re-entry). A substantial minority of jurisdictions finds a sublease in this situation.

The second (and less common) test considers the intention of the parties. The actual words used—*sublease* or *assignment*—are not conclusive (witness the *Ernst* case), though they may be persuasive (except in those cases, hardly unheard of, when both terms are used). Indeed, one occasionally gets the impression that courts claiming to honor the intention of the parties are in fact doing nothing more than inferring that "intention" from use of the words *sublease* or *assignment,* without the slightest basis for assuming that the parties knew the consequences of what they were saying. See, e.g., Jaber v. Miller, 239 S.W.2d 760 (Ark. 1951).

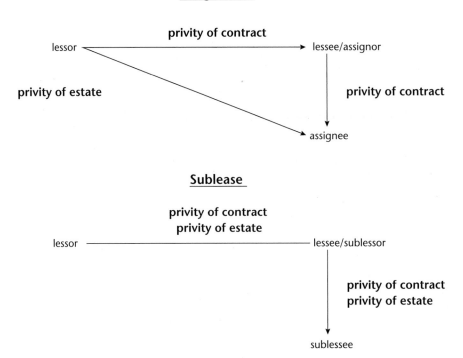

3. *Third-party beneficiary contract.* Restatement (Second) of Property, Landlord and Tenant, § 16.1 comment c at 120-121 (1977) provides as follows:

> At the time a transfer of an interest in the leased property is made, the transferor may exact a promise from the transferee that he will perform the promises in the lease which were made by the transferor. The exaction of such a promise does not relieve the transferor of liability on his promises. It does give him a direct remedy against his transferee if the transferee fails to perform the promises, which remedy will continue to be available even after the transferee has transferred the interest to someone else. If the holder of the benefits of the promises made by the transferor acquires enforcement rights as a third party beneficiary against the transferee by virtue of the transferee's promise to the transferor, then the transferee is in privity of contract with such third party beneficiary and a subsequent transfer by the transferee of an interest in the leased property will not affect that privity of contract liability.

This is a doctrine in contract law known as the *third-party beneficiary contract.* To illustrate it simply, suppose that in exchange for $20, *A* promises *B* (who paid the money) that *A* will wash *C*'s car. Although *B* is the promisee of *A*'s promise, *C* is the intended beneficiary, and if the local jurisdiction recognizes the third-party beneficiary contract doctrine (most do), then *C* has enforceable contract rights against *A*.

Go back to *Ernst*. In view of the third-party beneficiary contract doctrine, assuming that the jurisdiction recognized it, did it matter after all whether the Rogers-Conditt transfer was a sublease or an assignment?

4. *Problems*

(a) *L* leases to *T* for a term of three years at a monthly rent of $1,000. One year later *T* "subleases, transfers, and assigns" to *T1* for "a period of one year from date." Thereafter neither *T* nor *T1* pays rent to *L*. What rights has *L* against *T*? Against *T1*? See 1 American Law of Property §§ 3.57, 3.62 (1952 & Supp. 1977). Compare Ky. Rev. Stat. Ann. § 383.010(5) (Baldwin 2020). Suppose in the instrument of transfer there was a covenant (promise) whereby *T1* "agreed to pay the rents" reserved in the head lease. What effect might this have on *L*'s rights?

(b) *L* leases to *T* for a term of three years at a monthly rent of $1,000; the lease provides that "*T* hereby covenants to pay said rent in advance on the first of each month." The lease also provides that "*T* shall not sublet or assign without the permission of *L*." Six months later *T*, with the permission of *L*, transfers to *T1* for the balance of the term. Thereafter *T1* pays the rent directly to *L* for several months, then defaults. *L* sues *T* for the rent due. What result, and why? See South Bay Center, Inc. v. Butler, Herrick & Marshall, 250 N.Y.S.2d 863 (Sup. Ct. 1964); Buck v. J.M. McEntee & Sons, 275 P.2d 984 (Okla. 1954).

(c) *L* leases to *T* for a term of three years at a monthly rent of $1,000; in the lease "*T* covenants to pay the rent in advance on the first of each month" and also "covenants to keep the leased premises in good repair." Six months later *T* assigns her entire interest to *T1*, who agrees in the instrument of assignment to "assume all the covenants in the lease" between *L* and *T*; three months later *T1* assigns his entire interest to *T2*, and three months after that *T2* assigns his entire interest to *T3*. *T3* defaults on rent payments and fails to keep the premises in good repair. *L* sues *T*, *T1*, *T2*, and *T3*. What are the liabilities of the four tenants to *L* and as among themselves? See 1 American Law of Property, supra, § 3.61; 2 id. §§ 9.4, 9.5.

The head lease in *Ernst* contained a provision (paragraph 5 of the lease) prohibiting assignment or sublease without the lessors' approval. This is a so-called *consent clause* (sometimes called an *approval clause*), and it is a restraint on alienation. As we saw earlier (see page 304), the common law has long disfavored restraints on alienation, but the situation is different with respect to restraints on tenants' interests. The policy is thought to have less application to leasehold interests because landlords have a legitimate concern with protecting their reversionary interest and assuring that leasehold covenants are performed.

Consent clauses raise questions regarding the scope of the landlord's discretion to refuse consent to a proposed sublet or assignment. May the landlord refuse to give consent for any reason, or are there limitations on the scope of discretion? Some consent clauses themselves limit the landlord's discretion by expressly providing that the landlord may not withhold consent "unreasonably." Other clauses are silent on the question, providing no standard to guide the landlord's exercise of discretion. One question is, where the consent clause provides no standard, may the landlord refuse consent for any reason whatsoever? That is, may the landlord act unreasonably, or will the court imply a requirement of reasonableness? Another question is, when a reasonableness requirement exists, either on the basis of the language in the lease or as an implied term, what factors are acceptable reasons for denying consent? Consider the next case.

KENDALL v. ERNEST PESTANA, INC.

Supreme Court of California, 1985

709 P.2d 837

BROUSSARD, J. This case concerns the effect of a provision in a commercial lease[1] that the lessee may not assign the lease or sublet the premises without the lessor's prior written consent. The question we address is whether, in the absence of a provision that such consent will not be unreasonably withheld, a lessor may unreasonably and arbitrarily withhold his or her consent to an assignment.[2] This is a question of first impression in this court. . . .

The allegations of the complaint may be summarized as follows. The lease at issue is for 14,400 square feet of hangar space at the San Jose Municipal Airport. The City of San Jose, as owner of the property, leased it to Irving and Janice Perlitch, who in turn assigned their interest to respondent Ernest Pestana, Inc. Prior to assigning their interest to respondent, the Perlitches entered into a 25-year sublease with one Robert Bixler commencing on January 1, 1970. The sublease covered an original five-year term plus four 5-year options to renew. The rental rate was to be increased every 10 years in the same proportion as rents increased on the master lease from the City of San Jose. The premises were to be used by Bixler for the purpose of conducting an airplane maintenance business.

Bixler conducted such a business under the name "Flight Services" until, in 1981, he agreed to sell the business to appellants Jack Kendall, Grady O'Hara and Vicki O'Hara. The proposed sale included the business and the equipment, inventory and improvements on the property, together with the existing lease. The proposed assignees had a stronger financial statement and greater net worth than the current lessee, Bixler, and they were willing to be bound by the terms of the lease.

The lease provided that written consent of the lessor was required before the lessee could assign his interest, and that failure to obtain such consent rendered the lease voidable at the option of the lessor. Accordingly, Bixler requested consent from the Perlitches' successor-in-interest, respondent Ernest Pestana, Inc. Respondent refused to consent to the assignment and maintained that it had an absolute right arbitrarily to refuse any such request. The complaint recites that respondent demanded "increased rent and other more onerous terms" as a condition of consenting to Bixler's transfer of interest.

The proposed assignees brought suit for declaratory and injunctive relief and damages seeking, inter alia, a declaration "that the refusal of Ernest Pestana, Inc. to consent

---

1. We are presented only with a commercial lease and therefore do not address the question whether residential leases are controlled by the principles articulated in this opinion.

2. Since the present case involves an assignment rather than a sublease, we will speak primarily in terms of assignments. However, our holding applies equally to subleases. . . .

to the assignment of the lease is unreasonable and is an unlawful restraint on the freedom of alienation. . . ." The trial court sustained a demurrer to the complaint without leave to amend and this appeal followed.

The law generally favors free alienability of property, and California follows the common law rule that a leasehold interest is freely alienable. Contractual restrictions on the alienability of leasehold interests are, however, permitted. "Such restrictions are justified as reasonable protection of the interests of the lessor as to who shall possess and manage property in which he has a reversionary interest and from which he is deriving income." (Schoshinski, American Law of Landlord and Tenant (1980) § 8:15, at pp. 578-579. See also 2 Powell on Real Property, ¶ 246[1], at p. 372.97.)

The common law's hostility toward restraints on alienation has caused such restraints on leasehold interests to be strictly construed against the lessor. . . . This is particularly true where the restraint in question is a "forfeiture restraint," under which the lessor has the option to terminate the lease if an assignment is made without his or her consent. . . .

Nevertheless, a majority of jurisdictions have long adhered to the rule that where a lease contains an approval clause (a clause stating that the lease cannot be assigned without the prior consent of the lessor), the lessor may arbitrarily refuse to approve a proposed assignee no matter how suitable the assignee appears to be and no matter how unreasonable the lessor's objection. . . . The harsh consequences of this rule have often been avoided through application of the doctrines of waiver and estoppel, under which the lessor may be found to have waived (or be estopped from asserting) the right to refuse consent to assignment.

The traditional majority rule has come under steady attack in recent years. A growing minority of jurisdictions now hold that where a lease provides for assignment only with the prior consent of the lessor, such consent may be withheld *only where the lessor has a commercially reasonable objection to the assignment,* even in the absence of a provision in the lease stating that consent to assignment will not be unreasonably withheld. (See Rest. 2d Property, § 15.2(2) (1977); 21 A.L.R.4th 188 (1983).)

For the reasons discussed below, we conclude that the minority rule is the preferable position. . . .

The impetus for change in the majority rule has come from two directions, reflecting the dual nature of a lease as a conveyance of a leasehold interest and a contract. (See Medico-Dental etc. Co. v. Horton & Converse (1942) 21 Cal. 2d 411, 418, 132 P.2d 457.) The policy against restraints on alienation pertains to leases in their nature as *conveyances.* Numerous courts and commentators have recognized that "[i]n recent times the necessity of permitting reasonable alienation of commercial space has become paramount in our increasingly urban society." (Schweiso v. Williams [(1984) 150 Cal. App. 3d 883, 887, 198 Cal. Rptr. 238.)] . . .

One commentator explains as follows:

The common-law hostility to restraints on alienation had a large exception with respect to estates for years. A lessor could prohibit the lessee from transferring the estate for years to whatever extent he might desire. It was believed that the objectives served by allowing such restraints outweighed the social evils implicit in the restraints, in that they gave to the lessor a needed control over the person entrusted with the lessor's property and to whom he must look for the performance of the covenants contained in the lease. Whether this reasoning retains full validity can well be doubted. Relationships between lessor and lessee have tended to become more and more impersonal. Courts have considerably lessened the effectiveness of restraint clauses by strict construction and liberal applications of the doctrine of waiver. With the shortage of housing and, in many places, of commercial space as well, the allowance of lease clauses forbidding assignments and subleases is beginning to be curtailed by statutes. [2 Powell, supra, ¶ 246[1], at pp. 372.97-372.98, fns. omitted.]

The Restatement Second of Property adopts the minority rule on the validity of approval clauses in leases: "A restraint on alienation without the consent of the landlord of a tenant's interest in leased property is valid, *but the landlord's consent to an alienation by the tenant cannot be withheld unreasonably,* unless a freely negotiated provision in the lease gives the landlord an absolute right to withhold consent." (Rest. 2d Property, § 15.2(2) (1977), italics added.)[3] A comment to the section explains:

> The landlord may have an understandable concern about certain personal qualities of a tenant, particularly his reputation for meeting his financial obligations. The preservation of the values that go into the personal selection of the tenant justifies upholding a provision in the lease that curtails the right of the tenant to put anyone else in his place by transferring his interest, but this justification does not go to the point of allowing the landlord arbitrarily and without reason to refuse to allow the tenant to transfer an interest in leased property. [Id., com. a.]

Under the Restatement rule, the lessor's interest in the character of his or her tenant is protected by the lessor's right to object to a proposed assignee on reasonable commercial grounds. (See id., reporter's note 7 at pp. 112-113.) The lessor's interests are also protected by the fact that the original lessee remains liable to the lessor as a surety even if the lessor consents to the assignment and the assignee expressly assumes the obligations of the lease. . . .

The second impetus for change in the majority rule comes from the nature of a lease as a *contract.* As the Court of Appeal observed in Cohen v. Ratinoff, supra, "[s]ince Richard v. Degan & Brody, Inc. [espousing the majority rule] was decided, . . . there has been an increased recognition of and emphasis on the duty of good faith and fair dealing inherent in every contract." (Id., 147 Cal. App. 3d at p. 329, 195 Cal. Rptr. 84.) Thus, "[i]n every contract there is an implied covenant that neither party shall do anything which will have the effect of destroying or injuring the right of the other party to receive the fruits of the contract. . . ." (Universal Sales Corp. v. Cal. etc. Mfg. Co. (1942) 20 Cal. 2d 751, 771, 128 P.2d 665. . . .) "[W]here a contract confers on one party a discretionary power affecting the rights of the other, a duty is imposed to exercise that discretion in good faith and in accordance with fair dealing." (Cal. Lettuce Growers v. Union Sugar Co. (1955) 45 Cal. 2d 474, 484, 289 P.2d 785. See also, Larwin-Southern California, Inc. v. J.G.B. Inv. Co. (1979) 101 Cal. App. 3d 626, 640, 162 Cal. Rptr. 52.) Here the lessor retains the discretionary power to approve or disapprove an assignee proposed by the other party to the contract; this discretionary

---

3. This case does not present the question of the validity of a clause absolutely prohibiting assignment, or granting absolute discretion over assignment to the lessor. We note that under the Restatement rule such a provision would be valid if freely negotiated.

power should therefore be exercised in accordance with commercially reasonable standards. . . . Under the minority rule, the determination whether a lessor's refusal to consent was reasonable is a question of fact. Some of the factors that the trier of fact may properly consider in applying the standards of good faith and commercial reasonableness are: financial responsibility of the proposed assignee; suitability of the use for the particular property; legality of the proposed use; need for alteration of the premises; and nature of the occupancy, i.e., office, factory, clinic, etc.

Denying consent solely on the basis of personal taste, convenience or sensibility is not commercially reasonable. Nor is it reasonable to deny consent "in order that the landlord may charge a higher rent than originally contracted for." (Schweiso v. Williams, supra, 150 Cal. App. 3d at p. 886, 198 Cal. Rptr. 238.) This is because the lessor's desire for a better bargain than contracted for has nothing to do with the permissible purposes of the restraint on alienation—to protect the lessor's interest in the preservation of the property and the performance of the lease covenants. " '[T]he clause is for the protection of the landlord *in its ownership and operation of the particular property*—not for its general economic protection.' " (Ringwood Associates v. Jack's of Route 23, Inc. [(1977) 153 N.J. Super. 294, 379 A.2d 508, 512], quoting Krieger v. Helmsley-Spear, Inc. (1973) 62 N.J. 423, 302 A.2d 129, italics added.)

In contrast to the policy reasons advanced in favor of the minority rule, the majority rule has traditionally been justified on three grounds. Respondent raises a fourth argument in its favor as well. None of these do we find compelling.

First, it is said that a lease is a conveyance of an interest in real property, and that the lessor, having exercised a personal choice in the selection of a tenant and provided that no substitute shall be acceptable without prior consent, is under no obligation to look to anyone but the lessee for the rent. This argument is based on traditional rules of conveyancing and on concepts of freedom of ownership and control over one's property.

A lessor's freedom at common law to look to no one but the lessee for the rent has, however, been undermined by the adoption in [many jurisdictions] of a rule that lessors—like all other contracting parties—have a duty to mitigate damages upon the lessee's abandonment of the property by seeking a substitute lessee. Furthermore, the values that go into the personal selection of a lessee are preserved under the minority rule in the lessor's right to refuse consent to assignment on any commercially reasonable grounds. Such grounds include not only the obvious objections to an assignee's financial stability or proposed use of the premises, but a variety of other commercially reasonable objections as well. (See, e.g., Arrington v. Walter E. Heller Intl. Corp. (1975) 30 Ill. App. 3d 631, 333 N.E.2d 50 [desire to have only one "lead tenant" in order to preserve "image of the building" as tenant's international headquarters]; Warmack v. Merchants Natl. Bank of Fort Smith (Ark. 1981) 612 S.W.2d 733 [desire for good "tenant mix" in shopping center]; List v. Dahnke (Col. App. 1981) 638 P.2d 824 [lessor's refusal to consent to assignment of lease by one restaurateur to another was reasonable where lessor believed proposed specialty restaurant would not succeed at that location].) The lessor's interests are further protected by the fact that the original lessee remains a guarantor of the performance of the assignee. . . .

The second justification advanced in support of the majority rule is that an approval clause is an unambiguous reservation of absolute discretion in the lessor over assignments of the lease. The lessee could have bargained for the addition of a reasonableness clause to the lease (i.e., "consent to assignment will not be unreasonably withheld"). The lessee having failed to do so, the law should not rewrite the parties' contract for them. . . .

Numerous authorities have taken a different view of the meaning and effect of an approval clause in a lease, indicating that the clause is not "clear and unambiguous," as respondent suggests. As early as 1940, the court in Granite Trust Bldg. Corp. v. Great Atlantic & Pacific Tea Co. [(D. Mass. 1940)] 36 F. Supp. 77, examined a standard approval clause and stated: "It would seem to be the better law that when a lease restricts a lessee's rights by requiring consent before these rights can be exercised, *it must have been in the contemplation of the parties that the lessor be required to give some reason for withholding consent.*" (Id., at p. 78, italics added.) . . .

In light of . . . the increasing number of jurisdictions that have adopted the minority rule in the last 15 years, the assertion that an approval clause "clearly and unambiguously" grants the lessor absolute discretion over assignments is untenable. It is not a rewriting of a contract, as respondent suggests, to recognize the obligations imposed by the duty of good faith and fair dealing, which duty is implied by law in every contract.

The third justification advanced in support of the majority rule is essentially based on the doctrine of stare decisis. It is argued that the courts should not depart from the common law majority rule because "many leases now in effect covering a substantial amount of real property and creating valuable property rights were carefully prepared by competent counsel in reliance upon the majority viewpoint." (Gruman v. Investors Diversified Services [(1956) 247 Minn. 502, 78 N.W.2d 377, 381.] . . .) As pointed out above, however, the majority viewpoint has been far from universally held and has never been adopted by this court. Moreover, the trend in favor of the minority rule should come as no surprise to observers of the changing state of real property law in the 20th century. The minority rule is part of an increasing recognition of the contractual nature of leases and the implications in terms of contractual duties that flow therefrom. We would be remiss in our duty if we declined to question a view held by the majority of jurisdictions simply because it is held by a majority. . . .

A final argument in favor of the majority rule is advanced by respondent and stated as follows: "Both tradition and sound public policy dictate that the lessor has a right, under circumstances such as these, to realize the increased value of his property." Respondent essentially argues that any increase in the market value of real property during the term of a lease properly belongs to the lessor, not the lessee. We reject this assertion. . . . Respondent here is trying to get *more* than it bargained for in the lease. A lessor is free to build periodic rent increases into a lease, as the lessor did here. . . . Any increased value of the property beyond this "belongs" to the lessor only in the sense, as explained above, that the lessor's reversionary estate will benefit from it upon the expiration of the lease. We must therefore reject respondent's argument in this regard. . . .

In conclusion, both the policy against restraints on alienation and the implied contractual duty of good faith and fair dealing militate in favor of adoption of the rule that where a commercial lease provides for assignment only with the prior consent of the lessor, such consent may be withheld only where the lessor has a commercially reasonable objection to the assignee or the proposed use. Under this rule, appellants have stated a cause of action against respondent Ernest Pestana, Inc.

[Two justices dissented in *Kendall*, on the ground that the provisions of the agreement between the parties should be respected, especially because the lessor had relied upon the rule existing at the time of the lease. In the view of the dissent, the legislature had implicitly endorsed the common law rule overturned in *Kendall*; it was up to the legislature, not the court, to change the rule, and any change should be prospective only.]

Notes and Questions

1. *Consent clauses in commercial leases.* Parties who enter into commercial leases like that in *Kendall* are usually represented by counsel. Given this fact, was the court justified in reversing the default rule on consent clauses?

2. *Consent clauses in residential leases.* Should the rule in *Kendall* apply to residential leases? The opinion in the case leaves the question open (see footnote 1 on page 306), and a California statute that later codified the *Kendall* holding, Cal. Civ. Code § 1995.010, is limited to leases for other than residential purposes because, according to a Law Revision Commission Comment following that section, "residential real property leases involve different public policies than commercial real property leases." What are those different policies? In this respect, see Slavin v. Rent Control Bd. of Brookline, 548 N.E.2d 1226, 1228-1229 (Mass. 1990):

> [N]o State court has acted to create a reasonableness requirement in a case involving only a residential lease. . . .
>
> [An important] concern that appears to have motivated the commercial lease decisions is a desire to limit restraints on alienation in light of the fact that "the necessity of reasonable alienation of commercial building space has become paramount in our ever-increasing urban society." . . . [W]e are not persuaded that there is such a "necessity of reasonable alienation of [residential] building space" that we ought to impose on residential landlords a reasonableness requirement to which they have not agreed. We are mindful that valid arguments in support of such a rule can be made, but there are also valid counter-arguments, not the least of which is that such a rule would be likely to engender a plethora of litigation about whether the landlord's withholding of consent was reasonable. The question is one of public policy which, of course, the Legislature is free to address. We note that the Legislature has spoken in at least four States [Alaska, Delaware, Hawaii, and New York].

Do the court's reasons for not extending the reasonableness requirement to residential leases strike you as persuasive? Are there any other justifications for not requiring landlords of residential buildings to act reasonably in approving or rejecting subleases and assignments?

Given the reasoning in *Kendall*, one might think that the Supreme Judicial Court of Massachusetts would follow *Kendall* with respect at least to commercial leases. Not so! See Merchants Row Corp. v. Merchants Row, Inc., 587 N.E.2d 788, 789 (Mass. 1992). For another case rejecting the rule in *Kendall*, see First Federal Sav. Bank v. Key Markets, Inc., 559 N.E.2d 600 (Ind. 1990).

More recently, several states have followed *Kendall* in the case of commercial leases. See Newman v. Hinky Dinky Omaha-Lincoln, Inc., 427 N.W.2d 50 (Neb. 1988); Julian v. Christopher, 575 A.2d 735, 740 (Md. 1990).

Problems

1. Suppose the following situations arise in a jurisdiction following the rule in *Kendall*, or in any jurisdiction under a lease providing that "there shall be no sublease or assignment without landlord's consent, and such consent shall not be unreasonably withheld." What result?

(a) *L* leases to *T* for a term of five years. After two years, *T* wishes to transfer the lease to *T1*. *L* refuses consent because *T1* is a tenant in another of *L*'s buildings under a lease that is about to expire; *L* and *T1* have been actively negotiating a new lease, and *L* wants to avoid losing *T1* as a tenant in the other building. See Krieger v. Helmsley-Spear, Inc., 302 A.2d 129 (N.J. 1973), cited with apparent approval in *Kendall*.

Suppose instead that *T1* is not already a tenant of *L*, but rather is a prospective tenant who wants to use the leased property for a business that will compete with *L*'s business in the same area. See Norville v. Carr-Gottstein Foods Co., 84 P.3d 996 (Ala. App. 2004); Pay 'N Pak Stores, Inc. v. Superior Court, 258 Cal. Rptr. 816 (Cal. App. 1989).

(b) *L*, a Christian evangelical organization, owns a building that it uses as its headquarters. No religious services are held in the building. *L* leases space in the building to *T* for a term of three years. After one year, *T* wishes to transfer the lease to *T1*, an organization that proposes to use the leased space as a counseling center providing information on birth control and abortion. *L* refuses consent on the sole ground that it is fundamentally opposed to the aims and activities of *T1*. See American Book Co. v. Yeshiva Univ. Dev. Found., 297 N.Y.S.2d 156 (Sup. Ct. 1969).

(c) What if in any given situation *L* demands a fee in exchange for consenting to a transfer of the lease? See Giordano v. Miller, 733 N.Y.S.2d 94 (App. Div. 2001).

2. Suppose a jurisdiction following the majority rule and a lease providing that *L* may terminate if *T* transfers without the necessary consent. Unlike the situation in Problem 1, however, the lease prohibits only assignment without *L*'s permission. *T* wishes to assign to *T1*, but *L*—because she wishes to rent to *T1* on her own for a higher rent—refuses consent. *T* then transfers the lease to *T1* for the remainder of the original term, minus one day. *L* brings suit to terminate the head lease with *T* (which would terminate *T1*'s tenancy as well), arguing that the form of the transaction should be disregarded, that it was a subterfuge, that the parties clearly intended the transfer to be an assignment, and that the assignment was made without *L*'s consent. What result? See Walgreen Arizona Drug Co. v. Plaza Center Corp., 647 P.2d 643 (Ariz. 1982).

3. *L* leases to *T* for a term of five years at a monthly rent of $900; in the lease, *T* covenants to pay the rent and further covenants not to sublet or assign without *L*'s permission. Thereafter *T*, with *L*'s permission, assigns to *T1* (*T1* does not expressly assume the obligations of the lease); then *T1* assigns to *T2* without first obtaining *L*'s permission. *T2* defaults in rent payments, and *L* sues *T1* for the amount due. What result? See Restatement (Second) of Property, Landlord and Tenant § 16.1 comment g at 125 (1977) (expressing disapproval of the so-called Rule in Dumpor's Case, 76 Eng. Rep. 1110 (K.B. 1578), "which would terminate the prohibition against assignment when the landlord consents to an assignment unless he specifically reserves the right to prohibit future assignments").

4. *L* leases a building to *T* (a company that makes computers) for a period of 10 years; a clause in the lease states that *T* shall not transfer the lease without the permission of *L*. *T* subsequently merges into a corporation, *ABC*. Does the merger result in a transfer of the lease that triggers the permission requirement? Does it matter whether *T* and *ABC* are related (e.g., as parent and subsidiary)? Cf. Brentsun Realty Corp. v. D'Urso Supermarkets, Inc., 582 N.Y.S.2d 216 (App. Div. 1992) (merger into subsidiary not deemed to constitute an assignment under lease); Pacific First Bank v. New Morgan Park Corp., 876 P.2d 761 (Or. 1994) (merger into subsidiary effected transfer requiring landlord's consent, which could be withheld at his sole discretion); Standard Operations, Inc. v. Montague, 758 S.W.2d 442 (Mo. 1988) (merger not considered an assignment under lease). If a court were to require *T* to get the approval of *L*, and the applicable rule is that announced in the *Kendall* case, what considerations might *L* be obliged, or allowed, to take into account?

D. THE TENANT WHO DEFAULTS

Suppose a tenant *in possession* has defaulted—say by failing to pay rent or observe some other lease obligation—or is holding over after the termination of the lease (see page 286), and the landlord wishes to recover possession. Or suppose the tenant has *abandoned* the premises prior to the end of the tenancy, perhaps owing some back rent. What, in each case, may the landlord do? Consider the following materials.

1. The Tenant in Possession

BERG v. WILEY
Supreme Court of Minnesota, 1978
264 N.W.2d 145

ROGOSHESKE, J. Defendant landlord, Wiley Enterprises, Inc., and defendant Rodney A. Wiley (hereafter collectively referred to as Wiley) appeal from a judgment upon a jury verdict awarding plaintiff tenant, A Family Affair Restaurant, Inc., damages for wrongful eviction from its leased premises. The issues for review are whether the evidence was sufficient to support the jury's finding that the tenant did not abandon or surrender the premises and whether the trial court erred in finding Wiley's reentry forcible and wrongful as a matter of law. We hold that the jury's verdict is supported by sufficient evidence and that the trial court's determination of unlawful entry was correct as a matter of law, and affirm the judgment.

On November 11, 1970, Wiley as lessor and tenant's predecessor in interest as lessee executed a written lease agreement letting land and a building in Osseo, Minnesota, for use as a restaurant. The lease provided a 5-year term beginning December 1, 1970, and specified that the tenant agreed to bear all costs of repairs and remodeling, to "make no changes in the building structure" without prior written authorization from Wiley, and to "operate the restaurant in a lawful and prudent manner." Wiley also reserved the right "at [his] option [to] retake possession" of the premises "[s]hould the Lessee fail to meet the conditions of this Lease."[4] In early 1971, plaintiff Kathleen Berg took assignment of the lease from the prior lessee, and on May 1, 1971, she opened "A Family Affair Restaurant" on the premises. In January 1973, Berg incorporated the restaurant and assigned her interest in the lease to "A Family Affair Restaurant, Inc." As sole shareholder of the corporation, she alone continued to act for the tenant. [The prior lessee referred to by the court was Phillip Berg, Kathleen's brother, who ran a pool hall and served low-alcohol beer and small meals on the leased premises from December 1, 1970 (when the lease began), until February 20, 1971 (when Phillip assigned to Kathleen with the consent of Wiley). Kathleen then began remodeling the premises to make them suitable for a restaurant.]

The present dispute has arisen out of Wiley's objection to Berg's continued remodeling of the restaurant without procuring written permission and her consequent operation of the restaurant in a state of disrepair with alleged health code violations. Strained relations between the parties came to a head in June and July 1973. In a letter dated June 29, 1973, Wiley's attorney charged Berg with having breached lease items 5 and 6 by making changes in the building structure without written authorization and by operating an unclean kitchen in violation of health regulations. The letter demanded that a list of eight remodeling items be completed within 2 weeks from the date of the letter, by Friday, July 13, 1973, or Wiley would retake possession of the premises under lease item 7. Also, a June 13 inspection of the restaurant by the Minnesota Department of Health had produced an order that certain listed changes be completed within specified time limits in order to comply with the health code. The major items on the inspector's list, similar to those listed by Wiley's attorney, were to be completed by July 15, 1973.

During the 2-week deadline set by both Wiley and the health department, Berg continued to operate the restaurant without closing to complete the required items of remodeling. The evidence is in dispute as to whether she intended to permanently close the restaurant and vacate the premises at the end of the 2 weeks or simply close for about 1 month in order to remodel to comply with the health code. At the close of business on Friday, July 13, 1973, the last day of the 2-week period, Berg dismissed her employees, closed the restaurant, and placed a sign in the window saying "Closed for Remodeling." Earlier that day, Berg testified, Wiley came to the premises in her absence and attempted to change the locks. When she returned and asserted her right to continue in possession, he complied with her request to leave the locks unchanged. Berg also testified that at about 9:30 P.M. that evening, while she and four of her friends

---

4. The provisions of the lease pertinent to this case provide:

Item #5 The Lessee will make no changes to the building structure without first receiving written authorization from the Lessor. The Lessor will promptly reply in writing to each request and will cooperate with the Lessee on any reasonable request.

Item #6 The Lessee agrees to operate the restaurant in a lawful and prudent manner during the lease period.

Item #7 Should the Lessee fail to meet the conditions of this Lease the Lessor may at their [sic] option retake possession of said premises. In any such event such act will not relieve Lessee from liability for payment [of] the rental herein provided or from the conditions or obligations of this lease.

were in the restaurant, she observed Wiley hanging from the awning peering into the window. Shortly thereafter, she heard Wiley pounding on the back door demanding admittance. Berg called the county sheriff to come and preserve order. Wiley testified that he observed Berg and a group of her friends in the restaurant removing paneling from a wall. Allegedly fearing destruction of his property, Wiley called the city police, who, with the sheriff, mediated an agreement between the parties to preserve the status quo until each could consult with legal counsel on Monday, July 16, 1973.

Wiley testified that his then attorney advised him to take possession of the premises and lock the tenant out. Accompanied by a police officer and a locksmith, Wiley entered the premises in Berg's absence and without her knowledge on Monday, July 16, 1973, and changed the locks. Later in the day, Berg found herself locked out. The lease term was not due to expire until December 1, 1975. The premises were re-let to another tenant on or about August 1, 1973. Berg brought this damage action against Wiley and three other named defendants, including the new tenant, on July 27, 1973. A second amended complaint sought damages for lost profits, damage to chattels, intentional infliction of emotional distress, and other tort damages based upon claims in wrongful eviction, contract, and tort. Wiley answered with an affirmative defense of abandonment and surrender and counterclaimed for damage to the premises and indemnification on mechanics lien liability incurred because of Berg's remodeling. At the close of Berg's case, all defendants other than Rodney A. Wiley and Wiley Enterprises, Inc., were dismissed from the action. Only Berg's action for wrongful eviction and intentional infliction of emotional distress and Wiley's affirmative defense of abandonment and his counterclaim for damage to the premises were submitted by special verdict to the jury. With respect to the wrongful eviction claim, the trial court found as a matter of law that Wiley did in fact lock the tenant out, and that the lockout was wrongful.

The jury, by answers to the questions submitted, found no liability on Berg's claim for intentional infliction of emotional distress and no liability on Wiley's counterclaim for damages to the premises, but awarded Berg $31,000 for lost profits and $3,540 for loss of chattels resulting from the wrongful lockout. The jury also specifically found that Berg neither abandoned nor surrendered the premises. . . .

On this appeal, Wiley seeks an outright reversal of the damages award for wrongful eviction, claiming insufficient evidence to support the jury's finding of no abandonment or surrender and claiming error in the trial court's finding of wrongful eviction as a matter of law.

The first issue before us concerns the sufficiency of evidence to support the jury's finding that Berg had not abandoned or surrendered the leasehold before being locked out by Wiley. Viewing the evidence to support the jury's special verdict in the light most favorable to Berg, as we must, we hold it amply supports the jury's finding of no abandonment or surrender of the premises. While the evidence bearing upon Berg's intent was strongly contradictory, the jury could reasonably have concluded, based on Berg's testimony and supporting circumstantial evidence, that she intended to retain possession, closing temporarily to remodel. Thus, the lockout cannot be excused on the ground that Berg abandoned or surrendered the leasehold.

The second and more difficult issue is whether Wiley's self-help repossession of the premises by locking out Berg was correctly held wrongful as a matter of law.

Minnesota has historically followed the common-law rule that a landlord may rightfully use self-help to retake leased premises from a tenant in possession without incurring liability for wrongful eviction provided two conditions are met: (1) The landlord is legally entitled to possession, such as where a tenant holds over after the lease term or where a tenant breaches a lease containing a reentry clause; and (2) the landlord's means of reentry are peaceable. Mercil v. Broulette, 66 Minn. 416, 69 N.W. 218 (1896). Under the common-law rule, a tenant who is evicted by his landlord may recover damages for wrongful eviction where the landlord either had no right to possession or where the means used to remove the tenant were forcible, or both.

Wiley contends that Berg had breached the provisions of the lease, thereby entitling Wiley, under the terms of the lease, to retake possession, and that his repossession by changing the locks in Berg's absence was accomplished in a peaceful manner. In a memorandum accompanying the post-trial order, the trial court stated two grounds for finding the lockout wrongful as a matter of law: (1) It was not accomplished in a peaceable manner and therefore could not be justified under the common-law rule, and (2) any self-help reentry against a tenant in possession is wrongful under the growing modern doctrine that a landlord must always resort to the judicial process to enforce his statutory remedy against a tenant wrongfully in possession. Whether Berg had in fact breached the lease and whether Wiley was hence entitled to possession was not judicially determined. . . .

In each of our previous cases upholding an award of damages for wrongful eviction, the landlord had in fact been found to have no legal right to possession. In applying the common-law rule, we have not before had occasion to decide what means of self-help used to dispossess a tenant in his absence will constitute a nonpeaceable entry, giving a right to damages without regard to who holds the legal right to possession. Wiley argues that only actual or threatened violence used against a tenant should give rise to damages where the landlord had the right to possession. We cannot agree.

It has long been the policy of our law to discourage landlords from taking the law into their own hands, and our decisions and statutory law have looked with disfavor upon any use of self-help to dispossess a tenant in circumstances which are likely to result in breaches of the peace. We gave early recognition to this policy in Lobdell v. Keene, 85 Minn. 90, 101, 88 N.W. 426, 430 (1901), where we said:

> The object and purpose of the legislature in the enactment of the forcible entry and unlawful detainer statute was to prevent those claiming a right of entry or possession of lands from redressing their own wrongs by entering into possession in a violent and forcible manner. All such acts tend to a breach of the peace, and encourage high-handed oppression. The law does not permit the owner of land, be his title ever so good, to be the judge of his own rights with respect to a possession adversely held, but puts him to his remedy under the statutes.

To facilitate a resort to judicial process, the legislature has provided a summary procedure in Minn. St. 566.02 to 566.17 whereby a landlord may recover possession of leased premises upon proper notice and showing in court in as little as 3 to 10 days. As we recognized in Mutual Trust Life Ins. Co. v. Berg, 187 Minn. 503, 505, 246 N.W. 9, 10 (1932), "[t]he forcible entry and unlawful detainer statutes were intended to prevent parties from taking the law into their own hands when going into possession of lands and tenements. . . ." To further discourage self-help, our legislature has provided treble damages for forcible evictions, §§ 557.08 and 557.09, and has provided additional criminal penalties for intentional and unlawful exclusion of a tenant, § 504.25. In

Sweeney v. Meyers, 199 Minn. 21, 270 N.W. 906 (1937), we allowed a business tenant not only damages for lost profits but also punitive damages against a landlord who, like Wiley, entered in the tenant's absence and locked the tenant out.

In the present case, as in *Sweeney*, the tenant was in possession, claiming a right to continue in possession adverse to the landlord's claim of breach of the lease, and had neither abandoned nor surrendered the premises. Wiley, well aware that Berg was asserting her right to possession, retook possession in her absence by picking the locks and locking her out. The record shows a history of vigorous dispute and keen animosity between the parties. Upon this record, we can only conclude that the singular reason why actual violence did not erupt at the moment of Wiley's changing of the locks was Berg's absence and her subsequent self-restraint and resort to judicial process. Upon these facts, we cannot find Wiley's means of reentry peaceable under the common-law rule. Our long-standing policy to discourage self-help which tends to cause a breach of the peace compels us to disapprove the means used to dispossess Berg. To approve this lockout, as urged by Wiley, merely because in Berg's absence no actual violence erupted while the locks were being changed, would be to encourage all future tenants, in order to protect their possession, to be vigilant and thereby set the stage for the very kind of public disturbance which it must be our policy to discourage. . . .

We recognize that the growing modern trend departs completely from the common-law rule to hold that self-help is never available to dispossess a tenant who is in possession and has not abandoned or voluntarily surrendered the premises. Annotation, 6 A.L.R.3d 177, 186; 76 Dickinson L. Rev. 215, 227. This growing rule is founded on the recognition that the potential for violent breach of peace inheres in any situation where a landlord attempts by his own means to remove a tenant who is claiming possession adversely to the landlord. Courts adopting the rule reason that there is no cause to sanction such potentially disruptive self-help where adequate and speedy means are provided for removing a tenant peacefully through judicial process. At least 16 states have adopted this modern rule, holding that judicial proceedings, including the summary procedures provided in those states' unlawful detainer statutes, are the exclusive remedy by which a landlord may remove a tenant claiming possession. . . .

While we would be compelled to disapprove the lockout of Berg in her absence under the common-law rule as stated, we approve the trial court's reasoning and adopt as preferable the modern view represented by the cited cases. To make clear our departure from the common-law rule for the benefit of future landlords and tenants, we hold that, subsequent to our decision in this case, the only lawful means to dispossess a tenant who has not abandoned nor voluntarily surrendered but who claims possession adversely to a landlord's claim of breach of a written lease is by resort to judicial process. . . .

Applying our holding to the facts of this case, we conclude, as did the trial court, that because Wiley failed to resort to judicial remedies against Berg's holding possession adversely to Wiley's claim of breach of the lease, his lockout of Berg was wrongful as a matter of law. The rule we adopt in this decision is fairly applied against Wiley, for it is clear that, applying the older common-law rule to the facts and circumstances peculiar to this case, we would be compelled to find the lockout nonpeaceable for the reasons previously stated. The jury found that the lockout caused Berg damage and, as between Berg and Wiley, equity dictates that Wiley, who himself performed the act causing the damage, must bear the loss.

Affirmed.

Notes and Questions

1. *Self-help, at common law and today.* Under the common law, a landlord entitled to possession could resort to self-help without fear of civil liability—so long as he used no more force than reasonably necessary.

The modern view (and majority rule) on self-help appears to be that in *Berg v. Wiley*. See Randy D. Gerchick, Comment, No Easy Way Out: Making the Summary Eviction Process a Fairer and More Efficient Alternative to Landlord Self-Help, 41 UCLA L. Rev. 759, 777 (1994) (self-help banned by the majority of states). Nevertheless, some courts continue to permit the exercise of self-help, at least in commercial settings. See, e.g., Northfield Park Associates v. Northeast Ohio Harness, 521 N.E.2d 466 (Ohio App. 1987). Where self-help is allowed, of course, it must be accomplished without a breach of the peace.

2. *Prohibiting self-help eviction—a good idea?* Are limitations on self-help evictions a good thing for tenants? Consider the following:

> The movement to prohibit self-help evictions by landlords has long had a few critics, with the most prominent ones suggesting that landlords would pass the high costs of judicially evicting deadbeat tenants onto the tenants who paid their bills on time. Some passing on of these costs undoubtedly occurs, but the reputation revolution suggests a deeper criticism of the prohibitions on landlord self-help. Eviction via self-help typically creates no public records. Courts are not involved in a self-help eviction, and a landlord has no economic incentive to report such a dispossession to a credit bureau or any other information broker. Evictions via summary proceedings, on the other hand, necessarily generate public records, and it is those public records that will prove so damaging to tenants the next time they try to rent an apartment. From the perspective of facilitating tenant rehabilitation and second chances, a law prohibiting self-help by landlords will prove counterproductive. Many tenants who have trouble making rent payments will fail to appreciate the reputational repercussions of involvement in summary proceedings. For these tenants, the law's prohibition on self-help can be a particularly raw deal. This is a point overlooked by defenders of the prohibition on self-help. [Lior J. Strahilevitz, Reputation Nation: Law in an Era of Ubiquitous Personal Information, 102 Nw. U. L. Rev. 1667, 1679-1680 (2008).]

Professor Strahilevitz stresses the costs that prohibiting self-help impose on landlords and says those will be passed on to non-"deadbeat" tenants. What about the costs imposed on tenants of the risk of being wrongfully evicted? Consider how the reasons the court in *Berg* mentions for prohibiting self-help, especially the landlord's lack of objectivity regarding the basis for the eviction action, might bear on this question. Suppose, for example, the tenant was not paying rent because of an asserted violation of the warranty of habitability, which we will study in depth later in this chapter. From a strict cost-benefit perspective, the question is whether the error costs of allowing the landlord to be a judge in his own case outweigh the costs of having to go to housing court to procure eviction. There is also a distributive question about who is better positioned to bear the cost, the landlord or the tenant.

3. *Residential leases.* Berg v. Wiley involved a commercial lease, but the court's reasoning would appear to apply to all leases, residential and commercial alike. See also Simpson v. Lee, 499 A.2d 889 (D.C. App. 1985) (self-help prohibited in either instance). In some jurisdictions, the prohibition on self-help applies only to residential leases. Is there any reason to treat the two situations differently? See Case Note, 60 N.C. L. Rev. 885, 891-892 (1982) (loss of residence has greater psychological impact than loss of possession of place of business, and the need for immediate replacement of commercial space is less vital; moreover, in the commercial setting there is more likely to be equal bargaining power between the parties). See also Watson v. Brown, 686 P.2d 12 (Haw. 1984) (permits self-help in commercial tenancies, because of equality of bargaining power; expresses no opinion as to residential tenancies). Of what relevance is equal bargaining power?

4. *Bargaining around the prohibition.* In *Berg*, item 7 of the lease might be read to permit self-help by the landlord. Should the parties be permitted to waive the prohibition against self-help repossession? Courts appear to split on this question, but the Restatement view is that the prohibition cannot be contracted away. See Restatement (Second) of Property, Landlord and Tenant § 14.2 (1977).

Summary eviction proceedings. As *Berg* illustrates, courts have regularly relied on the availability of summary proceedings as one reason to abrogate the common law remedy of self-help. Summary proceedings (sometimes called *forcible entry* and *detainer statutes*) are an alternative to the cumbersome, time-consuming, common law procedure called *ejectment* (which still exists today, with statutory modifications). Today every state provides some form of summary proceeding.

The typical statute requires only a few days' notice to the tenant prior to bringing an eviction action, and the range of issues subject to litigation is kept narrow. However, summary eviction procedures can be time-consuming and expensive, even if uncontested, so that summary proceedings can be less summary than one might suppose.

Covid-19, eviction moratoria, and rent assistance. The Covid-19 pandemic has caused thousands of people to lose their jobs, their businesses, and their means of livelihood. As a result, many of these people can no longer afford to pay their rent. Under these extraordinary circumstances, more than a few jurisdictions, including the federal government, have enacted eviction moratoria measures. The federal CARES Act, signed into law on March 27, 2020, provides 120 days of eviction relief for tenants in federally backed housing. Specifically, tenants may not be served with an eviction notice until July 25, 2020, and the notice must give tenants 30 days to leave the property (August 24, 2020). See Office of Multifamily Housing Programs, HUD, Questions and Answers for Office of Multifamily Housing Stakeholders: Questions and Answers for Office of Multifamily Housing Stakeholders: Coronavirus (COVID-19), at https://www.hud.gov/sites/dfiles/Housing/documents/HUD_Multifamily_Corona_QA_FINAL.pdf (last visited June 1, 2020). The eviction moratorium does not relieve tenants of the obligation to pay rent. It merely forbids the landlord from evicting the tenant during that period for late payment. The eviction moratorium covers only certain categories of tenants, such as those in housing receiving federal subsidies including Section 8 housing, or those that have federally backed mortgages. Many states and municipalities enacted their own rent moratoria measures, the exact terms of which vary widely.

These moratoria are only temporary. Evictions are likely to begin once the moratoria expire. As we go the press, there are already reports of landlords filing eviction notices even before their states' moratoria deadlines have expired. See Landlords Lining Up to Evict Hundreds of Tampa Bay Tenants Once Moratorium Expires, available at https://www.tampabay.com/news/health/2020/05/23/landlords-lining-up-to-evict-hundreds-of-tampa-bay-tenants-once-moratorium-expires/.

The CARES Act also provides funding supporting rental assistance. Through this federal funding, many municipalities and local governments established rental assistance programs to support individuals and families impacted by Covid-19. In Los Angeles, for example, the COVID-19 Emergency Rental Assistance Program provides rent payments to property owners on behalf of an income-eligible household, up to $1,000 per month, for three months. See Los Angeles County Rent Assistance Programs, Los Angeles Development Authority, at https://wwwa.lacda.org/programs/rent-relief (last visited June 1, 2020).

2. The Abandoning Tenant

SOMMER v. KRIDEL
Supreme Court of New Jersey, 1977
378 A.2d 767

PASHMAN, J. We granted certification in these cases to consider whether a landlord seeking damages from a defaulting tenant is under a duty to mitigate damages by making reasonable efforts to re-let an apartment wrongfully vacated by the tenant. Separate parts of the Appellate Division held that, in accordance with their respective leases, the landlords in both cases could recover rents due under the leases regardless of whether they had attempted to re-let the vacated apartments. Although they were of different minds as to the fairness of this result, both parts agreed that it was dictated by Joyce v. Bauman, 113 N.J.L. 438, 174 A. 693 (E.&A. 1934), a decision by the former Court of Errors and Appeals. We now reverse and hold that a landlord does have an obligation to make a reasonable effort to mitigate damages in such a situation. We therefore overrule Joyce v. Bauman to the extent that it is inconsistent with our decision today.

Sommer v. Kridel

The case was tried on stipulated facts. On March 10, 1972 the defendant, James Kridel, entered into a lease with the plaintiff, Abraham Sommer, owner of the "Pierre

Apartments" in Hackensack, to rent apartment 6-L in that building.[5] The term of the lease was from May 1, 1972 until April 30, 1974, with a rent concession for the first six weeks, so that the first month's rent was not due until June 15, 1972.

One week after signing the agreement, Kridel paid Sommer $690. Half of that sum was used to satisfy the first month's rent. The remainder was paid under the lease provision requiring a security deposit of $345. Although defendant had expected to begin occupancy around May 1, his plans were changed. He wrote to Sommer on May 19, 1972, explaining

> I was to be married on June 3, 1972. Unhappily the engagement was broken and the wedding plans cancelled. Both parents were to assume responsibility for the rent after our marriage. I was discharged from the U.S. Army in October 1971 and am now a student. I have no funds of my own, and am supported by my stepfather.
>
> In view of the above, I cannot take possession of the apartment and am surrendering all rights to it. Never having received a key, I cannot return same to you.
>
> I beg your understanding and compassion in releasing me from the lease, and will of course, in consideration thereof, forfeit the 2 months' rent already paid.
>
> Please notify me at your earliest convenience.

Plaintiff did not answer the letter.

The Pierre Apartments
Hackensack

---

5. Among other provisions, the lease prohibited the tenant from assigning or transferring the lease without the consent of the landlord. If the tenant defaulted, the lease gave the landlord the option of re-entering or re-letting, but stipulated that failure to re-let or to recover the full rental would not discharge the tenant's liability for rent.

Subsequently, a third party went to the apartment house and inquired about renting apartment 6-L. Although the parties agreed that she was ready, willing and able to rent the apartment, the person in charge told her that the apartment was not being shown since it was already rented to Kridel. In fact, the landlord did not re-enter the apartment or exhibit it to anyone until August 1, 1973. At that time it was rented to a new tenant for a term beginning on September 1, 1973. The new rental was for $345 per month with a six week concession similar to that granted Kridel.

Prior to re-letting the new premises, plaintiff sued Kridel in August 1972, demanding $7,590, the total amount due for the full two-year term of the lease. Following a mistrial, plaintiff filed an amended complaint asking for $5,865, the amount due between May 1, 1972 and September 1, 1973. The amended complaint included no reduction in the claim to reflect the six week concession provided for in the lease or the $690 payment made to plaintiff after signing the agreement. Defendant filed an amended answer to the complaint, alleging that plaintiff breached the contract, failed to mitigate damages and accepted defendant's surrender of the premises. . . .

The trial judge ruled in favor of the defendant. Despite his conclusion that the lease had been drawn to reflect "the 'settled law' of this state," he found that "justice and fair dealing" imposed upon the landlord the duty to attempt to re-let the premises and thereby mitigate damages. He also held that plaintiff's failure to make any response to defendant's unequivocal offer of surrender was tantamount to an acceptance, thereby terminating the tenancy and any obligation to pay rent. . . . The Appellate Division reversed in a per curiam opinion.

Riverview Realty Co. v. Perosio

This controversy arose in a similar manner. On December 27, 1972, Carlos Perosio entered into a written lease with plaintiff Riverview Realty Co. The agreement covered the rental of apartment 5-G in a building owned by the realty company at 2175 Hudson Terrace in Fort Lee. As in the companion case, the lease prohibited the tenant from subletting or assigning the apartment without the consent of the landlord. It was to run for a two-year term, from February 1, 1973 until January 31, 1975, and provided for a monthly rental of $450. The defendant took possession of the apartment and occupied it until February 1974. At that time he vacated the premises, after having paid the rent through January 31, 1974.

The landlord filed a complaint on October 31, 1974, demanding $4,500 in payment for the monthly rental from February 1, 1974 through October 31, 1974. Defendant answered the complaint by alleging that there had been a valid surrender of the premises and that plaintiff failed to mitigate damages. The trial court granted the landlord's motion for summary judgment against the defendant, fixing the damages at $4,050 plus $182.25 interest.

The Appellate Division affirmed the trial court holding that it was bound by prior precedents, including Joyce v. Bauman, supra.

As the lower courts in both appeals found, the weight of authority in this State supports the rule that a landlord is under no duty to mitigate damages caused by a defaulting tenant. . . . This rule has been followed in a majority of states, and has been tentatively adopted in the American Law Institute's Restatement of Property. Restatement (Second) of Property, § 11.1(3) (Tent. Draft No. 3, 1975).

Nevertheless, while there is still a split of authority over this question, the trend among recent cases appears to be in favor of a mitigation requirement. . . .

River View Towers
2175 Hudson Terrace
Fort Lee

The majority rule is based on principles of property law which equate a lease with a transfer of a property interest in the owner's estate. Under this rationale the lease conveys to a tenant an interest in the property which forecloses any control by the landlord; thus, it would be anomalous to require the landlord to concern himself with the tenant's abandonment of his own property. Wright v. Baumann, 239 Or. 410, 398 P.2d 119, 120-21, 21 A.L.R.3d 527 (1968).

For instance, in Muller v. Beck, [94 N.J.L. 311, 110 A. 831 (Sup. Ct. 1920)], where essentially the same issue was posed, the court clearly treated the lease as governed by property, as opposed to contract, precepts.[6] The court there observed that the "tenant had an estate for years, but it was an estate qualified by this right of the landlord to prevent its transfer," 94 N.J.L. at 313, 110 A. at 832, and that "the tenant has an estate with which the landlord may not interfere." Id. at 314, 110 A. at 832. Similarly, in Heckel v. Griese, [12 N.J. Misc. 211, 171 A. 148 (Sup. Ct. 1934)], the court noted the absolute nature of the tenant's interest in the property while the lease was in effect, stating that "when the tenant vacated, . . . no one, in the circumstances, had any right to interfere with the defendant's possession of the premises." 12 N.J. Misc. at 213, 171 A. at 148, 149. Other cases simply cite the rule announced in Muller v. Beck, supra, without discussing the underlying rationale. . . .

Yet the distinction between a lease for ordinary residential purposes and an ordinary contract can no longer be considered viable. . . . This Court has taken the lead

---

6. It is well settled that a party claiming damages for a breach of contract has a duty to mitigate his loss. . . .

in requiring that landlords provide housing services to tenants in accordance with implied duties which are hardly consistent with the property notions expressed in Muller v. Beck, supra, and Heckel v. Griese, supra. . . . Application of the contract rule requiring mitigation of damages to a residential lease may be justified as a matter of basic fairness.[7] Professor McCormick first commented upon the inequity under the majority rule when he predicted in 1925 that eventually

> the logic, inescapable according to the standards of a "jurisprudence of conceptions" which permits the landlord to stand idly by the vacant, abandoned premises and treat them as the property of the tenant and recover full rent, will yield to the more realistic notions of social advantage which in other fields of the law have forbidden a recovery for damages which the plaintiff by reasonable efforts could have avoided. [McCormick, The Rights of the Landlord Upon Abandonment of the Premises by the Tenant, 23 Mich. L. Rev. 211, 221-22 (1925).]

Various courts have adopted this position.

The pre-existing rule cannot be predicated upon the possibility that a landlord may lose the opportunity to rent another empty apartment because he must first rent the apartment vacated by the defaulting tenant. Even where the breach occurs in a multi-dwelling building, each apartment may have unique qualities which make it attractive to certain individuals. Significantly, in Sommer v. Kridel, there was a specific request to rent the apartment vacated by the defendant; there is no reason to believe that absent this vacancy the landlord could have succeeded in renting a different apartment to this individual.

We therefore hold that antiquated real property concepts which served as the basis for the pre-existing rule, shall no longer be controlling where there is a claim for damages under a residential lease. Such claims must be governed by more modern notions of fairness and equity. A landlord has a duty to mitigate damages where he seeks to recover rents due from a defaulting tenant.

If the landlord has other vacant apartments besides the one which the tenant has abandoned, the landlord's duty to mitigate consists of making reasonable efforts to re-let the apartment. In such cases he must treat the apartment in question as if it was one of his vacant stock.

As part of his cause of action, the landlord shall be required to carry the burden of proving that he used reasonable diligence in attempting to re-let the premises. We note that there has been a divergence of opinion concerning the allocation of the burden of proof on this issue. While generally in contract actions the breaching party has the burden of proving that damages are capable of mitigation, here the landlord will be in a better position to demonstrate whether he exercised reasonable diligence in attempting to re-let the premises.

The Sommer v. Kridel case presents a classic example of the unfairness which occurs when a landlord has no responsibility to minimize damages. Sommer waited 15 months and allowed $4,658.50 in damages to accrue before attempting to re-let the apartment.

---

7. We see no distinction between the leases involved in the instant appeals and those which might arise in other types of residential housing. However, we reserve for another day the question of whether a landlord must mitigate damages in a commercial setting.

Despite the availability of a tenant who was ready, willing and able to rent the apartment, the landlord needlessly increased the damages by turning her away. While a tenant will not necessarily be excused from his obligations under a lease simply by finding another person who is willing to rent the vacated premises, see, e.g., Regent v. Dempsey-Tegler & Co., 70 Ill. App. 2d 32, 216 N.E.2d 500 (Ill. App. 1966) (new tenant insisted on leasing the premises under different terms); Edmands v. Rust & Richardson Drug Co., 191 Mass. 123, 77 N.E. 713 (1906) (landlord need not accept insolvent tenant), here there has been no showing that the new tenant would not have been suitable. We therefore find that plaintiff could have avoided the damages which eventually accrued, and that the defendant was relieved of his duty to continue paying rent. Ordinarily we would require the tenant to bear the cost of any reasonable expenses incurred by a landlord in attempting to re-let the premises, . . . but no such expenses were incurred in this case.

In Riverview Realty Co. v. Perosio, no factual determination was made regarding the landlord's efforts to mitigate damages, and defendant contends that plaintiff never answered his interrogatories. Consequently, the judgment is reversed and the case remanded for a new trial. Upon remand and after discovery has been completed, R. 4:17 et seq., the trial court shall determine whether plaintiff attempted to mitigate damages with reasonable diligence, . . . and if so, the extent of damages remaining and assessable to the tenant. As we have held above, the burden of proving that reasonable diligence was used to re-let the premises shall be upon the plaintiff.

In assessing whether the landlord has satisfactorily carried his burden, the trial court shall consider, among other factors, whether the landlord, either personally or through an agency, offered or showed the apartment to any prospective tenants, or advertised it in local newspapers. Additionally, the tenant may attempt to rebut such evidence by showing that he proffered suitable tenants who were rejected. However, there is no standard formula for measuring whether the landlord has utilized satisfactory efforts in attempting to mitigate damages, and each case must be judged upon its own facts. Compare Hershorin v. La Vista, Inc., 110 Ga. App. 435, 138 S.E.2d 703 (App. 1964) ("reasonable effort" of landlord by showing the apartment to all prospective tenants); Carpenter v. Wisniewski, 139 Ind. App. 325, 215 N.E.2d 882 (App. 1966) (duty satisfied where landlord advertised the premises through a newspaper, placed a sign in the window, and employed a realtor); Re Garment Center Capitol, Inc., 93 F.2d 667, 115 A.L.R. 202 (2 Cir. 1938) (landlord's duty not breached where higher rental was asked since it was known that this was merely a basis for negotiations); Foggia v. Dix, 265 Or. 315, 509 P.2d 412, 414 (1973) (in mitigating damages, landlord need not accept less than fair market value or "substantially alter his obligations as established in the pre-existing lease"); with Anderson v. Andy Darling Pontiac, Inc., 257 Wis. 371, 43 N.W.2d 362 (1950) (reasonable diligence not established where newspaper advertisement placed in one issue of local paper by a broker); Scheinfeld v. Muntz T.V., Inc., 67 Ill. App. 2d 8, 214 N.E.2d 506 (Ill. App. 1966) (duty breached where landlord refused to accept suitable subtenant); Consolidated Sun Ray, Inc. v. Oppenstein, 335 F.2d 801, 811 (8 Cir. 1964) (dictum) (demand for rent which is "far greater than the provisions of the lease called for" negates landlord's assertion that he acted in good faith in seeking a new tenant).

The judgment in Sommer v. Kridel is reversed. In Riverview Realty Co. v. Perosio, the judgment is reversed and the case is remanded to the trial court for proceedings in accordance with this opinion.

THE REST OF THE STORY . . .

Ezra Rosser, a law professor at American University Washington College of Law, interviewed James Kridel and kindly reported to us the following:

Kridel was a law student at the time his problems arose; once he graduated he worked on his case after hours at the firm that hired him. The litigation consumed seven years and about $500,000 in fees; the cost to print the briefs on appeal exceeded the $800 the case could have been settled for at the outset. After Kridel lost at one stage in the appeals process, a local newspaper wrote a story about *Sommer v. Kridel* with the title "Engagement Broke But Not Lease." A lengthy brief Kridel submitted relied in part on an Oregon case, prompting his adversary to dismiss the case as being from Oregon, "a state whose principal industries are logging and salmon." When Kridel eventually won (based in part on the Oregon case), he sent that lawyer a salmon and some wood wrapped in a copy of the court's ruling; the lawyer responded by sending back the message "Touché." One of the justices hearing Kridel's appeal had to recuse himself because his son had been in the army with Kridel and was going to lend money to Kridel if Kridel lost his case (the justice figured his son would borrow the funds from him!). A grandson of Justice Pashman, the author of the opinion in the case, ended up being a tenant of Kridel's.

Notes and Questions

1. *Rationales for the no-duty-to-mitigate rule.* Various justifications are given for the rule, jettisoned in *Sommer*, that a landlord is under no obligation to mitigate damages in the event of abandonment by a tenant: The tenant cannot by his own wrongdoing impose a duty on the landlord; the tenant has "purchased" an interest in real estate (and, presumably, is stuck with it); the landlord should not be forced into a personal relationship with a new tenant he does not wish to accept; the landlord should not be required to seek out new tenants "continually." See Annot., 75 A.L.R.5th 1, 42-62 (2000). The Restatement offers another consideration in support of its surprising position against a duty of mitigation: "Abandonment of property is an invitation to vandalism, and the law should not encourage such conduct by putting a duty of mitigation of damages on the landlord." Restatement (Second) of Property, Landlord and Tenant § 12.1 comment i at 392 (1977). Are any of these points compelling?

2. *Surrender and abandonment.* Suppose that in *Sommer* the landlord, Sommer, had been more sympathetic with James Kridel's predicament and agreed to terminate his tenancy prematurely. Such an agreement by landlord and tenant prematurely to terminate a tenancy is called a *surrender*, and if effected, a surrender relieves the tenant from liability for future rent (although the tenant remains liable for any past unpaid rent). Normally, an express surrender is subject to the Statute of Frauds, and if the lease had to be in writing, so must the surrender.

Abandonment is another way in which a surrender can be effected—through an *implied* surrender rather than an express surrender. Restatement (Second) of Property, Landlord and Tenant, supra, § 12.1 comment i, defines abandonment this way: "An abandonment of the leased property by the tenant occurs when he

vacates the leased property without justification and without any present intention of returning and he defaults in the payment of rent." The tenant's abandonment is considered to be an implied offer to surrender, which the landlord is free
to accept (thereby effecting a surrender) or reject.

3. *The landlord's options—the traditional view.* Traditionally, the landlord
had three options where the tenant abandoned:

> ▶ *Terminate the lease.* The landlord could treat the abandonment as an implied
> offer to surrender and accept the offer, thereby terminating the lease.
> ▶ *Leave premises vacant; recover accrued rent.* Rejecting the implied offer to sur-
> render and keeping the lease in effect, the landlord could leave the prem-
> ises vacant and later bring an action for accrued unpaid rent.
> ▶ *Mitigate damages; recover any difference in rent.* Rejecting the implied offer to
> surrender and keeping the lease in effect, the landlord could mitigate the
> tenant's damages by reletting the premises to a third party and bringing an
> action against the tenant to recover any difference in the rent.

Traditional view

4. *The modern rule and its rationale.* Although *Sommer* refers to the no-
mitigation rule as the majority rule, this is no longer accurate. A majority of juris-
dictions now impose a duty to mitigate. See Stephanie G. Flynn, Duty to Mitigate
Damages Upon a Tenant's Abandonment, 34 Real Prop., Prob. & Tr. J. 721 (2000).
Most of the jurisdictions now extend the duty to commercial leases. See, e.g.,
Austin Hill Country Realty v. Palisades Plaza, 948 S.W.2d 293 (Tex. 1997).

The rationales for the duty to mitigate are relevant to the question. The opinion in *Sommer* mentions "modern notions of fairness and equity." Considerations
of efficiency also enter in. In *Austin Hill Country Realty*, for example, the court
observed that the old common law rule (no duty to mitigate) "encourages both
economic and physical waste. . . . A mitigation requirement thus returns the property to productive use rather than allowing it to remain idle." Relatedly, it helps
prevent property damage. "If the landlord is encouraged to let the property remain
unoccupied, 'the possibility of physical damage to the property through accident
or vandalism is increased.'" 948 S.W.2d at 298. (Compare in this connection the
Restatement's views about vandalism, mentioned in Note 1 above.)

5. *Fulfilling the duty to mitigate—the "vacant stock" idea.* The court in
Sommer held that a landlord must treat abandoned premises as part of his "vacant
stock" (page 324); presumably, then, the landlord must make at least the same
effort to rent the abandoned premises as he makes to rent other vacant units. Is
this justified by the rationale that the rent the landlord "receives from the substitute tenant is . . . a gain *enabled* by the breach of contract by the first tenant"? See
Richard A. Posner, Economic Analysis of Law 134 (9th ed. 2014).

Security deposits. Most people have had (often unpleasant) experience with
security deposits. The purposes of such deposits—to protect the landlord in the
event a tenant defaults in rent, damages the premises, or otherwise breaches the
lease—are straightforward, but there is some evidence that things get bent in
practice. In principle, the landlord is obliged to return to the tenant, upon termination of the lease, the deposit less any amounts necessary to compensate for
defaults by the tenant. In practice, the landlord has an incentive to imagine all

sorts of reasons why he should be entitled to retain the deposit, and with money in hand he has leverage that permits abuse. This, at least, is the central concern; justified or not, it has led to a good deal of reform—most of it statutory. The following provisions are typical: limits are placed on the amount of deposits (e.g., two months' rent); deposits must be placed in a trust or escrow account; deposits are not to be commingled with other funds; the tenant's claim to a deposit is made prior to other creditors, including, in some instances, a trustee in bankruptcy; the landlord must pay interest on deposits; the landlord must submit an itemized list of deductions from a deposit; and penalties are levied for violations (e.g., double or treble the amount of the deposit, or some fixed sum).

E. THE LANDLORD'S DUTIES

This section discusses the duties of the landlord once a lease has begun. We give special emphasis to the landlord's duties with regard to the condition of the premises because this is the area in which there has been the greatest amount of doctrinal change in landlord-tenant law, especially residential landlord-tenant law, within the past 50 years. We begin, however, with the landlord's initial duty to deliver possession to the tenant.

1. The Duty to Deliver Possession

Suppose that L and T have entered into a lease to begin on the first of January. On that date, T arrives at the premises, ready to take possession, only to find a former tenant holding over. Is this L's problem, or T's? Could there be any question? Actually, the answer is yes, or maybe (or, better), it depends upon where this occurs. The jurisdictions are divided between two rules, with case support for both. Under the so-called *American rule*, the landlord is obligated only to deliver legal possession; i.e., the legal right to possession of the premises when the lease term begins. The upshot is that it is the tenant's responsibility, rather than the landlord's, to oust a trespasser or holdover. The tenant's remedies are against the person wrongfully in possession: he may sue to recover possession and damages.

Under the so-called *English rule*, the landlord must deliver not merely legal, but actual possession. Upon the landlord's default, the tenant may terminate the lease and sue for damages. Alternatively, the new tenant may continue the lease and sue for damages. See 1 American Law of Property § 3.37 (A.J. Casner ed. 1952).

The policy bases of the two rules? The American rule is thought "to be founded on the argument that the tenant has sufficient legal and equitable remedies available to protect himself against the third party wrongfully in possession and a greater incentive to use them than the landlord would have." Restatement (Second) of Property, Landlord and Tenant, supra, § 6.2 Reporter's Note at 245. The English rule, like much else of modern landlord-tenant law, is based on the view that the landlord has the greater ability to guard against the risk of trespassers and holdovers. Moreover, it is commonly said that most landlords these days, especially in the residential context, are more sophisticated about the eviction process and better able to bear costs thereof.

A majority of jurisdictions now follows the English rule. So also do the Restatement (Second) of Property, Landlord and Tenant § 6.2 (1977) and the Uniform Residential Landlord and Tenant Act (URLTA) § 2.103. The former permits the parties to agree otherwise; the latter, it appears, does not (see URLTA § 1.403).

2. Duties Regarding the Condition of the Premises

It is now common to say that a "revolution" has occurred in residential landlord-tenant law. As one commentator summarizes the change, "[t]he residential tenant, long the stepchild of the law has now become its ward and darling. Tenants' rights have increased dramatically; landlords' rights have decreased dramatically." Edward H. Rabin, The Revolution in Residential Landlord-Tenant Law: Causes and Consequences, 69 Cornell L. Rev. 517, 519 (1984). Beginning in the 1960s, courts began to develop legal doctrines aimed at addressing the appallingly bad housing conditions in many low-income areas of the nation's cities. Courts and commentators often characterize this revolution by saying that it involves rejection of a "property" model of leases in favor of a "contract" model. This characterization is somewhat inaccurate, however. The legal doctrines that form the core of the revolution are not always consistent with contract law—at least not entirely so. It is more accurate to say that these doctrines are a hybrid of traditional property and contract law. The clearest change that these doctrines signify is a rejection of the traditional common law approach to defining the landlord's duties regarding the care of the premises, an approach that was based on a model of leasehold covenants as independent.

THE ORIGINAL COMMON LAW APPROACH: INDEPENDENT COVENANTS

As we saw earlier, the common law treated a lease as both a conveyance of an estate and a contract. As a contract, the lease is a bundle of covenants, some of which the parties expressly made and others of which the law implied. For example, the law implied a *covenant of title* running from the landlord to the tenant. This made sense because at a time when no system of keeping records to land titles existed, the landlord was in the best position to know whether he had good legal title to convey to the tenant.

A major difference between landlord-tenant law and the law of contracts is that unlike contract law, leasehold covenants, whether express or implied, were considered independent of each other. That is, covenants had to be performed regardless of whether the other party's covenants had been performed. So, for example, even if a landlord had expressly covenanted to repair the premises and failed to perform the covenant, the tenant was still obligated to perform all of his covenants, including, notably, the covenant to pay rent.

There was one major exception to this independent covenants approach: the obligation to pay rent was dependent upon the tenant's having possession undisturbed by the landlord (or someone claiming through the landlord). An important covenant running from the landlord to the tenant that the common law implied was the *covenant of quiet enjoyment.*

Originally, this meant that the landlord promised not to interfere with the tenant's right to actually possess the land during the term of the lease. This covenant was so central to the parties' relationship that a breach of this covenant by the landlord (or anyone under the landlord's authority) would discharge the tenant's duty under the covenant to pay rent.

The covenant of quiet enjoyment was initially limited to cases in which the tenant was actually ousted physically. As time went on, however, courts expanded its scope to include actions by the landlord (and those acting under him) that so substantially interfered with the tenant's beneficial enjoyment of the premises that the tenant has no reasonable alternative but to vacate the premises. Under these circumstances, the courts said that there was a *constructive eviction.* For purposes of the tenant's obligation to pay rent, a constructive eviction was the equivalent of an actual eviction—it discharged the tenant's duty to pay rent. But the development of the constructive eviction doctrine opened further questions: What actions by the landlord might lead to a constructive eviction? Did *in*actions by the landlord count as well as positive acts, and if so, under what circumstances? What if the interfering acts were committed by third parties rather than by the landlord? How much interference with the tenant's beneficial enjoyment must occur before a tenant is justified in vacating the premises and claiming constructive eviction? We consider these and other questions in the section that follows.

Disputes between landlord and tenant regarding the condition of the premises arise in essentially two ways. First, the tenant might wish to vacate, or to stay but pay less (or no) rent. Second, the tenant (or an invitee of the tenant) might be injured by allegedly defective premises and claim damages against the landlord in tort. The materials below concentrate on the first sort of dispute, but give some attention to the second as well.

3. Quiet Enjoyment and Constructive Eviction

VILLAGE COMMONS, LLC v. MARION COUNTY PROSECUTOR'S OFFICE

Court of Appeals of Indiana, 2008
882 N.E.2d 210

RILEY, J. Appellants-Plaintiffs, Village Commons, LLC and Rynalco, Inc. (collectively, Landlord), appeals the trial court's judgment in favor of the Appellees-Defendants, Marion County Prosecutor's Office and Carl Brizzi, in his official capacity as Marion County Prosecutor (collectively, MCPO). We affirm.

Landlord raises three issues for our review: (1) Whether the exclusive-remedy provision of the lease between Landlord and the MCPO barred the MCPO from asserting that it was evicted by acts or omissions of the Landlord; (2) Whether the trial court's findings that the MCPO was both actually evicted and constructively evicted were clearly erroneous; and (3) Whether a provision limiting the MCPO's time to sue barred the MCPO's defenses and counterclaims.

Facts and Procedural History

On June 2, 1999, then Marion County Prosecutor Scott C. Newman executed a lease on behalf of the MCPO with Lombard Associate Limited Partnership (Lombard) to lease the basement of the Victoria Centre in Indianapolis, Indiana (the Lease). Sometime thereafter, Lombard sold the Victoria Centre to Landlord and assigned the Lease to Landlord. The MCPO's Grand Jury Division used the leased premises as its office and evidence storage space.

Pursuant to the provisions of the Lease, the MCPO was to rent 9,356 square feet of lower level space in the Victoria Centre for a period of seven years and five months, commencing on August 1, 1999. The payment obligations increased over time, beginning with zero dollars owed per month for the first five months, increasing to $8,576.33 per month for months seventy-eight through eighty-nine of the lease term.

Under the Lease provisions, Landlord was required to maintain all equipment used in common with other tenants—such as elevators, plumbing, heating and similar equipment—and to maintain the premises in good order, condition and repair. In the event of breach by Landlord, the lease provided that the MCPO could "sue for injunctive relief or to recover damages for any loss resulting from the breach, but [it] shall not be entitled to terminate this Lease or withhold, setoff or abate any rent due thereunder."

Beginning in 2001, there was a series of water intrusions from the outside and leaks from building equipment, which damaged property secured by the MCPO and affected the areas that the MCPO occupied or used. On March 11, 2001, there was a leak in the restroom area. On June 25, 2001, there was a leak in the MCPO's evidence room. On August 2, 2001, there was leak in what the MCPO refers to as its war room, a room that extends out from the building underneath a sidewalk adjacent to the building. On August 16, 2001, there was leak in the electrical conduit. On August 24 and 28, 2001, Landlord took an inventory of water spots on ceiling tiles and other water damage throughout the MCPO's leased area and noted several spots and other damage that had been caused by sweating pipes or leaks. On August 28 and September 10, 2001, leaks were again noted in the war room, which were either caused by cracks in the sidewalk or steam from Indianapolis Power and Light's underground pipes.

As a result of repeated water intrusions in the war room, Landlord hired Indoor Air Management (IAM) to conduct microbiological sampling and visual inspections. IAM reported visual signs of water damage in the war room and along dry wall. Landlord caulked and sprayed sealant on the sidewalk above the war room on several occasions, but these actions did not stop the leaking. The drywall was scheduled to be repaired, but another leak delayed the work. Landlord sought an estimate to remove and re-pour the concrete sidewalk above the war room on October 11, 2001. However, Landlord elected not to perform this work due to the estimated costs.

Another leak was discovered outside of an office on January 22, 2002, and was noticeably worse on January 29, 2002. On Memorial Day 2002, the main water supply pipe in the building's air conditioning system broke causing a leak in the evidence room. Approximately seventy boxes of evidence were damaged. The MCPO had to dedicate several person-hours to attend to the damaged evidence. On June 10, 2002, Mold Remediation Services (MRS) inspected the damaged evidence room and detected mold spores. MRS provided Landlord a quoted price for recommended work to address the microbial contamination. However, due to the estimated cost of the remediation services, Landlord did not hire MRS, but rather permitted its maintenance man to perform demolition and replace drywall. Landlord's maintenance man did not perform several of the tasks recommended by MRS.

On July 17, 2002, nearly one year after the original leak in the war room, Landlord's maintenance man again replaced ceiling tiles that showed signs of water damage. On July 19, 2002, IAM performed microbiological testing in the main evidence room, hallway, conference room and office of the Chief Deputy Prosecutor of the Grand Jury Division, Mark Hollingsworth (Hollingsworth). IAM informed the MCPO that additional demolition was necessary and that the boxes that were damaged should be discarded because of microbiological contamination.

On July 31, 2002, a new leak caused by the HVAC system was discovered in the break room. On August 2, 2002, IAM reported that moisture readings collected from drywall in the closet area were elevated. A wall in the war room had visible signs of water damage. Also, different types of mold spores were present inside the premises than those found outdoors. Surface testing reported excessive fungal growth. IAM recommended several actions to deal with the moisture and microbiological problems, many of which were previously recommended by MRS.

Landlord spoke with IAM and was advised regarding the possibility of allergic reactions for certain people to mold contamination. However, after this meeting Landlord advised the MCPO there were no health risks presented by the building conditions. At least one of the MCPO employees complained of suffering from unusual coughing and sneezing for a prolonged period of time. Another of the MCPO employees experienced headaches while working at the leased premises. The employee reported his symptoms to a physician, was reassigned outside of the leased premises, and the symptoms subsided. On August 13, 2002, Landlord and the MCPO met with an IAM employee to discuss IAM's report. IAM's employee explained to the MCPO there was an elevated mold count, but not the type of mold that requires a building to be quarantined.

On October 10, 2002, Hollingsworth instructed an employee to make daily inspections. The employee reported to Hollingsworth that there were moisture problems in three of the four rooms the MCPO Grand Jury Division used to store evidence. Landlord sent a letter to the MCPO on October 14, 2002, suggesting the MCPO move evidence that it was storing and other materials away from parts of the premises that were vulnerable to water damage. On November 25, 2002, there was a sewage leak in Hollingsworth's office. On January 9, 2003, a water intrusion was discovered in the women's restroom, causing it to be closed for approximately three weeks. The phone system for the MCPO Grand Jury Division went out on January 27, 2003, and MCPO employees took photographs of water damage on the phone board. On January 28, 2003, a major water intrusion was discovered in the main evidence room. An employee photographed a stream of water pouring from the ceiling.

On January 30, 2003, the MCPO elected to vacate the leased premises, and moved to a location where another of the MCPO's divisions was located. Also, January 2003, was the last month that the MCPO paid rent to Landlord, leaving three years and eleven months, or $380,477.37, unpaid according to the terms of the Lease.

On February 23, 2004, Landlord filed a Complaint against the MCPO, alleging that the MCPO breached the Lease, and sought the damages provided under the Lease. The MCPO filed its answer on April 14, 2004, asserting affirmative defenses and a counterclaim premised on a wrongful eviction theory. In its counterclaim, MCPO initially alleged that it had been constructively evicted in January 2003. On July 18, 2005, the MCPO sought leave to amend its counterclaim, stating that the January 2003 allegation had been an error in dates. To correct that error in the amended counterclaim, the MCPO changed an allegation that it was constructively evicted in August 2002.

On January 9 through 11, 2007, the trial court held a bench trial. Thereafter, the parties submitted proposed findings of fact and conclusions of law pursuant to Ind. Trial Rule 52(C). The trial court's judgment held that: (1) the MCPO's defenses and counterclaim were not barred by the Lease's exclusive-remedy provisions; (2) the MCPO was "actually" evicted in October 2002 and then "constructively" evicted in January 2003; and (3) assuming the Landlord could recover against the MCPO, the Landlord did not mitigate its damages reasonably. MCPO was awarded $7,664 and costs on its wrongful eviction counterclaim. . . .

Discussion and Decision

. . .

II. Exclusive-Remedy Provision

Landlord argues that the trial court's judgment is clearly erroneous because it ignored the exclusive-remedy provision of the Lease by concluding that the MCPO had been constructively evicted. Specifically, Landlord argues that the exclusive-remedy provision is permissible under Indiana law and the trial court erred by granting MCPO a remedy prohibited by that provision.

Indiana courts have recognized the contractual nature of leases and the applicability of the law of contracts to leases. The construction of a written contract is a question of law. When interpreting a contract, our paramount goal is to ascertain and effectuate the intent of the parties. This requires the contract to be read as a whole, and the language construed so as not to render any words, phrases, or terms ineffective or meaningless. Where the terms of a contract are clear and unambiguous, we will not construe the contract or look at extrinsic evidence, but will apply the contractual provisions.

The provision of the Lease which Landlord refers to as the exclusive-remedy provision, provides as follows:

> *Section 15.04. Default by Landlord and Remedies by Tenant.* It shall be a default under and breach of this Lease by Landlord if it shall fail to perform or observe any term, condition, covenant or obligation required to be performed or observed by it under this Lease for a period of thirty (30) days after notice thereof from Tenant; provided, however, that if the term, condition, covenant or obligation to be performed by Landlord is of such nature that the same cannot reasonably be performed within such thirty-day period, such default shall be deemed to have been cured if Landlord commences such performance within said thirty-day period and thereafter diligently undertakes to complete the same, and further failure to perform or observe any term, condition, covenant or obligation under this Lease is due to causes beyond the reasonable control of Landlord. Upon the occurrence of any such default, Tenant may sue for injunctive relief or to recover damages for any loss resulting from the breach, but Tenant shall not be entitled to terminate this Lease or withhold, setoff or abate any rent due thereunder.

Landlord encourages us to conclude that the remedy provision of the Lease is exclusive and bars any other remedy, such as the one utilized by the trial court. . . . [W]e conclude from the unambiguous language of the Lease that the MCPO did not have the right to terminate the Lease or withhold, setoff, or abate any rent due. However, this determination is not dispositive of the dispute before us.

III. Eviction

A. The Effects of Eviction on Obligations Under the Lease

The trial court found that the MCPO was actually evicted from the leased premises beginning in October of 2002, and was then constructively evicted as of January 28, 2003, due to repeated and un-remedied water intrusions. In explaining the theories of eviction, our supreme court stated the following:

> Eviction is either actual or constructive, actual when the tenant is deprived of the occupancy of some part of the demised premises, and constructive when the lessor, without intending to oust the lessee, does an act by which the latter is deprived of the beneficial enjoyment of some part of the premises, in which case the tenant has his right of election, to quit, and avoid the lease and rent, or abide the wrong and seek his remedy in an action for the trespass. But in every case of constructive eviction the tenant must quit the premises if he would relieve himself from liability to pay rent; and whether or not he is justifiable in so quitting is a question for the jury. [Talbott v. English, 156 Ind. 299, 307-308, 59 N.E. 857, 860 (1901).]

In further explaining the nature of actual eviction and the effects thereof on the obligations of a tenant, the *Talbott* court stated:

> It may be said that in every lease there is an implied covenant that the tenant shall have the right of possession, occupancy, and beneficial use of every portion of the leased premises. The tenant is regarded as having hired the use of the property as an entirety, and therefore if the landlord, after the grant, deprives the tenant of the possession and enjoyment of any part of the premises, the landlord shall not be entitled to any part of the rent during the time he thus deprives the tenant of this rights. The landlord may not apportion the rent by his own wrong. [Id. at 859.]

We have more recently articulated this concept by stating: "The general rule is that a tenant will be relieved of any obligation to pay further rent if the landlord deprives the tenant of possession and beneficial use and enjoyment of any part of the demised premises by actual eviction. . . . Stated differently, after termination *the lease and all liability under it for future rent are extinguished.*" Gigax v. Boone Village Ltd. Partnership, 656 N.E.2d 854, 858 (Ind. Ct. App. 1995) (emphasis in original).

In [Sigsbee v. Swathwood, 419 N.E.2d 789, 796 (Ind. Ct. App. 1981], we summarized the theory of constructive eviction by explaining: "If an act or omission by the lessor materially deprives the lessee of the beneficial use or enjoyment of the lease property, the lessee may elect to abandon the property and avoid further obligations under the lease. If the lessee so elects, the abandonment of the property must occur within a reasonable time after the act or omission." Thus, if a landlord commits acts or omissions sufficient to actually evict the tenant, the tenant is no longer obligated to pay rent. And likewise, if a landlord commits acts or omissions sufficient to constructively evict the tenant, and the tenant leaves within a reasonable period, the tenant is no longer obligated to pay rent under the lease.

Here, the trial court concluded that "it would be contrary to public policy to permit a landlord to completely eliminate a Tenant's remedy of constructive eviction if conditions are such that the leased property is unusable." However, we find that it is unnecessary to resort to a consideration of public policy to determine this dispute since the unambiguous terms of the exclusive-remedy provision did not prohibit Landlord from evicting the MCPO. The exclusive-remedy provision limited only the MCPO's ability to "terminate this Lease or withhold, setoff or abate any rent due thereunder." Upon the occurrence of eviction, either actual or constructive, it is the lessor's act or omission that ends the obligation to pay rent, not the lessee. Therefore, since we conclude below that the trial court's findings that the MCPO had been wrongfully evicted were not clearly erroneously, we hold that it was the Landlord's own act or omission that resulted in extinguishing MCPO's future rent payment obligations.

[B]. MCPO Was Wrongfully Evicted

Landlord contends that the trial court erred when it found that the MCPO had been evicted. Specifically, Landlord argues that the uncontroverted testimony, largely by the MCPO's own witnesses, contradict the findings and conclusions entered by the trial court, and therefore are clearly erroneous and should be reversed.

In reviewing the record, we observe that the trial court concluded that Landlord actually evicted the MCPO in October of 2002 when "Landlord informed the [MCPO] to refrain from using those portions of the leased space 'most vulnerable to water.'" We also observe the trial court concluded the MCPO was "constructively evicted as of January 28, 2003, due to repeated un-remedied water intrusions."

As we stated above, actual eviction occurs when a tenant is deprived of a material part of the leased premises, and constructive eviction occurs when an interference with possession so serious that it deprives the lessee of the beneficial enjoyment of the leased premises. When a transitory and fleeting interference by the lessor with the lessee's possession occurs, there is no eviction, but a mere trespass, for which the lessee is entitled to damages.

In challenging the trial court's conclusion of eviction, . . . Landlord argues that testimony by employees or agents of the MCPO, stating that each incident of water intrusions and related problems were temporary or eventually fixed, is uncontroverted evidence which shows that the trial court's findings of both actual and constructive eviction are clearly erroneous. To the contrary, when reviewing the record, we find substantial evidence supporting the trial court's findings that the water intrusions were recurring, which in turn supports a finding that they were not transitory or fleeting. Moreover, it was Landlord who suggested to the MCPO that it should move evidence and materials out of areas of the leased premises that were vulnerable to water, showing the Landlord's acknowledgement that water leaks would recur. Additionally, this evidence supports the trial court's findings that the MCPO was deprived of a material part of the leased premises by these water intrusions and related problems. . . .

Affirmed.

Notes and Questions

1. *The covenant of quiet enjoyment.* As the court notes in *Village Commons,* "in every lease there is an implied covenant that the tenant shall have the right of possession, occupancy, and beneficial use of every portion of the leased premises." (See page 334, quoting from an earlier decision.) Originally, the covenant of quiet enjoyment was developed to protect a tenant against wrongful eviction by the landlord or someone claiming under the landlord. The one exception to the independence of covenants was in cases of wrongful eviction. In such cases, the tenant could treat the lease and the obligation to pay rent as terminated. The tenant's obligation was dependent on not being evicted by the landlord.

Over time, the covenant was expanded to include other landlord breaches that interfered with tenants' beneficial enjoyment of the leased premises. This was obviously sensible—otherwise landlords could simply make tenants miserable, without actually ousting them. This expansion was limited, however, because early common law imposed on landlords no duty to provide suitable premises. The implied covenant of quiet enjoyment was breached only when the landlord's conduct had "the effect of depriving the lessee of the beneficial use of the demised premises, whether by positive acts of interference or by withholding something essential to full enjoyment *and included within the terms of the lease.*" 1 American Law of Property, supra, § 3.51 at 280 (emphasis added). But given the absence of a common law duty on the landlord's part, what if anything, would be "included within the terms of the lease"?

There were several possibilities. One was an explicit clause in the lease, or a statutory requirement, that might express certain landlord obligations (to provide heat, to make repairs, for example). Another possible source of a duty arose through *exceptions* to the general no-landlord-duty rule, of which there were several:

- ▶ *Furnished dwelling*: As to short-term leases of furnished dwellings, landlords had an implied duty to make and keep the premises habitable.
- ▶ *Latent defect*: Landlords had the duty to disclose latent defects in the premises that existed at the time the lease was entered into, were or should have been known by the landlord, and were not apparent on reasonable inspection by the tenant.
- ▶ *Common areas*: Landlords had a duty to maintain common areas used by all the tenants in a building.
- ▶ *Fraudulent misrepresentations*: Landlords had a duty to avoid fraudulent misrepresentations as to the condition of the leased premises.
- ▶ *Nuisance abatement*: In some jurisdictions, landlords were under a duty to abate immoral conduct and other nuisances that occurred on property owned by the landlord if they affected the leased premises.

There was no problem of landlord duty in *Village Commons,* because the lease in the case expressly required the landlord to maintain all equipment used in common with other tenants and to maintain the premises in good order, condition, and repair. It seems to be increasingly the case, however, that no such lease provisions are required, and no common law exceptions need be brought into play, in order to pin liability on landlords. Instead, the covenant of quiet enjoyment is taken to create, of itself, a duty upon the part of landlords to provide suitable premises. See, e.g., Reste Realty Corp. v. Cooper, 251 A.2d 268 (N.J. 1969); Max P. Rapacz, Origin and Evolution of Constructive Eviction in the United States, 1 DePaul L. Rev. 69 (1951).

2. *The idea of constructive eviction.* As noted above, the lease obligations of a tenant are dependent on not being wrongfully evicted by the landlord. Just what does "eviction" mean? As explained in *Village Commons* (see page 334), eviction might mean being physically removed or kept out by the landlord (such as changing the locks on the door), in which case there is an actual eviction. See Olin v. Goehler, 694 P.2d 1129 (Wash. App. 1985). But further to aid the cause of tenants, courts developed the idea of constructive eviction. If (a) the condition of the leased premises amounts to a breach of the covenant of quiet enjoyment, and (b) the breach is so substantial as to justify the tenant absenting the premises, and (c) the tenant thereafter leaves within a reasonable time, then it was as though the tenant has been evicted (the eviction was "constructive"). And once evicted, of course, the tenant is relieved of the obligation to pay rent. Q.E.D.

3. *Elements of the covenant of quiet enjoyment and constructive eviction.* To prove breach of the covenant of quiet enjoyment and constructive eviction, ~~Test~~ the tenant must establish three elements: (1) *wrongful conduct* by the landlord (or someone for whom the landlord is legally responsible); (2) *substantial interference* with the tenant's use and enjoyment; and (3) *vacation* of the premises in a timely fashion.

• Wrongful Conduct

Affirmative acts by the landlord that seriously interfere with the tenant's use or enjoyment of the premises are easy cases. There are two situations in which this element has proved to be more difficult for courts—*inactions* by the landlord and *acts of third parties.*

→ <u>Failure by the landlord to act.</u> In general, inaction by the landlord is wrongful only where the landlord is under a duty to act. Such a duty can exist on the basis, for example, of an express clause in the lease, such as a covenant to make repairs. Statutes may also impose a duty on the landlord to act in certain ways (e.g., provide heat). Apart from the lease and statutes and the limited exceptions to *caveat lessee* noted earlier, the early common law imposed no duty on the landlord to keep the premises in good repair or in habitable condition. As we have already mentioned, today courts treat the covenant of quiet enjoyment itself as the source of the landlord's duty to act.

→ <u>Acts of third parties.</u> The traditional rule is that landlords are not responsible for the acts of third parties. Today jurisdictions are divided on the question. Although some adhere to the traditional rule, others have held that the landlord is responsible for controlling the third party's conduct if the landlord has the legal authority to do so. In Blackett v. Olanoff, 358 N.E.2d 817 (Mass. 1977), for example, the court found a constructive eviction where loud noise from a bar near the tenant's apartment and which the landlord owned and leased to another party led the tenant to vacate his apartment after the landlord failed to take steps to abate the noise despite repeated requests to do so. The court found that the landlord had it within his control to correct the problem because the lease for the bar expressly provided that entertainment in the bar had to be conducted so that it would not disturb the nearby neighbors.

- **Substantial Interference**

The conduct must constitute such a major interference with the tenant's ability to use or enjoy the premises that a reasonable person would conclude that the property is uninhabitable or unfit for its intended use. Minor interferences, such as a single broken window, do not amount to constructive eviction. Was the interference in *Village Commons* so substantial as to render the premises unusable for commercial purposes?

- **Timely Vacation**

A tenant who vacates claiming a constructive eviction takes a real chance. On the one hand, the tenant must give the landlord notice of the defect and time to resolve the problem. If she leaves too soon, she cannot later successfully assert constructive eviction as an affirmative defense in an action by the landlord for unpaid rent. On the other hand, the covenant of quiet enjoyment is waivable, and if the tenant waits too long before vacating the premises, she will be considered to have waived any constructive eviction claim. Why do you suppose MCPO waited so long before finally moving out of its office? Was it reasonable under the circumstances for it to do so?

May the covenant of quiet enjoyment be breached if the tenant remains in possession (i.e., absent a constructive eviction)? The answer should be yes. Judicial decisions sometimes say that an eviction, actual or constructive, is necessary to constitute a *breach* of the covenant of quiet enjoyment, but they are incorrect. The covenant of quiet enjoyment and constructive eviction, although related, are distinct doctrines. Constructive eviction is a remedy for a breach of the covenant of quiet enjoyment, but it is not the only available remedy. So, the tenant should be, and usually is, able to stay in possession and sue for damages equal to the difference between the value of the property with and without the breach. See Echo Consulting Services, Inc. v. North Conway Bank, 669 A.2d 227 (N.H. 1995) (if breach is not so substantial as to work a constructive eviction, tenant may stay in possession and sue for compensatory damages); Stevan v. Brown, 458 A.2d 466 (Md. App. 1983) (same).

4. *Partial eviction—actual and constructive.* If there is an *actual eviction*, even though from a *part* of the premises only, the tenant is relieved of *all* liability for rent notwithstanding continued occupation of the balance. The rationale is that the landlord may not apportion his wrong. (Restatement (Second) of Property, Landlord and Tenant § 6.1 (1977) rejects this rule and provides that the tenant may receive an abatement in the rent but may not withhold all rent.) Is a tenant relieved of the obligation to pay rent when there is not an actual, but rather a *constructive*, partial eviction—say when some breach by the landlord makes only a part, but not all, of the premises uninhabitable—even though the tenant remains in undisturbed possession of the balance? In most jurisdictions the answer is no. See, e.g., Brine v. Bergstrom, 480 P.2d 783 (Wash. App. 1971). The lower courts in New York have gone back and forth on the question. See Minjak Co. v. Randolph, 528 N.Y.S.2d 554 (Sup. Ct. 1988) (accepting theory); Zweighaft v. Remington, 66 Misc. 2d 261 (Civ. Ct. 1971) (rejecting theory); East Haven Assocs., Inc. v. Gurian, 64 Misc. 2d 276 (Civ. Ct. 1970) (accepting the theory of constructive partial eviction).

Constructive eviction = no autonomous breach but if not breach tenant Sub breach remain in Can remain + sue possession + damages for damages

Problems

In each of the following cases, *T*, who has a term of years, vacates the leased premises prior to the end of the term and stops paying rent. In a subsequent suit by *L* for unpaid rent, *T* asserts a defense of constructive eviction, claiming that *L* breached the covenant of quiet enjoyment. What result on the facts described below?

(1) *L* fails to respond to repeated complaints from a nonsmoking tenant when cigarette smoke from neighboring units seeps into the tenant's unit. Compare DeNardo v. Corneloup, 163 P.3d 956 (Alaska 2007), with Merrill v. Bosser, 2005 WL 5680219 (Fla. Cir. Ct. 2005).

(2) The building in which *T* leases an apartment from *L* has been the site of criminal activity—acts of burglary and vandalism by unknown third parties. *L* installs deadbolt locks on all entrance doors and hires private security guards, but the problems continue. See Charlotte Eastland Mall, L.L.C. v. Sole Survivor, Inc., 608 S.E.2d 70 (N.C. App. 2004); Sciascia v. Riverpark Apts., 444 N.E.2d 40 (Ohio App. 1981); Annot., 43 A.L.R.5th 207 (1996).

(3) *T*, a professional spa offering a variety of therapeutic treatments, complained to *L* when the tranquility required for the success of its business was destroyed by hammering, sawing, "colorful language of construction workers," and by the joyful squeals of children waiting their turn at the hair parlor in the space immediately above the spa. *L* had understood that *T* required peace and tranquility to run its business. See 3000 B.C. v. Bowman Properties Ltd., 2008 WL 5544414 (Pa. Com. Pl. 2008), aff'd in part, vacated in part, remanded by 3000 B.C. v. Bowman, 990 A.2d 33 (Table) (Pa. Super. Ct. 2009).

4. The Implied Warranty of Habitability

THE EARLY COMMON LAW: *CAVEAT LESSEE*

As we have seen, the early common law was hardheaded, and hardhearted, about a tenant's rights and remedies. Absent some clause in the lease providing otherwise, the tenant took the premises "as is," and landlords were under no obligation to warrant their fitness. Apart from the few narrow exceptions that we briefly considered on page 336 in connection with the covenant of quiet enjoyment, there was no implied warranty of habitability. Tenants had to protect themselves. *Caveat lessee*—let the lessee beware!

With the 1960s there began a period of sweeping reform—most of it at first concerned with residential tenancies, much of it initiated by courts rather than legislatures—the implications and merits of which are still matters of dispute. The reforms have not so much replaced conventional doctrine as riddled it. A given jurisdiction might adopt one new reform but not another, or limit what it adopts to residential tenancies. A useful understanding of this area of landlord-tenant relations thus still requires some attention to the older rules as well as the newer ones.

HILDER v. ST. PETER

Supreme Court of Vermont, 1984
478 A.2d 202

BILLINGS, C.J. Defendants appeal from a judgment rendered by the Rutland Superior Court. The court ordered defendants to pay plaintiff damages in the amount of $4,945.00, which represented "reimbursement of all rent paid and additional compensatory damages" for the rental of a residential apartment over a fourteen month period in defendants' Rutland apartment building. Defendants filed a motion for reconsideration on the issue of the amount of damages awarded to the plaintiff, and plaintiff filed a cross-motion for reconsideration of the court's denial of an award of punitive damages. The court denied both motions. On appeal, defendants raise three issues for our consideration: first, whether the court correctly calculated the amount of damages awarded the plaintiff; secondly, whether the court's award to plaintiff of the entire amount of rent paid to defendants was proper since the plaintiff remained in possession of the apartment for the entire fourteen month period; and finally, whether the court's finding that defendant Stuart St. Peter acted on his own behalf and with the apparent authority of defendant Patricia St. Peter was error.

The facts are uncontested. In October, 1974, plaintiff began occupying an apartment at defendants' 10-12 Church Street apartment building in Rutland with her three children and new-born grandson.[8] Plaintiff orally agreed to pay defendant Stuart St. Peter $140 a month and a damage deposit of $50; plaintiff paid defendant the first month's rent and the damage deposit prior to moving in. Plaintiff has paid all rent due under her tenancy. Because the previous tenants had left behind garbage and items of personal belongings, defendant offered to refund plaintiff's damage deposit if she would clean the apartment herself prior to taking possession. Plaintiff did clean the apartment, but never received her deposit back because the defendant denied ever receiving it. Upon moving into the apartment, plaintiff discovered a broken kitchen window. Defendant promised to repair it, but after waiting a week and fearing that her two year old child might cut herself on the shards of glass, plaintiff repaired the window at her own expense. Although defendant promised to provide a front door key, he never did. For a period of time, whenever plaintiff left the apartment, a member of her family would remain behind for security reasons. Eventually, plaintiff purchased and installed a padlock, again at her own expense. After moving in, plaintiff discovered that the bathroom toilet was clogged with paper and feces and would flush only by dumping pails of water into it. Although plaintiff repeatedly complained about the toilet, and defendant promised to have it repaired, the toilet remained clogged and mechanically inoperable throughout the period of plaintiff's tenancy. In addition, the bathroom light and wall outlet were inoperable. Again, the defendant agreed to repair the fixtures, but never did. In order to have light in the bathroom, plaintiff attached a fixture to the wall and connected it to an extension cord that was plugged into an adjoining room. Plaintiff also discovered that water leaked from the water pipes of the upstairs apartment down the ceilings and walls of both her kitchen and back bedroom. Again,

---

8. Between October, 1974, and December, 1976, plaintiff rented apartment number 1 for $140.00 monthly for 18 months, and apartment number 50 for $125.00 monthly for 7 months.

defendant promised to fix the leakage, but never did. As a result of this leakage, a large section of plaster fell from the back bedroom ceiling onto her bed and her grandson's crib. Other sections of plaster remained dangling from the ceiling. This condition was brought to the attention of the defendant, but he never corrected it. Fearing that the remaining plaster might fall when the room was occupied, plaintiff moved her and her grandson's bedroom furniture into the living room and ceased using the back bedroom. During the summer months an odor of raw sewage permeated plaintiff's apartment. The odor was so strong that the plaintiff was ashamed to have company in her apartment. Responding to plaintiff's complaints, Rutland City workers unearthed a broken sewage pipe in the basement of defendants' building. Raw sewage littered the floor of the basement, but defendant failed to clean it up. Plaintiff also discovered that the electric service for her furnace was attached to her breaker box, although defendant had agreed, at the commencement of plaintiff's tenancy, to furnish heat.

In its conclusions of law, the court held that the state of disrepair of plaintiff's apartment, which was known to the defendants, substantially reduced the value of the leasehold from the agreed rental value, thus constituting a breach of the implied warranty of habitability. The court based its award of damages on the breach of this warranty and on breach of an express contract. Defendant argues that the court misapplied the law of Vermont relating to habitability because the plaintiff never abandoned the demised premises and, therefore, it was error to award her the full amount of rent paid. Plaintiff counters that, while never expressly recognized by this Court, the trial court was correct in applying an implied warranty of habitability and that under this warranty, abandonment of the premises is not required. Plaintiff urges this Court to affirmatively adopt the implied warranty of habitability.

Historically, relations between landlords and tenants have been defined by the law of property. Under these traditional common law property concepts, a lease was viewed as a conveyance of real property. See Note, Judicial Expansion of Tenants' Private Law Rights: Implied Warranties of Habitability and Safety in Residential Urban Leases, 56 Cornell L.Q. 489, 489-90 (1971) (hereinafter cited as Expansion of Tenants' Rights). The relationship between landlord and tenant was controlled by the doctrine of caveat lessee; that is, the tenant took possession of the demised premises irrespective of their state of disrepair. Love, Landlord's Liability for Defective Premises: Caveat Lessee, Negligence, or Strict Liability?, 1975 Wis. L. Rev. 19, 27-28. The landlord's only covenant was to deliver possession to the tenant. The tenant's obligation to pay rent existed independently of the landlord's duty to deliver possession, so that as long as possession remained in the tenant, the tenant remained liable for payment of rent. The landlord was under no duty to render the premises habitable unless there was an express covenant to repair in the written lease. Expansion of Tenants' Rights, supra, at 490. The land, not the dwelling, was regarded as the essence of the conveyance.

An exception to the rule of caveat lessee was the doctrine of constructive eviction. Lemle v. Breeden, 51 Haw. 426, 430, 462 P.2d 470, 473 (1969). Here, if the landlord wrongfully interfered with the tenant's enjoyment of the demised premises, or failed to render a duty to the tenant as expressly required under the terms of the lease, the tenant could abandon the premises and cease paying rent.

Beginning in the 1960's, American courts began recognizing that this approach to landlord and tenant relations, which had originated during the Middle Ages, had become an anachronism in twentieth century, urban society. Today's tenant enters into lease agreements, not to obtain arable land, but to obtain safe, sanitary and comfortable housing.

> [T]hey seek a well known package of goods and services—a package which includes not merely walls and ceilings, but also adequate heat, light and ventilation, serviceable plumbing facilities, secure windows and doors, proper sanitation, and proper maintenance. [Javins v. First National Realty Corp., 428 F.2d 1071, 1074 (D.C. Cir.), cert. denied, 400 U.S. 925, 91 S. Ct. 186, 27 L. Ed. 2d 185 (1970).]

Not only has the subject matter of today's lease changed, but the characteristics of today's tenant have similarly evolved. The tenant of the Middle Ages was a farmer, capable of making whatever repairs were necessary to his primitive dwelling. Additionally, "the common law courts assumed that an equal bargaining position existed between landlord and tenant. . . ." Note, The Implied Warranty of Habitability: A Dream Deferred, 48 UMKC L. Rev. 237, 238 (1980) (hereinafter cited as A Dream Deferred).

In sharp contrast, today's residential tenant, most commonly a city dweller, is not experienced in performing maintenance work on urban, complex living units. The landlord is more familiar with the dwelling unit and mechanical equipment attached to that unit, and is more financially able to "discover and cure" any faults and break-downs. Confronted with a recognized shortage of safe, decent housing, today's tenant is in an inferior bargaining position compared to that of the landlord. Park West Management Corp. v. Mitchell, 47 N.Y.2d 316, 324-25, 391 N.E.2d 1288, 1292, 418 N.Y.S.2d 310, 314, cert. denied, 444 U.S. 992, 100 S. Ct. 523, 62 L. Ed. 2d 421 (1979). Tenants vying for this limited housing are "virtually powerless to compel the performance of essential services." Id. at 325, 391 N.E.2d at 1292, 418 N.Y.S.2d at 314.

10-12 Church Street
Rutland, Vermont, 1999

In light of these changes in the relationship between tenants and landlords, it would be wrong for the law to continue to impose the doctrine of caveat lessee on residential leases. . . .

Therefore, we now hold expressly that in the rental of any residential dwelling unit an implied warranty exists in the lease, whether oral or written, that the landlord will deliver over and maintain, throughout the period of the tenancy, premises that are safe, clean and fit for human habitation. This warranty of habitability is implied in tenancies for a specific period or at will. Additionally, the implied warranty of habitability covers all latent and patent defects in the essential facilities of the residential unit.[9] Essential facilities are "facilities vital to the use of the premises for residential purposes. . . ." Kline v. Burns, 111 N.H. 87, 92, 276 A.2d 248, 252 (1971). This means that a tenant who enters into a lease agreement with knowledge of any defect in the essential facilities cannot be said to have assumed the risk, thereby losing the protection of the warranty. Nor can this implied warranty of habitability be waived by any written provision in the lease or by oral agreement.

In determining whether there has been a breach of the implied warranty of habitability, the courts may first look to any relevant local or municipal housing code; they may also make reference to the minimum housing code standards enunciated in 24 V.S.A. §§5003(c)(1)-5003(c)(5). A substantial violation of an applicable housing code shall constitute prima facie evidence that there has been a breach of the warranty of habitability. "[O]ne or two minor violations standing alone which do not affect" the health or safety of the tenant, shall be considered de minimis and not a breach of the warranty. In addition, the landlord will not be liable for defects caused by the tenant.

However, these codes and standards merely provide a starting point in determining whether there has been a breach. Not all towns and municipalities have housing codes; where there are codes, the particular problem complained of may not be addressed. In determining whether there has been a breach of the implied warranty of habitability, courts should inquire whether the claimed defect has an impact on the safety or health of the tenant.

In order to bring a cause of action for breach of the implied warranty of habitability, the tenant must first show that he or she notified the landlord "of the deficiency or defect not known to the landlord and [allowed] a reasonable time for its correction." King v. Moorehead, 495 S.W.2d [65, 76 (Mo. App. 1973)].

Because we hold that the lease of a residential dwelling creates a contractual relationship between the landlord and tenant, the standard contract remedies of rescission, reformation and damages are available to the tenant when suing for breach of the implied warranty of habitability. The measure of damages shall be the difference between the value of the dwelling as warranted and the value of the dwelling as it exists in its defective condition. In determining the fair rental value of the dwelling as warranted, the court may look to the agreed upon rent as evidence on this issue. . . .

We also find persuasive the reasoning of some commentators that damages should be allowed for a tenant's discomfort and annoyance arising from the landlord's breach of the implied warranty of habitability. See Moskovitz, The Implied Warranty of Habitability: A New Doctrine Raising New Issues, 62 Cal. L. Rev. 1444, 1470-73 (1974)

---

9. The warranty also covers those facilities located in the common areas of an apartment building or duplex that may affect the health or safety of a tenant, such as common stairways, or porches. . . .

(hereinafter cited as A New Doctrine); A Dream Deferred, supra, at 250-51. Damages for annoyance and discomfort are reasonable in light of the fact that

> the residential tenant who has suffered a breach of the warranty . . . cannot bathe as frequently as he would like or at all if there is inadequate hot water; he must worry about rodents harassing his children or spreading disease if the premises are infested; or he must avoid certain rooms or worry about catching a cold if there is inadequate weather protection or heat. Thus, discomfort and annoyance are the common injuries caused by each breach and hence the true nature of the general damages the tenant is claiming. [Moskovitz, A New Doctrine, supra, at 1470-71.]

Damages for discomfort and annoyance may be difficult to compute; however, "[t]he trier [of fact] is not to be deterred from this duty by the fact that the damages are not susceptible of reduction to an exact money standard." Vermont Electric Supply Co. v. Andrus, 132 Vt. 195, 200, 315 A.2d 456, 459 (1974).

Another remedy available to the tenant when there has been a breach of the implied warranty of habitability is to withhold the payment of future rent.[10] The burden and expense of bringing suit will then be on the landlord who can better afford to bring the action. In an action for ejectment for nonpayment of rent, 12 V.S.A. § 4773, "[t]he trier of fact, upon evaluating the seriousness of the breach and the ramification of the defect upon the health and safety of the tenant, will abate the rent at the landlord's expense in accordance with its findings." A Dream Deferred, supra, at 248. The tenant must show that: (1) the landlord had notice of the previously unknown defect and failed, within a reasonable time, to repair it; and (2) the defect, affecting habitability, existed during the time for which rent was withheld. See A Dream Deferred, supra, at 248-50. Whether a portion, all or none of the rent will be awarded to the landlord will depend on the findings relative to the extent and duration of the breach.[11] Javins v. First National Realty Corp., supra, 428 F.2d at 1082-83. Of course, once the landlord corrects the defect, the tenant's obligation to pay rent becomes due again.

Additionally, we hold that when the landlord is notified of the defect but fails to repair it within a reasonable amount of time, and the tenant subsequently repairs the defect, the tenant may deduct the expense of the repair from future rent. 11 Williston on Contracts §1404 (3d ed. W. Jaeger 1968); Marini v. Ireland, 56 N.J. 130, 146, 265 A.2d 526, 535 (1970).

In addition to general damages, we hold that punitive damages may be available to a tenant in the appropriate case. Although punitive damages are generally not recoverable in actions for breach of contract, there are cases in which the breach is of such a willful and wanton or fraudulent nature as to make appropriate the award

---

10. Because we hold that the tenant's obligation to pay rent is contingent on the landlord's duty to provide and maintain a habitable dwelling, it is no longer necessary for the tenant to first abandon the premises; thus, the doctrine of constructive eviction is no longer a viable or needed defense in an action by the landlord for unpaid rent. . . .

11. Some courts suggest that, during the period rent is withheld, the tenant should pay the rent, as it becomes due, into legal custody. See, e.g., Javins v. First National Realty Corp., supra, 428 F.2d at 1083 n.67; see also King v. Moorehead, supra, 495 S.W.2d at 77 (King requires the deposit of the rent into legal custody pending the litigation). Such a procedure assures the availability of that portion, if any, of the rent which the court determines is due to the landlord. King v. Moorehead, supra, 495 S.W.2d at 77; see A Dream Deferred, supra, at 248-250.

of exemplary damages. A willful and wanton or fraudulent breach may be shown "by conduct manifesting personal ill will, or carried out under circumstances of insult or oppression, or even by conduct manifesting . . . a reckless or wanton disregard of [one's] rights. . . ." Sparrow v. Vermont Savings Bank, 95 Vt. 29, 33, 112 A. 205, 207 (1921). When a landlord, after receiving notice of a defect, fails to repair the facility that is essential to the health and safety of his or her tenant, an award of punitive damages is proper. 111 East 88th Partners v. Simon, 106 Misc. 2d 693, 434 N.Y.S.2d 886, 889 (N.Y. Civ. Ct. 1980). . . .

In the instant case, the trial court's award of damages, based in part on a breach of the implied warranty of habitability, was not a misapplication of the law relative to habitability. Because of our holding in this case, the doctrine of constructive eviction, wherein the tenant must abandon in order to escape liability for rent, is no longer viable. When, as in the instant case, the tenant seeks, not to escape rent liability, but to receive compensatory damages in the amount of rent already paid, abandonment is similarly unnecessary. Under our holding, when a landlord breaches the implied warranty of habitability, the tenant may withhold future rent, and may also seek damages in the amount of rent previously paid.

In its conclusions of law the trial court stated that the defendants' failure to make repairs was compensable by damages to the extent of reimbursement of all rent paid and additional compensatory damages. The court awarded plaintiff a total of $4,945.00; $3,445.00 represents the entire amount of rent plaintiff paid, plus the $50.00 deposit. This appears to leave $1,500.00 as the "additional compensatory damages." However, although the court made findings which clearly demonstrate the appropriateness of an award of compensatory damages, there is no indication as to how the court reached a figure of $1,500.00. It is "crucial that this Court and the parties be able to determine what was decided and how the decision was reached." Fox v. McLain, 142 Vt. 11, 16, 451 A.2d 1122, 1124 (1982).

Additionally, the court denied an award to plaintiff of punitive damages on the ground that the evidence failed to support a finding of willful and wanton or fraudulent conduct. The facts in this case, which defendants do not contest, evince a pattern of intentional conduct on the part of defendants for which the term "slumlord" surely was coined. Defendants' conduct was culpable and demeaning to plaintiff and clearly expressive of a wanton disregard of plaintiff's rights. The trial court found that defendants were aware of defects in the essential facilities of plaintiff's apartment, promised plaintiff that repairs would be made, but never fulfilled those promises. The court also found that plaintiff continued, throughout her tenancy, to pay her rent, often in the face of verbal threats made by defendant Stuart St. Peter. These findings point to the "bad spirit and wrong intention" of the defendants, Glidden v. Skinner, 142 Vt. 644, 648, 458 A.2d 1142, 1144 (1983), and would support a finding of willful and wanton or fraudulent conduct, contrary to the conclusions of law and judgment of the trial judge. However, the plaintiff did not appeal the court's denial of punitive damages, and issues not appealed and briefed are waived.

We find that defendants' third claimed error, that the court erred in finding that both defendant Stuart St. Peter and defendant Patricia St. Peter were liable to plaintiff for the breach of the implied warranty of habitability, is meritless. Both defendants were named in the complaint as owners of the 10-12 Church Street apartment building. Plaintiff's complaint also alleged that defendant Stuart St. Peter acted as agent for defendant Patricia St. Peter. Defendants failed to deny these allegations; under V.R.C.P. 8(d) these averments stand as admitted.

Affirmed in part; reversed in part and remanded for hearing on additional compensable damages, consistent with the views herein.

Notes, Questions, and Problems

1. *Status of the implied warranty of habitability.* By latest count, the warranty of habitability has been adopted for residential leases in all but three jurisdictions (Alabama, Arkansas, and Wyoming). See 1 Milton R. Friedman, Friedman on Leases App. 10A (Patrick A. Randolph, Jr. ed. & rev. 5th ed. 2005). In most states, adoption has been effected through legislation rather than judicial reform, as in *Hilder*. A majority of jurisdictions have declined to extend the idea to an implied warranty of fitness or suitability for purpose in commercial leases. Even in the residential context, however, the warranty usually does not apply to all leases. Single family residences might be excluded, for example; or agricultural leases, or long-term leases. So too for casual leases by non-merchant landlords, as when a law professor goes off on sabbatical and rents her house to a visitor. See, e.g., Zimmerman v. Moore, 441 N.E.2d 690 (Ind. App. 1982) (single-family home rented by non-merchant landlord). The upshot is that the implied warranty of habitability does *not* render pointless the doctrines of quiet enjoyment, constructive eviction, and illegal leases considered earlier.

2. *Standard and breach of the warranty.* The standard of the implied warranty of habitability, and the shortcomings that amount to breaches of the standard, appear to vary among jurisdictions, but the differences are probably more nominal than real when it comes to actual cases. Generally speaking, an "adequate standard of habitability" has to be met, and a breach occurs when the leased premises are "uninhabitable" in the eyes of a reasonable person. Housing code provisions and their violation are compelling but usually not conclusive.

In short, the objective is safe and healthy housing; substantial compliance is required. But this means something more than merely avoiding slum conditions. For example, continued loud noise in an apartment building might be a breach. See, e.g., Millbridge Apts. v. Linden, 376 A.2d 611 (N.J. Dist. Ct. 1977). So too for failure of a central air conditioning system. See, e.g., Park Hill Terrace Assocs. v. Glennon, 369 A.2d 938 (N.J. App. Div. 1977). So too for bedbugs. See, e.g., Ludlow Properties, LLC v. Young, 780 N.Y.S.2d 853 (N.Y. City Civ. Ct. 2004). And second-hand smoke. See, e.g., Poyck v. Bryant, 820 N.Y.S.2d 774 (N.Y. City Civ. Ct. 2006).

3. *Mandatory or default rule?* Most jurisdictions agree with *Hilder* that the implied warranty of habitability cannot be waived, but a few might permit a "knowing" waiver by the tenant if "bargaining power" is essentially "equal." See Restatement (Second) of Property, Landlord and Tenant § 5.6 (1977). Consistent with this, most jurisdictions apply the warranty even to patent defects, though a few appear to exclude them at least so long as they do not violate housing code provisions. Why might it be that the warranty of habitability is typically a mandatory rule, rather than a default rule?

4. *Remedies for breach.* The implied warranty of habitability is based largely on contractual principles, and a number of cases agree with *Hilder* that in the case of breach a tenant may avail himself of all the basic contract remedies—damages, rescission, and reformation. There are some unique aspects of the tenant's remedies, however. In general, the following remedies are available to the tenant: (1) remain in possession and bring an action for damages for breach of the warranty (as in *Hilder*); (2) rescind the lease, thereby permitting the tenant to vacate the premises with no further obligation to pay rent; (3) remain in possession and withhold all or part of the rent (most jurisdictions allow the tenant to withhold all of the rent, even for a partial breach of the warranty; some require the tenant to deposit withheld rent in a separate escrow account until the dispute is finally resolved); and (4) repair the defects and deduct the costs of the repairs from rent payments. There is considerable disagreement about how to calculate the rent reduction or damages. Courts have used three different formulae:

→ 1. *Agreed rent—fair market rental value (FMRV) of premises in defective condition*

This is the most straightforward formula because it uses the agreed rent as the starting point. In *Hilder*, however, the court used a different verbal formula: "the difference between the value of the dwelling as warranted and the value of the dwelling as it exists in its defective condition." So,

→ 2. *FMRV of premises in compliant conditions—FMRV of premises in defective condition*

Why did the court use this formula, given the fact that the premises obviously were not in compliance with the warranty at the inception of the lease (notice, by the way, that the court said that the tenant may use the agreed rent as evidence to establish "fair rental value as warranted")? The obvious problem is that formula 1 may lead to zero damages because if the defects existed at the inception of the lease, and if the tenant was aware of them (as in *Hilder*), the agreed rent will tend to equal the value of the premises in their actual (i.e., noncompliant) condition. This would provide an indirect means of allowing the parties to waive a term that is presumably non-waivable. The aim of formula 2 is to avoid that possibility. Does this formula strike you as fair to both parties, or does it provide a windfall to the tenant?

→ 3. *Agreed rent—% of rent corresponding to lease value lost as a consequence of the landlord's breach*

Example: L charges T $600 per month for an apartment. The fair rental value of the premises in habitable conditions (under the warranty of habitability) is $1,000 per month. The fair rental value of the premises in this existing, non-complying condition is $500 per month. The percentage of value lost is 50%. Hence, the tenant is entitled to reduce the rent by $300 a month to $300 a month.

5. *The consequences of the warranty of habitability.* The warranty of habitability is certainly not without its critics. The most common criticism is that, contrary to the expectations of its supporters, the warranty does not improve the welfare of low-income tenants. Most of the work on the consequences of the warranty has been theoretical, but some empirical work has been done. An article

on several studies of landlord-tenant courts summarized several findings, among which are the following:

- The new doctrinal regime did not increase the number of eviction cases filed, indicating perhaps that there has not been an increase in tenant rent withholding.
- A very large percentage of eviction cases never reach open court. Landlord-tenant courts have high default rates. Apparently, once landlords get either the rent or possession, they drop the proceeding. Tenants apparently prefer to move rather than litigate.
- Of the small minority that do reach court, the vast majority are resolved with no reference to the condition of the premises. Tenants are seldom represented by counsel, tenants themselves appear to lack sufficient knowledge of the law to assert their rights under it. See David A. Super, The Rise and Fall of the Implied Warranty of Habitability, 99 Cal. L. Rev. 389, 434-436 (2011).

6. *Problems*

(a) *L* owns a high-rise apartment building. *L*'s entire maintenance and janitorial staff goes on strike for two weeks. The building's incinerators are inoperative as a consequence of the strike; tenants must take their garbage to the curb in paper bags supplied by *L*. City sanitation workers refuse to cross the striking employees' picket lines. Trash piles up to the height of the building's first-floor windows. The garbage exudes noxious odors and results in a declaration of a health emergency by the city. Routine maintenance and extermination service is not performed during the strike, and rats and vermin become a problem. Has *L* breached the implied warranty of habitability? See Park West Management Corp. v. Mitchell, 391 N.E.2d 1288 (N.Y.), cert. denied, 444 U.S. 992 (1979).

(b) *T* resides in a fancy apartment building on Manhattan's "fashionable" Upper East Side and pays a high rent for the privilege. *T*'s lease provides for a lot of fancy amenities: an attendant at the door, an elevator, a swimming pool and gym in the apartment building, and so on. State law requires that leased dwellings be fit for habitation, safe and healthy, and in accord with "the uses reasonably intended by the parties." Does the quoted language extend the implied warranty of habitability so as to encompass the services and amenities that *T* reasonably expected to get according to the terms of his lease? Why might it matter? See Solow v. Wellner, 658 N.E.2d 1005 (N.Y. 1995).

(c) *L* leases an apartment to *X*, a registered sex offender. *T*, who had already leased an adjacent apartment for a one-year term, learns of the lease to *X* and notifies *L* in writing that she wants *L* to terminate her tenancy. When *L* does not respond, *T* vacates and sues for return of her security deposit; *L* counterclaims for the balance of the rent due on the original lease. Did *L*, by leasing to *X*, breach the implied warranty of habitability? Is *T* free to vacate in any event? See Knudsen v. Lax, 842 N.Y.S.2d 341 (Cty. Ct. 2007).

(d) *L* offers a small run-down house for rent at $100 per month. *T* inspects the premises, finds a number of defects, and tells *L* that she will take the place as is, "but only at $50 a month because that's all it's worth in its condition." *L* agrees and *T* takes possession; subsequently she fails to pay any rent. In an eviction suit by *L*, may *T* assert breach of the implied warranty of habitability as a defense (and what are *T*'s damages)? See Haddad v. Gonzalez, 576 N.E.2d 658, 668 (Mass. 1991); Foisy v. Wyman, 515 P.2d 160 (Wash. 1973).

The illegal lease and retaliatory eviction doctrines. Along with the implied warranty of habitability, courts developed two cognate doctrines. The first is the *illegal lease* doctrine. This doctrine provides that a lease for premises that are subject to housing code violations that create unsafe or unsanitary conditions is illegal and therefore unenforceable. The upshot is that the landlord may not enforce provisions in the lease, including the covenant to pay rent. From the tenant's point of view, the chief attraction of the illegal lease defense was the leverage it provided: unlike a claim based on quiet enjoyment and constructive eviction, the tenant could withhold rent and still stave off the landlord's inevitable action to evict for nonpayment. The doctrine is a dead letter today, however, because it has been replaced by the warranty of habitability.

The second cognate doctrine—retaliatory eviction—is much more important. In a nutshell, this doctrine provides that a landlord cannot retaliate against a tenant for reporting housing code violations. Conventional common law doctrine gave landlords virtually unlimited freedom to terminate periodic tenancies and tenancies at will upon proper notice and to refuse to renew expired terms of years. The landlord's reasons were irrelevant and could be malevolent. This feature of the common law could easily undermine the warranty of habitability simply by getting rid of tenants who complained of a breach of the warranty. To avoid this result, most jurisdictions today, whether by statute or judicial decision, forbid retaliatory action by landlords. A fairly common approach is to create a rebuttable presumption of retaliatory purpose if the landlord seeks to terminate a tenancy, increase rent, or decrease services within some given period (commonly anywhere from 90 to 180 days) after a good-faith complaint or other action by a tenant based on the condition of the premises. Retaliatory acts beyond the stated period are also usually prohibited, but the tenant bears the burden of proof.

The (uncertain) impact of Covid-19 on the landlord's obligations. Suppose a landlord discovers an outbreak of Covid-19 cases in its building. What are its legal responsibilities and, beyond that, its ethical responsibilities? Should it shut the building down and decontaminate it? If this is residential property, where will the tenants go? Are they entitled to rent abatement or reduction? If the building is commercial property, will the landlord be liable for business interruption? Who is liable to pay for the cost of decontamination? What if the landlord doesn't shut down the building, decontaminate, or prevent infected persons from entering? What is its possible legal exposure? Is notice to other tenants sufficient? We don't know the answers to these questions, but we raise them to alert to some of the many uncertainties that now face landlords in the era of the Covid-19 virus. We expect that answers to some or all of questions like these will begin to emerge in the months ahead.

Review Problem

On January 1, 2011, Owen rented a small apartment to Alysha under a written 5-year lease for $1,000/month. The lease provided that the lessee could not assign or sublease without the lessor's express consent and that failure to obtain consent rendered the lease voidable at the lessor's option. It imposed no requirement that the lessor act reasonably. A little more than a year later, in February 2012, Alysha's employer relocated her to a different city. Alysha found someone, Britney, who was willing to take over her lease for the duration of its term. Alysha asked Owen to consent to her assigning her lease to Britney for the balance of the terms, on the same terms and conditions as the head lease. Britney had a good job and an excellent credit report, but Owen refused, simply saying that he "disliked turnover." Alysha went ahead anyway and assigned the lease to Britney.

Britney took possession of the apartment on March 1, 2012. Everything went smoothly for the first three months. She mailed monthly checks to Owen on the first of each month to pay the rent of $1,000, and Owen cashed each check. On May 25, the toilet and both the bathroom and kitchen sinks in the apartment backed up and became unusable. These were the only toilets and sinks in the apartment, and Britney was desperate for help. She contacted Owen immediately and asked him to fix the problems. Owen's only response was, "I'll see what I can do." Britney waited five days, but no one showed up. In the meantime she used a neighbor's apartment for her bathroom needs. By June 1, Britney had had enough. She stopped paying rent and sent Owen a letter stating that she intended to remain in possession but no longer pay rent until he properly repaired the toilet and sink problems. Owen's response was to bring an action against Alysha to terminate the head lease and another action against Britney to recover possession for failure to pay rent. What arguments do Alysha and Britney have in defense? How strong are these arguments?

PART IV

TRANSFERS OF LAND

By now you should understand the premium that the legal system puts on alienability, on the easy transfer and exchange of property rights. Generally speaking, free and voluntary exchange permits resources, land included, to move to higher valued uses. But free here means unfettered, not costless. Exchange is never costless because it takes place in a world full of friction and imperfect information. Transferors and transferees must search out mutually beneficial opportunities for exchange, must negotiate and enforce agreements, must confront risk and uncertainty, must obtain and secure that elusive thing called title. Presumably, the law strives to reduce these burdens—these transaction costs—but how well it succeeds is a matter of dispute, in the case of land transfers in particular. There is little question that the cost (including time expended) of transferring land ownership is greater per dollar value than the cost of transferring ownership of stocks or automobiles or diamond rings. Why? The reasons should become apparent in the next two chapters, which focus on land transactions.

CHAPTER 7

The Land Transaction

A. INTRODUCTION TO BUYING AND SELLING REAL ESTATE

While most real estate transactions share many elements in common, each deal presents its own complications and challenges. The following example illustrates the steps that will take place as Bob and Betty Byar go about buying a home. The first step for the Byars is to assess how much they can afford to pay, given their income and savings (lenders frequently require borrowers to contribute 10 to 20 percent of the purchase price as a down payment). The Byars might also contact a mortgage bank or financial institution to pre-qualify for a loan. Then the search for properties will begin, perhaps with the Byars using an Internet site such as www.realtor.com to learn about the market. But eventually, if they are like most home buyers, the Byars will consult a broker with access to Multiple Listing Service (MLS) listings and happy to show a variety of homes. The commission for the broker will typically be paid for by the seller.

Once the Byars find a house they want to buy, they'll begin negotiating a purchase and sale agreement. Usually it's best to hire an attorney to do this, but in some states brokers are permitted to provide the service. In any event, the agreement will probably be done in terms of a form contract such as the one on pages 354-367, which we will be referring to from time to time. The contract will set forth the legal description of the property, its price, provision for an earnest money deposit, and the date for the closing or settlement (the transfer of title).

Real estate contracts are almost always executory, meaning that title is not transferred immediately upon signing the agreement, because both buyers and seller must do certain things during the time between the contract and closing. The buyer will need to obtain a title search to satisfy herself and her lender that the seller can convey good title to the property. The title search is conducted by a title company in some states, by attorneys in others. Most contracts of sale also contain a mortgage contingency, which provides that if the purchaser cannot obtain a mortgage loan within a given time, she can rescind the contract and get back her deposit. For an example of a mortgage contingency clause, see paragraph 11 in the form contract. A second contingency found in many contracts is a clause allowing the buyer to obtain an inspection of the property and rescind the contract if the cost of remedying the problem exceeds some threshold. See paragraph 10 of the form contract. Sometimes this clause is the most heatedly negotiated part of the sales contract.

After the contract has been signed by both parties, either the Byars or the seller will order a title search. The Byars will also typically apply for a mortgage loan and have an inspector visit the property. The title company or lawyer who does the search will provide an abstract of title that will list any encumbrances (such as existing mortgages, liens, rights of way), as well as a listing of the preceding owners of the property. Assuming that the title abstract turns up nothing troubling, the transaction moves forward. If the Byars' application for a mortgage is approved by the lender, they are issued a mortgage commitment that is good for a specified period—typically a couple of months. If all of the other contingencies are satisfied, the Byars and their seller proceed to the closing and transfer of title.

In many states (New York, for example), the transfer of the deed takes place with all parties physically present; in some other states (California, for example), transfer is handled by a third-party escrow agent. The lender provides the proceeds of the loan to the seller, who uses that money and the additional funds paid by the Byars to (1) pay off any existing loans on the property, (2) pay the real estate brokers their commission, (3) pay the legal fees and other fees (such as title insurance) he has agreed to take care of, and (4) pocket the remaining proceeds. At the same time the lender advances the funds for the purchase, the seller transfers title to the property to the Byars by giving them a deed; they sign a promissory note for the loan; they execute a mortgage or deed of trust in favor of the lender and pay fees for the services provided by their lawyer, the title company, and any other parties involved in the transaction. In most instances, a title insurance company will record the deed and mortgage at the County Clerk's office. The company also will issue a policy of title insurance, which promises to defend against any adverse claims and pay a fixed amount if the title is later found to be flawed or unmarketable. The Byars are now the proud owners of a new home.

MULTI-BOARD RESIDENTIAL REAL ESTATE CONTRACT 5.0

1. THE PARTIES: Buyer and Seller are hereinafter referred to as the "Parties." Buyer(s) _____ (Please Print) Seller(s) _____ (Please Print)

If Dual Agency applies, complete Optional Paragraph 41.

2. THE REAL ESTATE: Real Estate shall be defined as the Property, all improvements, the fixtures and Personal Property included therein. Seller agrees to convey to Buyer or to Buyer's designated grantee, the Real Estate with the approximate lot size or acreage of _____ commonly known as:

_____
Address   City   State   Zip

County Unit # (if applicable) Permanent Index Number(s) of Real Estate
If Condo/Coop/Townhome Parking Is Included: # of space(s) ___; identified as Space(s) #_____; (*check type*) ❏ deeded space ❏ limited common element ❏ assigned space.

3. FIXTURES AND PERSONAL PROPERTY: All of the fixtures and included Personal Property are owned by Seller and to Seller's knowledge are in operating condition on the Date of Acceptance, unless otherwise stated herein. Seller agrees to transfer to Buyer all fixtures, all heating, electrical, plumbing and well systems together with the following items of Personal Property by Bill of Sale at Closing:

[*Check or enumerate applicable items*]

__ Refrigerator __ Central Air Conditioning __ Central Humidifier __ Light Fixtures, as they exist

__ Oven/Range/Stove __ Window Air Conditioners __ Water Softener (owned) __Microwave

__ Built-in or   __ Ceiling Fan(s) __ Sump Pumps __ All Window Treatments and Attached Shelving and Hardware

__Dishwasher __Intercom System __Electronic or Media __Existing Storms & Air Filter Screens

__ Garbage Disposal __ TV Antenna System __ Central Vac & Equipment __ Washer

__ Fireplace Screens/Doors/Grates __ Trash Compactor __ Satellite Dish __ Outdoor Shed

__ Security System (owned) __ Fireplace Gas Logs __ Garage Door Opener with Transmitters

__ Invisible Fence System, Collars & Box __ Dryer __ Planted Vegetation __ Gas Grill

__ Attached Gas __ Outdoor Playsets __ All Tacked Down Carpeting __ Carbon Monoxide Detectors

Other items included:

_____

Other items NOT included:

_____

Seller warrants to Buyer that all fixtures, systems and Personal Property included in this Contract shall be in operating condition at Possession, except:

_____

A system or item shall be deemed to be in operating condition if it performs the function for which it is intended, regardless of age, and does not constitute a threat to health or safety.

Home Warranty ❑ shall ❑ shall not be included at a Premium not to exceed $_____.

4. PURCHASE PRICE: Purchase Price of $_____ shall be paid as follows: Initial earnest money of $_____ by ❑ check, ❑ cash OR ❑ note due on _____, 20____ to be increased to a total of $_____ by _____, 20____. The earnest money shall be held by the [*check one*] ❑ Seller's Broker ❑ Buyer's Broker as "Escrowee," in trust for the mutual benefit of the Parties. The balance of the Purchase Price, as adjusted by prorations, shall be paid at Closing by wire transfer of funds, or by certified, cashier's, mortgage lender's or title company's check (provided that the title company's check is guaranteed by a licensed title insurance company).

5. CLOSING: Closing or escrow payout shall be on _____, 20___ or at such time as mutually agreed by the Parties in writing. Closing shall take place at the escrow office of the title company (or its issuing agent) that will issue the Owner's Policy of Title Insurance, situated nearest the Real Estate or as shall be agreed mutually by the Parties.

6. POSSESSION: Unless otherwise provided in Paragraph 39, Seller shall deliver possession to Buyer at the time of Closing. Possession shall be deemed to have been delivered when Seller has vacated the Real Estate and delivered keys to the Real Estate to Buyer or to the office of the Seller's Broker.

7. STATUTORY DISCLOSURES: If applicable, prior to signing this Contract, Buyer [*check one*] ❏ has ❏ has not received a completed Illinois Residential Real Property Disclosure Report; [*check one*] ❏ has ❏ has not received the EPA Pamphlet, "Protect Your Family From Lead in Your Home"; [*check one*] ❏ has ❏ has not received a Lead-Based Paint Disclosure; [*check one*] ❏ has ❏ has not received the IEMA Pamphlet "Radon Testing Guidelines for Real Estate Transactions"; [*check one*] ❏ has ❏ has not received the Disclosure of Information on Radon Hazards.

8. PRORATIONS: Proratable items shall include, without limitation, rents and deposits (if any) from tenants; Special Service Area or Special Assessment Area tax for the year of Closing only; utilities, water and sewer; and Homeowner or Condominium Association fees (and Master/Umbrella Association fees, if applicable). Accumulated reserves of a Homeowner/Condominium Association(s) are not a proratable item. Seller represents that as of the Date of Acceptance Homeowner/Condominium Association(s) fees are $_____ per _____ (and, if applicable, Master/Umbrella Association fees are $_____ per _____). Seller agrees to pay prior to or at Closing any special assessments (by any association or governmental entity) confirmed prior to the Date of Acceptance. Installments due after the year of Closing for a Special Assessment Area or Special Service Area shall not be a proratable item and shall be payable by Buyer. The general Real Estate taxes shall be prorated as of the date of Closing based on _____% of the most recent ascertainable full year tax bill. All prorations shall be final as of Closing, except as provided in Paragraph 20. If the amount of the most recent ascertainable full year tax bill reflects a homeowner, senior citizen or other exemption, a senior freeze or senior deferral, then Seller has submitted or will submit in a timely manner all necessary documentation to the appropriate governmental entity, before or after closing, to preserve said exemption(s).

9. ATTORNEY REVIEW: Within five (5) Business Days after the Date of Acceptance, the attorneys for the respective Parties, by Notice, may:

(a) Approve this Contract; or

(b) Disapprove this Contract, which disapproval shall not be based solely upon the Purchase Price; or

(c) Propose modifications except for the Purchase Price. If within ten (10) Business Days after the Date of Acceptance written agreement is not reached by the Parties with respect to resolution of the proposed modifications, then either Party may terminate this Contract by serving Notice, whereupon this Contract shall be null and void; or

(d) Propose suggested changes to this Contract. If such suggestions are not agreed upon, neither Party may declare this Contract null and void and this Contract shall remain in full force and effect.

Unless otherwise specified, all Notices shall be deemed made pursuant to Paragraph 9(c). If Notice is not served within the time specified herein, the provisions of this paragraph shall be deemed waived by the Parties and this Contract shall remain in full force and effect.

10. PROFESSIONAL INSPECTIONS AND INSPECTION NOTICES: Buyer may conduct at Buyer's expense (unless otherwise provided by governmental regulations) a home, radon, environmental, lead-based paint and/or lead-based paint hazards (unless separately waived), and/or wood destroying insect infestation inspection of the Real Estate by one or more licensed or certified inspection service(s).

(a) Buyer agrees that minor repairs and routine maintenance items of the Real Estate do not constitute defects and are not a part of this contingency. **The fact that a functioning major component may be at the end of its useful life shall not render such component defective for purposes of this paragraph.** Buyer shall indemnify Seller and hold Seller harmless from and against any loss or damage caused by the acts or negligence of Buyer or any person performing any inspection. The home inspection shall cover only the major components of the Real Estate, including but not limited to central heating system(s), central cooling system(s), plumbing and well system, electrical system, roof, walls, windows, ceilings, floors, appliances and foundation. A major component shall be deemed to be in operating condition if it performs the function for which it is intended, regardless of age, and does not constitute a threat to health or safety. If radon mitigation is performed, Seller shall pay for any retest.

(b) Buyer shall serve Notice upon Seller or Seller's attorney of any defects disclosed by any inspection for which Buyer requests resolution by Seller, together with a copy of the pertinent pages of the inspection reports within five (5) Business Days (ten (10) calendar days for a lead-based paint and/or lead-based paint hazard inspection) after the Date of Acceptance. If within ten (10) Business Days after the Date of Acceptance written agreement is not reached by the Parties with respect to resolution of all inspection issues, then either Party may terminate this Contract by serving Notice to the other Party, whereupon this Contract shall be null and void.

(c) Notwithstanding anything to the contrary set forth above in this paragraph, in the event the inspection reveals that the condition of the Real Estate is unacceptable to Buyer and Buyer serves Notice to Seller within five (5) Business Days after the Date of Acceptance, this Contract shall be null and void.

(d) Failure of Buyer to conduct said inspection(s) and notify Seller within the time specified operates as a waiver of Buyer's right to terminate this Contract under this Paragraph 10 and this Contract shall remain in full force and effect.

11. MORTGAGE CONTINGENCY: This Contract is contingent upon Buyer obtaining a firm written mortgage commitment (except for matters of title and survey or matters totally within Buyer's control) on or before _____, 20____ for a [*check one*] ❑ fixed ❑ adjustable; [*check one*] ❑ conventional ❑ FHA/VA (if FHA/VA is chosen, complete Paragraph 35) ❑ other _____ loan of ____% of Purchase Price, plus private mortgage insurance (PMI), if required. The interest rate (initial rate, if applicable) shall not exceed ____% per annum, amortized over not less than _____ years. Buyer shall pay loan origination fee and/or discount points not to exceed ____% of the loan amount. Buyer shall pay the cost of application, usual and customary processing fees and closing costs charged by lender. (Complete Paragraph 33 if closing cost credits apply.) Buyer shall make written loan application within five (5) Business Days after the Date of Acceptance. **Failure to do so shall constitute an act of Default under this Contract. If Buyer, having applied for the loan specified above, is unable to obtain such loan commitment and serves Notice to Seller within the time specified, this Contract shall be null and void. If Notice of inability to obtain such loan commitment is not served within the time specified, Buyer shall be deemed to have waived this contingency and this Contract shall remain in full force and effect. Unless otherwise provided in Paragraph 31, this Contract shall not be contingent upon the sale and/or closing of Buyer's existing real estate. Buyer shall be deemed to have satisfied the financing conditions of this paragraph if Buyer obtains a loan commitment in accordance with the terms of this paragraph even though the loan is conditioned on the sale and/ or closing of Buyer's existing real estate.** If Seller at Seller's option and expense, within thirty (30) days after Buyer's Notice, procures for Buyer such commitment or notifies Buyer that Seller will accept a purchase money mortgage upon the same terms, this Contract shall remain in full force and effect. In such event, Seller shall notify Buyer within five (5) Business Days after Buyer's Notice of Seller's election to provide or obtain such financing, and Buyer shall furnish to Seller or lender all requested information and shall sign all papers necessary to obtain the mortgage commitment and to close the loan.

    12. HOMEOWNER INSURANCE: This Contract is contingent upon Buyer obtaining evidence of insurability for an Insurance Service Organization HO-3 or equivalent policy at standard premium rates within ten (10) Business Days after the Date of Acceptance. If Buyer is unable to obtain evidence of insurability and serves Notice with proof of same to Seller within the time specified, this Contract shall be null and void. If Notice is not served within the time specified, Buyer shall be deemed to have waived this contingency and this Contract shall remain in full force and effect.

    13. FLOOD INSURANCE: Unless previously disclosed in the Illinois Residential Real Property Disclosure Report, Buyer shall have the option to declare this Contract null and void if the Real Estate is located in a special flood hazard area which requires Buyer to carry flood insurance. **If Notice of the option to declare this Contract null and void is not given to Seller within ten (10) Business Days after the Date of Acceptance or by the Mortgage Contingency deadline date described in Paragraph 11 (whichever is later), Buyer shall be deemed to have waived such option and this Contract shall remain in full force and effect.** Nothing herein shall be deemed to affect any rights afforded by the Residential Real Property Disclosure Act.

    14. CONDOMINIUM/COMMON INTEREST ASSOCIATIONS: (If applicable) The Parties agree that the terms contained in this paragraph, which may be contrary to other terms of this Contract, shall supersede any conflicting terms.

    (a) Title when conveyed shall be good and merchantable, subject to terms, provisions, covenants and conditions of the Declaration of Condominium/ Covenants, Conditions and Restrictions and all amendments; public and utility easements including any easements established by or implied from the Declaration of Condominium/Covenants, Conditions and Restrictions or amendments thereto; party wall rights and agreements; limitations and conditions imposed by the Condominium Property Act; installments due after the date of Closing of general assessments established pursuant to the Declaration of Condominium/Covenants, Conditions and Restrictions.

(b) Seller shall be responsible for payment of all regular assessments due and levied prior to Closing and for all special assessments confirmed prior to the Date of Acceptance.

(c) Buyer has, within five (5) Business Days from the Date of Acceptance, the right to demand from Seller items as stipulated by the Illinois Condominium Property Act, if applicable, and Seller shall diligently apply for same. This Contract is subject to the condition that Seller be able to procure and provide to Buyer, a release or waiver of any option of first refusal or other pre-emptive rights of purchase created by the Declaration of Condominium/Covenants, Conditions and Restrictions within the time established by the Declaration of Condominium/Covenants, Conditions and Restrictions. In the event the Condominium Association requires the personal appearance of Buyer and/or additional documentation, Buyer agrees to comply with same.

(d) In the event the documents and information provided by Seller to Buyer disclose that the existing improvements are in violation of existing rules, regulations or other restrictions or that the terms and conditions contained within the documents would unreasonably restrict Buyer's use of the premises or would result in financial obligations unacceptable to Buyer in connection with owning the Real Estate, then Buyer may declare this Contract null and void by giving Seller Notice within five (5) Business Days after the receipt of the documents and information required by Paragraph 14(c), listing those deficiencies which are unacceptable to Buyer. If Notice is not served within the time specified, Buyer shall be deemed to have waived this contingency, and this Contract shall remain in full force and effect.

(e) Seller shall not be obligated to provide a condominium survey.

(f) Seller shall provide a certificate of insurance showing Buyer and Buyer's mortgagee, if any, as an insured.

15. THE DEED: Seller shall convey or cause to be conveyed to Buyer or Buyer's designated grantee good and merchantable title to the Real Estate by recordable general Warranty Deed, with release of homestead rights (or the appropriate deed if title is in trust or in an estate), and with real estate transfer stamps to be paid by Seller (unless otherwise designated by local ordinance). Title when conveyed will be good and merchantable, subject only to: general real estate taxes not due and payable at the time of Closing; covenants, conditions and restrictions of record; and building lines and easements, if any, provided they do not interfere with the current use and enjoyment of the Real Estate.

16. TITLE: At Seller's expense, Seller will deliver or cause to be delivered to Buyer or Buyer's attorney within customary time limitations and sufficiently in advance of Closing, as evidence of title in Seller or Grantor, a title commitment for an ALTA title insurance policy in the amount of the Purchase Price with extended coverage by a title company licensed to operate in the State of Illinois, issued on or subsequent to the Date of Acceptance, subject only to items listed in Paragraph 15. The requirement to provide extended coverage shall not apply if the Real Estate is vacant land. The commitment for title insurance furnished by Seller will be conclusive evidence of good and merchantable title as therein shown, subject only to the exceptions therein stated. If the title commitment discloses any unpermitted exceptions or if the Plat of Survey shows any encroachments or other survey matters that are not acceptable to Buyer, then Seller shall have said exceptions, survey matters or encroachments removed, or have the title insurer commit to either insure against loss or damage that may result from such exceptions or survey matters or insure against any court-ordered removal of the encroachments. If Seller fails to have such exceptions waived or insured over prior to Closing, Buyer may elect to take the title as it then is with the right to deduct from the Purchase Price prior encumbrances of a definite or ascertainable amount. Seller shall furnish Buyer at Closing an Affidavit of Title covering the date of Closing, and shall sign any other customary forms required for issuance of an ALTA Insurance Policy.

    17. PLAT OF SURVEY: Not less than one (1) Business Day prior to Closing, except where the Real Estate is a condominium (see Paragraph 14) Seller shall, at Seller's expense, furnish to Buyer or Buyer's attorney a Plat of Survey that conforms to the current Minimum Standards of Practice for boundary surveys, is dated not more than six (6) months prior to the date of Closing, and is prepared by a professional land surveyor licensed to practice land surveying under the laws of the State of Illinois. The Plat of Survey shall show visible evidence of improvements, rights of way, easements, use and measurements of all parcel lines. The land surveyor shall set monuments or witness corners at all accessible corners of the land. All such corners shall also be visibly staked or flagged. The Plat of Survey shall include the following statement placed near the professional land surveyor seal and signature: "This professional service conforms to the current Illinois Minimum Standards for a boundary survey." A Mortgage Inspection, as defined, is not a boundary survey and is not acceptable.

    18. ESCROW CLOSING: At the election of either Party, not less than five (5) Business Days prior to Closing, this sale shall be closed through an escrow with the lending institution or the title company in accordance with the provisions of the usual form of Deed and Money Escrow Agreement, as agreed upon between the Parties, with provisions inserted in the Escrow Agreement as may be required to conform with this Contract. The cost of the escrow shall be paid by the Party requesting the escrow. If this transaction is a cash purchase (no mortgage is secured by Buyer), the Parties shall share the title company escrow closing fee equally.

    19. DAMAGE TO REAL ESTATE OR CONDEMNATION PRIOR TO CLOSING: If prior to delivery of the deed the Real Estate shall be destroyed or materially damaged by fire or other casualty, or the Real Estate is taken by condemnation, then Buyer shall have the option of either terminating this Contract (and receiving a refund of earnest money) or accepting the Real Estate as damaged or destroyed, together with the proceeds of the condemnation award or any insurance payable as a result of the destruction or damage, which gross proceeds Seller agrees to assign to Buyer and deliver to Buyer at Closing. Seller shall not be obligated to repair or replace damaged improvements. The provisions of the Uniform Vendor and Purchaser Risk Act of the State of Illinois shall be applicable to this Contract, except as modified by this paragraph.

20. REAL ESTATE TAX ESCROW: In the event the Real Estate is improved, but has not been previously taxed for the entire year as currently improved, the sum of three percent (3%) of the Purchase Price shall be deposited in escrow with the title company with the cost of the escrow to be divided equally by Buyer and Seller and paid at Closing. When the exact amount of the taxes to be prorated under this Contract can be ascertained, the taxes shall be prorated by Seller's attorney at the request of either Party and Seller's share of such tax liability after proration shall be paid to Buyer from the escrow funds and the balance, if any, shall be paid to Seller. If Seller's obligation after such proration exceeds the amount of the escrow funds, Seller agrees to pay such excess promptly upon demand.

21. SELLER REPRESENTATIONS: Seller represents that with respect to the Real Estate, Seller has no knowledge of nor has Seller received written notice from any governmental body regarding:

(a) zoning, building, fire or health code violations that have not been corrected;

(b) any pending rezoning;

(c) boundary line disputes;

(d) any pending condemnation or Eminent Domain proceeding;

(e) easements or claims of easements not shown on the public records;

(f) any hazardous waste on the Real Estate;

(g) any improvements to the Real Estate for which the required permits were not obtained;

(h) any improvements to the Real Estate which are not included in full in the determination of the most recent tax assessment; or

(i) any improvements to the Real Estate which are eligible for the home improvement tax exemption.

Seller further represents that:

1. There [*check one*] ❏ is ❏ is not a pending or unconfirmed special assessment affecting the Real Estate by any association or governmental entity payable by Buyer after date of Closing.

2. The Real Estate [*check one*] ❏ is ❏ is not located within a Special Assessment Area or Special Service Area, payments for which will not be the obligation of Seller after the year in which the Closing occurs.

If any of the representations contained herein regarding a Special Assessment Area or Special Service Area are unacceptable to Buyer, Buyer shall have the option to declare this Contract null and void. If Notice of the option to declare this Contract null and void is not given to Seller within ten (10) Business Days after the Date of Acceptance or by the Mortgage Contingency deadline date described in Paragraph 11 (whichever is later), Buyer shall be deemed to have waived such option and this Contract shall remain in full force and effect. Seller's representations contained in this paragraph shall survive the Closing.

22. CONDITION OF REAL ESTATE AND INSPECTION: Seller agrees to leave the Real Estate in broom clean condition. All refuse and personal property that is not to be conveyed to Buyer shall be removed from the Real Estate at Seller's expense prior to delivery of Possession. Buyer shall have the right to inspect the Real Estate, fixtures and included Personal Property prior to Possession to verify that the Real Estate, improvements and included Personal Property are in substantially the same condition as of the Date of Acceptance, normal wear and tear excepted.

23. MUNICIPAL ORDINANCE, TRANSFER TAX, AND GOVERNMENTAL COMPLIANCE:

(a) Parties are cautioned that the Real Estate may be situated in a municipality that has adopted a pre-closing inspection requirement, municipal Transfer Tax or other similar ordinances. Transfer taxes required by municipal ordinance shall be paid by the party designated in such ordinance.

(b) Parties agree to comply with the reporting requirements of the applicable sections of the Internal Revenue Code and the Real Estate Settlement Procedures Act of 1974, as amended.

24. BUSINESS DAYS/HOURS: Business Days are defined as Monday through Friday, excluding Federal holidays. Business Hours are defined as 8:00 A.M. to 6:00 P.M. Chicago time.

25. FACSIMILE OR DIGITAL SIGNATURES: Facsimile or digital signatures shall be sufficient for purposes of executing, negotiating, and finalizing this Contract.

26. DIRECTION TO ESCROWEE: In every instance where this Contract shall be deemed null and void or if this Contract may be terminated by either Party, the following shall be deemed incorporated: "and earnest money refunded to Buyer upon written direction of the Parties to Escrowee or upon entry of an order by a court of competent jurisdiction." There shall be no disbursement of earnest money unless Escrowee has been provided written direction from Seller and Buyer. Absent a direction relative to the disbursement of earnest money within a reasonable period of time, Escrowee may deposit funds with the Clerk of the Circuit Court by the filing of an action in the nature of Interpleader. Escrowee shall be reimbursed from the earnest money for all costs, including reasonable attorney fees, related to the filing of the Interpleader action. Seller and Buyer shall indemnify and hold Escrowee harmless from any and all conflicting claims and demands arising under this paragraph.

. . .

28. PERFORMANCE: Time is of the essence of this Contract. In any action with respect to this Contract, the Parties are free to pursue any legal remedies at law or in equity and the prevailing Party in litigation shall be entitled to collect reasonable attorney fees and costs from the non-Prevailing Party as ordered by a court of competent jurisdiction.

29. CHOICE OF LAW/GOOD FAITH: All terms and provisions of this Contract including but not limited to the Attorney Review and Professional Inspection Paragraphs shall be governed by the laws of the State of Illinois and are subject to the covenant of good faith and fair dealing implied in all Illinois contracts.

30. OTHER PROVISIONS: This Contract is also subject to those OPTIONAL PROVISIONS initialed by the Parties and the following attachments, if any:

_____

_____

OPTIONAL PROVISIONS (Applicable ONLY if initialed by all Parties)
31. SALE OF BUYER'S REAL ESTATE:

[Initials]

(A) REPRESENTATIONS ABOUT BUYER'S REAL ESTATE: Buyer represents to Seller as follows:

(1) Buyer owns real estate commonly known as (address): _____
_____.

(2) Buyer [*check one*] ❑ has ❑ has not entered into a contract to sell said real estate.

If Buyer has entered into a contract to sell said real estate, that contract:

(a) [*check one*] ❑ is ❑ is not subject to a mortgage contingency.

(b) [*check one*] ❑ is ❑ is not subject to a real estate sale contingency.

(c) [*check one*] ❑ is ❑ is not subject to a real estate closing contingency.

(3) Buyer [*check one*] ❑ has ❑ has not listed said real estate for sale with a licensed real estate broker and in a local multiple listing service.

(4) If Buyer's real estate is not listed for sale with a licensed real estate broker and in a local multiple listing service, Buyer [*check one*]

(a) ❑ Shall list said real estate for sale with a licensed real estate broker who will place it in a local multiple listing service within five (5) Business Days after the Date of Acceptance. [For information only] Broker: _____
Broker's Address: _____ Phone: _____.

(b) ❑ Does not intend to list said real estate for sale.

(B) CONTINGENCIES BASED UPON SALE AND/OR CLOSE OF BUYER'S REAL ESTATE:

(1) This Contract is contingent upon Buyer having entered into a contract for the sale of Buyer's real estate that is in full force and effect as of _____, 20___. Such contract should provide for a closing date not later than the Closing Date set forth in this contract. **If Notice is served on or before the date set forth in this subparagraph that Buyer has not procured a contract for the sale of Buyer's real estate, this Contract shall be null and void. If notice that Buyer has not procured a contract for the sale of Buyer's real estate is not served on or before the close of business on the date set forth in this subparagraph, Buyer shall be deemed to have waived all contingencies contained in this Paragraph 31, and this Contract shall remain in full force and effect.** (If this paragraph is used, then the following paragraph **must** be completed.)

(2) In the event Buyer has entered into a contract for the sale of Buyer's real estate as set forth in Paragraph 31(B)(1) and that contract is in full force and effect, or has entered into a contract for the sale of Buyer's real estate prior to the execution of this Contract, this Contract is contingent upon Buyer closing the sale of Buyer's real estate on or before _____, 20___. **If Notice that Buyer has not closed the sale of Buyer's real estate is served before the close of business on the next Business Day after the date set forth in the preceding sentence, this Contract shall be null and void. If Notice is not served as described in the preceding sentence, Buyer shall be deemed to have waived all contingencies contained in this Paragraph 31, and this Contract shall remain in full force and effect.**

(3) If the contract for the sale of Buyer's real estate is terminated for any reason after the date set forth in Paragraph 31(B)(1) (or after the date of this Contract if no date is set forth in Paragraph 31(B)(1)), Buyer shall, within three (3) Business Days of such termination, notify Seller of said termination. **Unless Buyer, as part of said Notice, waives all contingencies in Paragraph 31 and complies with Paragraph 31(D), this Contract shall be null and void as of the date of Notice. If Notice as required by this subparagraph is not served within the time specified, Buyer shall be in default under the terms of this Contract.**

(C) SELLER'S RIGHT TO CONTINUE TO OFFER REAL ESTATE FOR SALE: During the time of this contingency, Seller has the right to continue to show the Real Estate and offer it for sale subject to the following:

(1) If Seller accepts another bona fide offer to purchase the Real Estate while the contingencies expressed in Paragraph 31(B) are in effect, Seller shall notify Buyer in writing of same. Buyer shall then have _____ hours after Seller gives such Notice to waive the contingencies set forth in Paragraph 31(B), subject to Paragraph 31(D).

(2) Seller's Notice to Buyer (commonly referred to as a "kick-out" Notice) shall be in writing and shall be served on Buyer, not Buyer's attorney or Buyer's real estate agent. Courtesy copies of such "kick-out" Notice should be sent to Buyer's attorney and Buyer's real estate agent, if known. Failure to provide such courtesy copies shall not render Notice invalid. Notice to any one of a multiple-person Buyer shall be sufficient Notice to all Buyers. Notice for the purpose of this subparagraph only shall be served upon Buyer in the following manner:

(a) By personal delivery effective at the time and date of personal delivery; or

(b) By mailing to the addresses recited herein for Buyer by regular mail and by certified mail. Notice shall be effective at 10:00 A.M. on the morning of the second day following deposit of Notice in the U.S. Mail; or

(c) By commercial overnight delivery (e.g., FedEx). Notice shall be effective upon delivery or at 4:00 P.M. Chicago time on the next delivery day following deposit with the overnight delivery company, whichever first occurs.

(3) If Buyer complies with the provisions of Paragraph 31(D) then this Contract shall remain in full force and effect.

(4) If the contingencies set forth in Paragraph 31(B) are NOT waived in writing within said time period by Buyer, this Contract shall be null and void.

(5) Except as provided in Paragraph 31(C)(2) above, all Notices shall be made in the manner provided by Paragraph 27 of this Contract.

(6) Buyer waives any ethical objection to the delivery of Notice under this paragraph by Seller's attorney or representative.

(D) WAIVER OF PARAGRAPH 31 CONTINGENCIES: Buyer shall be deemed to have waived the contingencies in Paragraph 31(B) when Buyer has delivered written waiver and deposited with the Escrowee additional earnest money in the amount of $_____ in the form of a cashier's or certified check within the time specified. **If Buyer fails to deposit the additional earnest money within the time specified, the waiver shall be deemed ineffective and this Contract shall be null and void.**

(E) BUYER COOPERATION REQUIRED: Buyer authorizes Seller or Seller's agent to verify representations contained in Paragraph 31 at any time, and Buyer agrees to cooperate in providing relevant information.

32. CANCELLATION OF PRIOR REAL ESTATE CONTRACT: In the event either Party has entered into a prior real estate contract, this Contract shall be subject to written cancellation of the prior contract on or before _____ ____, 20____. **In the event the prior contract is not cancelled within the time specified, this Contract shall be null and void. Seller's notice to the purchaser under the prior contract should not be served until after Attorney Review and Professional Inspections provisions of this Contract have expired, been satisfied or waived.**

33. CREDIT AT CLOSING: Provided Buyer's lender permits such credit to show on the HUD-1 Settlement Statement, **and if not, such lesser amount as the lender permits,** Seller agrees to credit to Buyer at Closing $_____ to be applied to prepaid expenses, closing costs or both.

34. INTEREST BEARING ACCOUNT: Earnest money (with a completed W-9 and other required forms), shall be held in a federally insured interest bearing account at a financial institution designated by Escrowee. All interest earned on the earnest money shall accrue to the benefit of and be paid to Buyer. **Buyer shall be responsible for any administrative fee (not to exceed $100) charged for setting up the account.** In anticipation of Closing, the Parties direct Escrowee to close the account no sooner than ten (10) Business Days prior to the anticipated Closing date.

35. VA OR FHA FINANCING: If Buyer is seeking VA or FHA financing, this provision shall be applicable: **Required FHA or VA amendments and disclosures shall be attached to this Contract.** If VA, the Funding Fee, or if FHA, the Mortgage Insurance Premium (MIP) shall be paid by Buyer and [*check one*] ❑ shall ❑ shall not be added to the mortgage loan amount.

36. INTERIM FINANCING: This Contract is contingent upon Buyer obtaining a written commitment for interim financing on or before _____, 20____ in the amount of $_____. **If Buyer is unable to secure the interim financing commitment and gives Notice to Seller within the time specified, this Contract shall be null and void. If Notice is not served within the time specified, this provision shall be deemed waived by the Parties and this Contract shall remain in full force and effect.**

37. WELL AND/OR SEPTIC/SANITARY INSPECTIONS: Seller shall obtain at Seller's expense a well water test stating that the well delivers not less than five (5) gallons of water per minute and including a bacteria and nitrate (and lead test for FHA loans) and/or a septic report from the applicable County Health Department, a Licensed Environmental Health Practitioner, or a licensed well and septic inspector, each dated not more than ninety (90) days prior to Closing, stating that the well and water supply and the private sanitary system are in proper operating condition with no defects noted. Seller shall remedy any defect or deficiency disclosed by said report(s) prior to Closing, provided that if the cost of remedying a defect or deficiency and the cost of landscaping together exceed $3,000.00, and if the Parties cannot reach agreement regarding payment of such additional cost, this Contract may be terminated by either Party. Additional testing recommended by the report shall be obtained at Seller's expense. If the report recommends additional testing after Closing, the Parties shall have the option of establishing an escrow with a mutual cost allocation for necessary repairs or replacements, or either Party may terminate this Contract prior to Closing. Seller shall deliver a copy of such evaluation(s) to Buyer not less than one (1) Business Day prior to Closing.

38. WOOD DESTROYING INFESTATION: Notwithstanding the provisions of Paragraph 10, within ten (10) Business Days after the Date of Acceptance, Seller at Seller's expense shall deliver to Buyer a written report, dated not more than six (6) months prior to the date of Closing, by a licensed inspector certified by the appropriate state regulatory authority in the subcategory of termites, stating that there is no visible evidence of active infestation by termites or other wood destroying insects. Unless otherwise agreed between the Parties, if the report discloses evidence of active infestation or structural damage, Buyer has the option within five (5) Business Days of receipt of the report to proceed with the purchase or declare this Contract null and void.

39. POST-CLOSING POSSESSION: Possession shall be delivered no later than 11:59 P.M. on the date that is _____ days after the date of Closing ("the Possession Date"). Seller shall be responsible for all utilities, contents and liability insurance, and home maintenance expenses until delivery of possession. Seller shall deposit in escrow at Closing with _____, [*check one*] ❏ one percent (1%) of the Purchase Price or ❏ the sum of $_____ to be paid by Escrowee as follows:

(a) The sum of $_____ per day for use and occupancy from and including the day after Closing to and including the day of delivery of Possession, if on or before the Possession Date;

(b) The amount per day equal to three (3) times the daily amount set forth herein shall be paid for each day after the Possession Date specified in this paragraph that Seller remains in possession of the Real Estate; and

(c) The balance, if any, to Seller after delivery of Possession and provided that the terms of Paragraph 22 have been satisfied. Seller's liability under this paragraph shall not be limited to the amount of the possession escrow deposit referred to above. Nothing herein shall be deemed to create a Landlord/Tenant relationship between the Parties.

40. "AS IS" CONDITION: This Contract is for the sale and purchase of the Real Estate in its "As Is" condition as of the Date of Offer. Buyer acknowledges that no representations, warranties or guarantees with respect to the condition of the Real Estate have been made by Seller or Seller's Designated Agent other than those known defects, if any, disclosed by Seller. Buyer may conduct an inspection at Buyer's expense. **In that event, Seller shall make the Real Estate available to Buyer's inspector at reasonable times. Buyer shall indemnify Seller and hold Seller harmless from and against any loss or damage caused by the acts or negligence of Buyer or any person performing any inspection. In the event the inspection reveals that the condition of the Real Estate is unacceptable to Buyer and Buyer so notifies Seller within five (5) Business Days after the Date of Acceptance, this Contract shall be null and void. Failure of Buyer to notify Seller or to conduct said inspection operates as a waiver of Buyer's right to terminate this Contract under this paragraph and this Contract shall remain in full force and effect.** Buyer acknowledges that the provisions of Paragraph 10 and the warranty provisions of Paragraph 3 do not apply to this Contract.

41. CONFIRMATION OF DUAL AGENCY: The Parties confirm that they have previously consented to _____

(Licensee) acting as a Dual Agent in providing brokerage services on their behalf and specifically consent to Licensee acting as a Dual Agent with regard to the transaction referred to in this Contract.

42. SPECIFIED PARTY APPROVAL: This Contract is contingent upon the approval of the Real Estate by _____ _____ Buyer's Specified Party, within five (5) Business Days after the Date of Acceptance. In the event Buyer's Specified Party does not approve of the Real Estate and Notice is given to Seller within the time specified, this Contract shall be null and void. If Notice is not served within the time specified, this provision shall be deemed waived by the Parties and this Contract shall remain in full force and effect.

43. MISCELLANEOUS PROVISIONS: Buyer's and Seller's obligations are contingent upon the Parties entering into a separate written agreement consistent with the terms and conditions set forth herein, and with such additional terms as either Party may deem necessary, providing for one or more of the following: (*check applicable boxes*)

❑ Articles of Agreement for Deed or Purchase Money Mortgage ❑ Assumption of Seller's Mortgage ❑ Commercial/Investment ❑ Cooperative Apartment ❑ New Construction ❑ Short Sale ❑ Tax-Deferred Exchange ❑ Vacant Land.

Questions and Problem

1. *Additional information?* Read the Multi-Board Residential Real Estate Contract carefully. The contract does not disclose the seller's marital status. Why might the buyer want to know this?

The contract does not indicate whether the buyers intend to take title as joint tenants or tenants in common or tenants by the entireties. At the time the contract is executed, the buyers have equitable title and can enforce the contract by specific performance. If the seller tries to back out of the contract, and one of the buyers dies and the surviving buyer sues, would it matter what form of title the buyers intended to take?

Paragraph 15 of the Multi-Board Residential Real Estate Contract states that the seller shall convey "good and merchantable title" to the property. This is the most important phrase in the entire purchase agreement. The usual contract of sale requires the seller to furnish "marketable title." Is "good and merchantable title" satisfied by a title based on adverse possession?

Another question about Paragraph 15—suppose there is a recorded covenant restricting the land to a house of Georgian style or, if it is a vacant lot, a recorded easement cutting diagonally across the property. Is the buyer bound by the contract?

2. *Problem.* A wants to buy a house in a new development from the developer. The house is in the course of construction. The developer offers a standard form contract with this provision:

> The house will be completed substantially similar to a model house [the model house being identified]. But the builder may make substitution of material whenever the builder shall find it necessary or expedient and may make changes in construction the seller may find necessary.

The contract is conditioned on the ability of the seller to complete construction at current prices of material and labor. Otherwise, the seller may return the down payment and cancel the contract.

If completion of construction is delayed because of inclement weather, strikes, or for other reasons, the seller's time to perform is extended for a period commensurate with such delay.

Would you advise *A* to accept such a provision? Remember that a principle of modern contract law is that each party has an implied duty of good faith and fair dealing. See Milton R. Friedman and James Charles Smith, 1 Friedman and Smith on Contracts and Conveyances of Real Property § 1.7 (James Charles Smith ed. 8th ed. 2018).

B. THE CONTRACT OF SALE

1. The Statute of Frauds

The original English Statute of Frauds of 1677, sought to make people more secure in their property and their contracts by making deceitful claims unenforceable. The statute required that contracts for the sale and purchase of real property must be in writing in order to be legally enforceable. Every American state has adopted some version of the Statute of Frauds, either by statute or by judicial decision.

There are minimally three requirements for satisfying the Statute of Frauds: a memorandum of sale must be *signed* by the party to be bound, *describe* the real estate, and state the *price*. Courts have been somewhat flexible about what terms must be stated in the writing. For example, when a price has been agreed upon, most courts regard it as an essential term that must be set forth. But if no price was agreed upon, a court may imply an agreement to pay a reasonable price.

> **In Brief**
>
> There are three basic requirements under the Statute of Frauds:
>
> ▶ signature—the agreement must be signed by the party sought to be charged
> ▶ description—the agreement must describe the land covered by the contract
> ▶ price—the writing must state the contract price

Exceptions to the Statute of Frauds. Courts have created two principal exceptions to the Statute of Frauds: *part performance* and *estoppel.* Part performance allows the specific enforcement of oral agreements when particular acts have been performed by one of the parties to the agreement. Acts held to constitute part performance vary from jurisdiction to jurisdiction, depending primarily on how the court views the theoretical basis for the doctrine of part performance. One theory is that the acts of the parties substantially satisfy the evidentiary requirements of the Statute. Hence if the acts make sense only as having been performed pursuant to the oral contract, they constitute part performance. Such acts include the buyer's taking possession *and* paying all or part of the purchase price or making valuable improvements. Another theory of part performance is that it is a doctrine used to prevent injurious reliance on the contract; if the plaintiff shows that he would suffer irreparable injury if the contract were not enforced, then the buyer's taking of possession alone is sufficient to set the court in motion.

Estoppel applies when unconscionable injury would result from denying enforcement of the oral contract after one party has been induced by the other to seriously change his position in reliance on the contract. Estoppel, though originating in equity, has long been recognized as a defense in law. See Stewart E. Sterk, Estoppel in Property Law, 77 Neb. L. Rev. 756, 759-769 (1998).

HICKEY v. GREEN

Appeals Court of Massachusetts, 1982
442 N.E.2d 37, rev. denied,
445 N.E.2d 156 (1983)

CUTTER, J. This case is before us on a stipulation of facts (with various attached documents). A Superior Court judge has adopted the agreed facts as "findings." We are in the same position as was the trial judge (who received no evidence and saw and heard no witnesses).

Mrs. Gladys Green owns a lot (Lot S) in the Manomet section of Plymouth. In July, 1980, she advertised it for sale. On July 11 and 12, Hickey and his wife discussed with Mrs. Green purchasing Lot S and "orally agreed to a sale" for $15,000. Mrs. Green on July 12 accepted a deposit check of $500, marked by Hickey on the back, "Deposit on Lot . . . Massasoit Ave. Manomet . . . Subject to Variance from Town of Plymouth." Mrs. Green's brother and agent "was under the impression that a zoning variance was needed and [had] advised . . . Hickey to write" the quoted language on the deposit check. It turned out, however, by July 16 that no variance would be required. Hickey had left the payee line of the deposit check blank, because of uncertainty whether Mrs. Green or her brother was to receive the check, and asked "Mrs. Green to fill in the appropriate name." Mrs. Green held the check, did not fill in the payee's name, and neither cashed nor endorsed it. Hickey "stated to Mrs. Green that his intention was to sell his home and build on Mrs. Green's lot."

"Relying upon the arrangements . . . with Mrs. Green," the Hickeys advertised their house on Sachem Road in newspapers on three days in July, 1980, and agreed with a purchaser for its sale and took from him a deposit check for $500 which they deposited in their own account.[1] On July 24, Mrs. Green told Hickey that she "no longer intended to sell her property to him" but had decided to sell to another for $16,000. Hickey told Mrs. Green that he had already sold his house and offered her $16,000 for Lot S. Mrs. Green refused this offer.

The Hickeys filed this complaint seeking specific performance. Mrs. Green asserts that relief is barred by the Statute of Frauds contained in G.L. c. 259 § 1. The trial judge granted specific performance.[2] Mrs. Green has appealed.

---

1. On the back of the check was noted above the Hickeys' signatures endorsing the check "Deposit on Purchase of property at Sachem Rd. and First St., Manomet, Ma. Sale price, $44,000."

2. The judgment ordered Mrs. Green to convey Lot S to the Hickeys but, probably by inadvertence, it failed to include an order that it be conveyed only upon payment by the grantees of the admittedly agreed price of $15,000.

The present rule applicable in most jurisdictions in the United States is succinctly set forth in Restatement (Second) of Contracts, § 129 (1981). The section reads,

> A contract for the transfer of an interest in land may be specifically enforced notwithstanding failure to comply with the Statute of Frauds if it is established that the party seeking enforcement, in *reasonable reliance on the contract* and on the continuing assent of the party against whom enforcement is sought, *has so changed his position that injustice can be avoided only by specific enforcement* (emphasis supplied).[3]

The earlier Massachusetts decisions laid down somewhat strict requirements for an estoppel precluding the assertion of the Statute of Frauds. See, e.g., Glass v. Hulbert, 102 Mass. 24, 31-32, 43-44 (1869); Davis v. Downer, 210 Mass. 573, 576-577, 97 N.E. 90 (1912); Hazelton v. Lewis, 267 Mass. 533, 538-540, 166 N.E. 876 (1929); Andrews v. Charon, 289 Mass. 1, 5-7, 193 N.E. 737 (1935), where specific performance was granted upon a consideration of "the effect of all the facts in combination"; Winstanley v. Chapman, 325 Mass. 130, 133, 89 N.E.2d 506 (1949); Park, Real Estate Law, § 883 (1981). . . . Frequently there has been an actual change of possession and improvement of the transferred property, as well as full payment of the full purchase price, or one or more of these elements. . . .

The present facts reveal a simple case of a proposed purchase of a residential vacant lot, where the vendor, Mrs. Green, knew that the Hickeys were planning to sell their former home (possibly to obtain funds to pay her) and build on Lot S. The Hickeys, relying on Mrs. Green's oral promise, moved rapidly to make their sale without obtaining any adequate memorandum of the terms of what appears to have been intended to be a quick cash sale of Lot S. So rapid was action by the Hickeys that, by July 21, less than ten days after giving their deposit to Mrs. Green, they had accepted a deposit check for the sale of their house, endorsed the check, and placed it in their bank account. Above their signatures endorsing the check was a memorandum probably sufficient to satisfy the Statute of Frauds under A.B.C. Auto Parts, Inc. v. Moran, 359 Mass. 327, 329-331, 268 N.E.2d 844 (1971). Cf. Guarino v. Zyfers, 9 Mass. App. 874, 401 N.E.2d 857 (1980). At the very least, the Hickeys had bound themselves in a manner in which, to avoid a transfer of their own house, they might have had to engage in expensive litigation. No attorney has been shown to have been used either in the

---

3. Comments a and b to § 129, read (in part): "a. . . . This section restates what is widely known as the 'part performance doctrine.' Part performance is not an accurate designation of such acts as taking possession and making improvements when the contract does not provide for such acts, but such acts regularly bring the doctrine into play. The doctrine is contrary to the words of the Statute of Frauds, but it was established by English courts of equity soon after the enactment of the Statute. Payment of purchase-money, without more, was once thought sufficient to justify specific enforcement, but a contrary view now prevails, since in such cases restitution is an adequate remedy. . . . Enforcement has . . . been justified on the ground that repudiation after 'part performance' amounts to a 'virtual fraud.' A more accurate statement is that courts with equitable powers are vested by tradition with what in substance is a dispensing power based on the promisee's reliance, *a discretion to be exercised with caution* in the light of all the circumstances . . . [emphasis supplied].

"b. . . . Two distinct elements enter into the application of the rule of this Section: first, the extent to which the evidentiary function of the statutory formalities is fulfilled by the conduct of the parties; second, the reliance of the promisee, providing a compelling substantive basis for relief in addition to the expectations created by the promise."

transaction between Mrs. Green and the Hickeys or in that between the Hickeys and their purchaser.

There is no denial by Mrs. Green of the oral contract between her and the Hickeys. This, under § 129 of the Restatement, is of some significance.[4] There can be no doubt (a) that Mrs. Green made the promise on which the Hickeys so promptly relied, and also (b) she, nearly as promptly, but not promptly enough, repudiated it because she had a better opportunity. The stipulated facts require the conclusion that in equity Mrs. Green's conduct cannot be condoned. This is not a case where either party is shown to have contemplated the negotiation of a purchase and sale agreement. If a written agreement had been expected, even by only one party, or would have been natural (because of the participation by lawyers or otherwise), a different situation might have existed. It is a permissible inference from the agreed facts that the rapid sale of the Hickeys' house was both appropriate and expected. These are not circumstances where negotiations fairly can be seen as inchoate. . . .

Over two years have passed since July, 1980, and over a year since the trial judge's findings were filed on July 6, 1981. At that time, the principal agreed facts of record bearing upon the extent of the injury to the Hickeys (because of their reliance on Mrs. Green's promise to convey Lot S) were those based on the Hickeys' new obligation to convey their house to a purchaser. Performance of that agreement had been extended to May 1, 1981. If that agreement has been abrogated or modified since the trial, the case may take on a different posture. If enforcement of that agreement still will be sought, or if that agreement has been carried out, the conveyance of Lot S by Mrs. Green should be required now.

The case, in any event, must be remanded to the trial judge for the purpose of amending the judgment to require conveyance of Lot S by Mrs. Green only upon payment to her in cash within a stated period of the balance of the agreed price of $15,000. The trial judge, however, in her discretion and upon proper offers of proof of counsel, may reopen the record to receive, in addition to the presently stipulated facts, a stipulation or evidence concerning the present status of the Hickeys' apparent obligation to sell their house. If the circumstances have changed, it will be open to the trial judge to require of Mrs. Green, instead of specific performance, only full restitution to the Hickeys of all costs reasonably caused to them in respect of these transactions (including advertising costs, deposits, and their reasonable costs for this litigation) with interest. The case is remanded to the Superior Court Department for further action consistent with this opinion. The Hickeys are to have costs of this appeal.

So ordered.

---

4. Comment d of Restatement (Second) of Contracts, § 129, reads: "d. . . . Where specific enforcement is rested on a transfer of possession plus either part payment of the price or the making of improvements, it is commonly said that the action taken by the purchaser must be unequivocally referable to the oral agreement. But this requirement is not insisted on *if the making of the promise is admitted or is clearly proved.* The promisee *must act in reasonable reliance on the promise, before the promisor has* repudiated it, and the action must be such that the remedy of restitution is inadequate. If these requirements are met, *neither taking of possession nor payment of money nor the making of improvements is essential* . . ." (emphasis supplied).

Notes, Questions, and Problem

1. *The Statute of Frauds flaw in Hickey v. Green.* Which requirement(s) of the Statute of Frauds did the Hickeys fail to satisfy? Were there any writings that might have satisfied the requirements? What about the writing on their deposit check to Ms. Green?

2. *Problem.* O, owner of Blackacre, executes and delivers a deed of Blackacre to her daughter *A* as a gift. The deed is not recorded. Subsequently, *O* tells *A* that she would like Blackacre back, and *A*, a dutiful daughter, hands the deed back to *O* and says, "The land is yours again." *O* tears up the deed. Who owns Blackacre?

Suppose that, instead of as above, *O* executes and delivers a deed to her daughter conveying Blackacre to *O* and *A* as joint tenants. The deed is not recorded. Subsequently, *A* tells *O* she would like her son *B* to have her interest, and *O* agrees. To save the recording tax on two deeds, *A* "whites out" her name on the deed and replaces it with *B*'s name. This deed is then recorded. *O* dies. Who owns Blackacre? See Mann v. Mann, 677 So. 2d 62 (Fla. App. 1996).

3. *Electronic signatures.* The Electronic Signatures in Global and National Commerce Act of 2000, known as the E-sign Act, permits electronic signatures in transactions in or affecting interstate or foreign commerce. 15 U.S.C.A. §§ 7001-7031. Section 7006(5) defines an electronic signature as "an electronic sound, symbol, or process, attached to or logically associated with a contract or other record and executed or adopted by a person with the intent to sign the record."

2. Marketable Title

An implied condition of a contract of sale of land is that the seller must convey to the buyer a "marketable title." If the seller cannot convey a marketable title, the buyer is entitled to rescind the contract. Marketable title is "a title not subject to such reasonable doubt as would create a just apprehension of its validity in the mind of a reasonable, prudent and intelligent person, one which such persons, guided by competent legal advice, would be willing to take and for which they would be willing to pay fair value." Seligman v. First Natl. Invs., Inc., 540 N.E.2d 1057, 1060 (Ill. App. 1989).

LOHMEYER v. BOWER
Supreme Court of Kansas, 1951
227 P.2d 102

[In May 1949, Dr. K.L. Lohmeyer entered into a contract to buy from the Bowers lot number 37 in the Berkley Hills Addition to the city of Emporia. The contract provided that the Bowers would convey

> By Warranty Deed with an abstract of title, certified to date showing good merchantable title or an Owners Policy of Title Insurance in the amount of the sale price, guaranteeing said title to party of the second part [Dr. Lohmeyer], free and clear of all encumbrances except special taxes subject, however, to all restrictions and easements of record applying to this property, it being

understood that the first party shall have sufficient time to bring said abstract to date or obtain Report for Title Insurance and to correct any imperfections in the title if there be such imperfections.

The abstract of title showed that the original subdivider of the Berkley Hills Addition had, in 1926, imposed a restrictive covenant on lot 37 requiring any house erected on lot 37 to be two stories in height. Lot 37 had a one-story house on it.

Dr. Lohmeyer gave the abstract of title to a lawyer to examine, and from the lawyer Dr. Lohmeyer learned that the city of Emporia had a zoning ordinance providing that no frame building could be erected within three feet of a side or rear lot line. The frame house on lot 37 was located within 18 inches of the north line of the lot in violation of the ordinance. The Bowers had, in 1946, moved the house, which had been built elsewhere, onto lot 37. When Dr. Lohmeyer brought the zoning violation to the attention of the Bowers, they offered to purchase and convey to Lohmeyer two feet along the entire north side of lot 37. Dr. Lohmeyer refused their offer.

Dr. Lohmeyer brought suit to rescind the contract and demanded return of his earnest money. The Bowers answered, contesting Lohmeyer's right to rescind, and by cross-complaint asked specific performance of the contract. The trial court rendered judgment for the Bowers and decreed specific performance of the contract. Dr. Lohmeyer appealed that judgment.]

Parker, J. . . . From what has been heretofore related, since resort to the contract makes it clear appellees agreed to convey the involved property with an abstract of title showing good merchantable title, free and clear of all encumbrances, it becomes apparent the all decisive issue presented by the pleadings and the stipulation is whether such property is subject to encumbrances or other burdens making the title unmerchantable and if so whether they are such as are excepted by the provision of the contract which reads "subject however, to all restrictions and easements of record applying to this property."

The house on lot 37, Berkley Hills Addition,
which Dr. Lohmeyer backed out of buying, 1990.

Decision of the foregoing issue can be simplified by directing attention early to the appellant's position. Conceding he purchased the property subject to all restrictions of record he makes no complaint of the restrictions contained in the declaration forming a part of the dedication of Berkley Hills Addition nor of the ordinance restricting the building location on the lot but bases his right to rescission of the contract solely upon presently existing violations thereof. This, we may add, limited to restrictions imposed by terms of the ordinance relating to the use of land or the location and character of buildings that may be located thereon, even in the absence of provisions in the contract excepting them, must necessarily be his position for we are convinced, although it must be conceded there are some decisions to the contrary, the rule supported by the better reasoned decisions, indeed if not by the great weight of authority, is that municipal restrictions of such character, existing at the time of the execution of a contract for the sale of real estate, are not such encumbrances or burdens on title as may be availed of by a vendee to avoid his agreement to purchase on the ground they render his title unmerchantable. For authorities upholding this conclusion see Hall v. Risley & Heikkila, 188 Or. 69, 213 P.2d 818; Miller v. Milwaukee Odd Fellows Temple, 206 Wis. 547, 240 N.W. 193; Wheeler v. Sullivan, 90 Fla. 711, 106 So. 876; Lincoln Trust Co. v. Williams Bldg. Corp., 229 N.Y. 313, 128 N.E. 209; Maupin on Marketable Title to Real Estate, (3rd Ed.) 384 § 143; 175 A.L.R. anno. 1056 § 2; 57 A.L.R. anno. 1424 § 11(c); 55 Am. Jur. 705 § 205; 66 C.J. 860, 911 §§ 531, 591.

On the other hand there can be no question the rule respecting restrictions upon the use of land or the location and type of buildings that may be erected thereon fixed by covenants or other private restrictive agreements, including those contained in the declaration forming a part of the dedication of Berkley Hills Addition, is directly contrary to the one to which we have just referred. Such restrictions, under all the authorities, constitute encumbrances rendering the title to land unmerchantable. . . .

There can be no doubt regarding what constitutes a marketable or merchantable title in this jurisdiction. This court has been called on to pass upon that question on numerous occasions. See our recent decision in Peatling v. Baird, 168 Kan. 528, 213 P.2d 1015, and cases there cited, wherein we held:

> A marketable title to real estate is one which is free from reasonable doubt, and a title is doubtful and unmarketable if it exposes the party holding it to the hazard of litigation.
>
> To render the title to real estate unmarketable, the defect of which the purchaser complains must be of a substantial character and one from which he may suffer injury. Mere immaterial defects which do not diminish in quantity, quality or value the property contracted for, constitute no ground upon which the purchaser may reject the title. Facts must be known at the time which fairly raise a reasonable doubt as to the title; a mere possibility or conjecture that such a state of facts may be developed at some future time is not sufficient.

Under the rule just stated, and in the face of facts such as are here involved, we have little difficulty in concluding that the violation of section 5-224 of the ordinances of the city of Emporia as well as the violation of the restrictions imposed by the dedication declaration so encumber the title to lot 37 as to expose the party holding it to the hazard of litigation and make such title doubtful and unmarketable. It follows, since, as we have indicated, the appellees had contracted to convey such real estate to appellant by warranty deed with an abstract of title showing good merchantable title, free and clear of all encumbrances, that they cannot convey the title contracted for and that the trial court should have rendered judgment rescinding the contract. This, we may add is so, notwithstanding the contract provides the conveyance was to be made subject to all restrictions and easements of record for, as we have seen, it is the violation of the restrictions imposed by both the ordinance and the dedication declaration, not the existence of those restrictions, that render the title unmarketable. The decision just announced is not without precedent or unsupported by sound authority. . . .

Finally appellees point to the contract which, it must be conceded, provides they shall have time to correct imperfections in the title and contend that even if it be held the restrictions and the ordinance have been violated they are entitled to time in which to correct those imperfections. Assuming, without deciding, they might remedy the violation of the ordinance by buying additional ground the short and simple answer to their contention with respect to the violation of the restrictions imposed by the dedication declaration is that any changes in the house would compel the purchaser to take something that he did not contract to buy.

Conclusions heretofore announced require reversal of the judgment with directions to the trial court to cancel and set aside the contract and render such judgment as may be equitable and proper under the issues raised by the pleadings.

It is so ordered.

Notes and Questions

1. *The contract in* Lohmeyer. Look at the contract Dr. Lohmeyer signed. Would you have advised Dr. Lohmeyer not to sign it? First, the contract provides that Lohmeyer agrees to take the property subject to all restrictions and easements on record. Second, it provides that the sellers must provide Lohmeyer "with an abstract of title, certified to date showing good merchantable title *or* an Owners Policy of Title Insurance." Suppose that a title insurance company, of which you will learn more in Chapter 8, agreed to issue a policy of title insurance on the property, guaranteeing title, even though the title is legally unmarketable. Would Lohmeyer be entitled to rescind the contract? See Creative Living, Inc. v. Steinhauser, 355 N.Y.S.2d 897 (App. Div. 1974), aff'd without opinion, 365 N.Y.S.2d 987 (App. Div. 1975) (contract provided seller shall have a title such as a title insurer would insure; "[t]his provision in the contract made the title company the final judge of title and when the title company was prepared to insure title in accordance with the contract no further requirement had to be met").

2. *The purpose of marketable title.* What is the function of the concept of "marketable title"? Why do courts not rule that the seller must produce a complete chain of title from an unimpeachable source (a sovereign) and prove that no encumbrance exists? See William B. Stoebuck & Dale A. Whitman, The Law of Property § 10.12 (3d ed. 2000).

Why do public restrictions on land use, such as zoning or wetlands designations, make title unmarketable only if they are violated (see Truck South, Inc. v. Patel, 528 S.E.2d 424 (S.C. 2000) (wetlands); War Eagle, Inc. v. Belair, 694 S.E.2d 497 (N.C. App. 2010) (zoning); Wolf v. Commonwealth Land Title Ins. Co., 690 N.Y.S.2d 880 (App. Div. 1999) (zoning)), whereas private covenants make title unmarketable whether or not they are violated? See Michael J. Gamson & J. David Reitzel, Zoning Restrictions and Marketability of Title, 35 Real Est. L.J. 257 (2006).

3. *Effect of an easement.* Suppose there is a recorded sewage easement or easement for utility poles across the property. Does this make title unmarketable? Should it matter whether the easement is visible, or whether the easement diminishes or enhances the value of the property? See Rhodes v. Astro-Pac, Inc., 363 N.E.2d 347 (N.Y. 1977) (easement is an encumbrance, even though it does not diminish value of property); Ziskind v. Bruce Lee Corp., 307 A.2d 377 (Pa. Super. Ct. 1973) (knowledge of easement irrelevant; title unmarketable); Ludke v. Egan, 274 N.W.2d 641 (Wis. 1979) (easement known to purchaser, or open and obvious, does not make title unmarketable).

Equitable conversion. Both purchasers and sellers of real property are normally entitled to specific performance as a remedy for the other's breach of contract (see page 386). The doctrine of equitable conversion, simply put, is that if there is a specifically enforceable contract for the sale of land, equity regards as done that which ought to be done. The buyer is viewed in equity as the owner from the date of the contract (thus having the "equitable title"); the seller has a claim for money secured by a vendor's lien on the land. The seller is also said to hold the legal title as trustee for the buyer.

Risk of loss. Equitable conversion has been used by some courts to determine whether the seller or the purchaser takes the loss when the premises are destroyed between signing the contract of sale and the closing, and the contract has no provision allocating the risk of loss. Paine v. Meller, 31 Eng. Rep. 1088 (Ch. 1801), held that from the time of the contract of sale of real estate the burden of fortuitous loss is on the purchaser, even though the seller retains possession. This result was said to follow from equitable conversion, treating the purchaser as owner. Most courts are thought to follow this view. Some courts, however, have declined to apply equitable conversion and have held that the loss is on the seller until legal title is conveyed. In Massachusetts, the risk of loss is on the seller if the loss is substantial and the terms of the contract show that the building constituted an important part of the subject matter of the contract; if the loss is not substantial, either party can enforce the contract, though an abatement in purchase price may be given. In some other states, the risk of loss is placed on the party in possession, the view also taken by the Uniform Vendor and Purchaser Act (1935). See, e.g., Brush Grocery Kart, Inc. v. Sure Fine Market, Inc., 47 P.3d 680 (Colo. 2002). If the purchaser has the risk of loss, and the seller has insurance, in most states the seller holds the insurance proceeds as trustee for the buyer. See Bryant v. Willison Real Estate Co., 350 S.E.2d 748 (W. Va. 1986) (discussing the law of many states).

Inheritance. Equitable conversion has been applied in situations when one of the parties to a contract for the sale of land dies and the issue arises whether the decedent's interest is real property or personal property. If equitable conversion has occurred, the seller's interest is personal property (right to the purchase price), and the buyer is treated as owner of the land.

3. The Duty to Disclose Defects

STAMBOVSKY v. ACKLEY
New York Supreme Court, Appellate Division
First Department, 1991
572 N.Y.S.2d 672

RUBIN, J. Plaintiff, to his horror, discovered that the house he had recently contracted to purchase was widely reputed to be possessed by poltergeists, reportedly seen by defendant seller and members of her family on numerous occasions over the last nine years. Plaintiff promptly commenced this action seeking rescission of the contract of sale. Supreme Court reluctantly dismissed the complaint, holding that plaintiff has no remedy at law in this jurisdiction.

The unusual facts of this case, as disclosed by the record, clearly warrant a grant of equitable relief to the buyer who, as a resident of New York City, cannot be expected to have any familiarity with the folklore of the Village of Nyack. Not being a "local," plaintiff could not readily learn that the home he had contracted to purchase is haunted. Whether the source of the spectral apparitions seen by defendant seller are parapsychic or psychogenic, having reported their presence in both a national publication (Reader's Digest) and the local press (in 1977 and 1982, respectively), defendant is estopped to deny their existence and, as a matter of law, the house is haunted. More to the point, however, no divination is required to conclude that it is defendant's promotional efforts in publicizing her close encounters with these spirits which fostered the home's reputation in the community. In 1989, the house was included in a five-home walking tour of Nyack and described in a November 27th newspaper article as "a riverfront Victorian (with ghost)." The impact of the reputation thus created goes to the very essence of the bargain between the parties, greatly impairing both the value of the property and its potential for resale. The extent of this impairment may be presumed for the purpose of reviewing the disposition of this motion to dismiss the cause of action for rescission (Harris v. City of New York, 147 A.D.2d 186, 188-189) and represents merely an issue of fact for resolution at trial.

While I agree with Supreme Court that the real estate broker, as agent for the seller, is under no duty to disclose to a potential buyer the phantasmal reputation of the premises and that, in his pursuit of a legal remedy for fraudulent misrepresentation against the seller, plaintiff hasn't a ghost of a chance, I am nevertheless moved by the spirit of equity to allow the buyer to seek rescission of the contract of sale and recovery of his down payment. New York law fails to recognize any remedy for damages incurred as a result of the seller's mere silence, applying instead the strict rule of caveat emptor. Therefore, the theoretical basis for granting relief, even under the extraordinary facts of this case, is elusive if not ephemeral.

"Pity me not but lend thy serious hearing to what I shall unfold" (William Shakespeare, Hamlet, Act I, Scene V [Ghost]).

From the perspective of a person in the position of plaintiff herein, a very practical problem arises with respect to the discovery of a paranormal phenomenon: "Who you gonna' call?" as a title song to the movie "Ghostbusters" asks. Applying the strict rule of caveat emptor to a contract involving a house possessed by poltergeists conjures up visions of a psychic or medium routinely accompanying the structural engineer and Terminix man on an inspection of every home subject to a contract of sale. It portends that the prudent attorney will establish an escrow account lest the subject of the transaction come back to haunt him and his client—or pray that his malpractice insurance coverage extends to supernatural disasters. In the interest of avoiding such untenable consequences, the notion that a haunting is a condition which can and should be ascertained upon reasonable inspection of the premises is a hobgoblin which should be exorcised from the body of legal precedent and laid quietly to rest.

It has been suggested by a leading authority that the ancient rule which holds that mere nondisclosure does not constitute actionable misrepresentation "finds proper application in cases where the fact undisclosed is patent, or the plaintiff has equal opportunities for obtaining information which he may be expected to utilize, or the defendant has no reason to think that he is acting under any misapprehension" (Prosser, Torts § 106, at 696 (4th ed. 1971)). However, with respect to transactions in real estate, New York adheres to the doctrine of caveat emptor and imposes no duty upon the vendor to disclose any information concerning the premises (London v. Courduff, 141 A.D.2d 803) unless there is a confidential or fiduciary relationship between the parties (Moser v. Spizzirro, 31 A.D.2d 537, aff'd, 25 N.Y.2d 941; IBM Credit Fin. Corp. v. Mazda Motor Mfg. [USA] Corp., 152 A.D.2d 451) or some conduct on the part of the seller which constitutes "active concealment" (see, 17 E. 80th Realty Corp. v. 68th Assocs., 173 A.D.2d 245 (dummy ventilation system constructed by seller); Haberman v. Greenspan, 82 Misc. 2d 263 (foundation cracks covered by seller)). Normally, some affirmative misrepresentation (e.g., Tahini Invs. v. Bobrowsky, 99 A.D.2d 489 (industrial waste on land allegedly used only as farm); Jansen v. Kelly, 11 A.D.2d 587 (land containing valuable minerals allegedly acquired for use as campsite)) or partial disclosure (Junius Constr. Corp. v. Cohen, 257 N.Y. 393 (existence of third unopened street concealed); Noved Realty Corp. v. A.A.P. Co., 250 A.D. 1 (escrow agreements securing lien concealed)) is required to impose upon the seller a duty to communicate undisclosed conditions affecting the premises (contra, Young v. Keith, 112 A.D.2d 625 (defective water and sewer systems concealed)).

Caveat emptor is not so all-encompassing a doctrine of common law as to render every act of nondisclosure immune from redress, whether legal or equitable. . . . Where fairness and common sense dictate that an exception should be created, the evolution of the law should not be stifled by rigid application of a legal maxim.

The doctrine of caveat emptor requires that a buyer act prudently to assess the fitness and value of his purchase and operates to bar the purchaser who fails to exercise due care from seeking the equitable remedy of rescission (see, e.g., Rodas v. Manitaras, 159 A.D.2d 341). . . . It should be apparent, however, that the most meticulous inspection and search would not reveal the presence of poltergeists at the premises or unearth the property's ghoulish reputation in the community. Therefore, there is no sound policy reason to deny plaintiff relief for failing to discover a state of affairs which the most prudent purchaser would not be expected to even contemplate (see, Da Silva v. Musso, 53 N.Y.2d 543, 551).

The case law in this jurisdiction dealing with the duty of a vendor of real property to disclose information to the buyer is distinguishable from the matter under review. The most salient distinction is that existing cases invariably deal with the physical condition of the premises (e.g., London v. Courduff, supra) (use as a landfill); Perin v. Mardine Realty Co., 5 A.D.2d 685, aff'd, 6 N.Y.2d 920 (sewer line crossing adjoining property without owner's consent), defects in title (e.g., Sands v. Kissane, 282 A.D. 140 (remainderman)), liens against the property (e.g., Noved Realty Corp. v. A.A.P. Co., supra), expenses or income (e.g., Rodas v. Manitaras, supra (gross receipts)) and other factors affecting its operation. No case has been brought to this court's attention in which the property value was impaired as the result of the reputation created by information disseminated to the public by the seller (or, for that matter, as a result of possession by poltergeists).

Where a condition which has been created by the seller materially impairs the value of the contract and is peculiarly within the knowledge of the seller or unlikely to be discovered by a prudent purchaser exercising due care with respect to the subject transaction, nondisclosure constitutes a basis for rescission as a matter of equity. Any other outcome places upon the buyer not merely the obligation to exercise care in his purchase but rather to be omniscient with respect to any fact which may affect the bargain. No practical purpose is served by imposing such a burden upon a purchaser. To the contrary, it encourages predatory business practice and offends the principle that equity will suffer no wrong to be without a remedy.

Defendant's contention that the contract of sale, particularly the merger or "as is" clause, bars recovery of the buyer's deposit is unavailing. Even an express disclaimer will not be given effect where the facts are peculiarly within the knowledge of the party invoking it (Danaan Realty Corp. v. Harris, 5 N.Y.2d 317, 322; Tahini Invs. v. Bobrowsky, supra). Moreover, a fair reading of the merger clause reveals that it expressly disclaims only representations made with respect to the physical condition of the premises and merely makes general reference to representations concerning "any other matter or things affecting or relating to the aforesaid premises." As broad as this language may be, a reasonable interpretation is that its effect is limited to tangible or physical matters and does not extend to paranormal phenomena. Finally, if the language of the contract is to be construed as broadly as defendant urges to encompass the presence of poltergeists in the house, it cannot be said that she has delivered the premises "vacant" in accordance with her obligation under the provisions of the contract rider. . . .

In the case at bar, defendant seller deliberately fostered the public belief that her home was possessed. Having undertaken to inform the public-at-large, to whom she has no legal relationship, about the supernatural occurrences on her property, she may be said to owe no less a duty to her contract vendee. It has been remarked that the occasional modern cases which permit a seller to take unfair advantage of a buyer's ignorance so long as he is not actively misled are "singularly unappetizing" (Prosser, Torts § 106, at 696 (4th ed. 1971)). Where, as here, the seller not only takes unfair advantage of the buyer's ignorance but has created and perpetuated a condition about which he is unlikely to even inquire, enforcement of the contract (in whole or in part) is offensive to the court's sense of equity. Application of the remedy of rescission, within the bounds of the narrow exception to the doctrine of caveat emptor set forth herein, is entirely appropriate to relieve the unwitting purchaser from the consequences of a most unnatural bargain.

"... as a matter of law, the house is haunted."
AP/Wide World Photos

Accordingly, the judgment of the Supreme Court, New York County, entered April 9, 1990, which dismissed the complaint pursuant to CPLR 3211(a)(7), should be modified, on the law and the facts, and in the exercise of discretion, and the first cause of action seeking rescission of the contract reinstated, without costs.

SMITH, J., dissenting.

. . . [I]f the doctrine of caveat emptor is to be discarded, it should be for a reason more substantive than a poltergeist. The existence of a poltergeist is no more binding upon the defendants than it is upon this court.

Notes and Questions

1. *Modern majority view.* An increasing majority of states puts on the seller the duty to disclose all known defects, equating nondisclosure with fraud or misrepresentation. Caveat emptor is steadily being eroded. When the seller breaches

this duty, the buyer can rescind the contract or sue for damages after the closing. What should the seller's state of mind be for a buyer to maintain a successful action for nondisclosure? Compare Nystrom v. Cabada, 652 So. 2d 1266 (Fla. App. 1995), with Jensen v. Bailey, 76 So. 3d 980, 983 (Fla. App. 2011).

In most states, statutes have been enacted requiring the seller to deliver to prospective buyers a written statement disclosing facts about the property. The statutes set forth detailed information forms. The forms vary, but the required disclosure may include known significant structural defects, soil problems, underground sewage or storage tanks, presence of hazardous materials, alterations or repairs made without necessary permits, violations of building codes or zoning ordinances, and encroachments by neighbors. See, e.g., Cal. Civ. Code § 1102.6 (West 2020); Wis. Stat. Ann. § 709.03 (West 2020). Some statutes apply only to residential sellers and not to sellers of commercial property.

In each jurisdiction requiring disclosure, the defect must be "material" to be actionable. In Johnson v. Davis, 480 So. 2d 625 (Fla. 1985), the court held that the seller had a duty to disclose a leaky roof, and having failed to do so, the buyers were entitled to have the deposit returned. A leaky roof is one thing, but what about other problems, such as noise? Is a noisy air-conditioning system material? One of two tests of materiality is applied: (1) an objective test of whether a reasonable person would attach importance to it in deciding to buy, or (2) a subjective test of whether the defect "affects the value or desirability of the property to the buyer." Does either of these tests help in cases of noise?

2. *Stigma statutes.* Partly in response to cases finding sellers liable for failing to disclose conditions that "stigmatized" properties, several states have enacted statutes shielding sellers from a failure to disclose psychological or prejudicial factors that might affect market value, such as a murder within the house or that a former occupant died of AIDS. These statutes are known as *stigma statutes.* See, e.g., N.Y. Real Prop. Law § 443-a (McKinney 2020).

3. *Broker's duty to disclose.* One of the reasons so many states have passed statutes requiring sellers to disclose defects is the political pressure brought to bear on legislators by real estate brokers. In recent years, brokers have been subjected to liability under a number of theories. They have been found liable for fraud for either intentionally or negligently misrepresenting the condition of a property. See Powell v. Wold, 362 S.E.2d 796 (N.C. App. 1987) (intentional misrepresentation); Bloor v. Fritz, 180 P.3d 805 (Wash. App. 2008) (negligent misrepresentation); Tennant v. Lawton, 615 P.2d 1305 (Wash. App. 1980) (negligent misrepresentation).

4. *Disclosure of off-site conditions.* In Strawn v. Canuso, 657 A.2d 420 (N.J. 1995), the court held that the builder and selling brokers of new homes had the duty to disclose to potential buyers the existence of a landfill nearby that was suspected of containing toxic waste. The court said that professional sellers and brokers have a duty to disclose off-site as well as on-site conditions that are of sufficient materiality to affect the habitability, use, or enjoyment of the property and, therefore, render the property substantially less desirable or valuable to the objectively reasonable buyer. Although this duty appears to call for very broad disclosure, the court limited it somewhat by this comment:

> We do not hold that sellers and brokers have a duty to investigate or disclose transient social conditions in the community that arguably affect the

value of the property. In the absence of a purchaser communicating specific needs, builders and brokers should not be held to decide whether the changing nature of a neighborhood, the presence of a group home, or the existence of a school in decline are facts material to the transaction. Rather we root in the land the duty to disclose off-site conditions that are material to the transaction. [657 A.2d at 431.]

Within six months of the Supreme Court's decision in *Strawn*, the New Jersey legislature passed the New Residential Construction Off-Site Conditions Disclosure Act, N.J. Stat. Ann. §§ 46:3C-1 to 46:3C-12 (West 2020). The act effectively immunizes sellers of new homes from liability for nondisclosure of off-site conditions, provided they give buyers notice that lists of these conditions are available in the municipal clerk's office. Despite the immunity, the act permits buyers to maintain lawsuits based upon violations of certain statutes. The immunity provision is interpreted in Nobrega v. Edison Glen Assocs., 743 A.2d 864 (N.J. App. 2000).

Should the seller and broker have a duty to disclose other known off-site conditions that materially affect the value of the property, such as crimes or drug-dealing in the neighborhood?

Merger. An old doctrine says that when a buyer accepts a deed, the buyer is deemed to be satisfied that all the contractual obligations have been met. Thus the contract merges into the deed, and the deed is deemed the final act of the parties expressing the terms of their agreement. The buyer can no longer sue the seller on promises in the contract of sale not contained in the deed, but must sue the seller on the warranties, if any, contained in the deed. There are recognized exceptions to the doctrine, such as fraud and contractual promises deemed collateral to the deed. The merger doctrine principally applies to questions of title or quantity of land. The merger doctrine is now in disfavor and is becoming riddled with exceptions when the buyer does not intend to discharge the seller's contractual obligations by acceptance of the deed. The usual way of avoiding the doctrine is to say that the particular obligation of the seller is an independent or collateral obligation.

The implied warranty of quality. Recall the implied warranty of habitability in landlord-tenant law. (See pages 340-348.) The same development has occurred with respect to a warranty of quality in land sales contracts. At common law, the rule was caveat emptor. A builder who constructed a home and then sold it to a buyer was protected from liability even if the house was negligently constructed. Today a clear majority of jurisdictions holds that an implied warranty of quality exists in contracts for the sale of homes by builders, developers, or other "merchants" of housing. See, e.g., Albrecht v. Clifford, 767 N.E.2d 42 (Mass. 2002). Sales of real estate may also give rise to a similar warranty. Suits on the warranty can arise only after the closing has taken place and the plaintiff has accepted the deed.

In most states, the warranty does not impose strict liability. Hence the defendant is liable only if he failed to exercise the standard of skill and care customarily exercised by similar merchants. See, e.g., Lempke v. Dagenais, 547 A.2d 290 (N.H. 1988). Most courts hold that the warranty applies only to significant defects. See, e.g., Petersen v. Hubschman, 389 N.E.2d 1154 (Ill. 1979). Moreover, most courts hold that the warranty covers only latent or hidden defects. See, e.g., Lempke v. Dagenais, supra.

4. Remedies for Breach of the Sales Contract

In the event that the contract for sale is breached, three remedies are available to the nondefaulting party, whether the buyer or the seller: (1) damages, (2) retention of the deposit (sellers) or restitution of the deposit (buyers), or (3) specific performance of the contract. Generally, the winner may elect which remedy he or she prefers.

JONES v. LEE
Court of Appeals of New Mexico, 1998
971 P.2d 858

DONNELLY, J. Ihn P. Lee and Philomena Lee (Buyers) appeal from judgments determining that they breached a contract to purchase an Albuquerque, New Mexico, residence and awarding compensatory and punitive damages to Sam P. Jones and Sharon A. Jones (Sellers). . . . Following negotiations between the parties, on June 25, 1994, Buyers entered into a written real estate contract wherein they agreed to purchase Sellers' residence for $610,000. Sellers had listed the property for sale with Metro 100 Realtors. The purchase agreement entered into between Buyers and Sellers also listed Broker-Agents as Sellers' agents. Several weeks after signing the purchase agreement and tendering $6000 in earnest money, Buyers informed Sellers they were unable to consummate the agreement because of financial reasons. Buyers submitted a proposed termination agreement, dated August 23, 1994, to Sellers, whereby Buyers offered to void the contract in return for forfeiting their $6000 earnest money deposit.

Sellers rejected the proposed termination agreement and when it became clear that Buyers were not going to honor the purchase agreement, Sellers relisted the property for sale. Sellers ultimately sold the property in November 1994 to another purchaser for $540,000, $70,000 below the contract price originally agreed upon by the defaulting Buyers.

On April 12, 1995, Sellers filed suit against Buyers, seeking damages for breach of the real estate purchase agreement. . . . [The trial court awarded the sellers $70,000 in damages. Additionally, the trial court awarded the sellers special damages and punitive damages, for a total award of $157,118.94.]

I. Applicability and Measure of Damages

Buyers argue that the trial court erred in awarding compensatory and special damages to Sellers and that it utilized an incorrect measure in calculating the amount of damages to be awarded. On appeal, a reviewing court will not overturn the trial court's findings of fact or award of damages if there is substantial and competent evidence to support such determination, or unless it is clearly demonstrated that the trial court employed an incorrect measure of damages.

If a purchaser defaults on a contract to purchase realty, as a general rule, the seller has three alternative remedies. The sellers may (1) seek relief in equity for rescission, (2) offer to perform and bring an action for specific performance, or (3) elect to retain the realty and file suit seeking an award of damages. See Van Moorlehem v. Brown Realty Co., 747 F.2d 992, 994 (10th Cir. 1984). Here, Sellers elected to sue for damages. Where a party elects to sue for damages resulting from a breach of land sale contract, the burden is on that party to present competent evidence to support such claim for damages. The rationale underlying the award of damages in a breach of contract case is to compensate the non-defaulting party with just compensation commensurate with his or her loss.

Buyers accurately note that New Mexico follows the "loss of the bargain" rule in determining damages resulting from a purchaser's breach of a contract to buy realty. See Aboud v. Adams, 84 N.M. 683, 688-89, 507 P.2d 430, 435-36 (1973). The "loss of the bargain" rule . . . has been reaffirmed by our Supreme Court in Hickey v. Griggs, 106 N.M. 27, 30, 738 P.2d 899, 902 (1987). In *Hickey* the Court stated that when a purchaser breaches an executory real estate contract, the "vendor's measure of damages is the difference between the purchase price and the market value of the property at the time of the breach." *Hickey*, 106 N.M. at 30, 738 P.2d at 902.

Buyers argue that the trial court erred in calculating compensatory damages of $70,000 solely by determining the difference between the contract price agreed upon by the parties and the subsequent resale price of the property, without determining the fair market value of the property at the time of the breach. The parties stipulated that the fair market value on August 23, 1994, was $610,000; thus, Buyers argue that Sellers did not sustain any compensatory damages because "at the time of the breach . . . they held property worth exactly the same amount as the contract price[.]"

Buyers are correct that in order to apply the loss of the bargain rule, the trial court must determine the value of the property at the time of the breach and compare that amount with the contract price. *Aboud*, 84 N.M. at 689, 507 P.2d at 436; see also 5 Arthur L. Corbin, Corbin on Contracts § 1098A, at 535 (1964) (where purchaser defaults on purchase of realty, "the vendor's damages are the full contract price minus the market value of the land at date of breach and also minus any payment received").

. . . Where the market value at the time of the breach is the same as the contract price, the sellers are generally limited to the recovery of only nominal damages or forfeiture of any earnest money, unless the sellers have established that they have also incurred special damages resulting from such breach.

In the instant case, like *Aboud*, there was no finding determining the date of breach or the market value of the property at the time of the breach. These determinations are essential factors in applying the loss of the bargain rule and in calculating the amount of general damages resulting from a purchaser's breach of a real estate contract. Thus, we conclude that the cause must be remanded for adoption of express findings of fact in accordance with the rule.

. . . As indicated in *Aboud*, 84 N.M. at 689, 507 P.2d at 436, a subsequent sale of land may be considered evidence of the market value at the time of breach and should be considered with other evidence bearing on the issue. It is unclear from the appellate record, including our questioning and the attorneys' answers at oral argument, for what purpose and to what effect the parties agreed to the stipulation before the trial court concerning market value. It shall be for the trial court on remand to determine what effect to give the stipulation and to otherwise determine the market value at the time of breach, to compare that to the contract sale price, and to calculate general damages, if any.

II. Award of Special Damages

Buyers also challenge the trial court's award of special damages. Special damages may be awarded by the fact finder in a breach of contract case if the damages are shown to have resulted as the natural and probable consequence of the breach and, at the time of the formation of the contract, the breaching party reasonably knew or should have anticipated from the facts and circumstances that the damages would probably be incurred.

1. Solar System and Heating Warranty

Buyers challenge the trial court's special damages award of $1433 for an inspection of the solar system, $126 for a consultation on the solar system, and $300 for a heating warranty incident to the resale of the residence. The trial court found that these damages were reasonably foreseeable by a person in Buyers' situation when the contract was formed. We agree. Whether a situation is reasonably foreseeable is generally a question of fact to be determined by the fact finder from the evidence and circumstances.

. . . [T]he contract contemplated that an inspection would be made of the solar and heating systems, and these are major components of the residence, there was evidence in the record from which the trial court could reasonably determine that inspection of these systems and consultation with a specialist concerning such systems would be a reasonably foreseeable requirement imposed by a future purchaser. Similarly, our review of Paragraph 10 of the real estate sales agreement indicates the existence of evidence from which the trial court could find that Sellers may be required to pay for a heating warranty from a future purchaser. Paragraph 10 is a paragraph in the form contract indicating a list of warranties, the costs of which are sometimes borne by the sellers. The existence of this list in the contract is evidence upon which the trial court could find that the cost of the warranty was reasonably foreseeable.

2. Interest

After Buyers' default, Sellers relisted the property for sale and continued making payments on the first and second mortgages on the property until the subsequent sale. Sellers presented evidence that the interest payments on the mortgages totaled $4500. The trial court found that the mortgage interest that Sellers continued to pay on their residence following the breach by Buyers was foreseeable. However, the trial court acknowledged that Sellers enjoyed the benefit of the continued occupancy of the residence and therefore reduced this award of interest by one-half.

The trial court correctly determined that Sellers may be entitled to damages resulting from the payment of mortgage interest due to Buyers' breach of contract to purchase realty because such damages were reasonably foreseeable. Where a buyer defaults on a residential purchase agreement, thus forcing the seller to replace the property on the market for sale, the lapse of time between the original closing date and a subsequent sale may give rise to the incurring of special damages by the seller. See Shaeffer v. Kelton, 95 N.M. 182, 187, 619 P.2d 1226, 1231 (1980) (after default by purchaser plaintiff may recover interest payments on construction loan for period plaintiff sought to locate another buyer). . . .

III. Award of Punitive Damages

The trial court awarded punitive damages against Buyers for their conduct in attempting to persuade Sellers to agree to terminate the contract. The trial court found, among other things: Buyers and their family members engaged in acts of extremely poor judgment toward Sellers in their efforts to persuade Sellers to agree to a termination of the contract. One of these acts, Buyers' and their son's attempting to contact Mrs. Jones at her house, reasonably frightened Mrs. Jones but did not intimidate Sellers into agreeing to termination of the contract. Buyers made misrepresentations of fact regarding their financial situation in their efforts to persuade [Sellers] to agree to a termination of the contract.

At the time of their breach of the contract, Buyers had approximately $577,000 in a checking account, and earned income of more than $16,000.00 per month, plus bonuses. Buyers' failure to consummate the contract to purchase was wanton, utterly reckless and in utter disregard of their contractual obligations, and was sufficient to warrant the imposition of punitive damages. [Buyers'] conduct evidenced such a cavalier attitude toward their own obligations and the harm inflicted on [Sellers] as to establish their intent to harm Sellers. . . .

Notes and Questions

1. *Damages and timing.* As noted in *Jones*, the general rule upon the buyer's failure to perform is that the seller is entitled to damages measured by the difference between the contract price and the fair market value at the time of breach. See, e.g., White v. Farrell, 20 N.Y.3d 487 (N.Y. 2013). In cases of a rapidly declining market, where the seller will have more difficulty finding a new buyer, some courts have allowed damages to be calculated on the date the property is re-sold. Kuhn v. Spatial Design, Inc., 585 A.2d 967, 971 (N.J. App. 1991). In this respect, the court in *Kuhn* adopted the essence of the Uniform Commercial Code—which applies only to sales of goods—regarding sellers' damages. See, e.g., Gerald Korngold, Seller's Damages from a Defaulting Buyer of Realty: The Influence of the Uniform Land Transactions Act on the Courts, 20 Nova L. Rev. 1069 (1996).

2. *Specific performance.* Because courts assume that land, unlike other goods, is unique, they allow both specific performance for buyers and sellers in cases where the other has breached. But some courts have begun to depart from this general practice, applying ordinary contract (damages) remedies in appropriate cases. This is true, for example, in cases of sales of condominiums, presumably based upon the absence of uniqueness among homes in a development. See Centex Homes Corp. v. Boag, 320 A.2d 194 (N.J. Ch. 1974); but see Giannini v. First Natl. Bank of Des Plaines, 483 N.E.2d 924, 933 (Ill. App. 1985) (upheld the availability of specific performance for condominium purchasers, relying on the uniqueness of land).

3. *Retention of deposit.* Even in the absence of a forfeiture clause, a court will usually allow the seller to retain the buyer's deposit upon breach even when actual damages are less than the deposit. The rule of thumb is that a 10 percent "forfeiture" is reasonable. Courts will also typically enforce liquidated damages

provisions provided that they meet the standard tests of reasonableness. For buyers, the parallel remedy for seller breach is to seek restitution of the deposit.

C. THE DEED

1. Warranties of Title

Three types of deeds are used today: *general warranty deed, special warranty deed,* and *quitclaim deed.* They differ in the amount of protection they provide. A *general warranty deed* provides the greatest degree of protection, warranting title against all defects in title, whether they arose before or after the grantor took title. A *special warranty deed* comes next in terms of degree of protection. It contains warranties only against the grantor's own acts but not the acts of others. Thus, if the defect is a mortgage on the land executed by the grantor's predecessors in ownership, the grantor is not liable. A *quitclaim deed* contains no warranties of any kind. It merely conveys whatever title the grantor has, if any, and if the grantee of a quitclaim deed takes nothing by the deed, the grantee cannot sue the grantor.

Here is a general warranty deed:

GENERAL WARRANTY DEED

I, John Doe, grant to Nancy Roe and her heirs and assigns forever, for $10 and other good and valuable consideration, the following real estate situated in _____ County, State of _____, described as follows:

[Insert description of land]

To have and to hold the premises, with all the privileges and appurtenances belonging thereunto, to the use of the grantee and her heirs and assigns forever.

The grantor, for himself and his heirs and assigns, covenants (1) that the grantor is lawfully seized in fee simple of the premises, (2) that he has a good right to convey the fee simple, (3) that the premises are free from all encumbrances, (4) that the grantor and his heirs and assigns will forever warrant and defend the grantee and her heirs and assigns against every person lawfully claiming the premises or any part thereof, (5) that the grantor and his heirs and assigns will guarantee the quiet enjoyment of the premises to the grantee and her heirs and assigns, and (6) that the grantor and his heirs and

> **Sidebar**
>
> Habendum Clauses
>
> The clause beginning "To have and to hold" is known as the *habendum clause* (after the Latin *habendum et tenendum*). (Early deeds were written in Latin, the language of clerks (clerics).) The habendum clause had the function in feudal times of declaring of which lord the land was held and by what services. Modern deeds usually contain a habendum clause, which is unnecessary but may function to limit the estate granted in some way.

assigns will, on demand of the grantee or her heirs or assigns, execute any instrument necessary for the further assurance of the title to the premises that may be reasonably required.

Dated this _____ day of _____, 20 _____.

John Doe
_____
[signature of grantor]

Acknowledgment

State of _____

County of _____

I hereby certify that on this day before me, a notary public, personally appeared the above-named John Doe, who acknowledged that he voluntarily signed the foregoing instrument on the day and year therein mentioned.

In testimony whereof, I hereunto subscribe my name and affix my official seal on this _____ day of _____, 20 _____.

[*signature of notary*]
Notary Public in and for
_____ County,
State of _____
My commission
expires _____

Notes and Questions: The Deed

1. *Consideration.* It is customary to state in a deed that some consideration was paid by the grantee, in order to raise a presumption that the grantee is a bona fide purchaser entitled to the protection of the recording acts against prior unrecorded instruments. See page 416. It is neither customary nor necessary to state the exact consideration given. Do you see why?

2. *Acknowledgment.* In almost all states, a deed signed by the grantor, and delivered, is valid without an acknowledgment before a notary public. However, in order for the deed to be recorded in the courthouse, giving notice to the world of the grantee's interest, the deed must be acknowledged by the grantor (in some states, witnessing is permitted in place of acknowledgment). Therefore, as a matter of practice, all deeds prepared by professionals are acknowledged.

3. *Description of tract.* A deed must contain a description of the parcel of land conveyed that locates the parcel by describing its boundaries. Customary methods of description include (1) reference to natural or artificial monuments and, from the starting point, reference to directions and distances ("metes and bounds"); (2) reference to a government survey, recorded plat, or some other record; and (3) reference to the street and number or the name of the property.

There are many cases, particularly old ones, litigating the correct boundaries of a tract of land. When this country was settled, deed descriptions of land were very informal. They might refer to "Hester Quinn's farm" or to a tract "beginning at the old oak tree near the road and running 30 feet north, thence 70 feet east to the creek, thence south along the creek to an iron post, thence back to the beginning." In time, the reference points frequently disappeared.

4. *Seal.* An old saw says a deed to land is effective when it is signed, sealed, and delivered. The requirement of a signed document was initiated by the Statute of Frauds in 1677. The requirement of sealing is older, going back to the Norman Conquest, when a seal replaced the sign of the cross on documents. If a person had no seal, he borrowed someone else's. At common law, a "deed" was defined as a sealed instrument; a sealed instrument was required for the conveyance of a freehold. Most state legislatures have abolished the distinction between sealed and unsealed instruments. Where still extant, the requirement of a seal on transfers of real property is formal in the purest sense. Almost anything can be a seal: the word *seal*, the initials L.S. (standing for *locus sigilli*, the place of the seal), a ribbon, a scrawl, a scratch.

5. *Forgery and fraud.* A forged deed is void. The grantor whose signature is forged to a deed prevails over all persons, including subsequent bona fide purchasers from the grantee who do not know the deed is forged.

On the other hand, most courts hold that a deed procured by fraud is voidable by the grantor in an action against the grantee, but a subsequent bona fide purchaser from the grantee who is unaware of the fraud prevails over the grantor. The grantor, having introduced the deed into the stream of commerce, made it possible for a subsequent innocent purchaser to suffer loss. As between two innocent persons, one of whom must suffer by the act of the fraudulent third party, the law generally places the loss on the person who could have prevented the loss to the other.

Read closely the warranty clause of the general warranty deed set forth on pages 387-388, and you will see that it contains six express warranties:

1. *A covenant of seisin*—The grantor warrants that he owns the estate that he purports to convey.

2. *A covenant of right to convey*—The grantor warrants that he has the right to convey the property. In most instances this covenant serves the same purpose as the covenant of seisin, but it is possible for a person who has seisin not to have the right to convey (e.g., a trustee may have legal title but be forbidden by the trust instrument to convey it).

3. *A covenant against encumbrances*—The grantor warrants that there are no encumbrances on the property. Encumbrances include, among other items, mortgages, liens, easements, and covenants.

4. *A covenant of general warranty*—The grantor warrants that he will defend against lawful claims and will compensate the grantee for any loss that the grantee may sustain by assertion of superior title.

5. *A covenant of quiet enjoyment*—The grantor warrants that the grantee will not be disturbed in possession and enjoyment of the property by assertion of superior title. This covenant is, for all practical purposes, identical with the covenant of general warranty and is often omitted from general warranty deeds.

6. *A covenant of further assurances*—The grantor promises that he will execute any other documents required to perfect the title conveyed.

Observe that the first three covenants are phrased in the present tense and are called *present covenants*. The last three covenants are phrased in the future tense and are called *future covenants*. The distinction is this: a present covenant is broken, if ever, at the time the deed is delivered. Either the grantor owns the property at that time, or he does not; either there are existing encumbrances at that time, or there are none. A future covenant promises that the grantor will do some future act, such as defending against claims of third parties or compensating the grantee for loss by virtue of failure of title. A future covenant is not breached until the grantee or his successor is evicted from the property, buys up the paramount claim, or is otherwise damaged.

The statute of limitations begins to run on a breach of a present covenant at the date of delivery of the deed. It begins to run on a future covenant at the time of eviction or when the covenant is broken in the future.

BROWN v. LOBER

Supreme Court of Illinois, 1979
389 N.E.2d 1188

[In 1947, the owner of 80 acres of land conveyed it to William and Faith Bost, reserving a two-thirds interest in the mineral rights. In 1957, the Bosts conveyed the 80-acre tract to James R. Brown and his wife by a general warranty deed containing no exceptions. In 1974, the Browns contracted to sell the mineral rights to Consolidated Coal Co. for $6,000, but upon finding that the Browns owned only one-third of the mineral rights the parties had to renegotiate the contract to provide for payment of $2,000 for one-third of the mineral rights. The prior grantor had never made any attempt to exercise his mineral rights. The 10-year statute of limitations barred a suit on the present covenants, so the Browns sued the executor of the Bosts, who had died, seeking $4,000 damages for breach of the covenant of quiet enjoyment. The trial court ruled in favor of the defendant. The appellate court reversed, and the case is now before the supreme court.]

UNDERWOOD, J. . . . The question is whether plaintiffs have alleged facts sufficient to constitute a constructive eviction. They argue that if a covenantee fails in his effort to sell an interest in land because he discovers that he does not own what his warranty deed purported to convey, he has suffered a constructive eviction and is thereby entitled to bring an action against his grantor for breach of the covenant of quiet enjoyment. We think that the decision of this court in Scott v. Kirkendall, 88 Ill. 465 (1878), is controlling on this issue and compels us to reject plaintiffs' argument.

In Scott, an action was brought for breach of the covenant of warranty by a grantee who discovered that other parties had paramount title to the land in question. The land was vacant and unoccupied at all relevant times. This court, in rejecting the grantee's claim that there was a breach of the covenant of quiet enjoyment, quoted the earlier decision in Moore v. Vail, 17 Ill. 185, 191 (1855): "'Until that time, (the taking possession by the owner of the paramount title,) he might peaceably have entered upon and enjoyed the premises, without resistance or molestation, which was all his grantors covenanted he should do. They did not guarantee to him a perfect title, but the possession and enjoyment of the premises.'" 88 Ill. 465, 468.

Relying on this language in Moore, the Scott court concluded:

> We do not see but what this fully decides the present case against the appellant. It holds that the mere existence of a paramount title does not constitute a breach of the covenant. That is all there is here. There has been no assertion

of the adverse title. The land has always been vacant. Appellant could at any time have taken peaceable possession of it. He has in no way been prevented or hindered from the enjoyment of the possession by any one having a better right. It was but the possession and enjoyment of the premises which was assured to him, and there has been no disturbance or interference in that respect. True, there is a superior title in another, but appellant has never felt "its pressure upon him." [88 Ill. 465, 468-469.]

Admittedly, *Scott* dealt with surface rights while the case before us concerns subsurface mineral rights. We are, nevertheless, convinced that the reasoning employed in *Scott* is applicable to the present case. While plaintiffs went into possession of the surface area, they cannot be said to have possessed the subsurface minerals. "Possession of the surface does not carry possession of the minerals. . . . To possess the mineral estate, one must undertake the actual removal thereof from the ground or do such other act as will apprise the community that such interest is in the exclusive use and enjoyment of the claiming party." Failoni v. Chicago & North Western Ry. Co., 30 Ill. 2d 258, 262, 195 N.E.2d 619, 622 (1964).

Since no one has, as yet, undertaken to remove the coal or otherwise manifested a clear intent to exclusively "possess" the mineral estate, it must be concluded that the subsurface estate is "vacant." As in *Scott*, plaintiffs "could at any time have taken peaceable possession of it. [They have] in no way been prevented or hindered from the enjoyment of the possession by any one having a better right." (88 Ill. 465, 468.) Accordingly, until such time as one holding paramount title interferes with plaintiffs' right of possession (e.g., by beginning to mine the coal), there can be no constructive eviction and, therefore, no breach of the covenant of quiet enjoyment.

What plaintiffs are apparently attempting to do on this appeal is to extend the protection afforded by the covenant of quiet enjoyment. However, we decline to expand the historical scope of this covenant to provide a remedy where another of the covenants of title is so clearly applicable. As this court stated in Scott v. Kirkendall, 88 Ill. 465, 469 (1878): "To sustain the present action would be to confound all distinction between the covenant of warranty and that of seisin, or of right to convey. They are not equivalent covenants. An action will lie upon the latter, though there be no disturbance of possession. A defect of title will suffice. Not so with the covenant of warranty, or for quiet enjoyment, as has always been held by the prevailing authority." The covenant of seisin, unquestionably, was breached when the Bosts delivered the deed to plaintiffs, and plaintiffs then had a cause of action. However, despite the fact that it was a matter of public record that there was a reservation of a two-thirds interest in the mineral rights in the earlier deed, plaintiffs failed to bring an action for breach of the covenant of seisin within the 10-year period following delivery of the deed. The likely explanation is that plaintiffs had not secured a title opinion at the time they purchased the property. . . . Plaintiffs' oversight, however, does not justify us in overruling earlier decisions in order to recognize an otherwise premature cause of action. The mere fact that plaintiffs' original contract with Consolidated had to be modified due to their discovery that paramount title to two-thirds of the subsurface minerals belonged to another is not sufficient to constitute the constructive eviction necessary to a breach of the covenant of quiet enjoyment.

Accordingly, the judgment of the appellate court is reversed, and the judgment of the circuit court of Montgomery County is affirmed.

Questions

1. Suppose that the Browns buy up the two-thirds interest in the minerals for $10,000 and then sue the Bosts' executor on the covenant of general warranty. Can they recover?

2. *Knowledge of an encumbrance.* Suppose that the buyer has knowledge of an encumbrance on the property when he accepts a general warranty deed. Is the covenant against encumbrances breached?

There is considerable conflict among the authorities as to whether or not a visible or known easement is excepted from a covenant against encumbrances. A distinction is made in some cases between encumbrances which affect the title and those which simply affect the physical condition of the land. In the first class, it is universally held that the encumbrances are included in the covenant, regardless of the knowledge of the grantee. Those encumbrances relating to physical conditions of the property have, in many instances, been treated as excluded from the covenant. Some of these cases are decided upon the theory that, whenever the actual physical conditions of the realty are apparent, and are in their nature permanent and irremediable, such conditions are within the contemplation of the parties when contracting, and are therefore not included in a general covenant against encumbrances.

There seems to be a tendency toward the proposition that certain visible public easements, such as highways and railroad rights of way, in open and notorious use at the time of the conveyance, do not breach a covenant against encumbrances. However, it still seems to be the general rule, particularly in those cases involving private rights of way, that an easement which is a burden upon the estate granted and which diminishes its value constitutes a breach of the covenant against encumbrances in the deed, regardless of whether the grantee had knowledge of its existence or that it was visible and notorious.

Certainly, if the deed contains anything which would indicate that a known encumbrance was not intended to be within the covenant, the purchaser cannot complain that such an encumbrance was a breach of the covenant. However, with the possible exception of public easements that are apparent and in their nature permanent and irremediable, mere knowledge of the encumbrance is not sufficient to exclude it from the operation of the covenant. The intention to exclude an encumbrance should be manifested in the deed itself, for a resort to oral or other extraneous evidence would violate settled principles of law in regard to deeds. [Jones v. Grow Inv. & Mortgage Co., 358 P.2d 909, 910-911 (Utah 1961).]

2. Delivery

To be effective, a deed must be delivered with the intent that it be presently effective. Delivery is rarely an issue in commercial transactions. Either the grantor hands the deed to the grantee upon receipt of the purchase price, or the grantor puts the deed in the hands of a third party (an escrow agent) who hands over the deed upon closing the transaction. In the first case, the grantor intends to make an immediate transfer of title to the grantee. In the second, the grantor intends to transfer title when all conditions are fulfilled. If there is an enforceable contract of sale, the escrow agent is the agent of both the grantor and grantee. The grantor cannot recall the deed from the agent. When the agent delivers the deed to the grantee, if necessary to carry out the parties' intent and do equity, the title of the grantee will "relate back" to the date the grantor handed the deed to the agent. For example, if the grantor dies before the escrow agent delivers the deed, the delivery of the deed by the agent is treated as if it occurred before the grantor's death. By this fiction the rule that a will is required to pass title at death is avoided. Title is regarded as having been transferred to the grantee during the grantor's life.

Delivery problems almost never occur in commercial transactions. They are largely confined to donative transactions. Although some courts continue to require manual delivery of the deed to the grantee or a third person, see, e.g., Jones v. Phillips, 488 S.E.2d 692 (Ga. App. 1997), most courts recognize the doctrine of *constructive delivery*. According to this doctrine, delivery is deemed to have occurred where the grantor executes a deed and engages in conduct that indicates intent to transfer ownership. When the deed is handed over to the grantee but the extrinsic evidence shows that the deed is to "take effect" at the death of the grantor, a few courts have held that there is no delivery and that the transfer is testamentary and void. See William B. Stoebuck & Dale A. Whitman, The Law of Property § 11.3 at 830 (3d ed. 2000).

D. FINANCING REAL ESTATE TRANSACTIONS

1. Introduction to Mortgages

Let's go back to the Byars, whom we met on page 353. Recall that Bob and Betty applied for a loan to pay the balance of the purchase price beyond the down payment. Suppose Last National Bank agrees to make the loan. To assure repayment of the loan the Byars will provide two important documents to the bank: (1) a *promissory note*, indicating the purchasers' contractual commitment to repay; and (2) a *mortgage*, which secures the lender's note. The Byars are the mortgagors; the bank is the mortgagee. If the Byars fail to pay their note or do not otherwise perform their obligations, the bank can have the property sold ("foreclose the mortgage") and apply the proceeds of sale to the amount due on the note.

Title vs. lien theories of mortgages. Jurisdictions are divided over exactly what interest the lender receives under a mortgage. There are two theories of mortgages:

- ▶ *Title theory.* Some states adhere to the common law theory that the lender takes legal title to the land; the borrower has only the equity of redemption.
- ▶ *Lien theory.* Most states subscribe to the lien theory, which disregards the form and holds that the borrower keeps legal title and the lender has only a lien on the property.

Although this distinction used to count for a lot, the differences in practical application between lien and title states have almost entirely disappeared because title states have come to see that title passes to the mortgagee only for purposes of securing the debt and have interpreted the mortgage accordingly.

Changes in the home mortgage market. Mortgages are not what they used to be. Think of the relatively straightforward arrangement depicted in the classic movie "It's a Wonderful Life." A couple, say, the Byars, would borrow money from a local savings and loan association (S&L) to buy their home. The S&L would make the loan using money from funds deposited in customer savings accounts, would secure the loan with a mortgage, and, importantly, hold both the promissory note and the mortgage until the loan was fully paid or otherwise terminated. That world no longer exists. The mortgage market today is vastly more complex, as we will later explain. See pages 406-407.

2. Alternatives to Mortgages

The installment land sale contract. A mortgage is the usual instrument for securing repayment, but in some cases an arrangement known as an *installment land sale contract* may be used. In Section B of this chapter, beginning at page 368, we considered various aspects of the Contract of Sale. Don't confuse the Contract of Sale with the installment land sale contract device. Unlike the contract for the sale of land considered earlier, the installment land sale contract is a security device, a substitute for conventional mortgages. It is usually referred to as an *installment land contract*, or a *contract for deed*, or a *lease to own contract*. In each case, the device works like this: the buyer takes possession of the land immediately, but the seller contracts to deliver title to the buyer only after the buyer has paid the purchase price plus interest in regular installments over a fixed period of time.

There is little functional difference between a purchase money mortgage and an installment land sale contract, in that both are designed to secure payment of the sales price, yet all sorts of problems arise in practice. The installment contract commonly specifies that the property is transferred "as is," and provides that in the event of default the buyer forfeits the land and any payments already made. Financing is provided by the seller, not a bank or other institutional lender, and for this reason it is widely used in transfers of low-cost housing to buyers who have insufficient funds or an adequate credit record to qualify for loans from institutional lenders, to obtain a title search, to hire lawyers for advice at the outset—or to assist them in the case of default. Hence, even though many states provide protection for buyers by treating installment contracts just as they do mortgages, poorly informed buyers still regularly just walk away from their installment contract deals when they can no longer afford to make payments. Obviously, then, installment contracts are attractive to unscrupulous sellers, and use of the contracts has increased considerably in recent years.

A recent variation of the installment sale contract is the *lease-to-sell* arrangement. The basic difference between the two is that unlike an installment sale contract, in the typical lease-to-sell the tenant still needs to find financing to obtain title. Some leases require tenants to pay for any repairs (is this term legally enforceable in states with a non-waivable warranty of habitability?), and consumer-protection regulations like the federal Truth in Lending Act, which apply to installment sale contracts, do not apply to leases-to-sell. A report from the

National Consumer Law Center states that many such leases were "built to fail" and were predatory in nature. See http://www.nytimes.com/2016/07/14/business/dealbook/law-center-calls-seller-financed-home-sales-toxic-transactions.html.

HORNE v. HARBOUR PORTFOLIO

United States District Court for the Northern District of Georgia, 2018
304 F. Supp. 3d 1332

STORY, J. . . . This case arises out of contract for deed ("CFD") home purchase transactions extended by Harbour Portfolio VI, LP and Harbour Portfolio VII, LP (the "Harbour Defendants") to the Plaintiffs. Plaintiffs allege that these CFDs contained abusive credit terms. They also allege that the Harbour Defendants intentionally targeted Plaintiffs because of their race and that the Harbour Defendants actions had a disparate impact on Plaintiffs because they are African-American.

The Harbour Defendants purchased all, or nearly all, of its properties from Fannie Mae's portfolio of "real estate owned" properties, which are homes that went through foreclosure but were not purchased by third parties. These homes were often in poor or uninhabitable condition, but no repairs were made prior to selling them via the CFDs. The Harbour Defendants would mark up the sale price of the home to four or five times their purchase price. Under the terms of the CFDs, interest rates were 9.9% or 10% over a 30-year period. The CFDs also put the burden of home repairs, maintenance, property taxes, and homeowner's insurance on the buyer. Each CFD contained a forfeiture clause giving the Harbour Defendants the right, upon default, to elect to cancel the contract, keep all amounts paid, and evict the buyer.

Plaintiffs allege that the Harbour Defendants engaged in reverse redlining, the practice of issuing subprime loans to minority communities. They allege that the Harbour Defendants purchased homes located in communities that are majority African-American and designed a marketing scheme to draw primarily African-American buyers. The Harbour Defendants advertised by placing signs in front of the properties and through word of mouth. The Plaintiffs allege that the people most likely to see the signs or hear about the Harbour Defendants' properties were those already in the neighborhoods, i.e. African-Americans. Plaintiffs rely in large part on statistics to show both that the Harbour Defendants intentionally targeted African-American buyers and that their actions had a disparate impact on African-Americans.

Plaintiffs now bring multiple claims against the Harbour Defendants and others involved. Relevant to the currently pending motions, some or all of the Plaintiffs bring claims against the Harbour Defendants under the Fair Housing Act, the Equal Credit Opportunity Act, the Georgia Fair Housing Act, the Truth in Lending Act, the Georgia Fair Business Practices Act and the Unfair and Deceptive Practices Towards the Elderly Act, and the Georgia Residential Mortgage Act, and for equitable mortgage, declaratory judgment, unjust enrichment, and malicious eviction. . . .

The Harbour Defendants have filed a motion to dismiss the twelve claims brought against it. . . .

All Plaintiffs bring claims under the Fair Housing Act against the Harbour Defendants under theories of both intentional and unintentional discrimination for reverse redlining. "Redlining is the practice of denying the extension of credit to specific geographic areas due to the income, race, or ethnicity of its residents." *Hargraves v. Capital City Mortg. Corp.*, 140 F. Supp. 2d 7, 20 (D.D.C. 2000) (internal quotations omitted). Reverse redlining is "the practice of extending credit on unfair terms because of the plaintiff's race and geographic area." *Steed v. EverHome Mortg. Co.*, 308 Fed. Appx. 364, 369 (11th Cir. 2009) (citing *Hargraves*, 140 F. Supp. 2d at 20).

In *Steed*, the Eleventh Circuit applied the analysis of *Hargraves* in a reverse redlining case. To state a plausible reverse redlining claim, Plaintiffs must allege "that the defendants' lending practices and loan terms were unfair and predatory, and that the defendants either intentionally targeted on the basis of race, or that there is a disparate impact on the basis of race." *Steed*, 308 Fed. Appx. at 368 (internal quotations and citation omitted). "[P]redatory lending practices include exorbitant interest rates, equity stripping, acquiring property through default, repeated foreclosures, and loan servicing procedures that involve excessive fees." *Id.* at 369. "[W]hether the practices alleged occurred, and whether the practices were unfair and predatory, is a jury question." *Id.*

Plaintiffs have alleged that the Harbour Defendants engaged in predatory lending practices. They allege that the interest rates charged were 9.9% or 10%, while the prevailing interest rates for mortgage loans was around 4%; that the contracts included forfeiture clauses giving the Harbour Defendants the option to cancel the contract and keep all amounts paid; that the Harbour Defendants were able to reacquire the property through the default of the Plaintiffs; and that the Harbour Defendants have filed at least 71 eviction cases in Fulton, DeKalb, and Clayton County from 2011 to 2015. . . .

The Harbour Defendants argue that Plaintiffs have failed to allege a claim for disparate impact in light of *Texas Department of Housing & Community Affairs v. Inclusive Communities Project, Inc.*, 35 S. Ct. 2507 (2015). They argue that after *Inclusive Communities*, a plaintiff must (1) show statistically imbalanced lending patterns which adversely impact a minority group; (2) identify a facially neutral policy followed by the defendant during the same period of time; (3) show how that policy is artificial, arbitrary, and unnecessary; and (4) allege how that policy was a substantial cause of the adverse lending patterns. *Cobb Cty. v. Bank of Am. Corp.*, 183 F. Supp. 3d 1332, 1346 (N.D. Ga. 2016) (internal quotations omitted). While the Harbour Defendants argue that Plaintiffs have failed to meet their burden as to all four elements, the Court disagrees.

Plaintiffs have alleged that the Harbour Defendants had a policy of only purchasing homes from Fannie Mae and only advertising via yard signs and word of mouth. These are facially neutral policies. They have alleged that the homes available from Fannie Mae constituted less than one-quarter of foreclosure properties available during the relevant time period. This supports an inference, at the pleading stage, that the policy of purchasing from Fannie Mae was arbitrary because the Harbour Defendants could have purchased homes from other sources.

Plaintiffs have also pleaded facts that show a statistically imbalanced lending pattern that adversely impacts a minority group. They have alleged that a disproportionate concentration of the transactions by the Harbour Defendants occurred in high-minority census tracts. As alleged in the Second Amended Complaint, "Fannie Mae sales in Fulton and DeKalb County from 2011-2015 were located in census tracts that had a mean percentage of African-American residents of 71.37%." However, "the mean racial makeup of the census tracts where other (non-Fannie Mae) single family home sales occurred in Fulton and DeKalb County over the same time period was 48.37% African American." These facts support an inference at the pleading stage that the Harbour Defendants' customers were more likely to be members of a protected class than is true for the population of Fulton and DeKalb Counties as a whole.

Finally, the Harbour Defendants argue that Plaintiffs have not and cannot allege a robust causal connection between any alleged facially neutral policy and the alleged disproportionate racial outcome. The racial disparity in the relevant census tracts predates any involvement by the Harbour Defendants. Therefore, their conduct could not have caused the racial disparity. While it is true that the Harbour Defendants' policy of purchasing from Fannie Mae did not cause the racial imbalance in these areas, this argument misses the point. Plaintiffs do not argue that because of the policy, there are more African-Americans living in these areas. They argue that because the Harbour Defendants decided to purchase homes in areas with a higher concentration of African-Americans, African-Americans are more likely to be home buyers in this area and thus adversely impacted by the Harbour Defendants' alleged predatory lending practices.

Plaintiffs have alleged facts that, if true, would show that the Harbour Defendants' policy of only purchasing homes from Fannie Mae and only advertising those homes via yard signs and word of mouth caused a disproportionate impact on African-Americans. Plaintiffs have therefore stated a prima facie FHA claim under a theory of disparate impact.

The Harbour Defendants also argue that Plaintiffs have failed to state a claim for intentional discrimination under the FHA because they fail to allege that they were treated differently than similarly situated people outside of their protected class. In reverse redlining cases, however, courts have held that "if the plaintiff presents direct evidence that the lender intentionally targeted her for unfair loans on the basis of [membership in a protected class], the plaintiff need not also show that the lender makes loans on more favorable terms to others." *Matthews v. New Century Mortg. Corp.*, 185 F. Supp. 2d 874, 886-87 (S.D. Ohio 2002) (citing *Hargraves*, 140 F. Supp. 2d at 20). . . .

Plaintiffs have alleged that the Harbour Defendants intentionally targeted African-Americans by advertising properties via signs in front of each house for sale and via word of mouth, both of which were designed to reach the primarily African-American residents of communities where the Harbour Defendants purchased properties. This evidence, along with the evidence of the racial demographics of the relevant communities, is sufficient to state a claim for intentional targeting on the basis of race.

Plaintiffs have stated a prima facie case under the FHA under theories of both intentional targeting and disparate impact. The Harbour Defendants' Motion to Dismiss is therefore DENIED as to [the Fair Housing Act claims]. . . .

THE REST OF THE STORY . . .

The *Horne* litigation was settled in December 2018. The 12 households who were still living in their homes received a deed converting their contract for deed to a mortgage with title insurance, reduced interest rates, shorter repayment terms, in some cases principal reductions, and a lump sum cash payment. The four households who were evicted/no longer living in the home received separate lump sum cash payments. National Consumer Law Center, General Predatory Lending Briefs, Reports & Press Releases, Land Installment Contracts, available at https://www.nclc.org/predatory-mortgage-origination-and-lending/general-predatory-lending-policy-analysis/general-predatory-lending-briefs-reports-and-press-releases.html (last visited June 1, 2020).

Notes and Questions

1. *Treating installment land contracts and mortgages alike?* Are install-ment land contracts the equivalent of mortgages? Should they all be treated alike and subject to the same rules and procedures? That is the approach adopted by the Restatement (Third) of Property, Mortgages § 3.4(2) (1997), which states, "A contract for deed creates a mortgage." A comment to the Restatement identifies the benefit of this approach:

> [U]nder mortgage treatment the purchaser not only has the right to tardy redemption, but in addition, if no redemption occurs, the right in most juris-dictions to have the value of the land tested at a public foreclosure sale. If the property sells for more than the contract price, the purchaser has the right to the surplus. If the sale yields less than the contract debt the vendor, unless prohibited by statute, is entitled to a deficiency judgment.

Id., comment b.

Not all courts have adopted this approach. Some courts exercise discretion dis-tinguishing between those installment land contracts that should be treated the same as mortgages from those that should be enforced according to their terms. See Grombone v. Krekel, 754 P.2d 777 (Colo. App. 1988). Yet other courts hold that the borrower has no right of redemption under these contracts; consequently, the lender has the right to get the property back upon the borrower's default and eject the borrower. The lender is entitled to keep the payments already made by the borrower unless they so exceed the lender's damages as to amount to a for-feiture or penalty. See Stonebraker v. Zinn, 286 S.E.2d 911 (W. Va. 1982). Which approach seems most reasonable?

2. *Modern-day redlining.* *Horne* involved the practice of reverse redlining. Redlining itself began in the 1930s before anti-discrimination legislation was enacted. There is evidence that redlining history is repeating itself. A major study, based on 31 million records, found a pattern of denials of conventional mort-gage loans for people of color at rates far higher than their white counterparts across the country. See Aaron Glantz & Emmanuel Martinez, For People of Color, Banks Are Shutting the Door to Homeownership, Revealnews.org (Center for Investigative Reporting), Feb. 15, 2018, available at http://www.revealnews.org/ article/for-people-of-color-banks-are-shutting-the-door-to homeownership (last visited June 4, 2020).

Deed of trust. Under a deed of trust, the borrower conveys title to the land to a person (usually a third person but it may be the lender) to hold in trust to secure payment of the debt to the lender. The trustee is given the power to sell without going to court if the borrower defaults. (A mortgage that is not a deed of trust may also have a power of sale incorporated into it.) This arrangement is attractive to lenders because, as we will later discuss (see page 400), this method of foreclosure is quicker and cheaper than judicial foreclosure. Bear in mind, the deed of trust is not a trust. It is in effect a power of sale mortgage, and courts treat it as such.

Equitable mortgage. Under the doctrine of *equitable mortgage*, a court will treat a transaction that on its face is a deed, lease, or some other form of transfer as a

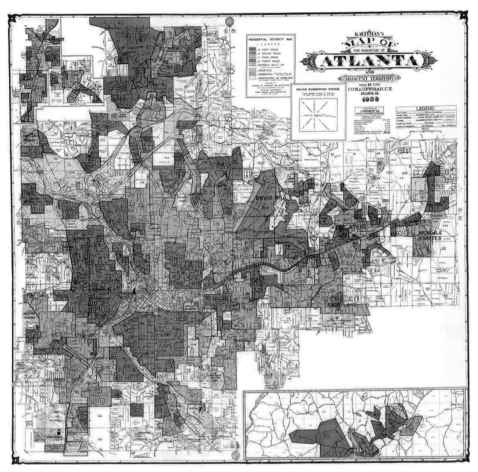

Map created by the federal Home Owner's Loan Corp. The dark gray area is defined
as "hazardous." The HOLC created maps like this for every major city in
the country between 1935 and 1940.

Source: Mapping Inequality, University of Richmond

mortgage. So, in Koenig v. Van Reken, 279 N.W.2d 590 (Mich. App. 1979), the plaintiff Helen Koenig owned a home, valued at $60,000, that was encumbered by three
mortgages totaling almost $26,000. The real estate taxes on her home had become
delinquent and foreclosure proceedings had begun on one of the mortgages. The
defendant Stanley Van Reken offered her a somewhat complicated arrangement,
the effect of which was that she transferred to him her equity in the home, worth
over $30,000, for less than $4,000 in a lease-back arrangement that effectively circumvented the right to redeem. The court applied the equitable mortgage doctrine.
"Although no set criterion has been established, the controlling factor in determining whether a deed absolute on its face should be deemed a mortgage is the intention of the parties." Id. at 592. Said the court, "Under Michigan law, it is well settled
that the adverse financial condition of the grantor, coupled with the inadequacy of
the purchase price for the property, is sufficient to establish a deed absolute on its
face to be a mortgage." Id.

3. Mortgage Foreclosure

The foreclosure process. When a borrower defaults on loan repayment, the lender may initiate foreclosure proceedings, permitting it to seize the property (say, a home) and selling it through some form of auction. The borrower can avoid foreclosure by paying off the debt, but how much must be repaid and when depend on several factors, including the presence of a *debt acceleration clause* in the loan agreement (in which case the entire loan balance must be paid), whether the parties can negotiate a new agreement to restructure the debt, and whether legal relief for foreclosure is provided by some applicable statute, such as under the federal CARES Act of 2020.

There are two methods of foreclosure, judicial and nonjudicial.

- *Judicial foreclosure*, which dominates, is a lawsuit that the lender initiates, ending in a court-supervised auction. It is costly and time-consuming.
- *Nonjudicial (power of sale) foreclosure*, which is permitted in about half the states, is available if the mortgage documents include a power of sale provision. It is more creditor friendly than a judicial foreclosure proceeding because there is no supervision by a court or other state third party. In many cases, the lender supervises the auction, although some states require a trustee.

Foreclosure cuts off the borrower's equity of redemption. (However, some states have enacted a *statutory* right of redemption, which permits the borrower to buy back the property for the price bid at the auction within some set period of time, say, six months, following foreclosure.) If the auction price is less than the loan balance, many states permit the lender to seek a *deficiency judgment* personally for the difference. Some states, however, either prohibit deficiency judgments or require lenders to bring deficiency actions at the same time as the foreclosure action. See Cal. Civ. Proc. Code § 580b (West 2020).

A common problem with foreclosure sales is the price bid at auction. Anyone can bid, but not uncommonly the only bidder is the lender, who has an incentive to bid low. The risk is that the lender will get the property at a price below fair market value but then sell it for its market value and keep the difference. This raises the questions whether courts should be willing to set aside foreclosure sales for inadequacy of price and, if so, under what circumstances?

MURPHY v. FIN. DEV. CORP.

Supreme Court of New Hampshire, 1985
495 A.2d 1245

DOUGLAS, J. The plaintiffs brought this action seeking to set aside the foreclosure sale of their home, or, in the alternative, money damages. The Superior Court (Bean, J.), adopting the recommendation of a Master (R. Peter Shapiro, Esq.), entered a judgment for the plaintiffs in the amount of $27,000 against two of the defendants, Financial Development Corporation and Colonial Deposit Company (the lenders).

The plaintiffs purchased a house in Nashua in 1966, financing it by means of a mortgage loan. They refinanced the loan in March of 1980, executing a new promissory note and a power of sale mortgage, with Financial Development Corporation as mortgagee. The note and mortgage were later assigned to Colonial Deposit Company.

In February of 1981, the plaintiff Richard Murphy became unemployed. By September of 1981, the plaintiffs were seven months in arrears on their mortgage payments, and had also failed to pay substantial amounts in utility assessments and real estate taxes. After discussing unsuccessfully with the plaintiffs proposals for revising the payment schedule, rewriting the note, and arranging alternative financing, the lenders gave notice on October 6, 1981, of their intent to foreclose.

During the following weeks, the plaintiffs made a concerted effort to avoid foreclosure. They paid the seven months' mortgage arrearage, but failed to pay some $643.18 in costs and legal fees associated with the foreclosure proceedings. The lenders scheduled the foreclosure sale for November 10, 1981, at the site of the subject property. They complied with all of the statutory requirements for notice. See RSA 479:25.

At the plaintiffs' request, the lenders agreed to postpone the sale until December 15, 1981. They advised the plaintiffs that this would entail an additional cost of $100, and that the sale would proceed unless the lenders received payment of $743.18, as well as all mortgage payments then due, by December 15. Notice of the postponement was posted on the subject property on November 10 at the originally scheduled time of the sale, and was also posted at the Nashua City Hall and Post Office. No prospective bidders were present for the scheduled sale.

In late November, the plaintiffs paid the mortgage payment which had been due in October, but made no further payments to the lenders. An attempt by the lenders to arrange new financing for the plaintiffs through a third party failed when the plaintiffs refused to agree to pay for a new appraisal of the property. Early on the morning of December 15, 1981, the plaintiffs tried to obtain a further postponement, but were advised by the lenders' attorney that it was impossible unless the costs and legal fees were paid.

At the plaintiffs' request, the attorney called the president of Financial Development Corporation, who also refused to postpone the sale. Further calls by the plaintiffs to the lenders' office were equally unavailing.

The sale proceeded as scheduled at 10:00 A.M. on December 15, at the site of the property. Although it had snowed the previous night, the weather was clear and warm at the time of the sale, and the roads were clear. The only parties present were the plaintiffs, a representative of the lenders, and an attorney, Morgan Hollis, who had been engaged to conduct the sale because the lenders' attorney, who lived in Dover, had been apprehensive about the weather the night before. The lenders' representative made the only bid at the sale. That bid of $27,000, roughly the amount owed on the mortgage, plus costs and fees, was accepted and the sale concluded.

Later that same day, Attorney Hollis encountered one of his clients, William Dube, a representative of the defendant Southern New Hampshire Home Traders, Inc. (Southern). On being informed of the sale, Mr. Dube contacted the lenders and offered to buy the property for $27,000. The lenders rejected the offer and made a counter offer of $40,000. Within two days a purchase price of $38,000 was agreed upon by Mr. Dube and the lenders and the sale was subsequently completed.

The plaintiffs commenced this action on February 5, 1982. The lenders moved to dismiss, arguing that any action was barred because the plaintiffs had failed to petition for an injunction prior to the sale. The master denied the motion. After hearing the evidence, he ruled for the plaintiffs, finding that the lenders had "failed to exercise good faith and due diligence in obtaining a fair price for the subject property at the foreclosure sale. . . ."

The master also ruled that Southern was a bona fide purchaser for value, and thus had acquired legal title to the house. That ruling is not at issue here. He assessed monetary damages against the lenders equal to "the difference between the fair market value of the subject property on the date of the foreclosure and the price obtained at said sale."

Having found the fair market value to be $54,000, he assessed damages accordingly at $27,000. He further ruled that "[t]he bad faith of the 'Lenders' warrants an award of legal fees." The lenders appealed. . . .

The . . . issue before us is whether the master erred in concluding that the lenders had failed to comply with the often-repeated rule that a mortgagee executing a power of sale is bound both by the statutory procedural requirements *and* by a duty to protect the interests of the mortgagor through the exercise of good faith and due diligence. . . .

The master found that the lenders, throughout the time prior to the sale, "did not mislead or deal unfairly with the plaintiffs." They engaged in serious efforts to avoid foreclosure through new financing, and agreed to one postponement of the sale. The basis for the master's decision was his conclusion that the lenders had failed to exercise good faith and due diligence in obtaining a fair price for the property.

This court's past decisions have not dealt consistently with the question whether the mortgagee's duty amounts to that of a fiduciary or trustee. This may be an inevitable result of the mortgagee's dual role as seller and potential buyer at the foreclosure sale, and of the conflicting interests involved. See Wheeler v. Slocinski, 82 N.H. 211, 214, 131 A. 598, 600 (1926).

We need not label a duty, however, in order to define it. In his role as a seller, the mortgagee's duty of good faith and due diligence is essentially that of a fiduciary. Such a view is in keeping with "[t]he 'trend . . . towards liberalizing the term [fiduciary] in order to prevent unjust enrichment.'" Lash v. Cheshire County Savings Bank, Inc., 124 N.H. 435, 438, 474 A.2d 980, 981 (1984) (quoting Cornwell v. Cornwell, 116 N.H. 205, 209, 356 A.2d 683, 686 (1976)).

A mortgagee, therefore, must exert every reasonable effort to obtain "a fair and reasonable price under the circumstances," Reconstruction Finance Corp. v. Faulkner, 101 N.H. 352, 361, 143 A.2d 403, 410 (1958), even to the extent, if necessary, of adjourning the sale or of establishing "an upset price below which he will not accept any offer." Lakes Region Fin. Corp. v. Goodhue Boat Yard, Inc., 118 N.H. 103, 107, 382 A.2d 1108, 1111 (1978).

What constitutes a fair price, or whether the mortgagee must establish an upset price, adjourn the sale, or make other reasonable efforts to assure a fair price, depends on the circumstances of each case. Inadequacy of price alone is not sufficient to demonstrate bad faith unless the price is so low as to shock the judicial conscience. . . .

We must decide, in the present case, whether the evidence supports the finding of the master that the lenders failed to exercise good faith and due diligence in obtaining a fair price for the plaintiffs' property.

We first note that "[t]he duties of good faith and due diligence are distinct. . . . One may be observed and not the other, and any inquiry as to their breach calls for a separate consideration of each." Wheeler v. Slocinski, 82 N.H. at 213, 131 A. at 600. In order "to constitute bad faith there must be an intentional disregard of duty or a purpose to injure." Id. at 214, 131 A. at 600-01.

There is insufficient evidence in the record to support the master's finding that the lenders acted in bad faith in failing to obtain a fair price for the plaintiffs' property. The lenders complied with the statutory requirements of notice and otherwise conducted the sale in compliance with statutory provisions. The lenders postponed the sale one time and did not bid with knowledge of any immediately available subsequent purchaser. Further, there is no evidence indicating an intent on the part of the lenders to injure the mortgagor by, for example, discouraging other buyers.

There is ample evidence in the record, however, to support the master's finding that the lenders failed to exercise due diligence in obtaining a fair price. "The issue of the lack of due diligence is whether a reasonable man in the [lenders'] place would have adjourned the sale," id. at 215, 131 A. at 601, or taken other measures to receive a fair price.

In early 1980, the plaintiffs' home was appraised at $46,000. At the time of the foreclosure sale on December 15, 1981, the lenders had not had the house reappraised to take into account improvements and appreciation. The master found that a reasonable person in the place of the lenders would have realized that the plaintiffs' equity in the property was at least $19,000, the difference between the 1980 appraised value of $46,000 and the amount owed on the mortgage totaling approximately $27,000.

At the foreclosure sale, the lenders were the only bidders. The master found that their bid of $27,000 "was sufficient to cover all monies due and did not create a deficiency balance" but "did not provide for a return of any of the plaintiffs' equity."

Further, the master found that the lenders "had reason to know" that "they stood to make a substantial profit on a quick turnaround sale." On the day of the sale, the lenders offered to sell the foreclosed property to William Dube for $40,000. Within two days after the foreclosure sale, they did in fact agree to sell it to Dube for $38,000. It was not necessary for the master to find that the lenders knew of a specific potential buyer before the sale in order to show lack of good faith or due diligence as the lenders contend. The fact that the lenders offered the property for sale at a price sizably above that for which they had purchased it, only a few hours before, supports the master's finding that the lenders had reason to know, at the time of the foreclosure sale, that they could make a substantial profit on a quick turnaround sale. For this reason, they should have taken more measures to ensure receiving a higher price at the sale.

While a mortgagee may not always be required to secure a portion of the mortgagor's equity, such an obligation did exist in this case. The substantial amount of equity which the plaintiffs had in their property, the knowledge of the lenders as to the appraised value of the property, and the plaintiffs' efforts to forestall foreclosure by paying the mortgage arrearage within weeks of the sale, all support the master's conclusion that the lenders had a fiduciary duty to take more reasonable steps than they did to protect the plaintiffs' equity by attempting to obtain a fair price for the property. They could have established an appropriate upset price to assure a minimum bid. They also could have postponed the auction and advertised commercially by display advertising in order to assure that bidders other than themselves would be present.

Instead, as Theodore DiStefano, an officer of both lending institutions testified, the lenders made no attempt to obtain fair market value for the property but were concerned *only* with making themselves "whole." On the facts of this case, such disregard for the interests of the mortgagors was a breach of duty by the mortgagees.

Although the lenders *did* comply with the statutory requirements of notice of the foreclosure sale, these efforts were not sufficient in this case to demonstrate due diligence. At the time of the initially scheduled sale, the extent of the lenders' efforts to publicize the sale of the property was publication of a legal notice of the mortgagees' sale at public auction on November 10, published once a week for three weeks in the Nashua Telegraph, plus postings in public places. The lenders did not advertise, publish, or otherwise give notice to the general public of postponement of the sale to December 15, 1981, other than by posting notices at the plaintiffs' house, at the post office, and at city hall. That these efforts to advertise were ineffective is evidenced by the fact that no one, other than the lenders, appeared at the sale to bid on the property. This fact allowed the lenders to purchase the property at a minimal price and then to profit substantially in a quick turnaround sale.

We recognize a need to give guidance to a trial court which must determine whether a mortgagee who has complied with the strict letter of the statutory law has nevertheless violated his additional duties of good faith and due diligence. A finding that the mortgagee had, or should have had, knowledge of his ability to get a higher price at an adjourned sale is the most conclusive evidence of such a violation.

More generally, we are in agreement with the official Commissioners' Comment to section 3-508 of the Uniform Land Transactions Act:

> The requirement that the sale be conducted in a reasonable manner, including the advertising aspects, requires that the person conducting the sale use the ordinary methods of making buyers aware that are used when an owner is voluntarily selling his land. Thus an advertisement in the portion of a daily newspaper where these ads are placed or, in appropriate cases such as the sale of an industrial plant, a display advertisement in the financial sections of the daily newspaper may be the most reasonable method. In other cases employment of a professional real estate agent may be the more reasonable method. It is unlikely that an advertisement in a legal publication among other legal notices would qualify as a commercially reasonable method of sale advertising. [13 Uniform Laws Annotated 704 (West 1980).]

As discussed above, the lenders met neither of these guidelines.

While agreeing with the master that the lenders failed to exercise due diligence in this case, we find that he erred as a matter of law in awarding damages equal to "the difference between the fair market value of the subject property . . . and the price obtained at [the] sale."

Such a formula may well be the appropriate measure where *bad faith* is found. See Danvers Savings Bank v. Hammer, 122 N.H. 1, 5, 440 A.2d 435, 438 (1982). In such a case, a mortgagee's conduct amounts to more than mere negligence. Damages based upon the *fair market value*, a figure in excess of a *fair* price, will more readily induce mortgagees to perform their duties properly. A "fair" price may or may not yield a figure close to fair market value; however, it will be that price arrived at as a result of due diligence by the mortgagee.

Where, as here, however, a mortgagee fails to exercise due diligence, the proper assessment of damages is the difference between a fair price for the property and the price obtained at the foreclosure sale. We have held, where lack of due diligence has been found, that "the test is not 'fair market value' as in eminent domain cases nor is the mortgagee bound to give credit for the highest possible amount which might be obtained under different circumstances, as at an owner's sale." Silver v. First National Bank, 108 N.H. 390, 392, 236 A.2d 493, 495 (1967) (quoting Reconstruction Finance Corp. v. Faulkner, 101 N.H. 352, 361, 143 A.2d 403, 410 (1958)) (citation omitted). Accordingly, we remand to the trial court for a reassessment of damages consistent with this opinion.

Because we concluded above that there was no "bad faith or obstinate, unjust, vexatious, wanton, or oppressive conduct," on the part of the lenders, we see no reason to stray from our general rule that the prevailing litigant is not entitled to collect attorney's fees from the loser. Harkeem v. Adams, 117 N.H. 687, 688, 377 A.2d 617, 617 (1977). Therefore, we reverse this part of the master's decision.

Reversed in part; affirmed in part; remanded.

GRANT S. NELSON & DALE A. WHITMAN, REAL ESTATE FINANCE LAW
§ 7.21 at 640-641
(5th ed. 2007)

All jurisdictions adhere to the recognized rule that mere inadequacy of the foreclosure sale price will not invalidate a sale, absent fraud, unfairness or other irregularity. Courts generally articulate two main standards for invalidating a foreclosure sale based on price. First, many courts state that inadequacy of the sale price is an insufficient ground unless it is so gross as to shock the conscience of the court, warranting an inference of fraud or imposition. Second, another significant group of courts require that, in the absence of some other defect in the foreclosure process, the price must be "grossly inadequate" before a sale may be invalidated. . . .

Under either the "shock the conscience" or "grossly inadequate" standards, unless other foreclosure defects exist, it is extremely difficult to get a sale set aside on mere price inadequacy. While some courts have found that sales for one-seventh and one-sixtieth of fair market value "shock the conscience," one commentator has noted with respect to his jurisdiction that "such sales have been upheld where the price paid for the property was only one-half, one-third, one-fourth, one-fifth, or even one-twentieth of its reasonable value." On the other hand, where other factors are present, such as chilled bidding, unusual hour of sale or any other indicia of unfairness, courts do set sales aside. For example, in a case where the mortgaged real estate sold for 3% of the fair market value, the court set aside the sale because of the additional factor that the mortgagee had informed the mortgagor of the incorrect sale date.

Notes and Questions

1. Murphy. In *Murphy*, how can the mortgagee determine an appropriate upset price? Specifically, what should the lenders have done to receive a higher bid?

2. *Foreclosure sales. Murphy* is unusual. Most courts usually uphold foreclosure sales despite low prices, in the absence of procedural irregularity that is prejudicial or that chilled bidding. See, e.g., Lo v. Jensen, 106 Cal. Rptr. 2d 443 (Cal. App. 2001); Lona v. Citibank, N.A., 134 Cal. Rptr. 3d 622 (Cal. App. 2011).

However, in the wake of the mortgage crisis of the first decade of the twenty-first century, about which we shall have more to say later, there have been a number of cases setting aside judgments based upon mistakes. See, e.g., Millennium Rock Mortgage, Inc. v. T.D. Service Co., 102 Cal. Rptr. 3d 544 (Cal. App. 2009) (disparity between legal description and address); CitiMortgage, Inc. v. Synuria, 86 So. 3d 1237 (Fla. App. 2012) (bank did not have agent at foreclosure sale). Also, in Lost Mountain Dev. Co. v. King, 2006 WL 3740791 (Tenn. App.), the court scrutinized a sale particularly stringently because of the deficiency judgment. What constitutes chilled bidding? For one view, see Justin Lischak Earley, Chilling the Bidding, 5 J. Marshall L.J. 99 (2011).

3. *Borrower's remedies.* If the foreclosure sale is defective, what are the borrower's remedies? Can the title of the purchaser at the sale be set aside? See Grant S. Nelson & Dale A. Whitman, Real Estate Finance Law § 7.22 (5th ed. 2007). The avalanche of mortgage foreclosures that began in 2007 as part of the mortgage crisis has spawned renewed interest in the subject of mortgage foreclosure and its reform. See, e.g., Aaron Byrkit, Reforming Foreclosure Disposition: A Tool for Tempering the Financial Meltdown, 63 Consumer Fin. L.Q. Rep. 275 (2009).

4. *Deeds in lieu of foreclosure.* Mortgage foreclosure can be an extremely costly proposition for borrowers and lenders alike. In instances where a borrower cannot repay its debt, it can frequently avoid foreclosure by tendering its deed to the lender in lieu of foreclosure. In most instances, the lender will agree to give up any claim for a deficiency judgment. When a mortgagor cannot pay its debt and the property's value is above the amount of the loan, he or she can always sell the property and pay off the loan. Similarly, when the debt is greater than the loan, he or she can offer a deed in lieu of foreclosure. Why would the parties ever go to the expense and trouble of foreclosure?

5. *Forfeiture for delinquent property taxes.* Rafaeli owed $8.41 in unpaid property taxes from 2011, which grew to $285.81 after interest, penalties, and fees. The county foreclosed on Rafaeli's property for the delinquency, sold the property at public auction for $24,500, and retained all the sale proceeds in excess of the taxes, interest, penalties, and fees. Rafaeli argued that the county committed an unconstitutional taking by retaining the surplus proceeds from the tax-foreclosure sale that exceeded the amount it owed in unpaid delinquent taxes, interest, penalties, and fees. In Rafaeli, LLC v. Oakland County, 2020 WL 4037642 (Mich. 7/20/2020), the Michigan Supreme Court agreed. The court stated that the property owner "had a cognizable, vested property right to collect th[e] surplus proceeds" and that the county's failure to return the surplus constituted a government taking under the Michigan Constitution entitling owner to just compensation. We will study the subject of takings in Chapter 12.

Subprime lending and the changing mortgage market. Until the mid-1980s, there was one mortgage market; today there are two. It used to be the case that a hypothetical home purchaser, such as the Byars, whom we met earlier, would borrow money from a local savings and loan association (S&L) to buy their house at a fixed interest rate.

This one-market structure began to change in the 1980s when two federally sponsored entities, the Federal National Mortgage Association (Fannie Mae) and the Federal Home Loan Mortgage Corporation (Freddie Mac), began creating mortgage-backed securities. This led to the creation of a secondary mortgage market. Hundreds of mortgage loans were purchased and pooled together; securities representing the pool were then issued to investors. The securities, typically guaranteed by Fannie Mae and Freddie Mac, were appealing to many investors who would otherwise have found home mortgage loans unattractive investments.

Along with the emergence of a secondary mortgage market, the types of mortgage loans offered to borrowers changed. With interest rates going up to 16 percent and higher, lenders began to offer adjustable rate loans. The initial rate would be below the market level but would gradually increase according to an index based on debt issued by the Federal Reserve Bank.

The market for home loans changed tremendously as well. No longer lending solely (or even mainly) to borrowers with high credit ratings and stable income profiles, lenders began making highly risky subprime loans. By 2005, risk-based lending was in full swing. These loans were made to borrowers who had low credit ratings, unstable income prospects, and for low, or no, down payments.

Subprime lending hit people of color especially hard, as lending institutions targeted communities of color, where borrowers commonly had limited access to credit. A unit within Wells Fargo in the mid-Atlantic area was specially tasked with aggressively seeking to make subprime loans in minority communities. See Michael Powell, Bank Accused of Pushing Mortgage Deals on Blacks, N.Y. Times, June 6, 2009, available at http://www.nytimes.com/2009/06/07/us/07baltimore .html (last visited June 3, 2020). The targeting of subprime loans to people of color was not confined to low income borrowers either. Black and Hispanic families with household annual incomes over $200,000 were more likely to receive a subprime loan than a white family with an annual income under $30,000. See Jacob William Faber, Racial Dynamics of Subprime Mortgage Lending at the Peak, 23 Housing Policy Debate 328 (2013). When the mortgage crisis that led to the Great Recession occurred in 2008, the neighborhoods where these subprime loans were heavily concentrated experienced high rates of foreclosure, and many of the former homeowners have never really recovered.

When the housing bubble burst, many borrowers found that they owed more on the loans than their homes were worth. These *underwater mortgages* literally had no equity. Borrowers stopped making payments, and foreclosures followed in large numbers. See Christopher K. Odinet, Foreclosed: Mortgage Servicing and the Hidden Architecture of Homeownership in America 32-39 (2019). Since then, the legal system has had to deal with the legal problems that ensued. The next case is an example.

COMMONWEALTH v. FREMONT INVESTMENT & LOAN

Supreme Judicial Court of Massachusetts, 2008
897 N.E.2d 548

BOTSFORD, J. The Commonwealth, acting through the Attorney General, commenced this consumer protection enforcement action against the defendant Fremont Investment & Loan and its parent company, Fremont General Corporation (collectively, Fremont), claiming that Fremont, in originating and servicing certain "subprime"[5] mortgage loans between 2004 and 2007 in Massachusetts, acted unfairly and deceptively in violation of G.L. c. 93A, § 2. Fremont appeals from a preliminary injunction granted by a judge in the Superior Court in favor of the Attorney General that restricts, but does not remove, Fremont's ability to foreclose on loans with features that the judge described as "presumptively unfair." All of the loans at issue are secured by mortgages on the borrowers' homes.

. . .

> ## Sidebar
>
> Adjustable-rate-mortgage (ARM) loans are what the term suggests. They set an attractive initial rate that results in low monthly payments, but after a few (one to three) years, the rate becomes adjustable, floating up or down during the remainder of the term. In times of tight money, the rate can become quite high, resulting in monthly payments that are much higher than the initial payments. When the initial rate is reset, "ARM reset shock" often occurs.

Fremont is an industrial bank chartered by the State of California. Between January, 2004, and March, 2007, Fremont originated 14,578 loans to Massachusetts residents secured by mortgages on owner-occupied homes. Of the loans originated during that time period, roughly 3,000 remain active and roughly 2,500 continue to be owned or serviced by Fremont. An estimated fifty to sixty per cent of Fremont's loans in Massachusetts were subprime.[6] Because subprime borrowers present a greater risk to the lender, the interest rate charged for a subprime loan is typically higher than the rate charged for conventional or prime mortgages. . . .

Fremont's subprime loan products offered a number of different features to cater to borrowers with low income. A large majority of Fremont's subprime loans were adjustable rate mortgage (ARM) loans, which bore a fixed interest rate for the first two or three years, and then adjusted every six months to a considerably higher variable rate for the remaining period of what was generally a thirty year loan. Thus, borrowers' monthly mortgage payments would start out lower and then increase substantially after the introductory two-year or three-year period. To determine loan qualification, Fremont generally required that borrowers have a debt-to-income ratio of less than or equal to fifty per cent—that is, that the borrowers' monthly debt obligations, including the applied-for mortgage, not exceed one-half their income. However, in calculating the debt-to-income ratio, Fremont considered only the monthly payment required for the introductory rate period of the mortgage loan, not the payment that would ultimately be required at the substantially higher "fully indexed" interest rate.[7]

---

5. "Subprime" loans are loans made to borrowers who generally would not qualify for traditional loans offered at the generally prevailing rate of interest for conventional mortgages.

6. The judge made this estimate based on the fact that sixty-four per cent of all Fremont's loans were adjustable rate mortgage loans (ARM loans), and 38.4 per cent were "stated income" loans, in which the borrower provided no documentation of his or her income. The judge inferred, based on the limited record available at the preliminary injunction stage, that all of the stated income loans were subprime ARM loans, and a majority of the remaining ARM loans were also subprime.

7. The "fully indexed" rate refers to the interest rate that represents the LIBOR rate at the time of the loan's inception plus the rate add specified in the loan documents. The judge noted that calculation of the debt-to-income ratio based on the fully indexed rate generally yields a ratio that exceeds fifty per cent.

As an additional feature to attract subprime borrowers, who typically had little or no savings, Fremont offered loans with no down payment. Instead of a down payment, Fremont would finance the full value of the property, resulting in a "loan-to-value ratio" approaching one hundred per cent. Most such financing was accomplished through the provision of a first mortgage providing eighty per cent financing and an additional "piggy-back loan" providing twenty per cent.

As of the time the Attorney General initiated this case in 2007, a significant number of Fremont's loans were in default. An analysis by the Attorney General of ninety-eight of those loans indicated that all were ARM loans with a substantial increase in payments required after the first two (or in a few cases, three) years, and that ninety per cent of the ninety-eight had a one hundred per cent loan-to-value ratio.

The judge granted a preliminary injunction . . . [having] determined that the Attorney General was likely to prevail on the claim that Fremont's loans featuring a combination of the following four characteristics qualified as "unfair" under G.L. c. 93A, § 2: (1) the loans were ARM loans with an introductory rate period of three years or less; (2) they featured an introductory rate for the initial period that was at least three per cent below the fully indexed rate; (3) they were made to borrowers for whom the debt-to-income ratio would have exceeded fifty per cent had Fremont measured the borrower's debt by the monthly payments that would be due at the fully indexed rate rather than under the introductory rate; and (4) the loan-to-value ratio was one hundred per cent, or the loan featured a substantial prepayment penalty (defined by the judge as greater than the "conventional prepayment penalty" defined in G.L. c. 183C, § 2) or a prepayment penalty that extended beyond the introductory rate period.

The judge reasoned that Fremont as a lender should have recognized that loans with the first three characteristics just described were "doomed to foreclosure" unless the borrower could refinance the loan at or near the end of the introductory rate period, and obtain in the process a new and low introductory rate. The fourth factor, however, would make it essentially impossible for subprime borrowers to refinance unless housing prices increased, because if housing prices remained steady or declined, a borrower with a mortgage loan having a loan-to-value ratio of one hundred per cent or a substantial prepayment penalty was not likely to have the necessary equity or financial capacity to obtain a new loan. The judge stated that, "[g]iven the fluctuations in the housing market and the inherent uncertainties as to how that market will fluctuate over time . . . it is unfair for a lender to issue a home mortgage loan secured by the borrower's principal dwelling that the lender reasonably expects will fall into default once the introductory period ends unless the fair market value of the home has increased at the close of the introductory period. To issue a home mortgage loan whose success relies on the hope that the fair market value of the home will increase during the introductory period is as unfair as issuing a home mortgage loan whose success depends on the hope that the borrower's income will increase during that same period."

The judge concluded that the balance of harms favored granting the preliminary injunction, and that the public interest would be served by doing so. The injunction he granted requires Fremont to do the following: (1) to give advance notice to the Attorney General of its intent to foreclose on any of its home mortgage loans; and (2) as to loans that possess each of the four characteristics of unfair loans just described and that are secured by the borrower's principal dwelling (referred to in the injunction as "presumptively unfair" loans), to work with the Attorney General to "resolve" their differences regarding foreclosure—presumably through a restructure or workout of the loan. If the loan cannot be worked out, Fremont is required to obtain approval for foreclosure from the court. The judge made clear that the injunction in no way relieved borrowers of their obligation ultimately to prove that a particular loan was unfair and foreclosure should not be permitted, or their obligation to repay the loans they had received.

2. Standard of review. . . .

Fremont's basic contention is that, while the terms of its subprime loans may arguably seem "unfair" within the meaning of G.L. c. 93A, § 2, if judged by current standards applicable to the mortgage lending industry, they did not violate any established concept of unfairness at the time they were originated; the judge, in Fremont's view, applied new rules or standards for defining what is "unfair" in a retroactive or ex post facto fashion—a result that is not in accord with the proper interpretation of c. 93A, § 2, and also represents "bad policy," because (among other reasons) lenders cannot know what rules govern their conduct, which will reduce their willingness to extend credit, hurting Massachusetts consumers. We do not agree that the judge applied a new standard retroactively.

Fremont highlights the judge's statement that at the time Fremont made the loans in question between 2004 and March of 2007, loans with the four characteristics the judge identified as unfair were not considered by the industry or more generally to be unfair; Fremont argues this acknowledgment by the judge is proof that the judge was creating a new definition or standard of unfairness. The argument lacks merit. First, the judge's statement that Fremont's combination of loan features were not recognized to be unfair does not mean the converse: that the loans were recognized to be fair. More to the point, at the core of the judge's decision is a determination that when Fremont chose to combine in a subprime loan the four characteristics the judge identified, *Fremont* knew or should have known that they would operate in concert essentially to guarantee that the borrower would be unable to pay and default would follow unless residential real estate values continued to rise indefinitely—an assumption that, in the judge's view, logic and experience had already shown as of January, 2004, to be unreasonable. The judge concluded that the Attorney General was likely to prove that Fremont's actions, in originating loans with terms that in combination would lead predictably to the consequence of the borrowers' default and foreclosure, were within established concepts of unfairness at the time the loans were made, and thus in violation of G.L. c. 93A, § 2. The record supports this conclusion.

. . .

The record here suggests that Fremont made no effort to determine whether borrowers could "make the scheduled payments under the terms of the loan." Rather, as the judge determined, loans were made in the understanding that they would have to be refinanced before the end of the introductory period. Fremont suggested in oral argument that the loans were underwritten in the expectation, reasonable at the time, that housing prices would improve during the introductory loan term, and thus could be refinanced before the higher payments began. However, it was unreasonable, and unfair to the borrower, for Fremont to structure its loans on such unsupportable optimism. As a bank and mortgage lender, Fremont had been warned repeatedly before 2004 (in the context of guidance on loan safety and soundness) that it needed to consider the performance of its loans in declining markets. See, e.g., Consumer Affairs and Business Regulation, Massachusetts Division of Banks,

Subprime Lending (Dec. 10, 1997) ("[M]ost subprime loans have been originated during robust economic conditions and have not been tested by a downturn in the economy. Management must ensure that the institution has adequate financial and operational strength to address these concerns effectively"). Fremont cannot now claim that it was taken by surprise by the effects of an economic decline, or that it should not be held responsible.

Finally, the conclusion that Fremont's loans featuring the four characteristics at issue violated established concepts of unfairness is supported by the consent agreement that Fremont entered into with the FDIC on March 7, 2007, the date Fremont stopped making loans. The consent agreement contains no admission of wrongdoing by Fremont, and we do not consider it as evidence of liability on Fremont's part. However, we view it as evidence of existing policy and guidance provided to the mortgage lending industry. The fact that the FDIC ordered Fremont to cease and desist from the use of almost precisely the loan features that are included in the judge's list of presumptively unfair characteristics indicates that the FDIC considered that under established mortgage lending standards, the marketing of loans with these features constituted unsafe and unsound banking practice with clearly harmful consequences for borrowers. Such unsafe and unsound conduct on the part of a lender, insofar as it leads directly to injury for consumers, qualifies as "unfair" under G.L. c. 93A, § 2.

. . .

Because the Attorney General, in the name of the Commonwealth, brings this case to carry out her statutory mandate to enforce the Consumer Protection Act, it is necessary to consider whether the preliminary injunction order promotes the public interest. Commonwealth v. Mass. CRINC, 392 Mass. 79, 88-89, 466 N.E.2d 792 (1984). Fremont argues that it does not, primarily because in Fremont's view, the order imposes new standards on lending practices that were considered permissible and acceptable when the loans were made. The result, Fremont claims, will be an unwillingness on the part of lenders to extend credit to Massachusetts consumers because they will be unwilling to risk doing business in an environment where standards are uncertain and the rules may change after the fact.

Our previous discussion, and rejection, of Fremont's claim that the judge retroactively applied new unfairness standards disposes of Fremont's public interest argument; we do not accept the premise that, in concluding that Fremont is likely to be found to have violated established concepts of unfairness, the judge's order has created an environment of uncertainty that lenders will shun. The injunction order crafted by the judge strikes a balance between the interests of borrowers who face foreclosure and loss of their homes under home loan mortgage terms that are at least presumptively unfair, on the one hand; and the interest of the lender in recovering the value of its loans to borrowers who received the benefit of those loaned funds and continue to have a contractual obligation to repay, on the other. The order does not bar foreclosure as a remedy for the lender, nor does it relieve borrowers of their obligations ultimately to repay the loans. Rather, it requires, where the mortgage loan terms include all four features deemed presumptively unfair, that Fremont explore alternatives to foreclosure in the first instance (a step that Fremont has indicated its desire to take in any event), and then seek approval of the court. If the court does not approve the foreclosure, that decision merely leaves the preliminary injunction in place until the Commonwealth has an opportunity to try to prove that the particular loan at issue actually violated c. 93A—a burden that is never shifted to Fremont. We conclude the order serves the public interest.

THE REST OF THE STORY . . .

Fremont Investment & Loan filed for Chapter 11 bankruptcy in June 2008. See Tiffany Kary, Fremont Files Bankruptcy After CapitalSource Sale (Bloomberg 2008). Since the beginning of 2008, 481 financial institutions have made it onto the Federal Deposit Insurance Corporation (FDIC) Failed Banks List. See http://www.fdic.gov/bank/individual/failed/banklist.html. Many others, including big names like Citibank, saw their capital reserves diminish quickly and applied for and received federal bailout money under the Troubled Asset Relief Program. Fannie Mae and Freddie Mac have been taken over by the federal government, their private investors' equity eliminated. Some major investment banks and insurance companies, such as Bear Stearns, Lehman Brothers, and AIG, essentially became insolvent and either have shut their doors or went into what amounts to federal receivership. While the causes of each institutional collapse are varied, subprime mortgages have played a direct or indirect role in many of them. Indeed, the bursting of the real estate bubble and the collapse of the subprime market contributed greatly to the credit crunch that launched the United States into its worst recession since the Great Depression. See Richard A. Posner, A Failure of Capitalism: The Crisis of '08 and the Descent into Depression (2009).

Notes and Questions

1. *Changes in the structure of the mortgage market.* Notice that in *Fremont* the loan applicants did not interact directly with bank employees. Instead, they applied through independent mortgage brokers who received fees upon the closing of the loans. Once the loan was originated, Fremont would typically sell it in the secondary mortgage market, and eventually it would be bundled into a mortgage-backed security. The process for getting a home was quite different 25 years ago; when applicants approached a savings and loan association directly, the institution made the underwriting decision and then held any loans made to maturity. How might the change in the structure of the mortgage market over the past quarter-century have contributed to the subprime crisis?

2. *The purchasers' motives.* Why would home purchasers seek loans that, according to the opinion in *Fremont*, were "doomed to foreclosure"? For an interesting perspective on the question, using insights from law and economics and cognitive psychology, see Oren Bar-Gill, The Law, Economics and Psychology of Subprime Mortgage Contracts, 94 Cornell L. Rev. 1073 (2009).

Covid-19 and foreclosure relief. As we noted earlier (see page xxix), local and state governments and the federal government responded to the Covid-19 pandemic with a variety of relief measures. Among these are moratoria on mortgage foreclosures. The landscape of these measures is widely varied and evolving. What we say here may be moot by the time you read this, but as of summer 2020, here are some generalizations.

A number of states have taken steps, usually initiated by executive order, to institute or authorize moratoria on foreclosure for limited periods of time, some of which were subject to limited extensions. For a state-by-state rundown, see A Guide to Mortgage and Rent Relief in Every State During the Coronavirus Emergency, http://moneywise.com/a/moneygeek-mortgage-rent-relief-by-state. Congress and federal agencies also have provided temporary relief for borrowers under the CARES Act (see page 319).

Property-related Covid-19 litigation has already been initiated, and more is likely to come. These lawsuits challenge different aspects of relief measures that states have taken. See, e.g., Friends of Danny DeVito v. Wolf, 2020 WL 1847100 (Pa. S. Ct. 4/13/2020) (challenge to governor's shutdown order as an unconstitutional taking rejected). For a brief overview of these measures, see Michael Allan Wolf, Powell on Real Property, Covid-19 Pandemic and Real Property Law: An Early Assessment of Relief Measures for Tenants and Residential Mortgagors (LexisNexis Matthew Bender 2020).

CHAPTER 8

Title Assurance

Return to the hypothetical home purchasers we discussed in the last chapter, the Byars. What the Byars are actually purchasing is title. A land sale is really a sale of title. This being the case, it is essential to the Byars that the seller, or vendor, have good legal title to convey. How can they protect themselves against title risks? That is the topic of this chapter.

Three main methods of title assurance are used in this country:

- *Title opinion based on a title search*
- *Title insurance*
- *Title covenants*

These methods are hardly mutually exclusive. In fact, it is common for a purchaser of land to use all three, adopting a kind of "belt-and-suspenders" approach. In this chapter we focus primarily on the first method, a professional opinion concerning title based on a title search. We will also briefly consider title insurance. We discussed title covenants earlier, on pages 387-388.

In a few localities, a method known as title registration is available. Under title registration, the state registers title and issues a title certificate to the owner, which is reissued to each new purchaser of the property.

Title searches rely on the public records office, where all instruments affecting land titles (deeds, mortgages, liens, wills, and so forth) are recorded. Public records are not always perfect, though, and purchasers commonly want further security. So private insurance companies sell title insurance to purchasers for a premium.

With title insurance companies serving as backup to the recording system, security of title in the United States ought to be, and is, very high. This, however, results less from any merits in our land title transfer system than from the ingenuity of professionals in the title industry, who manage to provide security in spite of the recording system's manifest and long-recognized defects.

A. THE RECORDING SYSTEM

1. Introduction

Public recording of deeds, mortgages, leases, and other instruments affecting land title began in this country in the Plymouth and Massachusetts Bay colonies around 1640. It was not an English custom. Today in every American state, statutes provide for land title records to be maintained by the county recorder (or other equivalent public official) in each county. The land title records include copies of documents filed with the recorder and indexes to these copied documents. (The original document presented for recordation is copied by the recorder and returned to the grantee.) Increasingly, jurisdictions are computerizing their land records, although the practice has only begun to affect the law of title.

Purposes of recordation: Recordation is generally not necessary for a deed or other instrument to be valid. A deed is valid and good against the grantor upon delivery without recordation. The recording system serves other functions:

→ Establishes a system of public recordation of land titles

Anyone—creditor, tax collector, prospective purchaser, or just plain curious—can ascertain who owns land in the county by searching the records.

→ Preserves in a secure place important documents

In most states, recorded copies of documents can be admitted directly into evidence in judicial proceedings, without producing or accounting for the original.

Generally, any kind of deed, mortgage, lease, option, or other instrument creating or affecting an interest in land can be recorded. A judgment or decree affecting title to land can also be recorded. In addition, wills and affidavits of heirship of an intestate are entitled to be recorded.

→ Protects purchasers for value and lien creditors against prior unrecorded interests

This is the most important function of recording statutes. In some circumstances, title to the same piece of land may be subject to more than one conflicting claim. Suppose:

> *Example 1. O* mortgages Blackacre to *A. O* subsequently conveys Blackacre to *B*, who does not know of the mortgage.

At common law, as between successive grantees, priority of title was determined by priority in time of conveyance. The theory was that once the grantor conveyed his interest to a grantee, the grantor no longer had an interest to convey to any subsequent grantee. So, in *Example 1*, at common law *B* takes the land subject to *A*'s mortgage. Equity, however, developed the doctrine of *bona fide purchaser*. In general, a bona fide purchaser is someone who purchases (i.e., provides valuable consideration for) an interest in land without notice of another interest already held by a third party. Under this doctrine, in *Example 1*, *B* would be protected against *A*'s mortgage if *A*'s mortgage were purely equitable and not a legal interest.

The recording acts in general have adopted and broadened the equitable doctrine of bona fide purchaser. Under the recording acts, *a subsequent bona fide purchaser is protected against prior unrecorded interests*. Thus a purchaser of property will want to search the records to make sure that there are no adverse prior recorded claims, and a purchaser records his deed in order to prevent a subsequent purchaser from a previous owner from prevailing over him. *But remember*: The common law rule of "prior in time, prior in effect," illustrated by *Example 1*, continues to control unless a person can qualify for protection under the applicable recording act.

2. The Indexes

When a buyer of land wishes to search out and find all the interests in a particular parcel of land, she must use an index to locate the relevant documents. Two types of indexes are currently used in the United States:

a. Grantor-Grantee Index

This is the most common type of index. Under this system separate indexes are kept for grantors and grantees. In the *grantor index*, all instruments are indexed alphabetically and chronologically under the grantor's surname. In the *grantee index*, all instruments are indexed under the grantee's surname. Thus a deed from Able to Baker will be indexed under Able's name in the grantor index and under Baker's name in the grantee index. Usually, many volumes compose the grantor index and similarly the grantee index. There may also be separate grantor and grantee indexes for each type of instrument—one index for deeds, one for mortgages, one for wills, one for liens, and so on. In our description of searching title below, we use the term *grantor index* to refer comprehensively to all the volumes indexing grantors. Similarly, the term *grantee index* refers to all volumes indexing grantees.

The reference in the index to a document sets forth its essentials: the grantor, the grantee, description of the land, kind of instrument, date of recording, and volume and page numbers where the instrument can be found set forth in full. The title searcher must, of course, examine the complete instrument; the index is merely a helpful method of locating the instrument among the many volumes in the recorder's office.

b. Tract Index

Some county recorder's offices use a tract index. These index documents by a parcel identification number assigned to the particular tract. The title search under this type of index is simple. Every document affecting the relevant tract is filed under its own parcel identification number, so a title searcher simply looks up the documents in that tract's file to examine the state of title.

How to search title. Searching title bears some resemblance to what the genealogist does in establishing kindred; first, trace backward for ancestors, and then under each ancestor fill in the names and relationships of his or her descendants. Similarly, in searching title you first go *backward* in time to an acceptable source or "root of title," then you search *forward* from that source. Since you use the grantee index to search backward and the grantor index to search forward, both indexes must be searched.

To illustrate, suppose your clients, the Byars, are purchasing from Dominguez. To find out how Dominguez received title, you look in the *grantee* index under Dominguez's name from the present time backward until you find a deed to Dominguez from Corleone in 1977. Now you want to know how Corleone received title, so you look, still in the grantee index, under Corleone's name from 1977 backward in time until you find a deed to Corleone from Baker in 1952. Now you want to know how Baker received title, and so you run Baker's name in the grantee index from 1952 backward in time to her source of title, Alvarez.

```
1980 - - - - - GRANTOR INDEX FEB. 2.81 THRU FEB. 20.81 - - - - - SUFFOLK COUNTY REGISTRY OF DEEDS

                                                                                          PAGE  180

MO-DY   GRANTOR                      GRANTEE              TOWN  BOOK PGE INST  DESCRIPTION

02-05   SECURITY PLANNERS LTD INC EAL   RELEASE                 9607 238 REL  U S TAX LIEN A515.35
02-05   SECURITY WAREHOUSE INC EAL      RELEASE                 9607 236 REL  U S TAX LIEN 8467,535
02-05   SECURITY WAREHOUSE INC EAL      RELEASE                 9609 237 REL  U S TAX LIEN 8442,251
02-05   SECURITY WAREHOUSE INC EAL      RELEASE                 9609 247 REL  U S TAX LIEN
02-05   SEGAL, EDITH      EAL           RELEASE                 9609 243 REL  U S TAX LIEN
02-05   SEGAL, MARY L.    EAL           RELEASE                 9609 241 REL  U S TAX LIEN
02-05   SEGAL, MARY L.    EAL           RELEASE                 9609 242 REL  U S TAX LIEN
02-05   SEGAL, MAX     EAL              RELEASE                 9609 243 REL  U S TAX LIEN
02-05   SEGAL, MICHAEL G.  EAL          RELEASE                 9609 242 REL  U S TAX LIEN
02-05   SEGAL, MICHAEL D.  EAL          RELEASE                 9609 241 REL  U S TAX LIEN
02-04   SEGAL, ROSALYN A.  EAL          AMENDMENT               9603 225 AMCT MASTER CNDMNM DEED
                                                                             9349,317 PLANS
02-03   SEGALINI, ROLAND JR  EAL        J N MCLAUGHLIN TR       9667 240 MTG  UNIT 400-21 OF THE
                                                                             CANTERBURY VILLAGE CNDMNM
02-12   SEGALINI, ROLAND JR  TR         M C MAGUIRE EAL     BRI 9676 306 DEED 57 DUSTIN ST LT 45 PL
                                                                             3500,516 PEING LT 3A PL
                                                                             1932,383
02-20   SEIDNER, MICHAEL A.             HOUSEHOLD FIN CORP  BRI 9693 242 MTG  SUMMIT AVE EALLSTON ST LT
                                                                             1 PL 2306,415
02-11   SEKENSKI, EDWARD A. JR  EAL     LEVY & SUSPENDED    CHE 9675 316 LES  WALTHAM DIST CT MADE
                                                                             FEB 11, 1981 BELLINGHAM
                                                                             ST 2 PCS
02-11   SEKENSKI, LINDA C.   EAL        LEVY & SUSPENDED    CHE 9675 316 LES  WALTHAM DIST CT MADE
                                                                             FEB 11, 1981 BELLINGHAM
                                                                             ST 2 PCS,
02-05   SELBY AUTO SUPPLY CO INC EAL    RELEASE                 9607 240 REL  U S TAX LIEN A443,434
02-05   SELLARO, FRANK    EAL           RELEASE                 9607 248 REL  U S TAX LIEN
02-09   SELWYN, BARBARA F.  EAL         SHAWMUT BK BOSTON N A   9671 113 MTG  19-21 RICKER TERR LT 30
                                                                             PL 2436 FND WDLSX #JUT
                                                                             OF CO
02-13   SELYA, ANNE    EAL              DISCHARGE               9677 193 DIS  MTG A640,419
02-13   SELYA, DAVID   EAL              DISCHARGE               9677 193 DIS  MTG A640,419
02-04   SEMINERIO, SANTINA   TR         A DESALVATORE EAL   BRI 9673 170 DEED MURDOCK&SPARHAWK STS LT 4
                                                                             PL D APRIL 4,1887
02-03   SENA, LAURA   EAL               NOTICE PETN         S B 9665 316 NOT  8 HUMPHREYS ST FCL TAX
                                                                             2143,090
02-02   SENNET, CAROL   EAL             C SENNETT EAL       T P 9665 234 DFED 1b2 SHERDIN ST LT 546 PL
                                                                             4710 LND
02-18   SEPULVEDA, PABLO                J A PRDROK JR       ROX 9660 135 DEED M ESTRELLA ST
02-06   SERVICENTER LTD   EAL           WESTINGHOUSE CR CORP ROX 9670 338 MTG  BROOKLINE AVE,FRANCISE
                                                                             BINNEY STS GEENWOOD RD PL
                                                                             C 1-25-1979
02-06   SERVICENTER LTD   EAL           WESTINGHOUSE CR CORP    9671 1   ASST ASST LEASE&RENTS ETC SEE
                                                                             INSTR
```

A page from the Grantor Index, Register of Deeds, Suffolk County, Massachusetts

Suppose you run the grantee index back to 1900, which is as far as you deem necessary, and you find that in 1900, record title was in Oh. Now you must switch to the *grantor* index and search that index *forward* in time under the name of each grantor (remember: you found the names of each grantor by running the grantee index). You start with Oh in the year 1900. You look under Oh's name in 1900, 1901, 1902, and so forth, until you find a deed from Oh to Alvarez, executed and recorded in 1915. You stop looking under Oh's name and start, with the volume for 1915, looking under Alvarez's name to find the first deed out from Alvarez, which is a deed from Alvarez to Baker executed in 1934 and recorded in 1939. You then run Baker name in the grantor index from 1934 (the date of execution of the deed) until you find, in 1952, the deed from Baker to Corleone, which was executed and recorded on the same day in 1952. You next run Corleone's name in the grantor index from 1952 until you find the deed from Corleone to Dominguez, executed and recorded in 1977. Finally, you run Dominguez's name in the grantor index from 1977 to the present.

So, now you have developed a chain of title that looks like this:

1900-1915	*Oh owns; conveys to Alvarez in 1915*
1915-1934	*Alvarez owns; conveys to Baker in 1934 by deed not recorded until 1939*
1934-1952	*Baker owns; conveys to Corleone in 1952*
1952-1977	*Corleone owns; conveys to Dominguez in 1977*

In running the grantor index under Oh's name from 1900 to 1915 (the first deed out, to Alvarez) you pick up any mortgages given by Oh, any attachments or lawsuits filed against Oh, and any conveyances by Oh of interests less than a fee simple. Similarly, with respect to each other owner, you pick up all of the claims against the particular owner by running the grantor index under the owner's name forward from the time of the *execution* of the first deed giving title to such owner to the time of *recording* of the first deed out from such owner.

Why must you search under Baker's name from 1934 (the date of execution of the A to B deed) rather than from 1939 (the date of recording)? The deed from Alvarez to Baker passed title to Baker in 1934. Baker thus could convey title to a person after that time.

The search sketched above, the minimum required in all jurisdictions without tract indexes, is the standard title search. This search produces a chain of title going back to a source deemed satisfactory. Many jurisdictions require a more extensive search of title, however. The more extensive searches and the problems they raise are examined in the discussion of Chain of Title Problems beginning at page 435.

How far back? How far back in the abysm of time a title searcher must search to find a satisfactory root of title varies both with local custom and with the identity of the client. In some jurisdictions, the practice is to go back to a sovereign, in others 60 years, and in still others a shorter period. The search is not ordinarily limited to the period of the statute of limitations because the statute may not have begun to run on various types of interests (such as a remainder, an easement, a covenant, or mineral rights).

LUTHI v. EVANS

Supreme Court of Kansas, 1978
576 P.2d 1064

PRAGER, J. On February 1, 1971, Grace V. Owens was the owner of interests in a number of oil and gas leases located in Coffey county. On that date Owens, by a written instrument designated "Assignment of Interest in Oil and Gas Leases," assigned to defendant International Tours, Inc. (hereinafter Tours) all of such oil and gas interests. This assignment provided as follows:

Assignment of Interest in Oil and Gas Leases

KNOW ALL MEN BY THESE PRESENTS:

That the undersigned Grace Vannocker Owens, formerly Grace Vannocker, Connie Sue Vannocker, formerly Connie Sue Wilson, Larry R. Vannocker, sometimes known as Larry Vannocker, individually and also doing business as Glacier Petroleum Company and Vannocker Oil Company, hereinafter called Assignors, for and in consideration of $100.00 and other valuable consideration, the receipt whereof is hereby acknowledged, do hereby sell, assign, transfer and set over unto International Tours, Inc., a Delaware Corporation, hereinafter called Assignee, all their right, title, and interest (which includes all overriding royalty interest and working interest) in and to the following Oil and Gas Leases located in Coffey County, Kansas, more particularly specified as follows, to-wit:

[The court omitted the description of the leases assigned, but, to make the case more understandable, we reproduce here the description of one of the leases referred to in the actual instrument:
WILEY (Phillips CP #50098)
Entire 7/8 Working Interest in Lease
Dated: June 8, 1936
From: Lillian Wiley
To: E.L. Harrigan and T.F. Harrigan
Recorded: Book 6L pages 137 and 138
Insofar as lease covers NE4 Sec. 14-23-14 (160 a.)
Similar descriptions of six other leases from Rossillon, Scott, Shotwell, Vannocker, McCartney, and Cochran are set forth in the instrument of assignment.]

together with the rights incident thereto and the personal property thereon, appurtenant thereto or used or obtained in connection therewith.

And for the same consideration the Assignors covenant with the Assignee, his heirs, successors or assigns: That the Assignors are the lawful owners of and have good title to the interest above assigned in and to said Lease, estate, rights and property, free and clear from all liens, encumbrances or adverse claims; That said Lease is valid and subsisting Lease on the land above described, and all rentals and royalties due thereunder have been paid and all conditions necessary to keep the same in full force have been duly performed, and that the Assignor will warrant and forever defend the same against all persons whomsoever, lawfully claiming or to claim the same. *Assignors intend to convey, and by this instrument convey, to the Assignee all interest of whatsoever nature in all working interests and overriding royalty interest in all Oil and Gas Leases in Coffey County, Kansas, owned by them whether or not the same are specifically enumerated above with all oil field and oil and gas lease equipment owned by them in said County whether or not located on the leases above described*, or elsewhere in storage in said County, but title is warranted only to the specific interests above specified, and assignors retain their title to all minerals in place and the corresponding royalty (commonly referred to as land owners royalty) attributable thereto. The effective date of this Assignment is February 1, 1971, at 7:00 o'clock A.M.

/s/ *Grace Vannocker Owens*
Connie Sue Vannocker
Larry R. Vannocker

(Acknowledgment by Grace Vannocker Owens before notary public with seal impressed thereon dated Feb. 5, 1971, appears here.) (Emphasis supplied.)

This assignment was filed for record in the office of the register of deeds of Coffey county on February 16, 1971.

It is important to note that in the first paragraph of the assignment, seven oil and gas leases were specifically described. Those leases are not involved on this appeal. In addition to the seven leases specifically described in the first paragraph, Owens was also the owner of a working interest in an oil and gas lease known as the Kufahl lease which was located on land in Coffey county. The Kufahl lease was not one of the leases specifically described in the assignment.

The second paragraph of the assignment states that the assignors intended to convey, and by this instrument conveyed to the assignee, "all interest of whatsoever nature in all working interests and overriding royalty interest in all Oil and Gas Leases in Coffey County, Kansas, owned by them whether or not the same are specifically enumerated above. . . ." The interest of Grace V. Owens in the Kufahl lease, being located in Coffey county, would be included under this general description.

On January 30, 1975, the same Grace V. Owens executed and delivered a second assignment of her working interest in the Kufahl lease to the defendant, J.R. Burris. Prior to the date of that assignment, Burris personally checked the records in the office of the register of deeds and, following the date of the assignment to him, Burris secured an abstract of title to the real estate in question. Neither his personal inspection nor the abstract of title reflected the prior assignment to Tours.

The controversy on this appeal is between Tours and Burris over ownership of what had previously been Owens's interest in the Kufahl lease. It is the position of Tours that the assignment dated February 1, 1971, effectively conveyed from Owens to Tours, Owens's working interest in the Kufahl lease by virtue of the general description contained in paragraph two of that assignment. Tours then contends that the recording of that assignment in the office of the register of deeds of Coffey county gave constructive notice of such conveyance to subsequent purchasers, including Burris. Hence, Tours reasons, it is the owner of Owens's working interest in the Kufahl lease.

Burris admits that the general description and language used in the second paragraph of Owens's assignment to Tours was sufficient to effect a valid transfer of the Owens interest in the Kufahl lease to Tours *as between the parties to that instrument*. Burris contends, however, that the general language contained in the second paragraph of the assignment to Tours, as recorded, which failed to state with specificity the names of the lessor and lessee, the date of the lease, any legal description, and the recording data, was not sufficient to give constructive notice to a subsequent innocent purchaser for value without actual notice of the prior assignment. Burris argues that as a result of those omissions in the assignment to Tours, it was impossible for the register of deeds of Coffey county to identify the real estate involved and to make the proper entries in the numerical index. Accordingly, even though he checked the records at the courthouse, Burris was unaware of the assignment of the Kufahl lease to Tours and he did not learn of the prior conveyance until after he had purchased the rights from Grace V. Owens. The abstract of title also failed to reflect the prior assignment to Tours. Burris maintains that as a result of the omissions and the inadequate description of the interest in real estate to be assigned under the second paragraph of the assignment to Tours, the Tours assignment, as recorded, was not sufficient to give constructive notice to a subsequent innocent purchaser for value. It is upon this point that Burris prevailed before the district court. On appeal, the Court of Appeals held the general description contained in the assignment to Tours to be sufficient, when recorded, to give constructive notice to a subsequent purchaser for value, including Burris.

At the outset, it should be noted that a deed or other instrument in writing which is intended to convey an interest in real estate and which describes the property to be conveyed as "all of the grantor's property in a certain county," is commonly referred to as a "Mother Hubbard" instrument. The language used in the second paragraph of the assignment from Owens to Tours in which the assignor conveyed to the assignee "all interest of whatsoever nature in all working interests . . . in all Oil and Gas Leases in Coffey County, Kansas," is an example of a "Mother Hubbard" clause. The so-called Mother Hubbard clauses or descriptions are seldom used in this state, but in the past have been found to be convenient for death bed transfers and in situations where time is of the essence and specific information concerning the legal description of property to be conveyed is not available. . . . The parties in this case agree, and the Court of Appeals held, that the second paragraph of the assignment from Owens to Tours, providing that the assignors convey to the assignee all interests in all oil and gas leases in Coffey County, Kansas, owned by them, constituted a valid transfer of the Owens interest in the Kufahl lease to Tours *as between the parties to that instrument*. We agree. We also agree with the parties and the Court of Appeals that a single instrument, properly executed, acknowledged, and delivered, may convey separate tracts by specific description and by general description capable of being made specific, where the clear intent of the language used is to do so. We agree that a subsequent purchaser, who has *actual* notice or knowledge of such an instrument, is bound thereby and takes subject to the rights of the assignee or grantor.

Sidebar

The source of the "Mother Hubbard" clause term is, of course, the old nursery rhyme. Recall that old Mother Hubbard had nothing more to give her poor dog. So, too, a Mother Hubbard clause leaves the grantor with nothing more to convey.

Above is the entry in the grantor index of the assignment from Owens to Tours. The land involved is described by reference to the United States Government Survey. Observe that land involved in the Wiley lease, referred to in the case, is described in the index as NE4 (northeast quarter) in 14-23-14 (Section 14, Township 23, Range 14). The other tracts were described by similar references. The Kufahl land did not come within the legal descriptions mentioned in the index.

This case involves a legal question which is one of first impression in this court. As noted above, the issue presented is whether or not the recording of an instrument of conveyance which uses a "Mother Hubbard" clause to describe the property conveyed, constitutes *constructive notice to a subsequent purchaser*. The determination of this issue requires us to examine the pertinent Kansas statutes covering the conveyance of interests in land and the statutory provisions for recording the same. . . .

The recordation of instruments of conveyance and the effect of recordation is covered in part by K.S.A. 58-2221, 58-2222, and 58-2223. These statutes are directly involved in this case and are as follows:

58-2221. *Recordation of instruments conveying or affecting real estate; duties of register of deeds.* Every instrument in writing that conveys real estate, any estate or interest created by an oil and gas lease, or whereby any real estate, may be affected, proved or acknowledged, and certified in the manner hereinbefore prescribed, may be recorded in the office of register of deeds of the county in which such real estate is situated: *Provided*, It shall be the duty of the register of deeds to file the same for record immediately, and in those counties where a numerical index is maintained in his or her office the register of deeds shall compare such instrument, before copying the same in the record, with the last record of transfer in his or her office of the property described and if the register of deeds finds such instrument contains apparent errors, he or she shall not record the same until he or she shall have notified the grantee where such notice is reasonably possible.

The grantor, lessor, grantee or lessee or any other person conveying or receiving real property or other interest in real property upon recording the instrument in the office of register of deeds shall furnish the register of deeds the full name and last known post-office address of the person to whom the property is conveyed or his or her designee. The register of deeds shall forward such information to the county clerk of the county who shall make any necessary changes in address records for mailing tax statements.

58-2222. *Same; filing imparts notice.* Every such instrument in writing, certified and recorded in the manner hereinbefore prescribed, shall, from the time of filing the same with the register of deeds for record, impart notice to all persons of the content thereof; and all subsequent purchasers and mortgagees shall be deemed to purchase with notice.

58-2223. *Same; unrecorded instrument valid only between parties having actual notice.* No such instrument in writing shall be valid, except between the parties thereto, and such as have actual notice thereof, until the same shall be deposited with the register of deeds for record.

. . . [W]e must also consider the Kansas statutes which govern the custody and the recordation of instruments of conveyance, and the duties of the register of deeds in regard thereto, as contained at K.S.A. 19-1201 through K.S.A. 19-1219. We will discuss only those statutes which we deem pertinent in the present controversy. . . . K.S.A. 19-1205 requires the register of deeds to keep a general index, direct and inverted, in his office. The register is required to record in the general index under the appropriate heading the names of grantors and grantees, the nature of the instrument, the volume and page where recorded, and, where appropriate, *a description of the tract.*

K.S.A. 19-1207 requires the register to keep a book of plats with an index thereof. K.S.A. 19-1209 provides that the county commissioners of any county may order the register of deeds to furnish a numerical index containing "the name of the instrument, the name of the grantor, the name of the grantee, *a brief description of the property*, and the volume and page in which each instrument indexed is recorded." K.S.A. 19-1210 makes it the duty of the register to make correct entries in the numerical index, of all instruments recorded concerning real estate, under the appropriate headings, and *"in the subdivision devoted to the particular quarter section described in the instrument making the conveyance."*[1]

. . . It . . . seems obvious to us that the purpose of the statutes authorizing the recording of instruments of conveyance is to impart to a subsequent purchaser notice of instruments which affect the title to a *specific tract of land* in which the subsequent purchaser is interested at the time. From a reading of all of the statutory provisions together, we have concluded that the legislature intended that recorded instruments of conveyance, to impart constructive notice to a subsequent purchaser or mortgagee, should describe the land conveyed with sufficient specificity so that the specific land conveyed can be identified. . . . A description of the property conveyed should be considered sufficient if it identifies the property or affords the means of identification within the instrument itself or by specific reference to other instruments recorded in the office of the register of deeds. Such a specific description of the property conveyed is required in order to impart constructive notice to a subsequent purchaser. . . .

Again, we wish to emphasize that an instrument which contains a "Mother Hubbard" clause, describing the property conveyed in the general language involved here, is valid, enforceable, and effectively transfers the entire property interest as between the parties to the instrument. Such a transfer is not effective as to subsequent purchasers and mortgagees unless they have *actual* knowledge of the transfer. If, because of emergency, it becomes necessary to use a "Mother Hubbard" clause in an instrument of conveyance, the grantee may take steps to protect his title against subsequent purchasers. He may take possession of the property. Also, as soon as a specific description can be obtained, the grantee may identify the specific property covered by the conveyance by filing an affidavit or other appropriate instrument or document with the register of deeds.

We also wish to make it clear that in situations where an instrument of conveyance containing a sufficient description of the property conveyed is duly recorded but not properly indexed, the fact that it was not properly indexed by the register of deeds will not prevent constructive notice under the provisions of K.S.A. 58-2222. From what we have said above, it follows that the recording of the assignment from Owens to Tours, which did not describe with sufficient specificity the property covered by the

---

1. Observe that the Kansas statutes require each county to maintain a grantor-grantee index ("a general index, direct and inverted"). The statutes give the counties the option of establishing, in addition, a tract ("numerical") index by quarter sections of the U.S. government survey. An index by quarter sections is better than no tract index at all, but such an index contains references to instruments affecting land in the quarter section other than the land the searcher is interested in.

   Where tract indexes are available, the jurisdictions are split over whether the title searcher must search the tract index as well as the grantor-grantee index and over whether the searcher can rely on the tract index alone and not search the grantor-grantee index. In some states, only recordation in the grantor-grantee index gives constructive notice. — EDS.

conveyance, was not sufficient to impart constructive notice to a subsequent purchaser such as J.R. Burris in the present case. Since Burris had no *actual* knowledge of the prior assignment from Owens to Tours, the later assignment to Burris prevails over the assignment from Owens to Tours.

The judgment of the Court of Appeals is reversed and the judgment of the district court is affirmed.

Notes and Questions

1. *Improper indexing.* Note that the Kansas court states in the third paragraph from the end of its opinion that "the fact that it [a deed] was not properly indexed by the register of deeds will not prevent constructive notice." 4 American Law Property § 17.25 (1952) states that:

> [T]he rule appears to be well established that in the absence of statutory provision to that effect, an index is not an essential part of the record. In other words, a purchaser is charged with constructive notice of a record even though there is no official index which will direct him to it.

Is this a sound rule? See Dyer v. Martinez, 54 Cal. Rptr. 3d 907 (Cal. App. 2007) (rejecting the rule on the ground that a title search could not have disclosed the *lis pendens* in the index); Howard Sav. Bank v. Brunson, 582 A.2d 1305 (N.J. Super. Ct. 1990) (rejecting rule). Suppose that a mortgagee records its mortgage, and the mortgage is properly indexed in the grantor-grantee index, but it is not recorded in the tract index. Is it "properly recorded" so as to provide constructive notice to subsequent mortgagees? See MidCountry Bank v. Krueger, 782 N.W.2d 238 (Minn. 2010) (mortgage properly recorded and provides constructive notice).

2. *Recourse for Tours?* In Luthi v. Evans, Grace Owens assigned her working interest in the Kufahl lease twice. The first assignee, Tours, lost to the second assignee, Burris. Does Tours have any claim against Owens? Under principles of restitution, Tours can have a constructive trust imposed upon Owens to prevent Owens's unjust enrichment. Since Owens sold Tours's oil and gas interest to Burris, Owens must give Tours the amount Owens received from Burris.

3. *Computerized indexes.* In recent years, in urban counties with many daily real estate transactions, recording clerks have begun to type the indexing information into a computer (and not enter it by hand, as was done in Luthi v. Evans). This enables the title searcher to search the grantor-grantee indexes by computer back to the date computer entries began. When older index books are consolidated, they will be consolidated into the computer (much as library card catalogs have been replaced by computer retrieval systems). In a few localities, the copies of deeds are micrographically stored, and the computer system permits the deed itself to be called up on the screen.

In some localities, computerized tract indexes have been established. This requires giving each parcel a parcel identification number (PIN). The tax assessor's number may be used as a PIN, or the PIN may be derived from aerial photography, surveyor's coordinates, or field inspection. Parcel identification numbers are not based on legal descriptions. Old records will probably not be computerized in public record offices because of the high cost, and complete computerization will take a generation or two to be phased in. Indeed, a more recent article reports between 8,000 and 10,000 electronic documents are recorded every day. See David E. Ewan & Mark Ladd, Race to the (Virtual) Courthouse: How Standards Drive Electronic Recording of Real Property Documents, Prob. & Prop., Feb. 2008, at 8. See also Brian Henry & Mary Dunn, Understanding Electronic Recording: Current Legislation and Trends, 38 Mich. Real Prop. Rev. 55 (2011).

3. Types of Recording Acts

Recall from our previous discussion (see page 416) that under the recording acts, a subsequent bona fide purchaser is protected against prior unrecorded interests. To gain the protection of a recording act, a purchaser must know which type of recording statute exists locally. There are three types of recording statutes:

- *Race*—as between successive purchasers of the same parcel of land, the person who records first wins.

Thus:

> *Example 2. O*, owner of Blackacre, conveys Blackacre to *A*, who does not record the deed. *O* subsequently conveys Blackacre to *B* for a valuable consideration. *B* actually knows of the deed to *A*. *B* records the deed from *O* to *B*. Under a race statute, *B* prevails over *A*, and *B* owns Blackacre.

This was the earliest type of recording statute. The virtue of a race statute for the title searcher is that it limits inquiry into matters off the record. The question of who knew what (in *Example 2*, whether *B* actually knew of the deed to *A*), which is often difficult to ascertain and harder to prove, is not relevant. Transfer of title is more efficient where off-record inquiries are eliminated. However, most states decided that this method was unfair precisely because it failed to take notice into account. Hence, race statutes applicable to conveyances exist today only in Louisiana and North Carolina.

- *Notice*—the subsequent bona fide purchaser has priority even though that person fails to record.

Thus:

> *Example 3. O*, owner of Blackacre, conveys Blackacre to *A*, who does not record the deed. *O* subsequently conveys Blackacre to *B* for a valuable consideration. *B* has no knowledge of *A*'s deed. Under a notice statute, *B* prevails over *A* even though *B* does not record the deed from *O* to *B*.

In *Example 2* above, if a notice statute were applicable, *B* would not prevail over *A* because *B* has notice of *A*'s prior deed.

The virtue of a notice statute is its fairness as between two conflicting claimants, but inasmuch as the question of whether the subsequent purchaser has notice depends on facts not on record, notice statutes are less efficient than race statutes. In *Example 3*, for instance, suppose that, after the conveyance to *B* and before *B* records, *A* records his deed. Thereafter *C* desires to purchase from *B*. *C*, searching title, would find *A*'s deed on record, and *C* then would have to ascertain from facts off the record whether *B* had notice of *A*'s deed. If *B* did not have notice, *B* prevails over *A*, and *C* can buy from *B* and, standing in *B*'s shoes, prevail over *A*.

The shelter rule. Why does *C* prevail over *A* in a notice jurisdiction when *A* records before *B* does? *A*'s recordation puts *C* on notice as to *A*'s deed so *C* cannot claim to be a subsequent purchaser without notice. The answer is: *C* claims protection under the *shelter rule*. A person who takes from a bona fide purchaser protected by the recording act has the same rights as his grantor. This rule is necessary if the recording act is to give *B* the benefit of his bargain by protecting his market.

The shelter rule does not extend to *B*'s grantor, *O*, however. If *O* repurchased Blackacre from *B*, *O* would not prevail over *A*. There is too much risk of undiscoverable collusion between *O* and *B* to permit *B* to transfer the property back to his grantor freed of *A*'s claim.

- *Race-notice*—a subsequent purchaser is protected against prior unrecorded instruments only if the subsequent purchaser (1) is without notice of the prior instrument and (2) records before the prior instrument is recorded.

The race-notice statute incorporates features of both a notice statute and a race statute. Thus:

> *Example 4. O*, owner of Blackacre, conveys Blackacre to *A*, who does not record the deed. *O* subsequently conveys Blackacre to *B*, who does not know of *A*'s deed. Then *A* records. Then *B* records. *A* prevails over *B* because, even though *B* had no notice of *A*'s deed, *B* did not record before *A* did.

The virtues of a race-notice statute, compared to a race or notice statute, are debatable. It has been suggested that a race-notice statute tends to eliminate lawsuits turning on extrinsic evidence about which deed was delivered first. In *Example 3*, for instance, whether *A* or *B* wins depends upon whether *O* delivered *A*'s deed or *B*'s deed first. Under a race-notice statute, the allegation that *B*'s deed was delivered after *A*'s (or *A*'s after *B*'s) is irrelevant if one of the deeds has been recorded; the first to record wins. It has also been suggested that a race-notice statute is preferable because, by punishing nonrecording, it provides motivation to record, making the public records complete.

About half the states have notice statutes, and half have race-notice statutes. Among the notice jurisdictions are Illinois, Massachusetts, Texas, and Virginia; among the race-notice ones are Georgia, Michigan, New Jersey, and New York.

Notice statute. Fla. Stat. Ann. § 695.01(1) (West 2020):

> No conveyance, transfer or mortgage of real property, or of any interest therein, nor any lease for a term of one year or longer, shall be good and effectual in law or equity against creditors or subsequent purchasers for a valuable consideration and without notice, unless the same be recorded according to the law.

In Brief

Three types of recording statutes:

▶ Race statute—The first purchaser (meaning anyone who has paid consideration for an interest in land) for value who records first, prevails (notice is irrelevant).

▶ Notice statute—A subsequent purchaser for value who takes without notice of third-party interests in the land prevails, regardless of whether he records.

▶ Race-notice statute—A subsequent purchaser for value who takes without notice of third-party interests in the land prevails only if he records before the prior instrument is recorded.

Race-notice statute. Cal. Civ. Code § 1214 (West 2020):

> Every conveyance of real property or an estate for years therein, other than a lease for a term not exceeding one year, is void as against any subsequent purchaser or mortgagee of the same property, or any part thereof, in good faith and for a valuable consideration, whose conveyance is first duly recorded, and as against any judgment affecting the title, unless the conveyance shall have been duly recorded prior to the record of notice of action.

Problems

1. *O* conveys Whiteacre to *A*, who does not record. *O* subsequently conveys to *B*, who purchases in good faith and for a valuable consideration, but does not record. *A* then records and conveys to *C*. *C* purchases in good faith and for a valuable consideration. *B* records. *C* records. Who prevails under a notice statute? A race-notice statute?

2. *O*, owner of Blackacre, which is worth $50,000, borrows $10,000 from *A* and gives *A* a mortgage on Blackacre. *A* does not record. *O* then borrows $14,000 from *B* and, after telling *B* of the prior mortgage to *A*, gives *B* a mortgage on Blackacre. *B* records. *O* then borrows $5,000 from *C* and gives *C* a mortgage on Blackacre. *C* has no notice of *A*'s mortgage. *C* records.

Subsequently, Blackacre is discovered to be contaminated with hazardous wastes, and its value plummets. *O* defaults. Upon foreclosure sale, Blackacre sells for $20,000. How should this amount be distributed among *A*, *B*, and *C*? Suppose all of the figures in this problem, except for the original worth of $50,000, were $5,000. How should the fund be distributed? The dissenting opinion of Dixon, J., in Hoag v. Sayre, 33 N.J. Eq. 552 (1881), suggesting that the parties should be given their expectations, is the starting point for discussion by most commentators. See 2 Grant Gilmore, Security Interests in Personal Property §§ 39.1-39.4 (1965); 4 American Law of Property § 17.33 (1952).

The actual copying by the recorder of a document into the records does not necessarily mean that the document is "recorded" within the terms of the recording act. If it is not authorized, it may not be "recorded" so as to give constructive notice. Almost without exception, statutes require that, in order for an instrument to enter the records, it must be acknowledged before a notary public or other official. In addition, some states require that a transfer tax must be paid before a deed is recorded. If the record does not show that the tax has been paid, a deed actually of record may be deemed not to be legally recorded.

MESSERSMITH v. SMITH
Supreme Court of North Dakota, 1953
60 N.W.2d 276

Morris, C.J. This is a statutory action to quiet title to three sections of land in Golden Valley County. The records in the office of the register of deeds of that county disclose the following pertinent facts concerning the title: For some time prior to May 7, 1946, the record title owners of this property were Caroline Messersmith and

Frederick Messersmith. On that date, Caroline Messersmith executed and delivered to Frederick Messersmith a quitclaim deed to the property which was not recorded until July 9, 1951. Between the date of that deed and the time of its recording the following occurred: On April 23, 1951, Caroline Messersmith, as lessor, executed a lease to Herbert B. Smith, Jr., lessee, which was recorded May 14, 1951. On May 7, 1951, Caroline Messersmith, a single woman, conveyed to Herbert B. Smith, Jr., by mineral deed containing a warranty of title, an undivided one-half interest in and to all oil, gas and other minerals in and under or that may be produced upon the land involved in this case. This deed was recorded May 26, 1951. On May 9, 1951, Herbert B. Smith, Jr., executed a mineral deed conveying to E.B. Seale an undivided one-half interest in all of the oil, gas and other minerals in and under or that may be produced upon the land. This deed was also recorded in the office of the Registry of Deeds of Golden Valley County, on May 26, 1951. Seale answered plaintiff's complaint by setting up his deed and claiming a one-half interest in the minerals as a purchaser without notice, actual or constructive, of plaintiff's claim. To this answer the plaintiff replied by way of a general denial and further alleged that the mineral deed by which Seale claims title is void; that it was never acknowledged, not entitled to record and was obtained by fraud, deceit and misrepresentation. The defendant Herbert B. Smith, Jr., defaulted.

For some time prior to the transactions herein noted, Caroline Messersmith and her nephew, Frederick S. Messersmith, were each the owner of an undivided one-half interest in this land, having acquired it by inheritance. The land was unimproved except for being fenced. It was never occupied as a homestead. Section 1 was leased to one tenant and Sections 3 and 11 to another. They used the land for grazing. One party had been a tenant for a number of years, paying $150 a year. The amount paid by the other tenant is not disclosed. The plaintiff lived in Chicago. Caroline Messersmith lived alone in the City of Dickinson where she had resided for many years. She looked after the renting of the land, both before and after she conveyed her interest therein to her nephew. She never told her tenants about the conveyance.

On April 23, 1951, the defendant Smith, accompanied by one King and his prospective wife, went to the Messersmith home and negotiated an oil and gas lease with Miss Messersmith covering the three sections of land involved herein. According to Miss Messersmith, all that was discussed that day concerned royalties. According to the testimony of Mr. Smith and Mr. King, the matter of the mineral deed was discussed.

Two or three days later, Smith and King returned. Again the testimony varies as to the subject of conversation. Miss Messersmith said it was about royalties. Smith and King say it was about a mineral deed for the purchase of her mineral rights. No agreement was reached during this conversation. On May 7, 1951, Smith returned alone and again talked with Miss Messersmith. As a result of this visit, Miss Messersmith executed a mineral deed for an undivided one-half interest in the oil, gas and minerals

Caroline Messersmith's house in 1997, after Frederick Messersmith moved out. This was the first house built on a platted street in Dickinson.

under the three sections of land. Smith says this deed was acknowledged before a notary public at her house. She says no notary public ever appeared there. She also says that Smith never told her she was signing a mineral deed and that she understood she was signing a "royalty transfer." The consideration paid for this deed was $1,400, which is still retained by Miss Messersmith. After leaving the house Smith discovered a slight error in the deed. The term "his heirs" was used for the term "her heirs." He returned to the home of Miss Messersmith the same day, explained the error to her, tore up the first deed, and prepared another in the same form, except that the error was corrected. According to Smith's testimony, he took the second deed to the same notary public to whom Miss Messersmith had acknowledged the execution of the first deed and the notary called Miss Messersmith for her acknowledgment over the telephone and then placed on the deed the usual notarial acknowledgment, including the notary's signature and seal. The notary, who took many acknowledgments about that time, has no independent recollection of either of these acknowledgments. It is the second deed that was recorded on May 26, 1951, and upon which the defendant, E.B. Seale, relied when he purchased from the defendant, Herbert B. Smith, Jr., the undivided one-half interest in the minerals under the land in question. . . .

The trial court found "that such deeds, or either of them, were not procured through fraud or false representation." The evidence does not warrant this court in disturbing that finding.

The determination that the mineral deed from Caroline Messersmith to Herbert B. Smith, Jr., was not fraudulently obtained by the grantee does not mean that the defendant, who in turn received a deed from Smith, is entitled to prevail as against the plaintiff in this action. At the time Miss Messersmith executed the mineral deed she owned no interest in the land, having previously conveyed her interest therein to the plaintiff. Smith in turn had no actual interest to convey to the defendant Seale. If Seale can assert title to any interest in the property in question, he must do so because the plaintiff's deed was not recorded until July 9, 1951, while the deed from Caroline Messersmith to Smith and the deed from Smith to the defendant Seale were recorded May 26, 1951, thus giving him a record title prior in time to that of the plaintiff. . . . The defendant Seale asserts that priority of record gives him a title superior to that of the plaintiff by virtue of the following statutory provision, Section 47-1941, NDRC 1943:

> Every conveyance of real estate not recorded as provided in section 47-1907 shall be void as against any subsequent purchaser in good faith, and for a valuable consideration, of the same real estate, or any part or portion thereof, whose conveyance, whether in the form of a warranty deed, or deed of bargain and sale, or deed of quitclaim and release, of the form in common use or otherwise, first is recorded, or as against an attachment levied thereon or any judgment lawfully obtained, at the suit of any party, against the person in whose name the title to such land appears of record, prior to the recording of such conveyance. The fact that such first recorded conveyance of such subsequent purchaser for a valuable consideration is in the form, or contains the terms, of a deed of quitclaim and release aforesaid, shall not affect the question of good faith of the subsequent purchaser, or be of itself notice to him of any unrecorded conveyance of the same real estate or any part thereof.

Section 47-1945, NDRC 1943, in part, provides:

> The deposit and recording of an instrument proved and certified according to the provisions of this chapter are constructive notice of the execution of such instrument to all purchasers and encumbrancers subsequent to the recording.

As against the seeming priority of record on the part of Seale's title, the plaintiff contends that the deed from Caroline Messersmith to Smith was never acknowledged and, not having been acknowledged, was not entitled to be recorded, and hence can confer no priority of record upon the grantee or subsequent purchasers from him.

It may be stated as a general rule that the recording of an instrument affecting the title to real estate which does not meet the statutory requirements of the recording laws affords no constructive notice. J.I. Case Co. v. Sax Motor Co., 64 N.D. 757, 256 N.W. 219; First National Bank v. Casselton Realty & Investment Co., 44 N.D. 353, 175 N.W. 720, 29 A.L.R. 911. The applicability of the rule is easily determined where the defect appears on the face of the instrument, but difficulty frequently arises where the defect is latent. Perhaps the most common instance of this nature arises when an instrument is placed of record bearing a certificate of acknowledgment sufficient on its face despite the fact that the statutory procedure for acknowledgment has not been followed. See Annotations 19 A.L.R. 1074; 72 A.L.R. 1039.

The certificate of acknowledgment on the mineral deed to Smith, while it is presumed to state the truth, is not conclusive as to the fact of actual acknowledgment by the grantor.

> **Note well**
>
> At the time of this case, North Dakota followed the *Zimmer* rule, according to which a subsequent purchaser has legally recorded her conveyance *only if* all prior conveyances in her chain of title are properly recorded. Zimmer v. Sundell, 296 N.W. 589 (Wis. 1941).

In Severtson v. Peoples, 28 N.D. 372, 148 N.W. 1054, 1055, this court, in the syllabus, said:

> 4. A certificate of acknowledgment, regular on its face, is presumed to state the truth; and proof to overthrow such certificate must be very strong and convincing, and the burden of overthrowing the same is upon the party attacking the truth of such certificate. 5. To constitute an acknowledgment, the grantor must appear before the officer for the purpose of acknowledging the instrument, and such grantor must, in some manner with a view to giving it authenticity, make an admission to the officer of the fact that he had executed such instrument. 6. Where, in fact, the grantor has never appeared before the officer and acknowledged the execution of the instrument, evidence showing such fact is admissible, even as against an innocent purchaser for value and without notice.

It avails the purchaser nothing to point out that a deed is valid between the parties though not acknowledged by the grantor—see Bumann v. Burleigh County, 73 N.D. 655, 18 N.W.2d 10—for Caroline Messersmith, having previously conveyed to the plaintiff, had no title. The condition of the title is such that Seale must rely wholly upon his position as an innocent purchaser under the recording act.

Before a deed to real property can be recorded its execution must be established in one of the ways prescribed by Section 47-1903, NDRC 1943. No attempt was made to prove the execution of this deed other than "by acknowledgment by the person executing the same." It is the fact of acknowledgment that the statute requires as a condition precedent to recording. Subsequent sections of Chapter 47-19, NDRC 1943, prescribe before whom and how proof of the fact of acknowledgment may be made. A general form of certificate of acknowledgment is set forth in Section 47-1927. The certificate on the mineral deed follows this form and states:

> On this 7th day of May, in the year 1951, before me personally appeared Caroline Messersmith, known to me to be the person described in and who executed the within and foregoing instrument, and acknowledged to me that she executed the same.

But Caroline Messersmith did not appear before the notary and acknowledge that she executed the deed that was recorded. In the absence of the fact of acknowledgment the deed was not entitled to be recorded, regardless of the recital in the certificate. The deed not being entitled to be recorded, the record thereof did not constitute notice of its execution, Section 47-1945, or contents, Section 47-1919. The record appearing in the office of the register of deeds not being notice of the execution or contents of the mineral deed, the purchaser from the grantee therein did not become a "subsequent purchaser in good faith, and for a valuable consideration" within the meaning of Section 47-1941, NDRC 1943.

In this case we have the unusual situation of having two deeds covering the same property from the same grantor, who had no title, to the same grantee. The only difference between the two was a minor defect in the first deed, for which it was destroyed. The evidence is conflicting as to whether or not the first deed was acknowledged. The second deed clearly was not. It is argued that the transaction should be considered as a whole, with the implication that if the first deed was actually acknowledged, the failure to secure an acknowledgment of the second deed would not be fatal to the right to have it recorded and its efficacy as constructive notice. We must again point out that the right which the defendant Seale attempts to assert is dependent exclusively upon compliance with the recording statutes. His claim of title is dependent upon the instrument that was recorded and not the instrument that was destroyed. Assuming that Smith is right in his assertion that the first deed was acknowledged before a notary public, we cannot borrow that unrecorded acknowledgment from the destroyed deed and, in effect, attach it to the unacknowledged deed for purposes of recording and the constructive notice that would ensue. . . .

The judgment appealed from is reversed.

On Petition for Rehearing

MORRIS, C.J. The respondent has petitioned for a rehearing and additional briefs have been filed. From the cases cited and statements of counsel, it appears that there may be a misapprehension concerning the scope of our opinion. We would emphasize the fact that at the time Caroline Messersmith signed and delivered the deed to Herbert B. Smith, Jr., she had no title to convey. Smith therefore obtained no title to convey to E.B. Seale who, as grantee of Smith, claims to be an innocent purchaser. The title had already been conveyed to Frederick Messersmith. The deed to Smith had never been acknowledged and was therefore not entitled to be recorded, although it bore a certificate of acknowledgment in regular form. Seale, whose grantor had no title, seeks through the operation of our recording statutes to divest Frederick Messersmith of the true title and establish a statutory title in himself.

We are here dealing with a prior unrecorded valid and effective conveyance that is challenged by a subsequent purchaser to whom no title was conveyed and who claims that the recording laws vest title in him by virtue of a deed that was not acknowledged in fact and therefore not entitled to be placed of record. This situation differs materially from a case where an attack is made by a subsequent purchaser on a prior recorded deed which actually conveyed title to the grantee but was not entitled to be recorded because of a latent defect. The questions presented by the latter situation we leave to be determined when they arise.

The petition for rehearing is denied.

THE REST OF THE STORY . . .

Caroline Messersmith's nephew Frederick, the last descendant of a pioneer family that settled Dickinson, North Dakota, moved back to Dickinson from Chicago and into the family home. Professor Michael J. Davis has sent us a copy of the *Dickinson Press*, Oct. 22, 1995, which carries a front-page story about Frederick, then age 85, unmarried and worth about $2 million. It relates that a guardian had been appointed for Frederick, ailing from senile dementia, and the guardian was trying to set aside Frederick's conflicting wills, earlier probated under North Dakota's unusual procedure permitting probate of a will before death. The guardian claimed undue influence by some of the beneficiaries, including the kindly neighbor to whom Frederick devised the land in Golden Valley County, deeded to Frederick by his aunt Caroline in 1946. Frederick died in 1998, and a legal brouhaha, involving the guardian, cousins, neighbors, charities, and, of course, lawyers, ensued.

Six years after the decision in *Messersmith*, the North Dakota legislature amended its recording act to provide that "[n]o action affecting any right, title, interest or lien, to, in or upon real property shall be commenced or maintained . . . in court on the ground that a recorded instrument was not entitled to be recorded." N.D. Cent. Code § 47-19-41 (2005).

Notes and Questions

1. *Question.* In denying the petition for rehearing, the court in *Messersmith* draws a distinction between the following two cases:

> *Example 5. O* conveys to *A*, who does not record. *O* subsequently conveys to *B*, who has no notice of *A*'s deed and gives a valuable consideration. *B*'s deed is entered into the records, but it has a defective acknowledgment. *B* conveys to *C*, who has no notice of *A*'s deed, gives a valuable consideration, and records his deed. This is the *Messersmith* case, where it is held that *B*'s deed is not "recorded" and therefore *C* is not a "subsequent purchaser in good faith . . . whose conveyance . . . first is recorded."
>
> *Example 6. O* conveys to *A* by a deed with a defective acknowledgment. *A* records his deed. *O* subsequently conveys to *B*, who records. The court in the last paragraph of the *Messersmith* opinion says this case "differs materially" from *Example 5* and leaves open the question whether *B* would prevail over *A*. (The majority rule in this situation is that when the defect does not appear on the face of the acknowledgment, the deed imparts constructive notice, but if the defect is patent, the deed does not give constructive notice. Of course, if *B* actually searched the record and found *A*'s deed, *B* would have actual notice; the issue of constructive notice arises only if *B* does not have actual notice.)

Does *B* have a more persuasive claim in *Example 6* than *C* does in *Example 5*? Which one can better protect himself against prior claims? See John C. Murray, Defective Real Estate Documents: What Are the Consequences? 42 Real Prop., Prob. & Tr. J. 367 (2007).

2. *Notice or race-notice—does it matter?* Would Seale have lost in *Messersmith* if North Dakota had a notice statute rather than a race-notice statute?

4. Chain of Title Problems

Earlier (see pages 417-419) we described the standard title search required against each owner: from the date of execution of the deed granting title to the owner to the date of recordation of the first deed by such owner conveying title to someone else. There are four well-known ambiguous situations in which a document may be recorded in the literal sense that it is physically located in the recorder's office but may be difficult or almost impossible for title searchers to find. In these instances, the question is whether physical recordation of the documents should equal legal recordation, such that the document is held to provide constructive notice to subsequent purchasers.

The four classic situations are: (1) prior document recorded too early; (2) prior document recorded too late; (3) the "wild deed"; and (4) deeds from a common grantor. We illustrate each of these problems with a simple hypothetical. We will then focus a bit more on the second two problems.

> *Example 7. X* owns Blackacre. *O*, who has no legal rights to Blackacre, deeds title to *A* in 2019; *A* records. In 2020, *X* deeds title in Blackacre to *O*, who records. In 2020, *O* deeds title to *B*, who records. Is *B* charged with constructive notice of the *O-A* deed?

Most courts today hold that a document recorded before the grantor obtained title (the *O-A* deed in *Example 7*) is not in the chain of title and therefore is not legally "recorded." See, e.g., Ryczkowski v. Chelsea Title & Guaranty Co., 449 P.2d 261 (Nev. 1969); Sabo v. Horvath, 559 P.2d 1038 (Alaska 1976). The reason is that the contrary rule would place an unreasonable burden on title searchers because a title searcher could locate the *O-A* deed only by searching in the grantor-grantee index under *O's* name for every year of *O's* life before 2020. Therefore, *B* is not charged with notice of the *O-A* deed.

> *Example 8. O* deeds to *A*, who does not record. *O* subsequently deeds to *B*, who knows of the conveyance to *A*. *B* records. *A* records. Later *B* conveys to *C*, a purchaser for value who has no actual knowledge of the deed from *O* to *A*. *C* records. Who prevails, *A* or *C*? The issue is: Does the deed from *O* to *A*, when recorded, give constructive notice to *C*?

This situation is essentially the same as in *Example 7* except that here the deed in question, the *O-A* deed, is recorded "too late" rather than "too early." The issue is whether a prior deed from an owner recorded after a later deed from the same owner gives constructive notice of the prior deed to subsequent purchasers from the grantee of the second deed. Most courts today reach the result as they do in the *Example 7* scenario, and basically for the same reason. See, e.g., Palamarg Realty Co. v. Rehac, 404 A.2d 21 (N.J. 1979); Morse v. Curtis, 2 N.E. 929 (Mass. 1885). But see Woods v. Garnett, 16 So. 390 (Miss. 1894) (the leading case for the opposite view).

The third problematic chain-of-title scenario is the "wild deed" problem:

> *Example 9. O* conveys to *A*, who does not record. *A* conveys to *B*, who records the *A*-to-*B* deed. *O* conveys to *C*, a purchaser for value who has no actual knowledge of the deeds from *O* to *A* and from *A* to *B*. *C* records. Who prevails, *B* or *C*? The issue is: Is the *A*-to-*B* deed properly "recorded" so as to give constructive notice to the world?

BOARD OF EDUCATION OF MINNEAPOLIS v. HUGHES

Supreme Court of Minnesota, 1912
136 N.W. 1095

BUNN, J. Action to determine adverse claims to a lot in Minneapolis. The complaint alleged that plaintiff owned the lot, and the answer denied this, and alleged title in defendant L.A. Hughes. The trial resulted in a decision in favor of plaintiff, and defendants appealed from an order denying a new trial.

The facts are not in controversy and are as follows: On May 16, 1906, Carrie B. Hoerger, a resident of Faribault, owned the lot in question, which was vacant and subject to unpaid delinquent taxes. Defendant L.A. Hughes offered to pay $25 for this lot. His offer was accepted, and he sent his check for the purchase price of this and two other lots bought at the same time to Ed Hoerger, husband of the owner, together with a deed to be executed and returned. The name of the grantee in the deed was not inserted; the space for the same being left blank. It was executed and acknowledged by Carrie B. Hoerger and her husband on May 17, 1906, and delivered to defendant Hughes by mail. The check was retained and cashed. Hughes filled in the name of the grantee, but not until shortly prior to the date when the deed was recorded, which was December 16, 1910. On April 27, 1909, Duryea & Wilson, real estate dealers, paid Mrs. Hoerger $25 for a quitclaim deed to the lot, which was executed and delivered to them, but which was not recorded until December 21, 1910. On November 19, 1909, Duryea & Wilson executed and delivered to plaintiff a warranty deed to the lot, which deed was filed for record January 27, 1910. It thus appears that the deed to Hughes was recorded before the deed to Duryea & Wilson, though the deed from them to plaintiff was recorded before the deed to defendant.

The questions for our consideration may be thus stated: (1) Did the deed from Hoerger to Hughes ever become operative? (2) If so, is he a subsequent purchaser whose deed was first duly recorded, within the language of the recording act?

1. The decision of the first question involves a consideration of the effect of the delivery of a deed by the grantor to the grantee with the name of the latter omitted from the space provided for it, without express authority to the grantee to insert his own or another name in the blank space. It is settled that a deed that does not name a grantee is a nullity, and wholly inoperative as a conveyance, until the name of the grantee is legally inserted. Allen v. Allen, 48 Minn. 462, 51 N.W. 473; Clark v. Butts, 73 Minn. 361, 76 N.W. 199; Id. 78 Minn. 373, 81 N.W. 11; Casserly v. Morrow, 101 Minn. 16, 111 N.W. 654. It is clear, therefore, and this is conceded, that the deed to defendant Hughes was not operative as a conveyance until his name was inserted as grantee.

Defendant, however, contends that Hughes had implied authority from the grantor to fill the blank with his own name as grantee, and that when he did so the deed became operative. This contention must, we think, be sustained. Whatever the rule may have been in the past, or may be now in some jurisdictions, we are satisfied that at the present day, and in this state, a deed which is a nullity when delivered because the name of the grantee is omitted becomes operative without a new execution or acknowledgment if the grantee, with either express or implied authority from the grantor, inserts his name in the blank space left for the name of the grantee. . . .

Unquestionably the authorities are in conflict; but this court is committed to the rule that in case of the execution and delivery of a sealed instrument, complete in all respects save that the blank for the name of the grantee is not filled, the grantee may insert his name in the blank space, provided he has authority from the grantor to do so, and, further, that this authority may be in parol, and may be implied from circumstances. We consider this the better rule, and also that it should be and is the law that when the grantor receives and retains the consideration, and delivers the deed in the condition described to the purchaser, authority to insert his name as grantee is presumed. Any other rule would be contrary to good sense and to equity. The same result could perhaps be reached by applying the doctrine of estoppel; but we prefer to base our decision on the ground of implied authority. Clearly the facts in the case at bar bring it within the principle announced, and we hold that Hughes, when he received the deed from Mrs. Hoerger, had implied authority to insert his name as grantee, in the absence of evidence showing the want of such authority. The delay in filling up the blank has no bearing on the question of the validity of the instrument when the blank was filled.

It is argued that holding that parol authority to fill the blank is sufficient violates the statute of frauds. This theory is the basis of many of the decisions that conflict with the views above expressed; but we do not think it sound. The cases in this state, and the Wisconsin, Iowa, and other decisions referred to, are abundant authority for the proposition that the authority of the grantee need not be in writing. Our conclusion is, therefore, that the deed to Hughes became operative as a conveyance when he inserted his name as grantee.

2. When the Hughes deed was recorded, there was of record a deed to the lot from Duryea & Wilson to plaintiff, but no record showing that Duryea & Wilson had any title to convey. The deed to them from the common grantor had not been recorded. We hold that this record of a deed from an apparent stranger to the title was not notice to Hughes of the prior unrecorded conveyance by his grantor. He was a subsequent purchaser in good faith for a valuable consideration, whose conveyance was first duly recorded; that is, Hughes' conveyance dates from the time when he filled the blank space, which was after the deed from his grantor to Duryea & Wilson. He was, therefore, a "subsequent purchaser," and is protected by the recording of his deed before the prior deed was recorded. The statute cannot be construed so as to give priority to a deed recorded before, which shows no conveyance from a record owner. It was necessary, not only that the deed to plaintiff should be recorded before the deed to Hughes, but also that the deed to plaintiff's grantor should be first recorded. Webb, Record of Title, § 158; 3 Washburn, Real Property, 292; Losey v. Simpson, 11 N.J. Eq. 246; Burke v. Beveridge, 15 Minn. 160 (205); Schoch v. Birdsall, 48 Minn. 443, 51 N.W. 382.

Our conclusion is that the learned trial court should have held on the evidence that defendant L.A. Hughes was the owner of the lot.

Order reversed, and new trial granted.

Questions

1. *Race, notice, race-notice—does it matter?* Minnesota at the time of the *Hughes* case was, and at present is, a race-notice jurisdiction. Minn. Stat. Ann. § 507.34 (West 2020). Would the result in the case be different in a notice jurisdiction? In a race jurisdiction? Although *actual* knowledge of a prior instrument by a subsequent purchaser is irrelevant under a race statute, whether a prior instrument has been first "recorded" (so as to give *constructive notice* of its contents) is important. Thus, the problems discussed under Chain of Title Problems, pages 435-441, can arise in a race jurisdiction as well as in notice and race-notice jurisdictions. See Lawing v. Jaynes, 206 S.E.2d 162 (N.C. 1974); Watterson v. Magee, 498 So. 2d 30 (La. App. 1986).

Would the result in *Hughes* be different if a tract index were used? See Andy Assocs., Inc. v. Bankers Trust Co., 399 N.E.2d 1160 (N.Y. 1979); Wash. Temple Church of God in Christ, Inc. v. Global Properties and Assocs., Inc., 865 N.Y.S.2d 641 (Sup. Ct. 2008).

2. *The Board's rights?* What are the rights of the Board of Education against Duryea & Wilson and against Carrie B. Hoerger?

3. *Importance of the operative date of the deed.* Suppose that the court had decided that the deed to Hughes became operative on May 17, 1906. What result? See B. Taylor Mattis, Recording Acts: Anachronistic Reliance, 25 Real Prop., Prob. & Tr. J. 17, 50-55 (1990).

The final chain of title problem involves deeds from a common grantor of multiple parcels. Thus:

> *Example 10. O*, owner of Blackacre and Whiteacre, conveys Blackacre to *A* by a deed that also transfers to *A* an easement over Whiteacre. *A* records the deed, and it is described in the index as a deed to Blackacre. *O* subsequently conveys Whiteacre to *B*, a purchaser for value who has no actual knowledge of the easement over Whiteacre conveyed to *A*. *B* records. Is Whiteacre subject to the easement? The issue is: Does the deed of Blackacre from *O* to *A* give constructive notice to purchasers of Whiteacre?

GUILLETTE v. DALY DRY WALL, INC.
Supreme Judicial Court of Massachusetts, 1975
325 N.E.2d 572

BRAUCHER, J. A recorded deed of a lot in a subdivision refers to a recorded plan, contains restrictions "imposed solely for the benefit of the other lots shown on said plan," and provides that "the same restrictions are hereby imposed on each of said lots now owned by the seller." A later deed of another lot from the same grantor refers to the same plan but not to the restrictions. The plan does not mention the restrictions, and the later grantee took without knowledge of them. We reject the later grantee's contention that it was not bound by the restrictions because they were not contained in a deed in its chain of title, and affirm a decree enforcing the restrictions.

The plaintiffs, owners of three lots in the subdivision, brought suit in the Superior Court to enjoin the defendant, owner of a lot in the same subdivision, from constructing a multifamily apartment building on its lot. The case was referred to a master, and his report was confirmed. A final decree was entered enjoining the defendant from "constructing any structures designed, intended, or suited for any purpose other than a dwelling for one family and which . . . [do] not conform to the restrictions contained in a deed from Wallace L. Gilmore to Pauline A. Guillette and Kenneth E. Guillette." The defendant appealed, and the case was transferred from the Appeals Court to this court under G.L. c.211A, § 10(A). The evidence is not reported.

We summarize the master's findings. Gilmore sold lots in a subdivision called Cedar Hills Section I in Easton to the plaintiffs, the defendant, and others. Two of the plaintiffs, the Walcotts, purchased a lot in August, 1967, by a deed referring to a plan dated in July, 1967. The plaintiff Guillette and her husband, now deceased, purchased a lot in May, 1968, by a deed referring to a plan dated in March, 1968. The 1967 and 1968 plans are the same for all practical purposes; neither mentions restrictions. The plaintiffs Paraskivas purchased a lot in June, 1968, by a deed referring to the 1968 plan. Each of these deeds and five other deeds to lots in the subdivision either set out the restrictions or incorporated them by reference. Only the Guillette deed and one other contained a provision restricting lots retained by the seller.[2] It was the intention of the

---

2. Paragraph 8 of the restrictions in the Guillette deed: "The foregoing restrictions are imposed solely for the benefit of the other lots shown on said plan, and may be modified or released at any time by an instrument in writing signed by the seller herein or the legal representative of said seller, and the owner or owners for the time being of each of said lots, said written instructions to be effective immediately upon recording thereof in the proper Registry of Deeds; *and the same restrictions are hereby imposed on each of said lots now owned by the seller*" (emphasis supplied). The italicized language is found only in the Guillette deed and one other. The master found that there had been no release.

grantor and the plaintiffs to maintain the subdivision as a residential subdivision to include only dwellings for one family.

The master further found that the defendant Daly Dry Wall, Inc. (Daly), purchased its lot from Gilmore in April, 1972, and that the deed to Daly contained no reference to any restrictions but did refer to the 1968 plan. Daly made no inquiry concerning restrictions and did not know of any development pattern. It had a title examination made. It learned of the restrictions in August, 1972. Subsequently it obtained a building permit for thirty-six apartment-type units.

In similar circumstances, where the common grantor has not bound his remaining land by writing, we have held that the statute of frauds prevents enforcement of restrictions against the grantor or a subsequent purchaser of a lot not expressly restricted. G.L. c.183, § 3. Houghton v. Rizzo, 361 Mass. 635, 639-642 (1972), and cases cited. Gulf Oil Corp. v. Fall River Housing Authy., 364 Mass. 492, 500-501 (1974). Where, as here, however, the grantor binds his remaining land by writing, reciprocity of restriction between the grantor and grantee can be enforced. See Snow v. Van Dam, 291 Mass. 477, 482 (1935), and cases cited. In such cases a subsequent purchaser from the common grantor acquires title subject to the restrictions in the deed to the earlier purchaser. Beekman v. Schirmer, 239 Mass. 265, 270 (1921). See Am. Law of Property, § 9.31 (1952); Tiffany, Real Property, §§ 858, 861 (3d ed. 1939); Restatement: Property, § 539, comment i (1944). Each of the several grantees, if within the scope of the common scheme, is an intended beneficiary of the restrictions and may enforce them against the others. . . .

The sole issue raised by the defendant is whether it is bound by a restriction contained in deeds to its neighbors from a common grantor, when it took without knowledge[3] of the restrictions and under a deed which did not mention them. It has, it says, only the duty to ascertain whether there were any restrictions in former deeds in its chain of title. See Stewart v. Alpert, 262 Mass. 34, 37-38 (1928). But the deed from Gilmore to the Guillettes conveyed not only the described lot but also an interest in the remaining land then owned by Gilmore. That deed was properly recorded under G.L. c.36, § 12, and cannot be treated as an unrecorded conveyance under G.L. c.183, § 4. As a purchaser of part of the restricted land, the defendant therefore took subject to the restrictions. See Houghton v. Rizzo, 361 Mass. 635, 642 (1972); Am. Law of Property, § 17.24 (1952).

The defendant argues that to charge it with notice of any restriction put in a deed by a common grantor is to "put every title examiner to the almost impossible task of searching carefully each and every deed which a grantor deeds out of a common subdivision." But our statutes provide for indexing the names of grantors and grantees, not lot numbers or tracts. G.L. c.36, §§ 25, 26. Lot numbers or other descriptive information, even though included in an index, do not change what is recorded. Cf. Gillespie v. Rogers, 146 Mass. 610, 612 (1888), and cases cited. In such a system the purchaser cannot be safe if the title examiner ignores any deed given by a grantor in the chain of title during the time he owned the premises in question. In the present case the defendant's deed referred to a recorded subdivision plan, and the deed to the Guillettes referred to the same plan. A search for such deeds is a task which is not at all impossible. Cf. Roak v. Davis, 194 Mass. 481, 485 (1907).

Decree affirmed with costs of appeal.

---

3. General Laws c.183, § 4, as appearing in St. 1941, c.85, denies protection to "persons having actual notice of" an unrecorded conveyance.

Note and Questions

1. *State of the authorities.* William B. Stoebuck & Dale A. Whitman, The Law of Property 896-897 (3d ed. 2000), says the cases are equally divided between the position of the Massachusetts court and the position that an easement or restrictive covenant on Whiteacre that appears in a prior deed of Blackacre from the common owner of Blackacre and Whiteacre is not in the purchaser's chain of title to Whiteacre. On the other hand, a more recent article suggests that the latter position is now the majority rule. See Herbert Hovenkamp, Post-Sale Restraints and Competitive Harm: The First Sale Doctrine in Perspective, 66 N.Y.U. Ann. Surv. Am. L. 487, 520 (2011) ("Most courts hold that the servitude must be properly recorded in the chain of title of all persons against whom subsequent enforcement is sought."). For cases taking this latter position, see Krueger v. Oberto, 724 N.E.2d 21 (Ill. App. 1999); Witter v. Taggart, 577 N.E.2d 338 (N.Y. 1991); Simone v. Heidelberg, 877 N.E.2d 1288 (N.Y. 2007); Spring Lakes, Ltd. v. O.F.M. Co., 467 N.E.2d 537 (Ohio 1984).

If you were practicing in Illinois, New York, or Ohio, how would you put the subdivider's covenants in the deeds, so as to give notice to all subsequent purchasers?

2. *Tract index.* Would the problem in *Example 8* arise if the jurisdiction had a tract index?

5. Persons Protected by the Recording System

The recording statute in each state must be read carefully to see who comes within the protection of the statute. Observe that the Florida statute (page 428) protects, against unrecorded conveyances or mortgages, "creditors or subsequent purchasers for a valuable consideration," and the California statute (page 429) protects "any subsequent purchaser or mortgagee" and "any judgment affecting the title." By judicial construction, the recording statutes have been held, almost universally, *not* to protect donees and devisees, even in race jurisdictions. As a result, it is sometimes necessary for a court to decide whether a person is a purchaser (and protected) or a donee (and not protected). This in turn may require the court to determine what is a valuable consideration for purposes of obtaining the protection of the recording act.

An examination of the cases leads to the conclusion that there is some disagreement as to how much a grantee must pay to be deemed a purchaser. Most courts require more than a nominal value, such as a "substantial" amount, or an amount "not grossly inadequate." See William B. Stoebuck & Dale A. Whitman, The Law of Property § 11.10 at 879 (3d ed. 2000). Why do you suppose that courts require more "consideration" here than is necessary to enforce a contract?

If a deed recites that it is for "$1 and other good and valuable consideration," this raises a presumption that the grantee is a purchaser for a valuable consideration, and places the burden of going forward to establish the falsity of the recital of consideration on the party attacking the deed.

LEWIS v. SUPERIOR COURT

California Court of Appeal, Second District, 1994
37 Cal. Rptr. 2d 63

[In early February 1992, Robert and Josephine Lewis contracted to buy a residence from Shipley for $2.3 million. After the Lewises opened escrow, and just a few days before they acquired title, Fontana Films recorded a *lis pendens* (notice of lawsuit affecting title to the property) against Shipley. The *lis pendens* was recorded on February 24, but not indexed until February 29, the day after the Lewises acquired title. Under the contract of sale, the Lewises paid Shipley $350,000 on February 25. Closing took place on February 28, and the deed from Shipley to the Lewises was recorded on that day. The Lewises gave Shipley their note for $1,950,000, which they paid in March 1992. Within the next year the Lewises spent an additional $1,050,000 in renovating the property. In September 1993, the Lewises were served in Fontana's lawsuit and learned about the *lis pendens*. The Lewises brought suit for summary judgment to remove the *lis pendens* and clear their title. The trial court denied the motion for summary judgment.

The Lewises appealed. The court of appeal held that the *lis pendens* was not properly recorded until it was indexed, which occurred the day after the title passed to the Lewises. The opinion of the court continues.]

Woods, J. . . . Relying on the case of Davis v. Ward, 109 Cal. 186, 41 P. 1010 (1895), [Fontana] contends that even if the Lewises took title before the indexing of the Fontana lis pendens, they nevertheless were not bona fide purchasers because they did not fully pay for the property until after indexing. [Fontana] appears to be making a make-weight argument that if the court determines that the date of recordation is not the effective date by reason of an absence of indexing until later, then the date for determining the Lewises' status is the date they paid $1,950,000 as the balance of the purchase price on the property. By then, [Fontana] contends, the deed had long since been indexed and the Lewises were chargeable with notice of the lis pendens.

. . . [We] conclude that the *Davis* case payment of value rule does not apply in the instant case for a number of reasons. . . .

In *Davis*, Ward mortgaged some property to Davis' predecessor. Apparently by mutual mistake, the mortgage identified the wrong parcel of land. Ward later sold half of the property to Fleming, who paid cash, and half to Brown, who paid part cash and part notes. (Davis v. Ward, supra, 109 Cal. at pp. 187-191.) Davis sued to have the mortgage reformed and foreclosed. Evidence at trial proved that Fleming and Brown both took without notice of the prior sale because the mortgage was recorded against the wrong property and could not have been discovered by searching the record of the property actually purchased. The evidence also showed, however, that when Brown received notice of Davis' claim—apparently by being sued—he had paid only $200 of the purchase price. (Id., at p. 190.) Fleming and Brown both won nonsuits on the ground that they were bona fide purchasers.

On appeal, the Supreme Court affirmed the nonsuit as to Fleming, the cash purchaser. However, it reversed Brown's nonsuit, holding that he was not a bona fide purchaser because he could not show that "the purchase money had been paid before notice." (109 Cal. at p. 189.) The court relied in part on Jewett v. Palmer, 7 Johnson Ch. 68 (1823 Ch.), where the court explained, "'A plea of a purchase for a valuable consideration, without notice, must be with the money actually paid; or else, according to

Lord Hardwicke, you are not hurt. The averment must be, not only that the purchaser had not notice at or before the execution of the deeds, but that the purchase money was paid before notice.'" (Davis v. Ward, supra, at p. 190.)

As we discuss in more detail below, the Supreme Court did not decide what remedy should be applied. It simply reversed a nonsuit, saying nothing about how the trial court should adjust the parties' rights.

(a). The payment of value rule stated in *Davis* cannot be reconciled with modern real property law and practice and should be strictly limited to its facts.

Davis was premised, in part, on Lord Hardwicke's assertion that a purchaser who loses his property is "not hurt" if he has not fully paid for the land. This claim is inconsistent with both equitable considerations and modern market expectations.

Any purchaser without notice who makes a down payment and unequivocally obligates himself to pay the balance has every reason to believe that, if he makes the payments when due, his right to the property will be secure. Such a purchaser may drastically alter his position on the basis of this understanding, such as by selling his prior residence, moving his family and making significant improvements to the property. If his property is taken, his injury remains even if his money is returned. Aside from ignoring this undeniable reality, *Davis* also ignores the ancient principle that real property is unique and its loss cannot be compensated in money. (Glynn v. Marquette, 152 Cal. App. 3d 277, 280, 199 Cal. Rptr. 306 (1984) (specific performance available in land sale contracts because it is assumed real property is unique).) . . . We discern that Lord Hardwicke was simply expostulating an erroneous rule of law.

While this court is bound to follow existing Supreme Court authority, we resist any attempt to apply an outdated theory to modern real property transactions. Since *Davis* was grounded on an archaic and misunderstood principle of real property conveyancing, we confine it to its facts and its narrow purpose. . . .

(b). *Davis* cannot rationally be applied to cases involving only constructive notice.

In *Davis*, Brown received actual notice of the litigation affecting his property; there was no constructive notice, and the court did not opine on what the effect of constructive notice would have been. . . .

One might argue that a buyer in this situation—someone who continues to pay his seller in the face of actual notice of a competing claim—should be at risk of losing his post-notice investment, if only because the assertion of the claim could give rise to a defense to the payment obligation (in other words, the buyer becomes a volunteer). But constructive notice should not have that effect, and nothing in *Davis* requires such a result.

Applying *Davis* to a case of constructive notice penalizes a completely innocent purchaser for simply living up to his payment obligations. This is a purchaser who is "innocent" in every sense of the recording statutes, because he has already acquired title and has already received whatever title information or title insurance he was entitled to under his purchase agreement. If constructive notice before payment threatens him with loss of title, he will have to undertake a title search before each and every payment—360 title searches for a typical 30-year note! Such an obviously absurd result is fundamentally contrary to the whole purpose of the recording statutes, but it would be the unavoidable result of holding that constructive notice is enough to trigger the *Davis* payment of value rule. . . .

(d). Because the court in *Davis* merely reversed Brown's nonsuit and remanded the case, it did not determine the proper remedy. However, the trial court, exercising its equitable powers, could have easily preserved all of the parties' interests in the property except Ward's, in recognition that Ward, as the wrongdoer, should be the one to sacrifice his interest—i.e., his claim against Brown for the balance of his purchase price. The likely and appropriate remedy would have been for Davis to acquire Ward's interest in the property. In other words, Davis would become the payee of Brown's note to Ward, and Brown's position would remain unchanged: he would continue to pay the note, but would make payments to Davis rather than Ward, whose interest would be extinguished. Under this approach, the wrongdoer is penalized, the aggrieved party is compensated and the innocent purchaser's rights are preserved. This result would be possible because, at least as far as the opinion reveals, by the time of trial Brown's note to Ward was still outstanding, so the trial court had something on which to act.

Davis reaches (or at least permits) this correct result, but for the wrong reasons. Davis should have prevailed not because Brown was not a good faith purchaser, but rather because Ward continued to hold an interest that, in equity, belonged to Davis, as the party damaged by Ward's wrongful conduct. . . .

(f). Applying *Davis* would unfairly penalize the Lewises for paying cash for the property, rather than financing the purchase price.

In *Davis*, the court recognized that if Ward had assigned the notes to a bank for value and without notice, "the defense of both Brown and the bank to this action would be complete, for in that event, the notes would have been payment." (Davis v. Ward, supra, 109 Cal. at p. 191.) In other words, the fact that the seller ends up being fully paid transforms the buyer into a good-faith purchaser when otherwise he would not be. This distinction makes no sense; from the buyer's perspective, he is in the same position, and equally obligated to repay a note over time, whether the seller or a bank holds the mortgage.

Here, the Lewises did not merely obligate themselves to pay the purchase price; they paid the price in cash before receiving notice of the litigation. Bringing this case within *Davis'* sweep would lead to a thoroughly anomalous result: the Lewises, cash buyers, would be at risk of losing their property, while another purchaser, who paid only a small down payment and financed the balance, would be considered a bona fide purchaser. No one could comfortably acquiesce in so unfair an outcome.

Disposition

Let a peremptory writ of mandate issue directing the superior court to vacate its order denying petitioners' motion for summary judgment, and thereafter issue a new and different order granting said motion and expunging the lis pendens. Petitioners to recover costs of these proceedings.

Notes

1. *Creditors.* A number of recording statutes protect "creditors" against unrecorded deeds and mortgages (see the Florida statute on page 428). Courts have interpreted these statutes to protect only creditors who have established a lien, such as by attachment or judgment, and not all creditors. Merely lending money to the record owner does not give priority over unrecorded instruments. In some states, lien creditors are construed to come within broad language extending protection to "all persons except parties to the conveyance."

In many states, a creditor is not protected until the creditor prosecutes a lawsuit to judgment and forecloses a lien or holds an execution sale. The buyer at the sale, who may be the creditor, is protected under the recording act as a subsequent bona fide purchaser for value if the buyer has no notice of the unrecorded claim at the time of sale.

2. *Quitclaim deeds.* In a few jurisdictions, a purchaser by quitclaim deed cannot claim the position of a bona fide purchaser without notice. This rests upon the idea that a refusal of the grantor to warrant title should create a strong suspicion that the title is defective. See Diversified, Inc. v. Hall, 23 S.W.3d 403 (Tex. App. 2000); Polhemus v. Cobb, 653 So. 2d 964 (Ala. 1995). It may even be held that a quitclaim deed in the chain of title puts all subsequent purchasers on inquiry notice. They must make further investigation about the deed. See Richardson v. Amresco Residential Mortgage Corp., 592 S.E.2d 65 (Va. 2004); Schwalm v. Deanhardt, 906 P.2d 167 (Kan. App. 1995). In a large majority of jurisdictions, however, a quitclaim deed is treated the same as a warranty deed for purpose of giving notice. There are many reasons why a grantor may use a quitclaim deed other than a questionable title.

6. Inquiry Notice

There are three kinds of notice a person may have with respect to a prior claim: *actual*, *record*, and *inquiry*. Actual notice arises where one is personally aware of a conflicting interest in real property, often due to another's possession of the property. The latter two are forms of constructive notice—notice that the law deems you to have regardless of your actual knowledge. Record notice consists of notice that one has based on properly recorded instruments. Inquiry notice is based on facts that would cause a reasonable person to make inquiry into the possible existence of an interest in real property. See generally Swanson v. Swanson, 769 N.W.2d 614 (N.D. 2011); Gorzeman v. Thompson, 986 P.2d 29 (Or. App. 1999).

> **In Brief**
>
> Three types of notice:
> - Actual—personal knowledge of the prior interest
> - Record—notice of a prior interest that would be revealed by an appropriate title search
> - Inquiry—notice based on a purchaser's duty to investigate relevant circumstances

WALDORFF INSURANCE AND BONDING, INC. v. EGLIN NATIONAL BANK

District Court of Appeal of Florida, First District, 1984
453 So. 2d 1383

SHIVERS, J. Waldorff Insurance and Bonding, Inc. (Waldorff) appeals the supplemental final judgment of foreclosure entered against it in favor of Eglin National Bank (Bank) on a condominium unit [in the 216-unit Gulf Terrace Condominium in Destin]. Appellant argues that the trial court erred in not finding its interest in the condominium unit superior to the liens of two mortgages held by the Bank. We agree and reverse.

Choctaw Partnership (Choctaw) developed certain properties in Okaloosa County by constructing condominiums. On June 8, 1972, Choctaw executed a promissory note and mortgage on these properties in the amount of $850,000. . . . [This mortgage was promptly recorded.] This note and mortgage was eventually assigned to appellee Bank on January 17, 1975. At that time, the principal balance remaining on this note and mortgage was $41,562.61.

Waldorff entered into a written purchase agreement with Choctaw for condominium unit 111 on April 4, 1973. Choctaw was paid $1,000 at that time as a deposit on Unit 111. The total purchase price of Unit 111 was to be $23,550. In April or May 1973, Waldorff began occupancy of the unit. Furniture worth $5,000 was purchased by Waldorff and placed in the unit. Waldorff continually occupied the unit for about 1½ years thereafter, paying the monthly maintenance fee, the fee for maid service, the fee for garbage pick-up, and paying for repairs to the unit. At the time of the hearing in this case on February 21, 1983, the furniture was still in the unit, the utility bills and monthly maintenance fees were paid by Waldorff, and Waldorff had the keys to the unit and controlled it.

On October 10, 1973, Choctaw executed a note and mortgage for the principal sum of $600,000 in favor of the Bank. Among the properties included in this mortgage was the condominium unit involved in the instant case, Unit 111.

On June 28, 1974, Choctaw executed yet another note and mortgage, this one in favor of the Bank for the principal sum of $95,000. This mortgage secured a number of units, one of which was Unit 111. Choctaw was apparently a client of Waldorff, and in 1974, Choctaw owed Waldorff over $35,000 for insurance premiums. Choctaw agreed to consider the purchase price of Unit 111 paid in full in return for cancellation of the debt owed by Choctaw to Waldorff. Waldorff "wrote off" the debt, and Choctaw executed a quitclaim deed to Unit 111 in favor of Waldorff. The deed was recorded in March 1975.

In 1976, the Bank brought a foreclosure action against Choctaw, Waldorff and others. A final judgment of foreclosure was entered in September 1976, but that judgment did not foreclose Waldorff's interest in Unit 111. Instead, the 1976 final judgment explicitly retained jurisdiction to determine the ownership of Unit 111. A hearing was held on February 21, 1983. The issue at this hearing was whether Waldorff's occupancy, together with the purchase agreement, was sufficient notice so as to make Waldorff's interest in Unit 111 superior to that of the Bank. At this hearing, evidence was taken concerning the agreements between Choctaw and Waldorff and Waldorff's occupancy of Unit 111. There was evidence that condominium units other than 111 were also occupied and that many of these units were occupied by persons who had no legal interest in the units, e.g., persons invited by Choctaw to occupy the units for a time as part of Choctaw's marketing campaign.

The trial court entered a supplemental final judgment of foreclosure which found that Waldorff's occupancy of Unit 111 was "equivocal" because Choctaw allowed at least 8 other condominium units to be furnished and used for occupancy by various persons. The trial court also found that Waldorff did not pay the consideration promised for Unit 111 because the debt owed by Choctaw to Waldorff was used as a bad debt write-off for federal income tax purposes rather than being credited to Choctaw. The trial court found that "even if defendant could establish some right to Unit 111 by occupancy, defendant failed to pay the agreed consideration for the quitclaim deed and, therefore, the conveyance is void." Based on these findings, the trial court held the Bank's mortgage liens superior to Waldorff's interest.

Gulf Terrace Condominium
Destin, Florida

A contract to convey legal title to real property on payment of the purchase price creates an equitable interest in the purchaser. Lafferty v. Detwiler, 155 Fla. 95, 20 So. 2d 338, 343 (1944); Felt v. Morse, 80 Fla. 154, 85 So. 656 (1920). Beneficial ownership passes to the purchaser while the seller retains mere naked legal title. Arko Enterprises, Inc. v. Wood, 185 So. 2d 734 (Fla. 1st DCA 1966); Tingle v. Hornsby, 111 So. 2d 274 (Fla. 1st DCA 1959). Subsequent successors to the legal title take such title burdened with the equitable interests of which they have either actual or constructive notice. Hoyt v. Evans, 91 Fla. 1053, 109 So. 311 (1926). In the instant case, it appears clear that the April 4, 1973, Agreement to Purchase entered into between Choctaw and Waldorff vested equitable title in Waldorff. Therefore, the interests acquired by the Bank pursuant to the October 1973 and June 1974 mortgages would be subordinate to Waldorff's equitable interest if the Bank had either actual or constructive notice of that interest.

In Blackburn v. Venice Inlet Co., 38 So. 2d 43 (Fla. 1948), the court stated:

It is settled law in Florida that actual possession is constructive notice to all the world, or anyone having knowledge of said possession of whatever right the occupants have in the land. Such possession, when open, visible and exclusive, will put upon inquiry those acquiring any title to or a lien upon the land so occupied to ascertain the nature of the rights the occupants really have in the premises. [38 So. 2d at 46.]

In the instant case, Waldorff was in open, visible and exclusive possession of Unit 111 at the time of the making of the October 1973 and June 1974 mortgages.

The trial court found, however, that Waldorff's possession of Unit 111 was "equivocal" because other units in the condominium project were occupied by persons who had no interest in the units. We do not agree with this analysis. Although many of the condominium units were held by a common grantor, Choctaw, the units were separate parcels intended to be alienated individually. The mortgage executed on June 28, 1974, which secures both the $95,000 note and the $600,000 note of October 10, 1973, described the property mortgaged in terms of individual units, specifically including Unit 111. The status of other units within the condominium project, therefore, is irrelevant to the question of the possession of Unit 111. The issue in the instant case concerned only the rights of the parties involved in Unit 111, not the condominium project as a whole or any other individual units.

Appellee argues, however, that it would have been difficult to ascertain whether any person physically occupying any of the units in the project had a claim of ownership interest in the unit being occupied. Although we agree that it would be more inconvenient for a prospective lender to make several inquiries rather than a single one, we do not find this argument persuasive. We find the ancient, but oft-cited, case of Phelan v. Brady, 119 N.Y. 587, 23 N.E. 1109 (N.Y. 1890), to be instructive in this matter. On May 1, 1886, Mrs. Brady took possession of a tenement building containing 48 apartments occupied by 20 different occupants as tenants from month to month. Her possession was pursuant to a contract for sale secured for her by her attorney. Three of the apartments were occupied by Mrs. Brady and her husband, who kept a liquor store in part of the building. Mrs. Brady began collecting rents immediately upon taking possession of the premises. Mrs. Brady's deed, however, was not recorded until August 26, 1886, subsequent to the recordation of Phelan's mortgage which had been executed by the record owner of the property on July 23, 1886. The court stated:

> At the time of the execution and delivery of the mortgage to the plaintiff, the defendant Mrs. Brady was in the actual possession of the premises under a perfectly valid, but unrecorded, deed. Her title must therefore prevail as against the plaintiff. It matters not, so far as Mrs. Brady is concerned, that the plaintiff in good faith advanced his money upon an apparently perfect record title of the defendant John E. Murphy. Nor is it of any consequence, so far as this question is concerned, whether the plaintiff was in fact ignorant of any right or claim of Mrs. Brady to the premises. It is enough that she was in possession under her deed and the contract of purchase, as that fact operated in law as notice to the plaintiff of all her rights. It may be true, as has been argued by plaintiff's counsel, that, when a party takes a conveyance of property situated as this was, occupied by numerous tenants, it would be inconvenient and difficult for him to ascertain the rights or interests that are claimed by all or any of them. But this circumstance cannot change the rule. Actual possession of real estate is sufficient to a person proposing to take a mortgage on the property, and to all the world, of the existence of any right which the person in possession is able to establish. [23 N.E. at 1110-1111.]

Moreover, cases citing Phelan v. Brady have stated that the possession involved there was not equivocal. Swanstrom v. Day, 46 Misc. 311, 93 N.Y.S. 192 (N.Y. Sup. Ct. 1905); Baker v. Thomas, 61 Hun. 17, 15 N.Y.S. 359 (N.Y. Sup. Ct. 1891).

We also agree with appellant that the trial court erred in finding that the conveyance of the property from Choctaw to Waldorff was void due to lack of consideration for the quitclaim deed. Although Waldorff may have erred in attempting to take a "bad debt" tax deduction after cancelling the debt Choctaw owed to Waldorff for insurance premiums, Choctaw was relieved from payment of that debt, and this constituted a valuable consideration flowing to Choctaw. Booth v. Bond, 56 Cal. App. 2d 153, 132 P.2d 520 (Cal. Dist. Ct. App. 1942); see generally Dorman v. Publix-Saenger-Sparks Theatres, 135 Fla. 284, 184 So. 886 (1939); 17 C.J.S. Contracts §§ 74, 87 (1963).

The parties agree that the 1972 mortgage lien is superior to Waldorff's interest in Unit 111. Appellee, however, stated at oral argument that it did not disagree with the proposition that a proper application of the funds from the 1976 foreclosure sale of the rest of the condominium project should first satisfy the 1972 mortgage. Our decision renders moot appellant's other points on appeal. Accordingly, the supplemental final judgment of foreclosure is reversed and the cause remanded for entry of a judgment consistent with this opinion.

Reversed and remanded.

Problem, Note, and Questions

1. *Problem.* You are the attorney for a prospective purchaser of a 50-unit apartment house. The present owner has shown the prospective purchaser copies of the leases on file in her office. Can the purchaser rely on these leases? Suppose that the landlord had orally extended tenant *A*'s one-year lease for two more years and has given tenant *B* a written option to renew for a five-year term, but the option does not appear in the landlord's records. Suppose also that tenant *C* has a five-year lease and has prepaid the rent, though there is nothing in the lease to indicate this. Will the prospective purchaser take subject to the aforementioned rights of tenants *A*, *B*, and *C*? See Gates Rubber Co. v. Ulman, 262 Cal. Rptr. 630 (Cal. App. 1989); Martinique Realty Corp. v. Hall, 166 A.2d 803 (N.J. Super. Ct. 1960). What would you advise the prospective purchaser to do? See 4 American Law of Property § 17.12 (1952).

2. *Red flags.* What types of red flags must be present for a subsequent purchaser to be on notice of a prior interest in a property? In some instances, courts will require quite a bit of reason for concern. For example, in Grose v. Sauvageau, 942 P.2d 398 (Wyo. 1997), Grose purchased property from Ryberg, but never recorded the quitclaim deed because of a variety of deficiencies in the document. After pigs repeatedly escaped from the subject property and injured horses on Sauvageau's farm, and after an unsuccessful City Council reelection campaign that engendered opposition from Grose, Sauvageau apparently sought to exact her revenge by searching title and discovering that there was no deed to show ownership of the property by Grose. Sauvageau then went to the record owner (Ryberg) and purchased the property. The Wyoming Supreme Court held that while Sauvageau "was well aware that the Groses had possession of the property and had made improvements upon it, she diligently searched the records only to discover that the Grose's possession of the property was entirely consistent with the rights of the record owner. Therefore, the Grose's possession of the property did not create a situation which would put Sauvageau on guard as to the possibility of an unrecorded instrument or an alternative claim to the property." Id. at 403. But see Horse Creek Conservation Dist. v. State ex rel. Wyoming Attorney General, 221 P.3d 306 (Wyo. 2009) (examination of record insufficient if one party has actual notice of unrecorded claim).

3. *Questioning inquiry notice.* Is the doctrine of inquiry notice sound? Does it make the transfer of land more costly and title less certain? Should the courts abolish inquiry notice and require actual notice?

4. *Negligence and title law.* Professor Stewart Sterk describes the development of title doctrine as increasingly importing negligence principles from tort law. With respect to inquiry notice, he observes that "a reasonable purchaser would have asked enough questions to discover the true owner's interest; if this purchaser did not, the purchaser was at fault, and is not protected by the true owner's failure to record." See Stewart E. Sterk, Strict Liability and Negligence in Property Theory, 160 U. Pa. L. Rev. 2129, 2143 (2012). As with tort cases, Sterk argues that importing negligence standards into property law creates incentives for the true owner to take precautions.

7. Marketable Title Acts

Marketable title acts, enacted in a large number of states, have as their purpose limiting title searches to a reasonable period, typically the last 30 or 40 years. The essential idea is quite simple: when one person has a record title to land for a designated period of time, inconsistent claims or interests are extinguished. Some of the acts take the form of a statute of limitations barring a claim not recorded within the designated period. Others declare that the record owner with a clear title going back for the designated period has marketable record title that is free and clear of adverse claims. Thus, except for the interests excepted from the statute, title searches may be safely limited to the number of years specified in the statute. Under a marketable title act, all claimants of interests in land, to be safe, must file a notice of claim every 30 to 40 years after the recording of their instruments of acquisition. See Uniform Marketable Title Act (1990) (30 years); Fla. Stat. Ann. §§ 712.01 et seq. (West 2020); Mich. Comp. Laws Ann. §§ 565.101 et seq. (West 2020); N.C. Gen. Stat. §§ 47B-1 et seq. (2020).

Some states, without general marketable title statutes, require the periodic re-recordation of certain types of interests in order to preserve them. If not re-recorded, the interests expire. The usual re-recordation period is 30 years. Interests affected by these special re-recordation requirements may include possibilities of reverter and rights of entry (see page 250), easements, covenants, and mineral interests. See Texaco v. Short, 454 U.S. 516 (1982) (upholding a retroactive Indiana statute requiring re-recordation of unused mineral interests every 20 years).

B. TITLE INSURANCE

Title insurance developed because of the inadequacies and inefficiencies of the public records in protecting private titles. Title insurance is bought by one premium paid at the time the policy is issued. The premium is based on the amount of insurance purchased, which ordinarily, in a homeowner's policy, is the amount of the purchase price of the property and, in a lender's policy, the amount of the loan. Title insurance has no fixed term and continues for as long as the insured maintains an interest in the property. Title insurance creates liability to the insured only and does not run with the land to subsequent purchasers. A subsequent purchaser must take out a new policy if the purchaser wants title insurance. In a nutshell, title insurance is the opinion of the insurer concerning the validity of title, backed by an agreement to make that opinion good if it should prove to be mistaken and loss results as a consequence.

In most states, title insurance companies are free to use whatever contract forms they choose. However, under pressure by large institutional lenders and by quasi-governmental corporations operating the secondary mortgage market (Federal National Mortgage Association, Federal Home Loan Mortgage Corporation, Government National Mortgage Association)—all of whom need uniform national forms—most title insurance companies today use uniform policy forms based upon forms developed by the American Land Title Association. ALTA has two basic forms of title insurance policies, a mortgagee's policy and an owner's policy. The mortgagee's policy insures the mortgage lender and not the homeowner. The homeowner who desires title insurance must take out a separate owner's policy.

The ALTA owner's policy basically covers four types of risk:

- risk that title is held by someone other than the insured party
- risk of a defect, lien, or encumbrance on the insured's title
- risk that title is unmarketable, and
- risk that the insured owner has no right of access to the land

Basically, title insurance guarantees that the insurance company has searched the public records and insures against any defects in the public records, unless such defects are specifically excepted from coverage in the policy.

Extended coverage, adding various kinds of protection, can be purchased for an increased premium. This coverage is actually not quite as broad as it seems because it is subject to both exclusions and exceptions. Virtually every policy contains standardized exclusions. The standard exclusions include: (1) losses arising from government regulations affecting the use, occupancy, or enjoyment of land (for example, zoning ordinances, subdivision regulations, and building codes), unless a notice of enforcement or violation is recorded in the public records; (2) claims of persons in possession not shown by the public records, as well as unrecorded easements, and implied easements (see pages 490-492); and (3) easements arising by prescription (see pages 501-503).

Policy exceptions are title defects (actual or potential) that relate to the specific property. These are usually defects that would be revealed by a survey or inspection.

The American Land Title Association's standard mortgage policy insuring the mortgage lender is substantially similar to the owner's policy. It varies principally in that it insures that the mortgage lien is valid, enforceable, and a first and prior lien against all other liens, including mechanics' liens. Almost all institutional lenders require title insurance (at the borrower's expense). Because all secondary-market purchasers of mortgages also require lender's title insurance, there has been an explosive growth of title insurance in the last 30 years.

The next case illustrates the problem of determining the scope of the coverage against the risk of unmarketable title.

LICK MILL CREEK APARTMENTS v. CHICAGO TITLE INSURANCE CO.

Court of Appeal of California, Sixth District, 1991
283 Cal. Rptr. 231

AGLIANO, P.J. Plaintiffs Lick Mill Creek Apartments and Prometheus Development Company, Inc., appeal from a judgment of dismissal entered after the trial court sustained, without leave to amend, the demurrer of defendants Chicago Title Insurance Company and First American Title Insurance Company to plaintiffs' first amended complaint. The trial court determined, based on undisputed facts alleged in the complaint, that title insurance policies issued by defendants did not provide coverage for the costs of removing hazardous substances from plaintiffs' property. For the reasons stated below, we conclude the trial court's ruling was correct and affirm the judgment. . . .

The real property which is the subject of this case comprises approximately 30 acres of land near the Guadalupe River in Santa Clara County. Prior to 1979, various corporations operated warehouses and/or chemical processing plants on the property. Incident to this use of the property, the companies maintained underground tanks, pumps, and pipelines for the storage, handling, and disposal of various hazardous substances. These hazardous substances eventually contaminated the soil, subsoil, and groundwater.

In 1979, Kimball Small Investments 103 (KSI) purchased the property. Between 1979 and 1981, the California Department of Health Services ordered KSI to remedy the toxic contamination of the property. KSI, however, did not comply with this order.

In early October 1986, plaintiffs acquired lot 1 of the property from KSI. In connection with this acquisition, plaintiffs purchased title insurance from Chicago Title Insurance Company (Chicago Title). The insurance policy issued was of the type known as an American Land Title Insurance Association (ALTA) policy (policy 1). Prior to issuing this policy, Chicago Title commissioned a survey and inspection of the property by Carroll Resources Engineering & Management (Carroll Resources). Plaintiffs subsequently purchased lots 2 and 3 from KSI and secured two additional ALTA policies (policies 2 and 3) from Chicago Title and First American Title Insurance Company (First American). The entire site was surveyed and inspected. During its survey and inspection, Carroll Resources noted the presence of certain pipes, tanks, pumps, and other improvements on the property. At the time each of the policies was issued, the Department of Health Services, the Regional Water Quality Control Board, and the Santa Clara County Environmental Health Department maintained records disclosing the presence of hazardous substances on the subject property.

Following their purchase of the property, plaintiffs incurred costs for removal and clean-up of the hazardous substances in order "to mitigate plaintiffs' damages and avoid costs of compliance with government mandate." Then, claiming their expenses were a substitute, i.e., a payment made under threat of compulsion of law, for restitution to the State Hazardous Substance Account (Health & Saf. Code, § 25300 et seq.) and "response costs" as defined under the Comprehensive Environmental Response, Compensation, and Liability Act (CERCLA) (42 U.S.C. § 9601 et seq.), plaintiffs sought indemnity from defendants for the sums expended in their cleanup efforts. Defendants, however, denied coverage.

Discussion . . .

Here the insuring clauses of policies 1, 2, and 3 are identical and provide the following: "Subject to the Exclusions From Coverage, the Exceptions Contained in Schedule

B and the Provisions of the Conditions and Stipulations Hereof [The Insurer] Insures, As of Date of Policy Shown in Schedule A, Against Loss or Damage, Not Exceeding the Amount of Insurance Stated in Schedule A, and Costs, Attorneys' Fees and Expenses Which the Company May Become Obligated to Pay Hereunder, Sustained or Incurred by the Insured by Reason of: ¶ (1) Title to the Estate or Interest Described in Schedule A Being Vested Otherwise Than as Stated Therein; ¶ (2) Any Defect in or Lien or Encumbrance on Such Title; ¶ (3) Lack of a Right of Access to and From the Land; or ¶ (4) Unmarketability of Such Title."

Marketability of Title

Plaintiffs first contend the policies in the instant case expressly insured that title to the subject property was marketable and, since the presence of hazardous substances on the property impaired its marketability, defendants were obliged to pay cleanup costs. Plaintiffs' position, however, is dependent upon their view that California courts have adopted a definition of marketable title that encompasses the property's market value. Our review of relevant authority establishes no support for this position. . . .

The case of Hocking v. Title Ins. & Trust Co., 37 Cal. 2d 644, 234 P.2d 625, 40 A.L.R.2d 1238 (1951), . . . illustrates the distinction between marketability of title and marketability of the land. In *Hocking*, the plaintiff purchased unimproved property and received a grant deed, describing it as two lots in a particular block according to a recorded subdivision map. However, because the subdivider had not complied with various local ordinances regarding subdivision of land, the city would not issue building permits until the plaintiff complied with the ordinances. The plaintiff sought damages from the title insurer claiming defective title. The *Hocking* court noted the distinction between the land and its title: "It is defendants' position that plaintiff confuses title with physical condition of the property she purchased and of the adjacent streets, and that 'One can hold perfect title to land that is valueless; one can have marketable title to land while the land itself is unmarketable.' The truth of this proposition would appear elementary. It appears to be the condition of her *land* in respect to improvements related thereto (graded and paved streets), rather than the condition of her *title* to the land, which is different from what she expected to get." (37 Cal. 2d at p. 651; italics in original.) Thus, the court held that the owner's inability to make economic use of the land due to the subdivider's violations of law did not render the title defective or unmarketable within the terms of the title insurance policy. "Although it is unfortunate that plaintiff has been unable to use her lots for the building purposes she contemplated, it is our view that the facts which she pleads do not affect the marketability of her *title* to the land, but merely impair the market *value* of the property. She appears to possess fee simple title to the property for whatever it may be worth; if she has been damaged by false representations in respect to the condition and value of the land her remedy would seem to be against others than the insurers of the title she acquired." (37 Cal. 2d at p. 652, italics in original.) Similarly, here plaintiffs have pled facts relating to marketability of the land rather than marketability of title.

Other jurisdictions have also recognized the distinction. In Chicago Title Ins. Co. v. Kumar, 24 Mass. App. 53, 506 N.E.2d 154, 156 (1987), the defendant had purchased property on which hazardous substances were discovered. The defendant sought payment for cleanup costs from its title insurer. (Ibid.) The insurer sought a declaration as to its obligations under the policy. The defendant owner filed a counterclaim, seeking a declaration that the presence of hazardous substances constituted a defect in title and the state's statutory power to impose a lien to secure payment of cleanup costs rendered his title unmarketable. (Ibid.) Relying on Hocking v. Title Ins. & Trust Co., supra, 37 Cal. 2d 644, 651, the court found in favor of the insurer, stating "the defendant confuses economic lack of marketability, which relates to physical conditions affecting the use of the property, with title marketability, which relates to defects affecting legally recognized rights and incidents of ownership. . . . The presence of hazardous material may affect the market value of the defendant's land, but, on the present record [since no lien had been recorded], it does not affect the title to the land." (506 N.E.2d at p. 157.)[4] . . .

We find no ambiguity in the insuring clause: defendants are obligated to insure plaintiffs against unmarketability of title on the subject property. Because marketability of title and the market value of the land itself are separate and distinct, plaintiffs cannot claim coverage for the property's physical condition under this clause of the insurance policies.

Encumbrance on Title

The policies in question insure plaintiffs against "any defect in or lien or encumbrance" on title. Although no lien had been recorded or asserted at the time the title insurance policies were issued, plaintiffs contend the presence of hazardous substances on the property constituted an encumbrance on title.

Encumbrances are defined by statute as "taxes, assessments, and all liens upon real property." (Civ. Code, § 1114.) Where a property is contaminated with hazardous substances, a subsequent owner of the property may be held fully responsible for the financial costs of cleaning up the contamination. (42 U.S.C. § 9607(a); Health & Saf. Code, §§ 25323.5, 25363.) A lien may also be imposed on the property to cover such cleanup costs. (42 U.S.C. § 9607(*l*).) Plaintiffs reason that because any transfer of contaminated land carries with it the responsibility for cleanup costs, liability for such costs constitutes an "encumbrance on title" and is covered. We disagree.

In United States v. Allied Chemical Corp., 587 F. Supp. 1205 (N.D. Cal. 1984), the plaintiff alleged a breach of warranty that property conveyed was free of encumbrance where hazardous substances were present on the property at the time it was conveyed. The court dismissed the plaintiff's cause of action, stating: "Plaintiff argues that the term 'encumbrance' is broad enough to include the presence of hazardous substances. However, the only authorities cited have interpreted 'encumbrance' to include only liens, easements, restrictive covenants and other such interests in or rights to the land held by third persons. (See Evans v. Faught, 231 Cal. App. 2d 698, 706. . . .) Plaintiff has given no authority establishing its broad argument that any physical condition, including the presence of hazardous substances, is an 'encumbrance' if 'not visible or known' at the time of conveyance. The court declines to interpret 'encumbrance' as broadly as plaintiff urges. The court finds that, under current law, the term 'encumbrance' does not extend to the presence of hazardous substances alleged in this case." (Id. at p. 1206.) (Accord Cameron v. Martin Marietta Corp., 729 F. Supp. 1529, 1532 (E.D.N.C. 1990).)

---

4. Plaintiffs did not purchase an environmental protection endorsement (ALTA form 8.1 policy).

In Chicago Title Ins. Co. v. Kumar, supra, 506 N.E.2d 154, the court also held that the presence of hazardous substances on the land at the time title was conveyed did not constitute an encumbrance. "The mere possibility that the Commonwealth may attach a future lien . . . , as a result of the release of hazardous material (existing but unknown at the time a title insurance policy is issued) when the Commonwealth has neither expended moneys on the property requiring reimbursement nor recorded the necessary statement of claim, is insufficient to create a 'defect in or lien or encumbrance on . . . title.'" (Id. at p. 156.)

In South Shore Bank v. Stewart Title Guar. Co., 688 F. Supp. 803 (D. Mass. 1988), the plaintiff sought a declaration that the title insurance company was liable for the cleanup costs related to hazardous substances on the property where there was no recorded lien at the time the policy was issued. The court held as a matter of law there was no coverage under the policy, stating "[p]laintiff has neither alleged nor offered any facts to show a defect in title. Hence, it has no cause of action against [the title insurer]." (Id. at p. 806.)

In Holmes v. Alabama Title Co., Inc., 507 So. 2d 922 (Ala. 1987), the landowners' parcels contained an abandoned coal mine. Surface fractures began to appear, indicating that methane gas might eventually escape. The landowners brought suit against their title insurers and others. The reviewing court found in favor of the insurers, reasoning: "The purpose of title insurance is not to protect the insured against loss arising from physical damage to property; rather, it is to protect the insured against defects in the title." (Id. at p. 925.) (Accord Title & Trust Co. of Florida v. Barrows, 381 So. 2d 1088, 1090 (Fla. Dist. Ct. App. 1979); Mafetone v. Forest Manor Homes, Inc., 34 A.D.2d 566, 310 N.Y.S.2d 17, 18 (1970); Edwards v. St. Paul Title Ins. Co., 39 Colo. App. 235, 563 P.2d 979, 980 (1977).) . . .

Exclusions in Policies 1 and 3

Plaintiffs contend the governmental regulation and police power exclusions included in policies 1 and 3 are inapplicable.[5] We need not decide this question, since we have found no coverage under the identical insuring clauses of each policy. . . .

As previously discussed, the language of the insuring clauses of all three policies unambiguously provides coverage only for defects relating to title. These clauses make no reference to the physical condition of the land. . . .

Disposition

The judgment is affirmed.

---

5. Policies 1 and 3 contain exclusions from coverage as follows: "Any law, ordinance or governmental regulation (including but not limited to building and zoning ordinances) restricting or regulating or prohibiting the occupancy, use or enjoyment of the land, or regulating the character, dimensions or location of any improvement now or hereafter erected on the land, or prohibiting a separation in ownership or a reduction in the dimensions or area of the land, or the effect of any violation of any such law, ordinance or governmental regulation." The police power exclusion states as follows: "Rights of eminent domain or governmental rights of police power unless notice of the exercise of such rights appears in the public records at Date of Policy."

Notes and Problem

1. *Recovery based on negligence.* In addition to actions based on contract, property owners often seek to recover against title companies based on negligence. Mistakes that might give rise to liability are illustrated by cases like Surace v. Commonwealth Land Title Ins. Co., 879 N.Y.S.2d 542 (App. Div. 2009), where the court held that a title insurer breached its policy and acted negligently by failing to record a mortgage in a timely fashion. But when an insurance commitment contains an error, the company may escape liability for damages that result from investment decisions by the insured. See, e.g., First Midwest Bank, N.A. v. Stewart Title Guaranty Co., 843 N.E.2d 327 (Ill. 2006) (title insurer not liable for negligence in failing to report covenant in title commitment because the insurer is not in the business of supplying information to guide business decisions). One article suggests that jurisdictions are evenly split on the issue of tort liability for title insurers. See James Bruce Davis, More Than They Bargained For: Are Title Insurance Companies Liable in Tort for Undisclosed Title Defects?, 45 Cath. U. L. Rev. 71 (1995). But see John C. Murray, Attorney Malpractice in Real Estate Transactions: Is Title Insurance the Answer?, 42 Real Prop., Prob. & Tr. J. 221 (2007) (suggesting that tort liability for title insurers is still the minority rule).

2. *Problem.* Plaintiff purchased a home and obtained a policy of title insurance with an exclusion for losses resulting from "[g]overnmental police power, and the existence or violation of any law or government regulation." According to the policy, the exclusion did not apply "to violations or the enforcement of these matters if notice of the violation or enforcement appears on Public Records at the Policy Date." One week after the plaintiff closed title on the property, it was demolished pursuant to a condemnation order of the city. The property had been listed in the city's condemnation records for one year prior to the purchase. May the plaintiff maintain an action under the policy? Compare Glenn v. First American Title Ins. Co., 2009 WL 1830745 (Mich. App.) (holding condemnation records were not "records that give notice to matters affecting title under state law"), with New England Credit Union v. Stewart Title Guarantee Co., 765 A.2d 450 (Vt. 2000) (holding that public records giving constructive notice regarding matters of real property are not limited to municipal land records).

C. TITLE REGISTRATION (THE TORRENS SYSTEM)

The recording system suffers from certain gaps. Certain title problems, adverse possession, for example, may not show up in the title records. Title insurance helps, but its coverage is limited, as we have just seen.

An entirely different approach to title assurance is title registration. Under title registration systems, the government determines title ownership and encumbrances using its land registration. With few exceptions, the government's determination is conclusive, providing indefeasible title to the person recorded on the register as the owner and of all other interests recorded on the register. The system does away with the need for proving a chain of title.

Under a title registration system (named the Torrens system, after the person who created it, Sir Robert Torrens), a lawsuit adjudicates title to be in the plaintiff, subject to any mortgage, easement, or other interest the court finds to exist. All other claims are wiped out. This adjudicated state of title is officially on a conclusive certificate of title. When the registered title is transferred, a new certificate is issued by the registrar after making a substantive review of what has happened to the title since the last certificate was issued.

The Torrens system used to exist in about twenty states, but today exists in jurisdictions in only five states. Theoretically, it is a superior system to the recording system, but in the United States, it suffered from several problems. First, the cost of the initial lawsuit adjudicating title proved prohibitive in many jurisdictions. Second, despite its supposed conclusiveness, courts or legislatures have made the certificate of title subject to exceptions for certain interests (e.g., tax liens, possessory claims, visible easements). Third, title insurance companies, a powerful lobby, have opposed title registration. See Thomas J. Miceli & C.F. Sirmans, Torrens vs. Title Insurance: An Economic Analysis of Land Title Systems, Illinois Real Estate Letter (Fall 1997). For a critical analysis of the operation of the Torrens system in Australia and the United States, see Paul Babie & John Orth, The Troubled Borderlands of Torrens Indefeasibility: Lessons from Australia and the United States, 7 Prop. L. Rev. 33 (2017).

> ### Sidebar
>
> Sir Robert Richard Torrens (1812-1884) was an Irish-born Australian parliamentarian, writer, and land reformer. He emigrated to South Australia after being appointed to a civil service post there, eventually becoming its Premier for a short while.
>
> Torrens is given credit for devising the land registration that bears his name, but one of his contemporaries, Anthony Forester, challenged that claim. See Letter to the editor, The Advertiser. 8 February 1932. p. 10, retrieved 3 March 2011. Forester, sometime parliamentarian/sometime newspaper editor, wrote a letter to the editor of a newspaper in which he stated that he had written "a series of leading articles" in the same newspaper pointing out "especially the absurd and apparently unfair practice of charging heavy fees for the retrospective investigation of title in every single transaction, although the same title had been investigated a dozen times before." Even so, it was Torrens's idea to do away with deeds altogether and replace them with the indefeasible certificate of title, which would be registered.

PART V

LAND USE CONTROLS

In Chapter 1 (see page 35) we introduced the concept of "externalities"; since then, we have considered the relevance of the concept in a number of settings. It takes only a moment's reflection to see that the presence of external costs and benefits becomes especially important to understanding the role of property institutions in controlling conflicting uses of land—the concern of this part. As the examples in Chapter 1's introduction should have suggested, land use activities present the paradigm case of externalities, and much of the law to be studied now can be fruitfully examined as responses to this central fact. But there is more to the subject than just that, and economic considerations should not provide the only perspective. History, a sense of changing times and attitudes, is especially important to understanding many of the major developments in land use. The same is true for politics, especially with regard to zoning and related devices. Finally, some of the most difficult issues presented in the following chapters involve fundamental questions of distributional justice and basic fairness.

The materials that follow are arranged chronologically. They begin, in Chapter 9, with the law of nuisance, the earliest formal legal method of controlling conflicting land uses; then turn in Chapter 10 to the law of servitudes that developed somewhat later; and then survey in Chapter 11 the law of zoning, a creature of the twentieth century. Zoning gives rise to the important problem of regulatory takings of property, examined together with eminent domain in Chapter 12.

All of these methods of land use control are alive and well. Each method has a different institution at its center. The content of nuisance law is set down, essentially but not entirely, by common law courts. Servitudes are defined primarily by private arrangements in light of market forces. Zoning is largely a legislative (and, thus, political) matter, and so too for eminent domain. Throughout the materials, however, courts and markets and legislative and administrative bodies always play some part, whatever the method of control.

CHAPTER 9

Judicial Land Use Controls: The Law of Nuisance

The law of nuisance is part torts and part property—torts because nuisance liability arises from negligent or otherwise wrongful activity, and property because the liability is for interference with the use and enjoyment of *land*. Nuisance law is a means by which common law judges resolve conflicting land uses. The guiding principle is an ancient maxim: *Sic utere tuo ut alienum non laedas*, meaning that one should use one's own property in such a way as not to injure the property of another. But what kind of guide is that? Suppose two neighbors are engaged in incompatible land uses, such that if *A* gets his way *B* can't get her way, and vice versa. *Sic utere* gets you nowhere. How, then, is the conflict to be resolved?

That question is what this chapter is about. What you learn will prove instructive in the subsequent chapters as well.

MORGAN v. HIGH PENN OIL CO.

Supreme Court of North Carolina, 1953
77 S.E.2d 682

Civil action to recover temporary damages for a private nuisance, and to abate such nuisance by injunction.

The salient facts appear in the numbered paragraphs which immediately follow. . . .

2. The land of the plaintiffs is a composite tract, which they acquired by two separate purchases antedating 3 August, 1945. It contains a dwelling-house, a restaurant, and accommodations for thirty-two habitable trailers. The dwelling-house existed at the time of the purchases of the plaintiffs, and has been occupied by them as their home since 3 August, 1945. The plaintiffs constructed the restaurant and the trailer accommodations immediately after they established their residence on the premises, and have been renting these improvements since their completion to third persons. They have been supplementing their income from these sources by taking lodgers in their dwelling. . . .

5. The High Penn Oil Company operated [an] oil refinery at virtually all times between 10 October, 1950, and the date of the rendition of the judgement in this action. . . .

9. The oil refinery is approximately 1,000 feet from the dwelling of the plaintiffs.

10. These structures are situated within a radius of one mile of the oil refinery: a church; at least twenty-nine private dwellings; four tourist and trailer camps; a grocery store; two restaurants; a nursery appropriated to the propagation of young trees, shrubs, and plants; three motor vehicle service stations; two motor vehicle repair shops; a railroad track; the terminus of a gasoline pipe line; numerous large storage tanks capable of storing sixty million gallons of gasoline; and the headquarters of at least four motor truck companies engaged in the transportation of petroleum products and other property for hire. Railway tank cars and motor tank trucks are filled with gasoline at the storage tanks for conveyance to various places at virtually all hours of the day and night. . . .

16. The evidence of the plaintiffs tended to show that for some hours on two or three different days during each week of its operation by the High Penn Oil Company, the oil refinery emitted nauseating gases and odors in great quantities; that the nauseating gases and odors invaded the nine acres owned by the plaintiffs and the other lands located within "a mile and three-quarters or two miles" of the oil refinery in such amounts and in such densities as to render persons of ordinary sensitiveness uncomfortable and sick; that the operation of the oil refinery thus substantially impaired the use and enjoyment of the nine acres by the plaintiffs and their renters; and that the defendants failed to put an end to the atmospheric pollution arising out of the operation of the oil refinery after notice and demand from the plaintiffs to abate it. The evidence of the plaintiffs tended to show, moreover, that the oil refinery was the only agency discharging gases or odors in annoying quantities into the air in the Friendship section. . . .

18. [The jury found the refinery to be a nuisance and set damages at $2,500. The trial judge entered a judgment to that effect and further enjoined the defendant from continuing the nuisance. The defendant appealed.]

ERVIN, J. . . . The High Penn Oil Company contends that the evidence is not sufficient to establish either an actionable or an abatable private nuisance. . . .

The law of private nuisance rests on the concept embodied in the ancient legal maxim *Sic utere tuo ut alienum non laedas*, meaning, in essence, that every person should so use his own property as not to injure that of another. . . . As a consequence, a private nuisance exists in a legal sense when one makes an improper use of his own property and in that way injures the land or some incorporeal right of one's neighbor. . . .

Much confusion exists in respect to the legal basis of liability in the law of private nuisance because of the deplorable tendency of the courts to call everything a nuisance, and let it go at that. . . . The confusion on this score vanishes in large part, however, when proper heed is paid to the sound propositions that private nuisance is a field of tort liability rather than a single type of tortious conduct; that the feature which gives unity to this field of tort liability is the interest invaded, namely, the interest in the use and enjoyment of land; that any substantial nontrespassory invasion

---

Sidebar

"Ervin, J." refers to Sam J. Ervin, Jr. In 1954, a year after the decision in *Morgan*, Sam Ervin was elected to the U.S. Senate; 20 years after that, he presided over the Senate Select Committee on Presidential Campaign Activities. "[T]o millions of Americans he was the hero of the unfolding drama of the Watergate affair that led, eventually, to the resignation of President Nixon in 1974." N.Y. Times, Apr. 24, 1985, at B12 (obituary).

of another's interest in the private use and enjoyment of land by any type of liability forming conduct is a private nuisance; that the invasion which subjects a person to liability for private nuisance may be either intentional or unintentional; that a person is subject to liability for an intentional invasion when his conduct is unreasonable under the circumstances of the particular case; and that a person is subject to liability for an unintentional invasion when his conduct is negligent, reckless or ultrahazardous. See Scope and Introduction Note to Chapter 40, American Law Institute's Restatement of the Law of Torts. . . .

An invasion of another's interest in the use and enjoyment of land is intentional in the law of private nuisance when the person whose conduct is in question as a basis for liability acts for the purpose of causing it, or knows that it is resulting from his conduct, or knows that it is substantially certain to result from his conduct. Restatement of the Law of Torts, section 825. . . . A person who intentionally creates or maintains a private nuisance is liable for the resulting injury to others regardless of the degree of care or skill exercised by him to avoid such injury. . . .

When the evidence is interpreted in the light most favorable to the plaintiffs, it suffices to support a finding that in operating the oil refinery the High Penn Oil Company intentionally and unreasonably caused noxious gases and odors to escape onto the nine acres of the plaintiffs to such a degree as to impair in a substantial manner the plaintiffs' use and enjoyment of their land. This being so, the evidence is ample to establish the existence of an actionable private nuisance, entitling the plaintiffs to recover temporary damages from the High Penn Oil Company. . . .

When the evidence is taken in the light most favorable to the plaintiffs, it also suffices to warrant the additional inferences that the High Penn Oil Company intends to operate the oil refinery in the future in the same manner as in the past; that if it is permitted to carry this intent into effect, the High Penn Oil Company will hereafter cast noxious gases and odors onto the nine acres of the plaintiffs with such recurring frequency and in such annoying density as to inflict irreparable injury upon the plaintiffs in the use and enjoyment of their home and their other adjacent properties; and that the issuance of an appropriate injunction is necessary to protect the plaintiffs against the threatened irreparable injury. This being true, the evidence is ample to establish the existence of an abatable private nuisance, entitling the plaintiffs to such mandatory or prohibitory injunctive relief as may be required to prevent the High Penn Oil Company from continuing the nuisance. . . .

For the reasons given, the evidence is sufficient to withstand the motion of the High Penn Oil Company for a compulsory nonsuit. . . .

Notes and Questions

1. *Unreasonableness.* Issues of "unreasonableness" have come to play an important role in the law of nuisance. Precisely what that role amounts to, however, is obscure. The opinion in *Morgan* states the textbook rules: an interference with use and enjoyment of land, in order to give rise to liability, must be substantial; it must also be *either* intentional and unreasonable *or* the unintentional result of negligent, reckless, or abnormally dangerous activity. See Restatement (Second) of Torts §§ 821F, 822 (1979).

Regarding the question of unreasonableness, the case of unintentional nuisance seems clear enough. Liability here is based on traditional tort categories—negligence, recklessness, abnormally dangerous activities—all of which "embody in some degree the concept of unreasonableness." Id. § 821B comment e, at 90. The intentional nuisance is another matter, and an important one given that most modern-day nuisances are intentional in the sense that the *Morgan* case and the Restatement use that term. Thus, situations giving rise to allegations of nuisance today typically involve interference with use and enjoyment of land—from air and water pollution, noise, odors, vibrations, flooding, excessive light (or inadequate light)—that continues over time and is known by the defendant to result from its activities. Despite the presence of intent in these instances, nuisance liability arises only if the resulting interference is substantial and unreasonable.

What does *unreasonable* mean in this context of an intentional tort? In one view, the term has a function here that is quite different from the role it plays in the law of negligence. Rather than inviting a comparison of whether the social benefits of the defendant's conduct outweigh its expected costs, the relevant inquiry is said to concern the *level* of interference that results from the conduct—particularly, whether the interference crosses some threshold that marks the point of liability. For example, in Jost v. Dairyland Power Coop., 172 N.W.2d 647 (Wis. 1969), the court upheld the exclusion of evidence offered by the defendant to show that the utility of its operations outweighed the gravity of the harm caused to the plaintiffs. Of the defendant's operation, a power plant, the court said, "Whether its economic or social importance dwarfed the claim of a small farmer is of no consequence in this lawsuit." Id. at 653.

The view of the *Jost* case is contrary to the Restatement's position that, to determine unreasonableness in a case of intentional nuisance, the court is to consider whether "the gravity of the harm outweighs the utility of the actor's conduct. . . ." Restatement (Second) of Torts, supra, § 826(1). See also id. § 827 (factors relevant to gravity of the harm are the extent and character of the harm, the social value of the plaintiff's use, its suitability to the locality in question, and the burden on the plaintiff of avoiding the harm); §828 (factors relevant to utility of the actor's conduct are its social value, its suitability to the locality in question, and the impracticality of the defendant preventing the harm). Which view dominates is not clear, though it can be said that relatively few courts have followed the Restatement explicitly. See Jeff L. Lewin, *Boomer* and the American Law of Nuisance: Past, Present, and Future, 54 Alb. L. Rev. 189, 212-214 (1990).

  2. *More on unreasonableness: trespass compared.* Typically, an intentional tort results in liability without regard to the amount of harm or the reasonableness of the activity causing it. Trespass, involving a *physical invasion* of land, is a case in point. While liability for unintentional trespass is virtually identical to that for unintentional nuisance,[1] the two torts differ markedly if the element of

---

1. See Restatement (Second) of Torts § 165 (1965):

> One who recklessly or negligently, or as a result of an abnormally dangerous activity, enters land in the possession of another or causes a thing or third person so to enter is subject to liability to the possessor if, but only if, his presence or the presence of the thing or the third person upon the land causes harm to the land, to the possessor, or to a thing or a third person in whose security the possessor has a legally protected interest.

See also Restatement (Second) of Torts, supra, § 821D comment e, at 102 (commenting on the similarity of the two torts). Since a physical invasion—e.g., by polluted water—can also interfere with use and enjoyment of land and thus be a nuisance, the choice of theory with regard to unintentional conduct is usually a matter of indifference, statutes of limitations and variations in the interest protected aside.

intent is present. In such an instance, trespass is treated like the other intentional torts; nuisance, on the other hand, is usually subjected to inquiries about reasonableness and amount of harm. Thus, unless the plaintiff can show a physical invasion by a tangible thing (that is, a trespass), the defendant can escape liability for intentional conduct on grounds of reasonableness or amount of harm that would be irrelevant if there has been a physical invasion by a tangible thing. This seems anomalous. Is there any sense to a system of rules that treats the intentional release of contaminated water onto neighboring land one way (trespass) and the intentional release of polluting gases another way (nuisance)? Some torts scholars have thought not, and at their urging the Restatement added a provision that an intentional invasion is "unreasonable" for purposes of nuisance law if, (1) as before, the gravity of the harm caused outweighs the utility of the actor's conduct; *or* if, (2) alternatively, "the harm caused by the conduct is serious and the financial burden of compensating for this and similar harm to others would not make the continuation of the conduct not feasible." Restatement (Second) of Torts, supra, § 826(b). See also id. § 829A ("an intentional invasion of another's interest in the use and enjoyment of land is unreasonable if the harm resulting from the invasion is severe and greater than the other should be required to bear without compensation"). Is alternative (2) a restatement of the threshold-level test of liability? Do the remedies available to a plaintiff differ under the two alternatives? See Jeff L. Lewin, Compensated Injunctions and the Evolution of Nuisance Law, 71 Iowa L. Rev. 775, 779-785 (1986). For a case explicitly rejecting alternative (2), see Carpenter v. Double R Cattle Co., Inc., 701 P.2d 222 (Idaho 1985).

Why should an activity that causes serious harm be excused from liability under alternative (2) if the obligation to pay would make continuation of the activity "not feasible"? Why should it be excused under alternative (1) simply because the utility of the conduct in question outweighs the harm it causes?

Section 826(b) of the Restatement moves intentional nuisance in the doctrinal direction of intentional trespass, though still there are differences. (Do you see them?) At times one finds a court taking the opposite approach, treating an intentional trespass like an intentional nuisance. A case in point is Martin v. Reynolds Metals Co., 342 P.2d 790 (Or. 1959), cert. denied, 362 U.S. 918 (1960). The plaintiffs in *Martin* were cattle ranchers who alleged that their herds were poisoned by fumes from the defendant's aluminum plant. The trial court found the defendant liable on a *trespass* theory; on appeal the defendant argued that trespass was inappropriate because there had been no physical invasion of the plaintiffs' land. The court rejected the argument, choosing "in this atomic age" to define a trespass "as any intrusion which invades the possessor's protected interest in exclusive possession, whether that intrusion is by visible or invisible pieces of matter or by energy which can be measured only by the mathematical language of the physicist." Id. at 793-794. But then, having found an intentional trespass, the court went on to apply a balancing test of reasonableness in order to determine liability. Trespass and nuisance were harmonized, but by subjecting both to the utilitarian calculus of intentional nuisance. Compare Wilson v. Interlake Steel Co., 649 P.2d 922 (Cal. 1982), holding that excessive noise alone will not support a trespass action absent some kind of physical invasion or physical damage to property. Intangible intrusions, the court said, must be approached on a nuisance theory.

As anomalous as it may at first seem, might the trespass-nuisance dichotomy in fact be sensible—at least as to the typical trespass (where *A* enters *B's* land) and the typical nuisance (where pollution, say, from *A's* operations interferes with neighbors *B, C, D, . . . N*)? Is there a way to generalize the difference between the typical fact settings of the two torts, so as to arrive at better doctrine? See Thomas W. Merrill, Trespass, Nuisance, and the Costs of Determining Property Rights, 14 J. Legal Stud. 13 (1985).

Lateral and subjacent support. Lateral support refers to that provided to one piece of land by the parcels of land surrounding it; subjacent support refers to support from underneath as opposed to the sides. The common law right of lateral support imposes a duty on neighboring land to provide the support that the subject parcel would need and receive under *natural* conditions; ordinarily, then, there is no right to support of *structures* on the land. A cause of action for interference with the right to lateral support does not arise until subsidence actually occurs or is threatened, and then it runs against the excavator (who may, of course, be a predecessor of the present possessor). Liability is absolute; negligence need not be shown. If, however, the supported land had been built upon in such a way that subsidence would not have occurred but for the improvements, there is no liability without negligence, at least so long as the excavator gives notice of his plans. Generally speaking, there is also no liability, absent negligence, if subsidence of improved or unimproved land is shown to have been caused by withdrawal of fluids (e.g., groundwater) or their release as a result of excavation.

The right of lateral support can be waived; it can also be expressly expanded, as by grant of a right to additional support. Moreover, a number of jurisdictions have statutes that enlarge or otherwise modify the common law right, in recognition of its unsuitability to modern, dense, high-rise building practices.

Issues of subjacent support arise when one person owns surface rights and another person owns some kind of subsurface rights, such as a mineral interest. The situation is analogous to that of lateral support, and the law pretty much tracks that outlined above.

BOOMER v. ATLANTIC CEMENT CO.

Court of Appeals of New York, 1970
257 N.E.2d 870

BERGAN, J. Defendant operates a large cement plant near Albany. These are actions for injunction and damages by neighboring land owners alleging injury to property from dirt, smoke, and vibration emanating from the plant. A nuisance has been found after trial, temporary damages have been allowed; but an injunction has been denied.

The public concern with air pollution arising from many sources in industry and in transportation is currently accorded ever wider recognition accompanied by a growing sense of responsibility in State and Federal Governments to control it. Cement plants are obvious sources of air pollution in the neighborhoods where they operate.

But there is now before the court private litigation in which individual property owners have sought specific relief from a single plant operation. The threshold question raised by the division of view on this appeal is whether the court should resolve the litigation between the parties now before it as equitably as seems possible; or whether, seeking promotion of the general public welfare, it should channel private litigation into broad public objectives.

A court performs its essential function when it decides the rights of parties before it. Its decision of private controversies may sometimes greatly affect public issues. Large questions of law are often resolved by the manner in which private litigation is decided. But this is normally an incident to the court's main function to settle controversy. It is a rare exercise of judicial power to use a decision in private litigation as a purposeful mechanism to achieve direct public objectives greatly beyond the rights and interests before the court.

Effective control of air pollution is a problem presently far from solution even with the full public and financial powers of government. In large measure adequate technical procedures are yet to be developed and some that appear possible may be economically impracticable.

It seems apparent that the amelioration of air pollution will depend on technical research in great depth; on a carefully balanced consideration of the economic impact of close regulation; and of the actual effect on public health. It is likely to require massive public expenditure and to demand more than any local community can accomplish and to depend on regional and interstate controls.

A court should not try to do this on its own as a by-product of private litigation and it seems manifest that the judicial establishment is neither equipped in the limited nature of any judgment it can pronounce nor prepared to lay down and implement an effective policy for the elimination of air pollution. This is an area beyond the circumference of one private lawsuit. It is a direct responsibility for government and should not thus be undertaken as an incident to solving a dispute between property owners and a single cement plant—one of many—in the Hudson River valley.

The cement making operations of defendant have been found by the court at Special Term to have damaged the nearby properties of plaintiffs in these two actions. That court, as it has been noted, accordingly found defendant maintained a nuisance and this has been affirmed at the Appellate Division. The total damage to plaintiffs' properties is, however, relatively small in comparison with the value of defendant's operation and with the consequences of the injunction which plaintiffs seek.

The ground for the denial of injunction, notwithstanding the finding both that there is a nuisance and that plaintiffs have been damaged substantially, is the large disparity in economic consequences of the nuisance and of the injunction. This theory cannot, however, be sustained without overruling a doctrine which has been consistently reaffirmed in several leading cases in this court and which has never been disavowed here, namely that where a nuisance has been found and where there has been any substantial damage shown by the party complaining an injunction will be granted.

The rule in New York has been that such a nuisance will be enjoined although marked disparity be shown in economic consequence between the effect of the injunction and the effect of the nuisance.

The problem of disparity in economic consequence was sharply in focus in Whalen v. Union Bag & Paper Co., 208 N.Y. 1, 101 N.E. 805. A pulp mill entailing an investment of more than a million dollars polluted a stream in which plaintiff, who owned a farm, was "a lower riparian owner." The economic loss to plaintiff from this pollution was small. This court, reversing the Appellate Division, reinstated the injunction granted by the Special Term against the argument of the mill owner that in view of "the slight advantage to plaintiff and the great loss that will be inflicted on defendant" an injunction should not be granted (p. 2, 101 N.E. p. 805). "Such a balancing of injuries cannot be justified by the circumstances of this case," Judge Werner noted (p. 4, 101 N.E. p. 805). He continued: "Although the damage to the plaintiff may be slight as compared with the defendant's expense of abating the condition, that is not a good reason for refusing an injunction" (p. 5, 101 N.E. p. 806).

Thus the unconditional injunction granted at Special Term was reinstated. The rule laid down in that case, then, is that whenever the damage resulting from a nuisance is found not "unsubstantial," viz., $100 a year, injunction would follow. This states a rule that had been followed in this court with marked consistency. . . .

Although the court at Special Term and the Appellate Division held that injunction should be denied, it was found that plaintiffs had been damaged in various specific amounts up to the time of the trial and damages to the respective plaintiffs were awarded for those amounts. The effect of this was, injunction having been denied, plaintiffs could maintain successive actions at law for damages thereafter as further damage was incurred.

The court at Special Term also found the amount of permanent damage attributable to each plaintiff, for the guidance of the parties in the event both sides stipulated to the payment and acceptance of such permanent damage as a settlement of all the controversies among the parties. The total of permanent damages to all plaintiffs thus found was $185,000. The basis of adjustment has not resulted in any stipulation by the parties.

This result at Special Term and at the Appellate Division is a departure from a rule that has become settled; but to follow the rule literally in these cases would be to close down the plant at once. This court is fully agreed to avoid that immediately drastic remedy; the difference in view is how best to avoid it.[2]

One alternative is to grant the injunction but postpone its effect to a specified future date to give opportunity for technical advances to permit defendant to eliminate the nuisance; another is to grant the injunction conditioned on the payment of permanent damages to plaintiffs which would compensate them for the total economic loss to their property present and future caused by defendant's operations. For reasons which will be developed the court chooses the latter alternative.

If the injunction were to be granted unless within a short period—e.g., 18 months—the nuisance be abated by improved methods, there would be no assurance that any significant technical improvement would occur.

The parties could settle this private litigation at any time if defendant paid enough money and the imminent threat of closing the plant would build up the pressure on defendant. If there were no improved techniques found, there would inevitably be applications to the court at Special Term for extensions of time to perform on showing of good faith efforts to find such techniques.

---

2. Respondent's investment in the plant is in excess of $45,000,000. There are over 300 people employed there.

Moreover, techniques to eliminate dust and other annoying by-products of cement making are unlikely to be developed by any research the defendant can undertake within any short period, but will depend on the total resources of the cement industry nation-wide and throughout the world. The problem is universal wherever cement is made.

For obvious reasons the rate of the research is beyond control of defendant. If at the end of 18 months the whole industry has not found a technical solution a court would be hard put to close down this one cement plant if due regard be given to equitable principles.

On the other hand, to grant the injunction unless defendant pays plaintiffs such permanent damages as may be fixed by the court seems to do justice between the contending parties. All of the attributions of economic loss to the properties on which plaintiffs' complaints are based will have been redressed.

The nuisance complained of by these plaintiffs may have other public or private consequences, but these particular parties are the only ones who have sought reme-dies and the judgment proposed will fully redress them. The limitation of relief granted is a limitation only within the four corners of these actions and does not foreclose pub-lic health or other public agencies from seeking proper relief in a proper court.

It seems reasonable to think that the risk of being required to pay permanent dam-ages to injured property owners by cement plant owners would itself be a reasonable effective spur to research for improved techniques to minimize nuisance.

The power of the court to condition on equitable grounds the continuance of an injunction on the payment of permanent damages seems undoubted. . . .

The damage base here suggested is consistent with the general rule in those nui-sance cases where damages are allowed. "Where a nuisance is of such a permanent and unabatable character that a single recovery can be had, including the whole dam-age past and future resulting therefrom, there can be but one recovery" (66 C.J.S. Nuisances § 140, p. 947). It has been said that permanent damages are allowed where the loss recoverable would obviously be small as compared with the cost of removal of the nuisance (Kentucky-Ohio Gas Co. v. Bowling, 264 Ky. 470 477, 95 S.W.2d 1). . . .

Thus it seems fair to both sides to grant permanent damages to plaintiffs which will terminate this private litigation. The theory of damage is the "servitude on land" of plaintiffs imposed by defendant's nuisance. (See United States v. Causby, 328 U.S. 256, 261, 262, 267, 66 S. Ct. 1062, 90 L. Ed. 1206, where the term "servitude" addressed to the land was used by Justice Douglas relating to the effect of airplane noise on prop-erty near an airport.)

The judgment, by allowance of permanent damages imposing a servitude on land, which is the basis of the actions, would preclude future recovery by plaintiffs or their grantees.

This should be placed beyond debate by a provision of the judgment that the payment by defendant and the acceptance by plaintiffs of permanent damages found by the court shall be in compensation for servitude on the land. . . .

The orders should be reversed, without costs, and the cases remitted to Supreme Court, Albany County to grant an injunction which shall be vacated upon payment by defendant of such amounts of permanent damage to the respective plaintiffs as shall for this purpose be determined by the court.

JASEN, J. (dissenting). I agree with the majority that a reversal is required here, but I do not subscribe to the newly enunciated doctrine of assessment of permanent damages, in lieu of an injunction, where substantial property rights have been impaired by the creation of a nuisance. . . .

I see grave dangers in overruling our long-established rule of granting an injunction where a nuisance results in substantial continuing damage. In permitting the injunction to become inoperative upon the payment of permanent damages, the majority is, in effect, licensing a continuing wrong. It is the same as saying to the cement company, you may continue to do harm to your neighbors so long as you pay a fee for it. Furthermore, once such permanent damages are assessed and paid, the incentive to alleviate the wrong would be eliminated, thereby continuing air pollution of an area without abatement. . . .

THE REST OF THE STORY . . .

On remand, the trial judge struck a middle-ground position on damages. On the one hand, he agreed with the plaintiffs that damages should not be limited to the decrease in fair-market value. On the other hand, he rejected their view that damages should be set at the level that plaintiffs would have demanded before they agreed to lift a permanent injunction. Instead, he considered the above-market prices that Atlantic had spent in acquiring other property in the neighborhood. The appellate division upheld this approach as reasonable.

The plaintiffs were not entirely satisfied with the outcome. Mr. Boomer and Mr. Millious believed that the court should have shut down the plant completely. Millious says that even though he now lives four or five miles away from the plant, there is still dust in the air occasionally. See Daniel A. Farber, The Story of *Boomer*: Pollution and the Common Law, 32 Ecology L.Q. 113, 128-129 (2005).

Notes and Questions

1. *The liability issue.* Why was a nuisance found in *Boomer*? In a subsequent case, Copart Indus., Inc. v. Consolidated Edison Co., 362 N.E.2d 968 (N.Y. 1977), the N.Y. Court of Appeals confronted a set of facts essentially identical to those in *Boomer*, yet found no nuisance. The court in *Copart* claimed to follow the Restatement. It considered the liability category of abnormally dangerous conditions to be inapplicable and concluded that neither intent nor negligence had been established. *Boomer* was distinguished on the ground that it involved an intentional and unreasonable invasion.

Do you agree with that characterization of the *Boomer* case? Notice the statement in *Boomer* that the trial court based liability simply on the fact that the plaintiffs' property had been damaged. Given that, which of the theories of nuisance liability discussed earlier (see pages 463-465) might *Boomer* reflect?

2. *The remedy issue: injunctions.* Is it accurate to characterize *Boomer* as saying that the court, in essence, denied injunctive relief and that it did so by "balancing the equities"? What do you think of the method of striking the balance? Consider the following from Mahoney v. Walter, 205 S.E.2d 692, 698 (W. Va. 1974):

> One of the chief problems with this doctrine [of balancing the equities] is that it compares the general loss to the public, such as loss of jobs, while it

only considers specific loss to the private land owner, i.e., the specific money damage to his property, notwithstanding he may be damaged in many general ways which cannot be translated into specific damages.

See also Comment, Equity and the Eco-System: Can Injunctions Clear the Air?, 68 Mich. L. Rev. 1254, 1284 n.158 (1970):

> Most cases in which injunctions are sought involve injury to only one or a few persons, but in the air pollution context many are being injured. If the plaintiff were to bring a class action, the weighing of the benefit which would result from granting the injunction would include all the members of the class. Class actions are sometimes difficult to bring, however, and it therefore seems appropriate as a general rule that if a judge can recognize harm to third persons from granting an injunction, he should be able to consider harm to third persons from not granting the injunction.

Is balancing the equities a sensible (or necessary) way to reach a decision about granting or denying injunctive relief; should one look instead at factors other than those suggested by the balancing doctrine (which are what)?

3. *The remedy issue: permanent damages.* Notice the nature of the relief awarded in *Boomer*. Does the fact that a court can award permanent damages dispel the concern that denial of injunctive relief relegates plaintiffs to a series of lawsuits? Do permanent damages have any other advantages? Any disadvantages? Consider the observation of the dissenting judge in *Boomer*, who argued that an award of permanent damages destroys any incentive on the part of the defendant to abate its pollution in the future—presumably even if new, cost-effective technology is developed. Is there any solution to this problem, other than periodic or temporary damages (which, of course, will give rise to a multiplicity of actions)?

4. *The remedy issue: injunction with compensation.* Another possible remedy is to grant the injunction, but only on condition that the plaintiff compensate the defendant for its losses. This was the remedy that the court ordered in Spur Industries, Inc. v. Del E. Webb Development Co., 494 P.2d 700 (Ariz. 1972) (enjoining feed lot operation, but requiring plaintiff to indemnify defendant). *Spur* has been a controversial decision, and other courts have not followed its approach.

Public nuisances. Morgan and *Boomer* both involved private nuisances, but nuisances may also be public. The Restatement of Torts defines a *public nuisance* as "an unreasonable interference with a right common to the general public." Circumstances said to bear on the issue of unreasonableness are: whether the conduct in question significantly interferes with public health, safety, peace, comfort, or convenience; whether the conduct is proscribed by statute or ordinance (as in *Spur*); and whether the conduct is of a continuing nature or has produced a permanent or long-lasting effect. See Restatement (Second) of Torts § 821B (1979). Essentially, though, the underlying bases of liability for public nuisance are the same as those for private nuisance—there must be substantial harm caused by intentional and unreasonable conduct or by conduct that is negligent, reckless, or abnormally dangerous. And, as with private nuisance, unreasonableness turns heavily on considerations of gravity and utility. Thus, as one early public nuisance case is said to have put it, *"Le utility del chose excusera le noisomeness del stink."* Quoted in id. § 826 comment a, at 120.

The difference between public and private nuisance lies in the interests protected: public nuisance protects public rights; private nuisance protects rights in the use and enjoyment of land. (It is possible, though, for the same conduct to create both a private and a public nuisance.)

Usually, the plaintiff in a public nuisance action is a governmental entity, such as a city, that sues on behalf of the general public. In theory, any member of the affected public may sue, but usually *only* if the person bringing suit can show "special injury" (or "special damage," or "particular damage")—injury or damage of a kind different from that suffered by other members of the public.

CHAPTER 10

Private Land Use Controls: The Law of Servitudes

In this chapter we study land use arrangements arising out of private agreements. Usually, but not always, the agreements involve two or more parcels of land, and the purpose of the agreements is to increase the total value of all the parcels involved. And usually, but not always, the effect of the agreements is to burden one parcel of land for the benefit of another parcel. For example, the owner of Tract 1 may have an easement to cross Tract 2 to reach a public road. Burdens and benefits are often reciprocal, as when all lots in a subdivision are restricted to residential use. These agreements create interests in land, binding and benefiting not only the parties to the agreement in question but also their successors. These interests are commonly called, as a class, *servitudes*.

A. CLASSIFYING SERVITUDES

Students, not to mention law professors and practicing lawyers, often find the law of servitudes complex and confusing. Servitude law's complexity stems largely from the fact that the same functional interest may be classified under different doctrinal labels, each with its own set of requirements. Traditional servitude doctrine classifies private use interests into four categories: easements, covenants, profits à prendre (or "profits" for short), and licenses. By far, the most important are the first two, easements and covenants. Covenants are further divided into another dichotomy: covenants enforceable at law (called "real covenants") and covenants enforceable in equity ("equitable servitudes").

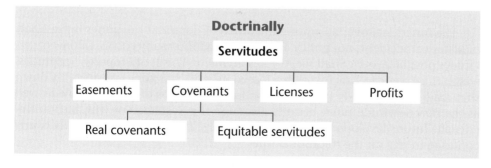

These labels can be misleading, however, because there is considerable functional overlap among interests bearing different labels. If we look at servitudes from a functional perspective—that is, what they do—they fall into these five categories:

Functionally

▸ A right to do some act on another person's land (e.g., a right of way)
▸ A right to enter onto someone's land and remove something attached to the land (e.g., remove minerals)
▸ A right to restrict an owner from using her land in some way (e.g., your neighbor cannot develop her land commercially)
▸ A right to compel an owner to perform some act on her own land (e.g., maintain a fence)
▸ A right to compel an owner to pay money to maintain certain facilities (e.g., a swimming pool available to residents)

What makes servitude law frustrating, both for teachers as well as their students, is that these two ways of classifying servitudes traditionally have overlapped to a considerable extent. So, putting the two boxes together, we come up with the following:

Doctrinally and Functionally

▸ A right to do some act on another person's land (e.g., a right of way) → **Easement**
▸ A right to enter onto someone's land and remove something attached to the land (e.g., remove minerals) → **Profit**
▸ A right to restrict an owner from using her land in some way (e.g., your neighbor cannot develop her land commercially) → **Easement** (a negative easement), *or* → **Real covenant**, *or* → **Equitable servitude**
▸ A right to compel an owner to perform some act on her own land (e.g., maintain a fence) → **Real covenant**, *or* → **Equitable servitude**
▸ A right to compel an owner to pay money to maintain certain facilities (e.g., maintain a swimming pool available to residents) → **Real covenant**, *or* → **Equitable servitude**

The functional overlap among the different doctrinal categories is the result of historical accident, not policy. Is a unified and internally consistent law of servitudes possible? As we shall see, the Restatement (Third) of Property, Servitudes, which the American Law Institute adopted in 2000, has gone considerably down that road. We will study both the traditional doctrines of servitude law as well as the new Servitude rules, because although the Restatement will likely influence the future development of Restatement law, for the time being many courts continue to rely on the traditional rules.

B. EASEMENTS

The primary modern forms of servitudes—easements, real covenants, and equitable servitudes—are largely products of the nineteenth century. In the days of common fields, there was little need for defining rights of way; people wandered where they wished through the unfenced countryside, causing little injury. But the English enclosure movement, which began in the sixteenth century and terminated common use rights, together with the Industrial Revolution, created the need for a new, systematic body of law dealing with easements of way as well as other servitudes regulating interdependent land uses.

In the nineteenth century, a general law of easements developed, replacing the hodgepodge of specific interests that courts recognized with nothing organizing them. The courts gradually classified easements in two different ways, along two vectors, if you will. The first vector concerns whether the easement is *affirmative* (or positive) or *negative* (i.e., restrictive) in character. The vast majority of easements are affirmative; that is, they give the interest holder a right to do an affirmative act on land that someone else owns. The early law also recognized a few types of negative easements—easements forbidding one landowner from doing something on his land that might harm a neighbor. But the courts were chary of creating new negative easements, for reasons we will discuss later, at pages 522-523, and strictly fenced them in.

In addition to the distinction between affirmative and negative easement, easements are also classified as *appurtenant* or *in gross*. Both types of easements give easement owners the right to make some specific use (or in the case of a negative easement, restrict some particular use) of land that they do not own. But remember, you cannot create an easement over your own land. (Make sure you understand why.) See Fitzpatrick v. Kent, 458 P.3d 943 (Idaho 2020). An easement appurtenant gives that right to whomever owns a parcel of land that the easement benefits. An easement in gross gives the right to some person without regard to ownership of land. Stated somewhat differently, an easement appurtenant benefits the easement owner in the use of land belonging to that owner, but an easement in gross benefits the easement owner personally rather than in connection with use of land that the person owns. If it is unclear which type of easement is intended by the parties, the law construes in favor of an easement appurtenant. For example, in a case where the sellers reserved an easement "for the watering of livestock owned by the sellers," the court held that the easement was appurtenant to the neighboring tract the sellers owned. Nelson v. Johnson, 679 P.2d 662 (Idaho 1984). See Restatement (Third) of Property, Servitudes § 4.5 (2000).

Classifying Easements

	Do an Affirmative Act	Restrict an Owner's Use
Benefits land	Affirmative (positive) Appurtenant	Negative Appurtenant
Benefits no land	Affirmative (positive) In gross	Negative In gross

In Brief	
Type of easement	Burdened/Benefitted land
Appurtenant	Burdened: Servient estate
	Benefitted: Dominant estate
In gross	Burdened: Servient estate

Easements appurtenant require both a *dominant tenement* (or estate) and a *servient tenement*. The easement attaches to and benefits the dominant tenement. Appurtenant easements are usually transferable. The easement transfers along with the dominant tenement to successive owners. However, appurtenant easement can be made personal to the easement owner only and not transferable to others.

Because an easement in gross does not benefit any land, it involves no dominant estate, only a servient estate. Easements in gross may be alienable or inalienable. Easements in gross are sometimes said to be "personal," but they are personal only in the sense that they do not attach to any parcel of land owned by the easement owner, not in the sense that they may not be transferred to another person.

1. Creation of Easements

An *easement*, being an interest in land, is within the Statute of Frauds (so too for *profits*). Creation of an easement generally requires a written instrument signed by the party to be bound thereby. However, in addition to the usual exceptions of fraud, part performance, and estoppel, an easement may, under certain circumstances, be created by implication or by prescription.

WILLARD v. FIRST CHURCH OF CHRIST, SCIENTIST
Supreme Court of California, 1972
498 P.2d 987

PETERS, J. In this case we are called upon to decide whether a grantor may, in deeding real property to one person, effectively reserve an interest in the property to another. We hold that in this case such a reservation vests the interest in the third party.

Plaintiffs Donald E. and Jennie C. Willard filed an action to quiet title to a lot in Pacifica against the First Church of Christ, Scientist (the church). After a trial, judgment was entered quieting the Willards' title. The church has appealed.

Genevieve McGuigan owned two abutting lots in Pacifica known as lots 19 and 20. There was a building on lot 19, and lot 20 was vacant. McGuigan was a member of the church, which was located across the street from her lots, and she permitted it to use lot 20 for parking during services. She sold lot 19 to one Petersen, who used the building as an office. He wanted to resell the lot, so he listed it with Willard, who is a realtor. Willard expressed an interest in purchasing both lots 19 and 20, and he and Petersen signed a deposit receipt for the sale of the two lots. Soon thereafter they entered into an escrow, into which Petersen delivered a deed for both lots in fee simple.

At the time he agreed to sell lot 20 to Willard, Petersen did not own it, so he approached McGuigan with an offer to purchase it. She was willing to sell the lot provided the church could continue to use it for parking. She therefore referred the matter to the church's attorney, who drew up a provision for the deed that stated the conveyance was "subject to an easement for automobile parking during church hours

Figure 10.1
A recent aerial photo of the lots involved in *Willard*. Lot 20 (the paved parking lot) is near the lower right and remains open.

for the benefit of the church on the property at the southwest corner of the intersection of Hilton Way and Francisco Boulevard . . . such easement to run with the land only so long as the property for whose benefit the easement is given is used for church purposes." Once this clause was inserted in the deed, McGuigan sold the property to Petersen, and he recorded the deed.

Willard paid the agreed purchase price into the escrow and received Petersen's deed 10 days later. He then recorded this deed, which did not mention an easement for parking by the church. While Petersen did mention to Willard that the church would want to use lot 20 for parking, it does not appear that he told him of the easement clause contained in the deed he received from McGuigan.

Willard became aware of the easement clause several months after purchasing the property. He then commenced this action to quiet title against the church. At the trial, which was without a jury, McGuigan testified that she had bought lot 20 to provide parking for the church, and would not have sold it unless she was assured the church could thereafter continue to use it for parking. The court found that McGuigan and Petersen intended to convey an easement to the church, but that the clause they employed was ineffective for that purpose because it was invalidated by the common law rule that one cannot "reserve" an interest in property to a stranger to the title.

The rule derives from the common law notions of reservations from a grant and was based on feudal considerations. A reservation allows a grantor's whole interest in the property to pass to the grantee, but revests a newly created interest in the grantor.[1] (4 Tiffany, The Law of Real Property (3d ed. 1939) § 972.) While a reservation could theoretically vest an interest in a third party, the early common law courts vigorously rejected this possibility, apparently because they mistrusted and wished to limit conveyance by

---

1. The effect of a reservation should be distinguished from an exception, which prevents some part of the grantor's interest from passing to the grantee. The exception cannot vest an interest in the third party, and the excepted interest remains in the grantor. (6 Powell, The Law of Real Property (Rohan ed. 1971) § 892.) [This citation to Powell is unhelpful. The useful reference is Powell on Real Property § 34.04[5] (Michael A. Wolf gen. ed. 2009).—Eds.]

deed as a substitute for livery by seisin.[2] (See Harris, Reservations in Favor of Strangers to the Title (1953) 6 Okla. L. Rev. 127, 132-133.) Insofar as this mistrust was the foundation of the rule, it is clearly an inapposite feudal shackle today. Consequently, several commentators have attacked the rule as groundless and have called for its abolition. (See, e.g., Harris, supra, 6 Okla. L. Rev. at p. 154; Meyers & Williams, Oil and Gas Conveyancing; Grants and Reservations by Owners of Fractional Mineral Interests (1957) 43 Va. L. Rev. 639, 650-651; Comment, Real Property: Easements: Creation by Reservation or Exception (1948) 36 Cal. L. Rev. 470, 476; Annot., Reservation or exception in deed in favor of stranger, 88 A.L.R.2d 1199, 1202; cf. 4 Tiffany, supra, § 974, at p. 54; 2 American Law of Property (Casner ed. 1952) § 8.29, at p. 254.)

California early adhered to this common law rule. (Eldridge v. See Yup Company (1860) 17 Cal. 44.) In considering our continued adherence to it, we must realize that our courts no longer feel constricted by feudal forms of conveyancing. Rather, our primary objective in construing a conveyance is to try to give effect to the intent of the grantor. . . . In general, therefore, grants are to be interpreted in the same way as other contracts and not according to rigid feudal standards. . . . The common law rule conflicts with the modern approach to construing deeds because it can frustrate the grantor's intent. Moreover, it produces an inequitable result because the original grantee has presumably paid a reduced price for title to the encumbered property. In this case, for example, McGuigan testified that she had discounted the price she charged Petersen by about one-third because of the easement. . . .

In view of the obvious defects of the rule, this court has found methods to avoid it where applying it would frustrate the clear intention of the grantor. In Butler v. Gosling (1900) 130 Cal. 422 [62 P. 596], the court prevented the reserved title to a portion of the property from vesting in the grantee by treating the reservation as an exception to the grant. In Boyer v. Murphy (1927) 202 Cal. 23 [259 P. 38], the court, noting that its primary objective was to give effect to the grantor's intention (id., at pp. 28-29), held that the rule was inapplicable where the third party was the grantor's spouse. (See Fleming v. State Bar (1952) 38 Cal. 2d 341, 345, fn. 2 [239 P.2d 866].) Similarly, the . . . courts of other states[3] have found ways of circumventing the rule.

---

2. Our late colleague and redoubtable historian Brian Simpson told us that the court's history is wrong. Livery of seisin was required to transfer a possessory freehold estate (page 197), whereas easements were created by grant; i.e., a sealed instrument. Professor Simpson believed the rule against creating easements in third parties is traceable to the principle that only parties to a deed can take advantage of it. The same principle underlies the rule that third parties cannot sue on a contract (unless they are in privity of estate with a party). See pages 524-527, 533. —EDS.

3. (See generally Harris, Reservations in Favor of Strangers to the Title, supra, 6 Okla. L. Rev. 127, 139-150.) Some courts, like the court in Butler v. Gosling, supra, mitigate the harshness of the rule by treating the reservation as an exception that retained the interest in the grantor. (See Lemon v. Lemon (1918) 273 Mo. 484, 201 S.W. 103.) While this approach did prevent the reserved interest from passing to the grantee, it did not achieve the grantor's intention of vesting that interest in the third party. Other courts gave effect to the grantor's intention by estopping those who claimed under a chain of title including the deed containing the reservation from challenging it on the basis of the common law rule. (See Beinlein v. Johns (1898) 102 Ky. 570, 19 Ky. L.R. 1969, 44 S.W. 128; Hodge v. Boothby (1861) 48 Me. 68; Dalton v. Eller (1926) 153 Tenn. 418, 284 S.W. 68.) This approach has the effect of emasculating the common law rule without expressly abandoning it. One court found that a reservation created a trust in favor of the stranger (Burns v. Bastien (1935) 174 Okla. 40, 50 P.2d 377), but this approach seems unduly elaborate to achieve the grantor's intent. Finally, several courts, like the court in Boyer, supra, will disregard the rule entirely when the stranger is the grantor's spouse. (See Saunders v. Saunders (1940) 373 Ill. 302, 26 N.E.2d 126, 129 A.L.R. 306; Du Bois v. Judy (1920) 291 Ill. 340, 126 N.E. 104; Derham v. Hovey (1917) 195 Mich. 243, 161 N.W. 883, 21 A.L.R. 999; Glasgow v. Glasgow (1952) 221 S.C. 322, 70 S.E.2d 432.) Thus, as in California, the rule has been riddled with exceptions in other states.

The highest courts of two states have already eliminated the rule altogether, rather than repealing it piecemeal by evasion. In Townsend v. Cable (Ky. 1964) 378 S.W.2d 806, the Court of Appeals of Kentucky abandoned the rule. It said: "We have no hesitancy in abandoning this archaic and technical rule. It is entirely inconsistent with the basic principle followed in the construction of deeds, which is to determine the intention of grantor as gathered from the four corners of the instrument." (Id., at p. 808.) (See also Blair v. City of Pikeville (Ky. 1964) 384 S.W.2d 65, 66; Combs v. Hounshell (Ky. 1961) 347 S.W.2d 550, 554.) Relying on *Townsend*, the Supreme Court of Oregon, in Garza v. Grayson (1970) 255 Ore. 413 [467 P.2d 960], rejected the rule because it was "derived from a narrow and highly technical interpretation of the meaning of the terms 'reservation' and 'exception' when employed in a deed" (id., at p. 961), and did not sufficiently justify frustrating the grantor's intention in some cases even though it is riddled with exceptions, we follow the lead of Kentucky and Oregon and abandon it entirely.

Willard contends that the old rule should nevertheless be applied in this case to invalidate the church's easement because grantees and title insurers have relied upon it. He has not, however, presented any evidence to support this contention, and it is clear that the facts of this case do not demonstrate reliance on the old rule. There is no evidence that a policy of title insurance was issued, and therefore no showing of reliance by a title insurance company. Willard himself could not have relied upon the common law rule to assure him of an absolute fee because he did not even read the deed containing the reservation. This is not a case of an ancient deed where the reservation has not been asserted for many years. The church used lot 20 for parking throughout the period when Willard was purchasing the property and after he acquired title to it, and he may not claim that he was prejudiced by lack of use for an extended period of time.

The determination whether the old common law rule should be applied to grants made prior to our decision involves a balancing of equitable and policy considerations. We must balance the injustice which would result from refusing to give effect to the grantor's intent against the injustice, if any, which might result by failing to give effect to reliance on the old rule and the policy against disturbing settled titles. The record before us does not disclose any reliance upon the old common law rule, and there is no problem of an ancient title. Although in other cases the balancing of the competing interests may warrant application of the common law rule to presently existing deeds, in the instant case the balance falls in favor of the grantor's intent, and the old common law rule may not be applied to defeat her intent.

Willard also contends that the church has received no interest in this case because the clause stated only that the grant was "subject to" the church's easement, and not that the easement was either excepted or reserved. In construing this provision, however, we must look to the clause as a whole which states that the easement "is given." Even if we assume that there is some ambiguity or conflict in the clause, the trial court found on substantial evidence that the parties to the deed intended to convey the easement to the church.

The judgment is reversed.

Notes and Questions

1. *Modern authority.* Restatement (Third) of Property, Servitudes § 2.6(2) (2000), provides that an easement can be created in favor of a third party, but contrary authority in a number of states is cited in the Reporter's Note. Cases

reaffirming the common law rule that a grantor cannot reserve an easement in favor of a third party include Tripp v. Huff, 606 A.2d 792 (Me. 1992); Estate of Thomson v. Wade, 509 N.E.2d 309 (N.Y. 1987); Beachside Bungalow Preservation Assn. of Far Rockaway, Inc. v. Oceanview Associates, LLC, 753 N.Y.S.2d 133 (App. Div. 2003). See also Note, Ancient, Antiquated & Archaic: South Carolina Fails to Embrace the Rule That a Grantor May Reserve an Easement in Favor of a Third Party, 52 S.C. L. Rev. 269 (2000).

2. *Drafting to avoid the common law rule.* How would you draft documents so as to carry out Genevieve McGuigan's intent and not violate the common law rule that an easement cannot be reserved in favor of a third party? If the church had lost, would the church's attorney who drew up the deed be liable for malpractice? See Jesse Dukeminier, Cleansing the Stables of Property: A River Found at Last, 65 Iowa L. Rev. 151, 174 (1979).

3. *Reservations and exceptions.* In *Willard*, the court held that an easement can be reserved in favor of a third party but stated in footnote 1 that an easement cannot be excepted in favor of a third party. What is the difference between an exception and a reservation? How did the court determine that Genevieve McGuigan had reserved rather than excepted an easement? (The deed said "subject to an easement.")

A *reservation* is a provision in a deed creating some *new* servitude which did not exist before as an independent interest. For example, O conveys Blackacre to A, reserving a 20-foot-wide easement of way along the south boundary of Blackacre. The easement did not exist as an independent interest prior to the conveyance by O. An *exception* is a provision in a deed that excludes from the grant some *preexisting* servitude on the land. For example, after the above conveyance, A conveys Blackacre to B, except for the easement previously reserved by O.

When the grantor attempted to reserve an easement at early common law, there were difficulties. A new right, such as some feudal obligation or the payment of rent, could be reserved if it was to issue out of the land granted, but the English courts held that an easement could not be reserved because it did not issue out of the land granted. English courts ultimately found a way around this obstacle by inventing the *regrant theory.* They held that an easement "reserved" by the grantor was not a reservation at all (which would be void), but a *regrant* of an easement by the grantee to the grantor. Thus a deed from O to A and her heirs, reserving an easement in O, was treated as if it were two deeds. The deed grants A a fee simple; then A is treated as granting an easement back to O.

The regrant theory may have been a brilliant way around the crabbed interpretation of what could be reserved in a grant, but it brought a new difficulty of its own. Because a reserved easement theoretically involved a regrant by the grantee, the Statute of Frauds required the deed to be signed by the grantee as well as by the grantor. In this country, where deeds are usually signed only by the grantor, this could have caused trouble. But American courts deftly held that the grantee had, by accepting the deed, made it her own and adopted the seal and signature of the grantor! Thus was a legal fiction invented to overcome a faulty premise.

Now that you understand the difference between a reservation and an exception, does the court's statement in footnote 1 that an exception cannot vest an easement in a third party make sense?

4. *Appurtenant or in gross?* Is the church's easement in the *Willard* case *appurtenant* or *in gross*? If the Christian Science Church sold the church on Hilton

Way and Francisco Boulevard to a Methodist Church, and erected a new church a block away to the west on Hilton Way, would the easement belong to the Methodist Church or to the Christian Science Church, or would the easement be extinguished?

An easement can have a duration comparable to any of the possessory estates. An easement can be in fee simple (perpetual duration), or for life, or for a term of years. How would you describe the duration of the easement in *Willard*?

Special issues with easements in gross. Easements in gross raise special concerns that appurtenant easements do not. Two in particular stand out.

→ *Assignability.* The transferability of easements in gross raises special problems. The benefits and burdens of appurtenant easements pass automatically to assignees of the land to which they are appurtenant, if the parties so intend and the burdened party has notice of the easement. Where the benefit is in gross, however, the benefit may not be assignable. The first Restatement of Property § 489 (1944) provided that an easement in gross can be assigned if it is of a commercial character (used primarily for economic benefit rather than personal satisfaction). Restatement (Third) of Property, Servitudes §§ 4.6(1)(c), 5.8 (2000), provides that all easements in gross are assignable regardless of their commercial character. Most recent cases permit any easement in gross to be assignable if the parties so intended. See O'Donovan v. McIntosh, 728 A.2d 681 (Me. 1999).

→ *Divisibility.* Assignability leads to a second question about easements in gross: may the benefit holder divide the benefit with another person? The general view is that an easement in gross is divisible when the creating instrument so indicates or when the easement is exclusive. The term "exclusive" in this context means that the easement owner has the sole right to engage in the activity that the easement permits.

Excessive division of the benefit of an easement in gross could lead to a substantial increase in the burden on the servient estate. Restatement (Third) of Property, supra, § 5.9, provides that easements in gross may be divided unless contrary to the intent of the parties creating the easement or unless the division unreasonably increases the burden on the servient estate. Accord, Orange County v. Citgo Pipeline Co., 934 S.W.2d 472 (Tex. Civ. App. 1996). On this view, the benefit of an easement in gross may be divided and utilized independently by its holders, assuming that this is not contrary to the intent of the original parties and that division would not place an unreasonable burden on the servient estate. However, the Restatement points out that division of benefits in gross is more likely than subdivision of appurtenant benefits to run counter to the servient owner's expectations because division permits independent use of the easement in gross by each of the transferees. Restatement (Third) of Property, supra, § 5.9 comment a. Under the Restatement's approach, the exclusivity or non-exclusivity of the easement is still relevant. "Division of an exclusive easement is less likely to be contrary to the intent of the parties than division of a non-exclusive easement." Id.

Licenses and easements by estoppel. An easement must be distinguished from a license. A *license* is oral or written permission given by the occupant of land allowing the licensee to do some act that otherwise would be a trespass. Licenses are very common: the plumber fixing a drain, the guest coming to dinner, and the purchaser of a theater ticket all have licenses. This privilege to use the land resembles an easement, but a license is revocable, whereas an easement is not.

There are two distinct exceptions to the rule that a license is revocable. First, a license coupled with an interest cannot be revoked. A license coupled with an interest is one that is incidental to ownership of a chattel on the licensor's land. For example, *O* grants to *A* the right to take timber from Blackacre, owned by *O*. *A* has an interest (a *profit*) and an irrevocable license to enter the land and take the timber. The irrevocability of a license coupled with an interest bears some resemblance to the doctrine of easements by necessity. (See pages 499-501.) The second exception is a license that becomes irrevocable under the rules of estoppel. A license that cannot be revoked is treated as an easement in Restatement (Third) of Property, Servitudes § 1.2(4) (2000).

MUND v. ENGLISH

Court of Appeals of Oregon, 1984
684 P.2d 1248

ROSSMAN, J. This case arises from a family dispute over the ownership of a well. Plaintiffs are the son and daughter-in-law of defendant. In 1977, plaintiffs and defendant, together with the deceased husband of defendant, purchased adjoining one acre parcels of property near Pendleton. In that year, a water well was drilled on defendant's property. Equipment and pipes were installed so that plaintiffs and defendant received water from the one well. In less than a year after the installation, the parties began to quarrel about their rights to the well and water. The fighting has continued since then, culminating in this suit for declaratory judgment and specific performance.

Plaintiffs contend that, from the beginning, their interest in the well was to have been a permanent and irrevocable interest. Defendant claims that plaintiffs' rights were not permanent and were subject to certain conditions. The trial court found for defendant. On de novo review, we agree with the trial court that plaintiffs failed to prove that the parties had agreed that defendant would deed a one-half interest in the well to plaintiffs, as well as a permanent easement over the land for the installation of the water system. There simply was no meeting of the minds. However, the facts clearly show that defendant did grant an irrevocable license to plaintiffs, and the trial judge was in error in refusing to allow plaintiffs' motion to amend the pleadings to conform to the evidence. Accordingly, we reverse. . . .

Defendant argues that an irrevocable license can only be established when there is proof of an agreement for a permanent easement which is taken out of the Statute of Frauds (requiring a writing) by part performance. Defendant says that the proof is lacking here. Defendant's argument misses the basis of an irrevocable license. Although it is true that, in most jurisdictions, an oral license may be revoked, Oregon has consistently held that, when a licensee makes valuable improvements on the basis of a promise, the licensor will not be permitted to assert that the license could be revoked.

An irrevocable license does not depend on proof of the agreement of the parties but arises by operation of law to prevent an injustice. . . .

. . . Defendant admits that she and her deceased husband granted plaintiffs the right to use the well and to install a pipeline to plaintiffs' property. The testimony of plaintiffs and defendant as to the permanency of this agreement is in direct dispute, and the testimony of the attorney who was to draft an agreement for the parties was indeterminant. The attorney admitted that he could not find a record of his meeting and that he had only a general recollection of the event. He recalled a lack of agreement as to whether the parties wanted a contract or a deed of easement, but he could not recall any specifics.

However, the circumstances here show a permanent arrangement. Plaintiffs and defendant shared the installation costs of the well and water system. Plaintiff Mr. Mund and defendant's husband worked together installing the system. The parties have continued to share operating expenses. Even more significantly, plaintiffs secured a $40,000 commercial loan in 1977 and constructed a residence on their property. There was, and is, no other source of domestic water for plaintiffs. The improvements made by plaintiffs clearly show their reliance on a permanent agreement. The law will not permit defendant to claim that she can withdraw the license to use the well.

Reversed and remanded for entry of a decree granting plaintiffs a one-half interest in the water well and water system on defendant's property, granting plaintiffs an easement over defendant's property for the purpose of access to the water system and requiring plaintiffs and defendant to share equally the cost of maintaining the system.

Notes and Questions

1. *The basis of easements by estoppel.* Section 2.10 of the Restatement (Third) states:

   If justice can be avoided only by establishment of a servitude, the owner or occupier of land is estopped to deny the existence of a servitude burdening the land when:

   (1) the owner or occupier permitted another to use that land under circumstances in which it was reasonable to foresee that the user would substantially change position believing that the permission would not be revoked, and the user did substantially change position in reasonable reliance on that belief; or
   (2) the owner or occupier represented that the land was burdened by a servitude under circumstances in which it was reasonable to foresee that the person to whom the representation was made would substantially change position on the basis of that representation, and the person did substantially change position in reasonable reliance on that representation.

Would the facts of *Mund* have warranted application of this provision? Did the case meet the standard that "justice can be avoided only by establishment of a servitude"?

2. *Status of the easement by estoppel/irrevocable license doctrines.* Most courts call the interest involved in *Mund* an "irrevocable license." Other courts call it an "easement by estoppel." The important point is the estoppel principle. So, § 2.10 comment e of the Restatement states, "Normally the change in position

that triggers application of the rule stated in this subsection is an investment in improvements either to the servient estate or to other land of the investor." See also id. illustration 5.

Some courts do not recognize either doctrine, on the basis that the Statute of Frauds requires a writing. In Henry v. Dalton, 151 A.2d 361 (R.I. 1959), the court explained:

> We are of the opinion that in reason and justice the better rule is expressed in the case of Crosdale v. Lanigan, 129 N.Y. 604, 29 N.E. 824. . . . The court stated the rule . . . as follows: "[A] parol license to do an act on the land of the licensor, while it justifies anything done by the licensee before revocation, is, nevertheless, revocable at the option of the licensor, and this, although the intention was to confer a continuing right and money had been expended by the licensee upon the faith of the license. This is plainly the rule of the statute. It is also, we believe, the rule required by public policy. It prevents the burdening of lands with restrictions founded upon oral agreements, easily misunderstood. It gives security and certainty to titles. . . ." [29 N.E. at 825.]
>
> The right which complainants seek to establish in the land of the respondent is essentially an easement and should be the subject of a grant, expressed in the solemnity of a written instrument. It is no hardship for one in the position of these complainants either to secure an easement in perpetuity in the manner provided by the statute, or, such being refused, to weigh the advantages inuring to them as against the uncertainty implicit in the making of expenditures on the basis of a revocable license.

3. *Duration of an irrevocable license.* For how long does a license made irrevocable by estoppel last? As long as necessary to prevent unjust enrichment by the licensor? That appeared to be the position of the first Restatement (the license remains irrevocable "to the extent reasonably necessary to realize upon [the] expenditures," Restatement of Property § 519(4) (1944)). Restatement (Third) of Property, however, abandons that position in favor of the view that "the irrevocable license is treated the same as any other easement," unless the parties intended or reasonably expected that it would remain irrevocable only so long as reasonably necessary to recover expenditures. Restatement (Third) of Property, Servitudes ch. 4 Introductory Note, at 496 (2000).

VAN SANDT v. ROYSTER
Supreme Court of Kansas, 1938
83 P.2d 698

ALLEN, J. The action was brought to enjoin defendants from using and maintaining an underground lateral sewer drain through and across plaintiff's land. The case was tried by the court, judgment was rendered in favor of defendants, and plaintiff appeals.

In the city of Chanute, Highland Avenue running north and south, intersects Tenth street running east and west. In the early part of 1904 Laura A.J. Bailey was the owner of a plot of ground lying east of Highland Avenue and south of Tenth Street. Running east from Highland avenue and facing north on Tenth Street the lots are numbered respectively, 19, 20, and 4. In 1904 the residence of Mrs. Bailey was on lot 4 on the east part of her land.

In the latter part of 1903 or the early part of 1904, the city of Chanute constructed a public sewer in Highland Avenue west of lot 19. About the same time a private lateral drain was constructed from the Bailey residence on lot 4 running in a westerly direction through and across lots 20 and 19 to the public sewer.

On January 15, 1904, Laura A.J. Bailey conveyed lot 19 to John J. Jones, by general warranty deed with the usual covenants against encumbrances, and containing no exceptions or reservations. Jones erected a dwelling on the north part of the lot. In 1920 Jones conveyed the north 156 feet of lot 19 to Carl D. Reynolds; in 1924 Reynolds conveyed to the plaintiff, who has owned and occupied the premises since that time.

In 1904 Laura A.J. Bailey conveyed lot 20 to one Murphy, who built a house thereon, and by mesne conveyances the title passed to the defendant, Louise H. Royster. The deed to Murphy was a general warranty deed without exceptions or reservations. The defendant Gray has succeeded to the title to lot 4 upon which the old Bailey home stood at the time Laura A.J. Bailey sold lots 19 and 20.

> ### Sidebar
>
> The residence on lot 4, locally known as "Gray's Mansion," was originally built in 1880 by Laura Bailey's husband, Mahlon Bailey, a surgeon who later became a prominent banker in Chanute. There are six red brick chimneys located at various points on the house. Reportedly, many townspeople bemoan the addition of these chimneys because they block the view of the ornate cupola. We are grateful to Professor Greg Vetter and his wife, Dr. Christy Vetter (a native of Chanute), for providing us with this information.

In March, 1936, plaintiff discovered his basement flooded with sewage and filth to a depth of six or eight inches, and upon investigation he found for the first time that there existed on and across his property a sewer drain extending in an easterly direction across the property of Royster to the property of Gray. The refusal of defendants to cease draining and discharging their sewage across plaintiff's land resulted in this lawsuit. . . .[4]

The drain pipe in the lateral sewer was several feet under the surface of the ground. There was nothing visible on the ground in the rear of the houses to indicate the existence of the drain or the connection of the drain with the houses.

As a conclusion of law the court found that "an appurtenant easement existed in the said lateral sewer as to all three of the properties involved in the controversy here." Plaintiff's prayer for relief was denied and it was decreed that plaintiff be restrained from interfering in any way with the lateral drain or sewer.

Plaintiff contends that the evidence fails to show that an easement was ever created in his land, and, assuming there was an easement created as alleged, that he took the premises free from the burden of the easement for the reason that he was a bona fide purchaser, without notice, actual or constructive.

Defendants contend: (1) That an easement was created by implied reservation on the severance of the servient from the dominant estate of the deed from Mrs. Bailey to Jones; (2) there is a valid easement by prescription.

---

4. Professor Vetter reports that several residents of Chanute have told him stories about Mss. Van Sandt and Royster dumping buckets of sewage on each other's front porch. The court mentioned only the Van Sandt sewage problem, but it is possible that both houses experienced clogging and that the court was either misinformed or simply did not report the full facts. —Eds.

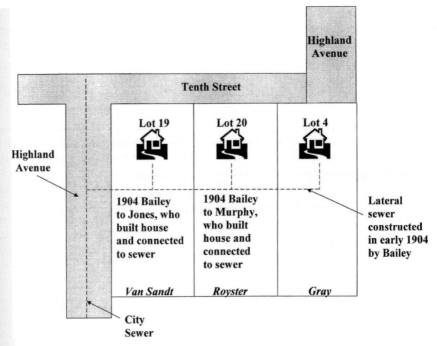

Figure 10-2

In finding No. 11, the court found that the lateral sewer "was an appurtenance to the properties belonging to plaintiff and Louise Royster, and the same is necessary to the reasonable use and enjoyment of the said properties of the parties."

As an easement is an interest which a person has in land in the possession of another, it necessarily follows that an owner cannot have an easement in his own land. (Johnston v. City of Kingman, 141 Kan. 131, 39 P.2d 924; Ferguson v. Ferguson, 106 Kan. 823, 189 Pac. 925.) However, an owner may make use of one part of his land for the benefit of another part, and this is very frequently spoken of as a quasi easement.

When one thus utilizes part of his land for the benefit of another part, it is frequently said that a quasi easement exists, the part of the land which is benefited being referred to as the "quasi dominant tenement" and the part which is utilized for the benefit of the other part being referred to as the "quasi servient tenement." The so-called quasi easement is evidently not a legal relation in any sense, but the expression is a convenient one to describe the particular mode in which the owner utilizes one part of the land for the benefit of the other. . . .

If the owner of land, one part of which is subject to a quasi easement in favor of another part, conveys the quasi dominant tenement, an easement corresponding to such quasi easement is ordinarily regarded as thereby vested in the grantee of the land, provided, it is said, the quasi easement is of an apparent, continuous and necessary character. [2 Tiffany on Real Property, 2d ed., 1272, 1273.]

A view of houses on lots 19, 20, and 4 (right to left) from the intersection of Highland Avenue and Tenth Street

Lot 4 (locally known as "Gray's Mansion")

Following the famous case of Pyer v. Carter, 1 Hurl & N. 916, some of the English cases and many early American cases held that upon the transfer of the quasi-servient tenement there was an implied reservation of an easement in favor of the conveyor. Under the doctrine of Pyer v. Carter, no distinction was made between an implied reservation and an implied grant.

The case, however, was overthrown in England by Suffield v. Brown, 4 De G.J. & S. 185, and Wheeldon v. Burrows, L. R. 12 Ch. D. 31. In the former case the court said:

> It seems to me more reasonable and just to hold that if the grantor intends to reserve any right over the property granted, it is his duty to reserve it expressly in the grant, rather than to limit and cut down the operation of a plain grant (which is not pretended to be otherwise than in conformity with the contract between the parties), by the fiction of an implied reservation. If this plain rule be adhered to, men will know what they have to trust, and will place confidence in the language of their contracts and assurances. . . . But I cannot agree that the grantor can derogate from his own absolute grant so as to claim rights over the thing granted, even if they were at the time of the grant continuous and apparent easements enjoyed by an adjoining tenement which remains the property of him the grantor. [pp. 190, 194.]

Many American courts of high standing assert that the rule regarding implied grants and implied reservations is reciprocal and that the rule applies with equal force and in like circumstances to both grants and reservations. (Washburn on Easements, 4th ed. 75; Miller v. Skaggs, 79 W. Va. 645, 91 S.E. 536, Ann. Cas. 1918 D. 929.)

On the other hand, perhaps a majority of the cases hold that in order to establish an easement by implied reservation in favor of the grantor the easement must be one of strict necessity, even when there was an existing drain or sewer at the time of the severance.

Thus in Howley v. Chaffee et al., 88 Vt. 468, 474, 93 Atl. 120, L.R.A. 1915 D. 1010, the court said:

> With the character and extent of implied grants, we now have nothing to do. We are here only concerned with determining the circumstances which will give rise to an implied reservation. On this precise question the authorities are in conflict. Courts of high standing assert that the rule regarding implied grants and implied reservations of "visible servitudes" is reciprocal, and that it applies with equal force and in like circumstances to both grants and reservations. But upon a careful consideration of the whole subject, studied in the light of the many cases in which it is discussed, we are convinced that there is a clear distinction between implied grants and implied reservations, and that this distinction is well founded in principle and well supported by authority. It is apparent that no question of public policy is here involved, as we have seen is the case where a way of necessity is involved. To say that a grantor reserves to himself something out of the property granted, wholly by implication, not only offends the rule that one shall not derogate from his own grant, but conflicts with the grantor's language in the conveyance, which, by the rule, is to be taken against him, and is wholly inconsistent with the theory on which our registry laws are based. If such an illogical result is to follow an absolute grant, it must be by virtue of some legal rule of compelling force. The correct rule is, we think, that where, as here, one grants a parcel of land by metes and bounds, by a deed containing full covenants of warranty and without any express reservation, there can be no reservation by implication, unless the

easement claimed is one of strict necessity, within the meaning of that term as explained in Dee v. King, 73 Vt. 375.

See, also, Brown v. Fuller, 165 Mich. 162, 130 N.W. 621, 33 L.R.A., n.s., 459, Ann. Cas. 1912 C 853. The cases are collected in 58 A.L.R. 837.

We are inclined to the view that the circumstance that the claimant of the easement is the grantor instead of the grantee, is but one of many factors to be considered in determining whether an easement will arise by implication. An easement created by implication arises as an inference of the intentions of the parties to a conveyance of land. The inference is drawn from the circumstances under which the conveyance was made rather than from the language of the conveyance. The easement may arise in favor of the conveyor or the conveyee. In the Restatement of Property, Tentative Draft No. 8, section 28, the factors determining the implication of an easement are stated:

> Sec. 28. Factors Determining Implication of Easements or Profits. In determining whether the circumstances under which a conveyance of land is made imply an easement or a profit, the following factors are important: *(a)* whether the claimant is the conveyor or the conveyee, *(b)* the terms of the conveyance, *(c)* the consideration given for it, *(d)* whether the claim is made against a simultaneous conveyee, *(e)* the extent of necessity of the easement or the profit to the claimant, *(f)* whether reciprocal benefits result to the conveyor and the conveyee, *(g)* the manner in which the land was used prior to its conveyance, and *(h)* the extent to which the manner of prior use was or might have been known to the parties.

Comment j, under the same section, reads:

> *The extent to which the manner of prior use was or might have been known to the parties.* The effect of the prior use as a circumstance in implying, upon a severance of possession by conveyance, an easement or a profit results from an inference as to the intention of the parties. To draw such an inference, the prior use must have been known to the parties at the time of the conveyance, or, at least, have been within the possibility of their knowledge at the time. Each party to a conveyance is bound not merely to what he intended, but also to what he might reasonably have foreseen the other party to the conveyance expected. Parties to a conveyance may, therefore, be assumed to intend the continuance of uses known to them which are in a considerable degree necessary to the continued usefulness of the land. Also they will be assumed to know and to contemplate the continuance of reasonably necessary uses which have so altered the premises as to make them apparent upon reasonably prudent investigation. The degree of necessity required to imply an easement in favor of the conveyor is greater than that required in the case of the conveyee (see comment b). Yet, even in the case of the conveyor, the implication from necessity will be aided by a previous use made apparent by the physical adaptation of the premises to it.

Illustrations:

> 9. *A* is the owner of two adjacent tracts of land, Blackacre and Whiteacre. Blackacre has on it a dwelling house. Whiteacre is unimproved. Drainage from the house to a public sewer is across Whiteacre. This fact is unknown to *A*, who purchased the two tracts with the house already built. By reasonable effort, *A* might discover the manner of drainage and the location of the drain. *A* sells Blackacre to *B*, who has been informed as to the manner of drainage

and the location of the drain and assumes that *A* is aware of it. There is created by implication an easement of drainage in favor of *B* across Whiteacre.

10. Same facts as in illustration 9, except that both *A* and *B* are unaware of the manner of drainage and the location of the drain. However, each had reasonable opportunity to learn of such facts. A holding that there is created by implication an easement of drainage in favor of *B* across Whiteacre is proper.

At the time John J. Jones purchased lot 19 he was aware of the lateral sewer, and knew that it was installed for the benefit of the lots owned by Mrs. Bailey, the common owner. The easement was necessary to the comfortable enjoyment of the grantor's property. If land may be used without an easement, but cannot be used without disproportionate effort and expense, an easement may still be implied in favor of either the grantor or grantee on the basis of necessity alone. This is the situation as found by the trial court.

Neither can it be claimed that plaintiff purchased without notice. At the time plaintiff purchased the property he and his wife made a careful and thorough inspection of the property. They knew the house was equipped with modern plumbing and that the plumbing had to drain into a sewer. Under the facts as found by the court, we think the purchaser was charged with notice of the lateral sewer. It was an apparent easement as that term is used in the books. (Wiesel v. Smira, 49 R.I. 246, 142 Atl. 148, 58 A.L.R. 818; 19 C.J. 868.)

The author of the annotation on Easements by Implication in 58 A.L.R. 832, states the rule as follows:

> While there is some conflict of authority as to whether existing drains, pipes, and sewers may be properly characterized as apparent, within the rule as to apparent or visible easements, the majority of the cases which have considered the question have taken the view that appearance and visibility are not synonymous, and that the fact that the pipe, sewer, or drain may be hidden underground does not negative its character as an apparent condition; at least, where the appliances connected with and leading to it are obvious.

As we are clear that an easement by implication was created under the facts as found by the trial court, it is unnecessary to discuss the question of prescription.

The judgment is affirmed.

Notes and Questions

1. *Easements implied from a prior existing use (or "quasi-easement").* As *Van Sandt* illustrates, courts will imply an easement on the basis of an apparent and continuous (or permanent) use of a portion of the tract existing when the tract is divided. The existing use is often described as a "quasi-easement." The easement is implied to protect the probable expectations of the grantor and grantee that the existing use will continue after the transfer. The inference that the parties intended to create an easement is not conclusive, however. It may be negated by contrary evidence. See Zotos v. Armstrong, 828 N.E.2d 551 (Mass. App. 2005).

2. *Requirements of an implied easement based on a prior existing use.* The usual requirements that must be satisfied in order for an easement to be implied from a preexisting use are: (1) initial unity of ownership of the now dominant and servient estates, followed by severance of the title to the dominant and servient estates; (2) an existing, apparent, and continuous use of one parcel for the benefit of the other, existing at the time of the severance; and (3) reasonable necessity

for that use. See *Favart v. Ouellette*, 2020 WL 2601921 (N.H. 2020). Necessity is a requirement because it reflects the probable intention of the parties as to whether the existing use is to continue.

Was the use in *Van Sandt* apparent?

3. *By grant or by reservation—who's claiming the easement, the grantee or the grantor?* Does it matter whether the easement is claimed by the grantor or the grantee? It may. Take these two cases:

> ### In Brief
>
> The traditional requirements for an easement implied from a prior existing use are as follows:
>
> ▶ Initial unity of ownership, followed by severance of title
> ▶ An existing, apparent, and continuous use of the servient parcel for the benefit of the dominant parcel at the time of the severance
> ▶ Reasonable necessity to continue the prior use at the time of severance

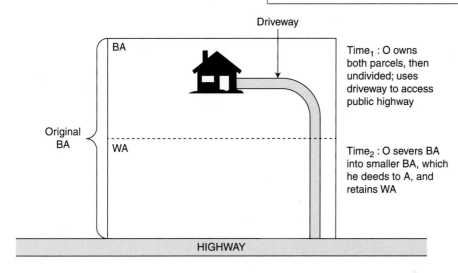

IMPLIED GRANT

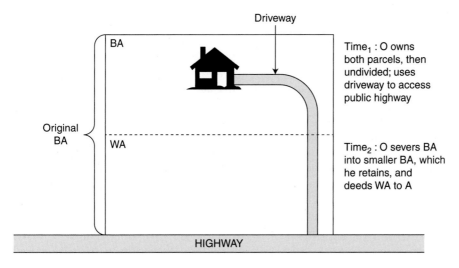

IMPLIED RESERVATION

The cases are the same except that the parties are reversed. In Case 1, *A*, the grantee from *O*, is the one who claims the easement over the parcel that *O* retained. In Case 2, the claimant is *O*, the grantor of Whiteacre, the servient parcel. In Case 2, *O* claims that she impliedly retained an easement over the parcel that she deeded to *A*. In this situation, some courts have been more reluctant to imply an easement, on the view that doing so detracts from what the deed apparently conveys to the grantee. So, several jurisdictions, including New York and Texas, follow the old rule that strict necessity is required for implied easements in favor of the grantor. See Houston Bellaire, Ltd. v. TCP LB Portfolio I, L.P., 981 S.W.2d 916 (Tex. Civ. App. 1998). Indeed, at least one court has ruled that reserved easements in favor of the grantor cannot arise on the basis of necessity at all, but only on the basis of a prior use. See Northland Realty, LLC v. Crawford, 953 A.2d 359 (Me. 2008). However, the weight of authority today holds that only reasonable necessity is required for an implied easement, regardless of whether the easement is implied in favor of the grantor or the grantee.

4. *Extinguishment of the implied easement.* If the dominant parcel and the servient parcel come into the same ownership, the easement is extinguished altogether. It will not be revived by a severance of the united title into the former dominant and servient parcels. If the united title is subsequently redivided, a new easement by implication can arise if the circumstances at that time indicate a new easement was intended.

OTHEN v. ROSIER

Supreme Court of Texas, 1950
226 S.W.2d 622

BREWSTER, J. Petitioner, Albert Othen, brought this suit to enforce a roadway easement on lands of respondents, Estella Rosier et al., claiming the easement both of necessity and by prescription.

The land of both parties is a part of the Tone Survey of 2493 acres, all of which was formerly owned by one Hill. [The Rosiers own tracts of 100 acres and 16.31 acres, over which Othen claims an easement. Along the west side of the Rosiers' 100 acres runs Belt Line Road, a public highway running north and south. Othen owns tracts of 60 acres and 53 acres, lying to the east of, and contiguous to, the Rosiers' land (see Figure 10-3).

The chronological order of the conveyances of these tracts is as follows. First, Hill conveyed the 100-acre tract on August 26, 1896; by mesne conveyances this tract came into the hands of the Rosiers in 1924. Second, Hill conveyed the 60-acre tract in 1897, and by mesne conveyances Othen acquired it in 1904. These two conveyances left Hill owning the 53-acre tract and the 16.31-acre tract (and possibly other land). On the same day, January 26, 1899, Hill conveyed the 53-acre tract and the 16.31-acre tract to separate purchasers, who conveyed the 53 acres to Othen in 1913 and the 16.31 acres to the Rosiers in 1924.]

The 1896 deed from Hill conveying the 100-acre parcel

. . . The Tone Survey touches three roads: the Belt Line Road, which runs along its west side; the Duncanville Road, which borders it on the south; and the Fish Creek Road, which is its north boundary. But Othen's 113 acres is not contiguous to any of them; so he must cross somebody else's land to get out to a highway. That he had accomplished before the happening which precipitated this litigation by going through a gate in the west line of his 60 acres and in the east line of Rosiers' 16.31 acres, a short but unproved distance south of the south line of Rosiers' 100 acres; thence west-northwesterly across the 16.31 acres into a fenced lane which runs along the south side of Rosiers' 100 acres; thence through this lane to a gate, which opens into the Belt Line Road. Near this gate and in the southwest corner of the 100 acres was the Rosiers' dwelling house, orchard, stock lots and barns. The Rosiers travel and use the lane above described for such purposes as go with the operation of a farm, as well as for their stock to travel to and from the 16.31 acres, which they use as a pasture and from which they get fire wood. On the 16.31 acres is a tenant house, which has been occupied some of the 18 or 20 years previous to the trial by tenants of the Rosiers; and they have made the same use of the lane as Othen has made. The south fence of this lane was built about 1895. Its north fence and the outside gate were constructed about 1906. Before Othen bought his 60 acres in 1904 he had lived on it for two years as a tenant and had moved away for about a year; and he has continuously used the disputed roadway to get to and from the highway from and to his home.

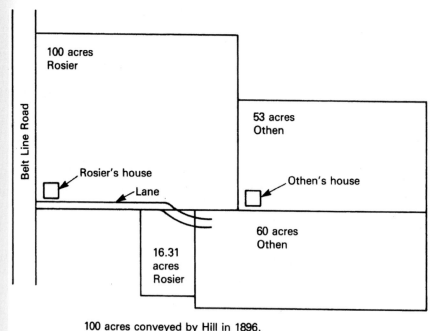

100 acres conveyed by Hill in 1896.
60 acres conveyed by Hill in 1897.
53 acres and 16.31 acres conveyed by Hill in 1899.

Figure 10-3

It seems undisputed that the Rosiers made whatever repairs were necessary to keep the land usable. And, so far as the record shows, nobody else recognized any obligation or claimed any right so to keep it. The surface waters flowing into the lane had cut out a large ditch which threatened to encroach across the roadway and render it impassable unless a bridge should be built across it, and these waters threatened erosion damage to Rosiers' cultivated land. To remedy that situation the Rosiers caused a levee 300 feet long to be constructed as close as possible to the south fence of the lane, with something like half of it in the lane and the other half curving southeasterly into the 16.31 acres. This levee impounded the waters draining southward off Rosiers' 100 acres and made the lane so muddy that for weeks at a time it was impassable except by horseback, thereby, Othen alleged, depriving him of ingress and egress to and from his farm. So he filed this suit praying a temporary writ of injunction enjoining the Rosiers from further maintaining this levee and a "mandatory writ of injunction commanding and enjoining and restraining the said defendant from further interfering with" his "use of such easement and roadway" and for damages.

The trial court found that Othen had an easement of necessity and adjudged it to him "upon, over and across" land of the Rosiers beginning at the northeast corner of the 16.31 acres and extending westward "along the said 16.31 acre tract and having a width of approximately 40 feet" to a point in its north boundary immediately east of the northwest corner of the 16.31 acres, thence across that boundary line and westward along the south boundary line of Rosiers' 100 acres to its southwest corner and into the Belt Line Road. The judgment further ordered the Rosiers "to take such action as is necessary to put said easement and roadway, so described, in as usable a condition as same was prior to the erection of said levee."

The Court of Civil Appeals . . . concluded that Othen has no easement either of necessity or by prescription and rendered judgment for the Rosiers, Chief Justice Bond dissenting. 221 S.W.2d 594. That conclusion is attacked here in two points of error.

In support of his claim to an easement of necessity, Othen quotes from 15 Tex. Jur., Sec. 16. p. 785, as follows:

> Furthermore, the grantor impliedly reserves for himself a right of way where he sells land surrounded by other land of which he is owner, and to which he can have access or egress only through the granted premises, and the servient estate is charged with the burden in the hands of any vendee holding under the conveyance.[5]

That statement is in line with the recent holding by this court in Bains v. Parker, 143 Texas 57, 182 S.W.2d 397: "Where a vendor retains a tract of land which is surrounded partly by the tract conveyed and partly by the lands of a stranger, there is an implied reservation of a right of way by necessity over the land conveyed where grantor has no other way out." In 28 C.J.S., Easements, §§ 34 and 35, pp. 694 et seq., it is made clear that before an easement can be held to be created by implied reservation it must be shown: (1) that there was a unity of ownership of the alleged dominant and servient estates; (2) that the roadway is a necessity, not a mere convenience; and (3) that

---

5. Blackstone put it this way: "[I]f a man grants me a piece of ground in the middle of his field, he at the same time tacitly and impliedly gives me a way to come to it; and I may cross his land for that purpose without trespass." 2 William Blackstone, Commentaries *36. — EDS.

the necessity existed at the time of severance of the two estates. And see 17 Am. Jur., Easements, §§ 43 and 49, pp. 953 and 963.

Under the foregoing authorities, Othen's claim to an implied reservation of an easement in a roadway means that when Hill, the original owner, sold the 116.31 acres to the Rosiers[6] it was then necessary, not merely convenient, for him to travel over it from the 113 acres now owned by Othen in order to get to and from the Belt Line Road. In determining that question we shall ignore the Duncanville Road to the South, which was established in 1910, as well as the Fish Creek Road to the north, although the record is silent as to when the latter came into existence.

As already stated, the entire Tone Survey of 2493 acres was owned by one Hill, in whom was unity of ownership of the lands now owned by the parties to this suit. On August 26, 1896, he sold the 100 acres in question to Rosiers' predecessors in title, retaining the south 60 acres now owned by Othen, which he conveyed on February 20, 1897. In the deed of date August 26, 1896, did he impliedly reserve the roadway easement from the 60 acres, which he retained over and across the 16.31 acres which he did not convey until January 26, 1899, thence on and along the south side of the 100 acres to the Belt Line Road? Obviously, no such easement arose as to the 16.31 acres over which the trial court decreed Othen a roadway, because Hill did not part with his title to it until two years and five months after he sold the 100 acres and about two years after he sold the 60 acres which Othen now owns; one cannot be said to have an easement in lands, the fee simple title to which is in himself. Alley v. Carleton, 29 Texas 74, 94 Am. Dec. 260. Under the record before us we cannot hold that petitioner has shown any implied easement as to the 100 acres by reason of the deed of August 26, 1896, because the record nowhere shows that the roadway along the south line of the 100 acres was a necessity on the date of that deed, rather than a mere convenience. The burden to prove that was on Othen. Bains v. Parker, supra. There was testimony that it was the only outlet to a public road since about 1900 and for the "last 40 years"; *but there was none as to the situation on August 26, 1896.* One Posey did testify that the owner of the "Othen land" (necessarily the 60 acres) in 1897 "came out up across the south side of the place to the road there," but he did not testify that it was then the only roadway out. On that proposition his testimony was: "Q. Now, then, *is* there any other outlet from Mr. Othen's place to a highway, outside of the road—to a public road? A. Well, I don't know of any." (Italics ours.) The record does not show just how much of the Tone Survey Hill owned when he conveyed the 100 acres on August 26, 1896, but it does appear from a stipulation of the parties that he owned as much as 1350 acres of it until January 26, 1899; and Othen's 53 acres and Rosiers' 16.31 acres were a part of that tract. So, for all the record shows, Hill may easily have been able to cross the 53 acres and around north of the 100 acres on to the Belt Line Road, or he may as easily have been able to go from the 16.31 acres southwesterly to that road across land which he still owned. Certainly Othen should have excluded any such possibility by proof if he would raise an implied reservation in derogation of the warranties in Hill's deed of date August 26, 1896. Rights claimed in derogation of the warranties are implied with great caution, hence they should be made clearly to appear. Sellers v. Texas Cent. Ry. Co., 81 Texas 458, 17 S.W. 32, 13 L.R.A. 657; Scarborough v. Anderson Bros. Const. Co. (Civ. App.), 90 S.W.2d 305 (er. dism.).

---

6. The court misspeaks here. As the court itself makes clear later in the opinion, Hill did not convey either the 100 acres or the 16.31 acres directly to the Rosiers, but to intermediate purchasers who then conveyed their respective parcels to the Rosiers in 1924.—EDS.

What we have said determines Othen's claim to a way of necessity; such an easement necessarily can arise only from an implied grant or implied reservation. This results from [the] rule that the mere fact that the claimant's land is completely surrounded by the land of another does not, of itself, give the former a way of necessity over the land of the latter, where there is no privity of ownership. . . .

It is dependent upon an implied grant or reservation, and cannot exist unless it is affirmatively shown that there was formerly unity of ownership of the alleged dominant and servient estates, for no one can have a way of necessity over the land of a stranger. Necessity alone, without reference to any relations between the respective owners of the land, is not sufficient to create such a right. [Ward v. Bledsoe (Civ. App.), 105 S.W.2d 1116.]

Petitioner's other point complains of the holding of the Court of Civil Appeals that, as a matter of law, he has no easement by prescription.

An important essential in the acquisition of a prescriptive right is an adverse use of the easement.

Generally, the hostile and adverse character of the user necessary to establish an easement by prescription is the same as that which is necessary to establish title by adverse possession. If the enjoyment is consistent with the right of the owner of the tenement, it confers no right in opposition to such ownership.

17 Am. Jur., Easements, Sec. 63, p. 974, citing cases from 22 jurisdictions, among which are Weber v. Chaney (Civ. App.), 5 S.W.2d 213 (er. ref.), and Callan v. Walters (Civ. App.), 190 S.W. 829. Therefore, the same authority declares in Sec. 67, at page 978,

The rule is well settled that use by express or implied permission or license, no matter how long continued, cannot ripen into an easement by prescription, since user as of right, as distinguished from permissive user, is lacking,

citing, among other cases, Klein v. Gehrung, 25 Texas Supp. 232, 78 Am. Dec. 565.

In Klein v. Gehrung, it is said: "The foundation of prescriptive title is the presumed grant of the party whose rights are adversely affected; but where it appears that the enjoyment has existed by the consent or license of such party, no presumption of grant can be made."

In Weber v. Chaney, supra, the Webers sued to require Chaney to reopen a road through his farm to public use. Before Chaney closed it such of the public as had occasion to do so used the road as if it had been an established highway. Chaney, his family, tenants and employees likewise used it. Although Chaney never made any objection to the public using the road, he at all times maintained three closed gates across it and the public usually closed them after passing through. It was held that this use by the public was a permissive use which, in the absence of any adverse claim of right against Chaney, could never ripen into a prescriptive right against him so as to constitute the road a public highway.

Callan v. Walters, supra, holds that where both the owner and the claimant were using a common stairway, each to get into his own building, the claimant's use was not adverse because not exclusive. "The use of a way over the land of another when the owner is also using the same is not such adverse possession as will serve as notice of a claim of right, for the reason that the same is not inconsistent with a license from the owner."

In Sassman v. Collins, 53 Texas Civ. App. 71, 115 S.W. 337 (er. ref.), Collins sued to enforce a roadway across Sassman's land, alleging that he had an easement therein both of necessity and by prescription. Collins and others did use the roadway to get to a public road but Sassman and his predecessors in title likewise used it for the same purpose. The court held that under those circumstances the use of the roadway by the claimant and others is presumed to be with the consent of the owner and not adverse. . . .

It is undisputed that the road along the Rosiers' 100 acres has been fenced on both sides since about 1906; that the gate opening from the lane into the Belt Line Road was erected at the same time and has been kept closed by the Rosiers and Othen as well as by all parties using the lane as an outlet to the road; that the Rosiers and their tenants have used the lane for general farm purposes as well as to haul wood from the 16.31 acres and to permit their livestock to get to and from the pasture. Under those facts, we conclude that Othen's use of the roadway was merely permissive, hence constituted only a license, which could not and did not ripen into a prescriptive right.

But Othen insists that he had prescriptive title of 10 years to the easement before the lane was fenced and the gate opening into the Belt Line Road was erected in 1906, because "at least since 1895 and probably since 1893 said roadway has been established and claimed by petitioner and others." Othen testified that about 1900 he moved onto the 113 acres in question as a tenant and lived there two years, moved away for about 11 months, then "bought it and moved back." It is obvious that he did not use the roadway in any way for any period of 10 years prior to 1906. The testimony as to its use by Othen's predecessors is, in our opinion, too vague and uncertain to amount to any evidence of prescriptive right to the roadway decreed by the trial court. For example, when Othen was asked to "tell the court what the condition of that passageway was there," he answered: "Well, in that day and time it was just prairie and there were some hog wallows which would hold water. You would just pick your place round about; if there was a hog wallow, go around it and come on in. But that was the general direction through there." Another witness, asked whether in 1901 there was a road "by the side of the present Rosier property," replied: "It was on the present Rosier property, and at that time went up through the edge of the field." When asked by Othen's counsel, "Do you know anything about where this road used to run?", Mrs. Rosier said: "Well, it didn't run up exactly next to the Belt Line like it is running now." It cannot be said that this showed only a slight divergence in the directions taken by the roadway before 1904, therefore Othen did not discharge his burden of showing that his predecessors' adverse possession was in the same place and within the definite lines claimed by him and fixed by the trial court. . . .

Moreover, since Hill did not part with his title to Othen's alleged dominant estate until 1897 (as to the 60 acres) and until 1899 (as to the 53 acres) and did not part with his title to 16.31 acres of the Rosiers' alleged servient estate until 1899, Othen could not under any circumstances have perfected prescriptive title to a roadway easement on the 16.31 acres prior to 1906.

> Since a person cannot claim adversely to himself, the courts uniformly maintain that the prescriptive period does not begin to run while the dominant and servient tracts are under the same ownership. [17 Am. Jur., Easements, Sec. 69, p. 980.]

It follows that the judgment of the Court of Civil Appeals is affirmed.

Notes, Questions, and Problem—Easements by Necessity

1. *Rationales for easements by necessity.* Two different rationales support implying an easement on the basis of necessity: (1) public policy and (2) the intent of the parties. In most cases, it does not matter which justification is given, but if the parties expressly provide that no way of necessity exists, the court must decide whether such a provision is valid. Compare Mersac, Inc. v. National Hills Condominium Assn., Inc., 480 S.E.2d 16 (Ga. 1997) (holding that retained parcel was land locked when developer inadvertently failed to retain an easement of access; the doctrine of implied reservation of easement by grantor was not recognized).

2. *Requirements of an easement by necessity.* Two requirements must conventionally be met in order for an easement to be implied on the basis of necessity: (1) initial unity of ownership of the now dominant and servient estates, followed by severance of the title to the dominant and servient estates; and (2) strict necessity at the time of severance.

3. *How much necessity?* There is some conflict in the cases over the degree of necessity required for an easement by necessity. Some courts, like the court in *Othen*, continue to adhere to the traditional requirement of strict necessity. See, e.g., Schwab v. Timmons, 589 N.W.2d 1 (Wis. 1999) (refusing to recognize an easement by necessity when allegedly "landlocked" parcel had access to a public road on foot, down a steep cliff; the fact that the cost of building a road over the cliff would be $700,000 was deemed irrelevant). Today most courts require only reasonable necessity, not a "physical or absolute necessity but a reasonable

---

In Brief

The traditional requirements for an easement implied from necessity are as follows:

- ▶ Initial unity of ownership, followed by severance of title
- ▶ Strict necessity at the time of severance

The modern—and now majority—view has relaxed the necessity requirement.

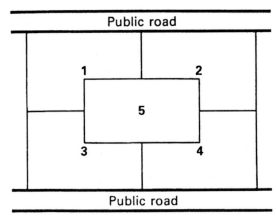

Figure 10-4

and practicable necessity." Palmer v. R.A. Yancey Lumber Corp., 803 S.E.2d 742 (Va. 2017).

4. *Problem. A* owns five adjoining tracts of forest land, numbered 1 through 5. All five lots had previously been owned by *O* as a single tract; *A* purchased each lot from *O* in a separate transaction, lot 1 first, lot 2 second, lot 3 third, lot 4 fourth, and finally lot 5. Lots 1 and 2 are bounded by a public road on the north. Lots 3 and 4 are bounded by a public road on the south. Lot 5 has no access to a public road except through one of the other four lots, as shown in Figure 10-4. Subsequently, *A* dies intestate. Her five children, *B, C, D, E,* and *F,* are her heirs. In the decree of distribution settling *A*'s estate, the court assigns lot 1 to *B,* lot 2 to *C,* lot 3 to *D,* lot 4 to *E,* and lot 5 to *F.* Nothing is said in the decree about lot 5 having an easement of way. Sometime later *F* sues the owners of lots 1 through 4, claiming an easement by necessity. What result? See 2 American Law of Property § 8.91 (1952). Cf. Horner v. Heersche, 447 P.2d 811 (Kan. 1968); McQuinn v. Tantalo, 339 N.Y.S.2d 541 (App. Div. 1973).

5. *Extinguishment of easement by necessity.* An easement by necessity endures only so long as it is necessary. If the dominant owner secures another way out from the landlocked parcel, the easement by necessity ceases. Thus, if *A,* owner of a landlocked parcel with an easement by necessity over *B*'s land, acquires an easement over *C*'s land enabling *A* to reach a public road, the easement by necessity disappears.

In Van Sandt v. Royster, page 484, suppose that the city constructs a public sewer on Tenth Street, and that the owner of lot 4 can connect with it. Does the owner of lot 4 lose the implied sewer easement over lots 19 and 20?

6. *Right of private condemnation.* In some states, mainly in the West, statutes give an owner of landlocked land the right to condemn an easement across neighboring land upon showing the requisite necessity. The condemnation is a judicial proceeding, and the landowner must pay damages to the owner of the land where the easement is sought. Under these statutes, it does not matter how the landlocking occurred; prior common ownership of the dominant and servient estates is not required.

Why should the servient owner of a common law easement by necessity receive no compensation, whereas the servient owner of a privately condemned easement by necessity receives compensation from the benefited owner?

Notes, Questions, and Problem—Easements by Prescription

1. *The theory and requirements of prescriptive easements.* Most courts analyze prescriptive easements by analogy to adverse possession. In this view, the requirements for a prescriptive easement are usually stated as follows: (1) the use must be adverse and hostile; (2) open and notorious; (3) continuous; and (4) for the statutory period.

In most states, the statutory period is the same as that required for adverse possession. A few courts use a different theory to explain prescriptive easements. This is the so-called lost grant theory. According to this theory, which derives from historical English law, if a use was shown to have existed for 20 years, courts presumed that the owner granted an easement to the user and that the grant had been lost. This presumption, which was only a legal fiction, could not be rebutted by evidence that no grant had in fact been made.

> **In Brief**
>
> The traditional requirements for a prescriptive easement are as follows:
>
> ▶ *Adverse and hostile use*
> ▶ *Open and notorious use*
> ▶ *Continuous use*
> ▶ *Use for the statutory period*

2. *The two theories compared: interrupting the statute of limitations.* Is there any practical difference between the two theories of prescriptive easements? In short, yes, in one situation—how to interrupt the running of the statute of limitations. The lost grant theory draws a confusing distinction between acquiescence and permission. Under lost grant theory, the owner of land is presumed to consent or acquiesce in the use; after all, the owner (or his predecessor) is thought to have granted the easement. On the other hand, if the use is made with the permission of the owner, the use is not adverse. To secure a prescriptive easement under lost grant theory, the claimant must show that the use was not permissive and also that the owner acquiesced (did not object).

Consider the fiction of the lost grant in relation to the following problem: To reach her land more easily, in 1992, *A* makes a road across *O*'s land. In 2003, *O* writes *A* a letter saying: "You are hereby notified that the portion of my land that you made into a road is my private property. No person has the right to cross this land, and you are liable to me in damages. I hereby forbid you to pass over any portion of my land, especially that portion that you unlawfully made into a road." *A* ignores *O*'s letter and continues to use the road for the prescriptive period of 20 years. In 2020, does *A* have a prescriptive easement? See Dartnell v. Bidwell, 98 A. 743 (Me. 1916) (holding that a letter interrupts prescription because it rebuts any claim of acquiescence or grant). Would a letter to a possessor stop adverse possession from running?

In a jurisdiction using the adverse possession theory, to prevent a prescriptive easement from being acquired, the owner must effectively interrupt or stop the adverse use. Suppose, under the preceding facts, that in 2010, *O* had erected a fence across the road, and that *A* tore down the fence and continued to use the road. Does *A* acquire a prescriptive easement in 2020? See Restatement (Third) of Property, Servitudes § 2.17 comment j illustration 35 (2000). Some states have statutes that allow landowners to interrupt an adverse use by simply giving written notice to persons using the owner's land of the owner's intent to dispute any claim arising from such use. See, e.g., Conn. Gen. Stat. § 47-38 (2020); Iowa Code Ann. §§ 564.4-564.7 (2020); R.I. Gen. Laws § 34-7-6 (2020).

3. *Exclusivity.* You may have noticed that in identifying the requirements of prescriptive easements in Note 1, we did not include *exclusive*, which is required for adverse possession. Exclusivity can be a confusing topic in prescriptive easement law. Among the courts that do include exclusivity as a requirement, most define it differently from the adverse possession requirement. "Exclusivity does not require a showing that only the claimant made use of the way, but that the claimant's right to use the land does not depend upon a like right in others." Page v. Bloom, 584 N.E.2d 813, 815 (Ill. App. 1991). Thus, in most states, the user can acquire a prescriptive easement even though the easement is also used by the servient owner.

In Othen v. Rosier, the court presumed that the use of the road by Othen was permissive rather than adverse because it was not exclusive. Why should this be presumed? In order to gain title by adverse possession, a person must show exclusive possession for the required period. There is good reason for this requirement when one is claiming exclusive ownership of the land ousting the legal owner. But why should it apply so as to bar a claim to a nonexclusive prescriptive easement to be used by the servient owner as well?

4. *Problem.* Adjacent to Conrad Hilton's home is a golf club. Every day several golf balls are driven onto Hilton's property, and the players come onto his property to retrieve them. If this continues, will the golf club acquire a prescriptive easement over Hilton's property? See MacDonald Properties, Inc. v. Bel-Air Country Club, 140 Cal. Rptr. 367 (Cal. App. 1977) (finding prescriptive easement where golfers hit and retrieved "several balls per day" on neighbor's land). If so, what should Hilton do to prevent a prescriptive easement from arising?

5. *Public easements.* Many courts today recognize public easements of access, relying on different theories.

Prescription. Some courts recognize public easements on the basis of prescription, i.e., long continuous use by the public under a claim of right. The landowner must be put on notice, by the kind and extent of use, that an adverse right is being claimed by the general public, not by individuals. This changes the traditional view that the public could not acquire a prescriptive easement.

Implied dedication. Other courts use the theory of implied dedication, rather than prescription, for public easements. Dedications may be express or implied. Express dedications are essentially grants and usually involve gratuitous transfers of land to a government body or the public at large. Subdivision maps, for example, commonly contain dedications of roads to the public. The theory of implied dedication owes something to the lost grant fiction, for it seeks a substitute for a grant in an implied dedication. It may be used where the landowner evidences an intent to dedicate, and the state accepts by maintaining the land used by the public. Or implied dedication theory may be used as a substitute for prescription.

Custom. Public access to beaches has become an increasingly important, and controversial, topic in recent years. The prescriptive easement doctrine has not been notably successful in providing public access, largely because most courts presume that public use of beaches is with the permission of the owner, and the burden of proving adverse use cannot be met. See City of Daytona Beach v. Tona-Rama, Inc., 294 So. 2d 73 (Fla. 1974). Because beach access is usually presumed to be with the permission of the owner, and because each individual beach access case must be litigated separately under the prescriptive easement doctrine, courts in some jurisdictions have turned to other doctrines with greater potential for opening the beaches. In Florida, Oregon, and Texas, courts have used the medieval doctrine of customary rights—uses that existed for so long that "the memory of man runneth not to the contrary"—and have held that long usage of beaches by the public is protected as a customary right. City of Daytona Beach v. Tona-Rama, Inc., supra; Stevens v. City of Cannon Beach, 854 P.2d 449 (Or. 1993), cert. denied, 510 U.S. 1207 (1994).

Public trust. Yet another theory upon which some courts have proceeded is the public trust doctrine, which we encountered in Chapter 1 (pages 58-65). As we saw there, the public trust doctrine has been used to provide public access to beaches. In most states today, the list of activities that the public enjoys under the doctrine includes recreation. In Raleigh Avenue Beach Assn. v. Atlantis Beach Club, 879 A.2d 112 (N.J. 2005), the court held that under New Jersey's public trust doctrine, a private beach club could not unreasonably exclude members of the public from the dry-sand portion of its beach for recreational purposes.

> **Sidebar**
>
> In Rockefeller Center, in New York City, a private street called Rockefeller Plaza is situated between the GE Building and the sunken skating rink. In order to preserve Rockefeller Center's right of ownership of the street, each year the street is closed to all traffic, even pedestrian, for one day—a Sunday in July is usually chosen as interfering least with tenants and visitors. Lawyers for Rockefeller Center believe that this formality is necessary to prevent the public from acquiring a permanent right of way in the street.

2. Scope of Easements

BROWN v. VOSS

Supreme Court of Washington, 1986
715 P.2d 514

BRACHTENBACH, J. The question posed is to what extent, if any, the holder of a private road easement can traverse the servient estate to reach not only the original dominant estate, but a subsequently acquired parcel when those two combined parcels are used in such a way that there is no increase in the burden on the servient estate. The trial court denied the injunction sought by the owners of the servient estate. The Court of Appeals reversed. Brown v. Voss, 38 Wash. App. 777, 689 P.2d 1111 (1984). We reverse the Court of Appeals and reinstate the judgment of the trial court.

A portion of an exhibit [Figure 10-5] depicts the involved parcels.

In 1952 the predecessors in title of parcel A granted to the predecessor owners of parcel B a private road easement across parcel A for "ingress to and egress from" parcel B. Defendants acquired parcel A in 1973. Plaintiffs bought parcel B on April 1, 1977 and parcel C on July 31, 1977, but from two different owners. Apparently the previous owners of parcel C were not parties to the easement grant.

When plaintiffs acquired parcel B a single family dwelling was situated thereon. They intended to remove that residence and replace it with a single family dwelling which would straddle the boundary line common to parcels B and C.

Plaintiffs began clearing both parcels B and C and moving fill materials in November 1977. Defendants first sought to bar plaintiffs' use of the easement in April 1979 by which time plaintiffs had spent more than $11,000 in developing their property for building.

Defendants placed logs, a concrete sump and a chain link fence within the easement. Plaintiffs sued for removal of the obstructions, an injunction against defendants' interference with their use of the easement and damages. Defendants counterclaimed for damages and an injunction against plaintiffs using the easement other than for parcel B.

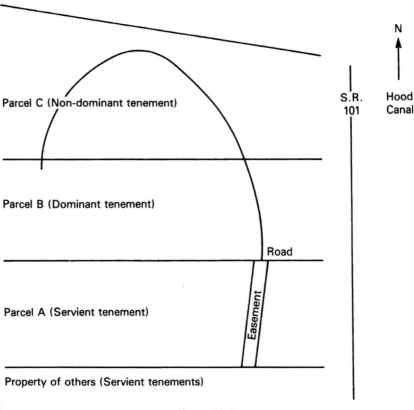

Figure 10-5
The original exhibit used in the case.

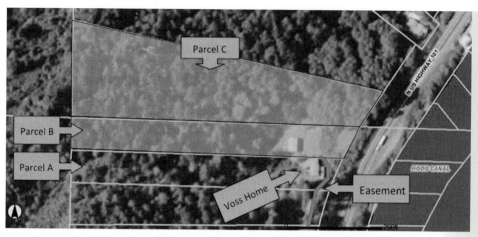

Figure 10-6
An aerial photograph providing a more accurate view.

The trial court awarded each party $1 in damages. The award against the plaintiffs was for a slight inadvertent trespass outside the easement.

The trial court made the following findings of fact:

VI

The plaintiffs have made no unreasonable use of the easement in the development of their property. There have been no complaints of unreasonable use of the roadway to the south of the properties of the parties by other neighbors who grant[ed] easements to the parties to this action to cross their properties to gain access to the property of the plaintiffs. Other than the trespass there is no evidence of any damage to the defendants as a result of the use of the easement by the plaintiffs. There has been no increase in volume of travel on the easement to reach a single-family dwelling whether built on tract B or on tracts B and C. There is no evidence of any increase in the burden on the subservient estate from the use of the easement by the plaintiffs for access to parcel C.

VIII

If an injunction were granted to bar plaintiffs' access to tract C across the easement to a single-family residence, Parcel C would become landlocked; plaintiffs would not be able to make use of their property; they would not be able to build their single-family residence in a manner to properly enjoy the view of the Hood Canal and the surrounding area as originally anticipated at the time of their purchase and even if the single-family residence were constructed on parcel B, if the injunction were granted, plaintiffs would not be able to use the balance of their property in parcel C as a yard or for any other use of their property in conjunction with their home. Conversely, there is and will be no appreciable hardship or damage to the defendants if the injunction is denied.

IX

If an injunction were to be granted to bar the plaintiffs' access to tract C, the framing and enforcing of such an order would be impractical. Any violation of the order would result in the parties back in court at great cost but with little or no damages being involved.

X

Plaintiffs have acted reasonably in the development of their property. Their trespass over a "little" corner of the defendants' property was inadvertent, and de minimis. The fact that the defendants' counter claim seeking an injunction to bar plaintiffs' access to parcel C was filed as leverage against the original plaintiffs' claim for an interruption of their easement rights, may be considered in determining whether equitable relief by way of an injunction should be granted.

Relying upon these findings of fact, the court denied defendants' request for an injunction and granted the plaintiffs the right to use the easement for access to parcels B & C "as long as plaintiffs' properties (B and C) are developed and used solely for the purpose of a single family residence." Clerk's Papers, at 10.

The Court of Appeals reversed, holding [that an injunction must issue]. . . .

The easement in this case was created by express grant. Accordingly, the extent of the right acquired is to be determined from the terms of the grant properly construed to give effect to the intention of the parties. See Zobrist v. Culp, 95 Wash. 2d 556, 561, 627 P.2d 1308 (1981); Seattle v. Nazarenus, 60 Wash. 2d 657, 665, 374 P.2d 1014 (1962). By the express terms of the 1952 grant, the predecessor owners of parcel B acquired a private road easement across parcel A and the right to use the easement for ingress to and egress from parcel B. Both plaintiffs and defendants agree that the 1952 grant created an easement appurtenant to parcel B as the dominant estate. Thus, plaintiffs, as owners of the dominant estate, acquired rights in the use of the easement for ingress to and egress from parcel B.

However, plaintiffs have no such easement rights in connection with their ownership of parcel C, which was not a part of the original dominant estate under the terms of the 1952 grant. As a general rule, an easement appurtenant to one parcel of land may not be extended by the owner of the dominant estate to other parcels owned by him, whether adjoining or distinct tracts, to which the easement is not appurtenant. E.g., Heritage Standard Bank & Trust Co. v. Trustees of Schs., 84 Ill. App. 3d 653, 40 Ill. Dec. 104, 405 N.E.2d 1196 (1980); Kanefsky v. Dratch Constr. Co., 376 Pa. 188, 101 A.2d 923 (1954); S.S. Kresge Co. of Mich. v. Winkleman Realty Co., 260 Wis. 372, 50 N.W.2d 920 (1952); 28 C.J.S. Easements § 92, at 772-73 (1941).

Plaintiffs, nonetheless, contend that extension of the use of the easement for the benefit of nondominant property does not constitute a misuse of the easement, whereas here, there is no evidence of an increase in the burden on the servient estate. We do not agree. If an easement is appurtenant to a particular parcel of land, any extension thereof to other parcels is a misuse of the easement. Wetmore v. Ladies of Loretto, Wheaton, 73 Ill. App. 2d 454, 220 N.E.2d 491 (1966). See also, e.g., Robertson v. Robertson, 214 Va. 76, 197 S.E.2d 183 (1973); Penn Bowling Rec. Ctr., Inc. v. Hot Shoppes, Inc., 179 F.2d 64 (D.C. Cir. 1949). As noted by one court in a factually similar case, "[I]n this context this classic rule of property law is directed to the rights of the respective parties rather than the actual burden on the servitude." National Lead Co. v. Kanawha Block Co., 228 F. Supp. 357, 364 (S.D. W. Va. 1968), aff'd, 409 F.2d 1309 (4th Cir. 1969). Under the express language of the 1952 grant, plaintiffs only have rights in the use of the easement for the benefit of parcel B. Although, as plaintiffs contend, their planned use of the easement to gain access to a single family residence located partially on parcel B and partially on parcel C is perhaps no more than technical misuse of the easement, we conclude that it is misuse nonetheless.

However, it does not follow from this conclusion alone that defendants are entitled to injunctive relief. Since the awards of $1 in damages were not appealed, only the denial of an injunction to defendants is in issue. Some fundamental principles applicable to a request for an injunction must be considered. (1) The proceeding is equitable and addressed to the sound discretion of the trial court. (2) The trial court is vested with a broad discretionary power to shape and fashion injunctive relief to fit the *particular facts, circumstances, and equities of the case before it.* Appellate courts give great weight to the trial court's exercise of that discretion. (3) One of the essential criteria for injunctive relief is actual and substantial injury sustained by the person seeking the injunction.

The trial court found as facts, upon substantial evidence, that plaintiffs have acted reasonably in the development of their property, that there is and was no damage to the defendants from plaintiffs' use of the easement, that there was no increase in the volume of travel on the easement, that there was no increase in the burden on the servient estate, that defendants sat by for more than a year while plaintiffs expended more than $11,000 on their project, and that defendants' counterclaim was an effort to gain "leverage" against plaintiffs' claim. In addition, the court found from the evidence that plaintiffs would suffer considerable hardship if the injunction were granted whereas no appreciable hardship or damages would flow to defendants from its denial. Finally, the court limited plaintiffs' use of the combined parcels solely to the same purpose for which the original parcel was used—i.e., for a single family residence.

Neither this court nor the Court of Appeals may substitute its effort to make findings of fact for those supported findings of the trial court. . . . Therefore, the only valid issue is whether, under these established facts, as a matter of law, the trial court abused its discretion in denying defendants' request for injunctive relief. Based upon the equities of the case, as found by the trial court, we are persuaded that the trial court acted within its discretion. The Court of Appeals is reversed and the trial court is affirmed.

DORE, J. (dissenting). The majority correctly finds that an extension of this easement to nondominant property is a misuse of the easement. The majority, nonetheless, holds that the owners of the servient estate are not entitled to injunctive relief. I dissent.

The comments and illustrations found in the Restatement of Property § 478 (1944) address the precise issue before this court. Comment e provides in pertinent part that "if one who has an easement of way over Whiteacre appurtenant to Blackacre uses the way with the purpose of going to Greenacre, the use is improper even though he eventually goes to Blackacre rather than to Greenacre." Illustration 6 provides:

> 6. By prescription, *A* has acquired, as the owner and possessor of Blackacre, an easement of way over an alley leading from Blackacre to the street. He buys Whiteacre, an adjacent lot, to which the way is not appurtenant, and builds a public garage one-fourth of which is located on Blackacre and three-fourths of

which is located on Whiteacre. *A* wishes to use the alley as a means of ingress and egress to and from the garage. He has no privilege to use the alley to go to that part of the garage which is built on Whiteacre, and he may not use the alley until that part of the garage built on Blackacre is so separated from the part built on Whiteacre that uses for the benefit of Blackacre are distinguishable from those which benefit Whiteacre.

The majority grants the privilege to extend the agreement to nondominant property on the basis that the trial court found no appreciable hardship or damage to the servient owners. However, as conceded by the majority, any extension of the use of an easement to benefit a nondominant estate constitutes a misuse of the easement. Misuse of an easement is a trespass. Raven Red Ash Coal Co. v. Ball, 184 Va. 534, 39 S.E.2d 231 (1946); Selvia v. Reitmeyer, 156 Ind. App. 203, 295 N.E.2d 869 (1973). The Browns' use of the easement to benefit parcel C, especially if they build their home as planned, would involve a continuing trespass for which damages would be difficult to measure. Injunctive relief is the appropriate remedy under these circumstances. *Selvia*, at 212, 295 N.E.2d 869; Gregory v. Sanders, 635 P.2d 795, 801 (Wyo. 1981). In Penn Bowling Rec. Ctr., Inc. v. Hot Shoppes, Inc., 179 F.2d 64, 66 (D.C. Cir. 1949), the court states:

> It is contended by appellant that since the area of the dominant and non-dominant land served by the easement is less than the original area of the dominant tenement, the use made by appellant of the right of way to serve the building located on the lesser area is not materially increased or excessive. It is true that where the nature and extent of the use of an easement is, by its terms, unrestricted, the use of the dominant tenement may be increased or enlarged. . . . But the owner of the dominant tenement may not subject the servient tenement to use or servitude in connection with other premises to which the easement is not appurtenant. See Williams v. James, Eng. Law. Rep. (1867), 2 C.P. 577. And when an easement is being used in such a manner, an injunction will be issued to prevent such use. Cleve et al. v. Nairin, 204 Ky. 342, 264 S.W. 741 [(1924)]; Diocese of Trenton v. Toman et al., 74 N.J. Eq. 702, 70 A. 606 [(1908)]; Shock v. Holt Lumber Co. et al., 107 W. Va. 259, 148 S.E. 73 [(1929)]. Appellant, therefore, may not use the easement to serve both the dominant and nondominant property, even though the area thereof is less than the original area of the dominant tenement.

See also Kanefsky v. Dratch Constr. Co., 376 Pa. 188, 101 A.2d 923 (1954). Thus, the fact that an extension of the easement to nondominant property would not increase the burden on the servient estate does not warrant a denial of injunctive relief.

The Browns are responsible for the hardship of creating a landlocked parcel. They knew or should have known from the public records that the easement was not appurtenant to parcel C. See Seattle v. Nazarenus, 60 Wash. 2d 657, 670, 374 P.2d 1014 (1962). In encroachment cases this factor is significant. As stated by the court in Bach v. Sarich, 74 Wash. 2d 575, 582, 445 P.2d 648 (1968): "The benefit of the doctrine of balancing the equities, or relative hardship, is reserved for the innocent defendant who proceeds without knowledge or warning that his structure encroaches upon another's property or property rights."

In addition, an injunction would not interfere with the Browns' right to use the easement as expressly granted, i.e., for access to parcel B. An injunction would merely require the Browns to acquire access to parcel C if they want to build a home that straddles parcels B and C. One possibility would be to condemn a private way of necessity over their existing easement in an action under RCW 8.24.010. See Brown v. McAnally, 97 Wash. 2d 360, 644 P.2d 1153 (1982).

I would affirm the Court of Appeals decision as a correct application of the law of easements. If the Browns desire access to their landlocked parcel they have the benefit of the statutory procedure for condemnation of a private way of necessity.

THE REST OF THE STORY . . .

All of the tracts involved in Brown v. Voss were on a wooded hillside overlooking Hood Canal. Professor Elizabeth Samuels has determined that Figure 10-5, reproduced in the court's opinion, is inaccurate or deceptive in several respects. In her article, Elizabeth Samuels, Brown v. Voss, in Stories Out of School: Teaching the Case of *Brown v. Voss*, 16 Cardozo L. Rev. 1445 (1995), she points out, first, that all three parcels fronted on, and had access to, State Road 101, which parallels Hood Canal. The map does not make this clear. Second, Parcel B is a long, narrow lot consisting of 1.4 acres. Parcel C is 5.05 acres, three and a half times larger. Third, the map suggests that the house would be located on Parcel B or straddling the property line. Brown testified at the trial that the exact location of the house had not been determined, and Professor Samuels, inspecting the property after the lawsuit, discovered that the Browns had prepared a large, flat area high up on Parcel C, which she thought was "a perfect site for a large house."

The Browns bought their two parcels directly from the sellers, without consulting a real estate broker or a lawyer. They started using the easement in November 1977 to clear their parcels and bring in fill. They did not tell the Vosses what they were going to build on their property or where they were going to build. They did not seek permission to use the easement to benefit Parcel C, because they assumed they could use the easement to service their entire tract. Throughout the dispute, the Browns did not attempt to bargain with the Vosses, because they thought the Vosses had no right about which it was necessary to bargain. They believed it was none of the Vosses' business what they were going to build on their tract.

Smarting from not knowing what was going on as the trucks were going in and out, and not being consulted about where the new road would go on the Browns' land, Voss got his dander up. He began raising objections. He disputed the location of the easement and complained that Brown and his contractors were trespassing, both through their driving off of the easement and by backing up and turning vehicles on a triangular piece of the Vosses' land where the easement joined Parcel B. Voss erected a chain link fence along the east side of the easement, which Brown believed encroached on the easement.

Brown was in no mood to negotiate. He hired a surveyor and invited Voss to join him in walking the property line between their tracts as well as the location of the easement, but he told Voss he was only to listen and not to talk with either him or the surveyor. Voss was highly offended by this. He thought Brown downright unneighborly. The quarreling continued for several months until the parties came to blows. Brown said Voss assaulted him, and Voss said Brown, who was 15 years younger, knocked him down. Voss unsuccessfully sought to have Brown prosecuted for assault, and the Browns' lawyer sent Voss a letter threatening legal action against him. A few months later the Browns filed their lawsuit to enjoin the Vosses from interfering with their easement. In the lawsuit, the Browns complained that the Vosses had intentionally placed logs and a concrete sump on the easement "preventing its full use."

After the lawsuit was filed, the Vosses hired a lawyer, who advised them to counterclaim for an injunction preventing the Browns from using the easement to reach Parcel C. The original dispute over location and misuse of the easement now turned into a legal issue of use of the easement by nondominant land. To the Browns, this counterclaim came as a bolt out of the blue—something Voss had never complained of before. The Browns' position in reply was that Parcels B and C had merged into one tract with one owner, that the parcel lines had disappeared, and that they had a right to use the easement to service their entire tract. They thought the traditional rule against use by nondominant land made no sense because, if they located their house straddling the former parcel lines, they would be permitted to enter one part of their house and not another. Moreover, the Browns had bought the two lots with the idea of building a large new home—a home that might be too large to erect on Parcel B alone—and they testified that they would not have bought these lots had they known of this limitation on the easement. They felt terribly wronged by this new claim by the Vosses, which they viewed as spiteful and entirely unreasonable. And in the trial their lawyer presented their position exactly this way.

The Vosses' lawyer believed the case turned solely on the rule that an easement cannot be extended to nondominant land. As a result, at the trial he did not let the Vosses tell their story—how they had tried to be good neighbors and how uncooperative the Browns had been. He viewed this as irrelevant. The Vosses' lawyer also made what was perhaps a crucial error: he did not offer into evidence a correct map of the properties, which would show that Parcel C had direct access to Route 101 and was not landlocked.

The trial and appeals dragged on for seven years. Finally, the Washington Supreme Court ruled that although the legal rule that an easement cannot be used for nondominant land is enforceable—in this case, only by an award of damages of $1—the trial court did not abuse its discretion in denying the Vosses injunctive relief. The Vosses' lawyer wrote them that they had won the case. Subsequently, when a bill for the Browns' legal costs arrived, they were rather surprised, but they paid it without complaint. By this time, the Browns were out of the picture.

The Browns were not able to build their dream house. They had bought Parcel B on an installment land contract and, after failing to make payments to the seller while the lawsuit was proceeding, the seller declared a forfeiture. The Browns lost Parcel C in a tax sale resulting from their failure to pay taxes on the property for three years. Dogged by financial reverses, the Browns pulled up stakes and moved to Alaska before the Washington Supreme Court handed down its decision. The owner of Parcel B, who had sold it to the Browns, now sold it to the Vosses, thereby merging Parcels A and B into common ownership, terminating the bitterly contested easement.

When Professor Samuels contacted Mr. Brown by telephone in Alaska, "[f]ifteen years after the lawsuit began, he continued to express frustration and anger with Mr. Voss, whom he called 'one of the scum-baggiest persons I've ever met' [and whose wife he called a 'bozo']. When he learned near the end of our conversation that Mr. Voss now owns Parcel B, he commented—after long moments of silence—that Mr. Voss did not deserve to have the property and that 'it's unfortunate we didn't bury him right there.'" Id. at 1487.

Notes and Questions

1. *The traditional rule.* According to the traditional rule, still followed in most jurisdictions, an easement may not be used in connection with a nondominant estate, and any such use is subject to an injunction. The Restatement (Third) of Property, Servitudes § 4.11 (2000), endorses the conventional rule. Brown v. Voss departs from the traditional rule and has been the subject of a fair amount of commentary, both pro and con. See, e.g., Lee Strang, Damages as the Appropriate Remedy for "Abuse" of an Easement: Moving Toward Consistency, Efficiency, and Fairness in Property Law, 15 Geo. Mason L. Rev. 933 (2008); Stewart E. Sterk, Property Rules, Liability Rules, and Uncertainty About Property Rights, 106 Mich. L. Rev. 1285, 1323-1327 (2008). What is your reaction to the court's analysis? Do you think Voss would have sold an extension of the easement to include lot C for only one dollar, the amount of damages that the court awarded?

2. *Subdividing the dominant parcel.* Suppose that the owner of the dominant tenement wants to subdivide her land into 100 subdivision tracts. Will each tract have the right to use the easement over the servient tenement? Restatement (Third) of Property, Servitudes § 4.10 (2000), says:

> [T]he holder of an easement or profit . . . is entitled to use the servient estate in a manner that is reasonably necessary for the convenient enjoyment of the servitude. The manner, frequency, and intensity of the use may change over time to take advantage of developments in technology and *to accommodate normal development of the dominant estate* or enterprise benefited by the servitude. Unless authorized by the terms of the servitude, the holder is not entitled to cause unreasonable damage to the servient estate or interfere unreasonably with its enjoyment. (Emphasis added.)

The comment to this section points out that what is normal development for an area changes over time, and what may be considered abnormal at any one time may become normal at a later time. Note also that under the Restatement provision quoted above the use of an easement may change over time to take advantage of new technological developments, unless language in the granting instrument provides otherwise. See, e.g., Center v. Bluebonnet, 264 S.W.3d 381 (Tex. App. 2008).

3. *Relocating an easement.* O grants A an easement of way over Blackacre to reach adjacent land owned by A. The easement location is fixed by mutual agreement. Subsequently, O proposes to change the location of the easement, at O's expense, in order to facilitate development of O's land. A objects. What result?

The established rule is that the location of an easement, once fixed by the parties, cannot be changed by the servient owner without permission of the dominant owner. See Davis v. Bruk, 411 A.2d 660 (Me. 1980) (advancing reasons why servient owner cannot unilaterally change location of easement). Restatement (Third) of Property, supra, § 4.8(3) changes this rule. It grants the servient owner the right to change the location of an easement, at his expense, if the change does not "(a) significantly lessen the utility of the easement, (b) increase the burdens on the owner of the easement in its use and enjoyment, or (c) frustrate the purpose for which the easement was created." Courts in about 20 states have adopted some form of unilateral easement relocation rule, while courts in about 15 other states have rejected the Restatement approach. See John A. Lovett, Diane B. Davies & James Charles Smith, A Deep Dive into Easements, The ACREL Papers 23 (Fall 2017).

4. *Scope of prescriptive easements.* A prescriptive easement is not as broad in scope as an easement created by grant, by implication, or by necessity. Although the uses of a prescriptive easement are not confined to the actual uses made during the prescriptive period, the uses made of a prescriptive easement must be consistent with the general kind of use by which the easement was created and with what the servient owner might reasonably expect to lose by failing to interrupt the adverse use. For example, a prescriptive easement acquired by pedestrian traffic or by herding livestock with men and horses across land has been held not usable by motor vehicles. "Anyone who does not think there is a significant difference between horses and motorcycles may wish to ponder why it is that carriages in Central Park are pulled by horses, not Hondas." Connolly v. McDermott, 208 Cal. Rptr. 796, 799 (Cal. App. 1984).

A Look Back

Go back to Othen v. Rosier (page 492). Does Brown v. Voss show a way out of the problem of the landlocked owner's dilemma in that case? We can note that the court in *Brown* protected the servient tenement with a liability rule (damages) rather than a property rule (injunction). Could not the same approach have been used in *Othen*?

3. Termination of Easements

PRESEAULT v. UNITED STATES

United States Court of Appeals, Federal Circuit, 1996
100 F.3d 1525

[Under the Transportation Act of 1920, in order to abandon a line, a railroad must receive permission of the Interstate Commerce Commission. In 1983, Congress enacted the Rails-to-Trails Act, 16 U.S.C. § 1247(d) (1994), which has two purposes: (1) preserving discontinued railroad corridors for future railroad use and (2) permitting public recreational use of discontinued railroad rights of way. The act gives the ICC[7] authority to authorize *abandonment* of the line *or* to permit *discontinuance* of rail service and transfer of the railroad right of way to a public or private group willing to maintain the right of way as a public trail. In this case, the railroad shut down service in 1970, and in 1975 removed the railroad tracks, but it never applied to the ICC for an abandonment order. In 1985, the railroad entered into an agreement with the state of Vermont and the city of Burlington that the latter would maintain the former railroad strip as a public trail. In 1986, the ICC approved the trails agreement and authorized the railroad to discontinue service. The owners of the underlying fee simple over which the tracks

---

7. The ICC Termination Act of 1995, 109 Stat. 803, abolished the ICC and transferred its responsibilities to the newly created Surface Transportation Board, with a saving clause for suits initiated before 1996.

formerly ran—the Preseaults—sued, claiming the Rails-to-Trails Act was unconstitutional. In Preseault v. Interstate Commerce Commission, 494 U.S. 1 (1990), the United States Supreme Court held that the act was constitutional as an appropriate exercise of congressional power to regulate interstate commerce, but further held that the Preseaults may have a remedy under the Fifth Amendment for a taking of their property as defined by state law:

> Determining what interest petitioners would have enjoyed under Vermont law, in the absence of the ICC's recent actions, will establish whether petitioners possess the predicate property interest that must underlie any takings claim. . . .
>
> The scope of the Commission's authority to regulate abandonments, thereby delimiting the ambit of federal power, is an issue quite distinct from whether the Commission's exercise of power over matters within its jurisdiction effected a taking of petitioner's property. . . . The Commission's actions may delay property owners' enjoyment of their reversionary interests, but that delay burdens and defeats the property interest rather than suspends or defers the vesting of those property rights. . . . Any other conclusion would convert the ICC's power to pre-empt conflicting state regulation of interstate commerce into the power to pre-empt the rights guaranteed by state property law, a result incompatible with the Fifth Amendment. [494 U.S. at 20, 22 (O'Connor, J., concurring).]

The Preseaults now bring suit claiming that the federal government, acting through the ICC, took their property when it authorized the conversion of the former railroad right-of-way to public trail use. They rely upon the traditional rule of takings law that permanent physical occupation of property by the government or the public is a taking of the owners' property. (See Loretto v. Teleprompter Manhattan CATV Corp., 458 U.S. 419 (1982), reproduced at page 643.)]

PLAGER, J. In this Takings case, the United States denies liability under the Fifth Amendment of the Constitution[8] for actions it took pursuant to the Federal legislation known as the Rails-to-Trails Act. The original parties to the case were the property owners, J. Paul and Patricia Preseault, plaintiffs, and the United States (the "Government"), defendant. The State of Vermont (the "State"), claiming an interest in the properties involved, intervened and, under the joinder rules of the Court of Federal Claims, entered its appearance as a co-defendant. The Court of Federal Claims, on summary judgment after hearings and argument, concluded that the law was on the Government's side, and rendered judgment against the complaining property owners. Preseault v. United States, 27 Fed. Cl. 69 (1992). The property owners appeal. . . .

A. Introduction and Summary

In brief, the issue in this case is whether the conversion, under the authority of the Rails-to-Trails Act and by order of the Interstate Commerce Commission, of a long unused railroad right-of-way to a public recreational hiking and biking trail constituted a taking of the property of the owners of the underlying fee simple estate. . . .

---

8. U.S. Const. amend. V ("nor shall private property be taken for public use, without just compensation").

B. Factual Background

The Preseaults own a fee simple interest in a tract of land near the shore of Lake Champlain in Burlington, Vermont, on which they have a home. This tract of land is made up of several previously separate properties, the identities of which date back to before the turn of the century. The dispute centers on three parcels within this tract, areas over which the original railroad right-of-way ran. The areas are designated by the trial court as parcels A, B, and C. Two of those parcels, A and B, derive from the old Barker Estate property. The third parcel, C, is part of what was the larger Manwell property.

The Rutland-Canadian Railroad Company, a corporation organized under the laws of Vermont, acquired in 1899 the rights-of-way at issue on parcels A, B, and C, over which it laid its rails and operated its railroad. . . .

Meanwhile, ownership of the properties over which the rights-of-way ran passed through the hands of successors in interest, eventually arriving in the hands of the Preseaults. A map of the Preseault tract, showing the various parcels and the areas subject to the railroad's rights-of-way, is reproduced [on the next page].

C. The Property Interests

In Preseault [v. Interstate Commerce Commission, 494 U.S. 1], Justice Brennan writing for the Supreme Court noted the importance of determining the nature of the interests created by these turn-of-the-century transfers:

> The alternative chosen by Congress [the Rails-to-Trails program] is less costly than a program of direct federal trail acquisition because, under any view of takings law, only some rail-to-trail conversions will amount to takings. Some rights-of-way are held in fee simple. Others are held as easements that do not even as a matter of state law revert upon interim use as nature trails.

Id. at 16. . . .

Clearly, if the Railroad obtained fee simple title to the land over which it was to operate, and that title inures, as it would, to its successors, the Preseaults today would have no right or interest in those parcels and could have no claim related to those parcels for a taking. If, on the other hand, the Railroad acquired only easements for use, easements imposed on the property owners' underlying fee simple estates, and if those easements were limited to uses that did not include public recreational hiking and biking trails ("nature trails" as Justice Brennan referred to them), or if the easements prior to their conversion to trails had been extinguished by operation of law leaving the property owner with unfettered fee simples, the argument of the Preseaults becomes viable.

The determinative issues in the case, then, are three: (1) who owned the strips of land involved, specifically did the Railroad by the 1899 transfers acquire only easements, or did it obtain fee simple estates; (2) if the Railroad acquired only easements, were the terms of the easements limited to use for railroad purposes, or did they include future use as public recreational trails; and (3) even if the grants of the Railroad's easements were broad enough to encompass recreational trails, had these easements terminated prior to the alleged taking so that the property owners at that time held fee simples unencumbered by the easements. . . .

The question of what estates in property were created by these turn-of-the-century transfers to the Railroad requires a close examination of the conveying instruments, read in light of the common law and statutes of Vermont then in effect. . . . With regard to the two parcels, A and B, derived from the Barker Estate, [the Railroad, exercising a power of eminent domain given it by the state, acquired its interest by a document called a Commissioner's Award. It surveyed and located the land it wanted for its tracks, and, since the land owners and the Railroad could not agree on the damages to be paid, three disinterested commissioners were appointed who fixed the damages and executed the Commissioner's Award. The document made no reference to an easement or a fee simple.] In her opinion, the trial judge concluded that . . . "the portion of the right-of-way consisting of the parcel of land condemned from the Barker Estate and taken by commissioner's award is indisputably an easement under the law of the State of Vermont." [Preseault v. United States, 24 Cl. Ct. 818 at 827 (1992).]

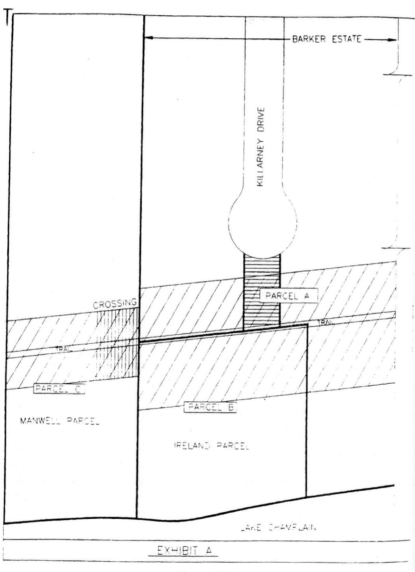

Figure 10-7
Map from Court's opinion

As a result of our independent examination of the question we conclude that there is little real dispute about this. . . . With few exceptions the Vermont cases are consistent in holding that, practically without regard to the documentation and manner of acquisition, when a railroad for its purposes acquires an estate in land for laying track and operating railroad equipment thereon, the estate acquired is no more than that needed for the purpose, and that typically means an easement, not a fee simple estate. . . .

Determining the provenance of the third parcel, C, derived from the Manwell tract, tests the above stated proposition even further. The operative instrument is a warranty deed, dated August 2, 1899, from Frederick and Mary Manwell to the Railroad. The deed contains the usual habendum clause found in a warranty deed, and purports to convey the described strip of land to the grantee railroad "to have and to hold the above granted and bargained premises . . . unto it the said grantee, its successors and assigns forever, to its and their own proper use, benefit and behoof forever." The deed further warrants that the grantors have "a good, indefeasible estate, in fee simple, and have good right to bargain and sell the same in manner and form as above written. . . ." In short, the deed appears to be the standard form used to convey a fee simple title from a grantor to a grantee.

But did it? . . .

At trial, the Preseaults argued that, although the Manwell deed purports to grant a fee simple, the deed was given following survey and location of the right-of-way and therefore it should be construed as conveying only an easement in accordance with Vermont railroad law. . . .

In Hill v. Western Vermont Railroad, 32 Vt. 68 (1859), . . . [t]he court observed that railroads acquire needed land either by order of a designated public body (through the exercise of eminent domain) or by consent of the landowner, although even in the latter case "the proceeding is, in some sense, compulsory." Id. at 75. Thus,

> in either mode of appropriating land for the purposes of the company, there is this implied limitation upon the power, that the company will take only so much land or estate therein as is necessary for their public purposes. It does not seem to us to make much difference in regard to either the quantity or the estate whether the price is fixed by the commissioners or by the parties.

Id. at 76. . . .

Thus it is that a railroad that proceeds to acquire a right-of-way for its road acquires only that estate, typically an easement, necessary for its limited purposes, and that the act of survey and location is the operative determinant, and not the particular form of transfer, if any. Here, the evidence is that the Railroad had obtained a survey and location of its right-of-way, after which the Manwell deed was executed confirming and memorializing the Railroad's action. On balance it would seem that, consistent with the view expressed in *Hill*, the proceeding retained its eminent domain flavor, and the railroad acquired only that which it needed, an easement for its roadway. Nothing the Government points to or that we can find in the later cases would seem to undermine that view of the case; the trial court's conclusion that the estate conveyed was an easement is affirmed. . . .

D. The Scope of the Railroad's Easement

We turn then to the question of whether the easements granted to the Railroad, to which the Preseaults' title was subject, are sufficiently broad in their scope so that the use of the easements for a public recreational trail is not a violation of the Preseaults' rights as owners of the underlying fee estate. Both the Government and the State argue that . . . the scope of the original easements, admittedly limited to railroad purposes, is properly construed today to include other public purposes as well, and that these other public purposes include a public recreational hiking and biking trail. Under that theory of the case, the establishment in 1986 of such a trail would be within the scope of the easements presumably now in the State's hands, and therefore the Preseaults would have no complaint. On the other hand, if the Government's use of the land for a recreational trail is not within the scope of the easements, then that use would constitute an unauthorized invasion of the land to which the Preseaults hold title. The argument on this issue assumes that the easements were still in existence in 1986, and for purposes of this part of the discussion we assume they were. . . .

In the absence of a Vermont case on point, we must seek the answer in traditional understandings of easement law, recognizing as we must that Vermont follows and applies common law property principles.

. . . [T]he scope of an easement [may be] . . . adjusted in the face of changing times to serve the original purpose, so long as the change is consistent with the terms of the original grant:

> It is often said that the parties are to be presumed to have contemplated such a scope for the created easement as would reasonably serve the purposes of the grant. . . . This presumption often allows an expansion of use of the easement, but does not permit a change in use not reasonably foreseeable at the time of establishment of the easement.

Richard R. Powell, 3 Powell on Real Property ¶ 34.12[2] (Patrick J. Rohan ed., 1996). . . .

When the easements here were granted to the Preseaults' predecessors in title at the turn of the century, specifically for transportation of goods and persons via railroad, could it be said that the parties contemplated that a century later the easements would be used for recreational hiking and biking trails, or that it was necessary to so construe them in order to give the grantee railroad that for which it bargained? We think not. Although a public recreational trail could be described as a roadway for the transportation of persons, the nature of the usage is clearly different. In the one case, the grantee is a commercial enterprise using the easement in its business, the transport of goods and people for compensation. In the other, the easement belongs to the public, and is open for use for recreational purposes, which happens to involve people engaged in exercise or recreation on foot or on bicycles. It is difficult to imagine that either party to the original transfers had anything remotely in mind that would resemble a public recreational trail.

Furthermore, there are differences in the degree and nature of the burden imposed on the servient estate. It is one thing to have occasional railroad trains crossing one's land. Noisy though they may be, they are limited in location, in number, and in frequency of occurrence. Particularly is this so on a relatively remote spur. When used for public recreational purposes, however, in a region that is environmentally attractive, the burden imposed by the use of the easement is at the whim of many individuals, and, as the record attests, has been impossible to contain in numbers or to keep strictly within the parameters of the easement. . . .

Most state courts that have been faced with the question of whether conversion to a nature trail falls within the scope of an original railroad easement have held that it does not. . . .

Given that the easements in this case are limited by their terms and as a matter of law to railroad purposes, we are unable to join the dissent's effort to read into Vermont law a breadth of scope for the easements that is well outside the parameters of traditional common law understanding. . . .

E. Abandonment

Even assuming for sake of argument that the . . . original conveyances [may be read so as to permit trail use,] . . . there remains yet a further obstacle to the Government's successful defense. The Preseaults contend that under Vermont law the original easements were abandoned, and thus extinguished, in 1975. If that is so, the State could not, over ten years later in 1986, have re-established the easement even for the narrow purposes provided in the original conveyances without payment of the just compensation required by the Constitution. . . .

Typically the grant under which such rights-of-way are created does not specify a termination date. The usual way in which such an easement ends is by abandonment, which causes the easement to be extinguished by operation of law. See generally Restatement of Property § 504. Upon an act of abandonment, the then owner of the fee estate, the "burdened" estate, is relieved of the burden of the easement. In most jurisdictions, including Vermont, this happens automatically when abandonment of the easement occurs. . . .

Vermont law recognizes the well-established proposition that easements, like other property interests, are not extinguished by simple non-use. As was said in Nelson v. Bacon, 113 Vt. 161, 32 A.2d 140, 146 (1943), "one who acquires title to an easement in this manner [by deed in that case] has the same right of property therein as an owner of the fee and it is not necessary that he should make use of his right in order to maintain his title." Thus in cases involving a passageway through an adjoining building (*Nelson*), or a shared driveway (Sabins v. McAllister, 116 Vt. 302, 76 A.2d 106 (1950), overruled in part on other grounds by Lague v. Royea, 152 Vt. 499, 568 A.2d 357 (1989)), the claimed easement was not extinguished merely because the owner had not made use of it regularly.

Something more is needed. The Vermont Supreme Court in *Nelson* summarized the rule in this way: "In order to establish an abandonment there must be in addition to nonuser, acts by the owner of the dominant tenement conclusively and unequivocally manifesting *either* a present intent to relinquish the easement or a purpose inconsistent with its future existence." *Nelson*, 32 A.2d at 146 (emphasis added); see also *Lague*, 152 Vt. at 503, 568 A.2d at 359; Barrett v. Kunz, 158 Vt. 15, 604 A.2d 1278 (1992). The record here establishes that these easements, along with the other assets of the railroad, came into the hands of the State of Vermont in the 1960s. The State then leased them to an entity called the Vermont Railway, which operated trains over them. In 1970, the Vermont Railway ceased active transport operations on the line which included the right-of-way over the parcels at issue, and used the line only to store railroad cars. In 1975 the Railroad removed all of the railroad equipment, including switches and tracks, from the portion of the right-of-way running over the three parcels of land now owned by the Preseaults. In light of these facts, the trial court concluded that under Vermont law this amounted to an abandonment of the easements, and adjudged that the easements were extinguished as a matter of law in 1975. . . .

The Government and the State argue that there are facts inconsistent with that determination, but we are not persuaded that any of them significantly undercut the trial court's conclusion. For example, when the Vermont Railway removed its tracks in 1975, it did not remove the two bridges or any of the culverts on the line, all of which remained "substantially intact." That is not surprising. The Railroad was under no obligation to restore the former easement to its original condition. Tearing out existing structures would simply add to its costs, whereas the rails that were taken up could be used for repairs of defective rails elsewhere on the line. It is further argued that, since the rail line continues to operate to a point approximately one and one-third miles south of the Preseaults' property, it is possible to restore the line to full operation. The fact that restoration of the northern portion of the line would be technically feasible tells us little. The question is not what is technically possible to do in the future, but what was done in the past.

Almost immediately after the tracks were removed, members of the public began crossing over the easement. Perhaps illustrating the difficulty in getting government paperwork to catch up with reality, or perhaps indicating that revenue collectors do not give up easily, the State of Vermont and Vermont Railway, as they had done before the removal of the tracks, continued to collect fees under various license and crossing agreements from persons wishing to establish fixed crossings. In January 1976, the Preseaults executed a crossing agreement with the Vermont Railway which gave the Preseaults permission to cross the right-of-way. In March 1976, the Preseaults entered into a license agreement with the State and the Vermont Railway to locate a driveway and underground utility service across the railroad right-of-way. As late as 1991, 985 Associates (through Paul Preseault) paid a $10 license fee to "Vermont Railroad" (sic), presumably pursuant to one of the 1976 agreements. The Preseaults paid "under protest." Much of this activity suggests that, initially at least, the adjacent property owners decided it was cheaper to pay a nominal license fee to the State than to litigate the question of whether the State had the right to extract the fee. In view of all the contrary evidence of physical abandonment, we find this behavior by the State's revenue collectors unconvincing as persuasive evidence of a purpose or intent not to abandon the use of the right-of-way for actual railroad purposes.

One uncontrovertible piece of evidence in favor of abandonment is that, in the years following the shutting down of the line in 1970 and the 1975 removal of the tracks, no move has been made by the State or by the Railroad to reinstitute service over the line, or to undertake replacement of the removed tracks and other infrastructure necessary to return the line to service. . . . Other events occurring after 1975 are also of little probative value.[9]

The trial judge in this case . . . concluded that as a fact the Railroad had effected in 1975 an abandonment of the easement running over parcels A, B, and C. . . . We affirm the determination of the trial court that abandonment of the easements took place in 1975. That determination provides an alternative ground for concluding that a governmental taking occurred.

---

9. Since the 1950s, Rutland Railway and later the Vermont Railway have licensed the Burlington Electric Light Department, a municipal utility, to install and maintain electrical transmission and distribution lines within the right-of-way. The City of Burlington installed a water line on the property under an agreement with the Vermont Railway. The Government says this occurred in 1974, but the Preseaults say it was in 1976.

F. The Taking

. . . The ICC in a January 1986 Order authorized Vermont Railway ex post facto to discontinue service and approved the agreement between the state and the city of Burlington for trail use by the former right of way. . . .

In due course an eight foot wide paved strip was established on the former right-of-way over parcels A, B, and C. The path is some 60 feet from the Preseaults' front door. On each side of the Preseaults' driveway, where it crosses the easement, two concrete posts and one metal post were installed to block automobile traffic. The city also erected two stop signs on the path and built a water main under and along the path. The Preseaults have been unable to build on the land under the easement or to construct a driveway connecting their land through parcels A and B to the nearest public street.

The path is used regularly by members of the public for walking, skating, and bicycle riding. On warm weekends up to two hundred people an hour go through the Preseaults' property. People using the path often trespass on the Preseaults' front yard. On one occasion Mr. Preseault was nearly run over by a cyclist as he walked across the path.

Thus, if the Preseaults have interests under state property law that have traditionally been recognized and protected from governmental expropriation, and if, over their objection, the Government chooses to occupy or otherwise acquire those interests, the Fifth Amendment compels compensation. The record establishes two bases on which the Preseaults are entitled to recover. One, if the easements were in existence in 1986 when, pursuant to ICC Order, the City of Burlington established the public recreational trail, its establishment could not be justified under the terms and within the scope of the existing easements for railroad purposes. The taking of possession of the lands owned by the Preseaults for use as a public trail was in effect a taking of a new easement for that new use, for which the landowners are entitled to compensation.

Two, as an alternative basis, in 1986 when the ICC issued its Order authorizing the City to establish a public recreational biking and pedestrian trail on parcels A, B, and C, there was as a matter of state law no railroad easement in existence on those parcels, nor had there been for more than ten years. The easement had been abandoned in 1975, and the properties were held by the Preseaults in fee simple, unencumbered by any former property rights of the Railroad. When the City, pursuant to federal authorization, took possession of parcels A, B, and C and opened them to public use, that was a physical taking of the right of exclusive possession that belonged to the Preseaults as an incident of their ownership of the land.

The Government argues that, since it was the City that actually established the trail, the United States should not be considered the responsible actor. If a taking occurred, says the Government, it was the City and the State who did it. . . .

In the case before us there was a . . . physical entry upon the private lands of the Preseaults, acting under the Federal Government's authority pursuant to the ICC's Order.

. . . [W]hen the Federal Government puts into play a series of events which result in a taking of private property, the fact that the Government acts through a state agent does not absolve it from the responsibility, and the consequences, of its actions.

Summary and Conclusion

. . .

Whether, at the time a railroad applies to abandon its use of an easement limited to railroad purposes, a taking occurs under an ICC order to "railbank" the easement for possible future railroad use, and allowing in the interim for use of the easement for trail purposes, is a question not now before us. We offer no opinion at this time on that question. We conclude that the occupation of the Preseaults' property by the City of Burlington under the authority of the Federal Government constituted a taking of their property for which the Constitution requires that just compensation be paid. The judgment of the Court of Federal Claims, holding the Government not liable, is reversed. The matter is remanded to that court for further proceedings consistent with this opinion.

[Three of the nine judges sitting en banc in this case dissented. In their view, the Railroad had not abandoned the easement because, even though the tracks were removed, there was no clear and unequivocal signal of intent to abandon. Lack of intent to abandon is confirmed by the crossing and license agreements entered into by the Railroad. On the scope of the easement, the dissenters thought a railroad easement can be used as a public trail that merely shifts the use from one public use to another and imposes no greater burden on the servient tenement.

Upon remand, a U.S. Court of Federal Claims judge awarded the Preseaults $234,000 plus interest from the time the government opened the nature trail. The Burlington (Vt.) Free Press, May 26, 2001, at 2B.]

Notes and Problem

1. *Methods of termination.* Easements can be terminated in a number of ways.

- *Release.* The easement owner may agree to release the easement. Because easements are interests in property, subject to the Statute of Frauds, normally a release requires a writing.
- *Expiration.* If the duration of an easement is limited in some way, it ends through expiration at the end of the stated period. Similarly, an easement created to end upon the occurrence of some event (sometimes called a *defeasible easement*) expires automatically if and when the stated event occurs. Easements by necessity end when the necessity that gave rise to it ends. See Note 5 on page 500.
- *Merger.* An easement ends by merger if the easement owner later becomes the owner of the servient estate.
- *Estoppel.* An easement may end through estoppel if the servient owner reasonably relies upon a statement or representation by the easement owner.
- *Abandonment.* As *Preseault* indicates, an easement may terminate by abandonment. Normally, mere non-use by the easement owner does not constitute abandonment, but in several states a prescriptive easement ends by abandonment upon non-use for the statutory period of time. See

Zadnichek v. Fidler, 894 So. 2d 702 (Ala. App. 2004) (holding non-use alone does not constitute abandonment of a right-of-way easement but suggesting that the benefitted owner's act of obtaining alternative means of access to the benefited parcel could constitute evidence of intent to abandon).

- *Condemnation.* An easement may terminate by condemnation if the government exercises its eminent domain power to take title to a fee interest in the servient estate for a purpose that is inconsistent with continued existence of the easement.

- *Prescription.* Finally, an easement may be terminated by prescription. If the servient owner wrongfully and physically prevents the easement from being used for the prescriptive period, the easement is terminated. Spiegel v. Ferraro, 541 N.E.2d 15 (N.Y. 1989); Faulconer v. Williams, 964 P.2d 246 (Or. 1998); Restatement (Third) of Property, Servitudes § 7.7 (2000).

2. *Intent to abandon?* Is it clear to you that in *Preseault* the railroad abandoned the easement by discontinuing railroad use? Abandonment requires not simply non-use, but an unequivocal act showing an intent to abandon. Was there such an act in the case?

3. *Abandonment of railroad rights-of-way.* In Brandt Revocable Trust v. United States, 572 U.S. 93 (2014), the Supreme Court faced the question of what happens when a federally granted statutory railroad right-of-way over public land was abandoned. Does it go to the federal government or to the private party who acquired the land underlying the right-of-way? In *Brandt*, the government conveyed a fee interest in a parcel of public land to the Brandt family in 1976, subject to the railroad's underlying right-of-way. Later, the railroad abandoned the easement, and the government claimed ownership. The Brandts resisted, arguing that the right-of-way was simply an easement, and, under ordinary common law rules, when it was terminated by abandonment the burden on their servient estate was removed, giving them clear title. The government responded that it had retained a reversionary interest all along, one that would become possessory in fee upon abandonment.

By an 8-1 vote, the Supreme Court held that prior case law provided a definitive construction of the 1875 federal act granting the government power to convey easements to railroads, and that under that construction, the statute gave no rights to the United States in the underlying land. Hence the government could not repurpose the abandoned right-of-way land for recreational trail use. See Danaya C. Wright, Rails to Trails: Conversion of Railroad Corridors to Recreational Trails, Powell on Real Property ch. 78A (Michael A. Wolf gen. ed. 2017).

4. Negative Easements

A *negative easement* is the right of the dominant owner to stop the servient owner from doing something on the servient land. English common law recognized only a small number of these. English courts did not recognize any other types of negative easements, however, in part because until 1925, England had no effective system of public records of land titles, making discovering of negative easements very difficult.

American courts also disfavored negative easements, although their approach has been a bit more welcoming. For example, in Petersen v. Friedman, 328 P.2d 264 (Cal. App. 1958), the court enforced an express easement of unobstructed view of the San Francisco Bay over a neighbor's house, compelling the neighbor to remove obstructing television aerials. In England, the right to an unspoiled view cannot exist as an easement. A solar easement, preventing a person from blocking a neighbor's solar collector, has also been recognized in this country.

The most noteworthy new negative easement is the conservation easement, developed in the last 40 years to preserve scenic and historic areas and open space. An owner of land can give a public body or a private charitable organization (such as a land trust) a conservation easement, preventing the servient owner from building on the land except as specified in the grant. The value of the conservation easement (which is usually the development value of the land) is deductible as a charitable gift on income tax returns. Statutes, such as the Uniform Conservation Easement Act, have been enacted in almost all states authorizing conservation easements.

Although the English law courts closed the books on negative easements 150 years ago, chancery soon thereafter began to enforce negative covenants between the parties as equitable servitudes (see page 528). Equitable servitudes became the equivalent of negative easements, but subject to a different set of rules developed in chancery. The American courts followed suit. Today negative restrictions on land are usually treated as equitable servitudes. American courts sometimes refer to equitable servitudes as negative easements, but that simply underlies both the similarity of these interests and equity's circumvention of the law. Restatement (Third) of Property, supra, § 1.2 comment h, treats negative easements as restrictive covenants.

C. COVENANTS RUNNING WITH THE LAND

In this section, we will study land use interests that are created by covenants, or promises. As we noted at the beginning of the chapter, traditional doctrine categorically distinguishes between two types of such interests—*real covenants* and *equitable servitudes*. More recently, however, the Restatement (Third) of Property, Servitudes (2000), discards this distinction, and many of the old rules with it, in an attempt to create a unified law of servitudes that is both more modern and more coherent. But the traditional distinction, with its rules, still survives in most jurisdictions. Hence we will first examine the traditional approach, and then briefly look at the Restatement's revisions.

BACKGROUND, BRIEFLY

After the law courts refused to recognize new types of negative easements, landowners looked for a new doctrinal basis for their attempts to impose restrictions on the use of land. They found one in the law of contracts, but with a twist. What the landowners wanted was judicial recognition of a contract right respecting land use enforceable not only against the promisor landowner, but against his successors in title as well.

Why were landowners so interested in imposing restrictions on the use of land? Suppose that *O* owns a large tract of land on which he wants to put several different uses—a factory, a residence, and a market. If *O* wishes to maximize the value of all parts of his tract, he will locate these uses so as to minimize the harms they might impose on each other. Because a factory produces smoke and a grocery produces traffic, *O* may place them at some distance from each other and from the residence.

Similarly, bargains among neighbors can serve to minimize the harmful impacts ("external costs") that arise from conflicting resource uses. Suppose, for example, *A* (owner of a vacant lot on Whiteacre) and *B* (owner of a vacant lot on Blackacre) are neighbors who reciprocally agree not to use their respective lots for factories. Presumably, the agreement between *A* and *B* maximizes their well-being (and society's too, if there are no third-party effects that *A* and *B* have neglected to take into account). The value of both Whiteacre and Blackacre for residential use is presumably greater than the value of the opportunities for industrial use that have been forgone.

There is a hitch, however. Such bargains are less likely to be struck if only the original promisor is bound and only the original promisee benefited. The promisee wants assurances that he and his successors in interest will be protected against the original promisor and her successors in interest. What is needed, then, is some sort of *property right* that is enforceable by and against subsequent purchasers of Whiteacre and Blackacre. A mere contract right—the right of the original promisee to sue the original promisor alone—will seldom be sufficient to enable the market to allocate conflicting land uses efficiently. Do you see why? The answer relates to the discussion of transaction costs at pages 36-37. See also James E. Krier, Book Review, 122 U. Pa. L. Rev. 1664, 1678-1680 (1974).

1. Covenants Enforceable at Law: Real Covenants—The Traditional Approach

In the early nineteenth century, contract rights and duties were not generally assignable. The law had, however, developed one exception to the rule of nonassignability. *Where there is privity of estate*, the judges held, the contract is enforceable by and against assignees. It had long been established that privity of estate existed between a landlord and a tenant and that most covenants in leases would run with the land. Landowners in England tried to persuade the law courts to expand the required relationship of privity of estate to include contracts between neighbors so that the contracts would be enforceable against successor landowners. These attempts ultimately failed. The courts concluded that privity of estate, required for the burden of a covenant to run at law to successors, was satisfied only by a landlord-tenant relationship. Keppell v. Bailey, 39 Eng. Rep. 1042 (Ch. 1834). So, only leasehold covenant burdens ran at law, and this is still true in England today.

Unlike the English courts, American courts did not define privity of estate to include only a landlord-tenant relationship. They permitted, under varying circumstances, covenants to run in favor of and against successor owners. They developed the American *real covenant*, a promise respecting the use of land that runs with the land *at law*. The cases on real covenants are in some disarray and are often obscure and disputed, but you will be able to understand the issues and the confusion if you pay close attention to the following analytic model:

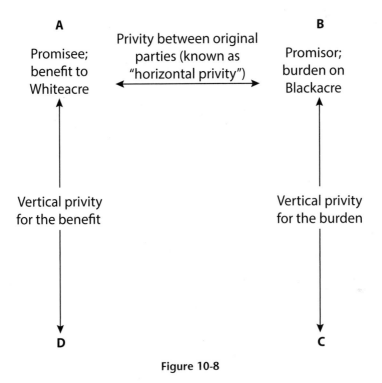

Figure 10-8

Suppose that B, owner of Blackacre, has promised A, owner of Whiteacre, that Blackacre shall not be used for industrial purposes. B sells Blackacre to C, and A sells Whiteacre to D. C constructs a factory on Blackacre. D sues C for damages. Will the covenant run to C and D? Let's start with the diagram in Figure 10-8.

If A, before any assignment, sues B, A is suing on the contract. There is privity of contract between A and B, and the law of contracts governs. No question arises whether a covenant runs. The question whether a covenant runs arises only when a person who is not a party to the covenant is suing or being sued.

Every covenant has two ends: the *benefit* end, originally held by A, and the *burdened* end, originally held by B. The burdened end concerns the duty to perform the promise. It is analogous to the servient estate in easement law. The benefited end concerns the right to enforce the promise and is the dominant estate. If *A* conveys Whiteacre to *D*, and *B* still owns Blackacre and constructs the factory, and *D* sues *B*, *D* must allege that the *benefit* runs to *D*. The burden remains with *B*, the original promisor. If *B* conveys Blackacre to *C*, who constructs the factory, and *A*, still owning Whiteacre, sues *C*, *A* must allege that the *burden* runs to *C*. If, as in the diagram above, both Whiteacre and Blackacre are conveyed to *D* and *C* respectively, and *D* sues *C*, *D* must allege that *both the burden and the benefit run*. It is important to keep in mind whether the running of the benefit or the running of the burden is involved in the case because the test for running of the burden is traditionally more onerous than the test for running of the benefit.

Traditionally, it has been easier for the benefit to run than the burden. It was thought that real covenants tend to impede the alienability of burdened land but less so of benefited land. Here are the traditional requirements for the burden and benefit of a real covenant to run:

1. *Horizontal privity.* This simply refers to privity between the original covenanting parties (*A* and *B* in Figure 10-8). The traditional rules are that horizontal privity is required for the *burden* to run but not for the *benefit*. Restatement of Property §§ 534, 548 (1944).

American courts define privity of estate to include two situations: (1) where the original parties have mutual simultaneous interests, such as an easement holder and the owner of the servient estate (sometimes called "simultaneous privity"); and (2) where the covenant is created during the course of a land transfer between the original parties, such as a covenant in the deed transferring the affected land (sometimes called "instantaneous privity"). So, in Figure 10-8, if *B*'s promise had been in a deed conveying Blackacre from *A* to *B*, *A* and *B* would be in privity of estate.

Restatement (Third), supra, § 2.4 eliminates the horizontal privity requirement altogether, and a growing number of courts are doing likewise. But many courts continue to adhere to the requirement on the burden side, and in still others there is ambiguity.

2. *Vertical privity.* Vertical privity concerns the relationship between the original party to the promise and his successor (on the burden side, in Figure 10-8, between *A* and *D*). On the *burden* side, the covenant is enforceable only against someone who has succeeded to the same estate as that of the original promisor. See Restatement of Property § 535 (1944). If the promisor had a fee simple, the party against whom enforcement is sought must have succeeded to that fee simple estate.

Courts made it easier for the benefit to run, that is, for successors to enforce the promise, however. A plaintiff who succeeded to *any interest* of the original promisee was considered in vertical privity with that promise and could enforce the promise. That is, the benefit runs to the successor in interest, regardless of what interest the successor acquired. So, for example, where a promisee who owns in fee simple leases the land, the

---

A Look Back

We encountered the concept of *privity of estate* previously in Chapter 6 (see pages 298-305) in discussing assignment and subleases by tenants.

lessee is entitled to enforce the promise (assuming the other requirements are met). An adverse possessor, however, could not because privity is lacking.

There are very few cases that actually hold that vertical privity is required on the benefit side. Restatement (Third), supra, § 5.2 eliminates the vertical privity requirement.

3. *Intent.* The original contracting parties must have intended to bind successors to their respective estates. This requirement is satisfied by language in the parties' agreement such as "*A*, on behalf of his heirs and assigns, covenants that . . ." and seldom poses a problem.

4. *"Touch and concern."* The promise must "touch and concern" the affected land. This basically means that the promise must relate in some way to the enjoyment, possession, or use of the affected land rather than being of personal concern to the original contracting parties. Restrictive covenants of the sort encountered in residential developments nearly always touch and concern. From the perspective of the touch and concern requirement, the most problematic covenants are affirmative covenants, usually involving the payment of money. Simple covenants to pay dues to homeowner associations are today nearly always enforced. Somewhat less certain are more complex monetary obligations to homeowner associations (or common interest communities, as they are also called). For example, in Streams Sports Club, Ltd. v. Richmond, 457 N.E.2d 1226 (Ill. 1983), the court held that a covenant requiring condominium owners to become dues-paying members of an adjacent sports club that the developer owned (and later sold to Streams Sports) touched and concerned the land because the owners had the right to enjoy the club facilities. However, in Midsouth Golf, LLC v. Fairfield Harbourside Condominium Assn., Inc., 652 S.E.2d 378 (N.C. App. 2007), the court held that a condominium association's recreational amenity fees covenant did not touch and concern the owners' properties.

5. *Notice.* The traditional statement of law is that notice is not a formal requirement for a real covenant to run with the land, and there are cases that so state. See, e.g., Dierberg v. Wills, 700 S.W.2d 461, 464 n.1 (Mo. App. 1985). This statement is problematic, however. In general, the recording statutes indirectly impose such a requirement. A real covenant is enforceable against a subsequent purchaser only if the purchaser has notice, record, actual, or inquiry, of the covenant.

A real covenant can be a *negative* promise (a promise not to do an act) or an *affirmative* promise (a promise to do an act).

Traditional Requirements for Real Covenants

	Burden	Benefit
Intent	yes	yes
Horizontal privity	yes	no
Vertical privity	yes	yes (lower standard)
Touch and concern	yes	yes
Notice	yes	no

Problems

1. *A* and *B*, neighboring landowners, decide that they will mutually restrict their lots to single-family residential use. They sign an agreement wherein each promises on behalf of herself, and her heirs and assigns, that her lot will be used for single-family residential purposes only. This agreement is recorded in the county courthouse under the name of each signer. *B* sells her lot to *C*. *C* builds an apartment house on his lot. *A* sues *C* for damages. What result? Suppose that *A* rather than *C* had built the apartment house. Is *C* entitled to damages against *A*?

2. *O*, owner of a two-acre parcel, divides that parcel and conveys one acre to *A*, keeping the other acre herself. The deed, properly recorded, included mutual covenants by *A*, on behalf of herself, her heirs, and assigns, and *O*, his heirs, and assigns, that the conveyed and retained parcels will be used for residential purposes only. Later, *B* takes *A*'s parcel by adverse possession and opens a restaurant on the premises. *O* brings an action against *B* for damages for breach of the covenant that *A* made. What result under the traditional rules?

3. Using the same facts as in Problem 2, suppose that instead *O* leased her parcel to *C* for five years. *A* opens a nursery school on her parcel. *C* brings an action against *A* for damages for breach of the covenant. What result under the traditional rules?

2. Covenants Enforceable in Equity: Equitable Servitudes—The Traditional Approach

Although in England the law courts, bound by the learning of the past, failed to respond positively to market demands for negative servitudes prohibiting some objectionable use enforceable against successor owners, the chancellor, by design or by result, came to the aid of the market in the famous case of Tulk v. Moxhay.

TULK v. MOXHAY
Court of Chancery, England, 1848
2 Phillips 774, 41 Eng. Rep. 1143

In the year 1808 the Plaintiff, being then the owner in fee of the vacant piece of ground in Leicester Square, as well as of several of the houses forming the Square, sold the piece of ground by the description of "Leicester Square garden or pleasure ground, with the equestrian statue then standing in the centre thereof, and the iron railing and stone work round the same," to one Elms in fee: and the deed of conveyance contained a covenant by Elms, for himself, his heirs, and assigns, with the Plaintiff, his heirs, executors, and administrators,

> that Elms, his heirs, and assigns should, and would from time to time, and at all times thereafter at his and their own costs and charges, keep and maintain the said piece of ground and square garden, and the iron railing round the

same in its then form, and in sufficient and proper repair as a square garden and pleasure ground, in an open state, uncovered with any buildings, in neat and ornamental order; and that it should be lawful for the inhabitants of Leicester Square, tenants of the Plaintiff, on payment of a reasonable rent for the same, to have keys at their own expense and the privilege of admission therewith at any time or times into the said square garden and pleasure ground.

The piece of land so conveyed passed by divers mesne conveyances into the hands of the Defendant, whose purchase deed contained no similar covenant with his vendor: but he admitted that he had purchased with notice of the covenant in the deed of 1808.

Charles Pepys, First Earl of Cottenham, by Charles Robert Leslie
Source: National Portrait Gallery, London

The Defendant having manifested an intention to alter the character of the square garden, and asserted a right, if he thought fit, to build upon it, the Plaintiff, who still remained owner of several houses in the square, filed this bill for an injunction; and an injunction was granted by the Master of the Rolls to restrain the Defendant from converting or using the piece of ground and square garden, and the iron railing round the same, to or for any other purpose than as a . . . square garden and pleasure ground in an open state, and uncovered with buildings. . . .

THE LORD CHANCELLOR [Cottenham]. . . . That this Court has jurisdiction to enforce a contract between the owner of land and his neighbour purchasing a part of it, that the latter shall either use or abstain from using the land purchased in a particular way, is what I never knew disputed. Here there is no question about the contract: the owner of certain houses in the square sells the land adjoining, with a covenant from the purchaser not to use it for any other purpose than as a square garden. And it is now contended, not that the vendee could violate the contract, but that he might sell the piece of land, and that the purchaser from him may violate it without this Court having any power to interfere. If that were so, it would be impossible for an owner of land to sell part of it without incurring the risk of rendering what he retains worthless. It is said that, the covenant being one which does not run with the land, this court cannot enforce it; but the question is, not whether the covenant runs with the land, but whether a party shall be permitted to use the land in a manner inconsistent with the contract entered into by his vendor, and with notice of which he purchased. Of course, the price would be affected by the covenant, and nothing could be more

Leicester Square, 1852

Leicester Square today

inequitable than the original purchaser should be able to sell the property the next day for a greater price, in consideration of the assignee being allowed to escape from the liability which he had himself undertaken.

That the question does not depend upon whether the covenant runs with the land is evident from this, that if there was a mere agreement and no covenant, this Court would enforce it against a party purchasing with notice of it; for if an equity is attached to the property by the owner, no one purchasing with notice of that equity can stand in a different situation from the party from whom he purchased. . . .

I think the cases cited before the Vice-Chancellor and this decision of the Master of the Rolls perfectly right, and, therefore, that this motion must be refused, with costs.

THE REST OF THE STORY . . .

The fascinating story behind Tulk v. Moxhay and the history of Leicester Square is told in James Charles Smith, Tulk v. Moxhay: The Fight to Develop Leicester Square, in Property Stories 171 (Gerald Korngold & Andrew P. Morriss eds. 2d ed. 2009). Professor Smith reports that the origin of the central restriction involved in the case was not the 1808 deed from Tulk to Elms but a certificate of partition executed earlier in 1789. The land of which the garden was a part was partitioned to pay the original owner's mortgagees. The court imposed the restrictions to protect land that the mortgagees acquired near the garden. Professor Smith speculates that had Moxhay's lawyers considered this fact they might have challenged Tulk's standing. Tulk owned none of the benefited land and hence was not an intended beneficiary of the judicial restriction. Id. at 178 n.24.

At the time of Tulk v. Moxhay, Leicester Square was changing from a residential to a commercial area, and the central garden had become an unkempt receptacle for rubbish. In 1851, James Wyld, a geographer, purchased the garden from Moxhay's widow. With the consent of the Tulk family, who received an option to purchase an undivided half of the garden at the end of 10 years, Wyld erected in the garden a building to house a 60-foot high plaster scale model of the earth. This building, called "Wyld's Monster Globe," dwarfed the surrounding houses. After 10 years this was pulled down, and John A. Tulk, grandson of the plaintiff in Tulk v. Moxhay, exercised the option to purchase. John A. Tulk hoped to convert the garden to building land, as Moxhay had tried to do formerly. After much public outcry, the garden was acquired by the government for a public park in 1874. Leicester Square today is the center of London's cinema district.

Notes, Questions, and Problems

1. *Tulk—Classifying the servitudes.* Examine each of the covenants made by Elms. How would you classify the rights and duties intended by the deed of conveyance? Is the covenant sued on really an easement of view in promissory form?

2. *Requirements of equitable servitudes.* Within a short time after the decision in Tulk v. Moxhay, English equity judges began developing a body of doctrinal requirements for covenants to be enforceable in equity, giving rise to the law of equitable servitudes. *An equitable servitude, enforceable by an injunction as in Tulk v. Moxhay, is a covenant respecting the use of land enforceable against successor owners or possessors in equity regardless of its enforceability at law.* The requirements for equitable servitudes to be enforceable are:

For the *burden* to run,

1) the promise must be *in writing* or be implied from a common plan of development (see Note 4 below)
2) the original parties must *intend* to bind successors
3) the promise must *"touch and concern"* the land
4) the successor in question must have *notice*

Neither horizontal nor vertical privity is required.
For the *benefit* to run,

1) the promise must be *in writing* or be implied from a common plan of development
2) the original parties must *intend* to benefit successors
3) the promise must *"touch and concern"* the land

Notice of the covenant is required for the *burden* of an equitable servitude to run with the land but is not required for the running of the *benefit*. However, equitable servitudes are enforceable against successors who give no consideration (donees, heirs, will beneficiaries), whether or not they have notice. A fundamental principle of the recording system is that only subsequent purchasers, and not donees, are protected against prior interests of which they have no notice. See page 441.

Traditional Requirements for Equitable Servitudes

	Burden	Benefit
Intent	yes	yes
Horizontal privity	no	no
Vertical privity	no	no, with exceptions
Touch and concern	yes	yes
Notice	yes	no

Vertical privity is not required for the *benefit* of an equitable servitude to run in nearly all jurisdictions. The basis for allowing someone who is not a successor of the original promisee to enforce the promise is as a third-party beneficiary. See Restatement (Third) of Property, Servitudes § 2.6 comment a (2000) ("The third-party-beneficiary doctrine provides the basis for recognizing that servitude benefits of all types can be created in favor of persons, either in gross or as holders of interests in land, who are not otherwise parties to the transaction"); Murawski v. Roland Well Drilling, 374 S.E.2d 207 (Ga. App. 1988). But see 328 Owners Corp. v. 330 West 86 Oaks Corp., 865 N.E.2d 1228 (N.Y. 2007) (requiring vertical privity on the benefit side).

3. *Is it a real covenant or an equitable servitude?* Students (and even some courts) are often confused about the distinction between real covenants and equitable servitudes. Given the different requirements for each under traditional doctrine, how does one know whether a covenant should be treated as one or the other? The simple answer is the remedy that the plaintiff is seeking—the traditional difference between real covenants and equitable servitudes relates to the remedy sought. The remedy for breach of a real covenant is damages in a suit at law. The remedy for breach of an equitable servitude is an injunction or enforcement of a lien in a suit in equity.

To see this, consider again Problem 1 on page 528: *A* and *B*, neighboring landowners, decide that they will mutually restrict their lots to single-family residential use. They sign an agreement wherein each promises on behalf of herself, and her heirs and assigns, that her lot will be used for single-family residential purposes only. This agreement is recorded in the county courthouse under the name of each signer. *B* sells her lot to *C*. *C* builds an apartment house on his lot. Suppose instead of seeking damages, *A* seeks an injunction against *C*. Would the result be the same as if *A* sought damages?

If you were the plaintiff in a case like this, would you rather have an injunction or damages? In the large majority of cases, the plaintiff seeks an injunction to enforce the covenant. Part of the reason is that if an injunction is granted, the plaintiff can, if the plaintiff wishes, "sell the injunction" to the defendant, as happened in Tulk v. Moxhay. By fixing the selling price of the injunction, the plaintiff can make his own determination of the amount of damages, whereas if the plaintiff sues for damages the jury determines the amount of damages.

4. *The Statute of Frauds and implying equitable servitudes from a common plan.* A real covenant is an interest in land within the meaning of the Statute of Frauds and must be created by a written instrument signed by the covenantor.

If the deed creating a real covenant is signed by the grantor only, and it contains a promise by the grantee, the promise is enforceable against the grantee. The grantee is bound by the act of accepting such a deed. A real covenant cannot arise by estoppel, implication, or prescription, as can an easement.

Similarly, an equitable servitude is an interest in land. But unlike a real covenant, it may be implied in equity under certain limited circumstances. An equitable servitude, which arises out of a promise, cannot be obtained by prescription.

Despite the Statute of Frauds, most courts have been willing to imply an equitable servitude where a developer of a residential subdivision has manifested a *common plan* or *common scheme* of restrictive servitudes throughout the development. The leading case is Sanborn v. McLean, 206 N.W.2d 496 (Mich. 1925), where the developers, intending to subject all 91 lots in their development to uniform servitudes restricting the lots to residential use, included express language to that effect in only 53 of the deeds. Some years later, the defendant purchased an apparently unrestricted lot and began to build a gas station in his back yard. The plaintiff and other restricted lot owners sued to enjoin the construction, and the court granted the injunction. The court held that an equitable servitude, which it misleadingly termed a "reciprocal negative easement," will be implied because the developer had a common plan to develop a residential subdivision. The evidence of this plan included sales literature, statements of the developer, but above all, the fact that 53 out of 91 lots were expressly restricted.

A few jurisdictions take the Statute of Frauds more seriously. In California, an equitable servitude must be created by a written instrument identifying the burdened lot; it will not be implied from the existence of restrictions on other lots in a subdivision. Riley v. Bear Creek Planning Comm., 551 P.2d 1213 (Cal. 1976). In Massachusetts, covenants will not be implied from a general plan, but if the covenants on the burdened lot are in writing a general plan may be used to show that the neighbors in the subdivision were intended as beneficiaries and may enforce the covenants. Snow v. Van Dam, 197 N.E. 224 (Mass. 1935).

3. The Restatement (Third) Approach—Unifying the Law of Servitudes

The Restatement (Third) of Property, Servitudes (2000), purports to modernize and rationalize the law of servitudes. The Restatement takes the position that there is, and ought to be, no difference in the rules applicable to real covenants and equitable servitudes. The Restatement drops the terms "real covenant" and "equitable servitude" and refers to these as covenants running with the land. Id. § 1.4. The same rules apply to all covenants running with the land. The court may enforce the covenant by "any appropriate remedy or combination of remedies, which may include declaratory judgment, compensatory damages, punitive damages, nominal damages, injunctions, restitution, and imposition of liens." Id. § 8.3. Moreover, the Restatement applies the same rules to easements and covenants (lumped together as "servitudes"), unless there is a sound reason for differentiation. For a summary of the irrational distinctions plaguing the old law of servitudes, see Susan F. French, Toward a Modern Law of Servitudes: Reweaving the Ancient Strands, 55 S. Cal. L. Rev. 1261 (1982); Uriel Reichman, Toward a Unified Concept of Servitudes, id. at 1179 (1982).

Under the Restatement, a servitude is created under four circumstances: (1) when the owner of land to be burdened "enters into a contract or makes a conveyance [that is] intended to create a servitude" that complies with the Statute of Frauds; (2) when the owner of land to be burdened conveys a lot in a common scheme development or common interest community subject to a recorded declaration of servitudes for the development; (3) if the requirements for creation of a servitude by estoppel, implication, necessity, or prescription are met; or (4) "if the requirements for creation of a servitude for public benefit [e.g., by condemnation] are met." Restatement (Third), supra, § 2.1. It goes on to provide that a servitude is valid unless it is illegal, unconstitutional, or violates certain public policies. Id. § 3.1. We will discuss these public policies later in this chapter (see pages 555-556).

4. Termination of Covenants

Covenants, like easements, can be terminated in a number of ways. They may be discharged by: (1) *merger* on the basis of unity of ownership of the benefit and burden by the same person; (2) a formal *release*, which is normally written and recorded; (3) *acquiescence*, which arises when the plaintiff has failed to enforce the servitude against other breaches and then seeks to enforce the servitude against the defendant; (4) *abandonment*, which resembles acquiescence except that it makes the servitude unenforceable as to the entire parcel rather than only as to the plaintiff immediately involved; (5) the equitable doctrine of *unclean hands*, according to which the court will refuse to enjoin a violation of a servitude that the plaintiff previously violated; (6) the equitable doctrine of *laches*, which involves an unreasonable delay by the plaintiff to enforce a servitude against the defendant causing prejudice to the defendant (laches does not extinguish the servitude but only bars enforcement); and (7) *estoppel*, if the defendant has relied upon the plaintiff's conduct, making it inequitable to allow the plaintiff to enforce the servitude. See Powell on Real Property § 60.10[1] (Michael A. Wolf gen. ed. 2009). Servitudes may also be terminated through the exercise of the government's eminent domain power (discussed on page 522) and on the basis of prescription.

Note that all the grounds for termination just listed deal with changes within the subdivision. What about changes outside the subdivision? May courts modify or terminate covenants on the basis of such changes? Consider the following case.

RIVER HEIGHTS ASSOCIATES L.P. v. BATTEN

Supreme Court of Virginia, 2004
591 S.E.2d 683

CARRICO, J.

Procedural Background

In a bill of complaint for declaratory judgment, Alice Batten and other owners of lots in the Carrsbrook Subdivision in Albemarle County (collectively, Batten) sought a declaration favoring the enforceability of restrictive covenants prohibiting commercial use of four unimproved lots in the same subdivision, namely, Lots 1, 2C, and 2D in Section C and Lot 1 in Section E. River Heights Associates Limited Partnership is the record owner of Lot 1, Section C, which it acquired in 1998, S.V. Associates is the record owner of Lots 2C and 2D, Section C, which it acquired in 1978, and First Gold Leaf Land Trust is the record owner of Lot 1, Section E, which it acquired in 1986. Batten named these record owners as the defendants in her bill of complaint.

Although the entities just listed hold title to the four lots in question, the briefs describe Wendell W. Wood and his wife, Marlene C. Wood, as the beneficial owners of the lots. While the Woods were not named as defendants below and are not parties to this appeal, the appellants in the case are referred to collectively in the briefs as "Wood," and we will follow the same practice.

Wood demurred to the bill of complaint on the grounds, inter alia, that Batten had failed to state a cause of action upon which relief could be granted and had failed to allege the existence of a controversy pursuant to Code § 8.01-184, a part of the declaratory judgment statutes, so as to confer jurisdiction over the claims asserted in the bill of complaint. The trial court overruled the demurrer on these grounds but sustained it on other grounds not pertinent here and allowed Batten to file an amended bill of complaint.

Batten filed an amended bill not differing in substance from her original bill. Wood filed an answer to the amended bill in which he denied the essential elements of Batten's claim for relief. In a section styled "Affirmative Defenses," Wood contended that Batten had failed to state a cause of action upon which relief could be granted, that the restrictive covenant was unenforceable, and that the covenant did not apply to his property. Wood also contended that he had no knowledge of the covenant.

Evidentiary Background

Carrsbrook Subdivision is located on the eastern side of U.S. Route 29 between the northern city limits of Charlottesville and the Rivanna River. The four lots here in dispute are located at the western edge of the subdivision and are the only lots with frontage on U.S. Route 29.

The restrictive covenants were established in a deed dated May 6, 1959, from Norman Kelsey and wife to Charles W. Hurt (the Kelsey-Hurt deed), which conveyed an unsubdivided 40-acre portion of "the land known as 'Carrsbrook.'" The conveyance was made subject to "certain restrictions . . . which shall be considered as covenants running with the land." Only one of the restrictions is pertinent here: "The property is to be used for residential purposes only and no rooming house, boarding house, tourist home, or any other type of commercial enterprise, or any church, hospital, asylum, or charitable institution shall be operated thereon" (the restrictive covenant).

In October 1960, Section C of Carrsbrook was subdivided into 19 lots, all made "subject to the restrictive covenants applicable to Carrsbrook Subdivision of record." [L]ot 1 . . . contain[s] 3.04 acres bordering Carrsbrook Drive, Indian Spring Road, and Route 29. Lot 2 . . . contain[s] 2.55 acres bordering Indian Spring Road and Route 29. A notation on the plat states that "[l]ots 1 & 2 restricted to non access on Rte. 29 if lots are used for residential purposes" (the plat note).

In 1962, Lot 2, Section C, was resubdivided into four lots, namely, 2A, 2B, 2C, and 2D. Lots 2C and 2D border Route 29. Lots 2A and 2B border only Indian Spring Road, leaving Lots 2C and 2D without direct access to the residential roads in the subdivision

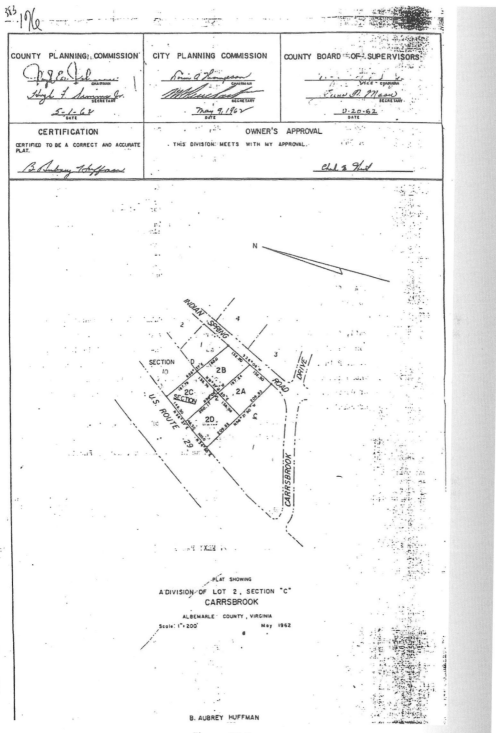

Figure 10-9
Map filed with the City Planning Commission showing the lots involved in the case

and Lots 2A and 2B without direct access to Route 29. In addition, Lots 2C and 2D, along with Lot 1C, are subject to the plat note.

In 1969, Albemarle County adopted its first comprehensive zoning ordinance. The lots in question were zoned to a depth of 200 feet from Route 29 in a B-1 classification, a commercial district in which residential use is prohibited. This zoning classification was continued in a comprehensive rezoning in 1980, with the result that presently the lots in question are zoned for commercial use but are subject to the restrictive covenant prohibiting such use.

When Carrsbrook Subdivision was created in 1969, Route 29 was a two-lane road with residences and small businesses located on each side of the road. In the area where the lots in question are located, Route 29 is today an eight- to ten-lane road that is highly developed commercially on both sides with shopping centers, hotels, restaurants, automobile dealerships, and other types of businesses. No residential uses have been implemented along Route 29 since 1959. There have been no changes within the Carrsbrook Subdivision other than the aging of homes and the maturing of trees.

The Trial Court's Decision

[T]he trial court held that the restrictive covenant against commercial use did apply to the four lots in question and that the covenant was enforceable. The court entered a final decree declaring the covenant enforceable and enjoining the use or operation of the lots in violation of the covenant, including developing the lots commercially in the future. We awarded Wood this appeal. . . .

Change of Conditions

Wood alleges that "[t]he trial court erred in failing to remove the residential restrictive covenant as to all four lots (Lots 1E, 1C, 2C, and 2D) in light of the overwhelming evidence that established a change of conditions so radical as practically to destroy the essential objects and purposes of the restriction."

Wood stresses the changes, outlined supra, that have taken place in the Route 29 corridor since Carrsbrook Subdivision was created in 1969, viz., the previous two-lane road with residences and small businesses strung along each side has become a heavily traveled eight- to ten-lane thoroughfare lined on each side with shopping centers, hotels, restaurants, automobile dealerships, and other types of businesses. Further, Wood also stresses the fact that "no residential houses have been built or used from the city limits of Charlottesville to the South Rivanna River on either the east or west side of Route 29 in the last thirty years."[10]

The test for determining whether changed conditions warrant the nullification of a restrictive covenant was enunciated in Deitrick v. Leadbetter, 175 Va. 170, 8 S.E.2d 276 (1940), as follows:

> "No hard and fast rule can be laid down as to when changed conditions have defeated the purpose of restrictions, but it can be safely asserted the changes must be so radical as practically to destroy the essential objects and purposes of the agreement."

---

10. Wood also stresses the zoning changes that have occurred along both sides of Route 29 since the restrictive covenant was created. However, in Ault v. Shipley, 189 Va. 69, 75, 52 S.E.2d 56, 58 (1949), this Court said that "a zoning law cannot constitutionally relieve land within the district covered by it from lawful restrictive covenants affecting its use for business purposes."

175 Va. at 177, 8 S.E.2d at 279 (quoting Rombauer v. Compton Heights Christian Church, 328 Mo. 1, 40 S.W.2d 545, 553 (1931)).

Wood takes the trial court to task, saying that the court "ignored the radical changes that have occurred in and around the subject properties since 1959, but rather focused myopically on whether or not there have been changes within the interior of the Subdivision." This is an unfair representation of what the trial court ruled in this case.

In a letter opinion, the trial court wrote: "[Wood has] failed to prove that radical changes both in and around the neighborhood have occurred such that the purpose of the restrictive covenant is destroyed." (Emphasis added.) Thus, it is clear the court did not focus upon conditions in Carrsbrook Subdivision alone but on conditions "around the neighborhood" as a whole.

This is in accord with Virginia law. In Booker [v. Old Dominion Land Co., 49 S.E.2d 314 (Va. 1948)], relief was sought from a restrictive covenant prohibiting commercial uses of residential lots in a subdivision. It was alleged that there had been a change of conditions so radical as to destroy the essential objectives and purposes of the covenant. These changes included the operation of a nearby zipper factory, the conversion of one of the lots into a hard-surfaced road leading to the factory, the widening of the road on which all the lots abutted from a two-lane roadway, carrying a small amount of traffic, to a heavily traveled four-lane federal highway, the construction nearby of a large shopping center, and the presence of a skating rink across the road from one of the lots.

The trial court refused to remove the restrictive covenant. This Court affirmed. We said that "if a radical change takes place *in the whole neighborhood* so as to defeat the purpose of the restrictions and render their enforcement inequitable and oppressive, equity will not compel observance of them by injunction." *Id.* at 317. (Emphasis added.)

Wood seemingly would have the rule the other way—ignore the circumstances within the property protected by a restrictive covenant and focus only upon the surrounding area. However, common sense tells us that when the issue is whether a restrictive covenant still serves its intended purpose and that purpose is to protect the lots in a particular subdivision from commercial uses, the conditions existing within the subdivision must be examined along with those existing in the surrounding area in order to determine the issue fairly. To ignore the conditions within the subdivision and to hold the covenant unenforceable solely because of changed conditions elsewhere would deny the lot owners the protection to which they are entitled according to a solemn covenant voluntarily made, and that would be grossly unfair.

What is required, therefore, is a leveling exercise in which fair consideration is given both to conditions in the subdivision and those in the surrounding area. Here, the facts are that there have been no changes within Carrsbrook Subdivision other than the aging of homes and the maturing of trees but there have been substantial changes within the surrounding area. After giving fair consideration to both situations, we are of opinion the changes are not so radical as to defeat the purpose of the covenant. . . .

Conclusion

For the reasons assigned, the judgment of the trial court will be affirmed.

Notes and Questions

1. *The changed conditions doctrine.* The changed conditions doctrine, of which *River Heights Associates* is a typical example, is a stringent one. As long as the restriction is of value to some land, courts usually will not terminate it, even though conditions have changed in such a way that the restriction decreases the value of other land.

2. *The appropriate remedy.* In most cases, when the court holds that the restriction has not terminated despite changed conditions, it enforces the covenant by injunctive relief. But is that the best remedy? We previously encountered the question whether an injunction or damages is the better remedy and what factors play into this choice of remedy, in Chapter 9, on nuisance. See Notes 3 and 4, at page 471. Generally, a court can enforce a restrictive covenant by an injunction or by an award of damages for breach. Which remedy is preferable, as a matter of fairness and efficiency, when conditions radically change? Should it matter whether multiple parties have the benefit of the covenant? For a searching discussion of this matter, see Glen O. Robinson, Explaining Contingent Rights: The Puzzle of "Obsolete" Covenants, 91 Colum. L. Rev. 546, 548-560, 570-576 (1991).

3. *The Restatement (Third) approach.* Restatement (Third) of Property, Servitudes § 7.10(2), provides: "If the purpose of the servitude can be accomplished, but because of changed conditions the servient estate is no longer suitable for uses permitted by the servitude, a court may modify the servitude to permit other uses under conditions designed to preserve the benefits of the original servitude." How does this compare with the traditional changed conditions doctrine, illustrated by *River Heights Associates*? Comment a goes on to state: "Where transaction costs are likely to be high because large numbers of people are involved . . . a court should be more ready to intervene than where transaction costs are likely to be low."

Section 7.10 applies to easements as well as to equitable servitudes and real covenants. This represents a major change in the law of easements, which traditionally did not recognize changed conditions as a basis for termination. The extension of the changed conditions doctrine to easements is part of the general objective of the Restatement to unify the law of servitudes.

5. Discriminatory Servitudes

SHELLEY v. KRAEMER

Supreme Court of the United States, 1948
334 U.S. 1

VINSON, C.J. These cases present for our consideration questions relating to the validity of court enforcement of private agreements, generally described as restrictive covenants, which have as their purpose the exclusion of persons of designated race or color from the ownership or occupancy of real property. . . .

On February 16, 1911, thirty out of a total of thirty-nine owners of property fronting both sides of Labadie Avenue between Taylor Avenue and Cora Avenue in the city of St. Louis, signed an agreement, which was subsequently recorded, providing in part:

> . . . the said property is hereby restricted to the use and occupancy for the term of Fifty (50) years from this date, so that it shall be a condition all the time and whether recited and referred to as (sic) not in subsequent conveyances and shall attach to the land, as a condition precedent to the sale of the same, that hereafter no part of said property or any portion thereof shall be, for said term of Fifty-years, occupied by any person not of the Caucasian race, it being intended hereby to restrict the use of said property for said period of time against the occupancy as owners or tenants of any portion of said property for resident or other purpose by people of the Negro or Mongolian Race.

. . .

On August 11, 1945, pursuant to a contract of sale, petitioners Shelley, who are Negroes, for valuable consideration received from one Fitzgerald a warranty deed to the parcel in question. The trial court found that petitioners had no actual knowledge of the restrictive agreement at the time of the purchase.

On October 9, 1945, respondents, as owners of other property subject to the terms of the restrictive covenant, brought suit . . . praying that petitioners Shelley be restrained from taking possession of the property and that judgment be entered divesting title out of petitioners Shelley and revesting title in the immediate grantor or in such other person as the court should direct. . . .

The Shelley House, at 4600 Labadie, St. Louis, Mo. The house is in the National Register of Historic Places.

The Supreme Court of Missouri sitting en banc reversed and directed the trial court to grant the relief for which respondents had prayed. That court held the agreement effective and concluded that enforcement of its provisions violated no rights guaranteed to petitioners by the Federal Constitution. . . .

. . .

Petitioners have placed primary reliance on their contentions, first raised in the state courts, that judicial enforcement of the restrictive agreements in these cases has violated rights guaranteed to petitioners by the Fourteenth Amendment of the Federal Constitution and Acts of Congress passed pursuant to that Amendment. Specifically, petitioners urge that they have been denied the equal protection of the laws. . . .

I.

. . .

It cannot be doubted that among the civil rights intended to be protected from discriminatory state action by the Fourteenth Amendment are the rights to acquire, enjoy, own and dispose of property. Equality in the enjoyment of property rights was regarded by the framers of that Amendment as an essential pre-condition to the realization of other basic civil rights and liberties which the Amendment was intended to guarantee. . . .

It is likewise clear that restrictions on the right of occupancy of the sort sought to be created by the private agreements in these cases could not be squared with the requirements of the Fourteenth Amendment if imposed by state statute or local ordinance. We do not understand respondents to urge the contrary. . . .

[T]he present cases . . . do not involve action by state legislatures or city councils. Here the particular patterns of discrimination and the areas in which the restrictions are to operate, are determined, in the first instance, by the terms of agreements among private individuals. Participation of the State consists in the enforcement of the restrictions so defined. The crucial issue with which we are here confronted is whether this distinction removes these cases from the operation of the prohibitory provisions of the Fourteenth Amendment. Since the decision of this Court in the Civil Rights Cases, 1883, 109 U.S. 3, the principle has become firmly embedded in our constitutional law that the action inhibited by the first section of the Fourteenth Amendment is only such action as may fairly be said to be that of the States. That Amendment erects no shield against merely private conduct, however discriminatory or wrongful.

We conclude, therefore, that the restrictive agreements standing alone cannot be regarded as a violation of any rights guaranteed to petitioners by the Fourteenth Amendment. So long as the purposes of those agreements are effectuated by voluntary adherence to their terms, it would appear clear that there has been no action by the State and the provisions of the Amendment have not been violated.

But here there was more. These are cases in which the purposes of the agreements were secured only by judicial enforcement by state courts of the restrictive terms of the agreements. . . .

II.

That the action of state courts and of judicial officers in their official capacities is to be regarded as action of the State within the meaning of the Fourteenth Amendment, is a proposition which has long been established by decisions of this Court. . . .

The action of state courts in imposing penalties or depriving parties of other substantive rights without providing adequate notice and opportunity to defend, has, of course, long been regarded as a denial of the due process of law guaranteed by the Fourteenth Amendment. . . .

But the examples of state judicial action which have been held by this Court to violate the Amendment's commands are not restricted to situations in which the judicial proceedings were found in some manner to be procedurally unfair. It has been recognized that the action of state courts in enforcing a substantive common-law rule formulated by those courts, may result in the denial of rights guaranteed by the Fourteenth Amendment, even though the judicial proceedings in such cases may have been in complete accord with the most rigorous conceptions of procedural due process. . . .

The short of the matter is that from the time of the adoption of the Fourteenth Amendment until the present, it has been the consistent ruling of this Court that the action of the States to which the Amendment has reference, includes action of state courts and state judicial officials. Although, in construing the terms of the Fourteenth Amendment, differences have from time to time been expressed as to whether particular types of state action may be said to offend the Amendment's prohibitory provisions, it has never been suggested that state court action is immunized from the operation of those provisions simply because the act is that of the judicial branch of the state government.

III.

. . .

We have no doubt that there has been state action in these cases in the full and complete sense of the phrase. The undisputed facts disclose that the petitioners were willing purchasers of properties upon which they desired to build homes. The owners of the properties were willing sellers; and contracts for sale were according consummated. It is clear that but for the active intervention of the state courts, supported by the full panoply of state power, petitioners would have been free to occupy the properties in question without restraint.

. . . The judicial action in each case bears the clear and unmistakable imprimatur of the State. . . . And when the effect of that action is to deny rights subject to the protection of the Fourteenth Amendment, it is the obligation of this Court to enforce the constitutional commands.

We hold that in granting judicial enforcement of the restrictive agreements in these cases, the States have denied petitioners the equal protection of the laws and that, therefore, the action of the state courts cannot stand. We have noted that freedom from discrimination by the States in the enjoyment of property rights was among the basic objectives sought to be effectuated by the framers of the Fourteenth Amendment. That such discrimination has occurred in these cases is clear. Because of the race or color of these petitioners they have been denied rights of ownership or occupancy enjoyed as a matter of course by other citizens of different race or color. . . .

. . .

The historical context in which the Fourteenth Amendment became a part of the Constitution should not be forgotten. Whatever else the framers sought to achieve, it is clear that the matter of primary concern was the establishment of equality in the enjoyment of basic civil and political rights and the preservation of those rights from discriminatory action on the part of the States based on considerations of race or color.

Seventy-five years ago this Court announced that the provisions of the Amendment are to be construed with this fundamental purpose in mind.

Upon full consideration, we have concluded that in these cases the States have acted to deny petitioners the equal protection of the laws guaranteed by the Fourteenth Amendment. Having so decided, we find it unnecessary to consider whether petitioners have also been deprived of property without due process of law or denied privileges and immunities of citizens of the United States.

For the reasons stated, the judgment of the Supreme Court of Missouri and the judgment of the Supreme Court of Michigan must be reversed.

THE REST OF THE STORY . . .

In his book *Five Chiefs*, retired Justice John Paul Stevens points out that Justices Reed, Jackson, and Rutledge, all of whom recused themselves in *Shelley*, likely did so because the deeds to their District of Columbia homes contained racially restrictive covenants. (We owe this point to Professor Josh Blackman, a member of the South Texas College of Law faculty.)

Notes and Questions

1. *Non-constitutional grounds for decision.* Could a court have declared the racially restrictive covenant in *Shelley* not only unenforceable but invalid on any non-constitutional grounds? Did the covenants in that case meet all of the common law requirements for covenants running with the land? See Carol M. Rose, Property Stories: *Shelly v. Kraemer*, in Property Stories 189, 200-204 (Gerald Korngold & Andrew P. Morriss eds. 2d ed. 2009).

2. *The signaling function of racial covenants.* Professors Richard Brooks and Carol Rose have established that with respect to racial covenants, *Shelley* changed very little. After the decision racial covenants continued to play an important role in perpetuating residential racial segregation in urban areas. They serve as important signals of neighbor racial preferences to real estate brokers and lenders. It was not until 1968, when the federal Fair Housing Act was first enacted, that this signaling function was seriously addressed. See Richard R.W. Brooks & Carol M. Rose, Saving the Neighborhood: Racially Restrictive Covenants, Law, and Social Norms (2013).

3. *The Fair Housing Act.* A covenant with a racially discriminatory effect may violate the federal Fair Housing Act, enacted as Title VIII of the Civil Rights Act of 1968, 42 U.S.C.A. §§ 3601-3631. Recall that the act makes it unlawful to refuse to sell or rent or otherwise make unavailable a dwelling to any person because of race, color, religion, sex, national origin, familial status, or handicap. See pages 291-293. Still, there may be ways around the prohibition. See Lior Jacob Strahilevitz, Information and Exclusion 55-71 (2011) (discussing "exclusionary amenities" and "exclusionary vibes" that circumvent anti-discrimination protection).

4. *Discrimination against group homes.* Covenants restricting property to "residential use only" or "single-family residence" have been the subject of considerable

litigation. Suppose that a private, not-for-profit corporation that assists mentally impaired persons purchases a house in a residential subdivision all the lots of which are restricted by covenant to "single-family" residences. The corporation plans to use the house as a group home for eight unrelated mentally impaired residents. The homeowner association charged with enforcing all restrictive covenants sues to enjoin such use on the ground that it would violate the restriction.

The situation poses two questions: (1) Does the use of the house as a group home fall within the meaning of the phrase "single-family residence"? On this question, the cases are mixed. Most courts have found that the intended use is permissible either on the theory that the restriction was intended to regulate an architectural style rather than the relationship among the structure's inhabitants (see, e.g., Blevins v. Barry-Lawrence County Assn. for Retarded Citizens, 707 S.W.2d 407 (Mo. 1986)), or that "single family" was intended to be interpreted to include groups of otherwise unrelated persons who function as a family. See, e.g., Berger v. State, 364 A.2d 993 (N.J. 1976). (2) Does such a restrictive term violate the federal Fair Housing Act or some other anti-discrimination statute? In Hill v. Community of Damien of Molokai, 911 P.2d 861 (N.M. 1996), the court, after first concluding that a group home for persons with AIDS fell within the meaning of a "single-family residence" covenant, held that the covenant violated § 3604(f)(1) of the FHA by discriminating on the basis of handicap. The court held that the covenant would impose no undue hardship on the neighbors and that the neighbors could reasonably accommodate the group home.

6. Common Interest Communities

Common interest communities, or CICs for short, are a form of residential ownership in which management of the development is separated from possession. There are three basic types of CICs—condominiums, cooperatives, and planned subdivisions, including gated communities.

Recent decades have witnessed a remarkable growth in the number of CICs. The number of community associations in the United States grew from 10,000 in 1970 and 222,500 in 2000 to 347,000 in 2020. More than 73.5 million Americans live in homeowners associations, condominium communities, cooperatives, and other planned communities. https://caionline.org/AboutCommunityAssociations/Pages/default.aspx.

Almost every state has adopted a statutory scheme for organizing a CIC. These statutes require a declaration of rules, called covenants, conditions, and restrictions, or CC&Rs for short, governing the community, which must be disclosed to purchasers. In most CICs, a homeowners association, in which all homeowners are automatically members, enforces the servitudes set forth in the declaration establishing the CIC. The association, governed by a board elected by its members, may adopt new regulations reasonably necessary to manage the common property, administer the servitude regime, protect community members from unreasonable interference in the enjoyment of their individual property, and carry out other functions set forth in the declaration establishing the CIC.

"The distinctive feature of a common-interest community," declares the Restatement (Third) of Property, Servitudes § 6.2 comment a (2000), "is the obligation that binds the owners of individual lots or units to contribute to the support of common property, or other facilities, or to support the activities of an association, whether or not the owner uses the common property or facilities, or agrees to join the association." Although the rules about servitudes covered earlier in this chapter are generally applicable to CICs, the homeowners association in addition has power to raise any funds reasonably necessary to carry out its functions. In most such communities, the power to levy assessments is enforceable by fines and a lien on the individual property.

In CICs, any requirement of horizontal or vertical privity is met because the original purchasers are all in privity with the developer and subsequent purchasers are in privity with the original purchasers. Any requirement that a covenant touch and concern the land is usually satisfied. Negative covenants restricting use are almost always held to touch and concern, as are affirmative covenants to pay dues to a homeowners association. But, because the rules of a CIC and the powers of the homeowners association can adversely affect the interests of individual members, courts have been called upon to determine whether individual members shall be protected from imposition by those who control the association. A major issue is by what standards the validity of the CIC's rules and regulations should be evaluated.

NAHRSTEDT v. LAKESIDE VILLAGE CONDOMINIUM ASSOCIATION, INC.

Supreme Court of California, 1994
878 P.2d 1275

KENNARD, J. A homeowner in a 530-unit condominium complex sued to prevent the homeowners association from enforcing a restriction against keeping cats, dogs, and other animals in the condominium development. The owner asserted that the restriction, which was contained in the project's declaration[11] recorded by the condominium project's developer, was "unreasonable" as applied to her because she kept her three cats indoors and because her cats were "noiseless" and "created no nuisance." Agreeing with the premise underlying the owner's complaint, the Court of Appeal concluded that the homeowners association could enforce the restriction only upon proof that plaintiff's cats would be likely to interfere with the right of other homeowners "to the peaceful and quiet enjoyment of their property."

Those of us who have cats or dogs can attest to their wonderful companionship and affection. Not surprisingly, studies have confirmed this effect. . . . But the issue before us is not whether in the abstract pets can have a beneficial effect on humans. Rather, the narrow issue here is whether a pet restriction that is contained in the recorded declaration of a condominium complex is enforceable against the challenge of a homeowner. As we shall explain, the Legislature, in Civil Code section 1354,

---

11. The declaration is the operative document for a common interest development, setting forth, among other things, the restrictions on the use or enjoyment of any portion of the development. (Civ. Code, §§ 1351, 1353.) In some states, the declaration is also referred to as the "master deed."

has required that courts enforce the covenants, conditions and restrictions contained in the recorded declaration of a common interest development "unless unreasonable."

Because a stable and predictable living environment is crucial to the success of condominiums and other common interest residential developments, and because recorded use restrictions are a primary means of ensuring this stability and predictability, the Legislature in section 1354 has afforded such restrictions a presumption of validity and has required of challengers that they demonstrate the restriction's "unreasonableness" by the deferential standard applicable to equitable servitudes. Under this standard established by the Legislature, enforcement of a restriction does not depend upon the conduct of a particular condominium owner. Rather, the restriction must be uniformly enforced in the condominium development to which it was intended to apply unless the plaintiff owner can show that the burdens it imposes on affected properties so substantially outweigh the benefits of the restriction that it should not be enforced against any owner. Here, the Court of Appeal did not apply this standard in deciding that plaintiff had stated a claim for declaratory relief. Accordingly, we reverse the judgment of the Court of Appeal and remand for further proceedings consistent with the views expressed in this opinion.

I.

Lakeside Village is a large condominium development in Culver City, Los Angeles County. It consists of 530 units spread throughout 12 separate 3-story buildings. The residents share common lobbies and hallways, in addition to laundry and trash facilities.

The Lakeside Village project is subject to certain covenants, conditions and restrictions (hereafter CC&R's) that were included in the developer's declaration recorded with the Los Angeles County Recorder on April 17, 1978, at the inception of the development project. Ownership of a unit includes membership in the project's homeowners association, the Lakeside Village Condominium Association (hereafter Association), the body that enforces the project's CC&R's, including the pet restriction, which provides in relevant part: "No animals (which shall mean dogs and cats), livestock, reptiles or poultry shall be kept in any unit."[12]

In January 1988, plaintiff Natore Nahrstedt purchased a Lakeside Village condominium and moved in with her three cats. When the Association learned of the cats' presence, it demanded their removal and assessed fines against Nahrstedt for each successive month that she remained in violation of the condominium project's pet restriction.

Nahrstedt then brought this lawsuit against the Association, its officers, and two of its employees, asking the trial court to invalidate the assessments, to enjoin future assessments, . . . and to declare the pet restriction "unreasonable" as applied to indoor cats (such as hers) that are not allowed free run of the project's common areas. Nahrstedt also alleged she did not know of the pet restriction when she bought her condominium. . . .

The Association demurred to the complaint. . . . The trial court sustained the demurrer as to each cause of action and dismissed Nahrstedt's complaint. Nahrstedt appealed.

---

12. The CC&R's permit residents to keep "domestic fish and birds."

Lakeside Village Condominiums, Culver City

A divided Court of Appeal reversed the trial court's judgment of dismissal. In the majority's view, the complaint stated a claim for declaratory relief based on its allegations that Nahrstedt's three cats are kept inside her condominium unit and do not bother her neighbors. According to the majority, whether a condominium use restriction is "unreasonable," as that term is used in section 1354, hinges on the facts of a particular homeowner's case. Thus, the majority reasoned, Nahrstedt would be entitled to declaratory relief if application of the pet restriction in her case would not be reasonable. . . .

On the Association's petition, we granted review to decide when a condominium owner can prevent enforcement of a use restriction that the project's developer has included in the recorded declaration of CC&R's. . . .

II.

Today, condominiums, cooperatives, and planned-unit developments with homeowners associations have become a widely accepted form of real property ownership. These ownership arrangements are known as "common interest" developments.

. . . [S]ubordination of individual property rights to the collective judgment of the owners association together with restrictions on the use of real property comprise the chief attributes of owning property in a common interest development. As the Florida District Court of Appeal observed in Hidden Harbour Estates, Inc. v. Norman (Fla. Dist. Ct. App. 1975) 309 So. 2d 180, a decision frequently cited in condominium cases: "[I]nherent in the condominium concept is the principle that to promote the health, happiness, and peace of mind of the majority of the unit owners since they are living in such close proximity and using facilities in common, each unit owner must give up a certain degree of freedom of choice which he [or she] might otherwise enjoy in separate, privately owned property. Condominium unit owners comprise a little democratic sub-society of necessity more restrictive as it pertains to use of condominium property than may be existent outside the condominium organization."

One significant factor in the continued popularity of the common interest form of property ownership is the ability of homeowners to enforce restrictive CC&R's against other owners (including future purchasers) of project units. (Natelson, Law of Property

Owners Associations 1989 § 1.3.2.1, p. 19. . . .) Generally, however, such enforcement is possible only if the restriction that is sought to be enforced meets the requirements of equitable servitudes or of covenants running with the land. . . .

When restrictions limiting the use of property within a common interest development satisfy the requirements of covenants running with the land or of equitable servitudes, what standard or test governs their enforceability? In California, as we explained at the outset, our Legislature has made common interest development use restrictions contained in a project's recorded declaration "enforceable . . . unless unreasonable." (Civil Code, § 1354, subd. (a).)

In states lacking such legislative guidance, some courts have adopted a standard under which a common interest development's recorded use restrictions will be enforced so long as they are "reasonable." (See Riley v. Stoves (1974) 22 Ariz. App. 223, 228, 526 P.2d 747, 752 [asking whether the challenged restriction provided "a reasonable means to accomplish the private objective"].) . . . Others would limit the "reasonableness" standard only to those restrictions adopted by majority vote of the homeowners or enacted under the rulemaking power of an association's governing board, and would not apply this test to restrictions included in a planned development project's recorded declaration or master deed. Because such restrictions are presumptively valid, these authorities would enforce them regardless of reasonableness. The first court to articulate this view was the Florida Fourth District Court of Appeal.

In Hidden Harbour Estates v. Basso (Fla. Dist. Ct. App. 1981) 393 So. 2d 637, the Florida court distinguished two categories of use restrictions: use restrictions set forth in the declaration or master deed of the condominium project itself, and rules promulgated by the governing board of the condominium owners association or the board's interpretation of a rule. The latter category of use restrictions, the court said, should be subject to a "reasonableness" test, so as to "somewhat fetter the discretion of the board of directors." Such a standard, the court explained, best assures that governing boards will "enact rules and make decisions that are reasonably related to the promotion of the health, happiness and peace of mind" of the project owners, considered collectively.

By contrast, restrictions contained in the declaration or master deed of the condominium complex, the Florida court concluded, should not be evaluated under a "reasonableness" standard. Rather, such use restrictions are "clothed with a very strong presumption of validity" and should be upheld even if they exhibit some degree of unreasonableness. Nonenforcement would be proper only if such restrictions were arbitrary or in violation of public policy or some fundamental constitutional right. The Florida court's decision was cited with approval recently by a Massachusetts appellate court in Noble v. Murphy (1993) 34 Mass. App. Ct. 452, 612 N.E.2d 266.

In Noble, managers of a condominium development sought to enforce against the owners of one unit a pet restriction contained in the project's master deed. The Massachusetts court upheld the validity of the restriction. The court stated that "[a] condominium use restriction appearing in originating documents which predate the purchase of individual units" was entitled to greater judicial deference than restrictions "promulgated after units have been individually acquired." The court reasoned that "properly-enacted and evenly-enforced use restrictions contained in a master deed or original bylaws of a condominium" should be insulated against attack "except on constitutional or public policy grounds." This standard, the court explained, best "serves the interest of the majority of owners [within a project] who may be presumed to have chosen not to alter or rescind such restrictions," and it spares overcrowded courts "the burden and expense of highly particularized and lengthy litigation."

Indeed, giving deference to use restrictions contained in a condominium project's originating documents protects the general expectations of condominium owners "that restrictions in place at the time they purchase their units will be enforceable." (Note, Judicial Review of Condominium Rulemaking (1981) 94 Harv. L. Rev. 647, 653; Ellickson, Cities and Homeowners' Associations (1982) 130 U. Pa. L. Rev. 1519, 1526-1527 [stating that association members "unanimously consent to the provisions in the association's original documents" and courts therefore should not scrutinize such documents for "reasonableness"].) This in turn encourages the development of shared ownership housing—generally a less costly alternative to single-dwelling ownership—by attracting buyers who prefer a stable, planned environment. It also protects buyers who have paid a premium for condominium units in reliance on a particular restrictive scheme.

III.

. . . Thus, when enforcing equitable servitudes, courts are generally disinclined to question the wisdom of agreed-to restrictions. . . . This rule does not apply, however, when the restriction does not comport with public policy. Equity will not enforce any restrictive covenant that violates public policy. (See Shelley v. Kraemer (1948) 334 U.S. 1, 68 S. Ct. 836, 92 L. Ed. 1161 [racial restriction unenforceable]; § 53, subd. (b) [voiding property use restrictions based on "sex, race, color, religion, ancestry, national origin, or disability"].) Nor will courts enforce as equitable servitudes those restrictions that are arbitrary, that is, bearing no rational relationship to the protection, preservation, operation or purpose of the affected land. (See Laguna Royale Owners Assn. v. Darger (1981) 119 Cal. App. 3d 670, 684, 174 Cal. Rptr. 136.)

These limitations on the equitable enforcement of restrictive servitudes that are either arbitrary or violate fundamental public policy are specific applications of the general rule that courts will not enforce a restrictive covenant when "the harm caused by the restriction is so disproportionate to the benefit produced" by its enforcement that the restriction "ought not to be enforced." (Rest., Property, § 539, com. f, pp. 3229-3230.) When a use restriction bears no relationship to the land it burdens, or violates a fundamental policy inuring to the public at large, the resulting harm will always be disproportionate to any benefit. . . .

With these principles of equitable servitude law to guide us, we now turn to Civil Code section 1354. As mentioned earlier, under subdivision (a) of section 1354 the use restrictions for a common interest development that are set forth in the recorded declaration are "enforceable equitable servitudes, unless unreasonable." In other words, such restrictions should be enforced unless they are wholly arbitrary, violate a fundamental public policy, or impose a burden on the use of affected land that far outweighs any benefit.

This interpretation of section 1354 is consistent with the views of legal commentators as well as judicial decisions in other jurisdictions that have applied a presumption of validity to the recorded land use restrictions of a common interest development. (Noble v. Murphy, supra, 612 N.E.2d 266, 270; Hidden Harbour Estates v. Basso, supra, 393 So. 2d 637, 639-640; Note, Judicial Review of Condominium Rulemaking, supra, 94 Harv. L. Rev. 647, 653.) As these authorities point out, and as we discussed previously, recorded CC&R's are the primary means of achieving the stability and pre-dictability so essential to the success of a shared ownership housing development. . . .

When courts accord a presumption of validity to all such recorded use restric-tions and measure them against deferential standards of equitable servitude law, it discourages lawsuits by owners of individual units seeking personal exemptions from the restrictions. This also promotes stability and predictability in two ways. It provides substantial assurance to prospective condominium purchasers that they may rely with confidence on the promises embodied in the project's recorded CC&R's. And it pro-tects all owners in the planned development from unanticipated increases in associa-tion fees to fund the defense of legal challenges to recorded restrictions.

How courts enforce recorded use restrictions affects not only those who have made their homes in planned developments, but also the owners associations charged with the fiduciary obligation to enforce those restrictions. (See Posey v. Leavitt (1991) 229 Cal. App. 3d 1236, 1247, 280 Cal. Rptr. 568; Advising Cal. Condominium and Homeowner Associations (Cont. Ed. Bar 1991) § 6.11, pp. 259-261.) When courts treat recorded use restrictions as presumptively valid, and place on the challenger the burden of proving the restriction "unreasonable" under the deferential standards applicable to equitable servitudes, associations can proceed to enforce reasonable restrictive covenants without fear that their actions will embroil them in costly and prolonged legal proceedings. Of course, when an association determines that a unit owner has violated a use restriction, the association must do so in good faith, not in an arbitrary or capricious manner, and its enforcement procedures must be fair and applied uniformly. . . .

There is an additional beneficiary of legal rules that are protective of recorded use restrictions: the judicial system. Fewer lawsuits challenging such restrictions will be brought, and those that are filed may be disposed of more expeditiously, if the rules courts use in evaluating such restrictions are clear, simple, and not subject to exceptions based on the peculiar circumstances or hardships of individual residents in condominiums and other shared-ownership developments.

Contrary to the dissent's accusations that the majority's decision "fray[s]" the "social fabric," we are of the view that our social fabric is best preserved if courts uphold and enforce solemn written instruments that embody the expectations of the parties rather than treat them as "worthless paper" as the dissent would. Our social fabric is founded on the stability of expectation and obligation that arises from the consistent enforcement of the terms of deeds, contracts, wills, statutes, and other writings. To allow one person to escape obligations under a written instrument upsets the expec-tations of all the other parties governed by that instrument (here, the owners of the other 529 units) that the instrument will be uniformly and predictably enforced. . . .

Refusing to enforce the CC&R's contained in a recorded declaration, or enforcing them only after protracted litigation that would require justification of their application on a case-by-case basis, would impose great strain on the social fabric of the common interest development. It would frustrate owners who had purchased their units in reli-ance on the CC&R's. It would put the owners and the homeowners association in the difficult and divisive position of deciding whether particular CC&R's should be applied to a particular owner. Here, for example, deciding whether a particular animal is "con-fined to an owner's unit and create[s] no noise, odor, or nuisance" is a fact-intensive determination that can only be made by examining in detail the behavior of the par-ticular animal and the behavior of the particular owner. Homeowners associations are ill-equipped to make such investigations, and any decision they might make in a particular case could be divisive or subject to claims of partiality.

Enforcing the CC&R's contained in a recorded declaration only after protracted case-by-case litigation would impose substantial litigation costs on the owners through their homeowners association, which would have to defend not only against owners contesting the application of the CC&R's to them, but also against owners contesting any case-by-case exceptions the homeowners association might make. In short, it is difficult to imagine what could more disrupt the harmony of a common interest development than the course proposed by the dissent.

IV.

Here, the Court of Appeal failed to consider the rules governing equitable servitudes in holding that Nahrstedt's complaint challenging the Lakeside Village restriction against the keeping of cats in condominium units stated a cause of action for declaratory relief. Instead, the court concluded that factual allegations by Nahrstedt that her cats are kept inside her condominium unit and do not bother her neighbors were sufficient to have the trial court decide whether enforcement of the restriction against Nahrstedt would be reasonable. For this conclusion, the court relied on two Court of Appeal decisions, Bernardo Villas Management Corp. v. Black (1987) 190 Cal. App. 3d 153, 235 Cal. Rptr. 509 and Portola Hills Community Assn. v. James (1992) 4 Cal. App. 4th 289, 5 Cal. Rptr. 2d 580, both of which had invalidated recorded restrictions covered by section 1354.

In *Bernardo Villas*, the manager of a condominium project sued two condominium residents to enforce a restriction that prohibited them from keeping any "truck, camper, trailer, boat . . . or other form of recreational vehicle" in the carports. In holding that the restriction was unreasonable as applied to the clean new pickup truck with camper shell that the defendants used for personal transportation, the Court of Appeal observed that parking the truck in the development's carport would "not interfere with other owners' use or enjoyment of their property."

Thereafter, a different division of the same district Court of Appeal used a similar analysis in *Portola Hills*. There, the court refused to enforce a planned community's landscape restriction banning satellite dishes against a homeowner who had installed a satellite dish in his backyard. After expressing the view that "[a] homeowner is allowed to prove a particular restriction is unreasonable as applied to his property," the court observed that the defendant's satellite dish was not visible to other project residents or the public, leading the court to conclude that the ban promoted no legitimate goal of the homeowners association.

At issue in both Bernardo Villas Management Corp. v. Black, supra, 190 Cal. App. 3d 153, 235 Cal. Rptr. 509, and Portola Hills Community Assn. v. James, supra, 4 Cal. App. 4th 289, 5 Cal. Rptr. 2d 580, were recorded use restrictions contained in a common interest development's declaration that had been recorded with the county recorder. Accordingly, the use restrictions involved in these two cases were covered by section 1354, rendering them presumptively reasonable and enforceable under the rules governing equitable servitudes. . . . In determining whether a restriction is "unreasonable" under section 1354, and thus not enforceable, the focus is on the restriction's effect on the project as a whole, not on the individual homeowner. Although purporting to evaluate the use restrictions in accord with section 1354, both *Bernardo Villas* and *Portola Hills* failed to apply the deferential standards of equitable servitude law just mentioned. Accordingly, to the extent they differ from the views expressed in this opinion, we disapprove *Bernardo Villas* and *Portola Hills.*

V.

Under the holding we adopt today, the reasonableness or unreasonableness of a condominium use restriction that the Legislature has made subject to section 1354 is to be determined not by reference to facts that are specific to the objecting homeowner, but by reference to the common interest development as a whole. As we have explained, when, as here, a restriction is contained in the declaration of the common interest development and is recorded with the county recorder, the restriction is presumed to be reasonable and will be enforced uniformly against all residents of the common interest development unless the restriction is arbitrary, imposes burdens on the use of lands it affects that substantially outweigh the restriction's benefits to the development's residents, or violates a fundamental public policy. . . .

We conclude, as a matter of law, that the recorded pet restriction of the Lakeside Village condominium development prohibiting cats or dogs but allowing some other pets is not arbitrary, but is rationally related to health, sanitation and noise concerns legitimately held by residents of a high-density condominium project such as Lakeside Village, which includes 530 units in 12 separate 3-story buildings.

Nahrstedt's complaint alleges no facts that could possibly support a finding that the burden of the restriction on the affected property is so disproportionate to its benefit that the restriction is unreasonable and should not be enforced.

. . . [W]e discern no fundamental public policy that would favor the keeping of pets in a condominium project. There is no federal or state constitutional provision or any California statute that confers a general right to keep household pets in condominiums or other common interest developments.

. . . For many owners, the pet restriction may have been an important inducement to purchase into the development. Because the homeowners collectively have the power to repeal the pet restriction, its continued existence reflects their desire to retain it.

. . . We reverse the judgment of the Court of Appeal, and remand for further proceedings consistent with the views expressed in this opinion.

ARABIAN, J., dissenting.

"There are two means of refuge from the misery of life: music and cats."[13]

I respectfully dissent. While technical merit may commend the majority's analysis, its application to the facts presented reflects a narrow, indeed chary, view of the law that eschews the human spirit in favor of arbitrary efficiency. In my view, the resolution of this case well illustrates the conventional wisdom, and fundamental truth, of the Spanish proverb, "It is better to be a mouse in a cat's mouth than a man in a lawyer's hands."

I find the provision known as the "pet restriction" contained in the covenants, conditions, and restrictions (CC&R's) governing the Lakeside Village project patently arbitrary and unreasonable within the meaning of Civil Code section 1354. Beyond dispute, human beings have long enjoyed an abiding and cherished association with their household animals. Given the substantial benefits derived from pet ownership,

---

13. Albert Schweitzer.

Natore Nahrstedt with Boo-Boo

the undue burden on the use of property imposed on condominium owners who can maintain pets within the confines of their units without creating a nuisance or disturbing the quiet enjoyment of others substantially outweighs whatever meager utility the restriction may serve in the abstract. It certainly does not promote "health, happiness [or] peace of mind" commensurate with its tariff on the quality of life for those who value the companionship of animals. Worse, it contributes to the fraying of our social fabric. . . .

From the statement of the facts through the conclusion, the majority's analysis . . . simply takes refuge behind the "presumption of validity" now accorded all CC&R's irrespective of subject matter. They never objectively scrutinize defendants' blandishments of protecting "health and happiness" or realistically assess the substantial impact on affected unit owners and their use of their property. . . .

Here, such inquiry should start with an evaluation of the interest that will suffer upon enforcement of the pet restriction. In determining the "burden on the use of land," due recognition must be given to the fact that this particular "use" transcends the impersonal and mundane matters typically regulated by condominium CC&R's, such as whether someone can place a doormat in the hallway or hang a towel on the patio rail or have food in the pool area, and reaches the very quality of life of hundreds of owners and residents. Nonetheless, the majority accept uncritically the proffered justification of preserving "health and happiness" and essentially consider only one criterion to determine enforceability: was the restriction recorded in the original declaration? If so, it is "presumptively valid," unless in violation of public policy.

Given the application of the law to the facts alleged and by an inversion of relative interests, it is difficult to hypothesize any CC&R's that would not pass muster. Such sanctity has not been afforded any writing save the commandments delivered to Moses on Mount Sinai, and they were set in stone, not upon worthless paper.

Moreover, unlike most conduct controlled by CC&R's, the activity at issue here is strictly confined to the owner's interior space; it does not in any manner invade other units or the common areas. Owning a home of one's own has always epitomized the American dream. More than simply embodying the notion of having "one's castle," it represents the sense of freedom and self-determination emblematic of our national character. Granted, those who live in multi-unit developments cannot exercise this freedom to the same extent possible on a large estate. But owning pets that do not disturb the quiet enjoyment of others does not reasonably come within this compromise. Nevertheless, with no demonstrated or discernible benefit, the majority arbitrarily sacrifice the dream to the tyranny of the "commonality."

. . . [T]he majority's . . . view, shorn of grace and guiding philosophy, is devoid of the humanity that must temper the interpretation and application of all laws, for in a civilized society that is the source of their authority. As judicial architects of the rules of life, we better serve when we construct halls of harmony rather than walls of wrath.

I would affirm the judgment of the Court of Appeal.

THE REST OF THE STORY . . .

After losing the lawsuit, Natore (who pronounced her name "Nature") Nahrstedt moved out of Lakeside Village, with her three cats, Boo-Boo, Dockers, and Tulip. Her legal bill was around $50,000. She commented, "I'm disappointed in their decision, but that doesn't mean that I'm not going to campaign to have it overturned by the Legislature." Condo Cat Fight Has Some Purring, Others Fleeing, available at http://articles.latimes.com/1994-09-04/local/me-34732_1_condo-cat. However, even without her lobbying efforts, the California legislature subsequently overturned the *Nahrstedt* decision in 2000, enacting Cal. Civ. Code § 1360.5. It states: "(a) No governing documents shall prohibit the owner of a separate interest within a common interest development from keeping at least one pet [defined as 'any domesticated bird, cat, dog, aquatic animal kept within an aquarium, or other animal as agreed to between the association and the homeowner'] within the common interest development, subject to reasonable rules and regulations of the association." Ms. Nahrstedt died on November 29, 2007.

Notes and Questions

1. *The court's reasonableness standard.* The court's reasonableness standard appears to give a presumption of validity to a restriction in the master declaration unless the restriction produces a result that is completely irrational for everyone in the CIC. Is this an accurate interpretation of the language of the California statute, which basically says that restrictions are valid and enforceable "unless unreasonable"? Or does the dissent have the better of the argument?

2. *The Restatement (Third) standard.* Rather than adopting a general reasonableness standard, as in *Nahrstedt*, Restatement (Third) of Property, Servitudes § 3.1 (2000) (see page 535) establishes a presumption that a servitude is valid unless it is "illegal, unconstitutional, or violates public policy." A servitude violates public policy if it (1) is arbitrary, spiteful, or capricious; (2) "unreasonably burdens

a fundamental constitutional right"; (3) "imposes an unreasonable restraint of alienation"; (4) imposes an unreasonable restraint on trade or competition; or (5) is unconscionable. Which approach, the Restatement's or the *Nahrstedt* court's, seems better to you? Consider this question in connection with the Problems below, pages 557-558.

3. *The business judgment rule.* In Lamden v. La Jolla Shores Clubdominium Homeowners Assn., 980 P.2d 940 (Cal. 1999), the court applied the business judgment rule to sustain the decision of a homeowner association board. When a condominium became infested with termites, the association's board decided to use spot treatment rather than to fumigate the entire building. When more termite infestation became apparent in one unit five years later, the unit owner brought an action against the board for damages allegedly resulting from the board's decision not to fumigate the whole building. Ruling for the board, the court stated that in making financial decisions all that was required of the board was that it exercise its discretion in good faith, after reasonable investigation, and in the best interests of the association and its members. The court distinguished *Nahrstedt* on the ground that the no-pets rule was an equitable servitude, governed by California Civil Code § 1354, whereas the board's action in *Lamden* involved no equitable servitude, only a financial decision.

Other courts have also applied the business judgment rule to homeowner associations. See America v. Sunspray Condo Assn., 61 A.3d 1249 (Me. 2013); Riverside Park Condominium Unit Owners Assn. v. Lucas, 691 N.W.2d 862 (N.D. 2005); Forest Close Assn., Inc. v. Richards, 845 N.Y.S.2d 418 (App. Div. 2007).

Condominiums and Cooperatives

Condominiums. Nahrstedt involved a condominium. The basic idea of a condominium is simple. Each unit (or interior space) in a condominium is owned *separately in fee simple* by an individual owner. The exterior walls, the land beneath, the hallways, and other common areas are owned by the unit owners as *tenants in common*. Because each unit is owned separately, each owner obtains mortgage financing by a separate mortgage on the owner's individual unit. Real estate taxes are assessed or allocated to each unit separately. The failure of one unit owner to pay mortgage interest or taxes does not jeopardize the other unit owners.

The declaration of condominium, filed before the first sale is made, will provide for an association of unit owners to make and enforce rules, to manage the common areas, and to set maintenance charges levied against unit owners. Each purchaser, by accepting a deed, becomes an association member and must abide by its bylaws. All 50 states have some form of condominium statute governing this type of shared ownership.

Each condominium unit owner is liable for a monthly charge to maintain common facilities and insure against casualty and liability. The condominium documents fix the fraction of each unit owner's pro rata burden of common expenses. This fraction also may govern the unit owner's voice in management and may be used by the tax assessor in apportioning the project's total value among the separate units. Enforcement of condominium obligations may be covered by the state condominium statute or the condominium declaration.

Cooperatives. New York City is probably the only housing market in the country with a substantial number of cooperative apartments. In a housing cooperative, the title to the land and building is held by a corporation; the residents own all the shares of stock in the corporation and control it through an elected board of directors. Each resident also has a long-term renewable lease of an apartment unit. Hence residents are both owners of the cooperative corporation (by virtue of stock ownership) and tenants of the corporation.

The cooperative property is usually subject to one blanket mortgage securing the money lender for the money borrowed to buy the land and erect the building. If one cooperator fails to pay his share of the mortgage interest or taxes, the other cooperators must make it up or the entire property may be foreclosed upon. Thus, in a cooperative more than a condominium, the investment of one person depends upon the financial stability of others. As a result, members of a cooperative have a strong incentive to screen applicants to ensure that they can carry their share of the collective mortgage.

Financial screening also provides an opportunity for social screening. New York courts have held that cooperative boards can deny entry to anyone for any reason and without giving any reason, provided the board does not violate federal and state civil rights laws. Weisner v. 791 Park Ave. Corp., 160 N.E.2d 720 (N.Y. 1959). Because cooperatives can screen prospective members, and because of long experience with the cooperative form of housing, they continue to flourish in New York City despite the growth of condominiums in the rest of the country. (In a condominium in New York, the boards typically can prevent entry only by exercising a preemptive option; they rarely screen applicants by social criteria.)

DOONESBURY © G.B. Trudeau.
Reprinted with permission of UNIVERSAL UCLICK.
All rights reserved.

Problems

In a CIC, the developer imposes the following restrictions. Which, if any, are invalid under the Restatement (Third) of Property § 3.1? Under the *Nahrstedt* version of the reasonableness requirement?

1. "No flag of any kind, including the American flag, may be displayed." See 4 U.S.C. § 5 Note (Pub. L. No. 109-243, 120 Stat. 572 (July 24, 2006)); Cal. Govt. Code § 434.5 (West 2020); Ky. Rev. Stat. Ann. § 2.042 (2020).

2. "No sign except house location number may be displayed, nor may Christmas lights be displayed outside of a house." See Osborne v. Power, 890 S.W.2d 570 (Ark. 1994); cf. City of Ladue v. Gilleo, 512 U.S. 43 (1994); Brian Jason Fleming, Note, Regulation of Political Signs in Private Homeowner Associations: A New Approach, 59 Vand. L. Rev. 571 (2006).

3. "No solar energy device shall be installed on the roof of any house." See Mass. Laws Ann. ch. 184, § 23C (2020); Fla. Stat. Ann. § 163.04 (2020).

4. "No house shall be used to provide day care for nonresidents of the house." See Woodvale Condominium Trust v. Scheff, 540 N.E.2d 206 (Mass. App. 1989); Cal. Health & Safety Code § 1597.40 (2020).

5. "No religious services or activities of any kind are allowed in the development's auditorium or any other common areas." When a number of association members met in the auditorium on Saturday morning for religious services, the association's board of directors sought to enjoin them from violating the restriction. Would it make a difference if a local state statute prohibited condominium associations from "unreasonably restrict[ing] any unit owner's right to peaceably assemble . . ."? Fla. Stat. Ann. § 718.123 (2005). See Neuman v. Grandview at Emerald Hills, Inc., 861 So. 2d 494 (Fla. App. 2003).

6. "No signs, billboards, or advertising without the prior approval of the architectural control committee." When a resident places on her door a Christmas wreath that features a peace symbol, the architecture control committee orders her to remove it.

7. "No smoking of cigarettes, cigars, or any other tobacco product, marijuana, or illegal substance anywhere within the boundaries of the complex. This prohibition shall include the outside common area, enclosed common area, exclusive use common area, and units within the complex."

8. A homeowners association mandates residents to keep their garage doors open from 8 A.M. to 4 P.M. on weekdays or face a $200 fine. See https://www.sacbee.com/news/nation-world/national/article193685849.html.

Airbnb and CICs. The recent rise of Airbnb and similar platforms has given rise to a spate of disputes involving several legal issues. One issue concerns CC&Rs that restrict short-term rentals. Are such covenants valid? In Adams v. Kimberley One Townhouse Owner's Assn., 352 P.3d 492 (Idaho 2015), a homeowners association voted to amend the declaration of the association's CC&Rs to prohibit leasing of units for less than six months. One of the owners sued to declare the retroactive restraint on alienation invalid. The Idaho Supreme Court found the retroactive restraint to be valid. It did not constitute an unreasonable restraint on alienation, nor did it exceed the scope of the association's powers to amend the declaration retroactively. Contra, Wilkinson v. Chiwawa Communities Assn., 327 P.3d 614 (Wash. 2014).

Another issue concerns whether short-term rentals violate covenants restricting property to "residential" use. Courts are divided over the question, but the majority hold that use of property for Airbnb and similar short-term rentals is residential use consistent with such covenants. See Timberwood Park Owners Assn., 2018 Tex. LEXIS 442 (Tex. 2018) (holding that VRBO rental did not violate

"residential purpose" deed restriction: "The phrase 'residential purposes' does not mean only the occupying of a premises for the purpose of making it one's 'usual' place of abode; a building is a residence if it is 'a' place of abode."); Vera Lee Revocable Trust v. O'Bryant, 537 S.W.3d 254 (Ark. 2018). But see Vonderhaar v. Lakeside Place Homeowners Assn., 2014 WL 3887913 (Ky. App. 2014) (finding short-terms rentals to be closer to hotel use and thus commercial in nature).

On gated communities, see Sheryll D. Cashin, Privatized Communities and the "Secession of the Successful": Democracy and Fairness Beyond the Gate, 28 Fordham Urb. L.J. 1675 (2001).

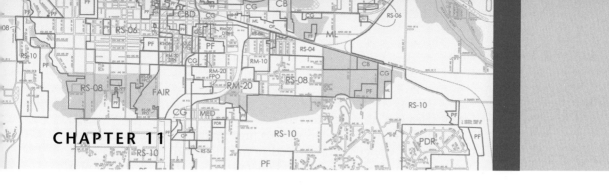

CHAPTER 11

Legislative Land Use Controls:
The Law of Zoning

A. INTRODUCTION

Although servitudes are one way to regulate land use, they are not the primary method of land use control in the United States today. Public, rather than private, land use control, in the form of zoning, is common throughout the United States.

BACKGROUND, BRIEFLY

Zoning developed during the early twentieth century in response to the rapid and dramatic changes in living conditions that resulted from urbanization between 1865 and 1900. "Industrialism, the main creative force of the 19th Century," Lewis Mumford observed in his great work, The City in History (1961), "produced the most degraded human environment the world had yet seen." Id. at 433. The extraordinary changes it brought—congestion, overcrowding, noise, tenement housing, factories belching smoke from soft coal, and foul odors—were beyond the corrective powers of the doctrines on nuisance and servitudes considered in Chapters 9 and 10. Courts, not wishing to hinder the development that was making the United States rich, were reluctant to declare anything a nuisance except a use highly objectionable in a particular context. Any number of injuries could be visited by one neighbor upon others, yet not be legal nuisances.

Restrictive covenants also were incapable of dealing effectively with relations among neighbors in urban areas. They were useful only in new subdivisions and other developments of large acreage occurring under a single owner, who imposed the covenants. At the turn of the century, most development was lot by lot. Hence, early in the twentieth century, social reformers and city planners turned to zoning, which was in theory designed to *prevent* harmful neighborhood effects.

The roots of zoning are traceable to the City Beautiful movement of the late nineteenth century. The City Beautiful movement was animated by the idea that cities should be made to replicate the moral and civic order of the village, an order that leaders of the movement believed was virtuous and uncorrupted. The core premise of the movement was that beauty could be an effective social control device.

One of the movement's leaders, the architect Daniel Burnham, staged the Chicago World's Fair in 1893, which through its enormous success fired up the City Beautiful movement. In 1901, the United States Congress was moved to produce, with Burnham's guidance, a new master plan for Washington, restoring and revitalizing L'Enfant's 1791 plan for the city. Other cities—Cleveland, Kansas City, Denver—followed with visionary city plans. The magnificent American railroad stations—Washington's Union Station, New York's Grand Central Terminal, and Kansas City's cavernous Union Station—are products of the City Beautiful movement. Within 20 years, however, the City Beautiful movement ran out of steam.

What survived the demise of the City Beautiful movement was a certitude that rational planning was actually possible and an optimistic belief that planning bodies could control the shortsighted and uncoordinated decisions of individual landowners, which had resulted in ugly and chaotic cities. In the early twentieth century, several American cities enacted ordinances reflecting this belief. The most important of these was New York City's 1916 zoning ordinance, the country's first comprehensive zoning program. This ordinance assigned several classes of land uses to different zones and restricted the height and bulk of buildings.

Zoning spread rapidly in the years after 1916, especially following the appearance of a model zoning statute in 1922, the Standard State Zoning Enabling Act. By 1925, 368 municipalities had zoning ordinances. With the spread of zoning came constitutional attacks—assertions that the new controls amounted to takings of property without compensation or worked deprivations of property without due process of law. By the mid-1920s, a few state courts had struck down zoning as unconstitutional, but others had upheld it. Everyone, especially city planners and realtors, wanted an answer from the United States Supreme Court. The answer came in the case that follows.

The 1893 World's Columbian Exposition in Chicago gave great impetus to the City Beautiful movement.

In 1924, a federal district court found the zoning ordinance of Euclid, Ohio unconstitutional:

> The plain truth is that the true object of the ordinance in question is to place all the property in an undeveloped area of 16 square miles in a strait-jacket. The purpose to be accomplished is really to regulate the mode of living of persons who may hereafter inhabit it. In the last analysis, the result to be accomplished is to classify the population and segregate them according to their income or situation in life. The true reason why some persons live in a mansion and others in a shack, why some live in a single-family dwelling and others in a double-family dwelling, why some live in a two-family dwelling and others in an apartment, or why some live in a well-kept apartment and others in a tenement, is primarily economic. It is a matter of income and wealth, plus the labor and difficulty of procuring adequate domestic service. Aside from contributing to these results and furthering such class tendencies, the ordinance has also an esthetic purpose; that is to say, to make this village develop into a city along lines now conceived by the village council to be attractive and beautiful. . . . Whether these purposes and objects would justify the taking of plaintiff's property as and for a public use need not be considered. It is sufficient to say that, in our opinion, and as applied to plaintiff's property, it may not be done without compensation under the guise of exercising the police power. [Ambler Realty Co. v. Village of Euclid, 297 F. 307, 316 (N.D. Ohio 1924).]

The judge knew his decision was an important one. "This case," he said, "is obviously destined to go higher." 297 F. at 308.

1. Constitutionality

VILLAGE OF EUCLID v. AMBLER REALTY CO.
Supreme Court of the United States, 1926
272 U.S. 365

SUTHERLAND, J. The Village of Euclid is an Ohio municipal corporation. It adjoins and practically is a suburb of the City of Cleveland. Its estimated population is between 5,000 and 10,000, and its area from twelve to fourteen square miles, the greater part of which is farm lands or unimproved acreage. It lies, roughly, in the form of a parallelogram measuring approximately three and one-half miles each way. East and west it is traversed by three principal highways: Euclid Avenue, through the southerly border, St. Clair Avenue, through the central portion, and Lake Shore Boulevard, through the northerly border in close proximity to the shore of Lake Erie. The Nickel Plate railroad lies from 1,500 to 1,800 feet north of Euclid Avenue, and the Lake Shore railroad 1,600 feet farther to the north. The three highways and the two railroads are substantially parallel.

Appellee is the owner of a tract of land containing 68 acres, situated in the westerly end of the village, abutting on Euclid Avenue to the south and the Nickel Plate railroad to the north. Adjoining this tract, both on the east and on the west, there have been laid out restricted residential plats upon which residences have been erected.

On November 13, 1922, an ordinance was adopted by the Village Council, establishing a comprehensive zoning plan for regulating and restricting the location of

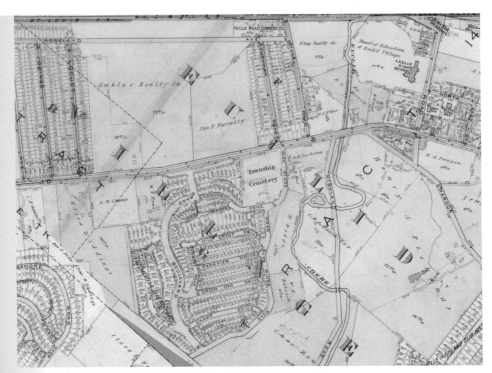

Euclid before zoning

trades, industries, apartment houses, two-family houses, etc., the lot area to be built upon, the size and height of buildings, etc.

The entire area of the village is divided by the ordinance into six classes of use districts, denominated U-1 to U-6, inclusive; three classes of height districts, denominated H-1 to H-3, inclusive; and four classes of area districts, denominated A-1 to A-4, inclusive. The use districts are classified in respect of the buildings which may be erected within their respective limits, as follows: U-1 is restricted to single family dwellings . . . ; U-2 is extended to include two-family dwellings; U-3 is further extended to include apartment houses, hotels, churches, schools, public libraries . . . ; U-4 is further extended to include banks, offices, studios, telephone exchanges, fire and police stations . . . ; U-5 is further extended to include [light industry]; U-6 is further extended to include . . . manufacturing and industrial operations of any kind other than, and any public utility not included in, a class U-1, U-2, U-3, U-4 or U-5 use. . . . Class U-1 is the only district in which buildings are restricted to those enumerated. In the other classes the uses are cumulative; that is to say, uses in class U-2 include those enumerated in the preceding class, U-1; class U-3 includes uses enumerated in the preceding classes, U-2 and U-1; and so on. . . . Appellee's tract of land comes under U-2, U-3, and U-6. The first strip of 620 feet immediately north of Euclid Avenue falls in class U-2, the next 130 feet to the north, in U-3, and the remainder in U-6. The uses of the first 620 feet, therefore, do not include apartment houses, hotels, churches, schools, or other public and semi-public buildings, or other uses enumerated in respect to U-3 to U-6, inclusive. The uses of the next 130 feet include all of these, but exclude industries, theatres, banks, shops, and the various other uses set forth in respect of U-4 to U-6, inclusive.

Annexed to the ordinance, and made a part of it, is a zone map, showing the location and limits of the various use, height and area districts, from which it appears that the three classes overlap one another; that is to say, for example, both U-5 and U-6 use districts are in A-4 area districts, but the former is in H-2 and the latter in H-3 height districts. . . .

The lands lying between the two railroads for the entire length of the village area and extending some distance on either side to the north and south, having an average width of about 1,600 feet, are left open, with slight exceptions, for industrial and all other uses. This includes the larger part of appellee's tract. . . .

The enforcement of the ordinance is entrusted to the inspector of buildings, under rules and regulations of the board of zoning appeals. Meetings of the board are public, and minutes of its proceedings are kept. It is authorized to adopt rules and regulations to carry into effect provisions of the ordinance. Decisions of the inspector of buildings may be appealed to the board by any person claiming to be adversely affected by any such decision. The board is given power in specific cases of practical difficulty or unnecessary hardship to interpret the ordinance in harmony with its general purpose and intent, so that the public health, safety and general welfare may be secure and substantial justice done. Penalties are prescribed for violations . . . The ordinance is assailed on the grounds that it is in derogation of § 1 of the Fourteenth Amendment to the Federal Constitution in that it deprives appellee of liberty and property without due process of law and denies it the equal protection of the law, and that it offends against certain provisions of the Constitution of the State of Ohio. The prayer of the bill is for an injunction restraining the enforcement of the ordinance and all attempts to impose or maintain as to appellee's property any of the restrictions, limitations or conditions. The court below held the ordinance to be unconstitutional and void, and enjoined its enforcement. 297 Fed. 307.

Before proceeding to a consideration of the case, it is necessary to determine the scope of the inquiry. The bill alleges that the tract of land in question is vacant and has been held for years for the purpose of selling and developing it for industrial uses, for which it is especially adapted, being immediately in the path of progressive industrial development; that for such uses it has a market value of about $10,000 per acre, but if the use be limited to residential purpose the market value is not in excess of $2,500 per acre; that the first 200 feet of the parcel back from Euclid Avenue, if unrestricted in respect of use, has a value of $150 per front foot, but if limited to residential uses, and ordinary mercantile business be excluded therefrom, its value is not in excess of $50 per front foot.

It is specifically averred that the ordinance attempts to restrict and control the lawful uses of appellee's land so as to confiscate and destroy a great part of its value; . . . that the ordinance constitutes a cloud upon the land, reduces and destroys its value, and has the effect of diverting the normal industrial, commercial and residential development thereof to other and less favorable locations.

The record goes no farther than to show, as the lower court found, that the normal, and reasonably to be expected, use and development of that part of appellee's land adjoining Euclid Avenue is for general trade and commercial purposes, particularly retail stores and like establishments, and that the normal, and reasonably to be expected, use and development of the residue of the land is for industrial and trade purposes. Whatever injury is inflicted by the mere existence and threatened enforcement of the ordinance is due to restrictions in respect of these and similar uses; to which perhaps should be added—if not included in the foregoing—restrictions in respect of apartment houses. . . .

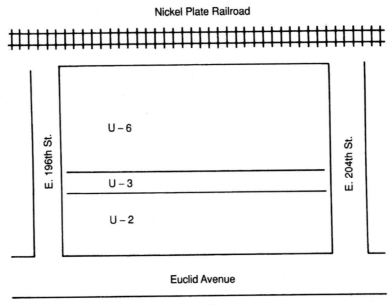

Figure 11-1
Ambler Realty Property

Building zone laws are of modern origin. They began in this country about twenty-five years ago. Until recent years, urban life was comparatively simple; but with the great increase and concentration of population, problems have developed, and constantly are developing, which require, and will continue to require, additional restrictions in respect of the use and occupation of private lands in urban communities. Regulations, the wisdom, necessity and validity of which, as applied to existing conditions, are so apparent that they are now uniformly sustained, a century ago, or even half a century ago, probably would have been rejected as arbitrary and oppressive. Such regulations are sustained, under the complex conditions of our day, for reasons analogous to those which justify traffic regulations, which, before the advent of automobiles and rapid transit street railways, would have been condemned as fatally arbitrary and unreasonable. And in this there is no inconsistency, for while the meaning of constitutional guaranties never varies, the scope of their application must expand or contract to meet the new and different conditions which are constantly coming within the field of their operation. In a changing world, it is impossible that it should be otherwise. . . . The ordinance now under review, and all similar laws and regulations, must find their justification in some aspect of the police power, asserted for the public welfare. The line which in this field separates the legitimate from the illegitimate assumption of power is not capable of precise delimitation. It varies with circumstances and conditions. A regulatory zoning ordinance, which would be clearly valid as applied to the great cities, might be clearly invalid as applied to rural communities. In solving doubts, the maxim *sic utere tuo ut alienum non laedas*, which lies at the foundation of so much of the common law of nuisances, ordinarily will furnish a fairly helpful clew. And the law of nuisances, likewise, may be consulted, not for the purpose of controlling, but for the helpful aid of its analogies in the process of ascertaining the scope of, the power. Thus the question whether the power exists to forbid the erection of a building of a particular kind or for a particular use, like the question whether a particular thing is a nuisance, is to be determined, not by an abstract consideration of the building or of the thing considered apart, but by considering it in connection with the circumstances and the locality. . . . A nuisance may be merely a right thing in the wrong place—like a pig in the parlor instead of the barnyard. If the validity of the legislative classification for zoning purposes be fairly debatable, the legislative judgment must be allowed to control. . . .

There is no serious difference of opinion in respect of the validity of laws and regulations fixing the height of buildings within reasonable limits, the character of materials and methods of construction, and the adjoining area which must be left open, in order to minimize the danger of fire or collapse, the evils of over-crowding, and the like, and excluding from residential sections offensive trades, industries and structures likely to create nuisances. . . .

Here, however, the exclusion is in general terms of all industrial establishments, and it may thereby happen that not only offensive or dangerous industries will be excluded, but those which are neither offensive nor dangerous will share the same fate. But this is no more than happens in respect of many practice-forbidding laws which this Court has upheld although drawn in general terms so as to include individual cases that may turn out to be innocuous in themselves. . . . The inclusion of a reasonable margin to insure effective enforcement, will not put upon a law, otherwise valid, the stamp of invalidity. Such laws may also find their justification in the fact that, in some fields, the bad fades into the good by such insensible degrees that the two are not capable of being readily distinguished and separated in terms of legislation. In the light of these considerations, we are not prepared to say that the end in view was not sufficient to justify the general rule of the ordinance, although some industries of an innocent character might fall within the proscribed class. It cannot be said that the ordinance in this respect "passes the bounds of reason and assumes the character of a merely arbitrary fiat." Purity Extract Co. v. Lynch, 226 U.S. 192, 204. Moreover, the restrictive provisions of the ordinance in this particular may be sustained upon the principles applicable to the broader exclusion from residential districts of all business and trade structures, presently to be discussed. We find no difficulty in sustaining restrictions of the kind thus far reviewed. The serious question in the case arises over the provisions of the ordinance excluding from residential districts, apartment houses, business houses, retail stores and shops, and other like establishments. This question involves the validity of what is really the crux of the more recent zoning legislation, namely, the creation and maintenance of residential districts, from which business and trade of every sort, including hotels and apartment houses, are excluded. Upon that question this Court has not thus far spoken. The decisions of the state courts are numerous and conflicting; but those which broadly sustain the power greatly outnumber those which deny altogether or narrowly limit it; and it is very apparent that there is a constantly increasing tendency in the direction of the broader view. . . .

The matter of zoning has received much attention at the hands of commissions and experts, and the results of their investigations have been set forth in comprehensive reports. These reports, which bear every evidence of painstaking consideration, concur in the view that the segregation of residential, business, and industrial buildings will make it easier to provide fire apparatus suitable for the character and intensity of the development in each section; that it will increase the safety and security of home life; greatly tend to prevent street accidents, especially to children, by reducing the traffic and resulting confusion in residential sections; decrease noise and other conditions which produce or intensify nervous disorders; preserve a more favorable environment in which to rear children, etc. With particular reference to apartment houses, it is pointed out that the development of detached house sections is greatly retarded by the coming of apartment houses, which has sometimes resulted in destroying the entire section for private house purposes; that in such sections very often the apartment house is a mere parasite, constructed in order to take advantage of the open spaces and attractive surroundings created by the residential character of the district. Moreover, the coming of one apartment house is followed by others, interfering by their height and bulk with the free circulation of air and monopolizing the rays of the sun which otherwise would fall upon the smaller homes, and bringing, as their necessary accompaniments, the disturbing noises incident to increased traffic and business, and the occupation, by means of moving and parked automobiles, of larger portions of the streets, thus detracting from their safety and depriving children of the privilege of quiet and open spaces for play, enjoyed by those in more favored localities — until, finally, the residential character of the neighborhood and its desirability as a place of detached residences are utterly destroyed. Under these circumstances, apartment houses, which in a different environment would be not only entirely unobjectionable but highly desirable, come very near to being nuisances.

If these reasons, thus summarized, do not demonstrate the wisdom or sound policy in all respects of those restrictions which we have indicated as pertinent to the inquiry, at least, the reasons are sufficiently cogent to preclude us from saying, as it must be said before the ordinance can be declared unconstitutional, that such provisions are clearly arbitrary and unreasonable, having no substantial relation to the public health, safety, morals, or general welfare. . . . Decree reversed.

VAN DEVANTER, MCREYNOLDS, and BUTLER, JJ., dissent.

THE REST OF THE STORY . . .

Real estate dealers and realty boards selected as a test case the zoning ordinance in tiny Euclid, Ohio (pop. 3,300 in 1920), a suburb of Cleveland (pop. 800,000). They thought it a favorable case for a broad holding for several reasons. First, it took three-quarters of the value out of part of the plaintiff's land. Second, the court might see tiny Euclid as interfering with the natural and desirable expansion of Cleveland. Third, the ordinance had six use districts, three height districts, and four area districts, making it difficult to justify as nuisance prevention.

Notes and Questions

1. *Euclidean zoning.* The zoning scheme of the Euclid ordinance is known today as *Euclidean zoning*. Districts are graded from "highest" (single-family residences) to "lowest" (the worst kind of industry). Under Euclidean zoning,

the uses permitted in each district are cumulative; higher uses are permitted in areas zoned for lower uses but not vice versa. Thus one can put a single-family house in an apartment district, and both uses in a commercial district, but not a commercial use in a residential district nor an apartment house in a single-family district. In an attempt to preserve large tracts for future industrial use, improving the fiscal base, some cities have turned to noncumulative zoning, prohibiting houses and commerce in industrial zones (often called *industrial parks*).

The terms "higher" and "lower" uses do not refer to economic value. *A*, whose lot is zoned residential, has a higher use than *B*, whose lot is zoned commercial, but *A*'s lot ordinarily has a lower value. Commercially zoned property usually sells at a higher price than residentially zoned property.

> **Sidebar**
>
> Justice George Sutherland, the author of the majority opinion in the *Euclid* case, was a noted judicial conservative on the Court, along with Justices Van Devanter, McReynolds, and Butler (who dissented in *Euclid*). In the 1930s, the four were collectively known as "the Four Horsemen." By managing to pick up a fifth vote, they struck down important New Deal legislation as depriving citizens of liberty or property without (substantive) due process of law. In *Euclid*, Justices Taft, Holmes, Brandeis, and Stone managed to get Justice Sutherland to join them as the swing vote. Why would Justice Sutherland endorse a seemingly radical reform like zoning?

2. *"As applied" constitutional challenges.* Notice that the plaintiff in *Euclid* did not challenge any specific provisions of the ordinance in question, but rather attacked the zoning law in its entirety. The Supreme Court in turn held zoning *in general* to be constitutional but added that concrete applications of specific provisions could prove to be arbitrary and unreasonable; such problems would be dealt with as they arose. Two years later, in Nectow v. City of Cambridge, 277 U.S. 183 (1928), the Court followed through on this warning by deciding that the zoning ordinance, as applied to the plaintiff's land, was arbitrary and unreasonable. After *Nectow*, the Supreme Court went out of the zoning business for nearly half a century, leaving the policing of zoning laws to state courts. In recent years, however, the Court has become active in the area once again. We shall have occasion to consider some of its opinions in the balance of this chapter and in the next.

3. *Zoning U.S.A.* "Today, zoning is virtually universal in the metropolitan areas of the United States. . . . Of cities with over 250,000 population only Houston, Texas, has not enacted a zoning ordinance." Robert C. Ellickson, Alternatives to Zoning: Covenants, Nuisance Rules, and Fines as Land Use Controls, 40 U. Chi. L. Rev. 681, 692 (1973). And Houston is an exception in only the strictest sense; "extensive government regulation belies the city's free market reputation in land use management. . . . [G]overnment policies have altered land use decisions for decades, and recent interventions continue the trend toward greater regulation." Teddy M. Kapur, Land Use Regulation in Houston Contradicts the City's Free Market Reputation, 34 Envtl. L. Rep. 10045 (2004). Moreover, Houston has in recent years turned increasingly to nuisance law to regulate undesirable land uses. See, e.g., Bradley Olson, Nuisance Laws Stoke Regulatory Arsenal, Hous. Chron., Apr. 10, 2009; Houston Using Nuisance

Laws on Business, Hous. Chron., Apr. 11, 2009. A recent study by two economists at the Federal Reserve Bank of Dallas suggests that the absence of zoning laws has kept land values in Houston stable, reducing volatility in housing prices. See Amber C. McCullagh & Robert W. Gilmer, Neither Boom Nor
Bust: How Houston's Housing Market Differs from Nation's, Federal Reserve
Bank of Dallas, Houston Branch (January 2008).

2. Zoning Authority and Legislation

Zoning is an exercise of the police power—essentially, the power of government
to protect health, safety, welfare, and morals. Generally speaking, the police power
is held to reside in the state, but in the case of zoning, all states have adopted
enabling acts that delegate zoning authority to local governments.

The Standard State Zoning Enabling Act is fairly representative of zoning
ordinances. It empowers municipalities to "regulate and restrict the height, number of stories, and size of buildings and other structures, the percentage of lot that
may be occupied, the size of yards, courts, and other open spaces, the density of
population, and the location and use of buildings, structures, and land for trade,
industry, residence, or other purposes." It permits the division of municipalities
into districts (zones) of appropriate number, shape, and area, and provides that
regulations may vary from district to district. The regulations must be made in
accordance with a comprehensive plan. Under the Standard Act, to enact a zoning ordinance a city must create a planning (or zoning) commission and a board
of adjustment (sometimes called a board of zoning appeals). The commission and
the board are composed of citizens appointed by the mayor. The commission,
advised by planning experts, has the function of recommending a comprehensive plan and a zoning ordinance to the city council. The zoning ordinance must
be enacted by the city council.

The board of adjustment plays a different role. It may grant a variance when
the zoning restrictions cause the owner practical difficulty or unnecessary hardship. It also may grant a special exception when specific requirements set forth in
the zoning ordinance are met.

The comprehensive plan is a statement of the local government's objectives
and standards for development. Usually made up of maps, charts, and descriptive
text, it shows the boundaries of height, area, bulk, and use zones, and the locations of streets, bridges, parks, public buildings, and the like. The plan is based on
surveys and studies of the city's present situation and future needs, the idea being
to anticipate change and promote harmonious development. Only about half
of the states require comprehensive plans. As to those with plan requirements,
judicial attitudes vary greatly. Some hold, absent very specific language in the
enabling legislation, that the plan need not be written down in a document separate from the zoning ordinance itself; some consider that the statement of purpose
in the zoning ordinance's preamble is evidence of an underlying plan to which the
ordinance conforms; some have found the scheme of regulations in the ordinance
to be "the plan." Even when a written plan exists, zoning regulations inconsistent
with it are not necessarily invalid, so long as they are considered reasonable and
in the public interest.

B. THE NONCONFORMING USE

JONES v. LUTKEN

Court of Appeals of Mississippi, 2011
62 So. 3d 455

GRIFFIS, J. This appeal reviews a circuit court's reversal of a local authority's zoning decision. The Washington County Board of Supervisors granted Mike Jones a permit for a permissible non-conforming use. A group of homeowners appealed to the Washington County Circuit Court, which reversed the Board of Supervisors' decision and denied the permit. On appeal, Jones argues that . . . the circuit court erred when it found the Board of Supervisors' decision arbitrary and capricious and unsupported by substantial evidence. Finding error, we reverse the circuit court's judgment and reinstate the decision of the Board of Supervisors.

Facts

In 2005, Jones leased property near Lake Washington, a large oxbow lake in Washington County. The lake is a popular vacation spot, and Jones catered to the vacationers. On the property, Jones operated an RV campground, ran a convenience store that sold fishing bait and refreshments, and maintained a few permanent cabins for rent.

In 2006, the Washington County Zoning Ordinance was enacted. Most of the land around Lake Washington, including Jones's land, was zoned R-2 residential (single-family residential). Jones's RV park, convenience store, and cabin-rental business were not in conformity with the new ordinance. However, the ordinance expressly provided for the continuation of non-conforming uses that existed at the time the ordinance was enacted. The ordinance, in pertinent part, reads:

> It is the intent of this Ordinance to allow nonconformities to continue. It is further the intent of this Ordinance that nonconformities shall not be enlarged upon, expanded, or extended, nor be used as grounds for adding other structures or uses prohibited elsewhere in the same district.

Washington County Zoning Ordinance § 3001(3)(a). Jones continued operating his business as a permissible non-conforming use. However, the ordinance prohibited Jones from expanding the non-conforming use.

At some time thereafter, Jones began selling portable cabins. These cabins were small manufactured buildings that could be loaded on trucks and transported. He displayed the cabins for sale on his land near his convenience store.

Jones sold several portable cabins. Most of the cabins sold were removed from his property. However, two of the cabins were placed on RV lots, which were on Jones's property, at the request of the purchasers. The purchasers paid rent for the lots like an RV user.

The Washington County Planning Director informed Jones that he could not display the cabins for sale and that he could not keep the two cabins on the RV lots. The director maintained that Jones was in violation of the zoning ordinance. The director determined that Jones's display of the cabins and his placement of the cabins on RV lots were impermissible expansions of his non-conforming use.

Jones then sought a permit from the Washington County Planning Commission. The Commission agreed with the director that the display of cabins for sale was an impermissible expansion. Thereafter, Jones ceased the display of cabins for sale. This decision was never challenged. However, the Commission disagreed with the director as to the two portable cabins placed on the RV lots.

The Commission found that the placement of the portable cabins was a permissible continuation of Jones's non-conforming use, not an expansion, and Jones was granted the permit to allow the portable cabins to remain.

A group of nearby homeowners appealed the Commission's decision to the Board of Supervisors. The Board of Supervisors affirmed the Commission's decision. The homeowners then filed a bill of exceptions and appealed the decision to the circuit court. The circuit court reversed the Board of Supervisors' decision.

Jones now appeals the circuit court's decision. . . .

Analysis

. . .

The circuit court ruled that the Board of Supervisors' decision was arbitrary and capricious and unsupported by substantial evidence. The circuit court found that the placement of the portable cabins on RV lots was an expansion of Jones's non-conforming use. Thus, the court concluded that the Board of Supervisors' decision to grant Jones the permit was contrary to the express language of the ordinance, which prohibits expansion of non-conforming uses.

The question facing the Board of Supervisors was whether placing the portable cabins on the RV lots was an expansion of Jones's non-conforming use or whether it was a permissible continuation of the non-conforming use. If it was an expansion, then the ordinance prohibited it. If it was a continuation, then the ordinance allowed it.

To answer this question, the nature of Jones's non-conforming use must be defined. Jones had an RV park, a convenience store, and a few permanent cabins available for rent on the land. The homeowners contend that Jones had an RV park, and nothing else, and that these portable cabins are not RVs; thus, their placement cannot be a continuation of the permissible non-conforming use. Jones argues that his non-conforming use should be construed as a commercial operation, rather than merely an RV park. If the non-conforming use is broadly defined as a commercial operation, then he claims it is easier to see how placing the portable cabins could be viewed as a continuation and not an expansion.

Even if the permissible non-conforming use is narrowly defined as an RV park and nothing else, there is a second difficult question—whether these portable cabins qualify as RVs under the ordinance. The ordinance defines RVs as "portable or mobile living unit[s] for temporary human occupancy away from the place of residence of the occupants." Washington County Zoning Ordinance § 203. This definition appears to be broad enough to include the portable cabins at issue.[1] If the cabins are RVs within

---

1. The homeowners point out that the next sentence in the ordinance states: "For the purpose of this Ordinance, such RV shall be considered a VEHICLE AND NOT A STRUCTURE." Washington County Zoning Ordinance § 203. The homeowners then argue that the portable cabins are structures, not vehicles; therefore, they cannot be RVs within the meaning of the ordinance. We do not agree with that reading of the ordinance. The first sentence defines RVs. The second sentence then states that, going forward, whenever the ordinance refers to a "structure" it is not referring to an RV, and whenever it refers to a "vehicle" it is referring to an RV in addition to whatever else qualifies as a "vehicle" under the ordinance. The second sentence does not modify the definition of an RV.

the meaning of the ordinance, then their placement on RV lots would not be an expansion of Jones's non-conforming use.

The Board of Supervisors was faced with these questions and had to interpret the zoning-ordinance language. The words "expansion" and "continuation" were not clearly defined, precise terms in the zoning ordinance. These words must be interpreted and applied within the context of a given factual scenario. It is the role of the Board of Supervisors to make these judgments, subject to limited appellate review.

"[I]n construing a zoning ordinance, unless manifestly unreasonable, great weight should be given to the construction placed upon the words by the local authorities." Hall v. City of Ridgeland, 37 So. 3d 25, 40 (Miss. 2010) (quoting Columbus & Greenville Ry. Co. v. Scales, 578 So. 2d 275, 279 (Miss. 1991)). As stated previously, where the question is "fairly debatable," the decision of the Board of Supervisors must be affirmed. Saunders v. City of Jackson, 511 So. 2d 902, 906 (Miss. 1987). Here, it is our opinion that the interpretation of the zoning-ordinance definition of RV could include the portable cabins. Accordingly, we find that the Board of Supervisors' decision was "fairly debatable" and that this interpretation was not manifestly unreasonable.

For these reasons, we find the circuit court committed error when it reversed the decision of the Board of Supervisors. Accordingly, we reverse the circuit court's judgment and reinstate the decision of the Board of Supervisors. . . .

Problems, Notes, and Questions

1. *Protecting nonconforming uses—a good idea?* Should nonconforming uses be protected? Imagine that you have been lawfully operating a concrete plant in a city for the past 15 years. The city has recently rezoned the area for light commercial and office use only. Your concrete plant is now a *preexisting nonconforming use.*

This is a problem of legal transitions. On the one hand, fairness seems to require legal protection for preexisting nonconforming uses. Owners of property with such uses have settled expectations based on the law that existed at the time their use began. On the other hand, the costs of protecting such uses are high. Legal protection of nonconforming uses can undermine the effectiveness of the zoning changes. See Christopher Serkin, Existing Uses and the Limits of Land Use Regulations, 84 N.Y.U. L. Rev. 1222 (2009). Professor Serkin points out that protecting owners from legal change can create perverse investment incentives. Property owners anticipating future regulatory changes lock in use of buildings or other property before the change occurs. This can trigger a race to develop and lead to inefficient overinvestment in property. Id. at 1283.

2. *The right to continue.* The Washington County Zoning Ordinance explicitly provides owners of land with preexisting nonconforming uses with a right to continue such uses, presumably indefinitely. Is this a good idea?

The right to continue has raised a number of legal issues. One concerns whether the owner may expand such a use. The Washington County ordinance distinguishes between continuance of a prior nonconforming use (permitted) and expansion of one (not permitted). Were the portable cabins in Jones v. Lutken a "continuation" or an "expansion" of Jones's preexisting nonconforming use? Can you tell? The court defers to the decision of the Board of Supervisors but tells us nothing the reasons for the board's decision. What do you suspect might have been the board's reasons?

Another issue concerns intensity of use. In Trip Associates, Inc. v. Mayor and City Council of Baltimore, 898 A.2d 449 (Md. App. 2006), the local zoning board of appeals restricted the number of days per week that an adult entertainment nightclub could continue its valid nonconforming use. The owner had legally operated his adult entertainment business on an unrestricted basis until a city ordinance declared such businesses nonconforming. He was directed to cease using his premises for adult entertainment, but the zoning appeals board permitted him to operate two days per week. He challenged the board's decision because he wanted to operate more frequently than two nights a week. The Court of Appeals defined the issue as whether using the valid nonconforming use more frequently than it was being used when its use became nonconforming was an "expansion" of use, in which case it was prohibited, or a "mere intensification of the use," which was permitted. The court ruled that it was an intensification and therefore permitted. There are decisions to the contrary. See, e.g., Williston Park v. 280 Hillside Park Rest. Corp., 390 N.Y.S.2d 637 (App. Div. 1977). Is the distinction between expansion and intensification any more helpful than that between continuation and expansion? Even in jurisdictions with an indefinite right to continue, certain events will cause termination. *Destruction* of a nonconforming use (by act of God or otherwise) usually terminates. So, too, does *abandonment*, which requires intent to abandon the nonconforming use. Some ordinances go even further and eliminate litigation over intent to abandon and prohibit the continuation of a nonconforming use if it is "discontinued" over a period of time, say, two years. See Pike Indus., Inc. v. Woodward, 999 A.2d 257 (N.H. 2010).

3. *Amortization.* In most states, local governments allow nonconforming uses to be phased out through a process known as *amortization.* The idea is to strike a balance between protecting the owner's investment and expectation and facilitating the goals of zoning. Amortization permits the preexisting nonconforming use to continue for a set period of time and then requires it to end. It enables the owner to earn back all or part of its investment in the use. To be valid the amortization process must be reasonable, but jurisdictions differ on what constitutes a reasonable amortization period. In AVR, Inc. v. City of St. Louis Park, 585 N.W.2d 411 (Minn. App. 1998), the court upheld a two-year amortization period.

4. *Zoning out Airbnb.* In Styller v. Aylward, 2018 Mass. LCR Lexis 194 (Mass. Land Ct. 2018), Styller, the owner of a large single-family home in a residential neighborhood, rented out his house on a short-term basis through Airbnb. One of his renters held a very large party in the course of which a guest was shot and killed. Styller was immediately served with a cease and desist order from the town to cease renting his house on a short-term basis without a special permit from the zoning board of appeals. The town amended its zoning bylaw explicitly to address such rentals. Styller argued that his short-term rental operation was a valid preexisting nonconforming use, but the board of zoning appeals disagreed. Styller appealed to the Land Court. That court found that Styller's short-term rentals were not a use permitted under the zoning laws in existence at the time Styller began his short-term rentals and, hence, could not be "grandfathered" as "as of right" uses.

5. *Vested rights.* Related to the law of nonconforming uses is the more general doctrine of vested rights. In the case of nonconforming uses, a preexisting operation is protected; plans to engage in some particular use are insufficient.

In the case of vested rights doctrine, a proposed use might be protected if suffi-cient commitments have been made—plans drawn, permits obtained, the site prepared, construction begun—in reliance on existing zoning requirements that are subsequently changed in a way that invalidates the proposed use. Vested rights doctrine varies in practice from jurisdiction to jurisdiction (some of which have statutes or ordinances on the question), but the critical variables include how far the developer has gone in obtaining governmental approvals, how much money has been invested in good faith, and on what the money has been spent. See gen-erally American Law of Zoning, supra, §§ 12:20-12:34.

C. ACHIEVING FLEXIBILITY IN ZONING

By segregating various classes of uses in tightly drawn districts, Euclidean zon-ing can work inequitable hardships and promote inefficient patterns of land use. Zoning laws can also inhibit socially and aesthetically desirable diversity. See Jane Jacobs, The Death and Life of Great American Cities 152-177, 222-269 passim (1961). On a number of grounds, then, there is a need to provide flexibility in zon-ing. The approach to nonconforming uses, considered in the last section, could be regarded as one way of doing so; this section surveys a number of others. They range from modest techniques to modify traditional zoning regulations, to dis-tinctly non-Euclidean approaches, to public control of land use.

As you study the materials that follow, note the differing requirements of each of the flexibility devices and the differing methods (and decision makers) they employ. Keep especially in mind that the power to regulate "flexibly" can be the power to favor, or disfavor, for illegitimate reasons.

1. Variances and Special Exceptions

The Standard State Zoning Enabling Act authorizes a board of adjustment to adopt two different means of avoiding undue hardships that might result from strict zoning enforcement: the *variance* and the *special exception*. The act states that the board may

> in appropriate cases and subject to appropriate conditions and safeguards, make special exceptions to the terms of the ordinance in harmony with its general purpose and intent . . . , [and may authorize] in specific cases such variance from the terms of the ordinance as will not be contrary to the public interest, where, owing to special conditions, a literal enforcement of the pro-visions of the ordinance will result in unnecessary hardship, and so that the spirit of the ordinance shall be observed and substantial justice done.

a. Variances

Commons v. Westwood Zoning Board of Adjustment, 410 A.2d 1138 (N.J. 1980). As is typical, New Jersey's enabling statute delegates to boards of adjust-ment the power to grant a variance, provided two conditions are met. First, the variance must be necessary to avoid imposing *undue hardship* on the owner of the land in question. (Undue hardship "involves the underlying notion that no effective use can be made of the property in the event the variance is denied.") To show hardship, the owner must first have made reasonable efforts to comply with the zoning ordinance—say by trying, in the case of an undersized lot, to sell it to, or buy additional land from, a neighbor, in either case at a fair price. And the owner's hardship must not have been self-inflicted, such as by earlier disposing of part of his land with the result that what was left fell short of area requirements. Second, "the grant of the variance must not substantially impinge upon the public good and the intent and purpose of the zoning plan and ordinance." This requires paying attention to "the manner in and extent to which the variance will impact upon the character of the area."

Weingarten wanted to build a one-family residence on the only undeveloped lot in a residential neighborhood. Because his lot did not meet the existing zoning ordinance's minimum lot size requirements (it had a frontage of 30 feet and a total area of 5,190 square feet, whereas the zoning ordinance required a frontage of 75 feet and total area of 7,500 square feet), Weingarten sought a variance, proposing to build a narrow but deep four-bedroom home. Neighbors opposed this plan, and the board of adjustment denied the variance, finding "that the applicant failed to demonstrate any evidence to establish hardship" and "that the granting of the variance would substantially impair the intent and purpose of the Zone Plan and Zoning Ordinance of the Borough of Westwood."

On appeal by Weingarten, the court held that the record did not support the board of adjustment's conclusions. The board could not base its decision on the size of the house, because the planned construction did not violate any of the traditional zoning purposes of light, air, and open space reflected in the ordinance. And while minimum lot size requirements, "conserving the value of the surrounding properties," and "aesthetic considerations" were all appropriate "desiderata of zoning," the board did not rest its decision on evidence about such matters, but instead simply drew conclusions that were unsupported by the facts.

"Until the 1947 amendment to the zoning ordinance the plaintiffs or their predecessors in title could have constructed a one-family house on the lot. Ownership commenced in 1927 when the Borough of Westwood had no zoning ordinance. Furthermore an attempt, albeit unsuccessful, had been made to acquire an additional ten-foot strip from Mr. Butler, owner of the property bordering to the south. A 40-foot frontage would have at least brought the property into conformity with one home in the neighborhood and within close proximity of the size of the lots of two other houses. In addition there had been discussion concerning the possible sale of the property to a neighbor, there being a substantial divergence in the offering and asking prices. Lastly, one could reasonably conclude that, if a variance were not granted, the land would be zoned into inutility. In view of all the above, it cannot be said that there was not any evidence to establish hardship.

"Passing to the [questions of impact on the public good and on the general zoning plan], the board of adjustment made only the conclusive statement that the variance would substantially impair the intent and purpose of the zone plan and ordinance. The manner in which the variance would cause that effect is not explained. The board found that the lot was the only 30-foot parcel in the block, that the applicant builder had never constructed a house on a 30-foot lot, and that the proposed house would be 19 feet in width. How these facts relate to the zone plan is not made clear. The proposed use, side yards and setback meet the requirements of the ordinance. The proposed sales price of the home would be within the range of the value of the houses in the neighborhood. The total acreage of the land, exceeding 5,000 square feet, is comparable to 17 other properties in the neighborhood."

The court remanded for further proceedings, noting not only that the board should address the problems noted by the court, but also that the applicant—who had the burden of proof—should submit plans for the proposed house.

Notes and Questions

1. *Conditional variances.* In granting a variance, zoning boards may impose reasonable conditions related to the use of the property that minimize the adverse impact of the use on neighbors. Such conditions may relate, for example, to fences, landscaping, outdoor lighting and noises, and enclosure of buildings. On the other hand, zoning boards may not condition a variance upon use of the property by the original applicants only, as this has no relation to ameliorating the effects of the proposed land use and is unrelated to the legitimate purposes of zoning. A variance thus must "run with the land." St. Onge v. Donovan, 522 N.E.2d 1019 (N.Y. 1988).

2. *Area versus use.* The *Commons* case involved a so-called area (or dimensional) variance, having to do with setback requirements and the like, as opposed to a use variance relaxing restrictions on permissible uses in a particular area (e.g., allowing a commercial use in a residential zone). The burden of proof is said to be greater for a use variance than for an area variance. See, e.g., Hertzberg v. Zoning Bd. of Adjustment of Pittsburgh, 721 A.2d 43 (Pa. 1998).

Why might this be? Does an area variance necessarily have less impact on the neighborhood than a use variance? And as between area and use, is it always clear which is which?

b. Special Exceptions

The second method of avoiding hardships from rigid zoning enforcement is the *special exception*. Special exceptions (sometimes called *conditional uses*) differ from variances in that while a variance is an administratively authorized departure from the terms of the zoning ordinance, "an exception is a use *permitted by the ordinance* in a district in which it is not necessarily incompatible, but where it might cause harm if not watched." Daniel R. Mandelker, Delegation of Power and Function in Zoning Administration, 1963 Wash. U. L.Q. 60, 62-63 (emphasis added). Typical exceptions require large amounts of land and involve uses that have the potential to cause injury to the surrounding area. Examples include airports, landfills, and hospitals. The harms involved might be noise or traffic. Hence the zoning board grants exceptions on a case-by-case basis, and only after satisfying itself that the proposed use will not cause harm in the specific location involved.

2. Zoning Amendments and the Spot Zoning Problem

State v. City of Rochester, 268 N.W.2d 885 (Minn. 1978). The case involves zoning amendments, another way to provide flexibility. A single tract of land in Rochester, Minnesota bordered single-family homes, multiple-family dwellings, and a vacant lot zoned for "institutional" use and owned by the Mayo Clinic. High-rise condominiums and the Mayo Clinic Complex were one block away and visible from the tract, and the central business district was three blocks away. The tract was zoned for low-density residential use (multiple-family dwellings), but the owner wanted to build a 49-unit "luxury condominium," so he applied to have the property rezoned for high-density residential use. The Rochester city council approved his application and passed an ordinance rezoning the property. It provided no written reasons or findings supporting the rezoning, but minutes from council meetings showed "that the council members believed the proposed condominium was needed to serve the city's expanded housing requirements. Council members stated that the Gooding property would be an ideal site since it was located within three blocks of the central business district and since high-density residential uses already across two streets from the property would be compatible with the proposed condominium and made development of the subject property for any other use unlikely."

Owners of the neighboring homes appealed the city council decision. They sought closer judicial scrutiny of the rezoning by arguing that it was an administrative or quasi-judicial act. The court rejected the opportunity to apply a higher level of review, saying:

"[W]e have consistently held that when a municipality adopts or amends a zoning ordinance, it acts in a legislative capacity under its delegated police powers. As a legislative act, a zoning or rezoning classification must be upheld unless opponents prove that the classification is unsupported by any rational basis related to promoting the public health, safety, morals, or general welfare, or that the classification amounts to a taking without compensation. . . . Our narrow scope of review reflects a policy decision that a legislative body can best determine which zoning classifications best serve the public welfare."

This left the plaintiffs with the job of convincing the court that the rezoning had no reasonable relation to promoting public health, safety, morals, or general welfare—a very tough sell. Given the proximity of the tract of land to commonly used services (city bus lines, public community centers, a child care center, a city library, the central business district, and a major shopping area) and the fact that the tract was surrounded by medium and high density residential uses, the court concluded that "[t]here was a rational basis for concluding that a six-story condominium would be compatible with existing uses in the neighborhood of the subject property." Plaintiffs' arguments that the new condominium would disrupt the neighboring single-family community's stability and character by increasing noise and traffic, and would make the homes lose some of their value, fell short. "All of these factors may make the reasonableness of the zoning change fairly debatable, but under our standard of review, that is not enough to justify the court's interfering with the council's legislative judgment in passing the ordinance."

Note

Spot zoning. The plaintiffs in *City of Rochester* claimed that the zoning amendment was invalid "spot zoning," defined by the court as "zoning changes, typically limited to small plots of land, which establish a use classification inconsistent with surrounding uses and create an island of nonconforming use within a larger zoned district, and which dramatically reduce the value for uses specified in the zoning ordinance of either the rezoned plot or abutting property." Id. at 891.

Spot zoning is invalid where a zoning amendment (1) singles out a small parcel of land for special and privileged treatment (2) only for the benefit of the landowner rather than in the public interest and (3) in a way that is not in accord with a comprehensive plan. Even if one or more of these factors is absent, spot zoning may be found invalid in some jurisdictions.

In Residential and Agricultural Advisory Committee, LLC v. Dyersville City Council, 888 N.W.2d 24 (Iowa 2016), the Dyersville City Council voted to rezone the area containing the *Field of Dreams* movie site from agricultural to commercial in order to facilitate the development of a baseball complex. A group of community members challenged the rezoning on several grounds, including illegal spot zoning. The Iowa Supreme Court disagreed, finding that although this was spot zoning, it was valid because the city council had a reasonable basis for its decision to rezone the land despite the surrounding property. "The *Field of Dreams* property has been a unique site for years. The baseball field on the Lansing farm has been used in the community for baseball and softball games, in addition to local and national tourism. Part of the location's charm is simply that it is a baseball field surrounded by farmland." Id. at 46.

Dyersville and other cases are discussed as examples of "the common law of zoning" in Michael Allan Wolf, A Common Law of Zoning, 61 Ariz. L. Rev. 771 (2019).

> ### Sidebar
>
> For those not familiar with the film, *Field of Dreams* was a 1989 production starring Kevin Costner and James Earl Jones about an Iowa farmer who builds a baseball field in the middle of his cornfield after hearing a voice whispering, "If you build it, he will come," and seeing a vision of a baseball diamond in his field. The film was nominated for three Academy Awards, including Best Picture.

D. EXPANDING THE AIMS OF ZONING

> The best laid schemes o' mice an' men
> Gang aft a-gley,
> An' lea'e us nought but grief an' pain
> For promised joy!—
>
> *Robert Burns,*
> To a Mouse (1785)

What are the appropriate objectives of zoning? Judging from Euclid v. Ambler, the early objectives seemed to be little more than the comprehensive control of nuisances. Thus the height, spacing, and location of buildings were controlled as means to provide light and air, to help avoid and control the dangers of fire, to prevent overcrowding, and to exclude offensive industries from areas where people lived.

But the picture that the *Euclid* Court painted was somewhat misleading. Recall, for example, that the Euclid ordinance excluded apartment buildings from areas zoned for single-family and two-family dwellings, a result the trial court characterized as economic segregation but that the Supreme Court managed to justify in the same terms as it did the more benign aspects of Euclidean zoning. The facts and holding in the case, then, could be read as a generous endorsement of social engineering in the name of public health, safety, and welfare.

Over the years since *Euclid*, the aims of zoning gradually expanded, no doubt for a host of reasons—population growth, increased pressures on the public fisc, the rise of activist government generally, racial prejudice, an expanding environmental consciousness, and so on. Zoning authorities began taking initiatives that the Court in *Euclid* would never have imagined. We shall concentrate on the rise of three factors in zoning: aesthetics, household composition, and the nature and size of local populations.

1. Aesthetic Regulation

STATE EX REL. STOYANOFF v. BERKELEY
Supreme Court of Missouri, 1970
458 S.W.2d 305

PRITCHARD, COMMISSIONER. Upon summary judgment the trial court issued a peremptory writ of mandamus to compel appellant to issue a residential building permit to respondents. The trial court's judgment is that the below-mentioned ordinances are violative of Section 10, Article I of the Constitution of Missouri, 1945, V.A.M.S., in that restrictions placed by the ordinances on the use of property deprive the owners of their property without due process of law. Relators' petition pleads that they applied to appellant Building Commissioner for a building permit to allow them to construct a single family residence in the City of Ladue, and that plans and specifications were submitted for the proposed residence, which was unusual in design, "but complied with all existing building and zoning regulations and ordinances of the City of Ladue, Missouri."

It is further pleaded that relators were refused a building permit for the construction of their proposed residence upon the ground that the permit was not approved by the Architectural Board of the City of Ladue. Ordinance 131, as amended by Ordinance 281 of that city, purports to set up an Architectural Board to approve plans and specifications for buildings and structures erected within the city and in a preamble to

> conform to certain minimum architectural standards of appearance and conformity with surrounding structures, and that unsightly, grotesque and unsuitable structures, detrimental to the stability of value and the welfare of surrounding property, structures and residents, and to the general welfare and

happiness of the community, be avoided, and that appropriate standards of beauty and conformity be fostered and encouraged.

It is asserted in the petition that the ordinances are invalid, illegal and void, "are unconstitutional in that they are vague and provide no standard nor uniform rule by which to guide the architectural board," that the city acted in excess of statutory powers (§ 89.020, RS Mo 1959, V.A.M.S.) in enacting the ordinances, which "attempt to allow respondent to impose aesthetic standards for buildings in the City of Ladue, and are in excess of the powers granted the City of Ladue by said statute."

Relators filed a motion for summary judgment and affidavits were filed in opposition thereto. Richard D. Shelton, Mayor of the City of Ladue, deposed that the facts in appellant's answer were true and correct, as here pertinent: that the City of Ladue constitutes one of the finer suburban residential areas of Metropolitan St. Louis, the homes therein are considerably more expensive than in cities of comparable size, being homes on lots from three fourths of an acre to three or more acres each; that a zoning ordinance was enacted by the city regulating the height, number of stories, size of buildings, percentage of lot occupancy, yard sizes, and the location and use of buildings and land for trade, industry, residence and other purposes; that the zoning regulations were made in accordance with a comprehensive plan "designed to promote the health and general welfare of the residents of the City of Ladue," which in furtherance of said objectives duly enacted said Ordinances numbered 131 and 281. Appellant also asserted in his answer that these ordinances were a reasonable exercise of the city's governmental, legislative and police powers, as determined by its legislative body, and as stated in the above-quoted preamble to the ordinances. It is then pleaded that relators' description of their proposed residence as "'unusual in design' is the understatement of the year. It is in fact a monstrosity of grotesque design, which would seriously impair the value of property in the neighborhood."

The affidavit of Harold C. Simon, a developer of residential subdivisions in St. Louis County, is that he is familiar with relators' lot upon which they seek to build a house, and with the surrounding houses in the neighborhood; that the houses therein existent are virtually all two-story houses of conventional architectural design, such as Colonial, French Provincial or English; and that the house which relators propose to construct is of ultramodern design which would clash with and not be in conformity with any other house in the entire neighborhood. It is Mr. Simon's opinion that the design and appearance of relators' proposed residence would have a substantial adverse effect upon the market values of other residential property in the neighborhood, such average market value ranging from $60,000 to $85,000 each.

As a part of the affidavit of Russell H. Riley, consultant for the city planning and engineering firm of Harland Bartholomew & Associates, photographic exhibits of homes surrounding relators' lot were attached. . . . [The surrounding houses consisted of a conventional frame residence, several of a Colonial style, and one of a Tudor style.] In substance Mr. Riley went on to say that the City of Ladue is one of the finer residential suburbs in the St. Louis area. . . . The homes are considerably more expensive than average homes found in a city of comparable size. The ordinance which has been adopted by the City of Ladue is typical of those which have been adopted by a number of suburban cities in St. Louis County and in similar cities throughout the United States, the need therefor being based upon the protection of existing property values by preventing the construction of houses that are in complete conflict with the general type of houses in a given area. The intrusion into this neighborhood of relators' unusual, grotesque and nonconforming structure would have a substantial adverse effect on market values of other homes in the immediate area. According to Mr. Riley the standards of Ordinance 131, as amended by Ordinance 281, are usually and customarily applied in city planning work and are:

(1) whether the proposed house meets the customary architectural requirements in appearance and design for a house of the particular type which is proposed (whether it be Colonial, Tudor English, French Provincial, or Modern), (2) whether the proposed house is in general conformity with the style and design of surrounding structures, and (3) whether the proposed house lends itself to the proper architectural development of the City; and that in applying said standards the Architectural Board and its Chairman are to determine whether the proposed house will have an adverse effect on the stability of values in the surrounding area.

Photographic exhibits of relators' proposed residence were also attached to Mr. Riley's affidavit. They show the residence to be of a pyramid shape, with a flat top, and with triangular shaped windows or doors at one or more corners. . . .

[R]elators' position is that "the creation by the City of Ladue of an architectural board for the purpose of promoting and maintaining 'general conformity with the style and design of surrounding structures' is totally unauthorized by our Enabling Statute." (§§ 89.020, 89.040, RS Mo 1959, V.A.M.S.) It is further contended by relators that Ordinances 131 and 281 are invalid and unconstitutional as being an unreasonable and arbitrary exercise of the police power (as based entirely on aesthetic values); and that the same are invalid as an unlawful delegation of legislative powers (to the Architectural Board).

Section 89.020 provides . . . [for regulation of lot size; height, size, spacing, and use of buildings; and population density—all for the purpose of promoting health, safety, and welfare.] Section 89.040 provides . . . [that regulations be made in accordance with a comprehensive plan and designed "to promote health *and the general welfare. . . . Such regulations shall be made with reasonable consideration, among other things, to the character of the district and its peculiar suitability for particular uses, and with a view to conserving the values of buildings and encouraging the most appropriate use of land throughout such municipality.*" (Italics added by the court.)]

Relators say that "Neither Sections 89.020 or 89.040 nor any other provision of Chapter 89 mentions or gives a city the authority to regulate architectural design and appearance. There exists no provision providing for an architectural board and no entity even remotely resembling such a board is mentioned under the enabling legislation." Relators conclude that the City of Ladue lacked any power to adopt Ordinance 131 as amended by Ordinance 281 "and its intrusion into this area is wholly unwarranted and without sanction in the law." As to this aspect of the appeal realtors rely upon the 1961 decision of State ex rel. Magidson v. Henze, Mo. App., 342 S.W.2d 261. That case had the identical question presented. An Architectural Control Commission was set up by an ordinance of the City of University City. In its report to the Building Commissioner, the Architectural Control Commission disapproved the Magidson application for permits to build four houses. It was commented that the proposed houses did not provide for the minimum number of square feet, and "In considering the existing character of

Houses in Ladue on the same street as the proposed Stoyanoff house

this neighborhood, the Commission is of the opinion that houses of the character proposed in these plans are not in harmony with and will not contribute to nor protect the general welfare of this neighborhood" (loc. cit. 264). The court held that § 89.020, RS Mo 1949, V.A.M.S., does not grant to the city the right to impose upon the landowner aesthetic standards for the buildings he chooses to erect.

As is clear from the affidavits and attached exhibits, the City of Ladue is an area composed principally of residences of the general types of Colonial, French Provincial and English Tudor. The city has a comprehensive plan of zoning to maintain the general character of buildings therein. The *Magidson* case, supra, did not consider the effect of §89.040, supra, and the italicized portion relating to the character of the district, its suitability for particular uses, and the conservation of the values of buildings therein. These considerations, sanctioned by statute, are directly related to the general welfare of the community. . . . In Marrs v. City of Oxford (D.C.D. Kan.) 24 F.2d 541, 548, it was said, "The stabilizing of property values, and giving some assurance to the public that, if property is purchased in a residential district, its value as such will be preserved, is probably the most cogent reason back of zoning ordinances." The preamble to Ordinance 131, quoted above in part, demonstrates that its purpose is to conform to the dictates of § 89.040, with reference to preserving values of property by zoning procedure and restrictions on the use of property. This is an illustration of what was referred to in Deimeke v. State Highway Commission, Mo., 444 S.W.2d 480, 484, as a growing number of cases recognizing a change in the scope of the term "general welfare." In the *Deimeke* case on the same page it is said, "Property use which offends sensibilities and debases property values affects not only the adjoining property owners in that vicinity but the general public as well because when such property values are destroyed or seriously impaired, the tax base of the community is affected and the public suffers economically as a result."

A 2001 rendering by architect Stephen Harby showing what the
Stoyanoff house might have looked like

Relators say further that Ordinances 131 and 281 are invalid and unconstitutional as being an unreasonable and arbitrary exercise of the police power. It is argued that a mere reading of these ordinances shows that they are based entirely on aesthetic factors in that the stated purpose of the Architectural Board is to maintain "conformity with surrounding structures" and to assure that structures "conform to certain minimum architectural standards of appearance." The argument ignores the further provisos in the ordinance: . . . and that unsightly, grotesque and unsuitable structures, *detrimental to the stability of value and the welfare of surrounding property, structures, and residents,* and *to the general welfare and happiness of the community,* be avoided, and that appropriate standards of beauty and conformity be fostered and encouraged. (Italics added.) Relators' proposed residence does not descend to the "'patently offensive character of vehicle graveyards in close proximity to such highways'" referred to in the *Deimeke* case, supra (444 S.W.2d 484). Nevertheless, the aesthetic factor to be taken into account by the Architectural Board is not to be considered alone. Along with that inherent factor is the effect that the proposed residence would have upon the property values in the area. In this time of burgeoning urban areas, congested with people and structures, it is certainly in keeping with the ultimate ideal of general welfare that the Architectural Board, in its function, preserve and protect existing areas in which structures of a general conformity of architecture have been erected. The area under consideration is clearly, from the record, a fashionable one. In State ex rel. Civello v. City of New Orleans, 154 La. 271, 97 So. 440, 444, the court said, "If by the term 'aesthetic considerations' is meant a regard merely for outward appearances, for good taste in the matter of the beauty of the neighborhood itself, we do not observe any substantial reason for saying that such a consideration is not a matter of general welfare. The beauty of a fashionable residence neighborhood in a city is for the comfort and happiness of the residents, and it sustains in a general way the value of property in the neighborhood." . . .

The denial by appellant of a building permit for relators' highly modernistic residence in this area where traditional Colonial, French Provincial and English Tudor styles of architecture are erected does not appear to be arbitrary and unreasonable when the basic purpose to be served is that of the general welfare of persons in the entire community.

In addition to the above-stated purpose in the preamble to Ordinance 131, it establishes an Architectural Board of three members, all of whom must be architects. Meetings of the Board are to be open to the public, and every application for a building permit, except those not affecting the outward appearance of a building, shall be submitted to the Board along with plans, elevations, detail drawings and specifications, before being approved by the Building Commissioner. The Chairman of the Board shall examine the application to determine if it conforms to proper architectural standards in appearance and design and will be in general conformity with the style and design of surrounding structures and conducive to the proper architectural development of the city. If he so finds, he approves and returns the application to the Building Commissioner. If he does not find conformity, or has doubt, a full meeting of the Board is called, with notice of the time and place thereof given to the applicant. The Board shall disapprove the application if it determines the proposed structure will constitute an unsightly, grotesque or unsuitable structure in appearance, detrimental to the welfare of surrounding property or residents. If it cannot make that decision, the application shall be returned to the Building Commissioner either with or without suggestions or recommendations, and if that is done without disapproval, the Building Commissioner may issue the permit. If the Board's disapproval is given and the applicant refuses to comply with recommendations, the Building Commissioner shall refuse the permit. Thereafter provisions are made for an appeal to the Council of the city for review of the decision of the Architectural Board. Ordinance 281 amends Ordinance 131 only with respect to the application initially being submitted to and considered by all members of the Architectural Board.

Relators claim that the above provisions of the ordinance amount to an unconstitutional delegation of power by the city to the Architectural Board. It is argued that the Board cannot be given the power to determine what is unsightly and grotesque and that the standards, "whether the proposed structure will conform to proper architectural standards in appearance and design, and will be in general conformity with the style and design of surrounding structures and conducive to the proper architectural development of the City . . ." and "the Board shall disapprove the application if it determines that the proposed structure will constitute an unsightly, grotesque or unsuitable structure in appearance, detrimental to the welfare of surrounding property or residents . . . ," are inadequate. . . . Ordinances 131 and 281 are sufficient in their general standards calling for a factual determination of the suitability of any proposed structure with reference to the character of the surrounding neighborhood and to the determination of any adverse effect on the general welfare and preservation of property values of the community. . . .

The judgment is reversed.

Notes

1. *Nuisance compared.* Courts, developing the law of nuisance, rarely declared an ugly site a nuisance. Obnoxious smells, deafening noises, yes, but unsightliness, no. There were no common standards to determine beauty; as the old saw puts it, beauty is in the eye of the beholder.

As we have seen, courts early viewed zoning under the police power as a form of nuisance control. Naturally, then, by an analogy to nuisance, they held that the police power can be exercised to further public health, safety, and general welfare, but not for purely aesthetic purposes. When billboards proliferated along highways in the first part of the twentieth century, and cities passed ordinances against them, courts first held these ordinances invalid, but, later, as public outrage against blaring billboards grew, courts held they could be regulated as menaces to public health and safety. After all, they might be blown down and fall on someone, they blocked sunlight and air, and the ground behind them might be used for dumping wastes (or doing other bad things). As the Missouri Supreme Court put it in the watershed case, "The sign boards . . . endanger the public health, promote immorality, constitute hiding places and retreats for criminals and all classes of miscreants." St. Louis Gunning Advertising Co. v. City of St. Louis, 137 S.W. 929, 942 (Mo. 1911), appeal dismissed, 231 U.S. 761 (1913). This disingenuous reasoning, of course, masked the real objection: billboards are ugly.

Not until the 1950s did courts begin to accept the legitimacy of zoning based exclusively on aesthetic considerations. In Berman v. Parker, 348 U.S. 26 (1954), an urban renewal case involving the use of the federal police power in the District of Columbia, the Supreme Court approved an expanded conception of the "public welfare." The values it represents, said the Court, "are spiritual as well as physical, aesthetic as well as monetary. It is within the power of the legislature to determine that the community should be beautiful as well as healthy, spacious as well as clean, well-balanced as well as carefully patrolled." Id. at 33. Perhaps a majority of jurisdictions today follow *Berman* and accept aesthetics as a legitimate police power goal in itself. But a good number still waffle on the issue, and a few are opposed to aesthetic regulation.

2. *The basis for the* Stoyanoff *holding.* Notice that the court in *Stoyanoff* did not rest its decision on the legitimacy of aesthetics as a zoning objective, relying instead largely on protection of property values. Professor Frank Michelman observes that this is "escapist reasoning that evades the real issues." Frank Michelman, Toward a Practical Standard for Aesthetic Regulation, 15 Prac. Law. 36 (1969). He explains:

> The effect on market value, after all, is derivative or symptomatic—not primary or of the essence. If the activities curbed by the regulation would otherwise make the surrounding property less valuable, it must be because those activities would radiate some kind of undesirable impact.
>
> If that impact is received and felt through visual sensibility, then the "economic" interest in question simply masks what has been referred to above as an "aesthetic" interest. In other words, without the aesthetic nuisance, there would be no market devaluation. [Id. at 36-37.]

3. *Sign codes.* The town of Gilbert, Arizona, enacted a sign code regulating the manner in which people may display outdoor signs. The code identified various categories of signs based on the type of information they conveyed, then subjected each category to different restrictions. One of the categories was "Temporary Directional Signs Relating to a Qualifying Event," defined as signs directing the public to a meeting of a nonprofit group. The code imposed more stringent restrictions on those signs than it did on signs conveying other messages, including "ideological signs" and "political signs." In Reed v. Town of Gilbert, 576 U.S. 155 (2015), the Supreme Court struck down Gilbert's sign code, deeming it to be a content-based restriction on freedom of speech that could be justified only by a compelling governmental interest. The town's asserted interests in public safety and aesthetic concerns, while legitimate, were not compelling, the Court concluded.

2. Controls on Household Composition

MOORE v. CITY OF EAST CLEVELAND

Supreme Court of the United States, 1977
431 U.S. 494

POWELL, J. East Cleveland's housing ordinance, like many throughout the country, limits occupancy of a dwelling unit to members of a single family. § 1351.02. But the ordinance contains an unusual and complicated definitional section that recognizes as a "family" only a few categories of related individuals, § 1341.08.[2] Because her family, living together in her home, fits none of those categories, appellant stands convicted of a criminal offense. The question in this case is whether the ordinance violates the Due Process Clause of the Fourteenth Amendment.

I.

Appellant, Mrs. Inez Moore, lives in her East Cleveland home together with her son, Dale Moore Sr., and her two grandsons, Dale, Jr., and John Moore, Jr. The two boys are first cousins rather than brothers; we are told that John came to live with his grandmother and with the elder and younger Dale Moores after his mother's death.

In early 1973, Mrs. Moore received a notice of violation from the city, stating that John was an "illegal occupant" and directing her to comply with the ordinance. When she failed to remove him from her home, the city filed a criminal charge. Mrs. Moore moved to dismiss, claiming that the ordinance was constitutionally invalid on its face. Her motion was overruled, and upon conviction she was sentenced to five days in jail and a $25 fine. The Ohio Court of Appeals affirmed after giving full consideration to her constitutional claims, and the Ohio Supreme Court denied review. . . .

II.

The city argues that our decision in Village of Belle Terre v. Boraas, 416 U.S. 1 (1974), requires us to sustain the ordinance attacked here. Belle Terre, like East Cleveland, imposed limits on the types of groups that could occupy a single dwelling unit. Applying the constitutional standard announced in this Court's leading land-use case, Euclid v. Ambler Realty Co., 272 U.S. 365 (1926), we sustained the Belle Terre ordinance on the ground that it bore a rational relationship to permissible state objectives.

But one overriding factor sets this case apart from Belle Terre. The ordinance there affected only unrelated individuals. It expressly allowed all who were related by "blood, adoption, or marriage" to live together, and in sustaining the ordinance we were careful to note that it promoted "family needs" and "family values." 416 U.S., at 9. East Cleveland, in contrast, has chosen to regulate the occupancy of its housing by slicing deeply into the family itself. This is no mere incidental result of the ordinance.

---

2. Section 1341.08 (1966) provides:

" 'Family' means a number of individuals related to the nominal head of the household or to the spouse of the nominal head of the household living as a single housekeeping unit in a single dwelling unit, but limited to the following:

"(a) Husband or wife of the nominal head of the household.

"(b) Unmarried children of the nominal head of the household or of the spouse of the nominal head of the household, provided, however, that such unmarried children have no children residing with them.

"(c) Father or mother of the nominal head of the household or of the spouse of the nominal head of the household.

"(d) Notwithstanding the provisions of subsection (b) hereof, a family may include not more than one dependent married or unmarried child of the nominal head of the household or of the spouse of the nominal head of the household and the spouse and dependent children of such dependent child. For the purpose of this subsection, a dependent person is one who has more than fifty percent of his total support furnished for him by the nominal head of the household and the spouse of the nominal head of the household.

"(e) A family may consist of one individual."

On its face it selects certain categories of relatives who may live together and declares that others may not. In particular, it makes a crime of a grandmother's choice to live with her grandson in circumstances like those presented here.

When a city undertakes such intrusive regulation of the family, neither *Belle Terre* nor *Euclid* governs; the usual judicial deference to the legislature is inappropriate. . . . [W]hen the government intrudes on choices concerning family living arrangements, this Court must examine carefully the importance of the governmental interests advanced and the extent to which they are served by the challenged regulation.

When thus examined, this ordinance cannot survive. The city seeks to justify it as a means of preventing overcrowding, minimizing traffic and parking congestion, and avoiding an undue financial burden on East Cleveland's school system. Although these are legitimate goals, the ordinance before us serves them marginally, at best. For example, the ordinance permits any family consisting only of husband, wife, and unmarried children to live together, even if the family contains a half dozen licensed drivers, each with his or her own car. At the same time it forbids an adult brother and sister to share a household, even if both faithfully use public transportation. The ordinance would permit a grandmother to live with a single dependent son and children, even if his school-age children number a dozen, yet it forces Mrs. Moore to find another dwelling for her grandson John, simply because of the presence of his uncle and cousin in the same household. We need not labor the point. Section 1341.08 has but a tenuous relation to alleviation of the conditions mentioned by the city.

III.

. . .

Our decisions establish that the Constitution protects the sanctity of the family precisely because the institution of the family is deeply rooted in this Nation's history and tradition. It is through the family that we inculcate and pass down many of our most cherished values, moral and cultural.

Ours is by no means a tradition limited to respect for the bonds uniting the members of the nuclear family. The tradition of uncles, aunts, cousins, and especially grandparents sharing a household along with parents and children has roots equally venerable and equally deserving of constitutional recognition. . . .

[T]he Constitution prevents East Cleveland from standardizing its children and its adults by forcing all to live in certain narrowly defined family patterns.

Reversed.

Notes and Question

1. *Belle* Terre. In Village of Belle Terre v. Boraas, 416 U.S. 1 (1974), the Supreme Court upheld a family zoning ordinance that apparently was aimed at preventing local college students from living together. It defined "family" as "[o]ne or more persons related by blood, adoption, or marriage" or up to two unrelated persons. Six unrelated college students challenged the regulation. Applying a rational basis test, the Court held that the regulation bore a reasonable relationship to legitimate state objectives of regulating noise, parking, and other density-related issues. The dissenting opinion argued that the strict scrutiny test should have been apply because the constitutional rights of association and privacy were involved.

The Court in *Moore* distinguished the instant case from *Belle Terre*. Was the Court's distinction persuasive?

2. *Family zoning in the state courts.* On issues of household composition, some state courts have taken a less deferential position than the Supreme Court did in *Belle Terre*. A notable example is McMinn v. Town of Oyster Bay, 488 N.E.2d 1240 (N.Y. 1985). The ordinance in *McMinn* restricted single-family housing to any number of people related by blood, adoption, or marriage, or two people not so related but over age 62. The court invalidated the ordinance on the basis of the due process provision in the New York state constitution. The objectives of the ordinance—controlling density, reducing traffic and noise—were legitimate, but the means were not. Occupancy restrictions based on biological or legal relationships, the court said, had no reasonable relationship to the city's objectives. But see City of Ladue v. Horn, 720 S.W.2d 745 (Mo. App. 1986) (upholding an ordinance, as applied to an unmarried couple with three children from prior marriages, defining "family" as two or more persons related by blood, adoption, or marriage).

CITY OF EDMONDS v. OXFORD HOUSE, INC.

Supreme Court of the United States, 1995
514 U.S. 725

GINSBURG, J. The Fair Housing Act (FHA or Act) prohibits discrimination in housing against, *inter alios*, persons with handicaps.[3] Section 3607(b)(1) of the Act entirely exempts from the FHA's compass "any reasonable local, State, or Federal restrictions regarding the maximum number of occupants permitted to occupy a dwelling." 42 U.S.C. § 3607(b)(1). This case presents the question whether a provision in petitioner City of Edmonds' zoning code qualifies for § 3607(b)(1)'s complete exemption from FHA scrutiny. The provision, governing areas zoned for single-family dwelling units, defines "family" as "persons [without regard to number] related by genetics, adoption, or marriage, or a group of five or fewer [unrelated] persons." Edmonds Community Development Code (ECDC) § 21.30.010 (1991).

The defining provision at issue describes who may compose a family unit; it does not prescribe "the maximum number of occupants" a dwelling unit may house. We hold that § 3607(b)(1) does not exempt prescriptions of the family-defining kind, i.e., provisions designed to foster the family character of a neighborhood. Instead, § 3607(b)(1)'s absolute exemption removes from the FHA's scope only total occupancy limits, i.e., numerical ceilings that serve to prevent overcrowding in living quarters.

I.

In the summer of 1990, respondent Oxford House opened a group home in the City of Edmonds, Washington for 10 to 12 adults recovering from alcoholism and drug addiction. The group home, called Oxford House-Edmonds, is located in a

---

3. The FHA, as originally enacted in 1968, prohibited discrimination based on race, color, religion, or national origin. See 82 Stat. 83. Proscription of discrimination based on sex was added in 1974. See Housing and Community Development Act of 1974, § 808(b), 88 Stat. 729. In 1988, Congress extended coverage to persons with handicaps and also prohibited "familial status" discrimination, i.e., discrimination against parents or other custodial persons domiciled with children under the age of 18. 42 U.S.C. § 3602(k).

neighborhood zoned for single-family residences. Upon learning that Oxford House had leased and was operating a home in Edmonds, the City issued criminal citations to the owner and a resident of the house. The citations charged violation of the zoning code rule that defines who may live in single-family dwelling units. The occupants of such units must compose a "family," and family, under the City's defining rule, "means an individual or two or more persons related by genetics, adoption, or marriage, or a group of five or fewer persons who are not related by genetics, adoption, or marriage." Edmonds Community Development Code (ECDC) § 21.30.010. Oxford House-Edmonds houses more than five unrelated persons, and therefore does not conform to the code.

Oxford House asserted reliance on the Fair Housing Act, 102 Stat. 1619, 42 U.S.C. § 3601 et seq., which declares it unlawful "to discriminate in the sale or rental, or to otherwise make unavailable or deny, a dwelling to any buyer or renter because of a handicap of . . . that buyer or renter." § 3604(f)(1)(A). The parties have stipulated, for purposes of this litigation, that the residents of Oxford House-Edmonds "are recovering alcoholics and drug addicts and are handicapped persons within the meaning" of the Act.

Discrimination covered by the FHA includes "a refusal to make reasonable accommodations in rules, policies, practices, or services, when such accommodations may be necessary to afford [handicapped] persons equal opportunity to use and enjoy a dwelling." § 3604(f)(3)(B). Oxford House asked Edmonds to make a "reasonable accommodation" by allowing it to remain in the single-family dwelling it had leased. Group homes for recovering substance abusers, Oxford urged, need 8 to 12 residents to be financially and therapeutically viable. Edmonds declined to permit Oxford House to stay in a single-family residential zone, but passed an ordinance listing group homes as permitted uses in multifamily and general commercial zones.

Edmonds sued Oxford House in the United States District Court for the Western District of Washington seeking a declaration that the FHA does not constrain the City's zoning code family definition rule. Oxford House counterclaimed under the FHA, charging the City with failure to make a "reasonable accommodation" permitting maintenance of the group home in a single-family zone. The United States filed a separate action on the same FHA-"reasonable accommodation" ground, and the two cases were consolidated. Edmonds suspended its criminal enforcement actions pending resolution of the federal litigation.

On cross-motions for summary judgment, the District Court held that ECDC § 21.30.010, defining "family," is exempt from the FHA under § 3607(b)(1) as a "reasonable . . . restrictio[n] regarding the maximum number of occupants permitted to occupy a dwelling." The United States Court of Appeals for the Ninth Circuit reversed; holding § 3607(b)(1)'s absolute exemption inapplicable, the Court of Appeals remanded the cases for further consideration of the claims asserted by Oxford House and the United States. Edmonds v. Washington State Building Code Council, 18 F.3d 802 (1994).

The Ninth Circuit's decision conflicts with an Eleventh Circuit decision declaring exempt under § 3607(b)(1) a family definition provision similar to the Edmonds prescription. See Elliott v. Athens, 960 F.2d 975 (1992). We granted certiorari to resolve the conflict, and we now affirm the Ninth Circuit's judgment.

II.

The sole question before the Court is whether Edmonds' family composition rule qualifies as a "restrictio[n] regarding the maximum number of occupants permitted to

Oxford House, Edmonds, Washington

occupy a dwelling" within the meaning of the FHA's absolute exemption. 42 U.S.C. § 3607(b)(1).[4] In answering this question, we are mindful of the Act's stated policy "to provide, within constitutional limitations, for fair housing throughout the United States." § 3601. We also note precedent recognizing the FHA's "broad and inclusive" compass, and therefore according a "generous construction" to the Act's complaint-filing provision. Trafficante v. Metropolitan Life Ins. Co., 409 U.S. 205, 209, 212 (1972). Accordingly, we regard this case as an instance in which an exception to "a general statement of policy" is sensibly read "narrowly in order to preserve the primary operation of the [policy]." Commissioner v. Clark, 489 U.S. 726, 739 (1989).

A

Congress enacted §3607(b)(1) against the backdrop of an evident distinction between municipal land use restrictions and maximum occupancy restrictions.

Land use restrictions designate "districts in which only compatible uses are allowed and incompatible uses are excluded." D. Mandelker, Land Use Law § 4.16, pp. 113-114 (3d ed. 1993) (hereinafter Mandelker). These restrictions typically categorize uses as single-family residential, multiple-family residential, commercial, or industrial. See, e.g., 1 E. Ziegler, Jr., Rathkopf's The Law of Zoning and Planning § 8.01, pp. 8-2 to 8-3 (4th ed. 1995); Mandelker § 1.03, p. 4; 1 E. Yokley, Zoning Law and Practice § 7-2, p. 252 (4th ed. 1978).

---

4. Like the District Court and the Ninth Circuit, we do not decide whether Edmonds' zoning code provision defining "family," as the City would apply it against Oxford House, violates the FHA's prohibitions against discrimination set out in 42 U.S.C. §§ 3604(f)(1)(A) and (f)(3)(B). [For these prohibitions, see pages 292-293, where § 3604 is set forth. — EDS.]

Land use restrictions aim to prevent problems caused by the "pig in the parlor instead of the barnyard." Village of Euclid v. Ambler Realty Co., 272 U.S. 365, 388 (1926). In particular, reserving land for single-family residences preserves the character of neighborhoods, securing "zones where family values, youth values, and the blessings of quiet seclusion and clean air make the area a sanctuary for people." Village of Belle Terre v. Boraas, 416 U.S. 1, 9 (1974); see also Moore v. City of East Cleveland, 431 U.S. 494 (1977). To limit land use to single-family residences, a municipality must define the term "family"; thus family composition rules are an essential component of single-family residential use restrictions.

Maximum occupancy restrictions, in contradistinction, cap the number of occupants per dwelling, typically in relation to available floor space or the number and type of rooms. See, e.g., Uniform Housing Code § 503(b) (1988); BOCA National Property Maintenance Code §§ PM-405.3, PM-405.5 (1993) (hereinafter BOCA Code); Standard Housing Code §§ 306.1, 306.2 (1991); APHA-CDC Recommended Minimum Housing Standards § 9.02, p. 37 (1986) (hereinafter APHA-CDC Standards). These restrictions ordinarily apply uniformly to all residents of all dwelling units. Their purpose is to protect health and safety by preventing dwelling overcrowding. See, e.g., BOCA Code §§ PM-101.3, PM-405.3, PM-405.5 and commentary; Abbott, Housing Policy, Housing Codes and Tenant Remedies, 56 B.U. L. Rev. 1, 41-45 (1976). . . .

Section 3607(b)(1)'s language—"restrictions regarding the maximum number of occupants permitted to occupy a dwelling"—surely encompasses maximum occupancy restrictions. But the formulation does not fit family composition rules typically tied to land use restrictions. In sum, rules that cap the total number of occupants in order to prevent overcrowding of a dwelling "plainly and unmistakably," see A.H. Phillips, Inc. v. Walling, 324 U.S. 490, 493 (1945), fall within § 3607(b)(1)'s absolute exemption from the FHA's governance; rules designed to preserve the family character of a neighborhood, fastening on the composition of households rather than on the total number of occupants living quarters can contain, do not.

B

Turning specifically to the City's Community Development Code, we note that the provisions Edmonds invoked against Oxford House, ECDC §§ 16.20.010 and 21.30.010, are classic examples of a use restriction and complementing family composition rule. These provisions do not cap the number of people who may live in a dwelling. In plain terms, they direct that dwellings be used only to house families. Captioned "USES," ECDC § 16.20.010 provides that the sole "Permitted Primary Use" in a single-family residential zone is "single-family dwelling units." Edmonds itself recognizes that this provision simply "defines those uses permitted in a single family residential zone."

A separate provision caps the number of occupants a dwelling may house, based on floor area:

> Floor Area. Every dwelling unit shall have at least one room which shall have not less than 120 square feet of floor area. Other habitable rooms, except kitchens, shall have an area of not less than 70 square feet. Where more than two persons occupy a room used for sleeping purposes, the required floor area shall be increased at the rate of 50 square feet for each occupant in excess of two. ECDC § 19.10.000 (adopting Uniform Housing Code § 503(b) (1988)).

This space and occupancy standard is a prototypical maximum occupancy restriction.

Edmonds nevertheless argues that its family composition rule, ECDC § 21.30.010, falls within § 3607(b)(1), the FHA exemption for maximum occupancy restrictions, because the rule caps at five the number of unrelated persons allowed to occupy a single-family dwelling. But Edmonds' family composition rule surely does not answer the question: "What is the maximum number of occupants permitted to occupy a house?" So long as they are related "by genetics, adoption, or marriage," any number of people can live in a house. Ten siblings, their parents and grandparents, for example, could dwell in a house in Edmonds' single-family residential zone without offending Edmonds' family composition rule.

Family living, not living space per occupant, is what ECDC § 21.30.010 describes. Defining family primarily by biological and legal relationships, the provision also accommodates another group association: five or fewer unrelated people are allowed to live together as though they were family. This accommodation is the peg on which Edmonds rests its plea for § 3607(b)(1) exemption. Had the City defined a family solely by biological and legal links, § 3607(b)(1) would not have been the ground on which Edmonds staked its case. It is curious reasoning indeed that converts a family values preserver into a maximum occupancy restriction once a town adds to a related persons prescription "and also two unrelated persons."

Edmonds additionally contends that subjecting single-family zoning to FHA scrutiny will "overturn Euclidian zoning" and "destroy the effectiveness and purpose of single-family zoning." This contention both ignores the limited scope of the issue before us and exaggerates the force of the FHA's antidiscrimination provisions. We address only whether Edmonds' family composition rule qualifies for § 3607(b)(1) exemption. Moreover, the FHA antidiscrimination provisions, when applicable, require only "reasonable" accommodations to afford persons with handicaps "equal opportunity to use and enjoy" housing. §§ 3604(f)(1)(A) and (f)(3)(B).

The parties have presented, and we have decided, only a threshold question: Edmonds' zoning code provision describing who may compose a "family" is not a maximum occupancy restriction exempt from the FHA under § 3607(b)(1). It remains for the lower courts to decide whether Edmonds' actions against Oxford House violate the FHA's prohibitions against discrimination set out in §§ 3604(f)(1)(A) and (f)(3)(B). For the reasons stated, the judgment of the United States Court of Appeals for the Ninth Circuit is

Affirmed.

THOMAS, SCALIA, and KENNEDY, JJ., dissent.

Note

What is a "group home"? "Group homes" is a generic term for any number of small, decentralized treatment facilities housing foster children, the mentally ill, the developmentally disabled, juvenile offenders, ex-drug addicts, alcoholics, and so on. Such people were once congregated in large public institutions, but group homes have become very common in recent years because they are less expensive than centralized facilities and are thought to provide more humane and effective treatment.

Not surprisingly, neighbors dislike group homes and commonly want them excluded from their neighborhood. A circular mailed out by a Michigan group listed some of the reasons neighbors give for not wanting a group home on their street. The reasons were portrayed like this:

> Our road is too wide / Our road is too narrow
> It's too dangerous in the country / It's too dangerous in the city
> The residents might hurt my kids / My kids might hurt the residents
> Our street ends in a cul-de-sac / Our street is a thru street

Other sorts of reasons were: we don't have sidewalks; there's water (someone else said quicksand) nearby; we let our dogs run free; the retarded stay up and scream all night; dust in our neighborhood would be a health hazard to the residents of the home. See Peter Margulies, Building Communities of Virtue: Political Theory, Land Use Policy, and the "Not in My Backyard" Syndrome, 43 Syracuse L. Rev. 945 (1992).

For a comprehensive analysis of the theories for determining fairness in siting "locally undesirable land uses" (LULUs), see Vicki Been, Locally Undesirable Land Uses in Minority Neighborhoods: Disproportionate Siting or Market Dynamics?, 103 Yale L.J. 1383 (1994); Vicki Been, What's Fairness Got to Do with It? Environmental Justice and the Siting of Locally Undesirable Land Uses, 78 Cornell L. Rev. 1001 (1993); Lynn E. Blais, Environmental Racism Reconsidered, 75 N.C. L. Rev. 75 (1996). LULUs have been disproportionately sited in neighborhoods populated by the poor and by people of color. These neighborhoods are now fighting back, using environmental protection and land use laws. For more on this, see Jon C. Dubin, From Junkyards to Gentrification: Explicating a Right to Protective Zoning in Low-Income Communities of Color, 77 Minn. L. Rev. 739 (1993).

> **Sidebar**
>
> Efforts of neighbors to keep group homes out of their neighborhoods are an example of the Not In My Back Yard (NIMBY) phenomenon. NIMBYism has a broad reach. Neighbors are reported to have objected to putting a dog run in a park, building a baseball field, building a middle school or a church or housing for the elderly or a planetarium or a nature trail, putting up a swing set in the yard, replacing wood window frames with aluminum ones, pruning a hedge (this dispute resulted in a double homicide), etc. See David M. Herszenhorn, Today, "Not in My Backyard" Can Cover Almost Anything, N.Y. Times, Apr. 16, 2000, at 29; Kathryn Shattuck, Beware the Cry of "Niyby": Not in *Your* Backyard!, N.Y. Times, May 11, 2000, at B1.

3. Exclusionary Zoning

All zoning is exclusionary by definition: Its central purpose is to minimize or eliminate unwanted effects—externalities—in a given district, whether the effects be caused by typical nuisances (*Euclid*'s pig in a parlor), by apartments or commercial uses in a high-class single family residential zone, or by group homes. Commonly, however, zoning measures like these aim not to ban uses (nuisances aside), but rather to relegate them to what the zoners regard as their proper place in the community. Contrast another kind of exclusionary zoning, the kind to which that phrase particularly refers today: measures whose purpose or effect is essentially to close an entire community to unwanted groups—typically people of low income who might put a heavy burden on the public fisc, yet at the same time contribute little to it, resulting in increased property taxes and reduced land values throughout the community. The attitude here is, "Let them go elsewhere, to some other city."

SOUTHERN BURLINGTON COUNTY NAACP v. TOWNSHIP OF MOUNT LAUREL

Supreme Court of New Jersey, 1975
336 A.2d 713, appeal dismissed and cert. denied,
423 U.S. 808 (1975)

HALL, J. This case attacks the system of land use regulation by defendant Township of Mount Laurel on the ground that low and moderate income families are thereby unlawfully excluded from the municipality. . . .

The implications of the issue presented are indeed broad and far-reaching, extending much beyond these particular plaintiffs and the boundaries of this particular municipality. . . .

Plaintiffs represent the minority group poor (black and Hispanic)[5] seeking such quarters. But they are not the only category of persons barred from so many municipalities by reason of restrictive land use regulations. We have reference to young and elderly couples, single persons and large, growing families not in the poverty class, but who still cannot afford the only kinds of housing realistically permitted in most places—relatively high-priced, single-family detached dwellings on sizeable lots and, in some municipalities, expensive apartments. We will, therefore, consider the case from the wider viewpoint that the effect of Mount Laurel's land use regulation has been to prevent various categories of persons from living in the township because of the limited extent of their income and resources. In this connection, we accept the presentation of the municipality's counsel at oral argument that the regulatory scheme was not adopted with any desire or intent to exclude prospective residents on the obviously illegal bases of race, origin or believed social incompatibility. . . .

I.

The Facts

Mount Laurel is a flat, sprawling township, 22 square miles, or about 14,000 acres, in area, on the west central edge of Burlington County. . . .

In 1950, the township had a population of 2,817, only about 600 more people than it had in 1940. It was then, as it had been for decades, primarily a rural agricultural area with no sizeable settlements or commercial or industrial enterprises. The populace

---

5. Plaintiffs fall into four categories: (1) present residents of the township residing in dilapidated or substandard housing; (2) former residents who were forced to move elsewhere because of the absence of suitable housing; (3) nonresidents living in central city substandard housing in the region who desire to secure decent housing and accompanying advantages within their means elsewhere; (4) three organizations representing the housing and other interests of racial minorities. The township originally challenged plaintiffs' standing to bring this action. The trial court properly held (119 N.J. Super. at 166, 290 A.2d 465) that the resident plaintiffs had adequate standing to ground the entire action and found it unnecessary to pass on that of the other plaintiffs. The issue has not been raised on appeal. . . .

generally lived in individual houses scattered along country roads. There were several pockets of poverty, with deteriorating or dilapidated housing (apparently 300 or so units of which remain today in equally poor condition). After 1950, as in so many other municipalities similarly situated, residential development and some commerce and industry began to come in. By 1960 the population had almost doubled to 5,249 and by 1970 had more than doubled again to 11,221. These new residents were, of course, "outsiders" from the nearby central cities and older suburbs or from more distant places drawn here by reason of employment in the region. The township is now definitely a part of the outer ring of the South Jersey metropolitan area, which area we define as those portions of Camden, Burlington and Gloucester Counties within a semicircle having a radius of 20 miles or so from the heart of Camden city. And 65% of the township is still vacant land or in agricultural use.

The growth of the township has been spurred by the construction or improvement of main highways through or near it. . . . This highway network gives the township a most strategic location from the standpoint of transport of goods and people by truck and private car. There is no other means of transportation.

The location and nature of development have been, as usual, controlled by the local zoning enactments. The general ordinance presently in force, which was declared invalid by the trial court, was adopted in 1964. We understand that earlier enactments provided, however, basically the same scheme but were less restrictive as to residential development. The growth pattern dictated by the ordinance is typical.

Under the present ordinance, 29.2% of all the land in the township, or 4,121 acres, is zoned for industry. This amounts to 2,800 more acres than were so zoned by the 1954 ordinance. . . .

Only industry meeting specified performance standards is permitted. The effect is to limit the use substantially to light manufacturing, research, distribution of goods, offices and the like. Some nonindustrial uses, such as agriculture, farm dwellings, motels, a harness racetrack, and certain retail sales and service establishments, are permitted in this zone. At the time of trial no more than 100 acres . . . were actually occupied by industrial uses. They had been constructed in recent years, mostly in several industrial parks, and involved tax ratables of about 16 million dollars. The rest of the land so zoned has remained undeveloped. If it were fully utilized, the testimony was that about 43,500 industrial jobs would be created, but it appeared clear that, as happens in the case of so many municipalities, much more land has been so zoned than the reasonable potential for industrial movement or expansion warrants. At the same time, however, the land cannot be used for residential development under the general ordinance.

The amount of land zoned for retail business use under the general ordinance is relatively small—169 acres, or 1.2% of the total. . . .

While the greater part of the land so zoned appears to be in use, there is no major shopping center or concentrated retail commercial area—"downtown"— in the township.

The balance of the land area, almost 10,000 acres, has been developed until recently in the conventional form of major subdivisions. The general ordinance provides for four residential zones, designated R-1, R-1D, R-2 and R-3. All permit only single-family, detached dwellings, one house per lot—the usual form of grid development. Attached townhouses, apartments (except on farms for agricultural workers) and mobile homes are not allowed anywhere in the township under the general ordinance. This dwelling development, resulting in the previously mentioned quadrupling of the population, has been largely confined to the R-1 and R-2 districts in two sections. . . . The result has been quite intensive development of these sections, but at a low density. The dwellings are substantial. . . . A variation from conventional development has recently occurred in some parts of Mount Laurel, as in a number of other similar municipalities, by use of the land use regulation device known as "planned unit development" (PUD). This scheme differs from the traditional in that the type, density and placement of land uses and buildings, instead of being detailed and confined to specified districts by local legislation in advance, is determined by contract, or "deal," as to each development between the developer and the municipal administrative authority, under broad guidelines laid down by state enabling legislation and an implementing local ordinance. The stress is on regulation of density and permitted mixture of uses within the same area, including various kinds of living accommodations with or without commercial and industrial enterprises. The idea may be basically thought of as the creation of "new towns" in virgin territory, full-blown or in miniature, although most frequently the concept has been limited in practice, as in Mount Laurel, to residential developments of various sizes having some variety of housing and perhaps some retail establishments to serve the inhabitants. . . .

These projects, three in the southwesterly sector and one in the northeasterly sector, are very substantial and involve at least 10,000 sale and rental housing units of various types to be erected over a period of years. Their bounds were created by agreement rather than legislative specification on the zoning map, invading industrial, R-1, R-1D, R-3 and even flood plain zones. If completed as planned, they will in themselves ultimately quadruple the 1970 township population, but still leave a good part of the township undeveloped. (The record does not indicate how far development in each of the projects has progressed.) While multi-family housing in the form of rental garden, medium rise and high rise apartments and attached townhouses is for the first time provided for, as well as single-family detached dwellings for sale, it is not designed to accommodate and is beyond the financial reach of low and moderate income families, especially those with young children. The aim is quite the contrary; as with the single-family homes in the older conventional subdivisions, only persons of medium and upper income are sought as residents.

A few details will furnish sufficient documentation. Each of the resolutions of tentative approval of the projects contains a similar fact finding to the effect that the development will attract a highly educated and trained population base to support the nearby industrial parks in the township as well as the business and commercial facilities. The approvals also sharply limit the number of apartments having more than one bedroom. Further, they require that the developer must provide in its leases that no school-age children shall be permitted to occupy any one-bedroom apartment and that no more than two such children shall reside in any two-bedroom unit. The developer is also required, prior to the issuance of the first building permit, to record a covenant, running with all land on which multi-family housing is to be constructed, providing that in the event more than .3 school children per multi-family unit shall attend the township school system in any one year, the developer will pay the cost of tuition and other school expenses of all such excess numbers of children. In addition, low density, required amenities, such as central air conditioning, and specified developer contributions help to push rents and sales prices to high levels. These contributions include fire apparatus, ambulances, fire houses, and very large sums of money for educational facilities, a cultural center and the township library.

Still another restrictive land use regulation was adopted by the township through a supplement to the general zoning ordinance enacted in September 1972 creating a new zone, R-4, Planned Adult Retirement Community (PARC). . . . The extensive development requirements detailed in the ordinance make it apparent that the scheme was not designed for, and would be beyond the means of, low and moderate income retirees. . . .

All this affirmative action for the benefit of certain segments of the population is in sharp contrast to the lack of action, and indeed hostility, with respect to affording any opportunity for decent housing for the township's own poor living in substandard accommodations, found largely in the section known as Springville (R-3 zone). . . . In 1968 a private non-profit association sought to build subsidized, multi-family housing in the Springville section with funds to be granted by a higher level governmental agency. Advance municipal approval of the project was required. The Township Committee responded with a purportedly approving resolution, which found a need for "moderate" income housing in the area, but went on to specify that such housing must be constructed subject to all zoning, planning, building and other applicable ordinances and codes. This meant single-family detached dwellings on 20,000 square foot lots. (Fear was also expressed that such housing would attract low income families from outside the township.) Needless to say, such requirements killed realistic housing for this group of low and moderate income families.

The record thoroughly substantiates the findings of the trial court that over the years Mount Laurel "has acted affirmatively to control development and to attract a selective type of growth" and that "through its zoning ordinances has exhibited economic discrimination in that the poor have been deprived of adequate housing and the opportunity to secure the construction of subsidized housing, and has used federal, state, county and local finances and resources solely for the betterment of middle and upper-income persons."

There cannot be the slightest doubt that the reason for this course of conduct has been to keep down local taxes on *property* (Mount Laurel is not a high tax municipality) and that the policy was carried out without regard for non-fiscal considerations with respect to *people*, either within or without its boundaries. This conclusion is demonstrated not only by what was done and what happened, as we have related, but also by innumerable direct statements of municipal officials at public meetings over the years which are found in the exhibits. . . .

This policy of land use regulation for a fiscal end derives from New Jersey's tax structure, which has imposed on local real estate most of the cost of municipal and county government and of the primary and secondary education of the municipality's children. The latter expense is much the largest, so, basically, the fewer the school children, the lower the tax rate. Sizeable industrial and commercial ratables are eagerly sought and homes and the lots on which they are situate are required to be large enough, through minimum lot sizes and minimum floor areas, to have substantial value in order to produce greater tax revenues to meet school costs. Large families who cannot afford to buy large houses and must live in cheaper rental accommodations are definitely not wanted, so we find drastic bedroom restrictions for, or complete prohibition of, multi-family or other feasible housing for those of lesser income.

This pattern of land use regulation has been adopted for the same purpose in developing municipality after developing municipality. Almost every one acts solely in its own selfish and parochial interest and in effect builds a wall around itself to keep out those people or entities not adding favorably to the tax base, despite the location of the municipality or the demand for varied kinds of housing. There has been no effective intermunicipal or area planning or land use regulation. All of this is amply demonstrated by the evidence in this case as to Camden, Burlington and Gloucester counties. . . .

One incongruous result is the picture of developing municipalities rendering it impossible for lower paid employees of industries they have eagerly sought and welcomed with open arms (and, in Mount Laurel's case, even some of its own lower paid municipal employees) to live in the community where they work. . . .

II.

The Legal Issue

The legal question before us, as earlier indicated, is whether a developing municipality like Mount Laurel may validly, by a system of land use regulation, make it physically and economically impossible to provide low and moderate income housing in the municipality for the various categories of persons who need and want it and thereby, as Mount Laurel has, exclude such people from living within its confines because of the limited extent of their income and resources. Necessarily implicated are the broader questions of the right of such municipalities to limit the kinds of available housing and of any obligation to make possible a variety and choice of types of living accommodations.

We conclude that every such municipality must, by its land use regulations, presumptively make realistically possible an appropriate variety and choice of housing. More specifically, presumptively it cannot foreclose the opportunity of the classes of people mentioned for low and moderate income housing and in its regulations must affirmatively afford that opportunity, at least to the extent of the municipality's fair share of the present and prospective regional need therefor. These obligations must be met unless the particular municipality can sustain the heavy burden of demonstrating peculiar circumstances which dictate that it should not be required so to do.[6]

We reach this conclusion under state law and so do not find it necessary to consider federal constitutional grounds urged by plaintiffs. We begin with some fundamental principles as applied to the scene before us.

Land use regulation is encompassed within the state's police power. . . .

It is elementary theory that all police power enactments, no matter at what level of government, must conform to the basic state constitutional requirements of substantive due process and equal protection of the laws. . . .

It is required that, affirmatively, a zoning regulation, like any police power enactment, must promote public health, safety, morals or the general welfare. (The last term seems broad enough to encompass the others.) Conversely, a zoning enactment which is contrary to the general welfare is invalid. . . .

. . . Frequently the decisions in this state . . . have spoken only in terms of the interest of the enacting municipality, so that it has been thought, at least in some quarters, that such was the only welfare requiring consideration. It is, of course, true that many cases have dealt only with regulations having little, if any, outside impact where the

---

6. While, as the trial court found, Mount Laurel's actions were deliberate, we are of the view that the identical conclusion follows even when municipal conduct is not shown to be intentional, but the effect is substantially the same as if it were.

local decision is ordinarily entitled to prevail. However, it is fundamental and not to be forgotten that the zoning power is a police power of the state and the local authority is acting only as a delegate of that power and is restricted in the same manner as is the state. So, when regulation does have a substantial external impact, the welfare of the state's citizens beyond the borders of the particular municipality cannot be disregarded and must be recognized and served. . . .

This brings us to the relation of housing to the concept of general welfare just discussed and the result in terms of land use regulation which that relationship mandates. There cannot be the slightest doubt that shelter, along with food, are the most basic human needs. . . .

It is plain beyond dispute that proper provision for adequate housing of all categories of people is certainly an absolute essential in promotion of the general welfare required in all local land use regulation. Further the universal and constant need for such housing is so important and of such broad public interest that the general welfare which developing municipalities like Mount Laurel must consider extends beyond their boundaries and cannot be parochially confined to the claimed good of the particular municipality. It has to follow that, broadly speaking, the presumptive obligation arises for each such municipality affirmatively to plan and provide, by its land use regulations, the reasonable opportunity for an appropriate variety and choice of housing, including, of course, low and moderate cost housing, to meet the needs, desires and resources of all categories of people who may desire to live within its boundaries. Negatively, it may not adopt regulations or policies which thwart or preclude that opportunity.

It is also entirely clear, as we pointed out earlier, that most developing municipalities, including Mount Laurel, have not met their affirmative or negative obligations, primarily for local fiscal reasons. . . .

In sum, we are satisfied beyond any doubt that, by reason of the basic importance of appropriate housing and the long-standing pressing need for it, especially in the low and moderate cost category, and of the exclusionary zoning practices of so many municipalities, conditions have changed, and . . . judicial attitudes must be altered . . . to require, as we have just said, a broader view of the general welfare and the presumptive obligation on the part of developing municipalities at least to afford the opportunity by land use regulations for appropriate housing for all.

We have spoken of this obligation of such municipalities as "presumptive." The term has two aspects, procedural and substantive. Procedurally, we think the basic importance of appropriate housing for all dictates that, when it is shown that a developing municipality in its land use regulations has not made realistically possible a variety and choice of housing, including adequate provision to afford the opportunity for low and moderate income housing or has expressly prescribed requirements or restrictions which preclude or substantially hinder it, a facial showing of violation of substantive due process or equal protection under the state constitution has been made out and the burden, and it is a heavy one, shifts to the municipality to establish a valid basis for its action or non-action. . . .

The substantive aspect of "presumptive" relates to the specifics, on the one hand, of what municipal land use regulation provisions, or the absence thereof, will evidence invalidity and shift the burden of proof and, on the other hand, of what bases and considerations will carry the municipality's burden and sustain what it has done or failed to do. Both kinds of specifics may well vary between municipalities according to peculiar circumstances.

We turn to application of these principles in appraisal of Mount Laurel's zoning ordinance, useful as well, we think, as guidelines for future application in other municipalities.

The township's general zoning ordinance . . . permits, as we have said, only one type of housing—single-family detached dwellings. This means that all other types—multi-family including garden apartments and other kinds housing more than one family, town (row) houses, mobile home parks—are prohibited. Concededly, low and moderate income housing has been intentionally excluded. . . .

Mount Laurel's zoning ordinance is also so restrictive in its minimum lot area, lot frontage and building size requirements, earlier detailed, as to preclude single-family housing for even moderate income families. . . . Again it is evident these requirements increase the size and so the cost of housing. The conclusion is irresistible that Mount Laurel permits only such middle and upper income housing as it believes will have sufficient taxable value to come close to paying its own governmental way. . . .

Without further elaboration at this point, our opinion is that Mount Laurel's zoning ordinance is presumptively contrary to the general welfare and outside the intended scope of the zoning power in the particulars mentioned. A facial showing of invalidity is thus established, shifting to the municipality the burden of establishing valid superseding reasons for its action and non-action. We now examine the reasons it advances.

The township's principal reason in support of its zoning plan and ordinance housing provisions, advanced especially strongly at oral argument, is the fiscal one previously adverted to, i.e., that by reason of New Jersey's tax structure which substantially finances municipal governmental and educational costs from taxes on local real property, every municipality may, by the exercise of the zoning power, allow only such uses and to such extent as will be beneficial to the local tax rate.

We have previously held that a developing municipality may properly zone for and seek industrial ratables to create a better economic balance for the community vis-à-vis educational and governmental costs engendered by residential development, provided that such was ". . . done reasonably as part of and in furtherance of a legitimate comprehensive plan for the zoning of the entire municipality." Gruber v. Mayor and Township Committee of Raritan Township, 39 N.J. 1, 9-11, 186 A.2d 489, 493 (1962). We adhere to that view today. But we were not there concerned with, and did not pass upon, the validity of municipal exclusion by zoning of types of housing and kinds of people for the same local financial end. We have no hesitancy in now saying, and do so emphatically, that, considering the basic importance of the opportunity for appropriate housing for all classes of our citizenry, no municipality may exclude or limit categories of housing for that reason or purpose. While we fully recognize the increasingly heavy burden of local taxes for municipal governmental and school costs on homeowners, relief from the consequences of this tax system will have to be furnished by other branches of government. It cannot legitimately be accomplished by restricting types of housing through the zoning process in developing municipalities. . . .

By way of summary, what we have said comes down to this. As a developing municipality, Mount Laurel must, by its land use regulations, make realistically possible the opportunity for an appropriate variety and choice of housing for all categories of people who may desire to live there, of course including those of low and moderate income. It must permit multi-family housing, without bedroom or similar restrictions, as well as small dwellings on very small lots, low cost housing of other types and, in general, high density zoning, without artificial and unjustifiable minimum requirements as to lot size, building size and the like, to meet the full panoply of these needs. Certainly when a municipality zones for industry and commerce for local tax benefit purposes, it without question must zone to permit adequate housing within the means of the employees involved in such uses. (If planned unit developments are authorized, one would assume that each must include a reasonable amount of low and moderate income housing in its residential "mix," unless opportunity for such housing has already been realistically provided for elsewhere in the municipality.) The amount of land removed from residential use by allocation to industrial and commercial purposes must be reasonably related to the present and future potential for such purposes. In other words, such municipalities must zone primarily for the living welfare of people and not for the benefit of the local tax rate.

. . . Frequently it might be sounder to have more of such housing, like some specialized land uses, in one municipality in a region than in another, because of greater availability of suitable land, location of employment, accessibility of public transportation or some other significant reason. But, under present New Jersey legislation, zoning must be on an individual municipal basis, rather than regionally. So long as that situation persists under the present tax structure, or in the absence of some kind of binding agreement among all the municipalities of a region, we feel that every municipality therein must bear its fair share of the regional burden. (In this respect our holding is broader than that of the trial court, which was limited to Mount Laurel-related low and moderate income housing needs.)

The composition of the applicable "region" will necessarily vary from situation to situation and probably no hard and fast rule will serve to furnish the answer in every case. Confinement to or within a certain county appears not to be realistic, but restriction within the boundaries of the state seems practical and advisable. (This is not to say that a developing municipality can ignore a demand for housing within its boundaries on the part of people who commute to work in another state.) Here we have already defined the region at present as "those portions of Camden, Burlington and Gloucester Counties within a semicircle having a radius of 20 miles or so from the heart of Camden City." The concept of "fair share" is coming into more general use and, through the expertise of the municipal planning adviser, the county planning boards and the state planning agency, a reasonable figure for Mount Laurel can be determined, which can then be translated to the allocation of sufficient land therefor on the zoning map. . . .

There is no reason why developing municipalities like Mount Laurel, required by this opinion to afford the opportunity for all types of housing to meet the needs of various categories of people, may not become and remain attractive, viable communities providing good living and adequate services for all their residents in the kind of atmosphere which a democracy and free institutions demand. They can have industrial sections, commercial sections and sections for every kind of housing from low cost and multi-family to lots of more than an acre with very expensive homes. Proper planning and governmental cooperation can prevent over-intensive and too sudden development, insure against future suburban sprawl and slums and assure the preservation of open space and local beauty. We do not intend that developing municipalities shall be overwhelmed by voracious land speculators and developers if they use the powers which they have intelligently and in the broad public interest. Under our holdings today, they can be better communities for all than they previously have been.

III.

The Remedy

. . . We are of the view that the trial court's judgment should be modified in certain respects. We see no reason why the entire zoning ordinance should be nullified. Therefore we declare it to be invalid only to the extent and in the particulars set forth in this opinion. The township is granted 90 days from the date hereof, or such additional time as the trial court may find it reasonable and necessary to allow, to adopt amendments to correct the deficiencies herein specified. It is the local function and responsibility, in the first instance at least, rather than the court's, to decide on the details of the same within the guidelines we have laid down. If plaintiffs desire to attack such amendments, they may do so by supplemental complaint filed in this cause within 30 days of the final adoption of the amendments.

We are not at all sure what the trial judge had in mind as ultimate action with reference to the approval of a plan for affirmative public action concerning the satisfaction of indicated housing needs and the entry of a final order requiring implementation thereof. Courts do not build housing nor do municipalities. That function is performed by private builders, various kinds of associations, or, for public housing, by special agencies created for that purpose at various levels of government. The municipal function is initially to provide the opportunity through appropriate land use regulations and we have spelled out what Mount Laurel must do in that regard. It is not appropriate at this time, particularly in view of the advanced view of zoning law as applied to housing laid down by this opinion, to deal with the matter of the further extent of judicial power in the field or to exercise any such power. . . . The municipality should first have full opportunity to itself act without judicial supervision. We trust it will do so in the spirit we have suggested, both by appropriate zoning ordinance amendments and whatever additional action encouraging the fulfillment of its fair share of the regional need for low and moderate income housing may be indicated as necessary and advisable. (We have in mind that there is at least a moral obligation in a municipality to establish a local housing agency pursuant to state law to provide housing for its resident poor now living in dilapidated, unhealthy quarters.) The portion of the trial court's judgment ordering the preparation and submission of the aforesaid study, report and plan to it for further action is therefore vacated as at least premature. Should Mount Laurel not perform as we expect, further judicial action may be sought by supplemental pleading in this cause.

The judgment of the Law Division is modified as set forth herein.

Notes and Questions

1. *Exclusionary zoning in general.* Exclusionary zoning is not just a thing of the past. For the last 50 years at least, suburban communities have resorted to various measures in an effort to restrict or bar particular uses—such as apartments, small houses on small lots, mobile homes—and to limit or foreclose entry by particular people, especially the poor and racial minorities.

Simple prejudice has much to do with exclusionary efforts, but—as the court in *Mount Laurel* indicates—fiscal concerns are also a powerful motivation. Ideally, *all* communities want low property taxes. Citizens obviously would rather spend their money in other ways, and they like the fact that low property taxes buoy up property values. Public officials want contented citizens who will keep them in office.

The straightforward way to achieve relatively low taxes is to have a handsome tax base (valuable property, especially nonresidential property), well-to-do residents, and low demand for such public services as water and sewer, schools, police and fire departments, public assistance programs, and so on. Translated into policy, this means measures to ensure a community of substantial and desirable industrial uses and expensive homes located in a low density manner (say on large lots). With such a policy in place, residents will necessarily tend to have high incomes; the typical family will have few children. Most of the workers in the local industries will be unable to live in the community or in other suburbs nearby (the other suburbs will be using exclusionary measures to pursue their own fiscal aims). They will reside in the central city.

2. *Exclusionary zoning techniques.* Putting aside blatant efforts to exclude racial minorities and the poor, and focusing on residential uses, there are a number of techniques a community might use to exclude people whose characteristics (low income, high service demand) would interfere with the ideal fiscal picture controls on minimum housing cost, minimum housing size, and minimum lot size. Related techniques include prohibitions on mobile homes and on multifamily housing.

3. *The basis of the* Mount Laurel *decision.* Notice that *Mount Laurel* is based on state, not federal, constitutional law. Justice Hall was aware that several decisions of the U.S. Supreme Court made federal constitutional law an uneasy basis for exclusionary zoning claims.

4. *The Fair Housing Act.* As City of Edmonds v. Oxford House on pages 590-594 should suggest, racially discriminatory exclusionary zoning practices violate the federal Fair Housing Act. On the Fair Housing Act generally, see pages 291-293. As we saw there, under the FHA, housing discrimination can be proven by "disparate impact." The first federal court decision to adopt that approach was in United States v. City of Black Jack, Missouri, 508 F.2d 1179 (8th Cir. 1974). In that case, an interfaith religious organization began planning Park View Heights to create alternative housing opportunities for persons of low and moderate income living in the inner-city areas of the city of St. Louis. It settled on an unincorporated part of St. Louis County, in what became Black Jack, Missouri. Within a few short weeks, area residents incorporated the area that included the site of the proposed Park View Heights project. The Black Jack City Council enacted an exclusionary zoning ordinance, with the result that the racial composition of Black Jack was virtually all white, in strong contrast with the racial composition of other parts of the St. Louis area. The Eighth Circuit held that the exclusionary zoning ordinance violated the FHA. The court stated that the challengers of the ordinance need to "prove no more than that the conduct of the defendant actually or predictably results in racial discrimination; in other words, that it has a discriminatory effect." Id. at 1184.

5. *After* Mount Laurel. It appears that the idea behind *Mount Laurel* was essentially one of deregulation: remove obstacles that local governments had put in the way of less costly housing and let the market respond. Newly constructed housing, even of modest residences, might be beyond the reach of low income

people, but the increased supply would let used housing trickle down to them at affordable prices.

Things did not work out quite that way. Communities read the *Mount Laurel* opinion closely. They saw, for example, that it applied only to "developing" communities. A number of communities claimed that they were not "developing." Others pleaded that their local ecology was too sensitive to fall fully under *Mount Laurel*'s dictates. Still others fudged, changing their ordinances in such a way as to create the appearance, but not the reality, of compliance. And a host of questions developed about how a "fair share" within a "region" was to be determined.

The township of Mount Laurel itself was grudging — indeed, less than honest — in complying with the court's mandate. It rezoned for low-cost housing three small, widely scattered areas (less than .25 percent of its land) suffering from high noise levels and proximity to industrial uses. This new ordinance was struck down as a complete failure to meet the township's constitutional obligations in Southern Burlington County NAACP v. Township of Mount Laurel, 456 A.2d 390 (N.J. 1983) — popularly known as *Mount Laurel II.*

Mount Laurel II gave the court a chance to address some of the issues left open in *Mount Laurel I.* In the eight years between the cases, the court had learned, it said, that without a strong judicial hand there would not be more housing but only paper, process, and litigation. It also learned, or so it seems, that its original idea of deregulation and an unconstrained market was wrong; rather the need was for measures that *required* the production of low and moderate income housing. So *Mount Laurel II* held, among other rulings, as follows:

Essentially, *every* municipality — not just developing ones — must provide a realistic opportunity for decent housing for its poor, except where (as in many urban areas) the poor represent a disproportionately large percentage of the population as compared to the rest of the region. Good-faith attempts on the part of municipalities would be insufficient; each community must provide its fair share, expressed in terms of number of units needed immediately and in the future. It would not be enough for municipalities to remove barriers to low cost construction; they were to undertake affirmative measures and to assist developers in obtaining state and federal aid. Affirmative measures might include inclusionary zoning devices — such as altering density limits in exchange for a developer's commitment to construct certain amounts of low and moderate income housing. Zones for mobile homes were to be created if necessary to meet the fair-share obligation. All future *Mount Laurel* litigation would be assigned to a group of three judges, appointed by the chief justice, a measure intended in part to ease the difficulties of calculating fair shares. Finally, the opinion confirmed a "builder's remedy" under which the trial court could allow a developer to go forth with a low income project even though the municipality had not granted a permit if the court found that the municipality had not fulfilled its *Mount Laurel* obligations.

"It is difficult to convey adequately the intensity of the public reaction to the *Mount Laurel* process since 1983," Professor John Payne reported. Where *Mount Laurel I* could be ignored because it was ineffective, *Mount Laurel II* worked, and it stirred up a fire storm. John M. Payne, Rethinking Fair Share: The Judicial Enforcement of Affordable Housing Policies, 16 Real Est. L.J. 20, 22 (1987). Governor Thomas Kean attacked *Mount Laurel II* as an undesirable intrusion on the home rule principle. Two years later, the New Jersey legislature, responding to the ongoing problem of exclusionary zoning and the controversy provoked by the builder's remedy, enacted a Fair Housing Act. N.J. Stat. Ann. §§ 52:27D-301 to 329 (2001). The statute put a moratorium on the builder's remedy. It also established an administrative agency, the Council on Affordable Housing (COAH), to determine fair-share obligations for each municipality subject to a *Mount Laurel* obligation. Municipalities that filed satisfactory plans to meet their obligations would receive a "substantive certification" from COAH, protecting them from builder's remedies for a period of 10 years. Uncertified municipalities were subject to suit under *Mount Laurel II*. COAH certification decisions could be appealed, but courts were to treat them with deference. New Jersey's Fair Housing Act was upheld by the New Jersey Supreme Court in Hills Dev. Co. v. Bernards Township, 510 A.2d 621 (N.J. 1986) (known as *Mount Laurel III*).

A particularly interesting feature of the Fair Housing Act provided for regional contribution agreements whereby any suburb might, with Council approval, compensate cities for agreeing to absorb up to half of the suburb's fair-share obligation. The legislation itself states that the purpose of the transfer option is to make use of the existing housing stock; suburban contributions would make it possible to rehabilitate substandard housing, presumably in the central cities. Regional contribution agreements proved to be quite popular—over 10,000 units were built or renovated after 1986. See State of New Jersey, Department of Community Affairs, COAH: Reports and Quick Facts (2009). In 2008, the New Jersey Legislature amended the Fair Housing Act to eliminate the regional contribution option.

What are the arguments—pro and con—for regional contribution agreements? See Editorial: RCAs, RIP, 193 N.J. L.J. 814 (2008); Charles M. Haar, Suburbs Under Siege: Race, Space, and Audacious Judges 113-116 (1996); Michael H. Schill, Deconcentrating the Inner City Poor, 67 Chi.-Kent L. Rev. 795 (1991).

Since the New Jersey Supreme Court dipped its toe (plunged into the deep end?) into exclusionary zoning, over 36,000 units of housing have been built or renovated pursuant to the *Mount Laurel* doctrine. See COAH: Reports and Quick Facts, supra. Some have argued that while the quantity of units built or rehabilitated is small compared to overall need (which is in the 600,000 to 700,000 range through 2014), "[s]omething is surely better than nothing." See John M. Payne, The Paradox of Progress: Three Decades of the Mount Laurel Doctrine, 5 J. of Planning Hist. 126, 134 (2006). Empirical studies of who is living in Mount Laurel housing suggest that they are not necessarily the people anticipated by Justice Hall in *Mount Laurel I*. See Naomi Bailin Wish & Stephen Eisdorfer, The Impact of Mount Laurel Initiatives: An Analysis of the Characteristics of Applicants and Occupants, 27 Seton Hall L. Rev. 1268 (1997).

6. *Inclusionary zoning.* Rather than trying to eliminate exclusionary zoning—which has proven to be difficult to accomplish—many communities are now embracing a different tactic: inclusionary zoning. The term includes a variety of devices. Some states and communities have adopted density bonuses, which permit developers to build at higher levels of density than the zoning code otherwise permits if they include a statutorily prescribed percentage of affordable housing in their projects. See Cal. Govt. Code § 65915 (West 2020); San Francisco Planning Code § 315.1 (2018). Other local communities use tax incentives to induce developers to build affordable housing.

CHAPTER 12

Eminent Domain and the Problem of Implicit Takings

"[N]or shall private property be taken for public use, without just compensation."

—U.S. Const., amend V.

The clause of the Fifth Amendment quoted above, known as the Takings Clause, concerns the ability of the government, federal, state, and local, to compel transfer of title to property via the exercise of the government's power of eminent domain. The Takings Clause applies to the federal government directly and applies to the states through the Due Process Clause of the Fourteenth Amendment. That the government has the power of eminent domain is, as we shall see, a point long beyond dispute. The language of the Takings Clause imposes constraints, however: the condemnation, as the action is called, must be "for public use" and with "just compensation."

This language limits not only the government's right literally to take property through the power of eminent domain, but its freedom to regulate property as well. In regulating through zoning or other means, the government might at times be said to have expropriated what it claimed only to control; so too in carrying out the myriad other activities that attend the modern state. Some of the most intractable issues in the jurisprudence of property concern the matter of just when—under what circumstances—such governmental activities should be regarded as takings.

A. THE POWER OF EMINENT DOMAIN: SOURCES AND RATIONALES

BACKGROUND, BRIEFLY

Source of and rationales for the eminent domain power. The origins of eminent domain can be traced back to ancient Rome. See Susan Reynolds, Before Eminent Domain 15-16 (2010). English sovereigns enjoyed similar powers. By the time of the American Revolution, the power of the British government to take private property for public uses was well established.

While never required to do so, the British Parliament has commonly paid compensation in the course of appropriating land for public purposes.

Early American practice regarding eminent domain was heavily influenced by the precedent of English experience. The power of government to take private property was recognized, though compensation was hardly universal in colonial times. Gradually, however, statutes came to provide for compensation, and constitutional provisions began to appear in the late 1700s.

Various rationales for the taking power have been offered over the years. Early civil law scholars argued that sovereign states had original and absolute ownership of property; individual possession derived from grants from the state and was held subject to an implied reservation that the state might resume its ownership. Another rationale, offered especially by natural law theorists, that eminent domain is an inherent attribute of sovereignty, necessary to the very existence of government. Each of these notions has been reflected to some degree in American law, the last being the most common rationale today.

A functional justification for the eminent domain power focuses on economic considerations. Specifically, as Judge Richard Posner points out, it functions as "an antimonopoly device." See Richard A. Posner, Economic Analysis of Law 56 (9th ed. 2014). When governments build large projects such as railroads, pipelines, airports, and the like, they face a strategic problem that, arguably, private developers typically do not. They must acquire very large parcels of land by assembling together smaller parcels from individual landowners. Usually, the location is site-specific—there is no other location that is suitable for the project (usually private developers have alternatives). Each owner of the individual parcels that the government must acquire has a monopoly on that parcel. The government, in turn, is in a monopoly position on the price to be paid to each landowner, creating a classic bilateral monopoly. The result in such situations commonly is a holdout, as one party or both engages in strategic behavior and bargaining goes on endlessly. But the government needs the land for a public use. Eminent domain is the power of the government to force a sale, so that the land can be put to a more valuable use.

B. PUBLIC USE (AND A NOTE ON JUST COMPENSATION)

The Fifth Amendment's mention of "public use" is read to mean that property may be taken *only* for such uses; the government may not condemn for "private" purposes, however willing it might be to pay compensation for the forced transfer. Quite obviously, then, the reach of the eminent domain power hinges directly on the breadth or narrowness of meaning attached to the term "public use."

KELO v. CITY OF NEW LONDON
Supreme Court of the United States, 2005
545 U.S. 469

STEVENS, J. In 2000, the city of New London approved a development plan that, in the words of the Supreme Court of Connecticut, was "projected to create in excess of 1,000 jobs, to increase tax and other revenues, and to revitalize an economically distressed city, including its downtown and waterfront areas." In assembling the land needed for this project, the city's development agent has purchased property from willing sellers and proposes to use the power of eminent domain to acquire the remainder of the property from unwilling owners in exchange for just compensation. The question presented is whether the city's proposed disposition of this property qualifies as a "public use" within the meaning of the Takings Clause of the Fifth Amendment to the Constitution.

I.

The city of New London (hereinafter City) sits at the junction of the Thames River and the Long Island Sound in southeastern Connecticut. Decades of economic decline led a state agency in 1990 to designate the City a "distressed municipality." In 1996, the Federal Government closed the Naval Undersea Warfare Center, which had been located in the Fort Trumbull area of the City and had employed over 1,500 people. In 1998, the City's unemployment rate was nearly double that of the State, and its population of just under 24,000 residents was at its lowest since 1920.

These conditions prompted state and local officials to target New London, and particularly its Fort Trumbull area, for economic revitalization. To this end, respondent New London Development Corporation (NLDC), a private nonprofit entity established some years earlier to assist the City in planning economic development, was reactivated. In January 1998, the State authorized a $5.35 million bond issue to support the NLDC's planning activities and a $10 million bond issue toward the creation of a Fort Trumbull State Park. In February, the pharmaceutical company Pfizer Inc. announced that it would build a $300 million research facility on a site immediately adjacent to Fort Trumbull; local planners hoped that Pfizer would draw new business to the area, thereby serving as a catalyst to the area's rejuvenation. . . . The Fort Trumbull area is situated on a peninsula that juts into the Thames River. The area comprises approximately 115 privately owned properties, as well as the 32 acres of land formerly occupied by the naval facility (Trumbull State Park now occupies 18 of those 32 acres). The development plan encompasses seven parcels. Parcel 1 is designated for a waterfront conference hotel at the center of a "small urban village" that will include restaurants and shopping. This parcel will also have marinas for both recreational and commercial uses. A pedestrian "riverwalk" will originate here and continue down the coast, connecting the waterfront areas of the development. Parcel 2 will be the site of approximately 80 new residences organized into an urban neighborhood and linked by public walkway to the remainder of the development, including the state park. This parcel also includes space reserved for a new U.S. Coast Guard Museum. Parcel 3, which is located immediately north of the Pfizer facility, will contain at least 90,000 square feet of research and development office space. Parcel 4A is a 2.4-acre site that will be used either to support the adjacent state park, by providing parking or retail services for visitors, or to support the nearby marina. Parcel 4B will include a renovated marina, as well as the final stretch of the riverwalk. Parcels 5, 6, and 7 will provide land for office and retail space, parking, and water-dependent commercial uses.

The NLDC intended the development plan to capitalize on the arrival of the Pfizer facility and the new commerce it was expected to attract. In addition to creating jobs, generating tax revenue, and helping to "build momentum for the revitalization of

Aerial view of the Fort Trumbull neighborhood, which remains largely vacant today—the marker at 79 Goshen Street is the Italian Dramatic Club and the large complex to the south is the former Pfizer plant, now owned by General Dynamics. (We owe this photo and information to Professor Andrew Kull, of the University of Texas at Austin Law School, with gratitude.)

downtown New London," the plan was also designed to make the City more attractive and to create leisure and recreational opportunities on the waterfront and in the park. . . .

II.

Petitioner Susette Kelo has lived in the Fort Trumbull area since 1997. She has made extensive improvements to her house, which she prizes for its water view. Petitioner Wilhelmina Dery was born in her Fort Trumbull house in 1918 and has lived there her entire life. Her husband Charles (also a petitioner) has lived in the house since they married some 60 years ago. In all, the nine petitioners own 15 properties in Fort Trumbull—4 in parcel 3 of the development plan and 11 in parcel 4A. Ten of the parcels are occupied by the owner or a family member; the other five are held as investment properties. There is no allegation that any of these properties is blighted or otherwise in poor condition; rather, they were condemned only because they happen to be located in the development area.

In December 2000, petitioners brought this action in the New London Superior Court. They claimed, among other things, that the taking of their properties would violate the "public use" restriction in the Fifth Amendment. After a 7-day bench trial,

Susette Kelo's house. The house has been moved to a different location in
New London. The lot on which her house originally stood is vacant.
Source: Institute for Justice

the Superior Court granted a permanent restraining order prohibiting the taking of the
properties located in parcel 4A (park or marina support). It, however, denied petitioners relief as to the properties located in parcel 3 (office space).

After the Superior Court ruled, both sides took appeals to the Supreme Court
of Connecticut. That court held, over a dissent, that all of the City's proposed takings were valid. It began by upholding the lower court's determination that the
takings were authorized by the State's municipal development statute. That statute
expresses a legislative determination that the taking of land, even developed land,
as part of an economic development project is a "public use" and in the "public
interest." Next, relying on cases such as Hawaii Housing Authority v. Midkiff, 467
U.S. 229 (1984), and Berman v. Parker, 348 U.S. 26 (1954), the court held that such

economic development qualified as a valid public use under both the Federal and State Constitutions. . . .

We granted certiorari to determine whether a city's decision to take property for the purpose of economic development satisfies the "public use" requirement of the Fifth Amendment.

III.

Two polar propositions are perfectly clear. On the one hand, it has long been accepted that the sovereign may not take the property of *A* for the sole purpose of transferring it to another private party *B*, even though *A* is paid just compensation. On the other hand, it is equally clear that a State may transfer property from one private party to another if future "use by the public" is the purpose of the taking; the condemnation of land for a railroad with common-carrier duties is a familiar example. Neither of these propositions, however, determines the disposition of this case. . . .

The disposition of this case . . . turns on the question whether the City's development plan serves a "public purpose." Without exception, our cases have defined that concept broadly, reflecting our longstanding policy of deference to legislative judgments in this field.

In Berman v. Parker, 348 U.S. 26 (1954), this Court upheld a redevelopment plan targeting a blighted area of Washington, D.C., in which most of the housing for the area's 5,000 inhabitants was beyond repair. Under the plan, the area would be condemned and part of it utilized for the construction of streets, schools, and other public facilities. The remainder of the land would be leased or sold to private parties for the purpose of redevelopment, including the construction of low-cost housing.

The owner of a department store located in the area challenged the condemnation, pointing out that his store was not itself blighted and arguing that the creation of a "better balanced, more attractive community" was not a valid public use. Writing for a unanimous Court, Justice Douglas refused to evaluate this claim in isolation, deferring instead to the legislative and agency judgment that the area "must be planned as a whole" for the plan to be successful. The Court explained that "community redevelopment programs need not, by force of the Constitution, be on a piecemeal basis—lot by lot, building by building." The public use underlying the taking was unequivocally affirmed:

> We do not sit to determine whether a particular housing project is or is not desirable. The concept of the public welfare is broad and inclusive. . . . The values it represents are spiritual as well as physical, aesthetic as well as monetary. It is within the power of the legislature to determine that the community should be beautiful as well as healthy, spacious as well as clean, well-balanced as well as carefully patrolled. In the present case, the Congress and its authorized agencies have made determinations that take into account a wide variety of values. It is not for us to reappraise them. If those who govern the District of Columbia decide that the Nation's Capital should be beautiful as well as sanitary, there is nothing in the Fifth Amendment that stands in the way.

In Hawaii Housing Authority v. Midkiff, 467 U.S. 229 (1984), the Court considered a Hawaii statute whereby fee title was taken from lessors and transferred to lessees (for just compensation) in order to reduce the concentration of land ownership. We unanimously upheld the statute and rejected the Ninth Circuit's view that it was a naked attempt on the part of the state of Hawaii to take the property of *A* and transfer it to *B* solely for *B*'s private use and benefit. Reaffirming *Berman*'s deferential approach to legislative judgments in this field, we concluded that the State's purpose of eliminating the "social and economic evils of a land oligopoly" qualified as a valid public use. Our opinion also rejected the contention that the mere fact that the State immediately transferred the properties to private individuals upon condemnation somehow diminished the public character of the taking. "[I]t is only the taking's purpose, and not its mechanics," we explained, that matters in determining public use . . . competition. 467 U.S., at 1015. . . .

. . . For more than a century, our public use jurisprudence has wisely eschewed rigid formulas and intrusive scrutiny in favor of affording legislatures broad latitude in determining what public needs justify the use of the takings power.

IV.

Those who govern the City were not confronted with the need to remove blight in the Fort Trumbull area, but their determination that the area was sufficiently distressed to justify a program of economic rejuvenation is entitled to our deference. The City has carefully formulated an economic development plan that it believes will provide appreciable benefits to the community, including—but by no means limited to—new jobs and increased tax revenue. As with other exercises in urban planning and development, the City is endeavoring to coordinate a variety of commercial, residential, and recreational uses of land, with the hope that they will form a whole greater than the sum of its parts. To effectuate this plan, the City has invoked a state statute that specifically authorizes the use of eminent domain to promote economic development. Given the comprehensive character of the plan, the thorough deliberation that preceded its adoption, and the limited scope of our review, it is appropriate for us, as it was in *Berman*, to resolve the challenges of the individual owners, not on a piecemeal basis, but rather in light of the entire plan. Because that plan unquestionably serves a public purpose, the takings challenged here satisfy the public use requirement of the Fifth Amendment.

To avoid this result, petitioners urge us to adopt a new bright-line rule that economic development does not qualify as a public use. Putting aside the unpersuasive suggestion that the City's plan will provide only purely economic benefits, neither precedent nor logic supports petitioners' proposal. Promoting economic development is a traditional and long accepted function of government. There is, moreover, no principled way of distinguishing economic development from the other public purposes that we have recognized. In our cases upholding takings that facilitated agriculture and mining, for example, we emphasized the importance of those industries to the welfare of the States in question; in *Berman*, we endorsed the purpose of transforming a blighted area into a "well-balanced" community through redevelopment; in *Midkiff*, we upheld the interest in breaking up a land oligopoly that "created artificial deterrents to the normal functioning of the State's residential land market." . . . It would be incongruous to hold that the City's interest in the economic benefits to be derived from the development of the Fort Trumbull area has less of a public character than any of those other interests. Clearly, there is no basis for exempting economic development from our traditionally broad understanding of public purpose. . . .

Just as we decline to second-guess the City's considered judgments about the efficacy of its development plan, we also decline to second-guess the City's determinations as to what lands it needs to acquire in order to effectuate the project. "It is not for the courts to oversee the choice of the boundary line nor to sit in review on the size of a particular project area. Once the question of the public purpose has been decided, the amount and character of land to be taken for the project and the need for a particular tract to complete the integrated plan rests in the discretion of the legislative branch." *Berman*, 348 U.S., at 35-36.

In affirming the City's authority to take petitioners' properties, we do not minimize the hardship that condemnations may entail, notwithstanding the payment of just compensation. We emphasize that nothing in our opinion precludes any State from placing further restrictions on its exercise of the takings power. Indeed, many States already impose "public use" requirements that are stricter than the federal baseline. Some of these requirements have been established as a matter of state constitutional law, while others are expressed in state eminent domain statutes that carefully limit the grounds upon which takings may be exercised. As the submissions of the parties and their amici make clear, the necessity and wisdom of using eminent domain to promote economic development are certainly matters of legitimate public debate. This Court's authority, however, extends only to determining whether the City's proposed condemnations are for a "public use" within the meaning of the Fifth Amendment to the Federal Constitution. Because over a century of our case law interpreting that provision dictates an affirmative answer to that question, we may not grant petitioners the relief that they seek.

The judgment of the Supreme Court of Connecticut is affirmed.

[Justice Kennedy concurred in the judgment, but added that even with a deferential standard of review, a taking should not survive the public use test if there is a clear showing that its purpose is "to favor a particular private party, with only incidental or pretextual public benefits. . . ." That a taking for economic development is not presumptively invalid, as petitioners had urged, "does not foreclose the possibility that a more stringent standard of review . . . might be appropriate for a more narrowly drawn category of takings."

Justice O'Connor dissented, joined by Chief Justice Rehnquist and Justices Scalia and Thomas (the latter also wrote a separate dissenting opinion). Justice O'Connor noted three categories of takings that had been held to satisfy the public use requirement in the past: transfers of private property to public ownership, as for a road; transfers to private parties such as common carriers, railroads, and the like, who make the property available for public use; and transfers to private parties as part of a program to serve a public purpose, as in *Midkiff* and Berman v. Parker (also discussed in the majority opinion). The third category is the most troubling, especially where, as here, the public purpose is economic development. *Midkiff* and *Berman* involved takings as part of programs to cure public harms—oligopoly in *Midkiff*, blight in *Berman*. *Kelo* goes beyond this, and too far, because "nearly any lawful use of real private property can be said to generate some incidental benefit to the public. . . . The beneficiaries are likely to be those citizens with disproportionate influence and power in the political process, including large corporations and development firms. As for the victims, the government now has license to transfer property from those with fewer resources to those with more."]

THE REST OF THE STORY . . .

The planned renovation of New London never occurred. In 2010, Pfizer pulled out of New London and relocated 1,400 jobs to another town. The developer could not obtain the necessary financing for the project, leading the city to abandon its redevelopment plan. Kelo sold her house, and the new owner moved the house to a new location. The original site of Kelo's house remains vacant, and one report describes the lot and most of the surrounding properties as "a barren wasteland of weeds, litter, and rubble." Jeff Benedict, Little Pink House: A True Story of Defiance and Courage 377 (2009).

Notes and Questions

1. *The meaning of "public use" after* Kelo. In the Supreme Court's most important pronouncement of the public-use requirement prior to *Kelo*, Justice O'Connor, writing for the majority, stated that the requirement was "coterminous with the scope of the sovereign's police powers" and that courts should review exercises of the eminent domain power only to assure that they are "rationally related to a conceivable public purpose." Hawaii Housing Auth. v. Midkiff, 467 U.S. 229, 240, 242-243 (1984). Prior to *Kelo*, courts interpreted that statement to mean that review for public use requires only the most deferential type of rationality review. According to this view, the public-use requirement is met as long as the court can conceive of some legitimate purpose that the legislature might have had in mind and that the taking can rationally be considered to achieve. Is this the same standard that the Court in *Kelo* adopts, or does the Court adopt a more demanding standard of review?

2. *An alternative approach—means versus ends.* In both *Midkiff* and *Kelo*, the Court's public-use analysis focused on ends. As long as the government is pursuing a legitimate public end, it has broad discretion over the means it chooses to achieve that end. However, there is another way to approach the question of public use—in terms of means rather than ends. The idea is to ask whether the power of eminent domain is really necessary to accomplish whatever aim the government has in mind. Professor Merrill has proposed just such a means-oriented approach, suggesting that the question to ask should be "where and how the government should get property, not what it may do with it." Thomas W. Merrill, The Economics of Public Use, 72 Cornell L. Rev. 61, 67 (1986). Merrill argues that this approach is more judicially manageable than the ends approach. Do you agree?

3. *Post-*Kelo *state constitutions/statutes.* *Kelo* produced an enormous political backlash, all of it opposed in one way or another to the use of eminent domain for economic development. The responses ranged from amendments to state constitutional prohibitions of the use of eminent domain for "private use" (e.g., New Hampshire) to adjustments in state and local eminent domain procedures. See Marc Mihaly & Turner Smith, *Kelo's* Trail: A Survey of State and Federal Legislative and Judicial Activity Five Years Later, 38 Ecology L.Q. 703 (2011).

"Just compensation." Courts have held that "just" compensation does not necessarily mean full compensation, but instead *market* compensation. The reason for the discrepancy between full and market compensation is that relocation costs, sentimental attachments, and other factors lead some owners to value their land more highly than the market rate. Why do courts award market value rather full value (meaning personal value)? The Supreme Court has explained: "Because of serious practical difficulties in assessing the worth an individual places on particular property at a given time, we have recognized the need for a relatively objective working rule." What are those "practical difficulties"?

Fair-market value means the amount that a willing buyer would pay to a willing seller. See United States v. Miller, 317 U.S. 369, 374 (1943). The problem is that in this context the seller is not a willing seller. Courts resolve the problem by using the various techniques that are ordinarily used to appraise the value of real estate, whether for tax purposes, listing a home for sale, or other purposes. These techniques include the following: (1) look at recent sale prices, if any, for the property in question; (2) look at recent sale prices of "comparables," i.e., other properties in the area that are considered comparable to the property in question; (3) use the capital value of the actual or potential rental value of the property in question; and (4) use the rebuilding cost of the building in question discounted on the basis of its age and wear and tear.

The law of just compensation is quite complex. Consider just two of a few of the nice issues that can arise:

→ Suppose that the government condemns part of a tract of land and that the government's use of that land will reduce the value of the rest of the tract remaining in the condemnee's hands. How is just compensation computed? See Julius L. Sackman, Nichols on Eminent Domain § 8A.02 (3d ed. 2005). Is compensation due if the government's use does not reduce the value of the condemnee's remaining land, but does reduce the rate at which it appreciates? See State v. Doyle, 735 P.2d 733 (Alaska 1987).

→ May a city downzone property, restricting its permissible uses, so as to be liable in a subsequent condemnation action only for fair-market value in light of the restrictive zoning? See Riggs v. Township of Long Beach, 538 A.2d 808 (N.J. 1988).

C. IMPLICIT TAKINGS

In a straightforward condemnation action, there is no question that the government is taking property; taking is the admitted purpose of the action. But, as you will see below, a long line of Supreme Court decisions hold that takings can also arise from other governmental activities, notwithstanding the government's insistence that no taking has occurred. An example would be a government regulation that requires the destruction of all specimens of a particular species of tree that are or might become infected with a certain infectious disease, and any such tree located within a certain radius of an apple orchard. The ostensible purpose of the statute is to prevent a public nuisance. A landowner with over 200 of these trees must cut them down, as a consequence of which the value of his land has declined very substantially. Has there been a taking, for which compensation must be paid?

The key issue in cases such as this is *whether* a taking has occurred in consequence of the governmental action, and the doctrine that deals with the issue is conventionally referred to, even by the Supreme Court, as the law of "regulatory takings." But that label is misleading. Many so-called regulatory takings have nothing whatsoever to do with regulation, and regulation is not treated as a distinctive category of activity in Supreme Court opinions. Takings by government regulation are just one member—albeit a substantial member—of a general class of all takings that arise outside the context of explicit takings by condemnation. We refer to this class as *implicit* takings. See James E. Krier & Stewart E. Sterk, An Empirical Study of Implicit Takings, 58 Wm. & Mary L. Rev. 35 (2016). Generally speaking, implicit takings arise when government action of any sort, regulatory or not, so restricts the use or enjoyment of private property that it is the functional equivalent of an explicit expropriation. We say "generally" because there are exceptions and complications, such that the problem of determining when there has been a compensable implicit taking, and when not, is one of the most controversial and nagging topics in all of property law. The first case we shall study, Pennsylvania Coal Co. v. Mahon, is generally considered to be the origin of implicit takings doctrine, and the Court's approach in that case is still relevant today.

1. The Standard Approach: Ad Hoc Balancing

PENNSYLVANIA COAL CO. v. MAHON

Supreme Court of the United States, 1922
260 U.S. 393

HOLMES, J. This is a bill in equity brought by the defendants in error to prevent the Pennsylvania Coal Company from mining under their property in such way as to remove the supports and cause a subsidence of the surface and of their house. The bill sets out a deed executed by the Coal Company in 1878, under which the plaintiffs claim. The deed conveys the surface, but in express terms reserves the right to remove all the coal under the same, and the grantee takes the premises with the risk, and waives all claim for damages that may arise from mining out the coal. But the plaintiffs say that whatever may have been the Coal Company's rights, they were taken away by an Act of Pennsylvania, approved May 27, 1921, P.L. 1198, commonly known there as the Kohler Act. The Court of Common Pleas found that if not restrained the defendant would cause the damage to prevent which the bill was brought, but denied an injunction, holding that the statute if applied to this case would be unconstitutional. On appeal the Supreme Court of the State agreed that the defendant had contract and property rights protected by the Constitution of the United States, but held that the statute was a legitimate exercise of the police power and directed a decree for the plaintiffs. A writ of error was granted bringing the case to this Court.

The result of "robbing pillars," as locals called it. We owe this to Professor Andrew Kull, of the University of Texas at Austin Law School. http://kullproperty.weebly.com/ pennsylvania-coal-co-v-mahon.html

The statute forbids the mining of anthracite coal in such way as to cause the subsidence of, among other things, any structure used as a human habitation, with certain exceptions, including among them land where the surface is owned by the owner of the underlying coal and is distant more than one hundred and fifty feet from any improved property belonging to any other person. As applied to this case the statute is admitted to destroy previously existing rights of property and contract. The question is whether the police power can be stretched so far.

Government hardly could go on if to some extent values incident to property could not be diminished without paying for every such change in the general law. As long recognized, some values are enjoyed under an implied limitation and must yield to the police power. But obviously the implied limitation must have its limits, or the contract and due process clauses are gone. One fact for consideration in determining such limits is the extent of the diminution. When it reaches a certain magnitude, in most if not in all cases there must be an exercise of eminent domain and compensation to sustain the act. So the question depends upon the particular facts. The greatest weight is given to the judgment of the legislature, but it always is open to interested parties to contend that the legislature has gone beyond its constitutional power.

This is the case of a single private house. No doubt there is a public interest even in this, as there is in every purchase and sale and in all that happens within the commonwealth. Some existing rights may be modified even in such a case. Rideout v. Knox, 148 Mass. 368. But usually in ordinary private affairs the public interest does not warrant much of this kind of interference. A source of damage to such a house is not a public nuisance even if similar damage is inflicted on others in different places. The damage is not common or public. Wesson v. Washburn Iron Co., 13 Allen 95, 103. The extent of the public interest is shown by the statute to be limited, since the statute ordinarily does not apply to land when the surface is owned by the owner of the coal.

Furthermore, it is not justified as a protection of personal safety. That could be provided for by notice. Indeed the very foundation of this bill is that the defendant gave timely notice of its intent to mine under the house. On the other hand the extent of the taking is great. It purports to abolish what is recognized in Pennsylvania as an estate in land—a very valuable estate—and what is declared by the court below to be a contract hitherto binding the plaintiffs. If we were called upon to deal with the plaintiffs' position alone, we should think it clear that the statute does not disclose a public interest sufficient to warrant so extensive a destruction of the defendant's constitutionally protected rights.

Justice Oliver Wendell Holmes

But the case has been treated as one in which the general validity of the act should be discussed. The Attorney General of the State, the City of Scranton, and the representatives of other extensive interests were allowed to take part in the argument below and have submitted their contentions here. It seems, therefore, to be our duty to go farther in the statement of our opinion, in order that it may be known at once, and that further suits should not be brought in vain.

It is our opinion that the act cannot be sustained as an exercise of the police power, so far as it affects the mining of coal under streets or cities in places where the right to mine such coal has been reserved. As said in a Pennsylvania case, "For practical purposes, the right to coal consists in the right to mine it." Commonwealth v. Clearview Coal Co., 256 Pa. St. 328, 331. What makes the right to mine coal valuable is that it can be exercised with profit. To make it commercially impracticable to mine certain coal has very nearly the same effect for constitutional purposes as appropriating or destroying it. This we think that we are warranted in assuming that the statute does.

Justice Louis Dembitz Brandeis

It is true that in Plymouth Coal Co. v. Pennsylvania, 232 U.S. 531, it was held competent for the legislature to require a pillar of coal to be left along the line of adjoining property, that, with the pillar on the other side of the line, would be a barrier sufficient for the safety of the employees of either mine in case the other should be abandoned and allowed to fill with water. But that was a requirement for the safety of employees invited into the mine, and secured an average reciprocity of advantage that has been recognized as a justification of various laws.

The rights of the public in a street purchased or laid out by eminent domain are those that it has paid for. If in any case its representatives have been so short sighted as to acquire only surface rights without the right of support, we see no more authority for supplying the latter without compensation than there was for taking the right of way in the first place and refusing to pay for it because the public wanted it very much. The protection of private property in the Fifth Amendment presupposes that it is wanted for public use, but provides that it shall not be taken for such use without compensation. A similar assumption is made in the decisions upon the Fourteenth Amendment. Hairston v. Danville & Western Ry. Co., 208 U.S. 598, 605. When the seemingly absolute protection is found to be qualified by the police power, the natural tendency of human nature is to extend the qualification more and more until at last private property disappears. But that cannot be accomplished in this way under the Constitution of the United States.

The general rule at least is, that while property may be regulated to a certain extent, if regulation goes too far it will be recognized as a taking. It may be doubted how far exceptional cases, like the blowing up of a house to stop a conflagration, go—and if they go beyond the general rule, whether they do not stand as much upon tradition as upon principle. Bowditch v. Boston, 101 U.S. 16. In general it is not plain that a man's misfortunes or necessities will justify his shifting the damages to his neighbor's shoulders. Space v. Lynn & Boston R.R. Co., 172 Mass. 488, 489. We are in danger of forgetting that a strong public desire to improve the public condition is not enough to warrant achieving the desire by a shorter cut than the constitutional way of paying for the change. As we already have said, this is a question of degree—and therefore cannot be disposed of by general propositions. But we regard this as going beyond any of the cases decided by this Court. The late decisions upon laws dealing with the congestion of Washington and New York, caused by the war, dealt with laws intended to meet a temporary emergency and providing for compensation determined to be reasonable by an impartial board. They went to the verge of the law but fell far short of the present act. Block v. Hirsh, 256 U.S. 135. Marcus Brown Holding Co. v. Feldman, 256 U.S. 170. Levy Leasing Co. v. Siegel, 258 U.S. 242.

We assume, of course, that the statute was passed upon the conviction that an exigency existed that would warrant it, and we assume that an exigency exists that would warrant the exercise of eminent domain. But the question at bottom is upon whom the loss of the changes desired should fall. So far as private persons or communities have seen fit to take the risk of acquiring only surface rights, we cannot see that the fact that their risk has become a danger warrants the giving to them greater rights than they bought.

Decree reversed.

BRANDEIS, J., dissenting. The Kohler Act prohibits, under certain conditions, the mining of anthracite coal within the limits of a city in such a manner or to such an extent "as to cause the . . . subsidence of any dwelling or other structure used as a human habitation, or any factory, store, or other industrial or mercantile establishment in which human labor is employed." Coal in place is land; and the right of the owner to use his land is not absolute. He may not so use it as to create a public nuisance; and uses, once harmless, may, owing to changed conditions, seriously threaten the public welfare. Whenever they do, the legislature has power to prohibit such uses without paying compensation; and the power to prohibit extends alike to the manner, the character and the purpose of the use. Are we justified in declaring that the Legislature of Pennsylvania has, in restricting the right to mine anthracite, exercised this power so arbitrarily as to violate the Fourteenth Amendment?

Every restriction upon the use of property imposed in the exercise of the police power deprives the owner of some right theretofore enjoyed, and is, in that sense, an abridgement by the State of rights in property without making compensation. But restriction imposed to protect the public health, safety or morals from dangers threatened is not a taking. The restriction here in question is merely the prohibition of a noxious use. The property so restricted remains in the possession of its owner. The State does not appropriate it or make any use of it. The State merely prevents the owner from making a use which interferes with paramount rights of the public. Whenever the use prohibited ceases to be noxious—as it may because of further change in local or social conditions—the restriction will have to be removed and the owner will again be free to enjoy his property as heretofore.

The restriction upon the use of this property can not, of course, be lawfully imposed, unless its purpose is to protect the public. But the purpose of a restriction does not cease to be public, because incidentally some private persons may thereby receive gratuitously valuable special benefits. Thus, owners of low buildings may obtain, through statutory restrictions upon the height of neighboring structures, benefits equivalent to an easement of light and air. Furthermore, a restriction, though imposed for a public purpose, will not be lawful, unless the restriction is an appropriate means to the public end. But to keep coal in place is surely an appropriate means of preventing subsidence of the surface; and ordinarily it is the only available means. Restriction upon use does not become inappropriate as a means, merely because it deprives the owner of the only use to which the property can then be profitably put. The liquor and the oleomargarine cases settled that. Mugler v. Kansas, 123 U.S. 623; Powell v. Pennsylvania, 127 U.S. 678. Nor is a restriction imposed through exercise of the police power inappropriate as a means, merely because the same end might be effected through exercise of the power of eminent domain, or otherwise at public expense. Every restriction upon the height of buildings might be secured through acquiring by eminent domain the right of each owner to build above the limiting height; but it is settled that the State need not resort to that power. If by mining anthracite coal the owner would necessarily unloose poisonous gasses, I suppose no one would doubt the power of the State to prevent the mining, without buying his coal fields. And why may not the State, likewise, without paying compensation, prohibit one from digging so deep or excavating so near the surface, as to expose the community to like dangers? In the latter case, as in the former, carrying on the business would be a public nuisance.It is said that one fact for consideration in determining whether the limits of the police power have been exceeded is the extent of the resulting diminution in value; and that here the restriction destroys existing rights of property and contract. But values are relative. If we are to consider the value of the coal kept in place by the restriction, we should compare it with the value of all other parts of the land. That is, with the value not of the coal alone, but with the value of the whole property. The rights of an owner as against the public are not increased by dividing the interests in his property into surface and subsoil. The sum of the rights in the parts can not be greater than the rights in the whole. The estate of an owner in land is grandiloquently described as extending *ab orco usque ad coelum*. But I suppose no one would contend that by selling his interest above one hundred feet from the surface he could prevent the State from limiting, by the police power, the height of structures in a city. And why should a sale of underground rights bar the State's power? For aught that appears the value of the coal kept in place by the restriction may be negligible as compared with the value of the whole property, or even as compared with that part of it which is represented by the coal remaining in place and which may be extracted despite the statute. Ordinarily a police regulation, general in operation, will not be held void as to a particular property, although proof is offered that owing to conditions peculiar to it the restriction could not reasonably be applied. But even if the particular facts are to govern, the statute should, in my opinion, be upheld in this case. For the defendant has failed to adduce any evidence from which it appears that to restrict its mining operations was an unreasonable exercise of the police power. Where the surface and the coal belong to the same person, self-interest would ordinarily prevent mining to such an extent as to cause a subsidence. It was, doubtless, for this reason that the legislature, estimating the degrees of danger, deemed statutory restriction unnecessary for the public safety under such conditions.

It is said that this is a case of a single dwelling house; that the restriction upon mining abolishes a valuable estate hitherto secured by a contract with the plaintiffs; and that the restriction upon mining cannot be justified as a protection of personal safety, since that could be provided for by notice. The propriety of deferring a good deal to tribunals on the spot has been repeatedly recognized. . . . May we say that notice would afford adequate protection of the public safety where the legislature and the highest court of the State, with greater knowledge of local conditions, have declared, in effect, that it would not? If public safety is imperiled, surely neither grant, nor contract, can prevail against the exercise of the police power. . . .

This case involves only mining which causes subsidence of a dwelling house. But the Kohler Act contains provisions in addition to that quoted above; and as to these, also, an opinion is expressed. These provisions deal with mining under cities to such an extent as to cause subsidence of—

(a) Any public building or any structure customarily used by the public as a place of resort, assemblage, or amusement, including, but not being limited to, churches, schools, hospitals, theatres, hotels, and railroad stations.

(b) Any street, road, bridge or other public passageway, dedicated to public use or habitually used by the public.

(c) Any track, roadbed, right of way, pipe, conduit, wire, or other facility, used in the service of the public by any municipal corporation or public service company as defined by the Public Service Company Law.

A prohibition of mining which causes subsidence of such structures and facilities is obviously enacted for a public purpose and it seems, likewise, clear that mere notice of intention to mine would not in this connection secure the public safety. Yet it is said that these provisions of the act cannot be sustained as an exercise of the police power where the right to mine such coal has been reserved. The conclusion seems to rest upon the assumption that in order to justify such exercise of the police power there must be "an average reciprocity of advantage" as between the owner of the property restricted and the rest of the community; and that here such reciprocity is absent. Reciprocity of advantage is an important consideration, and may even be an essential, where the State's power is exercised for the purpose of conferring benefits upon the property of a neighborhood, as in drainage projects, Wurts v. Hoagland, 114 U.S. 606; Fallbrook Irrigation District v. Bradley, 164 U.S. 112; or upon adjoining owners, as by party wall provisions, Jackman v. Rosenbaum Co., [260 U.S.] 22. But where the police power is exercised, not to confer benefits upon property owners, but to protect the public from detriment and danger, there is, in my opinion, no room for considering reciprocity of advantage. There was no reciprocal advantage to the owner prohibited from using his oil tanks in 248 U.S. 498; his brickyard, in 239 U.S. 394; his livery stable, in 237 U.S. 171; his billiard hall, in 225 U.S. 623; his oleomargarine factory, in 127 U.S. 678; his brewery, in 123 U.S. 623; unless it be the advantage of living and doing business in a civilized community. That reciprocal advantage is given by the act to the coal operators.

THE REST OF THE STORY . . .

The decision in *Pennsylvania Coal* turns out not to have had much impact on the coal companies' behavior. Prior to the Supreme Court's decision anthracite mining companies in eastern Pennsylvania generally compensated surface owners for any damage caused by subsidence, even if the owner had waived the support right. What made the Kohler Act objectionable to coal companies was its remedy of private injunctions. Another state statute, the Fowler Act, was connected with this feature in a curious way. The Fowler Act taxed coal companies on all anthracite coal, which they mined throughout the state, but coal companies did not have to pay the tax unless they wanted relief from obligations imposed on them under the Kohler Act. In *Pennsylvania Coal*, Mahon had sought an injunction against the coal company to prevent mining under his land. The Court's decision freed the companies from the tax under the Fowler Act, but apparently it did not change their practice of voluntarily compensating surface owners for damage caused by subsidence. Why do you suppose the companies paid that compensation? This information and a fascinating account of the background of the case is provided in William A. Fischel, Regulatory Takings: Law, Economics, and Politics 25-47 (1995).

Notes and Questions

1. *Takings tests.* As we noted previously, *Pennsylvania Coal* is still a very important case. It is the source of the idea that regulations may "go too far" and therefore cross the line between non-compensable regulations (exercises of the police power) and compensable takings (exercises of the eminent domain power). This is the idea behind the regulatory taking doctrine. The question is how to determine when a regulation crosses that line. Justice Holmes's opinion did not give us much guidance, but it did guide us some.

His test says, in essence, that when governmental regulation of a use that is not a nuisance imposes too great a burden on property owners, it cannot go forth without compensation. Notice, though, that the regulation itself might provide implicit compensation by way of what Justice Holmes called, on page 622, "an average reciprocity of advantage." The idea, of course, is that the apparent losers under a government program might not be losers at all (or not, at least, big losers) because they are simultaneously benefited by the very action that burdens them. Watch for this idea as it plays into later cases.

For a general assessment of *Pennsylvania Coal*'s significance, see William Michael Treanor, Jam for Justice Holmes: Reassessing the Significance of *Mahon*, 86 Geo. L.J. 813 (1998).

2. *Diminution in value.* The rule of decision in *Pennsylvania Coal* is usually referred to as the *diminution-in-value test*. What is its point?

Notice Justice Brandeis's response to the majority opinion of Justice Holmes. He attacks the diminution-in-value test head on: diminution relative to what? The diminution-in-value test is extraordinarily ambiguous. How much of a loss of value is too much? Is loss to be measured in absolute terms, or rather in relative ones? If the latter, relative to what?

3. *Conceptual severance.* Consider how Holmes and Brandeis differed in their approach to the last question in particular. Pennsylvania law recognizes three separate estates in mining property: in the surface, in the minerals, and in support of the surface. Holmes saw the Kohler Act as purporting to "abolish" the third estate entirely. See page 621. Brandeis, on the other hand, reasoned that the "rights of an owner as against the public are not increased by dividing the interests in his property"; the Kohler Act did not take all of a smaller thing (the third estate), but only a part "of the whole property." See page 624.

Which view is correct? The approach reflected in Holmes's view is referred to in the literature as *conceptual severance*, a term whose origin is an article by Professor Margaret Jane Radin, The Liberal Conception of Property: Cross Currents in the Jurisprudence of Takings, 88 Colum. L. Rev. 1667, 1676 (1988). The Supreme Court has not definitively stated its position on the use of conceptual severance for all purposes.

Consider, for example, Keystone Bituminous Coal Association v. DeBenedictis, 480 U.S. 470 (1987), a case that might rightly be called *Pennsylvania Coal* redux. The case arose out of a 1966 Pennsylvania statute designed, as was the Kohler Act involved in *Pennsylvania Coal*, to control subsidence from coal mining. Under the legislation, coal companies had to keep up to 50 percent of their coal in place, and repair subsidence damage even if surface owners had waived their rights. The Court held that the statute did not work a taking, despite its similarities to the Kohler Act, because its purpose was not just to balance private economic interests, but rather to protect the public interest in health, environmental quality, and fiscal integrity. In any event, the Court held, the coal companies had not shown a sufficient diminution in value, a point related to the matter of conceptual severance. The millions of tons of coal that had to remain in place under the Pennsylvania statute were not a separate segment of property, but only a low percent of the total coal owned by the companies. Never mind that Pennsylvania law recognized the "support estate" as a separate interest; "our takings jurisprudence forecloses reliance on such legalistic distinctions within a bundle of property rights." Id. at 500.

Chief Justice Rehnquist, joined by Justices Powell, O'Connor, and Scalia, dissented. In their view, the majority in *Keystone* had wrongly discounted *Pennsylvania Coal*, "the foundation of our 'regulatory takings' jurisprudence." Id. at 508.

Conceptual severance figures in the next case as well.

PENN CENTRAL TRANSPORTATION COMPANY v. CITY OF NEW YORK

Supreme Court of the United States, 1978
438 U.S. 104

BRENNAN, J. The question presented is whether a city may, as part of a comprehensive program to preserve historic landmarks and historic districts, place restrictions on the development of individual historic landmarks—in addition to those imposed by applicable zoning ordinances—without effecting a "taking" requiring the payment of "just compensation." Specifically, we must decide whether the application of New York City's Landmarks Preservation Law to the parcel of land occupied by Grand Central Terminal has "taken" its owners' property in violation of the Fifth and Fourteenth Amendments.

I.

A

Over the past 50 years, all 50 States and over 500 municipalities have enacted laws to encourage or require the preservation of buildings and areas with historic or aesthetic importance. These nationwide legislative efforts have been precipitated by two concerns. The first is recognition that, in recent years, large numbers of historic structures, landmarks, and areas have been destroyed without adequate consideration of either the values represented therein or the possibility of preserving the destroyed properties for use in economically productive ways. The second is a widely shared belief that structures with special historic, cultural, or architectural significance enhance the quality of life for all. Not only do these buildings and their workmanship represent the lessons of the past and embody precious features of our heritage, they serve as examples of quality for today. . . .

New York City, responding to similar concerns and acting pursuant to a New York State enabling Act, adopted its Landmarks Preservation Law in 1965. See N.Y.C. Admin. Code, ch. 8-A, § 205-1.0 et seq. (1976). The city acted from the conviction that "the standing of [New York City] as a world-wide tourist center and world capital of business, culture and government" would be threatened if legislation were not enacted to protect historic landmarks and neighborhoods from precipitate decisions to destroy or fundamentally alter their character. . . .

The New York City law is typical of many urban landmark laws in that its primary method of achieving its goals is not by acquisitions of historic properties, but rather by involving public entities in land-use decisions affecting these properties and providing services, standards, controls, and incentives that will encourage preservation by private owners and users. While the law does place special restrictions on landmark properties as a necessary feature to the attainment of its larger objectives, the major theme of the law is to ensure the owners of any such properties both a "reasonable return" on their investments and maximum latitude to use their parcels for purposes not inconsistent with the preservation goals. . . .

Final designation as a landmark results in restrictions upon the property owner's options concerning use of the landmark site. First, the law imposes a duty upon the owner to keep the exterior features of the building "in good repair" to assure that

Grand Central Terminal c. 1930
Source: Library of Congress

the law's objectives not be defeated by the landmark's falling into a state of irremediable disrepair. Second, the Commission must approve in advance any proposal to alter the exterior architectural features of the landmark or to construct any exterior improvement on the landmark site, thus ensuring that decisions concerning construction on the landmark site are made with due consideration of both the public interest in the maintenance of the structure and the landowner's interest in use of the property. . . .

Although the designation of a landmark and landmark site restricts the owner's control over the parcel, designation also enhances the economic position of the landmark owner in one significant respect. Under New York City's zoning laws, owners of real property who have not developed their property to the full extent permitted by the applicable zoning laws are allowed to transfer development rights to contiguous parcels on the same city block. See New York City, Zoning Resolution Art. I, ch. 2, § 12-10 (1978) (definition of "zoning lot"). A 1968 ordinance gave the owners of landmark sites additional opportunities to transfer development rights to other parcels. Subject to a restriction that the floor area of the transferee lot may not

Excavation for Grand Central Terminal, 1906
Source: Library of Congress

be increased by more than 20% above its authorized level, the ordinance permitted transfers from a landmark parcel to property across the street or across a street intersection. In 1969, the law governing the conditions under which transfers from landmark parcels could occur was liberalized, see New York City Zoning Resolutions 74-79 to 74-793, apparently to ensure that the Landmarks Law would not unduly restrict the development options of the owners of Grand Central Terminal. See Marcus, Air Rights Transfers in New York City, 36 Law & Contemp. Prob. 372, 375 (1971). The class of recipient lots was expanded to include lots "across a street and opposite to another lot or lots which except for the intervention of streets or street intersections f[or]m a series extending to the lot occupied by the landmark build-ing[, provided that] all lots [are] in the same ownership." New York City Zoning Resolution 74-79 (emphasis deleted). In addition, the 1969 amendment permits, in highly commercialized areas like midtown Manhattan, the transfer of all unused development rights to a single parcel.

B

This case involves the application of New York City's Landmarks Preservation Law to Grand Central Terminal (Terminal). The Terminal, which is owned by the Penn Central Transportation Co. and its affiliates (Penn Central), is one of New York City's most famous buildings. Opened in 1913, it is regarded not only as providing an ingenious engineering solution to the problems presented by urban railroad stations, but also as a magnificent example of the French beaux-arts style.

The Terminal is located in midtown Manhattan. Its south facade faces 42d Street and that street's intersection with Park Avenue. At street level, the Terminal is bounded on the west by Vanderbilt Avenue, on the east by the Commodore Hotel, and on the north by the Pan-American Building. Although a 20-story office tower, to have been located above the Terminal, was part of the original design, the planned tower was never constructed. The Terminal itself is an eight-story structure which Penn Central uses as a railroad station and in which it rents space not needed for railroad purposes to a variety of commercial interests. The Terminal is one of a number of properties owned by appellant Penn Central in this area of midtown Manhattan. The others include the Barclay, Biltmore, Commodore, Roosevelt, and Waldorf-Astoria Hotels, the Pan-American Building and other office buildings along Park Avenue, and the Yale Club. At least eight of these are eligible to be recipients of development rights afforded the Terminal by virtue of landmark designation.

On August 2, 1967, following a public hearing, the Commission designated the Terminal a "landmark" and designated the "city tax block" it occupies a "landmark site." The Board of Estimate confirmed this action on September 21, 1967. Although appellant Penn Central had opposed the designation before the Commission, it did not seek judicial review of the final designation decision.

On January 22, 1968, appellant Penn Central, to increase its income, entered into a renewable 50-year lease and sublease agreement with appellant UGP Properties, Inc. (UGP), a wholly owned subsidiary of Union General Properties, Ltd., a United Kingdom corporation. Under the terms of the agreement, UGP was to construct a multistory office building above the Terminal. UGP promised to pay Penn Central $1 million annually during construction and at least $3 million annually thereafter. The rentals would be offset in part by a loss of some $700,000 to $1 million in net rentals presently received from concessionaires displaced by the new building.

Appellants UGP and Penn Central then applied to the Commission for permission to construct an office building atop the Terminal. Two separate plans, both designed by architect Marcel Breuer and both apparently satisfying the terms of the applicable zoning ordinance, were submitted to the Commission for approval. The first, Breuer I, provided for the construction of a 55-story office building, to be cantilevered above the existing facade and to rest on the roof of the Terminal. The second, Breuer II Revised, called for tearing down a portion of the Terminal that included the 42d Street facade, stripping off some of the remaining features of the Terminal's facade, and constructing a 53-story office building. The Commission denied a certificate of no exterior effect on September 20, 1968. Appellants then applied for a certificate of "appropriateness" as to both proposals. After four days of hearings at which over 80 witnesses testified, the Commission denied this application as to both proposals.

The Commission's reasons for rejecting certificates respecting Breuer II Revised are summarized in the following statement: "To protect a Landmark, one does not tear it down. To perpetuate its architectural features, one does not strip them off." Breuer I, which would have preserved the existing vertical facades of the present structure, received more sympathetic consideration. The Commission first focused on the effect that the proposed tower would have on one desirable feature created by the present structure and its surroundings: the dramatic view of the Terminal from Park Avenue South. Although appellants had contended that the Pan-American Building had already destroyed the silhouette of the south facade and that one additional tower could do no further damage and might even provide a better background for the facade, the Commission disagreed, stating that it found the majestic approach from the south to be still unique in the city and that a 55-story tower atop the Terminal would be far more detrimental to its south facade than the Pan-American Building 375 feet away. Moreover, the Commission found that from closer vantage points the Pan-Am Building and the other towers were largely cut off from view, which would not be the case of the mass on top of the Terminal planned under Breuer I. . . .

Appellants did not seek judicial review of the denial of either certificate. . . . Instead, appellants filed suit in New York Supreme Court, Trial Term, claiming, inter alia, that the application of the Landmarks Preservation Law had "taken" their property without just compensation in violation of the Fifth and Fourteenth Amendments and arbitrarily deprived them of their property without due process of law in violation of the Fourteenth Amendment. Appellants sought a declaratory judgment, injunctive relief barring the city from using the Landmarks Law to impede the construction of any structure that might otherwise lawfully be constructed on the Terminal site, and damages for the "temporary taking" that occurred between August 2, 1967, the designation date, and the date when the restrictions arising from the Landmarks Law would be lifted. The trial court granted the injunctive and declaratory relief, but severed the question of damages for a "temporary taking."

Breuer I

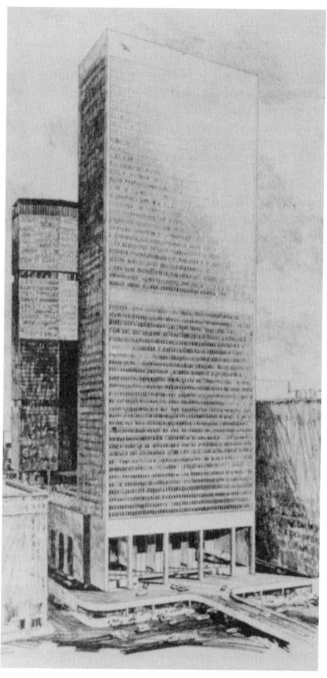

Breuer II

Appellees appealed, and the New York Supreme Court, Appellate Division, reversed. 50 A.D.2d 265, 377 N.Y.S.2d 20 (1975). The Appellate Division held that the restrictions on the development of the Terminal site were necessary to promote the legitimate public purpose of protecting landmarks and therefore that appellants could sustain their constitutional claims only by proof that the regulation deprived them of all reasonable beneficial use of the property. The Appellate Division held that the evidence appellants introduced at trial—"Statements of Revenues and Costs," purporting to show a net operating loss for the years 1969 and 1971, which were prepared for the instant litigation—had not satisfied their burden. . . .

The New York Court of Appeals affirmed. 42 N.Y.2d 324, 366 N.E.2d 1271 (1977). . . .

II.

The issues presented by appellants are (1) whether the restrictions imposed by New York City's law upon appellants' exploitation of the Terminal site effect a "taking" of appellants' property for a public use within the meaning of the Fifth Amendment, which of course is made applicable to the States through the Fourteenth Amendment, see Chicago, B. & Q. R. Co. v. Chicago, 166 U.S. 226, 239 (1897), and, (2), if so, whether the transferable development rights afforded appellants constitute "just compensation" within the meaning of the Fifth Amendment. We need only address the question whether a "taking" has occurred.

A

Before considering appellants' specific contentions, it will be useful to review the factors that have shaped the jurisprudence of the Fifth Amendment injunction "nor shall private property be taken for public use, without just compensation." The question of what constitutes a "taking" for purposes of the Fifth Amendment has proved to be a problem of considerable difficulty. While this Court has recognized that the "Fifth Amendment's guarantee . . . [is] designed to bar Government from forcing some people alone to bear public burdens which, in all fairness and justice, should be borne by the public as a whole," Armstrong v. United States, 364 U.S. 40, 49 (1960), this Court, quite simply, has been unable to develop any "set formula" for determining when "justice and fairness" require that economic injuries caused by public action be compensated by the government, rather than remain disproportionately concentrated on a few persons. See Goldblatt v. Hempstead, 369 U.S. 590, 594 (1962). Indeed, we have frequently observed that whether a particular restriction will be rendered invalid by the government's failure to pay for any losses proximately caused by it depends largely "upon the particular circumstances [in that] case." United States v. Central Eureka Mining Co., 357 U.S. 155, 168 (1958).

In engaging in these essentially ad hoc, factual inquiries, the Court's decisions have identified several factors that have particular significance. The economic impact of the regulation on the claimant and, particularly, the extent to which the regulation has interfered with distinct investment-backed expectations are, of course, relevant considerations. So, too, is the character of the governmental action. A "taking" may more readily be found when the interference with property can be characterized as a physical invasion by government, see, e.g., United States v. Causby, 328 U.S. 256 (1946), than when interference arises from some public program adjusting the benefits and burdens of economic life to promote the common good.

"Government hardly could go on if to some extent values incident to property could not be diminished without paying for every such change in the general law," Pennsylvania Coal Co. v. Mahon, 260 U.S. 393, 413 (1922), and this Court has accordingly recognized, in a wide variety of contexts, that government may execute laws or programs that adversely affect recognized economic values. Exercises of the taxing power are one obvious example. A second are the decisions in which this Court has dismissed "taking" challenges on the ground that, while the challenged government action caused economic harm, it did not interfere with interests that were sufficiently bound up with the reasonable expectations of the claimant to constitute "property" for Fifth Amendment purposes. See, e.g., United States v. Willow River Power Co., 324 U.S. 499 (1945) (interest in high-water level of river for runoff for tailwaters to maintain power head is not property); United States v. Chandler-Dunbar Water Power Co., 229 U.S. 53 (1913) (no property interest can exist in navigable waters).

More importantly for the present case, in instances in which a state tribunal reasonably concluded that "the health, safety, morals, or general welfare" would be promoted by prohibiting particular contemplated uses of land, this Court has upheld land-use regulations that destroyed or adversely affected recognized real property interests. See Nectow v. Cambridge, 277 U.S. 183, 188 (1928). Zoning laws are, of course, the classic example, see Euclid v. Ambler Realty Co., 272 U.S. 365 (1926) (prohibition of industrial use). . . .

B

In contending that the New York City law has "taken" their property in violation of the Fifth and Fourteenth Amendments, appellants make a series of arguments, which, while tailored to the facts of this case, essentially urge that any substantial restriction imposed pursuant to a landmark law must be accompanied by just compensation if it is to be constitutional. . . .

[Appellants] first observe that the airspace above the Terminal is a valuable property interest, citing United States v. Causby, supra. They urge that the Landmarks Law has deprived them of any gainful use of their "air rights" above the Terminal and that, irrespective of the value of the remainder of their parcel, the city has "taken" their right to this superadjacent airspace, thus entitling them to "just compensation" measured by the fair market value of these air rights.

Apart from our own disagreement with appellants' characterization of the effect of the New York City law, . . . the submission that appellants may establish a "taking" simply by showing that they have been denied the ability to exploit a property interest that they heretofore had believed was available for development is quite simply untenable. . . . "Taking" jurisprudence does not divide a single parcel into discrete segments and attempt to determine whether rights in a particular segment have been entirely abrogated. In deciding whether a particular governmental action has effected a taking, this Court focuses rather both on the character of the action and on the nature and extent of the interference with rights in the parcel as a whole—here, the city tax block designated as the "landmark site."

Secondly, appellants, focusing on the character and impact of the New York City law, argue that it effects a "taking" because its operation has significantly diminished the value of the Terminal site. Appellants concede that the decisions sustaining other land-use regulations, which, like the New York City law, are reasonably related to the promotion of the general welfare, uniformly reject the proposition that diminution in property value, standing alone, can establish a "taking," see Euclid v. Ambler Realty Co., 272 U.S. 365 (1926) (75% diminution in value caused by zoning law); Hadacheck v. Sebastian, 239 U.S. 394 (1915) (87 1/2% diminution in value), and that the "taking" issue in these contexts is resolved by focusing on the uses the regulations permit. Appellants, moreover, also do not dispute that a showing of diminution in property value would not establish a taking if the restriction had been imposed as a result of historic-district legislation, but appellants argue that New York City's regulation of individual landmarks is fundamentally different from zoning or from historic-district legislation because the controls imposed by New York City's law apply only to individuals who own selected properties. . . .

It is true, as appellants emphasize, that both historic-district legislation and zoning laws regulate all properties within given physical communities whereas landmark laws apply only to selected parcels. But, contrary to appellants' suggestions, landmark laws are not like discriminatory, or "reverse spot," zoning: that is, a land-use decision which arbitrarily singles out a particular parcel for different, less favorable treatment than the neighboring ones. In contrast to discriminatory zoning, which is the antithesis of land-use control as part of some comprehensive plan, the New York City law embodies a comprehensive plan to preserve structures of historic or aesthetic interest wherever they might be found in the city, and as noted, over 400 landmarks and 31 historic districts have been designated pursuant to this plan. . . .

Next, appellants observe that New York City's law differs from zoning laws and historic-district ordinances in that the Landmarks Law does not impose identical or similar restrictions on all structures located in particular physical communities. It follows, they argue, that New York City's law is inherently incapable of producing the fair and equitable distribution of benefits and burdens of governmental action which is characteristic of zoning laws and historic-district legislation and which they maintain is a constitutional requirement if "just compensation" is not to be afforded. It is, of course, true that the Landmarks Law has a more severe impact on some landowners than on others, but that in itself does not mean that the law effects a "taking." Legislation designed to promote the general welfare commonly burdens some more than others. The owners of the brickyard in *Hadacheck*, of the cedar trees in Miller v. Schoene, [276 U.S. 272 (1928),] and of the gravel and sand mine in Goldblatt v. Hempstead, were uniquely burdened by the legislation sustained in those cases. Similarly, zoning laws often affect some property owners more severely than others but have not been held to be invalid on that account. For example, the property owner in *Euclid* who wished to use its property for industrial purposes was affected far more severely by the ordinance than its neighbors who wished to use their land for residences.

In any event, appellants' repeated suggestions that they are solely burdened and unbenefited is factually inaccurate. This contention overlooks the fact that the New York City law applies to vast numbers of structures in the city in addition to the Terminal—all the structures contained in the 31 historic districts and over 400 individual landmarks, many of which are close to the Terminal. . . .

Appellants' final broad-based attack would have us treat the law as an instance, like that in United States v. Causby, in which government, acting in an enterprise capacity, has appropriated part of their property for some strictly governmental purpose. Apart from the fact that *Causby* was a case of invasion of airspace that destroyed the use of the farm beneath and this New York City law has in nowise impaired the present use of the Terminal, the Landmarks Law neither exploits appellants' parcel for city purposes nor facilitates nor arises from any entrepreneurial operations of the city. The situation is not remotely like that in *Causby* where the airspace above the property was in the flight pattern for military aircraft. The Landmarks Law's effect is simply to prohibit appellants or anyone else from occupying portions of the airspace above the Terminal, while permitting appellants to use the remainder of the parcel in a gainful fashion. . . .

C

Rejection of appellants' broad arguments is not, however, the end of our inquiry, for all we thus far have established is that the New York City law is not rendered invalid by its failure to provide "just compensation" whenever a landmark owner is restricted in the exploitation of property interests, such as air rights, to a greater extent than provided for under applicable zoning laws. We now must consider whether the interference with appellants' property is of such a magnitude that "there must be an exercise of eminent domain and compensation to sustain [it]." Pennsylvania Coal Co. v. Mahon, 260 U.S., at 413. That inquiry may be narrowed to the question of the severity of the impact of the law on appellants' parcel, and its resolution in turn requires a careful assessment of the impact of the regulation on the Terminal site.

. . . [T]he New York City law does not interfere in any way with the present uses of the Terminal. Its designation as a landmark not only permits but contemplates that appellants may continue to use the property precisely as it has been used for the past 65 years: as a railroad terminal containing office space and concessions. So the law does not interfere with what must be regarded as Penn Central's primary expectation concerning the use of the parcel. More importantly, on this record, we must regard the New York City law as permitting Penn Central not only to profit from the Terminal but also to obtain a "reasonable return" on its investment.

Appellants, moreover, exaggerate the effect of the law on their ability to make use of the air rights above the Terminal in two respects. First, it simply cannot be maintained, on this record, that appellants have been prohibited from occupying *any* portion of the airspace above the Terminal. While the Commission's actions in denying applications to construct an office building in excess of 50 stories above the Terminal may indicate that it will refuse to issue a certificate of appropriateness for any comparably sized structure, nothing the Commission has said or done suggests an intention to prohibit *any* construction above the Terminal. The Commission's report emphasized that whether any construction would be allowed depended upon whether the proposed addition "would harmonize in scale, material and character with [the Terminal]." Since appellants have not sought approval for the construction of a smaller structure, we do not know that appellants will be denied any use of any portion of the airspace above the Terminal.

Second, to the extent appellants have been denied the right to build above the Terminal, it is not literally accurate to say that they have been denied *all* use of even those pre-existing air rights. Their ability to use these rights has not been abrogated; they are made transferable to at least eight parcels in the vicinity of the Terminal, one or two of which have been found suitable for the construction of new office buildings. Although appellants and others have argued that New York City's transferable development-rights program is far from ideal, the New York courts here supportably found that, at least in the case of the Terminal, the rights afforded are valuable. While these rights may well not have constituted "just compensation" if a "taking" had occurred, the rights nevertheless undoubtedly mitigate whatever financial burdens the

A Survey of Transferable Development Rights Mechanisms in New York City

Department of City Planning

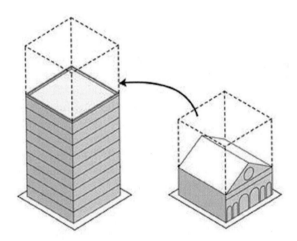

Development Rights Transfer
The landmarked building utilizes only a fraction of the permitted development rights
for the site, the remainder of which are transferred to the neighboring site within the
transfer area, which can now add to its development space.
Source: Department of City Planning, City of New York

law has imposed on appellants and, for that reason, are to be taken into account in considering the impact of regulation.

On this record, we conclude that the application of New York City's Landmarks Law has not effected a "taking" of appellants' property. The restrictions imposed are substantially related to the promotion of the general welfare and not only permit reasonable beneficial use of the landmark site but also afford appellants opportunities further to enhance not only the Terminal site proper but also other properties.

Affirmed.

REHNQUIST, J., with whom BURGER, C.J., and STEVENS, J., join, dissenting. . . .

I.

The Fifth Amendment provides in part: "nor shall private property be taken for public use, without just compensation." In a very literal sense, the actions of appellees violated this constitutional prohibition. Before the city of New York declared Grand Central Terminal to be a landmark, Penn Central could have used its "air rights" over the Terminal to build a multistory office building, at an apparent value of several million dollars per year. Today, the Terminal cannot be modified in *any* form, including the erection of additional stories, without the permission of the Landmark Preservation Commission, a permission which appellants, despite good-faith attempts, have so far been unable to obtain. Because the Taking Clause of the Fifth Amendment has not always been read literally, however, the constitutionality of appellees' actions requires a closer scrutiny of this Court's interpretation of the three key words in the Taking Clause — "property," "taken," and "just compensation."

A

Appellees do not dispute that valuable property rights have been destroyed. And the Court has frequently emphasized that the term "property" as used in the Taking Clause includes the entire "group of rights inhering in the citizen's [ownership]." United States v. General Motors Corp., 323 U.S. 373 (1945). The term is not used in the vulgar and untechnical sense of the physical thing with respect to which the citizen exercises rights recognized by law. [Instead, it] . . . denote[s] the *group of rights* inhering in the citizen's relation to the physical thing, *as the right to possess, use and dispose of it. . . .* The constitutional provision is addressed to *every sort of interest* the citizen may possess. Id., at 377-378 (emphasis added). While neighboring landowners are free to use their land and "air rights" in any way consistent with the broad boundaries of New York zoning, Penn Central, absent the permission of appellees, must forever maintain its property in its present state. The property has been thus subjected to a nonconsensual servitude not borne by any neighboring or similar properties.

B

Appellees have thus destroyed — in a literal sense, "taken" — substantial property rights of Penn Central. While the term "taken" might have been narrowly interpreted to include only physical seizures of property rights, "the construction of the phrase has not been so narrow. The courts have held that the deprivation of the former owner rather than the accretion of a right or interest to the sovereign constitutes the taking." Id., at 378. Because "not every destruction or injury to property by governmental action has been held to be a 'taking' in the constitutional sense," Armstrong v. United States, 364 U.S., at 48, however, this does not end our inquiry. But an examination of the two exceptions where the destruction of property does *not* constitute a taking demonstrates that a compensable taking has occurred here.

1

As early as 1887, the Court recognized that the government can prevent a property owner from using his property to injure others without having to compensate the owner for the value of the forbidden use. . . .

Thus, there is no "taking" where a city prohibits the operation of a brickyard within a residential area, see Hadacheck v. Sebastian, 239 U.S. 394 (1915), or forbids excavation for sand and gravel below the water line, see Goldblatt v. Hempstead, 369 U.S. 590 (1962). Nor is it relevant, where the government is merely prohibiting a noxious use of property, that the government would seem to be singling out a particular property owner.

The nuisance exception to the taking guarantee is not coterminous with the police power itself. The question is whether the forbidden use is dangerous to the safety, health, or welfare of others. . . .

Appellees are not prohibiting a nuisance. The record is clear that the proposed addition to the Grand Central Terminal would be in full compliance with zoning, height limitations, and other health and safety requirements. Instead, appellees are seeking to preserve what they believe to be an outstanding example of beaux-arts architecture. Penn Central is prevented from further developing its property basically because *too good* a job was done in designing and building it. The city of New York, because of its unadorned admiration for the design, has decided that the owners of the building must preserve it unchanged for the benefit of sightseeing New Yorkers and tourists.

Unlike land-use regulations, appellees' actions do not merely *prohibit* Penn Central from using its property in a narrow set of noxious ways. Instead, appellees have placed an *affirmative* duty on Penn Central to maintain the Terminal in its present state and in "good repair." Appellants are not free to use their property as they see fit within broad outer boundaries but must strictly adhere to their past use except where appellees conclude that alternative uses would not detract from the landmark. While Penn Central may continue to use the Terminal as it is presently designed, appellees otherwise "exercise complete dominion and control over the surface of the land," United States v. Causby, 328 U.S. 256, 262 (1946), and must compensate the owner for his loss. Ibid. "Property is taken in the constitutional sense when inroads are made upon an owner's use of it to an extent that, as between private parties, a servitude has been acquired." United States v. Dickinson, 331 U.S. 745, 748 (1947).

2

Even where the government prohibits a noninjurious use, the Court has ruled that a taking does not take place if the prohibition applies over a broad cross section of land and thereby "secure[s] an average reciprocity of advantage." Pennsylvania Coal Co. v. Mahon, 260 U.S., at 415. It is for this reason that zoning does not constitute a "taking." While zoning at times reduces *individual* property values, the burden is shared relatively evenly and it is reasonable to conclude that on the whole an individual who is harmed by one aspect of the zoning will be benefited by another.

Here, however, a multimillion dollar loss has been imposed on appellants; it is uniquely felt and is not offset by any benefits flowing from the preservation of some 400 other "landmarks" in New York City. Appellees have imposed a substantial cost on less than one one-tenth of one percent of the buildings in New York City for the general benefit of all its people. It is exactly this imposition of general costs on a few individuals at which the "taking" protection is directed. . . .

As Mr. Justice Holmes pointed out in Pennsylvania Coal Co. v. Mahon, "the question at bottom" in an eminent domain case "is upon whom the loss of the changes desired should fall." 260 U.S., at 416. The benefits that appellees believe will flow from preservation of the Grand Central Terminal will accrue to all the citizens of New York City. There is no reason to believe that appellants will enjoy a substantially greater share of these benefits. If the cost of preserving Grand Central Terminal were spread evenly across the entire population of the city of New York, the burden per person would be in cents per year—a minor cost appellees would surely concede for the benefit accrued. Instead, however, appellees would impose the entire cost of several million dollars per year on Penn Central. But it is precisely this sort of discrimination that the Fifth Amendment prohibits. . . .

C

Appellees, apparently recognizing that the constraints imposed on a landmark site constitute a taking for Fifth Amendment purposes, do not leave the property owner empty-handed. As the Court notes, the property owner may theoretically "transfer" his previous right to develop the landmark property to adjacent properties if they are under his control. Appellees have coined this system "Transfer Development Rights," or TDR's.

Of all the terms used in the Taking Clause, "just compensation" has the strictest meaning. The Fifth Amendment does not allow simply an approximate compensation but requires "a full and perfect equivalent for the property taken." Monongahela Navigation Co. v. United States, 148 U.S. 312, 326 (1893). . . .

Appellees contend that, even if they have "taken" appellants' property, TDR's constitute "just compensation." Appellants, of course, argue that TDR's are highly imperfect compensation. Because the lower courts held that there was no "taking," they did not have to reach the question of whether or not just compensation has already been awarded. The New York Court of Appeals' discussion of TDR's gives some support to appellants: "The many defects in New York City's program for development rights transfers have been detailed elsewhere. . . . The area to which transfer is permitted is severely limited [and] complex procedures are required to obtain a transfer permit." 42 N.Y.2d 324, 334-335, 366 N.E.2d 1271, 1277 (1977).

And in other cases the Court of Appeals has noted that TDR's have an "uncertain and contingent market value" and do "not adequately preserve" the value lost when a building is declared to be a landmark. French Investing Co. v. City of New York, 39 N.Y.2d 587, 591, 350 N.E.2d 381, 383, appeal dismissed, 429 U.S. 990 (1976). On the other hand, there is evidence in the record that Penn Central has been offered substantial amounts for its TDR's. Because the record on appeal is relatively slim, I would remand to the Court of Appeals for a determination of whether TDR's constitute a "full and perfect equivalent for the property taken." . . .

THE REST OF THE STORY . . .

The TDRs involved in *Penn Central* were unused for 40 years, but in 2015, the City of New York relaxed the zoning restrictions in the area around Grand Central, allegedly wiping out much if not all of the market value of the TDRs. The new owner of the TDRs filed suit, claiming that this rezoning, which provides more favorable treatment to neighboring property, is a taking of its TDRs, the very same TDRs that provided part of the justification for finding no taking in *Penn Central*. See Christopher Serkin, *Penn Central* Take Two, 92 Notre Dame L. Rev. 913 (2017).

Notes and Questions

1. *Conceptual severance, again.* Recall Note 3 on page 626. Does *Penn Central* reject conceptual severance?

2. *Factors in ad hoc review.* In *Pennsylvania Coal*, the Court engaged in an ad hoc form of review, identifying three relevant factors: (1) diminution in value;

(2) whether the regulation prevents a harm to the general public; and (3) whether the regulation secures an "average reciprocity of advantage." In *Penn Central*, the court also uses ad hoc review, referring to its analysis as "essentially *ad hoc*, factual inquiries." Compare with the *Pennsylvania Coal* factors the three factors Justice Brennan identifies as especially important:

▶ The economic impact of the regulation on the claimant
▶ The extent to which the regulation interferes with the owner's "distinct investment-backed expectations"
▶ The character of the governmental action

How do these factors compare with the *Pennsylvania Coal* factors? Is there any overlap between the two?

Consider the second factor—interference with the owner's "distinct investment-backed expectations." Both the factor and the phrase are drawn from Professor Frank Michelman's influential essay on takings, Property, Utility, and Fairness: Comments on the Ethical Foundations of "Just Compensation" Law, 80 Harv. L. Rev. 1165, 1229-1234 (1967). Is that factor different from the *Pennsylvania Coal* diminution-in-value test? Michelman saw the latter as calling for compensation when a claimant is deprived of "distinctly perceived, sharply crystallized, investment-backed expectations." Id. at 1223. His discussion suggests that *Pennsylvania Coal* is a case in point, for in *Pennsylvania Coal* the claimant had a distinct interest—the support estate—that was wiped out by the Kohler Act. What about the distinct interest of Penn Central in the air rights above Grand Central Terminal?

Does the timing of enactment of the landmark law matter? Suppose, for example, that the law had been enacted prior to Penn Central's purchase of Grand Central Terminal. Would that matter? See Palazzolo v. Rhode Island, 533 U.S. 606 (2001) (indicating that notice of an existing restriction would not necessarily bar a takings claim). We discuss *Palazzolo* infra at page 667.

Regarding the third factor, the character of the governmental action, part of the consideration is whether the government's action physically invaded the owner's space or was merely a regulation. Professor Thomas Merrill reads Justice Brennan's opinion more broadly, however. He suggests it can be read as saying that "a variety of considerations are relevant in assessing the character of the government action, including whether it is comprehensive, applies neutral and general criteria, does not single out particular owners for special treatment, and provides benefits to all members of the community." Thomas W. Merrill, The Character of the Governmental Action, 36 Vt. L. Rev. 649, 654-655 (2012).

3. *The relevant denominator.* In *Pennsylvania Coal* we encountered the "denominator problem"—determining the relevant property the value of which has diminished as a result of the regulation. In *Penn Central*, the Supreme Court regarded as the denominator the city tax block that was designated as the landmark site. Was this the proper denominator? Consider the approach taken by the New York Court of Appeals. That court stated:

> Numerous subways and bus routes pass through or near the terminal. Without the assistance of the city's transit system, now municipally owned and subsidized, the property [i.e., GCT], with or without a towering office structure atop it, would be of considerably decreased value. It is true that most city

property benefits to some extent from public transportation, but the benefit is peculiarly concentrated and great in the area surrounding Grand Central Terminal.

Absent this heavy public government investment in the terminal, the railroads, and the connecting transportation, it is indisputable that the terminal property would be worth but a fraction of its current economic value. [Penn Central Transportation Co. v. City of New York, 366 N.E.2d 1271, 1276 (N.Y. 1977).]

Does the photo on page 629, which shows Grand Central Terminal in its full setting while under construction, lend support to the Court of Appeals' analysis?

4. *TDRs.* Notice that the Court in *Penn Central* left unresolved the question whether TDRs can provide the "just compensation" required if a taking has occurred. See page 637. It appears to be the Court's view, however, that TDRs can ease the burden of a regulation such that it will not amount to a taking. Can you make sense of that line of thinking? If a given regulation without TDRs would be a taking but the same regulation with TDRs would not be a taking, isn't that just a roundabout way of saying that the TDRs do in fact amount to "just compensation," even though the value of the TDRs may fall short of the fair-market value ordinarily required in cases of condemnation? If so, the takings issue and the just-compensation requirement can be made, more or less, to disappear. See in this connection the concurring opinion of Justice Scalia in Suitum v. Tahoe Regional Planning Agency, 520 U.S. 725, 747-748 (1997): "Putting TDRs on the taking rather than the just-compensation side of the equation . . . is a clever, albeit transparent, device that seeks to take advantage of a peculiarity of our Takings-Clause jurisprudence: Whereas once there *is* a taking, the Constitution requires just (i.e. full) compensation, . . . a regulatory taking generally does not *occur* so long as the land retains substantial (albeit not its full) value."

2. Categorical Rules

LORETTO v. TELEPROMPTER MANHATTAN CATV CORP.

Supreme Court of the United States, 1982
458 U.S. 419

MARSHALL, J. This case presents the question whether a minor but permanent physical occupation of an owner's property authorized by government constitutes a "taking" of property for which just compensation is due under the Fifth and Fourteenth Amendments of the Constitution. . . . The New York Court of Appeals ruled that this appropriation does not amount to a taking. 53 N.Y.2d 124, 423 N.E.2d 320 (1981). Because we conclude that such a physical occupation of property is a taking, we reverse.

I.

Appellant Jean Loretto purchased a five-story apartment building located at 303 West 105th Street, New York City, in 1971. The previous owner had granted appellees Teleprompter Corporation and Teleprompter Manhattan CATV (collectively

Teleprompter) permission to install a cable on the building and the exclusive privilege of furnishing cable television (CATV) services to the tenants. The New York Court of Appeals described the installation as follows:

> On June 1, 1970 Teleprompter installed a cable slightly less than one-half inch in diameter and of approximately 30 feet in length along the length of the building about 18 inches above the roof top, and directional taps, approximately 4 inches by 4 inches by 4 inches, on the front and rear of the roof. By June 8, 1970 the cable had been extended another 4 to 6 feet and cable had been run from the directional taps to the adjoining building at 305 West 105th Street. [Id., at 135, 423 N.E.2d, at 324.]

Teleprompter also installed two large silver boxes along the roof cables. The cables are attached by screws or nails penetrating the masonry at approximately two-foot intervals, and other equipment is installed by bolts.

Initially, Teleprompter's roof cables did not service appellant's building. They were part of what could be described as a cable "highway" circumnavigating the city block, with service cables periodically dropped over the front or back of a building in which a tenant desired service. Crucial to such a network is the use of so-called "crossovers"—cable lines extending from one building to another in order to reach a new group of tenants. Two years after appellant purchased the building, Teleprompter connected a "noncrossover" line—i.e., one that provided CATV service to appellant's own tenants—by dropping a line to the first floor down the front of appellant's building.

Prior to 1973, Teleprompter routinely obtained authorization for its installations from property owners along the cable's route, compensating the owners at the standard rate of 5% of the gross revenues that Teleprompter realized from the particular property. To facilitate tenant access to CATV, the State of New York enacted § 828 of the Executive Law, effective January 1, 1973. Section 828 provides that a landlord may not "interfere with the installation of cable television facilities upon his property or premises," and may not demand payment from any tenant for permitting CATV, or demand payment from any CATV company "in excess of any amount which the [State Commission on Cable Television] shall, by regulation, determine to be reasonable." The landlord may, however, require the CATV company or the tenant to bear the cost of installation and to indemnify for any damage caused by the installation. Pursuant to § 828(1)(b), the State Commission has ruled that a onetime $1 payment is the normal fee to which a landlord is entitled. . . . The Commission ruled that this nominal fee, which the Commission concluded was equivalent to what the landlord would receive if the property were condemned pursuant to New York's Transportation Corporations Law, satisfied constitutional requirements "in the absence of a special showing of greater damages attributable to the taking."

Appellant did not discover the existence of the cable until after she had purchased the building. She brought a class action against Teleprompter in 1976 on behalf of all owners of real property in the State on which Teleprompter has placed CATV components, alleging that Teleprompter's installation was a trespass and, insofar as it relied on § 828, a taking without just compensation. She requested damages and injunctive relief. Appellee the City of New York, which has granted Teleprompter an exclusive franchise to provide CATV within certain areas of Manhattan, intervened. The Supreme Court, Special Term, granted summary judgment to Teleprompter and the city, upholding the constitutionality of §828 in both crossover and noncrossover situations. 98 Misc. 2d 944, 415 N.Y.S.2d 180 (1979). The Appellate Division affirmed without opinion. 73 App. Div. 2d 849, 422 N.Y.S.2d 550 (1979).

On appeal, the Court of Appeals . . . ruled that the law serves a legitimate police power purpose—eliminating landlord fees and conditions that inhibit the development of CATV, which has important educational and community benefits. Rejecting the argument that a physical occupation authorized by government is necessarily a taking, the court stated that the regulation does not have an excessive economic impact upon appellant when measured against her aggregate property rights, and that it does not interfere with any reasonable investment-backed expectations. . . .

II.

The Court of Appeals determined that § 828 serves the legitimate public purpose of "rapid development of and maximum penetration by a means of communication which has important educational and community aspects," and thus is within the State's police power. We have no reason to question that determination. It is a separate question, however, whether an otherwise valid regulation so frustrates property rights that compensation must be paid. We conclude that a permanent physical occupation authorized by government is a taking without regard to the public interests that it may serve. Our constitutional history confirms the rule, recent cases do not question it, and the purposes of the Takings Clause compel its retention.

A

In Penn Central Transportation Co. v. New York City, [438 U.S. 104 (1978)], the Court surveyed some of the general principles governing the Takings Clause. The Court noted that no "set formula" existed to determine, in all cases, whether compensation is constitutionally due for a government restriction of property. Ordinarily, the Court must engage in "essentially ad hoc, factual inquiries." Id., at 124. But the inquiry is not standardless. The economic impact of the regulation, especially the degree of interference with investment-backed expectations, is of particular significance.

> So, too, is the character of the government action. A "taking" may more readily be found when the interference with property can be characterized as a physical invasion by government, than when interference arises from some public program adjusting the benefits and burdens of economic life to promote the common good. [Ibid.]

As Penn Central affirms, the Court has often upheld substantial regulation of an owner's use of his own property where deemed necessary to promote the public interest. At the same time, we have long considered a physical intrusion by government to be a property restriction of an unusually serious character for purposes of the Takings Clause. Our cases further establish that when the physical intrusion reaches the extreme form of a permanent physical occupation, a taking has occurred. In such a case, "the character of the government action" not only is an important factor in resolving whether the action works a taking but also is determinative.

When faced with a constitutional challenge to a permanent physical occupation of real property, this Court has invariably found a taking. As early as 1872, in Pumpelly v. Green Bay Co., 13 Wall. 166, this Court held that the defendant's construction, pursuant to state authority, of a dam which permanently flooded plaintiff's property constituted a taking. A unanimous Court stated, without qualification, that "where real estate is actually invaded by superinduced additions of water, earth, sand, or other material, or by having any artificial structure placed on it, so as to effectually destroy or impair its usefulness, it is a taking, within the meaning of the Constitution." Id., at 181. More recent cases confirm the distinction between a permanent physical occupation, a physical invasion short of an occupation, and a regulation that merely restricts the use of property. In United States v. Causby, 328 U.S. 256 (1946), the Court ruled that frequent flights immediately above a landowner's property constituted a taking, comparing such overflights to the quintessential form of a taking:

> If, by reason of the frequency and altitude of the flights, respondents could not use this land for any purpose, their loss would be complete. It would be as complete as if the United States had entered upon the surface of the land and taken exclusive possession of it. [Id., at 261.] . . .

Although this Court's most recent cases have not addressed the precise issue before us, they have emphasized that physical *invasion* cases are special and have not repudiated the rule that any permanent physical *occupation* is a taking. The cases state or imply that a physical invasion is subject to a balancing process, but they do not suggest that a permanent physical occupation would ever be exempt from the Takings Clause. . . .

In short, when the "character of the governmental action," *Penn Central*, 438 U.S., at 124, is a permanent physical occupation of property, our cases uniformly have found a taking to the extent of the occupation, without regard to whether the action achieves an important public benefit or has only minimal economic impact on the owner.

B

The historical rule that a permanent physical occupation of another's property is a taking has more than tradition to commend it. Such an appropriation is perhaps the most serious form of invasion of an owner's property interests. . . .

Property rights in a physical thing have been described as the rights "to possess, use and dispose of it." United States v. General Motors Corp., 323 U.S. 373, 378 (1945). To the extent that the government permanently occupies physical property, it effectively destroys *each* of these rights. First, the owner has no right to possess the occupied space himself, and also has no power to exclude the occupier from possession and use of the space. The power to exclude has traditionally been considered one of the most treasured strands in an owner's bundle of property rights.[1] See *Kaiser Aetna*, 444 U.S., at 179-180; see also Restatement of Property § 7 (1936). Second, the permanent physical occupation of property forever denies the owner any power

---

1. The permanence and absolute exclusivity of a physical occupation distinguish it from temporary limitations on the right to exclude. Not every physical *invasion* is a taking. As PruneYard Shopping Center v. Robins, 447 U.S. 74 (1980), Kaiser Aetna v. United States, 444 U.S. 164 (1979), and the intermittent flooding cases reveal, such temporary limitations are subject to a more complex balancing process to determine whether they are a taking. The rationale is evident: they do not absolutely dispossess the owner of his rights to use, and exclude others from, his property.

The dissent objects that the distinction between a permanent physical occupation and a temporary invasion will not always be clear. This objection is overstated, and in any event is irrelevant to the critical point that a permanent physical occupation *is* unquestionably a taking. . . .

to control the use of the property; he not only cannot exclude others, but can make no nonpossessory use of the property. Although deprivation of the right to use and obtain a profit from property is not, in every case, independently sufficient to establish a taking, see Andrus v. Allard, supra, at 66, it is clearly relevant. Finally, even though the owner may retain the bare legal right to dispose of the occupied space by transfer or sale, the permanent occupation of that space by a stranger will ordinarily empty the right of any value, since the purchaser will also be unable to make any use of the property.

Moreover, an owner suffers a special kind of injury when a *stranger* directly invades and occupies the owner's property. . . . [P]roperty law has long protected an owner's expectation that he will be relatively undisturbed at least in the possession of his property. To require, as well, that the owner permit another to exercise complete dominion literally adds insult to injury. See Michelman, Property, Utility, and Fairness: Comments on the Ethical Foundations of "Just Compensation" Law, 80 Harv. L. Rev. 1165, 1228, and n.110 (1967). Furthermore, such an occupation is qualitatively more severe than a regulation of the *use* of property, even a regulation that imposes affirmative duties on the owner, since the owner may have no control over the timing, extent, or nature of the invasion.

The traditional rule also avoids otherwise difficult line-drawing problems. Few would disagree that if the State required landlords to permit third parties to install swimming pools on the landlords' rooftops for the convenience of the tenants, the requirement would be a taking. If the cable installation here occupied as much space, again, few would disagree that the occupation would be a taking. But constitutional protection for the rights of private property cannot be made to depend on the size of the area permanently occupied. Indeed, it is possible that in the future, additional cable installations that more significantly restrict a landlord's use of the roof of his building will be made. Section 828 requires a landlord to permit such multiple installations.

Finally, whether a permanent physical occupation has occurred presents relatively few problems of proof. The placement of a fixed structure on land or real property is an obvious fact that will rarely be subject to dispute. Once the fact of occupation is shown, of course, a court should consider the *extent* of the occupation as one relevant factor in determining the compensation due. For that reason, moreover, there is less need to consider the extent of the occupation in determining whether there is a taking in the first instance.

C

Teleprompter's cable installation on appellant's building constitutes a taking under the traditional test. The installation involved a direct physical attachment of plates, boxes, wires, bolts, and screws to the building, completely occupying space immediately above and upon the roof and along the building's exterior wall.[2]

---

2. It is constitutionally irrelevant whether appellant (or her predecessor in title) had previously occupied this space, since a "landowner owns at least as much of the space above the ground as he can occupy or use in connection with the land." United States v. Causby, supra, at 264.

The dissent asserts that a taking of about one-eighth of a cubic foot of space is not of constitutional significance. The assertion appears to be factually incorrect, since it ignores the two large silver boxes that appellant identified as part of the installation. Although the record does not reveal their size, appellant states that they are approximately 18" × 12" × 6", and appellees do not dispute this statement. The displaced volume, then, is in excess of 1 1/2 cubic feet. In any event, these facts are not critical; whether the installation is a taking does not depend on whether the volume of space it occupies is bigger than a breadbox.

Loretto's Apartment House
303 West 105th Street, New York City
Note the cable television line, a little left of center, dropping down the front of the building to the first floor.

In light of our analysis we find no constitutional difference between a crossover and a noncrossover installation. The portions of the installation necessary for both crossovers and noncrossovers permanently appropriate appellant's property. Accordingly, each type of installation is a taking.

Appellees raise a series of objections to application of the traditional rule here. Teleprompter notes that the law applies only to buildings used as rental property, and draws the conclusion that the law is simply a permissible regulation of the use of real property. We fail to see, however, why a physical occupation of one type of property but not another type is any less a physical occupation. Insofar as Teleprompter means to suggest that this is not a permanent physical invasion, we must differ. So long as the property remains residential and a CATV company wishes to retain the installation, the landlord must permit it.[3]

Teleprompter also asserts the related argument that the State has effectively granted a tenant the property right to have a CATV installation placed on the roof of his building, as an appurtenance to the tenant's leasehold. The short answer is that §828(1)(a) does not purport to give the *tenant* any enforceable property rights with respect to CATV installation, and the lower courts did not rest their decisions on this ground. Of course, Teleprompter, not appellant's tenants, actually owns the installation. Moreover, the government does not have unlimited power to redefine property rights. Finally, we do not agree with appellees that application of the physical occupation rule will have dire consequences for the government's power to adjust landlord-tenant relationships. This Court has consistently affirmed that States have broad power to regulate housing conditions in general and the landlord-tenant relationship in particular without paying compensation for all economic injuries that such regulation entails. In none of these cases, however, did the government authorize the permanent occupation of the landlord's property by a third party. Consequently, our holding today in no way alters the analysis governing the State's power to require landlords to comply with building codes and provide utility connections, mailboxes, smoke detectors, fire extinguishers, and the like in the common area of a building. So long as these regulations do not require the landlord to suffer the physical occupation of a portion of his building by a third party, they will be analyzed under the multifactor inquiry generally applicable to nonpossessory governmental activity. See Penn Central Transportation Co. v. New York City, 438 U.S. 104 (1978).[4]

III.

Our holding today is very narrow. We affirm the traditional rule that a permanent physical occupation of property is a taking. In such a case, the property owner entertains a historically rooted expectation of compensation, and the character of the invasion is qualitatively more intrusive than perhaps any other category of property regulation. We do not, however, question the equally substantial authority upholding

---

3. It is true that the landlord could avoid the requirements of § 828 by ceasing to rent the building to tenants. But a landlord's ability to rent his property may not be conditioned on his forfeiting the right to compensation for a physical occupation. . . .

4. If § 828 required landlords to provide cable installation if a tenant so desires, the statute might present a different question from the question before us, since the landlord would own the installation. Ownership would give the landlord rights to the placement, manner, use, and possibly the disposition of the installation. The fact of ownership is, contrary to the dissent, not simply "incidental"; it would give a landlord (rather than a CATV company) full authority over the installation except only as government specifically limited that authority. The *landlord* would decide how to comply with applicable government regulations concerning CATV and therefore could minimize the physical, esthetic, and other effects of the installation. Moreover, if the landlord wished to repair, demolish, or construct in the area of the building where the installation is located, he need not incur the burden of obtaining the CATV company's cooperation in moving the cable.

In this case, by contrast, appellant suffered injury that might have been obviated if she had owned the cable and could exercise control over its installation. The drilling and stapling that accompanied installation apparently caused physical damage to appellant's building. Appellant, who resides in the building, further testified that the cable installation is "ugly." Although § 828 provides that a landlord may require "reasonable" conditions that are "necessary" to protect the appearance of the premises and may seek indemnity for damage, these provisions are somewhat limited. Even if the provisions are effective, the inconvenience to the landlord of initiating the repairs remains a cognizable burden.

a State's broad power to impose appropriate restrictions upon an owner's *use* of his property.

Furthermore, our conclusion that § 828 works a taking of a portion of appellant's property does not presuppose that the fee which many landlords had obtained by Teleprompter prior to the law's enactment is a proper measure of the value of the property taken. The issue of the amount of compensation that is due, on which we express no opinion, is a matter for the state courts to consider on remand. . . .

BLACKMUN, J., with whom BRENNAN and WHITE, JJ., join, dissenting. . . . In a curiously anachronistic decision, the Court today acknowledges its historical disavowal of set formulae in almost the same breath as it constructs a rigid per se takings rule: "a permanent physical occupation authorized by government is a taking without regard to the public interests that it may serve." To sustain its rule against our recent precedents, the Court erects a strained and untenable distinction between "temporary physical invasions," whose constitutionality concededly "is subject to a balancing process," and "permanent physical occupations," which are "taking[s] without regard to other factors that a court might ordinarily examine."

In my view, the Court's approach "reduces the constitutional issue to a formalistic quibble" over whether property has been "permanently occupied" or "temporarily invaded." Sax, Takings and the Police Power, 74 Yale L.J. 36, 37 (1964). The Court's application of its formula to the facts of this case vividly illustrates that its approach is potentially dangerous as well as misguided. . . .

The Court's recent Takings Clause decisions teach that *nonphysical* government intrusions on private property, such as zoning ordinances and other land-use restrictions, have become the rule rather than the exception. Modern government regulation exudes intangible "externalities" that may diminish the value of private property far more than minor physical touchings. . . .

Precisely because the extent to which the government may injure private interests now depends so little on whether or not it has authorized a "physical contact," the Court has avoided per se takings rules resting on outmoded distinctions between physical and nonphysical intrusions. As one commentator has observed, a takings rule based on such a distinction is inherently suspect because "its capacity to distinguish, even crudely, between significant and insignificant losses is too puny to be taken seriously." Michelman, Property, Utility, and Fairness: Comments on the Ethical Foundations of "Just Compensation" Law, 80 Harv. L. Rev. 1165, 1227 (1967).

Surprisingly, the Court draws an even finer distinction today—between "temporary physical invasions" and "permanent physical occupations." When the government authorizes the latter type of intrusion, the Court would find "a taking without regard to the public interests" the regulation may serve. Yet an examination of each of the three words in the Court's "permanent physical occupation" formula illustrates that the newly created distinction is even less substantial than the distinction between physical and nonphysical intrusions that the Court already has rejected.

First, what does the Court mean by "permanent"? Since all "temporary limitations on the right to exclude" remain "subject to a more complex balancing process to determine whether they are a taking," the Court presumably describes a government intrusion that lasts forever. But as the Court itself concedes, § 828 does not require appellant to permit the cable installation forever, but only "[s]o long as the property remains residential and a CATV company wishes to retain the installation." This is far from "permanent."

. . . If § 828 authorizes a "permanent" occupation, and thus works a taking "without regard to the public interests that it may serve," then all other New York statutes that require a landlord to make physical attachments to his rental property also must constitute takings, even if they serve indisputably valid public interests in tenant protection and safety.[5]

The Court denies that its theory invalidates these statutes, because they "do not require the landlord to suffer the physical occupation of a portion of his building by a third party." But surely this factor cannot be determinative, since the Court simultaneously recognizes that temporary invasions by third parties are not subject to a per se rule. Nor can the qualitative difference arise from the incidental fact that, under § 828, Teleprompter, rather than appellant or her tenants, owns the cable installation. If anything, § 828 leaves appellant better off than do other housing statutes, since it ensures that her property will not be damaged esthetically or physically, without burdening her with the cost of buying or maintaining the cable.

In any event, under the Court's test, the "third party" problem would remain even if appellant herself owned the cable. So long as Teleprompter continuously passed its electronic signal through the cable, a litigant could argue that the second element of the Court's formula—a "physical touching" by a stranger—was satisfied and that § 828 therefore worked a taking. Literally read, the Court's test opens the door to endless metaphysical struggles over whether or not an individual's property has been "physically" touched. . . .

Third, the Court's talismanic distinction between a continuous "occupation" and a transient "invasion" finds no basis in either economic logic or Takings Clause precedent. In the landlord-tenant context, the Court has upheld against takings challenges rent control statutes permitting "temporary" physical invasions of considerable economic magnitude. . . .

For constitutional purposes, the relevant question cannot be solely *whether* the State has interfered in some minimal way with an owner's use of space on her building. Any intelligible takings inquiry must also ask whether the *extent* of the State's interference is so severe as to constitute a compensable taking in light of the owner's alternative uses for the property. Appellant freely admitted that she would have had no other use for the cable-occupied space, were Teleprompter's equipment not on her building.

The Court's third and final argument is that § 828 has deprived appellant of her "power to exclude the occupier from possession and use of the space" occupied by the cable. This argument has two flaws. First, it unjustifiably assumes that appellant's tenants have no countervailing property interest in permitting Teleprompter to use that space.[6] Second, it suggests that the New York legislature may not exercise its police power to affect appellant's common-law right to exclude Teleprompter even from one-eighth cubic foot of roof space. . . .

---

5. See, e.g., N.Y. Mult. Dwell. Law § 35 (McKinney 1974) (requiring entrance doors and lights); § 36 (windows and skylights for public halls and stairs); § 50-a (Supp. 1982) (locks and intercommunication systems); § 50-c (lobby attendants); § 51-a (peepholes); § 51-b (elevator mirrors); § 53 (fire escapes); § 57 (bells and mail receptacles); § 67(3) (fire sprinklers). See also Queenside Hills Realty Co. v. Saxl, 328 U.S. 80 (1946) (upholding constitutionality of New York fire sprinkler provision). . . .

6. It is far from clear that, under New York law, appellant's tenants would lack all property interests in the few square inches on the exterior of the building to which Teleprompter's cable and hardware attach. Under modern landlord-tenant law, a residential tenancy is not merely a possessory interest in specified space, but also a contract for the provision of a package of services and facilities necessary and appurtenant to that space. . . .

This Court now reaches back in time for a per se rule that disrupts that legislative determination. I would affirm the judgment and uphold the reasoning of the New York Court of Appeals.

THE REST OF THE STORY ...

On remand in *Loretto*, the New York Court of Appeals sustained the validity of the statutory provisions empowering the Commission on Cable Television to set compensation for the takings in question at $1. Loretto v. Teleprompter Manhattan CATV Corp., 446 N.E.2d 428 (N.Y. 1983). The Commission concluded that $1 was sufficient compensation because the presence of cable TV usually increases a building's value.

Notes and Questions

1. *"Per se" (or "categorical") rules.* As Justice Blackmun observes in his dissenting opinion (at page 650), the majority in *Loretto* decided the case in terms of a per se or categorical rule: a permanent physical occupation authorized by the government is a taking, period. As we shall see, the Court has developed a small number of such rules to determine whether a regulatory taking exists. Such categorical rules are the exceptions to the Court's usual balancing approach in regulatory takings cases. As we go through the remaining materials in this section, think about which approach—categorical rules or ad hoc balancing—is preferable.

One argument that Justice Marshall makes in favor of the *Loretto* categorical rule is that it avoids "difficult line-drawing problems." Do you agree? Consider the dissenting opinion of Justice Blackmun.

2. *"Permanent physical occupation" post-*Loretto. How common will cases of permanent physical occupation be? Judging from the history after *Loretto*, the answer is not very. The Court has interpreted the "permanent physical occupation" exception narrowly, it seems. In post-*Loretto* cases, the Court has held that where the owner has voluntarily permitted the initial occupation, government regulations that perpetuate the occupation do not effect a *Loretto*-like physical taking. See Yee v. City of Escondido, 503 U.S. 519 (1992) (rent control ordinance held not to constitute a per se taking); FCC v. Florida Power Corp., 480 U.S. 245 (1987) (federal order requiring utility companies to lease space on poles to cable companies not a per se taking where original lease was voluntary). As we shall see, however, in cases involving land use exactions, the Court arguably expanded the *Loretto* rule. See pages 680-681.

3. Loretto *and personal property.* Loretto itself involved real property. In Horne v. Department of Agriculture, 576 U.S. 350 (2015), the Supreme Court held that the per se rule for physical takings applies to personal property as well as to land. The case involved a government regulatory program designed to shore up the price of raisins by requiring farmers to hand over to the government a certain percentage of their raisin crop. The Court determined that this program constituted a categorical physical taking of personal property. The Court made a sharp

distinction between a physical taking of personal property and a regulation of its use. The latter does not effect a per se taking; indeed, the Takings Clause permits many forms of regulation of personal property (e.g., regulation of dangerous drugs). In dissent, Justice Sotomayor argued that this was a distinction without a difference.

More recently, in Maryland Shall Issue, Inc. v. Hogan, 2020 WL 3494322 (4th Cir. June 29, 2020), the Fourth Circuit held that *Horne* did not apply where a Maryland statute made it a crime to "manufacture, possess, sell, offer to sell, transfer, purchase, or receive" "rapid fire trigger activators" ("devices that, when attached to a firearm, increase its rate of fire or trigger activation"). The court distinguished *Horne* on the ground that unlike *Horne*, where the regulation required that the raisins actually be turned over to the government, here no *Loretto*-type physical appropriation occurred. Although the Maryland statute here "may make the personal property economically worthless, owners are 'aware of th[at] possibility' in areas where the State has a 'traditionally high degree of control.'" Id., quoting Lucas v. South Carolina Coastal Council, 505 U.S. 1003, 1027-1028 (1992). We discuss *Lucas* on pages 654-668. Is the court's distinction in *Maryland Shall Issue* persuasive?

BACKGROUND, BRIEFLY

In the late nineteenth and early twentieth centuries, the Supreme Court decided a series of cases that developed an important doctrine known as the *noxious use* or *public nuisance* doctrine. According to this doctrine, a regulation enacted pursuant to the state's police power for the purpose of abating a public nuisance is not a taking, even if it results in a substantial loss for the owner. See, e.g., Hadacheck v. Sebastian, 239 U.S. 394 (1915) (city ordinance prohibiting manufacture of bricks within city limits not a taking, notwithstanding decline in value of claimant's factory from $800,000 to $60,000); Mugler v. Kansas, 123 U.S. 623 (1887) (statute prohibiting manufacture of alcohol not a taking despite forcing claimant's brewery out of business). Though not without its defenders, the noxious use doctrine has been criticized as a basis for deciding when a regulation amounts to a taking. In his influential 1967 Harvard Law Review article, Professor Frank Michelman identified a "basic difficulty" with the doctrine: in the absence of a neutral benchmark, a regulation that purports to prevent public harms (and therefore triggers no compensation obligation) can just as easily be seen as one that extracts a benefit from an owner for the public (triggering a constitutional obligation to compensate the owner). See Michelman, Property, Utility, and Fairness, supra, at 1196-1197. Consider how the Supreme Court deals with this problem in the case that follows.

Think back to the diminution-in-value test of *Pennsylvania Coal* (stated on page 622): "if regulation goes too far it will be recognized as a taking." If, then, a regulation wipes out all value, won't this always be going "too far"? But what if the regulation claims to control a nuisance? Or what if the property owner had no "investment-backed expectations" (*Penn Central*, on page 645)? The following case addresses these questions.

LUCAS v. SOUTH CAROLINA COASTAL COUNCIL

Supreme Court of the United States, 1992
505 U.S. 1003

SCALIA, J. [South Carolina began managing its coastal zone in 1977, when it enacted a Coastal Zone Management Act (the federal government had enacted similar legislation in 1972). The 1977 law required owners of coastal land in "critical areas" (including beaches and immediately adjacent sand dunes) to obtain a permit from the South Carolina Coastal Council prior to committing the land to a use other than the use that the critical area was devoted to on September 28, 1977.

In 1986, petitioner Lucas paid $975,000 for two residential lots on an island off the coast of South Carolina. He intended to build single-family houses on the lots and, because no parts of the parcels were critical areas under the 1977 legislation, he did not need to get a permit. His plans to build, however, were halted by new legislation, the Beachfront Management Act, enacted by the state in 1988. The act had the direct effect of barring Lucas from building any permanent habitable structures on his two lots. A state trial court found that the act made Lucas's property "valueless."

Lucas filed suit in state court, claiming a taking. The trial court agreed, but the South Carolina Supreme Court reversed, holding that when a land use regulation is designed "to prevent serious public harm," no compensation is due regardless of the regulation's effect on the property's value. 305 S.C. 376, 383, 404 S.E.2d 895, 898 (1991).

The United States Supreme Court granted certiorari.]

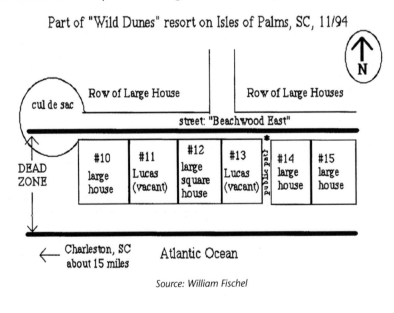

Part of "Wild Dunes" resort on Isles of Palms, SC, 11/94

Source: William Fischel

III.

A

Prior to Justice Holmes' exposition in Pennsylvania Coal Co. v. Mahon, 260 U.S. 393 (1922), it was generally thought that the Takings Clause reached only a "direct appropriation" of property, Legal Tender Cases, 12 Wall. 457, 551 (1871), or the functional equivalent of a "practical ouster of [the owner's] possession." Transportation Co. v. Chicago, 99 U.S. 635, 642 (1879). . . . Justice Holmes recognized in *Mahon*, however, that if the protection against physical appropriations of private property was to be meaningfully enforced, the government's power to redefine the range of interests included in the ownership of property was necessarily constrained by constitutional limits. . . . These considerations gave birth in that case to the oft-cited maxim that, "while property may be regulated to a certain extent, if regulation goes too far it will be recognized as a taking."

Nevertheless, our decision in *Mahon* offered little insight into when, and under what circumstances, a given regulation would be seen as going "too far" for purposes of the Fifth Amendment. In 70-odd years of succeeding "regulatory takings" jurisprudence, we have generally eschewed any "'set formula'" for determining how far is too far, preferring to "engag[e] in . . . essentially ad hoc, factual inquiries," Penn Central Transportation Co. v. New York City, 438 U.S. 104, 124 (1978) (quoting Goldblatt v. Hempstead, 369 U.S. 590, 594 (1962)). See Epstein, Takings: Descent and Resurrection, 1987 Sup. Ct. Rev. 1, 4. We have, however, described at least two discrete categories of regulatory action as compensable without case-specific inquiry into the public interest advanced in support of the restraint. The first encompasses regulations that compel the property owner to suffer a physical "invasion" of his property. In general (at least with regard to permanent invasions), no matter how minute the intrusion, and no matter how weighty the public purpose behind it, we have required compensation [citing *Loretto*, reproduced at page 643].

The second situation in which we have found categorical treatment appropriate is where regulation denies all economically beneficial or productive use of land. . . . As we have said on numerous occasions, the Fifth Amendment is violated when land-use regulation "does not substantially advance legitimate state interests *or denies an owner economically viable use of his land.*" [Agins v. City of Tiburon, 447 U.S. 255, 260 (1980).][7]

---

7. Regrettably, the rhetorical force of our "deprivation of all economically feasible use" rule is greater than its precision, since the rule does not make clear the "property interest" against which the loss of value is to be measured. When, for example, a regulation requires a developer to leave 90% of a rural tract in its natural state, it is unclear whether we would analyze the situation as one in which the owner has been deprived of all economically beneficial use of the burdened portion of the tract, or as one in which the owner has suffered a mere diminution in value of the tract as a whole. (For an extreme—and, we think, unsupportable—view of the relevant calculus, see Penn Central Transportation Co. v. New York City, 42 N.Y.2d 324, 333-334, 397 N.Y.S.2d 914, 920, 366 N.E.2d 1271, 1276-1277 (1977), aff'd, 438 U.S. 104 (1978), where the state court examined the diminution in a particular parcel's value produced by a municipal ordinance in light of total value of the taking claimant's other holdings in the vicinity.) Unsurprisingly, this uncertainty regarding the composition of the denominator in our "deprivation" fraction has produced inconsistent pronouncements by the Court. Compare Pennsylvania Coal Co. v. Mahon, 260 U.S. 393, 414 (1922) (law restricting subsurface extraction of coal held to effect a taking), with Keystone Bituminous Coal Assn. v. DeBenedictis, 480 U.S. 470, 497-502 (1987) (nearly identical law held not to effect a taking); see also id., at 515-520 (Rehnquist, C.J., dissenting); Rose, *Mahon* Reconstructed: Why the Takings Issue is Still a Muddle, 57 S. Cal. L. Rev. 561, 566-569 (1984). The answer to this difficult question may lie in how the owner's reasonable expectations have been shaped by the State's law of property—i.e., whether and to what degree the State's law has accorded legal recognition and protection to the particular interest in land with respect to which the takings claimant alleges a diminution in (or elimination of) value. In any event, we avoid this difficulty in the present case, since the "interest in land" that Lucas has pleaded (a fee simple interest) is an estate with a rich tradition of protection at common law, and since the South Carolina Court of Common Pleas found that the Beachfront Management Act left each of Lucas's beachfront lots without economic value.

We have never set forth the justification for this rule. Perhaps it is simply, as Justice Brennan suggested, that total deprivation of beneficial use is, from the landowner's point of view, the equivalent of a physical appropriation. See San Diego Gas & Electric Co. v. San Diego, 450 U.S., at 652 (Brennan, J., dissenting). "[F]or what is the land but the profits thereof[?]" 1 E. Coke, Institutes ch. 1, § 1 (1st Am. ed. 1812). Surely, at least, in the extraordinary circumstance when *no* productive or economically beneficial use of land is permitted, it is less realistic to indulge our usual assumption that the legislature is simply "adjusting the benefits and burdens of economic life," *Penn Central Transportation Co.*, 438 U.S., at 124, in a manner that secures an "average reciprocity of advantage" to everyone concerned. Pennsylvania Coal Co. v. Mahon, 260 U.S., at 415. And the *functional* basis for permitting the government, by regulation, to affect property values without compensation—that "Government hardly could go on if to some extent values incident to property could not be diminished without paying for every such change in the general law," id., at 413—does not apply to the relatively rare situations where the government has deprived a landowner of all economically beneficial uses.

On the other side of the balance, affirmatively supporting a compensation requirement, is the fact that regulations that leave the owner of land without economically beneficial or productive options for its use—typically, as here, by requiring land to be left substantially in its natural state—carry with them a heightened risk that private property is being pressed into some form of public service under the guise of mitigating serious public harm. . . . As Justice Brennan explained: "From the government's point of view, the benefits flowing to the public from preservation of open space through regulation may be equally great as from creating a wildlife refuge through formal condemnation or increasing electricity production through a dam project that floods private property." *San Diego Gas & Elec. Co.*, supra, 450 U.S., at 652 (Brennan, J., dissenting). The many statutes on the books, both state and federal, that provide for the use of eminent domain to impose servitudes on private scenic lands preventing developmental uses, or to acquire such lands altogether, suggest the practical equivalence in this setting of negative regulation and appropriation. . . .

We think, in short, that there are good reasons for our frequently expressed belief that when the owner of real property has been called upon to sacrifice *all* economically beneficial uses in the name of the common good, that is, to leave his property economically idle, he has suffered a taking.[8]

---

8. Justice Stevens criticizes the "deprivation of all economically beneficial use" rule as "wholly arbitrary," in that "[the] landowner whose property is diminished in value 95% recovers nothing," while the landowner who suffers a complete elimination of value "recovers the land's full value." This analysis errs in its assumption that the landowner whose deprivation is one step short of complete is not entitled to compensation. Such an owner might not be able to claim the benefit of our categorical formulation, but, as we have acknowledged time and again, "[t]he economic impact of the regulation on the claimant and . . . the extent to which the regulation has interfered with distinct investment-backed expectations" are keenly relevant to takings analysis generally. Penn Central Transportation Co. v. New York City, 438 U.S. 104 (1978). It is true that in at least *some* cases the landowner with 95% loss will get nothing, while the landowner with total loss will recover in full. But that occasional result is no more strange than the gross disparity between the landowner whose premises are taken for a highway (who recovers in full) and the landowner whose property is reduced to 5% of its former value by the highway (who recovers nothing). Takings law is full of these "all-or-nothing" situations.

Justice Stevens similarly misinterprets our focus on "developmental" uses of property (the uses proscribed by the Beachfront Management Act) as betraying an "assumption that the only uses of property cognizable under the Constitution are *developmental* uses." We make no such assumption. Though our prior takings cases evince an abiding concern for the productive use of, and economic investment in, land, there are plainly a number of noneconomic interests in land whose impairment will invite exceedingly close scrutiny under the Takings Clause. See, e.g., Loretto v. Teleprompter Manhattan CATV Corp., 458 U.S. 419, 436 (1982) (interest in excluding strangers from one's land).

David Lucas's lots, Isle of Palms, South Carolina
The lots are in the gated community of Wild Dunes.

B

The trial court found Lucas's two beachfront lots to have been rendered valueless by respondent's enforcement of the coastal-zone construction ban. Under Lucas's theory of the case, which rested upon our "no economically viable use" statements, that finding entitled him to compensation. Lucas believed it unnecessary to take issue with either the purposes behind the Beachfront Management Act, or the means chosen by the South Carolina Legislature to effectuate those purposes. The South Carolina Supreme Court, however, thought otherwise. In its view, the Beachfront Management Act was no ordinary enactment, but involved an exercise of South Carolina's "police powers" to mitigate the harm to the public interest that petitioner's use of his land might occasion. By neglecting to dispute the findings enumerated in the Act or otherwise to challenge the legislature's purposes, petitioner concede[d] that the beach/dune area of South Carolina's shores is an extremely valuable public resource; that the erection of new construction, *inter alia*, contributes to the erosion and destruction of this public resource; and that discouraging new construction in close proximity to the beach/dune area is necessary to prevent a great public harm. In the court's view, these concessions brought petitioner's challenge within a long line of this Court's cases sustaining against Due Process and Takings Clause challenges the State's use of its "police powers" to enjoin a property owner from activities akin to public nuisances. See Mugler v. Kansas, 123 U.S. 623 (1887) (law prohibiting manufacture of alcoholic beverages); Hadacheck v. Sebastian, 239 U.S. 394 (1915) (law barring operation of brick mill in residential area); Miller v. Schoene, 276 U.S. 272 (1928) (order to destroy diseased cedar trees to prevent infection of nearby orchards); Goldblatt v. Hempstead, 369 U.S. 590 (1962) (law effectively preventing continued operation of quarry in residential area).

It is correct that many of our prior opinions have suggested that "harmful or noxious uses" of property may be proscribed by government regulation without the requirement of compensation. For a number of reasons, however, we think the South

Carolina Supreme Court was too quick to conclude that that principle decides the present case. The "harmful or noxious uses" principle was the Court's early attempt to describe in theoretical terms why government may, consistent with the Takings Clause, affect property values by regulation without incurring an obligation to compensate—a reality we nowadays acknowledge explicitly with respect to the full scope of the State's police power. . . . "Harmful or noxious use" analysis was, in other words, simply the progenitor of our more contemporary statements that "land-use regulation does not effect a taking if it 'substantially advance[s] legitimate state interests.' . . ." Nollan [v. California Coastal Commn., 483 U.S. 825, 834 (1987)] (quoting Agins v. Tiburon, 447 U.S., at 260). . . .

The transition from our early focus on control of "noxious" uses to our contemporary understanding of the broad realm within which government may regulate without compensation was an easy one, since the distinction between "harm-preventing" and "benefit-conferring" regulation is often in the eye of the beholder. It is quite possible, for example, to describe in *either* fashion the ecological, economic, and aesthetic concerns that inspired the South Carolina legislature in the present case. One could say that imposing a servitude on Lucas's land is necessary in order to prevent his use of it from "harming" South Carolina's ecological resources; or, instead, in order to achieve the "benefits" of an ecological preserve. . . . Whether one or the other of the competing characterizations will come to one's lips in a particular case depends primarily upon one's evaluation of the worth of competing uses of real estate. . . . A given restraint will be seen as mitigating "harm" to the adjacent parcels or securing a "benefit" for them, depending upon the observer's evaluation of the relative importance of the use that the restraint favors. . . . Whether Lucas's construction of single-family residences on his parcels should be described as bringing "harm" to South Carolina's adjacent ecological resources thus depends principally upon whether the describer believes that the State's use interest in nurturing those resources is so important that *any* competing adjacent use must yield.[9]

When it is understood that "prevention of harmful use" was merely our early formulation of the police power justification necessary to sustain (without compensation) *any* regulatory diminution in value; and that the distinction between regulation that "prevents harmful use" and that which "confers benefits" is difficult, if not impossible, to discern on an objective, value-free basis; it becomes self-evident that noxious-use logic cannot serve as a touchstone to distinguish regulatory "takings"—which require compensation—from regulatory deprivations that do not require compensation. *A fortiori* the legislature's recitation of a noxious-use justification cannot be the basis for departing from our categorical rule that total regulatory takings must be compensated. If it were, departure would virtually always be allowed. The South Carolina Supreme Court's approach would essentially nullify *Mahon*'s affirmation of limits to the noncompensable exercise of the police power. Our cases provide no support for this: None of them that employed the logic of "harmful use" prevention to sustain a

---

9. In Justice Blackmun's view, even with respect to regulations that deprive an owner of all developmental or economically beneficial land uses, the test for required compensation is whether the legislature has recited a harm-preventing justification for its action. Since such a justification can be formulated in practically every case, this amounts to a test of whether the legislature has a stupid staff. We think the Takings Clause requires courts to do more than insist upon artful harm-preventing characterizations.

regulation involved an allegation that the regulation wholly eliminated the value of the claimant's land. . . .

Where the State seeks to sustain regulation that deprives land of all economically beneficial use, we think it may resist compensation only if the logically antecedent inquiry into the nature of the owner's estate shows that the proscribed use interests were not part of his title to begin with. This accords, we think, with our "takings" jurisprudence, which has traditionally been guided by the understandings of our citizens regarding the content of, and the State's power over, the "bundle of rights" that they acquire when they obtain title to property. It seems to us that the property owner necessarily expects the uses of his property to be restricted, from time to time, by various measures newly enacted by the State in legitimate exercise of its police powers. . . . And in the case of personal property, by reason of the State's traditionally high degree of control over commercial dealings, he ought to be aware of the possibility that new regulation might even render his property economically worthless (at least if the property's only economically productive use is sale or manufacture for sale), see Andrus v. Allard, 444 U.S. 51, 66-67 (1979) (prohibition on sale of eagle feathers). In the case of land, however, we think the notion pressed by the Council that title is somehow held subject to the "implied limitation" that the State may subsequently eliminate all economically valuable use is inconsistent with the historical compact recorded in the Takings Clause that has become part of our constitutional culture.

Where "permanent physical occupation" of land is concerned, we have refused to allow the government to decree it anew (without compensation), no matter how weighty the asserted "public interests" involved, Loretto v. Teleprompter Manhattan CATV Corp., 458 U.S., at 426—though we assuredly *would* permit the government to assert a permanent easement that was a pre-existing limitation upon the landowner's title. . . . We believe similar treatment must be accorded confiscatory regulations, i.e., regulations that prohibit all economically beneficial use of land: Any limitation so severe cannot be newly legislated or decreed (without compensation), but must inhere in the title itself, in the restrictions that background principles of the State's law of property and nuisance already place upon land ownership. A law or decree with such an effect must, in other words, do no more than duplicate the result that could have been achieved in the courts—by adjacent landowners (or other uniquely affected persons) under the State's law of private nuisance, or by the State under its complementary power to abate nuisances that affect the public generally, or otherwise.[10]

On this analysis, the owner of a lake bed, for example, would not be entitled to compensation when he is denied the requisite permit to engage in a landfilling operation that would have the effect of flooding others' land. Nor the corporate owner of a nuclear generating plant, when it is directed to remove all improvements from its land upon discovery that the plant sits astride an earthquake fault. Such regulatory action may well have the effect of eliminating the land's only economically productive use, but it does not proscribe a productive use that was previously permissible under relevant property and nuisance principles. The use of these properties for what are now expressly prohibited purposes was *always* unlawful, and (subject to other

---

10. The principal "otherwise" that we have in mind is litigation absolving the State (or private parties) of liability for the destruction of "real and personal property, in cases of actual necessity, to prevent the spreading of a fire" or to forestall other grave threats to the lives and property of others. Bowditch v. Boston, 101 U.S. 16, 18-19 (1880). . . .

constitutional limitations) it was open to the State at any point to make the implication of those background principles of nuisance and property law explicit. . . . In light of our traditional resort to "existing rules or understandings that stem from an independent source such as state law" to define the range of interests that qualify for protection as "property" under the Fifth (and Fourteenth) amendments, . . . this recognition that the Takings Clause does not require compensation when an owner is barred from putting land to a use that is proscribed by those "existing rules or understandings" is surely unexceptional. When, however, a regulation that declares "off-limits" all economically productive or beneficial uses of land goes beyond what the relevant background principles would dictate, compensation must be paid to sustain it.

The "total taking" inquiry we require today will ordinarily entail (as the application of state nuisance law ordinarily entails) analysis of, among other things, the degree of harm to public lands and resources, or adjacent private property, posed by the claimant's proposed activities, see, e.g., Restatement (Second) of Torts §§ 826, 827, the social value of the claimant's activities and their suitability to the locality in question, see, e.g., id., §§ 828(a) and (b), 831, and the relative ease with which the alleged harm can be avoided through measures taken by the claimant and the government (or adjacent private landowners) alike, see, e.g., id., §§ 827(e), 828(c), 830. The fact that a particular use has long been engaged in by similarly situated owners ordinarily imports a lack of any common-law prohibition (though changed circumstances or new knowledge may make what was previously permissible no longer so, see Restatement (Second) of Torts, supra, § 827, comment g). So also does the fact that other landowners, similarly situated, are permitted to continue the use denied to the claimant.

It seems unlikely that common-law principles would have prevented the erection of any habitable or productive improvements on petitioner's land. . . . The question, however, is one of state law to be dealt with on remand. We emphasize that to win its case South Carolina must do more than proffer the legislature's declaration that the uses Lucas desires are inconsistent with the public interest, or the conclusory assertion that they violate a common-law maxim such as *sic utere tuo ut alienum non laedas.* As we have said, a State, by *ipse dixit,* may not transform private property into public property without compensation. . . ." Webb's Fabulous Pharmacies, Inc. v. Beckwith, 449 U.S. 155, 164 (1980). Instead, as it would be required to do if it sought to restrain Lucas in a common-law action for public nuisance, South Carolina must identify background principles of nuisance and property law that prohibit the uses he now intends in the circumstances in which the property is presently found. Only on this showing can the State fairly claim that, in proscribing all such beneficial uses, the Beachfront Management Act is taking nothing.[11]

The judgment is reversed and the cause remanded for proceedings not inconsistent with this opinion.

---

11. Justice Blackmun decries our reliance on background nuisance principles at least in part because he believes those principles to be as manipulable as we find the "harm prevention"/ "benefit conferral" dichotomy. There is no doubt some leeway in a court's interpretation of what existing state law permits—but not remotely as much, we think, as in a legislative crafting of the reasons for its confiscatory regulation. We stress that an affirmative decree eliminating all economically beneficial uses may be defended only if an *objectively reasonable application* of relevant precedents would exclude those beneficial uses in the circumstances in which the land is presently found.

[Justice Kennedy concurred in the judgment, mentioning several points: (1) The majority opinion established a framework for remand but did not decide the ultimate question whether a temporary taking had actually occurred. (2) The finding that Lucas's property had no value was "curious." "I share the reservations of some of my colleagues about a finding that a beach front lot loses all value because of a development restriction." (3) "The finding of no value must be considered under the Takings Clause by reference to the owner's reasonable, investment-backed expectations. . . . There is an inherent tendency towards circularity in this synthesis, of course; for if the owner's reasonable expectations are shaped by what courts allow as a proper exercise of governmental authority, property tends to become what courts say it is. Some circularity must be tolerated in these matters, however, as it is in other spheres. . . . The definition, moreover, is not circular in its entirety. The expectations protected by the Constitution are based on objective rules and customs that can be understood as reasonable by all parties involved." (4) "In my view, reasonable expectations must be understood in light of the whole of our legal tradition. The common law of nuisance is too narrow a confine for the exercise of regulatory power in a complex and interdependent society."

Justice Souter filed a separate statement saying he would dismiss the writ of certiorari as having been improvidently granted. "The petition for review was granted on the assumption that the state by regulation had deprived the owner of his entire economic interest in the subject-property. Such was the state trial court's conclusion, which the state supreme court did not review. It is apparent now that in light of our prior cases . . . the trial court's conclusion is highly questionable. . . . [T]he Court is certainly right to refuse to take up the issue, which is not fairly included within the question presented. . . . This alone is enough to show that there is little utility in attempting to deal with this case on the merits."

In addition to the foregoing, there were two dissenting opinions, which follow.]

BLACKMUN, J., dissenting. Today the Court launches a missile to kill a mouse.

. . . Relying on an unreviewed (and implausible) state trial court finding that this restriction left Lucas' property valueless, this Court granted review to determine whether compensation must be paid in cases where the State prohibits all economic use of real estate. According to the Court, such an occasion never has arisen in any of our prior cases, and the Court imagines that it will arise "relatively rarely" or only in "extraordinary circumstances." Almost certainly it did not happen in this case. Nonetheless, the Court presses on to decide the issue, and as it does, it ignores its jurisdictional limits, remakes its traditional rules of review, and creates simultaneously a new categorical rule and an exception (neither of which is rooted in our prior case law, common law, or common sense). I protest not only the Court's decision, but each step taken to reach it. More fundamentally, I question the Court's wisdom in issuing sweeping new rules to decide such a narrow case. . . .

My fear is that the Court's new policies will spread beyond the narrow confines of the present case. For that reason, I, like the Court, will give far greater attention to this case than its narrow scope suggests—not because I can intercept the Court's missile, or save the targeted mouse, but because I hope perhaps to limit the collateral damage. . . .

If the state legislature is correct that the prohibition on building in front of the setback line prevents serious harm, then, under this Court's prior cases, the Act is constitutional. . . . The Court consistently has upheld regulations imposed to arrest a significant threat to the common welfare, whatever their economic effect on the owner. . . .

Petitioner never challenged the legislature's findings that a building ban was necessary to protect property and life. Nor did he contend that the threatened harm was not sufficiently serious to make building a house in a particular location a "harmful" use, that the legislature had not made sufficient findings, or that the legislature was motivated by anything other than a desire to minimize damage to coastal areas. . . .

Nothing in the record undermines the General Assembly's assessment that prohibitions on building in front of the setback line are necessary to protect people and property from storms, high tides, and beach erosion. Because that legislative determination cannot be disregarded in the absence of such evidence, . . . and because its determination of harm to life and property from building is sufficient to prohibit that use under this Court's cases, the South Carolina Supreme Court correctly found no taking.

. . . The Court creates its new takings jurisprudence based on the trial court's finding that the property had lost all economic value. This finding is almost certainly erroneous. Petitioner still can enjoy other attributes of ownership, such as the right to exclude others, "one of the most essential sticks in the bundle of rights that are commonly characterized as property." Kaiser Aetna v. United States, 444 U.S. 164, 176. Petitioner can picnic, swim, camp in a tent, or live on the property in a movable trailer. State courts frequently have recognized that land has economic value where the only residual economic uses are recreation or camping. . . . Petitioner also retains the right to alienate the land, which would have value for neighbors and for those prepared to enjoy proximity to the ocean without a house. . . .

Clearly, the Court was eager to decide this case. . . .

The Court does not reject the South Carolina Supreme Court's decision simply on the basis of its disbelief and distrust of the legislature's findings. It also takes the opportunity to create a new scheme for regulations that eliminate all economic value. From now on, there is a categorical rule finding these regulations to be a taking unless the use they prohibit is a background common-law nuisance or property principle. . . .

This Court repeatedly has recognized the ability of government, in certain circumstances, to regulate property without compensation no matter how adverse the financial effect on the owner may be. More than a century ago, the Court explicitly upheld the right of States to prohibit uses of property injurious to public health, safety, or welfare without paying compensation: "A prohibition simply upon the use of property for purposes that are declared, by valid legislation, to be injurious to the health, morals, or safety of the community, cannot, in any just sense, be deemed a taking or an appropriation of property." Mugler v. Kansas, 123 U.S., at 668-669 (1887). On this basis, the Court upheld an ordinance effectively prohibiting operation of a previously lawful brewery, although the "establishments will become of no value as property." . . .

The Court recognizes that "our prior opinions have suggested that 'harmful or noxious uses' of property may be proscribed by government regulation without the requirement of compensation," but seeks to reconcile them with its categorical rule by claiming that the Court never has upheld a regulation when the owner alleged the loss of all economic value. Even if the Court's factual premise were correct, its understanding of the Court's cases is distorted. In none of the cases did the Court suggest that the right of a State to prohibit certain activities without paying compensation turned on the availability of some residual valuable use. Instead, the cases depended on whether the government interest was sufficient to prohibit the activity, given the significant private cost.

These cases rest on the principle that the State has full power to prohibit an owner's use of property if it is harmful to the public. "[S]ince no individual has a right to use his property so as to create a nuisance or otherwise harm others, the State has not 'taken' anything when it asserts its power to enjoin the nuisance-like activity." *Keystone Bituminous Coal*, 480 U.S., at 491, n. 20. It would make no sense under this theory to suggest that an owner has a constitutionally protected right to harm others, if only he makes the proper showing of economic loss. . . .

Ultimately even the Court cannot embrace the full implications of its *per se* rule: It eventually agrees that there cannot be a categorical rule for a taking based on economic value that wholly disregards the public need asserted. Instead, the Court decides that it will permit a State to regulate all economic value only if the State prohibits uses that would not be permitted under "background principles of nuisance and property law."[12]

Until today, the Court explicitly had rejected the contention that the government's power to act without paying compensation turns on whether the prohibited activity is a common-law nuisance. The brewery closed in *Mugler* itself was not a common-law nuisance, and the Court specifically stated that it was the role of the legislature to determine what measures would be appropriate for the protection of public health and safety. See 123 U.S., at 661, 8 S. Ct., at 297. In upholding the state action in *Miller*, the Court found it unnecessary to "weigh with nicety the question whether the infected cedars constitute a nuisance according to common law; or whether they may be so declared by statute." 276 U.S., at 280, 48 S. Ct., at 248. Instead the Court has relied in the past, as the South Carolina court has done here, on legislative judgments of what constitutes a harm.

The Court rejects the notion that the State always can prohibit uses it deems a harm to the public without granting compensation because "the distinction between 'harm-preventing' and 'benefit-conferring' regulation is often in the eye of the beholder." Since the characterization will depend "primarily upon one's evaluation of the worth of competing uses of real estate," the Court decides a legislative judgment of this kind no longer can provide the desired "objective, value-free basis" for upholding a regulation. The Court, however, fails to explain how its proposed common-law alternative escapes the same trap.

The threshold inquiry for imposition of the Court's new rule, "deprivation of all economically valuable use," itself cannot be determined objectively. As the Court admits, whether the owner has been deprived of all economic value of his property will depend on how "property" is defined. The "composition of the denominator in our 'deprivation' fraction," is the dispositive inquiry. Yet there is no "objective" way to define what that denominator should be. "We have long understood that any land-use regulation can be characterized as the 'total' deprivation of an aptly defined

---

12. Although it refers to state nuisance and property law, the Court apparently does not mean just any state nuisance and property law. Public nuisance was first a common law creation, see Newark, The Boundaries of Nuisance, 65 L.Q. Rev. 480, 482 (1949) (attributing development of nuisance to 1535), but by the 1800s in both the United States and England, legislatures had the power to define what is a public nuisance, and particular uses often have been selectively targeted. See Prosser, Private Action for Public Nuisance, 52 Va. L. Rev. 997, 999-1000 (1966); J. Stephen, A General View of the Criminal Law of England 105-107 (2d ed. 1890). The Court's references to "common-law" background principles, however, indicate that legislative determinations do not constitute "state nuisance and property law" for the Court.

entitlement. . . . Alternatively, the same regulation can always be characterized as a mere 'partial' withdrawal from full, unencumbered ownership of the landholding affected by the regulation. . . ." Michelman, Takings, 1987, 88 Colum. L. Rev. 1600, 1614 (1988). . . .

Even more perplexing, however, is the Court's reliance on common-law principles of nuisance in its quest for a value-free takings jurisprudence. In determining what is a nuisance at common law, state courts make exactly the decision that the Court finds so troubling when made by the South Carolina General Assembly today: They determine whether the use is harmful. Common-law public and private nuisance law is simply a determination whether a particular use causes harm. See Prosser, Private Action for Public Nuisance, 52 Va. L. Rev. 997 (1966) ("*Nuisance* is a French word which means nothing more than harm"). There is nothing magical in the reasoning of judges long dead. They determined a harm in the same way as state judges and legislatures do today. If judges in the 18th and 19th centuries can distinguish a harm from a benefit, why not judges in the 20th century, and if judges can, why not legislators? There simply is no reason to believe that new interpretations of the hoary common-law nuisance doctrine will be particularly "objective" or "value free."[13] Once one abandons the level of generality of *sic utere tuo ut alienum non laedas*, one searches in vain, I think, for anything resembling a principle in the common law of nuisance.

Finally, the Court justifies its new rule that the legislature may not deprive a property owner of the only economically valuable use of his land, even if the legislature finds it to be a harmful use, because such action is not part of the "'long recognized'" "understandings of our citizens." These "understandings" permit such regulation only if the use is a nuisance under the common law. Any other course is "inconsistent with the historical compact recorded in the Takings Clause." It is not clear from the Court's opinion where our "historical compact" or "citizens' understanding" comes from, but it does not appear to be history.

The principle that the State should compensate individuals for property taken for public use was not widely established in America at the time of the Revolution.

> The colonists . . . inherited . . . a concept of property which permitted extensive regulation of the use of that property for the public benefit—regulation that could even go so far as to deny all productive use of the property to the owner if, as Coke himself stated, the regulation "extends to the public benefit . . . for this is for the public, and every one hath benefit by it." [F. Bosselman, D. Callies & J. Banta, The Taking Issue 80-81 (1973), quoting The Case of the King's Prerogative in Saltpetre, 12 Co. Rep. 12-13 (1606) (hereinafter Bosselman).]

See also Treanor, The Origins and Original Significance of the Just Compensation Clause of the Fifth Amendment, 94 Yale L.J. 694, 697, n. 9 (1985).

Even into the 19th century, state governments often felt free to take property for roads and other public projects without paying compensation to the owners. See M. Horwitz, The Transformation of American Law, 1780-1860, pp. 63-64 (1977)

---

13. "There is perhaps no more impenetrable jungle in the entire law than that which surrounds the word 'nuisance.' It has meant all things to all people, and has been applied indiscriminately to everything from an alarming advertisement to a cockroach baked in a pie." W. Keeton, D. Dobbs, R. Keeton & D. Owen, Prosser and Keeton on The Law of Torts 616 (5th ed. 1984) (footnotes omitted). . . .

(hereinafter Horwitz); Treanor, 94 Yale L.J., at 695. As one court declared in 1802, citizens "were bound to contribute as much of [land], as by the laws of the country, were deemed necessary for the public convenience." M'Clenachan v. Curwin, 3 Yeates 362, 373 (Pa. 1802). There was an obvious movement toward establishing the just compensation principle during the 19th century, but "there continued to be a strong current in American legal thought that regarded compensation simply as a 'bounty given . . . by the State' out of 'kindness' and not out of justice." Horwitz 65, quoting Commonwealth v. Fisher, 1 Pen. & W. 462, 465 (Pa. 1830). See also State v. Dawson, 3 Hill 100, 103 (S.C. 1836).

Although, prior to the adoption of the Bill of Rights, America was replete with land-use regulations describing which activities were considered noxious and forbidden, see Bender, The Takings Clause: Principles or Politics?, 34 Buffalo L. Rev. 735, 751 (1985); L. Friedman, A History of American Law 66-68 (1973), the Fifth Amendment's Takings Clause originally did not extend to regulations of property, whatever the effect. Most state courts agreed with this narrow interpretation of a taking. "Until the end of the nineteenth century . . . jurists held that the constitution protected possession only, and not value." Siegel, Understanding the Nineteenth Century Contract Clause: The Role of the Property-Privilege Distinction and "Takings" Clause Jurisprudence, 60 S. Cal. L. Rev. 1, 76 (1986); Bosselman 106. Even indirect and consequential injuries to property resulting from regulations were excluded from the definition of a taking. See *ibid.*; Callender v. Marsh, 1 Pick. 418, 430 (Mass. 1823).

Even when courts began to consider that regulation in some situations could constitute a taking, they continued to uphold bans on particular uses without paying compensation, notwithstanding the economic impact, under the rationale that no one can obtain a vested right to injure or endanger the public. . . .

In addition, state courts historically have been less likely to find that a government action constitutes a taking when the affected land is undeveloped. . . .

Nor does history indicate any common-law limit on the State's power to regulate harmful uses even to the point of destroying all economic value. Nothing in the discussions in Congress concerning the Takings Clause indicates that the Clause was limited by the common-law nuisance doctrine. Common-law courts themselves rejected such an understanding. They regularly recognized that it is "for the legislature to interpose, and by positive enactment to prohibit a use of property which would be injurious to the public." [Commonwealth v. Tewksbury, 11 Metc., at 57 (Mass. 1846).] Chief Justice Shaw explained in upholding a regulation prohibiting construction of wharves, the existence of a taking did not depend on "whether a certain erection in tide water is a nuisance at common law or not." [Commonwealth v. Alger, 7 Cush., at 104 (Mass. 1851).] . . .

In short, I find no clear and accepted "historical compact" or "understanding of our citizens" justifying the Court's new takings doctrine. Instead, the Court seems to treat history as a grab bag of principles, to be adopted where they support the Court's theory, and ignored where they do not. If the Court decided that the early common law provides the background principles for interpreting the Takings Clause, then regulation, as opposed to physical confiscation, would not be compensable. If the Court decided that the law of a later period provides the background principles, then regulation might be compensable, but the Court would have to confront the fact that legislatures regularly determined which uses were prohibited, independent of the common law, and independent of whether the uses were lawful when the owner purchased.

What makes the Court's analysis unworkable is its attempt to package the law of two incompatible eras and peddle it as historical fact. . . .

I dissent.

STEVENS, J., dissenting. . . . In my opinion, the Court is doubly in error. The categorical rule the Court establishes is an unsound and unwise addition to the law and the Court's formulation of the exception to that rule is too rigid and too narrow. . . .

[B]ecause of the elastic nature of property rights, the Court's new rule will . . . prove unsound in practice. In response to the rule, courts may define "property" broadly and only rarely find regulations to effect total takings. This is the approach the Court itself adopts in its revisionist reading of venerable precedents. We are told that—notwithstanding the Court's findings to the contrary in each case—the brewery in *Mugler*, the brickyard in *Hadacheck*, and the gravel pit in *Goldblatt* all could be put to "other uses" and that, therefore, those cases did not involve total regulatory takings.[14]

On the other hand, developers and investors may market specialized estates to take advantage of the Court's new rule. The smaller the estate, the more likely that a regulatory change will effect a total taking. Thus, an investor may, for example, purchase the right to build a multifamily home on a specific lot, with the result that a zoning regulation that allows only single-family homes would render the investor's property interest "valueless." In short, the categorical rule will likely have one of two effects: Either courts will alter the definition of the "denominator" in the takings "fraction," rendering the Court's categorical rule meaningless, or investors will manipulate the relevant property interests, giving the Court's rule sweeping effect. To my mind, neither of these results is desirable or appropriate, and both are distortions of our takings jurisprudence. . . .

THE REST OF THE STORY ...

On remand, the South Carolina Supreme Court held that the restrictions imposed by the Beachfront Management Act would not been authorized under the state's background nuisance law. Hence the act imposed a total taking, and the state could either abandon the law or condemn Lucas's property. However, the parties eventually settled the case. Lucas received $1,575,000 and transferred the two lots to the Coastal Council. Strapped for money, the Council sold the lots to—a developer! Eventually, houses were built on the two lots. For a full account of the case, see Vicki C. Been, Lucas v. The Green Machine: Using the Takings Clause to Promote More Efficient Regulation?, in Property Stories 299 (Gerald Korngold & Andrew Morriss eds. 2d ed. 2009).

---

14. Of course, the same could easily be said in this case: Lucas may put his land to "other uses"—fishing or camping, for example—or may sell his land to his neighbors as a buffer. In either event, his land is far from "valueless."

This highlights a fundamental weakness in the Court's analysis: its failure to explain why only the impairment of *"economically* beneficial or productive use" (emphasis added) of property is relevant in takings analysis. I should think that a regulation arbitrarily prohibiting an owner from continuing to use her property for bird watching or sunbathing might constitute a taking under some circumstances; and, conversely, that such uses are of value to the owner. Yet the Court offers no basis for its assumption that the only uses of property cognizable under the Constitution are *developmental* uses.

Notes and Questions

1. *Conceptual severance again.* Begin by returning to a subject already mentioned on several occasions in this chapter (see pages 626, 641). What is the status of conceptual severance after the Court's opinion in *Lucas*? Does Justice Scalia endorse the approach that the Court had taken in *Penn Central*? Stating the question differently, what is the denominator in the relevant fraction after *Lucas*? Consider what Justice Stevens has to say about that question.

2. *Rules and exceptions.* *Lucas* adds another per se rule along with *Loretto's* permanent physical occupation rule. But what Justice Scalia added with one hand, he took away with the other: he created an exception to the total economic wipe-out rule where the restriction stemmed from "background principles" of state nuisance law. How broad will that exception be? What will be the source(s) to which lower courts are to look to discover these background principles? Will they vary from state to state? Will they evolve over time? Notice that Justice Scalia relied on the Restatement of Torts as a source for identifying these nuisance principles. The Restatement basically defines nuisance according to an ad hoc balancing test. So, does Justice Scalia's exception swallow up his rule?

3. *Of missiles and mice.* Consider the opening words of Justice Blackmun's dissenting opinion in *Lucas*: "Today, the court launches a missile to kill a mouse." *Is* the target just a mouse? Is *Lucas* insignificant because regulatory programs rarely wipe out value altogether?

Related to the last question, can a state avoid the *Lucas* per se rule by leaving the owner with a token use of the property? In Palazzolo v. Rhode Island, 533 U.S. 606 (2001), a state law restricting wetlands development allowed an owner to build only one house on his 18-acre parcel, reducing its value from $3,150,000 to $200,000—a 94 percent decrease. The Court rejected the argument that this was a *Lucas*-type total taking: "A regulation permitting a landowner to build a substantial residence on an 18-acre parcel does not leave the property 'economically idle.'" Id. at 631.

4. *The temporal dimension of takings.* Suppose a local planning agency imposes a moratorium on development while studying the impact of growth on the area and preparing a comprehensive land use plan. During the period of the moratorium, undeveloped land has no market value whatsoever. Does this result in a per se taking under *Lucas*? An earlier decision by the United States Supreme Court suggested, but did not hold, that the answer is yes. See First English Evangelical Lutheran Church of Glendale v. County of Los Angeles, 482 U.S. 304 (1987).

Subsequently, in Tahoe-Sierra Preservation Council, Inc. v. Tahoe Regional Planning Agency, 535 U.S. 302 (2002), the Court held that a temporary moratorium on development did not constitute a *Lucas* per se taking. Justice Stevens's majority opinion expressly rejected the attempt to apply temporal conceptual severance, concluding that for purposes of a takings analysis, severing a property interest in terms of time is no more appropriate than severing it in terms of space.

More recently, in Arkansas Game & Fish Commn. v. United States, 568 U.S. 23 (2012), the Court unanimously held that the mere fact that flooding resulting from deviations by the Army Corps of Engineers from a flood control plan was temporary did not immunize the government from a takings claim. At the same time, the Court reaffirmed its preference for "situation-specific factual inquiries."

5. *Covid-19 business moratoria as temporal takings?* In Friends of Danny DeVito v. Wolf, 227 A.3d 872 (Pa. 2020), application for stay denied, ___ S. Ct. ___, 2020 WL 2177482 (U.S. 5/6/2020), the Pennsylvania Supreme Court rejected businesses owners' argument that the governor's executive order temporarily forcing them to close their businesses was a taking requiring compensation. The owners had made a *Lucas* argument that the effect of the moratorium was to deprive them of "all economically beneficial or productive use of [their] land." The Pennsylvania court rejected that argument, stating that the case was controlled instead by *Tahoe-Sierra* (see Note 4 above). This was "only a temporary loss of the use of the Petitioners' business premises," which did not deprive the owners' property of all its economic value.

The denominator problem redux. Beginning with *Pennsylvania Coal*, we have seen on multiple occasions the difficulty in, and importance of, identifying the relevant property interest at stake—the so-called denominator problem. We know that the impact of government restrictions on a parcel of land must be considered in light of the entire parcel over time, as opposed to just the restricted part for a limited time. But suppose state legislation consolidates two adjacent parcels owned by O, and subsequent regulatory restrictions allegedly deprive one of the former separate lots of all economically beneficial use. Can the two parcels be considered together as a whole in order to ward off the takings claim? Consider the case that follows.

MURR v. WISCONSIN
Supreme Court of the United States, 2017
137 S. Ct. 1933

KENNEDY, J. The classic example of a property taking by the government is when the property has been occupied or otherwise seized. In the case now before the Court, petitioners contend that governmental entities took their real property—an undeveloped residential lot—not by some physical occupation but instead by enacting burdensome regulations that forbid its improvement or separate sale because it is classified as substandard in size. The relevant governmental entities are the respondents.

Against the background justifications for the challenged restrictions, respondents contend there is no regulatory taking because petitioners own an adjacent lot. The regulations, in effecting a merger of the property, permit the continued residential use of the property including for a single improvement to extend over both lots. This retained right of the landowner, respondents urge, is of sufficient offsetting value that the regulation is not severe enough to be a regulatory taking. To resolve the issue whether the landowners can insist on confining the analysis just to the lot in question, without regard to their ownership of the adjacent lot, it is necessary to discuss the background principles that define regulatory takings.

The St. Croix River originates in northwest Wisconsin and flows approximately 170 miles until it joins the Mississippi River, forming the boundary between Minnesota and Wisconsin for much of its length. The lower portion of the river slows and widens to create a natural water area known as Lake St. Croix. Tourists and residents of the region have long extolled the picturesque grandeur of the river and surrounding area. . . .

Under the Wild and Scenic Rivers Act, the river was designated, by 1972, for federal protection. The law required the States of Wisconsin and Minnesota to develop "a management and development program" for the river area. In compliance, Wisconsin authorized the State Department of Natural Resources to promulgate rules limiting development in order to "guarantee the protection of the wild, scenic and recreational qualities of the river for present and future generations."

Petitioners are two sisters and two brothers in the Murr family. Petitioners' parents arranged for them to receive ownership of two lots the family used for recreation along the Lower St. Croix River in the town of Troy, Wisconsin. The lots are adjacent, but the parents purchased them separately, put the title of one in the name of the family business, and later arranged for transfer of the two lots, on different dates, to petitioners. The lots, which are referred to in this litigation as Lots E and F, are described in more detail below.

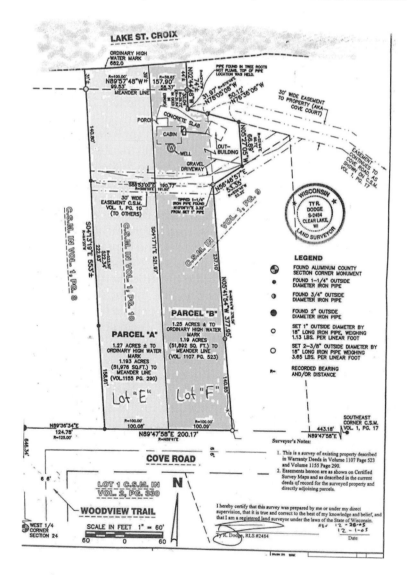

For the area where petitioners' property is located, the Wisconsin rules prevent the use of lots as separate building sites unless they have at least one acre of land suitable for development. A grandfather clause relaxes this restriction for substandard lots which were "in separate ownership from abutting lands" on January 1, 1976, the effective date of the regulation. The clause permits the use of qualifying lots as separate building sites. The rules also include a merger provision, however, which provides that adjacent lots under common ownership may not be "sold or developed as separate lots" if they do not meet the size requirement. The Wisconsin rules require localities to adopt parallel provisions, so the St. Croix County zoning ordinance contains identical restrictions. The Wisconsin rules also authorize the local zoning authority to grant variances from the regulations where enforcement would create "unnecessary hardship."

Petitioners' parents purchased Lot F in 1960 and built a small recreational cabin on it. In 1961, they transferred title to Lot F to the family plumbing company. In 1963, they purchased neighboring Lot E, which they held in their own names.

The lots have the same topography. A steep bluff cuts through the middle of each, with level land suitable for development above the bluff and next to the water below it. The line dividing Lot E from Lot F runs from the riverfront to the far end of the property, crossing the blufftop along the way. Lot E has approximately 60 feet of river frontage, and Lot F has approximately 100 feet. Though each lot is approximately 1.25 acres in size, because of the waterline and the steep bank they each have less than one acre of land suitable for development. Even when combined, the lots' buildable land area is only 0.98 acres due to the steep terrain.

The lots remained under separate ownership, with Lot F owned by the plumbing company and Lot E owned by petitioners' parents, until transfers to petitioners. Lot F was conveyed to them in 1994, and Lot E was conveyed to them in 1995. . . .

A decade later, petitioners became interested in moving the cabin on Lot F to a different portion of the lot and selling Lot E to fund the project. The unification of the lots under common ownership, however, had implicated the state and local rules barring their separate sale or development. Petitioners then sought variances from the St. Croix County Board of Adjustment to enable their building and improvement plan, including a variance to allow the separate sale or use of the lots. The Board denied the requests, and the state courts affirmed in relevant part. In particular, the Wisconsin Court of Appeals agreed with the Board's interpretation that the local ordinance "effectively merged" Lots E and F, so petitioners "could only sell or build on the single larger lot."

Petitioners filed the present action in state court, alleging that the state and county regulations worked a regulatory taking by depriving them of "all, or practically all, of the use of Lot E because the lot cannot be sold or developed as a separate lot." The parties each submitted appraisal numbers to the trial court. Respondents' appraisal included values of $698,300 for the lots together as regulated; $771,000 for the lots as two distinct buildable properties; and $373,000 for Lot F as a single lot with improvements. Petitioners' appraisal included an unrebutted, estimated value of $40,000 for Lot E as an undevelopable lot, based on the counterfactual assumption that it could be sold as a separate property.

The Circuit Court of St. Croix County granted summary judgment to the State, explaining that petitioners retained "several available options for the use and enjoyment of their property." For example, they could preserve the existing cabin, relocate the cabin, or eliminate the cabin and build a new residence on Lot E, on Lot F, or across both lots. The court also found petitioners had not been deprived of all economic value of their property. Considering the valuation of the property as a single lot versus two separate lots, the court found the market value of the property was not significantly affected by the regulations because the decrease in value was less than 10 percent.

The Wisconsin Court of Appeals affirmed. The court explained that the regulatory takings inquiry required it to "'first determine what, precisely, is the property at issue.'" Relying on Wisconsin Supreme Court precedent in Zealy v. Waukesha, 201 Wis. 2d 365, 548 N.W.2d 528 (1996), the Court of Appeals rejected petitioners' request to analyze the effect of the regulations on Lot E only. Instead, the court held the takings analysis "properly focused" on the regulations' effect "on the Murrs' property as a whole"—that is, Lots E and F together.

Using this framework, the Court of Appeals concluded the merger regulations did not effect a taking. In particular, the court explained that petitioners could not reasonably have expected to use the lots separately because they were "'charged with knowledge of the existing zoning laws'" when they acquired the property. Thus, "even if [petitioners] did intend to develop or sell Lot E separately, that expectation of separate treatment became unreasonable when they chose to acquire Lot E in 1995, after their having acquired Lot F in 1994." The court also discounted the severity of the economic impact on petitioners' property, recognizing the Circuit Court's conclusion that the regulations diminished the property's combined value by less than 10 percent. The Supreme Court of Wisconsin denied discretionary review. This Court granted certiorari.

[The Court then summarized its regulatory takings precedents, including Pennsylvania Coal v. Mahon and *Lucas*.]

This case presents a question that is linked to the ultimate determination whether a regulatory taking has occurred: What is the proper unit of property against which to assess the effect of the challenged governmental action? Put another way, "[b]ecause our test for regulatory taking requires us to compare the value that has been taken from the property with the value that remains in the property, one of the critical questions is determining how to define the unit of property 'whose value is to furnish the denominator of the fraction.'" Keystone Bituminous Coal Assn. v. DeBenedictis, 480 U.S. 470, 497, 107 S. Ct. 1232, 94 L. Ed. 2d 472 (1987).

[T]he answer to this question may be outcome determinative. This Court . . . has explained that the question is important to the regulatory takings inquiry. "To the extent that any portion of property is taken, that portion is always taken in its entirety; the relevant question, however, is whether the property taken is all, or only a portion of, the parcel in question." Concrete Pipe & Products of Cal., Inc. v. Construction Laborers Pension Trust for Southern Cal., 508 U.S. 602, 644, 113 S. Ct. 2264, 124 L. Ed. 2d 539 (1993).

Defining the property at the outset, however, should not necessarily preordain the outcome in every case. In some, though not all, cases the effect of the challenged regulation must be assessed and understood by the effect on the entire property held by the owner, rather than just some part of the property that, considered just on its own, has been diminished in value. This demonstrates the contrast between regulatory takings, where the goal is usually to determine how the challenged regulation affects the property's value to the owner, and physical takings, where the impact of physical appropriation or occupation of the property will be evident.

While the Court has not set forth specific guidance on how to identify the relevant parcel for the regulatory taking inquiry, there are two concepts which the Court has indicated can be unduly narrow.

First, the Court has declined to limit the parcel in an artificial manner to the portion of property targeted by the challenged regulation. In *Penn Central*, for example, the Court rejected a challenge to the denial of a permit to build an office tower above Grand Central Terminal. The Court refused to measure the effect of the denial only against the "air rights" above the terminal, cautioning that " '[t]aking' jurisprudence does not divide a single parcel into discrete segments and attempt to determine whether rights in a particular segment have been entirely abrogated."

In a similar way, in *Tahoe-Sierra*, the Court refused to "effectively sever" the 32 months during which petitioners' property was restricted by temporary moratoria on development "and then ask whether that segment ha[d] been taken in its entirety." That was because "defining the property interest taken in terms of the very regulation being challenged is circular." That approach would overstate the effect of regulation on property, turning "every delay" into a "total ban."

The second concept about which the Court has expressed caution is the view that property rights under the Takings Clause should be coextensive with those under state law. Although property interests have their foundations in state law, the *Palazzolo* Court reversed a state-court decision that rejected a takings challenge to regulations that predated the landowner's acquisition of title. The Court explained that States do not have the unfettered authority to "shape and define property rights and reasonable investment-backed expectations," leaving landowners without recourse against unreasonable regulations.

By the same measure, defining the parcel by reference to state law could defeat a challenge even to a state enactment that alters permitted uses of property in ways inconsistent with reasonable investment-backed expectations. For example, a State might enact a law that consolidates nonadjacent property owned by a single person or entity in different parts of the State and then imposes development limits on the aggregate set. If a court defined the parcel according to the state law requiring consolidation, this improperly would fortify the state law against a takings claim, because the court would look to the retained value in the property as a whole rather than considering whether individual holdings had lost all value.

As the foregoing discussion makes clear, no single consideration can supply the exclusive test for determining the denominator. Instead, courts must consider a number of factors. These include the treatment of the land under state and local law; the physical characteristics of the land; and the prospective value of the regulated land. The endeavor should determine whether reasonable expectations about property ownership would lead a landowner to anticipate that his holdings would be treated as one parcel, or, instead, as separate tracts. The inquiry is objective, and the reasonable expectations at issue derive from background customs and the whole of our legal tradition.

First, courts should give substantial weight to the treatment of the land, in particular how it is bounded or divided, under state and local law. The reasonable expectations of an acquirer of land must acknowledge legitimate restrictions affecting his or her subsequent use and dispensation of the property. A valid takings claim will not evaporate just because a purchaser took title after the law was enacted. A reasonable restriction that predates a landowner's acquisition, however, can be one of the objective factors that most landowners would reasonably consider in forming fair expectations about their property. In a similar manner, a use restriction which is triggered only after, or because of, a change in ownership should also guide a court's assessment of reasonable private expectations.

Second, courts must look to the physical characteristics of the landowner's property. These include the physical relationship of any distinguishable tracts, the parcel's topography, and the surrounding human and ecological environment. In particular, it may be relevant that the property is located in an area that is subject to, or likely to become subject to, environmental or other regulation.

Third, courts should assess the value of the property under the challenged regulation, with special attention to the effect of burdened land on the value of other holdings. Though a use restriction may decrease the market value of the property, the effect may be tempered if the regulated land adds value to the remaining property, such as by increasing privacy, expanding recreational space, or preserving surrounding natural beauty. A law that limits use of a landowner's small lot in one part of the city by reason of the landowner's nonadjacent holdings elsewhere may decrease the market value of the small lot in an unmitigated fashion. The absence of a special relationship between the holdings may counsel against consideration of all the holdings as a single parcel, making the restrictive law susceptible to a takings challenge. On the other hand, if the landowner's other property is adjacent to the small lot, the market value of the properties may well increase if their combination enables the expansion of a structure, or if development restraints for one part of the parcel protect the unobstructed skyline views of another part. That, in turn, may counsel in favor of treatment as a single parcel and may reveal the weakness of a regulatory takings challenge to the law.

State and federal courts have considerable experience in adjudicating regulatory takings claims that depart from these examples in various ways. The Court anticipates that in applying the test above they will continue to exercise care in this complex area.

The State of Wisconsin and petitioners each ask this Court to adopt a formalistic rule to guide the parcel inquiry. Neither proposal suffices to capture the central legal and factual principles that inform reasonable expectations about property interests. Wisconsin would tie the definition of the parcel to state law, considering the two lots here as a single whole due to their merger under the challenged regulations. That approach, as already noted, simply assumes the answer to the question: May the State define the relevant parcel in a way that permits it to escape its responsibility to justify regulation in light of legitimate property expectations? It is, of course, unquestionable that the law must recognize those legitimate expectations in order to give proper weight to the rights of owners and the right of the State to pass reasonable laws and regulations.

Wisconsin bases its position on a footnote in *Lucas*, which suggests the answer to the denominator question "may lie in how the owner's reasonable expectations have been shaped by the State's law of property—i.e., whether and to what degree the State's law has accorded legal recognition and protection to the particular interest in land with respect to which the takings claimant alleges a diminution in (or elimination of) value." 505 U.S., at 1017, n. 7. As an initial matter, *Lucas* referenced the parcel problem only in dicta, unnecessary to the announcement or application of the rule it established. In any event, the test the Court adopts today is consistent with the respect for state law described in *Lucas*. The test considers state law but in addition weighs whether the state enactments at issue accord with other indicia of reasonable expectations about property.

Petitioners propose a different test that is also flawed. They urge the Court to adopt a presumption that lot lines define the relevant parcel in every instance, making Lot E the necessary denominator. Petitioners' argument, however, ignores the fact that lot lines are themselves creatures of state law, which can be overridden by the State in the reasonable exercise of its power. In effect, petitioners ask this Court to credit the aspect of state law that favors their preferred result (lot lines) and ignore that which does not (merger provision). This approach contravenes the Court's case law, which recognizes that reasonable land-use regulations do not work a taking.

The merger provision here is likewise a legitimate exercise of government power, as reflected by its consistency with a long history of state and local merger regulations that originated nearly a century ago. Merger provisions often form part of a regulatory scheme that establishes a minimum lot size in order to preserve open space while still allowing orderly development.

When States or localities first set a minimum lot size, there often are existing lots that do not meet the new requirements, and so local governments will strive to reduce substandard lots in a gradual manner. The regulations here represent a classic way of doing this: by implementing a merger provision, which combines contiguous substandard lots under common ownership, alongside a grandfather clause, which preserves adjacent substandard lots that are in separate ownership. Also, as here, the harshness of a merger provision may be ameliorated by the availability of a variance from the local zoning authority for landowners in special circumstances.

Petitioners' insistence that lot lines define the relevant parcel ignores the well-settled reliance on the merger provision as a common means of balancing the legitimate goals of regulation with the reasonable expectations of landowners. Petitioners' rule would frustrate municipalities' ability to implement minimum lot size regulations by casting doubt on the many merger provisions that exist nationwide today.

Petitioners' reliance on lot lines also is problematic for another reason. Lot lines have varying degrees of formality across the States, so it is difficult to make them a standard measure of the reasonable expectations of property owners. Indeed, in some jurisdictions, lot lines may be subject to informal adjustment by property owners, with minimal government oversight. The ease of modifying lot lines also creates the risk of gamesmanship by landowners, who might seek to alter the lines in anticipation of regulation that seems likely to affect only part of their property.

Under the appropriate multifactor standard, it follows that for purposes of determining whether a regulatory taking has occurred here, petitioners' property should be evaluated as a single parcel consisting of Lots E and F together.

First, the treatment of the property under state and local law indicates petitioners' property should be treated as one when considering the effects of the restrictions. As the Wisconsin courts held, the state and local regulations merged Lots E and F. The decision to adopt the merger provision at issue here was for a specific and legitimate purpose, consistent with the widespread understanding that lot lines are not dominant or controlling in every case. Petitioners' land was subject to this regulatory burden, moreover, only because of voluntary conduct in bringing the lots under common ownership after the regulations were enacted. As a result, the valid merger of the lots under state law informs the reasonable expectation they will be treated as a single property.

Second, the physical characteristics of the property support its treatment as a unified parcel. The lots are contiguous along their longest edge. Their rough terrain and narrow shape make it reasonable to expect their range of potential uses might be limited. The land's location along the river is also significant. Petitioners could have anticipated public regulation might affect their enjoyment of their property, as the

Lower St. Croix was a regulated area under federal, state, and local law long before petitioners possessed the land.

Third, the prospective value that Lot E brings to Lot F supports considering the two as one parcel for purposes of determining if there is a regulatory taking. Petitioners are prohibited from selling Lots E and F separately or from building separate residential structures on each. Yet this restriction is mitigated by the benefits of using the property as an integrated whole, allowing increased privacy and recreational space, plus the optimal location of any improvements.

The special relationship of the lots is further shown by their combined valuation. Were Lot E separately saleable but still subject to the development restriction, petitioners' appraiser would value the property at only $40,000. We express no opinion on the validity of this figure. We also note the number is not particularly helpful for understanding petitioners' retained value in the properties because Lot E, under the regulations, cannot be sold without Lot F. The point that is useful for these purposes is that the combined lots are valued at $698,300, which is far greater than the summed value of the separate regulated lots (Lot F with its cabin at $373,000, according to respondents' appraiser, and Lot E as an undevelopable plot at $40,000, according to petitioners' appraiser). The value added by the lots' combination shows their complementarity and supports their treatment as one parcel.

The State Court of Appeals was correct in analyzing petitioners' property as a single unit. Petitioners allege that in doing so, the state court applied a categorical rule that all contiguous, commonly owned holdings must be combined for Takings Clause analysis. This does not appear to be the case, however, for the precedent relied on by the Court of Appeals addressed multiple factors before treating contiguous properties as one parcel. The judgment below, furthermore, may be affirmed on any ground permitted by the law and record. To the extent the state court treated the two lots as one parcel based on a bright-line rule, nothing in this opinion approves that methodology, as distinct from the result.

Considering petitioners' property as a whole, the state court was correct to conclude that petitioners cannot establish a compensable taking in these circumstances. Petitioners have not suffered a taking under *Lucas*, as they have not been deprived of all economically beneficial use of their property. They can use the property for residential purposes, including an enhanced, larger residential improvement. The property has not lost all economic value, as its value has decreased by less than 10 percent. See *Lucas*, supra, at 1019, n. 8 (suggesting that even a landowner with 95 percent loss may not recover).

Petitioners furthermore have not suffered a taking under the more general test of *Penn Central*. The expert appraisal relied upon by the state courts refutes any claim that the economic impact of the regulation is severe. Petitioners cannot claim that they reasonably expected to sell or develop their lots separately given the regulations which predated their acquisition of both lots. Finally, the governmental action was a reason able land-use regulation, enacted as part of a coordinated federal, state, and local effort to preserve the river and surrounding land.

. . .

Like the ultimate question whether a regulation has gone too far, the question of the proper parcel in regulatory takings cases cannot be solved by any simple test. Courts must instead define the parcel in a manner that reflects reasonable expectations about the property. Courts must strive for consistency with the central purpose of the Takings Clause: to "bar Government from forcing some people alone to bear public burdens which, in all fairness and justice, should be borne by the public as a whole." *Armstrong*, 364 U.S., at 49. Treating the lot in question as a single parcel is legitimate for purposes of this takings inquiry, and this supports the conclusion that no regulatory taking occurred here.

The judgment of the Wisconsin Court of Appeals is affirmed.

ROBERTS, C.J, with whom THOMAS and ALITO, JJ., join, dissenting.

The Murr family owns two adjacent lots along the Lower St. Croix River. Under a local regulation, those two properties may not be "sold or developed as separate lots" because neither contains a sufficiently large area of buildable land. The Court today holds that the regulation does not effect a taking that requires just compensation. This bottom-line conclusion does not trouble me; the majority presents a fair case that the Murrs can still make good use of both lots, and that the ordinance is a common-place tool to preserve scenic areas, such as the Lower St. Croix River, for the benefit of land-owners and the public alike.

Where the majority goes astray, however, is in concluding that the definition of the "private property" at issue in a case such as this turns on an elaborate test looking not only to state and local law, but also to (1) "the physical characteristics of the land," (2) "the prospective value of the regulated land," (3) the "reasonable expectations" of the owner, and (4) "background customs and the whole of our legal tradition." Our decisions have, time and again, declared that the Takings Clause protects private property rights as state law creates and defines them. . . . The majority's new, mal-leable definition of "private property"—adopted solely "for purposes of th[e] takings inquiry,"—undermines that protection.

I would stick with our traditional approach: State law defines the boundaries of distinct parcels of land, and those boundaries should determine the "private prop-erty" at issue in regulatory takings cases. Whether a regulation effects a taking of that property is a separate question, one in which common ownership of adjacent property may be taken into account. Because the majority departs from these settled principles, I respectfully dissent. . . .

Because a regulation amounts to a taking if it completely destroys a property's productive use, there is an incentive for owners to define the relevant "private prop-erty" narrowly. This incentive threatens the careful balance between property rights and government authority that our regulatory takings doctrine strikes: Put in terms of the familiar "bundle" analogy, each "strand" in the bundle of rights that comes along with owning real property is a distinct property interest. If owners could define the rel-evant "private property" at issue as the specific "strand" that the challenged regulation affects, they could convert nearly all regulations into per se takings.

And so we do not allow it. In *Penn Central* we held that property owners may not "establish a 'taking' simply by showing that they have been denied the ability to exploit a property interest." 438 U.S., at 130. . . . We rejected that narrow definition of the "property" at issue, concluding that the correct unit of analysis was the owners "rights in the parcel as a whole. Id. at 130-131. . . .

The question presented in today's case concerns the "parcel as a whole" language from *Penn Central*. This enigmatic phrase has created confusion about how to identify the relevant property in a regulatory takings case when the claimant owns more than one plot of land. Should the impact of the regulation be evaluated with respect to each individual plot, or with respect to adjacent plots grouped together as one unit? According to the majority, a court should answer this question by considering a number of facts about the land and the regulation at issue. The end result turns on whether those factors "would lead a landowner to anticipate that his holdings would be treated as one parcel, or, instead, as separate tracts."

I think the answer is far more straightforward: State laws define the boundaries of distinct units of land, and those boundaries should, in all but the most exceptional circumstances, determine the parcel at issue. . . .

Following state property lines is also entirely consistent with *Penn Central*. Requiring consideration of the "parcel as a whole" is a response to the risk that owners will strategically pluck one strand from their bundle of property rights—such as the air rights at issue in *Penn Central*—and claim a complete taking based on that strand alone. That risk of strategic unbundling is not present when a legally distinct parcel is the basis of the regulatory takings claim. State law defines all of the interests that come along with owning a particular parcel, and both property owners and the government must take those rights as they find them.

The majority envisions that relying on state law will create other opportunities for "gamesmanship" by landowners and States: The former, it contends, "might seek to alter [lot] lines in anticipation of regulation," while the latter might pass a law that "consolidates . . . property" to avoid a successful takings claim. But such obvious attempts to alter the legal landscape in anticipation of a lawsuit are unlikely and not particularly difficult to detect and disarm. . . .

Once the relevant property is identified, the real work begins. To decide whether the regulation at issue amounts to a "taking," courts should focus on the effect of the regulation on the "private property" at issue. Adjacent land under common ownership may be relevant to that inquiry. The owner's possession of such a nearby lot could, for instance, shed light on how the owner reasonably expected to use the parcel at issue before the regulation. If the court concludes that the government's action amounts to a taking, principles of "just compensation" may also allow the owner to recover damages "with regard to a separate parcel" that is contiguous and used in conjunction with the parcel at issue.

In sum, the "parcel as a whole" requirement prevents a property owner from identifying a single "strand" in his bundle of property rights and claiming that interest has been taken. . . . Instead, state law creates distinct parcels of land and defines the rights that come along with owning those parcels. Those established bundles of rights should define the "private property" in regulatory takings cases. While ownership of contiguous properties may bear on whether a person's plot has been "taken," *Penn Central* provides no basis for disregarding state property lines when identifying the "parcel as a whole."

The lesson that the majority draws from *Penn Central* is that defining "the proper parcel in regulatory takings cases cannot be solved by any simple test." Following through on that stand against simplicity, the majority lists a complex set of factors theoretically designed to reveal whether a hypothetical landowner might expect that his property "would be treated as one parcel, or, instead, as separate tracts." Those factors, says the majority, show that Lots E and F of the Murrs' property constitute a single parcel and that the local ordinance requiring the Murrs to develop and sell those lots as a pair does not constitute a taking.

In deciding that Lots E and F are a single parcel, the majority focuses on the importance of the ordinance at issue and the extent to which the Murrs may have been especially surprised, or unduly harmed, by the application of that ordinance to their property. But these issues should be considered when deciding if a regulation constitutes a "taking." Cramming them into the definition of "private property" undermines the effectiveness of the Takings Clause as a check on the government's power to shift the cost of public life onto private individuals. . . .

In departing from state property principles, the majority authorizes governments to do precisely what we rejected in *Penn Central*: create a litigation-specific definition of "property" designed for a claim under the Takings Clause. Whenever possible, governments in regulatory takings cases will ask courts to aggregate legally distinct properties into one "parcel," solely for purposes of resisting a particular claim. And under the majority's test, identifying the "parcel as a whole" in such cases will turn on the reasonableness of the regulation as applied to the claimant. The result is that the government's regulatory interests will come into play not once, but twice—first when identifying the relevant parcel, and again when determining whether the regulation has placed too great a public burden on that property.

. . . [T]he Takings Clause "prevents the public from loading upon one individual more than his just share of the burdens of government," Monongahela Nav. Co. v. United States, 148 U.S. 312, 325 (1893), by considering the effect of a regulation on specific property rights as they are established at state law. But the majority's approach undermines that protection, defining property only after engaging in an ad hoc, case-specific consideration of individual and community interests. The result is that the government's goals shape the playing field before the contest over whether the challenged regulation goes "too far" even gets underway.

Suppose, for example, that a person buys two distinct plots of land—known as Lots A and B—from two different owners. Lot A is landlocked, but the neighboring Lot B shares a border with a local beach. It soon comes to light, however, that the beach is a nesting habitat for a species of turtle. To protect this species, the state government passes a regulation preventing any development or recreation in areas abutting the beach—including Lot B. If that lot became the subject of a regulatory takings claim, the purchaser would have a strong case for a per se taking: Even accounting for the owner's possession of the other property, Lot B had no remaining economic value or productive use. But under the majority's approach, the government can argue that—based on all the circumstances and the nature of the regulation—Lots A and B should be considered one "parcel." If that argument succeeds, the owner's per se takings claim is gone, and he is left to roll the dice under the *Penn Central* balancing framework, where the court will, for a second time, throw the reasonableness of the government's regulatory action into the balance.

. . . [T]he majority's approach will lead to definitions of the "parcel" that have far more to do with the reasonableness of applying the challenged regulation to a particular landowner. . . . Reasonable government regulation should have been anticipated by the landowner, so the relevant parcel is defined consistent with that regulation. In deciding whether there is a taking under the second step of the analysis, the regulation will seem eminently reasonable given its impact on the pre-packaged parcel. . . .

Moreover, given its focus on the particular challenged regulation, the majority's approach must mean that two lots might be a single "parcel" for one takings claim, but separate "parcels" for another. This is just another opportunity to gerrymander the definition of "private property" to defeat a takings claim.

. . . The Murrs argued that the ordinance amounted to a taking of Lot E, but the State of Wisconsin and St. Croix County proposed that both lots together should count as the relevant "parcel." The trial court sided with the State and County, and the Wisconsin Court of Appeals affirmed. Rather than considering whether Lots E and F are separate parcels under Wisconsin law, however, the Court of Appeals adopted a takings-specific approach to defining the relevant parcel. Relying on what it called a "well-established rule" for "regulatory takings cases," the court explained "that contiguous property under common ownership is considered as a whole regardless of the number of parcels contained therein." And because Lots E and F were side by side and owned by the Murrs, the case was straight-forward: The two lots were one "parcel" for the regulatory takings analysis. The court therefore evaluated the effect of the ordinance on the two lots considered together.

As I see it, the Wisconsin Court of Appeals was wrong to apply a takings-specific definition of the property at issue. Instead, the court should have asked whether, under general state law principles, Lots E and F are legally distinct parcels of land. I would therefore vacate the judgment below and remand for the court to identify the relevant property using ordinary principles of Wisconsin property law.

After making that state law determination, the next step would be to determine whether the challenged ordinance amounts to a "taking." If Lot E is a legally distinct parcel under state law, the Court of Appeals would have to perform the takings analysis anew, but could still consider many of the issues the majority finds important. The majority, for instance, notes that under the ordinance the Murrs can use Lot E as "recreational space," as the "location of any improvements," and as a valuable addition to Lot F. These facts could be relevant to whether the "regulation denies all economically beneficial or productive use" of Lot E. . . .

I respectfully dissent.

[The separate dissenting opinion by Justice Thomas is omitted.]

Notes and Questions

1. *Conceptual aggregation?* As we have seen, Supreme Court takings doctrine provides that government restrictions on land use are to be considered in terms of their impact on an entire parcel of land as a whole, as opposed to just some affected portion of the parcel. The part may not be "conceptually severed" from the whole. The boundaries of the "parcel as a whole" are largely defined by state law. Suppose someone owns two such separate parcels adjacent to each other. Are states free to treat those two lots as one in measuring the impact of a land use restriction? In other words, may the two separate parcels be "conceptually aggregated"? In principle, the decision in *Murr* seems to say that they may, although many details remain unresolved.

2. *"Constitutional bottoms."* In his dissent, Chief Justice Roberts argues that as the first step in the case the Wisconsin courts should have considered how state law defines the boundaries of distinct parcels as a general matter, rather than using "a takings-specific definition of the property at issue." (See page 679.) Yet he seems to accept the principle of conceptual aggregation; beyond that, he agrees that the result reached (as opposed to the method used) by the majority in *Murr* is constitutionally acceptable. Why, then, did he dissent?

A possible explanation is this: If the Wisconsin courts had first considered that under state law each of the two co-owned lots in the case would ordinarily be defined as single parcels, then maybe they would have concluded that there was a taking, or maybe not. If they did find a taking, however, the U.S. Supreme Court would have no grounds for reversing the decision. The Takings Clause announces a "constitutional bottom," the degree to which states must protect private property at a minimum. States are free to provide more protection, but not less.

3. The Problem of Exactions

Exactions are local government measures that require developers to provide goods and services or pay fees as a condition to getting project approval. For a good account, see William A. Fischel, Regulatory Takings: Law, Economics, and Politics 341-351 (1995). Professor Fischel says that exactions were once small potatoes. Developers were willing to pay for sidewalks, sewer connections, and so forth in exchange for building permits, because these public goods yielded private benefits to the developers' projects. When communities wanted improvements that benefited everybody in the area generally—improvements not so directly linked to satisfying service demands created by new development itself—they relied on property taxes and government grants to provide the wherewithal.

But this situation changed, and eventually exactions became a common substitute means of funding public improvements. Fischel attributes the transformation to the dramatic expansion of land use regulation that began about 1970. Exactions are toothless without overlying regulations that limit development in the first place; for local communities, enacting regulations is like printing money, because the legal restrictions can be relaxed in exchange for goods and services. The politics of the strategy are pretty obvious, and finally exactions became so common and troublesome that the Supreme Court intervened.

The Court's first intervention came in Nollan v. California Coastal Commn., 483 U.S. 825 (1987). The Nollans owned a dilapidated bungalow on a beachfront lot, north and south of which were public beaches. They had bought the property under an obligation that they demolish and replace the bungalow with a larger house, and to do this they had to get a permit from the Coastal Commission. The Commission was willing to grant them the permit, but only on condition that the Nollans allow the public an easement to pass laterally along the beach behind their house, to go back and forth between the public beaches. The Nollans sued to have the condition invalidated, arguing that it was a taking. In a 5-4 decision, the Supreme Court declared the exaction a taking. Justice Scalia, writing for the majority, assumed that the Commission could have denied the permit outright for the purpose of ensuring "visual access" to the beaches and preventing overcrowding. But, he said, there was no "essential nexus" between the legitimate public purposes and the means imposed—the lateral access—to achieve them. He stated, "[U]nless the permit condition serves the same governmental purpose as the development ban, the building restriction is not a valid regulation of land but an 'out-and-out plan of extortion.'" Id. at 837 (citation omitted).

What the Court left unclear in *Nollan* was whether it was announcing a general requirement that all land use regulations satisfy some level of means-end instrumental fit or instead declaring a requirement that applied to exactions only. In the case that follows, the Court refined the *Nollan* requirement and indicated that exactions are a matter of special takings concern.

The second intervention answered one question that the Court left open in *Nollan*: just how much of a connection was required between the exaction and the government purpose? In Dolan v. City of Tigard, 512 U.S. 374 (1994), Florence Dolan sought a permit from the city to expand her plumbing store and to pave her parking lot. The city granted the permit subject to conditions that she either convey or dedicate two portions of her land: (1) one located in the floodplain of a creek adjacent to her property; and (2) a portion to be used as a link within a pedestrian/bicycle pathway. The Court found that the *Nollan* requirement was met because an essential nexus existed between these exactions and the government objectives. But the Court added another requirement: a "rough proportionality" must exist between the exaction and the impact of the proposed development. On the facts of the case, the Court concluded that the required proportionality did not exist. Why did Dolan have to provide property for the city's floodplain system? The requirement would make sense, the Court said, if her project would impact the existing system, but it would not. As to the second condition, it is true that Dolan's project would probably create more traffic, but the city failed to establish the relationship between the additional traffic and the pathway it sought. The city "must make some effort to quantify its findings in support of the dedication" beyond a conclusory statement, the Court said.

The Court's third and most recent intervention came in Koontz v. St. Johns River Water Management District, 570 U.S. 595 (2013). In that case the Court held that the *Nollan-Dolan* doctrine applies to monetary exactions as well as to mandated dedications of land. The Water Management District proposed permitting an owner to dredge his property on condition that he fund offsite mitigation projects on public land. In *Koontz*, in a 5-4 decision, the Court clarified that the *Nollan-Dolan* doctrine was a particular application of the unconstitutional conditional doctrine and that it applied equally if the permit condition required monetary payment rather than forced dedication of an easement or land. *Koontz* is insightfully discussed in Lee Anne Fennell & Eduardo M. Peñalver, Exactions Creep, 2013 S. Ct. Rev. 287.

Judicial takings. Up to this point all the government actions we have studied as involving takings have been either legislative or executive in nature. Suppose, for example, the change in law comes not from the legislature or a regulatory agency but from a court. If a court reverses or modifies common law precedents or reinterprets statutes or constitutions, should this type of government action be treated the same as legal changes effected by the other two branches for purposes of the Takings Clause? Suppose, for example, a state supreme court reinterprets its state's water law with the result of dramatically reallocating water rights. (See Robinson v. Ariyoshi, 753 F.2d 1468 (9th Cir. 1985) (holding that the reallocation was so extreme as to be unconstitutional), vacated on other grounds, 477 U.S. 902 (1986).) Does this constitute a judicial taking?

In Stop the Beach Renourishment, Inc. v. Florida Department of Environmental Protection, 560 U.S. 702 (2010), the United States Supreme Court was faced with this question. In that case the state of Florida had funded beach renewal projects to deposit new sand on eroded beaches. Once the project was completed, the state would set a fixed boundary line between private beachfront (or "littoral") property and state-owned property, replacing a line that moves over time through erosion or accretion. Hence, private beachfront owners' property would no longer expand if the beach expanded through accretion. A group of these owners sued the Florida Department of Environmental Protection, arguing that the department's order allowing the project to go forward violated the state constitution's takings clause.

The lower Florida court held that the project was unconstitutional because it would eliminate the right to receive accretions and "the right to have the property's contact with the water remain intact." It certified to the state supreme court the following question: "Has . . . the Beach and Shore Preservation Act [], been unconstitutionally applied so as to deprive the members of Stop the Beach Renourishment, Inc. of their riparian rights without just compensation for the property taken . . . ?" Save Our Beaches, Inc. v. Florida Department of Environmental Protection, 27 So. 3d 48, 60 (Fla. Dist. App. 2006). The Florida Supreme Court answered no and quashed the decision of the lower court. Walton County v. Stop the Beach Renourishment, Inc., 998 So. 2d 1102 (Fla. 2008).

On appeal, the United States Supreme Court affirmed. It held that the decision of the Florida Supreme Court "did not contravene the established property rights" (id. at 733) of littoral owners and thus had not violated the Takings Clause. Although the Court was unanimous on the result, it split on the question whether it should "determine whether, or when, a judicial decision determining the rights of property owners can violate the Takings Clause." Id. at 734. Four justices indicated that they might be prepared to recognize a cause of action for judicial takings, with Justice Scalia writing a plurality that relied on a textualist reading of the Takings Clause. He noted that the text "is not addressed to the action of a specific branch or branches" and declared that "[i]t would be absurd to allow a State to do by judicial decree what the Takings Clause forbids it to do by legislative fiat." Id. at 714. In a concurring opinion, Justice Kennedy, joined by Justice Sotomayor, agreed that there are constitutional limits to the judiciary's power to redefine property rights but that these limits are better established by the Due Process Clause than the Takings Clause. So the question of judicial takings remains unsettled for the time being. On the question whether the Takings or the Due Process Clause is the more appropriate vehicle for setting limits to judicial power to redefine established property rights, see Eduardo Moisés Peñalver & Lior Jacob Strahilevitz, Judicial Takings or Due Process?, 97 Cornell L. Rev. 305 (2012). See also Laura S. Underkuffler, Symposium: *Stop the Beach Renourishment v. Florida Department of Environmental Protection*: Judicial Takings: A Medley of Misconceptions, 61 Syracuse L. Rev. 203 (2011).

Appendix

ANSWERS TO REVIEW PROBLEMS
CHAPTER 2, PAGE 185

1. The facts of this Problem are taken from *Favorite v. Miller*, 407 A.2d 974 (Conn. 1978). The court began its analysis by noting, "when questions have arisen concerning the rights of the finder as against the person upon whose land the property was found, the resolution has turned upon the characterization given the property. Typically, if the property was found to be 'lost' or 'abandoned,' the finder would prevail, whereas if the property was characterized as 'mislaid,' the owner or occupier of the land would prevail." The court continued: "Lost property has traditionally been defined as involving an involuntary parting, i.e., where there is no intent on the part of the loser to part with the ownership of the property. . . . Abandonment, in turn, has been defined as the voluntary relinquishment of ownership of property without reference to any particular person or purpose, . . . while mislaid property is defined as that which is intentionally placed by the owner where he can obtain custody of it, but afterwards forgotten." The court noted that the distinctions among "lost," "mislaid," and "abandonment" rest on the intent or mental state of some unknown party who at some time in the past parted with the ownership or control of the property. The facts of this case point out one of the difficulties with this categorical approach. The events occurred over 200 years ago, so any conclusion as to the parties' mental states would be strictly conjectural and cannot form an adequate basis for determining the rights of the present parties.

The court then observed that other cases have held that except where the trespass was trivial, "the fact that the finder is trespassing is sufficient to deprive him of his normal preference over the owner of the place where the property was found." The basis of these decisions is deterrence—to deter parties from committing acts of trespass which might lead to breaches of the peace. In this case these decisions support Brown's claim over Abel's.

Further supporting Brown's claim is the fact that the fragment was found embedded nearly a foot beneath the surface. As the court in *Favorite* noted, cases such as *South Staffordshire Water Co. v. Sharman*, and *Elwes v. Brigg Gas Co.* hold in favor of the owner in quo on the basis of constructive possession.

The other aspect of the Problem is whether, assuming Brown's rights are superior to Abel's, Brown can recover the fragment from the museum. Assuming that the museum had no notice, actual or constructive, of the circumstances of the fragment's discovery, the museum is a bona fide purchaser. The question is whether Abel had the power to transfer good title in the fragment to the museum. The court in *O'Keefe v. Snyder* mentioned the possibility that the same question could be involved in that case. In a footnote the *O'Keefe* court quoted, UCC §2-403 governs that question. Under subsection (1), a seller in a transaction for the sale of goods can only transfer as good legal title as he has. Hence, a thief, who acquires void title by reason of the theft, cannot transfer good title even to a bona fide purchaser. That is the case here, where Abel by intentionally trespassing on Brown's land and taking the fragment that was buried in mud was a thief. So, Abel's subsequent sale to the Museum was void, and Brown is entitled to recover the fragment from the museum.

2. This is an adverse possession problem involving a boundary dispute arising from a mistake. The primary issue in such cases is the "hostility" requirement. In this respect the problem is somewhat similar to *Hollander v. World Mission Church*. The facts here are somewhat different from those in *Hollander*, however. In that case the boundary line described in the deed was wrong, and the court seems to indicate that the claimants relied, in part, on the erroneous deed description. Here there was no error in the deed description of the boundary line's location. Nevertheless, in *Hollander*, the court primarily emphasized the claimant's state of mind, specifically the fact that Hollander believed "that their property line ran up to the line of woods." In other words, hostility could be established even when possession was based on a mistake so long as the claimant had a definite intention to claim as his own the land up to a particular and definite line on the ground. Does this accept or reject the Maine doctrine? That's a good question. The opinion is very unclear about that. The court never mentions the Maine doctrine. In any event, the Maine doctrine is applied only by a distinct minority of courts these days. In a good majority of jurisdictions courts take an objective approach to the hostility requirement, and under that approach both Brianna and her parents would seem to have satisfied the requirement. They both used the strip of land in the usual way for owners of that kind of land in the area.

The other requirement for adverse possession that is at issue here is the continuity requirement. The limitation period is 10 years, and neither Brianna nor her parents have possessed the 1/2 acre strip of land that long. So, the issue is whether Brianna can tack her period of adverse possession to that of her parents. As *Howard v. Kunto* indicates, courts permit successive adverse possessors to tack their respective periods of adverse possession where there is privity of estate between them. The *Howard* court gave a liberal interpretation to privity, requiring only that transfer of possession between them be consensual. In this problem there is privity in the same sense as in *Howard*, i.e., even though the deed from Brianna's parents to her did not describe the half-acre strip, the transfer was completely volitional. Because all of the other elements of adverse possession would seem to be satisfied under these facts, Briana's claim to title of the strip of land via adverse possession ought to prevail.

CHAPTER 3, PAGE 220

Regarding all of the Problems, we assume *O* started out with a fee simple absolute.

1. After the conveyance, *A* has a fee simple subject to condition subsequent, and *O* has a right of entry in fee simple absolute. There are no other interests.

2. Assuming that building residences is a breach of the condition (which it almost certainly is), *A* has breached the condition subsequent, but the fee does

not automatically terminate. It terminates only if and when the right of entry is properly exercised. Who has the right of entry? In most states the right of entry is devisable by will, but, as the *Mahrenholz* case (page 214) indicates, there are a few states in which it is not. If the right of entry is devisable under local law, then *B* has it. If it is not devisable under local law, then *O*'s heirs (whoever they are) have it because a right of entry is descendible in all states. In either case, though, no one has taken steps to exercise the right, so *A*'s fee is still in effect.

3. After the conveyance, *A* has a fee simple determinable, and *O* has a possibility of reverter in fee simple absolute. A possibility of reverter does not have to be expressly stated to be created because it arises by operation of law.

4. Assuming that building a factory on Blackacre is a violation of the limitation, which it clearly is, *A* has violated the limitation with the result that the fee automatically terminates, without any action taken by *O* or anyone else. Title to Blackacre depends on succession to *O*'s possibility of reverter. If possibilities of reverter may be devised under local law (as most states permit), then *B* owns Blackacre in fee simple absolute. Otherwise, *O*'s heirs (whoever they are) hold the fee simple absolute as tenants in common.

5. After the conveyance, the Finger Lakes Land Trust has a fee simple subject to executory limitation, and Land Conservancy has an executory interest in fee simple absolute. It will become possessory if and when Greenacre is ever developed. In this respect, a fee simple subject to executory limitation operates the same way as a fee simple determinable. (Note that the executory interest is valid under the common law Rule Against Perpetuity because both interests were conveyed to charities.)

6. After the conveyance, *A* has a fee simple absolute. *A*'s promise creates a covenant, one which binds not only *A* but everyone who succeeds to ownership in Greenacre. The covenant does *not* make the fee subject to either a condition or a limitation. We will study covenants that "run with the land," as they are called, in Chapter 10.

7. The essential difference between a covenant, on the one hand, and a condition or limitation, on the other, concerns the effect of breach. As we have seen, in the case of both a condition and a limitation the effect of a breach or violation of the restriction is forfeiture of the fee simple, either automatically or upon the exercise of a right of entry. With a covenant, however, no forfeiture follows a breach. Rather, the person who holds the benefit of the covenant may either enjoin the breach or seek damages.

8. After the conveyance, *A* has a fee simple subject to executory limitation, and *B* has an executory interest. Note that *A*'s fee simple is defeasible only during *A*'s lifetime, i.e., in the event that *A* ever drinks alcohol or alcoholic beverages. Hence, *B*'s executory interest is valid under the common law Rule Against Perpetuities (*A* is the validating life). The state of title after the given events death depends on the alienability of executory interests. As we will see in Chapter 4, executory interests are generally alienable. So, *B*'s conveyance to *C* is valid, giving *C* the same executory interest that *B* had. When *A* subsequently drinks whiskey, that act causes the fee simple to terminate, and *C*'s executory interest now vests in possession as a fee simple absolute. *C* need not take any action for this to occur.

9. *A* has a life estate, and *B* has an indefeasibly vested remainder. The words of condition are mere surplusage. A possessory estate that is measured by the duration

of a person's life is, by definition, a life estate, not a fee simple subject to a condition. Similarly, the words of condition preceding *B*'s interest are redundant. It is certain that *A* will die; the only uncertainty is the timing of *A*'s death. A future interest that may that effect immediately following a life estate is a remainder, and *B*'s remainder is not subject to any conditions.

10. *A* has a life estate, and *B* has a vested remainder in a determinable fee simple. *O*'s successors in interest have a possibility of reverter. *B*'s remainder is not subject to any words of condition but rather words of limitation. Those words have the effect of making the possessory estate in which *B* has a future interest determinable, specifically, a determinable fee simple. Following every determinable fee simple there must be a possibility of reverter, regardless of whether it has been expressly reserved.

11. In Delaware, *A* has a fee tail, and *O* has a reversion. Delaware is one of the few states that still recognizes the fee tail. The words "and the heirs of his body" are words of limitation that denote a fee tail rather than a fee simple. Following every fee tail, there must be either a reversion or a remainder. *O* did not transfer a remainder here, so by operation of law, *O* retained a reversion. California does not recognize the fee tail. So, *A* takes a fee simple absolute, and *O* has nothing.

12. Massachusetts recognizes the fee tail, so in that state *A* would take a fee tail. *B* would have a remainder that takes effect if at *A*'s death *A* has no issue (children, grandchildren, etc.). When *A* died leaving two children, the remainder was terminated (could no longer take effect), and *A*'s fee tail then became absolute. So, when the two children later died leaving no issue, the remainder could not take effect. Rather, the children's interests in the fee simple absolute passed to their respective successors in interest; in this case, their spouses, who now each own a one-half interest in the fee simple absolute.

13. The correct answer is (c). *O* originally conveyed a fee simple determinable because the fee was subject to words of limitation. Thereafter, when *A* conveyed, she could only convey the same estate to *B*. *B*'s subsequent construction of an office building, in breach of the limitation, caused the fee immediately and automatically to terminate and simultaneously cause *O*'s possibility of reverter to take possession in fee simple absolute.

14. The correct answer is (a). *O* conveyed a fee simple absolute to *A*. A fee simple is fully devisable by will, so when *A*'s will devised his entire estate to his wife, *W*, that included the fee simple in Blackacre. A person's heirs take under an intestacy only to the extent that property has not otherwise been effectively transferred by gift or will.

CHAPTER 4, PAGE 235

Regarding all of the Problems, we assume *O* started out with a fee simple absolute.

1. After the conveyance, *A* has a life estate; *B* has a vested remainder for life; and there is a contingent remainder in fee simple absolute in *C*'s unascertained heirs. There is also a reversion in fee simple in *O*. Reversions, like possibilities of reverter, arise by operation of law and need not be expressly stated.

B's remainder is vested because we do not treat the expiration of *A's* preceding life estate as a condition precedent. In theory we could do so. The fact that we do not illustrates the common law's preference for early vesting. (One of the reasons for this preference was to reduce the incidence of invalid future interests under the Rule Against Perpetuities.) Another (more technical) way to classify the vested remainder for life is as a remainder vested subject to limitational defeasance. The limitation is *B's* death.

2. After the conveyance, *A* has a springing executory interest in fee simple absolute. *O* has a fee simple subject to an executory limitation (or subject to an executory interest, if you will). Immediately and automatically upon *A's* first wedding anniversary, if it ever occurs, *A's* executory interest will divest *O's* fee simple and become possessory in a fee simple absolute.

3. After the conveyance, *A* has a term of years followed by a contingent remainder in fee simple in which *X* and *Y* have an interest. There is also a reversion in fee simple in *O*. The remainder is contingent because it is subject to an unfulfilled condition precedent (attaining age 21).

4. *X's* attaining age 21 vests the contingent remainder in him or her, so that *X* now has a vested remainder in fee simple subject to partial divestment (also called subject to open) by *Y* and also subject to open because *A* is alive and may have more children some or all of whom may reach age 21. There is no reversion (the vesting of *X's* remainder simultaneously divests *O's* reversion). *Y* now has a shifting executory interest in fee simple which will vest if *Y* reaches age 21.

5. *X's* vested remainder is transmissible at death because it is not subject to any condition that *X* survive to the time of possession. So, it passes to *X's* successors in interest, i.e., *X's* devisees under any valid will or *X's* heirs. Those persons take *exactly the same* interest that *X* had. *Y* still has a shifting executory interest in fee simple. There is no reversion.

6. After the conveyance, *A* has a life estate; *X* has a vested remainder in fee simple subject to open; and there is a shifting executory interest in fee simple in *A's* unborn children. There is no reversion.

7. The birth of *Y* vests the remainder in him or her and simultaneously partially divests *X's* remainder (reducing *X's* share from 100 percent to 50 percent). Both *X's* and *Y's* remainders are subject to open (partial divestment) so long as *A* is still alive and capable of having more children. Once *A* dies, however, the class of *A's* children closes and *X's* and *Y's* interests become indefeasibly vested in fee simple absolute. With *A's* life estate terminated, *X* and *Y* take possession and own the property in fee simple absolute as tenants in common (each has an undivided interest—a concept that we will study in Chapter 5).

8. After the conveyance, *A* has a life estate; *B* has a remainder in fee simple that is vested subject to complete divestment; *C* has a shifting executory interest in fee simple absolute. There is no reversion.

9. After the conveyance, *A* has a life estate; *B* has a vested remainder in fee simple determinable; *O* has a possibility of reverter in fee simple absolute.

10. After the conveyance, *A* has a springing executory interest in fee simple absolute. *O* has a fee simple subject to executory limitation (or, if you will, an executory interest). If and when *A* graduates from college, *A's* executory interest will vest in possession, divesting *O's* fee simple.

11. *S* has a life estate, followed by a vested remainder in *T*'s children for their respective lives, followed by a contingent remainder (in a fee simple) in which *X*, *Y*, and *Z* have an interest. *T*'s successors in interest have a reversion. The contingent remainder in the grandchildren is valid under the Rule Against Perpetuities (RAP) because *T*'s children are the validating lives (more exactly, the last surviving child). All of those children were lives in being, and because this is a devise, no more children can be added to the class. So, all of *T*'s grandchildren to be born will be born no later than the death of the last surviving of *T*'s children, and as to the condition of survivorship, all of the grandchildren who survive *T*'s children (the condition) either will survive that child or die before that child no later than that child's death. Hence, the remainder is good.

12. *S* has a life estate, followed by a contingent remainder in *B*, followed by an alternative contingent remainder in *C*. There is also a technical reversion in *T*'s successors in interest. *B*'s contingent remainder is valid under the RAP because *B* is his own validating life. *C*'s contingent remainder is valid under the RAP with *B* as the validating life. *B* was a life in being, and no later than *B*'s death we will know whether or not *B* married *Z* by his 30th birthday (actually, we may know that sooner than *B*'s death). The same rationale applies to *C*'s contingent remainder.

13. The correct answer is (a). The difference between (a) and (b) is that in (b), there is a reversion. This is incorrect because reversions do not exist where there is a vested remainder in a fee simple. Options (c) and (d) are incorrect because the remainder in *S*'s children is vested (although not absolutely). It is vested because at least one of the beneficiaries is alive and the remainder is not subject to any condition precedent. The condition (survivorship of *S*) is stated in condition subsequent form.

14. The correct answer is (a). This is basically the same situation as Problem 14. Here, as there, the difference between (a) and (b) is that in (b), there is a reversion. This is incorrect because reversions do not exist where there is a vested remainder in a fee simple. Options (c) and (d) are incorrect because the remainder in *S*'s children is vested (although not absolutely). It is vested because at least one of the beneficiaries is alive and the remainder is not subject to any condition precedent. The condition (survivorship of *S*) is stated in condition subsequent form. The difference between this Problem and Problem 13 is the substance of the conditions. Here, the remainder is divested only if none of *A*'s children survive *A*, i.e., if even one of the children survive *A*, then the shares of the predeceased children are not divested but instead pass to their successors. In Problem 13, however, in order to take their shares, each individual child of *A* must survive *A*.

CHAPTER 6, PAGE 285

This is a residential landlord/tenant problem with two major parts, Alysha's lease assignment (and Owen's refusal to give consent to the assignment), which is raised by Owen's action to terminate the head lease, and Owen's duties to Britney for the various defects in the condition of the apartment, which is involved in Owen's action against Britney to recover possession for non-payment of rent.

Regarding the lease assignment, there are several issues. First, is there a duty that Owen act reasonably in acting on the approval clause of the lease? As the court in *Kendall v. Ernest Pestana, Inc.*, pointed out, the majority rule is that in the absence of a provision in the lease imposing a duty to act reasonably on the landlord, the landlord may arbitrarily refuse to give consent to a proposed assignment, no matter how objectively acceptable the proposed assignee may be. The court in *Kendall* changed that rule, but its new rule of reasonableness applies only to commercial, not residential leases. Even if there were a requirement that the landlord act reasonably here, it is at least arguable that Owen did so where the basis he gave for his refusal—that he disliked turnover—is arguably a legitimate business reason, rather than some arbitrary or capricious basis for refusal.

Assuming that there is no duty to act reasonably or that Owen did act reasonably, under the lease Owen had the power to terminate the head lease. Hence, he is entitled to cancel the head lease with Alyssa, which would invalidate the assignment to Britney. However, Owen cashed Britney's monthly checks to him. By doing so, he impliedly created a tenancy relationship with Britney. There are two possibilities: he may have confirmed the original lease that Alyssa assigned to Britney, or, alternatively, he created a series of new month-to-month tenancies with Britney. Either way, Owen and Britney are now in a landlord-tenant relationship.

This leads to the second major part of the problem—Owen's duties of care. The two doctrines raised here, of course, are the covenant of quiet enjoyment and the implied warranty of habitability. Regarding the covenant of quiet enjoyment, recall that there are two approaches, the traditional approach and the modern approach. Under the traditional approach the covenant does not itself create a duty of care on the landlord. Rather, the covenant is derivative of duties otherwise imposed by some source such as a promise by the landlord, or one of exceptions to caveat lessee. Under the modern approach, illustrated by the *Village Commons* case, the covenant itself creates a duty of care on the landlord. Under either approach, the covenant of quiet enjoyment may well have been breached here. Under the traditional approach, a court may reasonably interpret Owen's statement to Britney, "I'll see what I can do," as a promise to repair the toilet and sink problems. If that is the case, then Owen's breach of that promise furnishes the basis for a breach of the covenant of quiet enjoyment. It is also possible that the problems with the toilet and sink were latent, in which case the situation falls within one of the exceptions to caveat lessee, imposing a duty of care on Owen. Under the modern approach to the covenant of quiet enjoyment, the analysis is more straightforward. As the court stated in *Village Commons*, there is a breach of the covenant where an act or omission by the landlord materially deprives the tenant of the beneficial use or enjoyment of the premises. It seems quite likely that a court would find that non-working toilets and sinks such that the tenant must use someone else's facilities for the basics of life (i.e., going to the bathroom) fits this standard. But the real question here is the remedy. Had Britney vacated in a timely fashion, she would have been entitled to stop rent payment and assert the constructive eviction defense to Owen's action. But what she cannot do is remain in possession and withhold rent. Construction eviction requires that the tenant vacate. On the basis of the covenant of quiet enjoyment alone, then, Owen would prevail.

Britney's stronger argument is based on the implied warranty of habitability (IWH) doctrine, illustrated by *Hilder v. St. Peter.* As *Hilder* indicates, under IWH, landlords in residential leases are under a non-waivable duty to provide and maintain throughout the lease period premises that are safe, clean, and fit for human habitation. Defects in "essential facilities" are violations of the IWH, and "essential facilities" include those that are "vital to the use of the premises for residential purposes." That definition would almost surely include operative toilets and sinks. Assuming there is a substantial breach of the IWH here, what are Britney's remedies? The Notes following *Hilder* indicate that a tenant has a variety of available remedies, but for Britney's purposes what matters most is that in most jurisdictions she has the right to remain in possession and withhold rent. (There are variations on this among jurisdictions, but the basic remedy is rent withholding while remaining in possession.) Hence, Britney would prevail in Owen's action against her under the IWH.

Table of Cases

Italics indicate principal cases.

Author Index

Subject Index